CONTRACTS

CONTRACTS
Fourth Edition

E. ALLAN FARNSWORTH

**ALFRED McCORMACK PROFESSOR OF LAW
COLUMBIA UNIVERSITY**

REPORTER, RESTATEMENT (SECOND) OF CONTRACTS

ASPEN
PUBLISHERS

76 Ninth Avenue, New York, NY 10011
http://lawschool.aspenpublishers.com

Aspen Publishers
Attn: Permissions Department
76 Ninth Avenue, 7th Floor
New York, NY 10011-5201

Printed in the United States of America

ISBN 0-7355-4540-5 (PB)   15 14 13 12

Library of Congress Cataloging-in-Publication Data

Farnsworth, E. Allan (Edward Allan)
    Contracts / E. Allan Farnsworth. — 4th ed.
      p. cm.
    Includes index.
    ISBN 0-7355-2642-7 (CB : alk. paper) — ISBN 0-7355-4540-5 (SB : alk. paper)
    1. Contracts — United States.   I. Title.

KF801.F365 2004
346.7302 — dc22   2004045139

About Aspen Publishers

Aspen Publishers, headquartered in New York City, is a leading information provider for attorneys, business professionals, and law students. Written by preeminent authorities, our products consist of analytical and practical information covering both U.S. and international topics. We publish in the full range of formats, including updated manuals, books, periodicals, CDs, and online products.

Our proprietary content is complemented by 2,500 legal databases, containing over 11 million documents, available through our Loislaw division. Aspen Publishers also offers a wide range of topical legal and business databases linked to Loislaw's primary material. Our mission is to provide accurate, timely, and authoritative content in easily accessible formats, supported by unmatched customer care.

To order any Aspen Publishers title, go to *www.aspenpublishers.com* or call 1-800-638-8437.

To reinstate your manual update service, call 1-800-638-8437.

For more information on Loislaw products, go to *www.loislaw.com* or call 1-800-364-2512.

For Customer Care issues, e-mail *CustomerCare@aspenpublishers.com*; call 1-800-234-1660; or fax 1-800-901-9075.

Aspen Publishers
a Wolters Kluwer business

**To Karen
and other readers**

Summary of Contents

Summary of Contents

Contents

Contents

Contents

Preface

Perhaps books on contracts should not have prefaces. Langdell, in his preface to the first casebook in 1871, stressed the rationality of contract law, viewing law as a "science" and suggesting that if "the fundamental legal doctrines . . . could be so classified and arranged that each should be found in its proper place, and nowhere else, they should cease to be formidable from their number." Williston, in the preface to his treatise in 1920, emphasized the universality of contract law, aspiring "to treat the subject of contracts as a whole, and to show the wide range of application of its principles." These prefatory remarks were later scoffed at as exaggerating the rationality and the universality of the subject. Though these examples counsel silence, I follow tradition in venturing a few remarks on the reason for this treatise.

First, I have tried to write a book that would be of use to lawyers seeking a general treatment of some area of contrat law. I recalled the sort of book that I kept on my shelves after graduation from law school and had occasion to consult in the years that followed. To this end, I have attempted to feature matters that occur with some frequency in litigation, in arbitration, or otherwise in practice, to present them in such a way as to expose their practical significance, and to support the text with references that lead the reader to more thorough treatments of the subject.

Second, I have attempted to suggest some of the academic writing that might be of help as well of interest to lawyers. This includes material ranging from law and economics to legal philosophy. Although scholarly literature is sometimes regarded as remote from the daily practice of law, it is my hope that an occasional citation in the context of a practical problem may dispel this notion. More personal and theoretical treatment of many topics can be found through the citations to my book *Changing Your Mind: The Law of Regretted Decisions*.

In attempting to do these things, I have piled up many debts. Some are to colleagues and students, at Columbia and elsewhere, who have commented on chapters in draft. Of these, my longtime colleague and collaborator William F. Young requires particular mention. Other debts are to my student assistants. Those who have contributed to this edition include Lori A. Alvino, Diana Eng, Phineas Leahy, Craig E. Leen, Seth R. Meisels, Matthew A. Schwartz, Peng Tan, and John K. White, Jr., all of the Columbia School of Law. I remain grateful to those mentioned in the second edition: Steven L. Baglio, Gregory Gordon, Kyu Kahn, Spencer Lehv, Steven R. Meier, Donald More, Elizabeth A. Nowicki, Cynthia D. Richards, Douglas Stalgren, William J. Sushon, and Eva N. Valik, all of the Columbia School of Law, and to Arthur J. Mahoney, Patricia R. Sigman, and Rebecca Harrison Steele of the Stetson College of Law. The same holds true for those mentioned in the first edition: Mary Rose Alexander, Timothy Beeken, Leslie A. Bogen, Julia L. Brickell, Margret Ann Carfagno, Stephen Chawaga, Michael A. Clouser, D. Scott Coward, Paul Feuerman, Thomas D. Graber, Oliver J. Herzfeld, Kevin Koloff, Marlyn Ann Marincas, James Michael Meyer, C. Allen Parker, John V.N. Philip, Ruth Piekarski, Abraham D. Piontnica, Warren Scharf, and Cynthia Starnes, all of the Columbia School of Law. I am also indebted to the reference staff of the Columbia Law Library and Brian J. Donnelly for invaluable assistance. For financial support I am grateful to the Columbia University School of Law. Finally, I owe a debt to my publisher for its efforts to show that a law book can be handsome as well as useful.

E. Allan Farnsworth

March 2004

Acknowledgments

The American Law Institute has kindly given its permission for the reprinting of excerpts from the Restatement (Second) of Contracts (copyright 1981 by the American Law Institute) and the Restatement of Contracts (copyright 1932 by the American Law Institute). The American Law Institute and the National Conference of Commissioners on Uniform States Laws have kindly given their permission for the reprinting of parts of the Uniform Commercial Code, including Comments on which they hold the copyright. Thanks go to the Foundation Press for permission to adapt the introductory discussion in Chapter 1 of the Restatements of Contracts and much of the material in the Biographical Appendix from Farnsworth, Young & Sanger, Cases and Materials on Contracts (6th ed. 2001) and the introductory discussion in Chapter 1 of the Uniform Commercial Code from Farnsworth, Honnold, Harris, Mooney & Reitz, Cases and Materials on Commercial Law (4th ed. 1985), on which it holds the copyright. Thanks for copyrighted material also goes to the Board of Directors of the Columbia Law Review for permission to adapt Farnsworth, Legal Remedies for Breach of Contract, 70 Colum. L. Rev. 1145 (1970), in §12.4, and to the Yale Law Journal along with Fred B. Rothman & Co. for permission to adapt Farnsworth, "Meaning" in the Law of Contracts, 76 Yale L.J. 939 (1967), in §§7.7, 7.8, 7.9, 7.10 and 7.12.

Note on Citations

In this treatise, sections of the revised version of Article 2 of the Uniform Commercial Code are designated "UCC-R" and sections of the original version (the immediately previous version) are designated "UCC-O". The Restatement (Second) of Contracts is referred to simply as "Restatement Second," and the first Restatement of Contracts simply as "Restatement" or "first Restatement." Citations of cases are usually followed by an explanatory parenthetical phrase with a brief excerpt or other indication of the relevance of the case to the discussion. If a case is referred to more than once within a section, later citation is by cross-reference to refer the reader to the earlier parenthetical information. Of course the material in parentheses gives only a hint of the opinion itself, the only safe guide to the holding of the case. No notation is made of a higher court's refusal to review a case, including denial of certiorari by the United States Supreme Court.

CONTRACTS

PART I
INTRODUCTION

Chapter 1

Contracts and Contract Law in General

A.   THE MEANING AND ROLE OF CONTRACT

§1.1.   **The Meaning of *Contract*.**   Books on the law of contracts usually begin by explaining what lawyers mean by the word *contract*. Sometimes lawyers use the word, as it is used in common speech, simply to refer to a writing containing terms on which the parties have agreed. But they often use the word in a more technical sense to mean a *promise*, or a set of promises, that the law will *enforce* or at least recognize in some way.[1] The two italicized words in this definition indicate two limitations on the scope of the law of contracts.

The first limitation is that the law of contracts is confined to promises that the law will *enforce*. It is therefore concerned primarily with *exchanges* because, as will be explained later, courts have generally been unwilling to enforce a promise unless the promisee has given the promisor something in return for it.[2] In return for the promise the promisee may actually have rendered some

A definition of contract

Concern of contract law with exchanges

---

§1.1   [1]Restatement Second §1 defines a *contract* as "a promise or a set of promises for the breach of which the law gives a remedy, or the performance of which the law in some way recognizes as a duty." As we see later, a promise that is not directly enforceable may nevertheless indirectly receive legal recognition. See the discussions of the meaning of *unenforceable* and of other effects in §6.10 *infra* in connection with the statute of frauds.

[2]See the discussion of acceptance of the doctrine of consideration in §1.6 *infra*. See also §2.5 *infra*.

performance or may have given a promise to render some performance at a later time.[3] But conventional learning is that a promisor's mere promise to do something — a "bare" or "naked" promise for which the promisee has given nothing in return — is not enforceable.[4] So if nothing has been given in exchange for the promise, it has no legal consequences. And if it has no legal consequences, there is no contract. The main concern of the law of contracts, then, is with exchanges.

Concern of contract law with the future

The second limitation suggested by this definition is that the law of contracts is confined to *promises*. It is therefore concerned with exchanges that relate to the *future* because a "promise" is a commitment as to future behavior.[5] Examples of exchanges that do not include such a commitment (and so do not involve a contract in this sense) are the transaction of barter, in which the parties simply make a present exchange of, say, apples for oranges, and the present (or "cash") sale, in which the parties make a present exchange of, say, apples for money. Because no promise is given in either of these exchanges, there is no contract.[6] Such exchanges may give rise to interesting legal questions. For example, if the apples had been stolen by the seller from their rightful owner, a question might arise as to whether the buyer is entitled to keep them if the original owner claims them. But this is a question relating to conflicting rights of ownership of the apples themselves, and it is considered a question for the law of property rather than one for the law of contracts.[7] No question for the law of contracts arises unless the dispute is one over a promise — a commitment as to future behavior.

Example of cotton cases of 1973

Some idea of what the word *contract* means in practice can be gleaned from the cotton cases of 1973. That year saw a spectacular rise in the price of cotton on the American market. The causes were said to include large shipments to China, high-water and flood conditions in the cotton belt, late plantings forced by heavy rains, and the devaluation of the dollar. In the early months of the year, before planting, a cotton farmer makes a "forward" sales contract for delivery

---

[3] See the discussions of promise as consideration in a unilateral contract and of promise as consideration in a bilateral contract in §2.3 *infra*.

[4] That reliance may be an alternative, *see* §2.19 *infra*.

[5] Restatement Second §2(1) defines a *promise* as "a manifestation of intention to act or refrain from acting in a specified way, so made as to justify a promisee in understanding that a commitment has been made." See the discussion of the objective theory in §3.6 *infra*. For more on what is a promise, *see* E. Farnsworth, Changing Your Mind ch. 3 (1998).

[6] A present gift by, for example, delivery of apples is also not a contract, since it involves neither a promise nor an exchange.

[7] Even if the transaction involves a promise, the law of contracts is concerned only to the extent that the dispute involves the promise. For example, the stolen apples might have been delivered to the buyer pursuant to a prior agreement in which the seller had exchanged a promise to deliver apples for the buyer's promise to pay for them. But the dispute over who is entitled to the apples would still not be a dispute over either of those promises and would not be regarded as one for the law of contracts.

to the buyer of all cotton to be raised and harvested on a specified tract at a fixed price per pound, without guarantee of quantity or quality. The farmer can then use this contract to finance raising the crop. Early in 1973, cotton farmers made such contracts to sell at a price roughly equal to the price on the market at that time, some 30 cents a pound. By the time the cotton had been raised and was ready for delivery, however, the market price had risen to about 80 cents a pound. The farmers felt, as one judge later put it, "sick as an old hound dog who ate a rotten skunk." Many refused to perform the "forward" contracts that they had made at the lower price, and scores of lawsuits resulted throughout the cotton belt.[8] Not only were the farmers universally unsuccessful, but the decisions evoked little attention. One court put it simply, "The critical issue is whether . . . there was an enforceable promise to buy for each promise to sell. We believe there was."[9]

> **Executory exchanges of promises**

The farmers were bound by "contracts," that is, by *promises* — to sell cotton — that the law would *enforce*. The courts seemed to say that they would enforce them because something — a promise to buy — had been exchanged for each promise to sell. Yet these promises were still wholly executory, in the sense that neither party had begun to perform its promise. The farmers had not delivered anything and the buyers had not paid anything.[10] The principal goal of this chapter is to examine how and why the law came to enforce such purely executory exchanges of promises.

The two sections that follow begin this examination by tracing the development of the role of promise.

> **Importance of exchange to free enterprise**

§1.2. The Role of Exchange. Exchange is the mainspring of any economic system that relies as heavily on free enterprise as does ours. Such a system allocates resources largely by direct bilateral exchanges arranged by bargaining between individuals. In these exchanges each gives something to the other and receives in return something from the other.[1]

> **Other possible bases for economy**

Of course, it would be misleading to suggest that such exchanges are the only possible basis for an economic system. Anthropologists tell of primitive societies in which exchange played a minor role. In some the struggle for survival in an inhospitable environment made self-sufficiency the rule and cooperation the

---

[8]This summary is taken largely from one of those cases, Bolin Farms v. American Cotton Shippers Assn., 370 F. Supp. 1353 (W.D. La. 1974).

[9]J.L. McEntire & Sons v. Hart Cotton Co., 511 S.W.2d 179, 183 (Ark. 1974).

[10]The buyers had, however, relied on the farmers' promises by not making other arrangements to get cotton. As to whether the farmers' promises would have been enforceable if they had announced their intention not to deliver the cotton shortly after making their promises, and before any reliance, see the discussion of the protection of expectation in §1.6 *infra*.

§1.2 [1]*See* Johnson v. Scandia Assocs., 717 N.E.2d 24 (Ind. 1999) (quoting this section of this treatise).

exception.[2] In others notions of generosity led to obligations of sharing, based on a person's status as determined by such factors as kinship and age and reinforced by pressure from peers and from religion.[3] Furthermore, even contemporary developed societies rely to some extent on indirect exchanges that are channeled through the state, and communist societies were traditionally characterized by relatively heavy reliance on such exchanges.[4] In the United States we rely on such exchanges in, for example, our programs for construction of highways. And within large corporations or conglomerates the distribution of resources is arranged administratively by an internal hierarchy.

Adam Smith on exchange

In the main, however, our economy relies on direct bilateral exchanges between individuals and business entities. The central assumption behind this reliance was forcefully stated by Adam Smith in 1776. People, he reasoned, cannot gain the help of others by relying on their "benevolences." A person must "interest their self-love in his favour, and shew them that it is for their own advantage to do for him what he requires of them." One does this by bargaining in this way: "Give me that which I want, and you shall have this which you want." We thus obtain what we need from others by addressing ourselves "not to their humanity but to their self-love, and never talk to them of our own necessities but of their advantages."[5]

Function of bargain and markets

In a market economy, the terms of such direct bilateral exchanges are arrived at voluntarily by the parties themselves through this process of bargaining. Each party to an exchange seeks to maximize its own economic advantage on terms tolerable to the other party. Because of differences in value judgments and because of the division of labor, it is usually possible for each to realize a substantial advantage. "When the baker provides the dentist with bread and the dentist relieves the baker's toothache, neither the baker nor the dentist is harmed."[6] An economist would call this a "Pareto-superior" outcome, since at least one of the parties believes itself to be better off as a result and neither

---

[2] Probably no people have ever been so fiercely individualistic as Montesquieu's mythical Troglodytes, who resolved "that each individual should attend to his own interests, without troubling his mind about those of his neighbor." Montesquieu, The Persian Letters 23 (Bassorah ed. 1897). On the individualistic Ammassalik in Greenland, *see* Farnsworth, The Past of Promise: An Historical Introduction to Contract, 69 Colum. L. Rev. 576, 578-79 (1969).

[3] On the Zuni in New Mexico, *see* Farnsworth, The Past of Promise: An Historical Introduction to Contract, 69 Colum. L. Rev. 576, 579-80 (1969). *See also* Perillo, Exchange, Contract and Law in the Stone Age, 31 Ariz. L. Rev. 17 (1989).

[4] An attempt was made in early Soviet Russia to administer the economy without the institution of contract, to base centralized distribution of wealth on administrative norms. The experiment ended in failure, and Lenin wrote in 1921 that "we must now admit . . . if we do not want to hide our heads under our wings . . . [that] the private market proved to be stronger than we and . . . we ended up with ordinary purchase and sale, trade." Contracts were reintroduced and contract law was codified, largely along traditional lines. Loeber, Plan and Contract Performance in Soviet Law, in W. LaFave (ed.), Law in the Soviet Society 128-29 (1965).

[5] A. Smith, An Inquiry into the Nature and Causes of the Wealth of Nations 19 (1811 ed.).

[6] L. Von Mises, Human Action 666 (rev. ed. 1963).

6

believes itself to be worse off.[7] The economist might add that society as a whole benefits, since such exchanges tend to transfer resources to their highest valued, most productive uses and tend to maximize the efficient use of economic resources. Furthermore, the resulting economic system is one in which the making of decisions is widely dispersed among individual members of society, who control its resources.

The most primitive form of direct bilateral exchange is barter, the immediate exchange of goods by both parties. One party delivers apples to the other, and, in return, the other delivers oranges to the first at the same time. When a society comes to regard a particular form of wealth as money, there arises the present sale, in which goods are exchanged for money rather than for other goods. A seller delivers apples to a buyer, and, in return, the buyer pays the seller at the same time. But as we have seen, neither the transaction of barter nor that of present sale looks to the future — neither involves a promise.[8]

Exchanges without promise

What is the role of exchanges involving promises?

§1.3.   The Role of Promise.   The germ of promise was credit. The simplest form of credit transaction is the loan of money. From the loan it was but a short step to the sale on credit, in which performance on one side is deferred, the buyer merely promising to pay while the seller immediately performs. A seller delivers apples to a buyer, and, in return, the buyer promises to pay the seller at the end of the month. Credit became even more significant when specialization of labor generated a demand for services. Services usually take time to perform, so an exchange of services for payment cannot be simultaneous — an extension of credit by one of the parties is inevitable. If a builder is to put a new roof on an owner's house, either the builder must work in reliance on the owner's promise to pay or the owner must pay in reliance on the builder's promise to do the work.[1]

Rise of credit

But the loan and other credit transactions still left humankind short of a concept of promise, for the duty to which the loan gives rise was not generally regarded by primitive societies as arising out of the debtor's word alone. The debt may be seen as recoverable, not because of the debtor's promise to pay, but because the debtor, having received money on request, would otherwise be unjustly enriched. It has even been suggested that a breach by the debtor is regarded as a wrong with respect to the creditor's property, that the creditor's claim is founded, not on what the creditor is owed, but on what the creditor owns. The contemporary bank depositor displays this misconception of the

Credit not seen as involving promise

---

[7] R. Posner, Economic Analysis of Law 12 (6th ed. 2003) (*Pareto-superior transaction* "is one that makes at least one person in the world better off and no one worse off").

[8] See the discussion of a definition of *contract* in §1.1 *supra*.

§1.3   [1] The extension of credit is often minimized by providing for "progress payments" to be made by the owner as the work progresses.

transaction in referring to "my money" in the bank, rather than to the obligation that the bank owes the depositor.[2]

Executory exchanges of promises distinguished

The credit transaction was thus a far cry from the purely executory exchange of promises, in which each party merely makes a promise, looking to an exchange of performances at some later time. To conceive of enforcing such purely consensual transactions required a higher level of abstraction than that required for enforcing a debt arising out of the plaintiff's immediate performance.

Practical need for such exchanges

Such purely executory exchanges of promises did not become important in practice until a relatively advanced level of economic development had been attained. Economists tell us that parties engage in such exchanges instead of present exchanges for two main reasons. One is to transfer risks in order to take advantage of relative advantages in bearing those risks. The other is to protect investments that are specific to the exchange and that are made in reliance on the exchange in order to increase its value. As long as production and distribution remained in the hands of simple artisans, who themselves did all of the work required before consumption, there was little occasion for such transactions or for legal rules to support them. Indeed, a general theory of contract would have been something of a luxury in a society concerned with basic protection of life and property. Eventually, however, producers' operations became more complex, and they began buying raw materials from suppliers, employing others to work for them, and selling through distributors. Producers then saw the need to plan for the future in order to compete with other producers. An exchange of promises looking to a future exchange of performances would give a producer the basis for predictable calculation.

Function of contract law in executory exchanges

From the perspective of society as a whole, the function of the law of contracts might have been seen as furthering the general economic good by encouraging parties to enter into such productive transactions. From the perspective of the parties themselves, the function might have been viewed more narrowly as aiding them in planning for the future by protecting their expectations. From either perspective, it was essential to provide a general basis for the enforcement of promises that included *purely executory* exchanges of promises. The development of such a general basis closely paralleled the specialization of labor and the development of competitive markets.

Example of executory exchange of promises

Consider the simple example of a contract for future delivery against future payment. A seller promises to deliver apples to a buyer in six months, and in return the buyer promises to pay the seller $10,000 on delivery of the apples. If the seller should fail to deliver the apples in six months, the buyer will have to buy substitute apples in replacement. If the purchase can still be made at the

---

[2]According to a distinguished legal historian, a "vast gulf . . . to our minds divides the 'Give me what I own' and 'Give me what I am owed.'" F. Maitland, The Forms of Action at Common Law 38 (1936). As to the extent to which this view was characteristic of the early common law, see the discussion of the development of the action of debt in §1.5 *infra*.

contract price of $10,000, the buyer's only loss is the inconvenience in arranging the substitute transaction, and the economic importance of the agreement to the buyer is minimal. If, however, the price of apples has risen, so that the buyer must pay, say, $11,000 to have substitute apples delivered at the date for delivery under the contract, the loss will be increased by $1,000, and the economic importance of the agreement to the buyer is at least that amount. In making the contract, the buyer's expectation was that the transaction would provide protection against just such a rise in the market price. The seller, of course, had a comparable expectation of being protected against a falling market.

The decision to recognize purely executory exchanges of promises also allowed the parties to engage in more sophisticated planning for the future. They might extend the period to, say, five years; they might make the agreement cover many deliveries of apples under a long-term relationship; they might leave the quantity of apples flexible in terms of all that the buyer might "require" for an applesauce factory; they might let the price vary according to a formula based on published market quotations. Furthermore, recognition of such exchanges permitted an entirely new form of economic activity — speculation. The same contract for future delivery, used by the producer to plan for the future, could be used by the speculator to gamble on the future course of the market.

From the standpoint of contract law, the decision to recognize purely executory exchanges of promises opened a Pandora's box of problems. What could the law do to ensure that the exchange of promises was followed by the exchange of performances expected by the parties? In the event of nonperformance by one party, how were the other party's disappointed expectations to be valued? Were any limits to be placed on the expectations for which recovery would be allowed? These and related questions will be examined in later chapters.

But first let us see how purely executory exchanges of promises came to be enforced.

B. THE DEVELOPMENT OF A BASIS FOR ENFORCING PROMISES

§1.4. The Enforcement of Promises in Roman Law. The notion that a promise itself may give rise to an enforceable duty was an achievement of Roman law. But since the human mind is slow to generalize, it is not surprising that the history of contract law in Roman times is the account of the development of a number of discrete categories of promises that would be enforced, rather than the story of the creation of a general basis for enforcing promises.[1] Although a promise might be morally binding, it was not legally enforceable unless it

---

§1.4   [1]For an exhaustive description of the categories of Roman contracts, *see* A. Watson, The Law of Obligations in the Later Roman Republic (1984).

Margin notes:

More sophisticated transactions possible

Additional legal problems

Development of categories of enforceable promises

fell within one of these categories. In classical Roman law these included the "stipulation," the "real" contracts, and the "consensual" contracts.

Stipulation

The "stipulation" (*stipulatio*), which dates from a very early time in Roman law, turned on formalities. A party could make a binding promise called a "stipulation" in a ceremony in which the party observed a prescribed form of question and answer. Although the participation of both parties was required, only one party was bound. Therefore, the stipulation was not well suited to purely executory exchanges of promises, for which a pair of reciprocal stipulations would have been needed.

Real contracts

Nor was the category of "real" contracts suited to purely executory exchanges of promises. Real contracts were those, such as the contract of loan, in which the handing over of the subject matter made the recipient's promise to restore it binding. Since the validity of the contract depended on delivery by one of the parties, it was not adaptable to an exchange of promises in which there had been no performance on either side. Furthermore, as we have seen, the liability of the recipient under contracts of this sort did not necessarily have to be viewed as arising out of the promise itself.[2]

Consensual contracts

"Consensual" contracts were more flexible and did afford a legal basis for enforcing purely executory exchanges of promises. They differed from the stipulation in that they lacked its formalities, and they differed from real contracts in that agreement alone, without delivery, sufficed to make them binding. But in keeping with the pattern of evolution through the growth of exceptions, they were limited to four important types of contracts—sale, hire, partnership, and mandate.

Innominate contracts

These three categories of enforceable promises, however, sufficed to meet Roman needs through the classical period. The widespread use of promises was slow in coming, and even as late as the time of Justinian in the sixth century, the only expansion beyond the three categories of classical Roman law was to recognize a fourth category of "innominate" contracts. These were agreements under which one party promised to give or do something in exchange for a similar promise by the other party. Unlike both real and consensual contracts, they were not confined to specified classes of transactions and were therefore called "innominate." Moreover, unlike real contracts, the enforceability of the promise turned on some performance given in exchange and called a *quid pro quo*. But the innominate contracts were severely limited because they were binding only when one of the parties had completed performance. Until that happened either party could escape liability.

Lack of general basis for enforcement

None of these categories of contracts, then, resulted in the development of a general basis for enforcing promises that would include a purely executory exchange of promises in which there had been no formalities and no part performance. Roman law, having inherited the tendency of primitive societies to

---

[2]See the discussion of credit as not seen as involving promise in §1.3 *supra*.

10

view each type of transaction as a distinct complex of rights, never fully rid itself of this proclivity. The development of such a general basis for enforcing promises — the foundation of a general theory of contract — was therefore left to the great modern legal systems that arose in Europe during the Middle Ages: the common law system that grew up in England and the civil law systems that emerged on the European continent.[3]

How did the common law cope with this challenge?

§1.5.   **The Enforcement of Promises in Early English Law.**   Curiously, the common law began at a less advanced stage than that attained by Roman law. Although Roman law notions of contract were known in England, their influence there faded with the breakup of the Roman political system. English courts painfully had to reconstruct contract law during the Middle Ages. That they succeeded in doing so was all the more remarkable in view of the fact that, when they began, the English law of contracts was little more advanced than that of many primitive societies. "Surely," an American scholar wrote, "it would be hard to find a better illustration of the flexibility and power of self-development of the Common Law."[1]

    Beginnings of English contract law

No legal system has ever been reckless enough to make all promises enforceable. As a legal philosopher expressed it, some freedom to change one's mind is essential "for free intercourse between those who lack omniscience," and most of us "would shudder at the idea of being bound by every promise, no matter how foolish, without any chance of letting increased wisdom undo past foolishness."[2] In framing a basis for enforcing promises, however, one can approach the goal from two opposite extremes. One can begin with the assumption that promises are generally enforceable, and then create exceptions for promises considered undesirable to enforce. Or one can begin with the assumption that promises are generally unenforceable, and then create exceptions for promises thought desirable to enforce.

    Two possible assumptions

The common law courts chose this latter assumption, the same as that of Roman law: a mere promise does not give rise to an action. Their choice was scarcely surprising. It accorded well with the procedural niceties of common law courts, where recovery was not to be had unless the claim could be fitted within one of the established forms of action, and it suited the status-oriented society of the Middle Ages, which was anything but conducive to the flowering of promise. Furthermore, no great pressure existed for enforceability of promises, because contracts were not yet a significant part of the business of the common law courts. At the end of the twelfth century, a writer apologized

    Assumption of the common law courts

---

[3]On its development in civil law systems, *see* H. Kötz, European Contract Law (1997); F. Lawson, A Common Lawyer Looks at the Civil Law ch. 4 (1977).

§1.5   [1]Ames, The History of Assumpsit, 2 Harv. L. Rev. 252, 260 (1888).

[2]Cohen, The Basis of Contract, 46 Harv. L. Rev. 553, 573 (1932). As to why a promisor might want to be bound by a promise, *see* E. Farnsworth, Changing Your Mind ch. 1 (1998).

for the scant treatment of the subject in his treatise on English common law with the remark that "it is not the custom of the court of the lord king to protect private agreements, nor does it even concern itself with such contracts as can be considered to be like private agreements."[3]

Other courts more hospitable to promises

Competing jurisdictions, however, were more hospitable to actions for breach of promise. Under the law merchant (the body of rules then applied in the commercial courts), the courts in the medieval fairs and markets entertained actions, as commerce required, on promises made by merchants. Under canon law, the Church courts regarded a sworn promise (by which one pledged one's "faith," i.e., one's hope of salvation) as enforceable and its breach as a sin subject to ecclesiastical censures, including excommunication, and there was support for the position that even an unsworn promise was sacred and therefore enforceable.[4] And in equity, the Chancellor held that because a man was "damaged by the non-performance of the promise, he shall have a remedy."[5]

Success of common law courts

The general theory for enforcing promises that was ultimately fashioned by the common law courts succeeded less on its intrinsic merits than as an incident of the victories of those courts in their struggles to expand their own jurisdiction at the expense of their rivals. These victories were complete by the close of the sixteenth century. By that time the common law courts had so far succeeded in wresting jurisdiction from the commercial courts as to stifle the law merchant's practice of enforcing promises made by merchants in commerce. Although the Church courts had continued to enforce promises in the face of the prohibition of the Constitution of Clarendon of 1164, this business also dried up in the sixteenth century when the common law courts provided a forum for such causes.[6] And since, in equity, the Chancellor often intervened if he found the common law to be wanting, it is a tribute to the ingenuity and flexibility of the common law judges that they succeeded in moving fast enough to stay the Chancellor's hand. Credit for the development of the general basis for enforcing promises that we know today is therefore theirs and theirs alone.

Necessity of working within forms of action

The challenge faced and met by the common law courts in the fifteenth and sixteenth centuries was to develop a general basis for enforcing promises within the framework of the forms of action.[7] This they did, first by developing

[3]R. de Glanville, Treatise on the Laws and Customs of the Realm of England bk. 10, ch. 18 (G. Hall ed. 1965); *see also* bk. 10, ch. 8.

[4]Farnsworth, Parables About Promises: Religious Ethics and Contract Enforceability, 71 Fordham L. Rev. 695 (2002).

[5]Anon., Y.B. Pasch. 8 Edw. 4, fo. 4, pl. 11 (1468) (1640 ed.); C. Fifoot, History and Sources of the Common Law: Tort and Contract 304 (1949) (suit on promise to pay for services brought after performance). *Cf.* The Complete Works of Geoffrey Chaucer 537 (F. Robinson ed. 2d ed. 1957) ("Sometyme the world was so stedfast and stable that mannes word was obligacioun.").

[6]*See* Helmholz, Assumpsit and *Fidei Laesio*, 91 L.Q. Rev. 406 (1975).

[7]Under the formulary system, a plaintiff who sought relief in the common law courts had to state a case in accordance with one of a limited number of standard forms. According to Maitland's memorable description, "English law knows a certain number of forms of action, each with its

exceptions as the Romans had done, and then by fashioning those exceptions into something that the Romans had never achieved: a general basis for enforcing promises, including purely executory exchanges of promises. How was this brought about?

One possible vehicle for the development of a general basis for enforcing promises might have been a formal acknowledgment of liability, such as that on which the Roman stipulation was based. The common law action known as covenant that grew up in England near the end of the twelfth century became associated with such a formal acknowledgment in the form of a wax seal. Had the trend then been toward the relaxation of formalities, the action of covenant might have developed into a general contractual remedy. This possibility was foreclosed, however, by the middle of the fourteenth century, when it became settled that the seal was not merely evidentiary and therefore unless the plaintiff produced a writing under seal an action of covenant could not be maintained. With this turn of events, any hope that covenant might serve as a general ground for contractual liability vanished, since a sealed writing was little better suited to an informal exchange of promises than the Roman stipulation had been.

Unsuitability of action of covenant as general basis

Another possible avenue of evolution was through the concept of loan, which we have seen was familiar to most primitive societies. By the end of the twelfth century, this concept had given rise to the common law action known as *debt*, which would lie to recover a sum certain in money. But the defendant's liability in debt was not seen as based on a mere promise. It depended instead on the debtor's receipt of what the debtor had asked for — called a *quid pro quo* in imitation of the Romans — in the form of the loan. It was therefore thought to be unjust to allow the debtor to retain it without paying for it. The debtor's wrong was more in the nature of misfeasance than of nonfeasance.[8] Following this rationale, courts finally broadened the action of debt to allow recovery by anyone who had conferred a substantial benefit on the defendant, including one who had furnished personal services.

Development of action of debt

Suppose that an owner paid a builder $10,000 in return for the builder's promise to do specified work on the owner's house. If the builder failed to do the work, the action of debt was adequate to allow the owner to recover from the

Example of action of debt

---

own uncouth name. . . . The choice is not merely a choice between a number of queer technical terms, it is a choice between methods of procedure adapted to cases of different kinds. . . . The forms of action we have buried, but they still rule us from their graves." F. Maitland, The Forms of Action at Common Law 2 (1962).

[8]Scholars disagree over whether the action of debt was conceived of as proprietary in nature (*i.e.*, as founded on what the creditor *owned*, rather than on what the debtor *owed*). See the discussion of credit not being seen as involving promise in §1.3 *supra. See also* the critical discussion in A. Simpson, History of the Common Law of Contract 75-80 (1987). It seems clear, however, that it was based on notions of unjust enrichment, rather than of obligation arising out of mere promise.

builder. Since the promisor, the builder, had received a benefit in the amount of $10,000, recovery prevented the unjust enrichment of the promisor.[9]

Unsuitability of action of debt as general basis

But it was clear that, for there to be a *quid pro quo*, the benefit must have been actually conferred — a mere promise to confer it would not suffice. Therefore the action of debt was no better suited than were the innominate contracts of Roman law to the enforcement of a mere exchange of promises, such as a promise to deliver apples in the future in return for a promise to pay the price in the future. Moreover, the action of debt was subject to the further inconvenience — difficult for the modern mind to comprehend — that the defendant might avoid liability by a procedure known as "wager of law," in which the defendant denied the debt under oath accompanied by a number (usually 11) of oath-helpers, who swore that the defendant was telling the truth.

How was the common law to break out of this mold?

Availability of action of assumpsit for misfeasance

§1.6.   The Development of a General Basis for Enforcing Promises. The common law courts found the answer to this question in the law of torts. They had already recognized that liability in tort arose when a person undertook to perform a duty and then performed it in such a way as to cause harm to the obligee. The obligee could sue on the variety of the common law action of "trespass on the case" that came to be known as *assumpsit* (from the Latin, meaning that the defendant undertook). At the beginning of the fifteenth century it was available only if there had been misfeasance in the performance of the undertaking.

Example of action of assumpsit

This example was given in 1436: "If a carpenter makes a [promise to] me to make me a house good and strong and of a certain form, and he makes me a house which is weak and bad and of another form, I shall have an action of trespass on my case."[1] Such a case of misfeasance cried out for recovery. The promisee, who was left with a worthless house, had been harmed by relying on the promise. Justice could be done by requiring the promisor to pay compensation in an amount sufficient to put the promisee in as good a position as the promisee would have been in had the promise never been made. The promisee's claim to recovery based on the reliance interest was less compelling than that based on the restitution interest, since the reliance interest did not depend on any benefit received by the promisor (i.e., it was not founded on the concept of unjust enrichment). Nevertheless, the promisee's right to recovery seemed clear on principles developed in tort cases.

Extension of assumpsit to cases of nonfeasance

But might not a remedy lie when there had merely been nonfeasance, a failure by the promisor to perform the undertaking? At first the answer was no.

---

[9]The amount of recovery in debt at common law was not, however, limited to the value of the benefit conferred, but could be any definite amount of money or goods that the debtor had promised to pay. Ames, Parol Contracts Prior to Assumpsit, 8 Harv. L. Rev. 252, 260 (1894).

§1.6   [1]Y.B. 14 Hy. 6 [1679 ed.], p. 18, pl. 58 (1436), 3 W. Holdsworth, History of English Law 430 (4th ed. 1935).

In 1409 it was said: "Certainly it would lie [if the carpenter had built the house badly], because he would then answer for the wrong which he had done, but when a man makes a [promise] and does nothing under that [promise], how can you have an action against him without a [writing under seal]?"[2] Nevertheless, by the second half of the fifteenth century there was a growing inclination among common law judges, conscious of their rival jurisdictions, to make a major extension in the action of assumpsit by enforcing such promises, even where there had been only nonfeasance. But some limits had to be placed on which promises would be enforced, for the judges were not about to allow "that one shall have trespass for any breach of covenant in the world."[3] The courts were therefore forced to find a test to distinguish instances in which nonfeasance was actionable from those in which it was not.

Since the misfeasance cases that had originally given rise to the action in assumpsit were characterized by a detriment incurred by the promisee in reliance on the promise, it was natural to formulate an analogous test and to allow enforcement if the promisee had changed position on the faith of the promise and had been consequently damaged by its nonperformance. Doing nothing can make things worse.[4] Suppose, for instance, that a builder promised to do specified work on an owner's house in return for the owner's promise to pay the builder $10,000 on its completion, and, in reliance on the builder's promise, the owner rented and moved to another house to permit the builder to do the work. If the builder failed to do the work, the law could justify protecting the owner because of the detriment sustained. To the extent that the promisee incurred expenses in preparing to perform or suffered loss by forgoing other opportunities, a broken promise resulted in waste. Because the loss was purely economic, as contrasted with cases of misfeasance that had resulted in loss to person or property, the claim to recovery may have seemed less compelling. But in a society that depended on promises for cooperation, there was reason to protect those who relied on promises by placing the cost of that waste on those who broke them.

Requirement of reliance in cases of nonfeasance

This first major extension of the action of assumpsit fell short, however, of recognizing claims based on purely executory exchanges of promises, in which the claimant had not relied at all. As the sixteenth century drew to a close, the common law courts made a second and dramatic extension of the action of

Extension of assumpsit to executory exchanges of promises

[2]Y.B. Mich. 11 Hy. 4 [1605 ed.], p. 33, pl. 60 (1409), 3 W. Holdsworth, History of English Law 433-34 (4th ed. 1935).

[3]Y.B. Hil. 3 Hy. 6 [1679 ed.], p. 36, pl. 33 (1425), 3 W. Holdsworth, History of English Law 435 (4th ed. 1935).

[4]In 1499, Fyneux, C.J., said that "if a man covenants to build me a house by such a day, and he does nothing towards it, I shall have an action on my case upon this nonfeasance as well as if he had done it badly." For an example in addition to that given in the text, suppose that a builder promised to repair an owner's barn by December 1 and, when this was not done, the owner's livestock died from cold weather.

assumpsit by allowing such claims. It was held that even if one had given only a promise in exchange for the other's promise, one had nonetheless suffered a detriment by having one's freedom of action fettered: one was in turn bound by one's own promise. Suppose again that the builder promised to do specified work on the owner's house and, in return, the owner promised to pay the builder $10,000. On this reasoning, if the builder repudiated the bargain before the owner had done anything in reliance on the builder's promise, the owner had a claim for breach of contract. The reasoning is, of course, circular, since the conclusion that there was a detriment to the promisee, in this case the owner, assumed that the promisee was in turn bound by a promise, even though nothing but a promise had been given for it. Nevertheless, by the end of the sixteenth century the common law courts were enforcing exchanges of promises where no performance had been rendered on either side.[5]

Protection of expectation

This extension of the action of assumpsit had important implications for the measure of recovery in damages for nonperformance of a promise. Because the promisee had neither conferred a benefit upon the promisor nor incurred any detriment in reliance on the promisor's promise, recovery could not be measured by either benefit or detriment. Almost inevitably, courts protected the promisee by requiring the promisor to compensate the promisee for the promisee's disappointed expectation, that is to say, for the advantages that the promisee would have received had the promise been performed.[6]

Rationale for protecting expectation

Why, merely because the parties have exchanged promises, should the law protect one party's ephemeral expectation if the other repudiates before there has been any actual reliance on its promise? It has been contended that this protection of expectation has "a quasi-criminal aspect, its purpose being not so much to compensate the promisee as to penalize breach of promise by the promisor."[7] One explanation is that it is justified as the most effective way of

---

[5] Strangborough v. Warner, 74 Eng. Rep. 686 (K.B. 1588). That the American law of contract had not reached this stage as late as the eighteenth century, *see* Horwitz, The Historical Foundations of Modern Contract Law, 87 Harv. L. Rev. 917, 929-30 (1974), reprinted in M. Horwitz, The Transformation of American Law, 1780-1860, at 169 (1977) (explaining that in the eighteenth century "some American courts did not enforce executory contracts where there had been no part performance" and explaining that "pressure to enforce such contracts would not be great in a pre-market economy where contracts for future delivery were rare"). For criticism of this analysis, *see* Simpson, The Horwitz Thesis and the History of Contracts, 46 U. Chi. L. Rev. 533 (1979).

[6] Of course, at a much earlier date, disappointed expectations were protected in the absence of either benefit or detriment through the action of covenant. See the discussion of the unsuitability of covenant as a general basis in §1.5 *supra*.

[7] Fuller & Perdue, The Reliance Interest in Contract Damages (pt. 1), 46 Yale L.J. 52, 61 (1936). As the authors point out, "the force of argument will depend entirely upon the existing economic environment. It would be most forceful in a hypothetical society in which all values were available on the market and where all markets were 'perfect' in the economic sense. In such a society there would be no difference between the reliance interest and the expectation interest. The plaintiff's loss in foregoing to enter another contract would be identical with the expectation value of the contract he did make. The argument that granting the value of the expectancy merely compensates for that loss, loses force to the extent that actual conditions depart from those of such

16

protecting reliance. Unless agreements can be relied upon, they are of little use. A rule of law that only protected a promisee who had actually relied upon a promise would, in practice, tend to discourage reliance. The difficulties in proving and valuing reliance are such that a person in business would hesitate to rely on a promise if the legal sanction were important to him. These difficulties are especially acute when a party has relied by forgoing other opportunities, as in the case of the buyer who contracts with a seller for the future delivery of apples and who would have made arrangements to get them from another source had the seller not promised to deliver them. "To encourage reliance we must . . . dispense with its proof." Promises must be enforceable without regard to a showing of reliance "both in the sense that in some cases the promise is enforced although not relied upon . . . and in the sense that recovery is not limited to the detriment incurred in reliance."[8] The extension of the action of assumpsit to include the mere exchange of promise can be rationalized in this way. The result probably accords with the sense of justice of the average person in business.[9]

The action of assumpsit was still subject to one important restriction. It had been held that where the action of debt was available, the action of assumpsit was not. This proved a disadvantage to creditors, since in assumpsit the plaintiff was entitled to a jury trial, while in debt the defendant could resort to wager of law. The next important step in the common law's development of a law of contract was therefore to permit assumpsit to supplant debt. By the middle of the sixteenth century, it had been recognized that an action in assumpsit could be brought against a defendant who, being already indebted (*indebitatus*), expressly undertook (*assumpsit*) to pay a particular sum. This action in *indebitatus assumpsit* was also described as "general assumpsit," to distinguish it from the older action of "assumpsit," which was known as "special assumpsit" because of the specifics that had to be pleaded.[10] (Only special and not general assumpsit could be used for the enforcement of a purely executory contract, in which there had been an exchange of promises but no performance on either side.) Toward the end of the century, it began to be held that a debt alone, without a subsequent express promise, would support such an action of general assumpsit. The final triumph of this view came at the beginning of the seventeenth century in *Slade's Case*, in which the plaintiff sued for the price of a crop sold and delivered to the defendant. On a jury finding that "there was no

Supplanting of debt by indebitatus (general) assumpsit

---

a hypothetical society." *Id.* at 62. For a development of this analysis, *see* E. Farnsworth, Changing Your Mind ch. 6 (1998).

[8] 46 Yale L.J. at 62.

[9] *See* Weintraub, A Survey of Contract Practice and Policy, 1992 Wis. L. Rev. 1, 30-35.

[10] In *indebitatus assumpsit*, the plaintiff could state the origin of the debt in general terms, followed by a statement that, being indebted, the defendant promised to pay. This general statement of the source of the debt was the beginning of what later came to be known as the common counts of general assumpsit. *See* the discussion of the meaning of *quasi-contract* and *restitution* in §2.20 *infra*.

other promise or assumption, but only the said bargain," it was decided by all of the common law judges assembled to pass upon this important matter that every such bargain "imports in itself an assumpsit."[11] The creditor could sue in assumpsit as an alternative to debt, even though there was no subsequent promise. The creditor was at last assured of the benefits of jury trial in place of wager of law.

Use of term *consideration*

Over the course of the fifteenth and sixteenth centuries, the common law courts thus had succeeded in developing the action of assumpsit into a general basis for enforcing promises, including purely executory exchanges of promises. During the sixteenth century, the word *consideration*, which had earlier been used without technical significance, came to be used as a word of art to express the sum of the conditions necessary for an action in assumpsit to lie. It was therefore a tautology that a promise, at least if not under seal, was enforceable only if there was *consideration*, for this was to say no more than that it was enforceable only under those circumstances in which the action of assumpsit was allowed. In this way, however, the word *consideration* came to be applied to the test of enforceability of a promise and to be used to distinguish those promises that in the eyes of the common law were of sufficient significance to society to justify the legal sanctions of assumpsit for their enforcement.

Elements of consideration

It was, not surprisingly, neither a simple nor a logical test. Bound up in it were several elements. Most importantly, from the *quid pro quo* of debt, by way of the later extension of general assumpsit, came the notion that there must be a benefit to the promisor. From the reliance of special assumpsit came the notion that there must be a detriment to the promisee.

Acceptance of doctrine of consideration

The requirement of such an exchange found easy acceptance in a society entering a commercial age. The doctrine of consideration took care of the bulk of economically vital commercial agreements, even if it afforded no ground for the enforceability of gratuitous promises, for which nothing was given in exchange. "The large commercial interests of the new age sought a general sanction not for charitable gifts but for business enterprise. In such an environment it is not surprising that the judges should have required some material inducement to the defendant's undertaking."[12]

Doctrine of consideration as product of history

As a cornerstone for the law of contract, the doctrine of consideration has been widely criticized. It would be foolhardy to attempt to defend it by an exercise in logic, for it must be viewed in the light of its history and of the society that produced it. Nevertheless, in view of the difficulty that other societies have had in developing a general basis for enforcing promises, it is perhaps less

---

[11] Slade's Case, 76 Eng. Rep. 1074, 1077 (K.B. 1602). This landmark decision was handed down by all the judges of the central courts assembled in a special chamber, after argument by Sir Edward Coke, then Attorney General, for the plaintiff, and Sir Francis Bacon, Coke's bitter rival, for the defendant.

[12] C. Fifoot, History and Sources of the Common Law: Tort and Contract 399 (1949).

remarkable that the basis developed by the common law is logically flawed than that the common law succeeded in developing any basis at all.

Since contract law was still in its infancy when *Slade's Case* was decided at the start of the seventeenth century, we look briefly at the course of contract law over the ensuing four centuries.

§1.7. **Contract into the Twenty-first Century.** In 1861 Sir Henry Maine assured himself of immortality by declaring that "the movement of the progressive societies has hitherto been a movement *from Status to Contract*."[1] However, the development of the doctrine of consideration as a general basis for enforcing promises did not of itself give contract law any special impetus. True, the seventeenth and eighteenth centuries saw the recognition of the transferability of contract rights as a kind of property,[2] the enactment of legislation requiring a writing for some kinds of contracts,[3] and the shaping of the concept of the dependency of promises.[4] But the movement toward contract was a slow one for two centuries.

Slow growth for two centuries

It was not until the nineteenth century that economic conditions led contract law to its apogee, as the legal underpinning of a dynamic and expanding free enterprise system. One modern legal historian concluded that in America the years from 1800 to 1875 were, "above all else, the years of contract,"[5] and another called the nineteenth century "the golden age of the law of contract."[6] Contract expressed "energetic self-interest," and the law that governed it expressed "the nature of contract by insisting that men assert their interests, push them, and fight for them, if they were to have the help of the state."[7]

Contract reached a zenith in nineteenth century

It was generally supposed during this period that, as Adam Smith had proclaimed, freedom of contract—freedom to make enforceable bargains—would encourage individual entrepreneurial activity.[8] Lawmaking devoted much energy to creating the conditions for a market on which such bargains could be made. By the end of the century, the bargain test of consideration

Freedom of contract as supporting the market

---

§1.7 [1] H. Maine, Ancient Law 170 (1861).

[2] On the history of the assignability of contract rights, see §11.2 *infra*.

[3] On the enactment of the Statute of Frauds, see §6.1 *infra*.

[4] See the discussion of *Kingston v. Preston* in §8.9 *infra*.

[5] J. Hurst, Law and the Conditions of Freedom in the Nineteenth Century United States 18 (1956).

[6] L. Friedman, History of American Law 275 (2d ed. 1985) (adding that as late as Blackstone (1765), "contract occupied only a tiny corner of the temple of common law," so that "Blackstone devoted a whole volume to land law, but a few pages at most to informal, freely negotiated bargains").

[7] J. Hurst, Law and Economic Growth 301 (1964).

[8] See the discussion of Adam Smith on exchange in §1.2 *supra*. *Autonomy of the parties* is now a common substitute for the more traditional *freedom of contract*.

had taken shape and the objective theory of contract was in its ascendancy.[9] "The market took on legal definition mainly in the law of contract, and quite naturally in the temper of the time the law of contract dominated the nineteenth-century legal order."[10] From a utilitarian point of view, freedom to contract maximizes the welfare of the parties and therefore the good of society as a whole. From a libertarian point of view, it accords to individuals a sphere of influence in which they can act freely.

Reversal of trend toward freedom of contract

But, though contract provided opportunities for the realization of human wants, it did not shape those wants. "The cautious sense that contract alone was not a sufficient organizing principle for society never quite deserted us."[11] With the advent of the twentieth century, the tide in favor of freedom of contract began to be reversed. A contracts scholar characterized the individualism of our rules of contract law, epitomized in the notion of freedom of contract, as "closely tied up with the ethics of free enterprise capitalism and the ideals of justice of a mobile society of small enterprisers, individual merchants and independent craftsmen." As competitive capitalism has drifted toward monopoly and the free enterprise system has declined, "the meaning of contract has changed radically."[12] It was suggested that "the question is not so much one of status and contract as it is of a broader classification that embraces these concepts: standardized relations and individualized relations" and that in this sense there is now a "distinct veering back to status."[13]

Relation to ownership

Other changes accompanied this standardization of relations, which was caused, at least in part, by a concentration of private power. Some of the decline in the importance of contract in achieving social purposes resulted from a diminution in the extent to which society's material resources are subject to the control of private individuals. In a country with a centrally planned economy, such as that of the former Soviet Union, a substantial part of productive wealth is in theory owned by society as a whole, and the right to own property may be limited largely to goods for consumption. Even in a free-market economy, possibilities for private ownership are limited. To the extent that state ownership of a society's resources comes to replace private ownership,

---

[9]The bargain test of consideration is discussed in §2.2 *infra*. As to the objective theory, *see* the discussions of the objective theory in §3.6 *infra*, dealing with assent, and of the objectivist solution in §7.9 *infra*, dealing with interpretation.

[10]J. Hurst, Law and Economic Growth 285 (1964).

[11]Id. at 76.

[12]Kessler, Contracts of Adhesion — Some Thoughts About Freedom of Contract, 43 Colum. L. Rev. 629, 640 (1943). Furthermore, as Fuller and Perdue pointed out, "The enormous growth of the corporation . . . has meant a further decrease in the importance of contract as an organizing force, since the corporation and vertical integration tend to substitute for an organization resting on contract one resting on the relation of superior and inferior." Fuller & Perdue, The Reliance Interest in Contract Damages (pt. 1), 46 Yale L.J. 52, 63 n.13 (1936).

[13]Isaacs, The Standardizing of Contracts, 27 Yale L.J. 34, 39-40 (1917). *See generally* P. Atiyah, The Rise and Fall of Freedom of Contract (1979).

the individual's power to dispose of those resources is lessened, and the role of contract is diminished.[14]

Even without assuming ownership of resources, a society may severely restrict the individual's freedom to contract. It may dictate all of the terms of the contract, as many of our states have done for fire insurance and as the federal government has done for ocean bills of lading. Short of wholesale dictation of terms, the state may stipulate particular terms with the balance left to agreement, as has been done with life, accident, and health insurance; or it may merely prohibit or refuse to enforce particular terms, as in the case of laws fixing minimum wages or maximum interest rates. By methods such as these, entire industries, such as communications, transportation, banking, and insurance, have been brought under regulation. At the very least, the state may strive to ensure that those who are engaged in activities, such as the sale of goods, where there is relatively little governmental intervention do in fact bargain in acceptable ways and are not so powerful as to substitute coercion for bargain. To this end it may, for example, prohibit undesirable trade practices and limit the concentration of economic power.

Other limitations on freedom of contract

Most of these changes have come from legislatures rather than from courts. Legislation has sometimes given rise to special fields of law — separate and distinct from the general law of contract, which has traditionally been thought to govern agreements to furnish goods, money, land, or services. Thus the collective bargaining agreement is regarded as within the separate province of labor law, and the insurance policy is seen as within the separate province of insurance law. Even the contract for the sale of goods is often viewed as within the separate province of commercial, rather than contract, law. These special fields have been delineated from an amorphous residue developed largely through judicial decisions, the dominant primary source of general contract law. It is with this primary source and its evolution during the twentieth century that this treatise is largely concerned. But the shape of modern contract law is due in good part to the scholars whose treatises and other writings brought order out of the growing mass of cases.

General contract law and special fields

As the twentieth century drew to a close, those scholars drew attention to the increasing significance of the borderline between contract law — the law that concerns planning for the future — and tort law — the law that imposes liability to remedy wrongful violations of recognized interests.[15] Four examples are particularly worthy of attention. First, there has been an enhanced recognition

Borderline of contract and tort

---

[14]Such limitations vary from one country to the next. In Germany, the family of Thurn und Taxis became one of the most powerful in Europe through the private ownership of a postal system, an opportunity that would have been unavailable in the United States, where the postal system has always been public. 1 R. Ely, Property and Contract in Their Relations to the Distribution of Wealth 80-83 (1922).

[15]*See* Speidel, The Borderland of Contract, 10 N. Ky. L. Rev. 163 (1983).

of reliance on a promise as a basis for legal rights.[16] Second, there has been pressure to grant punitive damages in cases of breach of contract, pressure that is frequently rationalized on the ground that what is involved is not merely a breach of contract but also a tort.[17] Third, there has been an expanded awareness of the possibility of claims based on tortious interference with contractual relations, an awareness that has often led a party aggrieved by breach of contract to assert a tort claim against a third person as well as a contract claim against the other party.[18] Fourth, there has been an enhanced sensitivity to the possibility of claims by third persons against contracting parties, a sensitivity that has often led a third person aggrieved by a breach of contract to assert a claim based in tort as well as a claim as a contract beneficiary against the party in breach.[19]

Questions for twenty-first century

Further developments on all of these fronts can be expected in the twenty-first century. Here are three troublesome questions that they raise for the future of contract law. Will contract law maintain its integrity? Will it maintain its autonomy? Will it maintain its unity?

Integrity of contract law

Will contract law maintain its integrity? Samuel Williston echoed the views of many contract scholars of the nineteenth and early twentieth centuries when he wrote in the preface to his 1920 treatise that he aspired "to treat the subject of contracts as a whole, and to show the wide range of application of its principles."[20] Over the ensuing decades, however, some academics came to find Williston's imperialistic view of contract law unfashionable. In a dramatic — and dramatically premature — proclamation of "the death of contract," Professor Grant Gilmore reported that contract law was being reduced to a mere shadow of its former self because contract was "being reabsorbed into the mainstream of 'tort.'"[21] As pointed out above, the traditional borderline between contract and tort has come under increasing scrutiny in many contexts. But though attention will continue to be focused on the borderline, courts have become disenchanted with efforts to expand the boundaries of tort by extending the doctrine of "bad faith breach" beyond insurance contracts.[22] There is good reason to favor voluntary allocation of risks through contract over retroactive imposition of liability for tortious conduct.[23] Indeed, New York's highest court

---

[16] See §§2.19, 6.12 *infra*.

[17] See the discussion of departures from the rule in §12.8 *infra*.

[18] This topic is not dealt with in detail in this treatise. See footnote to the discussion of how economic analysis accords with the law's assumptions in §12.3 *infra*.

[19] See the discussion of analogous questions in §10.1 *infra*.

[20] S. Williston, The Law of Contracts iii (1920).

[21] G. Gilmore, The Death of Contract 87 (1974).

[22] See the discussion of the fall of bad faith breach in §12.8 *infra*.

[23] *See* R. Posner, Law and Legal Theory in England and America 95 (1996), reporting that a private rating of the risk of the nonenforceability of contracts placed the United States second best, after Switzerland and tied with the United Kingdom, with Iran, Venezuela, and Vietnam at the bottom.

has suggested that, at least as far as actions for breach of an express warranty are concerned, it is *tort* that is being absorbed into the mainstream of contract.

> This view of "reliance"—i.e., as requiring no more than reliance on the express warranty as being a part of the bargain between the parties—reflects the prevailing perception of an action for breach of express warranty that is no longer grounded in tort, but essentially in contract. . . . The express warranty is as much a part of the contract as any other term.[24]

There is little reason to suppose that contract law will cede any significant part of its present terrain to tort law during the twenty-first century.

Second, will contract law maintain its autonomy? Even if it maintains its integrity despite threatened incursions by the law of torts, it may lose its autonomy due to the infusion of alien influences. One of the most powerful of these influences has been that of economics. Contract law has proved fertile ground for the law and economics movement in the United States, which beginning with the analysis of the law of contract remedies has moved on to the examination of default rules.[25] The movement's impact on the courts and on practicing lawyers has fallen far short of its impact among academics, but this is likely to change, and for the better, as the new century progresses.[26] A different kind of alien influence comes from international unification. Since 1988 the United Nations Convention on Contracts for the International Sale of Goods has been in effect in the United States for international sales contracts.[27] In 1994 the Convention was joined by the UNIDROIT Principles of International Commercial Contracts, which has only the force of a restatement but has already been influential in international arbitrations.[28] Surely the body of American contract law will not be immune to these influences from abroad. But American contract law has never been truly autonomous, witness the influence of English law and through it of such civil law scholars as Pothier,[29] and it will doubtless benefit from them in the future as it has in the past.

Autonomy of contract law

---

[24]CBS Inc. v. Ziff Davis Publishing Co., 553 N.E.2d 997, 1001 (N.Y. 1990).

[25]See the discussion of the point that most contract rules are default rules in §1.10 *infra*.

[26]The enormous impact of the movement among scholars is evidenced by the fact that the most cited article in law journals is neither an article by a jurist nor one about law, but an article on economics by Nobel prize winner Ronald Coase. Coase, The Problem of Social Cost, 3 J.L. & Econ. 1 (1960). *See* E. Posner, Economic Analysis of Contract Law After Three Decades: Success or Failure?, 112 Yale L.J. 829 (2003), with responses by Ayres and Craswell; Symposium on Trends in Legal Citations and Scholarship, 71 Chicago-Kent L. Rev. 743 (1996). As to the lesser impact on courts, *see* Farnsworth, Law Is a Sometime Autonomous Thing, 21 Harv. J.L. & Pub. Poly. 95 (1998). See also the discussion of law and economics in §1.8 *infra*.

[27]See the discussion of the Vienna Convention in §1.9 *infra*.

[28]See the discussion of the UNIDROIT Principles in §1.8 *infra*.

[29]Pothier's Treatise on the Law of Obligations was translated into English in 1806 and was relied on by the Court of King's Bench in Taylor v. Caldwell, 122 Eng. Rep. 309 (1863). See the discussion of *Taylor v. Caldwell* in §9.5 *infra*.

Unity of contract law

Third, will contract law maintain its unity? More than three decades ago, a legal historian cited the growth of special fields of law described above in contrasting the role of contract in the nineteenth and twentieth centuries. He referred to "the rise and fall of contract," characterizing "pure" contract doctrine as "blind to details of subject matter and person" and suggesting that breadth of the subject was being whittled away by such specialized branches as consumer law, insurance law, and sale of goods law.[30] Will we come in the twenty-first century to speak of the law of contracts as we do of torts? This seems unlikely. In recent decades the generality of contract law has shown a surprising vitality, sometimes not undermined but reenforced by special fields. Thus many of the Uniform Commercial Code's specialized rules for the sale of goods, extended by analogy, found a place in the Restatement (Second) of Contracts and have been accepted by the courts as rules of general contract law.[31] Even though the possibility of fragmentation has been enhanced by the addition of a new article on leases, it seems unlikely that what we know as contract law will vanish in a flurry of fragmentation. One heartening development is that the requirement of good faith is being made consistent — or almost consistent — throughout the Code.[32]

Other questions

Other, more specific, questions might be asked. For example, what of encroachments by paternalism and public policy on the hallowed tenet of party autonomy?[33] What of the tension between form and substance?[34] What of such evolving fields as precontractual liability[35] and employment agreements?[36] And what of the impact of technological developments? Such questions will be addressed in later chapters, but a few words on electronic commerce will be useful here.

Electronic commerce

By the end of the twentieth century, electronic commerce was in widespread use, and the communication of information between computers in standardized formats had come to be known as electronic data interchange (EDI).[37] If,

---

[30] L. Friedman, Contract Law in America 20-21 (1965). With the arrival of Article 2A of the Uniform Commercial Code, lease law could be added.

[31] See the discussion of reasoning from the Code by analogy in §1.10 *infra*.

[32] Article 1 now contains a definition that applies to all of the Code Articles except Article 5, Letters of Credit. UCC 1-201(20). Article 5 remains out of step, adhering to a purely subjective standard of "honesty in fact." UCC 5-102(7).

[33] As to paternalism, see §4.28 (unconscionability) *infra*. As to public policy see §5.1 (public policy as a ground for unenforceability) *infra*.

[34] As to form, see §2.11 (peppercorns and the pretense of bargain), §2.16 (form: the seal), §6.1 (history and functions of the statute of frauds). As to substance, see §2.19 (reliance as a ground for recovery: promissory estoppel), §6.12 (reliance and the statute of frauds) *infra*.

[35] See §3.8 (intention not to be bound until later writing), §3.28 (precontractual liability).

[36] See the discussions of the example of at-will employment in §2.10 *infra* and of the employment cases in §7.17 *infra*.

[37] A broader definition of the term does not limit it to information in a standardized format and includes, for example, electronic mail. *See generally* B. Wright & J. Winn, The Law of Electronic Commerce (4th ed. looseleaf).

as often happens, EDI is used between regular trading partners, they can agree on rules to govern their EDI transmissions, and model agreements have been prepared for this purpose. These will not, however, obviate the need for more generally applicable rules in the form of legislation to deal with the problems raised by electronic commerce.[38] An initial step is to make sure that electronic contracting is not denied effect because of its form. The Uniform Electronic Transactions Act (UETA), promulgated in 1999 and adopted by most states, does this by providing that electronic signatures and records are not to be denied validity solely because they are electronic. A similar federal statute, the Electronic Signatures in Global and National Commerce Act, enacted in 2000 and known as "E-Sign," borrows significant provisions of UETA and preempts state laws on electronic authentication unless a state has adopted UETA in its recommended form.[39] Neither statute affects substantive contract law. Revised Article 2 of the Uniform Commercial Code takes advantage of the E-Sign provision that permits state laws, subject to some restrictions, to modify, limit, or supersede its provisions.[40] Some of the provisions of revised Articles 1 and 2 mimic E-Sign and UETA in order to promote harmonization and simplify advising.[41]

Because electronic commerce lacks the traditional indications of authenticity and integrity, such as a letterhead and a handwritten signature, an important practical problem is to devise a system to identify the sender of a message and to indicate that the message has not been altered.[42] A common solution to this problem involves a digital signature using two mathematically related cryptographic keys, one private and one public. The sender uses its private key to add to the message a digital signature in the form of data that is mathematically related to the contents of the message. The recipient uses the sender's public key not only to verify the authenticity of the message but also to determine that its contents have not been altered. The security of the system requires a legally recognized authority that can issue certificates to verify the authenticity and integrity of the message. Most states now have laws dealing with digital signatures.[43] In addition to these problems of authenticity and integrity, electronic commerce raises more traditional problems concerning the time that communications take effect and the requirement of a writing, which are dealt

Obviate = Prevent

Authentication

---

[38] For international initiatives, *see* UNCITRAL Model Law on Electronic Signatures (2001) (creating framework to give legal validity to electronic signatures); UNCITRAL Model Law for Electronic Commerce (1996) (dealing with such matters as formal legal requirements, attribution of messages, and time and place at which they take effect).

[39] 15 U.S.C. §§ 7001 et seq.

[40] UCC-R 2-108(4) (with stated exceptions, revised Article 2 "modifies, limits, and supersedes" E-Sign).

[41] See the discussions of the form of memorandum in §6.7 *infra* and of the means of signature in §6.8 *infra*.

[42] Of course, even traditional exchanges may raise troublesome problems of attribution of messages, many of which involve the law of agency.

[43] Utah was the first in 1995. *See* Utah Code Ann. §46-3-101 et seq.

with later.[44] Legal aspects of contracts generated by computers themselves are not dealt with in this treatise.[45]

We turn now to examine some secondary sources of contract law.

C. SOURCES AND ORGANIZATION OF CONTRACT LAW

Appearance of treatises

§1.8. Treatises, Restatements, and Scholarship. Compared to fields like tort law and criminal law, contract law is something of a parvenu. It did not become the subject of important treatises until the nineteenth century. Contracts scholars then struggled to fashion an orderly body of doctrine from the flood of new case law that had swelled from the trickle of the previous two centuries. By the middle of the twentieth century, however, the subject of contract law had been blessed by the publication of two of the most influential treatises to appear in any field of American law, first that of Samuel W. Williston[1] and later that of Arthur L. Corbin.[2]

Attention to generalities of contract law

Nineteenth-century treatises had devoted considerable attention to specific types of contracts, such as insurance, but had treated many of them as outside the scope of general contract law. When Williston launched his first edition in 1920, he deplored the tendency to exclude such contracts and sought to "treat the subject of contracts as a whole, and to show the wide range of application of its principles."[3] Contracts scholars, seeking organizing principles in their field, thus came to focus their attention on generalities common to most contracts, rather than on aspects peculiar to a few.

Contract law seen as essentially case law

Moreover, since the creative forces of contract law had traditionally been judicial rather than legislative, scholars tended to regard contract law as essentially case law and to seek these generalities in judicial decisions. In the accepted division of labor between judges and legislators, the former were seen as

---

[44] See the discussions of inapplicability if instantaneous in §3.22 *infra*, of the form of the memorandum in §6.7 *infra*, and of the test of intent to authenticate in §6.8 *infra*.

[45] *See* Hillman & Rachlinski, Standard-Form Contracting in the Electronic Age, 77 N.Y.U. L. Rev. 429 (2002); Radin, Humans, Computers, and Binding Commitment, 75 Ind. L.J. 1125 (2000).

§1.8 [1] S. Williston, Treatise on the Law of Contracts (1st ed. 1920) (in 4 volumes), now in a fourth edition. Two nineteenth-century American treatises were T. Parsons, The Law of Contracts (1853), and W. Story, A Treatise on the Law of Contracts Not Under Seal (1844).

William Story, son of the Supreme Court justice Joseph Story, was in his mid-twenties when he published his treatise. Before he reached thirty he abandoned the law and moved to Rome to devote himself to sculpture. In an account by Henry James, Story is quoted as saying that his "heart had gone over from Law to Art," though his mother thought him "mad" to "take such a leap in the dark." The Metropolitan Museum of Art has several of his pieces which "no one would buy," including his Libyan Sibyl. *See* 1 H. James, William Wetmore Story and His Friends 32 (1903).

[2] A. Corbin, Corbin on Contracts (1950-1960) (13 volumes), now in a revised edition.

[3] 1 S. Williston, Treatise on the Law of Contracts iii (1st ed. 1920).

charged with the declaration of general principles and the latter (with the notable exception of the Field civil code) with specialized deviations.[4] It was not entirely by accident that the first of the casebooks that were to revolutionize the method of teaching law was one on contracts.[5]

This emphasis on case law was reinforced by the American Law Institute. Formed in 1923 with a select membership of practitioners, judges, and law professors (now numbering several thousand), the Institute undertook to reduce the mass of case law to a body of readily accessible rules in the form of a Restatement of the Law, now made up of ten subjects. Contracts was one of the first subjects on which the Institute began work, and the Restatement of Contracts was completed in 1932. Williston acted as Reporter, with responsibility for preparing drafts. Corbin served as Special Adviser and Reporter for the chapter on Remedies. Other experts in the subject were formed into a Committee of Advisers, who conferred with the Reporter in producing drafts for submission to the Council of the Institute. These drafts, after discussion and revision by the Council, were then submitted as tentative drafts to the annual meetings of the Institute. Final promulgation depended on approval of the text by both the Council and the full meeting of Institute members.

Origin of Restatement of Contracts

The blackletter statements of general principles are accompanied by comments and illustrations. An initial plan for supplementing the Restatement by treatises citing and discussing case authority was dropped when experience proved that group production of such volumes was not feasible. However, the original Restatement of Contracts is characterized by what has been described as a "staccato" style,[6] which seemed suitable when its authors thought that it would be orchestrated by accompanying treatises.

Style of Restatement of Contracts

To what measure of authority is the Restatement entitled in the courts? This general question can have only a general answer. There is agreement among those who applaud the Restatement and those who deprecate it about the persuasiveness of an ideal restatement of the law. "A restatement, then, can have no other authority than as the product of men learned in the subject who have studied and deliberated over it. It needs no other and what could be higher?"[7] A former director of the Institute explained that if a court declines to follow the Restatement, "it will do so with the knowledge that the rule which it rejects has been written by the people who by training and reputation are supposed to be

Authority of Restatement

---

[4]General statutory provisions on contract law appear in states that adopted the civil code drafted in the nineteenth century by David Dudley Field. States with the Field civil code are California, Georgia, Montana, North Dakota, and South Dakota. Idaho adopted part of the code.

[5]C. Langdell, A Selection of Cases on the Law of Contracts (1871), discussed in Farnsworth, Contracts Scholarship in the Age of the Anthology, 85 Mich. L. Rev. 1406 (1987). *See also* Farnsworth, Casebooks and Scholarship: Confessions of an American Opinion Clipper, 42 Sw. L.J. 903 (1988).

[6]Wechsler, Foreword to Restatement (Second) of Contracts (Tentative Draft No. 1, 1964).

[7]Clark, The Restatement of the Law of Contracts, 42 Yale L.J. 643, 655 (1933).

eminently learned in the particular subject and that the specialist's conclusions have been discussed and defended before a body of very able critics." He called the Restatement "common law 'persuasive authority' with a high degree of persuasion."[8]

Origin of Restatement (Second) of Contracts

In 1952, the American Law Institute began the process of revising the Restatement to produce a "Restatement Second," and in 1962 it started such a revision of the Restatement of Contracts. Professor Robert Braucher of the Harvard Law School served as Reporter until his appointment to the Supreme Judicial Court of Massachusetts, when he was replaced by the author of this treatise. The Restatement (Second) of Contracts was published in 1981.[9] Its major changes in substance include an increased recognition of a party's reliance on the contract[10] and the introduction of a number of innovations by analogy to the Uniform Commercial Code.[11] In style, its fuller elaboration in text and comment contrasts with the style of its predecessor.

Departure from precedent

A continuing controversy centers on the desirability of departing in the Restatement from rules derived from existing precedents, in the interest of a more just regime of law. A notable example of such a departure from precedent in the original Restatement of Contracts was the creative formulation in §90 of the doctrine that is sometimes known as "promissory estoppel."[12] To some extent the expanded role of comments, to permit criticism as well as explanation, has helped to provide a vehicle for the expression of idealism.

Vitality of Restatement of Contracts

A more fundamental controversy relates to the vitality of the enterprise itself. Some have viewed the writing of Restatements with a marked lack of enthusiasm. An early critic complained of "the attempt to force a black letter sentence [to] do what it can never do — state pages of history and policy and honest study and deliberation."[13] But Braucher claimed that "the effort to restate the law of contracts in modern terms highlights the resilience of private autonomy in an era of expanding government activity. . . . Freedom of contract, refined and redefined in response to social change, has power as it always had."[14]

---

[8]Goodrich, Restatement and Codification, in David Dudley Field Centenary Essays 241, 244-45 (A. Reppy ed. 1949).

[9]It is cited in this treatise simply as "Restatement Second." Restatements of other subjects are specifically identified.

[10]*See* Knapp, Reliance in the Revised *Restatement:* The Proliferation of Promissory Estoppel, 81 Colum. L. Rev. 52 (1981).

[11]*See* Farnsworth, Ingredients in the Redaction of the *Restatement (Second) of Contracts*, 81 Colum. L. Rev. 1, 9-12 (1981).

[12]See the discussion of Restatement §90 in §2.19 *infra*.

[13]Clark, The Restatement of the Law of Contracts, 42 Yale L.J. 643, 646 (1933). For criticism of the restatement project, *see* Schwartz & Scott, The Political Economy of Private Legislatures, 143 U. Pa. L. Rev. 595 (1995).

[14]Braucher, Freedom of Contract and the Second Restatement, 78 Yale L.J. 598 (1969). The contracts Restatement accounts for nearly a fifth of all Restatement citations, which number over 150,000, and is second only to torts.

The appeal of restating widely shared principles of contract law has not been confined to the United States. In 1994, the International Institute for the Unification of Private Law (UNIDROIT), located in Rome, promulgated the UNIDROIT Principles of International Commercial Contracts.[15] Like the Restatement, the Principles are not intended for legislative enactment. They reflect concepts common to many legal systems as well as solutions that were thought desirable even if not yet generally adopted. Some of the concepts are drawn from civil law systems while others come from common law systems — including the Uniform Commercial Code and the Restatement (Second) of Contracts. The Principles may be applicable by agreement of the parties or, even in the absence of agreement, may be resorted to by arbitrators seeking appropriate rules for international disputes. Some of the more important aspects of the Principles are taken up in following chapters.

UNIDROIT Principles

As the twentieth century drew to a close, mainstream scholars produced new treatises[16] and revised old ones.[17] At the same time a vigorous and growing body of scholarship appeared on the scene, challenging in various ways traditional — or "neoclassical"[18] — scholarship as exemplified by the Restatement Second. In spite of its heterogeneity, this new body of scholarship is usually fitted under the rubric of "contract theory."[19] Much of this writing eschews descriptive analysis of what the law is and concentrates on normative analysis of what the law should be.

Rise of contract theory

---

[15] Principles of International Commercial Contracts (International Institute for the Unification of Private Law 1994). The Principles are cited in this treatise as "UNIDROIT Principles" followed by the number of the article (i.e., section). A similar project states principles of European contract law.

[16] These include, in addition to this one: J. Perillo, Calamari & Perillo on Contracts (5th ed. 2003); J. Murray, Murray on Contracts (3d ed. 1990). On English contract law, *see* P. Atiyah, An Introduction to the Law of Contract (6th ed. 2003); M. Furmston, Cheshire, Fifoot & Furmston's Law of Contract (14th ed. 2001); G. Treitel, The Law of Contract (10th ed. 1999); Chitty on Contracts (H. Beale gen. ed. 28th ed. 1999). *See also* A. Simpson, History of the Common Law of Contract (1987) (history of English contract law).

[17] *See* Corbin on Contracts (J. Perillo ed. rev. ed. 1993-); Williston on Contracts (R. Lord ed. 4th ed. 1990-2002).

[18] *See* Macneil, Contracts: Adjustment of Long-Term Economic Relations Under Classical, Neoclassical, and Relational Contract Law, 72 Nw. U.L. Rev. 854, 855 n.2 (1978) (*classical contract law* refers to "that developed in the 19th century and brought to its pinnacle by Samuel Williston," while *neoclassical contract law* refers to "body of contract law founded on that system in overall structure but considerably modified in some . . . of its detail," as epitomized by Article 2 of the Uniform Commercial Code and the Restatement Second).

[19] According to Gilmore, the idea that there was such a thing as a general law — or theory — of contract seems never to have occurred to the legal mind until Langdell somehow stumbled across it. G. Gilmore, The Death of Contract 6 (1974). It is far from clear, however, that Langdell thought he had a theory of contract, and the fascination with contract theory is due more to Gilmore than to Langdell.

Conventional idealism and relational law

Some of this scholarship is rooted in conventional idealism, in the tradition of Lon Fuller.[20] Important work along these lines has been done by Grant Gilmore[21] and Melvin Eisenberg.[22] Others have broken more sharply with the past, faulting traditional contract analysis for its preoccupation with exchanges that take the form of discrete transactions in contrast to longer term relationships, in which one party may become more dependent on the other. Thus it has been suggested that "discrete" (or "transactional") contracts should be distinguished from "relational" ones, and that it is

> useful to think of transactional and relational characteristics as creating a spectrum ranging from such extremes as the highly transactional horse selling epitome to the highly relational nuclear family or commune, As one moves towards the relational end of this spectrum . . . increasing aspects of the relation must be left to future determination.[23]

Critical legal studies

Writers associated with the critical legal studies movement espoused an extreme approach to contract law based on communitarian visions and notions of individual autonomy, with particularly heavy emphasis on altruism and solidarity. "[T]he modern law of contract . . . is hostile to personal authority as a source of order; it preaches equality in distrust. The mechanisms of egalitarian, self-interested bargaining and adjudication cannot be made to jibe with the illiberal blend of power and allegiance."[24] Feminist writers have also contributed analyses of contract law.[25]

Influence of other disciplines

Many contracts scholars have been heavily influenced by other disciplines.[26] Some have explored the historical foundations of contract law.[27] Others have

---

[20] Fuller's most influential writing in contract is Fuller & Perdue, The Reliance Interest in Contract Damages (pts. 1 & 2), 46 Yale L.J. 52, 373 (1936, 1937). See the discussion of the alternative of reliance in §12.8 *infra*.

[21] For a sample of Gilmore's wit and style, *see* G. Gilmore, The Death of Contract (1974).

[22] For a statement of Eisenberg's responsive model of contract law, in which principles of contract law should be based on considerations of fairness, as determined principally by conventional morality, and of policy, as determined principally by efficiency and administrability, *see* Eisenberg, The Responsive Model of Contract Law, 36 Stan. L. Rev. 1107, 1111 (1984).

[23] Macneil, Restatement (Second) of Contracts and Presentation, 60 Va. L. Rev. 589, 596 (1974).

[24] Unger, The Critical Legal Studies Movement, 96 Harv. L. Rev. 563, 624 (1983). *See* Kennedy, Form and Substance in Private Law Adjudication, 89 Harv. L. Rev. 1685, 1717-22 (1976) (discussing altruism and exchange, its "polar opposite concept for sharing and sacrifice").

[25] *See* Hadfield, An Expressive Theory of Contract: From Feminist Dilemmas to a Reconceptualization of Rational Choice in Contract Law, 146 U. Pa. L. Rev. 1235 (1998).

[26] In this respect, contracts scholarship followed in the path of the legal realists of the 1920s and 1930s.

[27] *See* P. Atiyah, The Rise and Fall of Freedom of Contract (1979); Horwitz, The Historical Foundations of Modern Contract Law, 87 Harv. L. Rev. 917 (1974), reprinted in M. Horwitz, The Transformation of American Law, 1780-1860 ch. 6 (1977), criticized in Simpson, The Horwitz

relied on the methods of sociology[28] or have drawn upon philosophy.[29] But by far the most pervasive influence has come from the field of economics.

The most significant member of the law and economics movement has been Richard Posner,[30] but much accessible writing of this kind in the field of contracts has come from other scholars as well.[31] By and large these scholars argue that society gains from the making and performance of some types of promises and that contract law should be designed to facilitate these gains. Such arguments are considered at many points in following chapters.

Law and economics

We now turn to the most significant single piece of legislation in the field of contracts — the Uniform Commercial Code.

§1.9.   Uniform Commercial Code. The origins of the Uniform Commercial Code lie in the law merchant, a specialized body of usages, or customs, that governed contracts dealing with commercial matters until the seventeenth century. The law merchant was applied by courts composed of merchants convened to pass on disputes that arose at the fairs that were the centers for much of early trade. Large amounts of this law were carried into the English common law of negotiable instruments and insurance. This was due in substantial part to Lord Mansfield, one of England's most noted judges, who became Chief Justice of the King's Bench in 1756. In controversies between merchants, he made it a point to ascertain and apply the usages of the trade, sometimes using a special jury of merchants to advise him on commercial practices. But the influence of the law merchant on the common law relating to the sale of goods was limited, and a complex body of English case law soon developed in this field.

Influence of the law merchant

This law was reduced to statutory form by the British Sale of Goods Act in 1893. The National Conference of Commissioners on Uniform State Laws entrusted to Williston the task of producing a similar statute for the American states. His draft of a Uniform Sales Act was approved by the Commissioners in 1906 and was eventually adopted by over 30 states. Like its British cousin, however, it had little to say about contractual problems arising out of the sale of goods, and these remained largely governed by case law.

Early statutes on sale of goods

At the close of the Second World War, the Commissioners joined forces with the American Law Institute in preparing a comprehensive Uniform

Origin of Uniform Commercial Code

Thesis and the History of Contracts, 46 U. Chi. L. Rev. 533 (1979); A. Simpson, History of the Common Law of Contract (1987).

[28] *See* Macaulay, Non-Contractual Relations in Business: A Preliminary Study, 28 Am. Soc. Rev. 55 (1963).

[29] *See* C. Fried, Contract as Promise: A Theory of Contractual Obligation (1981) (arguing that the moral basis of contract law is the "promise principle . . . by which persons may impose on themselves obligations where none existed before").

[30] R. Posner, Economic Analysis of Law ch. 4 (6th ed. 2003).

[31] *See* E. Posner, Economic Analysis of Contract Law After Three Decades: Success or Failure?, 112 Yale L.J. 829 (2003), with responses by Ayres and Craswell. As to the impact of economic analysis, see the discussion of the autonomy of contract law in §1.7 *supra*.

Commercial Code, to replace not only the Uniform Sales Act but also other uniform acts dealing with commercial matters. Karl Llewellyn was named as Chief Reporter.[1] A final Official Draft, with extensive comments, was approved by the two sponsoring organizations in 1952 and was promptly enacted in Pennsylvania, effective in 1954. In response to criticisms made in a study by the New York Law Revision Commission, the sponsors of the Code produced a revised text with comments in 1958. By 1961, 13 states, including Pennsylvania, had adopted this text. In 1962, New York adopted it, effective in 1964, and the complete success of the Code was assured. A number of states, however, made changes in the 1958 Official Text, and, in order to curb this tendency away from uniformity, a Permanent Editorial Board for the Code was established in 1961. The Board passed upon the amendments made or proposed by each state, and those it approved were incorporated in a 1962 Official Text. New articles on leases and funds transfers were added later. Some version of the Code has been enacted, with at most minor variations, in every state except Louisiana, which has extensively modified the provisions on sales.

Contents of the Code

The Code is divided into 11 substantive articles: Article 1, General Provisions; Article 2, Sales; Article 2A, Leases; Article 3, Negotiable Instruments; Article 4, Bank Deposits and Collections; Article 4A, Funds Transfers; Article 5, Letters of Credit; Article 6, Bulk Transfers;[2] Article 7, Warehouse Receipts, Bills of Lading and Other Documents of Title; Article 8, Investment Securities; Article 9, Secured Transactions; Sales of Accounts and Chattel Paper.[3] Our concern is almost exclusively with Articles 1 and 2, and with a few provisions of Article 9 that govern the assignment of contract rights and the delegation of

---

§1.9 [1] On the fate of a proposal by Llewellyn to use juries of merchants, as Mansfield did, and on his German sources for the Code, *see* Note, 97 Yale L.J. 156 (1987). See also the discussion of the Code's use of *merchant* in §1.10 *infra*.

Williston, who had drafted the Uniform Sales Act, found some of the changes in that area to be "not only iconoclastic but open to criticisms that I regard so fundamental as to preclude the desirability of enacting [the Sales Article] of the proposed Code." Williston, The Law of Sales in the Proposed Uniform Commercial Code, 63 Harv. L. Rev. 561, 561 (1950). Corbin was among those who took a different view. Corbin, The Uniform Commercial Code — Sales; Should It Be Enacted?, 59 Yale L.J. 821, 836 (1950) ("more than any previous code or restatement it provides within itself a method and principle of future growth").

For criticism of the drafting and revision process, *see* Schwartz & Scott, The Political Economy of Private Legislatures, 143 U. Pa. L. Rev. 595 (1995) ("theory suggests that a private legislature with a membership similar to that of the ALI and NCCUSL and procedures similar to theirs will have a strong status quo bias and sometimes will be captured by powerful interests").

[2] Most states have repealed Article 6 as recommended by the sponsors.

[3] It had originally been planned to add a new Article 2B, Licenses. When this effort failed, the National Conference of Commissioners on Uniform State Laws promulgated a Uniform Computer Information Transactions Act (UCITA) in 1999. It deals with "computer information transactions," including the creation and distribution of computer software, but excludes most other intellectual property. It has met with considerable opposition, particularly by consumer groups, and was amended in 2002 to make it more acceptable. It has been enacted by only Maryland and Virginia.

performance. The Code's original articles have been extensively revised during the half-century of the Code's existence.

Article 1 contains general provisions, including many definitions and some substantive provisions — notably the obligation of good faith[4] — that are of central importance to contract law. A revised version of Article 1 received final approval from the Code's sponsors in 2001. The revision makes not only substantive but organizational changes. A new Part B comprises ten new sections derived from sections of former Article 1. In addition to accommodating the possibility of electronic means of communication by the use of the term *record* in place of the term *writing*,[5] there are minor changes, including neutering of gender by elimination of all forms of the pronoun *he*.[6]

Article 1

Article 2 of the Code, which has the greatest importance for the law of contracts and which Llewellyn described as the "heart of the Code,"[7] is generally limited to "transactions in goods."[8] It does not apply to, say, contracts for the sale of land or for services.[9] Courts usually determine whether a transaction is one in goods, services, or land by looking for the "predominant factor" of the contract.[10]

Article 2

A revised version of Article 2 received final approval from the Code's sponsors in 2003. This brought to an end a contentious effort, with conflicting influences by consumer groups and business interests, that had begun more than a decade earlier. It was marked by the abandonment of an ambitious initial revision followed by the resignation in protest of the Reporter selected to draft it.[11] The resulting revision, much more modest and more satisfactory to business interests than that envisioned by the initial drafting group, makes some significant substantive changes but retains the organization of original Article 2.[12]

Revision of Article 2

---

[4] UCC 1-304. See the discussion of the duty of good faith in §7.17 *infra*.

[5] UCC 1-201(31) (defining *record* to include information "that is stored in an electronic or other medium and is retrievable in perceivable form").

[6] *See* UCC 1-106(2) ("words of any gender also refer to any other gender").

[7] Llewellyn, Why We Need the Uniform Commercial Code, 10 U. Fla. L. Rev. 367, 378 (1957).

[8] UCC 2-102. Some sections of Article 2 are explicitly limited to sales. *See* UCC 2-201 (statute of frauds applicable to "contract for the sale of goods"), treated in the discussion of sale of goods in §6.6 *infra*.

[9] G-W-L, Inc. v. Robichaux, 643 S.W.2d 392 (Tex. 1982) (Article 2 "not applicable to the construction and sale of a house").

[10] Bonebrake v. Cox, 499 F.2d 951 (8th Cir. 1974) (test is whether "predominant factor . . . is the rendition of service, with goods incidentally involved (e.g., contract with artist for painting) or is a transaction of sale, with labor incidentally involved (e.g., installation of water heater in a bathroom)").

[11] For an account by the Reporter, *see* Speidel, Revising UCC Article 2: A View from the Trenches, 52 Hastings L.J. 607 (2001).

[12] In this treatise sections of original Article 2 (immediately before revisions) are designated by "O" (e.g., "UCC-O 2-201"), while sections of the revised articles are designated by "R" (e.g., "UCC-R 2-201"). If the relevant part of a section is identical in both versions, neither designation

It deletes six sections (UCC-O 2-319 to 2-234) as "inconsistent with modern commercial practices" and adds two sections (UCC-R 2-313A and 2-313B), but none of these changes is central to the subject of contract law. The final obstacle to approval of revised Article 2 came with acceptance of a revised definition of *goods* in R 2-103(1)(k), under which the term "does not include information." The intention is that revised Article 2 will apply to a sale of "smart" goods such as an automobile that incorporates a computer program but will not apply to an electronic transfer of information not associated with goods. "Information" is not defined and the precise scope of the exception is left to the courts. In addition, many sections have undergone at least minor changes to accommodate the possibility of electronic means of communication[13] as well as to neuter the gender.

Vienna Convention

Since 1988, American exporters and importers have been subject to the United Nations (Vienna) Convention on Contracts for the International Sale of Goods (CISG).[14] The Convention, often called the *Vienna Convention* because of the site of the diplomatic conference at which it was put in final form, is a multilateral treaty. It applies only if the contract is one of international sale, defined as a contract for the sale of goods between parties whose places of business are in different countries, both of which have ratified the Convention.[15] When it applies it displaces much of Article 2 and makes some important changes in the applicable rules of contract law, including, for example, the abolition of the statute of frauds.[16] These changes are dealt with in the following chapters.

Approach of the Code

The Code made much less of an attempt than did the earlier codifications in Britain and the United States to follow existing formulations of the law. Very little of the language of the Uniform Sales Act was retained. In some respects, the Code took an entirely new approach to the law. One of the most important of the Code's innovations for our purposes is its reduction to statutory form of many of the rules of contract law relating to the sale of goods that had previously been left to case law. We shall have occasion to consider the soundness of many of these formulations.

---

is used (e.g., "UCC 2-201"). References to comments to Article 2 are to comments to original Article 2, the only comments available in final form when this treatise went to the publisher.

[13] *See* UCC-R 2-103(1)(f) (defining *electronic* as "relating to technology having electrical, digital, magnetic, wireless, optical, electromagnetic, or similar capabilities"); UCC-R 2-103(1)(g) (defining *electronic agent* as "a computer program or an electronic or other automated means used independently to initiate an action or respond to electronic records or performance in whole or in part, without review or action by an individual"); UCC-R 2-103(1)(h) (defining *electronic record* as "a record created, generated, sent, communicated, received, or stored by electronic means").

[14] The Convention is cited in this treatise as "CISG" followed by the number of the article (*i.e.*, section).

[15] CISG 1(1). The United States did not accept CISG 1(b), which would have given the Convention a broader application.

[16] See the discussion of no requirement for international contracts in §6.1 *infra*.

UCC 1-103 provides that the Code "must be liberally construed and applied to promote its underlying purposes and policies," one of which is "to make uniform the law among the various jurisdictions." In order to achieve this goal of uniformity, if a decision from another jurisdiction interprets the Code, a court will give it greater weight than would ordinarily be the case in order to avoid inconsistent applications of the Code.[17]

Uniform interpretation

One pervasive question in working with the Code is to what extent recourse may be had to prior drafts to aid interpretation. Earlier versions of the Code that have been enacted into law may, of course, be consulted. It is less clear that this is so for prior drafts that are merely the product of a drafting group unconnected with any legislature. The 1952 edition of the Code attempted to close the door on such drafting history by providing that "Prior drafts of text and comments may not be used to ascertain legislative intent." The comment to this provision explained that the reason for the prohibition was that the changes might be misleading, because matters were often "omitted as being implicit without statement and language has been changed or added solely for clarity."[18] However, the provision was deleted in the 1958 Official Text, leaving courts free to consult the drafting history of the Code when it seems relevant.[19]

Recourse to legislative history

A similar question is to what extent recourse should be had, in interpreting the Code, to the drafter's comments that follow each section.[20] The question arises because the comments, although styled as "official," have not been enacted into law by the state legislatures that have enacted the text, and in many states it is doubtful that they were even laid before the legislators in the form of a committee report. Yet the comments, written in an explanatory style, are easier to read than the text and often amplify it. The 1952 text of the Code provided that the comments "may be consulted in the construction and application of this Act but, if text and comment conflict, text controls," a provision that was deleted in the 1958 version for reasons unrelated to its substance.[21] The sponsors of the Code explain that to aid in uniform interpretation the comments "set forth the purpose of various provisions of this Act to promote uniformity, to aid in viewing the Act as an integrated whole, and to safeguard against misconstruction."[22] In practice, courts have given considerable weight to the comments — more than that ordinarily accorded an authoritative treatise

Recourse to comments

---

[17] Husker News Co. v. Mahaska State Bank, 460 N.W.2d 476 (Iowa 1990) (objectives of Code include uniform application).

[18] UCC 1-102(3)(g) cmt.2 (1952 ed.).

[19] *See* Mathis v. Exxon Corp., 302 F.3d 448 (5th Cir. 2002) (consulting history of comment to UCC 2-305); Northpark National Bank v. Bankers Trust Co., 572 F. Supp. 524 (S.D.N.Y. 1983) (consulting drafts of Article 4).

[20] References in this treatise to comments to Article 2 are to comments to original Article 2, the only comments available in final form when this treatise went to the publisher.

[21] UCC 1-102(3)(f) (1952 ed.); 1956 Recommendations, p. 3.

[22] General Comment at p. ix of 1972 edition.

or article but less than that accorded the text itself.[23] If the statutory provisions adopted by the legislature contradict the comments, the comments must clearly be rejected. The more difficult problem arises where the comments make assertions as to matters on which the text is silent, and here also courts have often rejected the comments.[24]

What can be said about the continued vitality of general principles of contract law in the face of the tendency toward specialization and the intrusion of legislation?

Variety of contracts

§1.10.   Adaptability of Contract Law.   Contracts come in endless variety. There are building contracts, employment contracts, contracts for the sale of land, contracts for the sale of goods, loan agreements, franchise agreements, collective bargaining agreements, insurance policies, theater tickets, and so on. They may involve small merchants or large corporations, governments or consumers. They may be short-term contracts for a single performance in the near future or long-term contracts under which a multitude of separate transactions are to take place. They may be negotiated face to face, over the telephone, by mail, or by electronic data exchange. They may be made in writing, orally, or even by gesture.

Problem of adaptability

How can a general body of contract law adapt itself to so many different types of transactions? In some instances the answer is that it has not succeeded in doing so and, as a result, separate fields such as insurance law and labor law have emerged. Indeed, one critic has denigrated the residuum of general contract law as "abstraction — what is left in the law relating to agreements when all particularities of person and subject matter are removed."[1] In many instances, however, the general rules of contract law have been successfully accommodated to the peculiarities of particular transactions, thus avoiding fragmentation into separate branches of law.[2]

Role of express provision and usage

Often the parties themselves make this accommodation by express provision at the time of their agreement, creating their own body of specialized rules for their particular situation. In other cases they have accomplished much the same

---

[23]Walker v. American Cyanamid Co., 948 P.2d 1123 (Idaho 1997) ("Court has frequently considered the comments . . . and has given the comments . . . and has given the comments substantial merit").

[24]Simmons v. Clemco Indus., 368 So. 2d 509 (Ala. 1979) (comments "have not been enacted by the legislature").

The comments also include extensive "Definitional Cross-References." A careful lawyer will not, however, rely on their completeness. Furthermore, only definitions in the strictest sense, of terms enclosed in quotation marks, are cross-referenced. There are no cross-references of terms defined in the course of stating a substantive rule. *See* UCC 2-606 on "What Constitutes Acceptance of Goods."

§1.10   [1]Friedman, Contract Law in America 20 (1965). For a different view, see that of Williston, quoted in the discussion of attention to the generalities of contract law in §1.8, *supra*.

[2]General rules of contract law have on occasion been applied in somewhat surprising situations. *See* Hentz v. Hargett, 71 F.3d 1169 (5th Cir. 1996) (plea bargains are "contractual").

result by tacitly subjecting themselves to a body of usages that can be shown to be regularly observed in transactions of that particular sort and that then serve as a body of specialized rules for the transaction at hand.

It is important to understand in this connection that the great bulk of the general rules of contract law, including those of the Uniform Commercial Code[3] and the Vienna Convention,[4] are subject to contrary provision by the parties. European legal systems have long had terms of art to distinguish between rules of law that the parties can vary by express provision or usage and rules of law that are beyond their power to modify. It has become common in English to refer to rules as *default* rules, by analogy to the default settings on a computer, since they are subject to contrary agreement but apply by default absent such agreement. Rules that are not subject to contrary agreement are often called *mandatory* rules.[5] Most rules of contract law are, then, default rules rather than mandatory rules.[6]

Most contract rules are default rules

The fact that most of its rules are default rules has been a source of both strength and weakness for contract law. To the extent that its general rules have admitted of departure, they have had an adaptability and a resilience that have enabled them to survive in an age when specialization has made it increasingly difficult to formulate such rules categorically. Many a court has approved and applied some general proposition of contract law with the aside that, had the parties not desired its application, they could have provided to the contrary. At the same time, the fact that the parties frequently exercise their power to depart from these general rules has significantly undermined the significance of the rules themselves. Many are more honored in the exception than in the application. The result is a heightened significance of the process of interpretation, by which the effect of the agreement actually reached by the parties is determined.[7]

Effect of this on contract law

In addition to the efforts of the parties themselves to shape the general rules of contract law to their particular needs, legislatures have played an important role in tailoring these rules to fit the peculiarities of the transaction. Notable examples have been the formulation of special rules for transactions involving merchants and for those involving consumers.

Legislative tailoring of rules

---

[3] UCC 1-302(a).

[4] CISG 6. The same is true under UNIDROIT Principles 1.1 ("Freedom of Contract").

[5] See UNIDROIT Principles 1.4 ("Mandatory Rules"). These are sometimes called "immutable rules," a term not in general international use.

[6] It has been argued, however, that as "more complex and refined terms are implied . . . , variation by express agreement becomes more difficult and costly" and "the courts' tendency to treat state-created rules as presumptively fair often leads to judicial disapproval of efforts to vary standard implied terms by agreement." Goetz & Scott, The Limits of Expanded Choice: An Analysis of the Interactions Between Express and Implied Contract Terms, 73 Cal. L. Rev. 261, 263-64 (1985).

[7] See Chapter 7 *infra*.

Concept of merchant in civil law systems

Although some of the European civil law systems have traditionally singled out for special treatment transactions involving those professionals called "merchants," the common law tradition has been to formulate general rules of contract law, applicable by their terms to those in business, as well as to others. The notion of special rules for merchants remained foreign to the American lawyer until the advent of the Uniform Commercial Code.[8]

Code's use of *merchant*

Not only did the drafters of the Code lay down special rules applicable only to contracts for the sale of goods, as opposed to other kinds of contracts, but they formulated special rules imposing higher standards on merchants than on other sorts of parties. Some of these rules apply if there is a transaction "between merchants,"[9] and others apply if only one party is a "merchant."[10] One is a merchant under UCC 2-104(1) if one deals in goods of the kind or otherwise holds oneself out by occupation "as having knowledge or skill peculiar to the practices or goods involved in the transaction." Under this provision, the required professional status may be based on specialized knowledge of either the goods or the practices involved.[11] A seller of goods from inventory "deals" in the goods. An artisan, such as a carpenter or a plumber, "holds himself out as having . . . skill peculiar" to goods with which the artisan works. But the knowledge that an ordinary person in business has of business "practices . . . involved in the transaction" is enough to make that person a "merchant," even absent specialized knowledge of the goods involved.[12] However, a few of the Code sections that lay down special rules for merchants do so only if the party is a merchant with respect to "goods of the kind" involved in the transaction, and under these sections knowledge of business practices alone would not suffice.[13]

Practicality of this distinction

It would be easy to imagine that the introduction of a definition of *merchant* would pose problems by requiring subtle distinctions at the borderline. For example, the comments tell us that a person is a merchant only when acting in a professional capacity: "banks or even universities . . . well may be 'merchants' "

---

[8] For a comparative discussion, *see* Schlesinger, The Uniform Commercial Code in the Light of Comparative Law, 1 Study of the Uniform Commercial Code (Report of New York Law Revision Commission for 1955) 87, 104-23 (N.Y. Leg. Doc. No. 65 (1955)).

[9] *See* UCC 2-201(2), providing that a failure to object to a confirmation within a fixed period satisfies the requirement of the statute of frauds in a transaction "between merchants."

[10] *See* UCC 2-314, under which "a warranty that the goods shall be merchantable is implied in a contract for their sale if the seller is a merchant with respect to goods of that kind."

[11] For an interesting account of the origins and fate of the Code's merchant rules, *see* Wiseman, The Limits of Vision: Karl Llewellyn and the Merchant Rules, 100 Harv. L. Rev. 465 (1987).

[12] *See* UCC 2-201(2), summarized *supra* note 9. Some courts have held that farmers are merchants. Rayle Tech v. Dekalb Swine Breeders, 133 F.3d 1405 (11th Cir. 1998) ("large hog producer . . . is a sophisticated purchaser and a 'merchant' "). Other courts have reached a contrary conclusion. Terminal Grain Corp. v. Freeman, 270 N.W.2d 806 (S.D. 1978) ("average farmer . . . is not a 'merchant' " under UCC 2-201(2)).

[13] Donald v. City Natl. Bank, 329 So. 92 (Ala. 1976) (bank was not merchant under UCC 2-314 with respect to boat sold after repossession).

but "a lawyer or bank president buying fishing tackle for his own use is not a merchant."[14] Judging from the litigation that has arisen from the definition, however, such distinctions have not often been the cause of controversy in practice. Litigation has been largely devoted to determining the circumstances in which a farmer is a "merchant" under the Code.[15]

Just as the general rules of contract law have traditionally applied to merchants as well as others, so too have they applied to consumers as well as others. Thus the Uniform Commercial Code, unlike the commercial codes of some civil law countries, does not exclude consumers. However, revised Article 2 modifies a few general rules of contract law where consumers are involved.[16] For example,[17] under consumer contracts it provides more rigorous requirements for disclaimers of implied warranties,[18] invalidates agreements for specific performance,[19] bars recovery of consequential damages from consumers,[20] and lays down different requirements for valid liquidated damages clauses.[21] The Code is not, however, a consumer protection statute, and it leaves it to other statutes to perform this role and provide special rules for transactions involving consumers to enhance their rights.[22] Such legislation varies widely from one jurisdiction to another but the Uniform Consumer Credit Code is typical. Under it, consumer transactions are limited to those in which a person acquires goods, services, or land "primarily for a personal, family, household, or agricultural purpose" of "a person other than an organization."[23] As in the case of the Uniform Commercial Code's use of *merchant*, this attempt at delineation of an area worthy of special rules appears not to have occasioned much controversy

Code's use of *consumer*

---

[14]UCC 2-104 cmt. 2. In addition, under the Code, one may be regarded as a merchant because of one's "employment of an agent or broker or other intermediary" that holds itself out by occupation as having the required knowledge or skill. UCC 2-104(1).

[15]For a transactional emphasis, *see* Sparks v. Stich, 522 N.Y.S.2d 707 (App. Div. 1987) (sellers "raised beef cattle, but only for sale on an annual basis," and "sale was more a part of the farm closing than an ongoing business transaction").

[16]*See* UCC-R 2-103(1)(c) & (d) (defining *consumer* and *consumer* contract). For a rare recognition of consumers under original Article 2, see the discussion of firm offers under the Code in §3.23 *infra*.

[17]For other examples, *see* UCC-R 2-502(1)(a) (giving consumer buyer a right to recover goods if seller repudiates or refuses to deliver); UCC-R 2-725(1) (invalidating agreements reducing period of limitation in consumer contracts).

[18]UCC-R 2-316(2) & (3). See the discussion of statutory reinforcement in §4.26 *infra*.

[19]UCC-R 2-716(1). See the discussion of power of parties in §12.6 *infra*.

[20]UCC-R 2-710(3). See the discussion of other loss in §12.9 *infra*.

[21]UCC-R 2-718(1). See the discussion of the difficulty of proof of loss in §12.18 *infra*.

[22]*See* UCC-R 2-1083(1)(b) (subjecting the Code to any applicable "rule of law that establishes a different rule for consumers").

[23]Uniform Consumer Credit Code 2.104(1)(b),(c). This definition is derived from the definition of *consumer goods* in UCC 9-102(23) and is its language is similar to that in the definition of *consumer* added by UCC-R 2-103(1)(c). For more on the Uniform Consumer Credit Code, see the discussion of legislation as common in §4.29 *infra*.

with respect to its borderline.[24] As to the substance of the rules in both cases, more will be said later.

Reasoning from the Code by analogy

Even where special rules have evolved for particular types of contracts, it would be a mistake to suppose that they bear no relation to the general body of contract law. For example, though Article 2 of the Code is generally limited to "transactions in goods"[25] Courts have, nonetheless, used these provisions as a basis for the application of similar rules in analogous cases.[26] The comments themselves invite such use, citing with approval cases in which courts have "recognized that the policies embodied in an act as applicable in reason to subject-matter that was not expressly included in the language of the act."[27] The Restatement Second also encourages courts to do this in specific instances, by formulating general principles of contract law derived from, or at least supported by, rules found in the Code — for example, the provisions on "good faith" and on "unconscionability."[28] This assimilation of rules from a specialized field of contract law into the body of general contract principles suggests the continuing vitality of those principles in spite of the twentieth-century tendency toward specialization.

We turn now to a brief summary of how this treatise is organized.

Organization in five parts

§1.11. Organization of This Treatise. This treatise is divided into five parts. Part I consists of this introductory chapter. Part II deals with the enforceability of promises, while Part III treats their scope and effect. Part IV investigates the rights of third persons under promises. Part V considers the enforcement of promises.

Part II deals with enforceability of promises

We begin our study of the enforceability of promises in Part II by examining, in Chapter 2, the cornerstone of liability in contract — the doctrine of consideration. The chapter also discusses two other important grounds of liability in transactions involving promises — reliance and restitution. Chapter 3 then takes up the process by which enforceable promises are made, a process that is

---

[24] For a case concerning this borderline, *see* Cape Conroe Ltd. v. Specht, 525 S.W.2d 215 (Tex. Civ. App. 1975) (purchaser of development lots was not "consumer" because he did not acquire "goods or services").

[25] See the discussion of the scope of Article 2 in §1.9 *supra*.

[26] Norcon Power Partners v. Niagara Mohawk Power Corp., 705 N.E.2d 656 (N.Y. 1998) ("policies underlying the UCC 2-609 counterpart should apply with similar cogency for the resolution of this kind of controversy," involving "long-term commercial contract between corporate entities . . . , which is complex and not reasonably susceptible of all security features being anticipated," but "Court needs to go no further").

However, cases analogizing from some provisions of Article 2, such as those on unconscionability and implied warranties, are not sound precedents in other situations, such as those involving the statute of frauds or the statute of limitations. Furthermore, Article 2A, Leases, eliminates the occasion for reasoning by analogy in lease cases.

[27] UCC 1-103 cmt. 1.

[28] On "good faith," *compare* UCC 1-304 *with* Restatement Second §205. On "unconscionability," *compare* UCC 2-302 *with* Restatement Second §208.

analyzed in terms of "offer" and "acceptance." Chapter 4 examines the extent to which courts will police the parties' agreement by restricting their freedom to make whatever agreement they please. It begins with the traditional doctrines that are designed to ensure the integrity of the agreement process (e.g., incapacity, mistake, misrepresentation, and duress) and moves to more recent developments (e.g., unconscionability and legislation). Chapter 5 considers the degree to which the interests of society at large may limit the power of individuals to make enforceable promises. Chapter 6 asks when the law requires that a promise be evidenced by a record such as a writing in order to be enforceable.

Part III inquires into the scope and effect of promises. Chapter 7 takes up the techniques by which courts ascertain the scope of contractual obligations undertaken by the parties — the techniques by which they find "the law of the contract." The focus is on interpreting the language used by the parties and on filling gaps not covered by that language. Chapter 8 deals with problems relating to the performance of contractual obligations, including the rules that govern performance in the absence of express provision by the parties. Its central concern is with the effect of a breach by one party on the remaining duties of the other party. Chapter 9 examines the effects of changed and mistaken circumstances under the doctrines of mistake, impracticability of performance, and frustration of purpose.

Part III deals with scope of promises

Part IV comprises two chapters dealing mainly with the rights of third persons under promises. Chapter 10 is concerned with contract beneficiaries — third persons who claim rights arising out of the contract itself. Chapter 11 is concerned in large part with assignees — third persons who claim rights arising out of a transfer subsequent to the making of a contract. The chapter also deals with problems arising out of the delegation of performance of a contract.

Part IV deals with rights of third persons

Finally we turn to enforcement. Part V consists of Chapter 12, which is devoted to the fundamental topic of remedies. Something will be said of specific relief, which compels the very performance that was promised. But enforcement of a promise does not usually entail requiring its actual performance, and much more will be said of substitutional relief, through the award of money damages in lieu of that performance. Notions of restitution and reliance also figure in the chapter.

Part V deals with the enforcement of promises

In the next chapter we discuss enforceability.

PART II
ENFORCEABILITY OF PROMISES

Chapter 2

Consideration and Other Grounds for Recovery

A. EXTENT OF LIABILITY

§2.1. Expectation, Reliance, and Restitution Interests. The preceding chapter traced the development of the doctrine of consideration as a means of enforcing promises. The present chapter is primarily concerned with the contours of that doctrine today and with alternative grounds for a promisor's liability. But the question of whether a promisor is liable is often bound up with

Significance of extent of liability

45

the question of the extent of that liability.[1] It is therefore useful to begin with a brief discussion of the relief to which a promisee may be entitled for breach of contract.[2]

Relief usually substitutional

Occasionally a court grants a promisee specific relief by ordering the promisor to perform the promise. But in our legal system such specific relief is the exception rather than the rule. Usually a court grants the promisee substitutional relief by awarding a sum of money intended to compensate for the harm to the promisee's interests caused by the promisor's failure to perform the promise. It is common to discuss the measure of this liability of the promisor in terms of the promisee's expectation, reliance, and restitution interests.

Recovery measured by expectation interest

In general, the amount of the award is measured by the promisee's *expectation interest* or, as it is sometimes said, "the benefit of the bargain." The court attempts to put the *promisee in the position in which the promisee would have been had the promise been performed* (i.e., had there been no breach). This is the measure generally used today in actions founded on promises that are enforceable because supported by consideration. But it is not the only possible measure of recovery.

Recovery measured by reliance interest

If the promisee changed its position to its detriment in reliance on the promise — as by incurring expenses in performing or preparing to perform — the court might award a sum of money intended to compensate for this loss. Recovery would then be measured by the promisee's *reliance interest*, in an attempt to put the *promisee back in the position in which the promisee would have been had the promise not been made.* Because such recovery does not take account of the promisee's lost profit, it is ordinarily less generous than recovery measured by the promisee's expectation interest.[3]

Recovery measured by restitution interest

If the promisee conferred a benefit on the promisor in the course of the transaction — as by delivering something to the promisor or improving the promisor's property — the court might award the promisee a sum of money intended to deprive the promisor of this benefit. Recovery would then be measured by the promisee's *restitution interest*, in an attempt to put the *promisor back in the position in which the promisor would have been had the promise not been made.* Because such recovery does not take account of either the promisee's lost profit or reliance by the promisee that produces no benefit to the promisor, it is ordinarily less generous than recovery measured by the promisee's expectation or reliance interest.

---

§2.1   [1] It is important not to confuse reliance as a *ground* for recovery and reliance as a *measure* of recovery. Compare §2.19 *infra* with §12.16 *infra*. As to why a promisor might want to be bound by a promise and the array of remedies available to accomplish this, *see* E. Farnsworth, Changing Your Mind chs. 1 & 11 (1998).

[2] This subject is developed in more detail in Chapter 12 *infra*. The expectation, reliance, and restitution interests are discussed in §12.1 *infra*.

[3] Courts generally have not taken account of lost opportunities in figuring the reliance interest. See the discussion of the reliance interest in §12.1 *infra*.

This brief discussion of measures of recovery serves as background for an exploration of our more immediate concern: the modern contours of the doctrine of consideration as a ground of liability.

B.   CONSIDERATION AS BARGAINED-FOR EXCHANGE

§2.2.   **The Bargain Test of Consideration.**   Among the limitations on the enforcement of promises, the most fundamental is the requirement of consideration.[1] For a time during the nineteenth century a "will theory," under which a promise was enforceable because the promisor had "willed" to be bound by the promise, was prevalent.[2] But that notion was to give way to one based on bargain. We have already seen how, out of the common law action of assumpsit, it came to be required that the promisee give something in exchange for the promise that is either a detriment to the promisee or a benefit to the promisor.[3] By the end of the nineteenth century, at least in the United States, the traditional requirement that the consideration be either a benefit to the promisor or a detriment to the promisee had begun to be replaced by a requirement that the consideration be "bargained for."[4] At first it was said that the benefit or detriment had to be bargained for. But when the first Restatement of Contracts was promulgated in 1933, it defined *consideration* with no mention of benefit or detriment, exclusively in terms of bargain.[5] The Restatement Second does the same and adds a definition. Something is said to be bargained for "if it is sought by the promisor in exchange for his promise and is given by the promisee in exchange for that promise."[6] The rise of this bargain test of consideration had two consequences.

Rise of bargain test of consideration

---

§2.2   [1] *See* In re Owen, 303 S.E.2d 351 (N.C. App. 1983) ("Consideration is the glue that binds the parties to a contract together."). That consideration is a matter of validity under CISG art. 4(a), *see* Geneva Pharms. Tech. Corp. v. Barr Labs., 201 F. Supp. 2d 236 (S.D.N.Y. 2002) (under article 4(a), "validity of an alleged contract is decided under domestic law"). UNIDROIT Principles 3.2 states that a "contract is concluded . . . by the mere agreement of the parties, without any further requirement" such as consideration, though it is arguable that the Principles cannot displace that requirement.

[2] *See* C. Fried, Contract as Promise 16 (1981) ("individual is morally bound to keep his promises"). *See generally* E. Farnsworth, Changing Your Mind ch. 4 (1998).

[3] See the discussion of the elements of consideration in §1.6 *supra*. It should not be forgotten that consideration is not required if no promise is to be enforced. Lack of consideration is not grounds for avoiding a contract that has been performed.

[4] *See generally* Eisenberg, The Principles of Consideration, 67 Cornell L. Rev. 640 (1982).

[5] Restatement §75.

[6] Restatement Second §71. *See* §3 (defining "bargain"), §79 (stating that if the requirement of consideration is met, there is no further requirement of "benefit to the promisor" or "detriment to the promisee"). The Uniform Commercial Code has no comparable provision.

Some promises made unenforceable

First, to the extent that it imposed a new requirement, that of bargain, the test made some promises unenforceable that might previously have been enforceable.[7] The requirement of bargain had little impact on transactions that took place in the marketplace, where bargain was an almost inevitable ingredient. But bargain might well be lacking in transactions taking place outside or on the periphery of the marketplace.[8] Exchanges in a family setting, for example, are often not arrived at by bargain, and promises made in such settings often turned out to be unenforceable under the bargain test. This consequence is scarcely startling, given nineteenth-century America's preeminent concern with the marketplace. New doctrines would have to be devised if such promises were to result in liability.

Some promises made enforceable

Second, to the extent that the test eliminated any requirement of benefit or detriment, it made some promises enforceable that might previously have been unenforceable.[9] It did so by shifting the concern of judges away from the substance of the exchange. Their sole inquiry now was into the process by which the parties had arrived at that exchange — was it the product of "bargain"? This development accorded well with the prevailing mood of nineteenth-century America, which placed its trust in free enterprise and in the dignity and creativity of the individual. Had not Adam Smith written that it was through the competitive process of "bargaining" that society could best take advantage of what he called man's "self-love"?[10] Under the bargain test a promise that had been exchanged as a result of that process satisfied the fundamental test of enforceability without anything more. Of course, if neither the benefit to one party nor the detriment to the other was relevant, that doctrine could scarcely serve as a safeguard against unfairness in the exchange. New doctrines would have to be developed if judges were to inquire into fairness.[11]

Here are some simple examples that meet the bargain test.

What can be consideration

§2.3.   What Can Constitute Consideration.   Virtually anything that anyone would bargain for in exchange for a promise can be consideration for that promise. The same consideration can support a number of promises.[1] Furthermore, as long as part of what is given in exchange for a promise is consideration it is immaterial that the rest is not.[2]

---

[7]Transactions lacking consideration under the bargain test are discussed in §§2.5-2.10 *infra.*

[8]See the discussion of the concern of contract law with exchanges in §1.1 *supra.*

[9]Transactions with consideration under the bargain test are discussed in §§2.11-2.15 *infra.*

[10]See the discussion of the concern of contract law with exchanges in §1.2 *supra.*

[11]For instances in which, even at the height of the emphasis on bargain, "courts often manipulated the bargain theory to serve the ends of justice," *see* Eisenberg, The Responsive Model of Contract Law, 36 Stan. L. Rev. 1107, 1116-17 (1984).

§2.3   [1]Restatement Second §80(1). The promises may be made by several different parties, although for the sake of simplicity we shall usually assume that only two parties are involved.

[2]Pruss v. Pruss, 514 N.W.2d 335 (Neb. 1994) ("fact that part of the stated consideration is insufficient . . . does not prevent another part of the consideration from operating as sufficient

Sometimes the consideration for a promise is some performance by the promisee, as when a seller delivers apples in return for a buyer's promise to pay at the end of the month. Such contracts are often called "unilateral" contracts because a promise is made on only one side.[3] The performance is usually the doing of something — some affirmative act — some action such as delivery of apples or payment of money. But it may also be the refraining from doing something — some inaction such as forbearance from collecting a debt.[4] It may even be a change in a purely intangible legal relation.[5]

Performance as consideration — unilateral contract

Usually, however, the consideration is a return promise,[6] as when a seller promises to deliver apples at the end of the month in return for a buyer's promise to pay at that time. Such contracts are often called "bilateral" contracts because promises are made on both sides. They are more common than unilateral contracts and make up the bulk of economically significant contracts today. The return promise is usually express but may be implied.[7]

Promise as consideration — bilateral contract

We have assumed so far that the performance or the return promise is given *to* the promisor and is given *by* the promisee. Although this is usually the case, it is not necessary as long as the performance or the return promise is bargained for. The consideration may "move" from the promisee *to* someone *other* than the promis*or*, or it may "move" to the promisor *from* someone *other* than the promis*ee*.

Need not move from promisee to promisor

To see how the consideration may "move" to someone other than the promisor, suppose that a bank says, "We promise you, seller, that we will pay you the price of apples if you deliver them to our customer, the buyer." The seller's performance is consideration for the bank's promise, and the seller (the promisee) can enforce that promise, even though the apples are not delivered to the bank (the promisor) but to the buyer (someone other than the promisor).[8]

Need not move to promisor

---

valid consideration"). *See* Restatement Second §80(2). See also note 1 to §2.13 *infra* and the discussion of nominal consideration in §2.11 *infra*.

[3] For a discussion of the utility of the terms "unilateral" and "bilateral," see the discussion of the abandonment of these terms in §3.4 *infra*.

[4] Hamer v. Sidway, 27 N.E. 256 (N.Y. 1891) (discussed in §2.4 *infra*).

[5] This may include "the creation, modification, or destruction" of that legal relation. Restatement Second §71.

[6] *See* Iacono v. Lyons, 16 S.W.3d 92 (Tex. App. 2000) (promises by two tourists to share winnings in Las Vegas "represent the respective benefits and detriments, or the bargained for exchange, necessary to satisfy the consideration requirement"). See also the discussions of the practical need for such exchanges in §1.3 *supra* and of the rationale for protecting expectation in §1.6 *supra*.

[7] See the discussion of the duty of reasonable efforts in §2.13 *infra*.

[8] Erftmier v. Eickhoff, 316 N.W.2d 754 (Neb. 1982) (benefit "need not be to the party contracting but may be to anyone else at his procurement or request"). Note that the consideration (delivery of the apples) might be regarded as being a detriment to the promisee (the seller) without being a benefit to the promisor (the bank). This is, of course, irrelevant under the bargain test of consideration. This rule is often applied in connection with promises of suretyship. *See* the discussion of the example of suretyship in §6.3 *infra*.

**Need not move
from promisee**

To see how the consideration may "move" from someone other than the promisee, suppose that a buyer says, "I promise you, bank, that I will pay you the price of apples if they are delivered to me by your customer, the seller." The seller's performance is consideration for the buyer's promise to pay, and the bank (the promisee) can enforce that promise, even though the apples are not delivered by the bank (the promisee) but by the seller (someone other than the promisee).[9]

**Rationale for
enforcing
exchanges of
promises**

The enforceability of exchanges of promise: prompts the question: Why should a promisee's mere return performance · /ithout more suffice to bind a promisor? Put differently, why should not the promisor be free to renege on the promise as long as the promisee has done nothing in reliance on it? English judges did not ask "why" when, beginning in the sixteenth century, they shaped the doctrine of consideration.[10] Since the enforcement of wholly executory exchanges of promises accords with the average person's sense of justice, there may be little practical purpose to the question, but for academics it has had an enduring fascination. Perhaps the most satisfying answer is that to encourage reliance of promises, "we must . . . dispense with its proof."[11] Promising is an important activity because a promise affords the promisee a basis for planning. But a promise will be of little use in planning unless it can be relied upon, and protecting a promisee's expectation is the most effective way of protecting a promisee's reliance. Although the law could protect reliance by enforcing promises only if the promisee proved reliance, reliance may be difficult to prove, and promisees might hesitate to rely on promises out of fear that the burden of proving reliance would complicate or prevent enforcement.[12] Difficulties of

---

[9] Marine Contractors Co. v. Hurley, 310 N.E.2d 915 (Mass. 1974) (retiring employee promised employer not to compete in consideration of early payment of retirement benefits by trust fund).

Note that the consideration (delivery of the apples) might be regarded as being a benefit to the promisor (the buyer) without being a detriment to the promisee (the bank). This is, of course, irrelevant under the bargain test of consideration.

Although subsection (2) of Restatement Second §71 speaks of something being bargained for when it "is given" by the *promisee* in exchange for the promise, subsection (4) makes it plain that this should not be understood as meaning that consideration can be given *only* by the promisee. For ease of expression, however, we shall usually follow the example of the Restatement in speaking only of the common situation, where it is the promisee that gives the consideration. For a situation in which the consideration is given *neither* to the promisor *nor* by the promisee, *see* Restatement Second §71 illus. 18.

[10] See §1.6 *supra*.

[11] L. Fuller & W. Perdue, The Reliance Interest in Contract Damages (pt. 1), 46 Yale L.J. 52, 62 (1936), expanded in E. Farnsworth, Changing Your Mind ch. 6 at 59 (1998) ("strength of a promisor's claim based on unproven lost opportunities turns in good measure on the plausibility of the assertion that the promsisee would have found and seized some supposed opportunity").

[12] *But see* P. Atiyah, Promises, Morals, and Law 40 (1981) (arguing that a promisor should have a chance to rebut a presumption of reliance by proving that the promisee had not relied before the promisor reneged).

Some promisees might even feign reliance or engage in wasteful reliance with a view to making legal sanctions available.

proof become acute when a party's reliance is negative – consisting in refraining from doing something rather than in doing something. A promisee's reliance on a promise typically consists in refraining from pursuing other opportunities to obtain a comparable commitment, often refraining from arranging for a comparable substitute for the promise on a market. Thus, the argument runs, a promisee should not be asked to produce proof of negative reliance. Better to favor the few who have not relied than to vex the many who have relied but will have trouble in proving it. A bright-line rule based on mere assent, it turns out, both protects expectation and at least covertly recognizes reliance.

An example of the application of the doctrine of consideration will now be helpful.

§2.4.   Example of Consideration. The venerable case of *Hamer v. Sidway*,[1] decided by the New York Court of Appeals in 1891, offers a simple and picturesque set of facts with which to test our understanding of the bargain test of consideration. When William E. Story II was 15 years old, his uncle, William E. Story, promised to pay him $5,000 if he would "refrain from drinking liquor, using tobacco, swearing and playing cards or billiards for money until he should become 21 years of age." The nephew refrained until age 21 and, when the $5,000 was not paid, suit was brought on the promise to pay $5,000. The defense was that there was no consideration for the uncle's promise. The court rejected the defense.[2]

Facts in Hamer v. Sidway

Was there consideration for the uncle's promise under the bargain test? This question can be divided into two subsidiary questions.[3] First, was something, either another promise or a performance, given in exchange for that promise? Here it was the nephew's performance that was given — his forbearance from engaging in the enumerated vices until he was 21.[4] Second, was the nephew's forbearance bargained for in the sense of both being sought by the uncle in exchange for his promise and being given by the nephew in exchange for that promise? It seems that this was so. Therefore, under the bargain test of consideration, the defense should fail. The uncle's promise was not unenforceable for lack of consideration. However, the example calls for two further observations.[5]

Analysis in terms of exchange and bargain

---

§2.4   [1]27 N.E. 256 (N.Y. 1891).

[2]For additional facts, *see* Hamer v. Sidway, 64 N.Y. Sup. Ct. (57 Hun.) 229 (1890) (revealing that the uncle had long planned a gift of $5,000 to his nephew and explaining the circumstances surrounding the nephew's transfer of his claim).

[3]First, of course, one must ask *whose* promise is sought to be enforced. The answer is obvious here, since only one party (the uncle) has made a promise. It would be less obvious if the nephew had promised to forbear.

[4]Therefore the nephew would not have been liable to the uncle if he had, say, begun to smoke when he was 19.

[5]The reader may also wonder about the liability of the uncle if the nephew had persisted in his forbearance but at age 19 had received a letter from his uncle purporting to revoke his promise. On this question, see §3.24 *infra*.

Promise could have been consideration

First, the result would have been the same if the uncle had bargained for and received the nephew's promise to forbear, rather than his actual forbearance, as consideration.[6] In general, if a performance would itself be consideration, a promise to render that performance can also be consideration.[7] But it must be the promise rather than the performance that is bargained for.[8]

Benefit and detriment irrelevant

Second, the bargain test of consideration does not require us to ask whether the nephew's forbearance was either a benefit to the uncle or a detriment to the nephew. It is arguable that it was both: that the uncle was benefited by having the pleasure of seeing his nephew and namesake abstain from the enumerated vices; and that the nephew suffered a detriment by denying himself the pleasures of those vices. The New York Court of Appeals took the view that the promise was enforceable on the latter ground, because of the detriment suffered by the nephew, rejecting the argument that by his abstinence the nephew had been "not harmed but benefited."[9] Given a sufficiently expansive definition of *benefit* and *detriment*, judges might have avoided inquiry into the substance of the exchange even without adoption of the bargain test. After all, if a promisor chooses to bargain for something it must be a benefit to the promisor, and if the promisor needs to bargain for something in order to extract it from the promisee, it must be a detriment to the promisee.[10]

Significance of doctrine

The principal significance of the doctrine of consideration lies in its role as one of the theoretical underpinnings of contract law.[11] Its practical importance is more limited, as is suggested by the ease with which its requirements can be satisfied, even in transactions that are on the periphery of the marketplace. Nevertheless, it does have important practical consequences in making some promises unenforceable, either because there is no exchange at all or because, although there is an exchange, there is no bargain.

---

[6] Schumm v. Berg, 231 P.2d 39 (Cal. 1951) (alternative holding: promise by mother of unborn illegitimate child to name it "Wallace" if boy and "Wally" if girl, after its father, actor Wallace Beery, was consideration for his promise to support the child).

[7] Restatement Second §75.

[8] Since, in the actual case, the uncle appeared to be bargaining for the nephew's forbearance, it would make no difference that (as the opinion suggests) the nephew may have promised to forbear. See the discussion of the offeror as "master of the offer" in §3.12 *infra*.

[9] Despite its age, *Hamer* is still very much alive, along with the notion that either a benefit or a detriment will suffice. *See* Weiner v. McGraw-Hill, 443 N.E.2d 441 (N.Y. 1982) ("any basic contemporary definition would include the idea that it consists of either a benefit to the promisor or a detriment to the promisee" as "elaborated in Hamer v. Sidway, the seminal case on the subject").

[10] *See* Hardesty v. Smith, 3 Ind. 39 (1851), and Chicago & Atl. Ry. v. Derkes, 3 N.E. 239 (Ind. 1885), both quoted in a footnote to the discussion of the reciprocal nature of the bargain in §2.6 *infra*.

[11] The first great issue in contract law is what kinds of promises the law should enforce — an issue usually subsumed under the heading of consideration." Eisenberg, The Responsive Model of Contract Law, 36 Stan. L. Rev. 1107, 1112 (1984).

What are the most significant types of promises that are unenforceable because of the doctrine of consideration?

C. TRANSACTIONS LACKING BARGAINED-FOR EXCHANGE

§2.5.   **Exchange Lacking: Gratuitous Promises.**   The most significant class of promises unenforceable for lack of consideration is made up of purely gratuitous (or gift) promises—promises for which there has been no exchange at all. Suppose that an employer promises an employee a gold watch as a present, but then reconsiders and refuses to deliver it. The employer's promise is not supported by consideration since there was no exchange—the employer received nothing in return.[1] It is therefore not enforceable unless there is some alternative basis for enforceability, as there was in the case of a gratuitous promise under seal before the seal was deprived of its effect.[2] Our common law tradition, in contrast to that of civil law systems, does not require us to define a special category of promises regarded as gratuitous.[3] As far as enforceability is concerned, what is significant is not that a promise is gratuitous but that it lacks consideration.

A gift (a present transfer of an interest in property) stands on a footing different from that of a promise to make a gift. Suppose that the employer, instead of merely making a promise, actually gives the employee the watch as a present, but then reconsiders and seeks the return of the watch. Here, because the employee's assertion of a right to keep the watch does not involve enforcement of a promise, the problem is not seen as one for the law of contracts. It is seen, instead, as one for the law of property.[4] Under that law, once the

Example of unenforceable gratuitous promise

Rule for completed gift contrasted

§2.5   [1]A promise to pay a larger sum of money, say $3, in return for a smaller sum of money, say $1, to be paid at the same time, is regarded as a promise to make a gift of the difference, here $2. See the discussion of a likely example of nominal consideration in §2.11 *infra*. This is not so, however, if the smaller sum is to be paid at an earlier time. *See* the discussion of the limitation on the rule in §4.23 *infra*.

[2]Stonestreet v. Southern Oil Co., 37 S.E.2d 676 (N.C. 1946) (gratuitous promise of reimbursement for half of cost of drilling a well held unenforceable). As to the effect of a seal, see the discussion of the unsuitability of the action of covenant as a general basis in §1.5 *supra* and §2.16 *infra*. The donee's acceptance of, or promise to accept, the gift is not consideration for a promise to make a gift. Briggs v. Miller, 186 N.W. 163 (Wis. 1922) (if "mere trouble involved in making an acceptance amounted to consideration, then there would in every conceivable offer and acceptance be involved a consideration"). *See* Restatement Second §71 illus. 7. Nor is the employee's gratitude consideration for the promise.

[3]On gratuitous promises in France and Germany, *see* J. Dawson, Gifts and Promises chs. 2 and 3 (1980).

[4]See the discussion of the concern of contract law with the future in §1.1 *supra*. The same would be true even if the employer had promised to make a gift of the watch before actually delivering it.

gift has been completed by the donor's delivery of the watch, the transfer is irrevocable and the donor cannot recover it.[5]

Justification based on substance

Why should the employer be able to revoke a promise to make a gift but not the gift itself? Why should delivery make a difference? [To say that the promise to make a gift is governed by the law of contracts while the gift is governed by the law of property is scarcely satisfactory.] One possible justification for the difference goes to substance. It can be argued that denial of relief in both instances evidences a policy of leaving parties to gratuitous transactions where they stand. Providing the legal machinery to dispense justice is costly, and it may not be warranted in the absence of the sort of exchange based on bargain that tends to enhance a society's total wealth. Gifts are not necessarily productive.[6]

Justification based on form

There is also some common sense to the requirement of delivery as a formality. It performs an "evidentiary" function by providing some proof of the fact that the donor intended to make a gift and of the fact that a gift was actually made. And it performs a "cautionary" function, by bringing home to the donor the significance of the act and preventing ill-considered and impulsive gifts.[7]

Promises lacking bargain distinguished

Whatever its justification, the distinction remains. It accounts for the most important type of promise that lacks consideration, the purely gratuitous promise—the promise for which there has been no exchange at all. The other significant classes of promise that fail in enforceability fail not for want of exchange, but for absence of bargain.[8]

What are these classes where bargain is absent?

Reciprocal nature of bargain

§2.6. Bargained-for Exchange Lacking: Analysis. For the requirement of a bargain to be met, there must be reciprocity. According to Holmes, an influential advocate of the requirement, what is required is that the promise and the consideration be in "the relation of reciprocal conventional inducement,

---

[5]A gift of a chattel could also be made by delivery of a sealed writing known as a "deed." *See* the discussion of the analogy of a gift of a chattel in §11.6 *infra*. Now that the effect of the seal has been abolished in most states (*see* the discussion of the decline of the seal in §2.16 *infra*), the efficacy of the delivery of an unsealed writing is unclear.

[6]*See generally* E. Farnsworth, Changing Your Mind chs. 7 & 8 (1998), revised from Farnsworth, Promises to Make Gifts, 43 Am. J. Comp. L. 359 (1995); Eisenberg, Donative Promises, 47 U. Chi. L. Rev. 1 (1979).

[7]For a classic discussion of the functions of formalities, *see* Fuller, Consideration and Form, 41 Colum. L. Rev. 799, 800-06 (1941).

[8]This analysis assumes that the concept of exchange is distinct from that of bargain and that some exchanges are the product of bargain while others are not. This is consistent with §75 of the first Restatement, which required that consideration be both "bargained for and given in exchange for the promise." Restatement Second §71, perhaps unfortunately, subsumes the requirement of exchange under the definition of bargain. Subsection (1) requires only that the consideration be "bargained for," and subsection (2) provides that something must be sought and given "in exchange" in order to be "bargained for."

each for the other."[1] In other words, "the promise and the consideration must purport to be the motive each for the other"; it is not enough that the promise induces the consideration or that the consideration induces the promise, "if the other half is wanting."[2] The Restatement Second reaffirms this by defining *bargain* to require that the consideration both be "*sought* by the *promisor* in exchange for his promise" and be "*given* by the *promisee* in exchange for his promise."[3] Where, as is common, a party makes a number of promises, the consideration given by the other party suffices as consideration for all of those promises.[4]

However, it is not required that the parties actually bargain over the terms of their agreement.[5] Nor is it required that they regard their relationship as adversarial or antagonistic. Nevertheless, the mere fact that there has been an exchange will not suffice.

Actual bargain not required

If we assume that there has been an exchange in which a promisor has made a promise and the promisee has made a promise or rendered some performance, the promisor's promise will still lack consideration if the promisee's action was not bargained for. Instances of such exchanges in which bargain is absent fall into two categories: first, those in which the promisor was *not seeking* to induce action by the promisee, and second, those in which the action that the promisee took was *not induced* by the promise (i.e., the promisee took action independently of the promise).

Two categories where bargain absent

The first category may itself be divided into two subcategories, in each of which the promisor, in making the promise, does not seek to induce action by the promisee, although the promisee takes or has taken some action that can be regarded as part of an exchange. The cases in the first subcategory are those of past consideration, in which the promisee has already taken the action at the time the promise is made (*see* §§2.7, 2.8 *infra*). The cases in the second subcategory are those of unsolicited action, in which the promisee takes the action after the promise is made, but the promisor did not seek to induce it (*see* §2.9 *infra*).

Promisor did not seek to induce action

The second category is made up of cases in which, although the promisor was seeking to induce action by the promisee and although the promisee did take such action, the action was not, in fact, induced by the promise. Generally, in these cases the promisee acts in ignorance of the promise (*see* §2.10 *infra*).

Action sought by promisor but not induced

---

§2.6 [1] O. Holmes, The Common Law 293-94 (1881). *See* G. Gilmore, The Death of Contract 19-21 (1974) (arguing that the "bargain theory" of consideration was a "newly-minted theory" proposed by Holmes when he lectured on contracts in 1881 and "enshrined" in the Restatement).

[2] Wisconsin & Mich. Ry. v. Powers, 191 U.S. 379, 386 (1903).

[3] Restatement Second §75.

[4] Reddy v. Community Found. of Man, 298 S.E.2d 906 (W. Va. 1982) (covenant "is not an isolated provision" since the "contract contains mutual promises, and that is adequate . . . on its face"). The consideration for an option contract is often part of a larger transaction. See the discussion of other consideration and reliance in §3.23 *infra*.

[5] See the discussion of standardized agreements in §4.26 *infra*.

Summary

Here is a summary of this analysis:

A. The promisor did not seek to induce the action taken by the promisee because
  1. the promisee had already taken the action at the time the promise was made (past consideration) (§§2.7, 2.8) or
  2. the promisee took action at the same time as or after the promise was made, but the promisor had not sought to induce that action when making the promise (unsolicited action) (§2.9).
B. The promisor did seek to induce the action taken by the promisee, but the action that the promisee took was not taken in response to the promise (§2.10).

First we examine cases where the promisor did not seek to induce the promisee's action because the promisee had already taken that action.

Past consideration cannot be consideration

§2.7. Past Consideration. Imagine an exchange consisting of a promise on one side and some action, either promise or performance, on the other. Only if that action has not yet been taken when the promise is made can the promisor be bargaining for it when making the promise. If the action has already been taken, the promisor cannot be seeking to induce it. Such "past consideration" — action already taken before a promise is made — cannot be consideration for the promise. Suppose that an employer promises an employee a gold watch "in return for your good work during the year just ended," but then reconsiders. The employee's "good work" in the past is no consideration for the employer's promise, and the promise is not enforceable. Although the employer may have made a promise, and the employee may have done work, the exchange was not the result of bargain. This principle has had its main impact in cases that have refused to enforce promises to pay pensions for past services.[1]

Possibility of restructuring the transaction

It is often possible for the parties to restructure the transaction to make the promise enforceable. The requirement of consideration will be met if the employer bargains for some future performance by the employee — remaining on the job for a stated time,[2] retiring within a stated time, refraining from

---

§2.7 [1] Feinberg v. Pfeiffer Co., 322 S.W.2d 163 (Mo. App. 1959) (dictum: recovery allowed on basis of reliance). The possibility of recovery by an employee on the basis of reliance on an employer's promise to pay a pension is discussed in §2.19 *infra*.

[2] Mabley & Carew Co. v. Borden, 195 N.E. 697 (Ohio 1935) ("In appreciation of the duration and faithful character of your services heretofore rendered . . . there will be paid in the event of your death, if still an employee of this Company . . . ."). *But cf.* Feinberg v. Pfeiffer Co., *supra* note 1 (no language "predicating plaintiff's right to a pension upon her continued employment"). As to whether it would make a difference if the employee were already bound to remain employed for the stated time, see §4.21 *infra*.

competing with the employer after retirement[3] — or for a return promise by the employee to do any of these things.[4]

The conclusion that past consideration cannot be consideration is inevitable under the bargain test. As we have seen in tracing the expansion of the action of assumpsit, courts had, by the middle of the sixteenth century, come to recognize that a debtor who was already liable on a promise in debt and who made a subsequent promise became liable in assumpsit (*indebitatus assumpsit*) on the subsequent promise.[5] Judges did not then distinguish between "past" and "present" consideration and were not troubled by the fact that there was nothing for the promisor to have sought in exchange for his subsequent promise. It was enough that the promisee had already done something, at the instance of the promisor that gave rise to liability in debt. With the holding in *Slade's Case*,[6] in 1602, that an action of assumpsit could be maintained without a subsequent promise, the need to find such a promise disappeared, along with any need to explain why that promise was enforceable though supported only by past consideration. Other situations were to arise later, however, in which it would be argued that a promise was enforceable though supported only by past consideration.

We turn now to those other situations.

Past consideration in the context of *Slade's Case*

§2.8. Moral Obligation.

By the latter half of the sixteenth century, courts had accepted the general principle that "past consideration" could not be consideration.[1] There was, however, pressure to allow exceptions for promises to perform what could be regarded as a "moral obligation." One such situation arose if a debtor promised to pay a debt that had been barred by the statute of limitations.[2] Although no longer under a legal obligation to pay the debt, the debtor might be thought to have a moral obligation to do so. Was a promise to perform that moral obligation enforceable? There was an obvious analogy to the enforcement of the debtor's subsequent promise prior to *Slade's*

Exception for debt barred by statute of limitations

---

[3] Langer v. Superior Steel Corp., 161 A. 571 (Pa. Super. 1932) ("as long as you live and preserve your present attitude of loyalty . . . and are not employed in any competitive occupation").

[4] Langer v. Superior Steel Corp., *supra* note 3 (alternative holding: by taking payments, employee "impliedly accepted the conditions," i.e., promised not to compete). Consideration may also be found in the employee's surrender of a claim against the employer or in a promise to do so. See §2.12 *infra*.

[5] See the discussion of the supplanting of debt by *indebitatus assumpsit* in §1.6 *supra*.

[6] 76 Eng. Rep. 1074 (K.B. 1602) (*see* the discussion of the supplanting of debt by *indebitatus assumpsit* in §1.6 *supra*).

§2.8 [1] Hunt v. Bate, 73 Eng. Rep. 605 (Q.B. 1568), discussed in A. Simpson, History of the Common Law of Contract 452-58 (1987).

[2] We are not here concerned with a promise, made as part of the original agreement, to extend the period of limitation. Such a promise would raise no problem of consideration, but it is generally regarded as void because contrary to a public policy against the pressing of stale claims. *See* UCC 2-725(1) (by "original agreement the parties may reduce the period of limitation [of four years] to not less than one year but may not extend it").

Case.[3] Courts concluded that here, too, the subsequent promise (to perform the debtor's moral obligation) was enforceable, and so it remains today.[4] Although judges may speak of "past consideration" or of "moral obligation" as consideration, they are really making an exception to the requirement of a bargained-for exchange.[5] Such promises as fall within that exception are simply enforceable *without* consideration, at least as that term is understood under the bargain test.[6]

Scope of exception

Today the exception extends to a promise to pay any antecedent contractual or quasi-contractual debt owed to the promisee.[7] Since the action is based on the new promise, rather than on the barred debt, recovery is limited to the terms of that promise. Therefore, if the promise is a conditional one or is one to pay only part of the debt, it is enforceable only to that extent.[8] The promise may be made before the period of limitations has run on the original debt, as well as afterward.[9] It may be inferred from an admission or acknowledgment of the debt (if not coupled with an indication of an intention not to pay),[10] or from a statement that the statute of limitations will not be pleaded as a defense (if not coupled with a denial of the debt and reservation of defenses),[11] or from a part payment of the debt (if made under such circumstances as indicate its recognition).[12] Frequent disputes over whether a subsequent promise had in fact been made led in 1828 to the enactment in England of Lord Tenterden's Act, requiring that the promise be in writing and signed, and then to similar legislation in most of the United States.[13] The requirement does not, however,

---

[3] See the discussion of past consideration in the context of *Slade's Case* in §2.7 *supra*.

[4] Little v. Blunt, 26 Mass. (9 Pick.) 488 (1830) ("debt barred by the statute of limitations is a good consideration for an express promise"). *See* Restatement Second §82.

[5] Sometimes the result was rationalized on the ground that the promise "revived" the barred debt or "waived" the bar of the statute, a locution that permitted the court to avoid the subject of consideration. The modern and better view, however, is that the old debt remains barred and that any new claim must be based on the new promise. *See* Restatement Second §82 cmt. *c*.

[6] The Restatement Second deals with the rule under the topic heading "Contracts without Consideration."

[7] Restatement Second §§82, 92. But it does not extend to "claims for damages for breach of a promissory bargain not performed on either side [nor to] tort claims not involving unjust enrichment." Restatement Second §82 cmt. *b*.

[8] Jones v. Jones, 242 F. Supp. 979 (S.D.N.Y. 1965) ("I promise you, if our efforts give the results expected, that I will fix you up very comfortably."); Brown v. Hebb, 175 A. 602 (Md. 1934) (acknowledgment of only $300 of $1,500 debt operated as promise as to only $300).

[9] Brown v. Hebb, *supra* note 8. In this situation, the debtor's subsequent promise may be supported by consideration in the form of the creditor's forbearance or promise to forbear.

[10] Cady v. Guess, 124 S.W.2d 213 (Ark. 1939) ("I think I may be able to send you $500 by October 10th and follow up with $100 a month until paid or as long as I live. I realize that this is a very sorry offer but don't see how I can do any better . . . .").

[11] Restatement Second §86(2)(c) & cmt. *f*.

[12] Jones v. Jones, *supra* note 8. The same result may follow from the payment of interest or the giving of a negotiable instrument or of collateral. Restatement Second §82(b) & cmt. *e*.

[13] 9 Geo. 4, ch. 14, §1 (1828), now replaced by Limitation Act, 1980, ch. 58, §30.

change the effect of part payments nor, of course, of promises that are otherwise supported by consideration.

A similar exception has traditionally been made if a debtor promises to pay a debt that has been discharged in bankruptcy proceedings or a debt that is not yet discharged but is dischargeable in bankruptcy proceedings begun before the promise is made.[14] In contrast to the case of a debt barred by the statute of limitations, however, the promise must be express and will not be inferred from, for example, a part payment. It is not clear whether this is merely an historical accident or a reflection of a stronger policy behind discharge in bankruptcy as compared with the bar of the period of limitations.[15] The bankruptcy law subjects such promises to additional requirements intended to ensure that the debtor was fully informed and that the promise was voluntary.[16]

Exception for debt discharged in bankruptcy proceedings

Situations also arise in which, although a promisor is allowed to avoid the promise under some rule designed for the promisor's protection, a new promise to perform the voidable obligation is enforceable. (This assumes, of course, that the new promise is not itself voidable for the same reason.) For example, a minor's promise is voidable for lack of capacity, but a promise on coming of age to perform that voidable promise is enforceable.[17] The result is frequently rationalized on the ground that the promisor has ratified or affirmed the original promise, electing not to exercise the power of avoidance. But it also can be regarded as an exception to the requirement of a bargained-for exchange — as an instance of a promise to perform a moral obligation that is enforceable without consideration.[18]

Exception for voidable promises

Lord Mansfield, who was no friend of the doctrine of consideration,[19] would have extended these exceptions to cover all situations in which it might be said that the promisor is under "moral obligation," even though there had never been a prior legal obligation. Near the end of the eighteenth century, he wrote, "Where a man is under a moral obligation, which no Court of Law or Equity

Mansfield's attempt at extension

[14] Stanek v. White, 215 N.W. 784 (Minn. 1927); Restatement Second §83.

[15] If it is the latter, it is curious that relatively few states have carried over to the case of bankruptcy the statutory requirement that the promise be in writing and signed.

[16] 11 U.S.C. §524(c), (d) (Bankruptcy Code).

[17] See the discussion of avoidance in §4.4 *infra*. See also the similar rules on mental incompetency (*see* the discussion of avoidance and ratification in §4.7 *infra*), misrepresentation (*see* the discussion of avoidance and ratification in §4.15 *infra*), duress (*see* the discussion of avoidance and ratification in §4.19 *infra*), and the statute of frauds (*see* the discussion of how the contract is not deprived of all effect in §6.10 *infra*). A distinction is sometimes made between a *voidable* contract (one that is voidable at the election of one party) and a *void* contract (one that has no legal effect because of some defect). The latter is not, at least under the traditional definition, a "contract" at all. *See* Restatement Second §7 cmt. *a*.

[18] *See* Restatement Second §85. A similar principle has been applied to enforce subsequent promises to perform obligations that were initially void, rather than merely voidable, because of some minor illegality, such as a violation of the usury laws (if the subsequent promise is to pay the untainted part). *See* the discussion of change in legislation in §5.5 *infra*.

[19] See the discussion of Lord Mansfield's view in §2.18 *infra*.

can inforce, and promises, the honesty and rectitude of the thing is a consideration."[20] But by the middle of the nineteenth century the Court of Queen's Bench had repudiated any such doctrine in England,[21] and Lord Mansfield's views on consideration fared no better in this country than in England.

Example of *Mills v. Wyman*

An early American example is *Mills v. Wyman*. Mills had cared for Wyman's 25-year-old son for several weeks, after the son had fallen ill on his return from a voyage at sea. Although the law did not make a father liable for the care of an adult child, the father, in gratitude, wrote Mills a letter promising to reimburse him for the expenses that he had incurred. When Wyman refused to pay, Mills sued. The Supreme Judicial Court of Massachusetts held that the father's promise was unenforceable. It distinguished "cases of debts barred by the statute of limitations, of debts incurred by infants, of debts of bankrupts" on the ground that subsequent promises "merely remove an impediment created by law to the recovery of debts honestly due" and are "not promises to pay something for nothing." Such promises as the father's, however, "the law of society has left . . . to the interior forum, as the tribunal of conscience has been aptly called."[22]

Arguments for and against moral obligation

Williston defended this traditional view as promoting certainty, arguing that the classes of promises that are enforceable must be clearly defined. "The test of moral consideration must vary with the opinion of every individual," and since it has been said that "there is a moral obligation to perform every promise, it would seem that if morality was to be the guide, every promise would be enforced."[23] In opposition, it has been urged that the solution to the problem of certainty lies not in rejecting the doctrine that moral obligation may be a basis for enforceability, "but in taming it by continuing the process of judicial exclusion and inclusion already begun in the cases involving infants' contracts, barred debts, and discharged bankrupts."[24] Such extensions have been made by a few courts and legislatures.

Example of *Webb v. McGowin*

One of the leading cases is *Webb v. McGowin*. Webb had saved McGowin's life by an act of heroism that left Webb badly crippled for life. Although the law gave Webb no claim against McGowin for his services,[25] Webb sued McGowin's estate alleging that McGowin had, in gratitude, promised (presumably orally) to pay him $15 every two weeks for the rest of Webb's life. Payments had been made for more than eight years, until after McGowin's death, but his executors

---

[20] Hawkes v. Saunders, 98 Eng. Rep. 1091 (K.B. 1782) (promise of executrix to pay legacy).

[21] Eastwood v. Kenyon, 113 Eng. Rep. 482 (K.B. 1840) ("enforcement of such promises at law, however plausibly reconciled by the desire to effect all conscientious engagements, might be attended with mischievous consequences to society," and suits and voluntary undertaking would be multiplied "to the prejudice of real creditors").

[22] 20 Mass. (3 Pick.) 207, 209-10 (1825).

[23] 1 S. Williston, Contracts §148 (1st ed. 1920). *See* Schnell v. Nell, 17 Ind. 29 (1861) ("moral consideration only will not support a promise").

[24] Fuller, Consideration and Form, 41 Colum. L. Rev. 799, 821, 822 (1941).

[25] See the discussion of the meaning of *gratuitous* in §2.20 *infra*.

refused to continue them.[26] The Court of Appeals of Alabama, noting that McGowin had "complied with this agreement up to the time of his death," held that the promise was enforceable, since McGowin, "having received a material benefit from the promisee, [was] morally bound to compensate him for the services rendered."[27]

Another leading case is *Estate of Hatten*. Mrs. Monsted, a widow, had furnished meals, transportation in her automobile, and similar services with increasing frequency in the several years before his death to Mr. Hatten, an elderly millionaire bachelor and family friend of over 25 years' standing. Hatten came to treat the Monsted home "as though it were his own" and told her that some day she would be "paid well" for her services. Although the law gave Monsted no claim against Hatten for her services, Hatten in gratitude wrote out a promissory note promising to pay her $25,000 in a year. When he died two months later, his administrator refused to pay. Monsted sued on the promise, claiming that the services were "of the reasonable value of $6,000." The Supreme Court of Wisconsin affirmed a judgment for Monsted in the amount of $25,000. The promise was enforceable on the ground "that a receipt by the promisor of an actual benefit will support an executory promise, and that a moral consideration may be sufficient to support an executory promise 'where the promisor originally received from the promisee something of value sufficient to arouse a moral as distinguished from a legal obligation.'"[28]

Example of *Estate of Hatten*

Restatement Second §86 states a flexible rule that purports to be based on this trend toward recognition of "moral obligation" as a basis for enforcement.

Restatement Second rule

(1) A promise made in recognition of a benefit previously received by the promisor from the promisee is binding to the extent necessary to prevent injustice.

(2) A promise is not binding under Subsection (1)
   (a) if the promisee conferred the benefit as a gift or for other reasons the promisor has not been unjustly enriched; or
   (b) to the extent that its value is disproportionate to the benefit.[29]

A few states have dealt with the problem by legislation. New York, for example, has enacted a statute that takes a distinctive approach. Under it, a written and signed promise

New York statute

[26] A letter to the author from counsel for the executors explains that no writing was alleged. It was the executors' position that McGowin had made no promise, but that, as president of the company that employed Webb, he had arranged out of gratitude to have the employer continue payments after Webb's workers' compensation payments ran out. McGowin's successor as president had the employer discontinue its payments. The case was settled after the sufficiency of Webb's complaint was upheld.

[27] 168 So. 196, 197, 198 (Ala. App. 1935).

[28] 288 N.W. 278, 287 (Wis. 1940) (relying on a questionable reading of the law relating to negotiable promissory notes).

[29] *Accord:* Worner Agency v. Doyle, 479 N.E.2d 468 (Ill. App. 1985) (promise to pay finder's fee for services "performed before the signing of the agreement"; Restatement Second not cited).

shall not be denied effect as a valid contractual obligation on the ground that consideration for the promise is past or executed, if the consideration is expressed in the writing and is proved to have been given or performed and would be a valid consideration but for the time when it was given or performed.[30]

Although the New York statute has the merit of providing a simple and clear means of making such promises enforceable, it has been criticized by the Reporter who drafted the Restatement Second rule as being both "too broad in scope and too restrictive in formal requirements."[31]

Breadth of statute

The facts of *Mills v. Wyman* illustrate this objection to the breadth of the statute. Under the New York statute the father's promise would be enforceable because it was made in a letter which presumably mentioned the past services. The illustrations to the Restatement Second, however, suggest that the father's promise still would be unenforceable because it was not made "in recognition of a benefit previously received by the *promisor*," but rather in recognition of a benefit received by his son.[32] The objection is also illustrated by the employer's promise to give an employee a gold watch "in return for your good work during the year just ended." Under the New York statute, the promise would be enforceable if made in a writing that complied with the statute. The comments to the Restatement Second, however, suggest that the promise would not be enforceable because "the enrichment of one party as a result of an unequal exchange is not regarded as unjust, and this Section has no application to a promise to pay or perform more or to accept less than is called for by a pre-existing bargain between the same parties."[33]

Restrictiveness of statute's formal requirements

The facts of *Webb v. McGowin* and *Estate of Hatten* illustrate the Reporter's objection to the restrictiveness of the statute's formal requirements. Under the New York statute, neither promise would be enforceable — McGowin's because it was not in writing and Hatten's because the writing did not mention the past services.[34] The illustrations to the Restatement Second, however, indicate that the promises in both cases would be enforceable. In the latter case, if the value of Monsted's services was materially less than the $25,000 promised, the

---

[30]N.Y. Gen. Oblig. L. §5-1105. California has a statute that provides that a "legal obligation resting upon the promisor, or a moral obligation originating in some benefit conferred upon the promisor, or prejudice suffered by the promisee, is also a good consideration for a promise, to an extent corresponding with the extent of the obligation, but no further or otherwise." Cal. Civ. Code §1606.

[31]Braucher, Freedom of Contract and the Second Restatement, 78 Yale L.J. 598, 605 (1969).

[32]See Restatement Second §86 illus. 1.

[33]This despite the fact that payments had been made for more than eight years.

[34]See Umscheid v. Simnacher, 482 N.Y.S.2d 295 (App. Div. 1984) (letter did not contain "unequivocal promise," nor was consideration "expressed" in it). And, conversely, if the promise had complied with these formalities, recovery would have been had for the full $25,000.

promise would not be binding "to the extent that its value is disproportionate to the benefit."[35]

Perhaps only two things can be said with assurance in this area. First, the trend is clearly in favor of increased enforceability of promises made in recognition of a "moral obligation." Second, the boundary between enforceability and unenforceability is likely to remain uncertain, as is suggested by the Restatement Second qualification, "to the extent necessary to prevent injustice."[36] In view of the negligible impact of these moral obligation cases on commercial life, however, this uncertainty is unlikely to cause concern in the marketplace.

Now we turn to cases of unsolicited action.

Trend toward enforceability; uncertainty of rules

§2.9. Unsolicited Action. Even if the promisee takes some action subsequent to the promise (so that there is no problem of past consideration), that action is not bargained for and cannot be consideration for the promise if it was unsolicited by the promisor. Under the bargain test, if the promise was gratuitous, subsequent action does not make the promise enforceable. And even if the promise was not gratuitous, subsequent action that differs from that sought by the promisor does not make the promise enforceable. Leaving this latter situation for the following chapter,[1] we discuss here only the case of the gratuitous promise.

Unsolicited action cannot be consideration

Suppose that a debtor is in default on a debt, and a friend of the debtor makes a gratuitous promise to the creditor to pay it. Knowing of this unenforceable promise, the creditor forbears from proceeding against the debtor for a month, during which time the debtor becomes insolvent. Can the creditor enforce the friend's promise to pay the debt on the ground that the creditor's forbearance was consideration? Under the bargain test, no. Although the friend may have had the benefit of the creditor's forbearance in exchange for the friend's promise,

Example of unsolicited action

---

[35] Illustration 12 to Restatement Second §86, which is said to be "based on Estate of Hatten," indicates that $25,000 would not be "disproportionate" to $6,000 in such a case. Compare Illustration 13 to §86, which is said in the Reporter's Note to be "based on" Estate of Gerke, 73 N.W.2d 506 (Wis. 1955), a case in which the promise was to leave the promisor's entire estate to the promisee, and recovery was limited on the ground that to allow the expectation measure would circumvent the statutory requirements of formalities for wills. The case also raises an interesting question as to the extent to which the liberalization of the rules relating to "moral obligation" undermines the requirement of a writing under statutes patterned after Lord Tenterden's Act, described in the discussion of the scope of the exception *supra*.

[36] Restatement Second §86 cmt. *f*. It is, for example, difficult to evaluate such factors as the fact that, had the promise not been enforced, at least in part, in Estate of Gerke, *supra* note 35, the amount claimed would have escheated to the state, and the fact that in Estate of Hatten, discussed *supra*, the decedent had no wife or children.

§2.9 [1] A simple example occurs if a promisor seeks a performance by the promisee, and instead the promisee merely promises to render that performance. See the discussion of the offeror as the "master of the offer" in §3.12 *infra*. See also the discussion of the interpretation of the offer to invite a promise in §3.24 *infra*. As to the situation in which someone other than the promisee takes the action sought by the promisor, see §3.11 *infra*.

the friend did not bargain for it when making that promise — the friend did not seek it in exchange.[2] (The result would be the same if the creditor first promised to forbear in response to the friend's promise.)

Presence of bargain is a question of fact

It is a question of fact whether, when making a promise, a promisor was bargaining for some action that was later taken by the promisee. How can bargaining be recognized? The answer to this question requires a closer look at the nature of the bargaining process in the context of the law of contract. Recall that we are speaking only of bargains involving promises and that by *promise* we mean a commitment by the promisor as to future behavior.[3] To determine whether a promisor is bargaining when making a promise, it is useful to look first at the promisor's *purpose* and then at the promisor's *means*.

Promisor's purpose must be to induce action in exchange

In principle, at least, the bargain test requires that the promisor's purpose in making that commitment be to induce some action in return — to induce an exchange. If the promisor is a seller of apples that wants to exchange apples for money, the seller's purpose in promising to deliver apples is to induce a promise to pay the price or to induce its actual payment. Although it is sometimes said that consideration should not be confused with motive, under the bargain test purpose is an element of bargain, which is in turn an element of consideration. Unless the promisor's purpose is to induce in exchange either a promise or a performance, the promisor is not bargaining, and nothing that is given in return can be consideration.

Promisor's use of condition

When bargaining, the means the promisor uses in attempting to induce an exchange is to condition the commitment or performance, threatening to withhold it unless the promisor gets the return commitment or performance sought. When a seller of apples says, "I promise to deliver these apples if you will promise to pay me $100," what the seller means is, "*If* you *do* make a commitment to pay me $100, you shall have my commitment to deliver these apples; *if* you *do not* make such a commitment, you shall have nothing." When the seller says, "I promise to deliver these apples if you pay me $100," what the seller means is, "*If* you *do* pay me $100, you shall have my commitment to deliver these apples; *if* you *do not* pay me $100, you shall have nothing."

Significance of condition to show bargain

In deciding whether a promisor was bargaining for a promise or performance in return for the promisor's own commitment, it is useful to ask whether the promisor conditioned the commitment on that promise or performance. If, for example, the debtor's friend promises the creditor to pay the debtor's debt "if you will promise to forbear from collecting it for a month," the conditional form of the promise seems to make it clear that the friend is bargaining for the creditor's promise to forbear. (Similarly, if the friend promises the creditor to

---

[2]Patel v. American Bd. of Psychiatry & Neurology, 975 F.2d 1312 (7th Cir. 1992) (Posner, J.: "Unbargained detriments are relevant not to contract but to estoppel."). As to the possibility that the promise might be enforceable on another ground, see §2.19 *infra*.

[3]See the discussion of the concern of contract law with the future in §1.1 *supra*.

pay the debt "if you forbear[4] from collecting it for a month," it seems clear that the friend is bargaining for the creditor's forbearance.)

However, a promisor may bargain without expressly conditioning the commitment in this way. Employees are often asked by their employers to promise not to compete with them after the employment is terminated.[5] Usually the promise is made as part of the employment agreement, and no problem of consideration arises. Occasionally, however, the employee makes the promise after the employment has begun. The employer then argues that it could have terminated the employment and that it was the employer's forbearance from doing so for which the employee bargained when making the promise. Courts have reached conflicting results, with some struggling to find a bargain where there is none.[6] Whether this conclusion is justified in a particular case depends on whether the possibility of termination by the employer was sufficiently likely to justify the conclusion that the employee was bargaining for the employer's forbearance.

Commitment may be impliedly conditioned

Even if a promisor expressly conditions the commitment, this may not suffice to show that the promisor is bargaining. In concluding that the debtor's friend is bargaining for the creditor's forbearance, we are assuming, as self-evident on the facts, that the friend's *purpose* in making the promise is to induce the creditor's promise to forbear in return. But the language of the condition alone is not determinative, for the same language may also be used where there is no bargain. A promise may be conditioned by the same words even though it is clearly gratuitous.

Language of condition not enough

An employer promises an employee the gift of a gold watch as a present "*if* you will stop by my office to pick it up." The employer uses the same language that it would use if bargaining — the promise is conditioned on the employee's stopping by the office. But it is evident that, in making the promise, the employer is not bargaining for the employee's stopping by the office; in making the promise, the employer's purpose is not to obtain that action, but simply to make a gift of the watch. Stopping by the office is merely a condition

Example of conditional gratuitous promise

---

[4] *But cf.* Whitten v. Greeley-Shaw, 520 A.2d 1307 (Me. 1987) (mistress's promise not to disturb married man was not consideration for his promise of support if "it was not sought after by [him], and motivated by his request that [she] not disturb him").

[5] Such promises are discussed in §5.3 *infra*.

[6] Iowa Glass Depot v. Jindrich, 338 N.W.2d 376 (Iowa 1983) (employee "retained his employment and prospered from it for several years" and "continued employment for an indefinite period of time is sufficient consideration"). *Contra:* George W. Kistler, Inc. v. O'Brien, 347 A.2d 311 (Pa. 1975) (continuation of employment "was not sufficient consideration for the covenant despite the fact that the employment relationship was terminable at the will of either party"). A similar question arises when an employee claims that forbearance from quitting under an employment at will is consideration for an employer's promise, made after hiring, of job security or benefits. Pine River State Bank v. Mettille, 333 N.W.2d 622 (Minn. 1983) ("by continuing to stay on the job, although free to leave, the employee supplies the necessary consideration for the offer").

of a gratuitous promise — an unenforceable gratuitous promise.[7] Though using the language of condition, the employer lacks the necessary purpose.

Analysis of example

Note that the question is not: Having decided to make the promise, did the promisor seek something in return? It may be that, having decided to promise the employee a gold watch as a gift, the employer sought to have the employee stop by the office to save the employer trouble or to show the employee's gratitude. Stopping by the office would still be only incidental to the promise. Rather, the question is: Did the promisor decide to make the promise in the first place in order to get something in return? (It may be helpful to ask: apart from the promise itself, would the promisor benefit from the exchange?) In the example it seems clear that the employer did not so decide. It would be a very strange employer who would use such a curious device merely to induce an employee to stop by the office.[8] That the situation is not always so simple, however, is shown by the 1845 case of *Kirksey v. Kirksey*.[9]

Example of *Kirksey*

In that case a man wrote to his recently widowed sister-in-law, "If you will come down and see me, I will let you have a place to raise your family."[10] The Supreme Court of Alabama concluded that this promise was a "mere gratuity," unsupported by consideration.[11] It regarded the sister-in-law's coming down as merely incidental to the promise. In other words, he could not give her a place to live unless she came down, and therefore, having already decided to make the promise, he merely sought this in return — his desire to have her come down did not induce him to make the promise. But this conclusion is not as compelling as in the example of the gold watch. His purpose in making the promise might have been to get her to come down so that she could live near

---

[7]Williston put a memorable example of a benevolent man who says to a tramp, "if you go around the corner to the clothing shop there, you may purchase an overcoat on my credit." He concluded that "no reasonable person would understand that the short walk was requested as the consideration for the promise, but that in the event of the tramp going to the shop the promisor would make him a gift." 1 S. Williston, Contracts §112 (1st ed. 1920).

An interesting variant occurs when the promisor makes a promise conditional on the promisee's doing something plainly detrimental to the *promisor* — a promise in the nature of a dare. *See* Cudahy Junior Chamber of Commerce v. Quirk, 165 N.W.2d 116 (Wis. 1969) (promise of $1,000 if offeree could show that "daily dose of four glasses [of fluoridated water] cannot cause 'dermatologic, gastrointestinal and neurological disorders'" proposed "a wager, unenforceable as against public policy"). On wagering contracts, see the discussion of the great variety of policies in §5.2 *supra*.

[8]Compare this promise by a father to his daughter: "If you will meet me at Tiffany's next Monday at noon, I will buy you the emerald ring advertised in this week's New Yorker." If one supposes that the father and daughter are estranged and that the daughter had refused to see the father, it is possible to make a case for bargain.

[9]8 Ala. 131 (1845).

[10]The promise was not very precise, but presumably she was to have the place for herself and her children at least until her family was raised.

[11]The brief and unsatisfying opinion is unusual in that it was written by a judge who disagreed with the decision of the court. As to promises within the family generally, see the discussion of family and social agreements in §3.7 *infra*.

him, and if that were so, her coming down would be bargained for and would be consideration.[12]

In applying the bargain test of consideration, however, courts have not been eager to inquire into the promisor's purpose.[13] If the promise was made in connection with a transaction in the marketplace, the court usually assumes that it was part of a bargain. Though a promisor may make a number of promises, a single consideration will suffice for all of them and the court will not inquire whether it was the motivation for each.[14] Though a promisor may have had several purposes, the court will not inquire into all of them as long as one of them — not even the principal one — was to induce an exchange.[15] As Holmes put it, "A man may promise to paint a picture for five hundred dollars, while his chief motive may be a desire for fame."[16] A court would be unlikely to question whether that promise was supported by consideration, but would simply assume that the $500 was at least part of the artist's inducement in making the promise. We discuss later the possibility that a court might entirely avoid the question of the promisor's purpose by holding the promise enforceable if there has been unsolicited reliance, even in the absence of consideration.[17] A final assessment of *Kirksey* must await that discussion.[18]

Next we examine cases of action that may have been sought by the promisor in return for the promise but that was not taken in response to the promise.

Reluctance to inquire into purpose

§2.10.   Action Not Taken in Response. Even if the promisee takes some action subsequent to the promise (so that there is no problem of past consideration), and even if the promisor sought that action in exchange for its promise (so that there is no problem of unsolicited reliance), that action is not bargained for unless it is given by the promisee in exchange for the promise. In other words, just as the *promisor's* purpose must be to induce an exchange, so the *promisee's* purpose must be to take advantage of the proposed exchange. In practice, the principal effect of this requirement is to deny enforcement of the promise if

Action not taken in response cannot be consideration

---

[12] *See* Hamer v. Sidway, 27 N.E. 256 (N.Y. 1891) (discussed in §2.4 *supra*); Devecmon v. Shaw, 14 A. 464 (Md. 1888) (uncle's promise to nephew, who had lived with his family and served as a clerk, to reimburse his expenses if he took a trip to Europe). Note that extreme imbalance in the exchange may be a factor arguing that such a promise is gratuitous. The promise in *Kirksey* would have looked less like a gratuitous one had it been to reimburse expenses, as in *Devecmon*.

[13] If the promisee's understanding of the promisor's purpose differs from the promisor's actual purpose, the former prevails as long as it is reasonable. *See* the discussion of the objective theory in §3.6 *infra*.

[14] See the discussion of the reciprocal nature of bargain in §2.6 *supra*.

[15] *See* Pasant v. Jackson Natl. Life Ins. Co., 52 F.3d 94 (5th Cir. 1995) ("promise that is supported by a mixture of gift and bargain is supported by adequate consideration").

[16] O. Holmes, The Common Law 293-94 (1881).

[17] In *Kirksey* the court resolved it in the promisor's favor, although the jury had given a verdict for the promisee. It is not clear why the court on appeal did not respect the jury's implicit finding of fact that the promise had not been gratuitous.

[18] See §2.19 *infra*.

the promisee takes the action sought by the promisor *without knowledge* of the promise.[1] As might be supposed, examples are infrequent.[2]

Example of cross offers

One example involves "cross offers." Suppose that two promisors, after preliminary negotiations to arrive at definite terms, independently dispatch promises that propose an identical agreement and that cross each other in transmission. Although each promisor may seek the other's promise in exchange for its own, neither *gives* a promise in exchange for the other's. Therefore neither promise is bargained for, neither can be consideration for the other, and neither is supported by consideration. There is no contract.[3]

Example of action in ignorance of reward

Another example involves offers of rewards. Suppose that an owner advertises a $100 reward for the return of a lost gold watch. If a finder of the watch, having read the advertisement, returns the watch to the owner, this action is bargained for, and the finder can enforce the owner's promise of a reward. But if the finder, unaware of the promise, notices the owner's name engraved on the watch and returns it, the action could not have been bargained for. Since the finder did not know of the owner's promise, the action could not have been given in exchange for it. The finder cannot, therefore, enforce the owner's promise.[4]

Example of at-will employment

A third example, and one of great practical importance, involves at-will employment.[5] Suppose that during the course of an at-will employment, either the employer or the employee makes a promise to the other, after which the employment continues. Where it is the employer that is the promisor, the promise is commonly one of job security and is often contained in a handbook distributed to employees. Is the employee's subsequent forbearance in not quitting the employment consideration for the employer's promise? It would be if it

---

§2.10 [1] For an exceptional case in which the court found that, though the promisee took the action sought by the promisor *with knowledge* of the promise, he was not motivated by the promise, *see* Shaw v. Philbrick, 151 A. 423 (Me. 1930) (forbearance to redeem a mortgage).

[2] Such cases as there are are often analyzed in terms of the requirement of mutual assent, rather than with that of consideration. *See* Restatement Second §23. We discuss them here because they seem properly to turn on an aspect of bargain.

[3] Tinn v. Hoffman & Co., 29 L.T.R. (N.S.) 271 (Ex. Ch. 1873) ("where the contract is to be made by the letters themselves, you cannot make it by cross offers"). *See* Restatement Second §23 illus. 4. Comment *d* to Restatement Second §23 suggests that, "theoretically, just as the offeror may assent in advance to an acceptance, so each of two offerors could assent in advance to a cross-offer," and the cross offers would then make a contract.

[4] Broadnax v. Ledbetter, 99 S.W. 1111 (Tex. 1907) (reward for return of escaped prisoner).

Although the Restatement Second makes no change in this rule, Comment *c* to §23 suggests that the recovery of the reward may be justified in the case of a standing offer by a governmental body on the grounds that such an offer is "intended to create a climate in which people do certain acts in the hope of earning unknown rewards" and that, furthermore, no consideration is required for the government's promise, which may be regarded as giving rise to a noncontractual obligation. Compare the formality of the seal treated in §2.16 *infra*. For more on rewards, *see* the discussion of acceptance by performance in §3.13 *infra*.

[5] See the discussion of employment cases in §7.17 *infra*.

were bargained for. But even assuming that the employer sought the employee's forbearance, there is rarely any evidence that the promise played any role in the employee not quitting — that the employee forbore in exchange for the promise. Nevertheless, a number of courts have departed from the traditional requirement that the consideration be given in exchange for the promise and held that the employer's promise is enforceable.[6] Where it is the employee that is the promisor, the promise is commonly one not to compete with the employer after the termination of the employment. Is the employer's subsequent forbearance in not firing the employee consideration for the employee's promise? Again, it would be if it were bargained for. But, again, even assuming that the employee sought the employer's forbearance, there is rarely any evidence that the promise played any role in the employer not firing the employee — that the employer forbore in exchange for the promise. Nevertheless, a number of courts have again departed from the traditional requirement that the consideration be given in exchange for the promise and held that the employee's promise is enforceable.[7] These cases represent a significant erosion of the requirement of bargain and illustrate the judicial aversion to inquiring into purpose in connection with consideration.[8]

This aversion to inquiring into purpose extends to the promisee as well as to the promisor.[9] As in the case of the promisor, if the promisee has several purposes for an action, the court need not inquire into all of them if one of them, and not necessarily the principal one, is to take advantage of the promise of an exchange. Even though the finder of the watch might have returned it if no reward had been promised, a court will ordinarily conclude that if the finder knew of the promise, the finder's purpose was at least in part to take advantage of the offer.[10] Only in rare cases has a promisee who knew of an offer been

Avoidance of question of purpose

---

[6] Pine River State Bank v. Mettille, 333 N.W.2d 622 (Minn. 1983) ("by continuing to stay on the job, although free to leave, the employee supplies the necessary consideration for the offer").

[7] Central Adjustment Bureau v. Ingram, 678 S.W.2d 28 (Tenn. 1984) (though there was no consideration when employee, already employed, signed covenant, "performance under the contract supplied the . . . consideration necessary to make the contract binding").

[8] Even if not supported by consideration, the promise might be enforceable on the ground of promissory estoppel if the promisee relied on the promise by not terminating the employment. But this also requires that the forbearance be in response to the promise. See the discussion of actual reliance required in §2.19 *infra*. It may be easier to show this in the handbook cases than in the restrictive covenant cases.

[9] See the discussion of reluctance to inquire into purpose in §2.9 *supra*.

[10] Jennings v. Radio Station KSCS, 708 S.W.2d 60 (Tex. App. 1986) (convict's listening to radio station was in response to its promise to pay $25,000 reward if it was caught playing fewer than three songs in a row because he stopped listening when station refused to pay). *See* Restatement Second §81(2).

That the promisee need not have the promise in mind when acting, *see* Simmons v. United States, 308 F.2d 160 (4th Cir. 1962) (fisherman who had heard of brewery's promise of prize to anyone who caught a tagged fish in its contest was entitled to prize although he did not have it in mind when he went fishing for pleasure). *But cf.* Hayes v. Plantations Steel Co., 438 A.2d

denied recovery on the ground that no part of the promisee's purpose was to take advantage of the offer.[11] This helps at least somewhat to explain the at-will employment cases.

This concludes our examination of transactions that lack some element of bargained-for exchange, and we turn to transactions in which courts have found some consideration under the bargain test.

D.   TRANSACTIONS WITH CONSIDERATION UNDER BARGAIN TEST

"Peppercorn theory"

§2.11.   Peppercorns and Pretense of Bargain. We have seen how the rise of the bargain test of consideration tended to shift the concern of judges from the substance of the exchange to the bargaining process.[1] This evoked the hyperbole that even a peppercorn — symbolic of something trifling in value — can be consideration as long as it is bargained for, a notion that has been dignified, sometimes derisively, as the "peppercorn theory" of consideration.[2] Although courts have not lost the habit of speaking of an "adequate," a "sufficient," or a "valuable" consideration,[3] the bargain test as epitomized in the Restatement imposes no such additional requirement.[4] Will a "peppercorn" then always suffice if it is bargained for? Will the bargain test tolerate any imbalance, no matter how extreme, in the exchange?

Risk affecting imbalance

A court can sometimes avoid this question, even though the imbalance appears extreme, by reasoning that the apparent imbalance is not a real one if

---

1091 (R.I. 1982) (employee's retirement was not consideration for employer's promise of pension where employee "had announced his intent to retire well in advance of any promise").

The evident reluctance of courts to deny recovery in borderline cases has also led them to allow recovery if the promisee learns of the offer after rendering part, but not all, of the requested performance and the promisee then completes performance with knowledge of the offer. Genessee County v. Pailthorpe, 224 N.W. 418 (Mich. 1929) (reward for giving information leading to arrest and conviction of murderer, some of which was given without knowledge of reward). Restatement Second §51 states this as the general rule unless the promisor manifests a contrary intention.

[11] Sheldon v. George, 116 N.Y.S. 969 (App. Div. 1909) (no recovery where diamonds were returned "under compulsion").

§2.11 [1] See the discussion of the rise of the bargain test of consideration in §2.2 *supra.*

[2] *See* Whitney v. Stearns, 16 Me. 394, 397 (1839) ("A cent or a pepper corn . . . would constitute a valuable consideration."). Reference to the peppercorn can be traced to the discussion of leases in 2 W. Blackstone, Commentaries on the Laws of England 440 (1766) ("in case of leases, always reserving a rent, though it be but a peppercorn: any of which consideration will, in the eye of the law, convert the gift . . . if not executed, into a contract").

[3] *See* Emberson v. Hartley, 762 P.2d 364 (Wash. App. 1988) (fn.2: distinguishing "adequacy" from "sufficiency").

[4] The first Restatement rejected any requirement of "adequacy," but spoke of the "sufficiency" of consideration. Restatement §§81 ("adequacy"), §19(c) ("sufficiency"). The Restatement Second not only rejects any requirement of "adequacy" but also abandons "sufficiency" as redundant. Restatement Second §79 cmt. *c* ("adequacy"); §19 cmt. *d.*

70

account is taken of the risks assumed by each party. This is especially true of aleatory promises, i.e., promises conditioned on the happening of a fortuitous event.[5] A common example is the promise of an insurer to pay a large sum of money, conditioned on the occurrence of some fortuitous and unlikely event, such as a fire, in return for the insured's payment of a much smaller sum as a premium. An extreme example is *Embola v. Tuppela*, which arose out of the promise of a destitute claimant to an Alaska gold mine that he would pay $10,000 if he succeeded in reclaiming his mine, in return for the promisee's payment of an additional $50 to enable him to go to Alaska and try. The Supreme Court of Washington held that his promise was enforceable. "The risk of losing the money advanced was as great in this case as if the same had been advanced under a grubstake contract."[6]

While such cases involve uncertainty in the value of the promise sought to be enforced, similar reasoning is applied to cases involving uncertainty in the value of the consideration. Thus in holding a dentist's promise to pay $4,000 for the good will of a deceased dentist's practice, the New York Court of Appeals reasoned that if a buyer "chooses to pay for the expectancy that customers will return to the seller's former location, believing the right to locate there is a valuable asset, so be it." As a general rule, "the adequacy of consideration is not a proper subject for judicial scrutiny."[7]

Risk affecting consideration

Suppose, however, that no such risk is involved, as when a seller promises to sell a farm in return for the buyer's promise to pay a dollar or the buyer's actual payment of a dollar. Is the seller's promise supported by consideration? To say that it is would not mean that the promise is necessarily enforceable. The imbalance in the exchange might still be used to support a showing, for example, of misrepresentation or duress by the buyer, of joking or mistake by the seller, of the seller's mental incompetency, or of the unconscionability of the bargain. Such defenses will be dealt with later.[8] Absent such a defense, however, it is difficult to imagine why the seller would agree to such an unequal exchange, and it is no surprise that the reports are devoid of cases in which competent

Unlikely example of nominal consideration

---

[5] Under an aleatory contract, one party's duty to perform is conditional on the occurrence of a fortuitous event; the other party takes the risk of having to perform, even though the event occurs and excuses the first party from rendering its performance. A contract is not aleatory if both parties' duties are conditioned on the same fortuitous event. *See* Restatement Second §379 cmt. *a*. The word comes from *alea*, Latin for dice.

[6] 220 P. 789, 790 (Wash. 1923). A "grubstake" contract is a contract under which the promise is one to pay a share of any profits.

[7] Apfel v. Prudential-Bache Sec., 616 N.E.2d 1095 (N.Y. 1993) (idea was consideration where buyer "has agreed that the idea has value," since court "will not ordinarily go behind that determination").

[8] See §§4.10 (misrepresentation), 4.16 (duress), 3.7 (joking), 9.2 (mistake), 4.6 (mental incompetency), 4.28 (unconscionability) *infra*. And even if no such defense is shown, so that the seller's promise is enforceable in an action at law for damages, the imbalance may still at least prevent its enforcement in a suit in equity for specific performance. See the discussion of unfairness in §12.7 *infra*.

sellers appear to have freely and seriously bargained to sell their farms for a dollar.[9] In practice the question whether payment of a nominal sum can be effective as consideration arises not in the context of such an exchange, but rather in the context of the disguised gratuitous promise — a promisor really intends to make a gratuitous promise and casts the transaction in the form of a bargain in order to make it enforceable.[10]

Likely example of nominal consideration

To be practical, then, we must restate the example in this way: a donor promises to make a gift of a farm to a donee, and, in order to make the promise enforceable, the donee gives a dollar to the donor. Is the donor's promise supported by consideration? There is some authority, including the first Restatement, that it is, at least if the transaction is cast in the form of a bargain.[11] The more modern view, however, mirrored in the Restatement Second, requires an actual bargain, not merely a pretense of bargain, and such extreme disparity in the exchange as here supposed would reveal the purported bargain to be a sham. Under this view the donor's promise is not supported by consideration.[12]

These conflicting views on the efficacy of a peppercorn have clashed in two significant situations, involving claims settlements and illusory promises. We take them up now.

Problem with invalid claims

§2.12.   Settlement of Invalid Claims as Consideration. Suppose that a claimant asserts a claim against another — perhaps in contract, in tort, or under a will — and the other promises to pay $1,000 if the claimant releases the claim or forbears or promises to forbear from pursuing it. If the claim is a valid one, and the promisor bargains for its settlement in return for his promise to pay $1,000, there is clearly consideration for the promise.[1] But what if it later turns out that the claim is invalid? Is settlement of an invalid claim enough of a peppercorn to support a promise?

---

[9] *Cf.* In re Good's Estate, 76 A. 98 (Pa. 1910) (sale for $500 of legacy worth about $2,600 upheld).

[10] The question has also arisen in the context of the firm offer or option contract, but this is now perceived as involving different issues. See the discussion of the effect of the abolition of the seal in §3.23 *infra*. The same holds true for releases. *See* Cochran v. Ernst & Young, 758 F. Supp. 1548 (E.D. Mich. 1991) (recital of payment of $1 was consideration for release of all claims).

[11] Illustration 1 to the first Restatement §84 reads: "A wishes to make a binding promise to his son B to convey to B Blackacre, which is worth $5,000. Being advised that a gratuitous promise is not binding, A writes to B an offer to sell Blackacre for $1. B accepts. B's promise to pay $1 is sufficient consideration."

[12] Illustration 5 to Restatement Second §71 reads: "A desires to make a binding promise to give $1,000 to his son B. Being advised that a gratuitous promise is not binding, A offers to buy from B for $1,000 a book worth less than $1. B accepts the offer knowing that the purchase of the book is a mere pretense. There is no consideration for A's promise to pay $1,000."

§2.12 [1] For the reasons suggested in a footnote to the discussion of the example of an unenforceable gratuitous promise in §2.5 *supra*, we assume that the claim is for not less than $1,000. The result is the same even though the promisor is not the person against whom the claim is asserted. See the discussion that consideration need not move to the promisor in §2.3 *supra*.

It may make sense to enforce the promise even if the claim is invalid. The law favors settlement by the parties of disputed claims in the interests of alleviating discord and promoting certainty. "Because litigation is considered injurious to society, . . . compromises which diminish litigation and promote a peaceful society are favored."[2] This can be done in two ways: first, by enforcing promises made to claimants in settlement of their claims; and second, by foreclosing any action by the claimant on the claim that has been settled. The second of these ways will be dealt with later.[3] Our concern here is with the first. We ask not whether the claimant is barred from enforcing the underlying claim, but whether the claimant can enforce the promise made in settlement. The policy favoring such compromises of disputed claims suggests that the claimant be allowed to enforce the promise, even if the settled claim later proves to be invalid.

Policy for enforcing promise

Most courts have taken a position favorable to compromise and have upheld promises made in settlement of invalid claims as long as the claim was disputed. A few courts have rejected this view, however, on the ground that there is no consideration for the promise if the claim that is settled turns out to be invalid. For example, a claimant's surrender of such a claim to a tract of land as he might have under a will was held not to be consideration for a promise by two devisees under the will to pay him $5,000, when it turned out that the claimant had no legal interest in the land. "No benefit accrued to him who made the promise, nor did any injury flow to him who received it."[4]

Occasional hostility

Courts following the prevailing view invariably require that the claim be asserted in good faith, that is, with an honest belief that it may fairly be determined to be valid.[5] Thus a claimant who contested his brother's will because "he was, as a brother, as much entitled to share in the estate as [his] brother and sister," but who "had not examined the will" and "wholly [failed] to show that there existed any ground, reasonable or otherwise, for a contest of the will,"

Requirement of good faith

---

[2] Hastings Pork v. Johanneson, 335 N.W.2d 802, 805 (N.D. 1983).

[3] See §§4.23 (pre-existing duty), 4.16 (duress), 9.3 (mutual mistake) *infra*.

[4] Renney v. Kimberly, 86 S.E.2d 217, 219 (Ga. 1955).

[5] Denburg v. Parker Chapin Flattau & Klimpl, 624 N.E.2d 995 (N.Y. 1993) (strong policy considerations "favor the enforcement of settlement agreements," so "party need only have a good-faith belief in the merit of its position"). Although Restatement Second §74(1) states as alternatives, first, a test of doubtfulness of the claim in fact and, second, one of good faith belief in the validity of the claim, the Restatement seems to assume a good faith belief if the claim is doubtful in fact.

In some circumstances, the initiation of civil process by one who does not have an honest belief in the validity of the claim may be actionable as malicious prosecution or malicious abuse of process under tort law and a threat to initiate such process may amount to duress. *See* the discussion of the threat of civil process in §4.17 *infra*. In those situations, and indeed in any situation in which the claimant does not have an honest belief in the claim, the refusal to enforce the promise can be justified on the ground of the policy against encouraging vexatious litigation, quite apart from the doctrine of consideration.

did not make his claim in good faith.[6] A claim that is neither valid nor asserted in good faith will not suffice as a peppercorn.

Requirement of doubtful claim

In addition to the requirement of the claimant's good faith, many courts have imposed a requirement that the claim itself have enough substance to be "doubtful," as opposed to unfounded, though there is little agreement on what is meant by "doubtful." One court gave the following graphic summary of the problem:

> It is difficult to reconcile the antinomous rules and statements which are applied to the "doubtful claims" and to find the words which will exactly draw the line between the compromise (on the one hand) of an honestly disputed claim which has some fair element of doubt and is therefore to be regarded as consideration and (on the other hand) a claim, though honestly made, which is so lacking in substance and virility as to be entirely baseless.... But ... we would say that if the claimant *in good faith*, makes a mountain out of a mole hill the claim is "doubtful." But if there is no discernable mole hill in the beginning, then the claim has no substance.[7]

Requirement in practice

In applying the requirement that the claim be at least doubtful, allowances have been made for the claimant's particular characteristics (such as age, intelligence, and education[8]), and courts have been willing to find doubt based on a claimant's misconception of the law[9] as well as a misunderstanding of the facts.[10] Many have so diluted the requirement, in fact, that the Restatement Second takes the position that good faith alone is enough.[11] As one court expressed it, "good faith is enough unless the claim is so obviously unfounded that the assertion of good faith would affront the intelligence of the ordinary and reasonable layman."[12] In practice the requirement that the claim be doubtful may have little significance, since it will be difficult for the claimant to show that the assertion of the claim was in good faith if the claim was not even doubtful in the minimal degree required by most courts. Courts have, however, been more receptive to the argument that a claim was worthless because the one who was

---

[6] Montgomery v. Grenier, 136 N.W. 9, 10, 11 (Minn. 1912).

[7] Duncan v. Black, 324 S.W.2d 483, 486-87 (Mo. App. 1959).

[8] Reed v. Kansas Postal Tel. Co., 264 P. 1065 (Kan. 1928) ("there could easily exist in the mind of the seventeen-year-old injured boy a reasonable doubt").

[9] Ralston v. Mathew, 250 P.2d 841 (Kan. 1952) (tort claim against church "was not obviously invalid or frivolous" although churches were not liable for their torts).

[10] Fiege v. Boehm, 123 A.2d 316 (Md. 1956) (claim of mother against putative father of illegitimate child for its support was not "frivolous" or "vexatious" although blood test later showed he was not father; no discussion of mother's possible bad faith by nondisclosure).

[11] Restatement Second §74(1)(b).

[12] Hall v. Fuller, 352 S.W.2d 559, 562 (Ky. 1961).

obligated was not financially viable than to the argument that the claim was not legally a valid one.[13]

If the claimant surrenders to the promisor a writing of a formal character embodying the claim, such as a negotiable instrument or a written guarantee, the argument in favor of enforceability of the promise made to settle the claim is enhanced. Even if the claim that the document surrenders is not disputed, consideration can be found in the execution and delivery of the document.[14]

Effect of formal writing

These cases on the settlement of claims show the interplay of the several theories of consideration. If a court chooses not to enforce the promise made in settlement of an invalid claim, it can find support in the argument that the relinquishment of such a claim is no detriment — no "legal" detriment, it is sometimes said — to the promisee, the claimant.[15] Somewhat less convincing is the argument that its settlement is no benefit to the promisor, which has at least managed to "buy its peace."[16] If, however, the court chooses to enforce the promise, it can find support in the bargain test for, as one court pointed out, the promisor "can hardly be heard to say that the claim . . . was obviously invalid and frivolous when it attached enough importance to it to make the contract in question."[17] But to the extent that a court is reluctant to let the parties determine which disputes should be settled, and wishes to use the doctrine of consideration to maintain at least minimal control, the most attractive rationale is that the doctrine requires a detriment to the promisee. We shall consider later, in another connection, whether the doctrine of consideration is an appropriate vehicle for control over claims settlements.[18]

Theories of consideration

We look next at the analogous problems posed by illusory promises.

§2.13.   Illusory Promises as Consideration.   Suppose that two parties exchange promises, but one of the promises appears on its face to be so insubstantial as to impose no obligation at all on the promisor — who says, in effect, "I will *if* I want to." Is such a facially insubstantial promise enough of a peppercorn to support the other party's promise?[1] The question arises because the promise appears to be conditional on an event that is entirely within the

Condition within promisor's control

---

[13]Newman & Snell's State Bank v. Hunter, 220 N.W. 665 (Mich. 1928) (bank's surrender of deceased husband's note was not consideration for widow's promise to pay his debt where both note and stock securing it were "worthless" because of insolvency of his estate and corporation).

[14]Mullen v. Hawkins, 40 N.E. 797 (Ind. 1895) (quitclaim deed by one who had no title was consideration). *See also* Restatement Second §74(2).

[15]For discussion of enforceability in terms of "legal detriment," *see* Keen v. Larson, 132 N.W.2d 350 (N.D. 1964).

[16]The argument that there is no benefit is stronger if the promisor is not the person against whom the claim is asserted. *See* note 1 *supra*.

[17]Ralston v. Mathew, *supra* note 9.

[18]See §4.23 *infra*.

§2.13   [1]This discussion assumes that there is no consideration other than the promise in question to support the other party's promise. Thus if a party has made more than one return promise, the fact that one of them is illusory is not fatal to the enforceability of the other party's

promisor's control. Such a promise differs from one that is conditional on an event that is beyond the promisor's control and that can therefore be consideration.[2] It also differs from one that is voidable or even unenforceable on grounds of public policy and that can nevertheless be consideration.[3]

Two responses

Courts have responded to facially insubstantial promises in two diametrically opposite ways. One way is to characterize the promise as an "illusory" one — a promise in form but not in substance — and to hold that it is not, even if bargained for, consideration for the other promise. The agreement is then not enforceable against either party. The other way is to read the facially insubstantial return promise so as to give it the substance that it appears to lack, so that it is not illusory, and to hold that it is consideration for the other promise. The agreement is then enforceable against both parties.

Refusal to enforce

The first response was once fashionable. Where, for example, a buyer promised only to buy all the coal that it "would want to purchase," in return for the seller's promise to sell all that the buyer ordered, the court relieved the seller from the bargain, holding that its promise was not supported by consideration since the buyer would not be liable on its return promise even if it ordered no goods. It was a promise, as the court characterized it, "to buy if it pleased, when it pleased, to buy if it thought it advantageous, to buy much, little, or not at all, as it thought best." The seller was not bound because the buyer's promise was illusory.[4] Similar reasoning was applied in a case in which a creditor promised only to forbear collection of a debt "until such time as I want my money," in return for the promise of the debtor's wife to pay if the debtor did not. When the creditor sued the wife, he lost because his promise imposed no duty on him to forbear and was not consideration for the wife's promise.[5] The same result has been reached if a party's duty is conditioned on some event that is entirely within its control. For example, a buyer's promise to buy a business was "conditioned upon the Buyer obtaining a new lease" from the owner of the premises where the business was carried on. When the buyer sued the seller, the buyer lost because his promise left him "free to get the lease or not as he willed" and was not consideration for the seller's promise.[6]

---

promise unless all of the return promises are illusory. Graphic Arts Finishers v. Boston Redev. Auth., 255 N.E.2d 793 (Mass. 1970) (promise to relocate business was consideration even though further promise to continue to operate business may have been within promisor's complete discretion). See the discussion of the reciprocal nature of bargain in §2.6 *supra* and, as to option contracts, the discussion of other consideration and reliance in §3.23 *infra*.

[2] *See* Restatement Second §76.

[3] As to voidable promises, see the discussion of avoidance compared in §2.14 *infra*. And as to unenforceable ones, see the discussion of the agreement as not necessarily void in §5.1 *infra*. *See also* Restatement Second §78.

[4] Wickham & Burton Coal Co. v. Farmers' Lumber Co., 179 N.W. 417, 419 (Iowa 1920).

[5] Strong v. Sheffield, 39 N.E. 330 (N.Y. 1895). (Since the case involved a negotiable promissory note, the result would be different under UCC 3-303(b), which lays down a special rule on consideration applicable to negotiable instruments.)

[6] Paul v. Rosen, 122 N.E.2d 603 (Ill. App. 1954).

In each of these cases the court characterized one party's promise as illusory, as undertaking no liability in any circumstances. To avoid holding the other party to a bargain with such extreme disparity in the exchange, the other party was not held at all. The reasoning sometimes involves what the New York Court of Appeals has described as "the not uncommon analytical error of engaging in a search for 'mutuality,' . . . rather than of seeking to determine the presence of consideration."[7]

Duty of good faith

More recently, however, courts have tended to respond by reading the apparently illusory promise so that it is not illusory.[8] Especially is this so if the agreement is an elaborate one entered into by both parties with the evident intention that it be enforceable. For example, an officer of a corporation promised as part of an agreement settling a dispute to devote to the corporation such time "as he in his sole judgment shall deem necessary" in return for the corporation's promise to employ him. In spite of the words "in his sole judgment," the court read his promise as requiring him "to act in good faith" in exercising his judgment, so that his promise was not illusory. It was therefore consideration for the corporation's promise, so that the officer could enforce that promise.[9] Similar reasoning was applied to the promise of a purchaser of land for a shopping center. The promise was conditioned on his obtaining leases for future occupancy that were "satisfactory to" the purchaser. Again the court read the promise as requiring the promisor "to exercise his judgment in good faith," so that the buyer's promise was not illusory. It was therefore consideration for the seller's promise, so that the buyer could enforce that promise.[10] Such decisions allow the parties to blur the sharp line drawn by the making of a contract.

Duty of reasonable efforts

In the preceding examples the agreement was salvaged simply by requiring that one of the parties perform in good faith. Sometimes courts have been willing to do more in order to salvage an agreement, and have found an "implied"

---

[7]Weiner v. McGraw-Hill, 443 N.E.2d 441, 444 (N.Y. 1982). Such mutuality is required only in the case of bilateral contracts. *See* the discussion of mutuality of obligation in §3.2 *infra*.

[8]Tanglewood Land Co. v. Byrd, 261 S.E.2d 655 (N.C. 1980) (provision in land sale contract for cancellation on "prior sale" interpreted to mean sale by another salesperson prior to the making of contract). To prevent a promise from being illusory, it is only necessary that it be binding in some circumstance. Wood County Grocer Co. v. Frazer, 284 F. 691 (8th Cir. 1922) (seller's promise to sell sugar at price between fixed minimum, which was the only price at which buyer had to accept, and fixed maximum, was not illusory because it was enforceable against seller if buyer was willing to pay maximum).

[9]Grean & Co. v. Grean, 82 N.Y.S.2d 787 (App. Div. 1948). The Uniform Commercial Code "rejects the uncommercial idea that an agreement that the seller may fix the price means that he may fix any price he may wish." UCC 2-305 cmt. 3. It provides instead that a "price to be fixed by the seller or by the buyer" means a price to be fixed "in good faith." UCC 2-305(2). Such a provision does not, therefore, make a promise illusory.

[10]Mattei v. Hopper, 330 P.2d 625 (Cal. 1958). As to the interpretation of "satisfaction" clauses, see the discussion of the nature of *satisfaction* in §8.4 *infra*. Rules for transactions in which a buyer may return goods that do not meet with its "approval" are stated in UCC 2-326.

return promise as consideration. A noted example is Cardozo's opinion in *Wood v. Lucy, Lady Duff-Gordon*. By an elaborate writing, Lady Duff-Gordon, a "creator of fashions," gave the exclusive right to market her designs for a period of at least a year to Wood, who was organized to do this. In return, she was to have half of anything that he derived from marketing them, but the agreement said nothing of any duty on his part to market them. When she broke her promise and dealt with others, he sued for damages. She argued that there was no consideration for her promise since he had made no promise to do anything in return. The court rejected her argument and found consideration on the ground that, although "he does not promise in so many words that he will use reasonable efforts to . . . market her designs, . . . such a promise is fairly to be implied." She had given him "an exclusive privilege," and the court would not "suppose that one party was to be placed at the mercy of the other."[11] The court could have avoided placing her at his mercy by refusing to enforce the agreement. Instead, it did so by imposing on him a duty to use "reasonable efforts" and, having done so, enforced the agreement.[12] The same line of reasoning has been used to uphold contracts for the sale of real property in which the buyer's obligation has been, for example, "contingent upon buyer being able to obtain mortgage" in a stated amount, the term being read so as to require the buyer to "make reasonable efforts to secure a suitable mortgage."[13] The processes of interpretation and implication by which courts flesh out the actual agreement of the parties will be discussed in more detail later.[14]

Disguised offers   Even if a promise is unenforceable because the promise given in return for it is illusory, the first promise is not necessarily without legal effect. It may amount to a disguised offer, since an offer is a kind of promise.[15] As we have seen, a seller that promises to sell all the goods that the buyer chooses to order is not bound to sell anything because the buyer's promise is illusory. If, however, the buyer then orders goods from the seller, the seller's promise may be regarded as a continuing or a "standing" offer, so that a new contract is formed each time that the buyer accepts by placing an order.[16] The seller can,

---

[11]118 N.E. 214, 218 (N.Y. 1917).

[12]This approach is followed, as to goods, by UCC 2-306(2), under which an "agreement by either the seller or the buyer for exclusive dealing in the kind of goods concerned imposes unless otherwise agreed an obligation by the seller to use best efforts to supply the goods and by the buyer to use best efforts to promote their sale."

That UCC 2-306(2) does not apply to a requirements buyer, as long as the seller is not bound to sell exclusively to the buyer, *see* MDC Corp. v. John H. Harland Co., 228 F. Supp. 2d 387 (S.D.N.Y. 2002) ("duty to use best efforts applies to exclusive agents only, and not to all requirements buyers").

[13]Lach v. Cahill, 85 A.2d 481 (Conn. 1951) (dictum).

[14]See Chapter 7 *infra*.

[15]See the discussion of the meaning of *offer* §3.3 *infra*.

[16]Brooklyn Bagel Boys v. Earthgrains Refrigerated Dough Prods., 212 F.3d 373 (7th Cir. 2000) (fn.4: what parties called a "Contract" was "akin to an offer . . . to manufacture bagels" and

of course, revoke the continuing offer at any time and is not then bound to fill later orders, even though still bound as to orders placed before revocation.[17] Similar reasoning was applied when a lumber company agreed to sell, and a purchaser agreed to purchase, a tract of land without timber rights, if the lumber company succeeded in acquiring the tract at a forthcoming sale. When the lumber company acquired the tract, the purchaser refused to accept a deed, and the lumber company sought specific performance. The court conceded that the lumber company's promise was illusory because it was conditioned on its purchase of the tract, an event entirely within its control, so that "at the time the contract was signed, it could not have been enforced against either party." Nevertheless, the court granted the lumber company specific performance on the ground that "the moment [the lumber company] acquired title to the real estate, it became equally binding on . . . both parties."[18] The same reasoning would allow a purchaser of real property that has completed arrangements for financing to enforce the agreement of sale against the vendor, even though the purchaser's promise might initially have been regarded as illusory because of the way in which it was conditioned on obtaining financing.[19]

Two important types of contract provisions that have raised questions as to the illusory nature of promises are clauses providing for termination and clauses fixing the quantity of goods sold in terms of the buyer's requirements or the seller's output. We discuss each in turn.

§2.14. **Termination Clauses.** Provisions that allow a promisor to put an end to its rights and duties by termination have evoked both of the responses described in the preceding section.[1] If the provision is read as giving the promisor the power to terminate at any time at will, without more, the promise will be held to be illusory. For another example, a license agreement for the manufacture of Orange Crush gave the licensee the exclusive right and the

Two responses to termination clauses

---

offeree "manifested its assent to the offer . . . by placing orders for the bagels"). See the discussion of language that suffices for an offer in §3.10 *infra*.

[17] Bernstein v. W.B. Mfg. Co., 131 N.E. 200 (Mass. 1921) (seller was "not bound to fill the balance of the order" after revocation).

[18] Obering v. Swain-Roach Lumber Co., 155 N.E. 712, 714 (Ind. App. 1927). The concession in the *Obering* case that the promise was illusory seems unnecessary, since even when the contract was made, the lumber company's promise bound it in the alternative to sell the land to the purchaser or not to acquire it. As to such alternative promises, see the discussion of promises that are arguably illusory in §2.15 *infra*.

[19] DiBenedetto v. DiRocco, 93 A.2d 474 (Pa. 1953) (alternative holding: even assuming that "agreement did not obligate plaintiff [purchaser] from the very beginning but should be interpreted as the mere grant of an option to him to purchase the property, he certainly became bound" when notice was given to vendor that necessary financial arrangements had been completed.).

§2.14 [1] On the Code's use of the words *termination* and *cancellation*, see the description in the footnote to the discussion of the example of a construction contract in §8.15 *infra*. As to termination clauses in franchise agreements, see the discussions of unconscionability as not limited to consumer contracts in §4.28 *infra* and of the franchise cases in §7.17 *infra*.

duty to manufacture the soft drink in a specified territory, but it provided that the licensee could at any time terminate the contract. In a suit by the licensee against the licensor, it was held that the licensee's promise was not consideration for the licensor's because the licensee "did not promise to do anything, and could at any time cancel the contract."[2] If, however, the provision is read as requiring the promisor to give notice a stated period of time before the termination becomes effective, the promise will not be held to be illusory. For example, a lease of a filling station provided that the lessee could at any time terminate the lease on ten days' notice. In a suit by the lessee against the lessor, it was held that the lessee's promise was consideration for the lessor's because the provision was not one "by which the lessee may terminate the lease at pleasure and without notice; at the very least the lessee bound itself to pay rent for the ten days."[3] Because of the traditional reluctance of courts to inquire into the fairness of the exchange, the brevity of the period has not been called into question, and it has even been argued that the mere requirement of giving notice of termination is enough to prevent the promise from being illusory.[4]

Termination on event

Even if a promisor has a power to terminate at will, the promise will not be held to be illusory if its exercise is conditioned on the occurrence of events beyond the promisor's control. A court inclined to salvage an agreement can do so by reading the provision in this way. For example, an agreement for the sale of real estate provided that "In the event that the buyer cannot make the settlement [i.e., pay the balance of the price], he may cancel the agreement." In an action by the purchaser against the vendor, it was held that the purchaser's promise was consideration for the vendor's because the purchaser "could have successfully defended only by proving that he was *unable* to complete the transaction, not merely that he did not *desire* to do so," and that turned on events beyond his control.[5] In an extreme example of such reasoning it was held that a provision giving the grantee of mineral rights the power to "in its sole discretion

---

[2] Miami Coca-Cola Bottling Co. v. Orange Crush Co., 296 F. 693 (5th Cir. 1924). Sometimes a buyer can enforce a seller's promise to sell even though that promise is not consideration for the buyer's return promise to buy. If the promise to sell is not consideration because it is terminable at the seller's will, the seller may nevertheless be regarded as having made a continuing or "standing" offer that the buyer may accept by submitting orders before termination. Compare the situation considered in the discussion of disguised offers in §2.13 *supra*, where the seller's promise is, by its own terms, enforceable and the question is whether the buyer's return promise is consideration for it.

[3] Lindner v. Mid-Continent Petroleum Corp., 252 S.W.2d 631, 632 (Ark. 1952). *See* Laclede Gas Co. v. Amoco Oil Co., 522 F.2d 33 (8th Cir. 1975) (contract not illusory where buyer could not terminate for one year and then only on anniversary date of first delivery and on 30 days' written notice).

[4] Johnson Lake Dev. v. Central Neb. Pub. Power & Irrigation Dist., 576 N.W.2d 806 (Neb. 1998) (because even slight restriction "such as the requirement that advance notice be given is sufficient," requirement of six months advance written notice sufficed). UCC 2-309(3) requires "reasonable notification" for termination, except on the happening of an agreed event.

[5] DiBenedetto v. DiRocco, 93 A.2d 474 (Pa. 1953) (alternative holding).

terminate . . . in the event it determines there is not sufficient promise of minerals . . . to justify the further expenditures of time or money" was not illusory because that power "may not be exercised capriciously or in bad faith."[6]

A troublesome borderline case is posed where a party can terminate at will, but only within some period after which the party loses the power of termination. Clearly, if the period expires without either party manifesting an intention not to be bound by the agreement, both will be bound.[7] The difficult question is whether the party who cannot terminate is bound even though the period has not expired. For example, a contract for sale of plate glass provided that the buyer could "cancel . . . before shipment." Nevertheless, it was held, in an action by the buyer against the seller, that the buyer's promise was consideration for the seller's because, since the seller "might have shipped at the same time that he accepted, there was one clear opportunity to enforce the contract, which the buyer could not have prevented or nullified."[8] It is unclear whether the result would have been the same if the buyer had been given a period of, say, ten days before shipment during which he had an unfettered power of termination.[9]

Termination within fixed period

A problem similar to that of the promise subject to termination is raised by the promise subject to avoidance on some ground such as lack of capacity, misrepresentation, or duress. Courts have generally characterized such agreements as "voidable" rather than "void," meaning that while one party can avoid the agreement, the other cannot. To support this result, they have been obliged to conclude that, while a promise made by one who lacks capacity or one obtained by fraud or duress may be voidable, it is nevertheless consideration for the other party's promise.[10]

Avoidance compared

We look now at the comparable questions raised by requirements and output contracts.

§2.15. Requirements and Output Contracts. Requirements and output contracts have also evoked both of the responses under discussion. A requirements contract is one under which the seller agrees to sell and the

Such contracts described

---

[6] Resource Mgt. Co. v. Weston Ranch & Livestock Co., 706 P.2d 1028, 1037 (Utah 1985).

[7] Sylvan Crest Sand & Gravel Co. v. United States, 150 F.2d 642 (2d Cir. 1945). Compare the "acceptance in escrow" mentioned in the footnote to the discussion of the point that the offer must be unconditional in §3.13 *infra*.

[8] Gurfein v. Werbelovsky, 118 A. 32, 33 (Conn. 1922).

[9] A case sometimes cited for the proposition that such a power of cancellation does not make a promise illusory is Sylvan Crest Sand & Gravel Co. v. United States, *supra* note 7. The court there said, "The alternative of giving notice was not difficult of performance, but it was a sufficient consideration to support the contract." But the court only enforced the promise subject to termination after the period had expired without termination.

[10] Holt v. Ward Clarencieux, 93 Eng. Rep. 954 (K.B. 1732) (infancy). *See* Restatement Second §78 and the discussion of voidable, not void, in §4.4 *infra*. See the discussions of partial unenforceability in §5.8 *infra* (unenforceability on grounds of public policy) and of who must sign in §6.8 *infra* (unenforceability because of statute of frauds).

buyer to buy all of the goods of a particular kind that the *buyer* may *require* in its business.[1] It assures the buyer of a source for those goods for the contract period.[2] An output contract is one under which the seller agrees to sell and the buyer to buy all of the goods of a particular kind that the *seller* may *produce* in its business. It assures the seller of an outlet for those goods for the contract period. Although agreements fixing the quantity of goods in terms of "requirements" or "output" have not posed serious problems under the requirement of definiteness,[3] they have often been challenged under the doctrine of consideration.

Promises arguably illusory

The argument in the case of a requirements contract is that the buyer's promise is illusory because it can perform without taking any goods at all, if it chooses instead to go out of the business that requires them.[4] A comparable argument is made as to the seller's promise under an output contract. A common answer has been that a promise reserving to the promisor a choice of alternative performances is nevertheless consideration, if each performance would have been consideration had it alone been bargained for, and that this is the case here.[5] Analysis in terms of "alternative promises" makes it tempting to abandon the bargain test and recur to the notion of "detriment" to the promisee, since it is difficult to imagine why a promise to go out of business would have been bargained for alone.[6] The analysis, however, misses the mark.

Imbalance of exchange

Take the case of a long-term requirements contract with a fixed price. (A comparable analysis can be made of such an output contract.) If the market price for the goods should fall, the contract will become less attractive to the buyer and its requirements may decrease to zero. If the market price should

---

§2.15 [1]Courts have not always insisted that the promise to buy exclusively from the seller be explicit. Laclede Gas Co. v. Amoco Oil Co., 522 F.2d 33 (8th Cir. 1975) (while distributor "did not expressly promise to purchase all the propane requirements," such a commitment necessarily follows from an intelligent practical reading of the agreement).

As long as the *seller* is not bound to sell exclusively to the buyer, the fact that the buyer is to buy exclusively from the seller does not make the contract one for "exclusive dealing" under UCC 2-306(2). MDC Corp. v. John H. Harland Co., 228 F. Supp. 2d 387 (S.D.N.Y. 2002) ("duty to use best efforts applies to exclusive agents only, and not to all requirements buyers").

[2]The buyer's requirements are usually fixed in terms of a period of time but may also be fixed in terms of a particular enterprise. R.A. Weaver & Assoc. v. Asphalt Constr., 587 F.2d 1315 (D.C. Cir. 1978) (contract to supply all crushed limestone required for particular project).

[3]Westesen v. Olathe State Bank, 204 P. 329 (Colo. 1922) (bank's promise to lend customer money up to $5,000 required for a trip was enforceable although "the exact sum he might require was not fixed"). *See* the discussion of the role of the drafter in §3.28 *infra*.

[4]Fort Wayne Corrugated Paper Co. v. Anchor Hocking Glass Corp., 130 F.2d 471 (3d Cir. 1942) ("the buyer in a requirements contract has no duty to have any requirements and a seller under an output contract has no duty to have any output" though "it may be assumed that good faith is required and that a party . . . cannot pretend not to have a requirement to avoid his obligation").

[5]See Restatement Second §77 for a statement of this rule on "alternative promises."

[6]Petroleum Refractionating Corp. v. Kendrick Oil Co., 65 F.2d 997 (10th Cir. 1933) ("question then is, would a discontinuance by the [seller under an output contract] to manufacture the grade of oil contracted for result in such a detriment to it as would constitute a consideration").

rise, the contract will become more attractive to the buyer and its requirements may increase dramatically. The imbalance of an exchange that subjects the seller to shifting demands within the buyer's control has not escaped the attention of courts.

One response has been to relieve the seller entirely, by concluding that the agreement is unenforceable because the buyer's promise is illusory. This has proved a tempting solution if the requirements of the buyer are particularly subject to variations in the market, as when the buyer buys for resale. "Thus," reasoned one court, "a foundry may purchase all the coal needed for the season; or a furnace company its requirements in the way of iron; or a hotel its necessary supply of ice. . . . So, too, a dealer in coal . . . may contract for such coal as he may need to fulfil his existing contracts. . . ." But, the court went on, when a seller agreed to supply lumber merchants with all the dock timber they would require for their trade in the Chicago market over a stated period of time, the buyers' promise was illusory since they "were at the time engaged in no manufacture or business that required dock oak lumber as an incidental supply, nor were they under any contract to deliver such lumber to third persons at fixed prices. They were lumber merchants pure and simple — middlemen" whose requirements could fluctuate freely with the market.[7] Courts have been more willing to enforce requirements contracts whose terms make the seller less vulnerable by providing, for example, a flexible price tied to the market or a maximum amount that the buyer may demand.[8]

One response: unenforceability

The opposite response is to hold the seller to the promise, but to eliminate the possibility of unfairness by using the process of implication to impose a limit on the amount that the buyer may demand.[9] The difficulty of fixing such a limit in the situation in which the buyer is new in the business and has had no prior requirements has led some courts to decline to enforce requirements contracts in such situations.[10]

Another response: implication

The Uniform Commercial Code uses this technique of implication in UCC 2-306(1):

Code response

> A term which measures the quantity by the output of the seller or the require-ments of the buyer means such actual output or requirements as may occur in good faith, except that no quantity unreasonably disproportionate to any stated estimate

---

[7]Crane v. C. Crane & Co., 105 F. 869, 871-72 (7th Cir. 1901).

[8]*See* McMichael v. Price, 58 P.2d 549 (Okl. 1936) (sand dealer's requirements of sand at price based on market price).

[9]Lima Locomotive & Mach. Co. v. National Steel Castings Co., 155 F. 77 (6th Cir. 1907) (seller's promise to supply manufacturer's requirements of castings would not obligate it "to supply castings not required in the usual course of that business").

[10]Pessin v. Fox Head Waukeshaw Corp., 282 N.W. 582 (Wis. 1938) (agreement to supply requirements of beer to distributor who had no established beer business was unenforceable). *But cf.* McMichael v. Price, *supra* note 8 (agreement to supply requirements of sand to wholesaler who had no established sand business but was experienced at selling sand was enforceable).

or in the absence of a stated estimate to any normal or otherwise comparable prior output or requirements may be tendered or demanded.

This provision attempts to eliminate the imbalance in the exchange by placing a limit on the buyer's requirements in terms of a stated estimate.[11] The background of this section suggests that its "except" clause operates only as an *upper* limit — as a ceiling and not as a floor.[12] At the same time, the provision attempts to meet the argument that consideration is lacking by conditioning the reduction or elimination of requirements on good faith.[13] Whether there may still be instances in which a promise to take one's requirements may be illusory is not clear.[14]

We turn now to the role of form in connection with the doctrine of consideration and to efforts aimed at its reformation.

E. FORM AND REFORM

Form and substance

§2.16. Form: The Seal. In separating enforceable from unenforceable promises, a legal system might look either to the form of the promise (i.e., to the manner in which it was made) or to its substance (i.e., to its terms).[1] Because most suggestions for reform in this area have emphasized form, we begin with a brief history of the importance of form in this context. We have already seen

---

[11]Orange & Rockland Util. v. Amerada Hess Corp., 397 N.Y.S.2d 814 (App. Div. 1977) (utility's demand "for more than double its contract estimates [of fuel oil] was, as a matter of law, 'unreasonably disproportionate' ").

[12]Empire Gas Corp. v. American Bakeries Co., 840 F.2d 1333 (7th Cir. 1988) ("The proviso does not apply, though the requirement of good faith does, where the buyer takes less rather than more of the stated estimate in a requirements contract.").

[13]Famous Brands v. David Sherman Corp., 814 F.2d 517 (8th Cir. 1987) (under Code "the prospective buyer's good faith in filling all of its requirements through the seller is deemed sufficient consideration to support the contract"). For the definition of *good faith, see* UCC 1-304 ("honesty in fact and the observance of reasonable standards of fair dealing); UCC-O 2-103(1)(b) (in case of merchant includes not only honesty in fact but "the observance of reasonable commercial standards of fair dealing in the trade"). For more on the meaning of *good faith* in this context, see the discussion of output and requirements in §7.17 *infra*.

[14]Take, for example, a promise by a wholesaler that deals in many kinds of goods to buy all requirements of goods of a very narrowly defined type in which the wholesaler has no established business.

§2.16 [1]For various views on the distinction between form and substance, *see* P. Atiyah & R. Summers, Form and Substance in Anglo-American Law 5-7 (1987) (distinguishing formal reasons from substantive reasons, notably " 'goal' reasons and 'rightness' reasons"); R. Unger, Law in Modern Society 203-16 (1976) (discussing "the compromise between formal and substantive justice"); Fuller, Consideration and Form, 41 Colum. L. Rev. 799, 799-800 (1941) (distinguishing objections "which touch the form rather than the content of the agreement" from those that touch "the significance of the promise").

a bit of this history, first in connection with the Roman stipulation[2] and later in connection with the English action of covenant.[3]

The action of covenant came to be used at common law to enforce "formal" contracts made under seal, as distinguished from "informal" or "simple" ones.[4] There were three requirements for making an enforceable promise under seal. First, there had to be a writing that designated the parties and contained a sufficiently definite promise. Second, the writing had to be sealed by the promisor. Third, the writing had to be delivered to the promisee. Once the sealed writing was delivered, the promise was enforceable, and it made no difference that the promisor might have received nothing in exchange for the promise. The seal was therefore a means for making an enforceable gratuitous promise.

Availability of action of covenant

It is misleading to say, as courts have sometimes done, that a seal "imports consideration" or that it raises a "presumption of consideration."[5] As we have seen, the action of covenant long antedated the general notion that an unsealed promise was enforceable if supported by consideration.[6] Far from deriving its effect from the doctrine of consideration, the seal was a distinct and independent alternative basis for the enforcement of a promise.[7] Indeed, so potent was the seal that at one time a person might be held on a sealed promise even though the seal had been lost or stolen and affixed without consent.[8]

Seal was distinct from consideration

In medieval England, the seal was a piece of wax affixed to the document and bearing an impression identifying the promisor, who did not have to sign it, although promisors came almost invariably to do so. At first its use was confined to the nobility, but later it spread to the commonalty.[9] With the growth of literacy and the use of the personal signature as a means of authentication, the required formality became so eroded that a seal could consist of any written or printed symbol, as long as it was intended by the promisor to serve as a seal.

Growth of the seal

---

[2] See the discussion of the stipulation in §1.4 *supra*.

[3] See the discussion of the unsuitability of the action of covenant as a general basis in §1.5 *supra*.

[4] Restatement Second §6 lists four types of contracts that are "formal" in the sense that they are subject to "special rules that depend on their formal characteristics and differ from those governing contracts in general": (1) contracts under seal; (2) recognizances; (3) negotiable instruments and documents; (4) letters of credit. All are discussed briefly in the Comment to §6. The last three are of no present concern.

[5] In re Conrad's Estate, 3 A.2d 697, 699 (Pa. 1938) ("well settled that a seal imports consideration").

[6] See the discussion of the unsuitability of the action of covenant as a general basis in §1.5 *supra*.

[7] A court, asked to grant equitable relief such as specific performance rather than a mere remedy at law such as damages, would generally look behind the seal and grant the requested relief only if there was something in the nature of a fair exchange. As to options under seal, see the discussion of the effect of the abolition of the seal in §3.23 *infra*.

[8] J. Ames, Lectures on Legal History 98 (1913). Fraud was no defense on a sealed instrument at common law.

[9] On the history of the seal, *see* 7 J. Wigmore, Evidence §2161 (Chadbourn rev. 1978).

The promisor did not have to affix the seal but could "adopt" a seal already placed on the instrument. The word *seal* or the words *locus sigilli* (the place of the seal) or the abbreviation *L.S.* were commonly printed near the place for signature on standard forms, so that the party signing might adopt them as a seal. It then became necessary to decide whether the promisor had in fact intended to adopt the symbol as a seal, and this detracted from the certainty that had been one of the seal's attractions.[10] To encourage a court to conclude that the promisor had done so, the form often contained a printed recital, such as "signed and sealed" or "witness my hand and seal."

Decline of the seal   With the erosion of the solemnity of the seal, its efficacy was called into question. According to Lon Fuller, legal formalities perform an "evidentiary" function, by providing trustworthy evidence of the existence and terms of the contract in the event of controversy, and a "cautionary" function, by bringing home to the parties the significance of their acts — inducing "the circumspective frame of mind appropriate in one pledging his future."[11] When it became doubtful that the seal performed either of these functions well, its effect on the enforceability of promises was abolished in roughly half of the states of the United States and seriously curtailed in the rest. The most recent of these assaults on the seal came in the Uniform Commercial Code which, as its commentary explains, "makes it clear that every effect of the seal which relates to 'sealed instruments' as such is wiped out insofar as contracts for sale [of goods] are concerned."[12] In jurisdictions where the seal was not entirely abolished, its effect might be limited to raising a rebuttable presumption of consideration or to making applicable a longer period of limitations. It is essential in such jurisdictions to consult the particular state statutes relating to the seal and the decisions applying those statutes.[13] In jurisdictions where the seal has been abolished, it has only historical interest, often as essential background for an understanding of later developments.

But has not consideration itself become as much a form as the seal?

Consideration as form   **§2.17.   Recitals.** It was Holmes who said that since courts do not ordinarily "inquire into the amount of . . . consideration . . . , consideration is as much a

---

[10]The promisor's delivery of a sealed writing generally sufficed to show adoption of the seal. Restatement Second §98.

[11]*See* Fuller, Consideration and Form, 41 Colum. L. Rev. 779, 800-01 (1941), which also discusses a third function, described as "channeling" (i.e., serving as "a simple and external test of enforceability" — "to mark or signalize the enforceable promise"). While the channeling function is not insignificant, it seems usually to be an unintended, or at least incidental, result of formalities directed at evidentiary or cautionary ends. *See also* E. Farnsworth, Changing Your Mind ch. 5 (1998).

[12]UCC 2-203 cmt.

[13]For an example of the continued vitality of the seal in some states, *see* Ga. Code Ann. §9-3-23 (20-year period of limitations for contract under seal).

form as a seal."[1] As far as nominal consideration is concerned, however, the contemporary doctrine of consideration requires more than mere form.[2] To what extent does this requirement extend to recitals as well?

Often the drafter of a contract hedges a promise with language intended to limit its legal effect by making some action by the promisee a condition of that promise. The drafter may say, for example, *"If you pay me $100,* I promise to deliver apples . . . ." Such language is generally given its intended effect, so that the promisor is under no duty to deliver apples unless the $100 is paid.[3] But what if the drafter goes further and tries to make it clear that there is consideration for the promise to deliver apples? Suppose the drafter says, *"In consideration of your payment of $100, receipt of which is hereby acknowledged,* I promise to deliver apples . . . ." Now the drafter has tried to do more than merely limit the legal effect of the promise. In order to make the promise to deliver apples enforceable, the drafter has recited two facts (that the consideration for the promise is the payment of $100 and that the $100 has been paid) that may or may not have occurred. What is the effect of such a recital?[4]

First, it is not within the drafter's power to transform something that *cannot* be consideration into consideration by reciting that it is given "in consideration." The employer cannot transform an unenforceable promise to give an employee a gold watch into an enforceable one simply by reciting, "In consideration of your past service, I promise . . . ."[5] Nor can the employer do so by reciting, "In consideration of my gratitude for your past service, I promise . . . ." Neither past service nor gratitude for past service can be consideration, and no recital can alter this. Such a recital does not impair the enforceability of a promise, however, if the promise is otherwise supported by consideration.[6]

Example of recital

No power over what cannot be consideration

§2.17 [1]Krell v. Codman, 28 N.E. 578, 578 (Mass. 1891). *See also* Holmes's discussion of consideration in Wisconsin & Mich. Ry. v. Powers, 191 U.S. 379, 386 (1903) (the promise and the consideration must be "the conventional inducements each for the other," and no matter "what the actual motive may have been, . . . the promise and the consideration must purport to be the motive each for the other, in whole or at least in part").

[2]See the discussion of a likely example of nominal consideration in §2.11 *supra.* That consideration might better be called a "technicality" rather than a "formality," *see* E. Farnsworth, Changing Your Mind ch. 5 (1998).

[3]As to whether it can be varied by a showing of a contrary oral agreement, see the discussion of lack of consideration in §7.4 *infra.*

[4]As to the effect of recitals generally, *see* the discussion of recitals in §7.10 *infra.*

[5]Moore v. Elmer, 61 N.E. 259 (Mass. 1901) (recital of past services as clairvoyant as consideration for promise to pay off mortgage). Nor can the employer turn the promise into an enforceable one by reciting, "In consideration of your accepting my gift, I promise . . . ." That a promisor cannot make a promise enforceable by reciting as consideration the payment of a dollar, when such a payment would not otherwise be consideration, *see* In re Greene, 45 F.2d 428 (S.D.N.Y. 1930) (recital of payment of $1 was not consideration for a promise to pay "hundreds of thousands of dollars").

[6]Thomas v. Thomas, 114 Eng. Rep. 330 (Q.B. 1842) (could be shown that promise to pay £1 a year and to make repairs was consideration in spite of recital "in consideration of such desire and of the premises," which could not have been consideration).

No power over truth

Second, neither is it within the drafter's power to change falsehood into truth by reciting that an act has been done as consideration in a promise if the act has not been done.[7] In spite of a recital that a performance has taken place (e.g., that the price has been paid), it can be shown that the performance has not taken place — that the recital is false.[8] And in spite of a recital that a promisor was seeking a stated promise (e.g., a promise to pay one dollar) or performance (e.g., payment of one dollar), it can be proved that the promisor was not bargaining for that performance or promise — that the recital is false and that there was merely a pretense of bargain.[9] A court that would refuse to enforce a promise on the ground that the claimed consideration was plainly a sham will not be dissuaded from doing so by a recital to the contrary. If a promise is otherwise supported by consideration, however, such a recital does not impair its enforceability.[10]

Power to furnish evidence of bargain

It is, however, within the drafter's power to furnish evidence that there was in fact a bargain by reciting that what was done was done in consideration of the promise. If it is unclear whether the promise is a conditional gratuitous promise or a promise supported by consideration, the evidence of bargain supplied by a recital of consideration may carry the day. The court that decided *Kirksey* would probably have found consideration for the brother-in-law's promise had it begun, *"In consideration of your coming down and seeing me,* I will . . . ," rather than "If you come down and see me, I will . . . ."[11]

Emphasis on substance over form

The law's attitude toward recitals is therefore similar to its attitude toward "nominal consideration." There is an underlying insistence on substance over form — an actual bargain as opposed to apparent bargain — that belies Holmes's assertion that consideration is as much a form as the seal.

With this brief excursion into form as a basis for enforcement of promises, we turn to reform of the bases for enforcement.

Lord Mansfield's view

§2.18. Reform of the Bases for Enforcement. Contemporary critics of the doctrine of consideration claim to trace their lineage back to Lord Mansfield,

---

[7] As to the important question of the applicability of this general statement to option contracts, however, *see* the discussion of the effect of recitals in §3.23 *infra*.

[8] Moorcroft State Bank v. Morel, 701 P.2d 1159 (Wyo. 1985) (recital that promise was in "consideration of the sum of One Dollar and other valuable consideration" received could be disproved). As to the possibility that a recital of "for value received" may have an effect under the statute of frauds, see the discussion of consideration as an essential term in §6.7 *infra*.

[9] Mount Sinai Hosp. v. Jordan, 290 So. 2d 484 (Fla. 1974) (recital that promise to donate money to charity was "in consideration of and to induce the subscriptions of others" was not effective). As to the effect of the parol evidence rule, see the discussion of the lack of consideration in §7.4 *infra*.

[10] Thomsen v. Glenn, 398 P.2d 710 (Nev. 1965) ("false recital [of receipt of $500] does not deprive the agreement of its legal operation"); Batsakis v. Demotsis, 226 S.W.2d 673 (Tex. Civ. App. 1949) (payment of 500,000 drachmae, apparently worth $750, could be shown despite recital of payment of $2,000).

[11] The prudent drafter might also add, "since I want you to be near me."

who mounted a memorable, if short-lived, attack on the doctrine in 1765. He advanced the heresy "that the ancient notion about the want of consideration was for the sake of evidence only: for when it is reduced into writing, there was no objection to the want of consideration."[1] Only 13 years later, Mansfield's heresy was extirpated from the common law by the House of Lords, which declared that if contracts "be merely written, and not specialties [e.g., under seal], . . . a consideration must be proved."[2] But Mansfield's heresy did not remain quiescent. The view that the formality of putting a promise in writing should operate as an alternative to consideration continued to have appeal, and it gained new vitality when the abolition of the seal gave the doctrine of consideration even greater prominence.

In 1937 the English Law Revision Committee recommended the enactment of a statute making a signed written promise enforceable without regard to consideration.[3] Although this recommendation has not been followed, a few of the American states have enacted legislation along similar lines. Pennsylvania has the most sweeping statute, under which any promise, even a purely gratuitous one, is not "unenforceable for lack of consideration, if the writing also contains an additional express statement, in any form of language, that the signer intends to be legally bound."[4] A more common variety of legislation, found in over a dozen states including California, makes a writing "presumptive evidence of consideration."[5] New York has enacted statutes making a writing a substitute for consideration in a limited number of situations, including promises supported only by "past consideration."[6]

Types of statutes

As John Dawson observed, in spite of "the intensity and depth of the hostility" that the doctrine of consideration has inspired, "even in the last hundred years little disposition has appeared to change the solutions in a basic way."[7] The limited success of efforts to reform the doctrine may therefore be attributable more to the fact that it has met with complacency than to the fact that it has found universal approval. For the most part, the doctrine works well enough in those areas of commercial life that are important to economic vitality. To the

Reason for lack of reform

---

§2.18   [1] Pillans & Rose v. Van Mierop & Hopkins, 97 Eng. Rep. 1035 (K.B. 1765). In the same case, he said, "In commercial cases amongst merchants, the want of consideration is not an objection." The idea that consideration may be dispensed with where merchants are involved is reflected in UCC 2-205. See the discussion of firm offers under the Code in §3.23 *infra*.

[2] Rann v. Hughes, 101 Eng. Rep. 1014n. (H.L. 1778).

[3] [English] Law Revision Committee, Report on the Statute of Frauds and the Doctrine of Consideration (Sixth Interim Report, Cmd. 5449, 1937), reprinted in 15 Can. B. Rev. 585 (1937).

[4] Pa. Stat. Ann. tit. 33, §6. This was originally promulgated as the *Uniform* Written Obligations Act by the National Conference of Commissioners on Uniform State Laws. But it was adopted only by Pennsylvania and Utah, and then repealed by Utah, after which it was renamed the *Model* Written Obligations Act. *See* E. Farnsworth, Changing Your Mind ch. 8 (1998).

[5] Cal. Civ. Code §1614.

[6] See the discussion of the New York statute in §2.8 *supra*.

[7] J. Dawson, Gifts and Promises 197, 224 (1980).

extent that it may enforce too many promises, it has been counteracted by other doctrines that permit a court to refuse to enforce promises.[8] To the extent that it may enforce too few promises, it has been supplemented by reliance as an alternative ground for enforcement.[9]

We turn now to reliance as an alternative ground for the enforcement of promises.

Importance of reliance outside the marketplace

§2.19. Reliance as a Ground for Recovery: Promissory Estoppel. We have seen that the promisee's unsolicited reliance is not consideration because it is not bargained for.[1] Promises made outside or on the periphery of the marketplace are particularly likely to lack this element of bargain. The failure of the doctrine of consideration to provide a more satisfactory basis for enforcing such promises might have brought greater pressure to reform the doctrine had it not been for the increasing recognition of reliance as an alternative ground for recovery.

Example of reliance

Suppose that an employer promises to pay an employee a pension of $500 a month upon retirement. Relying on the promise, the employee retires at an age when other employment is unavailable. If the employer then refuses to pay the pension, is the employee without recourse because the promise lacked consideration? Today, most courts would allow the employee to enforce the promise on the ground of reliance.[2] Suppose that a debtor is in default on a debt, and a friend makes a gratuitous promise to the creditor to pay it. Relying on the promise, the creditor forbears from proceeding against the debtor for a time during which the debtor becomes insolvent. If the friend refuses to pay the debt, is the creditor without recourse because the promise lacked consideration? Today, there is authority that the creditor can enforce the promise on the ground of reliance.[3]

Historical development of the doctrine

But it was not until the twentieth century that a generalized theory of recovery based on reliance developed, although reliance had figured in the history of consideration during the expansion of assumpsit.[4] Late in the nineteenth century, Holmes expressed the common law's traditional view of reliance: "It would cut up the doctrine of consideration by the roots, if a promisee could make a

---

[8] These are dealt with in Chapter 4.

[9] For attempts to fashion new theories of enforceability of promises, *see* Barnett, A Consent Theory of Contract, 86 Colum. L. Rev. 269 (1986), expanded in Barnett, Some Problems with Contract as Promise, 77 Cornell L. Rev. 1022 (1992); Gordley, Enforcing Promises, 83 Cal. L. Rev. 547 (1995).

§2.19 [1] See §2.9 *supra*.

[2] Feinberg v. Pfeiffer Co., 322 S.W.2d 163 (Mo. App. 1959).

[3] Restatement Second §85; W.B. Saunders Co. v. Galbraith, 40 Ohio App. 155, 178 N.E. 34 (1931) (creditor relied on widow's promise to pay husband's debt by not filing claim against his estate).

[4] See the discussion of the requirement of reliance in cases on nonfeasance in §1.6 *supra*. It is odd that after playing this part in the development of the doctrine of consideration, reliance played no important role for some four centuries.

gratuitous promise binding by subsequently acting in reliance on it."[5] Nevertheless, even during the nineteenth century, reliance on a gratuitous promise came to be recognized as a basis for recovery in a few categories of cases.

One category was made up of gratuitous promises to convey land. Courts enforced such promises if the promisee had relied by moving onto the land and making improvements (e.g., by putting up a building).[6]

Gratuitous promises to convey land

A second category consisted of gratuitous promises made by bailees in connection with gratuitous bailments. If, when the bailor delivered goods to the bailee, the bailee promised to obtain insurance on them but then failed to do so, the bailor's reliance by not obtaining insurance made the bailee's promise enforceable when the goods were later destroyed.[7] This was so although a gratuitous promise to obtain insurance that was not made in connection with a gratuitous bailment was not enforceable when it was followed by similar detrimental reliance.[8] The difference in result was ascribed to a distinction between "misfeasance," where a bailment was undertaken, and "nonfeasance," where one was not.[9]

Gratuitous promises by bailees

A third category was made up of promises to make gifts to charitable institutions ("charitable subscriptions").[10] Such a promise seems the archetype of the unenforceable gratuitous promise. However, as one court explained, "This promise was made to a charitable corporation, and for that reason we are not confined to . . . orthodox concepts. . . . There can be no denying that the strong desire on the part of the American courts to favor charitable institutions has established a doctrine which once would have been looked upon as legal heresy."[11] This desire to support private philanthropy also spawned a variety of tenuous arguments designed to show that such promises were supported by consideration. Sometimes courts found that the subscriber had bargained with the charitable organization, either for its act of proceeding with its work[12] or

Gratuitous promises to charities

---

[5] Commonwealth v. Scituate Sav. Bank, 137 Mass. 301, 302 (1884).

[6] Greiner v. Greiner, 131 Kan. 760, 293 P. 759 (1930). Reliance short of making improvements did not suffice. Although all these cases involved specific performance, presumably damages were also available. Contrast the doctrine of part performance under the statute of frauds, treated in the discussion of the land contract provision in §6.9 *infra*.

[7] Siegel v. Spear & Co., 234 N.Y. 479, 138 N.E. 414 (1923).

[8] Thorne v. Deas, 4 Johns. 84 (N.Y. Sup. Ct. 1809); Comfort v. McCorkle, 268 N.Y.S. 192 (Sup. Ct. 1933).

[9] Note the similar distinction between "misfeasance" and "nonfeasance" that was made during the growth of assumpsit. See the discussion of the extension of assumpsit to cases of nonfeasance in §1.6 *supra*.

[10] In the case of business subscriptions (e.g., promises to pay for stock to be issued), there is ordinarily no problem of finding consideration.

[11] Danby v. Osteopathic Hosp. Assn., 104 A.2d 903 (Del. Ch. 1954). *See* Jewish Fedn. v. Barondess, 560 A.2d 1353 (N.J. Super. 1989) (reliance is "questionable basis for enforcing a charitable subscription" and real basis "is one of public policy").

[12] I. & I. Holding Corp. v. Gainsburg, 12 N.E.2d 532 (N.Y. 1938) (hospital did humanitarian work as consideration for promise).

for its promise to use the funds in the way specified by the subscriber.[13] Sometimes they found that the subscriber had bargained with other subscribers for their similar promises, a finding that was encouraged if the first subscriber had appeared as the "bellwether" of the flock and promised a large sum if others would pledge a stated amount.[14] Now, however, it has come to be recognized that such promises are enforceable when relied on by the charitable institution, without resort to the doctrine of consideration.[15]

Gratuitous promises within the family

The fourth category consisted of gratuitous promises made within the family.[16] Because the pattern of the bargained-for exchange, so common in the marketplace, seems out of place within the family, promisors within a family may not actually bargain for something in return, even though they desire and expect it. In *Ricketts v. Scothorn*, for example, a grandfather went to the store where his granddaughter worked as a bookkeeper and gave her a promissory note, embodying his promise to pay her $2,000 on demand. He told her that he had "fixed out something that you have not got to work any more" and that "none of my grandchildren work, and you don't have to." She promptly quit work, but when he died several years later, his executor refused to honor his promise. In allowing the granddaughter to recover on the promise, the court reasoned, "Having intentionally influenced the plaintiff to alter her position for the worse on the faith of the note being paid when due, it would be grossly inequitable to permit the maker, or his executor, to resist payment on the ground that the promise was given without consideration." There was an "equitable estoppel."[17] Such decisions took much of the sting out of the requirement of consideration in family transactions. Courts no longer needed to search for a bargain in cases such as *Hamer v. Sidway*, in which one was found,[18] and *Kirksey*, in which one was not.[19]

Derivation of concept of estoppel

These decisions based on reliance, however, involved far more than a routine application of "equitable estoppel." That concept applied to a representation

---

[13] Allegheny College v. National Chautauqua County Bank, 159 N.E. 173 (N.Y. 1927) (college promised to set up memorial fund as consideration for promise).

[14] Congregation B'nai Sholom v. Martin, 173 N.W.2d 504 (Mich. 1969) ("in subscription agreement cases the mutual promises between subscribers . . . will constitute a consideration therefor").

Note that this is an instance in which the consideration does not "move" from the promisee, the charitable institution. *See* the discussion of the point that consideration need not move from the promisee in §2.3 *supra*.

[15] Some of the impetus came from Cardozo's noted dictum in Allegheny College v. National Chautauqua County Bank, *supra* note 13, "that we have adopted the doctrine of promissory estoppel as the equivalent of consideration in connection with our law of charitable subscriptions."

[16] This category overlaps the first category, since the land transactions within the first are often also family transactions within the fourth.

[17] 77 N.W. 365, 367 (Neb. 1898).

[18] 27 N.E. 256 (N.Y. 1891) (discussed in §2.4 *supra*).

[19] 8 Ala. 131 (1845), considered in the discussion of the example of *Kirksey* in §2.9 *supra*. The court that decided *Ricketts* would presumably have allowed recovery in this case.

of *fact* made by one party and relied on by the other. The estopped party was precluded from alleging or proving facts that contradicted its representation.[20] But cases like *Ricketts* involved a *promise*, not a representation of a fact. The promisor was "estopped" to raise the defense of lack of consideration in his promise. This type of estoppel came to be known as "promissory estoppel."[21]

In 1933, on the authority of such cases as these,[22] the American Law Institute promulgated §90 of the Restatement of Contracts, which was destined to become its most notable and influential rule.[23] It states, in terms generally applicable to all promises, the principle that courts had applied to the four narrow categories of promises just described:

Restatement §90

> A promise which the promisor should reasonably expect to induce action or forbearance of a definite and substantial character on the part of the promisee and which does induce such action or forbearance is binding if injustice can be avoided only by enforcement of the promise.

The following version appears as §90 in the Restatement Second:

> (1) A promise which the promisor should reasonably expect to induce action or forbearance on the part of the promisee or a third person and which does induce such action or forbearance is binding if injustice can be avoided only by enforcement of the promise. The remedy granted for breach may be limited as justice requires.
>
> (2) A charitable subscription or a marriage settlement is binding under Subsection (1) without proof that the promise induced action or forbearance.

Section 90 is the Restatement's most significant departure from its stated policy of following precedents[24] and has been the fountainhead of recovery based on

---

[20] For a case comparing equitable and promissory estoppel, *see* Mazer v. Jackson Ins. Agency, 340 So. 2d 770 (Ala. 1976) (developers' memorandum misrepresented effect of planning commission's memorandum). *See generally* E. Farnsworth, Changing Your Mind ch. 17 (1998).

[21] The first use of the term is attributed to Williston in Boyer, Promissory Estoppel: Requirements and Limitations of the Doctrine, 98 U. Pa. L. Rev. 459 (1950), citing 1 S. Williston, Contracts §139 (1st ed. 1920). It has been held that promissory estoppel is sufficiently equitable in nature that there is no right to trial by jury. Olson v. Synergistic Techs. Bus. Sys., 628 N.W.2d 142 (Minn. 2001) ("promissory estoppel is a creature of equity" and "elements of promissory estoppel evolved from the equitable cause of action unique to England's Chancery courts").

[22] A fifth category, the gratuitous agency cases, is sometimes added. "One who, by a gratuitous promise . . . which he should realize will cause another reasonably to rely upon the performance of definite acts of service by him as the other's agent, causes the other to refrain from having such acts done by other available means is subject to a duty to use care to perform such service or, while other means are available, to give notice that he will not perform." Restatement (Second) of Agency §378 (1958).

[23] It had been discussed on the floor of the Institute in 1926. *See* 4 Am. L. Inst. Proc., Appendix 85-114 (1926). On the history of §90, *see* Farnsworth, Contracts Scholarship in the Age of the Anthology, 85 Mich. L. Rev. 1406, 1454-62 (1987).

[24] See the discussion of departure from precedent in §1.8 *supra*.

reliance in a broad range of situations.[25] Most of these situations involve commercial transactions and are far removed from the traditional settings, such as that in *Ricketts*, in which the doctrine originated.[26] Although the rule that it states does not lend itself to precision, four requirements are of special interest.[27] First, there must have been a promise. Second, the promisor must have had reason to expect reliance on the promise. Third, the promise must have induced such reliance.[28] Fourth, the circumstances must have been such that injustice can be avoided only by enforcement of the promise.

First: promise　　　A promisor's liability when based on reliance, like a promisor's liability when based on consideration, is limited by the scope of the promise.[29] A claimant's first step in establishing liability under reliance is to show that there was a promise. Although some courts have held that the promise need not contain all the elements of an offer,[30] it must be "clear and definite," to use a phrase favored by courts.[31] The promise is rarely as clear as it was in *Ricketts*, where the grandfather's note read "I promise to pay." Thus the statement by a supplier

---

[25]Tour Costa Rica v. Country Walkers, 758 A.2d 795 (Vt. 2000) (in "reliance on a two-year commitment, [fledgling tour business] stopped soliciting business from other sources and declined other bookings"). For application of the doctrine in an unusual context, *see* Cohen v. Cowles Media Co., 479 N.W.2d 387 (Minn. 1992) (source's reliance on reporter's promise to keep source confidential).

That the Vienna Convention does not preempt a claim based on promissory estoppel, *see* Geneva Pharms. Tech. Corp. v. Barr Labs., 201 F. Supp. 2d 236 (S.D.N.Y. 2002) (no argument presented that "CISG had contemplated a similar 'reliance' principle in its determination of whether a contract had formed").

[26]Leading examples include the pension cases and the surety cases in the discussion of the example of reliance *supra* and the insurance cases in the discussion of promises to procure insurance *infra*. For a different example, *see* D & G Stout v. Bacardi Imports, 923 F.2d 566 (7th Cir. 1991) (supplier's promise to stay with liquor distributor).

[27]That all of the elements of §90, except the matter of avoidance of injustice, are matters of fact, *see* R.S. Bennett & Co. v. Economy Mechanical Indus., 606 F.2d 182 (7th Cir. 1979).

[28]The requirement of the first Restatement that the reliance be "of a definite and substantial character" has been dropped in the Restatement Second. This is partly because the Restatement Second allows a court to limit the remedy in the manner discussed below under the third heading. *See* Reporter's Note to Restatement Second §90. The requirement of the first Restatement that reliance be "on the part of the *promisee*" has been changed to permit reliance "on the part of the *promisee or a third person.*" *See* the discussion of the effect of reliance by the beneficiary in §10.3 *infra.*

[29]Local 1330, United Steel Workers v. United States Steel Corp., 631 F.2d 1264 (6th Cir. 1980) (manufacturer not liable on promise to continue plant in operation because conditional on profitability).

[30]Cyberchron Corp. v. Calldata Sys. Dev., 47 F.3d 39 (2d Cir. 1995) (there was "clear and unambiguous promise" where contractor directed subcontractor to proceed as if there had been agreement). See the discussions of the example of *Red Owl* and of the example of *Cyberchron* in §3.26 *infra.*

[31]D'Ulisse-Cupo v. Board of Directors of Notre Dame High School, 520 A.2d 217 (Conn. 1987) (such representations as "no problem with her teaching . . . the following year" and "everything looked fine for her return" were "neither sufficiently promissory nor sufficiently definite").

that "you can rest assured we will have an unending supply of remnants" was characterized not as a promise to the buyer but as "a mere expression of opinion of prediction concerning the future availability of . . . remnants."[32]

Second, the promisor must have had reason to expect the reliance that occurred, although the promisor may not have sought it (i.e., bargained for it). Even if the promisee relied on the promise, the promisor is not liable if the promisor had no reason to expect any reliance at all or had reason to expect reliance but not of the sort that occurred. The simplest case is that of a conditional gratuitous promise, for it is clearly reasonable for the promisor to expect that the promisee will take the action on which the promise is conditioned. Thus, in *Kirksey*, the promisor should reasonably have expected his sister-in-law to "come down and see me," and in the example of the employer's promise of a pension on retirement, the promisor should reasonably have expected the employee to retire. Even if the promise is not conditional, it may be reasonable for the promisor to expect reliance. Thus, the grandfather in *Ricketts* should have expected his granddaughter to quit work in reliance on his promise of $2,000. It would have been more difficult to show this expectation if he had not expressed his hope that it would enable her to stop working. The standard for testing expectation is an objective one, under which the promisor is bound if the promisor had reason to expect reliance, even if the promisor did not in fact expect it.[33]

Second: reason to expect reliance

Third, there must have been actual reliance on the promise.[34] And the reliance must have been of the sort to have been reasonably expected,[35] a requirement that courts have often transformed into a requirement that the reliance itself must be reasonable.[36] In *Ricketts* if, after the grandfather had

Third: reliance induced

---

[32] Major Mat Co. v. Monsanto Co., 969 F.2d 579, 583 (7th Cir. 1992).

[33] Local 1330, United Steel Workers v. United States Steel Corp., *supra* note 29 (union's "reliance upon a promise to keep these plants open on the basis of coverage of plant fixed costs was [not] within reasonable expectability"). On the objective theory, see §3.6 *infra*. Presumably the promisor is bound in the unlikely situation in which the promisor actually expected the reliance but had no reason to expect it.

[34] Section 90 does not say that the reliance must be "detrimental," though many cases assume that it must be.

For a case virtually dispensing with any requirement of detriment in the context of an employment contract, *see* Vastoler v. American Can Co., 700 F.2d 916 (3d Cir. 1983) ("jury could certainly find that when [employee] changed his position from an hourly worker responsible for his individual tasks to a salaried supervisor responsible for approximately fifty subordinate employees he was forced to absorb additional stress and trauma").

[35] *See* D & G Stout v. Bacardi Imports, 805 F. Supp. 1434 (N.D. Ind. 1992) (citing this sentence of this treatise and adding that "this principle does not require a promisee to prove that a promisor should have known of the precise form that the promisee's reliance would take; it merely requires that the general nature or extent of the promisee's reliance be reasonably expected"). Restatement Second §90 speaks of "*such* action or forbearance."

[36] Watkins & Son Pet Supplies v. Iams Co., 254 F.3d 607 (6th Cir. 2001) (if "written contract is completely integrated, it is unreasonable as a matter of law to rely on parol representations or promises within the scope of the contract made prior to execution").

expressed the hope that his granddaughter would stop working, she had relied by buying a gold watch or by adopting a lavish standard of living, it might have been difficult to show that he should reasonably have expected this sort of reliance. Until reliance occurs, the promise is not enforceable and can be revoked by the promisor. Since the reliance must have been *induced* by the promise, it cannot consist of action or forbearance that would have occurred in any event. If, in the example of the employer's promise of a pension on retirement, the employee had already made a firm decision to retire, the employee's action would not have been induced by the promise.[37] If, in *Ricketts*, the granddaughter had already made a firm decision to quit work, her action would not have been induced by the promise. If the claimed reliance consists of the promisee's forbearance rather than affirmative action, proof that this forbearance was induced by the promise requires a showing that the promisee could have acted.[38] The Restatement Second, however, continues the policy favoring charitable subscriptions by making such promises enforceable without proof of reliance. In that exceptional situation the promisor is bound immediately.[39]

Fourth: avoiding injustice

Fourth, the promise is not enforceable unless "injustice can be avoided only by enforcement." This vague qualification has been discussed in relatively few cases. In one of the more interesting the Supreme Court of Minnesota held that under §90 newspapers were bound by a reporter's promise to his source that he would keep the source confidential. The newspapers argued that "it is unjust to be penalized for publishing the whole truth," but the court responded that "it is not clear that this would result in an injustice in this case."

> Neither side in this case clearly holds the higher moral ground, but in view of the defendants' concurrence in the importance of honoring promises of confidentiality, and absent the showing of any compelling need in this case to break that

---

[37] Hayes v. Plantations Steel Co., 438 A.2d 1091 (R.I. 1982) (employer's promise of pension did not induce employee's retirement where "he made this decision on his own initiative" and "had reached that decision long before" promise was made).

[38] *See* Pitts v. McGraw-Edison Co., 329 F.2d 412 (6th Cir. 1964) (manufacturer's representative, whose relationship with the manufacturer was terminable at the manufacturer's will and was terminated by it, "in no way altered his position for the worse by reason of" the manufacturer's promise of a pension and "gave up nothing in accepting retirement that he would not have lost if he had refused to accept it").

[39] Salsbury v. Northwestern Bell Tel. Co., 221 N.W.2d 609 (Iowa 1974) (citing Restatement Second). *Contra:* Maryland Natl. Bank v. United Jewish Appeal Fedn., 407 A.2d 1130 (Md. 1979) (declining to follow Restatement Second); Congregation Kadimah Toras-Moshe v. DeLeo, 540 N.E.2d 691 (Mass. 1989) ("there is no injustice in declining to enforce the decedent's promise" to charity where rely), distinguished in King v. Trustees of Boston Univ., 647 N.E.2d 1196 (Mass. 1995) (whether pledge was supported by consideration or reliance properly submitted to jury). Of course, if a charitable subscription is enforced on the ground that the promises of other subscribers are consideration for it, no reliance by the charitable organization is necessary. See the discussion of gratuitous promises to charities *supra*.

promise, we conclude that the resultant harm to [the source] requires a remedy here to avoid an injustice.[40]

Only rarely have courts applied this vague qualification to deny recovery.[41]

Even if the requirements for enforceability of a promise are met, the Restatement Second states that recovery "may be limited as justice requires," language that is generally invoked in limiting recovery to damages based on the reliance interest.[42] Thus an employee may be allowed reliance damages when reliance on a promise of employment consists of quitting another job.[43] Williston, when drafting the first Restatement, had rejected any such notion. He argued, "Either the promise is binding or it is not. If the promise is binding, it has to be enforced as it is made."[44] Williston's choice was reinforced by the etymology of the term "promissory estoppel," although he generally avoided using that term in the Restatement.[45] If an "estoppel" precludes the promisor from showing that the promise "is lacking in one of the essential elements of a valid contract,"[46] as the court put it in *Ricketts v. Scothorn*, the ineluctable consequence is that the promise itself is enforceable, and the promisee may recover the value of the expectation interest. If, however, the ground of the promisee's recovery were regarded as the reliance interest, it would seem appropriate to limit recovery to the value of that interest — the cost to the promisee of the detriment

Recovery may be limited

---

[40] Cohen v. Cowles Media Co., *supra* note 25, at 391-92.

[41] Kiley v. First Natl. Bank, 649 A.2d 1145 (Md. App. 1994) (where depositors had benefit of bank's checking account terms "for some five years, justice certainly does not compel application of promissory estoppel"). For an example involving offer and acceptance, *see* the discussion of reluctance to protect the offeree in §3.25 *infra*.

[42] D & G Stout v. Bacardi Imports, *supra* note 26 (liquor distributor "had a business opportunity that all parties knew would be devalued once [supplier] announced its intention to go elsewhere" and "extent of that devaluation represents a reliance injury, rather than an injury to [distributor's] expectation of future profit"), on remand, D & G Stout v. Bacardi Imports, *supra* note 35 ("expenses associated with the warehouse are not recoverable because [distributor] would have incurred those costs even if it had remained as [supplier's] distributor" but "difference between [third party's] initial offer and the final sale price may be recovered as damages incurred in reliance"). On the meaning of the quoted language, *see* Restatement Second §139(2), treated in the discussion of Restatement Second §139 in §6.12 *infra*.

[43] Grouse v. Group Health Plan, 306 N.W.2d 114 (Minn. 1981) (promise of employment at will). *Contra:* White v. Roche Biomedical Laboratories, 807 F. Supp. 1212 (D.S.C. 1992) (denying recovery and noting that "numerous courts have reached a contrary result [to that in *Grouse*] under these or similar circumstances"), aff'd mem., 998 F.2d 1011 (4th Cir. 1993).

As to the applicability of the statute of frauds in such situations, see the discussion of other cases in §6.12 *infra*.

[44] 4 Am. L. Inst. Proc. app. 103-04 (1926). *See* Eisenberg, Donative Promises, 47 U. Chi. L. Rev. 1, 23-25 (1979).

[45] The only use of the term in the first Restatement comes in §178 cmt. *f*, in connection with the statute of frauds. Purists sometimes avoid the term "promissory estoppel" as supportive of Williston's view that damages must be based on expectation.

[46] 77 N.W. at 367.

that the promisee incurred in reliance on the promise.[47] The Restatement Second allows the court to proceed on either course, depending on what "justice requires" in the circumstances of the particular case. Although neither the black letter nor the comments state criteria for determining when the promisee should recover the value of the expectation interest and when "justice requires" that recovery be limited to the value of the reliance interest, a few are fairly obvious.[48] First, a lack of good faith on the part of the promisor will encourage a court to use the more generous expectation measure rather than the more restricted reliance measure.[49] Second, to the extent that there is a disparity between an expectation interest of large value and a reliance interest of small value, a court will tend to favor the latter.[50] Third, difficulty in calculating recovery on the basis of either measure will encourage a court to use the other. Thus, to the extent that calculation of the expectation measure is complicated by indefiniteness of the promise, recovery is likely to be limited to the reliance measure.[51] Conversely, to the extent that calculation of the reliance measure is complicated by difficulty in valuing the detriment, recovery of the expectation interest is likely.[52]

[47] *See* Seavey, Reliance upon Gratuitous Promises or Other Conduct, 64 Harv. L. Rev. 913 (1951). Comment *d* to Restatement Second §90 suggests that limitation to the promisee's restitution interest may also sometimes be appropriate, as in the case of gratuitous promises to convey land, where it might be appropriate to limit recovery to the value of the improvements (*see* §90 illus. 11). However, it seems questionable in such a case that recovery should be limited to their value to the *promisor* if the *promisee* had spent a greater amount on them in reliance on the promise.

[48] Comment *d* does say that "In the case of a promise to make a gift it would rarely be proper to award consequential damages which would place a greater burden on the promisor than performance would have imposed."

[49] *See* Restatement Second §90 ills. 8 & 9. See also the discussion of the duty of good faith in §7.17 *infra*.

[50] See note 28 *supra* for the effect of this on the previous requirement that reliance be substantial. To the extent that this criterion is given weight, however, it increases the significance of the court's choice between a theory of consideration (with recovery necessarily measured by the much larger expectation interest) and a theory of reliance (with recovery possibly limited to the much smaller reliance interest).

[51] Green v. Interstate United Mgt. Serv. Corp., 748 F.2d 827 (3d Cir. 1984) (limiting recovery to reliance damages was proper given "manifestly contingent nature" of promises). *See* Illustration 11 to Restatement Second §90, which suggests that for this reason the cases of improvements made in reliance on promises to give land may be particularly suitable instances for limitation of remedy. Similarly, if recovery were allowed in a case like *Kirksey*, it would presumably be limited to the amount of the sister-in-law's reliance.

[52] *See* Goldstick v. ICM Realty, 788 F.2d 456 (7th Cir. 1986) (Posner, J.: "much to be said for using the value of the promise as the measure of damages, simply on grounds of simplicity"). Consider the relative ease of calculating the expectation measure in Ricketts v. Scothorn or in the example of the employer's promise of a pension. Consider also the difficulty of calculating a reliance measure of damages in Hamer v. Sidway, *supra* note 18, if recovery in that case had been based on reliance rather than on consideration.

Gratuitous promises to procure insurance pose particularly difficult problems. Whether the expectation or the reliance measure is used, the promisor's liability will equal the amount of the loss, at least if the insured's lost opportunity to obtain other insurance is counted.[53] The promisor becomes, in effect, an insurer. Although courts have allowed recovery based on reliance in such cases,[54] they have been careful to make sure that all of the elements have been satisfied.[55]

What is the justification for this alternative ground of recovery? The possibility of an answer founded on principles of tort law is inescapable, particularly if recovery is limited to the reliance measure. Since one person has caused harm to another by making and then breaking a promise in circumstances that the promisor should reasonably have expected would cause such harm, the promisor could be seen as liable in tort for the harm caused. It has even been suggested that "what is happening is that 'contract' is being reabsorbed into the mainstream of 'tort.'"[56] Nevertheless, even if recovery is limited to the reliance measure, the promise is to that extent enforceable and is therefore a "contract" within our definition of the term.[57]

Recovery based on reliance will be considered again in the next chapter in connection with precontractual liability.[58] But first we take a brief look at restitution.

F.   RESTITUTION AS A GROUND FOR RECOVERY

§2.20.   Nature and Role of Restitution.   Finally, we turn to the possibility of a claim by one party based on the unjust enrichment of the other party — a kind of claim often dignified by a fiction as one based on a contract *implied in law*.[1] We briefly considered the possibility of such a claim in connection with

> **Promises to procure insurance**

> **Justification of reliance as a ground**

> **Relation to action of debt**

---

[53] The expectation measure would be the amount required to put the promisee in the position in which the promisee would have been had the insurance been procured, that is, the amount of the loss. The reliance measure would be the amount required to put the promisee in the position in which promisee would have been had the promise not been made, that is, the amount of the loss — if it is assumed that the promisee relied by forbearing to procure insurance elsewhere.

[54] Spiegel v. Metropolitan Life Ins. Co., 160 N.E.2d 40 (N.Y. 1959) (insurance agent liable on promise to wife-beneficiary to pay premium on her husband's life insurance).

[55] The cases cited *supra* note 8 reflect this concern.

[56] G. Gilmore, The Death of Contract 87 (1974). In reply, this account has been called "exaggerated," and it has been predicted that "bargain consideration has been and will remain for a long time to come a central feature of our law of contract." J. Dawson, Gifts and Promises 3 (1980).

[57] See the discussion of a definition of *contract* in §1.1 *supra*.

[58] See §§3.25, 3.26 *infra*.

§2.20   [1] Such claims should not be confused with claims based on what are sometimes called "contracts implied-in-fact," described in the the discussion of no formalities required in §3.10 *infra*. As to implied terms, see the discussion of how a court supplies an implied term in §7.16 *infra*.

the historical evolution of the common law action of debt.[2] We saw there that the lender's claim to recover on a loan was at first regarded as based, not on the borrower's promise to repay it, but on the notion that the borrower ought to disgorge the benefit received. After *Slade's Case* expanded the action of assumpsit, such claims based on restitutionary notions were replaced by claims based on the promise to repay.[3]

Meaning of
quasi-contract
and *restitution*

Money claims based on restitutionary notions continued to be pressed, however, in many other situations in which a party would arguably be unjustly enriched if allowed to retain without paying for it some benefit that had been conferred. A simple example is the claim for the return of money paid by mistake to one to whom it was not owed. Since these claims for the redress of unjust enrichment did not fit comfortably into either the category of contract or that of tort, they came to be described as claims in *quasi-contract*.[4] Recognizing that such claims are not based on the apparent intentions of the parties, the Supreme Court of Pennsylvania explained that liability "may be found in the absence of any expression of assent by the party to be charged and may indeed be found in spite of the party's contrary intention."[5] Some of these claims were originally characterized as being in *quantum meruit* (as much as the claimant deserved), one of what were known as the "common counts" into which the action of general assumpsit was divided after *Slade's Case*. Originally intended to enable a plaintiff to allege that the defendant was indebted to the plaintiff for work done, it gradually became a flexible basis for recovery where a benefit had been received by the defendant and it would be inequitable for the defendant to retain it.[6] This procedural term has persisted and is sometimes used inexactly as a synonym for the more general term *quasi-contract*, which refers to any money claim for the redress of unjust enrichment. *Restitution* is a still broader term, propagated by American scholars in the twentieth century to embrace all the remedies having that function, not only claims to money ("quasi-contractual" claims), but equitable relief involving specific restitution,[7] the constructive trust, the equitable lien, and subrogation.[8]

---

[2] See the discussion of the development of the action of debt in §1.5 *supra*.

[3] See the discussion of the supplanting of debt by *indebitatus* (general) *assumpsit* in §1.6 *supra*.

[4] The term *implied-in-law contract* is sometimes used instead of *quasi-contract*. See the discussion of silence as not generally acceptance in §3.14 *infra*.

[5] Schott v. Westinghouse Elec. Corp., 259 A.2d 443, 449 (Pa. 1969).

[6] *See* Aladdin Elec. Assocs. v. Town of Old Orchard Beach, 645 A.2d 1142 (Me. 1994) (*quantum meruit* "involves recovery for services or materials provided under an implied contract," while unjust enrichment "'describes recovery for the value of the benefit retained when there is no contractual relationship, but when, on the grounds of fairness and justice, the law compels performance of a legal and moral duty to pay.'").

[7] If the benefit conferred consists of the payment of money, however, equitable relief is not necessary to give specific restitution; a money judgment will do that.

[8] Restitution is the subject of a separate restatement. A Restatement (Third) of Restitution and Unjust Enrichment is being drafted. *See* Restatement of Restitution (1937), a small part of

The subject of restitution is far too complex to permit general treatment in this treatise. But since restitution problems are often inseparable from contract problems, a few basics are indispensable.[9] Suppose, for example, that two parties negotiate but never reach agreement. Can one recover from the other for benefits conferred in the course of those negotiations?[10] Or suppose that the parties do reach agreement, but that the agreement is unenforceable. Can one recover from the other for benefits conferred under the agreement if it is unenforceable because it is too indefinite?[11] Because one party lacked capacity?[12] Because one or both of the parties was mistaken?[13] Because the agreement is not evidenced by a writing as required by the statute of frauds?[14] Because it offends public policy?[15] Or suppose that the negotiations do result in a contract. Can one party recover from the other for benefits conferred under that contract if recovery on that basis would exceed recovery on the contract itself?[16] If the claimant is barred from recovery on the contract itself because of the claimant's own breach?[17] If the duties of both parties to render any further performance have been discharged because it has become impracticable for one party to perform?[18]

Examples of restitution problems in contract law

The Restatement of Restitution lays down the broad principle that a "person who has been unjustly enriched at the expense of another is required to make restitution."[19] We shall confine this preliminary consideration of that principle to a single inquiry: when does the law require one who has not requested a benefit to make restitution for it?[20]

General principle of restitution

To begin, the person claiming restitution must have conferred a benefit of some kind on the other party.[21] The benefit may result from the transfer of

Limitations on restitution

---

which was tentatively revised before work was discontinued. Restitution is also the subject of a four-volume treatise, G. Palmer, Law of Restitution (1978).

[9] For a list of the aspects of restitution discussed in this treatise, see the discussion of other aspects distinguished in §12.19 *infra*.

[10] See the discussions of liability for unjust enrichment and restitution for ideas appropriated in §3.26 *infra*.

[11] See the discussion of relief based on restitution in §3.30 *infra*.

[12] See §§4.5, 4.8 *infra*.

[13] See the discussion of avoidance in §9.4 *infra*.

[14] See §6.11 *infra*.

[15] See §5.9 *infra*.

[16] See §12.20 *infra*.

[17] See §8.14 *infra*.

[18] See the discussion of restitution in §9.9 *infra*.

[19] Restatement of Restitution §1. Note that in the situations we are about to discuss no promise is enforced.

[20] *See generally* 2 G. Palmer, Law of Restitution ch. 10 (1978).

[21] This situation should not be confused with that in which a promise is inferred from a person's conduct. *See* Peavey v. Pellandini, 551 P.2d 610 (Idaho 1976) (measure of recovery under contract inferred from conduct is "the reasonable value of the services rendered" and not the "actual benefit to the recipient"). *See also* the discussion of rules for services in §3.14 *infra*.

property or from services, including forbearance. Furthermore, even if a benefit has been conferred, a court may deny recovery on any of several grounds: the benefit may have been conferred "officiously"; it may have been conferred "gratuitously"; or it may not be "measurable."[22]

Meaning of officious

Officiousness is the term traditionally used to describe interference in the affairs of others that is not justified in the circumstances.[23] Recovery is denied for benefits officiously conferred so that one will not have to pay for something forced upon one against one's will. Suppose that a carpenter, seeing a house vacant and in need of repairs, makes repairs that would cost $1,000, in the belief that the owner will be willing to pay for them. When the owner refuses to pay, the carpenter sues the owner for $1,000. The carpenter will lose on the ground that the repairs were made officiously.[24] Conduct that intentionally deprives another person of the chance to make a contract with someone else is likely to be characterized as officious. Were the law otherwise, an unreasonable vigilance would be required of property owners in fending off underemployed artisans. Change the facts, however, so that the carpenter, having been called by the owner's neighbor to make repairs, makes an honest mistake and repairs the owner's house instead, while the owner — aware of the mistake — makes no protest. Now the case for denying recovery on the ground of officiousness vanishes, and the carpenter may be allowed restitution.[25] The circumstance that the claimant could have been expected to make a contract with the party benefited, as the carpenter could have done in the first hypothetical but not in the second, argues powerfully for officiousness.[26]

Life distinguished from property

Although the gist of the notion of officiousness is not difficult to grasp, the precise line between the "officious intermeddler" or "volunteer" and the

[22] For an excellent discussion, *see* Wade, Restitution for Benefits Conferred Without Request, 19 Vand. L. Rev. 1183 (1966); where the following helpful summary is given at page 1212: "One who, without intent to act gratuitously, confers a measurable benefit upon another, is entitled to restitution, if he affords the other an opportunity to decline the benefit or else has a reasonable excuse for failing to do so. If the other refuses to receive the benefit, he is not required to make restitution unless the actor justifiably performs for the other a duty imposed upon him by law."

[23] *See* Restatement of Restitution §2 cmt. *a.*

[24] Tom Growney Equip. v. Ansley, 888 P.2d 992 (N.M. App. 1994) (rule is founded on owner's "fundamental right" to determine whether and by whom its property shall be repaired).

The carpenter will lose even if the owner sells his house on his return for $1,000 more than he could have without the repairs. *See* Restatement of Restitution §112 illus. 3. Bailey v. West, 249 A.2d 414 (R.I. 1969) (where buyer of horse refused to accept it because it was lame and van driver left it with owner of horse farm who cared for and later sold it, buyer was not liable to owner of horse farm). *But cf.* Chase v. Corcoran, 106 Mass. 286 (1871) (owner who took back his lost boat was liable for finder's expenses in keeping and repairing it until owner was located). *Chase* is discussed in Levmore, Explaining Restitution, 71 Va. L. Rev. 65, 121-22 (1985).

[25] *See* Restatement (Third) of Restitution and Unjust Enrichment §9(2)(a) (Tent. Draft. No. 1, April 6, 2001) (restitution where recipient of benefit other than money "had notice of the claimant's mistake, yet failed to take reasonable steps to avert the resulting transfer").

[26] *See* Kull, Restitution and the Noncontractual Transfer, 11 J. Contr. Law 93, 105 (1997).

deserving claimant is difficult to draw, and no attempt will be made to draw it here. It is plain, however, that life stands on a different footing than does property. Suppose that a physician, seeing an injured and unconscious pedestrian, furnishes medical services worth $1,000 in the belief that the injured pedestrian will be willing to pay for them on regaining consciousness. The injured pedestrian, however, refuses to pay, and the physician sues for $1,000, claiming restitution of the benefit conferred. No court would condemn the physician as an "officious intermeddler" or "volunteer"; the right to recover is clear.[27] Make it a passing motorist, rather than a physician, however, who furnishes first aid rather than medical services, and the result will be different. The motorist, though not barred by the Scylla of officiousness, will be barred by the Charybdis of gratuitousness.[28]

Even if a benefit is not conferred officiously, recovery in restitution will be denied if it was conferred "gratuitously," that is, without expectation of compensation.[29] Thus, once having made a gift, one may not change one's mind and have restitution.[30] In general, if one's life or property is imperiled by impending disaster and another renders assistance in the emergency, the law presumes, in accordance with the mores of society, that the services were intended to be gratuitous.[31] The presumption may be rebutted if the services are excessively burdensome to the person rendering them, as when, for example, they continue for days or even weeks.[32] And the presumption does not apply if the person rendering the services does so in a professional or business capacity, as in the case of a physician or a hospital.

Meaning of gratuitous

An extension of this principle is applied to deny recovery if the claimant conferred a benefit in the expectation of compensation under a contract and now seeks restitution instead. It is often said that an express contract between the parties precludes recognition of an implied-in-law contract governing the

Compensation expected from another source

---

[27]Cotnam v. Wisdom, 104 S.W. 164 (Ark. 1907) (doctor rendered emergency services to unconscious patient who died without regaining consciousness).

[28]For an economic justification, *see* Landes & R. Posner, Salvors, Finders, Good Samaritans, and Other Rescuers: An Economic Study of Law and Altruism, 7 J. Legal Stud. 83, 110 (1978), reprinted in A. Kronman & R. Posner (eds.), The Economics of Contract Law 60-61 (1979).

[29]Brady v. State, 965 P.2d 1 (Alaska 1998) ("one who renders services in the expectation of gaining a future business advantage ordinarily cannot recover the value of those services").

[30]There is an exception if the donor is mistaken as to a material fact that induces the gift. *See* Wade, Restitution for Benefits Conferred Without Request, 19 Vand. L. Rev. 1183, 1191 (1966).

[31]For a case in which recovery in restitution was precluded for this reason, see the discussion of the example of *Webb v. McGowin* in §2.8 *supra*. The law of salvage in admiralty offers some interesting comparisons with these rules. *See* Wade, Restitution for Benefits Conferred Without Request, 19 Vand. L. Rev. 1183, 1208-12 (1966).

[32]As an example of such services, *see* the discussion of the example of Mills v. Wyman in §2.8 *supra*, where Mills may have had a claim in restitution against the *son*. Borderline cases include those of services rendered by close friends or members of the family. For a case in which recovery in restitution may have been precluded for this reason, see the discussion of the example of *Estate of Hatten* in §2.8 *supra*.

same subject matter.[33] Thus a party that has made a contract with another cannot simply disregard the contract and claim restitution from the other party for performance rendered under the contract. Nor can a party that has made a contract with another generally disregard the contract and claim restitution from a third person for performance rendered under the contract, even if the third person has benefited from that performance. Suppose that an owner of land makes a contract with a general contractor for the construction of a building, and the general contractor in turn makes another contract with a subcontractor for the plumbing work. Then suppose that the subcontractor does the plumbing work, but the general contractor fails to pay. If the owner has not yet paid the general contractor, does the subcontractor have a claim in restitution directly against the owner for the benefit conferred on the owner by the plumbing work? The answer is generally no. Although the subcontractor did not do the work gratuitously, since the subcontractor expected compensation from the general contractor and usually also has the protection afforded by a mechanics' lien,[34] the work was done with no expectation of compensation from the owner against whom the claim is made.[35] There is, however, a growing minority view that allows recovery in similar situations, especially if recovery from the person contracted with is precluded by bankruptcy or otherwise.[36]

Intimate relationships

Claims to restitution to avoid unjust enrichment arising out of family and other intimate relationships arise with increasing frequency. Such claims inevitably face the objection that benefits conferred in the course of such a relationship are conferred gratuitously. The Supreme Court of North Carolina

---

[33]Clark-Fitzpatrick, Inc. v. Long Island R.R., 516 N.E.2d 190 (N.Y. 1987) ("existence of a . . . written contract governing a particular subject matter ordinarily precludes recovery in quasi contract for events rising out of the same subject matter"). As to restitution as a remedy for breach of contract, see §12.10 *infra*.

[34]In all states statutes protect subcontractors by providing for what are known as "mechanics' liens." These statutes began to be enacted in the late eighteenth century to spur construction in a young and growing country. They protect laborers, suppliers of materials, subcontractors, contractors, and the like, who make improvements on real property by giving them a lien, i.e., a security interest, in that property to secure payment for the improvements. Public property is generally exempt. The subcontractor's lien is limited to the reasonable value of what was done, and in some states it may not exceed the amount then due from the owner to the general contractor. Typically the lien must be effected by serving notice on the owner and filing a statement in a public office within prescribed times.

Although the lien does not create any personal obligation from the owner to the subcontractor, it is enforceable through the sale of the owner's property in foreclosure proceedings, with the debt owed by the general contractor to the subcontractor payable out of the proceeds.

[35]Bennett Heating & Air Conditioning v. NationsBank, 674 A.2d 534 (Md. 1996) ("reported decisions involving claims by unpaid subcontractors against owners based on unjust enrichment . . . almost uniformly deny relief, and . . . do not turn on whether the owner has fully paid the general contractor").

[36]An influential case is Paschall's v. Dozier, 407 S.W.2d 150 (Tenn. 1966) (supplier of materials could recover from owners when supplier had "exhausted his remedies" against owner's daughter, who lived with them and made contract).

expressed conventional wisdom when it refused to grant a husband restitution against his wife on the ground that the rule denying recovery for "'a benefit voluntarily bestowed without solicitation or inducement' . . . is particularly applicable where a husband makes improvements to his wife's land because of the presumption that the improvements constitute a gift."[37] This presumption of gratuitousness can, however, be overcome.[38] In *Pyeatte v. Pyeatte*, for example, a husband and wife had an agreement that each would in turn work to provide sole support while the other was obtaining further education. After the wife had put the husband through law school, he told her that he wanted to dissolve the marriage. The Supreme Court of Arizona held that his promise was too indefinite to be enforceable. But it held that the wife was entitled restitution. The unenforceable agreement evidenced her expectation of compensation. And she had done more than "perform the usual and incidental activities of the marital relationship," having made "an extraordinary or unilateral effort" that inured solely to the benefit of her husband.[39] Courts have also been reluctant to grant restitution as between parties who are living together but not married, even though it can be argued that a person who confers a benefit in such a relationship, lacking the protection that the law affords to married persons, is less likely to be acting gratuitously.[40] But, as in the case of married couples, if the benefit conferred is out of the ordinary in the context of the relationship, an opposite conclusion is warranted.[41]

Finally, a claimant that has avoided the perils of officiousness and of gratuitousness must then show that the benefit conferred is "measurable." How is the benefit to be measured? Recall the example of the carpenter who, as the owner knew, mistakenly made repairs on the wrong house. Two different measures of the benefit conferred on the owner are possible. The first is that of "net enrichment." How much has the owner's total wealth been increased? How much more is the property now worth because of the repairs? If it could be shown that the price that the house will command on the market has been increased by, say, $1,000, then the benefit to the owner under this measure would be that amount. The second measure is that of "cost avoided." How

Meaning of
measurable

---

[37]Wright v. Wright, 289 S.E.2d 347, 354 (N.C. 1982) (adding, in response to the husband's equal protection argument, "that the same presumption of gift should apply whichever spouse furnishes improvements on the other spouse's land"). See the discussion of intimate implied-in-fact contracts in §3.10 *infra*.

[38]Estate of Cleveland v. Gorden, 837 S.W.2d 68 (Tenn. App. 1992) ("proof quickly dispels any notion that [niece] undertook to support her aunt gratuitously" where "ladies were not close relatives and had never lived together").

[39]661 P.2d 196, 203 (Ariz. 1982).

[40]Slocum v. Hammond, 346 N.W.2d 485 (Iowa 1984) (doctrine of unjust enrichment does not "invest this court with a roving mandate to sort through terminated personal relationships in an attempt to nicely judge and balance the respective contributions of the parties").

[41]Scott v. Rosenthal, 53 Fed. Appx. 137 (2d Cir. 2002) (girlfriend who had done years of graphic design for boyfriend's company).

much would the owner have had to pay someone else to have the repairs done? If it could be shown that the cost of obtaining such repairs on the market was, say, $1,000, then the benefit to the owner under this measure would be that amount.[42]

Net enrichment or cost avoided

The two measures of net enrichment and cost avoided often yield different results. In the typical case of repairs, not furnished in an emergency, the net enrichment is the same as or less than the cost avoided. The total value of the owner's house will be increased by no more than the cost of obtaining such repairs on the market. If the net enrichment is less than the cost avoided, recovery is usually limited to this smaller sum.[43] Services furnished in an emergency to save property from destruction or to prevent loss of life stand on a different footing. A clear case is that in which the physician saves the life of the unconscious patient. There the net enrichment (i.e., the value of that person's total life expectancy) far exceeds the cost avoided (i.e., the cost of such medical services on the market). The prevailing measure is again the smaller, the cost avoided.[44] A similar choice is made if the claim is for saving property from destruction, rather than for saving life.[45] And if it is not possible to determine the cost avoided, recovery is unlikely, although courts have occasionally allowed claimant's reasonable out-of-pocket expenses in such a case.[46] But it is usually possible to base the cost avoided on a market for services, because the requirement that the services not be rendered gratuitously tends to limit claimants to those who render services as a business or profession. Of those claimants who meet the other requirements for restitution, then, relatively few fail because of an inability to show a measurable benefit.

In the next chapter we examine the process of bargaining—offer and acceptance.

---

[42] See Restatement Second §371.

[43] Reimann v. Baum, 203 P.2d 387 (Utah 1949) (refusing to allow claimant costs of construction, "not limited to the extent of enhancement of land value, which cost could well exceed such enhancement").

[44] Bock v. American Growth Fund Sponsors, *supra* note 33 ("disgorging of all profits or benefits . . . is inappropriate" where employer fraudulently induces employee to accept employment at reduced compensation). Difficult questions may still arise in calculating the fee that the patient would otherwise have had to pay. *See* Cotnam v. Wisdom, *supra* note 27 (held error to consider the patient's ability to pay although doctors varied fees accordingly). *Contra:* In re Agnew's Estate, 231 N.Y.S. 4 (Surr. Ct. 1928) (financial standing considered).

[45] Chase v. Corcoran, *supra* note 24 (claim allowed for reasonable expenses of keeping and repairing lost boat).

[46] Chase v. Corcoran, *supra* note 24; Wade, Restitution for Benefits Conferred Without Request, 19 Vand. L. Rev. 1183, 1187-88 (1966). The claimant's out-of-pocket expenses are part of the reliance interest; they are an appropriate basis for a claim in restitution only to the extent that they measure the benefit conferred, in the sense of cost avoided. Generally the reliance interest will exceed the restitution interest. *See* the discussion of the reliance interest in §12.1 *infra*.

Chapter 3

The Bargaining Process: Offer and Acceptance

A.   THE BARGAINING PROCESS IN GENERAL

Two requirements

§3.1.   Requirements of Assent and of Definiteness. What requirements must the bargaining process meet if it is to result in a contract? Courts have had concerns along two lines. First, did both parties *assent* to be bound? Second, is their agreement *definite* enough to be enforceable?

Requirement of assent

The first requirement, that of assent, follows from the premise that contractual liability is consensual. Since it is difficult for a workable system of contract law to take account of assent unless there has been an overt expression of it, courts have required that assent to the formation of a contract be manifested in some way, by words or other conduct, if it is to be effective.[1] The requirement of a bargain imposed by the doctrine of consideration means that the parties' manifestations must have reference to each other, i.e., that they be reciprocal. Not only must the promisor seek the promise or performance that is the consideration in exchange for the promise, but the promisee must give it in exchange for that promise.[2]

Requirement of definiteness

The second requirement, that of definiteness, is implicit in the premise that contract law protects the promisee's expectation interest. In calculating the damages that will put the promisee in the position in which the promisee would have been had the promise been performed,[3] a court must determine the scope of that promise with some precision. In the less usual case in which the court orders specific performance or enjoins a threatened breach, it must know the scope of the promise with even greater precision in order to frame a decree, since failure to obey the decree will subject the promisor to the court's contempt power. If recovery is limited to the promisee's restitution or reliance interest, however, it is often unnecessary to inquire into the scope of the promise, as long as it is clear that the promise was broken.

Later in this chapter, the details of the requirements of assent and of definiteness will be explored, along with the possibility that they may not bar recovery based on the promisee's restitution or reliance interest. We look first, however, at some matters basic to the agreement process.

Moment when party becomes liable

§3.2.   Mutuality of Obligation. According to the orthodox catechism, there is a precise moment when a party becomes contractually bound on a promise. At that moment there is an abrupt transition from no liability to liability based on the promisee's expectation interest.

May not be determined

The commentary to the Code explains that the facts may "not disclose the exact point at which the deal was closed" even though "the actions of the parties indicate that a binding obligation has been undertaken."[1] Such uncertainty is

---

§3.1   [1] See the discussion of the objective theory in §3.6 *infra*.
[2] See the discussion of the reciprocal nature of bargain in §2.6 *supra*.
[3] See the discussion of recovery measured by the expectation interest in §2.1 *supra*.
§3.2   [1] UCC 2-204 cmt.

well under way

particularly likely if the dispute arises after performance is well under way. This does not mean that it is always necessary to determine that "exact point." As the Code puts it, "An agreement sufficient to constitute a contract of sale may be found even though the moment of its making is undetermined."[2] But it does mean that if a party has become contractually bound by a promise, there must have been some moment "at which the deal was closed," before which that party was not bound and after which it was.[3]

The orthodox catechism also has it that if both parties make promises, the moment when each becomes bound must be the same — unless both are bound, neither is bound.[4] The requirement applies only to bilateral contracts, where both parties make promises, and not to unilateral contracts, where only one party makes a promise.[5] Requiring mutuality of obligation for bilateral contracts serves the needs of the marketplace, where prices fluctuate according to supply and demand, for it eliminates the possibility that one party will be able to speculate on such changes at the expense of the other. Suppose that a seller and a buyer are negotiating a contract for the future delivery of apples at a fixed price. As long as neither is bound, the seller stands to lose if the market falls and to gain if it rises, while the buyer stands to gain if the market falls and to lose if it rises. As soon as both are bound, the reverse is true. It is the buyer that stands to lose if the market falls and to gain if it rises, and it is the seller that stands to gain if the market falls and to lose if it rises. In each case the risks are symmetrical.

If there is a period of time, however, during which one party is bound while the other party is not, the party not bound has, in effect, an option and can speculate at the expense of the party that is bound. If, for example, there is a period during which the seller is bound to sell apples at $100 but the buyer is not bound to buy them, the buyer has an option to buy at $100 during that period. If the market price rises to $110 during the period, the buyer can take advantage of the lower price at which the seller is bound under the option and insist upon delivery of apples for $100. But if the market price falls to $90 during the period, the buyer can ignore the option and take advantage of the lower market price by buying apples elsewhere, leaving the seller to sell the apples on the depressed market. The party that is not bound has the opportunity of speculating on market changes at the expense of the party that is bound. The unfairness of giving this advantage to one of the parties, at least if the other party has not agreed to it, suggests that neither party should be bound until both are bound. Because this reasoning assumes a market on which a party can speculate,

Requirement of mutuality

Risk of speculation

---

[2]UCC 2-204(2).

[3]Kleinschmidt Div. of SCM Corp. v. Futuronics Corp., 363 N.E.2d 701 (N.Y. 1977) (despite UCC 2-204, "if there be no basic agreement, the code will not imply one").

[4]For an early expression of the requirement, *see* Harrison v. Cage, 87 Eng. Rep. 736 (K.B. 1698) (either "all is a *nudum pactum*, or else the one promise is as good as the other").

[5]See the discussion of refusal to enforce in §2.13 *supra*.

it loses much of its force in the many situations in which the assumption is not borne out. Nevertheless, traditional analysis of the agreement process attaches great importance to the requirement of mutuality of obligation as a means of avoiding the opportunity for speculation.[6]

We shall postpone consideration of some reservations as to this requirement[7] and turn now to traditional analysis of the agreement process in terms of offer and acceptance.

Form of agreement process

§3.3. Offer and Acceptance. The outward appearance of the agreement process, by which the parties satisfy the requirement of bargain imposed by the doctrine of consideration, varies widely according to the circumstances. It may, for example, involve face-to-face negotiations, an exchange of letters or facsimiles, a transaction between computers,[1] or merely the perfunctory signing of a printed form supplied by the other party. Whatever the outward appearance, it is common to analyze the process in terms of two distinct steps:[2] first, a manifestation of assent that is called an *offer*, made by one party (the *offeror*) to another (the *offeree*); and second, a manifestation of assent in response that is called an *acceptance*, made by the offeree to the offeror.[3] Although courts apply this analysis on a case-by-case basis, depending on the circumstances, it gives a reassuring appearance of consistency.

Meaning of *offer*

What is an "offer"? It can be defined as a manifestation to another of assent to enter into a contract if the other manifests assent in return by some action, often a promise but sometimes a performance. By making an offer, the offeror thus confers upon the offeree the power[4] to create a contract. An offer is nearly

---

[6] *See* E. Farnsworth, Changing Your Mind ch. 19 (1998) for discussion of an anti-speculation principle.

[7] *See* §§3.23 to 3.26 *infra*. For a few exceptions, see the references collected in the discussion of avoidance compared in §2.14 *supra*.

§3.3 [1] *See* Forrest v. Verizon Communications, 805 A.2d 1007 (D.C. 2002) (a "contract is no less a contract simply because it is entered into via a computer"). See the discussion of click-wrap agreements in §4.26 *infra*.

[2] According to an English writer, it was not until the nineteenth century that "a doctrine of offer and acceptance was superimposed upon the eighteenth-century requirement of consideration and made to perform some of the same functions." Simpson, Innovation in Nineteenth Century Contract Law, 91 L.Q. Rev. 247, 258 (1975). Both the Vienna Convention and the UNIDROIT Principles show that the emphasis on offer and acceptance is not peculiar to the common law. *See* CISG part 2; UNIDROIT Principles ch. 2.

[3] Although there may be more than two parties, the discussion in this treatise will generally assume, for the sake of simplicity, that there are only two. At least two parties must be involved. One cannot make a contract with oneself. *See* Restatement Second §9; E. Farnsworth, Changing Your Mind ch. 1 (1998). Within large corporations or conglomerates, however, the distribution of resources is arranged administratively by an internal hierarchy without the use of contract and so without the need for a second party.

[4] As to the meaning of *power*, see footnote to the discussion of the meaning of *bilateral* and *unilateral* in §3.4 *infra*.

always a promise[5] and, in a sense, the action (promise or performance) on which the offeror conditions the promise is the "price" of its becoming enforceable. *Offer*, then, is the name given to a promise that is conditional on some action by the promisee *if* the legal effect of the promisee's taking that action is to make the promise enforceable. Empowerment of the offeree to make the offeror's promise enforceable is thus the essence of an offer. When does a promise empower the promisee to take action that will make the promise enforceable? In other words, when does a manifestation of assent amount to an offer? This is one of the main subjects of this chapter.

What is an "acceptance"? It can be defined as the action (promise or performance) by the offeree that creates a contract (i.e., makes the offeror's promise enforceable). *Acceptance*, then, is the name given to the offeree's action if the legal effect of that action is to make the offeror's promise enforceable. When does action by the promisee make the promise enforceable? In other words, when does the promisee's action amount to an acceptance? This is another of the main subjects of this chapter.

Meaning of acceptance

Because of the requirement of mutuality of obligation, both parties are free to withdraw from negotiations until the moment when both are bound. This is the moment when the offeree accepts the offer. It therefore follows, as we shall see later in more detail, that the offeror is free to revoke the offer at any time before acceptance.[6]

Freedom to revoke offer

We turn now to another facet of the traditional analysis.

§3.4. Bilateral and Unilateral Contracts. Traditional analysis of the bargaining process developed a dichotomy between "bilateral" and "unilateral" contracts. In forming a bilateral contract each party makes a promise: the offeror makes the promise contained in the offer, and the offeree makes a promise in return as acceptance. For example, a buyer offers to pay the price 30 days after delivery in return for a seller's *promise* to deliver apples.[1] In forming a unilateral contract only one party makes a promise: the offeror makes the promise contained in the offer, and the offeree renders some performance as acceptance.[2] For example, a buyer offers to pay the price 30 days after delivery

Meaning of bilateral and unilateral

---

[5] It is, however, possible to imagine an offer that is arguably not a promise. Suppose that B offers to A an immediate transfer of property in return for a promise: "These apples are yours if you promise to pay me $100." This rare species of agreement has been dubbed a "reverse unilateral contract," since it results from an offer of a performance for a promise, rather than an offer of a promise for a performance. *See* Restatement Second §55 & cmt. *a*.

[6] See the discussion of the principle of revocability in §3.17 *infra*.

§3.4 [1] See the discussions of the practical need for such exchanges in §1.3 *supra*, of the rationale for protecting expectation in §1.6 *supra*, and of a promise as consideration in §2.3 *supra*.

[2] For offers of prizes as examples, *see* Mears v. Nationwide Mut. Ins. Co., 91 F.3d 1118 (8th Cir. 1996) (offer to award cars for submitting winning slogans); Cobaugh v. Klick-Lewis, Inc., 561 A.2d 1248 (Pa. Super. 1989) (offer to award car "to anyone who made a hole-in-one at the ninth hole"). As to the possibility of a "reverse unilateral contract," see footnote to the discussion of the

Bilateral
Promise on both sides

Unilateral
Promise one side

Abandonment of these terms

in return for a seller's delivery of apples. Traditional analysis has it that in a bilateral contract there are promises on both sides (the buyer's promise to pay and the seller's promise to deliver); there are *duties* on both sides (the buyer's duty to pay and the seller's duty to deliver) and *rights* on both sides (the seller's right to payment and the buyer's right to delivery).[3] In a unilateral contract, however, there is a promise on only one side (the buyer's promise to pay); there is a *duty* on only one side (the buyer's duty to pay) and a *right* on the other side (the seller's right to payment).

The dichotomy between bilateral and unilateral plays a less important role in contemporary analysis of contracts. The Restatement Second abandons the use of the terms because of "doubt as to the utility of the distinction," which causes "confusion in cases where performance is complete on one side except for an incidental or collateral promise, as where an offer to buy goods is accepted by shipment and a warranty is implied."[4]

For example, if the seller delivers the apples, rather than promising to do so, the seller impliedly warrants that the apples are merchantable, so that it is not correct to say that the seller is under no duty and that the buyer has no right.[5] However, even the Restatement Second recognizes that an offeror may make an offer that "invites an offeree to accept by rendering a performance and does not invite a promissory acceptance."[6] The terms *bilateral* and *unilateral* will sometimes be used for convenience in this treatise, with the understanding that they are not without shortcomings.

Some other views of the agreement process will now be considered.

---

meaning of *offer* in §3.3 *supra*. It is also possible to have a contract in which the offeree both makes a promise and renders some performance as an acceptance: "I offer (promise) to sell you these apples for $100 if you pay $50 now and promise to pay $50 in 30 days."

[3]For the precise use of terms such as *right* and *duty*, the legal profession is indebted to Professor Wesley Newcomb Hohfeld, whose elaborate system of "Hohfeldian terminology" is set out in Hohfeld, Fundamental Legal Conceptions (1919). A is said to have a *right* that B shall do an act when, if B does not do the act, A can initiate legal proceedings that will result in coercing B. B in such a situation is said to have a *duty* to do the act. *Right* and *duty* are therefore correlatives, since in this sense there can never be a *duty* without a *right*. A *power* is the capacity to change a legal relationship. In this terminology the offeree has, before the contract is made, a *power* to create a contract by means of acceptance.

[4]Reporter's Note to Restatement Second §1. The Reporter's Note adds that "the effect of the distinction has been to exaggerate the importance of the type of bargain in which one party begins performance without making any commitment," although, as has been pointed out, the bulk of economically significant contracts are bilateral. See the discussion of a promise as consideration — bilateral contract in §2.3 *supra*.

[5]Under UCC 2-314, a warranty of merchantability is implied in every sale by a seller who is a merchant with respect to goods of the kind sold, unless that warranty has been disclaimed. Examples of "pure" unilateral contracts are a contract for sale of goods with all of the seller's warranties disclaimed and an insurance contract in which the premium has been fully paid.

[6]Restatement Second §45. See the discussion of Restatement Second §45 in §3.24 *infra*.

§3.5. **Another View of the Agreement Process.** Traditional analysis, in terms of an offer followed by an acceptance, may adequately describe the agreement process in simple transactions in which, for example, one party presents a printed form for the other to sign or both exchange letters or facsimiles. But it is difficult to accept this model as representative of the complex negotiations typical of substantial transactions — of "deals" for the long-term supply of energy, for the development of a shopping center, for the friendly takeover of a corporation, or the signing of a first-round draft choice. Major contractual commitments are typically set out in a lengthy document, or in a set of documents, signed by the parties in multiple copies and exchanged more or less simultaneously at a closing.[1] The terms are reached by negotiations, usually face-to-face over a considerable period of time and often involving corporate officers, bankers, engineers, accountants, lawyers, and others. The negotiations are a far cry from the simple bargaining envisioned by the classic rules of offer and acceptance, which evoke an image of single-issue, adversarial, zero-sum bargaining as opposed to multi-issue, problem-solving, gain-maximizing negotiation.[2]

During the negotiation of such deals there is often no offer or counteroffer for either party to accept, but rather a gradual process in which agreements are reached piecemeal in several "rounds" with a succession of drafts. There may first be an exchange of information and an identification of the parties' interests and differences, then a series of compromises with tentative agreement on major points, and finally a refining of contract terms. The negotiators may refrain from making offers because they want the terms of any binding commitment to be worked out by their lawyers, to whom things will be turned over once the original negotiators decide that they have settled those matters that they regard as important.[3] The drafts prepared by the lawyers are not offers because the lawyers lack authority to make offers.[4] When the ultimate

Limits of traditional analysis

Negotiation of substantial deals

---

§3.5 [1]*See* Keys v. Rehabilitation Centers, 574 So. 2d 579 (Miss. 1990) ("Where parties to a sales transaction assemble for a conventional closing, there are always a number of pages to be signed, and the law will view the closing as a single transaction, it being wholly irrelevant who signed what in which order or sequence."). An alternative to a closing is to put the documents in escrow and have them exchanged through the escrow agent.

[2]Negotiation aimed at the settlement of disputes may come closer to the zero-sum image. Such negotiations are not a central concern in this treatise.

[3]The lawyer's task has been described in the following way. "He is given an hour or an afternoon for what should be several days' careful work. He is told, or he understands without being told, that he is not to 'make it complicated.' He is not going to be popular if he tries to make the businessmen 'work out all the details.' Too often the attorney discovers that the businessmen really have not reached agreement on difficult issues, but have ignored them to avoid argument. If he wakes these sleeping dogs he may cause his client to lose a bargain that his client thinks is a good one. If he drafts an ambiguous document, avoiding hard issues, he exposes his client to serious risks, and his client will hold him responsible if any of the risks should materialize." Macaulay, The Use and Non-Use of Contracts in the Manufacturing Industry, 9 Prac. Law. 13, 16 (Nov. 1963).

[4]Moreover, the drafts may fail to be offers because of indefiniteness and lack of intent to make an offer.

agreement is reached, it is often expected that it will be embodied in a document or documents that will be signed by the parties at a closing.

Questions raised

If the parties sign at a closing, there is no question that they have given their assent to a contract, and there is therefore scant occasion to apply the classic rules of offer and acceptance. But if the negotiations fail and nothing is signed, a number of questions may arise that the classic rules of offer and acceptance do not address: May a disappointed party have a claim against the other party for having failed to conform to a standard of fair dealing? If so, what is the meaning of fair dealing in this context? And may the disappointed party get restitution? Be reimbursed for out-of-pocket expenses? Recover for lost opportunities? As deals have become larger and more complex, negotiations have become more complicated and prolonged, these questions have reached courts in increasing numbers, calling on courts for imaginative application of traditional contract doctrines. Later we shall see how successful courts have been in this.[5]

For the present, however, we turn to the traditional view of the contracting process and to the requirement of assent.

B. THE OBJECTIVE THEORY OF ASSENT

Actual or apparent intention

§3.6. Subjective and Objective Theories. When a court determines whether a party has assented to an agreement, is it the party's actual or its apparent intention that matters? This question provoked one of the most significant doctrinal struggles in the development of contract law, that between the subjective and objective theories.

Subjective theory

The subjectivists looked to the actual or subjective intentions of the parties. The subjectivists did not go so far as to advocate that subjective assent alone was *sufficient* to make a contract. Even under the subjective theory there had to be some manifestation of assent. But actual assent to the agreement on the part of both parties was *necessary*, and without it there could be no contract.[1] In the much-abused metaphor, there had to be a "meeting of the minds."[2]

Objective theory

The objectivists, on the other hand, looked to the external or objective appearance of the parties' intentions as manifested by their actions. One of the most influential objectivists, Judge Learned Hand, wrote in a memorable passage:

> A contract has, strictly speaking, nothing to do with the personal, or individual, intent of the parties. A contract is an obligation attached by the mere force of

---

[5]See the discussion of four grounds for liability in §3.26 *infra*.

§3.6 [1]See the discussion of the requirement of assent in §3.1 *supra*.

[2]Discussions of this topic would be improved if this metaphor were abandoned. Its origins appear to go back to faulty etymology, under which it was wrongly supposed that the word "agreement" was derived from *agregatio mentium*, a meeting of the minds. *See* Farnsworth, "Meaning" in the Law of Contracts, 76 Yale L.J. 939, 943-44 (1967).

law to certain acts of the parties, usually words, which ordinarily accompany and represent a known intent. If, however, it were proved by twenty bishops that either party when he used the words intended something else than the usual meaning which the law imposes on them, he would still be held, unless there were mutual mistake or something else of the sort.[3]

According to the objectivists, a party's mental assent was not necessary to make a contract. After all, was not contract law intended to protect *reasonable* expectations? If one party's actions, judged by a standard of reasonableness, manifested to the other party an intention to agree, the real but unexpressed state of the first party's mind was irrelevant. As Hand's colleague, Judge Jerome Frank, put it, "The objectivists transferred from the field of torts that stubborn anti-subjectivist 'the reasonable man.' "[4] As an analyst from the field of torts might be tempted to view it, the first party had through fault induced the other to believe that there was a contract.[5]

By the end of the nineteenth century, the objective theory had become ascendant and courts universally accept it today. In the words of a distinguished federal judge, " 'intent' does not invite a tour through [plaintiff's] cranium, with [plaintiff] as the guide."[6] True, one may still avoid liability by showing lack of intent to engage in the actions by which assent was apparently manifested as, for example, if one was falsely told that a writing had no legal effect[7] or was compelled to sign by such force that one was a "mere mechanical instrument."[8] But as long as one intended to engage in those actions, there is no further requirement that the actions were done with the intention of assenting to an agreement.[9] It is enough that the other party had reason to believe that the first party had that intention.[10]

Victory of objective theory

---

[3]Hotchkiss v. National City Bank, 200 F. 287, 293 (S.D.N.Y. 1911), aff'd, 201 F. 664 (2d Cir. 1912), aff'd, 231 U.S. 50 (1913).

[4]Ricketts v. Pennsylvania R.R., 153 F.2d 757, 760-61 (2d Cir. 1946) (concurring opinion).

[5]As to this view, see the discussion of the alternative of tort liability in §3.9 *infra*.

[6]Skycom Corp. v. Telstar Corp., 813 F.2d 810, 814 (7th Cir. 1987) (Easterbrook, J.) ("Wisconsin takes an objective view of 'intent' ").

[7]See the discussion of fraud in the factum or execution in §4.10 *infra*.

[8]See the discussion of physical compulsion or threat in §4.16 *infra*. Even in such cases, the same result will usually be reached under the objective theory, since the other party will usually have reason to know of these circumstances.

[9]Field-Martin Co. v. Fruen Milling Co., 298 N.W. 574 (Minn. 1941) (correcting an earlier "inadvertent misstatement" of same court "that a contract 'contemplates a meeting of the minds on a proposition'"). For a discussion of mistake in this context, see the discussion of other types of cases in §9.4 *infra*.

[10]Embry v. Hargadine, McKittrick Dry Goods Co., 105 S.W. 777 (Mo. App. 1907) ("though McKittrick may not have intended to employ Embry . . . , yet if what McKittrick said would have been taken by a reasonable man to be an employment, and Embry so understood it, it constituted a valid contract").

Although the other party often also actually believes that the first party had that intention, it should make no difference if, as in a routine transaction, the other party gave no thought to the

Promises, predictions, and opinions

Illustrative are cases in which the issue is whether a statement is a "promise" — an expression of a commitment to do something — or merely a "prediction" or "expression of opinion." The maker of the statement asserts, without contradiction, an intent only to make a prediction or express an opinion and not to undertake a commitment. The one to whom the statement was made asserts, without contradiction, a belief that the maker intended to undertake a commitment by making a promise.[11] Under the objective theory, the question then becomes whether the one to whom the statement was made had reason so to believe.[12]

Example of Anderson v. Backlund

In *Anderson v. Backlund*, a landlord sought to induce his tenant, who was behind in the rent, to put more cattle on the farm that he had rented. When the tenant hesitated for fear of a dry spell, the landlord assured him, "I will see there will be plenty of water because it never failed in Minnesota yet." The tenant bought more cattle, the water failed, and the tenant sued. Did the tenant have reason to believe that the landlord's statement was a promise? The court held that he did not, noting that the indefiniteness of the language "rather characterized the talk more as visiting or advice than a contract."[13] The fact that the maker of the statement has little or no control over the event to which the statement relates may be influential, but it is not determinative, for a promisor can always undertake a comimitment to pay if such an event does not occur. The landlord could, for example, have bound himself by promising his tenant that he would reimburse him for any loss due to a water shortage.[14]

Example of Hawkins v. McGee

In *Hawkins v. McGee*, a surgeon, in undertaking to perform a skin-grafting operation on a boy, said that the boy would be in the hospital "not over four [days]; then the boy can go home and it will be just a few days when he will be able to go back to work with a perfect hand." The court characterized these words as mere "expressions of opinion or predictions." But the surgeon had gone on to say, "I will guarantee to make the hand a hundred percent perfect hand." The court took account of evidence showing that the doctor "had repeatedly solicited" the opportunity to perform the operation as an "experiment in skin

---

matter. Furthermore, it seems preferable to state the test in terms of what the other party had reason to know or to believe, rather than in terms of a hypothetical "reasonable person." A court should be able to take account of the other party's particular circumstances, at least to the extent that the first party was or should have been aware of them.

[11] For more on what is a promise, *see* E. Farnsworth, Changing Your Mind ch. 3 (1998).

[12] Boston Car Co. v. Acura Auto. Div., 971 F.2d 811 (1st Cir. 1992) (language " '[i]t is our intention' . . . stands in conspicuous contrast to the other provisions . . . which are couched in promissory terms such as 'we agree' and 'you shall' "). As to the meaning of *promise*, see the discussion of the concern of contract law with the future in §1.1 *supra*. Many statements that might be characterized as predictions or expressions of opinion are clearly unenforceable because they are not regarded as reliable. See the discussion of opinion or knowledge in §4.14 *infra*.

[13] 199 N.W. 90, 91 (Minn. 1924).

[14] *See* O. Holmes, The Common Law 298 (1881) ("An assurance that it will rain tomorrow . . . may as well be a promise as one . . . that the promisor will pay the promisee one hundred dollars.").

grafting" and concluded that it was proper to submit the question of his liability on this statement to the jury.[15] Under the objective theory, the question for the jury would be whether the boy had reason to believe that the doctor was making a commitment that amounted to a promise.[16]

As these cases indicate, the objective theory tends to hold the parties to linguistic usage that is accepted as normal, a matter of fact that arguably falls within the province of a jury. The role of the jury in analogous cases involving the interpretation of contract language is discussed in a later chapter.[17]

Role of jury

We look next at the effect under the objective theory of an intention not to be legally bound.

§3.7.   Intention to Be Bound or Not. Parties to agreements, especially routine ones, often fail to consider the legal consequences of the actions by which they manifest their assent. The fact that one gives the matter no thought does not impair the effectiveness of one's assent, for there is no requirement that one intend or even understand the legal consequences of one's actions.[1] For example, one who signs a writing may be bound by it, even though one neither reads it nor considers the legal consequence of signing it. This rule, making a party's intention to be legally bound irrelevant, has the salutary effects of generally relieving each party to a dispute of the burden of showing the other's state of mind in that regard and of helping to uphold routine agreements.

Intention to be legally bound

A different rule applies, however, in those unusual instances in which one *intends* that one's assent have *no* legal consequences. Under the objective theory, a court will honor that intention if the other party has reason to know it. And it will honor it if the other party actually knows it.[2]

Intention not to be legally bound

[15] 146 A. 641, 643 (N.H. 1929) (new trial ordered on measure of damages). The Michigan statute requiring that such an agreement be evidenced by a signed writing, cited in a footnote to the discussion of other writing requirements in §6.2 *infra*, was enacted following Guilmet v. Campbell, 188 N.W.2d 601 (Mich. 1971) (jury question raised by statements such as operation "takes care of all your troubles" and "you can throw away your pill box"). As to the measure of damages in such cases, see the discussion of the example of Sullivan v. O'Connor in §12.17 *infra*.

[16] Problems similar to these arise under the "opinion or commendation" exception of UCC 2-313, which provides that "an affirmation merely of the value of the goods or a statement purporting to be merely the seller's opinion or commendation of the goods does not create a warranty."

[17] See the discussion of judge or jury in §7.14 *infra*.

§3.7   [1] According to Restatement Second §21 cmt. *a*, neither is it fatal that the parties are mistaken as to the legal effect of their agreement, unless it is their intention not to be legally bound. For more on mistake as to matters of law, see the discussion of matters of law in §4.14 *infra*.

[2] This means that one party's intention not to be legally bound prevails if it is actually known to the other party, regardless of what the other party might have reason to know. This can be rationalized under the objective theory, as formulated in the discussion of the objective theory in §3.6, on the ground that the other party cannot have reason to believe that the first party intends to assent to the agreement if the other party knows that the first party intends not to be legally bound. It would seem that one party's intention not to be legally bound should also prevail if the other party had the same intention but neither knew nor had reason to know the other's intention. For a related problem, see the discussion of the situation in which the same meaning is attached in §7.9 *infra*. Various combinations and permutations are dealt with in Restatement Second §20.

Intention shown by language

The easiest way for a party to make clear an intention not to be legally bound is to say so. In a number of commercial contexts, parties enter into agreements, commonly known as "gentlemen's agreements," that state that the parties are not legally bound, and it is beyond question that the parties can in this way turn an otherwise enforceable agreement into an unenforceable one.[3] The same result has been reached even though a written agreement is made as a sham, for the purpose of deceiving others, with an oral understanding that it will not be enforced.[4]

Intention shown by circumstances

Circumstances, rather than words, may also indicate a party's intention not to be bound. Thus the Supreme Court of Minnesota concluded that a reporter's promise to keep his source confidential was not enforceable because the court was "not persuaded that in the special milieu of media newsgathering a source and a reporter ordinarily believe they are engaged in making a legally binding contract."[5]

Agreements made in jest

If circumstances show that one has gone through the process of agreement solely for one's own amusement or that of others, the agreement will not be enforced. "No one has ever supposed that the actor who, as part of his lines in a play, went through the form of making a contract . . . incurred any obligation thereby."[6] In *Keller v. Holderman*, a man wrote a $300 check on a bank in which he had no funds and gave it for an old silver watch worth about $15. The seller sued on the promise represented by the check, but recovery was denied. When "the court below found that 'the whole transaction between the parties was a frolic and a banter, the plaintiff not expecting to sell, nor the defendant intending to buy the watch at the sum for which the check was drawn,' the conclusion should have been that no contract was ever made by the parties."[7] In a case that attracted media attention, a federal trial judge, confronted with a soft drink company's commercial purporting to offer Harrier jet for 7 million Pepsi Points, noted that explaining why a joke is funny "is a daunting task," but looked to "what an objective, reasonable person would have understood the commercial to convey," and concluded that the "tongue-in-cheek attitude of the commercial would not cause a reasonable person to conclude that a soft drink company would be giving away fighter planes as part of a promotion."[8]

---

[3] Dunhill Sec. Corp. v. Microthermal Applications, 308 F. Supp. 195 (S.D.N.Y. 1969) (underwriter's letter of intent stating that "no liability or obligation of any nature whatsoever is intended to be created as between any of the parties hereto").

[4] Nice Ball Bearing Co. v. Bearing Jobbers, 205 F.2d 41 (7th Cir. 1953) (sham contract for sale of stock to deceive seller's competitors not enforceable). As to the effect of the parol evidence rule on sham agreements, see the discussion of how one can show no agreement in §7.4 *infra*.

[5] Cohen v. Cowles Media Co., 457 N.W.2d 199, 203 (Minn. 1990), rev'd on other grounds, 501 U.S. 663 (1991), aff'd on remand on different grounds, 479 N.W.2d 387 (1992).

[6] National Bank v. Louisville Trust Co., 67 F.2d 7, 102-03 (6th Cir. 1933).

[7] 11 Mich. 248, 248-49 (1863).

[8] Leonard v. Pepsico, 88 F. Supp. 2d 116, 128, 127, 132 (S.D.N.Y. 1999) (Kimba Wood, J.), aff'd per curiam, 210 F.3d 88 (2d Cir. 2000). An agreement that results from an offer that has been made to call the offeree's bluff, as where the offeror acts to suggest that the offeree cannot

118

In *Lucy v. Zehmer*, however, the Supreme Court of Virginia invoked the objective theory to hold the Zehmers to a contract to sell their farm to Lucy for $50,000, despite their contention that they had entered into the transaction as a joke while drinking. Lucy successfully argued that, if they had been joking, he had neither known it nor had reason to know it, and that under the objective theory their secret intention was irrelevant.[9] In such a situation, as another court remarked, "the law will also take the joker at his word, and give him good reason to smile."[10]

Effect of objective theory

Courts have sometimes placed great weight on a family relationship between the parties as showing that legal consequences were not intended. The most notorious example is *Balfour v. Balfour*, an English case that denied a wife recovery on her husband's promise to pay her a stated monthly allowance while she remained in England for her health during his service in Ceylon. The opinion voiced the traditional attitude that "it would be of the worst possible example to hold that agreements such as this resulted in legal obligations which could be enforced in the Courts," for "each house is a domain into which the King's writ does not run and to which his officers do not seek to be admitted."[11] Such judicial hostility toward contracts between spouses has abated in recent decades, and it has never prevented spouses from making contracts with each other if they make clear their intention to do so.[12] Nevertheless, the fact that the parties to an agreement are members of the same family is entitled to weight as showing an intention not to be legally bound.[13] On similar reasoning, agreements of a social nature are generally supposed to be unenforceable, although these are rarely of such importance as to come before the courts.[14]

Family and social agreements

A more practical setting for this kind of controversy is that in which the parties make an agreement but leave one or more terms to be fixed by a later agreement between them. Their object in doing so is usually to postpone negotiations over

Agreements leaving terms for agreement

---

or will not pay the price, seems distinguishable. It is the essence of a bluff that the offeror will be bound in the unlikely event of acceptance. Ordinary business negotiations often have an element of bluffing. But for cases holding outright dares unenforceable, see footnote to the discussion of the example of a conditional gratuitous promise in §2.9 *supra*.

[9] 84 S.E.2d 516 (1954).

[10] Plate v. Durst, 24 S.E. 580, 581 (W. Va. 1896).

[11] [1919] 2 K.B. 571, 579 (C.A. 1919).

[12] On implied-in-fact agreements in the family, see the discussion of intimate implied-in-fact contracts in §3.10 *infra*. On considerations of public policy, see the discussion of the recent trend in §5.4 *infra*.

[13] Morrow v. Morrow, 612 P.2d 730 (Okl. App. 1980) (such arrangements as for care of invalid mother "are frequently gratuitous, founded in love and affection," and whether they "are contractual or not depends on the intent of the parties," but "party asserting the contract has the burden of setting aside our belief that most such arrangements are not contractual").

[14] Mitzel v. Hauck, 105 N.W.2d 378 (S.D. 1960) (to "spell out a contract [for use of a car] from this hunting trip of these young men, an enjoyable pastime with his friends as plaintiff described it, 'would transcend reality' ").

the missing terms until the occurrence of future events.[15] Common examples occur in connection with contracts for the sale of goods or the sale or rental of land in which the price or rent is left to be agreed upon at some later time, based on the state of the market at that time. The parties expect that they will reach agreement on the missing terms. What they expect to happen if they fail to do so is often unclear. Do they understand that in that event there will be no contract at all? Or do they understand that in that event there will be a contract with the missing term supplied as a matter of law?

Traditional premise

The first has been the traditional premise. "An agreement to be finally settled must comprise all the terms which the parties intend to introduce into the agreement. An agreement to enter into an agreement upon terms to be afterwards settled between the parties is a contradiction in terms."[16] But in many situations, if the parties are silent as to a term, the court will supply a term and enforce the agreement.[17] Should there not be an enforceable agreement with such a term supplied as a matter of law, even if the parties have not been able to agree on the term under "an agreement to agree"? Courts have generally resisted this course. As Kentucky's highest court explained, where "the parties were undertaking to fix the terms rather than to leave them to implication," the problem for the court "is not what the law would imply if the contract did not purport to cover the subject matter, but whether the parties, in removing this material term from the field of implication, have fixed their mutual obligations."[18] The point is well taken if it be supposed that the parties expected that a failure to agree on a missing term would result in no enforceable agreement at all, and that they intended to bargain over that term with that eventuality in mind. And this, of course, is the traditional premise.

Second premise possible

In recent decades, the second premise has gained favor, and courts have shown increasing willingness to find what is commonly called a "contract with open terms." The Uniform Commercial Code admits of this premise — that the parties understand that if they fail to reach agreement there will be a contract with the missing terms supplied as a matter of law. Under UCC 2-305, which deals with open-price terms, if the parties intend to "conclude a contract for sale even though the price is not settled" and "the price is left to be agreed by the parties and they fail to agree," the agreement is enforceable. The price is the same price as would be implied if "nothing is said as to price," that is, a "reasonable price at the time for delivery."[19] In other words, if the parties fail to agree, the law will fill the gap with the same terms that it would have supplied

---

[15] This is not the only possible object. They may merely be unwilling to take the time to bargain over the term before beginning performance and may wish to postpone, perhaps in the hope of avoiding, this aspect of the negotiations.

[16] Ridgway v. Wharton, 10 Eng. Rep. 1287, 1313 (H.L. 1857).

[17] See the discussion of the role of usages and implied terms in §3.28 *infra*.

[18] Walker v. Keith, 382 S.W.2d 198, 202 (Ky. 1964).

[19] Milex Prods. v. Alra Laboratories, 603 N.E.2d 1226 (Ill. App. 1992) ("there was sufficient evidence from which the trial court could conclude that the parties did intend to conclude the

had the parties been entirely silent as to that term. Bargaining with this eventuality in mind may be very different from bargaining on the assumption that a failure to agree would not result in a contract at all. On the latter assumption each party thinks, "If I do not make sufficient concessions to reach agreement, we will have no deal at all." On the former assumption, each thinks, "If I do not make sufficient concessions to reach agreement, we will still have a deal, with the usual terms supplied by courts in such deals." On this assumption, an agreement may not result unless each party believes that the agreement will be more favorable than one with the terms a court would supply.

Surely it should be up to the parties at the time of the initial agreement to indicate whether, if they ultimately fail to agree on missing terms, there is no contract at all or a contract with the missing terms supplied by law.[20] Although it is within their power to adopt either premise, they often fail to do so, leaving the court to divine their expectations. In that event the circumstance that one of the parties is to rely substantially on the agreement to agree argues for the second premise, since it is not lightly to be supposed that one party has undertaken such reliance on the mere hope that agreement with the other party can ultimately be reached.

Should be up to parties

It can be argued that the second premise is particularly likely to fit the expectations of the parties in the case of an open-price term in the archetypal Code transaction — the contract for sale of goods readily available on the market. Under the Code the price that the court will supply if the parties fail to agree on a price will be the market price at the time for delivery. If each party assumes that a failure to agree will result in no contract, the seller will be encouraged to agree to any price that is at least no lower than what the seller supposes could be gotten by selling the goods on the market, and the buyer to agree to any price that is at least no higher than what the buyer supposes would have to be paid for similar goods on the market. And if each party assumes that a failure to agree will result in a contract at the market price at the time for delivery, both seller and buyer will be encouraged to reach the same agreement as under the other assumption. The effect of the two assumptions on their bargaining will thus be substantially the same, and the parties' expectation that they will ultimately reach agreement will therefore be better served by the second premise, resulting in a contract at the market price at the time for delivery.[21]

Second premise if open-price term

We turn now to another practical instance of an intention not to be bound.

§3.8. Intention Not to Be Bound Until Later Writing. Parties to an agreement sometimes indicate that they intend to put it in a writing later.

Nature of the problem

---

contract [under UCC 2-305] even in the absence of a settled price"). For a provision with the same premise, *see* UNIDROIT Principles 2.14 ("Contract with terms deliberately left open").

[20] It is assumed here that a court would supply the missing terms and that the agreement would then be sufficiently definite to be enforceable. On the problem of indefiniteness, see §3.29 *infra*.

[21] This assumes that there are no complicating factors, such as the possibility before the delivery date of sale by the seller in a falling market or purchase by the buyer in a rising market.

Perhaps they reach an oral agreement, with or without an informal memorandum, and say that there is a "formal contract contemplated." Perhaps one, in answer to the other's letter, expresses agreement to the other's terms and proposes to "forward a contract." Perhaps the principal bargainers for each side have signed a "letter of intent," leaving details of a "final agreement" to be worked out by their lawyers. What is the effect of such an indication of a writing to be executed in the future? Does it postpone the making of a contract until the final writing is executed? Or is execution of the writing merely a formal step that confirms the existence of a contract that was made earlier when the initial agreement was reached?[1]

Intention controls   The question, as courts see it, is to determine when the parties intended to be bound. As the Supreme Judicial Court of Maine once said:

> If the party sought to be charged intended to close a contract prior to the formal signing of a written draft, or if he signified such an intention to the other party, he will be bound by the contract actually made, though the signing of the written draft be omitted. If on the other hand, such party neither had nor signified such an intention to close the contract until it was fully expressed in a written instrument and attested by signatures, then he will not be bound until the signatures are affixed . . . . [I]n other words: if the written draft is viewed by the parties merely as a convenient memorial, or record of their previous contract, its absence does not affect the binding force of the contract; if however, it is viewed as the consummation of the negotiation, there is no contract until the written draft is finally signed.[2]

Nearly a century later, the Seventh Circuit added:

> Under Illinois law, courts focus on the parties' intentions to determine whether an enforceable contract comes into being during the course of negotiations, or whether some type of formalization of the agreement is required before it becomes binding . . . . The fact that some matters may have been left for future agreement does not necessarily preclude a finding of intent to contract during preliminary negotiations . . . . Courts look to all circumstances surrounding the negotiations, including the actions of the principals both during and after, to determine what the parties intended.[3]

The difficulty comes when one party asserts that it had a particular intention but the other party claims neither to have known nor to have had reason to

---

§3.8   [1] See the comparison of the problem of the "formal contract contemplated" and that of the "agreement to agree" in a footnote to the reason for agreements with open terms in §3.29 *infra*.

[2] Mississippi & Dominion S.S. Co. v. Swift, 29 A. 1063, 1066-67 (Me. 1894) (exchange of correspondence showed that "a formal draft of the contract was in the minds of the parties, or at least in the mind of the defendants, as the only authoritative evidence of a contract").

[3] A/S Apothekernes Laboratorium v. I.M.C. Chem. Group, 873 F.2d 155, 157 (1989) (letter of intent "subject to our concluding an Agreement of Sale" acceptable to boards of directors of both parties "whose discretion shall in no way be limited").

know of that intention. Although Judge Friendly asserted that "[u]nder a view conforming to the realities of business life, there would be no contract . . . until the document is signed and delivered" and favored a rule requiring at least "clear and convincing proof" that the parties meant to be bound before the document was signed and delivered, most courts have not shared this reluctance to find a binding agreement.[4]

In some cases a party's language gives reason to know whether that party intends to be bound before a later writing is signed.[5] Courts have generally honored language such as "not binding until final agreement is executed" as showing an intent not to be bound.[6] On the other hand, use of terms such as "offer" and "acceptance" during negotiations may help to show that a binding agreement was intended.[7] However, the Supreme Court of Minnesota reached the opposite conclusion where, after an exchange of letters concerning the sale of a farm, the seller sent the buyer a draft of a contract, and the buyer returned it with changes and a suggestion that they could "close it right up" if the seller would sign and forward two copies of that version. The seller did so, but the buyer refused to sign. In explaining why there was no contract, the court said:

Reason to know from language

> The correspondence makes it clear that all through [the buyer] did not intend to become bound, and never expressed his assent to become bound, without the formal execution of the contract. . . . This is not a case where there has been a "mere reference to a future contract in writing" wanted by one or more of the parties as a memorial of something already finally agreed upon, but is rather one where the "reduction of the agreement to writing and its signature" has been made a condition precedent to its completion.[8]

More recently, the Second Circuit concluded that there was no contract where drafts provided that "when executed and delivered, [each agreement] will be a valid and binding agreement."[9]

---

[4]International Telemeter Corp. v. Teleprompter Corp., 592 F.2d 49, 57-58 (2d Cir. 1979) (concurrence). Judge Friendly admitted that this was not the view of the New York courts or the Restatement Second. *See* Restatement Second §27 (binding effect of agreement is not precluded by manifestation of parties' intent to adopt a subsequent written memorial of agreement).

[5]Doll v. Grand Union Co., 925 F.2d 1363 (11th Cir. 1991) (refusing "to allow a jury to infer an agreement to sign a lease when one of the parties specifically declared its intention not to be bound until a lease was drafted and signed"). See the discussion of intention shown by language in §3.7 *supra*.

[6]Reprosystem v. SCM Corp., 727 F.2d 257 (2d Cir. 1984) (drafts provided that "when executed and delivered, [each agreement] will be a valid and binding agreement").

It has been held, however, that "subject to formal contract" is not dispositive. Arnold Palmer Golf Co. v. Fuqua Indus., 541 F.2d 584 (6th Cir. 1976) ("subject to . . . preparation of the definitive agreement").

[7]V'Soske v. Barwick, 404 F.2d 495 (2d Cir. 1968) (not only did writer of letter "characterize it as an offer," but he specified the time limit within which it was to be operative").

[8]Massee v. Gibbs, 210 N.W. 872, 873 (Minn. 1926).

[9]Reprosystem v. SCM Corp., *supra* note 6.

Completeness and formality of writing

In their search for the intent of the parties, courts have often looked to the completeness and formality of the writing. The Supreme Court of Pennsylvania did this in concluding that a provision making a letter of intent "subject to agreement on a formal contract" did not prevent the letter from being binding where it spoke of "this offer" being "accepted" and where it "by its terms, formality and the extraordinary care in its execution, indicate[d] that the signatories intended to bind themselves to an enforceable contract."[10] In the same vein, the Sixth Circuit observed that the parties' obligations were "all described in unqualified terms," such as "will" and "shall."[11] If, however, the parties' agreement is evidenced only by an informal memorandum, its incompleteness or lack of detail, considering the size or nature of the transaction, may suggest an intention not to be bound until a more authoritative writing is signed. Where the parties signed a one-page "Memorandum of Understanding" of an agreement settling complicated lawsuits involving patents and manufacturing rights, the court noted that the caption did not use the word "agreement" or "contract," that "the typical formal language of a contract was not used, and that many essential issues were not included." It concluded that the memorandum was "so cursory in its treatment . . . as to convince us that the parties did not intend that document to be an enforceable agreement."[12] Even though a writing may not be so indefinite as to be unenforceable, indefiniteness — such as a lack of any provision for a fall-back standard — may suggest that the parties did not intend to be bound until a final agreement was executed.[13] The amount of specificity expected will depend on the nature of the parties[14] and on the magnitude and complexity of the transaction. In Judge Easterbrook's words:

> When a large-scale corporate transfer is afoot . . . the court will respect any evidence that only a formal contract binds; when a simple transaction for the lease of a machine is at issue . . . and the more formal agreement appears to be boilerplate, an objective reading of the documents more readily leads to the conclusion that a letter agreement is binding.[15]

[10]Field v. Golden Triangle Broadcasting, Inc., 305 A.2d 689, 693 (Pa. 1973). *But cf.* Hill v. McGregor Mfg. Co., 178 N.W.2d 553 (Mich. App. 1970) (writing prepared by lawyers did not use "the typical formal language of contract").

[11]Arnold Palmer Golf Co. v. Fuqua Indus., *supra* note 6, at 589.

[12]Hill v. McGregor Mfg. Corp., *supra* note 10, at 555.

[13]Joseph Martin Jr., Delicatessen v. Schumacher, 417 N.E.2d 541 (N.Y. 1981) (renewal clause providing for "annual rentals to be agreed upon" did not invite "recourse to an objective extrinsic event, condition or standard" and therefore was unenforceable). *See* Restatement Second §33(3).

[14]Banking & Trading Corp. v. Floete, 257 F.2d 765 (2d Cir. 1958) (since party was government agency subject to investigation and audit, "it was important that whenever [it] entered into contractual relationships its legal rights and obligations be clearly defined").

[15]Skycom Corp. v. Telstar Corp., 813 F.2d 810, 816 (7th Cir. 1987).

Although it has been said that the failure to spell out usual terms shows that the parties did not intend to be bound,[16] such an inference seems unjustified if there is no indication that those terms were to be the subject of further negotiations.[17] Indeed, if the contract is a common type and the term is sufficiently usual to be supplied by a court, an opposite inference might be drawn.[18]

Courts show particular concern with the extent to which the terms of the agreement are spelled out in writing. The fact that the parties' understanding is entirely oral may suggest an intention not to be bound, particularly given the size or nature of the transaction. In relatively small deals it may not be unusual for parties to rely on a handshake. But the purchase of a corporate jet, as a federal district court judge said, **Oral agreements**

> was no run-of-the-mill, over-the-counter transaction where terms and conditions of a sales contract are fairly well established and, in effect, are recognized as a custom of the trade [but rather] a structured, multifaceted deal of magnitude, with a purchase price of some $9,000,000 — no small change even in the life of a modern day giant corporation.[19]

The judge concluded that such a contract would be expected to be in writing and that the parties' oral agreement was not binding. Courts have occasionally insisted that some kinds of agreements, such as complex settlement agreements, be in writing even though they are not within the statute of frauds.[20]

In doubtful cases, courts have looked to many factors in deciding whether the parties intended their agreement to be binding, but no single factor is likely to be decisive. Here is a list of factors that has been popular for a century: **Lists of factors**

> whether the contract is of that class which are usually found to be in writing; whether it is of such nature as to need a formal writing for its full expression; whether it has few or many details; whether the amount involved is large or small; whether it is a common or unusual contract; whether the negotiations

[16] Banking & Trading Corp. v. Floete, *supra* note 14 (agreement failed to make appropriate variations in "terms upon which [government agency] customarily purchased rubber").

[17] Berg Agency v. Sleepworld-Willingboro, 346 A.2d 419 (N.J. Super. 1975) (key factor is "intent of the particular parties involved in the transaction at issue [and] presence or absence of essential contract provisions is but an element in the evidential panorama underlying a factual finding of intent and enforceability").

[18] Larwin-Southern Cal. v. JGB Inv. Co., 162 Cal. Rptr. 52 (Ct. App. 1979) ("usual and reasonable terms" can be looked to).

[19] Songbird Jet Ltd. v. Amax Inc., 605 F. Supp. 1097, 1102 (S.D.N.Y.) (also rejecting contention that statute of frauds was satisfied by part payment), aff'd mem., 779 F.2d 39 (2d Cir. 1985).

[20] Winston v. Mediafare Entertainment Corp., 777 F.2d 76 (2d Cir. 1985) (since purpose of settlement agreement "is to forestall litigation, prudence strongly suggests that [the] agreement be written in order . . . to avoid still further litigation").

themselves indicate that a written draft is contemplated as the final conclusion of the negotiations.[21]

More recently, the Second Circuit developed another list: (1) "a party's explicit statement that it reserves the right to be bound only when a written agreement is signed"; (2) "whether one party has partially performed, and that performance has been accepted by the party disclaiming the contract"; (3) "whether there was literally nothing left to negotiate or settle, so that all that remained to be done was to sign what had already been fully agreed to"; (4) "whether the agreement concerns those complex and substantial business matters where requirements that contracts be in writing are the norm rather than the exception."[22]

Proof of circumstances

The final decision is often left to the trier of the facts, based on all the circumstances.[23] Occasionally relevant circumstances are recited in the agreement itself.[24] Usually, however, they must be shown by extrinsic evidence. So, for example, where the negotiators have made a preliminary agreement before turning matters over to their lawyers, courts have sometimes reached the conclusion that the parties intended to be bound while the lawyers worked out the ultimate agreement and sometimes reached the opposite conclusion. Extrinsic evidence as to the extent of the lawyers' responsibility may be critical in such decisions.[25] If extrinsic evidence is offered, a question then arises as to the effect of the parol evidence rule, which applies to preliminary agreements no less than other agreements.[26] It is, however, difficult to see how the parol evidence rule, which comes into play only if there is an enforceable integrated agreement, could bar evidence to show that an agreement is enforceable, and it has been held that the rule does not exclude evidence bearing on enforceability of a preliminary agreement.[27]

---

[21] Mississippi & Dominion S.S. Co. v. Swift, *supra* note 2, at 1067. This list is incorporated in Restatement Second §27 cmt. *c*.

[22] R.G. Group v. Horn & Hardart Co., 751 F.2d 69, 75-76 (2d Cir. 1984) (franchise for 20 restaurants).

[23] Opdyke Inv. Co. v. Norris Grain Co., 320 N.W.2d 836 (Mich. 1982) ("such a factual inquiry should have been made only by a trial court fact-finder after consideration of all of the relevant evidence").

[24] Brassteel Mfg. Co. v. Mitsubishi Intl. Corp., 192 N.Y.S.2d 200 (Sup. Ct. 1959) (preliminary agreement recited that it would "serve as our understanding until the formal agreement is drawn up by our lawyer").

[25] *See* Karson v. Arnow, 224 N.Y.S.2d 891 (Sup. Ct. 1962) (lawyer told parties that unless they signed preliminary agreement, "how could he go back to Syracuse and have his girl type everything up then come back, and we had decided other things").

[26] Alaska N. Dev. v. Alyeska Pipeline Serv. Co., 666 P.2d 33 (Alaska 1983).

[27] Arnold Palmer Golf Co. v. Fuqua Indus., *supra* note 6 ("rule applies only after an integrated or a partially integrated agreement has been found"). In any event, evidence of prior negotiations should be admissible to show the meaning of such phrases as "formal contract to follow" and "subject to formal contract." On the admissibility of evidence of prior negotiations, see §7.12 *infra*.

If the parties have dealt with each other before in similar transactions involving preliminary agreements, their prior course of dealing may shed light on their intent.[28] The parties' behavior after making the preliminary agreement may also be given great weight. Even if not repeated so as to amount to a "course of performance" or "practical construction,"[29] a party's subsequent behavior, especially if inconsistent with the party's later contention, may be persuasive either as showing that the agreement was intended to be binding[30] or as showing that it was not.[31] A press release, for example, may indicate an intent to be bound[32] or the lack of such an intent.[33] A party's acquiescence in the other's reliance on the preliminary agreement may be a compelling justification for enforceability.[34]

Effect of parties' conduct

One reason for reducing an understanding to an authoritative writing is to have written evidence in the event of a dispute over its terms.[35] The need for such evidence is much less if the negotiations are by written correspondence instead of by face-to-face oral exchange. Therefore if the parties appear to have reached agreement by writtten correspondence, a court may be reluctant to conclude that there is no contract, even in the face of an express reference to a further writing. After an exchange of letters, a seller of apples telegraphed, "If satisfactory, answer and will forward contract," and the buyer telegraphed, "All right. Send contract as stated in our message." The New York Court of Appeals decided that the agreement was no "less obligatory upon both parties because they intended that it should be put into another form."[36]

Negotiations by correspondence

---

[28] May Metro. Corp. v. May Oil Burner Corp., 49 N.E.2d 13 (N.Y. 1943) (court looked to eight previous renewals of distributorship agreement).

[29] See UCC 1-303(a); Restatement Second §202(4) & cmt. g.

[30] California Food Serv. Corp. v. Great Am. Ins. Co., 182 Cal. Rptr. 67 (Ct. App. 1982) ("fact [seller of leasehold interest] allowed [purchaser] to take possession of the premises and to begin operating it as a restaurant strongly suggests both parties considered the terms of the letter of intent as being binding").

[31] Crellin Technologies v. Equipmentlease Corp., 18 F.3d 1 (1st Cir. 1994) (prospective borrower "tried valiantly to forge arrangements with other lending institutions — arrangements that would have left [prospective lender] out in the cold"). Subjectivists may take some satisfaction from such decisions, which must be premised on an actual intention shared by both parties and not on what one party knew or had reason to know. One party's subsequent conduct could not be relevant to what the other party had reason to know at an earlier time. See footnote to the discussion of the intention not to be legally bound in §3.7 supra.

[32] Arnold Palmer Golf Co. v. Fuqua Indus., supra note 6 (press release by party who later claimed memorandum was not binding said that parties "have agreed to cooperate in an enterprise").

[33] Reprosystem v. SCM Corp., supra note 6 (seller's press release and filing with SEC contradicted buyers' claim of binding agreement).

[34] Borg-Warner Corp. v. Anchor Coupling Co., 156 N.E.2d 513 (Ill. 1958) (acquirer spent large sums on survey of target's business under letter of intent).

[35] This is reinforced by the parol evidence rule, which makes such a writing the sole source of terms of the contract, to the exclusion of any other agreements that may have been reached during prior negotiations. See the discussion of the effect of the rule in §7.2 infra.

[36] Sanders v. Pottlitzer Bros. Fruit Co., 39 N.E. 75, 76 (N.Y. 1894).

We pursue our examination of the objective theory in a context that is of special interest — that of mistakes in expression and transmission.

Alternative of tort liability

§3.9.   **Criticism in Context of Mistake in Expression.**   The objective theory is today so widely and unquestioningly accepted as protecting the reasonable expectations of the parties that its implications tend to be overlooked. Well over half a century ago, one of its critics suggested that courts are too zealous in protecting the expectations of a party who mistakenly, although reasonably, believes that the other has assented. He thought it unfortunate that one party "is bound to the contract though the other party is notified of the mistake before the latter has changed his position or suffered any damage."[1] Not even the law of torts went that far. So he suggested that contractual liability be limited to situations in which there was subjective agreement and that liability in tort be imposed for the negligent use of language if a misunderstanding prevented such agreement. This would have an important effect on the amount of damages, since tort liability would protect only the promisee's reliance interest, while contractual liability protects the promisee's expectation interest.

Effect on mistake in language

Yet so complete is the acceptance of the objective theory that courts unhesitatingly allow recovery for loss of expectation if one party has simply made a mistake in the use of language. If a seller misspeaks and offers to sell "two hundred fifty" bushels of apples at a stated price, meaning to say "two hundred fifteen," a buyer that accepts, neither knowing nor having reason to know of the seller's mistake in expression, can recover for loss of expectation should the seller fail to deliver 250 bushels.[2] However, in granting recovery measured by the offeree's expectation interest, some courts have at least buttressed their opinions by pointing to reliance by the offeree.[3]

Effect on mistake in transmission

Furthermore, courts that faced the question usually extended the objective theory to bind an offeror whose offer had been mistakenly transmitted by a telegraph company. For example, where a seller's offer to sell at "two ten net cash" was mistakenly transmitted as "two net cash," the seller was held to a contract at the lower price, even though there was no showing of reliance by the buyer.[4] It was enough that the buyer neither knew nor had reason to know of the mistake in the offer as transmitted. As between offeror and offeree, it

§3.9   [1]Whittier, The Restatement of Contracts and Mutual Assent, 17 Cal. L. Rev. 441, 442 (1929), quoted as having "considerable force" as a matter of principle in Eisenberg, The Responsive Model of Contract Law, 36 Stan. L. Rev. 1107, 1120 (1984). The popularity of the objective theory is due in good part to the influence of Williston and the Restatement.

[2]As for the possibility of relief on the ground of mistake, see the discussion of other types of cases in §9.4 *infra*.

[3]Carnegie Steel Co. v. Connelly, 97 A. 774 (N.J. Sup. 1916) (seller relied, "having cut the rails to special lengths" pursuant to buyer's mistaken order).

[4]Ayer v. Western Union Tel. Co., 10 A. 495 (Me. 1887) ("the receiver of the offer may, . . . upon the strength of the telegram as received by him, have sold all the merchandise," but it did not appear that he had).

may have made sense to place on the offeror the loss caused by the offeree's reliance because, as sender of the telegram, the offeror had the better chance to shift the risk to the telegraph company by contract.[5] It was more questionable to place on the offeror, as the objective theory did, the loss of expectation of an offeree that may not have relied at all.[6]

Our analysis focuses now on the mechanics of assent in terms of offer and acceptance.

C.   THE MECHANICS OF ASSENT

§3.10.   **What Is an Offer.** According to traditional analysis, an offer is the penultimate communication in the making of a contract. We have seen that an offer is a manifestation of assent that empowers another to enter into a contract by manifesting assent in return.[1] Simple examples are: "I promise to deliver these apples if you promise to pay me $100"; "I promise to deliver these apples if you pay me $100."[2] An offer may invite more than one acceptance if, for example, a seller makes a continuing or "standing" offer to sell apples as the buyer may order them over a period of time.

Offer defined

No formalities are generally required for an offer.[3] It may be made by spoken or written words or by other conduct.[4] Sometimes a contract that results from words is described as "express," while one that results from conduct is described as "implied in fact," but the distinction as such has no legal consequences.[5]

No formalities required

[5] By federal statute a telegraph company may classify messages and vary its rates according to class, subject to the approval of the Federal Communications Commission. 47 U.S.C. §201. Pursuant to this power, such companies limit their liability for mistakes or delays but allow the sender to contract for greater liability under repeated message rates and special valuation.

[6] For an interesting case holding that there was no contract where an architect fraudulently gave one price for construction to the owner and a higher price to the builder, *see* Vickery v. Ritchie, 88 N.E. 835 (Mass. 1909).

§3.10 [1] See the discussion of the meaning of *offer* in §3.3 *supra*. According to Restatement Second §24, an offer is a "manifestation of willingness to enter into a bargain, so made as to justify another person in understanding that his assent to that bargain is invited and will conclude it."

[2] See the discussion of the promisor's use of a condition in §2.9 *supra*. As to the meaning of *promise*, see the discussion of the concern of contract law with the future in §1.1 *supra*, and for a rare instance in which the offer is not a promise, see footnote to the discussion of the meaning of *offer* in §3.3 *supra*.

[3] As to the formalities imposed by the statute of frauds, see Chapter 6 *infra*.

[4] For a contract inferred from conduct, *see* Smith-Scharff Paper Co. v. P.N. Hirsch & Co. Stores, 754 S.W.2d 928 (Mo. App. 1988) (though buyer "did not specifically request [seller] to conduct business in this fashion, [buyer] accepted the benefits of the practice . . . [and] could have told [seller] to stop").

[5] Carroll v. Lee, 712 P.2d 923 (Ariz. 1986) ("no difference in legal effect between an express contract and an implied contract").

Claims under implied-in-fact contracts should not be confused with claims under what are, by the use of a fiction, sometimes described as "implied-in-law" contracts. See the discussion of

Conduct that would lead a reasonable person in the other party's position to infer a promise in return for performance or promise may amount to an offer. One who holds out goods may be taken to be offering them for sale.[6] One who begins to perform services for another in apparent expectation of payment may be taken to be offering to furnish them for reasonable compensation. The question of fact in each case is whether a reasonable person in the position of the other party would understand that payment was expected for the services and that they were not gratuitous.[7]

Intimate implied-in-fact contracts

This question is particularly difficult if the parties are in an intimate or otherwise close relationship. The mere fact that personal services are performed in the home over a substantial period of time does not alter the situation, and courts have said that there is a rebuttable presumption of an intent to pay in such cases.[8] If there is a family relationship, however, courts have applied a presumption of gratuitousness similar to that applied in restitution cases.[9] The presumption can be rebutted if, for example, the services are unusually onerous and there are expressions of intent to pay.[10] The presumption also applies to an unmarried couple living together.[11] Again, the presumption can be

---

the relation to the action of debt in §2.20 *supra*. See also the discussion of how a court supplies a term in §7.16 *infra*.

[6] It has been held that in a self-service store the "merchant's act of stocking these self-service displays with goods thereby makes an offer to the shopper," which the shopper accepts by taking the goods from the shelf, even though it may be "common custom . . . for shoppers to change their minds and to return unwanted merchandise prior to paying for it." A contract of sale had therefore already been made when a bottle exploded as the customer started to put it in his shopping cart. Barker v. Allied Supermarket, 596 P.2d 870 (Okl. 1979).

[7] Whitfield v. Lear, 751 F.2d 90 (2d Cir. 1984) ("if a producer accepts a submitted idea with full knowledge that the offeror expects payment in the event of use, California courts impose liability under a theory of implied-in-fact contract").

[8] Buchweiser v. Estate of Laberer, 695 S.W.2d 125 (Mo. 1985) (it is "general rule that where no family relationship exists, the law presumes an intent to pay for services rendered," but trier of fact did not err in rejecting claim that there was evidence that recipient had paid for those services).

[9] Gibson v. McCraw, 332 S.E.2d 269 (W. Va. 1985) ("in the absence of an express contract . . . , services rendered between near relatives living in the same household are presumed to be gratuitous;" but "the mere fact of relationship by blood does not, of itself, trigger the presumption of gratuity").

[10] Estate of Beecham, 378 N.W.2d 800 (Minn. 1985) (daughter-in-law "rendered around the clock care for an elderly, chronically incontinent woman, seven days a week for nearly seven years," supporting $32,000 award from estate of $166,000).

[11] Morone v. Morone, 413 N.E.2d 1154 (N.Y. 1980) ("major difficulty with implying a contract from the rendition of services for one another by persons living together is that it is not reasonable to infer an agreement to pay for the services rendered when the relationship of the parties makes it natural that the services were rendered gratuitously"). *Accord:* Featherston v. Steinhoff, 575 N.W.2d 6 (Mich. App. 1997) (because neither party expected that cohabitant would be compensated for services, she did not overcome "presumption that these services were gratuitous").

rebutted.[12] In assessing attempts to rebut the presumption, courts might well consider that persons in such a relationship have more reason to create their own legal regime than do married persons, for whom the law provides a legal regime.

An offer is not effective until it reaches the offeree. This proposition is reinforced by the assumption that consideration requires a bargain, so that the acceptance must be in response to the offer.[13] The offer, however, need not be communicated directly by the offeror to the offeree. For example, it may be enough in the case of an offer of a reward that the offeree hears from a third person that a reward has been offered. But until the offer reaches the offeree, it is not effective and the offeror can withdraw it.[14]

Offer must reach the offeree

Whether a particular proposal amounts to an offer is a question of intention. The question most commonly arises when the maker of the proposal denies having had any intention to make an offer, while the one to whom the proposal was made claims to have believed that it was intended as an offer. Under the objective theory the issue then becomes whether the one to whom the proposal was made had reason to believe that it was intended as an offer.

Objective theory

Decisions on this question abound, but each turns on its own special facts. A court will look first to the language of the particular proposal. It will then take account of any prior communications between the parties. It will also consider such circumstances as the completeness of the suggested bargain and the number of persons to whom the proposal is addressed. Decisions of this kind make precedents of only limited value.

Limited value of precedents

Taken as a whole, however, such decisions show a reluctance, in doubtful cases, to characterize a proposal as an offer and to hold its maker to a contract. "It is true that there is much room for interpretation once the parties are inside the framework of a contract, but it seems that there is less in the field of offer and acceptance. Greater precision of expression may be required, and less help from the court given, when the parties are merely at the threshold of a contract."[15] Courts have reason for caution, since to hold the maker of a proposal to a contract exposes the maker to liability based on the recipient's expectation interest, even in the absence of any reliance.[16] Furthermore, as Judge Posner wisely observed, "the degree to which the reasonable recipient will think a vague offer intended to empower him to create by acceptance a legally enforceable contract depends on the courts' attitudes toward vague

Reluctance to find an offer

[12] Marvin v. Marvin, 557 P.2d 106 (Cal. 1976) ("nonmarital partner may recover in quantum meruit for the reasonable value of household services rendered less the reasonable value of support received if he can show that he rendered services with the expectation of monetary reward").

[13] See the discussion of how action not taken in response cannot be consideration in §2.10 *supra*.

[14] See the discussion of withdrawal distinguished in §3.17 *infra*.

[15] United States v. Braunstein, 75 F. Supp. 137, 139 (S.D.N.Y. 1947).

[16] See the discussion of the rationale for protecting expectation in §1.6 *supra*.

offers" and the "more willing the courts are to interpolate mssing terms, the more difficult it is for the recipient of a vague offer to interpret the intentions behind the offer."[17]

Examples

In a typical case, a prospective buyer wrote, "Will you sell me your store property . . . for the sum of $6,000.00?" The owner wrote back that "it would not be possible for me to sell it unless I was to receive $16,000 cash." The prospective buyer, regarding this as an offer, purported to accept. The Supreme Judicial Court of Maine held that the owner's letter was not an offer. His language was interpreted to mean, "I will not entertain an offer from you for less than $16,000," rather than "I will sell to you for $16,000."[18] A similar result was reached in a case in which a prospective seller wrote, "Do you want to buy 240 good 1000 lb. cattle at 8.25 must be sold by Friday." The Supreme Court of Kansas held that this was not an offer but a "mere inquiry."[19] How do courts tell an offer from a "mere inquiry" or, as it is sometimes quaintly put, "an offer to chaffer"? How do they draw the line between offers and preliminary negotiations that fall short of being offers?

Language that suffices for offer

The fact that the proposal itself uses the word *offer* or is sent in response to a request for an *offer* is deserving of weight, but it is not controlling, and a court may decide that what is called an *offer* is merely an invitation to the recipient to make an offer.[20] More important is whether the proposal contains language suggesting that it is within the power of the recipient to close the deal by acceptance. In *Fairmount Glass Works v. Crunden-Martin Woodenware Co.*, for example, a seller's answer to a buyer's inquiry as to prices read, "we quote you Mason fruit jars" at stated prices "for immediate acceptance." The court held that "there was more than a quotation of prices, although [seller's] letter uses the word 'quote' in stating the prices given . . . . We can hardly understand what was meant by the words 'for immediate acceptance,' unless the latter was intended as a proposition to sell at these prices if accepted immediately."[21] The fact that a proposal is very detailed suggests that it is an offer, while omission of many terms suggests that it is not. "The more terms the parties leave open, the

---

[17] Architectural Metal Sys. v.. Consolidated Sys., 58 F.3d 1227, 1229 (7th Cir. 1995).

[18] Owen v. Tunison, 158 A. 926 (Me. 1932). A similar result was reached in the celebrated English case of Harvey v. Facey, [1893] A.C. 552 (P.C. 1893), in which the prospective buyer telegraphed an owner of real property who had been negotiating for its sale to the town for £900, "Will you sell us Bumper Hall Pen? Telegraph lowest cash price . . . ." The owner telegraphed back, "Lowest price for Bumper Hall Pen £900." It was held that this was not an offer. The court reasoned that the owner stated the lowest cash price but did not answer the question of whether he would sell to the buyer at that price.

[19] Cox v. Denton, 180 P. 261 (Kan. 1919). Typically the proposal appears to be of a kind that would be sent to a number of prospective buyers.

[20] Moulton v. Kershaw, 18 N.W. 172 (Wis. 1884) ("we are authorized to offer Michigan fine salt" held not an offer because no limit on quantity).

[21] 51 S.W. 196, 197 (1899).

less likely it is that they have intended to conclude a binding agreement . . . ."[22] However, a proposal that would be insufficient by itself may be fleshed out by the incorporation of terms from prior communications. Clauses typical of a legally binding agreement also suggest that a proposal is an offer because they indicate that the author understood that there might be no other chance to insert them before the conclusion of a contract. In the *Fairmount Glass Works* case, for example, the proposal that was held to be an offer contained a clause providing "that we make all quotations and contracts subject to . . . delays or accidents beyond our control."[23]

Reservation of power to maker

On the other hand, the insertion into a proposal of a clause that reserves to its maker the power to close the deal is a compelling indication that the proposal is not an offer. A common example provides that the agreement is not binding until it has been approved at the home office of the maker of the proposal. Such a clause may be designed to allow the home office to review the text of the proposed agreement to make sure that the salesperson has made no changes from the standard form or, in the case of sales on credit, to allow the home office to check the other party's credit before being bound. Whatever its purpose, the clause prevents the proposal from being an offer and thereby delays the making of a contract,[24] a consequence that may trip up the author of the clause if the other party seeks to back out.[25]

Failure to limit quantity

A proposal will not usually be interpreted as an offer if such an interpretation would expose its maker to the risk of liability for performance far beyond the maker's means. Suppose, for example, that a seller of goods makes a proposal to sell goods without specifying an upper limit on the quantity, as in a catalog or price list. Were the proposal taken to be an offer, it would be possible for the offeree to accept in a quantity that the seller could not supply. In a leading case, a seller wrote, "we are authorized to offer Michigan fine salt, in full carload lots." The court, refusing to place an implied limit on the quantity in the proposal, read it as one "to sell any quantity . . . not less than one car-load." The recipient of such a proposal would not have reason to believe that its author intended exposure to the risk of being bound to deliver an unlimited quantity. The proposal was therefore not an offer.[26]

Effect of power in recipient

The risk disappears if the proposal specifies a range or an upper limit and gives the recipient the power to make a selection within it. Sometimes such an understanding can be based on usage, course of dealing, or a standard of

---

[22]UCC 2-204 cmt.

[23]51 S.W. at 197. The inclusion of such terms may, however, be explained merely by the author's desire to have the author's own terms govern, should the negotiations ripen into a contract.

[24]Kuzmeskus v. Pickup Motor Co., 115 N.E.2d 461 (Mass. 1953) ("This order is not binding unless authorized by an officer of the company, and purchaser's credit has been OK'd by Finance Company.").

[25]Kuzmeskus v. Pickup Motor Co., *supra* note 24 (buyer recovered deposit because no contract).

[26]Moulton v. Kershaw, *supra* note 20.

acceptance will cure vagueness ✗

reasonableness. On this basis a court may enforce a continuing or "standing" offer by which a seller, for example, engages to furnish a buyer with all the goods of a specified kind that the buyer "may order" over a period of time.[27] The mere fact that a proposal, standing alone, would not be definite enough to be enforceable as a contract does not prevent it from being an offer if the indefiniteness can be cured by the acceptance. The acceptance can cure the indefiniteness if, for example, the proposal leaves such matters as description or quantity to be specified in the acceptance.[28]

Failure to limit recipients

A similar situation occurs when a proposal for a limited quantity has been sent to more persons than its maker could accommodate. One who receives, from an owner interested in selling a tract of land, a proposal stating that "this is a form letter" or "I am writing to several people" would not usually have reason to believe that its author intended exposure to the risk of several acceptances resulting in several contracts for the single tract.[29] This rationale does not apply, however, if the proposal eliminates that risk by stating that it is "subject to prior sale."

Proposals made to the public

The same rationale extends to proposals made to the public through advertisements, posters, circulars, and the like, and these are generally held not to be offers. Otherwise, "supposing a shopkeeper were sold out of a particular class of goods, thousands of members of the public might crowd into the shop and demand to be served, and each one would have a right of action against the proprietor for not performing his contract."[30] A customer would not usually have reason to believe that the shopkeeper intended exposure to the risk of a multitude of acceptances resulting in a number of contracts exceeding the shopkeeper's inventory. (In the case of a proposal to the public it is tempting to put the reasonable person in the position of the author of the proposal and ask not what its recipient had reason to believe but what its author reasonably thought that a reasonable recipient would believe, which would have the advantage of treating all recipients alike.) Again, the rationale does not apply if the proposal is qualified by such language as "subject to prior sale," "first come first served," or "while they last."[31] Such qualifications must be expressed, however,

---

[27] Hopkins v. Racine Malleable & Wrought Iron Co., 119 N.W. 301 (Wis. 1909) (buyer could "purchase his supplies of irons wherever he chose" but "as he from time to time ordered a shipment . . . he became bound to pay for such shipment according to the terms of the offer"). See the discussion of the role of interpretation in §3.28 *infra*.

[28] See the discussion of the role of interpretation in §3.28 *infra*.

[29] Lonergan v. Scolnick, 276 P.2d 8 (Ct. App. 1954) ("This is a form letter.").

[30] Crawley v. Rex, [1909] Transvaal 1105, 1108 (S. Afr.). *But cf.* Donovan v. RRL Corp., 27 P.3d 702 (Cal. 2001) (without consideration of the general rule, "licensed automobile dealer's advertisements for the sale of a particular vehicle at a specific price" was an offer in light of statute governing such advertisements). Related problems of consumer abuse are dealt with by legislation relating to false advertising that is beyond the scope of this discussion.

[31] Lefkowitz v. Great Minneapolis Surplus Store, 86 N.W.2d 689 (Minn. 1957) (newspaper advertisement of three bargain furs "First Come First Served").

and will not ordinarily be read in by the court.[32] Of course, if the very nature of a proposal restricts its maker's potential liability to a reasonable number of people, there is no reason why it cannot be an offer. The nature of the proposal may be such that only a limited number of people can accept. An example is the offer of a reward for the return of lost property.[33] Or, although an unlimited number of people can accept, it may be that only a limited number can meet the conditions that the proposal imposes for the offeror's liability. An example is the offer of a reward for the furnishing of information that leads to the apprehension of a criminal.[34]

The reasoning behind these reward cases is not, however, applied to proposals to sell to the highest bidder. When an auctioneer puts property up for sale to the highest bidder, the auctioneer is taken, in the absence of a contrary understanding or usage, to be interested in entertaining offers in the form of bids, not in making an offer. Although only one of the many possible bidders could claim the property as the highest bidder, even the highest bid might be too low, and it would not be reasonable to assume an intention to sell in that case. The auctioneer's proposal is therefore not an offer, but each bid is an offer that the auctioneer may accept or reject. Under the Uniform Commercial Code, there is no contract until the auctioneer accepts by "the fall of the hammer or in other customary manner."[35] Such a typical auction is often described as being "with reserve"[36] to distinguish it from an auction "without reserve," in which putting up an item for bids amounts to a commitment, irrevocable for a reasonable time, to sell the item to the highest bidder.[37] Revised Article 2 abandons the terms "with reserve" and "without reserve," but retains the

Entertainment of bids

---

[32] For a discussion of French law, which treats advertisements as offers by reading in such a qualification, and of the problems raised where the personal qualities of the other party will play an important role under the contract, *see* 1 Formation of Contracts: A Study of the Common Core of Legal Systems 359 (R. Schlesinger ed. 1968).

[33] Another example is R.E. Crummer & Co. v. Nuveen, 147 F.2d 3 (7th Cir. 1945), in which the court found that a notice published in newspapers, promising to buy back bonds if they were sent to a New York bank, was an offer. "We cannot believe that the ordinary businessman could be expected to read the advertisement as an invitation to send bonds from wherever he might be to New York on the chance that when they got there the advertiser would accept his offer."

[34] Another example is Carlill v. Carbolic Smoke Ball Co., [1893] 1 Q.B. 256 (C.A. 1892), in which the court found that a newspaper advertisement promise to pay "£100 reward" to any person who caught the flu after buying and using the "carbolic smoke ball" was an offer. (The advertisement also stated that £1,000 had been deposited with a bank "showing our sincerity in the matter.") A large number of persons could accept by buying and using the smoke ball, but only a smaller number would meet the condition for liability of catching the flu.

[35] UCC 2-328(2).

[36] As to when an auction is without reserve, *see* Marten v. Staab, 543 N.W.2d 436 (Neb. 1996) (agreeing "that 'all auctions are presumed to be with reserve unless they are expressly stated to be without reserve' ").

[37] UCC-O 2-328(3) ("sale is with reserve unless the goods are in explicit terms put up without reserve").

distinction.[38] Even though the auctioneer may not withdraw the item in an auction "without reserve," a bidder may retract his bid before the auctioneer announces completion of the sale.[39] The rule for auctions "with reserve" is applied by analogy to construction contracts that are to be awarded on the basis of public bidding. Generally the owner merely "invites" offers, and it is the contractor's bid that is the offer.[40]

Who can accept an offer?

Only offeree can
accept

§3.11.   Who Can Accept an Offer. The offeror, it is often said, is "the master of the offer." The offeror may invite acceptance by one or more offerees, acting separately or together. But the offer can be accepted only by one that the offeror has invited to accept. "It is a rule of law, that if a person intends to contract with A, B cannot give himself any right under it."[1] (Under the objective theory it should be added that B can acquire such a right if B had reason to believe that the offeror intended to contract with B.) The general rule, consistent with the bargain requirement, is that only an offeree can accept an offer. If, for example, a buyer makes an offer to a seller to buy apples, no one other than that seller can accept the offer — not even one who has bought out the seller and taken over the seller's very business.[2] The rule applies even where the offeree could have accepted the offer and then transferred the contract to another.[3] But the seller cannot change the result by attempting to assign the offer or otherwise to transfer it to another who then purports to accept. Absent provision to the contrary in the offer itself, at least, an offer is not transferable.[4] (We shall not pause to consider the impact of the doctrine of the undisclosed principal under agency law.[5]) If the seller dies or loses the legal

---

[38]UCC-R 2-328(3) ("sale by auction is subject to the seller's right to withdraw the goods unless . . . it is announced in express terms that the right to withdraw the goods is not reserved").

[39]The rule is out of harmony with classic contract doctrine. If the putting up of an item is the offer and each bid an acceptance, making a contract conditional on no other bid being higher, how can the bidder withdraw his bid? If the bid is the offer, why can the auctioneer not reject it?

[40]Universal Constr. Co. v. Arizona Consol. Masonry & Plastering Contractors Assn., 377 P.2d 1017 (Ariz. 1963).

§3.11   [1]Pollock, C.B., in Boulton v. Jones, 157 Eng. Rep. 232, 233 (Ex. 1857).

[2]Boulton v. Jones, *supra* note 1 (order to seller could not be accepted by his former manager who had bought out seller's business).

[3]See the discussion of the meaning of *delegation* in §11.10 *infra*. If the offeree is a corporation, however, the fact that control of it has changed hands through sale of shares of its stock does not of itself impair its power to accept.

[4]Ott v. Home Sav. & Loan Assn., 265 F.2d 643 (9th Cir. 1958) (dictum: "the offeree, in whom the power of acceptance lies by virtue of the offer, has no assignable rights").

[5]An offeree that purports to act alone may instead be an agent that is acting for an undisclosed principal. Under agency law the undisclosed principal may not only be bound by the contract but may have rights under it. *See* Restatement (Second) of Agency §§186, 302 (1958).

capacity to make the contract, the offer is terminated because it can no longer be accepted.[6]

A purported acceptance by one who is not the offeree may itself amount to an offer. Thus if one, other than the seller to whom the offer was made, attempts to accept by shipping goods to the buyer, this amounts to an offer to sell the goods. If the buyer takes the goods with knowledge of the shipper's identity, the buyer accepts the offer.[7] If the buyer takes them in ignorance of the identity of the shipper, a problem is posed as to the effect of the buyer's mistake, and this will be dealt with later.[8]

Effect of purported acceptance

We look next to what is an acceptance.

§3.12.   **Offer May Invite Acceptance by a Promise or by Performance.** The offeror is often described as "the master of the offer" in the sense that, since the offeror confers on the offeree the power of acceptance, the offeror has control over the scope of that power and over how it can be exercised. The assumption that consideration requires a bargain supports this conclusion. The offeror enjoys a "freedom *from* contract" except on the offeror's own conditions. It is the offeree's acceptance that furnishes the consideration for the promise embodied in the offer. Because of the requirement of a bargain, that consideration must have been sought by the offeror in exchange for the offeror's promise.[1] What the offeror receives by way of acceptance of the offer must therefore be what the offeror sought in making the offer. If the offeror sought as consideration a return promise, the result will be a bilateral contract. If instead the offeror sought as consideration some performance, the result will be a unilateral contract.[2] Under the objective theory, however, the question is not what the offeror actually sought, but what the offeree had reason to believe the offeror sought or, to express it more succinctly if less precisely, what the *offer* sought. Did the offer seek acceptance by a promise or by performance?

Offeror as "master of offer"

Seeking acceptance by a promise has both advantages and disadvantages for the offeror. On the one hand, the offeror obtains the offeree's commitment to undertake the return performance and to be responsible for its completion and for any deficiencies, and the offeror is not bound until such a commitment has been received. On the other hand, the offeror is bound before receiving the return performance. Seeking acceptance by performance also has advantages and disadvantages for the offeror. On the one hand, the offeror

Advantages and disadvantages to offeror

---

[6]Restatement Second §48. If there is more than one offeree, a surviving offeree can still accept, and the offer may make the personal representative or distributee of a deceased offeree an additional offeree.

[7]Orcutt v. Nelson, 67 Mass. (1 Gray) 536 (1854) ("receipt of the goods . . . pursuant to this notice, and payment of the freight, are decisive proof of the assent of the [buyer] to the change").

[8]See the discussion of mistake as to identity in §9.4 *infra*.

§3.12   [1]See the discussion of two categories where bargain is absent in §2.6 *supra*.

[2]See the discussion of the meaning of *bilateral* and *unilateral* in §3.4 *supra*.

is not bound before receiving the return performance.[3] On the other hand, the offeror obtains from the offeree no commitment to undertake the return performance. These advantages and disadvantages for the offeror have correlative disadvantages and advantages for the offeree.

Example of Petterson v. Pattberg

Petterson v. Pattberg is instructive. A mortgagee offered to discharge the entire mortgage debt if the mortgagor paid a smaller lump sum by a stated date. The mortgagor raised the money and made a contract to sell the land free of the mortgage. He then took the money to the mortgagee's door and said, "I have come to pay off the mortgage." But before he could hand the money over, the mortgagee explained that his offer was no longer open because he had already sold his rights under the mortgage to someone else. The New York Court of Appeals held that the mortgagee was not bound by his promise to discharge the mortgage debt because his offer had not been accepted when he revoked it. "It is elementary that any offer to enter into a unilateral contract may be withdrawn before the act requested to be done has been performed."[4] By its terms, the offer sought performance, not a promise, so that even if the mortgagor's words and acts were regarded as signifying a promise to pay, this could not be acceptance, because the offer had not sought a promise. Had the offer sought a promise, the mortgagee would have risked being bound before receiving performance, and conversely, the mortgagor could have bound him without performing. But since the offer sought performance and not a promise, the mortgagee did not risk being bound before receiving performance, and conversely, the mortgagor could not bind the mortgagee without performing.

Cases where performance is sought

It is relatively rare for an offeror to seek acceptance by performance rather than by a promise. Particularly important are the handbook cases, in which an employee claims that an employer has, by distributing a handbook to employees, made an offer to modify the traditional at-will relationship and that the employee has accepted that offer by performing or by continuing to perform.[5] Most of the other situations in which an offeror has no interest in a bilateral contract are situations in which a commitment by the offeree would be of so little value to the offeror that the offeror has no interest in being bound in return for a promise.[6] The offeror of a reward or the sponsor of a prize contest, for example, wants to encourage activity by as many persons as possible but

---

[3]This statement is qualified somewhat in §3.24 *infra*.

[4]161 N.E. 428, 429 (N.Y. 1928). In 1937, New York enacted a statute precluding revocation, after tender of performance, of a written and signed offer to accept that performance in satisfaction of a claim. N.Y. Gen. Oblig. L. §15-503. But that statute might not have affected the result in the cited case because the court there said that payment had not been tendered.

[5]A leading case is Pine River State Bank v. Mettille, 333 N.W.2d 622 (Minn. 1983) (personnel handbook provisions, if they meet the requirements for formation of a unilateral contract, may become enforceable"). See the discussion of the employment cases in §7.17 *infra*.

[6]Even in such situations, the importance of unilateral contracts has been eroded by the increasing recognition of unbargained-for reliance. *See* §2.19 *supra*. For example, the case of Hamer v.

has no interest in being bound in return for their promises. The seller of real estate that offers to pay a commission to any broker that succeeds in producing a buyer wants to encourage activity by as many brokers as possible but does not want to be bound in return for their promises. In such situations, the offer is generally taken to seek acceptance by performance and not a promise, because performance is what the circumstances, including the language of the offer, give the offeree reason to believe the offeror is seeking. Further discussion of these atypical situations will be deferred.[7]

Typically, the offeror seeks a commitment from the offeree in the form of a promise in advance of performance. Perhaps the offeree's performance is to take place far enough in the future that the offeror is unwilling to rely (by performing, preparing to perform, or forgoing other opportunities) without such a commitment. The owner of land that makes an offer to pay a builder for putting up a building seeks the builder's promise to perform in order to be assured that the builder will undertake performance and will be responsible for its completion and for any deficiencies. Even if the offeree's performance is to take place soon after the offer is made, the offeror seeks a promise from the offeree to make sure that the offeree will be responsible for any deficiency in the performance that is rendered. Traditional contract doctrine recognized this preference for a promise by resolving doubts in favor of the interpretation that an offer invites acceptance by a promise rather than by performance.[8]

Reasons for inviting a promise

The Code's provisions on orders for prompt shipment of goods exemplify this preference of offerors for a promise by way of acceptance. Under UCC 2-206(1)(b):

Example of UCC 2-206(1)(b)

> Unless otherwise unambiguously indicated by the language or circumstances . . . an order or other offer to buy goods for prompt or current shipment shall be construed as inviting acceptance either by a prompt promise to ship or by the prompt or current shipment of conforming or non-conforming goods . . . .

The buyer that sends an order for prompt shipment of goods is regarded as seeking acceptance by a promise to ship rather than by shipment and is therefore bound by a contract as soon as the seller promises to ship.[9] Even if the seller ships instead of promising, a promise to ship conforming goods is implied by the shipment, so that the seller is liable if the goods are nonconforming. The buyer's offer is taken to seek acceptance by a promise, one that need not be expressed in words but that may be manifested by an attempt to perform. The

---

Sidway, discussed in §2.4 *supra*, might today have been decided in favor of the plaintiff on that basis.

[7] See §3.24 *infra*.

[8] *See* the first Restatement §31 ("in case of doubt it is presumed that an offer invites the formation of a bilateral contract . . . by a promise").

[9] *But cf.* Port Huron Mach. Co. v. Wohlers, 221 N.W. 843 (Iowa 1928) (dictum: sending order for goods "is an offer of a promise for an act").

seller that wants to avoid this liability can notify the buyer that the shipment of nonconforming goods is "offered only as an accommodation to the buyer." The shipment will then be taken not as a promise to ship conforming goods but as a counteroffer by the seller that the buyer is free to accept or reject.[10]

We now analyze just how that promise may be expressed.

Acceptance defined

§3.13. What Is an Acceptance.

We have seen that an offer is a manifestation of assent that empowers another to enter into a contract by manifesting assent in return.[1] If the offeree exercises this power by manifesting assent, the offeree is said to "accept" the offer. This acceptance is the final step in the making of a contract. Upon acceptance, the offeror is bound by the contract proposed by the offer. Whether the offer invites acceptance by a promise or by performance, the offeror is "the master of the offer" and acceptance must be on the terms of the offer. There are, however, limits to what the offeror can turn into an acceptance, and the offeror cannot, for example, turn an offeree's silence into acceptance.[2]

Acceptance by performance

If the offer invites acceptance by performance, the offeree cannot accept by promising the performance. Nor can the offeree accept by rendering a performance that does not conform to all of the terms of the offer. An offer of a reward, for example, cannot be accepted by one who does not do all that the terms of the reward require.[3] The case of *Petterson v. Pattberg*, discussed in the preceding section, is graphic: since the mortgagee's offer had invited the performance of payment of a stated sum, the mortgagor's raising that sum and taking it to the mortgagee's door did not count as acceptance.[4] If an offeree wishes to render the invited performance without accepting the offer, the offeree can do so by indicating this at or before the time of performance by, for example, saying that performance is gratuitous.[5] The rules that have developed to protect the offeree from revocation before performance is completed are discussed later in this chapter.[6]

Acceptance by a promise

Most offers invite acceptance by a promise rather than by performance, and most of the law of offer and acceptance has developed in connection with such offers.[7] Under the objective theory, the offeree's undisclosed intention is

[10]Corinthian Pharmaceutical Sys. v. Lederle Laboratories, 724 F. Supp. 605 (S.D. Ind. 1989) (nonconforming shipment as accommodation "constituted a counteroffer").

§3.13 [1]See the discussion of *offer* defined in §3.10 *supra*.

[2]See the discussion how the offeror cannot make silence acceptance in §3.14 *infra*.

[3]Blain v. Pacific Express Co., 6 S.W. 679 (Tex. 1887) (not liable for reward for arrest of two persons where claimant captured only one). For more on rewards, see the discussion of the example of action in ignorance of a reward in §2.10 *supra*.

[4]See the discussion of the example of *Petterson v. Pattberg* in §3.12 *supra*.

[5]*See* Restatement Second §53(3).

[6]See §3.24 *infra*.

[7]According to an English writer, application of the analysis of offer and acceptance to promises that invite acceptance by performance "has never been happy" and "only became canonical late in the nineteenth century in the celebrated case of Carlill v. Carbolic Smoke Ball Co. (1892),"

irrelevant, as long as the offeree's conduct gives the offeror reason to believe that the offeree intends to accept by making a promise.[8] An offeree that signs and returns a written contract cannot avoid liability by testimony that this was done with no intent to be bound. As Judge Easterbrook put it, "You can't escape contractual obligation by signing with your fingers crossed behind your back, even if that clearly shows your intent *not* to be bound."[9]

The fact that an offer invites acceptance by a promise does not mean that the promise must be in words. A promise may be implied from other conduct, such as a nod of the head, and in some circumstances beginning performance or even preparing for performance may as effectively indicate a commitment to finish as a promise in words.[10] As in the case of an offer that invites acceptance by performance, the offeree can, by an appropriate indication to the offeror, render the performance without accepting the offer.[11]

Promise need not be in words

According to UCC 2-206(1)(a):

Code rule

> Unless otherwise unambiguously indicated by the language or circumstances . . . an offer to make a contract shall be construed as inviting acceptance in any manner and by any medium reasonable in the circumstances . . . .

Although this provision might be read as saying that an ambiguous offer should be interpreted as inviting acceptance by either a promise or by performance, it makes more sense to read it as directed at the means by which acceptance by a promise may be expressed. May an offer in words be accepted by conduct as well as by words? May an offer by facsimile be accepted by letter?[12] This reading of the Code is consistent with the assumption that the typical offer

---

described in the discussion of the example of the *Carbolic Smoke Ball* case in §3.15 *infra*. Simpson, Innovation in Nineteenth Century Contract Law, 91 L.Q. Rev. 247, 262 (1975).

[8] Preston Farms & Ranch Supply v. Bio-Zyme Enters., 625 S.W.2d 295 (Tex. 1981) (by "continued purchases and payments [buyer] at least impliedly agreed to pay the specified interest"). See §3.6 *supra*. *See also* Restatement Second §53, which eliminates the requirement of "intent to accept" found in first Restatement §55. Restatement Second §19(2) provides instead that "conduct of a party is not effective as a manifestation of his assent unless he intends to engage in the conduct."

[9] Robbins v. Lynch, 836 F.2d 330, 332 (7th Cir. 1988).

[10] According to Restatement Second §62(2) a beginning of the invited performance "operates as a promise to render complete performance."

The first Restatement failed to recognize this, concluding that if an offeror wrote, "I will pay you $100 for plowing Flodden field, if you will promise me by next Monday to finish the work before the following Saturday," the offeree could accept by plowing rather than promising as long as the offeree finished and notified the offeror by Monday. Restatement §63 illus. *But see* Restatement Second §53(1). A better rationale is that the beginning of performance implied a promise to perform, committing the offeree to finish performance by Saturday and to be responsible for any deficiencies in the work. See the discussion of no formalities required in §3.10 *supra*.

[11] *See* Restatement Second §53(2).

[12] The Comments to UCC 2-206 do not suggest that the drafters gave careful attention to this distinction. Comment 1 leans toward the distinction suggested here by using *manner* narrowly to refer to "media of communication." Comment 2 goes on to explain that the rule on prompt

invites acceptance by a promise and accords with the precept that a promise need not be expressed in words.[13]

Three general requirements

The language or other conduct that will suffice as acceptance by a promise depends on the circumstances, and cases tend to turn on their special facts. When in doubt, courts may be somewhat more willing to find that an offeree has accepted an offer than that an offer has been made in the first place.[14] Three general requirements for an acceptance by a promise can be identified.

Must express commitment

First, there must be an expression of commitment. A mere acknowledgment of receipt of the offer or an expression of interest in it is not enough. A seller of goods was held not to have made a promise by writing to a customer, "Your order . . . is at hand and will receive our prompt and careful attention."[15] Where a response by a prospective purchaser's lawyer stated that "we are . . . ready to proceed with this transaction" and asked to "know the exact dollar amount that you expect to receive for your interest in the land," this was held not to be "an unequivocal, unconditional acceptance."[16]

Must be unconditional

Second, the commitment must not be conditional on any further act by either party. Since an acceptance is the ultimate step in making a contract, the commitment cannot be conditional on some final step to be taken by the offeror. A buyer of rubber that, in replying to the sellers' offer, insisted that the sellers "must promptly acknowledge" its order was held not to have accepted the offer. "The import of this proposal was that the [buyer] should not be bound until the [sellers] signified their assent to the terms set forth. When this assent was given and the acknowledgement made, this contract was then to come into existence . . . ."[17] Nor can the commitment be conditional on some decision to be made by the offeree. The offeree's promise to accept at some later time (a promise to make a promise) is not an acceptance, because it is conditional on a further step to be taken by the offeree at that time.[18] It has been held, however, that a promise that is to take effect automatically at some later time if a stated

---

shipment "rejects the artificial theory that only a single mode of acceptance is normally envisaged by an offer." If *mode* means *manner*, however, this is consistent with the reading suggested here.

[13]Restatement Second §32 seems to make a questionable extrapolation from the Code by stating that, "In case of doubt an offer is interpreted as inviting the offeree to accept either by promising to perform what the offeree requests or by rendering the performance, as the offeree chooses." Taken literally, this suggests that an offeree whose performance was incomplete or defective might choose to treat an offer as inviting performance and thereby escape liability on the ground that the offeree had never accepted by rendering the invited performance. However, §62(2) appears to eliminate this possibility by stating that in such a case an acceptance by performance operates as a promise to render complete performance. It would have been neater to have kept the first Restatement's preference for a promise as an accurate reflection of what the typical offeror seeks, and merely added a statement that a promise can be implied from performance.

[14]See the discussion of no formalities required in §3.10 *supra*.

[15]Courtney Shoe Co. v. E.W. Curd & Son, 134 S.W. 146 (Ky. 1911).

[16]Wucherpfennig v. Dooley, 351 N.W.2d 443 (N.D. 1984).

[17]Poel v. Brunswick-Balke-Collender Co., 110 N.E. 619, 622 (N.Y. 1915).

[18]However, the words, "Will accept. Send contract at once," were held to express an unconditional commitment in Billings v. Wilby, 96 S.E. 50 (N.C. 1918).

event has not occurred is effective as an acceptance at that time if the event has not occurred.[19] However, either party is free to withdraw before then. For example, an acceptance effective unless the offeree gives notice to the contrary within 30 days operates as an acceptance at the end of 30 days if the offeree has done nothing and if the offer is still open. But the offeror can revoke the offer until acceptance occurs at the end of the 30 days.[20]

Third, at least according to traditional contract doctrine, the commitment must be one on the terms proposed by the offer without the slightest variation. The offeree's promise, embodied in the acceptance, must be identical with the offeror's promise, embodied in the offer. Under traditional doctrine, the offeror as the master of the offer enjoys freedom from contract except on the terms of the offer. An offeree, having received an offer of land for cash, replied, "Your offer is accepted," and added, "please execute the enclosed deed . . . and send it to the Bank of Minnesota, St. Paul, with . . . instructions . . . to collect the amount due you, and deliver deed." When the offeror refused to convey the land, the offeree sued. He lost on the ground that an offer must be accepted "according to the terms" on which it was made, "without the introduction of any new terms."[21] Variations on this theme will be considered later.[22]

> **Must not vary terms of offer**

In addition to these three requirements, which courts have deduced from the nature of an acceptance, the offeror as the master of the offer may impose further requirements.[23] If, for example, the offer invites the offeree to make a specification of terms, the offeree must do so.[24] If the offer requires that the acceptance bear the signatures of a number of persons, it must be signed by all of them.[25] And if the offer insists that the offeree accept by words rather than other conduct, the offeree must do so. Thus when an offeror had written to a

> **Offer may impose requirements**

---

[19] Orr v. Doubleday, Page & Co., 119 N.E. 552 (N.Y. 1918) (acceptance of offer to renew lease would be "withdrawn" if stated events occurred). Fairness may require that the offeree notify the offeror that the event has not occurred. See the discussion of notice generally required in §3.15 *infra*.

[20] Hansen v. Bendert, 219 N.W. 883 (S.D. 1928) (party had "privilege of withdrawing from this contract for a period of thirty days"). Compare the cases described in the discussion of termination within a fixed period in §2.14 *supra*.

[21] Langellier v. Schaefer, 36 Minn. 361 (1887).

[22] See §3.21 *infra*. Of course, if the offeror allows the offeree a choice of, for example, quality or quantity, the offeree may select within that range. See the discussion of language that suffices for offer in §3.10 *supra*.

For an interesting case in which it was held that there was no contract made, either by owner's purported acceptance of "your tender" or by performance, where builder made alternative bids — one fixed-price and one cost-plus — and there was no way to tell which had been accepted, *see* Peter Lind & Co. v. Mersey Docks & Harbour Bd., [1972] 2 Lloyd's Rep. 234 (Com. Ct. 1972).

[23] Frank Crane Auctioneers v. Delchamps, 797 So. 2d 470 (Ala. App. 2001) (broker "could have accepted the offer only by complying with the terms of the offer and registering his prospect, as the postcard outlined").

[24] See the discussion of the effect of a power in the recipient in §3.10 *supra*.

[25] *But see* Shovel Transfer & Storage v. Pennsylvania Liquor Control Board, 739 A.2d 133 (Pa. 1999) ("in the absence of any express intention that the parties intended to be bound only

builder, "Upon an agreement to finish the fitting up of offices . . . in two weeks from date, you can begin at once," it was held that the builder had not accepted merely by purchasing materials and beginning work on them.[26] Although beginning performance or even preparing to perform may, in some circumstances, suffice to manifest the commitment required for acceptance, here the language of the offer indicated that the offeror wanted "an agreement" before work was commenced. When an offeror had signed a seller's form providing that "This contract is not binding . . . until accepted by signature of [seller's] Branch or District Manager," it was held that the offeror was not bound by the seller's beginning to manufacture the goods.[27] Although even preparation for performance may suffice to manifest the commitment required for acceptance, here the offeror had insisted — albeit with words put in the offeror's mouth by the offeree — on a signature of an officer. The offeror's control in this regard is, however, limited by the objective theory, under which the offeror's language may not have its intended effect if the offeree reasonably understands that the procedure prescribed by the offeror is not mandatory.[28] Even if an offeror that asks the offeree to "reply by return mail" intends to say that acceptance can be by no other means than return mail, this language may be interpreted to mean merely that acceptance, by whatever means, must arrive within such time as return mail would take.[29] To the extent that a provision is not advantageous to the offeror, it is not likely to be interpreted as a requirement. And there is authority that an offeror that has imposed such a requirement can later dispense with it.[30]

Effect of mutuality of obligation

As these examples suggest, it is usually the offeror that insists that it is not bound because the offeree has not complied with the requirements imposed by the offer. Under the principle of mutuality of obligation, however, it is open to the offeree to argue that it is not bound because of its own failure to comply with those requirements. Where, for example, an offeror had written to a city, "The signed acceptance of this proposal shall constitute a contract . . . ," it was held that the city council had not accepted merely by passing a resolution.[31] The offeree was not bound because what the offeror had invited was an acceptance

---

where [all] the signatures were affixed and absent any legal requirement for the signatures, an enforceable contract was formed between the parties").

[26]White v. Corlies & Tift, 46 N.Y. 467 (1871) (offer evidently delivered by hand).

[27]Venters v. Stewart, 261 S.W.2d 444 (Ky. 1953) (sale of storm doors and windows). *Accord:* Kuzmeskus v. Pickup Motor Co., 115 N.E.2d 46 (Mass. 1963). For more discussion of the "home office approval" clause, see the discussion of reservation of power to the maker in §3.10 *supra.*

[28]Allied Steel & Conveyors v. Ford Motor Co., 277 F.2d 907 (6th Cir. 1960) ("provision for execution and return of the acknowledgement copy . . . was not to set forth an exclusive method of acceptance but was merely to provide a simple and convenient method by which the assent . . . could be indicated").

[29]Tinn v. Hoffman & Co., 29 L.T.R. [N.S.] 271 (Ex. Ch. 1873) ("by return of post" means "you may reply . . . by any means not later than a letter . . . by return of post would reach us").

[30]Dickinson Resources v. Unocal Corp., 907 S.W.2d 453 (Tex. 1995) ("later writings reflect that [offeror] agreed to a modification of the terms of acceptance").

[31]Brophy v. City of Joliet, 144 N.E.2d 816 (Ill. App. 1957).

signed on the offeror's proposal. The party that inserts a "home office approval" clause on the form furnished to the other party desires just this kind of freedom from liability up to the time when the home office has done the invited act.[32] However, cases in which the offeree attempts to withdraw arise less often than those in which the offeror does so.

We now consider acceptance inferred from silence or exercise of dominion.

§3.14. Promise Inferred from Silence or Exercise of Dominion.

As a general rule, a promise will not be inferred from the offeree's mere inaction.[1] Thus an offeree's silence in the face of an offer to sell goods is not ordinarily an acceptance, because the offeror has no reason to believe from the offeree's silence that the offeree promises to buy.[2] The same is true if the offeror delivers the goods to the offeree, which retains them in silence. If there are additional circumstances, however, a promise may be inferred, resulting in a contract that is sometimes described as "implied-in-fact" as distinguished from "express."[3]

Silence not generally acceptance

If, for example, the offeree exercises dominion over the goods by acting inconsistently with the offeror's ownership, as by carrying them from the railroad station to the offeree's place of business, the offeree is taken to have accepted the offer and is bound to pay the price.[4] The same principle applies if dominion is exercised over real property.[5] It also applies if a creditor exercises dominion over a check that a debtor has offered in part or full payment.[6] The offeree's failure to notify the offeror of acceptance does not preclude the offeror from recovering, a result that is best explained on the ground that the offeror can waive the requirement of notice.[7]

Exercise of dominion is acceptance

It is possible that the offeree's exercise of dominion is a tortious interference with the offeror's property that gives the offeror a right to recover in conversion. The offeror need not, however, regard it as a tort and may ratify the wrongful

Exercise of dominion as tort

---

[32]See the discussion of reservation of power to the maker in §3.10 *supra*.

§3.14 [1]Haberl v. Bigelow, 855 P.2d 1368 (Colo. 1993) ("Typically, silence or inaction will be deemed acceptance of an offer only when the relationship . . . is such that an offeror is justified in expecting a reply or the offeree is under a duty to respond.").

[2]Marrero-Garcia v. Irizarry, 33 F.3d 117 (1st Cir. 1994) (residents who had refused to apply for water service and to post bond, had not by their silence accepted utility's offer of service, quoting this sentence).

[3]See the discussion of no formalities required in §3.10 *supra*, where the distinction is criticized as lacking legal consequences.

[4]Indiana Mfg. Co. v. Hayes, 26 A. 6 (Pa. 1893) (carload of refrigerators).

On implied-in-fact contracts for disclosure of ideas, *see* Reeves v. Alyeska Pipeline Serv. Co., 926 P.2d 1130 (Alaska 1996) (contract should not be implied when unsolicited idea is voluntarily received, though recipient has opportunity to prevent disclosure).

[5]Russell v. Texas Co., 238 F.2d 636 (9th Cir. 1956) (company used offeror's land for oil and gas operations).

[6]UCC 3-311, discussed in §4.23 *infra*.

[7]See the discussion of the offeror's control over the requirement in §3.15 *infra*. Restatement Second §56 reaches this result by excepting these cases from the general requirement of notice.

taking and recover instead in contract. As it is sometimes put, the offeror may "waive" the tort and recover in contract. The offeree, as tortfeasor, has no such choice.[8]

Liability in contract not restitution

Whether the exercise of dominion is tortious or not, the offeree's liability is in contract, according to the terms of the offer, and not merely for restitution. Under the Restatement Second formulation, however, liability will not be imposed if the terms are "manifestly unreasonable."[9] Statutes in a number of jurisdictions protect the recipient of unsolicited merchandise even if the recipient uses the merchandise.[10]

Rules for services

Analogous principles are applied to services. An offeree that takes the benefit of services offered is bound by the terms of the offer if the offeree had a reasonable opportunity to reject them.[11] In contrast to the situations just discussed, the offeree is expected not only to refrain from affirmative action that would appropriate the services to the offeror's use, but also to speak up in protest. Services, unlike property, cannot be returned, and the recipient of a nonreturnable benefit that silently watches another confer the benefit in apparent expectation of compensation is liable.[12] Although liability is for breach of contract rather than restitution, where services are concerned the contract liability will often be their reasonable value.

Rules severely tested

These traditional rules have been severely tested when offerees have been confronted with offers of goods or services under terms that the offeror may not have clearly and fully disclosed to the offeree. Such situations range from the conventional use of standard terms in fine print on the back of a form to more innovative situations, associated with the rise of mass market transactions, that have inspired to such colorful names as "shrink-wrap" and "click-wrap." They are discussed in the following chapter.[13]

Offeror cannot make silence acceptance

So fundamental is the tenet that mere silence is not acceptance that, even as the master of the offer, the offeror is powerless to alter the rule. The seller cannot turn the buyer's silence into acceptance by adding to the offer, "If I do

---

[8]The offeree's exercise of dominion might be tortious if, for example, the offeree takes goods shipped in a way that departs from the terms of the offer, as by taking them on credit when they are offered only for cash. In the ordinary case, in which the exercise of dominion is not tortious, the offeree can hold the offeror for any deficiency in the offeror's performance.

[9]Restatement Second §69(2).

[10]*See* N.Y. Gen. Bus. L. §396. *See also* 39 U.S.C. §3009 (making mailing of "unordered merchandise" and "dunning communications" for such merchandise "an unfair method of competition and an unfair trade practice" in violation of Federal Trade Commission Act). Even in the absence of legislation, the recipient is not expected to return unsolicited merchandise, and the length of time the recipient must keep it before throwing it away will depend on the circumstances.

[11]Collins v. Lewis, 149 A. 668 (Conn. 1930) (owner of cows took benefits of their care and feeding).

[12]Day v. Caton, 119 Mass. 513 (1876) (owner of land said nothing while neighbor built a wall that benefited both of them). For discussion of when a furnishing of services amounts to an offer, see the discussion of no formalities required in §3.10 *supra*.

[13]See §4.26 *infra*.

not hear from you in a week, I will take it that you have accepted my offer."[14] As it was neatly put by Karl Llewellyn, to give that effect to invited silence "in a systematics centering on overt manifestations is, one may suggest, almost lewd."[15] The same fate would befall an attempt by the offeror to make some usual and routine action or inaction of the buyer amount to acceptance. It will not avail the seller to add to the offer, for example: "If you go to work on Monday, I will take it that you have accepted my offer"; or, "If you do not go to work on Sunday, I will take it that you have accepted my offer."[16] By neither of these phrases can the offeror impose liability on the offeree that remains silent or continues in established ways.[17]

One effect of the rule that silence is not acceptance is that, unless the offer is sooner revoked, the offeree can speculate for a time by waiting for possible market changes without fear of being bound.[18] The offeree can benefit from the offer by deciding to accept it, but need not fear being bound by silently deferring that decision. Yet the principle of mutuality of obligation is not violated because the offeror has the power to revoke at any time before acceptance. Furthermore, if the subject matter of the contract invites speculation, the offer will lapse after a relatively short period.[19] If the offeror wishes additional protection, the offeror can, by express provision, shorten that period.

Possibility of speculation

There are, however, exceptional situations in which silence has been held to be acceptance. Although courts occasionally talk of a "duty to speak,"[20] a sounder rationale is that in these situations the offeror has reason to believe from the offeree's silence that the offeree assents. Each case turns on its own facts. Reliance by the offeror, although not of itself sufficient, is a significant factor. Sometimes the offeror relies by acting or by failing to act on the assumption that the offer has been accepted.[21] Sometimes the offeror relies because the very making of the offer ties the offeror's hands in such a way as to require the offeror

Exceptions where silence is acceptance

---

[14]J.C. Durick Ins. v. Andrus, 424 A.2d 249 (Vt. 1980) ("offeror cannot force the offeree to speak" by provision that insurance policy would be automatically accepted by insured's inaction).

[15]Llewellyn, Our Case-Law of Contract: Offer and Acceptance (pt. 2), 48 Yale L.J. 779, 801 n.35 (1939).

[16]*Cf.* J.H. Queal & Co. v. Peterson, 116 N.W. 593 (Iowa 1908) ("the mere fact of forbearance [to pursue a debt] is not sufficient evidence from which a promise to forbear may be presumed"). We are here concerned only with offers inviting promises. For an analogous problem arising out of offers inviting performance, see the discussion of the general rules for acceptance by performance in §3.13 *infra.*

[17]Central Ill. Pub. Serv. Co. v. Atlas Minerals, 146 F.3d 448 (7th Cir. 1998) (quoting this sentence of this treatise).

[18]See the discussion of the risk of speculation in §3.2 *supra.*

[19]See the discussion of the effect of speculative subject matter in §3.19 *infra.*

[20]Laredo Natl. Bank v. Gordon, 61 F.2d 906 (5th Cir. 1932) (where "offeree is under a duty to reply, the latter's silence will be regarded as an acceptance").

[21]Campione v. Adamar of N.J., 643 A.2d 42 (N.J. Super. 1993) (though silence is not ordinarily acceptance, when casino allowed patron to pursue hand with his $350 bet after casino had lowered the table limit to $100, it accepted his offer).

to forgo other opportunities to make the bargain sought.[22] Although courts have given weight to reliance, they have not confined recovery to the offeror's reliance interest, nor have they denied recovery where the only interest to be protected was the expectation interest. Other factors that may lead a court to conclude that silence is acceptance include prior dealings making it reasonable for the offeree to notify the offeror if the offeree does not intend to accept,[23] solicitation of the offer by a representative of the offeree,[24] and failure by the offeree to return property or something symbolic of agreement.[25] Subsequent conduct of the parties may also serve to confirm that there was acceptance.[26] It may be easier to show acceptance by silence in the case of a minor modification of an existing contract.[27]

Exceptional cases   In one leading case, a seller's salesperson took an order for 43,916 pounds of shortening on August 23 for prompt shipment "subject to acceptance by seller's authorized agent at point of shipment." The seller delayed until September 4, while the price of shortening rose from 7 and one-half to 9 cents a pound, and then refused to ship. The court held that it was for the jury to decide whether the delay, "in view of the past history of such transactions between the parties, including the booking, constituted an implied acceptance." The seller's salesperson had not only solicited the order, but had previously taken several orders from the buyer, "which orders in every case had been accepted and shipped not later than one week from the time they were given."[28] In another leading case a seller was allowed to recover the price of 2,350 eel skins that had been retained in silence by the buyer, a manufacturer of whips. Holmes wrote:

> The plaintiff was not a stranger to the defendant, even if there was no contract between them. He had sent eel skins in the same way four or five times before,

[22] This is particularly true of applications for insurance where the applicant has sent money with the application. *See* Moore v. Palmetto State Life Ins. Co., 73 S.E.2d 688 (S.C. 1952) (silent retention of application with 20-cent deposit by applicant who "would naturally not apply for the same insurance in some other company"). It may also apply to some cases in which sellers have sent goods to prospective buyers. *See* Hobbs v. Massasoit Whip Co., 33 N.E. 495 (Mass. 1893) (discussed *infra*).

[23] Hobbs v. Massasoit Whip Co., *supra* note 22; Ammons v. Wilson & Co., 170 So. 227 (Miss. 1936) (discussed *infra*). *See also* the discussion of how Subsection (2) incorporates terms by silence in §3.21 *infra*.

[24] Ammons v. Wilson & Co., *supra* note 23.

[25] Hobbs v. Massasoit Whip Co., *supra* note 22; Bohn Mfg. Co. v. Sawyer, 48 N.E. 620 (Mass. 1897) (silent retention of insurance policies). As to the possibility of an account stated, see the discussion of that subject in §4.24 *infra*.

[26] Bohn Mfg. Co. v. Sawyer, *supra* note 25 (offeree wrote letters about cancellation and substitution of insurance policies).

[27] Eimco Div. v. United Pac. Ins. Co., 710 P.2d 672 (Idaho App. 1985) ("general contractor had reason to understand that its assent" to subcontractor's proposed modification "would be manifested by silence and inaction"). As to the possibility of waiver, see the discussion of the reason for that concept in §8.5 *infra*.

[28] Ammons v. Wilson & Co., *supra* note 23.

and they had been accepted and paid for . . . . [S]ending them [imposed] on the defendant a duty to act about them; and silence on its part, coupled with a retention of the skins for an unreasonable time, might be found by the jury to warrant the plaintiff in assuming that they were accepted . . . .[29]

When must the offeree give the offeror notice of acceptance?

§3.15.   Notice of Acceptance.   If an offer invites acceptance by performance rather than a promise, the offeree must ordinarily notify the offeror that the offer has been accepted if the offeree has reason to believe that the offeror will not learn of the acceptance without notice.[1] The rule finds its most significant application in the guaranty cases. An offer to become a guarantor usually invites acceptance by the offeree's performance — lending money, delivering goods, or performing services on credit. If the offer is accepted, the offeror will want to take account of the resulting liability in planning for the future. If the offeree has reason to know that the offeror is uncertain whether the offer will be accepted and that the offeror is not likely to learn of acceptance without notice, notice is required.[2] In ordinary circumstances, however, notice to the guarantor is not necessary, a result that is encouraged by improved communications.[3]

> **Offer invites acceptance by performance**

Sometimes an offer that invites performance expressly dispenses with notice, or it is apparent from the circumstances that acceptance of the offer does not require notice. In *Carlill v. Carbolic Smoke Ball Co.*, a classroom favorite, a company had offered a "£100 reward" to anyone who caught the flu after using its smoke ball. When a consumer sued on this promise, the company defended on the ground that the consumer had not notified it of her acceptance. The court rejected this defense, reasoning that the company could not have wanted notices from all those who accepted its offer by using the smoke ball. "It follows from the nature of the thing that the performance . . . is sufficient acceptance without the notification of it, and a person who makes an offer in an advertisement of that kind makes an offer which must be read by the light of that common sense reflection."[4]

> **Example of *Carbolic Smoke Ball* case**

---

[29] Hobbs v. Massasoit Whip Co., *supra* note 22, at 495.

§3.15   [1] Restatement Second §54.

[2] In Bishop v. Eaton, 37 N.E. 665 (Mass. 1894), the court said, "Ordinarily, there is no occasion to notify the offeror of the acceptance . . . , and the promisor knows that he is bound when he sees that action has been taken on the faith of his offer. But if the act is of such a kind that knowledge of it will not quickly come to the promisor, the promisee is bound to give him notice of his acceptance within a reasonable time after doing that which constitutes the acceptance."

[3] Ross v. Leberman, 148 A. 858 (Pa. 1930) (involving "an understanding to underwrite one-third of the advances made for the corporation, in which [the guarantor] was interested").

[4] [1893] Q.B. 256 (C.A. 1892). For an entertaining illustrated account of the background of this case, *see* Simpson, Quackery and Contract Law: The Case of the Carbolic Smoke Ball, 14 J. Legal Stud. 345 (1985).

Offer invites acceptance by a promise

Where the offer invites acceptance by a promise rather than by performance, it is commonly said that the offeree must take appropriate steps to let the offeror know of acceptance.[5] If the promise is in words, it is often understood that communication of those words to the offeror is a necessary part of acceptance itself, so that there is no occasion for a further requirement of notice. If the promise is implied from conduct other than words, such as preparing for or beginning performance, the offeree is usually expected to give notice of acceptance or of the conduct amounting to acceptance if it would not otherwise come promptly to the offeror's attention. Such a requirement of notice will be read into the offer in the absence of any provision to the contrary.[6] The Code states broadly that notice of acceptance must be given if "the beginning of a requested performance is a reasonable mode of acceptance."[7] If, for example, a seller accepts a buyer's order of goods for prompt shipment by shipping the goods, it is reasonable to expect the seller to notify the buyer since the buyer will want to know whether its needs have been met.

Exceptions to general requirement

However, conduct other than words may give notice of acceptance by a promise, and in some instances performance or even preparation for performance may suffice. If, for example, the seller has reason to expect that the goods shipped will reach the buyer as quickly as would a separate notice, such a notice ought to be superfluous, even under the Code.[8] Furthermore, notice ought to be unnecessary if, by some other means, the offeror chances to learn of the acceptance as promptly as if notice had been given.[9]

Offeror's control over requirement

Where the offer invites acceptance by a promise, just as where it invites acceptance by performance, the offeror can impose more stringent requirements of notice. The offeror may also dispense with any requirement of notice, as sometimes happens when an offer is made on a form furnished by the offeree. For example, a seller's form provided that, after signature by the buyer, it "becomes a contract when . . . approved by an executive officer" of the seller at its home office. It was held that no notice of approval had to be sent to the

---

[5] *See* Restatement Second §56 ("it is essential to an acceptance by promise either that the offeree exercise reasonable diligence to notify the offeror of acceptance or that the offeror receive the acceptance seasonably"). The requirement of notice of acceptance is often stated in a more insistent form than where the offer seeks acceptance by performance. Compare Restatement Second §54.

[6] Petersen v. Thompson, 506 P.2d 697 (Or. 1973) (buyer of tractor who was to pick it up in the woods failed to notify seller for two to four weeks).

[7] UCC 2-206(2). The word *beginning* presumably covers situations like that in which a promise to ship conforming goods is implied by the seller's shipment of nonconforming goods. See §3.12 *supra*.

[8] Restatement Second §62 cmt. *b* states broadly that notice is unnecessary in "such standard cases as the shipment of goods in response to an order [because] the acceptance will come to the offeror's attention in normal course." But UCC 2-504(c) generally requires notice of shipment, although failure to give notice is ground for rejection of the goods only if loss or damage ensues.

[9] *See* Restatement Second §§54(2)(b), 56.

buyer.[10] Furthermore, since the requirement of notice is for the benefit of the offeror, it can be waived by the offeror, even though this may do some violence to the principle of mutuality of obligation.[11]

Whether the offer invites acceptance by a promise or by performance, the prevailing view is that if notice is required, it is enough if the offeree exercises reasonable care to let the offeror know of the acceptance, even if the offeror never actually learns of it.[12] The special problems that arise in connection with communications by mail will be discussed later.[13]

Reasonable care enough

If the offeree fails to give a required notice, the offeror need not show that the failure caused any loss. Regardless of loss, the offeror is not bound. There are two possible explanations for this. One is that notice is part of acceptance itself. According to this first explanation, there is no contract until the offeree gives notice. The other explanation is that notice is a condition of the continued effectiveness of the contract. According to this second explanation, there is a contract even before notice, but the offeror's duty under that contract is discharged if notice is not given within a reasonable time. This explanation has the advantage of terminating the offeror's power of revocation and protecting the offeree, which may rely on the offer after making a promise but before giving notice.[14] An interpretation of the offer to require notice as an essential part of acceptance is therefore more likely if the promise is to be manifested by words or other symbolic conduct that, as distinguished from preparing or beginning to perform, does not of itself involve reliance.[15] In any event, the question is likely to assume practical importance only if the offeror attempts to

Effect of failure to notify

---

[10] International Filter Co. v. Conroe Gin, Ice & Light Co., 277 S.W. 631 (Tex. Comm. App. 1925) (alternative holding). *See* C. Ashley, Law of Contracts 38 (1911) ("If one sends to a man on the opposite side of the river a letter containing a proposal calling for a counter promise, and says, 'Signify your acceptance by lighting a fire,' and the offeree does so in such a manner as unequivocally to indicate an intention to accept, surely a contract arises. This would be so even though a fog prevents the fire from being seen.").

[11] UCC 2-206(2) says that the offeror "*may* treat the offer as having lapsed."

[12] *See* UCC 1-202(d) ("taking such steps as may be reasonably required to inform the other person in ordinary course, whether or not the other person actually comes to know it"); Restatement Second §54(2)(a) ("exercises reasonable diligence to notify the offeror of acceptance").

[13] See §3.22 *infra*.

[14] This appears to be the rationale behind UCC 2-206(2), which allows the offeror to "treat the offer as having lapsed before acceptance." It might be more direct to say, as Restatement Second §54 does, that "the contractual duty of the offeror is discharged," but the thought appears to be the same. UCC 2-206 cmt. 3, however, appears to take a conflicting position. "The beginning of performance . . . can be effective as acceptance so as to bind the offeror only if followed within a reasonable time by notice to the offeror . . . . For the protection of both parties it is essential that notice follow in due course to constitute acceptance." The Comments should yield to the text, which is more authoritative and which states the preferable view.

[15] Kendel v. Pontious, 261 So. 2d 167 (Fla. 1972) (where prospective purchaser of real estate mailed offer to vendors, vendors had to "do more than indicate their acceptance . . . by signing"; they had to "set in motion some means by which knowledge of that acceptance would come to the purchasers").

revoke after the offeree has made a promise but before the offeree has given notice.[16]

We turn now from how the offeree's power of acceptance can be exercised to how that power can be terminated.

D.   TERMINATION OF THE POWER OF ACCEPTANCE

Four ways to terminate

§3.16.   Ways of Termination. After the offeror has conferred a power of acceptance on the offeree by making an offer, that power can be terminated in any of the following ways: (1) revocation of the offer by the offeror, (2) death or incapacity of the offeror, (3) lapse of the offer, or (4) rejection of the offer by the offeree. The next four sections analyze these four ways of termination in order.[1]

Renewal of power of acceptance

If the power of acceptance has been terminated because of revocation, lapse, or rejection, it may later be revived by the offeror. If, for example, an offeree rejects an offer to sell on the ground that the price is too high, the offeree's power of acceptance is terminated, but the offeror may revive it by replying, "Cannot reduce price."[2]

First we consider the termination of the power of acceptance by the offeror's revocation of the offer.

Withdrawal distinguished

§3.17.   Revocation of the Offer. Revocation of an offer must be distinguished from withdrawal. An offer can be withdrawn if notice of withdrawal reaches the offeree no later than the offer does.[1] This is a corollary of the principle that an offer is not effective until it has been communicated to the offeree.[2] But revocation of an offer after it has become effective is a different matter.

Rule of revocability

It is a fundamental tenet of the common law that an offer is generally freely revocable and can be countermanded by the offeror at any time before it has been accepted by the offeree. If the offer is divisible, as in the case of a standing

---

[16] Even under the first view, the offeree could be protected in this case if the offer were regarded as irrevocable during the period allowed for notice.

§3.16 [1] Though cases are rare, it is said that the power of acceptance can also be terminated by the death of a person or the destruction of a thing essential to performance or by supervening legal prohibition, depending on the terms of the offer and other circumstances. *See* Restatement Second §36 cmt. *c. See also* the discussions of supervening death or disability, supervening destruction, and supervening illegality in §9.5 *infra.*

[2] Livingstone v. Evans, [1925] 4 D.L.R. 769 (Alberta). *See* Restatement Second §23 illus. 6.

§3.17 [1] Miller v. United States, 62 F. Supp. 327 (Ct. Cl. 1945) (oral withdrawal before telegram containing offer arrived). It is useful to speak of *withdrawal* of an offer before it has become effective and of *revocation* of an offer after it has become effective. The distinction is important with respect to irrevocable offers. See the discussion of the effects of irrevocability in §3.23 *infra.*

[2] See the discussion of the point that the offer must reach the offeree in §3.10 *supra.*

offer that invites a series of acceptances, it is revocable as to any part not accepted. That the rule is not inevitable can be seen from the law of some civil law countries, including Germany, where an offer is irrevocable for a reasonable time, unless the offeror expresses a different intention.[3] However, the common law view that an offer is freely revocable is accepted throughout the United States, with rare exceptions.[4] The most important exception applies to offers in the form of bids to governmental entities, which are often irrevocable under statute or case law.[5] Both the Vienna Convention and the UNIDROIT Principles follow the common law view of free revocability.[6]

It is sometimes erroneously supposed that this rule of free revocability is a corollary of the doctrine of consideration. However, the revocability of offers unsupported by consideration does not necessarily follow from the revocability of ordinary promises unsupported by consideration. The rule of revocability is more properly regarded as a consequence of the aversion to allowing one party to speculate at the expense of the other. For if the offeror were not free to revoke the offer, the offeror would be bound though the offeree would not be bound, and this would subject the offeror to the risk that the offeree might speculate in a fluctuating market.[7] The rule of revocability was once also supported by the now-discredited notion, under the subjective theory of assent, that a contract required a "meeting of the minds."[8]

Reasons for rule

It is not uncommon for an offeror to transfer money or other property to the offeree as a "deposit," recoverable by the offeror if the offer is not accepted. Such a deposit does not limit the offeror's power of revocation, and ordinarily the offeror may recover the deposit on revoking the offer.[9] Sometimes, however, the parties agree that the property is to be retained by the offeree on revocation of the offer, an agreement that may be enforceable if it does not run afoul of the prohibition of penalties.[10] Nevertheless, the offer is still revocable even though the deposit be forfeited. Bidders on construction projects are usually required to post bid bonds, the sum to be forfeited by the lowest bidder should that bidder renege, and analogous rules apply to these. Thus the surety

Effect of deposit

---

[3] Formation of Contracts: A Study of the Common Core of Legal Systems 780-83 (R. Schlesinger ed. 1968).

[4] Restatement Second §42.

[5] *See* W. Keyes, Government Contracts §14.18 (2d ed 1996). For the California version of UCC 2-205, containing a provision, not limited to government contracts, making merchants' offers to supply goods to contractors irrevocable for ten days after the award of the prime contract, *see* Cal. Com. Code §2205(b). *See also* the Code provision on auctions without reserve treated in the discussion of the entertainment of bids in §3.10 *supra*.

[6] CISG 16(1); UNIDROIT Principles 2.4(1). But see the discussion of the difficulty of protecting the offeree in §3.23 *infra*.

[7] See the discussion of the risk of speculation in §3.2 *supra*.

[8] See the discussion of the subjective theory in §3.6 *supra*.

[9] *See* Restatement Second §44.

[10] See §12.18 *infra*.

on the bond is liable if the bidder attempts to revoke an irrevocable bid, unless of course the sum is a penalty.[11] But posting a bid bond cannot turn a revocable bid into an irrevocable one and the surety on the bond will not be liable if the bid is revocable.[12]

What is a revocation

What sort of manifestation of the offeror's intention suffices as a revocation of the offer? Just as the offeror need not say "offer" to offer, so too the offeror need not say "revoke" to revoke. It is enough that the offeror indicate an intention not to make the proposed contract. A subsequent offer, inconsistent with the original offer, may suffice to revoke the original offer.[13] Action without words may suffice if the action is inconsistent with an intention to contract. Equivocation by the offeror may raise a difficult question. In one case the offeree telephoned the offeror to say that it was ready to go through with a proposed real estate deal and would like to discuss it, to which the offeror replied, "Well, I don't know if we are ready. We have not decided, we might not want to go through with it." The court held that this language was sufficient to revoke the offer.[14] Judicial reluctance to force an agreement on parties whose assent is not clearly shown produces a tendency to resolve doubtful cases in favor of finding revocations, a tendency analogous to the tendency to resolve doubtful cases against finding offers.[15]

Effective on receipt

The revocation is not effective, however, until it is received by the offeree. In keeping with the objective theory, an uncommunicated change of mind does not suffice.[16] According to Holmes, "It would be monstrous to allow an inconsistent act of the offeror, not known or brought to the notice of the offeree, to affect the making of the contract."[17] A person who received the offer on behalf of the offeree is usually regarded as having the authority to receive a revocation of that offer.[18] The difficulties that arise out of attempts at revocation when the negotiations are by correspondence will be discussed in a later section.[19] Two other problems, however, remain.

[11] Daddario v. Town of Milford, 5 N.E.2d 23 (Mass. 1936) (where bid for construction of sewage treatment works was considered as an option, certified check was forfeited as liquidated damages).

[12] R.J. Taggert, Inc. v. Douglas County, 572 P.2d 1050 (Or. App. 1977) (bid bond not forfeited where bid was revocable).

[13] Norca Corp. v. Tokheim Corp., 643 N.Y.S.2d 139 (App. Div. 1996) (later offer with different price term revoked original offer before it was to expire by its terms).

[14] Hoover Motor Express Co. v. Clements Paper Co., 241 S.W.2d 851 (Tenn. 1951).

[15] See the discussion of reluctance to find an offer in §3.10 *supra*.

[16] No discussion of revocation would be complete without a reference to Cooke v. Oxley, 100 Eng. Rep. 785 (K.B. 1790), a confusing relic of the subjective era. It became the *bête noire* of the objectivists, who regarded it as standing for the proposition that an offeror of goods could prevent acceptance by the offeree by a mere change of mind, as by an uncommunicated sale of the goods to another.

[17] Brauer v. Shaw, 46 N.E. 617, 618 (Mass. 1897).

[18] Night Commander Lighting Co. v. Brown, 181 N.W. 979 (Mich. 1921) (revocation effective when given to same salesperson that took the order).

[19] See the discussion of the offeror's power to revoke in §3.22 *infra*.

One is that of indirect communication of revocation, a problem associated with *Dickinson v. Dodds*,[20] an English case that has achieved a notoriety somewhat exceeding its practical importance. It held that a revocation did not have to be communicated directly by the offeror to the offeree. It was enough that the offeree received reliable information to the effect that the offeror had taken definite action inconsistent with an intention to make the contract. The offer was one to sell land, and the offeree learned that the offeror had sold or contracted to sell the land to another person.[21] The first Restatement dignified the case with a separate section limiting the rule to these facts.[22] The Restatement Second has cast the rule in more general terms, extending it to any case in which "the offeror takes definite action inconsistent with an intention to enter into the proposed contract."[23]

Indirect revocation

The other remaining problem involves the revocation of a general offer, such as one made by a newspaper advertisement, a poster, or other general notification to the public. If the offeror can reasonably notify everyone who might accept the offer, revocation is not effective as to a particular offeree unless it has been communicated to that offeree.[24] Ordinarily, however, the maker of a general offer cannot do this. Even if the revocation receives publicity equal to that of the offer, it may not reach everyone. If that is so, giving equal publicity has been held to be enough, even as to an offeree that read the offer and missed the revocation.[25] Giving equal publicity ordinarily takes time, but even before the revocation has received equal notoriety, it is too late for an offeree that has seen the revocation to accept.

Revocation of general offer

What is the effect on the power of acceptance of the offeror's death or incapacity?

§3.18. Offeror's Death or Incapacity. It is generally accepted that the offeree's power of acceptance is terminated if the offeror dies before the offer

Effect of death or incapacity

---

[20] 2 Ch. Div. 463 (1876).

[21] The reporter stated that the offeree learned that the offeror "had been offering or agreeing to sell the property" to another, but the judges stated that the offeree learned that the offeror "was selling or had sold" or that the property had "been sold."

[22] Restatement §42 (limiting the rule to the case where "an offer is for the sale of an interest in land or in other things" and the offeror "sells or contracts to sell the interest to another person"). Corbin explained that the rule was so limited because some of Williston's advisers, not including Corbin, believed that the rule was not "fundamentally sound." Corbin, The Restatement of the Common Law by the American Law Institute, 15 Iowa L. Rev. 19, 36 (1929).

[23] Restatement Second §43.

[24] Long v. Chronicle Publishing Co., 228 P. 873 (Cal. App. 1924) (contestants who had participated in a contest "were not so numerous" but that, if changes were made in the rules, "the most natural thing to have been anticipated by each of the parties to the contract would have been an actual notification").

[25] Shuey v. United States, 92 U.S. 73 (1875) (too late to accept offer of reward for apprehension of alleged accomplice of John Wilkes Booth five months after notice of revocation was published).

has been accepted, regardless of whether the offeree has notice of the death.[1] Corbin, addressing this rule, denied

> any compelling necessity for [the rule's] existence. It may be said that you cannot contract with a dead man; but neither can you force a dead man to pay his debts contracted before his death. Yet the law has no difficulty, in the latter case, in creating legal relations with the dead man's personal representative, and there would be no greater difficulty in declaring the power of acceptance to survive as against the offeror's representative . . . .[2]

The offeror's supervening incapacity, as by adjudication or the appointment of a guardian, has the same effect as the offeror's death.

History of the rule   To the extent that the rule affects an offeree that has no reason to know of the offeror's death or incapacity, it is a glaring exception to the objective theory of assent. Under the original draft of the first Restatement, as written by Williston and his advisers, the unknown death of the offeror did not revoke the offer. But the Council of the American Law Institute changed the statement of the rule so that it does. Williston conceded, concluding that "though the amount of actual authority is not impressive, there is a very general opinion among lawyers that death, even though unknown, does revoke an offer and does revoke an agency." He noted that it was vital that the Restatement rule for contracts coincide with that for agency.[3] The Restatement Second preserves the rule, observing that it "seems to be a relic of the obsolete view that a contract requires a 'meeting of the minds,' and it is out of harmony with the modern doctrine that a manifestation of assent is effective without regard to actual mental assent."[4]

Authority for the rule   The leading case in support of the Restatement rule is well over a century old. It involved a standing offer to guaranty the prompt payment for merchandise that the offeree, a department store, might sell to one of its customers. For several months after the offeror's death the store sold merchandise to the customer. When the customer did not pay, the store sued the offeror's estate, claiming that each sale was an acceptance of an offer for a series of "unilateral" contracts. Even though the store had relied on the offer in ignorance of the offeror's death, the estate won on the theory that the store's power of acceptance was terminated when the offeror died. "It is no hardship to require traders, whose business it is to deal in goods, to exercise diligence so far as to ascertain whether a person upon whose credit they are selling is living."[5] The

---

§3.18   [1] As to the effect of the death or supervening incapacity of the offeree, see the discussion of the point that only the offeree can accept in §3.11 *supra*. For the rule in the case of a firm or irrevocable offer, see the discussion of the effects of irrevocability in §3.23 *infra*.

[2] Corbin, Offer and Acceptance, and Some of the Resulting Legal Relations, 26 Yale L.J. 169, 198 (1917).

[3] Am. L. Inst. Proc. 198 (1925).

[4] Restatement Second §48 cmt. *a*.

[5] Jordan v. Dobbins, 122 Mass. 168 (1877), followed in Beall v. Beall, 434 A.2d 1015 (Md. 1981) (death of husband terminated offer made by couple as tenants by entirety).

practical impact of the rule, however, is less than it was then, now that the typical offeror is a deathless corporate entity.

We next examine termination by lapse.

§3.19.   **Lapse of the Offer.** After some period of time an offer lapses, and the power to accept it thereby expires, if it has not already been terminated in some other way. As the master of the offer, the offeror may limit the period during which the offer is effective simply by so providing. Where an offer "to anyone who calls this show" was made during a nighttime television talk show, it was held that the offeror "limited his offer in time to remain only unlil the conclusion of the live . . . broadcast."[1] A more common example is the somewhat vague provision, "Reply by return mail."[2] The offeror may be more precise by saying, for example, "Reply within ten days."[3] However, if contained in a letter, even such a stipulation is ambiguous, both as to when the period begins to run (date of letter or time of its receipt) and as to when it ends (time of dispatch of acceptance or time of its receipt). The process of interpretation then determines whether the legal effect is to subject the offeror to uncertainty for ten days (date of letter to time of receipt of acceptance), to give the offeree ten days to decide (time of receipt of letter to time of dispatch of acceptance), or to do neither of these (e.g., date of letter to time of dispatch of acceptance).[4] The offeror can avoid such controversies by stating, for example, that the offer expires "if I have not heard from you within ten days of the date of this letter."

If the offer fails to specify a period, it lapses after a "reasonable" time.[5] What time is reasonable depends on the circumstances and involves balancing the offeree's interest in having time to make an informed decision against the offeror's interest in avoiding the risks of change during that time.[6] It may be affected by a course of dealing between the parties or by usage.[7]

Provision for lapse

Lapse after reasonable time

---

§3.19   [1]Newman v. Schiff, 778 F.2d 460, 466 (8th Cir. 1985).

[2]*See* Maclay v. Harvey, 90 Ill. 525 (1876) (where offeror's letter, saying "answer by return mail," was received on March 22, offeror was "entitled to expect a reply mailed . . . at the farthest, on the morning of the 24th"). *See also* the discussion of Restatement Second §41(3) *infra*.

[3]McKibben v. Mohawk Oil Co., 667 P.2d 1223 (Alaska 1983) ("please contact this office within twenty days of the date of this letter").

[4]Caldwell v. Cline, 156 S.E. 55 (W. Va. 1930) (acceptance was timely under offer that said "will give you eight days" to accept or reject, where letter dated January 29 containing offer arrived on February 2 and telegram of acceptance sent on February 8 arrived on February 9 because eight days did not begin to run until letter arrived).

[5]Starkweather v. Gleason, 109 N.E. 635 (Mass. 1915) (offer to buy stock could no longer be accepted five months after it was made, even though it said it could be accepted at "any time").

[6]Orlowski v. Moore, 181 A.2d 692 (Pa. Super. 1962) (shorter time suggested by offerors' knowledge of difficulty that offeree would have in obtaining money to avail himself of offer). *Cf.* Restatement Second §23 illus. 6.

[7]Piland Corp. v. REA Constr. Co., 672 F. Supp. 244 (E.D. Va. 1987) ("custom in the trade requires the successful bidder" to notify selected subcontractor "within a period of thirty days").

Effect of speculative subject matter

One important circumstance is the subject matter of the contract. If it is speculative in nature, it will not be supposed that the offeror intended to give the offeree an extended period to decide whether to accept. Thus, if the contract is one for the sale of something that undergoes rapid fluctuations in price, as is often the case for shares of stock or commodities, the reasonable time will be relatively short.[8] If, however, the contract is one for the sale of something that does not undergo rapid fluctuations in price, as is often the case for land, the reasonable time will be relatively long.[9]

Effect of means of transmission

Another important circumstance is the means by which the offer is transmitted. As a general rule, an offer made orally is understood to lapse when the conversation terminates. Thus, when an employee offered to resign during a conference with his employer, but she did not accept the offer and continued the conference, it was held that she could not accept his offer a few days later. "Ordinarily, an offer made by one to another in a face to face conversation is deemed to continue only to the close of their conversation, and cannot be accepted thereafter."[10] A similar understanding presumably applies to telephone conversations, but in the case of any conversation, the circumstances, including what is said by the parties, may and often do show that an oral offer survived the conversation.[11] A sense of urgency may be suggested if the offer is transmitted by expeditious means. A delay of a day in accepting a telegraphic offer of linseed oil, during a period when the market was unsettled and subject to sudden fluctuations, was held to be too long. The court thought it "clear that the intention of the plaintiff in making the offer by telegraph, to sell an article which fluctuates so much in price, must have been upon the understanding that the acceptance, if at all, should be immediate, and as soon after the receipt of the offer as would give a fair opportunity for consideration."[12] If the offer

---

[8] In Minnesota Linseed Oil Co. v. Collier White Lead Co., 17 F. Cas. 447 (D. Minn. 1876), the court said, "The delay here was too long, and manifestly unjust to the [offeror], for it afforded the [offeree] an opportunity to take advantage of a change in the market, and accept or refuse the offer as would best subserve its interests."

Restatement Second §41 cmt. *f* suggests that, "If the offeree makes use for speculative purposes of time allowed for communication, there may be a lack of good faith and an acceptance may not be timely even though it arrives within the time contemplated by the offeror." Illustration 8 gives an example of an offeree who uses the time saved by a telegram instead of a letter to speculate.

[9] In Kempner v. Cohn, 1 S.W. 869 (Ark. 1886), a letter containing an offer to sell land reached the offeree on February 2. The acceptance was mailed on February 7 and arrived on February 9. In holding that five days was not an unreasonable time to wait before deciding to accept, the court said: "The subject of negotiations was real estate, which requires more deliberation than if it had been a transaction in cotton or other article of merchandise. It is also less subject to sudden and violent fluctuations in price."

[10] Akers v. J.B. Sedberry, 286 S.W.2d 617, 621 (Tenn. App. 1955).

[11] Caldwell v. E.F. Spears & Sons, 216 S.W. 83 (Ky. 1919) (offer did not lapse before next day where in face-to-face conversation offeree said he wanted to talk with others and "will let you know").

[12] Minnesota Linseed Oil Co. v. Collier White Lead Co., *supra* note 8, at 449.

is by mail, the Restatement Second states that it "is seasonably accepted if an acceptance is mailed at any time before midnight on the day on which the offer is received," but the commentary cautiously adds that "in the absence of a significant speculative element in the situation, a considerably longer time may be reasonable."[13]

If the offer is an advertisement, the reasonable time may be very long. Where a reward was offered for information leading to the conviction of the crime of burning a specified building, it was held that a delay of up to three years, the statute of limitations for the offense, would not be fatal. Here the reward was not "wholly prospective" but was "for the discovery and punishment of crimes already committed . . . . So long as the statute of limitations continued to run against the offender, so long would this offer of a reward continue good."[14] The court distinguished a case in which newspaper advertisements were run for a week, advertising a reward for the apprehension and conviction of anyone setting fire to any building in Boston, and recovery was denied to a claimant who caught and helped to convict an incendiary who caused a fire three years and eight months later. In that case the court reasoned:

Lapse of general offer

> In that length of time, the exigency under which it was made having passed, it must be presumed to have been forgotten by most of the officers and citizens of the community, and cannot be presumed to have been before the public as an actuating motive to vigilance and exertion on this subject; nor could it justly and reasonably have been so understood by the plaintiffs.[15]

Delay of an offer in transit does not extend the time during which the offeree can accept if the offeree knows or has reason to know, as from the postmark or the date, of the delay. But if the delay is due to the fault of the offeror or the means of transmission adopted by the offeror, and the offeree neither knows nor has reason to know of it, the time within which the offeree can accept is extended by the delay.[16]

Effect of delay of offer

An acceptance that is not made until after the offer has lapsed may be treated by the original offeror as a counteroffer and may be accepted. There is no more reason here than in any other case to treat the offeror's mere silence as acceptance of that counteroffer. Nor can the offeror "waive" the delay by simply choosing to disregard it.[17] It has been suggested, however, that the offeror's failure to object and subsequent preparations for performance "may

Acceptance after lapse

---

[13] Restatement Second §41(3) & cmt. *e*.

[14] In re Kelly, 39 Conn. 159, 163 (1872).

[15] Loring v. City of Boston, 48 Mass. (7 Met.) 409, 414 (1844).

[16] Hapka v. Agribank, 555 N.W.2d 534 (Minn. App. 1996) ("delay in the communication of an offer does not extend the time period within which a contract can be accepted if the offeree knows or has reason to know of the delay"). *See* Restatement Second §49.

[17] Childs v. Adams, 909 S.W.2d 641 (Ark. 1995) (late acceptance "constitutes a counteroffer that must in turn be accepted to form a contract").

be evidence that acceptance was made within a reasonable time" if the offeror has not specified a period for acceptance.[18]

We next examine termination of the power of acceptance by rejection by the offeree.

Reason why rejection terminates

[handwritten margin note: don't have to worry about offeree rejecting & coming back later to accept]

§3.20.   Rejection by the Offeree. Rejection by the offeree terminates the power of acceptance.[1] If a seller offers to deliver goods to a buyer for $10,000, and the buyer replies, "I don't want your goods," the buyer's power of acceptance is terminated — the buyer cannot later accept. (If the buyer tried to, the purported acceptance might itself be an offer to the seller.) The rationale is that the offeror may rely on the rejection, by action (such as selling the goods elsewhere) or by inaction (such as failing to prepare to deliver them) or by merely failing to revoke the offer. The possibility of reliance is enough, and no actual reliance is required. The reasoning parallels that in support of holding an offeree that accepts by giving a promise, though the offeror's reliance in response to a rejection is not likely to be as difficult to prove as the offeror's reliance in response to an acceptance since reliance in response to a rejection is likely to be positive, consisting of exploring other opportunities, rather than negative.[2] Rejection has this effect even though the offerer has fixed a longer time after which the offer lapses. A manifestation of intention by the offeree is a rejection if it gives the offeror reason to believe that it is the offeree's intention not to accept the offer.[3]

Effect of counteroffer

This is usually the effect of a counteroffer, an offer "relating to the same matter as the original offer and proposing a substituted bargain differing from that proposed by the original offer."[4] The result is not inevitable, and on rare occasions an offeror may invite counteroffers and indicate that they will not be regarded as rejections.[5] But it is ordinarily reasonable for the offeror to believe that the offeree intends to take only one proposal under consideration at a time and therefore to believe that an offeree that makes a counteroffer does

---

The Vienna Convention and the UNIDROIT Principles state a different rule, under which a late acceptance is effective as an acceptance if the offeror so informs the offeree without undue delay. CISG 21(1); UNIDROIT Principles 2.9(1).

[18] Restatement Second §70 cmt. *b.*

§3.20   [1] Normile v. Miller, 326 S.E.2d 11 (N.C. 1985) ("original offer was rejected and ceased to exist"). If there is more than one offeree, rejection by one does not affect the power of another offeree to accept. As for the possibility that the offeror may renew the offer after its rejection, see the discussion of renewal of the power of acceptance in §3.16 *supra.* Restatement Second §38(1) adds that the rule is subject to contrary statement by the offeror, a qualification that is of little practical importance.

[2] See the discussion of the rationale for enforcing exchanges of promises in §2.3 *supra. See also* E. Farnsworth, Changing Your Mind ch. 18 (1998).

[3] Restatement Second §38(2) states that the offeree may avoid the effect of this rule by "manifesting an intention to take [the offer] under further advisement."

[4] *See* Restatement Second §39(1).

[5] *See* Restatement Second §39(2).

not intend to accept the original offer. Suppose that in the example just given, the buyer responds, "I'll give you $9,000 for your goods." Such a counteroffer rejects the seller's offer and terminates the buyer's power of acceptance, so that the buyer cannot later accept at $10,000.[6] But a mere request for modification, such as "Might you take $9,000?" does not ordinarily have the same effect.[7] Nor does a comment on terms, such as "Your asking price is rather high." Furthermore, the offeree may even succeed in making a counteroffer without rejecting the original offer, if the offeree is careful to indicate that the offer is not rejected. Thus the buyer might reply, "Keeping your offer under advisement, I am willing to offer you $9,000."[8] In this way the buyer could, without rejecting the offer received, tempt the seller to make a contract for $9,000, which might be preferable to a mere inquiry, which would at best tempt the seller to make an offer to sell for $9,000.

A particularly intractable problem is whether a purported acceptance that varies the terms of the offer is an acceptance or a counteroffer and a rejection. This is the subject of the next section.

§3.21.   **Battle of the Forms.**   We have seen that traditional contract doctrine requires that the offeree's commitment be one on the terms proposed by the offer with no variation.[1] An attempt to add to or change the terms of the offer turns the offeree's response from an acceptance into a counteroffer and a rejection of the offer.[2] This rule is sometimes called the "mirror image" rule because it requires that an acceptance be the mirror image of the offer. It has been applied even though the variation is unintentional, as when the offeree makes a mistake in repeating the terms of the offer.[3]

The mirror image rule

Courts have, however, developed techniques to mitigate the harshness of the mirror image rule. One technique is to interpret the offeree's language relating to the variation as a "mere suggestion," which the offeror might accept or reject,

Techniques for mitigation

---

[6]Minneapolis & St. Louis Ry. v. Columbus Rolling-Mill Co., 119 U.S. 149 (1886) ("Please enter our order for twelve hundred tons rails" rejected offer for 2,000 to 5,000 tons rails).

[7]Stevenson, Jaques & Co. v. McLean, L.R. 5 Q.B.D. 346 (1880) ("Please wire whether you would accept forty for delivery over two months, or if not, longest limit you would give."). *See* Restatement Second §39 illus. 2.

[8]*See* Restatement Second §39 illus. 3. An offer purporting to relate to a different matter may avoid the consequences of a counteroffer.

§3.21   [1]Cook's Pest Control v. Rebar, 852 So. 2d 730 (Ala. 2002) (no acceptance where consumers "countered with an arbitration provision of their own"). See the discussion of how the acceptance must be unconditional in §3.13 *supra*.

[2]In re Pago Pago Aircrash, 637 F.2d 704 (9th Cir. 1981) (where airline's offer of settlement "was contingent on . . . release of all the defendants," response that made release conditional "added a new term, rendering [the] response a qualified acceptance and a new proposal").

[3]United States v. Braunstein, 75 F. Supp. 137 (S.D.N.Y. 1947) (offer of 9,599 boxes of raisins at "ten cents per pound" accepted as one "for 9599 boxes raisins at 10 cents per box"). Mere differences in understanding of terms are generally resolved under the objective theory of assent and do not pose problems under the mirror image rule. *See* §§3.6 *supra*, 7.9 *infra*.

and to find an acceptance on the offeror's terms coupled with a further offer by the original offeree to modify that contract.[4] Where an employee, in manifesting assent to an offer of reinstatement, added notations reserving the right to see his personnel file, alleging mistakes in that file, and complaining of financial problems, the court found a "grumbling acceptance" that, "though unenthusiastic to be sure," was "an acceptance nevertheless."[5] Another technique is to read the offer as already containing by interpretation or implication the apparent variation made by the offeree and to find an acceptance of a contract on the offeree's terms, which are also regarded as those of the offeror.[6] Where a city accepted a contractor's bid "subject to EPA approval," it was held that the acceptance was unconditional because the city's invitation to bid included the condition of the EPA's satisfaction and therefore the contractor's "bid included the condition of EPA approval."[7] Finally, the rule does not seem appropriate in the case of a variation, such as a price concession, that is solely to the offeror's advantage.

Impact on sale of goods

Even as mitigated by these techniques, however, the impact of the mirror image rule on negotiations for the sale of goods has caused concern. A study of Wisconsin businesses, for instance, revealed that most firms have their own forms with standard terms for such transactions:

> Typically, these terms and conditions are lengthy and printed in small type on the back of the forms . . . . If the seller does not object to this planning and accepts the order, the buyer's "fine print" will control. If the seller does object, differences can be settled by negotiation . . . . However, the seller may fail to read the buyer's . . . fine print and may accept the buyer's order on the seller's own acknowledgement-of-order form.

The seller's form will then have different terms that favor the seller. The buyer's clerk who handles the seller's form has neither the time nor training to analyze the small print on back of the many forms received each day.

> The face of the acknowledgment — where the goods and the price are specified — is likely to correspond with the face of the purchase order. If it does, the two forms are filed away. At this point, both buyer and seller are likely to assume they have planned an exchange and made a contract. Yet they have done neither,

---

[4]Valashinas v. Koniuto, 124 N.E.2d 300 (N.Y. 1954) (seller's proposal of a closing date was "no more than a suggestion, request or overture"). *See* Restatement Second §59 & cmt. *a*.

[5]Panhandle Eastern Pipe Line Co. v. Smith, 637 P.2d 1020, 1023 (Wyo. 1981).

As to the assent required for an employee's agreement to arbitrate, *see* Leodori v. Cigna Corp., 814 A.2d 1098 (N.J. 2003) ("must reflect that an employee has agreed clearly and unambiguously to arbitrate the disputed claim").

[6]Rule v. Tobin, 719 A.2d 869 (Vt. 1998) (because "acceptance only clarified what [offerees] were already entitled to by law, it was unconditional").

[7]Safeco Ins. Co. v. City of White House, 36 F.3d 540, 547 (6th Cir. 1994).

as they are in disagreement about all that appears on the back of their forms. This practice is common enough to have a name. Law teachers call it "the battle of the forms."[8]

Though it would be impractical for either party on receipt of such a preprinted form to read and consider its terms, it is inevitable that the forms will contain terms on which there has been no agreement. In practice, most of these transactions are carried out without incident, even though there may be no contract. But how is contract law to resolve those disputes that do arise?

Disputes arise in two types of situations. [First, because of altered circumstances, such as a change in market price, one of the parties later seizes upon the discrepancies in the forms as an excuse for not performing.][9] [Second, after shipment of the goods by the seller and their receipt by the buyer, a dispute arises over some aspect of performance, often the quality of the goods, and it becomes necessary to determine the contract terms that govern the dispute.][10] In devising rules for the battle of the forms, these two types of situations produce opposing tensions. Relaxing the requirement that the acceptance match the offer may reduce the number of situations in which a party can seize upon a discrepancy in the forms as an excuse for not performing. But at the same time it will produce uncertainty where, as is more often the case, there has been performance and the dispute is over the terms that govern disputes over some aspect of that performance.

Two types of disputes

In disputes over some aspect of performance, traditional contract doctrine favors the party who fires the "last shot" in the battle of the forms. Performance by both parties makes it clear that there is a contract, and since each subsequent form is a counteroffer, rejecting any prior offer of the other party, the resulting contract must be on the terms of the party who sends the last counteroffer, which is then accepted by the other party's performance. In practice it is usually the seller that fires the last shot, a "confirmation of sale" form, in answer to the buyer's "purchase order" form. [Traditional contract doctrine therefore tends to favor the seller.]

Favors one who fires the last shot

The drafters of the original version of Article 2 recast the rules for the battle of the forms. The result, UCC-O 2-207, turned out to raise as many questions as it answers.[11] It begins with a major concession to the original offeror:

UCC-O 2-207 changes mirror image rule

[8] Macaulay, Non-Contractual Relations in Business: A Preliminary Study, 28 Am. Soc. Rev. 55, 58-59 (1963).

[9] For a description of the precipitous market drop that appears to have motivated the buyer's refusal to perform, *see* Poel v. Brunswick-Balke-Collender Co., 139 N.Y.S. 602, 607 (Sup. Ct. 1912).

[10] *See* Matter of Doughboy Indus., 233 N.Y.S.2d 488 (App. Div. 1962) (arbitration clause in seller's form not part of contract).

[11] *See* Roto-Lith v. F.P. Bartlett & Co., 297 F.2d 497 (1st Cir. 1962) (describing section as "not too happily drafted"); Southwest Engrg. Co. v. Martin Tractor Co., 473 P.2d 18 (Kan. 1970) (describing section as "murky bit of prose").

> (1) A definite and seasonable expression of acceptance or a written confirmation which is sent within a reasonable time operates as an acceptance even though it states terms additional to or different from those offered or agreed upon, unless acceptance is expressly made conditional on assent to the additional or different terms.

The drafters intended this provision to reduce the number of situations in which a party can seize upon a discrepancy in the forms as an excuse for not performing. Under subsection (1), such a discrepancy does not prevent a purported acceptance from creating a contract unless the offeree takes pains expressly to say that it does. The consequences are twofold: first, there is a contract; and second, the contract is on the offeror's terms. The additional terms are merely new offers by the original offeree to modify the contract thus formed. The advantage has shifted from the party that fires the last shot to the one that makes the first offer. Since a seller's catalog or price list is not usually regarded as an offer,[12] the first offer is likely to be the buyer's purchase order, so that the advantage has shifted from the seller to the buyer. Although the language of the subsection does not distinguish negotiations by letter or facsimiles from those by printed forms, the purpose underlying the section is less compelling when such forms are not involved.[13]

Application when variation is material

Subsection (1) may result in a contract on the offeror's terms even though the variation of acceptance from offer is a material one. The words *additional to* or *different from* seem to cover cases in which the acceptance omits a term contained in the offer, those in which the acceptance contains a term omitted in the offer, and those in which the acceptance and the offer contain conflicting terms. One writer argued, however, that the subsection should be read so that, in the case of conflicting terms, the terms would cancel each other out. This "knock-out" rule would give a contract consisting, not of the offeror's terms, but of the terms as to which there is no conflict, with the gap left by the conflicting terms to be filled by other sections of the Code.[14] There is, however, little reason to suppose that the drafters of the Code intended such a startling departure from the notion that the offeror is the master of the offer.

---

[12] See the discussion of failure to limit quantity in §3.10 *supra*.

[13] *See* Columbia Hyundai v. Carll Hyundai, 484 S.E.2d 468 (S.C. 1997) (UCC-O 2-207 inapplicable where "parties met and negotiated the provisions of their contract . . . for several months").

[14] In their first edition, Professors White and Summers advanced the interpretation that conflicting terms in an offer and acceptance knock each other out. J. White & R. Summers, Law Under the Uniform Commercial Code §1-2 (1st ed. 1972). The interpretation was based in part on UCC-O 2-207 cmt. 6 ("Where clauses on confirming forms sent by both parties conflict each party must be assumed to object to a clause of the other conflicting with one on the confirmation sent by himself"). In later editions, however, the authors disagree over the "knock-out" doctrine. "One of us (White) would turn to the foregoing comment and find that the two terms cancel one another . . . . Summers believes that Comment 6 is not applicable." J. White & R. Summers, Uniform Commercial Code §1-3 (5th ed. 2000).

There must be limits to the scope of subsection (1), however, for surely a buyer should not be taken to accept the seller's offer of two carloads at $10,000 each if the buyer replies, "I accept one carload at $5,000." Perhaps a reply from the offeree that varies terms, such as quantity or price, that are usually subject to bargaining, is not an "expression of acceptance" even if the offeree uses the word *accept*.[15]

Limits to "expression of acceptance"

Having made this major concession to the offeror in subsection (1), the drafters added a sop to the offeree in subsection (2):

Subsection (2) incorporates terms by silence

> (2) The additional terms are to be construed as proposals for addition to the contract. Between merchants such terms become part of the contract unless:
> (a) the offer expressly limits acceptance to the terms of the offer;
> (b) they materially alter it; or
> (c) notification of objection to them has already been given or is given within a reasonable time after notice of them is received.

Since the additional terms in the offeree's acceptance are regarded as proposals for addition to the contract,[16] the offeror may choose to accept them and modify the contract. What subsection (2) adds is that, if both parties are merchants, the offeror's mere silence will sometimes amount to such an acceptance.[18] This is, however, subject to the important qualification that the terms do not "materially alter" the contract. In other words, if the offeree adds a term that does materially alter the contract, subsection (1) holds the offeree to a contract on the offeror's terms and subsection (2) does not make the offeror's silence an acceptance of the added term. According to the commentary to UCC-O 2-207:

> Examples of typical clauses which would normally "materially alter" the contract and so result in surprise or hardship if incorporated without express

[15]Lambert v. Kysar, 983 F.2d 1110 (1st Cir. 1993) ("alteration of the quantity term amounted to a rejection of the original offer, rather than a mere modification or supplementation of the boilerplate language in the original offer form").

[16]A careful reading of UCC-O 2-207 might suggest that a distinction is to be made between "additional" and "different" terms and that only "additional" terms are subject to subsection (2). Support for this appears in Reaction Molding Technologies v. General Elec. Co., 588 F. Supp. 1280 (E.D. Pa. 1984) (subsection (2) "does not apply to different (as opposed to additional) terms"). But UCC-O 2-207 cmt. 3 suggests that this further erosion of the offeree's position was not intended: "Whether or not additional or different terms will become part of the agreement depends upon the provisions of subsection (2)."

[17]Twin Disc v. Big Bud Tractor, 772 F.2d 1329 (7th Cir. 1985) (buyer "expressly assented to the additional terms [disclaimers] 'by unequivocal behavior, clearly indicating a willingness to be bound by the terms'").

[18]Courts have sometimes confused UCC-O 2-207(2), under which terms may be incorporated in a contract by silence, with UCC 2-201(2), under which the statute of frauds may be satisfied by silence (see the discussion of a writing in confirmation under the code in §6.8 *infra*). Marlene Indus. Corp. v. Carnac Textiles, 380 N.E.2d 239 (N.Y. 1978) (error in applying UCC 2-201(2), which deals solely with question whether contract "is enforceable in the face of a Statute of Frauds defense").

awareness by the other party are: a clause negating such standard warranties as that of merchantability or fitness for a particular purpose in circumstances in which either warranty normally attaches; a clause requiring a guaranty of 90% or 100% deliveries in a case such as a contract by a cannery, where the usage of the trade allows greater quantity leeway; a clause reserving to the seller the power to cancel upon the buyer's failure to meet any invoice when due; a clause requiring that complaints be made in a time materially shorter than customary or reasonable . . . . Examples of clauses which involve no element of unreasonable surprise and which therefore are to be incorporated in the contract unless notice of objection is seasonably given are: a clause setting forth and perhaps enlarging slightly upon the seller's exemption due to supervening causes beyond his control . . . ; a clause fixing a reasonable time for complaints within customary limits . . . ; a clause providing for interest on overdue invoices or fixing the seller's standard credit terms where they are within the range of trade practice and do not limit any credit bargained for; a clause limiting the right of rejection for defects which fall within the customary trade tolerances for acceptance "with adjustment" or otherwise limiting remedy in a reasonable manner . . . .[19]

A vast amount of litigation has been devoted to determining whether particular terms result in such "surprise or hardship"[20] as to materially alter the contract[21] or whether they do not,[22] a question that courts have often treated as one of fact[23] but sometimes as one of law.[24] A particularly important dispute concerns whether the addition of an arbitration clause materially alters a contract.[25] Furthermore, subsection (2) contains the means by which the offeror can defeat even the limited concession that the subsection makes to the offeree, for if "the offer expressly limits acceptance to the terms of the offer" the offeror's silence will not be acceptance of even an immaterial term.[26] The offeror that fails to take

---

[19]UCC-O 2-207 cmts. 4 & 5.

[20]For factors to be considered in "surprise," *see* American Ins. Co. v. El Paso Pipe & Supply Co., 978 F.2d 1185 (10th Cir. 1992) (error to include "hardship with unreasonable surprise").

[21]Altronics of Bethlehem v. Repco, 957 F.2d 1102 (3d Cir. 1992) (provision excluding consequential damages).

[22]Sethness-Greenleaf, Inc. v. Green River Corp., 65 F.3d 64 (7th Cir. 1995) (Easterbrook, J.: payment terms on seller's invoice were more generous than "the default terms of the UCC" and "were not so surprising as to 'materially alter' the parties' agreement).

[23]Transamerica Oil Corp. v. Lynes, 723 F.2d 758 (10th Cir. 1983) (whether a term excluding consequential damages materially alters the contract "is a question that must be determined in the light of the facts of the case and the parties' expectations").

[24]Clifford-Jacobs Forging Co. v. Capital Engrg. & Mfg. Co., 437 N.E.2d 22 (Ill. App. 1982) ("as a matter of law, . . . no reasonable surprise occurred" by seller's addition of pricing provision).

[25]One view is that it does materially alter the contract. Marlene Indus. Corp. v. Carnac Textiles, *supra* note 18 (textile industry: "it is clear that an arbitration clause is a material addition").

Another view is that the question is one of fact, to be decided according to the circumstances of each case. Dorton v. Collins & Aikman Corp., 453 F.2d 1161 (6th Cir. 1972) (textile industry: whether clause materially altered oral offer "can be resolved only . . . on further findings of fact").

[26]Egan Mach. Co. v. Mobil Chem. Co., 660 F. Supp. 35 (D. Conn. 1986) (language "clearly" limited acceptance to terms of offer).

advantage of this provision can still prevent incorporation of a term by giving notice of objection to it.[27] Thus UCC-O 2-207 concedes much to the offeror in subsection (1) and little to the offeree in subsection (2), an imbalance that might well provoke a court to think twice before concluding that an alteration is "material."

Given this state of affairs, an offeree may well consider accepting the invitation in subsection (1) to employ an "acceptance . . . expressly made conditional on assent to the additional or different terms" that it contains.[28] Such an "acceptance" does not operate as an acceptance but as a counteroffer. There is therefore no contract unless the original offeror accepts the counteroffer.[29] This does not, however, restore to the offeree the advantage enjoyed under the common law by firing the "last shot" before performance.[30] This is because of the effect of subsection (3) on conduct by the parties.

Under subsection (3):

> (3) Conduct by both parties which recognizes the existence of a contract is sufficient to establish a contract for sale although the writings of the parties do not otherwise establish a contract. In such case the terms of the particular contract consist of those terms on which the writings of the parties agree, together with any supplementary terms incorporated under any other provision of this Act.

Since this provision applies to situations where the parties go ahead and perform, even though their exchange of writings has not resulted in a contract, it covers cases where no contract results from the writings because the offeree has expressly made acceptance conditional on assent to additional or different terms.[31] Thus the offeree that has taken the precaution of avoiding the trap laid in subsection (1) has not succeeded in having a contract on the offeree's own terms only in avoiding a contract on the offeror's terms. The offeree is bound

Margin notes:

Acceptance "expressly made conditional"

Subsection (3) gives contract by conduct

---

[27]*But cf.* Advance Concrete Forms v. McCann Constr. Specialties Co., 916 F.2d 412 (7th Cir. 1990) (buyer that continued to make purchases on credit waived any objection to credit term).

[28]For language held sufficient to come within the exception in subsection (1), *see* Construction Aggregates Corp. v. Hewitt-Robins, 404 F.2d 505 (7th Cir. 1968) (acceptance "predicated on the following clarifications, additions or modifications" was "expressly made conditional on assent to the additional or different terms").

[29]For a case in which the counteroffer was accepted, *see* Construction Aggregates Corp. v. Hewitt-Robins, *supra* note 28 (where original offeror telephoned to object to only one of the changes in the counteroffer, this "was an acquiescence in the remaining terms of the counteroffer").

[30]*See* Diamond Fruit Growers v. Krack Corp., 794 F.2d 1440 (9th Cir. 1986) (in order not to "reinstate to some extent the common law's last shot rule," there must be "a specific and unequivocal expression of assent on the part of the offeror when the offeree conditions its acceptance on assent to additional or different terms").

[31]Dresser Indus. v. Gradall Co., 965 F.2d 1442 (7th Cir. 1992) (rejecting contention that "supplementary terms" includes "only those terms expressly provided by the U.C.C." and not "terms that may be implied from the parties' course of performance, course of dealing, and usage of trade").

instead by a contract consisting of terms common to both writings, together with any others supplied by the Code.[32]

Avoidance of subsection (3)

The offeree that wishes a contract on the offeree's own terms might flatly reject the offer and make a counteroffer. By not making any "expression of acceptance" under subsection (1), the offeree has arguably avoided UCC-O 2-207 altogether and so is not bound by subsection (3). Subsequent performance by the original offeror ought in that case to be taken as an acceptance of all the terms of the offeree's counteroffer.[33] This tactic may be especially attractive where, as will usually be the case, the offeree is a seller that regards the terms that would be supplied by the Code as excessively favorable to the buyer.

Effect on confirmations

Thus far, the discussion of UCC-O 2-207 has been in terms of a variant acceptance. However, the section also purports to deal with a variant confirmation, and the commentary says that one of the two typical situations with which it is intended to deal is the one "where an agreement has been reached either orally or by informal correspondence between the parties and is followed by one or both of the parties sending formal acknowledgements or memoranda embodying the terms so far as agreed upon and adding terms not discussed."[34] It is difficult to see what subsection (1) means in this context when it says that "a written confirmation . . . operates as an acceptance," nor does its "unless" clause seem to be applicable to confirmations.[35] Subsection (3) also seems inapplicable to a case involving confirmation of an agreement that has already been reached. It is only subsection (2) that appears meaningful in the case of a confirmation, and its effect would be to allow the silence of the recipient of the confirmation to operate as acceptance of an offer "for addition to the contract" of a term that does not "materially alter it."[36]

Vienna Convention

The Vienna Convention contains a more traditional solution than does the original version of Aricle 2. Under article 19(1) and (2), "a reply to an offer which purports to be an acceptance" can operate as an acceptance only if any "additional or different terms . . . do not materially alter the terms of the offer." And article 19(3) provides that variations in such matters as "price, payment, quality and quantity of the goods, place and time of delivery, extent of one party's

---

[32]Transwestern Pipeline Co. v. Monsanto Co., 53 Cal. Rptr. 2d 887 (Ct. App. 1996) ("governing rule is that one party should not be able to impose its terms and conditions on the other simply because it fired the last shot").

[33]Herm Hughes & Sons v. Quintek, 834 P.2d 582 (Utah App. 1992) (UCC-O 2-207 not applicable when reply "not only added additional terms, but directly contradicted [the] offer, specifically in its treatment of payment terms").

[34]UCC-O 2-207 cmt. 1.

[35]For a court struggling with the use of "confirmation" in subsection (1), see Echo, Inc. v. Whitson Co., 121 F.3d 1099 (7th Cir. 1997) (Code must mean "that the confirmation makes the agreement legally enforceable.").

[36]Since the same rule applies to this situation regardless of whether a communication is a confirmation of an earlier contract or an acceptance of an offer, a court need not decide whether there was an earlier contract. *But see* UCC-O 2-207 cmt. 6 (quoted in note 12 *supra*).

liability to the other or the settlement of disputes" are to be regarded as material.[37] Since, then, most variations will be material, only in rare situations will the Convention depart from the mirror-image rule. In such a situation — where the acceptance contains additional or different terms that do *not* materially alter the terms of the offer — the additional or different terms become part of the contract unless the offeror without undue delay objects to the discrepancy.

The UNIDROIT Principles contain similar provisions.[38] But they have no counterpart to article 19(3) of the Convention, leaving what is "material" to "the circumstances of each case," with a suggestion that an important factor is whether the additional or different terms "come as a surprise to the offeror."[39] The Principles go on, however, to provide a special "knock-out" rule for the situation where both parties use standard terms. If agreement is reached except on those terms, the resulting contract contains the agreed terms and "any standard terms which are common in substance." Either party can, however, avoid this knock-out rule by indicating, either in advance or later without undue delay "that it does not intend to be bound by such a contract."[40]

UNIDROIT Principles

Revised Article 2 makes sweeping changes in the rules governing the battle of the forms. It asks first whether a contract has been formed and then, if that question is answered in the affirmative, it asks what the terms of that contract are. The first question is dealt with in UCC-R 2-204 and 2-206, and the second question is dealt with in a completely recast UCC-R 2-207.

Revised Artice 2 asks two questions

In answer to the first question, UCC 2-204 continues to provide that a "contract for the sale of goods may be made in any manner sufficient to show agreement" and a new UCC-R 2-206(3) adds that a "definite and seasonable expression of acceptance in a record operates as an acceptance even if it contains terms additional to or different from the offer." In rejecting the mirror image rule, this subsection is similar to UCC-O 2-207(1), but is limited to an acceptance "in a record," omits any reference to a "confirmation," and does not contain the "unless" clause of its predecessor. As under UCC-O 2-207(1), there must be limits to UCC-R 206(3), and a reply from an offeree that varies such essential terms as quantity or price is unlikely to be held to be an "expression of acceptance."[41]

Is there a contract?

In answer to the second question, UCC-R 2-207 provides that if there is a contract, the terms of the contract are (a) "those that appear in the records of both parties," (b) "terms to which both parties agree," and (c) "terms supplied or incorporated" under the Code. The contract may have resulted from

What are the terms of the contract?

---

[37] *See* Chateau des Charmes Wines v. Sabate USA, 328 F.3d 528 (9th Cir. 2003) (forum selection clause came under art. 19(3).

[38] UNIDROIT Principles 2.11 "Modified acceptance" (based on CISG 19(1) & (2)), 2.12. *See* UNIDROIT Principles 2.12 "Writings in confirmation."

[39] UNIDROIT Principles 2.11 cmt. 2.

[40] Article 2.22 "Battle of the forms."

[41] See the discussion of limits to "expression of acceptance" *supra*.

offer and acceptance, from conduct by both parties recognizing the contract's existence, or in any manner confirmed by a record containing terms additional to or different from those of the contract. If both parties send records, the resulting contract contains neither party's variant terms. Courts will no longer be asked to determine whether terms "materially alter" a contract.[42] However, by asking a court to determine under (b) whether a party "agrees" to the other party's terms, the revised section gives courts discretion in including or excluding terms in a manner different from the more mechanical rules of the original section. A court might, for example, find that parties agreed to arbitration even though the arbitraton provisions in their forms differed in minor respects.

Not limited to battle of forms

The revised section is not limited to cases in which there has been a battle of the forms.[43] Where, however, forms are exchanged the section is intended to give no preference to either the first form, as did UCC-O 2-207 or the last form, as did the common law. Performance after agreement will not normally amount to assent to the terms in the other party's record. Where, however, only one party has sent a record and there has been no agreement, the other party's performance will normally be considered as acceptance of the terms in the record. Thus a seller that delivers goods in response to a buyer's purchase order, without sending an acknowledgement or acceptance, will be bound by the terms of the purchase order. If a party insists in a record that its own terms are a condition to contract formation, as under the "unless" clause of UCC-O 2-207(1), no contract will be formed unless that party acknowledges the existence of a contract by subsequently performing or otherwises or the other party agrees to the first party's terms.

We look next to some special problems raised when parties contract by correspondence.

Several questions presented

§3.22.   Contracts by Correspondence. It is more difficult to work out the mechanics of assent if the parties are at a distance and communicate by mail or some other means that takes time. Suppose that the offeree has dispatched an acceptance that has not yet been received by the offeror. Is it too late for the offeror to reconsider and revoke the offer? Is it too late for the offeree to reconsider and reject the offer? Is there a contract even if the acceptance is lost in transit and never received by the offeror? These questions are further complicated if either party has relied on what it assumes to be the state of affairs. The common law has tended, however, to answer such questions without regard to reliance, on the simple assumption that there must be a single moment that is decisive in all cases — a moment after which the offeror's power to revoke

---

[42]See the discussion of how subsection (2) incorporates terms by silence *supra*.

[43]The revised section is not intended to take a position on the reasoning in Hill v. Gateway or the contrary reasoning in Step-Saver Data Sys. v. Wyse Technology. See the discussion of shrink-wrap agreements in §4.26 *infra*.

is terminated, after which the offeree's power to reject is at an end, and after which any further risks of transmission are on the offeror.[1]

The question that has been most often presented is that of the offeror's power to revoke. Suppose that a seller mails an offer to an offeree, and the offeree accepts by return mail. But while the acceptance is in transit, the offeror telephones the offeree to revoke the offer. Is the acceptance effective on dispatch, so that the revocation comes too late, and there is then a contract? Or is the acceptance effective only on receipt, so that the revocation comes in time, and there is then no contract? The Court of King's Bench addressed that question in 1818 in *Adams v. Lindsell*,[2] once one of the most celebrated cases in the field of contracts. The case involved an offer that had been sent by mail to sell wool. It held that, once the buyers had dispatched their letter of acceptance, it was too late for the offerors to revoke. The rule of *Adams v. Lindsell*, sometimes called the "mailbox rule," has met with general approval in the United States.[3] Several explanations have been advanced. It has been argued that the offeror that makes an offer by mail authorizes the post office to receive the acceptance as the offeror's agent.[4] It has also been argued that mailing the acceptance puts it irrevocably out of the offeree's control.[5] A more convincing explanation is

Offeror's power to revoke

§3.22   [1] In this context, "dispatch" occurs when the communication is put out of the sender's possession. Giving a letter to one's employee to be mailed will not suffice. "Receipt" occurs when the communication comes into the possession of the addressee or is delivered to a person or place authorized by the addressee for such communications. The addressee need not have read it or even seen it.

The Vienna Convention provides that an acceptance becomes effective and a contract is concluded "at the moment the indication of assent reaches the offeror." CISG 18(2), 23. But this apparent rejection of the mailbox rule is tempered by a provision that retains the most important effect of that rule, providing "an offer may be revoked [only] if the revocation reaches the offeree before he has dispatched an acceptance." CISG 16(1). UNIDROIT Principles 2.4(1) is based on CISG 18(2).

[2] 106 Eng. Rep. 250 (K.B. 1818). A curious feature of the case is that, though the offerors had sold the wool to another buyer while the acceptance was in transit, they had taken no steps to notify the offerees until after the acceptance had been received. It would seem, therefore, that revocation had been too late in any event. The explanation appears to lie in Cooke v. Oxley, described in a footnote to the discussion of effective on receipt in §3.17 *supra*, which suggested that an offeror could revoke the offer by a mere change of mind. The decision in Adams v. Lindsell may have been partly due to a desire to confine the supposed rule of Cooke v. Oxley as much as possible.

[3] *See* Restatement Second §63.

[4] Lucas v. Western Union Tel. Co., 109 N.W. 191 (Iowa 1906), in which the court asserted that "the post office became the agent" of the offeror when he mailed the offer and that he "impliedly authorized its acceptance through the same agency." The post office does not, however, owe a fiduciary duty to the sender of a letter and is an independent contractor, not an agent.

[5] Mactier's Admrs. v. Frith, 6 Wend. 103 (N.Y. 1830) ("a letter written would not be an acceptance so long as it remained in the possession or under the control of the writer"). As to how the offeree can show that the acceptance was mailed, *see* Cushing v. Thomson, 118 N.H. 292, 386 A.2d 805 (1978) (offeree put acceptance "in the outbox" and "it was customary office procedure for the letters to be sent out the same day").

that the rule curtails the offeror's freedom to revoke by ending it at the earliest feasible time.[6] Ending the offeror's power to revoke at the time of dispatch of the acceptance binds the offeror while the acceptance is in transit, even though the offeror does not know that the offer has been accepted and even though the offeree may not yet have relied on the contract. But allowing the offeror to revoke until the acceptance is received would aggravate the already vulnerable situation of the offeree, which may have relied, even though unable to prove it (for example, if reliance is by inaction). The mailbox rule is extended to protect the offeree against termination by the offeror's death as well as by revocation.

Acceptance must be invited

As the master of the offer, the offeror can vary the mailbox rule by so providing. And even if the offer is silent, an acceptance is not effective on dispatch to terminate the offeror's power of revocation unless, as the Restatement Second puts it, it is "made in a manner and by a medium invited by" the offer.[7] If the acceptance is not as invited, the rule does not apply, and the acceptance is not effective until receipt. Courts have not hesitated to apply the mailbox rule when an offer by mail was accepted by mail or an offer by telegram was accepted by telegram, as long as the acceptance was correctly addressed and properly dispatched.[8] It has even been applied when an offer delivered by hand was accepted by mail, on the ground that the offeror must have expected the offeree to take the offer, which did not lapse for 14 days, some distance to his residence and then use the mail.[9] Whether to apply the rule to an acceptance by telegram of an offer by mail[10] or an acceptance by mail of an offer by telegram[11] turned on such circumstances as the relative reliability and speed of the two means of communication.

Inapplicability if instantaneous

The rule has no application to substantially instantaneous means of communication, such as telephone, telex, facsimile, and electronic mail. The increasing use of such means has diminished the practical importance of the rule.[12]

---

[6] Restatement Second §63 cmt. *a.*

[7] Restatement Second §63. Restatement Second §67 states a generous rule under which an acceptance sent improperly or by a means not invited is nevertheless "treated as operative on dispatch" if received as soon as a properly dispatched acceptance would have been. Under UCC 1-201(36), "send" includes causing "to be received any record or notice whthin the time it would have arrived if properly sent."

[8] Trevor v. Wood, 36 N.Y. 307 (1867) (offer by telegram accepted by telegram).

[9] Henthorn v. Fraser, [1892] 2 Ch. 27. Giving the acceptance to one's own messenger is not effective, although the messenger's mailing of the acceptance may be.

[10] *See* Stephen M. Weld & Co. v. Victory Mfg. Co., 205 F. 770 (E.D.N.C. 1913) (acceptance on dispatch of telegram). *But see* Lucas v. Western Union Tel. Co., *supra* note 4 (acceptance on receipt of telegram).

[11] *See* Farmers Produce Co. v. McAlester Storage & Commn. Co., 150 P. 483 (Okl. 1915) (acceptance on dispatch of letter accepting counteroffer by telegram).

[12] For a contrary view as to electronic mail, *see* Note, 25 Hofstra L. Rev. 971 (1997). See the discussion of electronic commerce in §1.7 *supra.*

Under the general rule that a revocation is not effective until it reaches the offeree, a revocation by mail is not effective until receipt.[13] Where an offeror faxed an offer on June 20 and mailed a revocation on August 9, a federal district court held that an acceptance faxed on August 17 "was effective only if it was sent before the August 9 revocation was received."[14] If an offeror mails an offer and the next day mails a revocation, the offeror may nevertheless be bound if the offeree puts an acceptance in the mail after receipt of the offer but before receipt of the revocation.

Revocation not effective until receipt

Although the effect of the mailbox rule in *Adams v. Lindsell* was to bind the offeror, courts have generally assumed that it also applies to bind the offeree. On this assumption, once the offeree has dispatched an acceptance, it is too late for the offeree to reconsider and reject the offer or withdraw the acceptance.[15] This is not a necessary assumption, since it would be possible to deprive the offeror of the power to revoke the offer upon dispatch of the acceptance, while leaving the offeree free to reject the offer or withdraw the acceptance until its receipt, at least as long as the offeror receives the rejection or withdrawal first.

Offeree's power to reject

Such a rule would, however, offend the principle of mutuality of obligation. This can be seen from a consideration of the overtaking rejection or withdrawal, as where a letter is overtaken by a facsimile. If the mailbox rule is applied to terminate the offeror's power to revoke but is not applied to terminate the offeree's power to reject or withdraw, the result is to give the offeree the power to nullify the acceptance while it is in transit. In effect, the offeree has an option contract during that time and, although the offeror is bound, the offeree can speculate by watching the market and deciding whether to send an overtaking rejection or withdrawal. If the principle of mutuality of obligation is to be respected and speculation to be avoided, the mailbox rule is preferable here too.[16] By analogy, dispatch of the acceptance also protects the offeror in the event of the offeree's death while the acceptance is in transit.

Example of overtaking rejection

In the case of the overtaking rejection or withdrawal, it is unnecessary to decide whether it is the dispatch or the receipt of the rejection that terminates the offeree's power to accept, since both take place after the dispatch and before the receipt of the acceptance. Consider, however, the case of the acceptance

Example of overtaking acceptance

---

[13] L. & E. Wertheimer v. Wehle-Hartford Co., 9 A.2d 279 (Conn. 1939).

[14] Etablissement Asamar Ltd. v. Lone Eagle Shipping Ltd., 882 F. Supp. 1409, 1412 (S.D.N.Y. 1995).

[15] Morrison v. Thoelke, 155 So. 2d 889 (Fla. App. 1963) (telephone call overtook letter). *See* Restatement Second §63.

[16] The rare case in which a rejection does not mention the acceptance can be dealt with by estoppel. If the offeree overtakes a letter of acceptance by a facsimile that says simply, "Reject your offer," application of the mailbox rule to bind the offeror would be hard on the offeror if the offeror relies on the facsimile before receiving the letter. The offeree should then be estopped to enforce the contract. *See* Restatement Second §63 cmt. *c* & illus. 7.

that overtakes a rejection. The Restatement Second states that, as a general rule, the power to accept ends on offeror's receipt of the rejection, so that the offeree is bound.[17] This protects the offeror that has relied on the overtaking acceptance and passed up another deal. Suppose, however, that the offeree's acceptance does not overtake the rejection. Here it would be unfair to bind an offeror that has made another deal before the acceptance arrives. Under the Restatement Second solution, the purported acceptance is not an acceptance, but only a counteroffer, unless it overtakes the rejection, regardless of actual reliance by the offeror.

Risks of transmission

The mailbox rule has also been used to allocate the risk of transmission of the acceptance.[18] Is there a contract even if the acceptance is lost in transit and is never received by the offeror? Authority favors placing the risk on the offeror once the acceptance has been dispatched.[19] This rule, like those on revocation and rejection or withdrawal, is stated without regard to whether there has been reliance by the offeree. Llewellyn justified it on the ground that:

> the ingrained usage of business is to answer letters which look toward deals, but the usage is not so clear about acknowledging letters which close deals. The absence of an answer to a letter of offer is much more certain to lead to an inquiry than is the absence of an answer to a letter of acceptance, so that the party bitten by the mischance has under our rule a greater likelihood of being aware of uncertainty and of speedily discovering his difficulty.[20]

The Restatement Second justifies the rule with more diffidence by saying merely that it has been extended to cover this situation in "the interest of simplicity and clarity."[21] The offeror that is unwilling to bear the risk can provide otherwise in the offer.[22]

Other applications of rule

In addition to the three applications already mentioned, the mailbox rule has been pressed into service to determine the place where a contract is made by

---

[17] Restatement Second §40. A receipt rule for rejections appears in CISG 17 and UNIDROIT Principles 2.5.

[18] On the risks of transmission of the offer, see the discussion of the effect of mistake on transmission in §3.9 *supra*.

[19] Household Fire & Carriage Accident Ins. Co. v. Grant, 4 Exch. Div. 216 (C.A. 1897). *See* Restatement Second §63.

[20] Llewellyn, Our Case-Law of Contract: Offer and Acceptance (pt. 2), 48 Yale L.J. 779, 795 n.23 (1939).

[21] Restatement Second §63 cmt. *b*.

[22] Lewis v. Browning, 130 Mass. 173 (1881) ("If I do not hear from you . . . I shall conclude 'No.'").

correspondence,[23] the time when it is made,[24] and related matters.[25] However, there is good authority that it does not apply to option contracts.[26] Furthermore, it is not applied to matters of performance and so does not protect the debtor whose check to a creditor is lost in the mail.[27]

How can the offeree be protected from the risk of revocation?

E. PROTECTION OF THE OFFEREE

§3.23.   *Options, Option Contracts,* and *Firm Offers.* An offeree may need time to decide whether to accept the offer and, during that time, may need to spend money and effort. Even if the offeror is willing to assure the offeree that the offer will be held open for that time, the traditional common law rules make it difficult to protect the offeree against the offeror's power of revocation. Not only does the common law posit that offers are generally revocable, but the offeror's mere promise not to revoke the offer — or its mere statement that the offer is not revocable — has traditionally been regarded as unenforceable unless under seal or supported by consideration.[1] The doctrine of consideration, combined with the rule of free revocability, makes it impossible for the offeror to give the offeree the desired protection merely by saying so. The result has been increasingly subjected to criticism, especially where irrevocability does not expose the offeror to a substantial risk of speculation by the offeree.[2] It

Difficulty of protecting offeree

---

[23] Under Restatement (Second) of Conflict of Laws §188(2)(a) (1971), the "place of contracting" is one of "the contacts to be taken into account" in choosing the law applicable to the contract, if the parties have not made an effective choice.

The place where the acceptance is spoken generally determines the place of contracting by telephone, even though the Restatement Second generally assimilates acceptance by telephone, or another medium of instantaneous two-way communication, to the rules applicable where the parties are in the presence of each other. *See* Restatement Second §63 & cmt. *d.* The problem has little practical importance except in connection with the place of contracting.

[24] It may, for example, be important to know whether a contract of insurance was made before or after the occurrence of the event insured against. *See* Tayloe v. Merchants' Fire Ins. Co., 50 U.S. (9 How.) 390 (1850) (house burned down while acceptance was in the mail).

[25] See the discussion of provision for lapse in §3.19 *supra,* where entirely different considerations are involved.

[26] *See* Restatement Second §63(b).

[27] *Cf.* Dalton Buick, Oldsmobile, Pontiac, Cadillac v. Universal Underwriters Ins. Co., 512 N.W.2d 633 (Neb. 1994) ("deposit-acceptance rule operates at the stage during which a contract is being formed; here, we are concerned with the meaning of the language of a contract [requiring monthly report by insured,] which has been formed").

§3.23   [1] Hill v. Corbett, 204 P.2d 845 (Wash. 1949) (offer not made irrevocable by the language "the first parties do hereby grant unto the second parties the option to extend the lease").

[2] *See* J. Dawson, Gifts and Promises 213 (1980) ("difficulties were all manufactured by treating offers as a subordinate form of promise").

is rejected by both the Vienna Convention and the UNIDROIT Principles.[3] The conventional way for the offeree to overcome the obstacles imposed by the common law and get the desired protection is by means of an option.

Options and *option contracts*

An irrevocable offer is commonly called an *option.* Like any other offer, an option imposes no duty on the offeree. The offeree has unfettered discretion to either accept the offer or not.[4] An offeree that accepts the offer is said to "exercise" the option. An option is itself a contract, sometimes called an *option contract* to distinguish it from the main contract to be formed on acceptance of the offer.

Effect of abolition of seal

Before the abolition of the seal, the offeror could make an option by promising under seal not to revoke the offer.[5] Now that the seal has been generally abolished, the offeror can still make an option if the promise not to revoke is supported by consideration. The consideration may consist of either a promise or a performance.[6] Often it consists of a sum of money that is small in relation to the opportunity that speculation affords the offeree and the risk that speculation imposes on the offeror. Whatever hostility may have been shown to the device of nominal consideration in general,[7] courts have tolerated that device as a means of making an offer irrevocable and upheld options for which the peppercorn is as little as a dollar.[8] Nevertheless, the prudent lawyer would

---

[3]CISG 16(2)(a); UNIDROIT Principles 2.4(2)(a). Both of these formulations provide that one means of indicating that an offer is irrevocable is by "stating a fixed time for acceptance." In a common law system, this would probably be read as fixing a time when the offer lapsed and not as fixing a period of irrevocability. To some extent this provision undercuts the acceptance of the common law of free revocability, treated in the discussion of the reason for the principle in §3.17 *supra*.

[4]*See* Syrovy v. Alpine Resources, 859 P.2d 51 (Wash. 1993) (not an option contract where "contract creates an installment schedule where payment is mandatory, rather than optional").

[5]Thomason v. Bescher, 97 S.E. 654 (N.C. 1918) ("these options . . . , binding on the parties because in the form of a covenant under seal, serve their purpose in keeping the offer open for the time specified and preventing a withdrawal"). The practice of courts of equity to look behind the seal and to grant relief only if there was something in the nature of a fair exchange was not applied by most courts to options under seal. See footnote to the discussion of how the seal was distinct from consideration in §2.16 *supra*.

The offeror may put the promise in this form: "If you pay me $100, I promise not to revoke my offer to sell you apples for $10,000 for a period of 30 days." Or the offeror may put it in this form: "If you pay me $100, I will sell you apples for $10,000 on condition that you accept my offer within 30 days." The effect is the same.

[6]Gleeson v. Frahm, 320 N.W.2d 95 (Neb. 1982) (if "full or partial performance by the holder of the option is [not] required to exercise the option . . . , the holder may exercise by promising to perform, in which case the contract becomes bilateral — both parties are bound by their promises to perform the contract").

[7]See the discussion of a likely example of nominal consideration in §2.11 *supra*.

[8]Mier Co. v. Hadden, 111 N.W. 1040 (Mich. 1907) ("a valuable consideration was paid for the contract").

A single sum may even serve as consideration for an irrevocable divisible offer, one that invites a series of acceptances. That the offeree's payment of a deposit does not make an offer irrevocable,

do well to advise the client not to invite litigation by paying an absurdly small amount for an option.

A promise not to revoke an offer may also be supported by consideration other than money. Thus an option may be part of a larger transaction as, for example, when an option to renew a lease or to purchase the premises is given the lessee as part of the lease.[9] Even if the option is not part of a larger transaction, something other than the payment of money, such as some action by the offeree in preparation for consummating the transaction, may be consideration. But the difficulty of convincing a court that action of this kind was bargained for by the offeror counsels resort to the conventional device of a money payment.[10] The offeree's reliance on a promise not to revoke the offer may also afford a basis for protection.[11] But the difficulty of proving reliance and the possibility that recovery may be limited to the amount of losses incurred in reliance again counsel resort to the payment of money.[12]

Other consideration and reliance

If a sum of money is paid as consideration for an option, this fact is usually recited. Courts have differed as to the effect of such a recital if no payment has in fact been made. Some courts have held the recital to be of no effect,[13] adhering to the general principle that mere words cannot change falsehood into truth.[14] Others have held that the recital makes the offer irrevocable, either as a binding acknowledgment of payment or as a promise to pay.[15]

Effect of recitals

The Restatement Second favors the enforceability of what it calls *option contracts*.[16] As the commentary explains, even when

Option contracts under Restatement Second

> gross disproportion between the payment and the value of the option . . . indicates that the payment was not in fact bargained for but was a mere formality or pretense . . . , such a nominal consideration is regularly held sufficient to support a short-time option proposing an exchange on fair terms. The fact that the option

---

even if the deposit is to be forfeited on revocation, see the discussion of the effect of a deposit in §3.17 *supra*.

[9] Estate of Claussen, 482 N.W.2d 381 (Iowa 1992) (because real estate contract "was intended to be a single, non-severable agreement," option was supported by consideration). That separate consideration is not needed, see the discussion of reluctance to inquire into purpose in §2.9 *supra*.

[10] *See* Bard v. Kent, 122 P.2d 8 (Cal. 1942) (lessee's checking figures and having an architect do sketches was not consideration for option to extend a lease).

[11] Kucera v. Kavan, 84 N.W.2d 207 (Neb. 1957) (reliance on "option" to buy farm by entering into possession and making improvements).

[12] Thus it seems not to have been argued that the reliance on a promise not to revoke an offer consisted of forbearing from accepting at an earlier time, before revocation.

[13] Bard v. Kent, *supra* note 10 (false recital that $10 had been paid was not consideration).

[14] See the discussion of no power over truth in §2.17 *supra*.

[15] Real Estate Co. v. Rudolph, 153 A. 438 (Pa. 1930) (false recital that $1 had been paid "can only mean that [the offeror] acknowledges the receipt of that sum").

[16] Restatement Second §25 ("option contract is a promise which meets the requirements for the formation of a contract and limits the promisor's power to revoke an offer").

is an appropriate preliminary step in the conclusion of a socially useful transaction provides a sufficient substantive basis for enforcement, and a signed writing taking a form appropriate to a bargain satisfies the desiderata of form.[17]

The offer is irrevocable, however, only if it is for a "short term" and if the exchange is on "fair terms." If the option is for a term long enough to produce a substantial risk of speculation, more than a pretense of bargain is to be required. The section also puts the Restatement's stamp of approval on a signed writing that "recites a purported consideration for the making of the offer," but again only if it "proposes an exchange on fair terms within a reasonable time." The commentary adds, "The signed writing has vital significance as a formality, while the ceremonial manual delivery of a dollar or a peppercorn is an inconsequential formality." The attempt is to make a recital of consideration as effective a formality as was the seal, where options are concerned.

Firm offers under the Code

UCC 2-205 goes further in providing for *firm offers*, as the Code chooses to call irrevocable offers. The offer need only be "in a signed writing which by its terms gives assurance that it will be held open." It is then irrevocable "during the time stated or if no time is stated for a reasonable time." In keeping with the policy of shielding the offeror from excessive risk of speculation, the period of irrevocability may not exceed three months.[18] In order to prevent imposition on consumers, only a merchant can make a firm offer.[19] Even a merchant must separately sign the firm offer clause if it is on a form supplied by the other party.[20] These Code provisions are, of course, limited to the sale of goods.[21]

Effects of irrevocability

If an offer is irrevocable, a purported revocation by the offeror has no effect on the offeree's power of acceptance. The offeree can accept despite the purported revocation and can sue for breach of the contract if the offeror fails to

---

[17] Restatement Second §87 cmt. *b*.

[18] Mid-South Packers v. Shoney's, 761 F.2d 1117 (5th Cir. 1985) (proposal was, "at most, a 'firm offer,'" not a requirements contract, and was revocable after three months). A firm offer for a longer period can presumably be made as a paid-for option.

[19] This requirement was prompted by the fact that door-to-door sellers would otherwise be able to exact firm offers to buy on credit from consumers, giving a seller time to check a consumer's credit while the consumer was bound. See the discussion of reservation of power to maker in §3.10 *supra*.

[20] Initials will suffice as a signature. UCC 1-201(37).

[21] Under a New York statute an irrevocable offer of any sort can be made by a signed writing "which states that the offer is irrevocable." N.Y. Gen. Oblig. L. §5-1109. This statute is subject to the provisions of UCC 2-205, which presumably means, although it is less than clear, that it is totally inapplicable in the case of a sale of goods so that the restrictions of that section apply.

As to other legislation generally altering the requirement of consideration, see the discussion of the types of statutes in §2.18 *supra*. See also the discussion of auctions "without reserve" in connection with the entertainment of bids in §3.10 *supra*.

perform.[22] The same is true of the offeror's death or incapacity.[23] It is also said that the offeree's power of acceptance is not terminated by rejection, but this is generally said in the context of a paid-for option contract that has been rejected by a counteroffer.[24] It is less clear that one who has gratuitously made a firm offer by a signed writing under the Code should be held to it if the offeree has flatly rejected it, especially if the offeror has relied on the rejection.[25] An irrevocable offer, like any other offer, can be withdrawn if notice of withdrawal reaches the offeree no later than the offer does.[26] And the power of acceptance may terminate, as under any other offer, by lapse.[27] The transferability of the offeree's right under an irrevocable offer and the consequent effect of the offeree's death or supervening legal incapacity are governed by rules that are discussed later in connection with contracts in general.[28]

The next two sections deal with situations in which courts have protected the offeree even though the offeror has not said that the offer is irrevocable.

§3.24.   **Reliance on Offer That Invites Performance.**   We have seen that if an offer invites acceptance by performance, it can be accepted only by performance and not by a promise.[1] If the usual rules governing offer and acceptance were applied, the offeror could revoke the offer at any time until acceptance; until then the offeree would have no way to avoid vulnerability to revocation. Despite the limited practical importance of such offers, the development of the law governing the offeree's vulnerability in this situation has, as will be seen, significantly influenced the law governing offers in general.

The problem of the offeree's vulnerability becomes particularly acute if the invited performance takes time, as it does in the most durable and influential

Revocation of offers for unilateral contracts

Brooklyn Bridge hypothetical

---

[22]That specific performance is available, *see* Caras v. Parker, 309 P.2d 104 (Cal. App. 1957) (on "buyer's acceptance of the offer, there is then created the contract of sale and it is this contract which gives rise to the remedy of specific performance").

[23]Martin Enters. v. Janover, 528 N.Y.S.2d 855 (App. Div. 1988) ("option may survive the death . . . and devolve upon the estate, unless the terms of the option confine performance to the person who originally held it").

[24]Restatement Second §37 states a general rule that "the power of acceptance under an option contract is not terminated by rejection."

[25]*Cf.* Holt v. Stofflet, 61 N.W.2d 28 (Mich. 1953) (holder of option in lease "estopped" to exercise it after offerors contracted to sell to others since holder "took the initiative in suggesting and encouraging" the offerors to do this). *See* Illustration 2 to Restatement Second §37, which suggests that the rules on discharge will protect an offeror that relies on an offeree's assurance that the offeree will not exercise an option.

Both the Vienna Convention and the UNIDROIT Principles provide that even an irrevocable offer is terminated when a rejection reaches the offeror, but it is doubtful that this provision should apply if the offer is irrevocable because paid for. CISG 17; UNIDROIT Principles 2.5.

[26]See the discussion of the principle of revocability in §3.17 *supra.*

[27]See §3.18 *supra.*

[28]See §9.6 *infra.*

§3.24   [1]See the discussion of acceptance by performance in §3.13 *supra.*

hypothetical in American legal education. In the words of the scholar who propounded it:

> Suppose A says to B, "I will give you $100 if you walk across the Brooklyn Bridge." . . . B starts to walk across the Brooklyn Bridge and has gone about one-half of the way across. At that moment A overtakes B and says to him, "I withdraw my offer." Has B then any rights against A? Again, let us suppose that after A has said, "I withdraw my offer," B continues to walk across the Brooklyn Bridge and completes the act of crossing. Under these circumstances, has B any rights against A?

Traditional contract doctrine

According to traditional contract doctrine, the propounder reasoned, B had no rights against A:

> What A wanted from B, what A asked for, was the act of walking across the bridge. Until that was done, B had not given to A what A had requested. The acceptance by B of A's offer could be nothing but the act on B's part of crossing the bridge. It is elementary that an offeror may withdraw his offer until it has been accepted. It follows logically that A is perfectly within his rights in withdrawing his offer before B has accepted it by walking across the bridge — the act contemplated by the offeror and the offeree as the acceptance of the offer.[2]

If the offer invites performance and not a promise, neither preparation for performance[3] nor beginning performance itself[4] protects the offeree against the offeror's exercise of this power. The offeree may have a claim for restitution if a benefit has been conferred upon the offeror, but the offeree has no claim in contract.

Interpretation of offer to invite promise

A court may avoid this harsh result by interpreting the offer as seeking a promise, if its language will bear that interpretation, and then inferring a promise to cross the bridge from B's beginning to cross it, or even from B's preparing to cross it.[5] On this theory, B will be liable to A if B does not finish

---

[2]Wormser, The True Conception of Unilateral Contracts, 26 Yale L.J. 136, 136-37 (1916).

[3]A notorious example is Petterson v. Pattberg, 161 N.E. 428 (N.Y. 1928), described in §3.12 *supra*.

[4]Bartlett v. Keith, 90 N.E.2d 308 (Mass. 1950) ("acceptance of an offer to a unilateral contract must be by all the acts contemplated by the offer").

[5]A leading case is Davis v. Jacoby, 34 P.2d 1026 (Cal. 1934), in which an elderly man with a dying wife wrote her niece, Caro, and the niece's husband, Frank: "If Frank could come out here and be with me and look after my affairs . . . Caro will inherit everything . . . ," adding "Will you let me hear from you as soon as possible . . . ." Caro and Frank wired back, "Cheer up — we will soon be there . . . ," and had made arrangements to do so when the offeror committed suicide. The court held that this "was an offer to enter into a bilateral as distinguished from an unilateral contract," and that it was accepted by the answering letter. Inferring a promise from commencement of performance is more difficult to justify if there is a substantial risk that the offeree will not succeed in performing, as in a variation on Wormser's hypothetical in which A offers B $100 if B will climb a flagpole.

crossing the bridge, but this is a point of only theoretical interest if A revokes and is sued by B. Because such an interpretation protects B's justifiable reliance on A's offer, there is reason to prefer it to an interpretation under which the offer invites performance.[6]

A court may also avoid this harsh result by finding that the offer sought a series of acceptances by performance, leading to a series of unilateral contracts. If, for example, A had said to B, "I will give you $100 for each time that you walk across the Brooklyn Bridge up to a maximum of $1,000," and had revoked during B's seventh crossing, a court could award B $600 on the ground that the offer proposed a series of ten unilateral contracts, of which six had been made at the time of revocation.[7] A practical example is a standing offer of guaranty that looks to a series of extensions of credit, each of which is a separate acceptance of the offer and creates a new contract with the guarantor unless the guarantor has sooner revoked the offer.[8]

Interpretation of offer as divisible

The Restatement made a frontal attack on traditional contract doctrine by propounding a different rule in §45 — a section that has become as influential here as §90 did in connection with promissory estoppel. The rule, as revised, now appears in Restatement Second §45:

Restatement Second §45

(1) Where an offer invites an offeree to accept by rendering a performance and does not invite a promissory acceptance, an option contract is created when the offeree tenders or begins the invited performance or tenders a beginning of it.

(2) The offeror's duty of performance under any option contract so created is conditional on completion or tender of the invited performance in accordance with the terms of the offer.

The rule protects the offeree as soon as the offeree relies by beginning performance. When B has begun to cross the bridge, A's offer becomes irrevocable — "the beginning of performance . . . furnishes consideration for an option contract."[9] The rationale, as expressed in the comments to the first Restatement, is that the "main offer includes as a subsidiary promise, necessarily implied, that if part of the requested performance is given, the offeror will

---

[6] *See* Padbloc Co. v. United States, 161 Ct. Cl. 369 (1963) ("We know . . . that there are many situations in which the outline of the transaction appears unilateral but a [request for] a return promise can fairly be implied from all the circumstances.").

[7] The same is true of an agreement for the sale of goods that is interpreted as a standing offer to sell or an agreement for employment at will that is interpreted as a standing offer of employment. See footnote to the discussion of two responses to termination clauses in §2.14 *supra*.

[8] Offord v. Davies, 142 Eng. Rep. 1336 (Com. Pl. 1862) ("we consider each discount as a separate transaction").

[9] Restatement Second §45 cmt. *d.* Since crossing the bridge takes time, B cannot "tender" it so as to come within the branch of the rule that applies when "the offeree tenders . . . the invited performance or tenders a beginning of it." See the definition of tender in note 12 *infra*.

not revoke his offer and that if tender is made it will be accepted. Part performance or tender may thus furnish consideration for the subsidiary promise."[10] By coupling the offer with an option contract, the rule violates the principle of mutuality of obligation and subjects the offeror to the risk of speculation by the offeree. But the instances in which the rule has been invoked, however, have been far removed from the sort of transaction on a fluctuating market where speculation is a real risk, and the rule has generally met with judicial approval.[11] If the performance is one that can be tendered, the offeree is also protected under §45 by tendering the invited performance or a beginning of it, even though the offeror refuses to receive it.[12] Although reliance by mere preparation as distinguished from performance is not recognized by §45, it may have a similar effect under Restatement Second §87(2), discussed in the next section of the treatise.[13] The offeror, however, remains the master of the offer to the extent that the offeror can vary the rule of §45 by express provision.[14]

Requirement of completion of performance

It is curious that the Restatement insists upon completion of performance by the offeree as a condition of the right to recover, even though the offeror's attempt to revoke indicates that the offeror does not wish completion.[15] It would be consistent with the principle of mitigation of damages to refuse the offeree recovery of any amount that could have been avoided had the offeree ceased performance on revocation.[16] The offeree's right to recover anything

---

[10] First Restatement §45 cmt. *b*.

[11] Marchiondo v. Scheck, 432 P.2d 405 (N.M. 1967) (real estate brokerage). For a case decided before the promulgation of §45, *see* Brackenbury v. Hodgkin, 102 A. 106 (Me. 1917) (offer of elderly woman to leave her farm to her daughter and son-in-law if they would move there and take care of her during her life was an offer of a "unilateral contract" that they "accepted" by moving there and beginning to take care of her).

Even the propounder of the Brooklyn Bridge hypothetical recanted 34 years later. "Since that time I have repented, so that now, clad in sackcloth, I state frankly, that my point of view has changed. I agree, at this time, with the rule set forth in the Restatement . . . ." Book Review, 3 J. Legal Ed. 145, 146 (1950). On the history of §45, *see* Farnsworth, Contracts Scholarship in the Age of the Anthology, 85 Mich. L. Rev. 1406, 1449-54 (1987). *See generally* Tiersma, Reassessing Unilateral Contracts: The Role of Offer, Acceptance and Promise, 26 U.C. Davis L. Rev. 1 (1992).

[12] Tender is an offer to perform coupled with a present ability of immediate performance. The person to whom the tender is made must accept it in order for there to be performance. There can be a tender of money, goods, a deed, or the like, but not, strictly speaking, of services or other performance that takes time. (The mortgagor could have tendered the money in the situation described in the discussion of the example of *Petterson v. Pattberg* in §3.12 *supra*.)

[13] See the discussion of Restatement Second §87(2) in §3.25 *infra*.

[14] *But see* McGrath v. Rhode Island Retirement Bd., 88 F.3d 12 (1st Cir. 1996) (though generally offeror can reserve "the power to revoke the offer until the offeree's performance is complete, . . . this logic is not inevitable" and once employee fulfills service requirements for retirement benefits, employee acquires contractual right to those benefits).

[15] Restatement Second §45 cmt. *e* qualifies the text by explaining that "the condition may be excused, for example, if the offeror prevents performance, waives it, or repudiates."

[16] B could therefore recover $100 minus any amount that could be saved by stopping performance on A's revocation. See the discussion of stopping work in §12.12 *infra*. *See also* Baumgartner

would, of course, be conditional on an ability to complete performance absent revocation.[17] The question would vanish if the offeree's reliance interest were the limit of recovery under §45, as it may be under §90, but this possibility has been largely ignored.[18]

The popularity of the Brooklyn Bridge hypothetical has been due in part to the lack of more practical illustrations. The problem does not arise unless the offer, instead of inviting acceptance by a promise, invites acceptance by some continuing performance — as in continuing guaranty cases or in reward cases.[19] But the problem is often avoided in continuing guaranty cases by finding that the offer invites a series of unilateral contracts. And it is unlikely to arise in reward cases, because an offer of a reward is usually a general offer and is therefore difficult to revoke.[20] The major area for the practical application of §45 has been in the real estate brokerage cases, which are analogous to the conventional reward cases.

Lack of practical illustrations

Most owners, in listing their property with a broker, use an "open" listing, under which the property is listed with more than one broker, and the one that is fortunate enough to effect the sale claims a commission much as the bounty hunter claims a reward.[21] The incentive for each broker to make a substantial effort is small and brokers' reliance on open listings has not been accorded legal

Real estate brokerage transaction

---

v. Meek, 272 P.2d 552, 556 (Cal. App. 1954) (completion of performance by broker not necessary where owner repudiated offer to pay commission for arranging sale because unnecessary for broker "to spend additional money and time trying to find a buyer who could not have viewed the property").

[17] B could therefore not recover anything if it could be shown that B could not have finished crossing the bridge had there been no revocation.

[18] This, in effect, is what the court did in Offord v. Davies, *supra* note 8. *See* Fuller & Perdue, The Reliance Interest in Contract Damages (pt. 2), 46 Yale L.J. 373, 410-17 (1937) ("where the promisee's reliance before revocation was not extensive, and is readily convertible into money, this treatment [in §45] of the case will seem unduly drastic when it is recalled that the obligation imposed is unilateral, and that the promisor had no means of compelling the promisee to complete the act if he had chosen to abandon it").

[19] The problem has not been reported in litigation involving the other major type of unilateral contract, that arising out of employment at will. See the discussion of cases where performance is sought in §3.12 *infra*.

[20] See the discussion of revocation of a general offer in §3.17 *supra*. Furthermore, the claimant would have to have performed or at least have been able to perform. One practical example is the offer to leave property by will in return for support for life. *See* Davis v. Jacoby, *supra* note 5; Brackenbury v. Hodgkin, *supra* note 11.

[21] "[T]he very essence of a brokerage commission is that it is dependent upon success and that it is in no way dependent upon, or affected by, the amount of work done by the broker. A brokerage commission is earned if the broker, without devoting much, or any, time to hunting up a customer succeeds in procuring one; and it is equally true, on the other hand, not only that no commission is earned if a broker is not successful but a broker is not entitled to any compensation no matter how much time he has devoted to finding a customer, provided a customer is not found." Cadigan v. Crabtree, 61 N.E. 37 (Mass. 1901).

protection under §45.[22] The owner that wishes a broker to use more diligent efforts will give the broker the exclusive right to sell the property for a period of time under either an "exclusive agency" or an "exclusive right to sell."[23] What is the broker's situation if, after the broker has invested time and effort in trying to arrange a sale, the owner attempts to revoke? It is possible, in accord with the general rule applicable to exclusive arrangements,[24] to protect the broker by interpreting the owner's offer as seeking a promise by the broker to use best efforts and then by inferring such a promise from the broker's beginning performance, the owner's promise to pay a commission being subject to the condition that the broker succeed. Some courts have held the owner on this ground.[25] Others have treated the situation as coming within §45 and have held that the owner is bound by an option contract as soon as the broker has taken substantial steps,[26] analogous to B's beginning to cross the Brooklyn Bridge. (The possibility that the broker's efforts might be merely preparation rather than performance seems not seriously to have been considered.[27]) Whichever ground is adopted, recovery depends, at least in theory, on proof that the broker could have found a buyer had the broker been permitted to do so.[28]

Is the offeree ever given similar protection if the offeree relies on an offer that invites a promise rather than performance?

Reluctance to protect offeree

§3.25. Reliance on Offer That Invites a Promise. The preceding section discussed the development of a rule to protect an offeree from the risk of revocation before acceptance when the offer invites acceptance by performance. If the offer invites a promise, the need for such protection is less evident because the offeree can eliminate the risk simply by making the promise before doing anything in reliance on the offer. Courts have therefore been reluctant

---

[22] The broker, in any event, must have arranged a sale or at least have been able to do so. For a case applying the rule of §45 to a nonexclusive offer to a broker to pay a commission for arranging a sale to a specified prospect, *see* Marchiondo v. Scheck, *supra* note 11.

[23] These differ in that the owner retains the right to sell the property itself under an "exclusive agency" but not under an "exclusive right to sell." There is also an arrangement, called a "multiple listing," that attempts to combine the virtues of open and exclusive listings by having the owner list the property with a member of the local real estate board who promises to use best efforts and, in turn, to sublist the property with other members of the board. The broker splits the commission if another broker arranges a sale.

[24] See the discussion of the duty of reasonable efforts in §2.13 *supra*.

[25] Harris v. McPherson, 115 A. 723 (Conn. 1922) (when the broker "used reasonable efforts to procure a purchaser . . . and expended money and time in so doing" there "was such an acceptance of the offer . . . as created a contract").

[26] Baumgartner v. Meek, *supra* note 16.

[27] That preparation might also protect the broker, see the discussion of Restatement Second §87(2) in §3.25 *infra*.

[28] Brady v. East Portland Sheet Metal Works, 352 P.2d 144 (Or. 1960) ("it was essential for [broker] to show . . . that she probably would have sold the property"). Since the asking price is often inflated to permit bargaining, it may be difficult for the broker to show that a sale could have been arranged at that price.

to protect an offeree that has relied before making the invited promise. The language of Restatement Second §90 limiting enforcement of a promise to situations in which "injustice can be avoided only by enforcement of the promise" will ordinarily bar a claim based on that section.[1] It has been held, for example, that even if a prospective purchaser of land relies on the offer by spending money on having the title searched, the prospective purchaser has no remedy if the offeror revokes the offer before acceptance.[2] An offeree may get restitution if, in relying on the offer, the offeree has conferred a benefit on the offeror. Thus a prospective purchaser of land can generally get back a down payment if the negotiations fail to result in a contract.[3] But neither the offeree's reliance interest nor the offeree's expectation interest has traditionally been accorded protection.

The most significant change in this reluctance to protect the offeree has come in connection with bids on construction contracts. A general contractor, planning to bid on a construction contract, solicits bids from subcontractors and uses the most favorable one in making up its own bid. A problem arises if the contractor is awarded the contract but, before the contractor has a chance to notify the subcontractor whose bid the contractor has used, the subcontractor attempts to revoke its bid. The subcontractor's reason might be another better opportunity, a sudden rise in costs, or a mistake in figuring its bid. Three solutions commend themselves. Each assumes that the subcontractor's bid is an offer that invites acceptance by a promise from the contractor.

Revocability of subcontractors' bids

The first solution is to treat the subcontractor's offer as one that invites acceptance by the general contractor's promise after the award of the main contract and is revocable until such acceptance. This solution leaves the general contractor only the practical sanction of refusing to do further business with a subcontractor that revokes a bid on which the general contractor has relied.

Revocable until acceptance after award

The second solution is to treat the subcontractor's offer as one that invites the general contractor's promise after the award of the main contract but is, in contrast to the first solution, irrevocable until the general contractor has had a reasonable time to make that promise following the award. This arrangement binds the subcontractor but not the general contractor. It makes the subcontractor even more vulnerable to "bid shopping," a practice, regarded as unethical in the industry, in which the general contractor takes the lowest subcontractor's bid to competing subcontractors to try to get an even lower price. This

Irrevocable on use of bid

---

§3.25   [1] See the discussion of avoiding injustice in §2.10 *supra*.

[2] Friedman v. Tappan Dev. Co., 126 A.2d 646 (N.J. 1956) ("offeror had no reason to believe the offeree would cause a search of the title to be made before acceptance of the offer; and the offeree knew the risk in this regard").

[3] If there is no contract for the sale of goods because the price fails to be fixed, "the buyer must return any goods already received or if unable to do so must pay their reasonable value at the time of delivery and the seller must return any portion of the price paid on account." UCC 2-305(4). See the discussion of restitution in §3.26 *infra*.

solution aggravates any imbalance of bargaining power already favoring the general contractor.[4]

Contract on use of bid

The third solution is to ⌈treat the subcontractor's offer as one that invites acceptance by the general contractor's promise at the time it makes its own bid, rather than after the award as in the first two solutions.⌉ This promise by the general contractor may be implied from its use of the subcontractor's bid. The resulting contract would, of course, be subject to an implied condition that the general contractor receive the award. This solution would bind both parties and prevent bid shopping, but it raises practical problems. Subcontractors may have difficulty in proving that their bids were used by the general contractor if the general contractor does not list subcontractors in its own bid or notify them of the use of their bids. The contractor may not even use actual subcontractors' bids but may discount the lowest bids in anticipation of bid shopping or may "doctor" bids by combining figures from several of them. Subcontractors' bids may pose problems of definiteness or may need modification to meet the general contractor's needs.[5] And the general contractor may need additional time to check the subcontractors' reputations and financial responsibility. Indeed, since general contractors are rarely willing to make such commitments explicitly, it seems unlikely that this is the parties' understanding in the ordinary case.

Example of *Baird*

A notable opinion by Judge Learned Hand in *James Baird v. Gimbel Bros.* expounded traditional contract doctrine. Hand concluded that the subcontractor, which had discovered a mistake in its bid before the bid had been accepted by the general contractor, could revoke it in spite of reliance by the general contractor. The offer could not "be regarded as an option, giving the plaintiff the right seasonably to accept . . . if its bid was accepted, but not binding it to take and pay if it could get a better bargain elsewhere. There is not the least reason to suppose that the defendant meant to subject itself to such a one-sided obligation."[6] The notion of estoppel based on reliance, which had grown up in connection with purely gratuitous promises, was inappropriate where the parties were bargaining and the offer sought acceptance by a promise.

Example of *Drennan*

The Supreme Court of California made a dramatic departure from this traditional analysis in the landmark case of *Drennan v. Star Paving Co.* In that case Star Paving had telephoned a $7,131 bid for the paving work on a school job to Drennan, a general contractor who was preparing to bid on the job. Since Star's bid was lowest, Drennan used it in computing his own bid, listing Star's name as the paving subcontractor. Drennan was awarded the contract and stopped

---

[4]For an illuminating, if dated, study of the construction industry in Indiana, *see* Schultz, The Firm Offer Puzzle: A Study of Business Practice in the Construction Industry, 19 U. Chi. L. Rev. 237 (1952) (concluding that this solution would add further to the existing imbalance in favor of the general contractor and that it would be better if the bid were revocable, leaving the matter to be worked out by the parties).

[5]Of course, these problems are not entirely avoided if the second solution is adopted.

[6]64 F.2d 344, 346 (2d Cir. 1933). The general contractor could overcome this objection by having the subcontractor promise not to revoke its bid and then relying on this explicit promise.

by Star's office the next day, only to be told before accepting that Star had made a mistake in figuring its bid and could not do it for less than $15,000. Drennan found another paving subcontractor that did the work for $10,948 and then sued Star for the $3,817 difference. In an opinion by Justice Traynor, the court held that Drennan was entitled to this amount. It rejected the third solution suggested above — that there was "a bilateral contract binding on both parties" when Drennan used Star's bid — on the ground that there was no evidence to support this interpretation.[7] But it reasoned that, although Star had made no express promise to keep its offer open, such a subsidiary promise should be implied "to preclude the injustice that would result if the offer could be revoked after the offeree had acted in detrimental reliance thereon."[8] Drennan's reliance on this implied subsidiary promise made it binding and made the offer — the main promise — irrevocable.[9] The notion of estoppel based on reliance was not limited to purely gratuitous promises. Although *Drennan* might be faulted for tipping the scale too far in favor of the general contractor, it has been followed by later cases.[10] Courts have, however, been careful to point out that irrevocability lasts only long enough to give the general contractor a reasonable opportunity to accept and that the general contractor that abuses the rule by "bid shopping" loses its protection.[11]

Whatever stance a court might take, the parties themselves can determine the outcome. As the master of its offer, it is a simple matter for the subcontractor to reject the rule in *Drennan* by stating that its bid is revocable, assuming that the general contractor will accept such a bid.[12] If the general contractor has sufficient bargaining power, it might insist that the subcontractor adopt the rule in *Drennan* by stating that its bid is irrevocable so that the general

Autonomy of parties

---

[7]333 P.2d 757, 759 (Cal. 1958).

[8]See the discussion of Restatement §45 in §3.24 *supra*, including Comment *b* to §45 in the first Restatement quoted there.

[9]333 P.2d at 760. The court rejected the argument that Drennan's use of Star Paving's bid was consideration for the subsidiary promise not to revoke, on the ground that there was "no evidence that defendant offered to make its bid irrevocable in exchange for plaintiff's use of its figures in computing his bid." As to the difficulty encountered in showing that action of this kind is bargained for, see the discussion of other consideration and reliance in §3.23 *supra*.

[10]Loranger Constr. Corp. v. E.F. Hauserman Co., 384 N.E.2d 176 (Mass. 1978) (Braucher, J.: "doctrine is not as novel" as contended).

The mere fact that the offer is one for the sale of goods, so that the subcontractor could have made a firm offer in writing under UCC 2-205, should not change the result. See the discussion of option contracts under the Restatement Second in §3.23 *supra*. *But see* Gibson, Promissory Estoppel, Article 2 of the U.C.C., and the Restatement (Third) of Contracts, 73 Iowa L. Rev. 659, 696-706 (1988).

[11]Pavel Enters. v. A.S. Johnson Co., 674 A.2d 521 (Md. 1996) (general contractor's "reasonable expectation had dissipated in the span of a month" and injustice can be avoided without enforcement of promise if general engages "in bid shopping, chopping or peddling").

[12]*But see* Lyon Metal Prods. v. Hagerman Constr. Corp., 391 N.E.2d 1152 (Ind. App. 1979) (trial court could have found justifiable reliance though "offer expressly stated it was subject to withdrawal or modification 15 days after the date it was given").

contractor's reliance will make it so. The general contractor might also use the traditional legal device of an option supported by consideration, but this is seldom done.[13]

General contractor not bound

Courts have, however, rebuffed attempts by subcontractors to hold general contractors liable on the rationale in *Drennan*. As the Supreme Court of Minnesota said:

> [T]he subcontractor does not rely on the general and suffers no detriment. A subcontractor submits bids to all or most of the general contractors that it knows are bidding on the project . . . . The subcontractor engages in the same work and expense in preparing its bid regardless of who wins the general contract and whether the subcontractor wins the contract on which it bid . . . . [Furthermore], the nature of the bidding process compels allowing the general sufficient leeway to maintain its flexibility in executing subcontracts and selecting the subcontractors it will hire for a project.[14]

Restatement Second §87(2)

Restatement Second §87(2) generalizes from *Drennan*:

> An offer which the offeror should reasonably expect to induce action or forbearance of a substantial character on the part of the offeree before acceptance and which does induce such action or forbearance is binding as an option contract to the extent necessary to avoid injustice.[15]

Although the cases holding subcontractors to their bids have granted the full expectation measure of recovery,[16] §87(2) takes a more flexible approach than §45 and invites enforcement only "to the extent necessary to avoid injustice." It remains to be seen what influence it will have in extending the rationale of the *Drennan* case to analogous situations in which an offeree relies on an offer in making a related contract.[17] Section 87(2) gives some support to a claim based

---

[13]The general contractor might also try to protect itself by requiring subcontractors to post bid bonds. But if the subcontractor's bid is revocable, the general contractor may not be able to enforce the bond if the subcontractor revokes. See the discussion of the effect of a deposit in §3.17 *supra*.

[14]Holman Erection Co. v. Orville E. Madsen & Sons, 330 N.W.2d 693, 698 (Minn. 1983).

[15]Both the Vienna Convention and the UNIDROIT Principles have provisions similar to that of §87(2). CISG 16(2)(b); UNIDROIT Principles 2.4(2)(b).

[16]It would often be difficult to grant the reliance measure of recovery like in *Drennan* cases by attempting to put the general contractor back in the position in which it would have been if the subcontractor had not bid. If the general contractor had used a higher bid than another subcontractor, the general contractor might not have been awarded the contract and would have then allocated its resources differently. The uncertainties of such speculation have led courts to base recovery on expectation, by allowing the difference between the bid of the defaulting subcontractor and the next higher bidder.

[17]For a case ignoring §87(2) but applying §90 to an employer that revoked an offer of employment after a prospective employee had quit a previous job, *see* Grouse v. Group Health Plan, 306 N.W.2d 114 (Minn. 1981) ("measure of damages is not so much what he would have earned . . . as

on reliance before a beginning or tender of performance gives rights under §45, as in the hypothetical of B's preparing to cross the Brooklyn Bridge and in the case of a broker that uses efforts to find a purchaser.[18]

We turn now to more far-reaching suggestions for protection of the parties during the negotiating process.

§3.26.   **Precontractual Liability.**   Courts have traditionally accorded parties the freedom to negotiate without risk of precontractual liability. If the negotiations *succeed* and result in ultimate agreement, a party that has behaved improperly can be deprived of the bargain on the ground of misrepresentation, duress, undue influence, or unconscionability. But if the negotiations *fail* because of similar behavior, courts have been reluctant to impose precontractual liability. Although a duty of fair dealing is now generally imposed on the parties to an existing contract, that duty is not so formulated as to extend to negotiations before the contract is made.[1] Under an existing contract each party, though free to refuse to negotiate a modification, is bound, once negotiations have begun, by a duty of good faith and fair dealing imposed by that contract.[2] In sharp contrast, courts traditionally take a view of the precontractual period that assures a broad freedom of negotiation and relieves a party of the risk of liability arising during negotiation. As a general rule, a party to precontractual negotiations may break them off without liability at any time and for any reason — a change of heart, a change of circumstances, a better deal — or for no reason at all. The only cost of doing so is the loss of that party's own investment in the negotiations in terms of time, effort, and expense.

The problem of liability arising out of unsuccessful negotiations is commonly viewed in the optic of offer and acceptance though, as has been pointed out, the classic sequence of offer and acceptance is often absent in important contract negotiations.[3] Under the basic rules of offer and acceptance, there is no contractual liability until a contract is made by the acceptance of an offer. Prior to acceptance, the offeror is free to back out by revoking the offer. No sympathy is lost on the offeree if the offer is revoked, for an offeree is regarded as amply protected by the power to accept before revocation. An offeree that chooses to rely on the offer without accepting it is seen as taking the risk that the

Traditional freedom of negotiation

Optic of offer and acceptance

---

what he lost in quitting the job he had and in declining at least one other offer of employment elsewhere").

[18] Strata Prod. Co. v. Mercury Exploration Co., 916 P.2d 822 (N.M. 1996) (reliance served to make 120-day option irrevocable and offeree "was free to accept the original, unilateral contract offer simply by undertaking the performance"). See the discussions of Restatement Second §45 and of a real estate brokerage transaction in §3.24 *supra*. See also the discussion of the example of *Petterson v. Pattberg* in §3.12 *supra*.

§3.26   [1] UCC 1-304; Restatement Second §205 cmt. *c*.

[2] See the discussions of legislative reform and of remedies of the victim of bad faith in §4.22 *infra*.

[3] See the discussion of the limits of traditional analysis in §3.5 *supra*.

reliance will go uncompensated.[4] This "freedom from contract" is enhanced by the judicial reluctance to read a proposal as an offer in the first place.[5]

"Aleatory view" of negotiations

Courts have been even more reluctant to impose liability if no offer has been made at the time that the negotiations are broken off. At the root of this reluctance is the common law's "aleatory view" of negotiations: a party that enters negotiations in the hope of the gain that will result from ultimate agreement bears the risk of whatever loss results if the other party breaks off the negotiations. That loss includes out-of-pocket costs the disappointed party has incurred, any worsening of its situation, and any opportunities that it has lost as a result of the negotiations. All this is hazarded on a successful outcome of the negotiations; all this is lost on failure. As an English judge expressed it, the disappointed party "undertakes this work as a gamble, and its cost is part of the overhead expenses of his business which he hopes will be met out of the profits of such contracts as are made . . . ."[6] This aleatory view of negotiations rests on a concern that limiting the freedom of negotiation might discourage parties from entering negotiations. With rare exceptions, courts have resisted suggestions that parties may in some circumstances come under a duty to bargain in good faith.[7]

Rare exceptions

In a few narrow fields of economic activity one is not free to refuse to deal with another. Businesses described as "public utilities" — such as telephone companies, gas and electric companies, and railroads — are considered to be under "a duty to serve without discrimination and on proper terms all who request [their] service" and are liable in tort for breach of that duty.[8] The duty "is the result partly of historical development, partly of the nature of the services which they render and partly of their less competitive and more monopolistic character."[9] The assessment of damages is facilitated by the fact that the terms of the contract that should have been made are standard

[4]Drennan v. Star Paving Co., 333 P.2d 757 (Cal. 1958), described in the discussion of the example of *Drennan* in §3.25 *supra*, represents a limited inroad into the traditional freedom of negotiation. However, it extends protection only to offerees, not to offerors, and it does not protect a promisee if the promise falls short of being an offer.

[5]See the discussion of reluctance to find an offer in §3.10 *supra*.

[6]William Lacey (Hounslow) Ltd. v. Davis, [1957] 1 W.I.R. 932, 934 (Q.B).

[7]These suggestions go back to the German scholar Jhering, who in 1861 formulated a doctrine of *culpa in contrahendo* (fault in negotiating) under which "damages should be recoverable against the party whose blameworthy conduct during negotiations for a contract brought about its invalidity or prevented its perfection," though "the party who has relied on the validity of the contract to his injury will not be able to recover the value of the promised performance, the expectation interest," but rather "his 'negative interest' or reliance damages." Kessler & Fine, *Culpa in Contrahendo*, Bargaining in Good Faith, and Freedom of Contract, 77 Harv. L. Rev. 401, 401-02 (1964). *But see* Racine & Laramie v. California Dept. of Parks & Recreation, 14 Cal. Rptr. 2d 335 (Ct. App. 1992) (doctrine of *culpa in contrahendo* "has never been accepted in Anglo-American jurisprudence").

[8]Restatement of Torts §763 (1939).

[9]Restatement of Torts §763 cmt. *a* (1939).

terms.[10] In addition to these atypical examples of duty to serve the public, there are instances in which a refusal to deal may have legal consequences if it is improperly motivated. If, for example, the purpose of the refusal is to restrain trade or gain a monopoly, it may be wrongful under either the common law relating to business torts[11] or under statutes in the fields of antitrust and trade regulation.[12] And if the purpose of the refusal is improper discrimination, it may be wrongful under one of the antidiscrimination laws,[13] though such liability is also generally in tort rather than contract. Furthermore, federal law requires employers and unionized employees to engage in collective bargaining in "good faith."[14] The collective bargaining agreement is, however, a special sort of contract, in good part because of "the compulsory character of the bargaining relationship" in which the employer is required to bargain with the union that represents a majority of the employees, to the exclusion of all other unions.[15]

A rare exception in which a court imposed a duty to bargain in good faith is *Heyer Products Co. v. United States*. Heyer, the disappointed low bidder on a government contract, sued the government, alleging that it had awarded the contract to a higher bidder in order to retaliate against Heyer for testimony at a Senate hearing. The United States Court of Claims held that, while the government "could accept or reject an offer as it pleased," it had an obligation to honestly consider [Heyer's bid] and not to wantonly disregard it." For breach of this duty it would be liable to Heyer for its expenses in preparing its bid, although not for its lost profits.[16] The rule must be regarded with caution, having been framed in context of an invitation to bid on a government contract

Example of *Heyer Products*

---

[10] A related sort of liability has been imposed on life insurers. If the insurer takes an unreasonable length of time to act on an application and the applicant dies during the period of delay, the insurer has been held liable. Rosin v. Peninsular Life Ins. Co., 116 So. 2d 798 (Fla. App. 1960). The theory is often one of liability in tort for negligence, with damages predicated on the assumption that, had the insurer promptly rejected the application, the applicant would have obtained an identical policy elsewhere.

[11] *See* 2 F. Harper, F. James & O. Gray, Law of Torts §6.13 (2d ed. 1986).

[12] *See* 7 P. Areeda & H. Hovenkamp, Antitrust Law ch. 14 (2d ed. 1986).

[13] Gray v. Serruto Builders, 265 A.2d 404 (N.J. Super. 1970) (court, on a showing of violation of a fair housing law, ordered defendant to offer an apartment when available and awarded damages for mental suffering).

[14] National Labor Relations Act, 29 U.S.C. §158(d). The duty does not, however, "compel either party to agree to a proposal or require the making of a concession." Thus, in implementing this provision, the National Labor Relations Board may order a party to cease and desist from refusing to bargain, but it may not order a party to include a particular term in the agreement. *See* H.K. Porter Co. v. NLRB, 397 U.S. 99 (1970).

[15] *See* Summers, Collective Agreements and the Law of Contracts, 78 Yale L.J. 525, 530-33 (1969).

[16] 140 F. Supp. 409, 412, 413 (Ct. Cl. 1956). Heyer was, however, unable to prove its allegations. Heyer Prods. Co. v. United States, 177 F. Supp. 251 (Ct. Cl. 1959). Recovery of bid preparation costs was approved in King v. Alaska State Hous. Auth., 633 P.2d 256 (Alaska 1981).

where the bidder's power to revoke its bid is restricted.[17] But though the court noted that recovery could be had only on proof of "a fraudulent inducement for bids,"[18] subsequent decisions have required only "arbitrary and capricious" behavior for recovery of bid preparation costs.[19]

Four grounds for liability

In recent decades, courts have shown increasing willingness to impose pre-contractual liability. The possible grounds can be grouped under four headings: (1) unjust enrichment resulting from the negotiations; (2) a misrepresentation made during the negotiations; (3) a specific promise made during the negotiations; (4) an agreement to negotiate in good faith.[20]

Liability for unjust enrichment

The duty to make restitution of benefits received during negotiations is sometimes a compelling ground for precontractual liability. A negotiating party may not with impunity unjustly appropriate such benefits to its own use. To prevent such unjust enrichment, the law imposes liability measured by the injured party's restitution interest. Claims to restitution commonly involve either ideas disclosed or services rendered during negotiations.

Restitution for ideas appropriated

The clearest cases are those that involve misappropriation of ideas. Suppose, for example, that the owner of a business, in the course of negotiating for the sale of the business to a prospective buyer, discloses an idea in confidence in order to enable the buyer to appraise the value of the business, and when the negotiations fail the buyer makes use of the owner's idea. The buyer may be liable for misappropriation of the owner's idea on several grounds of which restitution is only one. The misappropriation may be a breach of a contract, either express or implied-in-fact, though this is rarely the case in the situation discussed here.[21] A more usual ground for imposing liability is that the idea is regarded as the owner's "property," the traditional rationale when the idea is

---

[17] See the discussion of the rule of revocability in §3.17 *supra*. However, *Heyer Products* was extended in New England Insulation Co. v. General Dynamics Corp., 522 N.E.2d 997 (Mass. App. 1988) ("no reason in principle why [misrepresentation cases] should not apply to private contractors").

[18] 140 F. Supp. at 414.

[19] See King v. Alaska State Hous. Auth., *supra* note 16 ("standard consistently relied on by the Court of Claims has been that . . . of 'arbitrary and capricious' behavior").

[20] See generally S. Burton & E. Andersen, Contractual Good Faith ch. 8 (1995); Farnsworth, Precontractual Liability and Preliminary Agreements: Fair Dealing and Failed Negotiations, 87 Colum. L. Rev. 217, 229-39, 263-69 (1987) (from which part of this section of the treatise is adapted).

[21] Where the subject matter of the negotiations is the idea itself, the parties may understand that compensation is to be paid if the idea is disclosed and then used. Sikes v. McGraw-Edison Co., 665 F.2d 731 (5th Cir. 1982) (idea for lawn trimmer).

But where, as in negotiations over the sale of a business, the subject matter is not the idea itself and its disclosure is merely incidental, such an understanding would be anomalous. Faris v. Enberg, 158 Cal. Rptr. 704 (Ct. App. 1979) (developer of idea for sports quiz show who disclosed idea in negotiations to hire sports announcer could not recover under contract implied-in-fact because developer "never thought of selling his sports quiz show idea to anyone").

a trade secret.[22] Another ground, accepted by some courts, is that the misappropriation is a breach of a confidential relation,[23] though if the negotiations were at arm's length, the relationship between negotiating parties cannot be characterized as "confidential" for this purpose.[24] Finally, a party may have a claim based on restitution of the benefit that the other party gained from an idea that is novel and concrete.[25] Recovery based on restitution is measured by the benefit to the party that appropriated the idea, while at least in principle recovery based on a property right or on a confidential relation is measured by the loss to the party from which the idea was appropriated. In practice, however, recovery on all three grounds tends to be measured by the benefit to the party that appropriated the idea as the only feasible measure.[26]

A party may also seek restitution for services rendered, as distinguished from ideas misappropriated, during unsuccessful negotiations. But the mere circumstance that the party's services benefited the other party does not give a claim to restitution, for under the aleatory view of negotiations, a court may treat benefit as well as loss as being at risk in the negotiations. The time, efforts, and activities expended during negotiations are, as one court put it, "the common grist of negotiations aimed toward consummation of an agreement," and "the endeavors by either side, if they fail, do not warrant a claim that one party has been unjustly enriched at the expense of the other." Each side's efforts were for the purpose of advancing its own interests,[27] a conclusion that is sometimes buttressed by the statement that it is only "*unjust* enrichment which is to be avoided" by the law of restitution.[28]

Restitution for services rendered

A particularly appealing kind of claim to restitution is that presented by an architect or builder that has rendered services to a developer during the planning stages of a development, only to have the developer award the contract to

Example of *Hill v. Waxberg*

---

[22] How J. Ryan & Assoc. v. Century Brewing Assn., 55 P.2d 1053 (Wash. 1936) (phrase "The Beer of the Century" became "a property right").

[23] Capital Films Corp. v. Charles Fries Prods., 628 F.2d 387 (5th Cir. 1980) ("screenings to potential film distributors . . . can support . . . finding that a confidential or type of fiduciary relationship exists").

[24] Faris v. Enberg, *supra* note 21 (negotiation did not give rise to "confidential relationship").

[25] Matarese v. Moore-McCormack Lines, 158 F.2d 631 (2d Cir. 1946) (device for loading cargo).

[26] How J. Ryan & Assoc. v. Century Brewing Assn., *supra* note 22 (value of property right or services depends on "value of the idea to the user").

[27] Songbird Jet Ltd. v. Amax, 581 F. Supp. 912 (S.D.N.Y. 1984) ("no reasonable business executive would expect payment for his own preliminary activities").

[28] Rutledge v. Housing Auth., 411 N.E.2d 82, 86 (Ill. App. 1980) (contractor and architect "were gambling on the successful completion of the structure"). *See* Restatement (Third) of Restitution and Unjust Enrichment §23 cmt. *c* (Tent. Draft No. 2, April 1, 2002) (such precontractual performance "rests on a self-interested calculation by which the anticipated reward to the performing party is the enhanced likelihood of a future return," and if the return is not realized, there is no question of unjust enrichment, though "fact that the defendant has been benefited at the plaintiff's expense may influence a court to find that an implied promise was made").

another. An example is *Hill v. Waxberg*, which arose when Hill asked Waxberg, a contractor, to help him prepare for the construction of a building on Hill's lot. It was understood that if the financing could be arranged through the Federal Housing Authority as contemplated, Hill would give Waxberg the building contract. At Hill's request, Waxberg made several trips to confer with the architects, hired a third party to secure a drill log on the property, surveyed the property, and was instrumental in getting the data for the FHA. He expected to be compensated for this out of the profits from the contemplated contract. When the FHA issued the commitment, Hill and Waxberg began negotiations for the building contract but were unable to agree. Hill then made a contract with another contractor, and Waxberg sued him for the reasonable value of his services and his expenditures. It was held that Waxberg was entitled to recover in restitution for "the value of the benefit which was acquired," because:

> something in the nature of an implied contract results where one renders services at the request of another with the expectation of pay therefor, and in the process confers a benefit on the other . . . . It makes no difference whether the pay expected is in the form of an immediate cash payment, or in the form of profits to be derived from a contract, the consummation of which would or should be anticipated by reasonable men. . . .[29]

However, few other courts have entertained claims for restitution of benefits conferred during failed negotiations.[30] Because a party's expenses during negotiation typically result in no benefit on the other party, such expenses have not often given rise to claims to restitution.[31]

Liability for misrepresentation   Misrepresentation, another possible basis of precontractual liability, has been no more popular than restitution has been. A negotiating party may not with impunity fraudulently misrepresent its intention to come to terms. Such an assertion is one of fact — of a state of mind — and if fraudulent, it may be actionable in tort.

Example of Markov   *Markov v. ABC Transfer & Storage Co.* is a rare exception. There, a lessor of warehouse facilities intentionally misrepresented to the lessee that it intended to renew the existing lease for another three years, while "it was at the same time

---

[29] 237 F.2d 936, 938-39 (9th Cir. 1956).

[30] For an exception, *see* Longo v. Shore & Reich, 25 F.3d 94 (2d Cir. 1994) (employee entitled to recover "for the reasonable value of the services and equipment she provided" when no agreement was concluded.

[31] *See* Reprosystem v. SCM Corp., 727 F.2d 257 (2d Cir. 1984) (prospective purchasers of foreign subsidiaries failed to show that their activities during negotiations benefited parent by increasing profits from subsidiaries); Burst v. Adolph Coors Co., 503 F. Supp. 19 (E.D. Mo. 1980) (applicant for franchise failed to show that information in application was of benefit to franchisor), aff'd per curiam, 650 F.2d 930 (8th Cir. 1981). *But see* Atacs Corp. v. Trans World Communications, 155 F.3d 659 (3d Cir. 1998) (where "unknown variables cloud a reasonably certain calculation of lost profits," appropriate to measure "fair value" of subcontractor's contribution to contractor's teaming agreement "in order to protect the subcontractor's restitution interest").

quietly negotiating for a sale of the premises." The lessor's motive was to have the premises occupied during the negotiations for their sale and to be assured that, should those negotiations fail, the lease could be renewed. When, only a few weeks before the lease expired, the purchaser gave the startled lessee a notice to vacate the premises, the lessee claimed damages from the lessor for fraud. The Supreme Court of Washington concluded that the lessor had fraudulently promised "to renew the lease . . . and to negotiate the amount of rentals in good faith" and explained that it is enough to show fraud "if the promise is made without care or concern whether it will be kept."[32] The court upheld an award of damages based on the lessee's reliance losses. The award included not only extra expense incurred by the lessee as a result of its precipitous move to another warehouse, but also profits lost to the lessee when its principal customer left because no preparations had been made for that move.[33] The court thus counted in the lessee's reliance damages its lost opportunity of continuing to serve its principal customer. The lessee's problems of proof were minimized because the opportunity that was lost involved the continuation of an existing arrangement.

Implicit in the act of negotiating is a representation of a serious intent to reach agreement with the other party. The rationale of the *Markov* case therefore generally applies, even in the absence of any explicit representation, if a party enters into negotiations without serious intent to reach agreement. It also applies if a party, having lost that intent, continues in negotiations or fails to give prompt notice of its change of mind. It supports recovery in other situations as well. Thus, for example, a negotiating party that misrepresents its authority to act as agent for another could be held liable for reliance damages if negotiations failed when the other party discovered the misrepresentation.[34] Indeed, it would seem that a party to failed negotiations might have a claim based on any misrepresentation, including one by nondisclosure, that upon being discovered caused the negotiations to fail.[35]

Lack of serious intent

But few such actions have been brought, perhaps because parties are rarely tempted to make misrepresentations of the sort made in *Markov*. While it is a common negotiating technique for a party to overstate its willingness to break off negotiations, a party would seldom have reason to overstate its eagerness to negotiate. One possible reason is suggested by *Markov*. In other less likely scenarios, a party might negotiate with a competitor in order to prevent it from

Few such actions

[32] 457 P.2d 535, 537-38, 539 (Wash. 1969).

[33] The measure of damages for fraudulent misrepresentation generally affords the injured party the "pecuniary loss suffered . . . as a consequence of . . . reliance" and, if proved with sufficient certainty, "the benefit of his contract." Restatement (Second) of Torts §549.

[34] For support, *see* Restatement (Second) of Agency §330, which states that for a tortious misrepresentation of authority there is liability "in an action of tort for loss caused by reliance upon such misrepresentation."

[35] For a reference to a Swiss case that provides an interesting example of such a claim, see note 46 *infra*.

taking advantage of another deal, or with an old customer in order to avoid telling it that its business was no longer wanted. Few other reasons suggest themselves.[36] And even when such misrepresentations are made, the injured party may be discouraged by the difficulty of proving fraudulent intent.[37]

Liability for specific promise

In recent decades, courts have begun to go beyond these two grounds of unjust enrichment and misrepresentation and base liability on a specific promise that has been made in order to interest the other party in the negotiations and that the other party has relied on. A negotiating party may not with impunity break such a promise. The franchise cases are instructive. A prospective franchisee, in reliance on a franchisor's promise of a franchise, may make substantial expenditures for advertising and other preparation before receiving a franchise. If the franchisor then refuses to grant a franchise, what rights has the disappointed prospective franchisee? In recent decades courts have shown a willingness to allow the franchisee to recover expenses incurred in preparing to do business.[38]

Example of *Red Owl*

The leading decision in this line is *Hoffman v. Red Owl Stores,* decided by the Supreme Court of Wisconsin in 1965. Hoffman, who owned a bakery, sought a franchise from Red Owl, which owned a supermarket chain. Red Owl assured him that he would be granted a franchise if he took steps to gain experience, and that the $18,000 he had to invest would be sufficient. Over the course of more than two years, he made extensive preparations that included the sale of his bakery, the acquisition and sale of a small grocery store, a move to another town, and a down payment on a lot — each time on assurances of a franchise by Red Owl's representative. The negotiations finally collapsed when Hoffman refused to make a substantially larger financial contribution than had originally been contemplated, and he sued to recover his expenses in reliance on the assurance of a franchise. Because Red Owl had made no offer and the terms of the franchise that might have ultimately been granted were not determined, the court addressed "the question of whether the promise necessary to sustain a cause of action for promissory estoppel must embrace all essential details of a proposed transaction between promisor and promisee so as to be the equivalent of an offer that would result in a binding contract between the parties if the promisee were to accept the same." The court concluded that this was not

---

[36]For an allegation that a party engaged in negotiations as a ruse to acquire a pay-T.V. transmission license, *see* Skycom Corp. v. Telstar Corp., 813 F.2d 810 (7th Cir. 1987).

[37]*See* Zeman v. Lufthansa German Airlines, 699 P.2d 1274 (Alaska 1985) (granting summary judgment to defendant as to fraud claims because of failure to show "reckless indifference" required by *Markov*).

[38]Goodman v. Dicker, 169 F.2d 684 (D.C. Cir. 1948) (recovery based on reliance allowed against franchisor's distributors in spite of their contention that franchise would have been terminable at will by franchisor). In Chrysler Corp. v. Quimby, 144 A.2d 123 (Del. 1958), however, the court went further and also allowed recovery based on lost profits for 90 days, where 90-day notice was required for termination. A curious attempt to reconcile these two cases with respect to the measure of damages appears in Restatement Second §90 illus. 8 & 9.

necessary and "that injustice would result here if plaintiffs were not granted some relief because of the failure of defendants to keep their promises which induced plaintiffs to act to their detriment." Because it was impossible to put a value on Hoffman's lost expectation, his recovery was measured by his reliance interest. The court held that the profits from the small grocery store that were lost on its sale should not be included.[39]

The case affirms that liability based on a specific promise has a place in the law of precontractual liability, even though the promise falls short of being an offer. By allowing recovery based on reliance against a party that had made no offer, the court went beyond the holding in *Drennan* and beyond the rule of the Restatement Second that is derived from it. It can be argued that the case for liability is even stronger where there is no offer, for there is nothing for the promisee to accept as an alternative to acting in reliance on the promise. Because liability is imposed even though there is no offer, a negotiating party cannot avoid it simply by a contrary provision in its offer, although the party might, by the use of appropriate language, so caution its bargaining partner that reliance would not be protected. Indeed, although the court spoke of promissory estoppel, the decision might have been fitted into that field of liability for blameworthy conduct that we know as tort, instead of that field of liability based on obligations voluntarily assumed that we call contract. Subsequent plaintiffs have often failed to show either that the defendant made a promise or that the plaintiff's reliance on that promise was reasonable.[40] But the rationale of *Red Owl* remains viable.

Significance of Red Owl

The rationale was the basis of the Second Circuit's decision in *Cyberchron Corp. v. Calldata Systems Development*. After extended negotiations between Grumman, which had a defense contract, and Cyberchron, which sought to be Grumman's subcontractor to supply a "rugged computer work station," Grumman delivered a purchase order. However, Cyberchron did not accept it because the parties were unable to agree on provisions concerning the weight of the work station. In mid-July of 1990, a Grumman representative directed Cyberchron to proceed with production of the station as if there had been agreement on the weight issue, asserting that the terms of the purchase order would be determined later. The dispute over the weight issue was never resolved and in late September Grumman abruptly broke off the negotiations and arranged to obtain the work station elsewhere. Cyberchron sued and prevailed on the ground of promissory estoppel. The Second Circuit accepted the district court's determination that "starting in mid-July there was . . . a clear and unambiguous promise" and that "Grumman's conduct exerting pressure

Example of Cyberchron

[39] 133 N.W.2d 267, 274-77 (Wis. 1965).

[40] *See* Reprosystem v. SCM Corp., 727 F.2d 257 (2d Cir. 1984) (prospective purchaser of foreign subsidiaries "can neither point to any clear and unambiguous promise made by [parent] to the effect that it would consummate the deal, nor show that they reasonably relied on any promise implied from [parent's] conduct during the negotiations").

on Cyberchron to produce the units at great expense, and then abruptly terminating the transaction to purchase heavier, inferior equipment at a later date from another company was unconscionable."[41] The Second Circuit allowed damages measured by Cyberchron's reliance on that promise.

Suggestions of general obligation

Some scholarly writers have generalized from the cases decided on the grounds of misrepresentation and specific promise to argue that a general obligation of fair dealing may arise out of the negotiations themselves, at least if the disappointed party has been led to believe that success is in prospect. Thus it has been suggested that if courts follow *Red Owl*, "it will no longer be possible for one party to scuttle contract negotiations with impunity when the other has been induced to rely to his detriment on the prospect that the negotiations will succeed."[42] American courts, however, have been unreceptive to these arguments and have declined to find a general obligation that would preclude a party from breaking off negotiations, even when success was in prospect. Their reluctance to do so is supported by the formulation of a general duty of good faith and fair dealing in both the Uniform Commercial Code and the Restatement Second that, at least by negative implication, does not extend to negotiations.[43] European courts have been more willing than American ones to accept scholarly proposals for precontractual liability based on a general obligation of fair dealing. But even in Europe it is difficult to find cases that actually impose precontractual liability where an American court would clearly not do so on other grounds.[44] The UNIDROIT Principles impose liability for negotiation in bad faith,[45] but the same result could be reached in the illustrations given under one of the grounds recognized by American courts.[46]

Neglect in United States

It is perhaps not surprising that American courts have rarely been asked to hold that a general obligation of fair dealing arises out of the negotiations themselves when they have reached a point where one of the parties has relied on a successful outcome. It may be that parties to negotiations are often unaware

---

[41] 47 F.3d 39, 45 (2d Cir. 1995).

[42] Summers, "Good Faith" in General Contract Law and the Sales Provisions of the Uniform Commercial Code, 54 Va. L. Rev. 190, 225 (1968).

[43] City of San Antonio v. Forgy, 769 S.W.2d 293 (Tex. App. 1989) (under "Restatement rule good faith in negotiations of contract is not within the scope of the concept").

[44] European authorities are discussed in Farnsworth, Precontractual Liability and Preliminary Agreements: Fair Dealing and Failed Negotiations, 87 Colum. L. Rev. 217, 239-42 (1987), cited in rejecting "this theory of liability" in Copeland v. Baskin Robbins, 117 Cal. Rptr. 2d 875 (Ct. App. 2002).

[45] UNIDROIT Principles 2.15 "Negotiations in bad faith" ("party who negotiates or breaks off negotiations in good faith is liable for the losses caused to the other party"). There is no comparable provision in the Vienna Convention.

[46] Illustration 1 involves negotiation with no intention of concluding a contract and is similar to *Markov*. Illustration 3 is based on a Swiss case (discussed in Farnsworth, Precontractual Liability and Preliminary Agreements: Fair Dealing and Failed Negotiations, 87 Colum. L. Rev. 217, 235 (1987)) that could also be decided on the ground of misrepresentation by nondisclosure. Illustration 4 is based on *Red Owl*. Illustration 2 does not involve breaking off negotiations.

of the possibility of recovery for lost opportunities.[47] But it may also be that they are not greatly dissatisfied with the common law's aleatory view of negotiations and feel that claims are fairly treated under the existing grounds of liability. As long as these grounds are not often invoked and have not been pushed to their limits, there will be little pressure to add a general obligation of fair dealing.[48]

Furthermore, there is ample justification for judicial reluctance to impose a general obligation of fair dealing on parties to precontractual negotiations. The common law's aleatory view of negotiations well suits a society that does not regard itself as having an interest in the outcome of the negotiations. The negotiation of an ordinary contract differs in this way from the negotiation of a collective bargaining agreement, in which society sees itself as having an interest in preventing labor strife. Although it is in society's interest to provide a regime under which the parties are free to negotiate ordinary contracts, the outcome of any particular negotiation is a matter of indifference. There is no reason to believe that imposition of a general obligation of fair dealing would improve the regime under which such negotiations take place. The difficulty of determining a point in the negotiations at which the obligation of fair dealing arises would create uncertainty. An obligation of fair dealing might have an undesirable chilling effect, discouraging parties from entering into negotiations if chances of success were slight. The obligation might also have an undesirable accelerating effect, increasing the pressure on parties to bring negotiations to a final if hasty conclusion. With no clear advantages to counter these disadvantages, there is little reason to abandon the present aleatory view.[49]

Justification for reluctance

The hard question for American courts is not whether a court should undertake on its own to resolve a dispute over fair dealing in precontractual negotiations, but whether it should undertake to resolve it when the parties have explicitly agreed that it do so. Is the rule that there is no obligation of good faith and fair dealing during precontractual negotiations merely a default rule out of which the parties can contract? As to this, courts have disagreed.

Agreements to negotiate

---

[47] Supporting recovery for opportunities lost in reliance on a promise, *see* D & G Stout v. Bacardi Imports, 923 F.2d 566 (7th Cir. 1991) (where liquor distributor passed up chance to sell distributorship in reliance on importer's promise not to take its line to another distributor, devaluation of distributor's business opportunity when importer broke its promise "represents a reliance injury, rather than an injury to . . . expectation"). In *Bacardi*, however, the opportunity lost was not similar to the promised one.

[48] If our courts were to impose a general obligation of fair dealing, could the parties disclaim that obligation? Under UCC 1-302(b), parties are powerless to disclaim the duty of good faith imposed by the Code under every contract, and it is hard to see why they should fare any better in the precontractual context. But a nondisclaimable duty would conflict with contemporary judicial tolerance of attempts to disclaim precontractual liability.

[49] "If the utility of contract as an instrument of self-government is not to be seriously weakened, parties must be free to break off preliminary negotiations without being held to an accounting." Kessler & Fine, *Culpa in Contrahendo*, Bargaining in Good Faith, and Freedom of Contract: A Comparative Study, 77 Harv. L. Rev. 401, 412 (1964).

Example of *Itek*

A seminal case favoring enforceability of agreements to negotiate in good faith is *Itek Corp. v. Chicago Aerial Industries.* After negotiations looking to the sale of CAI's assets to Itek, the parties executed a "letter of intent" confirming the terms of the sale and providing that the parties "shall make every reasonable effort to agree upon and have prepared as quickly as possible a contract . . . embodying the above terms and such other terms and conditions as the parties shall agree upon." The letter of intent added that if the parties failed to reach ultimate agreement, "they shall be under no further obligation to one another." When CAI, evidently having received a more favorable offer, telegraphed Itek that it was not going ahead with the transaction, Itek sued CAI for breach of contract. The trial court granted summary judgment for CAI, but the Supreme Court of Delaware reversed, reasoning that:

> it is apparent that the parties obligated themselves to "make every reasonable effort" to agree upon a formal contract, and only if such effort failed were they absolved from "further obligation" for having "failed" to agree upon and execute a formal contract. We think these provisions . . . obligated each side to attempt in good faith to reach final and formal agreement.

Since there was evidence that in order to accept a more favorable offer, "CAI willfully failed to negotiate in good faith and to make 'every reasonable effort' to agree upon a formal contract, as it was required to do," it was error to grant summary judgment.[50]

Example of *Channel*

A similar result was reached in *Channel Home Centers v. Grossman,* which arose out of a dispute over leasing a store in a mall. After several months of negotiations, the prospective lessor signed a letter of intent that covered most of the significant lease terms and provided that the prospective lessor would "withdraw the Store from the rental market and only negotiate . . . the leasing transaction to completion." When the prospective lessor broke off the negotiations and leased the store to a competitor of the prospective tenant, the prospective tenant sought an injunction. The trial court denied the injunction on the ground that the letter of intent was unenforceable, but the United States Court of Appeals for the Third Circuit reversed, concluding that the record supported "a finding that the parties intended to enter into a binding agreement to negotiate in good faith" and that "the agreement had sufficient specificity to make it an enforceable contract."[51]

Trend favors enforceability

Although not all courts have shared this willingness to enforce agreements to negotiate,[52] the view taken in *Itek* and *Channel* has gained a substantial

---

[50]248 A.2d 625, 629 (Del. 1968).

[51]795 F.2d 291, 300 (3d Cir. 1986).

[52]For an extreme statement, *see* Honolulu Waterfront Ltd. v. Aloha Tower Dev., 692 F. Supp. 1230 (D. Haw. 1988) ("overwhelming weight of authority holds that courts will not enforce an agreement to negotiate").

following, and the trend clearly favors enforceability.[53] At least this is so where the parties have reached agreement on a significant number of the major terms of the ultimate agreement.

From the requirement of assent we turn to that of definiteness.

F.   THE REQUIREMENT OF DEFINITENESS

§3.27.   Definiteness in General.   We have seen that the requirement of definiteness is implicit in the principle that the promisee's expectation interest is to be protected.[1] The Restatement Second states that the terms of a contract must "provide a basis for determining the existence of a breach and for giving an appropriate remedy."[2] The Uniform Commercial Code provides: "Even though one or more terms are left open a contract for sale does not fail for indefiniteness if the parties have intended to make a contract and there is a reasonably certain basis for giving an appropriate remedy."[3] If the parties specify what is required as performance, courts are prepared to prescribe the consequences of nonperformance. Furthermore, it is enough that the requirement of definiteness is met when the time for performance arrives. It need not be met at the time agreement is reached.[4] In Cardozo's words, "Indefiniteness must reach the point where construction becomes impossible."[5] But what the Supreme Court of Wisconsin described as the "so called 'liberality' " of this provision does not eliminate the fundamental requirement that the parties must have reached agreement.[6]

Restatement and Code requirements

Simple examples of agreements that do not meet the requirement are those in which the description of the subject matter is inadequate, as where the description or quantity of goods to be sold is lacking.[7] However, the requirement applies to the agreement of the parties and not to the offer, so that even if the offer leaves such matters as description or quantity of the goods to the offeree's specification in the acceptance, that specification may avoid any indefiniteness

Examples of indefiniteness

[53]Copeland v. Baskin Robbins, *supra* note 44 ("we disagree with those who say the courts . . . are ill-equipped to determine whether people are negotiating with each other in good faith"), citing Farnsworth, Precontractual Liability and Preliminary Agreements: Fair Dealing and Failed Negotiations, 87 Colum. L. Rev. 217, 263-69 (1987).

§3.27   [1]See the discussion of the requirement of definiteness in §3.1 *supra*. As to the requirement of certainty in proof of damages, see §12.15 *infra*.

[2]Restatement Second §33(2).

[3]UCC 2-204(3).

[4]See the discussions of a third party to fix the term and of the role of the drafter in §3.28 *infra*.

[5]Heyman Cohen & Sons v. Lurie Woolen Co., 133 N.E. 370, 371 (N.Y. 1921).

[6]Novelly Oil Co. v. Mathy Constr. Co., 433 N.W.2d 628, 629 (Wis. 1988).

[7]Witt v. Realist, Inc., 118 N.W.2d 85 (Wis. 1962) (there was "complete uncertainty, as to the quantity, if any, to be ordered").

in the agreement.[8] Before turning to other examples, it will help to consider why parties are not more precise in setting out the terms of their agreements.

Indefiniteness caused by haste

One common reason is that they do not want to take the time or the trouble to do so. This is especially true of routine transactions. A seller and a buyer that make an agreement to sell goods may specify the quantity and type of goods and the price, but may not bother to say anything about the time or place for delivery or payment. Their failure to speak out on these matters is not fatal to the enforceability of their agreement, however, because default rules enable courts to supplement expressed terms with implied ones.[9] Such default rules are especially well established for contracts for the sale of goods, for which hasty bargaining is often the rule, and are contained in the Uniform Commercial Code.[10]

Indefiniteness caused by reluctance

Another common cause of indefiniteness is the parties' reluctance to raise difficult issues for fear that the deal might fall through.[11] The seller of goods may say nothing about responsibility for their quality for fear that the buyer will insist on an express warranty. The buyer may say nothing on the subject for fear that the seller may insist on a disclaimer of warranties. Again, their failure to speak out is not fatal to the enforceability of their agreement because a court will supply a term, the Uniform Commercial Code's implied warranty of merchantability.[12]

Indefiniteness caused by unforeseeability

A third cause of indefiniteness is the parties' inability at the time of agreement to foresee all of the problems that may arise. Instead of a simple, discrete transaction to be consummated in the near future, there may be a complex of transactions to be spread over a period of time. For example, instead of an agreement for the immediate sale of a stated quantity of apples, it may be an agreement for the supply over five years of all of the apples that the buyer might "require" for an applesauce factory. The extent to which the requirement of definiteness can be accommodated to such situations, having characteristics that were described earlier as "relational,"[13] will affect in an important way the utility of contract law in contemporary economic life.

Failure to agree distinguished

It is essential to distinguish one other cause of incompleteness of agreement — a failure to agree. If the seller and the buyer of apples do discuss the

---

[8] That the detail of a proposal may bear on whether it is an offer, see the discussion of reluctance to find an offer in §3.10 *supra*. As to specification after the making of the agreement, see the discussion of a third party to fix the term in §3.28 *infra*.

[9] See §7.16 *infra*.

[10] *See* UCC 2-309(1) (if not agreed upon, time for delivery "shall be a reasonable time"); UCC 2-308 (unless otherwise agreed, "place for delivery of goods is the seller's place of business" or if it has none its "residence"); UCC 2-310 (unless otherwise agreed "payment is due at the time and place at which the buyer is to receive the goods").

[11] See §3.5 *supra*.

[12] UCC 2-314(1) (unless excluded or modified "warranty that the goods shall be merchantable is implied in a contract for their sale if the seller is a merchant with respect to goods of that kind").

[13] See §3.5 *supra*.

matter of the seller's responsibility for their quality and are unable to agree on how that matter is to be resolved, the incompleteness of their agreement in that respect will be fatal to the enforceability of their agreement — not because of lack of definiteness, but because of lack of assent. There is a critical distinction between remaining silent on such a matter and discussing it but failing to agree.[14]

We move now from causes of indefiniteness to explore in greater detail the requirement of definiteness itself.

§3.28.   **Examples of Indefiniteness.** The impact of the requirement of definiteness can be seen from a typical case, in which an architectural draftsman sued his employer on the employer's promise to pay "a fair share of my profits" in addition to a stated salary. The New York Court of Appeals denied recovery of profits on the ground that their amount was a matter of "pure conjecture" and "may be any amount from a nominal sum to a material part according to the particular views of the person whose guess is considered. Such an executory contract must rest for performance on the honor and good faith of the parties making it."[1]

Typical example

The first step in deciding whether the requirement of definiteness has been met is to interpret the language of the agreement. Rejecting the argument that the parties to a complex government bid had not reached agreement on one aspect, a federal judge wrote: "The design of the contract can be picked from the terms and words of the invitation, objectively read with the aid of contract construction (which are distillates of the common experience and the common sense of justice)."[2] Take, for example, an employment agreement that says nothing of duration except for specifying a yearly salary. If the language specifying the salary is interpreted as also fixing the duration as one year, the problem of indefiniteness is eliminated.[3] If it is not so interpreted, however, the agreement may be unenforceable for indefiniteness of duration.[4]

Role of interpretation

---

[14]See §3.30 *infra*. It is, of course, possible that after the seller and the buyer have disagreed over the term dealing with the seller's responsibility for quality, they may agree to say nothing on that matter in their agreement. In that case, there is no lack of assent as to that matter.

§3.28   [1]Varney v. Ditmars, 111 N.E. 822, 824 (N.Y. 1916). The court in *Varney* suggested, however, that if the draftsman's work was worth more than his salary, he would be entitled to restitution measured by the difference. 111 N.E. at 825. *See* Pyeatte v. Pyeatte, 661 P.2d 196 (Ariz. App. 1982) (though "sufficient mutual understanding regarding critical provisions of their agreement did not exist," wife was entitled to restitution for having conferred benefits on husband by "financial subsidization of [his] legal education — with the agreement and expectation that she would be compensated by his reciprocal efforts"). See also the discussion of relief based on restitution in §3.30 *infra*.

[2]WPC Enters., Inc. v. United States, 323 F.2d 874, 879 (Ct. Cl. 1963).

[3]Dennis v. Thermoid Co., 25 A.2d 886 (N.J. 1942) (trial court found from circumstances that the employment was on a yearly basis). That this is not the usual interpretation, see the discussion of the employment cases in §7.17 *infra*.

[4]See the discussion of reasonable time for duration *infra*.

Role of incorporation

Furthermore, a court can often piece together enough terms to satisfy the requirement from preliminary negotiations, including prior communications, and from references to external sources of terms, including trade and other standard terms.[5] A striking example involved a vendor who had conveyed land to a purchaser under a contract in which the purchaser promised "to erect a First Class Theatre" on the land. Three years later, the purchaser sold the land to a third party without having built a theater on it, and the seller sued for damages resulting from a failure to enhance the value of his nearby properties. The Supreme Court of California held the contract sufficiently definite to entitle the vendor to the relief that he sought. The term *First Class Theatre* could be made definite by reference to another theater that the purchaser operated in the same city and to the city building code and fire laws, which provided minimum standards for theater construction.[6] The Supreme Court of Idaho similarly held that a description of land was sufficient to justify specific performance where the claimant's "sketch used natural monuments such as trees, as well as structures like the shop, the home, and a trailer home to plot out his parcel," and all parties "knew the exact location of [his] property and knew he wished to keep those particular five acres."[7]

Role of usages and implied terms

Even without explicit incorporation, an agreement may be fleshed out by usages to which the parties are subject, by a course of dealing between the parties prior to their agreement, or by a course of performance between them after their agreement.[8] Indefiniteness may also be cured by the addition of such implied terms as will be supplied by courts,[9] including the parties' implied obligations of good faith and fair dealing.[10]

Reference to "reasonableness"

Some of the most troublesome cases arise when performance is defined by reference to a variant of a purported standard of "reasonableness." Courts have sometimes struggled, especially if there has been reliance on the agreement, to find an external standard that suffices to make such a reference sufficiently definite. Thus, where an employer promised its employee "reasonable recognition" in return for his turning over rights to his future inventions, the Supreme Judicial Court of Maine held that the employer was liable under the agreement, even though it had taken the precaution of providing that "the bases and amount of recognition to rest entirely with the employer." The court stressed

---

[5] See the discussion of terms as not part of the offer in §4.26 *infra*.

[6] Bettancourt v. Gilroy Theatre Co., 261 P.2d 351, 353-54 (Cal. App. 1953). See the discussion of the remedy sought *infra*.

[7] Thorn Springs Ranch v. Smith, 50 P.3d 975, 980 (Idaho 2002).

[8] Mears v. Nationwide Mut. Ins. Co., 91 F.3d 1118 (8th Cir. 1996) (indefiniteness in agreement to award "His and Her's Mercedes" as prizes could "be made certain by the subsequent actions or declarations of the parties"). See §7.13 *infra*.

[9] H.C. Schmieding Produce Co. v. Cagle, 529 So. 2d 243 (Ala. 1988) ("contract does not fail for indefiniteness, because . . . open terms may be supplemented by the UCC's 'gap-filler' provisions"). See §7.16 *infra*.

[10] See the discussion of the duty of good faith in §7.17 *infra*.

that the agreement also said that it was "to be interpreted in good faith on the basis of what is reasonable and intended and not technically."[11] The decision makes an interesting contrast with the New York case discussed above, in which the court refused to enforce the employer's agreement to pay his employee "a fair share of my profits."[12]

Similar problems are posed by agreements to sell goods at a "reasonable" price, by which both parties seek to avoid the risk of market fluctuations before delivery. Under UCC 2-305(1), the parties can make a contract for sale even though nothing is said as to price, the price then being a reasonable price at the time for delivery.[13] A similar principle has been applied to agreements for the sale of stock[14] or land,[15] where reasonableness can usually be determined by reference to a market.[16]

Sale at "reasonable" price

Where no time is specified for performance of a duty such as that to deliver goods or pay the price, courts have had little difficulty in supplying a term requiring performance within a "reasonable" time.[17] What is reasonable in such a case depends on all the circumstances.[18] Thus where no time was specified for delivery by a "small boutique company" of a "unique and exotic" Ferrari priced at $1,325,000, it was held that the "six-month period between the execution of the contract and the arrival of the first [Ferrari] was reasonable under the

Reasonable time for performance

[11]Corthell v. Summit Thread Co., 167 A. 94, 82 (Me. 1933).

[12]Although the parties there used the word *fair*, the court suggested that neither *fair* nor *reasonable* was sufficiently definite in that context. 111 N.E. at 823-24.

[13]See the discussion of a second premise as possible in §3.7 *supra*.

The Vienna Convention contains an awkward compromise. Article 55 expresses the view that an enforceable contract can be made even though it "does not expressly or implicitly fix or make provision for determining the price." In that event, the price is to be based on "the price generally charged at the time of the conclusion of the contract," as distinguished from the reference in UCC 2-305(1) to "a reasonable price at the time for delivery." However, article 14 appears to be more restrictive, providing that an offer is sufficiently definite if it "expressly or implicitly fixes or makes provision for determining . . . the price." Article 5.7 of the UNIDROIT Principles contains a provision inspired by article 55 of the Vienna Convention.

[14]IUE AFL-CIO Pension Fund v. Barker & Williamson, 788 F.2d 118 (3d Cir. 1986) (applying "modern view" of UCC 2-305 to sale of stock).

[15]Portnoy v. Brown, 243 A.2d 444 (Pa. 1968) (contract giving lessee right to purchase leased property at "current market value at the end of the final term" was specifically enforceable).

[16]As to what is a "reasonable price," *see* TCP Indus. v. Uniroyal, 661 F.2d 542 (6th Cir. 1981) (Code does not require seller to "price at fair market price under a contract with an open price term"). That a market price is not necessarily a "reasonable" price, *see* Spartan Grain & Mill Co. v. Ayers, 517 F.2d 214 (5th Cir. 1975) (prices for chicken feed not necessarily unreasonable simply because higher than those charged by other sellers, since seller also committed itself to buy all buyer's eggs).

[17]*See* UCC 2-309(1) (if not provided, time for any action "shall be a reasonable time").

[18]First Natl. Bank of Bluefield v. Clark, 447 S.E.2d 558 (W. Va. 1994) (where contract for developers to buy unsold limited partnership shares specified no time, it was reasonable to expect performance after two years). *See* E. Shepherdstown Developers v. J. Russell Fritts, Inc., 398 S.E.2d 517 (W. Va. 1990) (delay of 40 months before offering to close on sale of land was unreasonable).

circumstances." Courts have been much more reluctant, however, to cure indefiniteness as to duration in employment agreements by reading in a "reasonable" duration,[19] a result that may be justified on the ground that the indefiniteness goes to the central question of the quantity of work to be done and there is no satisfactory external standard of reasonableness to answer it.[20]

Third party to fix term

The parties may, if they choose, avoid the risk of having the issue of what is "reasonable" litigated in court by providing for a binding decision by an independent third party, such as an arbitrator or appraiser. Such provisions delegating to a third party the power to fix a term — usually price — have generally been held to meet the requirement of definiteness.[21]

Party to fix term

Sometimes the parties leave an important term to be fixed unilaterally by one of the parties. A long-term contract for oil or gas, for example, may provide that the price is to be the producer's posted price, the price offered to all its distributors nationwide.[22] Or a contract for the sale of goods, for example, may provide that the buyer can make a later selection within a specified range of seller's stock according to grade, color, weight, or the like. If the party with the power to select turns out to be the plaintiff, no problem arises.[23] But if it is the defendant that has the power and has refused to make the selection, a question of definiteness arises. Some support can be found for each of three solutions.[24] First, the agreement is not enforceable against that party.[25] Second, the agreement is enforceable, and recovery is to be based on whatever selection would have minimized the damages.[26] Third, the agreement is enforceable, and recovery is to be based on a selection made in good faith by the plaintiff. The

---

[19] Eidsmore v. RBB, 30 Cal. Rptr. 357, 363 (Ct. App. 1994).

[20] Plaskitt v. Black Diamond Trailor Co., 164 S.E.2d 645 (Va. 1968) (agreement to pay salesman commissions during unspecified time was at will and not for reasonable time). On the judicial preference for employment "at will," see the discussion of the employment cases in §7.17 *infra*.

[21] See the discussion of examples of indefiniteness in §3.27 *supra*.

[22] A leading case is Foley v. Classique Coaches, [1934] 2 K.B. 1, in which the parties agreed on the sale of gasoline "at a price to be agreed . . . from time to time" and that "any dispute or difference . . . shall be submitted to arbitration." The court interpreted the agreement to call for the fixing of the price by arbitrators in the event of a failure to agree and held the agreement enforceable. See the discussion of UCC 2-305 in §9.7 *infra*.

[23] Richard Short Oil Co. v. Texaco, Inc., 799 F.2d 415 (8th Cir. 1986) (producer's posted price satisfied UCC 2-305). Under a "most favored nation [customer] clause" a party undertakes an analogous duty, to offer the other party terms no less favorable than those offered to its most favored customer.

[24] Fairmount Glass Works v. Crunden-Martin Woodenware Co., 51 S.W. 196 (Ky. 1899) (buyer sued for breach of contract for glass jars under which it had right to select sizes).

[25] Wilhelm Lubrication Co. v. Brattrud, 268 N.W. 634 (Minn. 1936) (seller denied enforcement of contract for oil under which buyer had right to select weight). The result in this case would be different under the Code. See note 26 *infra*.

[26] Dolly Parker Motors v. Stinson, 245 S.W.2d 820 (Ark. 1952) (seller held entitled to damages based on his "smallest profit" for buyer's breach of contract for car, under which he had right to specify model and other details).

Code favors this third solution,[27] placing, as the Eighth Circuit explained it, the responsibility on the buyer under a supply agreement "to identify the products it wished to buy."[28] The situation in which a term is left to the agreement of both parties is discussed in the following section.

The extent to which the indefiniteness hinders the court in granting the particular remedy sought is an important factor in deciding whether enforcement will be refused.[29] A host of opinions can be found to support the proposition that less definiteness is required to support an award of damages than a decree of specific performance.[30] The reason is that a decree of specific performance must itself be formulated with precision because the severity of the sanction of contempt makes it imperative that the court and the parties be certain of its limits. As one court put it, "The precise act that the court would say must be specifically performed does not appear in this contract."[31] Even where damages are sought, the effect of indefiniteness on the ability to estimate loss depends on the measure of damages involved. It is usually easier to estimate damages based on the reliance interest than on the expectation interest.[32] Furthermore, though damages based on the expectation interest were sought in the case involving the sale of land for a theater,[33] the California court's task was eased because the damages sought for the defendant's failure "to erect a First Class Theatre" were based on the failure to enhance the value of the plaintiff's nearby properties. This loss would be affected little by the details of theater design that were left indefinite. A different result might be expected in a suit by an owner against a builder for damages for failure to perform an agreement "to erect a First Class Theatre" on the owner's land.[34]

Importance of remedy sought

Careful drafting of the agreement can ordinarily satisfy the requirement of definiteness. For example, if over a long term a seller wants to be assured of an outlet for a product, and a buyer wants to be assured of a source of supply, but neither wants to take the risk of a shift in the market, several means are open to them to make a legally enforceable agreement that will allow the price of the

Role of drafter

---

[27] UCC 2-311 provides that if a party's specification is not seasonably made, the other party may "perform in any reasonable manner or . . . treat the failure to specify . . . as a breach." The other party would be bound by the general obligation of good faith under UCC 1-304. *Cf.* UCC 2-305 (a price to be fixed means a price to be fixed "in good faith").

[28] Family Snacks of N.C. v. Prepared Prods. Co., 295 F.3d 864, 869 (8th Cir. 2002).

[29] See the discussion of the Restatement and Code requirements in §3.27 *supra*.

[30] Kruse v. Hemp, 853 P.2d 1373 (Wash. 1993) (if "specific performance is sought, rather than legal damages, a higher standard of proof must be met").

[31] Howard v. Beavers, 264 P.2d 858, 861 (Colo. 1954). Contrast this situation with that described in the discussion of the uncertainty of damages in §12.6 *infra*, where the agreement is definite but the uncertainty as to damages gives rise to an argument for specific performance.

[32] See the discussion of the significance of the alternative in §12.16 *infra*.

[33] Bettancourt v. Gilroy Theatre Co., *supra* note 6.

[34] *See* Klimek v. Perisich, 371 P.2d 956 (Or. 1962). In such a case, proof of damages would probably require a showing of what it would have cost the owner to have another builder do the same job, for which a fairly specific set of specifications would be required.

goods to fluctuate. They may leave the price term "open" so that the price will be "a reasonable price at the time of delivery."[35] They may use an "escalator clause," under which the price will be fixed according to a formula tied in some way to the market.[36] If they wish to leave the quantity flexible, they may fix it in terms of the buyer's "requirements" or the seller's "output"[37] or give the parties options or powers of termination.[38] Obligations that are difficult to define with precision may be expressed in such terms as "good faith" or "best efforts"[39] and "reasonable" or "honest satisfaction."[40]

Sensitivity to problems of drafter

Judges steeped in the tradition that a court should not "make a contract for the parties" still bridle at undertaking the "paternalistic task" of curing the drafter's failings.[41] This is particularly likely in the case of a discrete transaction, such as a sale of a stated quantity of goods to take place in the near future. In such a situation it is usually easy to satisfy the requirement of definiteness, and a court may regard the requirement as imposing on the parties a desirable measure of discipline in the interest of the efficient administration of justice. In Judge Richard Posner's words:

> If people want courts to enforce their contracts they have to take the time to fix the terms with reasonable definiteness so that the courts are not put to an undue burden of figuring out what the parties would have agreed to had they completed their negotiations. The parties have the comparative advantage over the court in deciding on what terms a voluntary transaction is value-maximizing; that is the premise of a free enterprise system.[42]

If, however, the parties plan a more complex relationship, such as the sale of all of the buyer's requirements of a stated kind of goods extending over a period of time, the requirement of definiteness poses a more serious obstacle to the enforceability of their agreement. Courts have shown an increasing sensitivity to the practical problems faced by the contract drafter in such situations and have been more tolerant of indefiniteness that seems endemic to the transaction.[43]

---

[35] UCC 2-305.

[36] On proof of market price, *see* UCC 2-723, 2-724.

[37] See §2.15 *supra* and the discussion of output and requirements contracts in §7.17 *infra*.

[38] See §2.14 *supra* and the discussion of termination in §7.17 *infra*.

[39] See the discussions of the duty of good faith in §2.13 *supra* and of the duty of good faith and of the duty of best efforts in §7.17 *infra*.

[40] See the discussions of the duty of reasonable efforts in §2.13 *supra* and of the nature of *satisfaction* in §8.4 *infra*.

[41] Walker v. Keith, 382 S.W.2d 198, 204 (Ky. 1964) (described in the discussion of the reluctance to extend the premise in §3.29 *infra*).

[42] Goldstick v. ICM Realty, 788 F.2d 456, 461 (7th Cir. 1986).

[43] DiMario v. Coppola, 10 F. Supp. 2d 213 (E.D.N.Y. 1998) (Weinstein, J.: modern courts "are willing to enforce fair contracts 'even where many terms are missing' to reflect the expectations of honest business people").

Judicial tolerance of indefiniteness can be seen in one area of real estate law. In *Hedges v. Hurd*, the court had before it a printed form of "earnest money receipt," prepared by a real estate broker and signed by the vendor and the purchaser. It described the property and set out the purchase price, the down payment, the terms for payment of the balance, and other details, but it called for the execution of a second and more detailed agreement, on whose terms the parties had not yet agreed.[44] In holding the agreement sufficiently definite to be enforceable, the court adverted to the "tremendous volume of real estate transactions in our state" and noted that such earnest money receipts were used in a "high percentage" of them. It found the reason for this "in the real estate practice that has grown up," in which property is handled through a broker, as an intermediary that shows the property to various prospects, so that the vendor may not see the purchaser until the deal is consummated.

Real estate transactions

> Ordinarily, no one is particularly interested or has the time to work out a contract . . . in minute detail. At this state, the parties are interested only in the execution of a simple agreement which will have some effective legal significance as to both.[45]

The court's task of supplying terms in such cases is made easier by the circumstance that the terms of commonplace real estate transactions are relatively standard.[46] But there are limits, and courts have occasionally regarded such receipts as too indefinite to be enforceable[47] or too indefinite to be specifically enforceable where specific relief was sought.[48]

Judicial tolerance of indefiniteness is also evident in connection with long-term contracts. An example is *Mantell v. International Plastic Harmonica Corp.*, which involved a two-year exclusive distributorship agreement for plastic harmonicas in a specified territory. The agreement provided for a price not greater than that charged any other distributor, but it did not fix the price because the plastic harmonica had not yet been perfected. New Jersey's highest court held that the agreement was enforceable at a "reasonable" price:

Long-term contracts

> In the very nature of the exclusive sales and distribution contract, it is not usually practicable to fix prices and the quantum of goods sold; and the rules

---

[44]For more on a "formal contract contemplated," see §3.8 *supra*.

[45]289 P.2d 706, 707 (Wash. 1955).

[46]*See* 289 P.2d at 709-10 (concurrence: "terms of such executory contracts are now so generally standardized that bona fide disagreement on the terms not covered by the earnest-money receipt and agreement is quite unlikely").

[47]Peterson v. Conida Warehouses, 575 P.2d 481 (Idaho 1978) ("earnest money agreement . . . was so unsettled, ambiguous and devoid of necessary terms and conditions as to be unenforceable").

[48]Luke v. Conrad, 526 P.2d 181 (Idaho 1974) (error to order specific performance where "Earnest Money Agreement was incomplete").

of certainty and definiteness which govern the ordinary contract of sale have no application . . . . Contracts of this category are to be given a practical interpretation in an area of conventional action that, due to unpredictable market conditions, production factors, and so on, ordinarily does not permit of greater certainty and definiteness in the particulars mentioned.[49]

The trend favors taking account of the practicalities of the situation and relaxing the requirement of definiteness to accommodate more complex and sophisticated transactions.[50]

Agreements with open terms pose special problems, now to be examined.

Reason for agreements with open terms

§3.29.   Indefiniteness in Agreements with Open Terms. Particularly perplexing problems of indefiniteness are posed when the parties make what purports to be an enforceable agreement but leave one or more terms to be fixed by later agreement between them. As was pointed out earlier, their object in doing so is usually to postpone negotiations over the missing terms until the occurrence of future events, as when the price for goods to be sold or the rent for land to be leased is left to be agreed upon at a later time. Although the parties expect that they will reach agreement on the missing terms, what they expect to happen if they fail to reach agreement is often unclear. They may understand that there will be no contract at all or they may understand that there will be a contract with the missing term supplied as a matter of law.[1] If the latter is their understanding, a question arises whether the agreement is one with open terms sufficiently definite to be enforceable or whether it is a mere unenforceable "agreement to agree."[2]

---

[49]55 A.2d 250, 255-56 (N.J. 1947). *See* Laveson v. Warner Mfg. Corp., 117 F. Supp. 124 (D.N.J. 1953) (price element in sales agency contract "is not of the essence" because it is passed on, together with the agent's commission, to the third party purchaser and the parties are both interested in a substantial volume of sales with a fair profit to both, in addition to which the price "cannot be finally fixed . . . at the very beginning of the sales agency"); Allied Disposal v. Home Serv., 595 S.W.2d 417 (Mo. App. 1980) (applying *Mantell* to contract "for an exclusive system of system of service").

[50]*See* Higbee v. Sentry Ins. Co., 253 F.3d 994 (7th Cir. 2001) ("any lawyer could tell you that a lack of agreement on minor, immaterial terms, and a party's subjective and unarticulated belief that she would not be bound by an oral agreement, do not preclude a finding that a contract has been formed"). See also the discussion of the negotiation of substantial deals in §3.5 *supra*.

§3.29 [1]See the discussions of an intention to be legally bound and an intention not to be legally bound in §3.7 *supra*.

[2]The problem of the "formal contract contemplated," discussed in §3.8 *supra*, differs from that of the "agreement to agree" in that the former involves a question of whether the parties intended to be bound at the time of the initial agreement, while the latter involves a question of whether, assuming they intended to be bound, their intention is to be given effect.

The Uniform Commercial Code answers the question in the affirmative in the case of an open-price term. As has already been explained, the Code allows the parties to make a contract for sale "even though the price is not settled," the price then being a reasonable price at the time for delivery.[3] In response to the argument that such an agreement would be too indefinite to be enforceable, the commentary explains that the Code "rejects in these instances the formula that 'an agreement to agree is unenforceable' . . . and rejects also defeating such agreements on the ground of 'indefiniteness.' "[4]

Code solution

Courts have, however, been reluctant to extend this solution to analogous open rental terms that are often found in agreements under which the lessee has an option to renew the lease at the end of the term. If the length of the term makes it undesirable for the parties to fix the rental for the renewal period at the time of the initial agreement, they may leave it for agreement at the time of renewal, on the basis of experience during the first term and market conditions at the time of renewal. Such an open rental term is usually fatal to the enforceability of the agreement for renewal. So it was held where the option provided that "rental will be fixed in such amount as shall actually be agreed upon by the lessors and the lessee with the monthly rental fixed on the comparative basis of rental values as of the date of the renewal with rental values at this time reflected by the comparative business conditions of the two periods." The court observed that the reference to "comparative business conditions" was "very broad indeed" and did not clearly refer to "local conditions, national conditions, or conditions affecting the lessee's particular business." It declined to undertake the "paternalistic task" of supplying a term "when the parties could so easily provide any number of workable methods by which rents could be adjusted."[5] Although support can be found for this traditional view in cases involving other types of agreement as well,[6] there is increasing authority to the contrary, and the lessee's reliance during the initial term of the lease may encourage a court to reject the argument of indefiniteness.[7]

Reluctance to extend premise

---

[3] UCC 2-305, treated in the discussion of a second premise as possible in §3.7 *supra*.

[4] UCC 2-305 cmt. 1.

[5] Walker v. Keith, 382 S.W.2d 198, 204 (Ky. 1964).

[6] Transamerica Equip. Leasing Corp. v. Union Bank, 426 F.2d 273 (9th Cir. 1970) ($600,000 loan agreement in which the parties left some terms to be negotiated); Bonk v. Boyajian, 274 P.2d 948 (Cal. App. 1954) (lessee's option to buy land provided "monthly payments on the balance due to be agreed upon at the time of purchase"); Willmott v. Giarraputo, 157 N.E.2d 282 (N.Y. 1959) (option to buy land provided "the payment of interest and amortization of principal shall be mutually agreed upon at the time of entering into a more formal contract"); Ansorge v. Kane, 155 N.E. 683 (N.Y. 1927) (contract to buy land provided "sum to be paid on signing of contract . . . to be agreed on").

[7] City of Los Angeles v. Superior Court, 333 P.2d 745 (Cal. 1959) ("the court could fix a reasonable rental for Wrigley Field, if this should ever become necessary"). The problem can be avoided by providing for rental to be fixed by an appraiser or arbitrator. The American Arbitration Association has promulgated rules for arbitration in real estate valuation disputes.

Relatively unimportant terms

When parties fail to agree, a court may be more willing to supply a term if the court regards the term as relatively unimportant. This seems a particularly appropriate response if the failure to agree is not born of a desire to await future developments, but rather is merely the result of an unwillingness to take the time to bargain over the term before beginning performance. A striking example is *Purvis v. United States ex rel. Associated Sand & Gravel Co.*, in which a subcontractor and a general contractor had been unable to agree on the compensation for one item of the concrete work, and the subcontractor undertook to do the job subject to their future agreement. No agreement was reached because the subcontractor insisted that it should be paid the actual cost of that item in addition to the contract price, while the contractor insisted that the item was already included in the contract price. The contractor contended that it was therefore liable only for the reasonable value of the work. The Ninth Circuit noted that the price of the item "was somewhat less than nine one-thousandths of the price of the whole job" and concluded that to accede to the contractor's contention would result in "a very small tail wagging a very large dog."[8] Having decided that the agreement was enforceable, the court supplied a term to "do what is fair in the circumstances" — it split the difference and allowed the subcontractor half of what it claimed. Other courts have arrived at similar solutions in like circumstances.[9]

Cure by concession

In some situations it is within the power of one party to make the agreement enforceable even without the other party's agreement. If the term subject to agreement is also one that is subject to complete concession by the party that wants to have the agreement performed, that party's concession has been held to cure the indefiniteness. For example, all that was left to agreement in an option to buy land were the terms on which the stated price was payable. The option was held to be enforceable where the purchaser "tendered himself as ready, willing, and able to pay the agreed price therefor, either in cash or upon such terms as [the vendor] might impose," and later actually tendered cash.[10]

Example of *Sun Printing*

Such a situation was discussed by Cardozo in *Sun Printing & Publishers Assn. v. Remington Paper & Power Co.* The controversy arose out of a contract for the sale of 1,000 tons of paper each month for 16 months. The price for each of the first four months was stated in the agreement. For the remaining 12 months, the agreement contemplated one or more renegotiations, under which both the price and the period of its duration were to be agreed on by the parties, but the price was not to be higher than that charged by a named Canadian supplier. At the end of four months, in a rising market, the seller

---

[8] 344 F.2d 867, 869 (9th Cir. 1965).

[9] Rego v. Decker, 482 P.2d 834 (Alaska 1971) (option to purchase land left security for payment of price to agreement; case remanded to allow trial court to condition decree of specific performance by vendor on purchaser furnishing "adequate security").

[10] Morris v. Ballard, 16 F.2d 175 (D.C. Cir. 1926).

refused to make further deliveries and the buyer, after demanding delivery and offering to pay the Canadian supplier's price for the month of delivery, sued for breach of contract. The New York Court of Appeals held that the agreement was unenforceable. Because the parties were to agree on both the price and the period of its duration, the price would not automatically change when the Canadian supplier's price changed. If the Canadian price should rise, the buyer's concession that the price should be that price prevailing in one month would not, Cardozo explained, "bind it to proceed at the price prevailing in another." And if the Canadian price should fall, "without an agreement as to time, the maximum would be lowered from one shipment to another." The parties had guarded "against the contingency of failing to come together as to price" but not "against the contingency of failing to come together as to time."[11] On the court's own reasoning, had the buyer offered to pay the Canadian supplier's *highest* price *for the month of delivery or any preceding month* during the period subject to agreement, instead of merely offering to pay the Canadian supplier's price *for the month of delivery*, there would appear no reason to refuse to enforce the agreement.[12]

We consider now some techniques to mitigate the effects of the requirement of definiteness.

§3.30.   **Mitigating Doctrines.**   Several mitigating doctrines soften the impact of the requirement of definiteness. If, for example, only part of the agreement is indefinite, the remaining part may be regarded as "divisible" or "severable" and may be enforced according to its terms.[1] This is only appropriate, however, if the exchange of performances under the enforceable part is fair in the light of what the parties originally bargained for. Reliance on the agreement may influence a court in reaching such a solution, but it is not a prerequisite. Relief may also be awarded under an indefinite agreement if the agreement can be regarded as a standing offer to be accepted by a series of performances. For example, an agreement for the sale of goods that is indefinite as to amount may give rise to a series of contracts to pay the stated price as goods are delivered and accepted.[2] Or an employment agreement that is indefinite

Relief based on terms of agreement

[11] 139 N.E. 470, 471 (N.Y. 1923). Since the court viewed the indefiniteness as one of time as well as price, UCC 2-305 does not compel a different result.

[12] The following excerpt gives interesting insights into practice, although it overlooks this point. "The standard contract used by manufacturers of paper to sell to magazine publishers has a pricing clause which is probably sufficiently vague to make the contract legally unenforceable. The house counsel of one of the largest paper producers [in Wisconsin] said that everyone in the industry is aware of this because of a leading New York case concerning the contract, but that no one cares." Macaulay, Non-Contractual Relations in Business: A Preliminary Study, 28 Am. Soc. Rev. 55, 60 (1963).

§3.30 [1] Wilhelm Lubrication Co. v. Brattrud, 268 N.W. 634 (Minn. 1936) (wholly executory agreement enforceable as to sale of grease but not as to oil). Divisibility is taken up in other contexts in §§5.8 and 8.13 *infra*.

[2] *See* UCC 2-607(1).

as to duration may give rise to a series of contracts to pay at the specified rate as each unit of work is performed.

Relief based on restitution

The mitigating doctrines just discussed give relief based on the terms of the agreement. Part performance of an agreement that is unenforceable for indefiniteness may also result in a claim in restitution.[3] If, for example, a contract of sale is unenforceable for failure to fix the price, "the buyer must return any goods already received or if unable to do so must pay their reasonable value at the time of delivery and the seller must return any portion of the price paid on account."[4] Or if an employer's promise to pay an employee a share of the profits in addition to a wage is unenforceable for indefiniteness, the employee may have restitution of the reasonable value of any services performed in excess of the wages paid.[5]

Relief based on reliance

Some courts have gone further and allowed recovery based on the reliance, as distinguished from the restitution, interest. In *Kearns v. Andree* a buyer agreed to purchase a house if the seller made specified alterations. After the seller had made them, the buyer refused to take the house, and the seller sold it to another buyer after having to modify some of the alterations. Although the agreement of sale was too indefinite to be enforceable, the seller was allowed to recover "the reasonable value of the services which he has performed, without regard to the extent of the benefit conferred on the other party" on the ground that "the services have been requested and have been performed by the plaintiff in the known expectation that he would receive compensation and neither the extent nor the presence of benefit . . . is of controlling significance."[6] In *Wheeler v. White*, White and Wheeler made an agreement under which White was to obtain or make a loan to finance the construction of a building on Wheeler's land. White later urged Wheeler to proceed with the demolition of existing buildings and reassured him that he would make the loan himself if money was not available elsewhere. Pursuant to these promises, Wheeler prepared the site for the new buildings. White then refused to perform, and Wheeler, unable to raise the money himself, sued White for the amount spent in reliance. In allowing recovery, the court said that "where there is actually no contract the promissory estoppel theory may be invoked, thereby supplying a remedy which will enable the injured party to be compensated for his foreseeable, definite and

---

[3]This is distinguishable, however, from a subsequent course of performance that makes the agreement sufficiently definite so that it is fully enforceable. See the discussion of the role of usages and implied terms in §3.28 *supra*.

[4]UCC 2-305(4). This provision only applies, however, if the parties intend not to be bound unless the price is fixed. See the discussions of the second possible premise §3.7 *supra* and of anomalous cases in §9.7 *infra*.

[5]Bragdon v. Shapiro, 77 A.2d 598 (Me. 1951); Varney v. Ditmars, 111 N.E. 822 (N.Y. 1916) (dictum).

[6]139 A. 695, 697 (Conn. 1928). No recovery was allowed for the cost of work to adapt the house for the second purchaser.

substantial reliance."[7] The agreement being too indefinite to support recovery based on the expectation interest, courts have limited recovery to the reliance interest in these cases.[8] They constitute another exception to the traditional principle of mutuality of obligation, under which neither party is bound until the moment when both are bound.

In the next chapter we consider how courts police the bargains that private parties make.

---

[7] 398 S.W.2d 93, 97 (Tex. 1965). See the discussion of liability for a specific promise in §3.26 *supra*.

[8] This is in contrast to the situation where there is reliance on an offer that seeks a promise. See §3.25 *supra*.

Chapter 4

Policing the Agreement

A. POLICING IN GENERAL

§4.1. Three Perspectives. This chapter is concerned with the extent to which courts "police" agreements against unfairness by placing limits on their enforceability. Such an interference in the bargaining process requires

Competing policies

217

courts to consider competing policies. On the side of enforcing the bargain as made stand the policies favoring the autonomy of the parties, the protection of justified expectations, and the stability of transactions. On the other side stand the policies favoring the prevention of unfairness and the protection of the parties from overreaching. No single formula has evolved to reconcile these competing policies, and often the factors that contribute to a particular decision can be separated, if at all, only with difficulty. Nevertheless, it is possible to distinguish three different perspectives from which courts view the task of policing agreements: substance, status, and behavior.

Reluctance to police substance

Of these three, courts have been most reluctant to view the problem in the first perspective, that of substantive unfairness. The rise of the bargain theory contributed to this reluctance by helping to strip from the doctrine of consideration any vestige of concern with the substance of the exchange on which the parties had agreed, thereby eliminating a possible basis for policing the agreement for substantive unfairness.[1] The doctrine of consideration shields the improvident promisor from liability if the promise is gratuitous, but not if the promisor has received something, however small, by way of bargained-for exchange.[2] One legal scholar identified three reasons for the willingness of courts to enforce the bargain of the parties without inquiring into substance:

> (1) The efficient administration of the law of contracts requires that courts shall not be required to prescribe prices. (2) The test of enforceability should be certain and should not be beclouded by such vague terms as "fair" or "reasonable" as tests of validity. (3) There is still the somewhat old-fashioned theory that persons of maturity and sound mind should be free to contract imprudently as well as prudently.[3]

Furthermore, judges are aware that they are not well equipped to redress fundamental imbalances in the distribution of wealth. Another scholar, Melvin Eisenberg, conceded the bargain principle's "conceptual simplicity and the ease with which it can be administered," since for its application "it need only be determined whether a bargain was made and, if so, what remedy is required to put the innocent party in the position he would have been in had the bargain been performed." But he concluded that while placing limits on the principle "involves costs of administration," failing to do so "involves still greater costs to the system of justice."[4]

Example of reluctance

In a case exemplifying the reluctance of courts to police for substantive unfairness, a federal district court held that the fact that a buyer for resale was to make a gross profit ranging roughly from 40 percent to 80 percent on parts purchased from a supplier for delivery to a government contractor did not affect

---

§4.1   [1] See the discussion of some promises made unenforceable in §2.2 *supra*.

[2] See the discussion of the "peppercorn theory" in §2.11 *supra*.

[3] Patterson, An Apology for Consideration, 58 Colum. L. Rev. 929, 953 (1958).

[4] Eisenberg, The Bargain Principle and Its Limits, 95 Harv. L. Rev. 741, 800-01 (1982).

the enforceability of the buyer's contract with the supplier. Even if it were shown that the buyer was to have received "a far greater profit than the [supplier] for a much smaller contribution, the [supplier] would nevertheless be bound by his agreement by the familiar rule that relative values of the consideration in a contract between business men dealing at arm's length without fraud will not affect the validity of the contract." To ask the court to decide

> in every case involving such a contract whether the compensation paid a middleman . . . is reasonable . . . would, in effect, impose price regulatory functions on the court . . . . I do not believe that it is the function of the court to interfere by determining the validity of a contract between ordinary business men on the basis of its beliefs as to the adequacy of consideration.[5]

As we shall see, the traditional reluctance of common law courts to police   **Status and** agreements for substantive unfairness was never shared by courts of equity[6]   **behavior** and over the years this traditional reluctance has declined.[7] Nevertheless, the established perspectives for policing agreements have been those of status and behavior rather than of substance.[8] That of *status* focuses on the characteristics of the party involved. Classic examples are the restrictions on the capacity of specified classes of persons, such as minors and the mentally incompetent, whose power to contract has been limited in order to shield them from the consequences of unwise bargains. The perspective of *behavior* focuses on how the parties acted during the bargaining process. Classic examples are the rules that allow a party to avoid the contract on the ground that the party has been induced to make the contract by misrepresentation or duress, the most flagrant examples of misbehavior during the bargaining process.

We first examine status.

B.   STATUS

§4.2.   Incapacity in General.   Even though individuals differ markedly   **Capacity** in their ability to represent their own interests in the bargaining process, one   **generally assumed** is generally assumed to have full power to bind oneself contractually. Only in extreme instances is one's power regarded as impaired because of an inability to participate meaningfully in the bargaining process.[1] One whose power is

---

[5] Black Indus. v. Bush, 110 F. Supp. 801, 805-06 (D.N.J. 1953). The fact that the government was the ultimate purchaser did not alter the result.

[6] See the discussion of policing in equity in §4.27 *infra*.

[7] See the discussion of application beyond sale of goods in §4.28 *infra*.

[8] For types of decisions, including *unfairly influenced* and *ill-considered* decisions, that occasion regret on the part of the promisor, *see* E. Farnsworth, Changing Your Mind ch. 2 (1998).

§4.2   [1] For discussion of subtler effects of differences in capacity, *see* Eisenberg, The Limits of Cognition and the Limits of Contract, 47 Stan. L. Rev. 211 (1995).

so impaired is said to lack capacity to contract and is subject to special rules that allow one to avoid the contracts that one makes in order to give protection from one's own improvident acts and from imposition by others. What kinds of defects are recognized as impairing the power to contract?

Kinds of defects

Two principal kinds of defects are today recognized as impairing the power to contract: immaturity and mental infirmity. In addition, the common law regarded a woman's marriage as depriving her for the life of her husband of separate legal identity, including the capacity to contract, but this disability was largely removed by statutes enacted in the nineteenth century, long before women were given the right to vote.[2] Limits on a person's power to contract that are not based on any supposed disadvantage in participating in the bargaining process will not be dealt with here. For example, the effect of an agreement by a corporation that exceeds its corporate powers is beyond the scope of this discussion.[3]

Competing policies

As with other instances of policing, the law relating to capacity to contract involves difficult choices between competing policies — on the one side favoring protection of the party that lacks capacity and on the other favoring protection of the other party's expectation, reliance, and restitution interests. Furthermore, the question may not be whether a particular rule would work toward a desired end, but whether its application comes at too great a price. Case-by-case analysis of incompetency may be too costly and too productive of uncertainty. Arbitrary rules may be better suited to enabling others to identify and avoid contractual arrangements with members of the protected class — who may, incidentally, find limitations on their participation in commercial life a mixed blessing at best.

We consider how these competing policies are resolved in connection with immaturity and mental incompetency.

Twenty-one at common law

§4.3.   The Test of Immaturity. With respect to immaturity, the law has tenaciously adhered to an arbitrary standard — the attainment of a prescribed age at the time of the making of the contract — ignoring the obvious differences in maturity among individuals of the same age. At common law that age was 21. Before the age of majority, one is a "minor" or an "infant" who lacks the capacity to contract and who therefore can avoid one's contracts, regardless of their fairness. A minor's apparent age or maturity is irrelevant, as is the other party's knowledge of the minor's age.[2] One's incapacity is not terminated by

---

[2] *See generally* E. Farnsworth, Changing Your Mind ch. 1 (1998).

[3] *See* R. Clark, Corporate Law §16.1 (1986).

§4.3   [1] Gastonia Personnel Corp. v. Rogers, 172 S.E.2d 19 (N.C. 1970).

[2] As to the effect of misrepresentation of age, see the discussion of the exception for misrepresentation in §4.5 *infra*. For a test not based on age, *see* Code of Maimonides, bk. 12 (The Book of Acquisition) 123 (I. Klein trans. 1951) (test is whether one "if given a stone will throw it away but if given a nut will take it").

emancipation by one's parents or by marriage, nor is it affected by participation in business.[3] One cannot, during one's minority, surrender one's power of avoidance.[4]

As the New York Court of Appeals observed in the nineteenth century,

Suggestions for reform

> a protracted struggle has been maintained in the courts, on the one hand to protect infants or minors from their own improvidence and folly, and to save them from the depredations and frauds practiced upon them by the designing and unprincipled, and on the other to protect the rights of those dealing with them in good faith and on the assumption that they could lawfully make contracts.[5]

The resulting rules evidence an indulgence toward minors that is not always easy to justify. In contrast to rules that shield minors from responsibility for torts or crimes, these rules may disadvantage minors by discouraging others from contracting with them. In practice a minor may be required to find an adult who is willing to undertake the obligation on behalf of or jointly with the minor.[6] In Lord Mansfield's words, "miserable must the condition of minors be, excluded from the society and commerce of the world."[7] The rules may also work hardship on those who have dealt fairly with minors. As the Supreme Court of New Hampshire put it:

> A stranger must think it strange that a minor in certain cases may be liable for his torts and responsible for his crimes and yet is not bound by his contracts. . . . However, the common law conception that a minor does not possess the discretion and experience of adults and therefore must be protected from his own contractual follies generally holds sway today.[8]

Nevertheless, substantial areas of commercial activity have developed that could scarcely survive without the patronage of those who are known to be minors.[9]

Statutes in most states have modified the law relating to minors in its details though not in its broad contours. The most prevalent reform has been the

Reduction in age to 18

---

[3]Kiefer v. Fred Howe Motors, 158 N.W.2d 288 (Wis. 1968). Emancipation involves the parent's surrender of the right to the child's services and the renunciation of parental duties. Marriage emancipates a minor. As to participation in business, see the discussion in the summary in §4.5 *infra*.

[4]Elkhorn Coal Corp. v. Tackett, 88 S.W.2d 943 (Ky. 1935) ("one deed voidable for infancy . . . is not ratified by the execution of another voidable for the same reason").

[5]Henry v. Root, 33 N.Y. 526, 536 (1865).

[6]*But cf.* Amado v. Ken-Mac Motors, 119 A.2d 125 (R.I. 1955) (sale of automobile to adult brother was mere "pretense").

[7]Zouch v. Parsons, 97 Eng. Rep. 1103, 1106-07 (K.B. 1765).

[8]Porter v. Wilson, 209 A.2d 730, 731 (N.H. 1965).

[9]For a discussion of the commercial importance of minors, *see* Edge, Voidability of Minors' Contracts: A Feudal Doctrine in a Modern Economy, 1 Ga. L. Rev. 205, 227-32 (1967).

lowering of the arbitrary age limit from 21 to 18 years, a step that mirrored the reduction in the voting age.[10] This had the important practical effect of eliminating the great bulk of minors whose transactions generated litigation when the age of majority was 21, though it did nothing to change the effects of minority. In addition, a few states have enacted statutes making exceptions for minors engaged in business.[11] But of the variety of suggestions that have been made to draw a less arbitrary line than that of age alone, none has won general support.

What are the legal effects of a contract made by a minor?

Voidable, not void

§4.4.   Effects of Minority.   Common law courts early announced the prevailing view that a minor's contract is "voidable" at the instance of the minor.[1] By this is meant that there is a contract if no further action is taken at the minor's instance, but that the effects of the contract can be avoided if appropriate steps are taken on the minor's behalf. This may be done by simply setting up minority as a defense in an action brought by the other party or by bringing an action to set aside the transaction or recover benefits conferred on the other party under it. The minor may avoid the contract even if it has been fully performed on both sides, as where the minor has received and paid for goods.[2] However, the other party is bound unless the minor avoids the contract. The contract is neither "void" nor voidable at the other party's instance, and the minor's voidable promise is consideration for the other party's promise.[3] The result is to allow the minor to enforce transactions that have proved advantageous while avoiding those that have proved disadvantageous. There are also important consquences for good faith purchasers.[4]

Avoidance

The power of avoidance is personal to the minor and can be exercised only by the minor or by the minor's legal representatives including, in some instances, a parent or other guardian during minority and, in the event of the minor's death, an executor or administrator or heirs.[5] The exercise of the power is known as

---

[10] See N.M. Stat. Ann. §28-6-1; N.Y. Gen. Oblig. L. §3-101; N.C. Gen. Stat. §48A-2.

[11] See Ga. Code Ann. §13-3-21 (minor engaging in profession, trade, or business "as an adult" by permission of parent or guardian is bound); Kan. Stat. Ann. §38-103 (minor bound if other party has "good reasons to believe" minor was of age because of engaging in business "as an adult").

§4.4   [1] 8 W. Holdsworth, History of English Law 51 (1926).

[2] The same is true of executed transactions, such as a conveyance of land, in which no promise is involved.

[3] Holt v. Ward Clarencieux, 93 Eng. Rep. 954 (K.B. 1732) ("we are all of opinion that this contract is not void, but only voidable at the option of the infant"). See the discussion of avoidance compared in §2.14 *supra*.

[4] Under the Uniform Commercial Code, as against a good faith purchaser of a negotiable instrument known as a *holder in due course*, a minor's transfer of ownership by negotiation cannot be avoided, though the minor's promise on the instrument is subject to a *real* defense and remains voidable. UCC 3-202(a), 3-305(a),(b). Nor can a minor's transfer of ownership in personal property be avoided as against a good faith purchaser. UCC 2-403.

[5] Crockett Motor Co. v. Thompson, 6 S.W.2d 834 (Ark. 1928) (parent as guardian).

disaffirmance. A minor may generally disaffirm a contract either before or after reaching majority.[6] Any manifestation of an unwillingness to be bound by the contract will suffice as a disaffirmance of it. Disaffirmance may be by words, written or oral,[7] or by other conduct, including the plea of minority as a defense or the commencement of an action to set aside the transaction.[8] The entire contract must be disaffirmed, not merely the portions that are burdensome to the minor.[9]

The surrender of the power of avoidance is known as *ratification*. An effective ratification cannot be made by one who is not yet of age, for the act of ratification would itself be voidable.[10] Any manifestation of an undertaking to be bound by the original transaction will suffice as a ratification. The undertaking need not be supported by consideration. As we have seen, a new undertaking to perform such a voidable duty can be regarded as an example of a promise to perform a "moral obligation," a promise that is enforceable without consideration, analogous to one to pay a debt barred by the statute of limitations.[11] Ratification may be by words, written or oral,[12] or by other conduct such as performance or acceptance of the other party's performance under the contract.[13]

Ratification

The effect of mere silence by the minor after reaching majority has proved especially troublesome. The principle of mutuality of obligation would seem to require a prompt election by the minor on coming of age.[14] As a Texas court explained:

Effect of silence

> By holding the right of election open [in]definitely, the minor would be enabled, after majority, to speculate upon fluctuations in value, to affirm or

---

[6] McNaughton v. Granite City Auto Sales, 183 A. 340 (Vt. 1936) (automobile).

[7] Tracy v. Brown, 163 N.E. 885 (Mass. 1928) (minor disaffirmed contract to buy automobile by saying "I was under age, and I want my money back, and the automobile is down there in the garage").

[8] Del Santo v. Bristol County Stadium, 273 F.2d 605 (1st Cir. 1960) (minor disaffirmed release by bringing suit on released claim).

[9] Putman v. Deinhamer, 70 N.W.2d 652 (Wis. 1955) (minor cannot disaffirm cancellation provisions of insurance policy without disaffirming rest of policy).

[10] *See* Oubre v. Entergy Operations, 522 U.S. 422 (1998) (Scalia, J., dissenting, citing this treatise: "an infant cannot ratify his voidable contract until he reaches majority"). This rule may cause trouble if a minor who has not performed seeks specific performance before reaching majority.

[11] See the discussion of the exception for a debt barred by the statute of limitations in §2.8 *supra*.

[12] Courts have, however, been more reluctant than in the case of a debt barred by the statute of limitations to find such a new undertaking from a mere acknowledgment of the duty, as by a part payment. Lee v. Thompson, 168 So. 848 (Fla. 1936) ("A mere acknowledgement is not sufficient. It must be a direct promise to pay or discharge the contract in question.").

[13] Jones v. Dressel, 623 P.2d 370 (Colo. 1981) (trial court, as matter of law, properly determined that minor ratified contract for skydiving services by using them after reaching majority). *See generally* E. Farnsworth, Changing Your Mind ch. 19 (1998).

[14] See the discussion of the requirement of mutuality of obligation in §3.2 *supra*.

disaffirm, as his subsequent interest might dictate; whereas the other party would be helpless until the minor might see fit to act. The protection which the rule affords is against the deleterious effects of contracts made during minority. Beyond that date he . . . should be required to act within a reasonable time in all cases where not to require it would be inequitable or unjust to the other party.[15]

Of course, most transactions involving minors pose no substantial risk of speculation, and courts have been indulgent with minors in this respect. Although it is often said that the minor must act within a reasonable time after coming of age, the minor is rarely precluded from avoidance by delay, as long as there has been no demonstrable reliance on the transaction by the other party.[16] If the minor has received goods that would have to be returned on avoidance, such reliance might be found in depreciation or damage that has occurred during the delay.[17] If the minor has conveyed real property, such reliance might be found in the other party's expenditures for improvements.[18]

Assuming that the minor can avoid, what is the minor's obligation to make restitution to the other party for the benefits received?

No right to full restitution

§4.5. Restitution on Minor's Avoidance. Since a minor may avoid even after having received some or all of the other party's performance under a contract, a court must often determine the extent to which the minor is accountable for the benefit conferred by that performance. At the very least, the minor is expected to return what remains of anything that was received from the other party. The minor is also expected to return what remains of anything acquired from third persons in exchange for what the minor received from the other party.[1] But what if the minor received services, such as transportation or lessons, that cannot be returned? Or what if the minor received goods, such as an automobile or a house trailer, that have been resold or damaged or that have depreciated with use? Is the minor accountable for the difference between the value of whatever remains and its original value? The traditional answer has been that the minor is not accountable for such loss or depreciation. A minor who has used services is not accountable for anything. A minor who has smashed an automobile or house trailer need only return the wreck. Even if a minor has

---

[15]Walker v. Stokes Bros. & Co., 262 S.W. 158, 160 (Tex. Civ. App. 1924).

[16]Cassella v. Tiberio, 80 N.E.2d 426 (Ohio 1948) (delay of 11 years did not preclude avoidance of contract as surety since "the contract is wholly executory and . . . the infant has received no benefits").

[17]That the other party usually has no claim on avoidance for such depreciation or damage, see the discussion of no right to full restitution in §4.5 *infra*.

[18]Martin v. Elkhorn Coal Corp., 13 S.W.2d 780 (Ky. 1929) (minor "stood by with full knowledge of his rights, living in the immediate vicinity of the property for more than eight years after he became of age," while the purchaser of mineral rights "incurred great expense in the installation of its mine operations").

§4.5 [1]Whitman v. Allen, 121 A. 160 (Me. 1923) (if minor "does not restore, it is his duty to explain the reason therefor" or "be charged with the value of what he received or of its substitute").

squandered or destroyed what has been received, the loss is regarded as "the result of the very improvidence and indiscretion of infancy which the law has always in mind."[2]

[The law in this area would surely be simpler and arguably fairer if the minor were accountable in full for the benefit received.] The New York Court of Appeals admitted:

> That young men, nearly twenty-one years of age, actively engaged in business, can at will revoke any or all of their business transactions and obligations, thereby causing loss to innocent parties dealing with them, upon the assumption or even the assurance that they were of age, has not appealed to some courts, and has been adopted without much enthusiasm by others.[3]

It was the New Hampshire Supreme Court that early distinguished itself by making the most sweeping judicial departure from the traditional rule and allowing restitution in full. It held, for example, that a minor who was a milk dealer was liable for the reasonable value of milk supplied to him in the course of his business.[4] While a few courts have followed the New Hampshire view, in most states the other party's right to full restitution depends on whether that party can bring the case within one of several exceptions.

The most universal of these exceptions to the traditional rule holds the minor accountable for the reasonable value of what are called *necessaries*, a doctrine that the Supreme Court of North Carolina said was "put on the ground that unless an infant can get credit for necessaries he may starve."[5] According to Lord Coke, these include "necessary meat, drinke, apparell, necessary physicke, and such other necessaries, and likewise for his good teaching or instruction, whereby he may profit himselfe afterwards."[6] What types of things can be necessaries is generally regarded as a question of law. Whether a thing is a necessary in a particular situation is often a question of fact that "depends on the social position and situation in life of the infant as well as upon his own fortune and that of his parents."[7] Goods or services furnished an unemancipated minor are not necessaries unless a parent or guardian has failed to supply the minor's needs, and the parent or guardian is accorded considerable latitude in

The New Hampshire view

Exception for necessaries

---

[2] Utterstrom v. Myron D. Kidder, Inc., 124 A. 725, 726 (Me. 1924). As to rental value, *see* Loomis v. Imperial Motors, 396 P.2d 467 (Idaho 1964) (declining to assess car's rental value "on the grounds of quasi-contract"). The better view is that, although one is under a duty to return what remains in one's hands, its return is not a condition of one's bringing suit to recover what one has given up. *See* Restatement Second §14 cmt. *c*.

[3] Sternlieb v. Normandie Natl. Sec. Corp., 188 N.E. 726, 726 (N.Y. 1934).

[4] Bartlett v. Bailey, 59 N.H. 408 (1879).

[5] Turner v. Gaither, 83 N.C. 357, 361 (1879).

[6] E. Coke on Littleton 259 (1628).

[7] International Text-Book Co. v. Connelly, 99 N.E. 722, 725 (N.Y. 1912).

this regard for, said an eighteenth-century English judge, "no man shall take upon him to dictate to a parent what clothing the child shall wear, at what time they shall be purchased, or of whom."[8] The term clearly includes such needed food, clothing, and shelter as are appropriate to the minor's situation[9] and its scope is enlarged if the minor is emancipated, particularly if by marriage.[10] Courts have also included such items as essential medical care and legal services.[11] Considerable litigation has been engendered by claims that education is a necessary, occasionally with surprising hostility to such claims. It seems unlikely that the New York Court of Appeals would today adhere to its dictum that though a "common school education is doubtless necessary in this country, because it is essential to the transaction of business and the adequate discharge of civil and political duties," a "classical or professional education, however, has been held not to come within the term."[12] Claims that an automobile or other motor vehicle is a necessary have been equally controversial, with the traditional response denying such claims[13] rejected by some courts.[14] A contract of loan for the purpose of paying for necessaries is treated as a contract for necessaries on the reasoning that the lender succeeds by subrogation to the rights of the person who furnished the necessaries.[15] The minor may recover any excess over the reasonable value of the necessaries, and if no necessaries have yet been furnished under the contract, the minor is free to disaffirm it.[16] Although the liability for necessaries is in restitution for their reasonable value and not on the contract itself, the party seeking recovery must have contracted with the minor. Thus if the goods or services are furnished, not on the minor's own credit, but on the credit of a parent or guardian, the minor is not liable.[17]

Exception for minor as plaintiff

A second exception is made in a substantial number of states in cases where the minor, as plaintiff, seeks recovery of money paid, as distinguished from

---

[8] Bainbridge v. Pickering, 96 Eng. Rep. 776, 776 (1779).

[9] Ragan v. Williams, 127 So. 190 (Ala. 1930) (house occupied by minor emancipated by marriage and his family was necessary).

[10] Merrick v. Stephens, 337 S.W.2d 713 (Mo. App. 1960) (if "minor is emancipated and does not have the parental roof for shelter, and if he is married (or marrying), with a wife for whom he is obligated to furnish shelter and lodging, the purchase or lease of a home can, depending upon the individual circumstances, become a *necessity*").

[11] Cole v. Wagner, *supra* note 8 (emergency hospital care was necessary).

[12] International Text-Book Co. v. Connelly, *supra* note 7, at 725 (five-year correspondence course in steam engineering was not a necessary).

[13] Russell v. Baffe Plywood Co., 68 A.2d 691 (Vt. 1949) (trucks bought for hauling logs, where married minor could have worked on father's farm, were not necessaries).

[14] Rose v. Sheehan Buick, 204 So. 2d 903 (Fla. App. 1967) (automobile bought by minor for "school, business and social activities" was a necessary).

[15] Price v. Sanders, 60 Ind. 310 (1878).

[16] Gregory v. Lee, 30 A. 53 (Conn. 1894) (college student's contract for room).

[17] Foster v. Adcock, 30 S.W.2d 239 (Tenn. 1930) (doctor's contract was with parent not with five-year-old child).

cases where the minor, as defendant, merely sets up minority as a defense. To this extent, as Chancellor Kent expressed it, "the privilege of infancy is to be used as a shield and not as a sword."[18] The result is that one who furnishes goods or services to a minor for cash is entitled to restitution in full in the event of avoidance, while one who furnishes them on credit is not. The airline that gets cash for the ticket is protected.[19] The automobile dealer that gets a down payment is, in that amount, protected.[20] From the minor's point of view, to the extent that one pays cash, one is fully accountable for the benefit received, while to the extent that one has used credit, one is not. One is, in short, protected against improvident commitment but not the improvident outlay of cash.

A third exception is made in some states if the minor has made a misrepresentation of age. The reasoning is that a minor is liable for torts and a fraudulent misrepresentation of age is actionable as a tort if it induced reliance by the other party.[21] Since the reliance induced is the furnishing of the goods or services, the loss suffered by the other party as a result of that party's failure to get restitution in full on avoidance is loss caused by the misrepresentation, and restitution in full is thereby achieved.[22] Even the courts that follow this reasoning, however, have balked at applying it to a misrepresentation consisting merely of a printed recital of majority on a standard form supplied by the other party.[23] And many courts have entirely rejected the reasoning on the ground that to treat a misrepresentation of age as a tort would involve indirect enforcement of the contract.[24] A few courts have gone to the opposite extreme and held that a minor is estopped by the misrepresentation to assert minority as a defense and is therefore liable not merely for restitution, but

Exception for misrepresentation

[18] 2 J. Kent, Commentaries on American Law 240 (3d ed. 1836), quoted in Rice v. Butler, 55 N.E. 275 (N.Y. 1899). *Accord:* Petit v. Liston, 191 P. 660 (Or. 1920) (minor who has made payment and used motorcycle "ought not to be permitted to recover the amount actually paid without allowing the vendor of the goods compensation for the use and depreciation"). *Contra:* Halbman v. Lemke, 298 N.W.2d 562 (Wis. 1980) (rejecting "'sword-shield' dichotomy," absent misrepresentation of age, as well as argument that minor should make "restitution" for diminished value of unsalvageable car by offset against price paid).

[19] Vichnes v. Transcontinental & Western Air, 18 N.Y.S.2d 603 (Sup. Ct. 1940).

[20] Petit v. Liston, *supra* note 18, followed in Dodson v. Shrader, 824 S.W.2d 545 (Tenn. 1992) (adopting "modified form of the Oregon rule"). Courts applying the exception sometimes measure the benefit to the minor by the value of the use of the automobile and sometimes by the depreciation in value of the automobile.

[21] Byers v. Lemay Bank & Trust Co., 282 S.W.2d 512 (Mo. 1955) (misrepresentation in obtaining loan). For the prevailing view, however, *see* Gillis v. Whitley's Discount Auto Sales, 319 S.E.2d 661 (N.C. App. 1984) ("minor's [mis]representation of his age does not bar him from disaffirming his contract").

[22] Keser v. Chagnon, 410 P.2d 637 (Colo. 1966) (counterclaim in tort by automobile dealer).

[23] Kiefer v. Fred Howe Motors, 158 N.W.2d 288 (Wis. 1968) (no intent to defraud shown).

[24] Sternlieb v. Normandie Natl. Sec. Corp., *supra* note 3 (misrepresentation in purchasing stock that became worthless). See the note to the discussion of voidable, not void in §4.4 *supra*.

on the contract itself.[25] But the conventional response is that of the Supreme Court of North Carolina in a century-old decision that estoppel would "hold out the temptation to infants, and to others who hope to profit by debauching them, to resort to this disreputable method of enabling the one to squander, and the other to extort, the patrimony intended to prepare a child for future usefulness."[26]

Summary

Even though a court does not accept the New Hampshire view, then, an automobile dealer that has sold an automobile to a minor has a claim on avoidance to restitution in full — in some states if the minor can show that it was a necessary, in some states if the minor has sold it for cash, and in some states if the minor has misrepresented his or her age. Yet the fact that these are exceptions to a general rule denying restitution in full is testimony to the law's continued indulgence with regard to minors. As the New York Court of Appeals once lamented:

> As long as young men and women, under twenty-one years of age, having the semblance and appearance of adults, are forced to make a living and enter into business transactions, how are the persons dealing with them to be protected if the infant's word cannot be taken or recognized at law? Are business men to deal with young people at their peril?[27]

Although the reduction in the age of majority to 18 has helped to lessen the bite of this complaint, the answer is still that, with exceptions already noted, persons must indeed deal with minors at their peril.

Mental infirmity poses comparable problems, which we now consider.

Difficulty of subject

§4.6. **The Test of Mental Incompetency.** According to the Supreme Court of Arkansas, "Perhaps no branch of jurisprudence is more elusive than that dealing with one's mental capacity to contract."[1] The intrinsic elusiveness of this subject is compounded by a patchwork of statutes that, as is the case for minors, vary considerably from one jurisdiction to another.

---

[25]Johnson v. McAdory, 88 So. 2d 106 (Miss. 1956) (misrepresentation in purchase of automobile).

[26]Carolina Interstate Bldg. & Loan Assn. v. Black, 25 S.E. 975, 976 (N.C. 1896).

[27]Sternlieb v. Normandie Natl. Sec. Corp., *supra* note 3, at 728.

§4.6   [1]Waggoner v. Atkins, 162 S.W.2d 55, 58 (Ark. 1942).

For opposing views on whether the issue of incapacity is for court or arbitrator, *compare* Spahr v. Secco, 330 F.3d 1266 (10th Cir. 2003) (defense "goes to both the entire contract and the specific agreement to arbitrate"), *with* Primerica Life Ins. Co. v. Brown, 304 F.3d 469 (5th Cir. 2002) (incapacity is "defense to his entire agreement" and not "specific challenge to the arbitration clause").

Although the older cases were concerned mainly with "lunacy" and "insanity," it is now recognized that incapacity due to mental infirmity may result from a variety of causes, including mental retardation, mental illness, brain damage, brain deterioration due to old age, and the use of alcohol or drugs.[2] The mere presence of such a disability, however, does not itself impair the capacity to contract. In the colorful words of the Supreme Court of Arkansas, the fact that a man may have been "filthy, forgetful and eccentric, . . . believed in witchcraft, and had dogs eat at the same table with him . . . does not establish lack of capacity."[3] Something more must be shown, and it has been difficult to formulate a single test of that additional element to encompass diverse types of mental disorders.

Mental disability alone not enough

The traditional test is a "cognitive" one. Did the party lack the capacity to understand the nature and consequences of the transaction in question?[4] Was the party unable to know what he or she was doing and to appreciate its effects? Since it is competency at the time the agreement was made that is critical, it is enough if the party had a "lucid interval" at that moment.[5] The cognitive test has been attacked as unscientific, and one legal scholar has condemned it as setting up a standard that is "ambiguous, self-contradictory and practically meaningless" and that "defies accurate verbal formulation."[6] Nevertheless, the cognitive test is almost universally accepted by courts. In view of the difficulty in applying the test, it is especially significant that it is irrelevant whether the other party knew or had reason to know of the mental disability.[7]

Cognitive (understanding) test

The principal challenges to the cognitive test have come from instances in which mentally infirm persons understand the nature and consequences of their actions, but nevertheless lack effective control of them, a situation characteristic of manic-depressives. Should a "volitional" test be applied in such cases, as an alternative to the cognitive one? In a seminal lower court New York case, a previously frugal and cautious businessman passed from the depressed to the manic phase of a manic-depressive psychosis and suddenly refused to see his psychiatrist, went on a buying spree, and embarked on ambitious construction projects. As part of one of these projects he contracted, against his lawyer's advice, to buy land for $51,500. Two weeks later he was sent to a mental hospital, and he later sued to rescind the contract. The court concluded that he

Volitional test

---

[2] Edmunds v. Chandler, 127 S.E.2d 73 (Va. 1962) (intelligence quotient of 51 resulting from childhood injury).

[3] Simmons First Natl. Bank v. Luzader, 438 S.W.2d 25, 30 (Ark. 1969) (quoting this statement with approval).

[4] Lloyd v. Jordan, 544 So. 2d 957 (Ala. 1989) ("incapable of understanding and appreciating the nature and effect of the . . . form that he signed").

[5] Critchfield v. Easterday, 26 App. D.C. 89 (1905); McPeck v. Graham, 49 S.E. 125 (W. Va. 1904).

[6] Green, Judicial Tests of Mental Incompetency, 6 Mo. L. Rev. 141, 147, 165 (1941).

[7] Orr v. Equitable Mortgage Co., 33 S.E. 708 (Ga. 1899) ("the mere fact that the other party to an alleged contract did not know of the incapacity would not restore the capacity to contract"). But see the possible effect of knowledge in the discussion of restitution in full in §4.8 *infra*.

understood the transaction since the "manic-depressive psychosis affects motivation rather than ability to understand." It nevertheless held that "capacity to understand is not . . . the sole criterion. Incompetence to contract also exists when a contract is entered into under the compulsion of a mental disease or disorder but for which the contract would not have been made."[8]

Restatement Second position

§10

The Restatement Second takes a compromise position by adding to the traditional cognitive test a qualified volitional test: "if by reason of mental illness or defect . . . he is unable to act in a reasonable manner in relation to the transaction and the other party has reason to know of his condition."[9] The qualification that the other party have reason to know of the condition — one that does not figure in the Restatement Second's formulation of the cognitive test — was reaffirmed by the New York Court of Appeals in *Ortelere v. Teachers' Retirement Board*, the leading case applying the volitional branch of the Restatement Second formulation. In balancing the interest in "stability in contractual relations and protection of the expectations of parties who bargain in good faith" against that in protecting "persons who may understand the nature of the transaction but who, due to mental illness, cannot control their conduct . . . , there should be relief only if the other party knew or was put on notice as to the contractor's mental illness."[10]

Intoxication or drug use

Intoxication may also render a party unable to understand the nature and consequences of the transaction. Intoxication is usually voluntary, however, and courts have often reprobated the party who seeks to avoid on this ground. "As for a drunkard who is *voluntarius daemon*," moralized Lord Coke, "he hath . . . no privilege thereby."[11] Under the rule stated in the Restatement Second, inability to understand by reason of intoxication makes a contract voidable only if the other party has reason to know of the inability,[12] but the behavior of the intoxicated party will ordinarily be enough to satisfy this requirement. The same rules presumably apply to the effects of drugs.

Types of evidence

Courts have not had an easy time evaluating evidence of mental incompetency. The party who seeks relief on that ground bears the burden of persuasion. The trier of the facts may consider the circumstances surrounding the transaction in dispute, the party's general behavior in that and similar transactions, the opinions of lay persons who have observed the party's behavior, the opinions

---

[8] Faber v. Sweet Style Mfg. Corp., 242 N.Y.S.2d 763, 767, 768 (Sup. Ct. 1963).

[9] Restatement Second §15(1). That section was disapproved in Estate of McGovern v. State Employees' Retirement Board, 517 A.2d 523 (Pa. 1986) (declining to adopt "new tests" of §15, which require "post-hoc determination of reasonableness").

[10] 250 N.E.2d 460, 465 (N.Y. 1969).

[11] E. Coke on Littleton 247a (1628). A few courts have taken the view that voluntary drunkenness is never a defense. Burroughs v. Richman, 13 N.J.L. 233 (1832) ("Drunkenness may be insanity, but it is voluntary. It is no excuse from the consequences of crime; why should it be against those of acts affecting property?").

[12] Restatement Second §16. (A similar rule is stated for inability "to act in a reasonable manner.")

of psychiatric experts, and past records of treatment and hospitalization⟩ As might be expected, judges differ considerably in their willingness to accept expert opinion when it departs from their own perception of the facts. A leading scholar found a growing recognition that the dominant factor is "whether the court sees *the particular transaction in its result* as that which a reasonably competent man might have made."[13] If it does, it is unlikely to upset the transaction.[14] If, however, the court regards the transaction as unfair, evidence of incapacity is more likely to be believed.[15]

An adjudication of incompetency and the appointment of a guardian is everywhere a conclusive determination of one's incapacity to contract at the time of the adjudication. This much is essential to the purpose of the guardianship in safeguarding the ward's estate. In many jurisdictions, the adjudication is conclusive as to capacity at later times as well, unless the guardianship has been terminated by a subsequent judicial order of restoration. Other courts, however, hold with good reason that the adjudication raises only a rebuttable presumption of incompetency at a later time, a presumption that can be overcome by proof that the person had recovered and was competent, even though there has been no judicial order of restoration.[16] A mere court order for admission to a hospital should be even less conclusive, although the fact of involuntary hospitalization may at least raise some doubt as to competency.

Effect of adjudication

Mental infirmity that falls short of that required for incompetency may nevertheless suffice to preclude equitable relief.[17] And it may combine with other circumstances showing overreaching or substantive unfairness to make a contract voidable for misrepresentation,[18] duress,[19] or undue influence.[20]

Infirmity short of incompetency

What are the legal effects of a determination that a party lacked capacity on the ground of mental infirmity at the time he made the contract?

§4.7. Effects of Mental Incompetency.[1]

It was once the view that an agreement made by a mental incompetent was void. This conclusion accorded

Void or voidable

---

[13] Green, Proof of Mental Incompetency and the Unexpressed Major Premise, 53 Yale L.J. 271, 307 (1944).

[14] *See* Cundick v. Broadbent, 383 F.2d 157 (10th Cir. 1967) (expert testimony disregarded where contract was "not unconscionable, unfair or inequitable").

[15] Krasner v. Berk, 319 N.E.2d 897 (Mass. 1974) (Braucher, J.: where "agreement . . . was an improvident one for a doctor who was about to consider whether he should give up his practice . . . the judge could find that he was not competent to make it").

[16] Fugate v. Walker, 265 S.W. 331 (Ky. 1924).

[17] See the discussions of the significance of factors other than substance in §4.27 *infra* and of unfairness in §12.7 *infra*.

[18] See §4.14 *infra*.

[19] See §4.18 *infra*.

[20] See §4.20 *infra*.

§4.7 [1] This section is concerned only with the effects of mental incompetency at the time the contract is made. As to its effects after the contract is made, *see* the discussion of supervening death or disability in §9.5 *infra*.

with the view that a contract required a subjective "meeting of the minds." As the United States Supreme Court rationalized in the nineteenth century, "a lunatic, or a person *non compos mentis*, has nothing which the law recognizes as a mind, and . . . cannot make a contract which may have any efficacy as such."[2] Today, however, it is generally held that such an agreement is not void but only voidable at the instance of the mentally incompetent party.[3] In a few states the rule of total nullity is preserved by statute, and in many more states a contract made by an incompetent during guardianship following an adjudication is void.[4]

Avoidance and ratification

Where the contract is voidable, the power of avoidance is personal to the incompetent.[5] It can be exercised: by the incompetent's legal representatives, including a guardian or committee; by the incompetent in the event of recovery; and by an executor or administrator or heirs in the event of the incompetent's death.[6] The rules on disaffirmance are generally similar to those for minors. The power of avoidance may be lost by ratification, which may be express or by conduct or by delay in disaffirmance.[7] There is, however, authority that in order to avoid the contract the incompetent must return whatever has been received and not, as in the case for minors, just whatever remains of what has been received.[8] This section is concerned only with the effects of mental incompetency at the time the contract is made. As to its effects after the contract is made, *see* the discussion of supervening death or disability in §9.5 *infra*.

Comparison with minors

Although the rules on disaffirmance and ratification are similar for minors and mental incompetents, their impact is often different in practice because of the greater uncertainty in applying the test of mental incompetency. A recognition of the uncertainty produced by doubts as to the existence and duration of the disability is reflected in the rules on restitution.

We now turn to them.

Restitution in full

§4.8. Restitution on Mental Incompetent's Avoidance.

The mental incompetent's power of avoidance, like the analogous power of a minor, can be

---

[2] Dexter v. Hall, 82 U.S. (15 Wall.) 9, 20 (1872).

[3] *See* Restatement Second §15.

[4] John P. Bleeg Co. v. Peterson, 215 N.W. 529 (S.D. 1927). (This question is not the same as the one considered in the discussion of the effect of adjudication in §4.6 *supra* (i.e., whether the adjudication is conclusive or only presumptive as to incompetency), though the rule that an agreement is void is sometimes regarded as a corollary of the rule that the adjudication is conclusive.)

[5] *But cf.* Rattner v. Kleiman, 36 S.W.2d 249 (Tex. Civ. App. 1931) (vendor's inability to convey good title because of mental incompetency unknown to vendee at time of contract would justify vendee's refusal to perform).

[6] Norfolk Southern Corp. v. Smith, 414 S.E.2d 485 (Ga. 1992) (incompetent after recovery).

[7] Bunn v. Postell, 33 S.E. 707 (Ga. 1899) (administrator ratified by taking possession of property and using it as property of estate). On the rules for minors, see §4.4 *supra*.

[8] Hauer v. Union State Bank, 532 N.W.2d 456 (Wis. App. 1995) (dictum: "two types of incapacity are essentially dissimilar," and contractual act of incompetent is voidable "only if avoidance accords with equitable principles").

exercised if the other party has fully performed the contract before learning of the disability. But the other party is under a greater disadvantage in the case of mental incompetency because the test of mental infirmity gives rise to more uncertainty than does that of immaturity. It is, therefore, not surprising that the other party's rights to restitution are greater as against a mental incompetent than as against a minor.[1] The minor is ordinarily accountable only for the benefits that remain in the minor's hands.[2] However, the mental incompetent is generally required, as a condition of relief, to make restitution in full to the extent of any benefit received.[3] Even if the incompetent has dissipated or squandered it during incompetency, so that it cannot be returned in kind, the incompetent must restore the status quo by making compensation in money.[4] Courts have not required full restitution, however, if the other party acted unfairly and with knowledge of the incompetency.[5] Furthermore, a court will exercise its discretion in allowing avoidance and may dispense with the requirement of full restitution if the incompetent derived little or no benefit from what was received.[6]

The incompetent must, in any case, make restitution for necessaries received, including those received by dependents.[7] This is important where restitution might otherwise be denied on the ground that the other party knew of the incompetency or that the contract was "void," rather than merely voidable. The test of what is a "necessary" is similar to that in the case of a minor[8] and extends to legal services, such as those rendered in an attempt, even if

Liability for necessaries

---

§4.8   [1]*See* Coburn v. Raymond, 57 A. 116 (Conn. 1904) ("one thing to hold that he who does not discover the tangible, definite, and ascertainable status of minority must suffer the consequences, and quite another to say that he who fails to detect the existence of the subtle, elusive and sporadic condition of mental unsoundness, and to correctly measure its degree, cannot be heard in court of equity to plead his ignorance and good faith").

[2] See the discussion of no right to full restitution in §4.5 *supra*.

[3] Hauer v. Union State Bank, 532 N.W.2d 456 (Wis. App. 1995) (infancy doctrine, under which disaffirming minor "may recover the purchase price without liability for use, depreciation or other diminution in value," does not apply to cases of mental incompetency).

[4] Sparrowhawk v. Erwin, 246 P. 541 (Ariz. 1926) (incompetent and husband borrowed money and husband spent it).

[5] Tubbs v. Hilliard, 89 P.2d 535 (Colo. 1939) (assignee knew of mental incapacity of assignor and dealings were "unconscionable"). If the other party has knowledge of the incompetency, that party may find itself in a worse position than a party against whom a contract is voidable for misrepresentation. See the discussion of the requirement of restitution in §4.15 *infra*.

[6] Jordan v. Kirkpatrick, 95 N.E. 1079 (Ill. 1911) (where incompetent borrowed money and husband spent it, "the lunatic, having no responsibility for the transaction and receiving no benefit therefrom, should receive the protection of the court of equity"). *Contra:* Sparrowhawk v. Erwin, *supra* note 4 (immaterial who received the benefit as long as other party "in good faith and at the request of the incompetent parted with consideration").

[7] Linch v. Sanders, 173 S.E. 788 (W. Va. 1934) (necessaries furnished incompetent's family after he was judicially declared insane and guardian appointed).

[8] In re Weber's Estate, 239 N.W. 260 (Mich. 1931) (nursing services to incompetent). See the discussion of the exception for necessaries in §4.5 *supra*.

unsuccessful, to have the incompetent released from confinement or adjudged competent.[9]

We turn now from the perspective of status to that of behavior, and we consider how courts police abuse of the bargaining process.

C. BEHAVIOR

Common forms of abuse

§4.9. Abuse of the Bargaining Process in General. Assuming competent parties, the traditional concern of courts in policing has been with abuse of the bargaining process rather than with the substance of the resulting bargain. The two most common kinds of claims of abuse are those arising from misleading conduct and from coercive conduct. Both kinds of claims tempt courts to pass moral judgment on the propriety of bargaining behavior. Our concern is with the effect of such misbehavior on the enforceability of promises.

Law as to deception

In a system of contract law based on supposedly informed assent, it is in the interest of society as well as of the parties to discourage misleading conduct in the bargaining process. To this end both tort and contract law provide remedies for misrepresentation, sometimes affording the recipient of the misrepresentation a choice between the two.[1] The relevant rules of tort law trace their origins to the common law action of deceit. They allow the recipient of the misrepresentation to recover from its maker damages that, at their most generous, are based on the value that the bargain would have had to the recipient had it been as represented.[2] Most of the relevant rules of contract law are derived from the action for rescission that was originally brought in equity. They allow the recipient of the misrepresentation to undo the transaction by avoiding it, and they seek to restore the parties to the positions in which they found themselves before they made the agreement.[3] In contrast to the tort rules, they ask only what types of behavior are not tolerable as the basis of a bargain, not what types are actionable in damages.

Premises as to deception

A contracting party's power to avoid the contract plainly threatens the security of transactions. Since the remedy of avoidance is not available for the other party's mere failure to perform the contract, its justification in the case of misrepresentation must proceed from the premise that deception in the bargaining process is significantly different from such a failure later to perform.

---

[9]Kay v. Kay, 89 P.2d 496 (Ariz. 1939) (attorney's fees and expenses incurred to restore incompetent to capacity).

§4.9 [1]As to the effect of a choice, see the discussion of avoidance and ratification in §4.14 *infra*. A misrepresentation, particularly one by a seller of goods, may also give rise to liability for breach of warranty. *See* UCC 2-313.

[2]This is the majority or "loss of bargain" rule, as opposed to the minority or "out of pocket" rule, which only compensates for loss sustained.

[3]Occasionally the contract rules have other consequences, such as allowing reformation of a writing to conform to a representation. *See* the discussion of reformation for fraud in §7.5 *infra*.

Wherein lies that difference? One possible assumption is that misleading conduct involves a moral wrong of a sort not involved in mere nonperformance. The focus would then be on the culpability of the maker of the misrepresentation. Another possible assumption is that misleading conduct produces harm of a sort not involved in mere nonperformance. The focus would then be on the unfairness to the recipient of the misrepresentation. Since courts allow avoidance for nonfraudulent as well as fraudulent misrepresentation, though they are occasionally more generous in allowing relief if fraud is shown,[4] it seems clear that the second assumption is the prevailing one.

[Coercive behavior,] the second type of abuse, is a particularly odious form of overreaching in a system of contract law based on assent supposedly freely given. It is more objectionable than misleading behavior since the recipient of a misrepresentation at least has the possibility of investigating the truth of the assertion. The common law courts developed the doctrine of duress to deal with coercive behavior. The rules on duress, like those on misrepresentation, allow the injured party to undo the transaction by avoiding it. They seek to restore the parties to the positions in which they found themselves before they made the agreement. In contrast to misrepresentation, however, there is traditionally no tort of duress, so obtaining assent to a contract by duress does not of itself give rise to an action for damages.[5] A related doctrine of undue influence grew up in courts of equity to give relief to victims of unfair transactions that were induced by improper persuasion.[6] Furthermore, in the common law courts there developed a rule known as the *pre-existing duty rule*, a curious appendage of the doctrine of consideration that had the incidental effect of protecting some victims of coercion.[7] This rule has now largely been overshadowed by the law of duress as a result of an extraordinary expansion of that law to afford protection from a wide variety of threats that would not formerly have amounted to duress.[8]

Coercive behavior poses a problem not posed by misleading behavior. Since misleading behavior has come to include nonfraudulent as well as fraudulent misrepresentation, all misleading behavior, with few exceptions, is regarded as an abuse of the bargaining process. This is not true of coercive behavior, however, for coercion is inherent in the bargaining process itself. As we have seen, every offer involves a kind of a threat in order to induce a response by the offeree.[9] The seller that offers to deliver cotton if the buyer promises to pay

Law as to coercion

Premises as to coercion

---

[4] See the discussion of the question of detriment in §4.13 *infra*. See also the notes to the discussions of avoidance and ratification and of remedies on avoidance in §4.15 *infra*.

[5] Cimarron Pipeline Constr. v. United States Fidelity & Guar. Ins. Co., 848 P.2d 1161 (Okl. 1993) ("we are not compelled to recognize the doctrine of economic duress as a general tort theory").

[6] See the discussion of development in §4.20 *infra*.

[7] See the discussion of the illustration of the rule in §4.21 *infra*.

[8] See the discussion of the remedies of a victim of bad faith in §4.22 *infra*.

[9] See the discussion of the promisor's use of condition in §2.9 *supra*.

$10,000 is saying, in effect, "If you do not promise to pay $10,000, you shall not have my promise to deliver the cotton." It is not usual, however, to think of such an offer as a threat, for a society in which one is largely free to dispose of what one owns could scarcely condemn withholding one's cotton unless one's price is met. Such threats are an inevitable part of the bargaining process in a free enterprise economy. The buyer need not promise to pay $10,000, but the buyer that does surely cannot get out of the bargain by claiming that it was induced by a threat. The problem then becomes one of singling out those threats that amount to abuse of the bargaining process. How are improper threats identified? One possibility would be to look at the maker of the threat and ask whether the maker was in some sense culpable. Another possibility would be to look at the victim of the threat and ask whether the victim was unfairly harmed. As we shall see, the trend is toward emphasizing the unfairness of the result of the threat to the victim, as opposed to the culpability of the maker.[10]

The law dealing with misleading behavior will be discussed first.

Fraud in factum or execution

§4.10.   The Elements of Misrepresentation. A distinction is drawn between misrepresentation that goes only to the "inducement" and misrepresentation that goes to the "execution" (or the "factum"). In the typical case, as when a seller misrepresents the quality of goods, the misrepresentation is said to go to the "inducement." The effect of such a misrepresentation is to make the contract voidable at the instance of the recipient. In rare cases, however, the misrepresentation is regarded as going to the very character of the proposed contract itself, as when one party induces the other to sign a document by falsely stating that it has no legal effect. Such a misrepresentation is said to go to the "execution" (or the "factum"[1]). If the other party neither knows nor has reason to know of the character of the proposed agreement, the effect of such a misrepresentation is that there is no contract at all [2] — what is sometimes anomalously described as a "void," as opposed to a voidable, contract.[3] The same result would follow from the general principles relating to assent.[4] The distinction is mainly of significance to such third parties as good faith purchasers, who generally take property free of claims and defenses based

---

[10] See the discussion of the significance of unfairness in §4.17 *infra*.

§4.10   [1] *See* Restatement Second §163 ("misrepresentation as to the character or essential terms of a proposed contract"). A plea that the defendant had not executed a document was a plea of *non est factum*. That fraud in the factum is for the court not the arbitrators, *see* Oakwood Mobile Homes v. Barger, 773 So. 2d 454 (Ala. 2000) ("challenge to the very existence of a contract is not subject to arbitration").

[2] Harkrider v. Posey, 24 P.3d 821 (Okl. 2000) ("fraud in the inducement creates a valid contractual relationship" until rescission, whereas "fraud *in esse contractus,* fraud in the execution, or fraud *in factum* . . . results in a contract which is a nullity").

[3] If a "contract" is defined in terms of an enforceable promise, a "void contract" is not a "contract" at all.

[4] See the discussion of the victory of the objective theory in §3.6 *supra*.

on misrepresentation if the misrepresentation goes only to the inducement, but not if it goes to the factum or the execution.[5] Only rarely, however, is a misrepresentation seen as going to the very nature of the contract itself. Even the identity of the other party is not usually regarded as sufficiently central, so that a mere misrepresentation as to identity, as when a buyer of goods obtains credit by impersonating a person of means, may make the contract voidable but is not ordinarily seen as preventing a manifestation of assent.[6]

In the great bulk of cases, the misrepresentation is seen as going only to the inducement, with the result that the contract is voidable. The requirements for avoidance can be grouped under four headings.[7] First, there must be an assertion that is not in accord with the facts. Second, the assertion must be either fraudulent or material. Third, the assertion must be relied on by the recipient in manifesting assent. Fourth, the reliance of the recipient must be justified.[8] Although the tort rules will not be discussed here, it is worthy of note that, just as the consequences of a misrepresentation are less severe in contract than in tort law, so too is the availability of relief less restricted.[9]

Fraud in inducement

We now turn to these four headings in order.

§4.11. Assertion Not in Accord with Facts. The essence of deception is a false representation as to fact, as distinguished from a mere nonperformance of a promise.[1] It must therefore be asserted that something is a fact at the time the assertion is made. The assertion may be one of a past event ("I have put this machine in running order"), as well as one of a present circumstance ("This machine is in running order"), but cannot be one of a future event ("I will put this machine in running order"). An assertion limited to a future event may be a promise that imposes liability for breach of contract or a mere prediction that

Assertion as to fact

---

[5] Fraud "that induced the obligor to sign the instrument with neither knowledge nor reasonable opportunity to learn of its character or its essential terms" is a *real* defense to an asserted obligation on a negotiable instrument, i.e., a good defense even when the instrument is in the hands of a good faith purchaser known as a *holder in due course.* UCC 3-305(a)(1),(b). *See* the discussion of the use of a promissory note in §11.8 *infra. Cf.* UCC 2-403(1) (good faith purchaser of goods takes good title from one with "voidable title"). In addition, at least in principle, the recipient of a misrepresentation may ratify the contract if it is voidable but not if it is "void." See the discussion of avoidance and ratification in §4.15 *infra.*

[6] UCC 2-403(1)(a); Phelps v. McQuade, 115 N.E. 441 (N.Y. 1917) (buyer of jewelry on credit impersonated "man of financial responsibility").

[7] *See* Barrer v. Women's Natl. Bank, 761 F.2d 752 (D.C. Cir. 1985) (Restatement Second §164 "provides helpful guidance" concerning these conditions).

[8] As to the burden of proof, *see* Ashmore v. Herbie Morewitz, Inc., 475 S.E.2d 271 (Va. 1996) (claimant must adduce "clear and convincing evidence," which is "that degree of proof which will produce . . . a firm belief or conviction concerning the allegations").

[9] Chicago Park Dist. v. Chicago & N.W. Transp. Co., 607 N.E.2d 1300 (Ill. App. 1992) ("proper analysis of how fraud affects or discharges a contractual obligation is not identical to the classical tort definition of fraudulent misrepresentation as a cause of action to recover damages").

§4.11 [1] See the discussion of premises as to deception in §4.9 *supra.*

does not, but it is not a misrepresentation as to that event.[2] Nevertheless, a promise or a prediction may carry with it by implication an assertion that facts exist from which the promised or predicted consequences will follow, and this may amount to a misrepresentation as to those facts. If, for example, a seller of a machine states that the machine will attain a specified level of performance when it is put into use, it may be inferred that its present design and condition make it capable of achieving that level.[3] This may be so even if the claim is a mere prediction, not binding as a promise.

Examples of facts   Ordinarily the fact that is asserted is some characteristic of the subject matter of the transaction, such as the quality of cotton being sold, but this is not necessarily the case. An assertion as to the contents or legal effect of a writing that is to evidence or embody the contract is an assertion of fact.[4] So, too, is an assertion as to one's own state of mind, such as one's opinion or intention,[5] for, as the noted dictum of an English judge graphically expressed it, "the state of a man's mind is as much a fact as the state of his digestion."[6] Whether the recipient is justified in relying on the assertion in any of these cases is a separate question that will be discussed later.[7]

Assertion by words   The assertion may take the form of any conduct,[8] but it is commonly a statement in spoken or written words. Whether such a statement is false depends on the meaning of these words in all the circumstances. When, for example, a seller of a resort that had lost money each year said that it was making "good money," the statement was "a false representation of a past or existing material fact."[9] What is asserted includes what may fairly be inferred. Thus a "half truth" that is true as to the facts stated, but fails to include a qualification necessary to prevent a false inference, is a misrepresentation.[10] For example, a

---

[2]If the speaker has no intention to do what is said, however, the statement may be a misrepresentation of the speaker's intention. *See* the discussion of promissory fraud in §4.14 *infra*. As to the distinction between a "promise" and a "prediction," *see* the discussion of promises, predictions, and opinions in §3.6 *supra*.

[3]Clements Auto Co. v. Service Bureau Corp., 444 F.2d 169 (8th Cir. 1971) (tort: representation that data processing system would provide information that "would constitute an effective and efficient tool to be used in inventory control" was not only "a prediction of what the system will do" but also "a statement of the inherent capabilities" of the system).

[4]Ten-Cate v. First Natl. Bank, 52 S.W.2d 323 (Tex. Civ. App. 1932) (party read aloud only part of writing).

[5]Markov v. ABC Transfer & Storage Co., 457 P.2d 535 (Wash. 1969) (tort: "There are times when the law demands of one an honest declaration of future intentions.").

[6]Lord Bowen in Edgington v. Fitzmaurice, L.R. 29 Ch. Div. 459, 483 (1882).

[7]See §4.14 *infra*.

[8]For example, drawing a check generally amounts to a representation that there are sufficient funds in the account on which it is drawn. Klockner v. Keser, 488 P.2d 1135 (Colo. App. 1971).

[9]Spiess v. Brandt, 41 N.W.2d 561 (Minn. 1950).

[10]Kannavos v. Annino, 247 N.E.2d 708 (Mass. 1969) (vendor advertised property as multifamily housing suitable for investment without revealing that zoning ordinance prohibited such use).

true statement that an event has occurred may invite a false inference that the situation has not changed since then.

An assertion may also take the form of concealment, an affirmative act that is intended or known to be likely to keep another from learning a fact. A seller of a building may, for example, conceal a defect from a prospective buyer by painting it over or by preventing the buyer from making an inspection. That conduct amounts to an assertion that the defect does not exist and is therefore a misrepresentation.[11] Or an offeror may read a written offer to the offeree and omit part of it. That conduct amounts to an assertion that the omitted part is not contained in the writing, and it is therefore a misrepresentation.[12]

Assertion by concealment

Where simple nondisclosure, as opposed to concealment, is involved, courts have had great difficulty in dealing with the extent to which candor, as distinguished from honesty, is required. The classic example is *Laidlaw v. Organ*, a case precipitated by the Treaty of Ghent, which ended the War of 1812 and with it the British blockade of New Orleans. Organ, who had learned the surprising news that the treaty had been signed hours before the news was known to the general public,[13] went directly to Laidlaw and bought a large quantity of tobacco, confident that the price of that commodity would rise with the lifting of the blockade. When the price went up 30 to 50 percent, Laidlaw sought to avoid the contract for fraud. In a noted if questionable dictum, Chief Justice Marshall stated that Organ "was not bound to communicate" what he had learned: "It would be difficult to circumscribe the contrary doctrine within proper limits, where the means of intelligence are equally accessible to both parties."[14]

Effect of nondisclosure

Nevertheless, the "contrary doctrine" has gained ground in the ensuing years. As the Supreme Court of Wisconsin wrote, "Courts have departed from or relaxed the 'no duty to disclose' rule by carving out exceptions to the rule and by refusing to adhere to the rule when it works an injustice."[15] Although one can still find statements that "businessmen dealing at arm's length are

Three situations

[11] DeJoseph v. Zambelli, 139 A.2d 644 (Pa. 1958) (alternate holding: vendor of house concealed termite infestation by painting basement to look like a "white sepulcher").

[12] Ten-Cate v. First Natl. Bank, *supra* note 4.

[13] News that the Treaty of Ghent had been signed on December 24, 1814 did not reach New Orleans until after Andrew Jackson had won the Battle of New Orleans on January 8, 1815. Organ bought on January 19. On the night before the sale, three men brought a letter from the British fleet bearing news of the peace treaty. The brother of one of them told Organ the news and took a one-third interest in the profits from his subsequent purchase. Organ went to Laidlaw's firm "soon after sunrise" on Sunday morning. Laidlaw's man asked Organ "if there was any news which was calculated to enhance the price," but there was no evidence of any answer. The writing evidencing the contract was given to Organ between 8 A.M. and 9 A.M. The news was made public in a handbill at 8 A.M.

[14] 15 U.S. (2 Wheat.) 178, 195 (1817). (The statement was dictum because the court reversed a judgment for Organ on the ground of an erroneous instruction to the jury.)

[15] Ollerman v. O'Rourke Co., 288 N.W.2d 95, 102 (Wis. 1980) (tort). *See* Restatement Second §161.

rarely under a duty to speak,"[16] courts have made substantial inroads on this principle, as have legislatures in such areas as the sale of stock and lending to consumers.[17] There are three situations in which courts have regarded a failure to disclose a fact as an assertion that the fact does not exist. In all of these the notion of nondisclosure of a fact necessarily implies that the fact is known to the person expected to disclose it. If the failure to disclose is unintentional, as when it is due to inadvertence or forgetfulness, it amounts to a nonfraudulent misrepresentation and will give a right to avoidance only if it is material. The contours of two of these three situations are relatively easy to describe.

Relation of trust or confidence

The first occurs if there is a relation of trust and confidence between the parties that entitles one of them to a disclosure of the fact in question. The relation need not involve one who is a true fiduciary as a matter of law (such as a trustee, an agent, a guardian, or an executor or administrator)[18] but may, for example, be one involving trust and confidence as a matter of fact (as between members of the same family, between physician and patient, or between member of the clergy and parishioner).[19] The one in whom trust and confidence is reposed is expected to speak up.

Need to correct

The second situation occurs if one who has made an assertion later acquires knowledge that bears on the earlier assertion. If, for example, one later learns that what was once true is no longer true, one is expected to speak up.[20] The same is expected if one learns that one has created a false impression.[21]

Mistake in basic assumption

The third situation is more troublesome. It is the situation in *Laidlaw v. Organ*, where one party knows that the other is laboring under a

---

[16]Simpson Timber Co. v. Palmberg Constr. Co., 377 F.2d 380, 385 (9th Cir. 1967) (tort: party not required to disclose unless "information was peculiarly within the scope of its own knowledge and not readily obtainable" by the other party).

[17]Leading examples are statutes protecting the purchasers of stock and consumer borrowers.

[18]In re Allegheny Intl., 954 F.2d 167 (3d Cir. 1992) (because corporate executives are fiduciaries, their "non-disclosure of a material fact is actionable"). This rule requiring disclosure should not be confused with the more stringent rule that applies when a true fiduciary makes a contract with a beneficiary relating to matters within the scope of the fiduciary relation. See the discussion of rare exceptions in §4.27 *infra*. In such a situation the contract is voidable by the beneficiary unless "it is on fair terms, and . . . all parties beneficially interested manifest assent with full understanding of their legal rights and of all relevant facts that the fiduciary knows or should know." Restatement Second §173.

[19]Vai v. Bank of America, 364 P.2d 247 (Cal. 1961) (husband failed to disclose to wife).

[20]Morykwas v. McKnight, 194 N.W.2d 522 (Mich. App. 1971) (vendor of trailer park failed to disclose problem raised by health officials which "rendered inaccurate or misleading prior representations").

Similarly, one who makes a nonfraudulent and nonmaterial misrepresentation and then learns facts that, had they been known at the time, would have made the misrepresentation fraudulent or material, is expected to speak up to prevent it from having the effect of being fraudulent or material. *See* Restatement Second §161(c) & cmt. *c*.

[21]Lomerson v. Johnston, 20 A. 675 (N.J. Eq. 1890) (creditor failed to correct wife's false impression that husband was in danger of imminent arrest).

misapprehension in some regard, although the first party has done nothing to contribute to it. To what extent is a party that has acquired information, perhaps at some cost, expected to share it with another? Clearly that party may reasonably expect the other party to take normal steps to inform itself and to draw its own conclusion. One party is not expected to compensate for the other's indolence, inexperience, ignorance, or bad judgment. But what of the paradigmatic case of the homeowner who knows that the house is riddled with termites and that the prospective buyer is unaware of this? Courts have been increasingly willing to hold that failure to disclose this fact amounts to an assertion that it is not riddled with termites.[22] The Restatement Second recognizes this trend by generally making a party's nondisclosure of a fact equivalent to an assertion that the fact does not exist if "he knows that disclosure of the fact would correct a mistake of the other party as to a basic assumption on which the party is making the contract."[23] According to the Supreme Court of North Dakota,

> in cases of passive concealment by the seller of defective real property, there is an exception to the rule of caveat emptor, . . . which imposes a duty on the seller to disclose material facts which are known or should be known to the seller and which would not be discoverable by the buyer's exercise of ordinary care and diligence.[24]

Whether a mistake is one as to a "basic assumption" is a question also confronted in connection with the law of mistake.[25] The concept has proved broad enough to give the relief for nondisclosure well beyond the termite cases.[26]

Indeed the concept is too broad, for surely a party cannot be expected to correct all known mistakes of the other party, even if they go to what might be

Limit of fair dealing

---

[22]A leading case is Obde v. Schlemeyer, 353 P.2d 672 (Wash. 1960) (though parties were "dealing at arms length," vendors "had a duty to inform the [purchasers] of the termite condition . . . regardless of the latter's failure to ask any questions relative to the possibility of termites"). *See* Restatement Second §161 illus. 5. *See also* Restatement (Second) of Torts §551 illus. 3 (1977). A leading case to the contrary is Swinton v. Whitinsville Sav. Bank, 42 N.E.2d 808 (Mass. 1942) (tort).

[23]Restatement Second §161(b).

[24]Holcomb v. Zinke, 365 N.W.2d 507, 512 (N.D. 1985) (defective sewage, water, and heating systems).

[25]See the discussion of basic assumption in §9.3 *infra*. As to the effect of a provision that a party bears the risk of mistake, see the discussion of three situations in §9.3 *infra*.

[26]AMPAT/Midwest v. Illinois Tool Works, 896 F.2d 1035 (7th Cir. 1990) (Posner, J.: "seller who has reason to know that the failure of his product to perform in the manner warranted is due to defect in the product can neither keep silent while knowing the nature of the problem nor pretend that the failure is really due to improper installation by the buyer or to an isolated problem that will be corrected by the shipment of replacement product" without committing fraud).

A party is not expected to disclose defects that the other party has reason to know or suspect. Christopher v. Evans, 361 N.W.2d 193 (Neb. 1985) ("water problem" was "fact not only within the reach of [purchasers] but actually grasped by them").

regarded as basic assumptions. A purchaser of land, for example, is not expected to disclose to the vendor circumstances, such as the presence of valuable minerals, that make the property worth more than the vendor supposes.[27] As a federal judge explained, "It may be some reflection of the business ethics fostered by a system of individual competition that the parties to a contract are permitted to deal at arm's length. I can buy my neighbor's land for a song, although I know and he doesn't that it is oil bearing. That isn't dishonest, it is 'smart business' and the just reward of my superior individualism."[28] The Restatement Second attempts to distinguish such situations by limiting relief based on nondisclosure to cases in which the nondisclosure "amounts to a failure to act in good faith and in accordance with reasonable standards of fair dealing."[29] Thus the prospective purchaser that learns of the minerals by surreptitiously trespassing on the vendor's land is expected to disclose this information,[30] even though the prospective purchaser that has obtained the same information from government surveys is not expected to do so. A court is more likely to expect a party to disclose if that party is in a position to have special knowledge or a special means of knowledge not generally available to those in the position of the other party.[31] This may explain why the burden is more often imposed on sellers than on buyers. Even in such a situation, however, it may be that the unwitting party should have been aware of the risk and should have inquired of the other party about it, so as to have either the truth or a claim based on express misrepresentation.

Mistake as to writing

A variation on the same theme occurs if one party knows that the other party is laboring under a mistake as to the contents or effect of a writing intended to evidence or embody their agreement. Is the first party expected to make the disclosure necessary to correct the mistake? The prevailing view is that the first party is expected to do so and that a failure to disclose amounts to a misrepresentation.[32] We discuss whether the other party is justified in relying on that misrepresentation and making the contract without reading the writing as a separate question later.[33]

We next consider the requirement that the misrepresentation be fraudulent or material.

[27] Neill v. Shamburg, 27 A. 992 (Pa. 1893) (oil).

[28] Blair v. National Sec. Ins. Co., 126 F.2d 955, 958 (3d Cir. 1942).

[29] Restatement Second §161(b).

[30] Phillips v. Homfray, L.R. 6 Ch. App. 770 (1871) (coal).

[31] The facts recited *supra* note 13 might be helpful to Laidlaw if the case were to arise today.

[32] Hollywood Credit Clothing Co. v. Gibson, 188 A.2d 348 (D.C. 1963) (seller failed to disclose that price in writing was higher than consumer had agreed to). *Accord:* Home Owners' Loan Corp. v. Stevens, 179 A. 330 (Conn. 1935) (seller of mortgage interest failed to disclose that buyer's clerk had mistakenly filled in too high a price). *See* Restatement Second §303(c).

[33] See the discussion of failure to read a writing in §4.14 *infra*.

§4.12. Fraudulent or Material. If the recipient of a misrepresentation seeks to hold the maker liable in tort for damages, tradition has it that the recipient must show that the misrepresentation was both fraudulent and material.[1] If, however, the recipient seeks merely to avoid the contract, it is said to be enough to show that the misrepresentation was either fraudulent or material.[2] We examine these alternatives of fraud and materiality in turn.

Fraudulent or material

In order that a misrepresentation be *fraudulent* for this purpose, it must be both consciously false and intended to mislead. As will be seen at the end of this section, however, the precise contours of these requirements are less significant in cases of avoidance than might appear at first.

Meaning of fraudulent

The knowledge required of the untrue character of the assertion is sometimes referred to as *scienter.* There is clearly scienter if the maker of the assertion knows, or even believes without actually knowing, that the facts are otherwise than as stated.[3] It is enough if the assertion carries with it, expressly or by implication, a representation that it is made on some particular basis, such as personal knowledge or investigation, and the maker knows that this is not the case.[4] Knowledge of or belief in the untruth of the assertion is not necessary. Courts have held that it suffices if the maker simply lacks confidence in its knowledge of the facts but nevertheless chooses — "recklessly," as is sometimes said — to assert them as of its own knowledge, rather than to confine the assertion to opinion.[5] However, the mere fact that a person of ordinary care and intelligence in the position of the maker would have recognized the assertion as false is not enough.[6]

Scienter

In addition to scienter, there must be intent to mislead. This requirement is met if the maker acts either with the desire to mislead another or in the belief that the other is substantially certain to be misled. If, for example, the maker knows that the statement is misleading because it is subject to two interpretations, it is enough if the statement is made either with the desire that it be understood in the false sense or in the belief that it is substantially certain to be

Intent to mislead

---

§4.12 [1]*See* Restatement (Second) of Torts §525 (1977). Liability in tort for negligent misrepresentation is now sometimes allowed. *See* §552. As to liability for even an innocent misrepresentation, *see* §552C.

[2]Miller v. Celebration Mining Co., 29 P.3d 1231 (Utah 2001) (whether "misrepresentation was made knowingly, it was material to the agreement"). *See* Restatement Second §164 (carrying forward alternative requirements of first Restatement).

[3]Petersen v. Mecham, 397 P.2d 295 (Utah 1964) (knowingly false representation of net income of motel).

[4]Pumphrey v. Quillen, 135 N.E.2d 328 (Ohio 1956) (tort: broker's statement as to construction of house).

[5]Zager v. Setzer, 88 S.E.2d 94 (N.C. 1955) ("representation . . . was recklessly made . . . when he was consciously ignorant whether it was true or false").

[6]The watershed is the great tort case of Derry v. Peek, 14 App. Cas. 337 (H.L. 1889) ("making a false statement through want of care falls far short of . . . fraud"). The problem does not often arise in contract cases, where it is unnecessary to show fraud if the misrepresentation is material. Materiality might, of course, form the basis for an inference as to knowledge.

so understood. It is not necessary that the maker have any particular recipient in mind at the time the misrepresentation is made. For example, in the case of a merchant that furnishes false information to a credit agency, it is enough if the merchant has reason to expect that the information will reach any of a class to which the recipient belongs.[7]

Material   Even if the misrepresentation is not fraudulent, the contract is voidable if the misrepresentation is material.[8] The requirement of materiality is usually met by showing that the misrepresentation would have been likely to have induced a reasonable recipient to make the contract.[9] If this cannot be shown, it may still be possible to meet the requirement by showing that the maker knew that, for some special reason, the misrepresentation was likely to induce the particular recipient to make the contract.[10] A person who is aware of another's idiosyncrasies and preys upon them cannot complain if the resulting contract is held to be voidable.

Fraud without materiality   In principle, it may make sense to allow avoidance for a fraudulent misrepresentation without concern for its materiality. Surely the policy favoring the security of transactions gives feeble support to the maker of the fraudulent misrepresentation. The first Restatement justified relief on moral grounds: "The law gives no privilege to cunning sharpers to induce foolish or ignorant persons by means of representations . . . to which wiser persons would attach no importance."[11] But although there is no shortage of cases allowing avoidance where the misrepresentation was both material and fraudulent, or material but not fraudulent, it is difficult to find cases that have done so where the misrepresentation was fraudulent but not material. Under the definition of *material* just suggested, such a case would have to involve a misrepresentation that succeeded in inducing the recipient to make the contract, even though it would not have been likely to have induced a reasonable recipient to do so and even though the maker knew of no special reason why it was likely to induce the particular recipient to do so. The rarity of such cases means that in practice the test for avoidance, as distinguished from recovery of damages in tort, is one of the materiality of the misrepresentation without regard to whether it is fraudulent.[12]

The requirement of reliance is next.

---

[7]Petersen v. Mecham, *supra* note 3 (misrepresentation made to real estate broker).

[8]Kessler v. National Enters., 238 F.3d 1006 (8th Cir. 2001) (if made without knowledge of falsity, "the misrepresentation must be material" for avoidance).

[9]Northern Heel Corp. v. Compo Indus., 851 F.2d 456 (1st Cir. 1988) (materiality "is not what a disappointed party says it is" but "demands an objective cross-matching of the significance of a fact to the essence of the transaction").

[10]Restatement Second §162(2) states that it is enough if "the maker knows that it is likely to induce the recipient" to manifest assent, a statement taken from Restatement (Second) of Torts §526(2)(b) (1977).

[11]Restatement §471 cmt. *i*. See the discussion of premises as to deception in §4.9 *supra*.

[12]The unimportance of fraud for rescission has been heightened by cases, to be discussed shortly, that have held that even where the contract has been fully performed fraud is not necessary

§4.13. Reliance. A party cannot avoid a contract on the ground of a misrepresentation unless the party relied on it in manifesting assent.[1] However, a variety of factors may have induced the party to make the contract, and the misrepresentation need not have been the sole or even the predominant one. It is not even necessary that the party would not have acted in the same way had there been no misrepresentation, as long as the misrepresentation substantially contributed to the party's decision.[2] If the misrepresentation was material, it is assumed that this is the case in the absence of a contrary showing.[3]

Requirement of reliance

A close question may be presented if the recipient made an independent investigation of the fact asserted. If it appears that the recipient relied solely on the investigation, rather than the misrepresentation, the recipient is not entitled to relief.[4] Some courts have held that an "as is" clause is sufficient to bar relief, even for a fraudulent misrepresentation,[5] though there is authority to the contrary.[6] Other courts have gone so far as to give effect to a recital of a "full investigation," as the New York Court of Appeals did in a leading case where it gave effect to recital that a purchaser of a leasehold had "inspected the premises," was "thoroughly acquainted with their condition," and was not "relying on any statement or representation, not embodied in this

Effect of investigation

---

for avoidance. *See* the discussion of disaffirmance and ratification in §4.15 *infra. But see* the suggestion of the significance of fraud in the discussion of premises as to deception in §4.9 *supra.*

§4.13 [1] Leasco Corp. v. Taussig, 473 F.2d 777 (2d Cir. 1972) (alternative holding: misleading earnings statement did not induce buyer to buy stock because of sources of information available to him as corporate officer). Reliance may consist of refraining from acting as well as acting. For example, an offeror may refrain from revoking an offer in reliance on a misrepresentation. For this reason, the situation in which a bidder had made a mistake in calculating a bid and the mistake is actually known to the other party is best treated as a case of misrepresentation by nondisclosure rather than as one of mistake. *See* Tyra v. Cheney, 152 N.W. 835 (Minn. 1915) (one cannot "snap up an offer or bid knowing that it was made in mistake"). As these cases suggest, not only must the recipient rely on the misrepresentation, but the reliance must be justified, so that a recipient who should have known better than to rely may be barred from relief. *See* §4.14 *infra.*

[2] Light v. Jacobs, 66 N.E. 799 (Mass. 1903) ("it is not necessary that the false representations should have been the sole, or even the predominant motive; it is enough if they had material influence"). Restatement Second §167 uses the phrase "if it substantially contributes to his decision to manifest his assent."

[3] See the discussion of material in §4.12 *supra.*

[4] Andrus v. Irick, 394 P.2d 304 (Idaho 1964) (purchasers of land who investigated availability of water claimed by vendor did not rely on representations but on "their own independent investigation").

[5] O'Connor v. Scott, 533 So. 2d 241 (Ala. 1988) (even if there were misrepresentations, vendor may limit liability for condition of premises by using "as is" clause). As to the effect of such provisions in cases of mistake, see the discussion of three situations in §9.3 *infra.*

[6] Dunbar Med. Sys. v. Gammex Inc., 216 F.3d 441 (5th Cir. 2000) ("as is" clause did not demonstrate "parties' clear intent to waive fraudulent inducement claims or disclaim reliance on representations about specific matters in dispute").

contract."[7] Other courts strongly disagree.[8] But if it appears that the recipient relied on both the investigation and the misrepresentation — as where the investigation tended to confirm the misrepresentation but was somewhat inconclusive — it is clear that the recipient is not precluded from avoiding.[9]

Question of detriment

Once reliance is shown, must it also be shown that it was to the recipient's detriment? Although detriment in the sense of pecuniary injury is an inevitable element of an action in tort for damages caused by a misrepresentation,[10] it is not an inevitable requirement for rescission. If rescission is sought, the question is whether the petitioner has a sufficient interest to justify upsetting the finality of the transaction. "Courts . . . do not," Joseph Story argued, "sit for the purpose of enforcing moral obligations or correcting unconscientious acts which are followed by no loss or damage."[11] The question is not often presented because in most cases there is no difficulty in finding detriment — the recipient has obtained the thing expected, but has found that it is worth less than the recipient was led to expect. Even if the recipient has obtained something of equivalent value that is substantially different from what was expected, courts have had no difficulty in finding sufficient detriment.[12]

Value as expected

But what if the recipient obtains what was expected, and it is as valuable as the recipient was led to expect? A court might conclude that the policy favoring

---

[7] Danann Realty Corp. v. Harris, 157 N.E.2d 597, 598 (N.Y. 1959) (tort: misrepresentation as to operating expenses).

As to the effectiveness of a merger clause, see the discussion of a merger clause as ineffective in §7.4 *infra*. As to the effectiveness of a provision purporting to relieve a principal from responsibility for the misrepresentations of its agent, *see* Restatement (Second) of Agency §260 (1958).

[8] Snyder v. Lovercheck, 992 P.2d 1079 (Wyo. 1999) (rejecting *Danann*). *Accord:* Manufacturers Hanover Trust Co. v. Yanakas, 7 F.3d 310 (2d Cir. 1993) ("many state court decisions since *Plapinger* . . . have ruled that the mere general recitation that a guarantee is 'absolute and unconditional' is insufficient"); Gibson v. Capano, 699 A.2d 68 (Conn. 1997) (absent "claim of mistake, fraud or unconscionability, a clause disclaiming reliance . . . on the seller's representations" is valid); Gibb v. Citicorp Mort., 518 N.W.2d 910 (Neb. 1994) (declining to follow *Danann* where vendor coupled disclaimer with "as is" clause). *Cf.* Matsuura v. Alston & Bird, 166 F.3d 1006 (9th Cir. 1999) ("Delaware Court is likely to interpret a release to bar a claim for fraudulent inducement of that release, if ever, only if the parties clearly and affirmatively expressed their intent to do so"); Pinken v. Frank, 704 F.2d 1019 (8th Cir. 1983) ("fraudulent inducement exception to the parol evidence rule is not rendered inapplicable by . . . a provision that no verbal agreement affecting the validity of the written contract will be recognized").

[9] Holcomb v. Hoffschneider, 297 N.W.2d 210 (Iowa 1980) (tort: if "purchaser intends to purchase a number of acres or by dimensions . . . the purchaser is damaged if the seller fraudulently misrepresents the acreage or dimensions" even if the purchaser knows boundaries from visual inspection). *See* Restatement Second §167 cmt. *b*. As to whether reliance without investigation is justified, see the discussion of the requirement of justification in §4.14 *infra*.

[10] *See* 2 F. Harper, F. James & O. Gray, Law of Torts §7.15 (2d ed. 1986); W. Prosser & P. Keeton, Law of Torts §110 (5th ed. 1984).

[11] J. Story, Equity Jurisprudence §203 (1st ed. 1836).

[12] *See* McCleary, Damage as Requisite to Rescission for Misrepresentation, 36 Mich. L. Rev. 1, 227, 235 (1937).

the security of transactions outweighs the policy favoring protection of a recipient who cannot show a substantial disappointment in reasonable expectations. On the whole, however, courts have not done so. For example, if I know that you will not deal with me and I misrepresent my identity to induce you to make a contract, most courts will allow you to avoid the transaction even though it is a fair one and you cannot show any detriment. The same result was reached in an interesting case in which a man thought he was buying a $5,000 mink coat for only $4,000 to give to a woman friend, only to discover that the store had concealed from him the fact that the woman was contributing the additional $1,000. The Supreme Court of California reasoned that since the man's motives "were clearly noneconomic, the general social interest in the stability of transactions is overridden by the interest in not having a seller make intentional misrepresentations which mislead a would-be donor into the erroneous belief that he alone is purchasing . . . a fully paid for gift."[14] The court did not feel required to speculate whether the buyer's disappointed expectations consisted in his failure to have made a purely chivalrous gesture or in his failure to get the mink at a bargain price. One advantage of dispensing with any requirement of detriment is that it eliminates the need for such speculation. Whether the courts that have dispensed with the requirement of detriment would be so willing to do so if the misrepresentation were nonfraudulent, however, is unclear.

We consider now the requirement that the reliance be justified.

§4.14. **Reliance Must Be Justified.** In order to avoid a contract on the ground of misrepresentation, the recipient must show not only reliance on the misrepresentation, but also that the reliance was justified.[1] The common law, wrote James Kent, "does not go to the romantic length of giving indemnity against the consequences of indolence and folly."[2] Thus the recipient may be barred from avoiding the contract if the misrepresentation was obviously false or if it could not be expected to be taken seriously. Courts are, however, particularly indulgent if the recipient is weak or credulous, even if the falsity of the representation would be obvious to a normal

Requirement of justification

---

[13] The same is true where one acts through an undisclosed agent to conceal one's identity.

[14] Earl v. Saks & Co., 226 P.2d 340, 346 (Cal. 1951). *See* E. Cahn, The Moral Decision 123-35 (1955) (discussing this case).

[15] See the discussion of premises as to deception in §4.9 *supra*. According to Comment *c* to Restatement Second §306, "In general, the recipient of a misrepresentation need not show that he has actually been harmed by relying on it in order to avoid the contract." But see the treatment of "cure" in the discussion of disaffirmance and ratification in §4.15 *infra*.

§4.14 [1] In re Topco, Inc., 894 F.2d 727 (5th Cir. 1990) (purchaser of debtor's assets "could not reasonably rely on the representations made by the debtor"). *See* Restatement Second §164(1) ("upon which the recipient is justified in relying").

[2] 2 J. Kent, Commentaries on American Law 380 (1st ed. 1827). *See* the discussion of misrepresentation of opinion and intention, *infra*.

person.[3] Furthermore, the recipient's failure to take steps to discover the facts before making the contract will not generally preclude avoidance. Courts incline to condemn the maker's misrepresentation rather than the victim's credulity. Thus failure to investigate has been excused on the ground that "one who deceives another to his prejudice ought not to be heard to say in defense that the other party was negligent in taking him at his word."[5] The Supreme Court of Pennsylvania, however, refused to follow this reasoning and held that a wife could not avoid a prenuptial agreement during divorce proceedings on the ground that her husband, when they stated their assets for the agreement over ten years earlier, had misrepresented the value of her engagement ring at $21,000. The wife took the ring to a jeweler after their separation, she discovered that it was not a diamond, as she had assumed, but a cubic zirconium worth much less than $32,000. The court concluded that she "had sufficient opportunity to inform herself fully of the nature and extent of her own assets"[6] Furthermore, one who begins an investigation and does not finish it or fails to conduct it properly may be less charitably treated than one who fails entirely to investigate.[7] In determining the effect of a recipient's fault, courts can be expected to distinguish between representations that are fraudulent and those that are not.[8]

Failure to read writing

An important and vexing aspect of the problem of fault is raised if the recipient has relied on a misrepresentation as to a writing without troubling to read the writing. No simple pattern emerges from the cases. Some courts have denied relief on the basis of the recipient's "clear neglect in signing the contract without ascertaining its contents."[9] However, the trend is in the other direction, particularly if some artifice has been used to prevent the recipient from reading the writing or if consumers are involved. There is appeal in the argument that, as the Supreme Court of Michigan expressed it, the fact that the fraud worked because the victim was "careless . . . did not render it any less a fraud."[10] The

---

[3] Sarvis v. Vermont State Colleges, 772 A.2d 494 (Vt. 2001) (declining to fault college "for failing to discover [instructor's] criminal background" since latter "cannot enforce the contract where his own actions hampered [college's] inquiry").

[4] Koral Indus. v. Security-Connecticut Life Ins. Co., 802 S.W.2d 650 (Tex. 1990) ("Failure to use due diligence to suspect or discover someone's fraud will not act to bar the defense of fraud to the contract."). Restatement Second §172 attempts to describe the exceptional case, in which avoidance is barred by the recipient's fault, by requiring that the fault amount "to a failure to act in good faith and in accordance with reasonable standards of fair dealing."

[5] Spiess v. Brandt, 41 N.W.2d 561, 570 (Minn. 1950).

[6] Porreco v. Porreco, 811 A.2d 566, 572 (Pa. 2002).

[7] McCormick & Co. v. Childers, 468 F.2d 757 (4th Cir. 1972) (by beginning investigation of patentability of chicken deboning machine, buyer of business "was charged with knowledge of everything that a proper investigation would disclose").

[8] See the discussion of premises as to deception in §4.9 *supra*.

[9] Dowagiac Mfg. Co. v. Schroeder, 84 N.W. 14, 14 (Wis. 1900).

[10] Schupp v. Davey Tree Expert Co., 209 N.W. 85, 86 (Mich. 1926) (homeowner failed to read contract with tree service).

same tolerance can be found where the remedy sought is reformation of the writing.[11]

Three recurring and troublesome applications of the requirement that the reliance be justified involve assertions of opinion, assertions as to matters of law, and assertions of intention. We consider them in that order.

A party engaged in contract negotiations often expresses an opinion as to the subject of those negotiations.[12] A party may, for example, express a belief in existence or quantity or a judgment as to quality or value. It is sometimes incorrectly suggested that such statements of opinion can be distinguished from statements of fact. There is no such distinction because a statement of opinion is one of fact — of the fact that a person is of the state of mind asserted. There is, however, an important distinction between a statement as to a matter that is one of opinion only and a statement that purports to be based on knowledge. If I say, in effect, no more than "I will hazard the opinion that . . . ," I make a statement of opinion only. But if I say, in effect, "I have reason to hold the opinion that . . . ," I assert both that I hold a particular opinion as to a matter and that my opinion is based on my knowledge as to it. Such an assertion is not one of opinion only. The extent to which an assertion will be regarded merely as one of the maker's opinion, and not as one of the maker's knowledge, is essentially a question of interpretation, which may depend on the circumstances in which the language was used. The form of the statement is important but not decisive. To the extent that the subject of the statement is not susceptible of knowledge or that points of view may be expected to differ on the matter, the statement is more likely to be one of opinion.[13] For example, a seller's statement of quality is more likely to be taken as one of opinion than is a seller's statement of quantity,[14] and a seller's statement of value is more likely to be so understood than a seller's statement of market price.[15]

Cordell v. Greene Fin. of Georgetown, 953 F. Supp. 1391 (M.D. Ala. 1996) ("illiterate plaintiff may rely upon the representation of the other party as to what the instrument contains"); Saylor v. Handley Motor Co., 169 A.2d 683 (D.C. 1961) (buyer of car failed to read contract with blank spaces). Factors that affect such decisions are analyzed in Comment, 34 Mich. L. Rev. 705 (1936).

[11] See the discussion of failure to read a writing in §7.5 *infra*.

[12] See the discussion of examples of facts in §4.11 *supra*.

[13] Harris v. Delco Prods., 25 N.E.2d 740 (Mass. 1940) (statement of well driller that he would get "good sweet water" was one of opinion only because it concerned "matters not susceptible of actual knowledge").

[14] Bertram v. Reed Auto. Co., 49 S.W.2d 517 (Tex. Civ. App. 1932) (tort: for "automobile selling agent to describe his offering merely as a 'dandy,' a 'bear-cat,' a 'good little car,' a 'good automobile,' or even a 'sweet job' is nothing"). Cases involving statements as to the quality of goods sold will now generally be actions for breach of warranty under UCC 2-313 ("an affirmation merely of the value of the goods or a statement purporting to be merely the seller's opinion or commendation of the goods does not create a warranty").

[15] Byers v. Federal Land Co., 3 F.2d 9 (8th Cir. 1924) (statement that value of land was $35 per acre was one of opinion only).

**Facts implied
from opinion**

Sometimes a statement of opinion implies that the maker knows facts that justify holding that opinion, or at least that the maker knows of no facts incompatible with it. Such a statement is not just one of the maker's opinion only, but one made to some extent as based on the maker's knowledge. If, therefore, the facts are other than as impliedly asserted, the statement may be grounds for avoidance.[16] Whether the recipient is justified in relying on the implied assertion is then determined as in the case of any other assertion of fact.[17]

Opinion only

Statements of opinion only, that carry with them no implied assertions of fact, are generally regarded as not to be taken seriously, and the recipient is not usually justified in relying on them. According to Kent, "Every person reposes at his peril in the opinion of others, when he has equal opportunity to form and exercise his own judgment."[18] This general rule is not, however, without exception. One exception covers the case in which the maker stands in such a relation of trust and confidence, whether the maker is strictly speaking a fiduciary or not, to the person whose opinion is asserted that the recipient is justified in relying on the opinion.[19] Another exception covers the case in which the recipient reasonably believes that, as compared with the recipient, the person whose opinion is asserted has special knowledge, skill, judgment, or objectivity with respect to the subject of the opinion.[20] And another exception covers the case in which the recipient is for some special reason particularly susceptible to a misrepresentation of the sort involved.[21]

**Second: Matters
of law**

Assertions as to matters of law have produced considerable confusion, most of which could have been avoided if they had simply been subjected to the general rules relating to reliance on other assertions.[22] Such an assertion may

---

However, a gross misrepresentation of value may not be regarded as one of opinion only. Benedict v. Dickens' Heirs, 177 A. 715 (Conn. 1935) (purchaser's statement that land worth at least $2,500 was not worth more than $15 to him was not one of opinion only).

[16] Spiess v. Brandt, *supra* note 5 (unqualified affirmation by vendor of resort that it was making "good money" was affirmation as of own knowledge).

[17] It is assumed that the facts in question are not disclosed or otherwise known to the recipient.

[18] 2 J. Kent, Commentaries on American Law 381 (1st ed. 1827). *See* UCC 2-313, *supra* note 14.

[19] Hassman v. First State Bank, 236 N.W. 921 (Minn. 1931) (purchaser of land relied on opinion of vendor's agent whom purchaser regarded as "financial adviser").

[20] Vokes v. Arthur Murray, Inc., 212 So. 2d 906 (Fla. App. 1968) (dance studio had "superior knowledge" as to whether widow, aged 51, had "dance potential").

The opinion need not be that of the maker of the representation, but may be that of a third party whose disinterest gives a special objectivity. Where a seller misrepresents itself as a disinterested third party by bidding on the seller's goods at auction without having reserved the liberty to do so, UCC 2-328(4) gives the buyer the choice of avoiding the sale or taking the goods at the price of the last good faith bid.

[21] Adan v. Steinbrecher, 133 N.W. 477 (Minn. 1911) ("gullible young man" relied on statements of manager of "roadhouse" that its value was $35,000 and that it was "a big paying proposition").

[22] *See* National Conversion Corp. v. Cedar Bldg. Corp., 246 N.E.2d 351 (N.Y. 1969) (dictum: "the modern rule extends . . . to cover a false opinion of law if misrepresented as a sincere opinion, as in the case of any other opinion").

or may not be one of opinion only. An assertion of one's opinion as to a matter of law may, as may any other statement of opinion, carry the implication that one knows facts justifying holding that opinion or, at least, that one knows no facts incompatible with that opinion. Such an assertion may, on the other hand, be an assertion of opinion only, on which the recipient is justified in relying only in exceptional circumstances. A lawyer's statement of belief that a client will prevail in a forthcoming appeal almost certainly is one of opinion only; a lawyer's statement that a party has prevailed in a particular case almost certainly is not.[23] In making a contract one is ordinarily expected to draw one's own legal conclusions and seek one's own independent legal advice. However, one is not conclusively presumed to know the law.[24] Thus, if a lawyer states an opinion on the law to a layperson, the layperson is entitled to take account of the lawyer's special expertise and to assume the lawyer's professional honesty, and the layperson may justifiably rely on the opinion even though the two have an adverse relation in negotiating the contract.[25] The same principle may even apply to a representation, at least as to routine matters, by one who is not a lawyer, for example, by a real estate broker or insurance agent.[26] Courts have occasionally refused to recognize that a statement of the law of a foreign country or even a different state can be one of opinion,[27] but it is difficult to justify this, except perhaps on the pragmatic ground that the recipient is less likely to be able to draw independent conclusions as to such law and is therefore more likely to rely.

Assertions of intention have also been troublesome. An assertion of intention, like one of opinion, is one of fact, since it asserts a state of mind.[28] But such assertions, like those of opinion, are often not to be taken seriously. Whether the recipient was justified in relying on the assertion is a question of fact that will turn on, among other things, the recipient's expectation that the intention can and will be carried out.

Third: Intention

[23] Seeger v. Odell, 115 P.2d 977 (Cal. 1941) (misrepresentation by purchaser of land that vendor had no title to land was not one of opinion only). Note the argument by Jessel, M.R., that a statement that a "lady is unmarried, is a statement of fact, neither more nor less; and it is not the less a statement of fact, that in order to arrive at it you must know more or less of the law." Eaglesfield v. Marquis of Londonderry, 4 Ch. D. 693, 703 (C.A. 1876).

[24] Cases in which the contrary is asserted are generally old ones, such as Platt v. Scott, 6 Blackf. 389 (Ind. 1843) (since it is "considered that every person is acquainted with the law, . . . no one can, therefore, complain of the misrepresentations of another respecting it").

[25] Sainsbury v. Pennsylvania Greyhound Lines, 183 F.2d 548 (4th Cir. 1950) (lawyer for alleged tortfeasor misrepresented to accident victim that as a serviceman his recovery would be limited).

[26] Safety Cas. Co. v. McGee, 127 S.W.2d 176 (Tex. 1939) (claims adjuster misrepresented Workmen's Compensation Law).

[27] Hembry v. Parreco, 81 A.2d 77 (D.C. 1951) (tort: contractor's statement that owner of truck would need no further licensing to use it on job in another jurisdiction was not one of opinion only).

[28] Berkeley Bank v. Meibos, 607 P.2d 798 (Utah 1980) (bank made misrepresentation by "statements of fact as to the bank's then-present intention that it would not look to the farmers to repay the loan made to the co-op"). See the discussion of examples of facts in §4.11 *supra*.

Unreliable statements of intention

In some situations, courts have accorded the maker considerable latitude in misrepresenting intention if the statement is of the kind that is generally regarded as unreliable. If, for example, a prospective purchaser of land misrepresents the intended use of the land in order to conceal from the vendor some special advantage that the purchaser will get from its purchase and that, if known to the vendor, would cause the vendor to demand a higher price, the court may nevertheless refuse to allow the vendor to avoid the contract on the ground that the purchaser's conduct did not offend reasonable standards for dealing in the trade.[29] The result will probably be different, however, if the purchaser misrepresents the intended use in order to conceal from the vendor some harm to the vendor's other interests that will be caused if the purchaser carries out its actual intention.[30]

Promissory fraud

Even a promise may amount to a misrepresentation of intention, in what is sometimes called *promissory fraud.* When the circumstances make it reasonable to do so, a promisee may properly interpret a promise as implying an assertion that the promisor intends to do what has been promised.[31] If the other requisites are present, such an implied assertion may be grounds for avoidance. It is thus a greater wrong to promise what one is not going to do than to fail to do what one has promised. The mere failure of the promisor to perform will not suffice to prove that the assertion was untrue; it must be shown that when the promise was made, the promisor did not intend to perform it.

The remedies available for misrepresentation are explored next.

Avoidance and ratification

§4.15. Effects of Misrepresentation. Misrepresentation in the inducement makes the resulting contract voidable at the instance of the recipient.[1] The recipient may avoid the contract by disaffirming it and then assert the misrepresentation either by raising it as a defense to an action brought to enforce

---

[29] Finley v. Dalton, 164 S.E.2d 763 (S.C. 1968) (misrepresentation characterized as not "material" and did not induce recipient to sell). Restatement Second §171 states that one is not justified in relying on an assertion that is one of intention only "if, in the circumstances, a misrepresentation of intention is consistent with reasonable standards of dealing."

[30] Adams v. Gillig, 92 N.E. 670 (N.Y. 1910) (buyer of portion of vacant lot represented that he intended to build houses on it when he intended to build garage).

[31] Entron v. General Cablevision, 435 F.2d 995 (5th Cir. 1970) (tort: supplier of cable television system said work could be completed in 60 days, when it knew or should have known that it could not do so or lacked knowledge as to its ability to perform). *See generally* E. Farnsworth, Changing Your Mind ch. 3 (1998).

If one promises to pay, knowing that one is insolvent and will probably be unable to pay, one is regarded as fraudulently misrepresenting one's intention. Manly v. Ohio Shoe Co., 25 F.2d 384 (1928). The Uniform Commercial Code, however, lays down a special rule as to a buyer's misrepresentations of solvency or intent to pay in UCC 2-702(2).

§4.15 [1] That the victim of fraud must avoid the entire contract even though it is divisible, *see* Filet Menu v. C.C.L. & G., 94 Cal. Rptr. 2d 438 (Ct. App. 2000) ("a divisible contract is still only a single contract").

the contract or by bringing an action based on avoidance (or "rescission") of the contract. One cannot avoid, however, if one has already ratified the contract. Although there was once authority for the proposition that avoidance for a non-fraudulent misrepresentation was precluded if the contract was fully performed by both parties, this view is now rejected.[2] The remedy of a seller of goods in the case of a buyer's misrepresentation of solvency has, however, been severely restricted by the Uniform Commercial Code.[3] Ratification may be express or by conduct inconsistent with avoidance, for example by the recipient's use of property obtained under the contract as though it were the recipient's own.[4] Ratification has also been found in the commencement of an action in tort for damages based on the misrepresentation, a result that is often explained on the ground that there has been an "election of remedies."[5] That doctrine's harsh results have, however, been tempered by liberal exceptions,[6] and the better view is that one is not disadvantaged by asking for both kinds of relief in the alternative.[7] In order not to do too much violence to the principle of mutuality of obligation, the recipient is also precluded from avoiding the contract by failing to disaffirm within a reasonable time after discovering the falsity of the representation.[8] Because a party's delay may allow that party to speculate, a party may be precluded from avoiding a contract, even if the other party has not relied on the contract during the delay.[9] Avoidance may also be precluded

[2] A leading case upholding avoidance of an executed transaction where no fraud was shown is Seneca Wire & Mfg. Co. v. A.B. Leach & Co., 159 N.E. 700 (N.Y. 1928). The opposite view was explained on the ground that "equity will refuse a specific [performance] in many cases where it would not rescind." Thompson v. Jackson, 24 Va. (3 Rand.) 504, 508 (1825). See the discussion of premises as to deception in §4.9 *supra*.

[3] UCC 2-702(2).

[4] Fryer v. Campbell, 43 P.2d 994 (Wyo. 1935) (buyer of motion picture equipment continued to operate it after discovery of fraud). That in general the recipient cannot affirm the contract in part and disaffirm it in part, *see* Restatement Second §383.

[5] Donovan v. Curts, 222 N.W. 743 (Mich. 1929) (purchaser of stock who sued in tort "chose that remedy with full knowledge of the facts, and in so doing irrevocably fixed the status of her rights").

[6] It has been held, for example, that the recipient is not precluded from avoidance if the tort action fails because the statute of limitations has run. Schenck v. State Line Tel. Co., 144 N.E. 592 (N.Y. 1924).

[7] *See* UCC 2-721 (neither rescission nor a claim of rescission of the contract for material misrepresentation or fraud "shall bar or be deemed inconsistent with a claim for damages or other remedy").

[8] Link Assocs. v. Jefferson Standard Life Ins. Co., 291 S.E.2d 212 (Va. 1982) (recipient "must act within a reasonable time and with great punctuality" and "duty of prompt disaffirmance is not dependent upon the proof of harm . . . caused by the delay"). *See* Restatement Second §381.

[9] Merrill v. DeMott, 951 P.2d 1040 (Nev. 1997) (ratification "does not require the showing of detrimental reliance necessary for estoppel"). *See generally* E. Farnsworth, Changing Your Mind ch. 19 (1998).

if, after the misrepresentation is made, the facts come into accord with it, so that it is "cured."[10]

Remedies on avoidance

On avoidance, the recipient is entitled to restitution, either in kind, if it is possible to return what the recipient has given to the other party, or in the form of a money judgment based on the benefit that the recipient has conferred.[11] Courts have also allowed the recipient incidental or consequential damages caused by the misrepresentation.[12] Equitable relief is available to impose a constructive trust on or to cancel a conveyance of property handed over to the other party or to subject property benefited by services to an equitable lien.[13]

Requirement of restitution

The recipient is, in turn, generally required to make restitution of what the recipient has received, either in kind, if this is possible[14] or, in some situations, through payment of an equivalent sum of money. Payment of money has been allowed, for example, if what was received was disposed of before the recipient learned of the falsity of the misrepresentation.[15] The recipient may also be required to account for the use of what the recipient is returning upon avoidance[16] and for any increase in value of what is returned to the recipient through repairs or improvements made by the other party.[17] Restitution is not required to the extent that it has become impossible because of defects that were the subject of the misrepresentation.[18] In an action at law, as distinguished from equity, courts have insisted that restitution be tendered before an action based on disaffirmance is commenced, at least unless the other party has indicated

---

[10]Johnson v. Seymour, 44 N.W. 344 (Mich. 1890) (vendor who fraudulently failed to disclose mortgage cured misrepresentation by later discharging it). According to Restatement Second §165, the "cure" does not preclude avoidance if "the recipient has been harmed by relying on the misrepresentation." This is in contrast to the general rule that the recipient need not show harm in order to avoid. See the discussion of the question of detriment in §4.13 *supra*.

[11]Ogden Martin Sys. v. San Bernardino County, 932 F.2d 1284 (9th Cir. 1991) (where contractor spent nearly $3.5 million to prepare environmental impact report, there was "genuine issue of material fact as to whether the County received a benefit"). See the discussion of premises as to deception in §4.9 *supra*.

[12]Katz v. Van Der Noord, 546 So. 2d 1047 (Fla. 1989) (purchaser's attorney fees under contract provision).

[13]Falk v. Hoffman, 135 N.E. 243 (N.Y. 1922) (constructive trust on proceeds of stock obtained by fraud). The Uniform Commercial Code gives the buyer who disaffirms a contract for the sale of goods a security interest in the goods, including a power to sell them, to secure any part of the price that has been paid. UCC 2-711(3), 2-721.

[14]American Exch. Bank v. Smith, 23 P.2d 414 (Wash. 1933) (buyer of automobile required to have it repaired after it had been wrecked).

[15]Bellefeuille v. Medeiros, 139 N.E.2d 413 (Mass. 1957) (purchaser of business sold some property and lost some in flood; "the rule is more liberal in equity").

[16]Miller v. Sears, 636 P.2d 1183 (Alaska 1981) (fiduciary: purchaser of house whose use continued after giving notice of rescission "must pay the seller for the reasonable value of his use").

[17]Walker v. Gait, 171 F.2d 613 (5th Cir. 1948) (improvements to real property).

[18]Faulkner v. Klamp, 20 N.W. 220 (Neb. 1884) (sick mule died).

that a tender would be refused.[19] Since a court in an action at law can render a judgment conditional on restitution being made, there is every reason to apply the equity rule to actions at law today.[20]

Other consequences

Misrepresentation may have consequences other than avoidance and liability in tort. Under the ancient doctrine of "equitable estoppel" or "estoppel *in pais*," from which the name *promissory estoppel* is derived, the maker of a misrepresentation was precluded from alleging or proving facts that contradicted the representation.[21] If the misrepresentation goes to the contents or effect of a writing, the writing may be reformed.[22] Furthermore, misleading conduct that falls short of misrepresentation may nevertheless be considered as one factor in connection with some other aspect of a court's power to police the agreement under, for example, the concept of undue influence[23] or that of unconscionability.[24] A discussion of the myriad rules and regulations designed to protect consumers from deception, as well as the special agencies created to enforce them, is beyond the scope of this treatise.

We turn now from misleading to coercive conduct.

§4.16. The Elements of Duress. Coercive behavior may take the form of physical compulsion or of threat. Under the general principles of contract law relating to assent, if a victim acts under physical compulsion, for instance, by signing a writing under such force that the victim is "a mere mechanical instrument," the victim's actions are not effective to manifest assent.[1] Such duress by physical compulsion results in no contract at all or in what is sometimes anomalously described as a "void contract."[2] More difficult and

Physical compulsion or threat

---

[19]Maumelle Co. v. Eskola, 865 S.W.2d 272 (Ark. 1993) (in "action at law, the tender must be done at or prior to the time of the commencement of the action" and "must be complete and unequivocal").

[20]Thorstenson v. Arco Alaska, 780 P.2d 371 (Alaska 1989) (though tender "is ordinarily a prerequisite to an action at law for rescission," employer "will be adequately protected if the trial court grants [employee] a reasonable time to tender back his termination allowance").

[21]The law-French term *in pais* comes from the French *en pays* ("in the country"), used to distinguish this kind of estoppel from preclusion by an admission in a court of record. For a comparison with promissory estoppel, *see* the discussion of the derivation of the concept of estoppel in §2.19 *supra*. *See generally* E. Farnsworth, Changing Your Mind ch. 17 (1998).

[22]See the discussion of reformation for fraud in §7.5 *infra*.

[23]See the discussion of "unfair" persuasion in §4.20 *infra*.

[24]See the discussion of factors in determining unconscionability in §4.28 *infra*.

§4.16 [1]We know this more from dicta than from holdings. *See* Fairbanks v. Snow, 13 N.E. 596 (Mass. 1887) (dictum by Holmes, J.). The quoted phrase appears in Restatement §494(b) and in Restatement Second §174 cmt. *a*. See the discussion of the victory of the objective theory in §3.6 *supra*.

[2]If *contract* is defined in terms of an enforceable promise, a "void contract" is not a "contract" at all. Duress that "nullifies the obligation of the obligor" is a *real* defense to an asserted obligation on a negotiable instrument, i.e., a good defense even when the instrument is in the hands of a good faith purchaser (known as a *holder in due course*). UCC 3-305(a)(1),(b). See the discussion of the use of a promissory note in §11.8 *infra*.

important questions arise when the coercion is by threat rather than by physical compulsion.

Duress by threat

The requirements for a showing of duress by threat can be grouped under four headings. First, there must be a threat. Second, the threat must be improper. Third, the threat must induce the victim's manifestation of assent. Fourth, it must be sufficiently grave to justify the victim's assent.[3]

Meaning of *threat*

First, what is a threat? A threat is a manifestation of an intent to inflict some loss or harm on another. It need not be expressed in words but may be inferred from words or other conduct. Thus if one person strikes or imprisons another, the conduct may amount to duress because of the threat of further blows or continued imprisonment that is implied. But a mere prediction of the probable consequences of a course of action may not amount to a threat.[4] The distinction is not unlike the distinction between a promisor that is bargaining for something in return and one that is not bargaining but should reasonably expect reliance.[5]

When threat is improper

Second, when is a threat improper? The kind of threat with which we are concerned is one that is made to induce the victim to manifest assent to a contract. But not all such threats are improper for, as we have seen, an offer may be regarded as such a threat.[6] The problem then becomes one of distinguishing impermissible threats from legitimate offers. As has been pointed out,[7] the seller that offers to deliver cotton to the buyer if the buyer promises to pay $10,000, but not otherwise, is not ordinarily thought of as making an improper threat. But what if cotton is scarce? If the buyer's need is desperate? If $10,000 is exorbitant? If the seller is already bound by a contract to deliver the same cotton to the buyer for $5,000? The limits on the kinds of threats that will be tolerated in the name of bargain are discussed in the next section.

When threat induces assent

Third, when does a threat induce the manifestation of assent? The requirement is simply one of causation. Did the threat actually induce assent on the part of the victim? Threats that would induce assent on the part of one person may not induce it in the case of another. The requirement is less often a subject of controversy than is the analogous requirement for misrepresentation.[8]

When threat is sufficient

Fourth, when is a threat sufficiently grave to justify the victim in succumbing to it? The early common law imposed a very strict test. According to Lord Coke, the victim might avoid a contract only:

---

[3]*See* Restatement Second §175(1) (the manifestation of assent must be "induced by an improper threat by the other party that leaves the victim no reasonable alternative").

[4]Fox v. Piercey, 227 P.2d 763 (Utah 1951) (fire chief "merely advised [fireman] of what the latter knew . . . would have been the inevitable result of his discharge" for misconduct).

[5]See the discussion of reason to expect reliance required in §2.19 *supra*.

[6]See the discussion of the promisor's use of a condition in §2.9 *supra*.

[7]See the discussion of premises as to coercion in §4.9 *supra*.

[8]King Enters. v. Manchester Water Works, 453 A.2d 1276 (N.H. 1982) (voluntariness of settlement "evidenced by the fact that the settlement terms were significantly more favorable to the plaintiff than the terms originally proposed by the defendant"). As to the requirement for misrepresentation, see the discussion of the requirement of reliance in §4.13 *supra*.

1. for fear of losse of life, 2. of losse of member, 3. of mayhem, and 4. of imprison-ment; otherwise it is for fear of battery, which might be very light, or for burning of his houses, or taking away, or destroying of his goods or the like, for there he may have satisfaction in damages.[9]

Assent in the face of that kind of fear was sometimes said to be "voluntary." The notion that the victim of a threat to property might always be expected to refuse to assent and resort to an action for damages gave way in the eighteenth century with the recognition of "duress of goods," the wrongful detention of the victim's property.[10] This presaged a "radical change" in the doctrine of duress[11] and paved the way to a more liberal doctrine of "economic duress," or "business compulsion,"[12] under which the threat went, not to the victim's person, but to the victim's economic interests. The requirement of the gravity of the threat is discussed in the section after the next.

We now examine in more detail the second requirement, that of impropriety of the threat.

§4.17. **The Impropriety of the Threat.** What threats are improper? As we have seen, courts first recognized as improper threats of [physical harm and later included threats of wrongful detention of goods.] In these early cases, the action threatened was ordinarily a crime or at least a tort, and it was natural to characterize the threat itself as "unlawful," or at least as "wrongful."[2] Indeed, the cases are filled with such misleading dicta as, "where the party threatens nothing which he has not a legal right to perform there is no duress."[3] Although cases arising out of threats of torts or crimes still reach the courts today, it is clear that the doctrine of duress has expanded well beyond these traditional situations and that a threat may be improper even though the one who makes it has a legal right to do the threatened act.[4]

Threat need not be wrongful

[9]E. Coke, Second Institute 482-83 (1642). *Accord:* Rubenstein v. Rubenstein, 120 A.2d 11 (N.J. 1956) (threats included gangster violence and arsenic poisoning).

[10]Astley v. Reynolds, 93 Eng. Rep. 939 (K.B. 1732) (detention of pawned plate until excess interest was paid).

[11]Tallmadge v. Robinson, 109 N.E.2d 496, 499 (Ohio 1952).

[12]The term *business compulsion* has sometimes been used to suggest a questionable distinction from the doctrine of duress. *See* Ramp Bldg. Corp. v. Northwest Bldg. Co., 4 P.2d 507 (Wash. 1931) ("The modern doctrine of 'business compulsion' differs somewhat from the well recognized principle of duress.").

§4.17 [1]See the discussion of when a threat is sufficient in §4.16 *supra*.

[2]Of course, if the crime or tort involved is a relatively minor one, the claim of duress may fail, even though the threat is improper, on the ground that it did not in fact induce assent or that the victim had a reasonable alternative.

[3]Hackley v. Headley, 8 N.W. 511, 513 (Mich. 1881).

[4]Centric Corp. v. Morrison-Knudsen Co., 731 P.2d 411 (Okl. 1986) ("Economic duress may be found if the act is done under circumstances which are considered wrongful even if there was a legal right to perform the threatened act.").

Difficulty of generalization

A perceptive scholar warned that the "history of generalization in this field offers no great encouragement for those who seek to summarize results in a single formula."[5] It may therefore be prudent to begin, as has been fashionable since the time of Lord Coke's list, with a discussion of the categories of threats that have been held to be improper.[6]

Threat of criminal prosecution

A threat to instigate criminal prosecution has generally been regarded as an improper means of inducing the victim of the threat to make a contract.[7] The question ordinarily arises in the context of a threat to instigate prosecution for embezzlement unless the victim of the threat repays or promises to repay the sum allegedly embezzled. The victim of the threat may not be the alleged embezzler but a relative or friend.[8] The impropriety lies in the use for "private benefit . . . of the criminal process of the court provided for the prosecution of crime and the protection of the public."[9] On this ground, the threat is improper even if the person who makes it honestly believes that the one whose prosecution is threatened is guilty and even if that person is in fact guilty.[10] Where it is established that the sum promised or paid was actually due, however, it has been suggested that "relief for duress will be given only for the purpose of restoring the excess over what is reasonably and justly due, and to the extent that such excess is shown to exist."[11]

Threat of civil process

A threat to use civil process, including that implied in its commencement, poses more difficult problems. The policy that favors free access to the judicial system militates against characterizing such threats as improper, even if the claim involved later proves to be without foundation. There are some circumstances, however, in which such a threat may be regarded as improper. It may be that the person who made the threat did not believe that there was a reasonable basis for the threatened process, knew that the threat would involve a misuse

---

[5] Dawson, Economic Duress — An Essay in Perspective, 45 Mich. L. Rev. 253, 289 (1947).

[6] Coke's list is quoted in the discussion of when a threat is sufficient in §4.16 *supra*. For lists, *see* Restatement Second §176; first Restatement §493.

[7] Warner v. Warner, 394 S.E.2d 74 (W. Va. 1990) ("when a person can establish that a threat to prosecute a criminal claim, irrespective of the individual's guilt or innocence, destroyed her ability to exercise her free will, duress may exist").

[8] Tiffany & Co. v. Spreckels, 262 P. 742 (Cal. 1927) (alternative holding: promise of husband of alleged conspirator); Port of Nehalem v. Nicholson, 259 P. 900 (Or. 1927) (promise of brother-in-law of alleged embezzler).

[9] Gorringe v. Reed, 63 P. 902, 905 (Utah 1901).

[10] FDIC v. White, 76 F. Supp. 2d 736 (N.D. Tex. 1999) ("threat of criminal prosecution may constitute duress whether or not the threatened party is actually guilty").

[11] Dawson, Economic Duress — An Essay in Perspective, 45 Mich. L. Rev. 253, 283 (1947). If the person that made the threat has a claim to restitution, that claim should be honored, but it is questionable whether that person should be able to take advantage of, say, a promissory note executed in response to the threat. Restatement Second §176 cmt. *c* says that the "guilt or innocence of the person whose prosecution is threatened is immaterial in determining whether the threat is improper, although it may be easier to show that the threat actually induced assent in the case of guilt."

of the process, or realized the demand was exorbitant.[12] Such threats have been held to be duress if defense of the threatened action is not a reasonable alternative.[13]

A threat by a party to a contract not to perform a contract duty is not, of itself, improper, and an agreement of modification or rescission induced by such a threat may be binding on both parties. The parties to a contract are, however, regarded as bound by a duty of good faith and fair dealing, and such a threat may be improper if it amounts to a breach of that duty.[14] According to the commentary to the Uniform Commercial Code,

Threat to break contract

> extortion of a "modification" without legitimate commercial reason is ineffective as a violation of the duty of good faith. . . . The test of "good faith" between merchants or as against merchants includes observance of reasonable commercial standards of fair dealing in the trade" (Section 2-103), and may in some situations require an objectively demonstrable reason for seeking a modification. But such matters as a market shift which makes performance come to involve a loss may provide such a reason even though there is no such unforeseen difficulty as would make out a legal excuse from performance under Sections 2-615 and 2-616.[15]

When, for example, a subcontractor refused to deliver goods needed by a general contractor to fulfill a government contract unless the general contractor both paid more than the contract price for the goods and awarded the subcontractor a second subcontract, the threat was held to amount to duress.[16] A similar result has been reached even though the agreement is not legally enforceable, so that the threatened act is not a breach of contract. Duress may be found if, for example, an employer who has the right to terminate the employment at will threatens to fire an employee as a means of obtaining some unrelated advantage, such as the release of a claim or the sale of shares of stock.[17]

As courts have continued to expand the concept of duress far beyond its origins, it has become increasingly difficult to define with precision the proper limits of bargaining. Judges have been caught up in making moral judgments of the most delicate sort, as suggested by the assertion in the commentary to the

Significance of unfairness

---

[12] Leeper v. Beltrami, 347 P.2d 12 (Cal. 1959) (foreclosure of mortgage as means of extorting money).

[13] For an extensive discussion, *see* Dawson, Duress Through Civil Litigation, 45 Mich. L. Rev. 571, 679 (1947).

[14] Applied Genetics Intl. v. First Affiliated Sec., 912 F.2d 1238 (10th Cir. 1990) ("Wyoming Supreme Court would permit a party to assert duress because of a bad faith threat when the legal remedy is clearly inadequate"). *See* UCC 1-304; Restatement Second §205. See also the discussion of the duty of good faith in §7.17 *infra*.

[15] UCC 2-209 cmt. 2.

[16] Austin Instrument Co. v. Loral Corp., 272 N.E.2d 533 (N.Y. 1971).

[17] Laemmar v. J. Walter Thompson Co., 435 F.2d 680 (7th Cir. 1970) (employer threatened to terminate employment unless employee sold it stock).

first Restatement that "acts . . . that are wrongful in a moral sense, if made use of as a means of causing fear vitiate a transaction induced by that fear."[18] One scholar urged that this preoccupation with morality be avoided by shifting the emphasis from the impropriety of the threat to the unfairness of the resulting exchange and that courts should concern themselves with "excessive and unjustified gains that are directly traceable to disparity in bargaining power."[19] It may be true that courts are better suited to passing on unfairness than on impropriety. Surely if the propriety of the threat is questionable, courts are prone to support a conclusion of no duress with an assertion that the resulting bargain was not unfair.[20] The Restatement Second follows this approach by dividing improper threats into two categories.[21] The first category comprises the more traditional kinds of improper threats that have been discussed up to now. They are regarded as "so shocking that courts will not inquire into the fairness of the resulting exchange . . . or . . . in themselves necessarily involve some element of unfairness." The second category comprises a group of "threats in which the impropriety consists of the threat in combination with resulting unfairness."[22]

Legitimacy of use of power

On the one hand, hard bargaining between experienced adversaries ought not to be discouraged. A party will ordinarily be held to an agreement even though that party's adversity has been taken advantage of, as long as the contract has been shaped by prevailing market forces.[23] If, however, the party has been induced to make a contract by a threat to exercise a power for illegitimate ends, the transaction is suspect.[24] For example, a threat not to deal with another is ordinarily not duress, but other circumstances may call the resulting agreement into question. One such circumstance exists if the threatened act, were the maker to carry it out, would harm the victim without significantly benefiting the maker, and would therefore be done maliciously and out of pure vindictiveness.[25] An obvious example is a threat to make public embarrassing information concerning the victim unless the victim makes the proposed contract.[26] Another

---

[18] Restatement §492 cmt. g.

[19] Dawson, Economic Duress — An Essay in Perspective, 45 Mich. L. Rev. 253, 290 (1947).

[20] Hellenic Lines v. Louis Dreyfus Corp., 372 F.2d 753 (2d Cir. 1967) (maker of threat was "demanding . . . only a promise to arbitrate, hardly a shocking request").

[21] Restatement Second §176.

[22] Restatement Second §176 cmt. a.

[23] A good example is United States v. Bethlehem Steel Corp., 315 U.S. 289 (1942) (not duress for shipbuilder to take advantage of government's wartime need for ships; strong dissent by Frankfurter).

[24] See Restatement Second §176(2)(c) ("what is threatened is . . . a use of power for illegitimate ends").

[25] See Restatement Second §176(2)(a) ("the threatened act would harm the recipient and would not significantly benefit the party making the threat").

[26] Perkins Oil Co. v. Fitzgerald, 121 S.W.2d 877 (Ark. 1938) (employer's threat that if injured employee did not sign release, it would discharge his stepfather and prevent his employment elsewhere).

such circumstance arises if the effectiveness of the threat is enhanced because the maker has achieved an advantage over the victim by unfair dealings.[27] An example is a seller's refusal to supply goods after manipulative conduct at the bargaining stage has left the buyer at the seller's mercy.[28] Other examples of this general principle can be expected to be identified by courts as cases present themselves.[29]

Assuming that a threat is improper, when will it be regarded as sufficiently grave to justify the victim in succumbing to it?

§4.18. The Gravity of the Threat. What threats are sufficiently grave to justify the victim in succumbing? The standard has shifted over the years. The early common law showed its concern for control over claims of duress by imposing a stubbornly objective requirement that the threat be sufficient to overcome the will of "a person of ordinary firmness."[1] The pendulum then swung to a more subjective standard under which the threat need only have deprived the particular victim of *free will*.[2] Difficulties in giving meaning to the term *free will* have now caused the pendulum to swing back to yet another standard, under which the threat must have left the particular victim "no reasonable alternative."[3] This question, of the required gravity of the threat, is best considered in the context of actual cases.

Shifting standard of gravity

As we have seen, a threat to commence an ordinary civil action to enforce a claim to money may be improper, but such a threat does not usually amount to duress because the victim usually has a reasonable alternative to succumbing to the threat. The victim can simply assert its rights in the threatened action.[4] If the threatened civil action involves the seizure of property, the use of oppressive

Threat of civil process

---

[27] *See* Restatement Second §176(2)(b) ("the effectiveness of the threat . . . is significantly increased by prior unfair dealing").

[28] Hochman v. Zigler's Inc., 50 A.2d 97 (N.J. Eq. 1946) (landlord encouraged tenant to find purchaser for tenant's business and then threatened not to execute lease unless he got nearly half of price).

[29] S.S. & O. Corp. v. Township of Bernards Sewerage Auth., 301 A.2d 738 (N.J. 1973) (sewerage authority threatened not to make connection to housing development unless developer paid excessive rate).

§4.18 [1] 1 W. Blackstone, Commentaries on the Law of England 131 (1765), relying on 2 H. Bracton, On The Law and Customs of England 65 (Thorne tr. 1968) ("nor is it the fear of the weak and timid, but such as may occur in a resolute man"). Coke showed concern for such control: one asserting duress must "shew some just cause for feare, for feare of it selfe is internall and secret." E. Coke on Littleton 253b (1628).

[2] Austin Instrument Co. v. Loral Corp., 272 N.E.2d 533 (N.Y. 1971) (threat deprived victim of "its free will").

[3] Leeper v. Beltrami, 347 P.2d 12 (Cal. 1959) (duress where victim "had no reasonable alternative"). *See* Restatement Second §175(1) (duress must leave "the victim no reasonable alternative").

[4] Shockley v. Wickliffe, 148 S.E. 476 (S.C. 1929) (threat of suit on discharged debt).

tactics, or the possibility of emotional consequences, however, that alternative may not be a reasonable one.[5]

Threat to withhold performance

A threat to withhold goods belonging to the victim, as the term "duress of goods" suggests,[6] may leave the victim no reasonable alternative.[7] The same may be true for a threat to withhold goods, services, land, or money to which the victim is entitled under a contract.[8] Such a threat will not amount to duress if the victim can procure a suitable substitute on the market as a reasonable alternative to succumbing to the threat.[9] However, the victim's reliance on the contract may have made it particularly vulnerable to a threat of this kind, by increasing the victim's dependence on the maker of the threat. Courts have traditionally assumed that a reasonable alternative was available in the case of a threat not to pay money,[10] but more recent decisions have rejected this assumption and found duress on a showing of particular necessity.[11] A suit for specific performance may be a reasonable alternative if the threat is one to withhold land and in other situations when such relief is available. The mere availability of legal remedy is not, however, decisive if it will not afford adequate relief because, for example, of delay or uncertainty.[12]

What is reasonable alternative

What is a reasonable alternative depends on all the circumstances, including the victim's age and background, the relationship of the parties, and the availability of disinterested advice.[13] "Persons of a 'weak or cowardly nature' are the very ones that need protection. The courageous can usually protect

---

[5] Leeper v. Beltrami, *supra* note 3 (filing of *lis pendens* clouded title to real property, preventing its sale).

[6] See the discussion of when a threat is sufficient in §4.16 *supra*.

[7] Murphy v. Brilliant Co., 83 N.E.2d 166 (Mass. 1948) (threat to retain victim's boat).

[8] Austin Instrument Co. v. Loral Corp., *supra* note 2 (other suppliers of gear parts not available).

[9] Tri-State Roofing Co. v. Simon, 142 A.2d 333 (Pa. Super. 1958) (other roofing subcontractors available). Even if the modification proposed by the party making the threat is more favorable to the victim than the substitute arrangements that the victim could make on the market, the victim is not expected to succumb in order to avoid loss. See the discussion of what is an appropriate substitute in §12.12 *infra*.

[10] A much-cited case following this view is Hackley v. Headley, 8 N.W. 511 (Mich. 1881), in which it was said that to make the applicability of the doctrine of duress turn on whether the victim was in "pecuniary straits" would be "a most dangerous, as well as a most unequal doctrine."

[11] Totem Marine Tug & Barge v. Alyeska Pipeline Serv. Co., 584 P.2d 15 (Alaska 1978) (debtor "deliberately withheld payment of an acknowledged debt, knowing that [creditor facing bankruptcy] had no choice but to accept an inadequate sum in settlement of that debt").

[12] Rissman v. Rissman, 213 F.3d 381 (7th Cir. 2000) ("litigation (especially an appraisal action . . .) would have been a sensible option"); Wou v. Galbreath-Ruffin Realty Co., 195 N.Y.S.2d 886 (Suup. Ct. 1959) (eviction proceedings were "inadequate" where tenant refused, shortly before demolition of building, to perform promise to vacate).

[13] Silsbee v. Webber, 50 N.E. 555 (Mass. 1898) (Holmes, J.: "it does not matter that the motive would not have prevailed with a differently constituted person"); Rubenstein v. Rubenstein, 120 A.2d 11 (N.J. 1956) ("age, sex, capacity, relation of the parties and all the attendant circumstances must be considered").

themselves. Capricious and timid persons are generally the ones that are influenced by threats, and it would be a great injustice to permit them to be robbed by the unscrupulous because they are so unfortunately constituted."[14] Where the threat is one of minor vexation only, ignoring it or tolerating it may be a reasonable alternative to succumbing to the proposed contract, but whether this can be expected turns on all the circumstances.[15]

What are the legal consequences of duress?

§4.19. Effects of Duress. Duress by threat, like misrepresentation in the inducement,⸢makes the resulting contract voidable at the instance of the victim.⸥ If, as occasionally happens, the assent of the victim is obtained by the duress of a third person rather than that of the other party to the contract, the victim can still avoid the contract unless the other party to the contract in good faith and without reason to know of the duress either gives value or relies materially on the contract.[2] The victim of duress may assert it either by raising duress as a defense to an action brought to enforce the contract or by bringing an action based on avoidance ("rescission") of the contract.[3] The victim is barred from avoidance, however, if the victim has ratified the contract. In order not to do too much violence to the principle of mutuality of obligation, the victim may also be precluded from avoiding the contract by failing to disaffirm within a reasonable time.[4] The time does not begin to run, however, until the threat has ceased.[5]

On disaffirmance the victim is entitled to restitution, either in kind, if it is possible to restore what the victim has given to the other party, or in the form of a money judgment based on the benefit that the victim has conferred. In

Avoidance and ratification

Restitution

[14] Parmentier v. Pater, 13 Or. 121, 130 (1885).

[15] Kaplan v. Kaplan, 182 N.E.2d 706 (Ill. 1962) (wife's threats to publicize husband's affair with other woman held not to be duress).

§4.19 [1] Although duress evolved at common law and misrepresentation was shaped largely in equity, their effects are surprisingly similar. As in the case of misrepresentation, if property obtained by duress is resold to a good faith purchaser, the good faith purchaser takes the property free of the victim's power of avoidance. UCC 2-403 (goods), 3-305 (negotiable instruments). *See* the note to the discussion of avoidance and ratification in §4.15 *supra*.

That in general the victim cannot avoid the contract in part, *see* Restatement Second §383. That duress is traditionally not a tort, see the discussion of the law as to coercion in §4.9 *supra*.

[2] In that case the other party is protected for reasons analogous to those that apply to the good faith purchaser. *See* Restatement Second §175(2) & cmt. *e*.

[3] That the burden of proof, as with defenses generally, is on the victim, *see* Great Am. Indem. Co. v. Berryessa, 248 P.2d 367 (Utah 1952).

[4] Abbadessa v. Moore Business Forms, 987 F.2d 18 (1st Cir. 1993) (by accepting benefits of resignation agreements and by failing to notify employer promptly of intention to repudiate, employees "treated the agreements as binding").

[5] Austin Instrument Co. v. Loral Corp., 272 N.E.2d 533 (N.Y. 1971) (contractor's delay in disaffirming as against subcontractor excused because "it feared another stoppage of deliveries which would again put it in an untenable position").

return, the victim must make restitution.[6] <u>Equitable relief</u> is available to assert a constructive trust on or to cancel a conveyance of property handed over or to subject property benefited by services furnished to an equitable lien.

Coercion as a factor

Coercive behavior that does not amount to duress may nevertheless be considered as one factor in connection with some other aspect of a court's power to police the agreement under, for example, the concept of undue influence[7] or that of unconscionability.[8]

It is to the concept of undue influence that we now turn.

Development

§4.20. Undue Influence. The concept of ⌐undue influence⌐ developed in courts of equity to give relief to victims of unfair transactions that were induced by improper persuasion.[1] In contrast to the common law notion of duress, the essence of which was simple fear induced by threat, the equitable concept of undue influence was aimed at the protection of those affected with a weakness, short of incapacity, against improper persuasion, short of misrepresentation or duress, by those in a special position to exercise such persuasion. By the end of the nineteenth century it had been carried over to actions at law as well as equity.[2] Like duress, undue influence makes a contract voidable and may serve as a defense or as the basis of a claim in restitution.[3] Two elements are commonly <u>required</u>: first, a special relation between the parties; second, improper persuasion of the weaker by the stronger.

Relationship of trust or confidence

A finding of undue influence is generally said to require a special relation between the parties that makes one of them peculiarly susceptible to persuasion by the other. It is generally agreed that, because the doctrine of undue influence does not apply prior to the establishment of the relationship, it does not

---

[6]But the victim need not restore that which was wrongfully withheld. First Natl. Bank v. Pepper, 454 F.2d 626 (2d Cir. 1972) ("Where duress of . . . goods has been found, it has never been suggested that [the maker of the threat] should receive back . . . the very property to which he had no right."). The victim is accountable for benefits that have depreciated in value or been squandered. That making restitution is not a condition of bringing an action, *see* Perkins Oil Co. v. Fitzgerald, 121 S.W.2d 877 (Ark. 1938). For similar rules for misrepresentation, see the discussion of the requirement of restitution in §4.15 *supra*.

[7]See the discussion of "unfair" persuasion in §4.20 *infra*.

[8]See the discussion of factors in determining unconscionability in §4.28 *infra*.

§4.20 [1]Much of the law of undue influence developed in connection with gratuitous transfers, including transfers by will, rather than with contracts. In a piquant case decided by Chancellor Francis Bacon in 1617, a woman with the quaint name of Mrs. Death "did so work upon [the] simplicity and weakness" of a man of some 80 years "by her dalliance and pretence of love . . . and by sundry adulterous courses with him and by sorcery" that he executed a will and deed, after which she "used him in a most cruel manner reviling him and causing him to be whipped and suffered him to be loathsomely and uncleanly in bed." Bacon set the transfers aside. Joy v. Bannister (Chan. 1617), in Bacon's Reports 33 (Ritchie ed. 1932).

[2]An example is Adams v. Irving Natl. Bank, 116 N.Y. 606 (1889) (jury verdict affirmed on "the equitable principle which renders voidable contracts obtained by undue influence").

[3]Avoidance is subject to the same rules that apply in cases of duress. See §4.19 *supra*.

apply to the agreement that establishes the relationship itself.[4] The mere fact that the victim is weak, infirm, or aged does not suffice in the absence of such a relationship, but it may be a factor in showing that such a relationship existed. The classical case involves a relation of trust or confidence in which the weaker party is justified in assuming that the stronger will not act in a manner inconsistent with the weaker's welfare.[5] Examples include the relations between parent and child,[6] member of the clergy and communicant, physician and patient,[7] husband and wife, and — according to some courts — one engaged person and the other.[8] In an illustrative case, the mother of a child born out of wedlock testified that during a period of emotional distress following the birth of the child, representatives of the maternity home, including her individual counsellor, had sought her agreement to give up the child. The Texas court observed that her counsellor was "a person to whom plaintiff was encouraged to look for guidance" and upheld a jury verdict based on this testimony, which was "rendered credible by the fact that an unwed mother who has just given birth is usually emotionally distraught and peculiarly vulnerable to efforts, well meaning or unscrupulous, to persuade her to give up her child."[9]

The protection afforded by the doctrine has been extended beyond relations characterized by trust and confidence to those in which the weaker party is for some reason under the domination of the stronger.[10] In one such case a schoolteacher alleged that after he had been arrested on criminal charges of homosexual activity, questioned by the police, booked, released on bail, and gone for 40 hours without sleep, the superintendent of the school district and the principal of his school came to his apartment to ask for his resignation. The California court noted the possibility "that exhaustion and emotional turmoil may wholly incapacitate a person from exercising his judgment" and held that

Relationship of domination

[4]Johnson v. Gudmundsson, 35 F.3d 1104 (7th Cir. 1994) (since no confidential relationship exists either before lawyer undertakes client's business or after relation has been dissolved, "consequences flowing from [lawyer's] failure to rebut the presumption of undue influence do not 'relate back' to services he may have performed . . . before the commencement of the attorney-client relationship").

[5]See Restatement Second §177 (party "who by virtue of the relation between them is justified in assuming that (the other) person will not act in a manner inconsistent with his welfare").

[6]But cf. Crider v. Crider, 635 N.E.2d 204 (Ind. App. 1994) (fn.4: suggesting that presumption of parental domination "should only be with respect to a minor child living in the parent's household"); Rebidas v. Murasko, 677 A.2d 331 (Pa. Super. 1996) ("mere existence of kinship, or a family tie, . . . is merely one factor").

[7]The first two relationships are reversible. Yount v. Yount, 43 N.E. 136 (Ind. 1896) (undue influence by adult son on mother who was "weak and enfeebled in mind by reason of age").

[8]Randolph v. Randolph, 937 S.W.2d 815 (Tenn. 1996) ("agreement to marry gives rise to a confidential relationship").

[9]Methodist Mission Home v. B., 451 S.W.2d 539, 543-44 (Tex. Civ. App. 1970).

[10]See Restatement Second §177 ("a party who is under the domination of the person exercising the persuasion").

the pleadings sufficed to show the required relation of "a dominant subject to a servient object."[11]

"Unfair" persuasion

Once the requisite relation is shown, it must then be shown that the assent of the weaker party was induced by unfair persuasion on the part of the stronger.[12] What are the limits of persuasion in this context? The degree of persuasion that will be characterized as "unfair" depends on a variety of circumstances, but the ultimate question is whether the result was produced by means that seriously impaired the free and competent exercise of judgment. A particularly important factor in showing unfairness in persuasion is imbalance in the resulting bargain. As one authority has expressed it, "Transactions must be judged not only in terms of motive but in terms of their effects."[13] Other factors include the unavailability of independent advice, the lack of time for reflection, and the susceptibility of the weaker party.[14] In the case of the schoolteacher, the court concluded that:

> the representatives of the school board undertook to achieve their objective by overpersuasion and imposition to secure plaintiff's signature but not his consent to his resignation through a high-pressure carrot-and-stick technique — under which they assured plaintiff they were trying to assist him, he should rely on their advice, there wasn't time to consult an attorney, if he didn't resign at once the school district would suspend and dismiss him from his position and publicize the proceedings, but if he did resign the incident wouldn't jeopardize his chances of securing a teaching post elsewhere.[15]

In the case of the unwed mother, the court noted that:

> she was subjected to an intensive campaign, extending over a five-day period, designed to convince her to give up her baby, rather than to insure that her decision, whatever it might be, would be based on a consideration of all relevant factors, [and she] was told, falsely, that she had no right to keep her child, . . . was accused of being selfish and told that if she "was any kind of person" she would consent to the adoption of her baby.[16]

---

[11] Odorizzi v. Bloomfield School Dist., 54 Cal. Rptr. 533, 540 (Ct. App. 1966).

[12] It is sometimes said that once the required relationship is established, the burden shifts to the dominant party to show that there was no unfair persuasion. McCullough v. Rogers, 431 So. 2d 1246 (Ala. 1983) (confidential relationship raises "presumption of undue influence").

[13] Dawson, Economic Duress — An Essay in Perspective, 45 Mich. L. Rev. 253, 264 (1947).

[14] In Odorizzi v. Bloomfield School Dist., *supra* note 11, at 541, the court said, "The pattern usually involves several of the following elements: (1) discussion of the transaction at an unusual or inappropriate time, (2) consummation of the transaction in an unusual place, (3) insistent demand that the business be finished at once, (4) extreme emphasis on untoward consequences of delay, (5) the use of multiple persuaders by the dominant side against a single servient party, (6) absence of third-party advisers to the servient party, (7) statements that there is no time to consult financial advisers or attorneys."

[15] 54 Cal. Rptr. at 543.

[16] 451 S.W.2d at 544.

Because the unfair persuasion required falls short of what is required for mis- **Comparison with**
representation or duress, undue influence affords protection in some situations **misrepresentation**
where those other doctrines would not. However, the extraordinary expansion **and duress**
of the scope of duress has to a considerable extent undercut the importance of
the concept of undue influence.[17]

In the sections that follow, we see how courts have used the doctrine of
consideration to police bargains involving modification and discharge.

D.   POLICING OF MODIFICATION AND DISCHARGE

§4.21.   Modification and the Pre-Existing Duty Rule. Suppose that **Illustration of rule**
a contractor agrees to construct a building and, after the work has begun,
threatens to walk off the job unless the owner promises to pay an additional
sum. The owner, in urgent need of the building and despairing of finding
another contractor quickly, promises to pay the sum in return for the contractor's
finishing the work. On completion of the building, the owner refuses to pay
more than the original contract price. Is the modification enforceable, so that
the contractor can recover the additional sum from the owner? Today a natural
response would be to analyze the problem in terms of duress. It is only relatively
recently, however, that the common law doctrine of duress has been broadened
to encompass such situations.[1] The traditional analysis of the problem proceeds,
instead, in terms of the doctrine of consideration. Under that doctrine the
owner would prevail on the ground that there was no consideration for the
new promise. All that the contractor did in return for the new promise was
to perform a duty that the contractor owed under an existing contract, and
under the pre-existing duty rule, performance of a pre-existing duty is not
consideration.[2]

The logic of the pre-existing duty rule is far from inexorable. To one schooled **Questionable**
in the contemporary bargain theory of consideration, it might seem just as **logic of rule**
logical to conclude that performance, even by one who is already under a duty
to perform, is consideration for a promise if the performance is bargained for a

---

[17]*See* Eckstein v. Eckstein, 379 A.2d 757 (Md. App. 1978) (where "husband and his lawyer
were dealing with an emotionally and mentally unstable [wife], we think that the conclusion that
the execution of the agreement was obtained by duress is inescapable").

§4.21   [1]See the discussion of a threat to break a contract in §4.17 *supra*. In evaluating the possible responses to such threats, it may be significant that the rule making penalties unenforceable
reduces a party's ability to provide sanctions for such threats in the contract itself.

[2]Lingenfelder v. Wainwright Brewing Co., 103 Mo. 578, 15 S.W. 844 (1891) (architect for
brewery).

Note that since the rule is an adjunct of the doctrine of consideration, it does no more than
make a party's new promise enforceable. It differs from duress in that it does not allow the party
to avoid and seek restitution based on any performance the party has rendered. See the discussion
of the remedies of a victim of bad faith in §4.22 *infra*.

second time, after it has once been refused. Furthermore, it requires no great stretch of the imagination to view performance by a promisee that is reluctant to perform both as a benefit to the promisor, which has reason to want a bird in the hand, and as a detriment to the promisee, which might prefer to take its chances on being sued for damages. It is sometimes argued that, because the promisee was already under a duty to render the performance, there is no "legal" detriment; but to say that the detriment is not "legal" begs the question.[3]

Applicability of rule

Whatever its logic, the pre-existing duty rule has been applied to a wide variety of modification agreements. These include not only promises of owners to pay contractors more for construction but also, for example, promises of employers to pay employees more for their work[4] and promises of buyers to pay sellers more for their goods.[5] The rule applies, all the more forcefully, to a modification under which the promisee gives in return only a promise to perform a pre-existing duty and not the actual performance of it — as when what the owner bargains for and the contractor gives is the contractor's promise to finish the work (not the actual finishing of the work).[6] Furthermore, the rule applies if the pre-existing duty is one imposed by law, instead of by contract.[7] For example, a police officer, who is under a legal duty to capture a criminal or to return lost property, cannot claim a reward that has been offered for doing so.[8]

Duty to third party

Some courts have gone so far as to apply the pre-existing duty rule where the duty was owed, not to the promisor, but to a third party.[9] Suppose, for example, that the contractor, having agreed with the owner to construct the building, makes another agreement with a subcontractor to have the plumbing done. The subcontractor then tells the owner, with whom the subcontractor

---

[3] On the notion of "legal" detriment, *see* the discussion of theories of consideration in §2.12 *supra*. The use of this notion to support the pre-existing duty rule, which has been increasingly subjected to criticism, has not reflected creditably on the concept of detriment as a basis of consideration.

[4] Alaska Packers' Assn. v. Domenico, 117 F. 99 (9th Cir. 1902) (seamen).

[5] Rexite Casting Co. v. Midwest Mower Corp., 267 S.W.2d 327 (Mo. App. 1954) (specially manufactured aluminum castings).

[6] Schlesinger v. Woodcock, 35 P.3d 1232 (Wyo. 2001) ("promise to pay a debt already due is not sufficient consideration for a creditor's promise to forbear the time of payment"). Restatement Second §73 states the rule that *performance* of a legal duty is not consideration. Then §75 makes it clear that a *promise* is not consideration if the promised performance *would not* itself be consideration. For more on the pre-existing duty rule under the Restatement Second, see the discussion of judicial reform in §4.22 *infra*.

[7] Gonsalves v. Regent Intl. Hotels, 447 N.E.2d 693 (N.Y. 1983) (hotel under duty to provide safe for guest).

[8] Denney v. Reppert, 432 S.W.2d 647 (Ky. 1968) (employees of robbed bank gave information leading to capture of robbers).

[9] The leading case is McDevitt v. Stokes, 192 S.W. 681 (Ky. 1917) (driver who had contract with owner to drive horse in noted trotting race was promised $1,000 by owner of horse's blood kin if driver would drive horse to victory).

has no contract and to whom the subcontractor owes no duty, that no plumbing will be put in unless the owner promises to pay the subcontractor a stated sum. The owner, in order to get the building finished on time, makes the promise in return for the subcontractor's doing the work. Then, when the plumbing work is done, the owner refuses to pay. Some courts have held that the owner's promise is unenforceable under the pre-existing duty rule because the subcontractor did no more than what was already its duty to the general contractor.[10] However, even under this view, the promise is enforceable if the general contractor was so in breach of the contract with the subcontractor that the latter was no longer under a duty to perform it.[11] Furthermore, other courts have declined to apply the pre-existing duty rule if the duty was owed to a third party. The Restatement also adopts this position.[12]

Although the pre-existing duty rule is a serious impediment to modification of contracts, there are two well-recognized techniques by which the parties can avoid its application. One is for the promisee to do or promise to do something in addition to performing the pre-existing duty. Consideration may be found, for example, in the contractor's agreement to change the specifications of the house or to advance the date for completion.[13] It may also be found in the contractor's agreement to continue work in spite of an asserted excuse for nonperformance if the contractor honestly, even if erroneously, believes that circumstances, such as unforeseen difficulty, afford an excuse.[14] Since a court will not generally inquire into the fairness of the exchange, even a "horse, hawk, or robe," in the quaint phrase of Lord Coke, is sufficient.[15] The other technique is for both parties to agree to rescind the original contract, leaving them free of any obligation, and then to make a new contract on the desired terms. This assumes that at the time of the agreement of rescission neither party has fully performed, so that the surrender by each party of its remaining rights will be consideration for the other's surrender of its rights.[16] If, for example, the owner and the contractor first agree on a rescission of their original contract, they can enter into any new

> **Techniques to avoid rule**

---

[10] Schaefer v. Brunswick Laundry, 183 A. 175 (N.J.L. 1936) (owner promised subcontractor to pay costs due to delay from strike).

[11] Joseph Lande & Son v. Wellsco Realty, 34 A.2d 418 (N.J.L. 1943) ("general contractor was in substantial default").

[12] Restatement Second §73 (limited to "a legal duty owed to a *promisor*"). Illustration 12 to that section repudiates the reasoning in McDevitt v. Stokes, *supra* note 9.

[13] King v. Duluth, Missabe & N. Ry., 63 N.W. 1105 (Minn. 1895) (contractor promised to complete work on time although owner's delays excused it from doing so).

[14] Melotte v. Tucci, 66 N.E.2d 357 (Mass. 1946) (promise of vendor of house to indemnify purchaser from any expense in installing gas and electric meters was supported by purchaser's surrender of invalid claim that existing meters were in breach of contract, "a claim . . . made in good faith and not frivolous, vexatious or unlawful"). For limits on the defense, see the discussions of the requirement of good faith and the requirement of doubtful claim discussed in §2.12 *supra*.

[15] For the origin of this phrase, *see* the discussion of the limitation on the rule in §4.23 *infra*.

[16] See the discussion of an agreement of rescission in §4.24 *infra*.

Judicial hostility to rule

contract they wish.[17] In theory, this must leave both parties with at least an instant of freedom, during which they are no longer bound by the old contract and are under no duty to make a new one. If the parties use this technique, a court will not generally inquire into the fairness of either the rescission or the new agreement.

Courts have become increasingly hostile to the pre-existing duty rule. A scholar characterized the rule as, "on the whole, that adjunct of the doctrine of consideration which has done most to give it a bad reputation."[18] Although it serves in some instances to give relief to a promisor that has been subjected to overreaching, it serves in other instances to frustrate the expectations of a promisee that has fairly negotiated a modification. It does not, for example, distinguish between the situation in which the contractor's demand for more money is motivated merely by opportunism and greed[19] and the situation in which the demand is prompted by the discovery of circumstances or the occurrence of events that makes the contractor's performance much more burdensome.[20] It is, therefore, not surprising to find that courts have often labored mightily to bring cases within some exception to the rule. They have been vigilant to spot a "horse, hawk, or robe."[21] They have been alert to find an agreement of rescission, followed by a new contract, on facts that might have suggested only a modification.[22] Some have spun out still other theories of the existence of consideration,[23] and others have dispensed with the requirement of consideration altogether if the promisee has relied upon the promise.[24]

Given all this dissatisfaction with the rule, what of attempts at reform?

---

[17] Schwartzreich v. Bauman-Basch, 131 N.E. 887 (N.Y. 1921) (employer and employee rescinded old contract and made new one at higher salary).

[18] Patterson, An Apology for Consideration, 58 Colum. L. Rev. 929, 936 (1958).

[19] See Alaska Packers' Assn. v. Domenico, *supra* note 4 (pre-existing duty rule applied where seamen refused on arrival in Alaska at start of salmon canning season to work unless given substantial raise).

[20] See Davis & Co. v. Morgan, 43 S.E. 732 (Ga. 1903) (pre-existing duty rule applied where employee reported better opportunity to employer, "saying that of course he would not go without consent").

[21] An important situation in which this reasoning is used arises where a creditor promises to extend the time when money is due. If interest is payable on the loan, the creditor's promise has been held to be supported by the debtor's implied promise to pay interest during the period of the extension. Adamson v. Bosick, 259 P. 513 (Colo. 1927).

[22] See Martiniello v. Bamel, 150 N.E. 838 (Mass. 1926) (jury could have drawn inference that owner and contractor rescinded old contract and made new one).

[23] One questionable exception is that if one party has already broken the contract, then a promise by the other "to secure to himself the actual performance of the work in place of a right to collect damages" is supported by consideration. Swartz v. Lieberman, 112, 80 N.E.2d 5, 6 (Mass. 1948) (quoted with approval; when party said it "would have" to charge more and the other agreed, this brought case within exception).

[24] Canada v. Allstate Ins. Co., 411 F.2d 517 (5th Cir. 1969) (insurance company relied on modification of termination provision by paying agent's successor; pre-existing duty rule not discussed).

§4.22.   **Reform of the Rule.**   Dissatisfaction with the pre-existing duty **Judicial reform**
rule has led a few courts to abandon it overtly. Again, take the case of the contractor that agrees to construct a building and then threatens to walk off the
job unless the owner promises to pay an additional sum. Now suppose that the
contractor's action is prompted by discovery of unforeseen subsoil conditions
that make construction much more expensive than was anticipated, but that fall
short of excusing the contractor from performing under the rules on mistake or
impracticability. It may be important to the owner, as well as to the contractor,
that the owner be able to make an enforceable promise to pay an additional
sum, for if the owner cannot, the contractor may choose to risk default.[1] In
these circumstances, some courts have concluded that, because of "unforeseen
difficulties," the owner's promise to pay the additional sum is enforceable, even
though all the owner gets in return is the contractor's promise to perform or performance of the original contract. In the words of Maryland's highest court, "it
would be making an exceedingly technical distinction to hold that the promise
would have been binding if the original contract had been expressly rescinded,
but that it is not binding because there was no express or actual rescission."
The exception to the pre-existing duty rule should be restricted, however, "to
cases where the refusal to perform was equitable and fair, and the difficulties
were substantial, unforeseen and not within the contemplation of the parties
when the original contract was made."[2] This view is endorsed by the Restatement Second,[3] which has been followed by a significant number of courts.[4] A
few other courts have abandoned the pre-existing duty rule without regard to
"unforeseen difficulties."[5]

See Restatement Second §89 ("promise modifying a duty under a contract not fully performed
on either side is binding . . . to the extent that justice requires enforcement in view of material
change of position in reliance on the promise"). Minor modifications involving conditions may be
effective under the concept of waiver. See §§8.5, 8.19 *infra*.

§4.22   [1] *See* R. Posner, Gratuitous Promises in Economics and Law, 6 J. Legal Stud. 411,
421 (1977) ("If the [owner] merely declares his intention of paying the builder a higher price,
but is free to renege, the builder may decide not to complete performance but instead to take
his chances in bankruptcy court. Yet the promisor dare not pay him the extra price in advance in
exchange for the builder's promise to continue . . . if the contractor is financially shaky for other
reasons. . . . ").

[2] Linz v. Schuck, 67 A. 286, 289 (Md. 1907).

[3] Restatement Second §89 ("promise modifying a duty under a contract not fully performed
on either side is binding . . . if the modification is fair and equitable in view of circumstances not
anticipated by the parties when the contract was made"). This section appears in a topic devoted
to "contracts without consideration."

[4] Angel v. Murray, 322 A.2d 630 (R.I. 1974) ("We believe that [§89] is the proper rule of law
and find it applicable to the facts of this case.").

[5] This is the case in Wisconsin, at least where the contract is partly or wholly unperformed on
both sides. Everlite Mfg. Co. v. Grand Valley Mach. & Tool Co., 171 N.W.2d 188 (Wis. 1969). This
departure from the rule developed out of the fiction that the consideration for the original contract
is "imported" into and becomes the consideration for the modification. Brown v. Everhard, 8 N.W.

Legislative reform The rule has also been the subject of legislative reform. Statutes in a few states make a signed writing a substitute for consideration to support a modification of a contract.[6] Uniform Commercial Code 2-209(1) completely abrogates the rule as to contracts for the sale of goods: "An agreement modifying a contract within this Article needs no consideration to be binding."[7] Although no writing is needed under this provision of the Code, the statute of frauds section of the Code must be satisfied if the contract as modified is within its provisions.[8] Furthermore, although the Code abandons the requirement of consideration for modifications, a modification, in order to be effective, must still meet the test of good faith imposed by the Code. According to the comments, as was noted earlier, "extortion of a 'modification' without legitimate commercial reason is ineffective as a violation of the duty of good faith."[9] In fashioning this solution to the problem of the enforceability of modifications, the drafters of the Code discarded the trappings of the doctrine of consideration to bare the real abuse of the bargaining process — coercion. The result is remarkably consistent with the liberalized rules on duress.[10] Both the Vienna Convention and the UNIDROIT Principles have provisions similar to that of UCC 2-209(1),[11] although it is by no means clear that the Convention, as contrasted with the Principles, imposes a duty of good faith as does the Code.[12]

Advantage of Code solution The Code solution has much to commend it. It may be true that the pre-existing duty rule does make unenforceable some promises that ought not to be enforced because they were extorted with no legitimate reason from one who was especially vulnerable due to having relied on a contract with the promisee. However, the rule is blind to the particulars of the case and strikes down modifications without regard to such circumstances. In doing away with the rule, the Code adds a flexible requirement of good faith, with an objective component of

---

725 (Wis. 1881). Minnesota and New Hampshire have also abandoned the rule. See the discussion of outright rejection of the rule in §4.25 *infra*.

[6] *See* Mich. Comp. Laws Ann. §566.1; N.Y. Gen. Oblig. L. §5-1103.

[7] As to the meaning of "modify" under a federal statute, *see* MCI Telecommunications Corp. v. American Tel. & Tel. Co., 114 S. Ct. 2223 (1994) (Scalia, J.: "modify," under Communications Act, "connotes moderate change").

[8] UCC 2-209(3). For more on this, *see* the discussion of modification and rescission in §6.2 *infra*. A writing is the most common but not the only way of satisfying the statute of frauds section. See §6.9 *infra*.

[9] UCC 2-209 cmt. 2, quoted in the discussion of a threat to break a contract in §4.17 *supra*. The comment asserts that "a mere technical consideration [cannot] support a modification made in bad faith." Although an effective rescission would appear to relieve the parties of their contractual duty of good faith (*see* the discussion of the traditional freedom of negotiation in §3.26 *supra*), a rescission in bad faith would presumably not be effective.

[10] *But see* Kelsey-Hayes Co. v. Galtaco Redlaw Castings Corp., 749 F. Supp. 794 (E.D. Mich. 1990) (rejecting argument "that the common law doctrine of economic duress . . . has been subsumed by the Uniform Commercial Code's 'good faith' test").

[11] CISG 29(1); UNIDROIT Principles 3.2.

[12] See the discussion of international solutions in §7.17 *infra*.

fair dealing in the case of a merchant. This is the same standard as that suggested earlier under the liberalized rules on duress.[13] In applying this requirement, courts have ruled that the "legitimate commercial reason" referred to in the Code commentary must be a reason beyond the control of the party seeking the modification, such as a drastic market shift.[14] This expanded concept of duress would make promises voidable in precisely those situations in which the pre-existing duty rule can be justified.[15] And since this concept of duress is not limited to contracts for the sale of goods, it makes sense to extend the Code solution to contracts of all kinds. The trend is plainly in this direction.

The imposition of a duty of good faith in the negotiation of contract modification has two important advantages for the victim of bad faith. First, it allows the victim to unravel the transaction by avoiding the modification and seeking restitution for any performance rendered.[16] In contrast, the pre-existing duty rule does no more than to make the victim's new promise unenforceable, with no right to avoid the modification and seek restitution for any performance that the victim may have rendered under it.[17] It does not, for example, give the owner the right to get its money back if the contractor has already been paid the additional sum promised. Second, it gives the victim the right to recover damages if the other party's breach of the duty of good faith resulted in a *failure* to arrive at a modification.[18] Damages should ordinarily be based on the victim's reliance losses, as in the analogous case of precontractual liability for breach of an agreement to negotiate in good faith.[19] In contrast, neither the concept of duress nor the pre-existing duty rule allows affirmative relief.[20]

Remedies of victim of bad faith

---

[13]Though the Code states no requirement that the threat to break the contract leave the victim no reasonable alternative, it would make sense to infer such a requirement. United States v. Stump Home Specialties Mfg., 905 F.2d 1117 (7th Cir. 1990) (dictum by Posner, J.: "sensible course would be to enforce contract modifications (at least if written) regardless of consideration and rely on the defense of duress to prevent abuse").

[14]T & S Brass & Bronze Works v. Pic-Air, 790 F.2d 1098 (4th Cir. 1986) ("legitimate commercial reason is one outside the control of the party seeking the modification").

[15]Two early examples of cases where the pre-existing duty rule was relied on to refuse enforcement of a promise obtained by particularly outrageous threats are Alaska Packers' Assn. v. Domenico, 117 F. 99 (9th Cir. 1902) (threat by seamen at start of canning season not to work), and Lingenfelder v. Wainwright Brewing Co., 15 S.W. 844 (Mo. 1891) (threat by architect, when building under construction, not to supervise).

[16]*See* Austin Instrument Co. v. Loral Corp., 272 N.E.2d 533 (N.Y. 1971), described in the discussion of a threat to break a contract in §4.17 *supra*. See also §4.19 *supra*.

[17]Even if the promisor pays without knowing that its promise is unenforceable under the pre-existing duty rule, it seems unlikely that the promisor can recover its payment on the ground of a mistake of law. *See* Restatement of Restitution §45 (1937) (generally no restitution where benefit conferred upon another to satisfy "an honest claim of the other"). *But cf.* §47 (restitution of benefit conferred under promise erroneously believed to be binding by one who "did not obtain the benefit expected by him in return").

[18]See the discussion of agreements to negotiate in §3.26 *supra*.

[19]See the discussion of the law as to coercion in §4.9 *supra*.

[20]That this is so for duress, see the discussion of the law as to coercion in §4.9 *supra*.

Next we examine the impact of the pre-existing duty rule on the settlement of claims.

§4.23.   Claims Settlements.   We noted earlier that the law favors settlement by the parties of disputed claims — at least if fairly bargained for — and that this policy supports the enforceability of a promise made to a claimant that is willing to settle a disputed claim, even if the claim later turns out to be invalid.[1] The same policy suggests that a claimant who has settled a claim should be foreclosed from later pursuing it in violation of the settlement agreement.

If a creditor with a claim for $1,000 against a debtor takes $800 "in full satisfaction" of the debt and purports to "discharge" the debt in its entirety, it might be thought that no question of consideration is raised. Consideration is required for the enforceability of a promise, but not for the efficacy of an executed transfer (such as the payment of the $800) nor, it might seem, for the discharge of the debt. A question of consideration might arise if the creditor *promised* to discharge the debt at some future time and if the enforceability of that promise were at issue. But why should such a question arise if the creditor gives a present discharge?

In *Pinnel's Case*, decided in 1602, Lord Coke declared that "payment of a less sum on the [due] day in satisfaction of a greater, cannot be any satisfaction for the whole."[2] Coke did not base his conclusion on the doctrine of consideration and, in any event, the case went off on a pleading point. However, his dictum was followed in *Foakes v. Beer*,[3] decided in 1884 by the House of Lords, which assumed that consideration was necessary for the discharge of a duty. Once this assumption was made, it followed naturally enough from the pre-existing duty rule that a debtor that was under a duty to pay a $1,000 debt could not discharge it by paying $800.

The "rule of *Foakes v. Beer*," as it is often called, took firm root in the United States. It extends not only to the discharge of a debtor's money debt to a creditor, but also to a discharge of an obligor's duty to an obligee and to a partial discharge of, or reduction in, such a duty. It has been applied, for example, to allow a landlord who accepted less rent than was due in full satisfaction of what was

---

§4.23   [1] See the discussion of the policy for enforcing the promise in §2.12 *supra*.

[2] 77 Eng. Rep. 237 (C.P. 1602).

[3] L.R. 9 A.C. 605 (H.L. 1884). For criticism of the case, *see* E. Farnsworth, Changing Your Mind ch. 15 (1998) ("No logic compelled the House of Lords to subject this branch of the law to the requirement of consideration, a requirement that had evolved to deal with persons who make promises . . . ."); Ferson, The Rule in Foakes v. Beer, 31 Yale L.J. 15, 23 (1921) ("rule lived because the discharge was mistaken for a contract" and "to maintain a supposed consistency, consideration was held essential to the discharge"); G. Gilmore, The Death of Contract 33 (1974) (quoting Williston, "the best that could be said for the rule is that it had 'at least' the merit of being logically consistent with other rules").

The Vienna Convention and the UNIDROIT Principles appear to reject the rule by providing that a contract can be terminated by mere agreement, with no exception for a contract that remains executory on only one side. CISG 29; UNIDROIT Principles 3.2.

Policy favoring settlement

Consideration required for discharge

Rule of Foakes v. Beer

Scope of rule

due under the lease to recover the balance.[4] If, however, the obligor has relied on the discharge of its duty, as a tenant may have done at least with respect to payments of rent accepted by a landlord, consideration may be dispensed with, as it may be under the pre-existing duty rule generally.[5]

The criticism heaped on the pre-existing duty rule approaches obloquy when the rule is applied, as it was in *Foakes v. Beer*, to prevent the settlement of claims. It is widely regarded as frustrating the justified expectations of the parties and as being at variance with commercial understanding. The New Hampshire Supreme Court observed in 1907 that "the absurdity of the results of the rule . . . has been commented upon in case after case; but persistence in error under the shadow of a great name [Lord Coke] still calls that right which is recognized to be wrong."[6] Coke himself laid the foundation for a major limitation on the rule when he allowed that, although the mere payment of a lesser sum cannot discharge a greater debt, "the gift of a horse, hawk, or robe, & c. in satisfaction is good." The problem is to find something in addition to or in place of the part performance. Coke gave two examples. One was payment at an earlier time: "the payment and acceptance of parcel [i.e., part] before the day in satisfaction of the whole would be a good satisfaction in regard of circumstance of time." Another was payment at another place: payment at York of only part of what is due at Westminster will satisfy the debt "for the expences to pay it at York, is sufficient satisfaction."[7]

The obligee is also considered to have received something different from mere part performance of the obligor's duty if the obligee receives part performance from a third party, and such performance can therefore be consideration for a discharge in full if it is so accepted by the obligee. The same is true of a third party's promise of part performance. If, therefore, the creditor takes "in full satisfaction" of the debt $800, or even a promise of $800, from a friend of the debtor rather than from the debtor itself, the $1,000 debt is discharged.[8] This does not, however, extend to the situation in which the third party acts as the obligor's agent or to the situation in which the third party purports to do so and the obligee later ratifies the act. Nor does it extend to the case in which a debtor simply offers payment by means of a check drawn by a third person.[9]

But the most significant class of cases in which an obligee is considered to have received something other than mere part performance of the obligor's duty consists of cases in which the obligor's performance involves giving up

Limitation on rule

Part performance by third party

Surrender of a defense

---

[4] Levine v. Blumenthal, 186 A. 457 (N.J. Super. 1936), aff'd per curiam, 189 A. 54 (N.J. 1937) (reduction of rent during depression).

[5] See the discussion of judicial hostility to the rule in §4.21 *supra*.

[6] Frye v. Hubbell, 68 A. 325, 332 (N.H. 1907).

[7] 77 Eng. Rep. at 237-38. See the discussion of techniques to avoid the rule in §4.21 *supra*.

[8] Welsh v. Loomis, 105 P.2d 500 (Wash. 1940) (creditor took $150 check of debtor's husband as payment in full of debt of over $200).

[9] *See* Restatement Second §278 cmt. *c*.

a defense that the obligor asserts as to that duty. Suppose, for example, that a debt is unliquidated because the debtor asserts that the debt is only $600 because of a partial defense to the $1,000 claim.[10] The debtor's payment of $800, $200 more than the debtor admits, can then supply the consideration for the discharge of the $1,000 debt.[11] The situation is analogous to that in which a promise is made in consideration of the surrender of a claim.[12] Just as the claim in that situation must be asserted in good faith and perhaps must also be "doubtful," the defense here must be asserted in good faith[13] and perhaps must also be "doubtful."[14] Disenchantment with the pre-existing duty rule, however, may result in less rigor in the enforcement of the requirement of doubtfulness here.[15] Some courts have gone so far as to hold that if the claim is unliquidated, the debtor's payment of no more than is admittedly due — $600 in the example just given — can be consideration for a discharge of the balance of the debt,[16] though there is authority to the contrary.[17] This problem often arises when a debtor tenders a check as "payment in full" or "in full satisfaction," commonly noted on the check itself. Such disputes are governed by UCC 3-311, added in the 1990 revision of Article 3.[18]

We now look at the forms of transactions resulting in discharge, along with some efforts at reform in this area.

Vocabulary of discharge

§4.24.   Discharge Supported by Consideration. Although no particular form is required for an agreement to discharge a duty, several recurring types of consensual transactions have evolved for this purpose. It is useful to know something about them, even though it is the substance of the transaction rather than its characterization that determines its efficacy. Some of these transactions involve exceptions to the requirement that a discharge be supported by consideration. They will not be discussed until the following section. In the transactions to be discussed here, the requirement of consideration is

---

[10] For the meaning of *unliquidated*, see the discussion of question of interpretation in §4.24 *infra*.

[11] DeJean v. United Airlines, 839 P.2d 1153 (Colo. 1992) (dispute over seniority rights).

[12] See §2.12 *supra*. The same is true of forbearance to assert a defense or a promise to forbear to assert one.

[13] Mackiewicz v. J.J. & Assocs., 514 N.W.2d 613 (Neb. 1994) (it is "essential that there be a bona fide dispute" and there was "no evidence that there ever was any dispute").

[14] Brunswick Corp. v. Levin, 276 A.2d 532 (Pa. 1971) (there must be "a reasonable dispute").

[15] For a rare complete departure from the requirement, *see* Sherwin-Williams Co. v. Sarrett, 419 So. 2d 1332 (Miss. 1982) (quoting with approval: "immaterial whether the creditor's claim is liquidated or disputed").

[16] Marton Remodeling v. Jensen, 706 P.2d 607 (Utah 1985) ("general rule . . . is that an accord and satisfaction of a single claim is not avoided merely because the amount paid . . . is only that which the debtor concedes to be due").

[17] Whittaker Chain Tread Co. v. Standard Auto Supply Co., 103 N.E. 695 (Mass. 1913).

[18] Contemporaneous revision of former UCC 1-207, the precursor of UCC 1-308, made it clear that that section did not apply to such disputes. *See* UCC 1-308(b).

satisfied. Although, for the most part, these transactions involve no exceptional legal principles, they have generated a considerable vocabulary of their own.[1] Unless otherwise indicated, the transactions discussed in these two sections may be used to discharge duties, such as tort duties, that do not arise out of contract.

In some transactions the consideration for the discharge consists of a performance or a promise that differs from what is due under the existing duty and that is accepted by the obligee in satisfaction of that duty. Such transactions can be divided into three principal types: substituted performance, substituted contract (including novation), and accord followed by satisfaction.

Something accepted in substitution

The term *substituted performance* is used to describe the transaction if what the obligee accepts is a performance, whether offered by the obligor or a third party. An example is an obligee's taking goods in satisfaction of a debt. As long as the performance differs in some way from what is due — as does a "horse, hawk, or robe" — there is consideration for the discharge.[2]

Substituted performance

The term *substituted contract* is used to describe the transaction if what the obligee accepts is a promise, whether offered by the obligor or a third party. An example is an obligee's taking a promise to deliver goods in satisfaction of a debt. Again, as long as the promised performance differs in some way from what is due, there is consideration for the discharge.[3]

Substituted contract

The term *novation* is used to describe a substituted contract that discharges a duty by adding a party who was neither the obligor nor the obligee of that duty.[4] The party added may be an obligor, as when a creditor takes a third party's promise to pay in satisfaction of the debt. Since the promise is that of a third party, it differs from the existing duty and is consideration for the discharge of that duty, even if the promised performance is only part of that owed by the original debtor.[5] The party added may instead be an obligee, as when the original creditor takes the debtor's promise to pay a third party in satisfaction of the debt. Since the promise is one to render performance to a third party, it,

Novation

---

§4.24   [1] For the sake of simplicity, the terminology used in the Restatement Second is followed here.

[2] *See* Restatement Second §278. If performance is by a third party, even part performance will suffice. See the discussion of part performance by a third party in §4.23 *supra*. The obligee has, however, a power to refuse performance by a third party by disclaimer, a power analogous to that of a contract beneficiary. See the discussion of disclaimer by a beneficiary in §10.3 *infra*. For the origin of the phrase quoted in text, see the discussion of techniques to avoid the rule in §4.21 *supra*.

[3] *See* Restatement Second §279.

[4] *See* Restatement Second §280. It is probably too late in the day to question the utility of the term, given the confusion that it has engendered. Sometimes *novation* is used to refer to any substituted contract, a usage not followed by the Restatement Second.

Transactions more complex than the simple novations described here, some involving more than three parties, are possible and are sometimes called "compound" novations.

[5] Pink v. Busch, 691 P.2d 456 (Nev. 1984) ("novation may be inferred by the creditor's acceptance of part performance from the new obligors").

too, differs from the existing duty and is consideration for the discharge of that duty, even if the promised performance is only part of that owed to the original creditor.[6]

Effect of substituted contract

The effect of a substituted contract is to discharge the original duty and to replace it with a new duty based on the substituted contract. The obligee, therefore, has no right to enforce the original duty, even on breach by the obligor of the substituted contract. The obligee is confined to its remedies under the substituted contract that has replaced that duty.[7] If, for example, a creditor takes a debtor's promise to deliver goods in satisfaction of the debt, and the debtor does not deliver the goods, the creditor's only remedy is for breach of the substituted contract to deliver goods. The creditor has given up the right to enforce the debt. When an earlier contract is completely replaced by a new contract in this way, the earlier contract is sometimes said to be "merged" into the later one.[8]

Accord

If the obligee is unwilling to give up its rights on the original duty until the obligor has actually performed the new promise, the obligee can make what is called an *accord*, rather than a substituted contract. An accord is a contract under which the obligee promises to accept a stated performance in satisfaction of the obligor's existing duty. If, for example, a creditor promises to take the debtor's delivery of goods in satisfaction of the debt, and the debtor promises to deliver the goods, there is an accord.[9] Not until performance, which is called *satisfaction*, however, is the original duty discharged. Discharge in this way is therefore said to be by *accord and satisfaction*. Until satisfaction by performance, the original duty is suspended and cannot be enforced by the obligee. If satisfaction is not forthcoming when it is due, the obligee has a

---

[6]The situation described here is distinguishable from that treated in the discussion of a duty to a third party in §4.21 *supra*. There an obligor, already under an existing duty to render performance to an obligee, makes a new promise to a third party to render the same performance to the obligee. In the novation described here, the new promise is to render performance to the third party.

[7]Haskins Law Firm v. American Natl. Property & Casualty Co., 304 Ark. 684, 804 S.W.2d 714 (1991) ("upon the execution of a valid and legally substituted agreement the original agreement merges into it and is extinguished, and failure to perform the substituted agreement will not revive the old agreement").

[8]Superior Concrete Pumping v. David Montoya Constr., 773 P.2d 346 (N.M. 1989) ("one contract will not merge into the other unless it is plainly shown such was the intent").

[9]This is a typical accord, in which the consideration for the obligee's promise to accept the new performance in satisfaction of the duty is the obligor's return promise to render that performance. An accord may also take the form of an option contract, in which the obligee's promise to accept the new performance in satisfaction is made enforceable in some other way, as by the payment of a nominal sum, and the obligor has the option of rendering that performance but does not promise to do so. *See* Restatement Second §281 illus. 2. There is no accord if the obligee does nothing more than make a revocable offer to accept the new performance in satisfaction of the duty, although the duty may be discharged if the performance is rendered before the offer is revoked.

choice. The obligee may enforce either the original duty or the accord.[10] In the example given, the obligee could either sue on the original debt or sue for breach of the contract to deliver goods. An accord, like a substituted contract, may bring in a new party. A common example of such an accord is a composition among creditors, under which each creditor of the embarrassed debtor agrees to accept part payment as full satisfaction in consideration of the similar promises of other creditors.[11]

Whether a contract is an accord or a substituted contract is a question of interpretation, subject to the general rules that apply to such questions.[12] In resolving doubts in this regard, a court will be less likely to suppose that an obligee was willing to accept a mere promise in satisfaction of an original duty that was clear than in satisfaction of one that was doubtful. It will therefore be less likely to find a substituted contract and more likely to find an accord if the original duty was one to pay money, if it was undisputed, if it was liquidated, and if it was matured.[13] A creditor owed an unquestioned debt that is already due is unlikely to assent to a substituted contract that discharges that debt in return for the debtor's promise to deliver goods in the future; the creditor is more likely to assent to an accord that will allow the creditor to enforce the debt if the goods are not forthcoming.

Question of interpretation

Instead of compromising or liquidating a disputed or unliquidated debt by a substituted contract or an accord, a debtor and creditor may merely reach an understanding in the nature of a computation. A manifestation by both parties to a stated sum as an accurate computation of the debt may result in an *account stated*. An account stated must be founded upon previous transactions that have given rise to the relation of debtor and creditor. It is usually based on a

Account stated

---

[10]Watkins v. Williams, 877 P.2d 19 (Mont. 1994) ("accord was not satisfied because [drawers] stopped payment" on check and refused to tender another). *See* Restatement Second §281. The term *executory accord* is sometimes used to underscore the point that the accord itself does not discharge the duty. It also reflects an historical anachronism, now generally rejected, under which an unperformed accord was not a defense to an action on the underlying duty.

[11]Under the usage suggested in Restatement Second §280, the word *novation* is reserved for a substituted contract that brings in a new party, and is not used to describe an accord that brings in a new party.

[12]McFaden v. Nordblom, 30 N.E.2d 852 (Mass. 1940); Johnson v. Utile, 472 P.2d 335 (Nev. 1970).

UCC 3-310(b) provides that, unless otherwise agreed, when a creditor takes a debtor's personal check in satisfaction of an obligation, "the obligation is suspended" to that extent "until dishonor of the check or until it is paid or certified," and if it is dishonored "the obligee may enforce either the instrument [i.e., the check] or the obligation." This section, in effect, lays down a rule of interpretation under which, in the absence of contrary agreement, a personal check is regarded as an accord rather than a substituted contract. (It lays down a different rule for a check on which a bank is liable, such as a cashier's or a certified check.)

[13]*See* Restatement Second §279 cmt. *c*, and §281 cmt. *e*. The Restatement Second abandons the rule of the first Restatement §419, which stated a rule of interpretation in this regard. A debt is described as "disputed" if its existence is contested, "unliquidated" if its amount is contested, and "unmatured" if payment is not yet due.

number of items and, if each party is indebted to the other, may be founded on the difference between their indebtedness. Opinions have differed as to the effect of an account stated on the existing debt. The first Restatement reflected Williston's view that the account discharged that debt, creating a new debt in its place.[14] The Restatement Second, however, takes the view that an account stated "does not itself discharge any duty" and is merely "an admission by each party of the facts asserted and a promise by the debtor to pay according to its terms."[15] For a discharge, a substituted contract or an accord must be found.[16] However, because it is usually the creditor that submits the statement of account to the debtor, it is usually the creditor that invokes the doctrine and the dispute goes not to the debtor's discharge but to the debtor's liability.[17] The debtor's retention of the statement without objection for an unreasonably long time operates as a promise to pay according to the terms of the account.[18] This promise may then be enforceable as a promise to pay an antecedent debt[19] or as a result of the creditor's reliance.[20]

Other forms with consideration

In the transactions described so far, the consideration for the discharge of the duty consists of a performance or a promise that is accepted by the obligee in satisfaction of that duty. There are three other forms of consensual transactions for the discharge of duties in which the consideration is of a different sort. These forms can be described as agreement of rescission, release, and contract not to sue.

Agreement of rescission

An *agreement of rescission* is limited to the discharge of contract duties. The parties to a bilateral contract that is at least partly unperformed on each side may agree to a discharge of all remaining duties of performance on both sides. Under an agreement of rescission, consideration is provided by each party's

---

[14] Restatement §422. *See* 3 S. Williston, Contracts §1862 (1st ed. 1920).

[15] Restatement Second §282. This reflect's Corbin's view. *See* 6 A. Corbin, Contracts §1314 (1962).

[16] *See* Eimco-BSP Serv. Co. v. Valley Inland Pac. Constructors, 626 F.2d 669 (9th Cir. 1980) ("there is no absolute rule against settling an unliquidated claim through an account stated" but the parties must "expressly agree to reduce the unliquidated claim to a definite amount").

[17] For an exception, *see* Zinn v. Fred R. Bright Co., 76 Cal. Rptr. 663 (Ct. App. 1969) (debtor employer "rendered the account by issuing its check" and employee's assent was implied though he died before presenting check for payment).

[18] Stan's Lumber v. Fleming, 538 N.W.2d 849 (Wis. App. 1995) ("evidence in this case demonstrates a classic account stated scenario" where seller regularly sent bills that were not disputed by buyer).

On acceptance by silence in general, see §3.15 *supra*. The party sending a statement cannot impose a time on the recipient merely by a clause on the statement reciting that objections must be made within that time.

[19] As to the doctrine of consideration and a promise to pay an antecedent debt, see the discussion of the scope of the exception in §2.8 *supra*.

[20] *See* Restatement Second §282 cmt. *c* (promise may "become binding as the result of reliance under the rule stated in §90" or "as a promise to pay an antecedent indebtedness under the rule stated in §82").

discharge of the other's remaining duties, regardless of the fairness of this exchange.[21] If one party has fully performed, so that it owes no remaining duties that can be discharged as consideration for the discharge of the other party's remaining duties, no agreement of rescission is possible. For an agreement of rescission, the parties need not use the word *rescission*. The agreement may even be inferred from conduct — like an implied-in-fact contract — if it indicates mutual abandonment.[22] If a party has already rendered some performance of the contract, a question arises as to whether the party is entitled to compensation, either by way of restitution or at the contract rate, for that performance. This is a question of interpretation to be determined on the facts of each case.[23]

The term *release* has traditionally been reserved for a formal written statement reciting that the obligor's duty is immediately discharged, although it has sometimes been used more loosely to refer to any consensual discharge.[24] Such writings are often used for the discharge of tort as well as contract duties. A release was traditionally made under seal, and in some jurisdictions the statute that generally deprives the seal of its effect does not apply to releases under seal.[25] A release may also be supported by consideration or by the obligor's reliance. If it is assumed that the parties intend to treat a release as a formal instrument, it should be subject to the same requirement of delivery as a contract under seal.[26]

Release

Sometimes, however, the obligee does not manifest an intention to discharge the obligor, but instead makes a contract under which the obligee promises not to sue the obligor. Such an agreement is called a *contract not to sue*.[27] A

Contract not to sue

---

[21] *See* Restatement Second §283. *Agreement of rescission* is preferable to *rescission*, since the latter term is sometimes used to refer to the exercise by one party of a power of avoidance (e.g., "rescind on grounds of fraud"). It is preferable to *contract of rescission*, since that term would exclude transactions in which there is no promise but only an immediate discharge on both sides. An agreement of "partial rescission," which would discharge less than all the parties' remaining duties of performance, is best treated as a modification. See the discussion of techniques to avoid the rule in §4.21 *supra*.

[22] Admiral Plastics Corp. v. Trueblood, Inc., 436 F.2d 1335 (6th Cir. 1971) (where both parties are in breach, "mutual delinquency gives rise to the presumption of mutual assent to a rescission").

[23] Copeland Process Corp. v. Nalews, Inc., 312 A.2d 576 (N.H. 1973) (involves "interpretation of the terms of the agreement of rescission").

[24] *See* Restatement Second §284. It seems useful to preserve the traditional usage since such writings are frequently used. In the narrow sense, a promise to discharge in the future an existing duty merely creates a new duty that can itself be discharged by the parties and is not a release. And a purported release of a duty that does not yet exist is not a release but a promise to discharge a duty in the future. However, no words of art are required for a release.

[25] *See* Restatement Second ch. 4, topic 3, statutory note. See also the statutes cited in the discussion of outright rejection of the rule in §4.25 *infra*, making a written release effective without consideration. A release is usually authenticated by a signature.

[26] See the discussion of the availability of the action of covenant in §2.16 *supra*.

[27] *See* Restatement Second §285. "Contract not to sue" is preferable to the more traditional "covenant not to sue," to avoid any suggestion that it must be under seal.

contract not to sue the obligor for a limited time bars an action to enforce the duty during that time. A contract never to sue the obligor discharges the obligor immediately, in spite of its terms, in order to avoid circuity of action.[28]

We look now at the forms of transactions that involve exceptions to the requirement that a discharge be supported by consideration.

Effect of dissatisfaction with rule

§4.25. Discharge Unsupported by Consideration. As has already been pointed out, much criticism has been heaped on the pre-existing duty rule when it has been applied to prevent the settlement of claims, as in the case of *Foakes v. Beer*.[1] In the wake of this dissatisfaction, courts have sometimes evaded the rule as applied to settlements by characterizing the transaction as not involving a promise, thus making consideration irrelevant. And in a few states courts or legislatures have flatly rejected the rule, at least in this context.

Theory of gift

A particularly appealing basis for evasion is the law of property governing gifts. A gift of tangible personal property, such as a horse, is irrevocable upon delivery, and consideration is irrelevant because there is a completed transfer.[2] The temptation to build on this simple example has proved irresistible to courts disenchanted with the rule of *Foakes v. Beer*. Suppose, for example, that a seller is under a duty to deliver a horse to a buyer that is under a duty to pay for it. If the seller says on delivering the horse but before payment that this is done as a gift, the seller's statement will be given effect. Because there has been a delivery of the horse, the buyer's duty to pay for it is discharged.[3] Consideration is irrelevant. Or if, before the seller delivers the horse but after payment, the buyer should tell the seller to keep it as a gift, the buyer's statement will be given effect. Although there has been no delivery of the horse, it would have been a simple matter for the seller to have delivered the horse to the buyer under the contract and for the buyer to have redelivered the horse to the seller as a gift. Since the law does not insist on the formality of delivery and redelivery, the seller's duty to deliver the horse is discharged.[4] Consideration is again irrelevant.

Delivery of writing

Since a creditor's right is intangible, the creditor cannot ordinarily make a gift of it to the debtor by delivery. However, some rights are so bound up

---

[28]Otherwise the obligee could sue and recover from the obligor, in breach of the contract not to sue, and the obligor could then recover the same amount from the obligee in an action for breach of that contract. In the case of co-obligors, a contract not to sue one co-obligor bars levy of execution on the promisee's property during the agreed time, but it does not bar an action or the recovery of judgment against any of the co-obligors. *See* Restatement Second §§295, 285(3) & cmt. *b*.

§4.25 [1]See the discussion of the rule in Foakes v. Beer in §4.23 *supra*. *See generally* E. Farnsworth, Changing Your Mind ch. 15 (1998).

[2]See the discussion of the rule for a completed gift contrasted in §2.5 *supra*.

[3]*See* Restatement Second §275, which extends the rule to the furnishing of services as well as to transfers of real and personal property.

[4]*See* Restatement Second §276.

in a writing that a delivery of the writing is regarded as delivery of the right that it represents. Before the abolition of the seal, if the creditor surrendered to the debtor a sealed instrument representing a debt with the intention of discharging the debt, the surrender had that effect.[5] This holds true today for a negotiable instrument, such as a promissory note, which can also be discharged by surrender.[6] The Restatement Second states the rule broadly so as to apply to any "writing of a type customarily accepted as a symbol or as evidence of [the obligee's] right."[7] The creditor can also discharge the debt without surrendering the writing if the creditor cancels or destroys it with the intention of discharging the debt.[8]

A few cases have gone so far as to apply this reasoning to a right that is not bound up in a writing. In one notable example, a seller, who was owed over $800 for goods sold, took a dollar from the buyer, noted on his books a "gift to balance account as to the rest, and gave the buyer a receipt 'in full.'" The New York Court of Appeals held that the requirement of delivery had been met, and "the gift of the debt was valid," even though the writing that was delivered was not evidence of the debt but of the discharge.[9] Few courts have, however, been willing so to distort the rules applicable to gifts.

Extension if no writing

The courts of Minnesota and New Hampshire have faced the problem directly. They have flatly rejected the rule of *Foakes v. Beer* and along with it the pre-existing duty rule as a whole. In those states a creditor can, by accepting part payment, discharge in full a debt that is undisputed and liquidated.[10] In a small number of states, a sealed release still retains its traditional effect.[11] A few other states have enacted statutes that make a writing a substitute for consideration in discharging a debt, giving the writing the effect that a sealed release had at common law.[12] Furthermore, the occasional state statutes mentioned

Outright rejection of rule

---

[5] *See* Restatement Second §274.

[6] UCC 3-604(a)(i) (person entitled to enforce instrument may discharge obligation of party to pay it "by an intentional voluntary act, such as surrender of the instrument").

[7] Restatement Second §279. For a comparable rule as to assignments, see the discussion of comparison with the delivery of a chattel in §11.6 *infra*. To the extent that the rules on discharge differ from those on assignments, a creditor's purported "assignment" of the debt to the debtor should be treated as an attempted discharge.

[8] *See* Restatement Second §279. *Cf.* UCC 3-604(a)(i) (cancellation or destruction of negotiable instrument).

[9] Gray v. Barton, 55 N.Y. 68 (1873).

[10] In Minnesota the rejection was presaged by dictum in Rye v. Phillips, 282 N.W. 459 (Minn. 1938) (creditor accepted livestock and cash in full satisfaction of debt), and confirmed by an alternative holding in Winter Wolff & Co. v. Co-op Lead & Chem. Co., 111 N.W.2d 461 (Minn. 1961) (creditor accepted debtor's check in full satisfaction of debt). In New Hampshire the rule was rejected in Frye v. Hubbell, 68 A. 325 (N.H. 1907) (mortgagee accepted part payment in full satisfaction of mortgage debt).

[11] See the discussion of a release in §4.24 *supra*.

[12] *See* Cal. Civ. Code §1524 ("part performance . . . expressly accepted . . . in writing, in satisfaction").

earlier, which abrogate the pre-existing duty rule by making a signed writing a substitute for consideration in connection with modifications, apply to cases of discharge as well.[13] It is doubtful that UCC 2-209(1), which abolishes the pre-existing duty rule in contracts for the sale of goods, also applies to cases of discharge as well as of modification.[14]

Remaining restraints

Even where the pre-existing duty rule is abolished in connection with discharge of a duty, there remain the restraints imposed by the rules on duress and undue influence, along with the duty to act in good faith.[15] Lest the reader's sympathy for "poor" and "weak" debtors, such as tenants paying rent and consumers paying for goods, obscure the full dimensions of the problem, it should be recalled that there are also "overreaching" debtors, such as tortfeasors and insurance companies settling claims and employers paying wages. Viewed from this perspective, the possibility of discharge by the creditor's oral statement, without more, poses obvious perils not unlike those inherent in the enforcement of gift promises. The compromise adopted by statutes that give effect to a written discharge may thus be justified if the required formality is thought to have a sufficient evidentiary and cautionary effect.[16]

Duties to pay damages

The discussion, up to this point, has treated alike duties of all kinds. Courts have, however, been somewhat more willing to uphold the discharge without consideration of a duty if the duty is one to pay damages for breach, rather than a duty of performance. The term *renunciation* is sometimes used to describe the obligee's surrender of its rights against the obligor after breach.

Renunciation at common law

Although the limits of renunciation at common law are far from clear, a number of cases support discharge of a duty to pay damages for partial breach of contract by a renunciation, written or oral, by the obligee on acceptance from the obligor of some performance under the contract.[17] If, for example, an owner, on taking delivery of a house, tells the builder that the owner will not hold the builder responsible for stated defects in performance, the builder's

---

[13] See the discussion of legislative reform in §4.22 *supra*. Both the Michigan and New York statutes cited there say "to change or modify, or to discharge."

[14] UCC 2-209(1) says only "modifying," while (2) and (4) speak of "modification or rescission." The comparable language of Restatement Second §89 is "modifying a duty under a contract not fully performed on either side."

[15] The meaning of good faith in this context, however, is far from clear. It can scarcely mean that there must be a good faith dispute, for this would amount to a return to the pre-existing duty rule. And if failure to act in good faith amounts to duress in such a case, as is suggested in the discussion of a threat to break the contract in §4.17 *supra*, the duty to act in good faith would appear to add little to the doctrine of duress.

[16] On the functions of formalities, see the discussion of the decline of the seal in §2.16 *supra*.

[17] See Restatement Second §277(2) ("A renunciation by the obligee on his acceptance from the obligor of some performance under a contract discharges without consideration a duty to pay damages for a breach that gives rise only to a claim for damages for partial breach of contract."). Under UCC 2-607(3)(a), a buyer's failure to notify the seller of breach "within a reasonable time after he discovers or should have discovered" it discharges without consideration the seller's duty to pay damages.

duty to pay damages for those defects may be held to be discharged without consideration by the owner's renunciation.[18]

The common law rules have become less significant with the enactment of the Uniform Commercial Code, which provides a simple method of renunciation. Under UCC 1-306, "A claim or right arising out of an alleged breach may be discharged in whole or in part without consideration by a agreement of the aggrieved party in an authenticated record." Because this section is in Article 1 of the Code, its applicability is not limited to contracts for the sale of goods.[19] Furthermore, an analogous provision has found its way into the Restatement Second.[20]

Renunciation under the Code

Our attention shifts now to the questions raised by some more recent techniques for policing agreements.

E. CONTEMPORARY CONTROLS

§4.26. Standardized Agreements. Traditional contract law was designed for a paradigmatic agreement that had been reached by two parties of equal bargaining power by a process of free negotiation. Today, however, in routine transactions the typical agreement consists of a standard form containing terms prepared by one party and assented to by the other with little or no opportunity for negotiation. Commonplace examples range from automobile purchase orders and credit card agreements to confirmations for goods ordered over the telephone and license agreements for software acquired online. Sometimes basic terms relating to quality, quantity, and price are negotiable. But the standard terms the standard terms — the *boilerplate*[1] — are not subject to bargain. They must simply be adhered to if the transaction is to go forward.

Use of standard forms

As with goods, standardization and mass production of contracts may serve the interest of both parties. Since standard forms can be tailored to fit office routines and mechanical equipment, they simplify operations and reduce costs. The product of the skilled drafter becomes available throughout the enterprise and frees sales and office personnel from responsibility for contract terms.

Advantages of standardization

---

[18] Renunciation may also be inferred from conduct. Kandalis v. Paul Pet Constr. Co., 123 A.2d 345 (Md. 1956) (failure by purchasers of house to object to defects when they accepted deed "waived" defects if they were visible).

[19] If UCC 2-209(1) were applied to cases of discharge as well as of modification, the impact of UCC 1-306 would be unclear. See the discussion of outright rejection of the rule *supra*.

[20] Restatement Second §277(1). The Restatement Second, in contrast to the Code, speaks only of "renunciation" and not of "waiver." The Code's use of the term *waiver* is unfortunate, since it suggests excuse of a condition rather than discharge of a duty to pay damages. Waiver is discussed in §§8.5, 8.19 *infra*.

§4.26 [1] From the iron or steel plates assembled to make a boiler.

Because a judicial interpretation of one standard form serves as an interpretation of similar forms, standardization facilitates the accumulation of experience. It helps to make risks calculable and, as one scholar put it, "increases that real security which is the necessary basis of initiative and the assumption of tolerable risks."[2] A leading commentator on the phenomenon wrote:

> It is to be noted that uniformity of terms of contracts typically recurring in a business enterprise is an important factor in the exact calculation of risks. Risks that are difficult to calculate can be excluded altogether. Unforeseeable contingencies affecting performance, such as strikes, fire, and transportation difficulties can be taken care of . . . . Standardized contracts have thus become an important means of excluding or controlling the [danger that a court or jury will be swayed by "irrational factors" to decide against a powerful defendant]. In this respect they are a true reflection of the spirit of our time with its hostility to irrational factors in the judicial process, and they belong in the same category as codifications and restatements.[3]

Two types of imposition

Dangers are inherent in standardization, however, for it affords a means by which one party may impose terms on another unwitting or even unwilling party. Several circumstances facilitate this imposition. First, the party that proffers the form has had the advantage of time and expert advice in preparing it, almost inevitably producing a form slanted in its favor. Second, the other party is usually completely or at least relatively unfamiliar with the form and has scant opportunity to read it—an opportunity often diminished by the use of fine print and convoluted clauses. Third, bargaining over terms of the form may not be between equals or, as is more often the case, there may be no possibility of bargaining at all. The form may be used by an enterprise with such disproportionately strong economic power that it simply dictates the terms. Or the form may be a take-it-or-leave-it proposition, often called a *contract of adhesion*,[4] under which the only alternative to complete adherence is outright rejection.[5] It would, indeed, defeat the purpose of standardization if the other party were free to negotiate over its terms. This impact of the phenomenon of standardization in reducing the possibility of negotiation over terms has prompted one observer to suggest that, in contrast to the "movement *from*

[2]Cohen, The Basis of Contract, 46 Harv. L. Rev. 553, 588 (1933).

[3]Kessler, Contracts of Adhesion — Some Thoughts About Freedom of Contract, 43 Colum. L. Rev. 629, 631-32 (1943).

[4]The term *contract of adhesion* was imported into the United States by Edwin Patterson, The Delivery of a Life-Insurance Policy, 33 Harv. L. Rev. 198, 222 (1919); *see* Patterson, The Interpretation and Construction of Contracts, 64 Colum. L. Rev. 833, 856-57 (1964). It was coined as *"contrat d'adhésion"* in R. Saleilles, De la déclaration de volonté 229 (1901).

[5]Disproportionately strong economic power is not necessary to the dictation of terms on a take-it-or-leave-it basis, as is illustrated when a large corporation, in order to park its truck, adheres to the terms of a small operator of a parking lot.

Status to Contract" that Sir Henry Maine detected in 1861,[6] there is now a "distinct veering back to status."[7]

Courts steeped in traditional contract doctrine have not been receptive to the argument that a party should be relieved of an agreement on the grounds of such imposition. A party that signs an agreement is regarded as manifesting assent to it and may not later complain about not having read or understood it, even if the agreement is on the other party's standard form. Since the requirement of bargain under the bargain theory of consideration is plainly met by simple adherence, the doctrine of consideration offers no ground for such relief. And since the objective theory of contracts imposes no requirement that one intend or even understand the legal consequences of one's actions, one is not entitled to relief merely because one neither read the standard form nor considered the legal consequence of adhering to it. As Maryland's highest court put it, "the law presumes that a person knows the contents of a document that he executes and understands at least the literal meaning of its terms."[8] This principle has been applied to standard forms,[9] and it has been adhered to even when the party seeking to be relieved of the agreement is poorly educated or illiterate.[10] Nevertheless, in hard cases, courts have strained to avoid applying this principle and, in doing so, they have developed several techniques.

Traditional response

One of these techniques is to interpret the language of the term to favor the weaker party. In a representative case from the Supreme Court of Pennsylvania, a tenant in an apartment building, who was injured in a fall on the lawn, sued the owner for negligent maintenance. The owner relied on a clause in the lease that excluded liability for injury arising out of the tenant's use of "elevators, hatches, openings, stairways, fire escapes, hallways . . . or . . . sidewalks," but that did not specifically mention lawns. The court interpreted the clause strictly against the owner, noting that "a lawn and a sidewalk are clearly different locations."[11] The technique of interpretation is aided by rules under which terms are generally interpreted against the drafter,[12] and separately negotiated terms are given greater weight than standardized terms and handwritten

1. Interpretation of terms

---

[6] H. Maine, Ancient Law 170 (1861), quoted in the discussion of slow growth for two centuries in §1.7 *supra*.

[7] Isaacs, The Standardizing of Contracts, 27 Yale L.J. 34, 40 (1917), quoted in the discussion of reversal of the trend toward freedom of contract in §1.7 *supra*.

[8] Merit Music Serv. v. Sonneborn, 225 A.2d 470, 474 (Md. 1967) (handwritten clauses added to standard form lease signed by tavern owners).

[9] Heller Fin. v. Midwhey Powder Co., 883 F.2d 1286 (7th Cir. 1989) (no reason to treat "adhesion contracts or form contracts differently").

[10] Mitchell Nissan, Inc. v. Foster, 775 So. 2d 138 (Ala. 2000) (car buyer with "only a sixth-grade reading level" was bound by arbitration clause where he "did not tell a representative of [seller] that he was unable to read or to understand any portion of the contract").

As to fraud, see the discussion of failure to read a writing in §4.14 *supra*.

[11] Galligan v. Arovitch, 219 A.2d 463, 464, 465 (Pa. 1966).

[12] See the discussions of *contra proferentem* and of standardized agreements in §7.11 *infra*.

or typed terms greater weight than printed ones.[13] Karl Llewellyn, however, pointed out the shortcomings of this technque, for it invites "the draftsman to recur to the attack. Give him time, and he will make the grade." Furthermore, it does "not face the issue" and fails "to accumulate either experience or authority in the needed direction: that of marking out for any given type of transaction what the *minimum decencies* are which a court will insist upon." Because it is a tool "of intentional and creative misconstruction" that purports to interpret but does not really do so, it seriously embarrasses "later efforts at true construction, later efforts to get at the true meaning of . . . wholly legitimate contracts and clauses," resulting in "unnecessary confusion and unpredictability. . . . Covert tools are never reliable tools."[14]

2. Writing not an offer

A second judicial technique in dealing with standard forms is to refuse to hold a party to the entire *form* on the ground that it was not of a type that would reasonably appear to the recipient to contain the terms of a proposed contract. Even under the objective theory, it can be reasoned that such a writing is not an offer at all. As a New York court said of a claim check given to a patron by a railroad's parcel checking service, "In the mind of the bailor the little piece of cardboard . . . did not arise to the dignity of a contract by which he agreed that in the event of the loss of the parcel, even through the negligence of the bailee itself, he would accept therefor a sum which perhaps would be but a small fraction of its actual value."[15] If there is no contract on the basis of the form, there is then one implied by the relationship of the parties in the absence of agreement. Even a sign calling attention to the effect of the writing or repeating its terms may not succeed, if not itself called to the customer's attention, in turning the writing into an offer or amounting to an offer itself.[16] The argument that the writing is not an offer is particularly compelling with respect to tickets, passes, and stubs but is unlikely to carry the day as to writings, such as steamship tickets, insurance policies, and warehouse receipts, that can reasonably be expected to contain contractual terms.[17]

3. Term not part of the offer

A third judicial technique in dealing with standard forms is to refuse to hold a party to an offensive *term* on the ground that, although the writing may plainly have been an offer, the term was not one that an uninitiated reader ought reasonably to have understood to be a part of that offer.[18] This result is especially easy to reach if the term is on the reverse side of the form

---

[13] See the discussion of more special rules in §7.11 *infra*.

[14] Llewellyn, Book Review, 52 Harv. L. Rev. 700, 702 (1939).

[15] Healy v. New York Cent. & Hudson River R.R., 138 N.Y.S. 287, 290 (App. Div. 1912), aff'd mem., 105 N.E. 1086 (N.Y. 1914).

[16] Berrios v. United Parcel Serv., 627 A.2d 701 (N.J. Super. 1992) ("majority of jurisdictions have held [parking ticket] limitations . . . to be ineffective where the motorist had not been aware of the liability limitation" and driver testified "she was unaware of any sign").

[17] D'Aloisio v. Morton's, Inc., 172 N.E.2d 819 (Mass. 1961) (customer bound by "storage receipt and contract" for mink coat that was not merely "means of identification").

[18] See the discussion of the role of interpretation in §3.28 *supra*.

and the reference, if any, to terms on the reverse side is itself in fine print or otherwise inadequate. In the colorful language of the Supreme Court of Pennsylvania:

> One of the most hateful acts of the ill-famed Roman tyrant Caligula was that of having the laws inscribed upon pillars so high that the people could not read them. Although the warrant of attorney [on the back of] the numerous sheets of the contract at bar was within the vision of the defendant, it was placed as to be completely beyond her contemplation of its purport.[19]

A similar technique has been used where the term was in a separate document, not attached to the signed writing but incorporated by a reference regarded by the court as insufficient.[20] The size of the type and other factors affecting legibility of both the reference and the term itself play an important part in determining whether a reference to a term makes it part of the contract.[21] One can well sympathize with the distinguished nineteenth-century New Hampshire judge who lamented, "Seldom has the art of typography been so successfully diverted from the diffusion of knowledge to the suppression of it."[22]

Statutes have reinforced these traditional judicial techniques. The Uniform Commercial Code sometimes requires that a term be "conspicuous," which it defines as being "so written, displayed, or presented that a reasonable person against which it is to operate ought to have noticed it."[23] Occasionally the Code requires that a term be "separately signed" as a protection against inadvertent incorporation.[24] UCC 2-316(1) provides that express warranties and

Statutory reinforcement

---

[19]Cutler Corp. v. Latshaw, 97 A.2d 234, 237 (Pa. 1953) (Musmanno, J.).

[20]In re Estate of Kokjohn, 531 N.W.2d 991 (Iowa 1995) ("common thread throughout these cases is a requirement that the reference be clear and specific").

[21]In Cutler Corp. v. Latshaw, *supra* note 19, the court stressed that the language "subject to conditions on reverse side" was in "small type" and that the clause on the reverse side was in "very small type." 97 A.2d at 235-36.

[22]DeLancy v. Insurance Co., 52 N.H. 581, 588 (1873) (Doe, J.).

[23]UCC 1-201(10); UCC-R 2-103(1)(b). UCC 1-201(10) goes on to set out several specific methods for making a term conspicuous, such as using type that is larger or contrasting in type, font, or color, but the ultimate test is "whether attention can reasonably be expected to be called" to the term. Cmt. 10. UCC-R 2-103(1)(b) states a special rule for situations where the sender of an electronic record intends "to evoke a response by an electronic agent." In that situation the presentation of the term must be capable of evoking a response from "a reasonably configured electronic agent." It goes on to state that an electronic record that is intended to evoke a response from an electronic agent is conspicuous if it is so placed that the "agent cannot proceed without taking action with respect to the particular term."

The determination of whether a term is conspicuous is "a decision for the court" under UCC 1-201(10).

[24]*See* UCC 2-205 (firm offer in "a form supplied by the offeree must be separately signed by the offeror"); UCC 2-209(2) ("except as between merchants," no-oral-modification clause in "a form supplied by the merchant must be separately signed by the other party"). See the discussion of *firm offers* under the Code in §3.23 *supra*.

disclaimers of warranties are to be "construed wherever reasonable as consistent with each other" but that the disclaimer "is inoperative to the extent that such construction is unreasonable."[25] UCC 2-316(2) explicitly requires that to exclude or modify the implied warranty of merchantability "the language must mention merchantability" and in the case of a writing or other record "must be conspicuous," and to exclude or modify any implied warranty of fitness the exclusion must be in a writing or other record and be "conspicuous," and UCC-R 2-316(2) also requires that a consumer contract include specific language in order to exclude of modify an implied warranty.[26] Scattered state statutes deal with such matters as the size of type,[27] and a few require that "plain language" be used.[28] The UNIDROIT Principles contain a provision under which a term contained in standard terms that could not reasonably have been expected must be expressly accepted to be effective.[29] Subsection (3) of Restatement Second §211, captioned "Standardized Agreements," states a more general rule under which, if "the other party has reason to believe that the party manifesting . . . assent would not do so if he knew that the writing contained a particular term, the term is not part of the agreement."[30] This is an exception to Subsection (1), which states that if "a party . . . signs or otherwise manifests assent to a writing and has reason to believe that like writings are regularly used to embody terms of agreements of the same type, he adopts the writing . . . with respect to the terms included in the writing." Although both the Restatement Second and the UNIDROIT Principles have provisions dealing with standard terms, revised Article 2, like original article 2, is silent on the subject.[31]

Terms coming too late

Furthermore terms may come too late if they are communicated only after a contract has been made. Thus writings dispensed by coin-operated machines have also been held to come too late to alter the terms of the contract already

---

[25] UCC 2-316(1).

[26] For the implied warranty of merchantability: "The seller undertakes no responsibility for the quality of the goods except as otherwise provided in this contract." For the implied warranty of fitness: "The seller assumes no responsibility that the goods will be fit for any particular purpose for which you may be buying these goods, except as otherwise provided in the contract."

[27] See N.Y.C.P.L.R. §4544 (portion of consumer contract printed in type smaller than stated size not admissible in evidence); Wis. Stat. Ann. §422.303(2) (consumer credit sale contract must use type of stated size).

[28] See N.Y. Gen. Oblig. L. 5-702 (consumer contracts up to $50,000 must be written "in a clear and coherent manner using words with common and every day meanings").

[29] UNIDROIT Principles 2.20 ("Surprising terms").

[30] Lauvetz v. Alaska Sales & Serv., 828 P.2d 162 (Alaska 1991) (adopting "the analysis of Section 211 with regard to standardized form agreements outside the insurance context").

[31] See Restatement Second §211, UNIDROIT Principles arts. 2.19 – 2.22. The Uniform Computer Information Transactions Act contains a definition of a *standard form* that is used, in turn, in defining a *mass market license*. UCITA §102(60) (*standard form* is one "containing terms prepared for repeated use" with "no negotiated change of terms" except for such matters as price and quantity), §102(43) (*mass market license* is "standard form used in mass market transaction").

made.[32] Courts have held that terms on an invoice received after a contract has been made are ineffective.[33]

On similar reasoning, the Third Circuit has held that a disclaimer of warranties on a "box top license" printed on packages of software acquired by a terminal manufacturer from a software producer came too late to be effective because a contract had already been formed by telephone orders confirmed by purchase orders before shipment.[34] The application of this reasoning to so-called "shrinkwrap" licenses, contained in plastic packaging of computers and software, has been controversial. The Seventh Circuit applied different reasoning to a case of a telephone sale of a boxed computer.

Shrink-wrap agreements

> A customer picks up the phone, orders a computer, and gives a credit card number. Presently a box arrives, containing the computer and a list of terms, said to govern unless the customer returns the computer within 30 days. Are these terms effective as the parties' contract, or is the contract term-free because the order-taker did not read any terms over the phone and elicit the customer's assent?

The court held that the consumer buyer was bound by an arbitration clause contained in the box even though there was no reference to them on the outside of the box. It was enough that the buyer could repack and return the computer after reading the terms if there were any objections to them. The contract was not concluded over the telephone. It was not concluded until the buyer accepted the seller's terms by failing to take action after delivery. Judge Frank Easterbrook noted that payment preceding the revelation of terms is common in such fields as air transportation and insurance, and gave the following justification for what appeared to be a departure from the traditional rules of offer and acceptance.

> Practical considerations support allowing vendors to enclose the full legal terms with their products. Cashiers cannot be expected to read legal documents to customers before ringing up sales. If the staff at the other end of the phone for direct-sales operations . . . had to read the four-page statement of terms before taking the buyer's credit card number, the droning voice would anesthetize rather than enlighten many potential buyers. Others would hang up in a rage over the waste of their time . . . . Customers as a group are better off when vendors skip

---

[32] Steven v. Fidelity & Cas. Co., 377 P.2d 284 (Cal. 1962) (insured not bound by restriction under air travel insurance sold through automatic vending machine since "he must purchase the policy before he even knows of its provisions").

[33] Even though a proposal for modification of a contract of sale needs no consideration under UCC 2-209(1) (see the discussion of legislative reform in §4.22 *supra*), terms so located are unlikely to be regarded as such a proposal. Diepeveen v. Larry Voight, Inc., 99 A.2d 329 (N.J. Super. 1953) (disclaimer on invoice ineffective when sent after oral contract of sale).

[34] Step-Saver Data Sys. v. Wyse Technology, 939 F.2d 91 (3d Cir. 1991). The court held that the disclaimer was not incorporated under UCC-O 2-207.

costly and ineffectual steps such as telephonic recitation, and use instead a simple approve-or-return device.[35]

Furthermore, reading the terms over the telephone would not avoid disputes over whether what had been read over the telephone corresponded to the contents of the writing. Revised Article 2 is silent with respect to terms on or in packaging and is not intended to take a position on these cases.[36]

Click-wrap agreements

Problems of assent have also begun to arise in agreements for the delivery of software programs to a computer or a disk. These have come to be known as a "clickwrap" (or "click-through") agreements because they typically present the user with a proposed electronic form agreement to which the user can assent by clicking on an icon identified for that purpose. There is no impediment to such an agreement as long as the traditional requirements for assent are met.[37] "Browsewrap" agreements, which typically provide that merely using a web site for the purchase of goods or services constitutes assent to terms available on the site, are more problematic. The Second Circuit has held that the mere act of downloading was not assent to an online software license agreement containing an arbitration clause. The court found that doing so was not a manifestation of assent where the users "were responding to an offer that did not carry an immediately visible notice of the existence of the license terms or require nonambiguous manifestation of assent to those terms."[38]

Problem of inequality

None of these traditional judicial techniques is adequate, at least in theory, to protect an unfortunate person who has actual knowledge — who realizes that the other party intends the writing to be a contract, who reads the terms that the other party means to include, or who understands how the other party would have them interpreted. This lack of equality between a person who is meticulous or who chances to have knowledge and a person who is blissfully unknowing is a patent point for dissatisfaction with all three techniques. The Restatement Second attempts to reduce the inequality by maintaining that a

---

[35] Hill v. Gateway 2000, 105 F.3d 1147, 1148, 1149 (7th Cir. 1997), following ProCD v. Zeidenberg, 86 F.3d 1447 (7th Cir. 1996) (Easterbrook, J.: "Notice on the outside, terms on the inside, and a right to return the software for a refund if the terms are unacceptable . . . may be a means of doing business valuable to buyers and sellers alike.").

See generally Einhorn, Shrink-Wrap Licenses: The Debate Continues, 38 Idea 383 (1998); Hillman Rolling Contracts, 71 Fordham L. Rev. 743 (2002); Hillman & Rachlinski, Standard-Form Contracting in the Electronic Age, 77 N.Y.U. L. Rev. 429 (2002); Maher, The Shrink-Wrap License: Old Problems in a New Wrapper, 34 J. Copyright Soc. 292 (1987); Radin, Humans, Computers, and Binding Commitment, 75 Ind. L.J. 1125 (2000).

[36] UCC-R 2-207 says nothing about such terms and does not pass on the reasoning in *Step-Saver,* under which the contract is made before delivery so that such terms would not be part of the contract unless incorporated by UCC-R 2-207 or the reasoning in *Hill,* under which a so-called "rolling contract" is not made until acceptance of the seller's terms after delivery.

[37] Caspi v. Microsoft Network, 732 A.2d 528 (N.J. Super 1999) (forum selection clause enforceable where potential subscriber could use services only after clicking "I agree").

[38] Specht v. Netscape Communications Corp., 306 F.3d 17, 31 (2d Cir. 2002).

standardized agreement "is interpreted wherever reasonable as treating alike all those similarly situated, without regard to their knowledge or understanding of the standard terms of the writing."[39] Nevertheless, the potential for such inequality is inherent in the rationale behind each of the three techniques.

This potential for inequality arises because each technique is based on a finding that assent is lacking—that there is no assent to be bound by the writing, no assent to be bound by particular terms of the writing, or no assent to the meaning of those terms advanced by the author of the writing. In a notable and trenchant criticism, Llewellyn attacked the traditional notion of assent as applied to standard forms:

Llewellyn on standardization

> Instead of thinking about "assent" to boiler-plate clauses, we can recognize that so far as concerns the specific, there is no assent at all. What has in fact been assented to specifically are the few dickered terms, the broad type of the transaction, and but one thing more. That one thing more is a blanket assent (not a specific assent) to any not unreasonable or indecent terms the seller may have on his form, which do not alter or eviscerate the reasonable meaning of the dickered terms.[40]

Judicial decisions that are overly protective of a weaker party may merely have the wasteful effect of encouraging the stronger party to make repeated revisions in response.

Llewellyn's points, that the traditional techniques were at least ostensibly unconcerned with fairness and that all of those techniques could be avoided by the clever drafter, are illustrated by *O'Callaghan v. Waller & Beckwith Realty Co.*, decided by the Supreme Court of Illinois in 1958. O'Callaghan was injured when she fell in the courtyard of her apartment building and sued her landlord. The landlord claimed that the action was barred by an exculpatory clause in the lease, and the court agreed. It observed that the clause "does not appear to be amenable to the strict construction to which such clauses are frequently subjected." The lessee argued that "due to a shortage of housing there is a disparity of bargaining power between lessors of residential property and their lessees that gives landlords an unconscionable advantage over tenants," but to this the court replied that there was no evidence that O'Callaghan was concerned about the clause or attempted to negotiate over it or to rent an apartment elsewhere. "The use of a form contract does not of itself establish disparity of bargaining power." The court noted that the housing shortage had "produced an active and varied legislative response" that suggested "that the legislature has taken all of the remedial action that it thought necessary or desirable," and that the legislature's imposition of rent control as part of its response "made it impossible for

Example of *O'Callaghan*

[39] Restatement Second §211(2). The impact of §211(3) is similar, since it appears to take no account of the actual knowledge of the assenting party: "Where the other party has reason to believe that the party manifesting such assent would not do so if he knew that the writing contained a particular term, the term is not part of the agreement."

[40] K. Llewellyn, The Common Law Tradition 370 (1960).

**Example of
Henningsen**

a lessor to negotiate for an increased rental in exchange for the elimination of an exculpatory clause . . . . In our opinion the subject is one that is appropriate for legislative rather than judicial action."[41] Two judges dissented.

A contrasting case in the search for a doctrine to deal with unfairness is *Henningsen v. Bloomfield Motors*, decided by the Supreme Court of New Jersey in 1960. Claus Henningsen bought a new car from a dealer. Ten days after it had been delivered, his wife Helen was injured when the steering mechanism failed while she was driving it. The Henningsens sued both the dealer and the manufacturer for breach of an implied warranty of merchantability. The defendants claimed that the warranty had been disclaimed by a provision on the back of the purchase order, among eight and one-half inches of fine print, which purported to disclaim liability for breach of warranty and substitute for it a warranty that defective parts would be replaced for a limited period. The court held that the Henningsens were not bound by the disclaimer. The court did not ignore traditional judicial techniques. It noted that, though the front of the purchase order referred to the terms on the back, the dealer "did not specifically call attention" to the clause, adding that, in any case, it could not as a matter of interpretation be concluded "that an ordinary layman would realize what he was relinquishing in return for what he was being granted." The main thrust of the court's opinion, however, went beyond these traditional techniques. The form, "a standardized form designed for mass use" by the Automobile Manufacturers Association whose members accounted for nearly all of the automobiles sold in the United States, "is imposed upon the automobile consumer" who "takes it or leaves it." The court continued:

> The status of the automobile industry is unique. Manufacturers are few in number and strong in bargaining position . . . . From the standpoint of the purchaser, there can be no arms length negotiating on the subject. Because his capacity for bargaining is so grossly unequal, the inexorable conclusion which follows is that he is not permitted to bargain at all. He must take or leave the automobile on the warranty terms dictated by the maker. He cannot turn to a competitor for better security.[42]

The clause was, therefore, invalid.

Further discussion of the problems involved in this landmark decision is deferred to the treatment of unconscionability that follows the next section.

Policing in equity

§4.27. Precursors of Unconscionability. Courts of equity did not share the reluctance of common law courts to police bargains for substantive unfairness. Though mere "inadequacy of consideration" alone was not a

---

[41] 155 N.E.2d 545, 546, 547 (Ill. 1958) (Schaefer, J.). Other states have reached contrary conclusions as to residential leases. Ransburg v. Richards, 770 N.E.2d 393 (Ind. App. 2002) (commercial lease cases are "not controlling in a case concerning a residential lease").

[42] 161 A.2d 69, 92, 87, 94 (N.J. 1960).

ground for withholding equitable relief,[1] a contract that was "inequitable" or "unconscionable" — one that was so unfair as to "shock the conscience of the court" — would not be enforced in equity.[2] In one such case, a man promised to give a 20 percent interest in all property that he might later acquire in Alaska in return for the promisee's payment of $1,000 and his cancellation of an $11,225 debt of questionable collectability. When the promisor acquired property worth over $750,000, the promisee sought specific performance. The Supreme Court of Missouri refused it. Though the fairness of the bargain was to be judged as of the time that the bargain was made,[3] in equity as at common law, here the "inadequacy of consideration" for the promise sought to be enforced was "so gross as to render the contract unconscionable."[4]

The case of *Campbell Soup Co. v. Wentz* has had a special impact, as will be seen in the next section. Campbell contracted with the Wentz brothers for the entire crop of Chantenay carrots to be grown on 15 acres of their farm during the season at a contract price of $30 a ton for January delivery. When adverse weather conditions made Chantenay carrots virtually unobtainable and drove the market price up to $90 a ton, the Wentzes began to sell their carrots to others. Campbell sought to enjoin these sales and to compel specific performance. The Third Circuit, reviewing the terms of the printed contract supplied by Campbell, concluded that it had "been drawn by skilful draftsmen with the buyer's interests in mind." Particularly offensive was a clause that excused Campbell from taking any carrots under stated circumstances considered as beyond its control, but prohibited the Wentzes from selling them elsewhere without the permission of Campbell. The court characterized this term as "carrying a good joke too far" and concluded that, even though the clause was irrelevant to the harshness complained of, the "sum total" of the contract provisions "drives too hard a bargain for a court of conscience to assist." The court denied relief with the explanation that "a party who has offered and succeeded in getting an agreement as tough as this one is, should not come to a chancellor and ask court help in the enforcement of its terms. That equity does not enforce unconscionable bargains is too well established to require elaborate citation."[5]

Example of Campbell Soup v. Wentz

---

§4.27 [1] Lord Eldon stated the traditional view: "Inadequacy of price is quite out of the question . . . . [U]nless the inadequacy of price is such as shocks the conscience . . . it is not itself a sufficient ground for refusing a specific performance." Coles v. Trecothick, 32 Eng. Rep. 592, 597 (Ch. 1804).

[2] See the discussion of discretionary limitations in §12.4 *infra.*

[3] Tuckwiller v. Tuckwiller, 413 S.W.2d 274 (Mo. 1967) (where woman with Parkinson's disease, aged 73, died some weeks after promising to devise a farm worth $34,400 in return for promise of lifetime care, contract was fair "viewed from the standpoint of the parties at the time of the agreement").

[4] Marks v. Gates, 154 F. 481, 483 (9th Cir. 1907).

[5] 172 F.2d 80, 83-84 (3d Cir. 1948). Under an arrangement between Campbell and the Wentzes, Campbell received all the carrots and paid $30 a ton to the Wentzes and paid $60 per ton into court pending the outcome of the litigation. As a result of the court's decision, the Wentzes received the

Significance of
factors other than
substance

The threshold for denial of equitable relief, however, defies precise formulation. One authority posited that a court may withhold equitable relief if "the contract itself is unfair, one-sided, unjust [or] unconscionable."[6] According to an English judge's much-quoted dictum, courts of equity would not enforce a bargain "such as no man in his senses and not under delusion would make on the one hand, and as no honest and fair man would accept on the other."[7] Usually, however, the bargain is infected with something more than substantive unfairness. It is typically mixed with an absence of bargaining ability that does not fall to the level of incapacity or with an abuse of the bargaining process that does not rise to the level of misrepresentation, duress, or undue influence. Often the bargain is obtained, as one writer put it, "by sharp and unscrupulous practices, by overreaching, by trickery, by taking undue advantage of [one's] position, by non-disclosure of material facts, or by . . . other unconscientious means."[8] Such circumstances have sometimes been characterized by the vague term *constructive fraud*.[9] Taken as a whole, the decisions that have refused to grant equitable relief on such grounds are consistent with the belief that persons of sound discretion who are not imposed upon are able to uphold their interests in the bargaining process.

Example of
*Woollums v.
Horsley*

Woollums v. Horsley is instructive in this regard. Horsley sued for specific performance of a contract by which Woollums was to sell him all the mineral rights in his Kentucky mountain farm of some 200 acres for 40 cents an acre, though these rights proved to have been worth closer to $15 an acre by the time of the trial. The Supreme Court of Kentucky denied specific performance, explaining, "Equity should not help out such a harsh bargain." But it also adverted to the abilities of the parties to bargain. Woollums was "about sixty years old, uneducated, afflicted with disease disabling him from work" and "knew but little of what was going on in the business world," while Horsley was "a man of large and varied experience in business, who was then buying mineral rights in that locality by the thousands of acres, and who was evidently familiar with all that was then going on . . . in that section." The court also noted some features of the bargaining process. Horsley "had a thorough knowledge of the [mineral value] of lands generally in that section, and of the developments then in progress or near at hand," including "the probability of the building of a railroad in that locality in the near future." But he assured Woollums "that he

---

full $90 a ton. The "skilful draftsmen" subsequently revised Campbell's form so that it withstood a similar challenge in Campbell Soup Co. v. Diehm, 111 F. Supp. 211 (E.D. Pa. 1952).

[6] J. Pomeroy, Equity Jurisprudence §1405a (5th ed. 1941).

[7] Lord Hardwicke in Earl of Chesterfield v. Janssen, 28 Eng. Rep. 82, 100 (Ch. 1750).

[8] J. Pomeroy, Equity Jurisprudence §1405a (5th ed. 1941).

[9] "By constructive frauds are meant such acts or contracts, as, though not originating in any actual evil design . . . to perpetuate a positive fraud . . . , are yet, by their tendency to deceive . . . other persons, or to violate . . . confidence, or to impair . . . the public interests, deemed equally reprehensible with positive fraud. . . ." 1 J. Story, Commentaries on Equity Jurisprudence §258 (1st ed. 1836).

would never be bothered by the contract during his life time" and "lulled [him] in the belief that the Rip Van Winkle sleep of that locality in former days was to continue."[10] Because equitable relief is most commonly sought in connection with transactions in land, most of the decisions denying equitable relief have, like *Woollums v. Horsley*, involved contracts for the sale of land, which one writer called "the only thing that relatively unsophisticated people have which is worth tricking them out of."[11]

In principle, denial of equitable relief leaves open the possibility of an award of damages in an action at law, though it seems that this alternative is not often pursued by suitors disappointed in equity.[12] Occasionally, courts have been persuaded to issue an equitable decree cancelling or rescinding the transaction, thus precluding relief at law as well as in equity. For example, the Supreme Court of Virginia held that a sister was entitled to a decree rescinding a deed to her brother of land containing timber worth over ten times the price of $275. The court found *constructive* fraud because of the 'confidential relationship' of the parties and the 'gross inadequacy in price,'" even though neither party had known of the presence of the timber at the time of the agreement.[13] Nevertheless, the general principle is that the standards for fairness of bargains that were fashioned in equity do not preclude the enforcement of bargains at law.[14]

In a few exceptional situations, however, common law courts came to accept equity's concern with substantive unfairness. One of these situations involved what are known as "fiduciary" relationships, such as those between trustee and beneficiary, principal and agent, or attorney and client. If a fiduciary made a contract with the beneficiary concerning matters within the scope of their relationship, courts of equity demanded that it be on fair terms and that the beneficiary's assent be with full knowledge of the facts and full understanding of the beneficiary's legal rights. This requirement was carried over into actions at law, and if such a bargain fails to meet these standards it is voidable, just as it would be for fraud or duress.[15] Other exceptions are the doctrine of undue influence[16] and the policy against forfeitures,[17] which also originated in

Availability of damages

Rare exceptions

---

[10]20 S.W. 781, 781, 782 (Ky. 1892). See the discussion of unfairness in §12.7 *infra*.

[11]Leff, Unconscionability and the Code — The Emperor's New Clause, 115 U. Pa. L. Rev. 485, 536 (1967) (arguing that real estate is special, not only because of the uniqueness of land, but because the agreement is likely to represent an economically significant "once-in-a-lifetime" transaction for one or both parties).

[12]See the discussion of the list of limitations in §12.7 *infra*.

[13]Jackson v. Seymour, 71 S.E.2d 181, 184 (Va. 1952).

[14]The classic case is Day v. Newman, 30 Eng. Rep. 36 (Ch. 1788) (relief denied both parties because the disadvantaged party "has no right to ask the Court to prevent the consequences of his own solemn act; but on the other hand, most certainly this is too hard a bargain for the Court to assist in").

[15]See Restatement Second §173.

[16]See §4.20 *supra*.

[17]See the discussion of the history as to penalties in §12.18 *infra*.

equity and were carried over into actions at law. In general, however, equitable concepts of fairness were confined to cases where relief was sought in equity.

The development of a general standard of fairness for law as well as equity had to await the advent of the Uniform Commercial Code.

UCC 2-302

§4.28.   Unconscionability. The equitable concept of unconscionability inspired one of the most innovative sections of the Uniform Commercial Code — UCC 2-302, which deals with unconscionable contracts and terms, provides in Subsection (1):

> If the court as a matter of law finds the contract or any clause of the contract to have been unconscionable at the time it was made the court may refuse to enforce the contract, or it may enforce the remainder of the contract without the unconscionable clause, or it may so limit the application of any unconscionable clause as to avoid any unconscionable result.[1]

Thus the Code recognizes a doctrine of unconscionability that is not limited to equity and that invites courts to police bargains overtly for unfairness instead of resorting to what Llewellyn called "covert tools."[2] In the words of the comments to the Code:

> This section is intended to enable courts to police explicitly against the contracts or clauses which they find to be unconscionable. In the past such policing has been accomplished by adverse construction of language, by manipulation of the rules of offer and acceptance or by determinations that the clause is contrary to public policy or to the dominant purpose of the contract.[3]

Llewellyn, who is credited with authorship of UCC 2-302, described it as "perhaps the most valuable section in the entire Code."[4] As scholars lavished more ink on this section than on any comparable passage in the Code,[5] the doctrine of unconscionability rapidly gained wide acceptance.

Application beyond sale of goods

Although UCC 2-302 is not one of the general articles of the Code and so strictly speaking governs only "transactions in goods," it has wisely been applied, either by analogy or as an expression of a general doctrine, to many other kinds of contracts,[6] including contracts that fall under other articles of the

---

§4.28 [1] UCC-O 2-302. UCC-R 2-302 replaces "clause" with "term."

[2] See the discussion of Llewellyn on standardization in §4.26 *supra*.

[3] UCC 2-302 cmt. 1.

[4] 1 N.Y.L. Revision Commn., Hearings on the Uniform Commercial Code 121 (1954).

[5] A provocative discussion of UCC 2-302 is Leff, Unconscionability and the Code — The Emperor's New Clause, 115 U. Pa. L. Rev. 485 (1967).

[6] Weaver v. American Oil Co., 276 N.E.2d 144 (Ind. 1971) ("Caveat lessee [of gas station lease] is no more the current law than caveat emptor. . . . The analogy is natural."); Zapatha v. Dairy Mart, 408 N.E.2d 1370 (Mass. 1980) (viewing legislative statements of policy on unconscionability "as fairly applicable to all aspects of the franchise agreement . . . by analogy.").

Code.[7] The Restatement Second contains a section on unconscionability patterned after the Code's and applicable to contracts generally,[8] and several
uniform laws contain similar provisions applicable to contracts within their
purview.[9] We begin our exploration of this doctrine with some observations on
the procedure for determining unconscionability.

UCC 2-302 makes it clear that the determination of unconscionability is
to be made by "the court as a matter of law" and not by a jury.[10] Because
unconscionability was historically a matter for equity where there was no jury,
it has been held that the Code does not deny a constitutional right to trial by
jury.[11] Under UCC 2-302(2):

> When it is claimed or appears to the court that the contract or any clause thereof
> may be unconscionable the parties shall be afforded a reasonable opportunity to
> present evidence as to its commercial setting, purpose and effect to aid the court
> in making the determination.[12]

It has therefore been held error for a court to preclude either party from
presenting such evidence by granting summary judgment when there are unre-
solved issues of fact relating to unconscionability.[13] The party asserting the
defense of unconscionability must prove it.[14] How is a court to determine
whether that proof has been made?

Nowhere among the Code's many definitions is there one of *unconscionability*. That the term is incapable of precise definition is a source of both strength

**Procedure for
determining
unconscionability**

**Lack of a
definition**

---

[7]Unico v. Owen, 232 A.2d 405 (N.J. 1967) (secured transaction under Article 9). *Contra:* In
re Advance Printing & Litho Co., 277 F. Supp. 101 (W.D. Pa.), aff'd, 387 F.2d 952 (3d Cir. 1967)
(secured transaction under Article 9); Hernandez v. S.I.C. Finance Co., 448 P.2d 474 (N.M. 1968)
(same). The article on leases has an unconscionability provision in UCC 2A-108. It would be
unfortunate if the addition of this provision were to discourage extension of UCC 2-302 to other
articles by analogy. For an example of the application of UCC 2-302 by analogy before its time
had come, see the discussion of the *Williams* case in note 22 *infra*.

[8]Restatement Second §208.

[9]*See* Uniform Consumer Credit Code §5.108; Uniform Consumer Sales Practices Act §4;
Uniform Land Transactions Act §1-311; Uniform Residential Landlord and Tenant Act §1.303.
See also N.Y. Real Prop. Law §235-c (leases of real property). Such statutes sometimes add detail
to the Code version. For examples, see note 52 *infra*.

[10]*See* UCC 2-302 cmt. 3 (the "section is addressed to the court, and the decision is to be made
by it").

[11]County Asphalt v. Lewis Welding & Engrg. Corp., 444 F.2d 372 (2d Cir. 1971) ("the
discretionary power to grant equitable relief according to the 'conscience' of the chancellor
was . . . unmistakably a matter for the equity side rather than the law side of the court").

[12]For the origins of the provision, *see* Leff, Unconscionability and the Code — The Emperor's
New Clause, 115 U. Pa. L. Rev. 485, 541-43 (1967).

[13]Luick v. Graybar Elec. Co., 473 F.2d 1360 (8th Cir. 1973) (error to grant summary judgment
against party claiming that clause was unconscionable since "he should be given a reasonable
opportunity to present evidence on this issue").

[14]Zapatha v. Dairy Mart, *supra* note 6 (franchisees "failed to sustain their burden of showing"
unconscionability.

and weakness. The comments to UCC 2-302 give only the most general guidance on the meaning of the term. They tell the reader that the "basic test is whether, in the light of the general commercial background and the commercial needs of the particular trade or case, the clauses involved are so one-sided as to be unconscionable under the circumstances existing at the time of the making of the contract."[15] The commentary then gives a series of examples based on pre-Code cases, confirming the reader's suspicion that the term is undefinable. UCC 2-302 does at least make it clear that any unfairness in the terms is to be judged at the time the contract is made and not at some later time.[16] The analogous provision of the UNIDROIT Principles on "gross disparity," in contrast, lists at least a few factors relevant to the determination of whether a contract or term "unjustifiably gave the other party an excessive advantage."[17]

Earlier equity cases not helpful

The most noted of these pre-Code cases is *Campbell Soup Co. v. Wentz*,[18] in which the court refused to grant equitable relief to a buyer of carrots. Though such equity cases may help to confirm the paternity of the unconscionability doctrine, they shed little light on the standards for determining unconscionability.[19] The typical equity cases involved suits for specific performance against vendors of land that complained of the harshness of the bargain as a whole.[20] Most of the UCC 2-302 cases involve actions for damages against buyers of goods that object to the unfairness of a particular clause in a form contract.

Example of *Williams v. Walker-Thomas*

A typical example is *Williams v. Walker-Thomas Furniture Co.*, decided by the federal Court of Appeals for the District of Columbia in 1965, an early but still notable application of the Code's unconscionability doctrine. Walker-Thomas sold Williams a $514 stereo set on credit, knowing that Williams received only a $218 monthly government check for herself and seven children and that she already owed the seller $164 for other items she had bought under similar contracts. Under the contract, the seller reserved a security interest in the stereo, with the right to repossess it if Williams defaulted. The controversy centered on a clause providing that, until her entire debt for all items purchased

---

[15] UCC 2-302 cmt. 1.

[16] Glopak Corp. v. United States, 851 F.2d 334 (Fed. Cir. 1988) ("fact that the actual application of the clause had an adverse effect . . . would not justify retroactively invalidating it as unconscionable"). That a different rule may apply to antenuptial agreements, *see* Newman v. Newman, 653 P.2d 728 (Colo. 1982) ("antenuptial agreement . . . may become voidable for unconscionability occasioned by circumstances existing at the time of the marriage dissolution"). *Contra:* Simeone v. Simeone, 581 A.2d 162 (Pa. 1990) (rejecting suggestion "that prenuptial agreements should be examined with regard to whether their terms remain reasonable").

[17] UNIDROIT Principles 3.10(1). However, these factors include, in addition to the nature and purpose of the contract, only taking unfair advantage of the other party.

[18] See the discussion of the example of Campbell Soup v. Wentz in §4.27 *supra*.

[19] For an especially strong expression of this view, *see* Leff, Unconscionability and the Code – The Emperor's New Clause, 115 U. Pa. L. Rev. 485, 537-38 (1967) (hope that "the mass of equity cases [will] help to define the kinds of contracts and contract clauses" that are unconscionable is "bootless").

[20] See the discussion of the example of Woollums v. Horsley in §4.27 *supra*.

was fully paid, any payments made would be spread "pro rata" over all outstanding accounts. The effect was to give the seller the right to repossess all the items if Williams failed to make a payment at any time before her entire debt for all of them was fully paid.[21] The court held that the trial judge erred in declining to determine whether the doctrine of unconscionability was applicable, and it remanded the case for such a determination.[22]

What, in the absence of a definition, have courts taken "unconscionability" to mean? The most durable answer is probably that of the court in *Williams v. Walker-Thomas*: "Unconscionability has generally been recognized to include an absence of meaningful choice on the part of one of the parties together with contract terms which are unreasonably favorable to the other party.[23] Over subsequent decades, there has been relatively little refinement of this description. Courts continue to focus on both "unreasonably favorable" terms and "an absence of meaningful choice." It has become fashionable to designate the former as "substantive" and the latter as "procedural" unconscionability.[24] Procedural unconscionability is broadly conceived to encompass not only the employment of sharp bargaining practices[25] and the use of fine print and convoluted language,[26] but a lack of understanding[27] and an inequality of bargaining power,[28] a term that is often used to include bargaining

Factors in determining unconscionability

---

[21] Such a clause is called a "dragnet" (or "anaconda") clause.

[22] 350 F.2d 445 (D.C. Cir. 1965). Though the contract was made before the effective date of the Code, the court regarded enactment of the Code as "persuasive authority for following the rationale of the cases from which the section is explicitly derived." The case has generally been treated as a Code case.

[23] 350 F.2d at 449. Though the court referred to "the possible unconscionability of the contracts," the appropriate remedy, if any, was presumably to refuse to enforce the offensive clause.

[24] For the origin of these terms, *see* Leff, Unconscionability and the Code — The Emperor's New Clause, 115 U. Pa. L. Rev. 485, 487 (1967) (referring to "bargaining naughtiness as 'procedural unconscionability,' and to evils in the resulting contract as 'substantive unconscionability.' ").

[25] UCC 2-302 cmt. 1 says that the principle on which the section is based is "the prevention of oppression and unfair surprise." It is not clear whether "oppression" refers to procedure or substance.

[26] John Deere Leasing Co. v. Blubaugh, 636 F. Supp. 1569 (D. Kan. 1986) ("provisions on the back side of the lease are in very light-colored, fine print" and "paper on which the lease is drawn is extremely lightweight, which allows the darker print on the front page to show through to the back, making it difficult to see the fine print"). But the mere fact that a contract is a standardized agreement does not make it unconscionable. *Compare* Restatement Second §208 (unconscionable contract or term) *with* §211 (standardized agreements). *See* §4.26 *supra*.

[27] Weaver v. American Oil Co., *supra* note 6 (gas station operator who "had left high school after one and a half years and spent his time . . . working at various skilled and unskilled labor oriented jobs . . . was not one who should be expected to know the law or understand the meaning of technical terms").

[28] Martin v. Joseph Harris Co., 767 F.2d 296 (6th Cir. 1985) ("relative bargaining power is an appropriate consideration in determining unconscionability under the . . . Code"); Shell Oil Co. v. Marinello, 307 A.2d 598 (N.J. 1973) ("the provisions . . . are the result of [franchisor's] disproportionate bargaining position and are grossly unfair").

skill.[29] But inequality of bargaining power is not by itself enough for, as Comment 1 to UCC 2-302 says, the principle underlying the section is not one "of disturbance of allocation of risks because of superior bargaining power."[30] On the whole, judges have been cautious in applying the doctrine of unconscionability, recognizing that the parties often must make their contract quickly, that their bargaining power will rarely be equal, and that courts are ill-equipped to deal with problems of unequal distribution of wealth in society. Most cases of unconscionability involve a combination of procedural and substantive unconscionability, and it is generally agreed that if more of one is present, then less of the other is required.[31] A court will weigh all elements of both substantive and procedural unconscionability and may conclude that the contract is unconscionable because of the overall imbalance. If the procedural unconscionability alone rises to the level of misrepresentation, duress, or undue influence, however, the contract may be voidable without regard to substantive unconscionability.

Procedural unconscionability and adhesion contracts

Courts have resisted applying the doctrine where there is only procedural unconscionability without substantive unfairness.[32] Thus the mere fact that the contract is one of adhesion is not generally regarded as fatal, especially where there is no element of surprise in the term. As Robert Braucher put it: "No doubt the contracts between the [mortgagors] and the bank were 'adhesion' contracts, but we are not prepared to hold that they were unconscionable in the aspects here in issue. . . . Customers who adhere to standardized contractual terms ordinarily 'understand that they are assenting to the terms not read or not understood, subject to such limitations as the law may impose.'"[33] More recently, the United States Supreme Court has observed, "Common sense dictates that a [commercial cruise ticket] will be a form contract the terms of which are not subject to negotiation, and that an individual purchasing the ticket will not have bargaining parity with the cruise line." But the court rejected the lower court's "determination that a nonnegotiated forum-selection clause in a form ticket contract is never enforceable simply because it is not the subject of

[29] Kerr-McGee Corp. v. Northern Utils., 673 F.2d 323 (10th Cir. 1982) (not unconscionable where "experienced negotiators for both parties entered into an agreement after several months of give and take").

[30] See Hydraform Prods. Corp. v. American Steel & Aluminum Corp., 498 A.2d 339 (N.H. 1985) (quoting UCC 2-302 cmt. 1 and explaining that the issue "tends to turn on whether the bargaining power is so disparate that the weaker party is left without any genuine choice").

[31] Armendariz v. Foundation Health Psychcare Servs., 6 P.3d 669 (Cal. 2000) ("the more substantively oppressive the contract term, the less evidence of procedural unconscionability is required").

[32] Communications Maintenance v. Motorola, 761 F.2d 1202 (7th Cir. 1985) (since there was "no substantive unconscionability we do not reach the issue of whether there was procedural unconscionability").

[33] Carpenter v. Suffolk Franklin Sav. Bank, 346 N.E.2d 892, 900 (Mass. 1976), quoting Restatement Second §211 cmt. b.

bargaining."[34] [A court will often buttress its conclusion that a provision in an adhesion contract is not unconscionable by stressing that the goods or services were not essential or could have been procured elsewhere.[35]

It has also been held that substantive unconscionability alone is not enough.[36] There has, however, been some reluctance to concede that a plainly oppressive term can be legitimized by fairness in bargaining, and New York's highest court has envisioned "exceptional cases where a provision of the contract is so outrageous as to warrant holding it unenforceable on the ground of substantive unconscionability alone."[37]

Substantive unconscionability

It is not surprising that the parties that have successfully invoked the doctrine of unconscionability have often been consumers.[38] But this has not always been the case.[39] The doctrine has, for example, been successfully invoked by gas station operators and other franchisees. In deciding these cases, most of which have involved provisions for the franchisor's termination of the relationship,[40] courts have emphasized the imbalance in the relationship between the parties. As the Supreme Court of New Jersey observed: "The dealer, particularly if he has been operating the station for a period of years and built up its business and clientele, when the time for renewal of the lease and dealer

Not limited to consumer contracts

---

[34]Carnival Cruise Lines v. Shute, 499 U.S. 585, 593 (1991) (Blackmun, J.). In 1992, *Shute* was overruled by a federal statute that invalidates agreements purporting to limit liability or to oust a court of competent jurisdiction as to claims by ship passengers for death or personal injury resulting from negligence. 46 App. U.S.C.A. §183c.

That a "clickwrap" contract to which one assents on line by clicking a box indicating that one has read, understood, and agreed to its terms, is not an unenforceable adhesion contract, *see* DeJohn v. The TV Corp., 245 F. Supp. 2d 913 (N.D. Ill. 2003) (rejecting argument that party was left "with no choice to agree to the dictated terms of the agreement without negotiation").

[35]Dean Witter Reynolds v. Superior Court, 259 Cal. Rptr. 789 (Ct. App. 1989) ("any claim of 'oppression' may be defeated if the complaining party had reasonably available alternative sources of supply").

[36]Wade v. Austin, 524 S.W.2d 79 (Tex. Civ. App. 1975) (both procedural and substantive abuse "must generally be present to produce a finding of unconscionability").

[37]Gillman v. Chase Manhattan Bank, 534 N.E.2d 824, 829 (N.Y. 1988) (dictum). *See* Restatement Second §208 cmt. *c* ("Theoretically, it is possible for a contract to be oppressive when taken as a whole, even though there is no weakness in the bargaining process and no single term which is itself unconscionable."). *See generally* Eisenberg, The Bargain Principle and Its Limits, 95 Harv. L. Rev. 741, 752 (1982) ("there have been strong indications that the doctrine of unconscionability authorizes a review of . . . fairness of terms").

[38]Vasquez v. Glassboro Serv. Assn., 415 A.2d 1156 (N.J. 1980) ("migrant farmworker has even less bargaining power than a residential tenant").

[39]Gianni Sport Ltd. v. Gantos, Inc., 391 N.W.2d 760 (Mich. App. 1986) (sustaining claim of clothing manufacturer that retailer's cancellation clause was unconscionable because " 'big sharks' in the garment industry were able to impose these clauses [on] small independent manufacturers").

[40]For franchise cases that did not, *see* Johnson v. Mobil Oil Corp., 415 F. Supp. 264 (E.D. Mich. 1976) (provision limiting liability of oil company so as to exclude consequential damages was unconscionable); Weaver v. American Oil Co., *supra* note 6 (provision that lessee of gas station would hold oil company harmless and indemnify it for any negligence of oil company on leased premises was unconscionable).

agreement comes around, cannot afford to risk confrontation with the oil company. He just signs on the dotted line."[41] Many courts, however, have not shared this attitude toward franchisees.[42] And courts have generally been chary about using the doctrine of unconscionability to protect merchants and similar professionals, declining to apply the doctrine in favor of sophisticated corporations.[43] As the Ninth Circuit said in rejecting an airline's claim of unconscionability in connection with a contract for the purchase of aircraft, "it makes little sense in the context of two large, legally sophisticated companies to invoke the . . . unconscionability doctrine."[44]

Arbitration clauses

At the close of the twentieth century, courts began to be confronted with myriad attacks on arbitration clauses on the ground of unconscionability. Courts have particularly solicitous of employees who have been required to sign arbitration agreements. In *Armendariz v. Foundation Health Psychcare Services*, decided by the Supreme Court of California in 2000, the court refused to enforce agreements by employees to arbitrate wrongful termination claims. After dealing with minimum requirements for arbitration of statutory claims, the court turned to more general objections on the ground of unconscionability where an arbitration agreement is imposed on an employee as a condition of employment with no opportunity to negotiate. The court concluded that "an arbitration clause imposed in an adhesive context lacks basic fairness and mutuality if it requires one contracting party, but not the other, to arbitrate all claims arising out of the same transaction or occurrence."[45] The agreement lacked a "modicum of bilaterality" because the agreement limited the employee to arbitration when the employee was claimant but no such limitation was imposed on the employer "when it seeks to prosecute a claim against the employee, without at least some reasonable justification for such one-sidedness based on 'business realities.'"[46] Consumers as well as employees have often succeeded

---

[41] Shell Oil Co. v. Marinello, *supra* note 28, at 601 ("provision giving Shell the absolute right to terminate on 10 days notice is void" and Shell could not terminate except for "good cause").

Only a few courts have characterized the franchise relationship as a fiduciary one. Carter Equip. Co. v. John Deere Indus. Equip. Co., 681 F.2d 386 (5th Cir. 1982) (existence of fiduciary relationship was "question of fact for the jury").

[42] Corenswet, Inc. v. Amana Refrigeration, 594 F.2d 129 (5th Cir. 1979) (rejecting argument that the "good faith obligation, like the Code's unconscionability provision, can properly be used to override or strike express contract terms" and holding that "Code does not *ipso facto* bar unilateral arbitrary terminations of distributorship agreements" and that it had not been shown that provision in appliance distributorship for "termination by either party 'at any time for any reason' on ten days' notice" was unconscionable).

[43] Hydraform Prods. Corp. v. American Steel & Aluminum Corp., *supra* note 30 (buyer's president "was not an innocent in the industry," and while seller may have been the larger company, buyer "had access to [seller's] competitors" and was not without "alternative to dealing with [seller]").

[44] Continental Airlines v. Goodyear Tire & Rubber Co., 819 F.2d 1519, 1527 (9th Cir. 1987).

[45] *Supra* note 31 at 694.

[46] *Supra* note 31 at 692.

in such attacks on arbitration clauses.[47] Lack of "mutuality," as in *Armendariz*, is a common ground,[48] though it is not always fatal.[49] Other grounds include [lack of consent to the clause,[50] prohibitive expense of arbitration,[51] and preclusion of class representation.][52] Courts have not, however, uniformly condemned arbitration clauses in employment agreements and consumer contracts.[53]

What remedies does the Code provide for unconscionability? The Code's statement of remedies betrays the historical origins of the doctrine. [The underlying notion is that a court may withhold relief just as it might refuse specific performance, not that a party may avoid the contract as a party might for misrepresentation or duress] Thus a court may refuse to enforce the entire contract or it may refuse to enforce or limit the application of an unconscionable term.[54] In cases where unconscionability has been found to infect an arbitration clause,

Remedies for unconscionability

---

[47]Villa Milano Homeowners Assn. v. Il Davorge, 102 Cal. Rptr. 2d 1 (Ct. App. 2000) (developer cannot use arbitration clause, hidden in "prolix form" in "deliberate attempt to circumvent statutory protections for home buyer").

[48]Ting v. AT&T, 319 F.3d 1126 (9th Cir. 2003) ("'bilaterality' is a requirement in all California arbitration agreements").

[49]Harris v. Green Tree Fin. Corp., 183 F.3d 173 (3d Cir. 1999) (terms of arbitration clause in secondary mortgage contract were not "so unreasonably favorable to [mortgagee] as to make the clause substantively unconscionable").

[50]Circuit City Stores v. Najd, 294 F.3d 1104 (9th Cir. 2002) (employee had right to opt out of agreement by returning a form).

[51]Mendez v. Palm Harbor Homes, 45 P.3d 594 (Wash. App. 2002) (arbitration clause in contract for sale of mobile home may be stricken when it is shown that "prohibitive costs are likely to render the arbitral forum inaccessible").

[52]Ting v. AT&T, *supra* note 48 ("class-action ban violates California's unconscionability law"); Szetela v. Discover Bank, 118 Cal. Rptr. 2d 862 (Ct. App. 2002) (no-class-action provision of arbitration clause added by credit card company was unconscionable as violating "fundamental notions of fairness"), followed in Ingle v. Circuit City Stores, 328 F.3d 1165 (9th Cir. 2003) ("one-sided provision proscribing an employee's ability to initiate class-wide arbitration operates solely to" employer's advantage), but distinguished in Lozano v. AT&T Wireless, 216 F. Supp. 2d 1071 (C.D. Cal. 2002) (agreement in *Szetela* "also specifically precluded pursuit of claims in a private attorney general capacity"), and rejected in Hutcherson v. Sears Roebuck & Co. 793 N.E.2d 886 (Ill. App. 2003) ("not convinced by the court's analysis in *Szetela*"). But cf. AutoNation USA Corp. v. Leroy, 105 S.W.3d 190 (Tex. App. 2003) (arbitration clause was not unconscionable on ground that it would preclude consumer buyer from maintaining class action on small claim where she did not argue that she would be deprived of substantive rights).

As to whether the availability of class arbitration is for court or arbitrator, *see* Green Tree Fin. Corp. v. Bazzle, ___ U.S. ___ (2003) (Breyer, plurality: whether contracts forbid class arbitration "is a matter for the arbitrator to decide"), followed in Pedcor Mgt. Co. Welfare Benefit Plan v. Nations Personnel of Texas, 343 F.3d 355 (5th Cir. 2003) (arbitration agreement "as in *Green Tree* does not clearly forbid class action").

[53]Hughes Training v. Cook, 254 F.3d 588 (5th Cir. 2001) (party seeking relief from adhesion contract must generally show that it is unconscionable and it is "not unfair for the arbitration agreement to include a standard of review that allowed the district court to assess the arbitrator's legal and factual conclusions").

[54]These provisions of UCC 2-302 are followed in other formulations of the unconscionability doctrine, as in Restatement Second §208.

courts have sometimes severed the offensive part of the clause and held the remainder enforceable.[55] Sometimes, however, as in *Armendariz*, they have found that the unconscionability permeates the entire clause and have stricken it in its entirety.[56] There the court reasoned that, given the agreement's lack of mutuality, there was "no single provision a court can strike or restrict in order to remove the unconscionable taint from the agreement," so that the court "would have to, in effect, reform the contract . . . by augmenting it with additional terms." Although, as the following discussion will show, courts have usually confined their attention to unconscionable clauses themselves, they have sometimes refused to enforce entire contracts[57] and have occasionally even read their mandate to permit them to add terms.[58] But courts have declined, just as a court of equity would have before the Code, to entertain damage suits based on unconscionability.[59] Because the remedies for unconscionability are cast in terms of withholding relief instead of avoidance, there is no inherent requirement that the claimant make restitution, as the claimant must in the case of avoidance for misrepresentation or duress.[60]

Applicability to price term

In the typical unconscionability case, the court passes judgment on the validity of a particular clause, as the trial court was directed to do in *Williams v. Walker-Thomas*. Courts have been more reluctant to pass judgment on the fairness of the price term.[61] In principle, of course, every term is part of the

---

[55] Little v. Auto Stiegler, 63 P.3d 979 (Cal. 2002) ("arbitration agreement is valid and enforceable once the unconscionable appellate arbitration provision is deleted").

As to the effect of a severability clause, *compare* Anders v. Hometown Mortgage Servs., 346 F.3d 1024 (11th Cir. 2003) ("Alabama law . . . gives full force to severability clauses"), *with* Sosa v. Paulos, 924 P.2d 357 (Utah 1996) (substantively unconscionable clauses in arbitration agreement not severable despite severability clause because negotiation of agreement was procedurally unconscionable).

[56] *Supra* note 31 at 697 (also noting that agreement had "both an unlawful damages provision and an unconscionably unilateral arbitration clause," indicating "a systematic effort to impose arbitration on an employee . . . as an inferior forum that works to the employer's advantage").

[57] American Home Improvement v. MacIver, 201 A.2d 886 (N.H. 1964) (alternative holding: contract not enforceable because of unconscionable price).

[58] Vasquez v. Glassboro Serv. Assn., *supra* note 38 (because of unconscionability of contract providing for housing of migrant farm worker, "public policy requires the implication of a provision for a reasonable time to find alternative housing"). If supplying a term to prevent unconscionability means that a contrary provision in the contract will not be effective, it involves considerations distinct from those in supplying a term generally (*see* §7.16 *infra*).

[59] Cowin Equip. Co. v. General Motors Corp., 734 F.2d 1581 (11th Cir. 1984) ("No case has been cited in which a damage award was based on an unconscionable contract"); Dean Witter Reynolds v. Superior Court, *supra* note 36 (California's general statute on unconscionability "merely codifies the *defense* of unconscionability").

[60] See *infra* note 64.

[61] Morris v. Capitol Furniture & Appliance Co., 280 A.2d 775 (D.C. 1971) ("markup of more than 100%" on furniture did not make contract unconscionable because buyer did not show "absence of a meaningful choice . . . plus contract terms which are unreasonably favorable to the other party"). This may seem odd because the equity cases that preceded the Code's doctrine

bargain as a whole and is, in a sense, part of the price. But the price term is somewhat peculiar, for rarely can a party claim surprise as to price, and in some situations price may actually be negotiable. Moreover, it is no simple matter for the court to make a judgment as to the fairness of the price term. Surely a seller's markup should not of itself be controlling.[62] Should a comparison of seller's price with prices charged by other sellers in similar transactions be determinative?[63] What of the seller's profit on the particular item or on the operation as a whole? What of the return on assets or on the seller's investment?[64] Furthermore, if the court should find the price term unconscionable, it usually cannot simply strike the clause and enforce the rest of the contract, as it can often do with other clauses.[65] For these reasons, it is not surprising that courts have tended to avoid square holdings that an excessive price without more is unconscionable.[66] Nor is it surprising that most of the cases in which price has been stressed as an element of unconscionability have emphasized elements of procedural unconscionability,[67] nor that all have involved consumers.

---

of unconscionability usually involved some judgment as to the inadequacy of the price. See the discussion of policing in equity in §4.27 *supra*.

[62] Shaffer v. Superior Court, 39 Cal. Rptr. 2d 506 (Ct. App. 1995) ("if a law firm's profit margin were relevant to the analysis of the conscionability of its fees, a veritable Pandora's Box of questions and problems would be opened"). Most courts have, however, been satisfied with crude calculations in price unconscionability cases. *See* Maxwell v. Fidelity Fin. Servs., 907 P.2d 51 (Ariz. 1995) ("we certainly cannot conclude that the contract as a whole is not unconscionable, given the $6,500 price of a water heater for a modest residence, payable at 19.5 percent interest, for a total time payment price of $14,860.43").

[63] *See* Uniform Consumer Credit Code §5.108 (listing as a factor in a determination of unconscionability "gross disparity between the price of the property or services obtained on credit] and the value of the property or services measured by the price at which similar property or services are readily obtainable in credit transactions by like consumers").

[64] Both profit and return on investment require a relatively complicated calculation based on the seller's records. *See* Patterson v. Walker-Thomas Furniture Co., 277 A.2d 111 (D.C. 1971) (elements of unconscionability "must be particularized in some detail before a merchant is required to divulge his pricing policies through interrogatories or through the production of records in court").

[65] For example, in Frostifresh Corp. v. Reynoso, 274 N.Y.S.2d 757 (N.Y.C. Civ. Ct. 1966), the trial court held that since the buyers had not returned the refrigerator freezer, they should reimburse the seller for its cost, $348, with no allowance for such items as commissions, service charges, or overhead. In Frostifresh Corp. v. Reynoso, 281 N.Y.S.2d 964 (Dist. Ct. 1967), the trial court's judgment was reversed and remanded for calculation of cost "plus a reasonable profit, in addition to trucking and service charges necessarily incurred and reasonable finance charges." *See* Jones v. Star Credit Corp., 298 N.Y.S.2d 264 (Sup. Ct. 1969) (buyers who had paid more than $600 of $1,234.80 price of home freezer with "maximum retail value of approximately $300" were relieved from making further payments).

[66] A leading case on price unconscionability is Perdue v. Crocker Natl. Bank, 702 P.2d 503 (Cal. 1985) ("it is clear that the price term, like any other term . . . , may be unconscionable"). That case involved the claimed unconscionability of a bank's $6 charge for checks drawn on insufficient funds and held that the parties should be given an opportunity to present evidence on this.

[67] Frostifresh v. Reynoso, *supra* note 65 (high-pressure sale in Spanish to Spanish-speaking buyers with contract in English).

Applicability to limitation of remedies

Clauses limiting the remedies of a buyer of goods have often been challenged on grounds of unconscionability and are given special attention by the Uniform Commercial Code.[68] A clause limiting the buyer's remedies to liquidated damages in a small amount may be challenged as unconscionable.[69] A clause limiting or excluding liability for consequential damages is unenforceable if "the limitation or exclusion is unconscionable," and such a limitation for personal injury due to consumer goods is prima facie unconscionable.[70] And a clause limiting a buyer's remedies to repair and replacement of goods may be invalid under a provision, not couched in terms of unconscionability, preserving a buyer's other remedies if circumstances cause this limited remedy "to fail of its essential purpose."[71]

In the next section we take up legislative initiatives designed to protect consumers against unfair contract terms.

Legislation common

§4.29. Consumer Legislation. The Uniform Commercial Code was not initially intended to deal with problems of consumer protection, though consumer interests have been better represented in its revisions, including that of Article 2.[1] Increasing awareness of the need to protect contracting parties against unfair terms has, however, resulted in a plethora of other legislation, both state and federal, to supplement the protections afforded by the common law and the Uniform Commercial Code. Most of this legislation, such as the Uniform Consumer Credit Code, is designed to protect consumers,[2] though other parties, such as franchisees, are protected under some federal and state statutes.[3] The discussion here will be confined to consumer legislation.

---

[68]That such provisions are generally enforceable, *see* Martin Rispens & Son v. Hall Farms, 621 N.E.2d 1078 (Ind. 1993) ("Indiana courts have rejected claims that contractual limitations of remedy are substantively unconscionable").

[69]*See* UCC 2-718 cmt. 1.

[70]UCC 2-719(3).

[71]UCC 2-719(2).

§4.29   [1]See the discussion of the Code's use of *consumer* in §1.10 *supra.*

[2]Attempts at unification of consumer protection law have had relatively little success. The Uniform Consumer Credit Code, first proposed by the National Conference of Commissioners on Uniform State Laws in 1968 and then revised in 1974, has been adopted in only eleven states.

Formulas for distinguishing consumer transactions from other transactions vary. The Uniform Commercial Code uses a definition of *consumer* that turns on particular use. UCC 9-102(23) (*consumer goods* are those "used or bought for use primarily for personal, family, or household purposes"), adapted in UCC-R 2-103(1)(c) (*consumer* is individual who buys goods intended "to be used primarily for personal, family, or household purposes"). The Magnuson-Moss Act, discussed *infra*, lays down a definition of *consumer product* that turns on general use. Magnuson-Moss Act 15 U.S.C.A. §101(1) ("normally used for personal, family, or household purposes"). *See* the discussion of the use of *consumer* in §1.10 *supra.*

[3]Federal legislation known as the Automobile Dealers' Day in Court Act was enacted in 1956 for the protection of automobile dealers (15 U.S.C.A. ch. 27) and federal legislation known as the Petroleum Marketing Practices Act was enacted in 1978 for the protection of service station operators (15 U.S.C.A. ch. 55 subch. 1).

In contrast with UCC 2-302, which condemns unconscionable terms in general, consumer legislation is usually directed at specific terms, such as finance charges or warranty disclaimers, singled out as likely to be unfair.[4] Statutes deal with such terms in two principal ways. Some attempt to control the terms directly, by limiting the parties' freedom to determine them in a way unfavorable to the consumer. Others leave the parties free to determine the terms but attempt to give the consumer an informed choice as to whether to make the contract, by requiring that the terms be clearly disclosed in advance.[5] Legislatures have sometimes delegated to government agencies some discretion in administering both types of statutes.[6]

Two main types

Most legislation designed to control terms has done so by specifying terms that are considered unfair and then prohibiting them. Classic examples are statutes that prohibit employers from fixing wages below a minimum level or prohibit public utilities from fixing rates above a maximum. Occasionally, however, legislation has taken a different course and has specified terms that are considered fair and then required them. A classic example is legislation prescribing standard terms for insurance policies.[7]

First type: control of terms

Common examples of consumer legislation of this type include state statutes that prohibit provisions setting finance charges in excess of a specified rate,[8] fixing balloon payments,[9] or cutting off defenses on assignment.[10] A few states have enacted statutes prohibiting disclaimers of implied warranties, such as the one attacked in *Henningsen.*[11] Legislation requiring specified terms is less common, though a number of states have statutes providing for application of payments in such a way as to prevent sellers from such repossessions as took place in *Williams.*[12]

Examples of control

---

[4]The Uniform Consumer Credit Code, however, contains a general provision on unconscionability in §5.108.

[5]These two categories are not exhaustive. Thus federal and state laws often allow a consumer who has entered into a contract as a result of home solicitation a "cooling-off" period, typically three days, to change his or her mind and avoid the transaction. *See* Uniform Consumer Credit Code §3.502; Fed. Trade Commn. Rule, Cooling-Off Period for Door-to-Door Sales, 16 C.F.R. §429.1.

[6]*See infra* notes 14 & 16.

[7]*See* R. Keeton & A. Widiss, Insurance Law §2.8 (1988). For such controls in other fields, *see* Cal. Civ. Code §§1812.50-1812.69 (dance studios); N.Y. Gen. Bus. Law §394-c (dating bureaus).

[8]*See* Uniform Consumer Credit Code §§2.201, 2.202, 2.401. Such statutes replace any usury statutes that would otherwise apply.

[9]*See* Uniform Consumer Credit Code §3.308. A balloon payment provision is one in an installment contract fixing one installment substantially in excess of the other ones. If the balloon payment is the final one, as it usually is, the earlier payments will be deceptively low.

[10]See the discussion of statutes protecting consumers in §11.8 *infra*.

[11]*See* Md. Com. Law Code Ann. §2-316.1; Mass. Ann. Laws ch. 106, §2-316A; Miss Code Ann. §§11-7-18, 75-2-719(4). See also the discussion of the example of *Henningsen* in §4.26 *supra*.

[12]*See* Uniform Consumer Credit Code §3.303 (payments under debts secured by cross-collateral "deemed . . . to have been applied first to the payment of the debts arising from the sales first made"). See also the discussion of the example of Williams v. Walker-Thomas in §4.28 *supra*.

Second type: disclosure of terms

On the whole, however, legislatures have favored the second type of solution—disclosure of terms, rather than control of terms—as more consistent with a market economy.[13] Given adequate information, the premise runs, a consumer will make an informed choice. It can be argued that elaborate and burdensome disclosure requirements tell the sophisticated consumer little that such a consumer does not already know and tell the unsophisticated consumer little that such a consumer can or will use.[14] Nevertheless, disclosure requirements have proved an attractive compromise between the extremes of protection through control of terms and no protection at all. Two examples are especially significant.

Example of Truth in Lending Act

The first is the Truth in Lending Act, enacted in 1968.[15] It is designed to allow a consumer contemplating the purchase of goods or services on credit to make an informed choice as to whether to buy on credit and, if so, among sources of credit. It therefore requires a creditor, before extending credit to the consumer, to disclose any finance charge as an annual percentage rate, together with other essential terms.[16] It is essentially a disclosure statute, however, and leaves the creditor free to impose any charges for credit that state law permits.

Example of Magnuson-Moss Act

Another federal disclosure statute is the Magnuson-Moss Act, enacted in 1975.[17] It is designed to prevent a consumer who is contemplating the purchase of durable goods from being confused or misled as to the warranties of the manufacturer or seller. Where it applies, it controls if there is a conflict with the Uniform Commercial Code. It requires a supplier of a consumer product who gives a written warranty to designate it as either a "full" or a "limited" warranty.[18] In either case, the supplier cannot disclaim implied warranties;[19] and, if the supplier designates a written warranty as "full," it must meet stated

---

[13] See the discussion of statutory reinforcement in §4.26 *supra*.

[14] *See* Kripke, Gesture and Reality in Consumer Credit Reform, 44 N.Y.U. L. Rev. 1, 3 (1969) (characterizing support of legislation requiring disclosure of finance charges as a "put-on"); Jordan & Warren, A Proposed Uniform Code for Consumer Credit, 8 B.C. Ind. & Com. L. Rev. 441, 449 (1967) (describing solutions such as disclosure as "largely middle-class solutions . . . to what has increasingly become a lower-class problem").

[15] The act is Title I of the Consumer Protection Act of 1968, 15 U.S.C.A. §§1601-1665. It was amended in 1988 to require more detailed and uniform disclosures by credit and charge card issuers. The act empowers the Board of Governors of the Federal Reserve System to promulgate regulations to implement the act, and the board has done so in Regulation Z, 12 C.F.R. 226. Many states also have general consumer credit disclosure statutes. Current versions of statutes and regulations can be found in CCH Consumer Credit Guide.

[16] Truth in Lending Act §§127, 128.

[17] The Magnuson-Moss Act is Title I of the Magnuson-Moss Warranty-Federal Trade Commission Improvement Act, 15 U.S.C.A. §§2301-2312. The act empowers the Federal Trade Commission to promulgate regulations to implement the act, and these can be found in 16 C.F.R. 700-702.

[18] Magnuson-Moss Act §103. (This provision is limited to products costing more than $10.)

[19] Magnuson-Moss Act §108. But this section leaves it open to a supplier who makes a limited warranty to limit implied warranties "in duration to the duration of a written warranty of reasonable duration."

requirements, including an undertaking to provide a remedy without charge by repair, replacement, or refund.[20] This act too is essentially a disclosure statute.[21] Thus a supplier's written warranty need not conform to the requirements for a full warranty if it is designated as limited. Moreover, a supplier need not make any written warranty, and, if the supplier does not, the act does not limit the power to disclaim warranties.

Advocates of consumer legislation such as the Truth in Lending Act and the Magnuson-Moss Act have recognized the shortcomings of the conventional private lawsuit as a means of enforcement. The amount in dispute is often small, and many consumers are deterred from pursuing their rights by ignorance, apathy, and inability to pay for legal services. One kind of solution is to "sweeten the pot" by allowing the consumer a civil penalty or multiple (e.g., treble) damages[22] and attorney's fees and other costs of litigation.[23] Another is to give each consumer the support of others by allowing them to join with claimants similarly situated in a class action.[24] Yet another is to reduce the cost of litigation by instituting a system of informal dispute-settlement procedures.[25]

Remedies by private lawsuit

Beyond encouraging consumers to press their own claims, consumer legislation often provides for investigation and enforcement by the government. Thus a public official or agency may be empowered to enjoin violations and other objectionable practices[26] or to seek criminal sanctions.[27]

Remedies by public action

---

[20] Magnuson-Moss Act §104.

[21] Nevertheless, some provisions go beyond mere disclosure. For example, §104 provides that a warrantor who gives a full warranty must repair a defective product without charge within a reasonable time and that, if repeated efforts at repair do not succeed, the consumer must be given a choice of refund or replacement.

[22] See Truth in Lending Act §130(a); Uniform Consumer Credit Code §5.201.

[23] See Magnuson-Moss Act §110(d)(2).

[24] See Magnuson-Moss Act §110(e); Truth in Lending Act §130.

[25] See Magnuson-Moss Act §110(a), which entrusts the Federal Trade Commission with the power to prescribe rules for "informal dispute settlement mechanisms," and the Commission's regulation on Informal Dispute Settlement Procedures, 16 C.F.R. pt. 703.

[26] See Magnuson-Moss Act §110, which confers such powers on the Attorney General and the Federal Trade Commission.

[27] See Truth in Lending Act §112, which make a willful and knowing violation a crime.

Chapter 5

Unenforceability on Grounds
of Public Policy

A. INTRODUCTION

§5.1. Public Policy as a Ground for Unenforceability. The principle of freedom of contract rests on the premise that it is in the public interest to accord individuals broad powers to order their affairs through legally enforceable agreements. In general, therefore, [parties are free to make such agreements as they wish, and courts will enforce them without passing on their substance.] Occasionally, however, a court will decide that this interest in party autonomy is outweighed by some other interest and will refuse to enforce the agreement or some part of it. This chapter is concerned with the rules that guide courts in reaching such decisions.

Relation to freedom of contract

---

§5.1 [1]There is a classic statement of this in Printing & Numerical Registering Co. v. Sampson, L.R. 19 Eq. 462 (1875) (Jessel, M.R.: "It must not be forgotten that you are not to extend arbitrarily these rules which say that a given contract is void as being against public policy, because if there is one thing which more than another public policy requires it is that men of full age and competent understanding shall have the utmost liberty of contracting, and that their contracts when entered into freely and voluntarily shall be held sacred and shall be enforced by courts of justice.").

[2]Sternamen v. Metropolitan Life Ins. Co., 62 N.E. 763 (N.Y. 1902) ("The power to contract is not unlimited. While as a general rule there is the utmost freedom of action in this regard, some restrictions are placed upon the right by legislation, by public policy, and by the nature of things. Parties cannot make a binding contract in violation of law or of public policy.").

Reluctance to aid promisee

A court may be moved by two considerations in refusing to enforce an agreement on grounds of public policy. First, it may see its refusal as an appropriate sanction to discourage undesirable conduct, either by the parties or by others.[3] Second, it may regard enforcement of the promise as an inappropriate use of the judicial process to uphold an unsavory agreement.[4] Both of these considerations turn on reluctance to aid the promisee rather than on solicitude for the promisor.[5] For this reason, they differ from the considerations discussed in the preceding chapter in connection with misrepresentation, duress, and undue influence. Though the rules dealt with there are intended to assure that bargaining has taken place in a manner compatible with the public interest in party autonomy, they reflect more solicitude for the promisor than reluctance to aid the promisee.

Agreement not necessarily void

When a court refuses to enforce an agreement on grounds of public policy, it sometimes characterizes the agreement as "void." Lord Mansfield expressed this view:

> The principle of public policy is this; *ex dolo malo non oritur actio* [no right of action arises from one's own fraud]. No court will lend its aid to a man who founds his cause of action upon an immoral or an illegal act. . . So if the plaintiff and defendant were to change sides, and the defendant was to bring his action against the plaintiff the latter would then have the advantage of it; for where both are equally in fault, *potior est conditio defendentis* [the condition of the defendant is the stronger].[6]

Although courts are fond of repeating the maxim *in pari delicto potior est conditio defendentis* ("where both parties are equally in fault, the position of the defendant is the stronger"), a court will not necessarily condemn the entire agreement as unenforceable by both parties merely because it offends public policy. A court may hold instead that the agreement can be enforced by one of the parties though it cannot be enforced by the other.[7] Or it may hold that part of the agreement is enforceable, though another part of it is not.[8] It is therefore

---

[3] Sirkin v. Fourteenth St. Store, 108 N.Y.S. 830 (App. Div. 1908) ("I think nothing will be more effective in stopping the growth and spread of this corrupting and now criminal custom [of commercial bribery] than a decision that the courts will refuse their aid to a guilty vendor or vendee.").

[4] Bank of the United States v. Owens, 27 U.S. (2 Pet.) 527 (1829) ("no court of justice can in its nature be made the handmaid of iniquity").

[5] Coppell v. Hall, 74 U.S. (7 Wall.) 542 (1868) ("The defense is allowed, not for the sake of the defendant, but of the law itself.").

[6] Holman v. Johnson, 98 Eng. Rep. 1120, 1121 (K.B. 1775).

[7] For examples, see the discussions of frustration of policy in §5.5 *infra* and of enforceability by the other party in §5.6 *infra*.

[8] See §5.8 *infra*.

more accurate to say that the agreement or some part of it is unenforceable by one or both parties than to say that it is "void."[9]

Courts are also fond of condemning the unenforceable agreement as "illegal."[10] This is misleading insofar as it suggests that some penalty is necessarily imposed on one of the parties, apart from the court's refusal to enforce the agreement. In some cases, the conduct that renders the agreement unenforceable is also a crime, but this is not necessarily or even usually so. It is therefore preferable to attribute unenforceability to grounds of public policy rather than to "illegality."

Agreement not necessarily illegal

How does a court determine that all or part of an agreement is unenforceable on grounds of public policy? Occasionally the legislature simplifies the court's task by saying explicitly in a statute that agreements or portions of agreements that violate the statute are unenforceable. Statutes dealing with gambling and usury, for example, often state that agreements that violate their provisions are "void."[11] The court's function is then merely statutory interpretation.[12] In most cases, however, the court alone must decide whether a contravention of public policy is grave enough to warrant unenforceability.

Function of court

If the agreement involves the commission of a serious crime or tort, it may be clear that unenforceability is warranted; and if the agreement involves only a trivial contravention of policy, it may be clear that unenforceability is unwarranted. In doubtful cases, however, the court's decision must rest on a delicate balancing of factors for and against enforcement of the particular agreement. Enforcement should not be refused unless the potential benefit in deterring misconduct or avoiding an inappropriate use of the judicial process outweighs the factors favoring enforceability.[13]

Balancing of interests

---

[9] Kedzie & 103rd Currency Exch. v. Hodge, 619 N.E.2d 732 (Ill. 1993) (payee's noncompliance with plumbing license law did not make obligation entirely void so as to bar claim of holder in due course of check).

Although it is sometimes said that one who is not a party to the contract cannot assert the defense that the contract is contrary to public policy, these statements are usually found where the defense is asserted by a stakeholder (see the discussion of situations against the public interest in §5.9 *infra*) or one who has assumed another's obligation (see the discussion of the example of assumption in §10.9 *infra*).

[10] Crichfield v. Bermudez Paving Co., 51 N.E. 552 (Ill. 1898) (if performance "has an evil tendency or furnishes a temptation to use improper means, the contract is illegal").

[11] *See* Cal. Civ. Code °§1916-2 (usury); Ill. Rev. Stat. ch. °38 §28-7 (gambling).

[12] The usury laws have posed particularly difficult problems of interpretation. For a simple illustration of the difficulty of drawing a line, *see* Embola v. Tuppela, 220 P. 789 (Wash. 1923) (if "principal sum advanced is to be repaid only on some contingency that may never take place, the sum so advanced is considered an investment, and not a loan, and the transaction is not usurious"), treated in connection with the discussion of risk affecting imbalance in §2.11 *supra*.

[13] Town of Newton v. Rumery, 480 U.S. 386 (1987) (rejecting *per se* rule of invalidity for release-dismissal agreements because "promise is unenforceable [only] if the interest in its enforcement is outweighed . . . by a public policy harmed by the agreement").

Factors favoring enforcement

One of the factors that a court will weigh in favor of enforceability is the public interest in protecting the justified expectations of the parties.[14] Another factor is any forfeiture that will result by loss of the reliance interest if enforcement is denied.[15] Because restitution is generally unavailable when enforcement is denied on grounds of public policy,[16] the case for enforcement becomes stronger if the claimant's reliance has resulted in a benefit to the other party. A court will also weigh a party's excusable ignorance of the contravention of public policy, though exceptions are not often made on the basis of such ignorance alone.[17]

Factors opposing enforcement

The force of the argument against enforcement depends on the strength of the public policy involved and the likelihood that refusal of enforcement will further that policy. In addition, a court will take account of the seriousness and deliberateness of any misconduct that has occurred and of the closeness of the connection between that misconduct and the agreement.[18]

Relationship to policy

An agreement challenged on grounds of public policy may be related to that policy in many ways. Most commonly, one of the promises under the agreement involves conduct that offends the policy. Sometimes the promise is one to engage in that conduct, as where the promise is one to commit a tort. Sometimes the promise is one that tends to induce the other party to engage in such conduct. This tendency may result because the promise is made in return for the promisee's engaging or promising to engage in the conduct, as when the promise is one to pay for the commission of a tort. Or it may result because the promise is conditioned on the promisee's engaging in such conduct, as when a seller's promise to deliver goods is conditioned on the buyer's committing a tort. In such cases it is the tendency to induce misconduct that makes the promise unenforceable, and whether the conduct actually takes place makes no difference.[19]

Conduct need not be against policy

In other situations, a promise to engage in conduct may offend public policy though the conduct itself does not, as does a promise to vote in a particular way. And an attempt to induce conduct may offend public policy though the

---

[14] Mincks Agri Ctr. v. Bell Farms, 611 N.W.2d 270 (Iowa 2000) (concluding "that the policy underlying the licensing requirements is strong; only a refusal to enforce the contracts will further that policy"). Restatement Second §178(2)(c) lists as a factor "any special public interest in the enforcement of the particular term." Comment *e* refers to "any interest that . . . third parties may have in the enforcement of the term." *See* illus. 18 & 19.

[15] Yank v. Juhrend, 729 P.2d 941 (Ariz. App. 1986) (buyer of land denied cancellation of note and deed of trust on ground that seller violated subdivision laws because "forfeiture is generally abhorred by the law").

[16] See §5.9 *infra*.

[17] For a very limited exception, see the discussion of excusable ignorance in §5.7 *infra*.

[18] These factors are elaborated for the case where a statute is involved in the discussion of the factors in a court's decision in §5.5 *infra*.

[19] Myers v. Western-Southern Life Ins. Co., 849 F.2d 259 (6th Cir. 1988) (party "need only show that the purpose of the contract provision is to create a situation which tends to operate to the detriment of the public interest; he need not demonstrate that the public interest has actually been harmed").

conduct itself does not, as when a promise is made in return for voting in a particular way.[20]

In refusing enforcement on grounds of public policy, courts have not limited themselves to these relationships between the agreement and the policy involved. Many other relationships are possible. But as the connection between the agreement and the policy becomes tenuous, a court will be more likely to disregard an offense to the policy as "remote" or "collateral" and will not refuse enforcement unless serious misconduct is involved.[21] Such misconduct is sometimes characterized as involving "serious moral turpitude."[22]

Sometimes a court can avoid the balancing of interests described here by interpretation of the agreement. Given a choice between two reasonable interpretations of an agreement, a court will prefer the one under which the agreement involves no contravention of public policy and is enforceable to the one under which it involves such a contravention and is not enforceable.[23] Such reasoning is often invoked to support the strict interpretation of restrictive covenants.[24] It is epitomized in the maxim *ut res magis valeat quam pereat* ("that the thing may rather have effect than perish").[25] Since the issue is one of enforceability of the agreement, the parol evidence rule does not bar extrinsic evidence that bears on this issue. Though the writing purports to be a complete integration, it still may be shown that the writing is unenforceable on grounds of public policy.[26]

Furthermore, the issue is sufficiently related to "fundamental concepts of morality and fair dealing"[27] that a court should not, as litigants have sometimes urged, ignore it merely because the claimant can plead its case without disclosing any contravention of public policy.[28] Indeed, even if neither party raises

Many possible relationships

Interpretation affected by public policy

Fundamental nature of issue

---

[20]Livingston v. Page, 52 A. 965 (Vt. 1902) (promise by candidate to pay for support by newspaper).

[21]See the discussion of *McConnell* in §5.6 *infra*.

[22]For a discussion of "moral turpitude," *see* Pullman Palace-Car Co. v. Central Transp. Co., 65 F. 158 (E.D. Pa. 1894).

[23]Perbal v. Dazor Mfg. Corp., 436 S.W.2d 677 (Mo. 1968) ("Where an agreement is susceptible of two constructions, one of which renders the contract invalid and the other sustains its validity, the latter construction is preferred.").

[24]Atlanta Center Ltd. v. Hilton Hotels Corp., 848 F.2d 146 (11th Cir. 1988) ("preferred interpretation [of restrictive covenant] is the one that least restricts competition, thereby posing the least affront to the public policy").

[25]In addition, a court may manifest hostility to the purpose of the provision concerned. *See* Kendall v. Ernest Pestana, Inc., 709 P.2d 837 (Cal. 1985) ("common law's hostility toward restraints on alienation" has led to their strict construction). See also the discussion of more special rules in §7.11 *infra*.

[26]See the discussion of the point that one can show no agreement in §7.4 *infra*.

[27]McConnell v. Commonwealth Pictures Corp., 166 N.E.2d 494, 497 (N.Y. 1960).

[28]Oscanyan v. Arms Co., 103 U.S. 261 (1880) ("the objection . . . could not be obviated or waived by any system of pleading [and was] one which the court itself was bound to raise").

the issue, the court will do so on its own initiative and refuse enforcement if justified by the record, at least if the contravention is serious.[29]

In the following sections we consider some policies that courts have developed without the intervention of legislation.

B. POLICIES DEVELOPED BY COURTS

Policies in precedents

§5.2. Some Judicially Developed Policies. In a famous dictum, a nineteenth-century English judge cautioned that public policy is "a very unruly horse, and when once you get astride it you never know where it will carry you. It may lead you from the sound law. It is never argued at all but when other points fail."[1] Nonetheless, judges themselves first developed the policies on which they denied enforcement of agreements. Most of these policies are now firmly rooted in precedents accumulated over centuries.[2]

Great variety of policies

These policies have many bases. Some are grounded on moral values, as are the policies against impairment of family relationships[3] and against gambling.[4] Some are based on economic notions, as are the policies against restraint of trade[5] and against restraints on alienation of property.[6] Some arise from a desire to protect the institutions of government, as do the policies against encouraging

---

[29]Oscanyan v. Arms Co., *supra* note 28 ("if it should appear from the opening statement . . . that there could be no recovery, the court should not hesitate to so declare").

§5.2 [1]Burrough, J., in Richardson v. Mellish, 130 Eng. Rep. 294, 303 (Ex. 1824).

[2]*See* Anaconda Fed. Credit Union v. West, 483 P.2d 909 (Mont. 1971) ("public policy can be enunciated by . . . the courts at any time and whether there is a prior expression or not the courts can refuse to enforce any contract which they deem to be contrary to the best interests of citizens as a matter of public policy").

[3]See §5.4 *infra*. For an example of a policy grounded on a desire to protect citizens, *see* Bowman v. Parma Bd. of Educ., 542 N.E.2d 663 (Ohio App. 1988) ("employment separation agreement clause purporting to prohibit a school district from disclosing pedophilia on the part of a school teacher to a school district that subsequently employs him is void as against public policy").

[4]Although wagering and gaming agreements were generally enforceable under the English common law, they have been condemned in most American states, sometimes because thought to encourage shiftlessness, poverty, and immorality, and sometimes because regarded as too frivolous to be worthy of judicial attention. Cudahy Junior Chamber of Commerce v. Quirk, 165 N.W.2d 116 (Wis. 1969) (challenge to pay Jaycees $1,000 if they could prove that statements critical of fluoridation were false was unenforceable because "participants in a wager may not use the court to settle their dispute").

[5]See §5.3 *infra*.

[6]*See* Proctor v. Foxmeyer Drug Co., 884 S.W.2d 853 (Tex. App. 1994) (option provision, though drafted as restraint on use, "operates indirectly as a restraint on alienation").

litigation[7] or otherwise interfering with the judicial process[8] and those against improperly influencing legislators and other government officials.[9] These policies are of such great variety that it is not possible to deal with most of them in any detail in this chapter.

Furthermore, policies vary over time. As the interests of society change, courts are called upon to recognize new policies, while established policies become obsolete or are comprehensively dealt with by legislation.[10] As a justice of the United States Supreme Court said in the nineteenth century, "The standard of such policy is not absolutely invariable or fixed, since contracts which at one stage of our civilization may seem to conflict with public interest, at a more advanced stage are treated as legal and binding."[11] To take an example given later by the Supreme Court of Michigan, "The curb of the ancient rule of champerty, and its fellow 'maintenance' . . . has long been rendered obsolete by modern judicial procedure and an independent judiciary."[12]

[One policy that has endured is that against the commission or inducement of torts and similar wrongs.] A promise that involves committing a tort[13] or a

Policies change with time

Policy against wrongs

---

[7]Plumlee v. Paddock, 832 S.W.2d 757 (Tex. App. 1992) ("sharing of fees with a layman by a lawyer is prohibited by statute, as well as by disciplinary rule" and "Penal Code makes barratry an offense for the attorney as well as the other party"). See the discussion of assignments against public policy in §11.4 *infra*.

[8]For an example, *see* Garden State Plaza Corp. v. S.S. Kresge Co., 189 A.2d 448 (N.J. Super. 1963) (clause forbidding resort to prior negotiations for the purpose of interpretation is void as against public policy because it would have court "wearing judicial blinders").

[9]On this ground courts have refused to enforce contingent fee agreements for obtaining special legislation or favorable action by government agencies. Ewing v. National Airport Corp., 115 F.2d 859 (4th Cir. 1940) (contingent fee agreement for securing passage of special legislation was unenforceable because such arrangements "are especially regarded with disfavor by the courts" and claimant "used personal and political influence").

The federal government and all states now regulate legislative lobbying by statute. *See* 2 U.S.C. §§261-270.

[10]For example, gambling agreements, which were originally condemned by the courts (*supra* note 4), have now been generally prohibited by legislation. The same is true of agreements tending to obstruct justice or in violation of a public duty. *See* Model Penal Code §§240-242 (1980).

On the other hand, arbitration agreements, which once were generally unenforceable, have now been validated by legislation in most jurisdictions. *See* °9 U.S.C. §2.

See also the discussion of *Marvin* in §5.4 *infra* and the discussion of the modern role of free assignability in §11.2 *infra*.

[11]Pope Mfg. Co. v. Gormully, 144 U.S. 224, 233-34 (1892) (Brown, J.).

[12]Grant v. Stecker & Huff, 1 N.W.2d 500, 501 (Mich. 1942).

[13]Sayres v. Decker Auto Co., 145 N.E. 744 (N.Y. 1924) (agreement by seller of automobile to defraud insurance company by giving buyer incorrect bill of sale was unenforceable). *Cf.* United States v. King, 840 F.2d 1276 (6th Cir.) ("parent's contract allowing a third person to burn, assault or torture his child is void"). *See* Restatement Second §§192, 194. Contracts in which the promise involves committing a crime are discussed in §§5.5, 5.6 *infra*.

breach of a fiduciary duty[14] is therefore unenforceable as against public policy. So is a promise made in return for such a wrongful act or in return for a promise to commit such a wrongful act.[15] This reasoning, however, does not extend to a promise to indemnify another against the consequences of his committing a tort, as long as the tortious action is only an undesired possibility and the promise does not tend to induce its commission.[16]

Exemption from liability for wrong

Courts have had difficulty in applying the policy against the inducement of wrongs to agreements by which one party is exempted from tort liability to the other. A party clearly cannot exempt itself from liability in tort for harm that it causes intentionally or recklessly.[17] However, a party generally can exempt itself from liability or limit its liability in tort for harm caused by negligence, as long as the provision is not unconscionable.[18]

Exceptions as to negligence

In exceptional cases, however, courts have held such an agreement unenforceable because the agreement affects the public interest and the other party is a member of the protected class. Two examples of this exception have long been recognized. First, an employer cannot exempt itself from liability in negligence to its employee.[19] Second, a common carrier or a public utility cannot exempt itself from liability in negligence to one it has contracted to serve in that capacity, although it may be allowed to limit its liability to a reasonable agreed value in return for a lower rate.[20] A number of courts have now

---

[14]Corti v. Fleisher, 417 N.E.2d 764 (Ill. App. 1981) (provision in contract between lawyer and his firm that lawyer had right to clients' files when he left firm was unenforceable because it deprived clients to whom he had fiduciary duty of right to counsel of their choice). *See* Restatement Second §193. However, this rule does not apply if the person to whom the fiduciary duty is owed effectively consents, so that no violation of a fiduciary duty results.

[15]Williams v. Wilson, 181 F. Supp. 351 (E.D. Ark. 1960) (promise to pay for theft of trade secrets was unenforceable).

[16]Jewett Publishing Co. v. Butler, 34 N.E. 1087 (Mass. 1893) (contract by which author agreed to indemnify publisher for any damages resulting from publication of book was enforceable where there was no showing of an intention to publish libelous matter).

[17]Martin Marietta Corp. v. International Telecommunications Satellite Org., 991 F.2d 94 (4th Cir. 1993) ("under Maryland law, a party . . . cannot waive liability for gross negligence").

[18]O'Callaghan v. Waller & Beckwith Realty Co., 155 N.E.2d 545 (Ill. 1958), discussed in §4.26 *supra* ("Clauses that exculpate the landlord from the consequences of his negligence have been sustained in residential as well as commercial leases."). *But see* UCC 1-302(b) ("obligations of good faith, diligence, reasonableness, and care . . . may not be disclaimed by agreement"). Statutes in many states invalidate exculpatory clauses in specified types of contracts. For a discussion of the strict interpretation of such clauses against the party claiming exemption, see the discussion of interpretation of terms in §4.26 *supra*.

[19]Pittsburgh, C.C. & St. L. Ry. v. Kinney, 115 N.E. 505 (Ohio 1916) (exculpatory clause in employment contract of Pullman car cleaner was "clearly in conflict with the sound and humane public policy of the state").

[20]Curtiss-Wright Flying Serv. v. Glose, 66 F.2d 710 (3d Cir. 1933) ("policy of law . . . that common carriers, in dealing with passengers, cannot compel them to . . . release [carriers'] legal liability for their own negligence" applies to air transportation).

added a third category by refusing to enforce exculpatory clauses in residential leases.[21]

In 1963 the Supreme Court of California fashioned a broad test in the influential case of *Tunkl v. Regents of University of California*, in holding unenforceable a standardized release from liability for negligence imposed as a condition for admission to a charitable research hospital. The court emphasized six things. First, the hospital was in a "business of a type generally thought suitable for public regulation." Second, its service was "of great importance to" and often "a matter of practical necessity for" the public. Third, it held itself out as generally "willing to perform this service for any member of the public." Fourth, it had "a decisive advantage of bargaining strength." Fifth, its "standardized adhesion contract" made no provision for protection against negligence on payment of "additional reasonable fees." Sixth, the other party's "person or property" was placed under its "control . . . subject to the risk of carelessness."[22] Not all courts have followed *Tunkl*.[23] Those that have done so have often given weight to a public interest evidenced by state regulation[24] and have generally balked at striking down exculpatory clauses in contracts involving activities, ranging from ski jumping to scuba diving, that are recreational in nature and that are known to be hazardous.[25]

Courts are not in entire agreement as to whether a seller of a product can exempt itself from the strict liability imposed for physical harm caused by the product's unreasonably dangerous condition.[26] Although such provisions generally will be held unenforceable, there is no good reason why this should result under, for example, a fairly negotiated contract between two merchants for the sale of an experimental product.[27] The extent to which a party can

---

[21] Henrioulle v. Marin Ventures, 573 P.2d 465 (Cal. 1978) ("In holding that exculpatory clauses in residential leases violate public policy, this court joins an increasing number of jurisdictions.").

[22] 383 P.2d 441, 445-46 (Cal. 1963).

[23] Wolf v. Ford, 644 A.2d 522 (Md. 1994) (in case involving stockbroker contract, we "expressly decline . . . to adopt the six-factor test set forth in *Tunkl*").

[24] *See* Emory Univ. v. Porubiansky, 282 S.E.2d 903 (Ga. 1981) (since "practice of dentistry is a profession licensed and controlled by the state" it is against public policy "to allow one who procures a license . . . to relieve himself by contract of the duty to exercise reasonable care").

Regulation is especially significant when the negligence involves a violation of a statutory duty. *See* Hunter v. American Rentals, 371 P.2d 131 (Kan. 1962) (where statute required trailers to have adequate safety hitch, lessor "in the business of renting trailers to the general public . . . owed a duty, not only to [lessee] but also to the general public, to see that the trailer hitch was properly installed and the trailer properly attached thereto in order that the same might be safely driven on the highway").

[25] Boehm v. Cody County Chamber of Commerce, 748 P.2d 704 (Wyo. 1987) (mock gunfight).

[26] Sterner Aero v. Page Airmotive, 499 F.2d 709 (10th Cir. 1974) (though buyer of rebuilt airplane engine was "expert in the field of aviation generally," seller could not assert contractual disclaimer provision as a valid defense to strict liability).

[27] Keystone Aeronautics Corp. v. R.J. Enstrom Corp., 499 F.2d 146 (3d Cir. 1974) (dictum: "Pennsylvania law does permit a freely negotiated and clearly expressed waiver of [Restatement

exempt itself from the consequences of its misrepresentation, particularly if the misrepresentation is not fraudulent, is also unclear.[28]

Rules of reason   In many instances, the rules condemning an agreement on grounds of public policy are formulated as rules of reason instead of absolute ones. An agreement choosing the law governing the contract may be unenforceable if "there is no . . . reasonable basis for the parties' choice."[29] An agreement fixing damages for a breach of contract may be unenforceable if not "reasonable in the light of the anticipated or actual harm caused by the breach and the difficulties of proof of loss."[30] An agreement imposing a restraint on the alienation of property may be unenforceable if not "reasonable under the circumstances."[31]

The next sections consider in more detail two judicially developed policies that have often been before the courts in recent decades: the policies against restraint of trade and against impairment of family relationships.

Role of legislation   **§5.3.   The Policy Against Restraint of Trade.** One of the oldest and best established of the policies developed by courts is that against restraint of trade.[1] Federal antitrust laws and related state statutes have so completely occupied this field that the common law rules are now of little consequence in most respects, such as the creation of monopolies and agreements fixing prices or tying purchases of one product to another. Nevertheless, the rules governing one type of agreement in restraint of trade — the promise to refrain from competition — have traditionally been left to judicial development.[2] In some states statutes now embody those rules.[3]

Rule of reason   In a sense, every promise that relates to business dealings operates as a restraint of trade by restricting the promisor's future activity. Such a promise is not regarded as against public policy and therefore unenforceable, however, unless the restraint imposed is unreasonably detrimental to a freely competitive private economy. This rule of reason is inevitably imprecise and leaves cases

---

(Second) of Torts] §402A between business entities of relatively equal bargaining strength"). This does not mean that third parties would be affected.

[28]Turkish v. Kasenetz, 27 F.3d 23 (2d Cir. 1994) (rejecting argument "that this doctrine applies only to clauses that completely exempt a party from liability [for fraudulent conduct], not to those that limit liability"). Restatement Second §196 broadens the rule of the first Restatement §573 to make unenforceable "a term unreasonably exempting a party" in the case of an innocent as well as a fraudulent misrepresentation. This is consistent with the rule of UCC 2-316(1), under which an express warranty prevails over an inconsistent disclaimer. As to the possibility that a clause in the nature of a merger clause might be effective to preclude extrinsic evidence of fraud see the discussion of a merger clause as ineffective in §7.4 *infra*.

[29]Restatement (Second) of Conflict of Laws §187(2)(a).

[30]Restatement Second §356.

[31]Restatement of Property §406(c).

§5.3   [1]*See* Restatement Second §186.

[2]A related type of agreement that has been left to the courts is one imposing a restraint on the alienation of land, mentioned in the discussion of the great variety of policies in §5.2 *supra*.

[3]*See* Cal. Bus. & Prof. Code °§§16600-02; Fla. Stats. °§542.335.

to be resolved on their particular facts, including general economic conditions. Courts view a promise in the light of its potential as well as its actual effects, taking account of the protection of the promisee's legitimate interests, the hardship to the promisor, and any injury to the public. A restraint that is reasonable and therefore enforceable in some circumstances may be unreasonable and therefore unenforceable in others. The imprecision of the rule is compounded because most claimants seek injunctive relief on the ground that damages cannot be proved with sufficient certainty[4] and, if the court denies such relief, it often fails to indicate whether damages could have been recovered had they been proved.[5] Nowhere has judicial activism in the service of public policy been more at war with judicial laissez faire in the name of freedom of contract.

In applying this rule of reason to promises to refrain from competition, courts have fashioned a requirement of ancillarity. To serve an interest of the promisee that is worthy of protection and that can outweigh the hardship to the promisor and any injury to the public, the restraint that the promise imposes must be *ancillary* to an appropriate transaction or relationship.[6] A *direct* or *nonancillary* restraint serves no such interest and is necessarily unreasonable. The promise that imposes the restraint is therefore unenforceable *per se*. If, for example, one merchant pays another in return for the other's naked promise not to compete in the same city, the restraint is nonancillary because it is not attached to any other transaction, and the promise is unenforceable.[7]

Unreasonable if not ancillary

An important example of a nonancillary restraint is one imposed by a promise not to bid at an auction or similar bidding competition.[8] The principle applies not only to a promise to refrain from bidding, but also to a promise to bid so as to affect the result adversely, even though the number of bidders is not diminished.[9] But the principle does not invalidate an agreement between two or more persons to bid for their collective benefit, because such a restraint is ancillary to a relationship of joint venture.[10]

Example of bidding restraints

---

[4]See the discussion of the uncertainty of damages in §12.6 *infra*.

[5]For an exception, *see* Cullman Broadcasting Co. v. Bosley, 373 So. 2d 830 (Ala. 1979) ("liquidated damages . . . should have been awarded . . . notwithstanding the fact that injunctive relief might have been inappropriate").

[6]JAK Prods. v. Wiza, 986 F.2d 1080 (7th Cir. 1993) ("Presumably when a covenant is merely part of a larger employment agreement, its relatively diminished stature reduces the likelihood of abuse where it simply eliminates a competitor."). *See* Restatement Second §187.

[7]Dyson Conveyor Maintenance v. Young & Vann Supply Co., 529 So. 2d 212 (Ala. 1988) (agreement between employers for "no switching" of employees was void because of "no underlying employer/employee agreement").

[8]Fletcher v. Johnson, 102 N.W. 278 (Mich. 1905) (such an agreement is unenforceable even though "the parties did not design to buy the property for less than its value").

[9]Frank v. Blumberg, 78 F. Supp. 671 (E.D. Pa. 1948) (party agreed to "make only a puffing bid").

[10]Longworth v. Kavanaugh, 228 S.W. 83 (Mo. 1921) (parties agreed to form single corporation to take franchise).

Restraints in sales of businesses

One of the most common situations in which courts find ancillarity arises when the seller of a business promises not to compete with the buyer.[11] In the seminal case, the Court of King's Bench in 1711 upheld a covenant ancillary to a baker's assignment of his lease.[12] The court applied a rule of reason that was reformulated more than a century later to ask

> whether the restraint is such only as to afford a fair protection to the interests of the party in favour of whom it is given, and not so large as to interfere with the interests of the public.[13]

Today such restraints are held justified by the buyer's need to protect the value of the good will purchased with the business.[14] Absent such a promise, the seller is bound by an implied promise not to solicit former customers or otherwise destroy the good will that he has sold, but is not precluded from opening a new business in competition with the buyer.[15] An analogous situation arises if a corporation's business depends heavily on the good will of one or more officers or significant shareholders. If such a person, on the sale of the corporation's business, promises the purchaser not to compete with the business, a court will treat the promise as ancillary to the sale.[16] Or if such a person, on the sale of that person's stock in the corporation, promises the corporation not to compete with it, a court will treat the promise as ancillary to the sale.[17]

Post-employment restraints

Another common situation in which courts find ancillarity arises when an employee promises an employer not to compete with the employer after the employment ends.[18] The justification for such restraints is the public interest in a workable employer-employee relationship with efficient use of employees. In general, therefore, post-employment restraints are sustained only if the employer stands to lose its investment in confidential information relating to some process or method — sometimes loosely called a "trade secret"[19] — or

---

[11]*See* Restatement Second §188(2)(a).

[12]Mitchel v. Reynolds, 24 Eng. Rep. 347, 352 (K.B. 1711).

[13]Horner v. Graves, 131 Eng. Rep. 284, 287 (C.P. 1831) (held: "far larger than is necessary").

[14]Chambers-Dobson v. Squier, 472 N.W.2d 391 (Neb. 1991) (covenant in contract for sale of business "is frequently necessary to make goodwill . . . a transferable asset and ensure that the buyer receives the full value of acquired goodwill").

[15]Mohawk Maintenance Co. v. Kessler, 419 N.E.2d 324 (N.Y. 1981) ("purchaser acquires no legal right to expect that the seller will refrain from engaging in a competing enterprise," but seller must not actively interfere "with the purchaser's relationship with his newly acquired customers").

[16]Greene County Tire & Supply v. Spurlin, 338 S.W.2d 597 (Tenn. 1960) (one of three shareholders).

[17]Hopkins v. Crantz, 54 N.W.2d 671 (Mich. 1952) (owner of nearly half of stock).

[18]*See* Restatement Second §188(2)(b). *But cf.* Lenox v. Sound Entertainment, 470 So. 2d 77 (Fla. App. 1985) (disk jockey was not "employee" but "independent contractor" so his covenant was invalid under Florida statute).

[19]What is a "trade secret" is determined by state law. The term is defined in the Restatement (Third) of the Law of Unfair Competition §39 (1995) as "any information that can be used in the

in customer lists or similar information.[20] Against this interest in a workable relationship, courts balance the public interest in individual economic freedom, free dissemination of ideas, and reallocation of labor to areas of greatest productivity.[21] Because post-employment restraints are often the product of unequal bargaining power and may inflict unanticipated hardship on the employee, they are scrutinized with more care than are covenants in the sale of a business. As the Supreme Court of West Virginia explained, a post-employment restraint "imposes a restraint upon a person's freedom to work for himself," while a "restriction imposed upon the seller of a business affords a person the freedom to sell something that has been acquired by virtue of their labor."[22]

Courts have sustained covenants not to compete when ancillary to types of transactions other than the two just discussed.[23] A partner's covenant not to compete with the partnership after leaving it is treated much the same as an employee's post-employment covenant.[24] The same is true for a participant in a joint venture.[25] Courts have also upheld a franchisee's covenant not to compete with the franchisor after the franchise is ended.[26]

A covenant made after a transaction is completed or a relationship is ended comes too late to be ancillary to it. In the case of a continuing relationship such as employment, however, it is enough if the promise is made before the termination of the relationship,[27] though the requirement of consideration may

Other examples of ancillarity

Time for ancillarity

---

operation of a business or other enterprise and that is sufficiently valuable and secret to afford an actual or potential economic advantage over others." The Uniform Trade Secrets Act, adopted by a majority of states, has a more elaborate definition in §1(4). *See generally* Bone, A New Look at Trade Secret Law: Doctrine in Search of Justification, 86 Cal. L. Rev. 241 (1998).

An employer may have an interest protectable by a restrictive covenant even if the process or method is not, strictly speaking, a "trade secret." AMP Inc. v. Fleischhacker, 823 F.2d 1199 (7th Cir. 1987) ("restrictive covenant may protect material, such as confidential information revealed to an employee during the course of employment, which does not constitute a trade secret").

[20] Reddy v. Community Health Found. of Man, 298 S.E.2d 906, 916 (W. Va. 1982) (situations "most likely to give rise to such an injury" include those where employer stands to "have his trade secrets or customer lists converted by the employee").

[21] For an analysis in economic terms, *see* Reddy v. Community Health Found. of Man, *supra* note 20, relying heavily on Rubin & Shedd, Human Capital and Covenants Not to Compete, 10 J. Legal Stud. 93 (1981).

[22] Weaver v. Ritchie, 478 S.E.2d 363, 367 (1996).

[23] *See* Janice Doty Unltd. v. Stoecker, 684 F. Supp. 973 (N.D. Ill. 1988) (ancillary to agreement between placement service and family for placement of domestic worker).

[24] Restatement Second §188(2)(c).

[25] *See* Restatement Second §188, cmt. *h*.

[26] Piercing Pagoda v. Hoffner, 351 A.2d 207 (Pa. 1976) ("franchisor had a protectable interest in the sale of his franchise to the [franchisees], such that a reasonable covenant not to compete effective upon termination of the franchise would be enforceable").

[27] Marine Contractors Co. v. Hurley, 310 N.E.2d 915 (Mass. 1974) (covenant of resigning employee was not unenforceable merely because it was negotiated at end of employment). *Cf.* Chenault v. Otis Engrg. Corp., 423 S.W.2d 377 (Tex. Civ. App. 1967) (covenant in leave of absence agreement was "ancillary to and connected with . . . employment status").

be a problem in this situation.[28] Such a continuing relationship has been held sufficient, though it is terminable at will and not, in the strict sense, a contract.[29]

Three other requirements

To be valid, a restraint not only must be ancillary, but also must meet three other requirements. First, it must protect some legitimate interest of the promisee. Second, its scope must be reasonable in the light of that interest. Third, it must not cause unreasonable hardship to the promisor or injury to the public.[30]

1. Legitimate interest of promisee

If the restraint is ancillary to the sale of a business and its good will, the employer has a legitimate interest in the protection of that good will. The type of activity that can validly be proscribed is therefore generally limited to that of the business sold.[31] If the restraint is ancillary to an employment contract "the central inquiry must always be the extent to which the employee may unjustly enrich himself by appropriating an asset of the employer for which the employee has not paid and using it against that very employer."[32]

2. Reasonableness of scope

To be valid, the restraint must also be reasonable in its scope as judged in the light of its protection of the promisee's legitimate interests. The scope of the restraint has three aspects: type of activity, geographical area, and time.[33] If a covenant not to compete proscribes types of activity that in any of these respects go beyond those necessary to protect the legitimate interests of the promisee, it is unreasonable.[34] In the case of a covenant ancillary to the sale of a business, the type of activity must generally be limited to that

---

[28] As to the requirement of consideration, see the discussion of the example of at-will employment in §2.10.

[29] Abel v. Fox, 654 N.E.2d 591 (Ill. App. 1995) (covenant in connection with at-will employment is "not a 'naked' restraint on trade," quoting this treatise).

As to the protection of an at-will employee against abuse of such a clause, *see* Hopper v. All Pet Animal Clinic, 861 P.2d 531 (Wyo. 1993) ("if an employer hired an employee at will, obtained a covenant not to compete, and then terminated the employee, without cause, to arbitrarily restrict competition, we believe such conduct would constitute bad faith").

[30] It has been suggested that a three-part inquiry is involved: "A covenant not to compete is reasonable only if it (1) is no greater than is required for the protection of the buyer; (2) does not impose an undue hardship upon the seller; and (3) is not injurious to the public." Weaver v. Ritchie, *supra* note 22, at 370.

[31] John T. Stanley Co. v. Lagomarsino, 53 F.2d 112 (S.D.N.Y. 1931) (promise not to engage in business of selling soap was unenforceable when seller's business had been limited to fats, grease, and bones).

[32] Reddy v. Community Health Found. of Man, *supra* note 20, at 916.

[33] That it is the totality of the restraint that is relevant, *see* Briggs v. R.R. Donnelley & Sons Co., 589 F.2d 39 (1st Cir. 1978) (impact of lack of geographical limitation "is softened by the short [three-year] time period involved"); Van Dyck Printing Co. v. DiNicola, 648 A.2d 898 (Conn. Super. 1993) ("time and geographical restrictions are to be reviewed as intertwined").

[34] In determining the promisee's interests, a court may take account of the nature of the competition that has actually occurred. Briggs v. R.R. Donnelley & Sons Co., *supra* note 33 ("any theoretical [geographical] overbroadness becomes academic under the actual facts of this case," in which companies for which employee worked after he left "did in fact compete substantially with his former employer").

of the business sold.[35] In the case of a post-employment restraint, it must generally be limited to the type of business carried on by the employer.[36] Similarly, the restraint may not cover a greater geographical area[37] or a longer time[38] than is necessary to protect the promisee's legitimate interests. Courts have, however, sometimes been generous in passing on the area of the restraint[39] and have occasionally even upheld a restraint unlimited as to time.[40]

Courts have come to view their function as one of "balancing" the legitimate interest of the promisee against the hardship to the promisor and the injury to the public in order to determine the permissible scope of a restraint.[41] In the case of a post-employment restraint, the hardship to the promisor consists of the restriction on the former employee's ability to earn a living.[42] Applying the balancing test in a picturesque setting, the Supreme Court of Nebraska rejected the contention of an aerial crop spraying service that flying a crop-spraying plane was "an avocation, not a vocation," done "more for the thrill of the helmet, the goggles, the roar of the engine and the white scarf trailing out of the open cockpit than for the living wage [that the pilot] would make to feed his family."[43] A few courts have been more tolerant of restrictions when the employee voluntarily quits the employment or is fired for good cause than when the employee is fired without cause.[44]

3. Hardship to promisor and injury to public

---

[35] John T. Stanley Co. v. Lagomarsino, 53 F.2d 112 (S.D.N.Y. 1931) (promise not to engage in business of selling soap was unenforceable where business sold had been limited to fats, grease, and bones).

[36] Karpinski v. Ingrasci, 268 N.E.2d 751 (N.Y. 1971) (employee's promise not to practice dentistry unenforceable where practice had been limited to oral surgery).

[37] Howard Schultz & Assocs. v. Broniec, 236 S.E.2d 265 (Ga. 1977) (while restrictions that "relate to the territory in which the employee was employed . . . generally will be enforced," those that "relate to the territory in which the employer does business . . . generally are unenforceable absent a showing by the employer of the legitimate business interests sought to be protected").

[38] Schneller v. Hayes, 28 P.2d 273 (Wash. 1934) (agreement by optician not to engage in business in same city unenforceable where unlimited as to time).

[39] Tasco, Inc. v. Winkel, 281 N.W.2d 280 (Iowa 1979) ("reasonable minds might disagree" where "very specialized" employer "operated throughout the United States" and "would go wherever the business was and . . . would sell any place").

[40] Karpinski v. Ingrasci, *supra* note 36 (unlimited time not fatal where geographical limitation was reasonable). Courts have sometimes read in a reasonable time. As to divisibility, see §5.8 *infra*.

[41] Miller Mechanical v. Ruth, 300 So. 2d 11 (Fla. 1974) ("courts employ a balancing test to weigh the employer's interest in preventing the competition against the oppressive effect on the employee").

[42] Chavers v. Copy Prods. Co., 519 So. 2d 942 (Ala. 1988) (though employee is "highly skilled working man, he is . . . still only a working man, and . . . the only trade he knows and by which he can support himself and his family is copier maintenance and repair").

[43] Boisen v. Petersen Flying Serv., 383 N.W.2d 29, 33 (Neb. 1986).

[44] This is easier to justify if equitable relief is in question. Central Adjustment Bureau v. Ingram, 678 S.W.2d 28 (Tenn. 1984) (even under at-will agreement, "discharge which is arbitrary,

The argument that a restrictive covenant is injurious to the public has often been advanced by lawyers and by physicians, usually with success by the former[45] but not by the latter.[46] The possibility that a court will treat a covenant as divisible and sustain the part not offensive to public policy is discussed later.[47]

In the next section we take up another policy developed by the courts — that against impairment of family relations.

Focus on marriage relationship

§5.4.   **The Policy Against Impairment of Family Relations.** Just as courts shaped the law to implement what they perceived to be the policy against restraint of trade, they also fashioned rules to carry out what they saw as the policy against the impairment of family relations. The discussion here is confined to the marriage relationship, which courts have long regarded as lying "at the foundation of our civilization."[1] In the florid language of an eighteenth-century English judge, "matrimony [was] one of the first commands given by God to mankind after the Creation, repeated again after the Deluge, and ever since echoed by the voice of Nature to all mankind."[2] We consider in particular the validity of agreements restraining the freedom of unmarried persons to marry, of agreements changing the incidents of the marriage relationship, of agreements tending to encourage divorce or separation, and of agreements between persons living together without being married. Agreements to marry are not included,[3] nor are agreements involving the relationship between parents and children[4] and surrogacy agreements.[5]

Recent trend

The law on agreements relating to the marriage relationship bears out the observation made earlier in this chapter that as the interests of

---

capricious or in bad faith clearly has a bearing on whether a court of equity should enforce a non-competition covenant").

[45] It is considered to be contrary to public policy to deprive a client of the right to employ a lawyer of the client's choosing. Dwyer v. Jung, 336 A.2d 498 (N.J. Super.) ("lawyer restrictions are inimical to the public interest"), aff'd mem., 348 A.2d 208 (N.J. Super. 1975).

[46] Bauer v. Sawyer, 134 N.E.2d 329 (Ill. 1956) (Schaefer, J.: where parties stipulated that there were 70 doctors serving area, court was "unable to say that the reduction of this number by one will cause such injury to the public as to justify as in refusing to enforce this contract").

[47] See §5.8 *infra*.

§5.4   [1] Estate of Duncan, 285 P. 757, 758 (Colo. 1930).

[2] Low v. Peers, 97 Eng. Rep. 138, 141 (Ex. Ch. 1770).

[3] In most states, "heartbalm" statutes bar or limit actions for breach of a promise to marry. *See* Cal. Civ. Code °§43.5; Pa. Stat. Ann. tit. °48, §171.

[4] On the validity of custody agreements, which involve special problems because the interests of a third person are involved, *see* Restatement Second §191.

[5] The most notorious case is In re Baby M, 537 A.2d 1227 (N.J. 1988) (simple surrogacy contract's "basic premise, that the natural parents can decide in advance of birth which one is to have custody of the child, bears no relationship to the settled law that the child's best interests shall determine custody"). *But cf.* Johnson v. Calvert, 851 P.2d 776 (Cal. 1993) (gestational surrogate contract with woman in whom couple's fertilized egg had been implanted by hetrological artificial

society change, courts are called upon to recognize new policies and discard obsolete ones.[6] We have already seen that judicial reluctance to enforce contracts between spouses has never prevented them from making contracts with each other as long as they make clear their intention to do so.[7] Changes in attitudes toward marriage and toward women have been reflected in a greater willingness to grant parties the same freedom of contract in connection with the marriage relationship that they enjoy in other areas, at least as long as the agreement is not an unfair one in the circumstances.

When one party to an agreement seeks to restrain the other party's freedom to marry, the one seeking to impose the restraint sometimes attempts this by having the other promise not to marry. More commonly, however, the one who seeks to impose the restraint conditions his or her own duty under the agreement on the other's not marrying. Because the common law regarded the freedom to marry as of concern to society as well as to the individual,[8] it subjected such agreements, whichever their form, to a rule of reason analogous to that applicable to agreements in restraint of trade.[9] Whether a court will enforce an agreement in restraint of marriage thus turns on whether the restraint is "reasonable."[10] As with an agreement in restraint of trade, the restraint must serve some legitimate purpose to be reasonable. A restraint that serves no purpose other than to discourage marriage will not be upheld.[11] For example, a court may enforce a contract that gives a person who undertakes to care for another a right to receive property when the other dies, on condition that the one providing the care does not marry, thereby becoming obligated to care for an additional person.[12] And a court may enforce a contract that gives a person who is being supported by another the right to support, on condition

Agreements in restraint of marriage

---

insemination did "not implicate the policies underlying the statutes governing termination of parental rights"). Some states have statutes dealing with such agreements. *See* Mich. Comp. Laws °§722.855 ("surrogate parentage contract is void and unenforceable").

[6] See the discussion of how policies change with time in §5.2 *supra*. For a good example, *see* Marvin v. Marvin, discussed *infra* ("mores of the society have indeed changed so radically in regard to cohabitation that we cannot impose a standard based on alleged moral considerations that have apparently been so widely abandoned by so many").

[7] See the discussion of family and social agreements in §3.7 *supra*.

[8] On this ground courts have refused to enforce contracts of marriage brokerage. Morrison v. Rogers, 46 P. 1072 (Cal. 1896) ("a marriage brokerage contract is invalid, as being contrary to public policy," because it inhibits "freedom of choice essential to a happy marriage").

[9] See the discussion of rules of reason in §5.3 *supra*.

[10] Barnes v. Hobson, 250 S.W. 238 (Tex. Civ. App. 1923) (validity "should be determined with reference to the reasonableness of such restraint under the circumstances of the particular case").

[11] McCoy v. Flynn, 151 N.W. 465 (Iowa 1915) (man's promise to pay woman $5,000 if she remained unmarried for three years, made in connection with settlement of her suit for breach of promise to marry, was unenforceable since no reason was shown for the restraint).

[12] Smith v. Nyburg, 16 P.2d 493 (Kan. 1932) (agreement under which parents promised to leave property to daughter, aged 18, if she would postpone contemplated marriage until she was 21 was enforceable).

that the one receiving the support does not marry and thereby acquire another provider.[13] As with an agreement in restraint of trade, the restraint must not be unlimited or "general," and its reasonableness will turn on its extent and duration.[14] Some courts, however, have been less critical of unlimited restraints on second marriages than of such restraints on first marriages.[15]

Agreements changing marriage relationship

An agreement between parties already married or about to marry is not necessarily invalid because it changes the incidents of the marriage relationship.[16] Spouses may, for example, validly contract for one of them to furnish services beyond those that would otherwise be required.[17] And they may validly contract to divide property that they have acquired or will acquire.[18] If, however, the court regards the incident as essential to the relationship and the change as offensive to public policy, it will refuse to enforce the agreement.[19]

Agreements limiting support

A particularly important application of this principle comes under agreements that limit the duty of support that the husband owes the wife. Courts have traditionally held such agreements unenforceable as unreasonably impairing an essential incident of marriage, whether they affect the duty of support during the marriage[20] or only after separation or divorce.[21] But a court will enforce a fair agreement limiting the duty of support if it is not made until the

---

[13] Indeed, alimony awarded by a court is conditioned in this way. Marshall v. Marshall, 163 A. 874 (Md. 1932) (distinguishing alimony from payment under agreement).

[14] Barnes v. Hobson, *supra* note 10 (where uncle promised to leave property to niece, aged 16, if she would keep house for him and not marry until she was 22, "the restraint . . . was not general but partial only [and] the question remaining as to its validity is one as to the reasonableness of the restraint").

[15] Cowan v. Cowan, 75 N.W.2d 920 (Iowa. 1956) ("tendency is . . . to uphold restraints on second marriages, either because it is said the 'public policy' rule does not apply to such marriages, or on the more limited ground, found in the facts of the cases, that the restraints imposed are under the circumstances reasonable and intended to serve a proper and meritorious purpose"). *See* Restatement Second §189 cmt. *a*.

[16] That such an agreement is unenforceable for lack of consideration under the pre-existing duty rule, *see* Borelli v. Brusseau, 16 Cal. Rptr. 2d 16 (Ct. App. 1993) ("performance of a personal duty created by the contract of marriage does not constitute a new consideration").

[17] Department of Human Resources v. Williams, 202 S.E.2d 504 (Ga. App. 1973) (wife's surrender of "legal right [to seek outside employment] to become a personal attendant to her [totally disabled] husband is sufficient consideration for the express contract of employment"). But see the discussion of family and social agreements in §3.7 *supra*.

[18] Marriage of Dawley, 551 P.2d 323 (Cal. 1976) (antenuptial agreement relating to property not contrary to public policy).

[19] Comment *a* to Restatement Second §190 gives two reasons for this. "One is that there is a public interest in the relationship, and particularly in such matters as support and child custody, that makes it inappropriate to subject it to modification by the parties. Another is that the courts lack workable standards and are not an appropriate forum for the types of contract disputes that would arise if such promises were enforceable."

[20] Cord v. Neuhoff, 573 P.2d 1170 (Nev. 1978) (postnuptial agreement limiting husband's duty to support wife during marriage as well as upon its dissolution was unenforceable).

[21] In re Marriage of Winegard, 278 N.W.2d 505 (Iowa 1979) ("Public policy will not allow a party to a marriage contract to avoid his or her resulting obligation of support.").

parties have separated or contemplate an immediate separation.[22] And many courts have now departed from tradition and upheld agreements limiting the duty of support after separation or divorce, even if they are made before marriage, as long as they are fair.[23] Some courts have insisted on full disclosure as essential to fairness,[24] though this is not universal.[25] And there is authority for imposing a test of fairness at the time of the implementation of agreement as well as at the time of its making.[26] Courts have occasionally held that engaged parties are in a confidential relationship so that the doctrine of undue influence applies.[27] The Supreme Court of Pennsylvania has abandoned the requirement of fairness, noting "a shift away from the former paternalistic approach of protecting women towards a newer approach of equal treatment," and holding that prenuptial agreements "should be evaluated under the same criteria as are applicable to other types of contracts."[28] The Supreme Court of Iowa voiced sympathy for this view, observing, with respect to the division of property, that the "gradual minimization of the extent to which we will review the terms of an agreement for fairness and equity may reflect the difficulty and arbitrariness of the task" and concluding that an agreement is fair when its provisions "are mutual or the division of property is consistent with the financial condition of the parties at the time of execution." The court declined "to so grossly interfere with the parties' freedom to contract" as "to declare invalid any prenuptial agreement that constitute[s] a bad fiscal bargain for one party."[29]

Roughly half the states have enacted the Uniform Premarital Agreement Act, promulgated in 1983. The Act allows the parties to a premarital agreement to contract with respect to "the modification or elimination of spousal support"

Uniform Act

[22]Allen v. Withrow, 110 S.E.2d 663 (Ga. 1959) ("where . . . the husband and wife were living in a state of separation, and the wife was suing the husband for divorce and alimony, they could enter into a valid and enforceable contract settling the issue as to alimony"). *See* Restatement Second §190(1); Uniform Marriage and Divorce Act §306.

[23]The seminal case is Posner v. Posner, 257 So. 2d 530 (Fla. 1972) (dictum: "inadequate and disproportionate provision for the wife . . . will not vitiate an antenuptial agreement").

[24]Ryken v. Ryken, 461 N.W.2d 122 (S.D. 1990) (rejecting contention that court "should impose upon Wife . . . an obligation to find out what the Husband owned," since "burden on the other spouse to disclose his assets is relatively small since that spouse knows what he owns better than anyone else").

[25]In re Marriage of Spiegel, 553 N.W.2d 309 (Iowa 1996) (property only: "We have never required that a party have precise valuations of the others assets; a general knowledge of the true nature and extent of the other's properties is sufficient.").

[26]Lewis v. Lewis, 748 P.2d 1362 (Haw. 1988) (unconscionability of support provision, in contrast to property settlement, to be determined at time of divorce).

[27]Rosenberg v. Lipneck, 389 N.E.2d 385 (Mass. 1979) (parties to antenuptial agreement "occupy a relationship of mutual trust and confidence and as such must exercise the highest degree of good faith, candor, and sincerity"). See the discussion of a relationship of trust or confidence in §4.20 *supra*.

[28]Simeone v. Simeone, 581 A.2d 162, 165 (Pa. 1990).

[29]In re Marriage of Spiegel, *supra* note 25, at 315, 316 (agreement made before effective date of Uniform Prenuptial Agreement in Iowa).

as well as "any other matter, including their personal rights and obligations, not in violation of public policy or a statute imposing a penalty."[30] At common law, however, such an agreement may be subject to attack on another ground — that it tends to encourage divorce or separation.

Agreements encouraging dissolution

Although married persons are free to terminate their relationships by divorce or separation, courts will not enforce an agreement that tends unreasonably toward dissolution of a marriage. Thus a promise by one already married to marry another is clearly unenforceable, though it is conditioned on dissolution of the first marriage.[31] Courts have had difficulty in fashioning a coherent test to determine whether, in less obvious cases, a particular promise tends unreasonably to "encourage divorce." Much depends on the particular circumstances, including the state of the marriage when the promise is made.[32] Agreements made before separation or its contemplation that fix the rights of the parties upon divorce or separation may be challenged on this ground. Although most courts will not regard such an agreement as tending unreasonably to encourage dissolution of the marriage merely because it predetermines property rights,[33] a court may refuse on this ground to enforce an agreement that eliminates or dramatically reduces the husband's traditional duty of support upon divorce or separation.[34]

Agreements affecting non-marital relationships

Courts have been particularly perplexed by the legal problems raised by persons who, instead of marrying, have simply lived together and made agreements — sometimes known as "living-together agreements" — affecting some aspects of their relationship. Courts traditionally looked with disfavor

---

[30] UPAA §3. Under §2, such an agreement "must be in writing and signed by both parties." Under §6, it cannot be enforced against a party who "did not execute the agreement voluntarily" or — if the agreement was unconscionable when made — who "was not provided a fair and reasonable disclosure of the property or financial obligations of the other party," who did not waive, in writing, any right to disclosure beyond that provided, and who neither had nor had reason to have knowledge of the relevant information. The UPAA has been adopted by a number of states.

[31] Reynolds v. Estate of Reynolds, 230 S.E.2d 842 (Ga. 1976) (agreement by married man to give stock to woman in return for her promise to marry him).

[32] For a case holding postnuptial agreement unenforceable as tending to encourage divorce, *see* Stern v. Stern, 243 A.2d 319 (Pa. 1968) (husband, regardless of whether he contested divorce, was to make payments to wife unless no final decree was entered within six months and wife was to share in proceeds of sale of their home unless there was a reconciliation).

[33] Marriage of Dawley, *supra* note 18 (there is no requirement "that parties to an antenuptial agreement must contemplate a lifelong marriage," and such an agreement determining property rights in the event of dissolution is unenforceable only if "the *terms* of the agreement promote or encourage the dissolution of [the] marriage").

[34] Estate of Duncan, *supra* note 1 (antenuptial contract establishing "companionate marriage" and providing that, upon marital discord, wife would relinquish all claims against husband in return for $100 for each year they had lived together "was a wicked device to evade the laws applicable to marriage relations, property rights, and divorces, and . . . was nothing more . . . than an attempt . . . to legalize prostitution").

upon such "cohabitation contracts" because they have regarded them not only as immoral but also as a threat to the institution of marriage.[35] However, there has been a marked change in this attitude, highlighted by a noted California case decided in 1976.

Lee Marvin, a movie actor, and Michelle Marvin, a former entertainer, had lived together for seven years, during which she had taken his name and he had taken title to all property acquired. She sued, alleging a contract in which they had agreed to hold themselves out as husband and wife, and, in return for her rendering services "as a companion, homemaker, housekeeper and cook," she was to "share equally any and all property accumulated as a result of their efforts whether individual or combined." In *Marvin v. Marvin*, the Supreme Court of California held that she had stated "a cause of action for breach of an express contract." The Court noted the "substantial increase in the number of couples living together without marrying" and observed that "many young couples live together without the solemnization of marriage, in order to make sure that they can successfully later undertake marriage." The court concluded that "a contract between nonmarital partners is unenforceable only *to the extent* that it *explicitly* rests upon the immoral and illicit consideration of meretricious sexual services" and that a contract concerning earnings, property, or expenses is not invalid merely because "a man and a woman live together without marriage, and engage in a sexual relationship" or because "the parties may have contemplated the creation or continuation of a nonmarital relationship when they entered into it."[36]

Marvin has not found universal favor. Some courts have denied recovery, balking at spelling out the terms of an implied contract. Thus the New York Court of Appeals concluded that for a court "to attempt through hindsight to sort out the intentions of the parties and affix jural significance to conduct carried out within an essentially private and generally noncontractual relationship runs too great a risk of error.[37] Other courts have allowed recovery but grounded it on status rather than on contract. Thus the Supreme Court of Washington adopted "a general rule requiring a just and equitable distribution of property following a meretricious relationship," looking for guidance to the laws governing the distribution of marital property.[38] But *Marvin* has had a substantial impact in many jurisdictions,[39] an impact that has carried over to claims arising out

Example of
Marvin

Impact of ***Marvin***

---

[35] Hewitt v. Hewitt, 394 N.E.2d 1204 (Ill. 1979) ("enhancing the attractiveness of a private arrangement over marriage . . . contravenes the . . . policy of strengthening and preserving the integrity of marriage").

[36] 557 P.2d 106, 109, 112, 113, 122, 123 (Cal. 1976).

[37] Morone v. Morone, 413 N.E.2d 1154, 1157 (N.Y. 1980).

[38] Connell v. Francisco, 898 P.2d 831, 834-35 (Wash. 1995).

[39] Watts v. Watts, 405 N.W.2d 303 (Wis. 1987) ("public policy does not necessarily preclude an unmarried cohabitant from asserting a contract claim against the other party . . . so long as the claim exists independently of the sexual relationship").

of contracts between persons of the same sex.[40] It has also carried over to restitutionary claims.[41] Courts have held that the circumstance that the man, at least, is married does not require a different result.[42] Whether courts will go beyond *Marvin* and uphold agreements in which sexual intercourse is at least some part of the agreement remains to be seen.[43] The common requirement that the agreement not be too closely connected with sexual intercourse has prompted some interesting judicial flights of fancy.

From this discussion of policies developed by the courts, we turn to a discussion of policies derived by courts from legislation.

C. POLICIES DERIVED FROM LEGISLATION

Increasing role of legislation

§5.5. Judicial Derivation of Policies from Legislation. Although many important public policies were first recognized by judges, the declaration of public policy has become increasingly the province of legislators. Legislators are usually more responsive to the public than are judges and have facilities for factual investigations that judges do not. For example, bargains tending to encourage litigation and improperly to influence legislators and other government officials have come under extensive legislative control.[1] Thus legislation supplements or replaces the common law of maintenance and champerty in many states,[2] and penal laws condemn bribery and corrupt influence, perjury and other falsification in official matters, and obstruction of government operation.[3] Older laws prohibiting usury have been supplemented by newer ones

---

[40]Whorton v. Dillingham, 248 Cal. Rptr. 405 (Ct. App. 1988) (*Marvin* extended to homosexual male plaintiff).

[41]Watts v. Watts, *supra* note 39 ("unmarried cohabitants may raise claims based on unjust enrichment following the termination of their relationships where one of the parties attempts to retain an unreasonable amount of the property acquired through the efforts of both"). On restitutionary claims by married and unmarried cohabitants, see the discussion of intimate relationships in §2.20 *supra*.

[42]*Marvin* is an example (male defendant was married, but female plaintiff, "being unmarried could neither be convicted of adulterous cohabitation nor of aiding and abetting defendant's violation").

[43]For a case that goes beyond *Marvin*, *see* Whorton v. Dillingham, *supra* note 40 (as distinguished from *Marvin*, "here the parties' sexual relationship was an express rather than implied, part of the consideration" and issue is "whether the sexual component . . . is severable").

§5.5 [1]See the discussion of the great variety of policies in §5.2 *supra*.

[2]*See* Mass. Ann. Laws ch. °221 §§43-44B (attorneys prohibited from soliciting business); N.Y. Jud. Law °§474-a (contingent fees regulated in actions for medical malpractice).

[3]*See* Model Penal Code §§240-243. As to statutes regulating lobbying, see footnote to the discussion of the great variety of policies in §5.2 *supra*.

dealing with consumer transaction[4] and older laws prohibiting gambling have been subjected to more modern exceptions.[5]

When legislators make conduct a crime, however, they seldom deal explicitly with the enforceability of contracts involving that conduct.[6] The legislation, even with the usual aids to its interpretation, commonly serves only to indicate a policy that the legislature regarded as significant. It is for the court to balance that policy against the policy favoring respect for party autonomy and determine whether unenforceability should be added to the sanctions provided by the legislature.

Function of court

If a statute expressly prohibits making the agreement or engaging in the agreed conduct, courts have often assumed that the agreement is unenforceable. This was the traditional judicial response to agreements made on Sunday in violation of statutes prohibiting the transaction of business on Sunday[7] and to agreements requiring performance on Sunday in violation of statutes prohibiting doing work on Sunday.[8] However, this response is not inevitable. A court may conclude that the sanction explicitly provided by the legislature is adequate to further the statute's underlying policy, without the additional sanction of unenforceability.[9]

Agreement or conduct prohibited

In deciding such cases, courts have sometimes attempted to distinguish cases in which the proscribed conduct is merely *malum prohibitum* ("wrong because prohibited") from those in which it is *malum in se* ("wrong in itself").[10] Jeremy Bentham wisely deprecated this distinction, "which being so shrewd and sounding so pretty, and being in Latin, has no sort of an occasion to have any meaning to it: accordingly it has none."[11] There is no simple substitute for the balancing process that a court must undertake in these cases.

Malum prohibitum or malum in se

---

[4]*See* Uniform Consumer Credit Code §§2.201, 2.202, 2.401.

[5]*See* N.J. Stat. Ann. °§5:12 (authorizing casino gambling in Atlantic City); N.Y. Rac. Pari-Mut. Wag. & Breed. Law °§§518-532 (authorizing off-track pari-mutuel betting). As to the common law on gambling, see the discussion of the great variety of policies in §5.2 *supra*.

[6]Common exceptions are gambling and usury laws, which often provide that proscribed contracts are "void." *See* N.Y. Gen. Oblig. Law §§5-411 (gambling), 5-511 (usury).

[7]Sauls v. Stone, 241 So. 2d 836 (Ala. 1970) (agreement made on Sunday for sale of business held unenforceable).

[8]Ewing v. Halsey, 272 P. 187 (Kan. 1928) (agreement by "Halsey's Flying Circus" to put on performance on Sunday was unenforceable, and Halsey was not liable for damages when he failed to appear).

[9]Daynard v. Ness, Motley, Loadholt, Richardson & Poole, 188 F. Supp. 2d 115 (D. Mass. 2002) ("public policy concerns inherent in the regulation of fee-splitting agreements are not significantly undermined through enforcement of this contract"). Revised Article 2 includes a new provision under which failure to comply with an array of listed laws, for example a "blood shield" statute insulating from liability a nonnegligent supplier of defective blood, "has only the effect specified in that law." UCC 2-108(3).

[10]Gardner v. Reed, 42 So. 2d 206 (Miss. 1949) (making contract for sale of fertilizer without complying with statutory requirements, such as registration as dealer and payment of inspection fees, "was not malum in se but merely malum prohibitum").

[11]J. Bentham, Comment on the Commentaries 80 (C. Everett ed. 1928).

Factors in court's decision

The Supreme Court of Indiana has listed five factors to be considered by a court engaged in this process:

> (i) the nature of the subject matter of the contract . . . ; (ii) the strength of the public policy underlying the statute . . . ; (iii) the likelihood that refusal to enforce the bargain or term will further that policy . . . ; (iv) how serious or deserved would be the forfeiture suffered by the party attempting to enforce the bargain . . . ; and (v) the parties' relative bargaining power and freedom to contract . . . .[12]

A court may be aided by the history and purpose of the legislation for, even if the legislature did not deal explicitly with the question of unenforceability, it may be helpful to search for the "intention of the legislature" on the matter.[13] A disparity between a relatively modest criminal sanction and a much greater forfeiture that will result if enforcement is refused may suggest that the policy in question is not substantial enough to justify the refusal.[14] Furthermore, the court may look beyond the particular statutory provision to the entire legislative scheme. If it finds, for example, that similar statutes in the same field contain explicit provisions making comparable agreements unenforceable, it may infer from the absence of such a provision in the statute at hand that the additional sanction of unenforceability is inappropriate.[15]

Frustration of policy

It has been said that the defense of illegality "is not automatic but requires . . . a comparison of the pros and cons of enforcement" and a consideration of "the reciprocal dangers of overdeterrence and underdeterrence."[16] Sometimes refusal to enforce the agreement will not further the policy that occasioned enactment of the statute.[17] In some situations it may even frustrate it. For example, if the legislation was enacted to protect a class of persons to which the claimant belongs in a situation like that before the court, refusal to enforce the agreement is usually inappropriate.[18] Furthermore, refusal to

---

[12] Fresh Cut v. Fazli, 650 N.E.2d 1126, 1130 (Ind. 1995).

[13] Gates v. Rivers Constr. Co., 515 P.2d 1020 (Alaska 1973) (where "the predecessor to the present statute expressly made such contracts void and of no effect . . . , repeal of the former section coupled with the new enactment evinces an intent on the part of Congress that such contracts are no longer to be 'void and of no effect'").

[14] DeCato Bros. v. Westinghouse Credit Corp., 129 N.H. 504, 529 A.2d 952 (1987) (lender's violation of statute requiring disclosure of interest, punishable as misdemeanor, was "not so repugnant as to entitle [borrower] to . . . the free use of a large amount of money").

[15] As to the significance in connection with licensing statutes, see the discussion of a regulatory or other purpose in §5.6 *infra*.

[16] Northern Ind. Pub. Serv. Co. v. Carbon County Coal Co., 799 F.2d 265, 273 (7th Cir. 1986).

[17] Miller v. Radikopf, 228 N.W.2d 386 (Mich. 1975) (statute prohibiting lottery did not make agreement to split winnings from Irish Sweepstakes unenforceable because "nonenforcement . . . might tend to discourage people from agreeing to split their legal winnings [but] would not tend to discourage people from buying or selling Irish Sweepstakes tickets").

[18] See the discussion of when the agreement may be enforceable by the other party in §5.6 *infra*.

enforce the agreement may frustrate the policy of the statute, though it was not enacted to protect persons such as the claimant. For example, federal immigration and nationality laws prohibit aliens to enter into employment agreements except in prescribed circumstances, and it has been held that an alien cannot recover earnings under an agreement made in violation of these laws.[19] However, a more enlightened court held that the alien can recover, recognizing that the purpose of legislation, "safeguarding of American labor from unwanted competition, . . . would not be furthered by permitting employers knowingly to employ excludable aliens and then, with impunity, to refuse to pay them for their services [and that] to so hold could well have the opposite effect from the one intended."[20] Furthermore, if the court finds abusive or oppressive conduct on the part of the other party, it may justify enforcement on the ground that the parties are not *in pari delicto*.[21]

Legislation in broad sense

The term *legislation* is used here in the broadest sense, to include not only statutes and constitutions[22] but also local ordinances and administrative regulations[23] and even codes of professional conduct.[24] A court should be alert, however, to the possibility that a minor ordinance or regulation may not indicate a sufficiently significant or broad interest to outweigh the interest in enforcement of the agreement.

Change in legislation

In general, the relevant legislation is that in effect at the time the agreement was made.[25] Therefore, courts have usually held that if a promise is unenforceable on grounds of public policy when made, it does not become enforceable if the legislature later changes the law, unless the legislature manifests an intent to validate such promises.[26] This is a questionable rule if the reason for the change

---

[19] Short v. Bullion-Beck & Champion Mining Co., 57 P. 720 (Utah 1899) (employee could not recover for services rendered under contract in violation of statute prohibiting work in mill for more than eight hours a day).

[20] Gates v. Rivers Constr. Co., *supra* note 13, at 1022.

[21] *See* Trees v. Kersey, 56 P.3d 765 (Idaho 2002) (court may enforce where "parties are not equally at fault by reason of the fact that one party commits fraud, or there is duress, oppression, or undue influence"). This exception, however, traditionally allows restitution rather than enforcement. See the discussion of not equally in the wrong in §5.9 *infra*.

[22] Wm. R. Clarke Corp. v. Safeco Ins. Co., 938 P.2d 372 (Cal. 1997) ("pay-*if*-paid" provision that applied regardless of reason for nonpayment was unenforceable as contrary to policy underlying state constitutional right to mechanic's lien).

[23] Lund v. Bruflat, 292 P. 112 (Wash. 1930) (city ordinance requiring licensing of plumbers).

[24] Matter of Cooperman, 633 N.E.2d 1069 (N.Y. 1994) (lawyer's nonrefundable retainer fee agreement violated Code of Professional Responsibility).

[25] Although the relevant law is ordinarily also that of the place where the conduct occurred, *see* Lewkowicz v. El Paso Apparel Corp., 625 S.W.2d 301 (Tex. 1981) ("contract made in consideration of compounding a criminal offense is void because it is in contravention of the [Texas] Penal Code and public policy" and fact that conduct occurred in Mexico was "no less abhorrent than had it been committed in Texas").

[26] Interinsurance Exch. v. Ohio Cas. Ins. Co., 373 P.2d 640 (Cal. 1962) (provision excluding permissive users from automobile insurance policy did not become enforceable on change in statute that prohibited such provisions).

is a dissatisfaction with the underlying policy. Many courts have adhered to it, however, even where the promisor ratified or made a new promise after the change.[27] This is in contrast to their general willingness to recognize a ratification or new promise in other types of cases.[28] For example, if a promise to pay a debt is unenforceable because the rate of interest is usurious, a new promise to pay the debt with no more than the legal rate of interest "purges" the usury and is enforceable.[29] In the converse situation, in which the promise is enforceable when made but the performance is subsequently prohibited by law, the promisor may be excused from performing on the ground of impracticability.[30] But if the promisor nonetheless performs, courts have not generally allowed recovery under the contract.[31]

In the next section we consider situations in which it is clear that refusal of enforcement will further the policy underlying the relevant legislation, but it is questionable whether refusal is justified in view of the forfeiture that would result.

Three types of cases

§5.6. Application to Commercial Bribery, Unlicensed Claimants, and Improper Use. The general principles discussed in the preceding section are especially difficult to apply when a party seeking to recover the price of goods delivered or services rendered is met with the defense that recovery is precluded on grounds of public policy. Though the court may be convinced that refusal to enforce the agreement will further the policy in question, it must take account of the obvious possibility of forfeiture when it weighs the factors for and against enforcement.[1] In determining the extent of the possible forfeiture, the court will consider whether the agreement is divisible, so that it can be enforced in part,[2] and whether restitution is available.[3] Unless the court concludes that the strength of the public policy is sufficient to justify the resulting forfeiture, it should not deny enforcement. In this section we consider

---

[27] Handy v. St. Paul Globe Publishing Co., 42 N.W. 872 (Minn. 1889) (agreement to publish newspaper on Sunday was "incapable of being ratified," even after amendment of law to except newspapers).

[28] Central Labor Council v. Young, 240 P. 919 (Wash. 1925) (new promise to pay over sums collected in performing agreement to sell tickets to illegal lottery was enforceable).

[29] Whittemore Homes v. Fleishman, 12 Cal. Rptr. 235 (Ct. App. 1961) (abandonment of original agreement and "execution of a new obligation for the amount of the original debt . . . bearing only legal interest purges the original usury"). *See* Restatement Second §86 cmt. *h* ("promise to pay the original debt with interest that is not usurious in substitution for the usurious interest is enforceable").

[30] See the discussions of supervening illegality in §9.5 and of examples of a basic assumption in §9.6 *infra*.

[31] Tocci v. Lembo, 92 N.E.2d 254 (Mass. 1950) (contractor barred from recovery for work done after construction was prohibited).

§5.6   [1] See the discussion of the balancing of interests in §5.1 *supra*.

[2] See §5.8 *infra*.

[3] See §5.9 *infra*.

338

three recurring types of cases that present this <u>problem of possible forfeiture:</u> cases in which <u>commercial bribery</u> is involved, cases in which the <u>claimant is unlicensed,</u> and cases in which the <u>claimant knew that his performance would be put to an improper use.</u> In each of these situations, be it noted, there is nothing in the terms of the agreement itself that offends public policy.

In the typical case involving commercial bribery, a seller that sues for the price of goods delivered is met with the defense that the agreement is unenforceable because the seller bribed the buyer's agent to induce him to make the agreement.[4] Statutes in a number of states specifically make such commercial bribery a crime.[5]

Commercial bribery cases

In the controversial case of *Sirkin v. Fourteenth St. Store*, a seller of hosiery sued a store for the purchase price of hosiery delivered to it. The store's defense was that the [seller had obtained the contract by bribing the store's purchasing agent,] in violation of a New York statute that made such bribery a misdemeanor. The trial court rejected this defense, but the Appellate Division of the New York Supreme Court reversed. Although the statute did not expressly make the contract unenforceable, <u>it evidenced "the public policy of the state, [and] it was the duty of the court to be guided thereby in administering the law."</u> The court opined that "<u>nothing will be more effective in stopping the growth and spread of this corrupting</u> and now criminal custom than a decision that the courts will <u>refuse their aid to a guilty vendor."[6]</u> A strong dissent declared it "no part of our duty to assume legislative power and prescribe an additional punishment."[7] The harsh result has not prevented the case from being cited with approval.[8]

Example of *Sirkin*

Half a century later, the New York Court of Appeals considered another example of a defense based on commercial bribery in *McConnell v. Commonwealth Pictures Corp.* A movie distributor, desiring distribution rights for motion pictures from a producer, agreed to pay McConnell $10,000 on the execution of the contract plus a percentage of gross receipts if McConnell succeeded in negotiating a contract for the rights with the producer. The enterprising McConnell succeeded by agreeing to pay the producer's agent the $10,000 as a bribe. When the distributor discovered that McConnell had paid the $10,000 to the producer's agent, it refused to pay McConnell his percentage of the gross receipts, and McConnell sued the distributor. He argued that [there was nothing improper about his contract with the distributor, since it did not contemplate his paying a bribe.] Furthermore, in contrast to *Sirkin*, the contract on which suit was brought was not obtained by payment of a

Example of *McConnell*

---

[4]The agreement under which the other party's agent is to pay the bribe is clearly unenforceable because it involves a breach of the agent's fiduciary duty to the principal. See the discussion of the policy against wrongs in §5.2 *supra*.

[5]*See* N.J. Stat. Ann. °§2C: 21-10; N.Y. Penal Law °§180.00-180.08.

[6]108 N.Y.S. 830, 833-34 (App. Div. 1908).

[7]108 N.Y.S. at 838.

[8]It is the basis of Restatement Second §178 illus. 12.

bribe. Nevertheless, the court found "a direct connection between the illegal transaction and the obligation" and held for the distributor on the ground that, as in *Sirkin*, the interest in enforcement was outweighed by the public policy against commercial bribery.[9] Holmes once said, "If the contract was legal, it would not be made illegal by misconduct on the part of the plaintiff in carrying it out."[10] However, *McConnell* shows that this is not a safe generalization.[11]

Unlicensed claimant cases

Cases of the second type, those involving unlicensed claimants, also contradict Holmes's generalization. In cases of this second type, a party who seeks to recover the price of goods delivered or services performed under an agreement is met with the defense that the party failed to comply with a licensing requirement. Although most of the leading cases involve licensing requirements, analogous problems arise under registration and similar requirements. In such cases, as in the licensing cases, sometimes the defense has succeeded,[12] and sometimes it has failed.[13]

Regulatory or other purpose

In deciding the licensing cases, courts have traditionally distinguished between requirements that have a regulatory purpose and those that do not. A court may regard the policy underlying a licensing requirement that has a regulatory purpose as sufficiently strong to justify a refusal to enforce the agreement, even though forfeiture will result.[14] A court will not, however, regard the policy underlying a requirement designed merely to raise revenue as sufficiently strong to justify a refusal.[15] In deciding whether the purpose is regulatory, a court will consider the entire legislative scheme, including any legislative

---

[9] 166 N.E.2d 494, 497 (N.Y. 1960) (5-2).

[10] Barry v. Capen, 23 N.E. 735 (Mass. 1890).

[11] *See* United States v. Acme Process Equip. Co., 385 U.S. 138 (1966) (government not bound by contract with general contractor whose key employees had accepted compensation for awarding subcontracts in violation of Anti-Kickback Act, since such kickbacks would be passed on to the government).

[12] Brooks v. R.A. Clark's Garage, 378 A.2d 1144 (N.H. 1977) (failure of garage to give customer written estimate as required by consumer protection statute barred garage from recovering for repairs).

[13] Taylor Thiemann & Aitkin v. Hayes, 418 S.E.2d 897 (Va. 1992) (lobbying contract not unenforceable because "Lobbying Act . . . does not require . . . registration prior to the execution of a contract for those services" and "illegality, if any, occurred after the contract was executed, when [lawyer] failed to register before taking action within the scope of the Lobbying Act").

[14] Capital Constr. Co. v. Plaza West Coop. Assn., 604 A.2d 428 (D.C. 1992) (though "strictness with which we have adhered to this rule has sometimes led to 'seemingly harsh results' . . . we have deferred to 'the legislature's intentional exposure of unlicensed contractors' . . . in order to carry out the legislative purpose of protecting homeowners from fraudulent and unscrupulous practices").

[15] M. Arthur Gensler, Jr., & Assocs. v. Larry Barrett, Inc., 499 P.2d 503 (Cal. 1972) (at most, failure to apply for amended building permit "affected only the revenue-raising provisions of the code and not those directed at public protection").

declaration of purpose and provisions for examination, apprenticeship, posting a bond, and license revocation.[16]

Balancing of interests

Even if the court concludes that the purpose is regulatory, it will not refuse to enforce the agreement <u>unless the policy underlying the licensing requirement clearly outweighs the interest in enforcing the agreement</u>. Courts have been increasingly reluctant to refuse enforcement on the ground of mere noncompliance with some regulatory law. A court may disregard the noncompliance if the regulation is intended to serve only an economic interest, and not an interest in health or safety,[17] if the penalty provided by the legislature for violation is relatively modest,[18] or if there has been substantial compliance with the licensing requirement.[19] And it may infer, from the legislation's silence on the question of unenforceability when compared with explicit provisions in similar legislation, that this additional sanction is inappropriate.[20]

Enforceability by other party

That an agreement is unenforceable by an unlicensed party does not necessarily mean that it is unenforceable by the other party. If the regulatory legislation is designed to protect persons in a particular class, a court may conclude that the policy underlying the legislation will best be served by allowing a claimant who is a member of that class to hold the unlicensed party in damages for any defective performance.[21] It may also conclude that

---

[16] Benjamin v. Koeppel, 650 N.E.2d 829 (N.Y. 1995) ("attorney registration system more closely resembles a revenue-raising measure").

[17] Rush-Presbyterian-St. Luke's Medical Center v. Hellenic Republic, 980 F.2d 449 (7th Cir. 1992) ("We do not think that a permit requirement designed to prevent the oversupply of competent services should be equated to a license requirement designed to protect people from incompetent practitioners."); John E. Rosasco Creameries v. Cohen, 11 N.E.2d 908 (N.Y. 1937) (although milk dealer was unlicensed, violation of statute did "not endanger health or morals").

[18] Rush-Presbyterian-St. Luke's Medical Center v. Hellenic Republic, *supra* note 17 ("Proportionality is the cornerstone of a rational system of sanctions" and "forfeiture of $200,000 is an excessive punishment for an offense punishable by a fine of only $10,000 and so lightly regarded by the state that it has not sought to impose the fine even though it learned of the violation years ago."); John E. Rosasco Creameries v. Cohen, *supra* note 17 (violations were punishable as misdemeanors, by fine of up to $200 and imprisonment of up to six months, whereas denial of enforcement will "punish the plaintiff to the extent of a loss of approximately $11,000 and permit the defendants to evade the payment of a legitimate debt").

[19] Asdourian v. Araj, 696 P.2d 95 (Cal. 1985) (contractor operated as sole proprietorship using own name instead of name of business under which he obtained license).

On the effect of fraud on the part of the other party, *see* Trees v. Kersey, 56 P.3d 765 (Idaho 2002) (applying exception where "parties are not equally at fault by reason of the fact that one party commits fraud, or there is duress, oppression, or undue influence").

[20] Mountain States Bolt, Nut & Screw Co. v. Best-Way Transp. Co., 568 P.2d 430 (Ariz. App. 1977) (where legislature expressly barred recovery by improperly licensed contractors, but did not do so in the case of deficiently licensed carriers, such a carrier was not barred from recovering for services). *See* Restatement Second §181.

[21] Hedla v. McCool, 476 F.2d 1223 (9th Cir. 1973) (owners could recover damages for delay caused by inadequacy of plans furnished by architects who were unlicensed where owners did not know this).

the claimant is entitled, in the alternative, to restitution of any payments made.[22]

Improper use cases

In the third type of case, a party that sues for the price of a performance rendered is met with the defense that, although the performance could have been put to a proper use, the party knew that the other party intended to put it to a use forbidden by law. Most of the cases have involved claims by sellers for the price of goods delivered. If the seller did not know of the purpose when the contract was made, the seller can recover the price[23] or have damages for the breach.[24] If the seller refuses to deliver the goods, however, the buyer has no claim for breach of contract.[25]

Knowledge alone not enough

A few courts have taken the position that mere knowledge of improper use is enough to bar the seller from recovering the price.[26] However, most courts have allowed sellers to recover the price of goods delivered, even if they knew of the buyer's intended use.[27] A seller that sells a gun, knowing that the buyer intends to use it to hunt out of season, can generally recover the price. The result would presumably be different if the improper use threatens grave social harm, as when the seller of the gun knows that the buyer intends to use it to commit a murder. As a justice of the United States Supreme Court opined a few years after the end of the Civil War, a seller of goods to a contractor for the Confederate States

> cannot be permitted to stand on the nice metaphysical distinction that, although he knows that the purchaser buys the goods for the purpose of aiding the rebellion, he does not sell them for that purpose. The consequences of his acts are too serious and enormous to admit of such a plea.[28]

And even if the improper use threatens no grave social harm, if the seller has acted to further that use, a court will deny recovery. Thus where a seller of

---

[22]Truitt v. Miller, 407 A.2d 1073 (D.C. 1979) (owners of house entitled to restitution of payments made to unlicensed home improvement contractor before they knew he was not licensed).

[23]Lipault Co. v. Iowa Novelty Co., 204 N.W. 252 (Iowa 1925) (seller could recover price for goods where he did not know that buyer bought them for resale as gambling devices).

[24]Gold Bond Stamp Co. v. Bradfute Corp., 463 F.2d 1158 (2d Cir. 1972) (where trading stamp company was unaware that "it was participating in an illegal sales promotion, [and] its participation in the operation of the promotion was minimal," it could recover additional expenses caused by promoter's breach).

[25]Church v. Proctor, 66 F. 240 (1st Cir. 1895) (buyer could not recover damages for seller's breach of contract to sell fish that buyer intended to misbrand to deceive customers).

[26]Advance Whip & Novelty Co. v. Benevolent Protective Order of Elks, 170 A. 95 (Vt. 1934) (seller of goods ordinarily used for gaming purposes could not recover price where it knew goods were to be used in Vermont in violation of statute).

[27]Carroll v. Beardon, 381 P.2d 295 (Mont. 1963) (purchase money mortgage resulting from sale of house of prostitution from one madam to another was not unenforceable since "bare knowledge of the purpose for which the property is sold is not enough"). *See* Restatement Second §182.

[28]Hanauer v. Doane, 79 U.S. (12 Wall.) 342, 347 (1871) (Bradley, J.).

342

candy and silverware facilitated the buyer's illegal lottery of the silverware by concealing tickets in some of the packages of the candy, the New York Court of Appeals held that seller could not recover the price of the goods delivered. Because the seller had acted "to aid or further the unlawful design" of the buyer, the court followed "the not unfamiliar English cases" that had held that if a seller of goods to be smuggled into England "has so packed the goods as to facilitate the smuggling, he is regarded as *particeps criminis* and cannot recover."[29]

We look next at the techniques courts sometimes use to mitigate the effects of unenforceability.

D.   MITIGATING TECHNIQUES

§5.7.   Mitigation in General.   In some cases, refusal to allow a party to enforce an agreement on grounds of public policy seems unduly harsh. We have seen that a court may be able to avoid this result by so interpreting the language of the agreement as to avoid any contravention of public policy and make the agreement enforceable.[1] And even if the court refuses to enforce the agreement, a party that has done nothing in reliance on the agreement will lose no more than its expectation. But a party that has relied on the agreement, as by performing or preparing to perform, before receiving the return performance will suffer forfeiture through loss of its reliance interest.[2] To the extent that the party's reliance has conferred a benefit on the other party, there may also be unjust enrichment. In such cases, courts have used several techniques to mitigate the harshness of the result.

Function of mitigation

One of these techniques is to allow a party to recover damages for breach of the agreement if the party was excusably ignorant, and the other party was not, of facts that would render the agreement unenforceable.[3] Thus a party that makes an agreement with an unlicensed party may be allowed to recover on the ground of excusable ignorance of the fact that the licensing requirement was not met.[4] On learning the truth, the innocent party is expected to withdraw

Excusable ignorance

---

[29] Hull v. Ruggles, 56 N.Y. 424, 428-29 (1874).

§5.7   [1] See the discussion of how interpretation is affected by public policy in §5.1 *supra*.

[2] See the discussion of the preference against forfeiture in §8.4 *infra*.

[3] Weinsklar Realty Co. v. Dooley, 228 N.W. 515 (Wis. 1930) (one party was ignorant that other had signed contract on Sunday in violation of statute).

Restatement Second §180 states circumstances under which a promisee who is "excusably ignorant of facts or of legislation of a minor character" may enforce a promise that would otherwise be unenforceable.

[4] Hedla v. McCool, 476 F.2d 1223 (1973) (owners could recover damages for delay caused by inadequacy of plans furnished by architects who were unlicensed where owners did not know this). If this is the basis of recovery, the plaintiff need not show that it is in a class intended to be protected by the statute. See the discussion of frustration of policy in §5.5 *supra*.

from the transaction promptly and render no further performance.[5] Though a party's ignorance may be excusable even if not induced by the other party, a court will give weight to any misrepresentations made by the other party. If, however, the other party is also excusably ignorant, a court will not enforce the agreement against the other party.[6]

We turn now to the two most important techniques for mitigation: treating the agreement as divisible and allowing restitution.

Partial unenforceability

§5.8. Divisibility. Although, as mentioned earlier, courts often make sweeping condemnations of agreements as entirely "void" on grounds of public policy,[1] they just as often avoid an "all or nothing" decision by holding agreements unenforceable only in part. Sometimes one of the parties can enforce the agreement, though the other cannot.[2] Sometimes a party can get damages for breach of the agreement, though the party is barred from specific performance.[3]

Unenforceability as to part on each side

In other instances a court will divide the performances on both sides into corresponding pairs of part performances, and it will enforce the agreement as to one pair, reasoning that this part of the agreement does not materially advance the improper purpose.[4] Such an agreement is said to be "divisible" or "severable." When an unlicensed plumber contracted to do work and furnished materials in violation of an ordinance that required a plumber to be licensed to furnish services as a plumber, the Supreme Court of Washington held that the agreement was divisible, so that the plumber could enforce it with respect to the materials but not the work.[5] When a seller contracted to sell machines, some of which were of a type that violated the gambling laws, the Supreme Court of California held that the agreement was divisible, so that the seller could enforce it with respect to those machines delivered that were not to be used for gambling but not the others.[6]

---

[5]Bond v. Charlson, 374 N.W.2d 423 (Minn. 1985) (though purpose of Blue Sky Laws is to protect investing public from fraudulent sales of securities, that purpose "is not served by permitting one who loses his innocence to await the outcome of his investment before invoking the securities act").

[6]As to the possibility of restitution in that situation, see the discussion of excusable ignorance in §5.9 *infra*. On the effect of ignorance generally, see the discussion of factors favoring enforcement in §5.1 *supra*.

§5.8 [1]See the discussion of the agreement as not necessarily void in §5.1 *supra*.

[2]See the discussions of frustration of policy in §5.5, of enforceability by the other party in §5.6, and of unenforceability as to part on one side in §5.7 *supra*. Thus a promise that is unenforceable on grounds of public policy can be consideration for another promise.

[3]See the discussion of the rule of reason in §5.3 *supra*. See also §12.7 *infra*.

[4]*See* Restatement Second §183.

[5]Lund v. Bruflat, 292 P. 112 (Wash. 1930) (unlicensed plumber could recover sum that represents "materials entering into the building of which [owners] received the benefit, and is clearly severable from the illegal contract for plumbing services").

[6]Keene v. Harling, 392 P.2d 273 (Cal. 1964) (contract for sale of coin-operated machine business, including some illegal bingo-type machines, was divisible).

Whether an agreement is divisible for this purpose is a question of substance **Two requirements**
and is not determined by the mere form of the agreement. As in other situ- **for divisibility**
ations where the concept of divisibility is invoked, two requirements must be
met.[7] First, it must be possible to apportion the parties' performances into
corresponding pairs of part performances. This process of apportionment is
essentially one of calculation, and the agreement is not divisible unless calculation is feasible. Under a contract for the sale of goods, it is enough if the price
of separate items is separately stated in the agreement or in a price list on which
the agreement was based, or if it can be reliably ascertained from stated prices
for components or from a total price for similar items.[8] Second, it must be
proper to regard the parts of each pair as agreed equivalents. This means that
the parts of the pair must be of roughly equivalent value to the injured party
in terms of that party's expectation with respect to the total agreed exchange.[9]
Fairness requires that the recipient of only a fraction of the expected performance should not be asked to pay that fraction of the price unless it appears that
the value to the recipient of the performance received is roughly that fraction
of the value of full performance. Since the rule is based on considerations of
fairness, it is necessarily somewhat imprecise and flexible. Moreover, an agreement is not necessarily divisible for this purpose, even though it is divisible for
some other purpose.[10]

Furthermore, courts impose two additional limitations on divisibility if part **Two additional**
of the agreement offends public policy. One is that the impropriety must not **limitations**
affect the entire agreement; it must not be an integrated scheme to contravene
public policy.[11] The other is that the party seeking enforcement must not have
engaged in serious misconduct.[12] Though a court may enforce part of a divisible
contract in favor of a party who has done nothing in reliance on it, a court is
more likely to do so in favor of a party who has already relied on the agreement,
as by preparation or performance.[13] In such a case a court will also take account
of the availability of restitution as an alternative means of avoiding forfeiture.

---

[7] See the discussion of the two requirements in §8.13 *infra*.

[8] Keene v. Harling, *supra* note 6 (part of price of coin-operated machine business to be allocated
to illegal bingo-type machines determined from the market price of the illegal machines as given
monthly in a national trade publication).

[9] *See* Restatement Second §183 cmt. *b*.

[10] See the discussion of the importance of the context in §8.13 *infra*.

[11] Graham Oil Co. v. Arco Prods. Co., 43 F.3d 1244 (9th Cir. 1994, 1995) ("severance is
inappropriate when the entire [arbitration] clause represents an 'integrated scheme to contravene
public policy,'" quoting this section).

[12] Artache v. Goldin, 519 N.Y.S.2d 702 (App. Div. 1987) (as "non professional employee in
the defendant's dental practice, the plaintiff could be found less culpable than the defendant" in
violation of fee-splitting prohibition).

[13] Murray Walter, Inc. v. Sarkisian Bros., 486 N.Y.S.2d 396 (App. Div. 1985) (where party
seeking enforcement has substantially performed, "refusal to enforce the indemnification clause
would work a substantial forfeiture").

Unenforceability as to part on one side

Sometimes a court can divide one party's performance into two parts, only one of which contravenes public policy, but it cannot divide the other party's performance into corresponding equivalents. If the party against whom enforcement is sought is the party who desired the inclusion of the term, the court may face a difficult choice between holding the entire agreement unenforceable and holding the agreement enforceable with the exception of the offensive term. Though refusing to enforce the entire agreement may seem extreme if the offensive part is relatively small, enforcing the agreement without the term against the party who sought its inclusion will deprive that party of part of the expected performance, with no concession in return. However, if this part of the performance is not a material part of the agreed exchange, a court will often enforce the rest of the agreement in favor of a claimant who did not engage in serious misconduct.[14]

Examples

Common examples occur when an agreement contains a restrictive covenant or an exculpatory or penalty clause that is unenforceable on grounds of public policy. Though a court will refuse to enforce that term, it will generally enforce the rest of the agreement, even though the result is to make the contract more favorable to the party who was to be bound by the clause.[15] Another example occurs when an agreement contains a term that is unenforceable because, by conditioning one party's duty on the occurrence of an event that is contrary to public policy, it encourages the other party to cause that event to occur. If the occurrence of the event is not a material part of the agreed exchange and the party seeking enforcement did not engage in serious misconduct, a court may enforce the agreement without the offensive term.[16]

Blue-pencil rule

Troublesome questions arise when a party argues that a term of an agreement is unenforceable only in part and seeks to have the other part enforced. This occurs most commonly in connection with covenants not to compete.[17] In the nineteenth century, an English court accepted such an argument where a covenant in a sale of a business included London and other places in England and Scotland. It refused to enforce the covenant outside of London, but held that "the stipulation as to not practicing in London is valid and is not affected by the illegality of the other part."[18] This was the origin of the "blue-pencil" rule, under which a court could sustain part of an overly broad covenant not to compete if it could reduce the scope to what was reasonable merely by excising

---

[14]See Restatement §184.

[15]Wright v. Robinson, 468 So. 2d 94 (Ala. 1985) ("void provision for a confession of judgment . . . does not render an entire agreement void"). As to the comparable treatment of provisions for penalties, see the discussion of the consequences of the distinction in §12.18 *infra*.

[16]Pierce v. Hand, Arendall, Bedsole, Greaves & Johnston, 678 So. 2d 765 (Ala. 1996) (retired law partner's right to deferred compensation was enforceable even though conditioned on his compliance with unreasonable restraint). *See* Restatement Second §185.

[17]This is sometimes erroneously referred to as "reformation," when what is involved is merely partial enforcement.

[18]Mallan v. May, 152 Eng. Rep. 967, 973 (Ex. 1843).

some of the words, as it might do by editing the language with a blue pencil.[19] As a corollary of the rule, however, a court would not save a covenant by reducing its scope if this could not be done by merely excising words. For example, if a covenant said "ten years," a court would not save it by reducing the time to three years.[20]

In recent decades, however, many courts have rejected this aspect of the **More liberal rule** blue-pencil rule and have reduced the scope of covenants, even though the offending language cannot be simply "blue-pencilled" out.[21] Thus the Supreme Court of Tennessee, observing that the "most recent trend . . . has been to abandon the 'blue pencil' rule in favor of a rule of reasonableness," upheld a lower court's reduction of the length of a post-employment covenant from two years to one.[22]

This more liberal approach creates a risk that drafters of covenants not to **Possibility of** compete will write excessively broad clauses, confident that courts will cut **abuse** them down to what they consider reasonable and then uphold them. This risk is especially prevalent in connection with employment agreements, in which the employer's bargaining position is usually dominant and the agreement is often on a standard form. Courts have shown themselves alert to this risk by refusing to reduce the scope of a clause, absent a showing that it was drafted in good faith and in accordance with standards of fair dealing in view of the circumstances at the time the contract was made.[23] Furthermore, in reducing the scope of a clause, the court may fix a lesser restraint than it would have allowed the parties themselves to fix in their agreement.[24] Courts have not, however, extended the more liberal approach to other types of clauses, such as penalty clauses, that offend public policy.[25]

In the final section of this chapter, we take up the allowance of restitution as a technique for mitigation.

---

[19] Licocci v. Cardinal Assocs., 445 N.E.2d 556 (Ind. 1983) (covenant that restricted competition in three ways was enforceable as to two); Karpinski v. Ingrasci, 268 N.E.2d 751 (N.Y. 1971) (covenant not to practice "dentistry and/or Oral Surgery" held void as to dentistry but enforceable as to oral surgery under "blue pencil" rule).

[20] Beit v. Beit, 63 A.2d 161 (Conn. 1948) (where "parties intended the covenant to apply to all of New London county, not to a portion of it left wholly indefinite by the terms of the agreement," covenant was wholly unenforceable).

[21] BDO Seidman v. Hirshberg, 712 N.E.2d 1220 (N.Y. 1999) (referring to blue-pencil rule as a "now-discredited doctrine").

[22] Central Adjustment Bureau v. Ingram, 678 S.W.2d 28, 37 (Tenn. 1984).

[23] Central Adjustment Bureau v. Ingram, *supra* note 22 (if there is credible evidence "that a contract is deliberately unreasonable and oppressive, then the covenant is invalid.").

[24] Jenkins v. Jenkins Irrigation, 259 S.E.2d 47 (Ga. 1979) ("when it becomes necessary . . . to prescribe the territory, the proscribed area usually should not be as extensive as the parties could have validly negotiated").

[25] Cad Cam, Inc. v. Underwood, 521 N.E.2d 498 (Ohio App. 1987) ("refusing to extend the scope of the holding in [restrictive covenant case] to embrace the situation in which a trial court finds a damages provision . . . to be a penalty provision").

**Restitution
generally
unavailable**

§5.9. Restitution. Courts generally do not grant restitution under agreements that are unenforceable on grounds of public policy.[1] A party that is barred for this reason from enforcing the other party's promise is usually also barred from getting restitution for any performance rendered in return for the unenforceable promise.[2] Furthermore, the other party is usually also barred from getting restitution for performance rendered under the return promise.[3] In general, a court will simply leave the parties as it finds them, even though this may result in a benefit to one of them. However, in a number of exceptional situations restitution is allowed.[4]

**Disproportionate
forfeiture**

One of these exceptions is made in favor of a party who would otherwise suffer a forfeiture that is disproportionate to the contravention of public policy involved. In applying this exception, a court will take account of such factors as the deliberateness of the claimant's involvement in any misconduct, the gravity of that misconduct, and the strength of the public policy.[5] A court is particularly likely to invoke this exception in the case of technical rules or regulations.[6] On the other hand, if the transaction involves the threat of grave social harm, no forfeiture will be regarded as disproportionate.

**Excusable
ignorance**

Another exception is made in favor of a claimant who is excusably ignorant of facts or of legislation of a minor character that is the basis of the unenforceability.[7] It has already been mentioned that such excusable ignorance may enable the claimant to enforce the agreement, but this is so only if the other party

---

§5.9 [1]Barrett Builders v. Miller, 576 A.2d 455 (Conn. 1990) (Peters, C.J.: "contractor who has failed to comply with the requirements of the Home Improvement Act" is not entitled to "recover in quasi contract"). *See* Restatement Second §197. Of course, a party that can enforce an agreement in spite of an argument based on public policy can seek restitution instead.

For an account of "the legendary [English] case of a highwayman against his comrade of the road for a partnership account of his plunder," *see* Riddell, A Legal Scandal Two Hundred Years Ago, 16 A.B.A.J. 422 (1930).

[2]Landi v. Arkules, 835 P.2d 458 (Ariz. App. 1992) (purpose of licensing statute "to avoid unscrupulous and unqualified persons from performing investigative services . . . would be undermined if defendants were assured of receiving compensation for their services despite their unlicensed status").

[3]Design-4 v. Masen Mountainside Inn, 372 A.2d 640 (N.J. Super. 1977) (motel owners who knew that designer was unlicensed could not recover sums paid because "the law leaves the parties where it finds them").

[4]*See* Wade, Restitution of Benefits Acquired Through Illegal Transactions, 95 U. Pa. L. Rev. 261 (1947).

[5]Edwards v. City of Renton, 409 P.2d 153 (Wash. 1965) (builder of shopping center who agreed with city to install traffic light in return for reimbursement of cost, in violation of state bidding and budgeting statutes, was entitled to restitution). *See* Restatement Second §197.

[6]Commercial Trust & Sav. Bank v. Christensen, 535 N.W.2d 853 (S.D. 1995) ("trial court properly allowed restitution for taxes and installment payments" by lessees who "were excusably ignorant of the technical requirement that agricultural land leases not exceed twenty years").

[7]*See* Restatement Second §198(a).

is not excusably ignorant.[8] If the other party is also excusably ignorant, the claimant cannot enforce the agreement, but he is entitled to restitution under this exception.

An exception is also made in favor of a claimant not equally in the wrong with the party from whom the claimant seeks restitution.[9] Such a claimant is said to be not *in pari delicto* (equally in the wrong) with the other party.[10] Courts have applied this exception in favor of the victim of misrepresentation or oppression by the other party.[11] A gambler who is cheated in an illegal gambling transaction is not *in pari delicto* with the gambler who has cheated, and the cheated gambler can get restitution of what has been lost. As the Supreme Court of North Carolina said of the victim of a shell game, "Surely, the artless fool, who seems to have been alike bereft of his senses and his money, is not to be deemed a partaker in the same crime, *in pari delicto*, with the juggling knave who gulled and fleeced him."[12] A mere misrepresentation concerning the potential gains to be made from the transaction may not suffice, but the abuse of the bargaining process need not rise to the level that would give a right to avoidance.[13] It may be enough that the other party occupies a special position of trust or confidence[14] or makes a business of engaging in improper transactions.[15] Courts have also

Not equally in the wrong

---

[8]See the discussion of excusable ignorance in §5.7 *supra*. That a party who has the right to enforce the contract can choose restitution instead, *see* Kneeland v. Emerton, 183 N.E. 155 (Mass. 1932) (buyer of stock could recover price where he was ignorant of seller's failure to comply with state statute requiring filing of notice).

[9]Restatement Second §198.

[10]This is because of the maxim *in pari delicto potior est conditio defendentis*. See the discussion of the agreement as not necessarily void in §5.1 *supra*. On the utility of such maxims, *see* Lissenden v. C.A.V. Bosch, Ltd., [1940] App. Cas. 412, 435 (Wright, L.J.: "These general formulae are found in experience often to distract the Court's mind from the actual exigencies of the case, and to induce the Court to quote them as offering a ready made solution.").

[11]Trees v. Kersey, 56 P.3d 765 (Idaho 2002) (applying exception where "parties are not equally at fault by reason of the fact that one party commits fraud, or there is duress, oppression, or undue influence").

[12]Webb v. Fulchire, 25 N.C. (3 Ired.) 485, 487 (1843).

[13]Karpinski v. Collins, 60 Cal. Rptr. 846 (Ct. App. 1967) ("small dairyman whose economic survival was dependent upon his ability to obtain a Grade A milk contract in a locality where such contracts were extremely scarce" could recover secret rebates that he paid creamery in violation of statute, on ground that he was not *"in pari delicto . . .* since [he] was only slightly at fault and [creamery was] grievously at fault"). Compare §§4.10 (misrepresentation), 4.16 (duress), 4.20 (undue influence) *supra*.

[14]Peyton v. Margiotti, 156 A.2d 865 (Pa. 1959) (where lawyer who took contingent fee for obtaining pardon for criminal was unsuccessful, client was entitled to recover fee since "parties were not equal"). For a poignant case, *see* Liebman v. Rosenthal, 57 N.Y.S.2d 875 (Sup. Ct.), aff'd mem., 59 N.Y.S.2d 148 (App. Div. 1945) (Parisian was not *in pari delicto* with intermediary whom he paid to bribe Portuguese consul in Bayonne, France, to enable Parisian and family to escape from Nazis, and he could have restitution when intermediary absconded with funds).

[15]Watts v. Malatesta, 186 N.E. 210 (N.Y. 1933) (professional gambler could not offset his losses when sued by amateur because "in the eye of the law the professional gambler and his customer . . . are not *in pari delicto*").

applied this exception if the claimant is considered less in the wrong because of belonging to a class that the public policy is designed to protect.[16] It has already been pointed out that a court may rely on this circumstance to permit the claimant to enforce the agreement.[17] However, even if the court does not permit enforcement, it may allow the claimant restitution.[18] Courts have not generally invoked this exception when the claimant has engaged in serious misconduct.[19]

Withdrawal from transaction

Yet another exception is made in favor of a claimant who has withdrawn from the transaction before its improper purpose has been achieved. Such a party is said to have acted within the *locus poenitentiae* (time for repentance).[20] The term is somewhat misleading, since only withdrawal and not actual repentance is required. In the words of the Supreme Court of West Virginia,

> If there was a turning back, that becomes paramount and the reasons for the change of action are inconsequential . . . . Penalties are imposed for wrongful conduct, not for improper intentions uncrystallized.[21]

Courts often justify the rule on the ground that it encourages a party to abandon an improper goal before it has been achieved.[22] Furthermore, a court may not consider allowing restitution a misuse of official authority if the claimant has repented in time. To come within this exception, the claimant must actually withdraw from the transaction by refusing any further participation or benefits. It is not enough if circumstances beyond the claimant's control, such as the other party's nonperformance, have prevented achievement of

---

[16]Capo v. Century Life Ins. Co., 610 P.2d 1202 (N.M. 1980) (debtor entitled to restitution of premiums paid in violation of statute making it illegal for lender to coerce purchase of insurance from particular broker since if statute "is designed for coercion of one party and the protection of another, the party so protected may have his remedy even though the transaction is completed").

[17]See the discussion of frustration of policy in §5.5 *supra*. A party who can enforce the agreement may have restitution as an alternative remedy. See §12.20 *infra*.

[18]Sykes v. Thompson, 76 S.E. 252 (N.C. 1912) (father entitled to restitution of money paid to prevent prosecution of sons on charges that he later found were false). *See* Restatement Second §198 cmt. *b* ("if the other party's conduct is especially reprehensible, the court may decide that it is more important to deprive him of his ill-gotten gains").

[19]Union Exch. Natl. Bank v. Joseph, 131 N.E. 905 (N.Y. 1921) (Cardozo, J.: man not entitled to restitution of money paid to stifle charge of felony against brother-in-law since he was "wrongdoer when he stifled a charge of crime" and possible innocence of brother-in-law would make no difference).

[20]Town of Meredith v. Fullerton, 139 A. 359 (N.H. 1927) ("until the illegal purpose [of town board in granting license] has been executed, there is a *locus poenitentiae* during which either party may repent and withdraw"). *See* Restatement Second §199(a) (party must withdraw from transaction "before the improper purpose has been achieved").

[21]Aikman v. City of Wheeling, 195 S.E. 667, 669 (W. Va. 1938).

[22]Town of Meredith v. Fullerton, *supra* note 20 ("The underlying reason . . . is to protect society from the influence of contracts made in disregard of the public weal . . . by interrupting the progress of illegal undertakings before the evil purpose has been fully consummated.").

the improper purpose.[23] Courts have sometimes been tolerant in determining when the improper purpose has been so substantially achieved that it is too late to repent.[24] If the claimant has already engaged in serious misconduct, the possibility of restitution may be foreclosed.[25]

A somewhat similar exception is made if granting restitution will put an end to a situation that is contrary to the public interest.[26] For example, an improper transaction may leave property in the hands of a person whose control renders its status so uncertain as seriously to restrain its alienation. Therefore, if two gamblers deposit money with a stakeholder under an unenforceable wagering agreement, both parties can get restitution from the stakeholder, even after the subject of the wager has occurred and the *locus poenitentiae* has ended.[27] The stakeholder, however, is not liable to the loser for anything that the stakeholder has paid over before notice by the loser of his claim to restitution.

In the next chapter we consider the requirement of a writing under the statute of frauds.

Situation against public interest

---

[23] Bigos v. Bousted, [1951] 1 All E.R. 92 (K.B. 1950) (reason "for this illegal contract not having come to fruition was [not] repentance" but the other party's failure to perform).

[24] Woel v. Griffith, 253 A.2d 353 (Md. 1969) (though contract for sale of real estate had been made on Sunday in violation of law, purchasers could recover their deposit since contract was still executory).

[25] Stone v. Freeman, 82 N.E.2d 571 (N.Y. 1948) ("when an agent receives money to be spent for illegal purposes, his principal may not recover back so much of that money as the agent has failed so to spend, particularly when the illegal purpose has been partly . . . attained").

[26] Ware v. Spinney, 91 P. 787 (Kan. 1907) (principal entitled to recover from agent money not spent for improper purpose). *See* Restatement Second §199(b).

[27] Gehres v. Ater, 73 N.E.2d 513 (Ohio 1947) (loser at craps who pledged $540 bond to secure $225 gambling debt was not barred from recovering from winner in conversion since only "where payment has been made or where a contract in violation of the gambling laws . . . has been executed by performance is the loser in a gaming transaction precluded from rescinding the transaction and recovering his money or property").

Chapter 6

The Requirement of a Writing: The Statute of Frauds

A. INTRODUCTION

§6.1. History and Functions of the Statute. It would be difficult to imagine a question more important to a person expecting to make agreements in an unfamiliar legal system than this: When is a writing needed for an enforceable agreement? The answer will determine both one's willingness to give unwritten assurances and one's insistence that the other party put its undertaking in writing. This question whether a writing is needed for an enforceable agreement should not be confused with the question whether a writing excludes evidence of prior negotiations. The latter is governed by the parol evidence rule and is discussed in a later chapter.[1] The former, which is discussed here, is governed by "statutes of frauds," patterned after the English Statute of Frauds of more than three centuries ago. We therefore begin with a discussion of that statute and its background.

Significance of writing requirement

---

§6.1 [1]See §7.2 *infra*. The somewhat analogous requirement of a writing under a no-oral-modifications clause is discussed in §7.6 *infra*.

Reason for Statute in England

With the development of the action of general assumpsit by the beginning of the seventeenth century, informal contracts had become generally enforceable. In contrast to formal contracts, such as those under seal, informal contracts might be oral.[2] However, the trial of an action based on an oral contract raised problems: parties were not permitted to testify, jurors might rely on their own knowledge of the facts, and judges had no effective mechanism to control arbitrary jury verdicts. These circumstances tempted plaintiffs to procure false testimony. To prohibit those "many fraudulent practices, which are commonly endeavoured to be upheld by perjury and subornation of perjury,"[3] Parliament enacted "An Act for Prevention of Frauds and Perjuries"[4] commonly known as the Statute of Frauds, in 1677.

Scope of Statute

Section 4 of the act listed five classes of contracts on which "no action shall be brought . . . unless the agreement . . . , or some memorandum or note thereof, shall be in writing, and signed by the party to be charged therewith, or some other person . . . by him lawfully authorized." Included were contracts: (1) "to charge any executor or administrator upon any special promise, to answer damages out of his own estate" (the *executor-administrator* provision); (2) "to charge the defendant upon any special promise to answer for the debt, default or miscarriages of another person" (the *suretyship* provision); (3) "to charge any person upon any agreement made upon consideration of marriage" (the *marriage* provision); (4) for the "sale of lands, tenements or hereditaments, or any interest in or concerning them" (the *land contract* provision); (5) "not to be performed within the space of one year from the making thereof" (the *one-year* provision). Section 17 contained special provisions applicable to contracts in a sixth class, those for the sale of goods (the *sale of goods* provision).

Enactment of statutes in United States

In most states the Statute of Frauds was not part of the English common law that was received on independence, but virtually all states enacted their own versions of the Statute.[5] Most of these American statutes of frauds imposed, in varying formulations, writing requirements for all six of the classes of contracts that were covered by the English Statute and often add other classes as well.[6]

---

[2] *See* J. Baker, An Introduction to English Legal History 288 (2d ed. 1979) ("Wager of law, for all its defects, had protected the innocent defendant from fraudulent claims by unscrupulous tradesmen," but after Slade's Case in 1602 "there was little protection against such claims except the good discretion of the jury."). The development of the action of general assumpsit is discussed in §1.6 *supra*. On formal contracts, see §2.16 *supra*.

[3] These words are from the introductory clause.

[4] Stat. 29 Car. 2, c.3. The Statute attempted to prevent fraud in the proof of many different kinds of transactions. It dealt with such matters as deeds, wills, trusts in land, and leaseholds in addition to contracts, but it is remembered for its provisions on contracts.

[5] Only Louisiana, Maryland, and New Mexico failed to enact a version of §4 of the original Statute, and judicial decisions in Maryland and New Mexico have held that the English statute was received in those states.

[6] See the discussion of the six provisions adopted in most states in §6.2 *infra*.

In 1954, after 277 years, Parliament repealed most of the Statute of Frauds.[7] Only the suretyship provision and the land contract provision were retained. Among the reasons given by the English Law Reform Committee for repeal were these: the classes of contracts within the Statute "seem to be arbitrarily selected and to exhibit no relevant common quality"; the requirement of a writing is "out of accord with the way in which business is normally done" and "promotes more frauds than it prevents"; and the Statute was the product of a time when "essential kinds of evidence were excluded (e.g., the parties themselves could not give evidence), and objectionable types of evidence were admitted (e.g., juries were still in theory entitled to act on their own knowledge of the facts in dispute)" and has become "an anachronism" now that the parties can freely testify.[8]

Repeal of Statute in England

The rules for international contracts contained in the Vienna Convention and the UNIDROIT Principles reflect the absence of writing requirements for commercial contracts in most civil law countries as well as the repeal of the sale of goods provision in England. The Convention, which displaces the Uniform Commercial Code with respect to contracts for the sale of goods within the Convention's scope, provides that such a contract "need not be concluded in or evidenced by writing and is not subject to any other requirement as to form."[9] The UNIDROIT Principles follow suit by stating that "Nothing in these Principles requires a contract to be concluded in or evidenced by a writing."[10]

No requirement for international contracts

Statutes of frauds remain in this country despite their many critics. During the period England was moving to abolish most of the Statute, including the sale of goods provision, the drafters of the Uniform Commercial Code were deciding to retain that part of the Statute, albeit in a less rigorous form.[11] The sale of goods provision survived attempts to delete it during the revision of Article 2 and remains, though with an elevated dollar threshold.[12] The different attitude toward the Statute in England may reflect differences in trial practice. In England trial by jury in contract actions is now unusual, being within the

Statutes remain in United States

---

[7] Law Reform (Enforcement of Contracts) Act, 1954, 2 & 3 Eliz. 2, c.34.

[8] Report of the [English] Law Revision Committee on the Statute of Frauds and the Doctrine of Consideration 6-7 (Sixth Interim Report, Cmd. 5449, 1937), reprinted in 15 Can. B. Rev. 585 (1937).

[9] CISG art. 11. At the insistence of the Soviet Union, article 96 of the Convention permits a ratifying country that has a writing requirement to make a reservation under which article 11 "does not apply where any party has his place of business" in that country. The United States did not avail itself of this reservation.

[10] UNIDROIT Principles art. 1.2.

[11] Supp. No. 1 to the 1952 Official Draft of Text and Comments of the Uniform Commercial Code 98 (1955) explained that "the spread of literacy, the rise of metropolitan living, the drive toward internal records, and the Code's removal of those unwise misinterpretations which so largely influenced the English decision, leave reasonable room for some Statute of Frauds in the sales field." The resulting sale of goods provision is discussed in §6.6 *infra*.

[12] UCC-R 2-201, described in §6.6 *infra*.

discretion of the judge, so that most cases that would formerly have been within the Statute no longer go to a jury. Furthermore, in England counsel fees are included in the costs assessed against the losing party, which makes it more likely that the technicalities and uncertainties of the Statute would discourage litigants from suing on otherwise meritorious claims.

Functions of statute

Attempts at justifying the statute of frauds in this country stress the functions of a formality such as a writing.[13] Its original purpose was evidentiary, providing some proof that the alleged agreement was actually made, and all its provisions perform this function to some degree. A few provisions perform other functions as well. The suretyship provision performs an important cautionary function, by bringing home to the promisor the significance of the promise and preventing ill-considered and impulsive promises.[14] The land contract provision performs a significant channeling function, by furnishing a simple test of enforceability to mark off unenforceable agreements from enforceable ones.[15] It is noteworthy that the most durable and well-regarded of the statute's provisions are those that fulfill more than just the original evidentiary purpose.

Effectiveness of statute

During its long life, the statute has occasioned an enormous amount of litigation, and critics have disagreed over how well it has served its purposes. One English jurist opined that the statute "promotes fraud rather than prevents it,"[16] and another thought that had it "been always carried into execution according to the letter, it would have done ten times more mischief than it has done good, by protecting, rather than by preventing, frauds."[17] An American critic agreed that the statute's provisions "are no longer preventing fraud, if they ever did, but rather are a cause of fraud."[18] On the other side, Karl Llewellyn argued that "after two centuries and a half the statute stands, in essence better adapted to our needs than when it first was passed."[19] Another observer suggested that

---

[13] See discussion of justification based on form in §2.5 *supra*.

[14] See the discussion of the cautionary function in §6.3 *infra*.

[15] See the discussion of its history and functions in §6.5 *infra*.

[16] Marvin v. Wallis, 119 Eng. Rep. 1035, 1038 (Ch. 1856).

[17] Simon v. Metivier, 96 Eng. Rep. 347, 348 (K.B. 1766) (Wilmot, J.).

[18] Willis, The Statute of Frauds — A Legal Anachronism (pt. 2), 3 Ind. L.J. 528, 541 (1928). Even Goethe, no stranger to the law, took a dig at insistence on a writing:

Mephistopheles . . . .   One small request — I'm sure you'll understand.; It's just in case — I'd like a line or two in your own hand.

Faust.   Poor pedant! Must it be in writing too? Is man's plighted word a thing unknown to you?

Faust (Part One) lines 1714-17 (D. Luke trans. 1987).

[19] Llewellyn, What Price Contract? — An Essay in Perspective, 40 Yale L.J. 704, 747 (1931). On Llewellyn's views on the statute of frauds and its fate, *see* Wiseman, The Limits of Vision: Karl Llewellyn and the Merchant Rules, 100 Harv. L. Rev. 465, 515-19, 529-34, 538-39 (1987). *See also* Phillippe v. Shapell Indus., 743 P.2d 1279 (Cal. 1987) (quoting "the memorable malaprop attributed to motion picture producer Samuel Goldwyn: 'An oral contract isn't worth the paper it's written on.'").

the statute was justified by "the thousands of uncontested current transactions where misunderstanding and controversy are avoided by the presence of a writing which the statute at least indirectly aided to procure."[20] After more than three centuries, the statute still plays to mixed reviews.[21]

Although the statute is not likely to be subjected to wholesale repeal in this country, it has been the subject of constant erosion. Courts have long been receptive to pleas that the statute should be narrowly interpreted so as not to cover the contract in question.[22] They have more recently become receptive to arguments that, even if the statute covers the contract in question, the statute's requirement of a writing has been met[23] or the claimant's reliance on the contract dispenses with the requirement.[24] This process of erosion promises to continue in the future.

Erosion of statute in United States

The remainder of this chapter deals with three questions: (1) What contracts are covered by the statute? (When the statute applies to a contract, the contract is said to be "within" the statute.) (2) How may the statute be complied with? (When the statute is complied with, it is said to be "satisfied.") (3) What are the effects of a failure to comply with the statute?

Three questions

We begin with the first.

B.   WHAT CONTRACTS ARE WITHIN THE STATUTE

§6.2.   Scope of the Statute. What contracts are within the typical American statute of frauds? Most states enacted provisions covering the five classes of contracts that came within §4 of the English Statute of 1677. Although these provisions vary in detail, both in text and in judicial interpretation, their general outline is widely shared. The Restatement Second summarizes them as follows:

Six provisions adopted in most states

> (a) a contract of an executor or administrator to answer for a duty of his decedent (the executor-administrator provision);
>
> (b) a contract to answer for the duty of another (the suretyship provision);
>
> (c) a contract made upon consideration of marriage (the marriage provision);

---

[20]Vold, The Application of the Statute of Frauds Under the Uniform Sales Act, 15 Minn. L. Rev. 391, 394 (1931).

[21] See Braucher, The Commission and the Law of Contracts, 40 Cornell L.Q. 696, 705 (1955) ("a cautious approach to the Statute of Frauds seems to be in harmony with American professional opinion").

[22]This is particularly notable in connection with the one-year provision. Goldstick v. ICM Realty, 788 F.2d 456 (7th Cir. 1986) ("Courts tend to take the concept of 'capable of full performance' quite literally . . . because they find the one-year limitation irksome."). See the discussion of its inapplicability if performance is possible in §6.4 *infra.*

[23]See the discussion of admissions in court proceedings in §6.7 *infra.*

[24]See §6.12 *infra.*

(d) a contract for the sale of an interest in land (the land contract provision);

(e) a contract that is not to be performed within one year from the making thereof (the one-year provision).[1]

In addition, a sixth provision (the sale of goods provision), in original Article 2 of the Uniform Commercial Code, covers contracts "for the sale of goods for the price of $500 or more,"[2] raised in revised Article 2 to "$5,000 or more."[3]

Four provisions of special importance

There are few guides to what the framers of the English Statute of 1677 intended in selecting these classes. Besides, as an English judge has pointed out, "It is now two centuries too late to ascertain the meaning of §4 by applying one's own mind independently to the interpretation of its language. Our task is a much more humble one; it is to see how that section has been expounded in decisions and how the decisions apply to the present case."[4] Because the classes of contracts that come within the statute have not been appreciably revised in more than three centuries, it is not surprising that the scope of the statute seems somewhat arbitrary. In terms of modern commercial activity, the statute fails to cover many significant and complex agreements, while many of the agreements that it does cover no longer seem worth singling out for this purpose. Nevertheless, four of the six traditional provisions continue to be of importance in practice: the suretyship provision, the one-year provision, the land contract provision, and the sale of goods provision. They will be dealt with in that order in the four sections that follow. The remaining two provisions will not be discussed in detail: the executor-administrator provision will be treated briefly in connection with the suretyship provision;[5] the marriage provision (which has been so interpreted as not to apply to mutual promises to marry)[6] is of minor importance and will be omitted.[7]

Additional provisions

In addition to the provisions derived from the English Statute, many states have added provisions covering other types of agreements. One of the more important covers contracts to make a testamentary disposition or contracts not

---

§6.2　[1] Restatement Second §110.

[2] UCC-O 2-201.

[3] UCC-R 2-201. The raise was less than inflation would have justified.

[4] Hanau v. Ehrlich, [1911] 2 K.B. 1056, 1069 (C.A. 1911) (Buckley, L.J.).

[5] See the discussion of the contract of an executor or administrator in §6.3 *infra*.

[6] Withers v. Richardson, 21 Ky. (5 T.B. Mon.) 94 (1827) ("It would be imputing to the legislature too great an absurdity, to suppose that they had enacted that all our courtships, to be valid, must be in writing."). Furthermore, "heartbalm" statutes in many states bar actions for breach of a promise to marry. See the discussion of the focus on the marriage relationship in §5.4 *supra*.

[7] The main importance of the marriage provision is in connection with marriage settlements. A promise by a prospective spouse to transfer property to the other spouse in consideration of marriage or of a promise to marry is within this provision. Dienst v. Dienst, 141 N.W. 591 (Mich. 1913) (woman promised man to leave all her property to him on her death if he would engage to marry her).

to be performed before the end of a lifetime.[8] It will be discussed in connection with the one-year provision.[9] Another covers contracts to pay brokers for arranging the sale of real estate or of a business opportunity.[10] It will be touched upon in connection with the effect of full performance and the availability of restitution.[11] Furthermore, in addition to the sale of goods provision, the Uniform Commercial Code contains a statute of frauds applicable to leases[12] and, until deleted in revised Article 1, contained a residual section applicable to contracts for the sale of personal property not otherwise covered.[13]

Moreover, legislators have an abiding faith in formality and there are many other requirements of a writing that are not presented in the traditional form of a statute of frauds and that may not be governed by the rules generally applicable to such a statute.[14] For example, arbitration statutes generally require a writing for an enforceable arbitration agreement,[15] and the Uniform Commercial Code requires a writing for an enforceable security agreement in personal property that is not in the secured party's possession.[16] In addition, most states require a writing for a new promise that removes the bar of the statute of limitations,[17] and some states require a writing for a new promise or acknowledgment that removes the bar of bankruptcy[18] for a ratification that precludes the defense of infancy.[19] These requirements are proliferating, a somewhat

Other writing requirements

---

[8] *See* Mass. L. Ann. c. 259 §§5, 5A ("agreement to make a will"); N.Y. Gen. Oblig. Law §5-701(a)(1) (contract under which performance "is not to be completed before the end of a lifetime"); N.Y. Est., Powers & Trusts Law §13-2.1(a)(2) ("contract to make a testamentary provision").

[9] See the discussions of performance on death and the lifetime provision in §6.4 *infra*.

[10] *See* Cal. Civ. Code §1624(a)(4); N.Y. Gen. Oblig. Law §5-701(a)(10).

[11] See the discussions of the brokerage provision in §6.9 *infra* and of restitution as contrary to policy in §6.11 *infra*.

[12] UCC 2A-201.

[13] Former UCC 1-206(1) (not enforceable "beyond five thousand dollars in amount or value of remedy"). Under subsection (2), however, this provision does not apply to contracts for the sale of goods or of securities. See the discussion of the statute of frauds in §11.3 *infra*.

[14] *See* Phillippe v. Shapell Indus., 743 P.2d 1279 (Cal. 1987) ("legislative preference for written contracts is stronger than ever before," giving examples of writing requirements for consumer contracts). Minnesota, for example, has a statute that requires that a cohabitation agreement concerning property or finances be "written." Minn. Stat. Ann. §513.075.

[15] *See* 9 U.S.C.A. §2; Cal. Civ. Proc. Code §1281; N.Y.C.P.L.R. §7501. While the traditional statute of frauds require a *signed* writing, some other statutes, such as these, require only that the agreement be "written."

[16] UCC 9-203(b)(3) ("authenticated a security agreement"). According to cmt. 3 to that section, this is "an evidentiary requirement in the nature of a Statute of Frauds." See the discussion of the statute of frauds in §11.3 *infra*. Statutes regulating retail installment sales also commonly require a writing.

[17] These statutes are derived from Lord Tenterden's Act, enacted in England in 1828 and are generally read to require the promise or acknowledgment itself to be in writing. See the discussion of the scope of the exception in §2.8 *supra*.

[18] See the discussion of the exception for a debt discharged in bankruptcy proceedings in §2.8 *supra*.

[19] See the discussion of ratification in §4.4 *supra*.

curious phenomenon in view of the erosion of the traditional statute of frauds, but they will not be discussed in this chapter.

Requirements as cumulative

All of these requirements have traditionally been regarded as cumulative: if more than one applies to a single contract, all must be met. If one of the requirements is more exacting, that requirement must be met.[20] However, a number of courts departed from this view in cases involving the one-year provision and the Code's sale of goods provision, which is notably less exacting than the other provisions of the statute,[21] and revised Article 2 adds a specific provision to this effect.[22]

Promise to sign writing

The statute of frauds may also apply to a promise to sign a writing. If an agreement is within the statute, a promise to sign a writing evidencing the agreement is also within the statute.[23]

Modification and rescission

The mere fact that a written agreement is within the statute of frauds does not prevent its modification by a subsequent oral agreement.[24] If, however, the agreement as modified is within the statute, the statute must be satisfied in order for that new agreement to be enforceable.[25] This would be so even if the original agreement did not come within the statute. But if the original agreement came within the statute and was satisfied by a writing, there is no reason why the same writing may not also satisfy the statute as to the modified agreement as long as no essential terms were modified.[26] If the modification agreement is unenforceable because the statute is not satisfied, the original contract stands unmodified.[27] On similar reasoning, an agreement of rescission that discharges all remaining duties on each side does not come within

---

[20] Riley v. Capital Airlines, 185 F. Supp. 165 (D.C. Ala. 1960) (within one-year and sale of goods provisions). For exceptions, see the discussions of leases in §6.5 *infra* and of the land contract provision in §6.9 *infra*.

[21] Roth Steel Prods. v. Sharon Steel Corp., 705 F.2d 134 (6th Cir. 1983) (Code is "comprehensive statutory scheme" and generally, when "irreconcilable conflict exists between a special statute and a general statute, the special statute prevails"). As to the respect in which the Code's version of the statute is less exacting, see the discussion of history in §6.6 *infra*.

[22] UCC-R 2-201(4) ("contract that is enforceable under this section is not unenforceable merely because it is not capable of performance within one year or any other period after its making").

[23] Strong v. Hall, 453 P.2d 425 (Or. 1969) ("an oral agreement to sign an agreement which the statute of frauds requires to be in writing is . . . unenforceable").

[24] Lieberman v. Templar Motor Co., 140 N.E. 222 (N.Y. 1923) (written contract not to be performed within a year, modified by oral contract that was performable within a year). See the discussion of oral modifications as valid in §7.6 *infra*.

[25] UCC 2-209(3) (statute "must be satisfied if the contract as modified is within its provisions"). See the discussion of the Code's relaxation of the writing requirement in §6.7 *infra*. *See also* Restatement Second §149. As to the effect of part performance, see the discussion of the sale of goods provision in §6.9 *infra*, and as to the effect of reliance, see the discussion of other cases in §6.12 *infra*.

[26] Because UCC 2-201 requires only that the quantity term be in the writing, a sensible reading of UCC 2-209(3) would require a new writing only if the quantity were modified.

[27] However, the commentary to the Restatement Second suggests that "it is possible for the parties to include in a single agreement two separate contracts, one to rescind a prior contract

the statute, since after the agreement no unperformed promise remains.[28] If the modification or rescission involves a new transfer of property in goods or land, however, the sale of goods provision or the land contract provision may apply independently to the agreement.[29] The impact of <u>reliance</u> on the modification is discussed later in this chapter.[30] The effect of a provision that a written agreement cannot be orally modified or rescinded is discussed in the next chapter.[31]

We turn now to the suretyship provision.

§6.3.   Contracts to Answer for the Duty of Another. One of the most important and durable provisions of the statute of frauds requires a writing for a contract to answer for another person's duty or, as the English Statute of 1677 expressed it, a "promise to answer for the debt, default or miscarriages of another."[1] The provision applies, with some important exceptions, to all contracts of suretyship and to promises to sign contracts of suretyship.[2] It does not, however, apply to involuntary suretyship resulting from another's assumption of a duty as a principal.[3] For example, a partner who retires from a partnership remains liable on partnership debts, but if the remaining partners agree to assume those debts, the retiring partner is liable only as a surety. Nevertheless, the suretyship provision does not preclude the retiring partner

Scope in general

---

and the other to make a new contract; in such a case they may intend the rescission to be effective even though the new contract is unenforceable." Restatement Second §149 cmt. *b*.

[28] Dave Zerwas Co. v. James Hamilton Constr. Co., 876 P.2d 653 (N.M. 1994) (rejecting argument that "whole purpose behind the Statute of Frauds would be abrogated were this Court to allow the cancellation of an exclusive listing contract through performance alone"). *See* Restatement Second §148 (noting that "Statute may, however, apply to a contract to rescind a transfer of property").

[29] See §§6.5, 6.6 *infra*.

[30] See the discussion of reliance on modification agreements in §6.12 *infra*.

That the statute applies to ratification if the contract ratified is within the statute, *see* Jones v. Melrose Park Natl. Bank, 592 N.E.2d 562 (Ill. App. 1992) ("law is clear that 'the same formality is required for ratification as for original authorization'").

[31] See §7.6 *infra*.

§6.3   [1] Stat. 29 Car. 2, c.3, §4 (1677). *See* Restatement (Third) of Suretyship and Guaranty §11. Comment *a* cites statutes in all states except Louisiana, Maryland, and New Mexico, the last two having incorporated the English statute by judicial decision. See the discussion of enactment of statutes in the United States in §6.1 *supra*. That this provision does not bar an action in tort for misrepresentation, see the discussion of other effects in §6.10 *infra*.

However, some states have an additional provision, derived from a provision in Lord Tenterden's Act of 1828 (see the discussion of the scope of the exception in §2.8 *supra*), that requires a signed writing for an action based on a misrepresentation as to the credit of a third person. *See* Cal. Civ. Proc. Code §1974.

[2] *See* Restatement Second §117.

[3] Were the rule otherwise, the retiring partner's oral promise to pay debts of the partnership would be unenforceable as a result of the retirement coupled with the assumption. *See* Restatement Second §119. See also the discussion of assumption by a delegate in §11.11 *infra*.

being held on debts contracted orally. Nor does the provision apply to contracts of suretyship on negotiable instruments.[4]

Evidentiary function

Like other provisions of the statute, the suretyship provision serves an evidentiary function. Indeed, because a surety receives from the obligee nothing in exchange that might serve to evidence the surety's promise, it can be argued that there is a special need for written evidence of that promise. Furthermore, though in many instances the principal pays the surety for its undertaking, in others the surety's motivation is purely gratuitous. As the Supreme Judicial Court of Massachusetts explained more than a century and a half ago:

> The object of the statute manifestly was, to secure the highest and most satisfactory species of evidence, in a case, where a party, without apparent benefit to himself enters into stipulations of suretyship, and where there would be great temptation, on the part of a creditor, in danger of losing his debt by the insolvency of his debtor, to support a suit against the friends or relatives of a debtor . . . by means of false evidence; by exaggerating words of recommendation, encouragement to forbearance, and requests for indulgence, into positive contracts.[5]

Cautionary function

In addition to this evidentiary role, the provision serves a cautionary function. By bringing home to the prospective surety the significance of the promise, it guards against ill-considered promises. Otherwise the surety might lightly undertake the obligation, unwisely assuming that there is only a remote possibility that the principal will not perform.

Suretyship described

A brief discussion of suretyship will help at this point. A *surety* is a person who is liable for the duty of another person, who is called the *principal* (or principal debtor). (A person whose liability for the duty of another person is conditioned on the failure of the other person to perform is sometimes termed a *guarantor*, especially if bound by a separate instrument, but this terminology will not be followed here, and the word *surety* will be used in its broad sense to include a guarantor.[6]) Both the principal and the surety are thus under a

---

[4] Under the Uniform Commercial Code, one who has not signed a negotiable instrument is not liable on it. UCC 3-401(a). One who signs a negotiable instrument as a surety is known as an "accommodation party." The instrument need not contain the terms of the contract, which are set out in UCC 3-419. Furthermore, "the obligation of an accommodation party may be enforced notwithstanding any statute of frauds." UCC 3-419(b). *See* Restatement Second §120. However, a promise not evidenced by a signature on the instrument is governed by general contract law. Thus, for example, a promise to sign a negotiable instrument as an accommodation party is within the suretyship provision.

[5] Nelson v. Boynton, 44 Mass. (3 Met.) 396, 399 (1841).

[6] *See* Restatement (Third) of Suretyship and Guaranty §1 cmt. *c* (Restatement uses "secondary obligor" because distinctions between sureties and guarantors "have been the subject of extended debate, not all of which is illuminating" and rights, as distinguished from duties, associated with suretyship status "are the same for sureties as for guarantors").

duty to a third person, the *obligee* (or creditor), to render the same performance.[7] But the obligee is entitled to only one performance, and as between the two obligors it is the principal rather than the surety that should render it.[8]

Suretyship differs from indemnity, which requires only two parties. Under a contract of indemnity, one party (the *indemnitor*) promises to hold another party (the *indemnitee*) harmless from loss or damage of some kind, irrespective of the liability of any third person. In a contract of indemnity, the promise runs to an obligor or a prospective obligor rather than to an obligee, as is typically the case in a contract of suretyship.[9]

Indemnity distinguished

Suretyship is often a means by which a creditor obtains security for the payment of a debt. For example, suppose that one person (A) wishes to obtain a loan from another (C). In order to get the creditor (C) to extend credit, the debtor (A) may not only promise to pay the price but may have a third person (B) add an additional promise to pay the creditor (C) the price. Both promisors (A and B) are then under a duty to the creditor (C) to render the same performance, payment of the full price, and as between the two promisors (A and B) one of them (A), rather than the other (B), should perform. The relationship is one of suretyship: the first debtor (A) is the principal, the other debtor (B) is the surety, and the person to whom the debt is owed (C) is the obligee (or creditor). The surety's (B's) promise is to answer for the duty of another (A) and so comes within the suretyship provision. A person may be a surety, even though that person's promise is to perform only part of the duty owed by the principal.[10]

Example of suretyship

---

[7]Two parties are under a duty to render the same performance if performance by either one discharges the other's duty as well as that of the party who has performed. If C lends $100 to two persons and each of them promises to repay the $100, they are under the same duty. But if C lends $100 to two persons and each of them promises to repay $50 of the $100, they are not under the same duty. (Payment of $50 by one of them will not discharge the other's duty to pay $50.)

[8]Pursuing the example given in note 7 *supra*, in which C lends $100 to two persons and each of them promises to repay the $100, one is principal and the other is surety if as between them the former rather than the latter should pay the $100. (Contrast the situation in which as between them each is to pay $50.)

[9]*See* Restatement (Third) of Suretyship and Guaranty §11(3)(b) & cmt..

[10]Thus if a creditor (C) lends $100 to a debtor (A), a person (B) who promises to pay only $50 of the debt may be a surety as to that amount. But a person who promises a different performance is not a surety, even though the purpose of that person's promise is to make it more certain that the debtor will perform. Thus, if a creditor (C) lends $100 to a debtor (A), a person (B) is not a surety if that person (B) merely warrants that the debtor's (A's) promise is not voidable on the ground of minority. King v. Summitt, 73 Ind. 312 (1881) ("a guaranty that the note is genuine . . . differs entirely from a promise to pay the debt"). The rule that a promise to sign a contract of suretyship is within the suretyship provision is therefore, in a sense, an exception.

Whether a transaction has given rise to a suretyship relationship is a question of substance rather than form, and a court may find such a relation though it is far less evident than in the transaction just described.[11]

Surety's duty may arise later

In the example just given, the duties of the principal and the surety arise at the same time, and the consideration for the promises of both the principal and the surety is the making of the loan to the principal. If the creditor has already made the loan to the principal when the surety makes its promise, the duty of the surety arises after that of the principal has come into existence, and the consideration for the surety's promise may be, for example, the creditor's extension of the time in which the loan is to be repaid. Of course, if the surety is a compensated surety (one who receives a fee from the principal), there is no problem in finding consideration whether the surety's duty arises simultaneously with that of the principal or at a later time.

Must be principal duty

But regardless of when the surety's duty arises, there can be no suretyship relationship unless there is a principal duty. A duty that is voidable by the principal will suffice for this purpose. Indeed, one common instance of suretyship occurs when the creditor insists on a surety because the principal is a minor and can avoid on this ground.[12]

Situations where duty is original

We turn next to two recurring situations in which courts have held that there is no suretyship relation on the ground that there is no duty owed by a principal. The conclusion that the promisor is not a surety in these situations is sometimes expressed by saying that the promisor's liability is "original" rather than "collateral."[13] In the words of the English Statute of 1677, the promise is not to perform the duty "of another."

Extension of credit to promisor distinguished

One situation in which courts have held that a promisor is not a surety because of the absence of any principal duty occurs when the obligee delivers goods or performs services to the other relying solely on the credit of the promisor.[14] Thus if B makes an oral offer to C to pay for C's services if C will render them to A, B's offer is not one to be surety for A but to be solely liable. If C accepts by

---

[11] For example, a contract to buy a right from the creditor to whom the debt is owed does not ordinarily give rise to a suretyship relation. But if the buyer's promise is conditional on the debtor's default, the circumstances may indicate that the buyer is in reality guaranteeing that the debtor will pay the debt. If that is so, a court should treat the buyer's contract as one of suretyship. *See* Restatement Second §122; Restatement (Third) of Suretyship and Guaranty §11(2)(c).

[12] Dexter v. Blanchard, 93 Mass. (11 Allen) 365 (1865) (rejecting "assumption that there was in fact no debt due . . . because [debtor] was a minor [and such a debt] is voidable only").

[13] For a discussion of this terminology, *see* Publishers Advertising Assoc. v. Wessel Co., 747 F.2d 1076 (7th Cir. 1984) ("whether a promise is original or collateral is a question of fact" subject to "the clearly erroneous standard").

[14] *See* Isaacs, The Economic Advantages and Disadvantages of the Various Methods of Selling Goods on Credit, 8 Cornell L.Q. 199 (1923) (describing the differences in the legal consequences of various transactions, such as those described here, as "surprising to the man of business").

rendering the services, B is liable but A is not. Since there is no principal duty, B is not a surety, and the suretyship provision does not apply to B's promise.[15] Whether an offeror (B) has offered to be solely liable or to be liable only as a surety for a third person (A) may raise a difficult question of interpretation.[16] If, however, the circumstances are such that the third person (A) comes under no duty to the offeree (C), the offeror (B) is not a surety no matter how the offer is interpreted.[17] And, in any case, even if B offers to become a surety, B does not become one unless C accepts the offer.

Another situation in which courts have held that a promisor is not a surety because of the absence of a principal duty occurs when there is a novation.[18] If A owes C a debt and C accepts B's oral promise either to pay the debt or to do something else in immediate satisfaction of A's duty to pay it, the transaction is a novation. At the moment that B becomes bound on the promise, A's duty is discharged. Since there is no longer any duty of A for which B can be surety, B's promise is not within the suretyship provision.[19]

Novation distinguished

In the situations just described, the promise in question is not within the statute because the promisor is not a surety. There are also some exceptional situations in which a promise is not within the suretyship provision, even though the promisor is a surety. We turn now to these exceptions.[20]

Situations where provision not applicable to sureties

One important situation in which a promise is not within the suretyship provision, though the promisor is a surety, occurs when the obligee neither knew nor had reason to know that the promisor was a surety.[21] It would plainly be unfair to bar the obligee from enforcing a promise for lack of a writing if the obligee had no reason to know that a writing was required. If the surety's promise is conditional in form (e.g., "I will pay if X does not"), the creditor has

Not applicable if obligee had no reason to know

---

[15]City of Highland Park v. Grant-Mackenzie Co., 115 N.W.2d 270 (Mich. 1962) (employer's promise to hospital to pay for care to employee was original).

[16]City of Highland Park v. Grant-Mackenzie Co., *supra* note 15 ("in interpreting the language used by the parties their prior dealings were properly given consideration"). The obligee's subsequent conduct is often given considerable weight, more so when the obligee has treated the offeror as a surety than when the obligee has done the opposite.

[17]Duca v. Lord, 117 N.E.2d 145 (Mass. 1954) (oral promise to pay for repairs to library if trustees did not do so was not within statute because trustees were not liable for repairs and promise was not conditional on trustees assuming that liability).

[18]See the discussion of novation in §4.24 *supra*.

[19]Hill v. Grat, 141 N.E. 593 (Mass. 1923) (promisor "at his own request had been substituted for [original debtor] and the promise therefore was an independent, original agreement to pay his own debt"). *See* Restatement Second §115. It should be noted that since A has been discharged, C would have no remedy at all if C could not enforce B's promise because of the statute of frauds.

[20]Courts are not always careful, however, in making this distinction, and they sometimes speak of these exceptional cases as if suretyship was not involved.

[21]*See* Restatement Second §112.

reason to know that the promisor is a surety.[22] Even if the surety's promise is unconditional in form (e.g., "I will pay"), the obligee usually knows or has reason to know that the consideration that the obligee furnishes is for the benefit of only one of the two obligors, and this will give the obligee reason to know that the other is a surety.[23] Thus if C delivers goods to A and both A and B orally promise C to pay the price, and it is understood between A and B that B is surety for A, C has reason to know that B is a surety because C knows or has reason to know that the goods are for A's benefit. B's oral promise is therefore unenforceable because of the suretyship provision. But if C delivers goods to A and both A and B orally promise C to pay the price, and it is understood between A and B that A will turn the goods over to B and that A is surety for B, the circumstances give C reason to know that a suretyship relation exists but no reason to know that A is the surety. Unless for some other reason C knows or has reason to know of the understanding between A and B, A's promise is not within the suretyship provision.[24]

Not applicable if promisor owes independent duty

Another situation in which a promise is not within the suretyship provision, even though the promisor is a surety, arises when the promised performance is one that the promisor is under a duty to render irrespective of the promise. Since such a promise binds the surety to do no more than the surety is already bound to do, courts have characterized it as a promise to answer for the surety's own "independent" duty, rather than for that "of another" within the meaning of the statute.[25] For example, if a debtor owes a creditor $1,000 and gives that sum to a third person directing that it be used to pay the debt, the third person, as trustee, owes the creditor a duty to pay the $1,000. If the third person then orally promises the creditor to pay the debt, the suretyship provision does not bar enforcement of the oral promise.[26] Similarly, if a partner promises to pay a debt of the partnership, the suretyship provision does not apply because a partner is liable for partnership debts irrespective of any

---

[22] For the purposes of this chapter, this is the only significance of the distinction that is sometimes made between a surety and a guarantor. See the discussion of suretyship described *supra*.

[23] *See* Restatement Second §114. According to the Restatement Second, the independent duty may be owed to the promisee or to someone else. In the latter case it is sufficient if the promisee reasonably, though mistakenly, believes the promisor owes the duty. Comment *a* to the section adds that the duty may exist when the promise is made or may arise subsequently. The duty need not be contractual.

[24] *See* Restatement Second §112 illus. 11; Restatement (Third) of Suretyship and Guaranty §11(3)(a). B's promise is not within the suretyship provision either, since B is in fact the principal debtor. B's promise may be within the sale of goods provision, but that provision does not bar recovery of the price of goods that have been received and accepted. See the discussion of the sale of goods provision in §6.9 *infra*.

[25] *See* Restatement Second §114.

[26] Holmes v. Hughes, 226 P. 424 (Ariz. 1924) (debtor's bank promised creditor to pay him $3,000 of $5,000 debtor had on deposit). *See* Restatement Second §114(a).

promise.[27] The exception applies only to the extent that the surety's promise coincides with the independent duty. Thus, in the example just given, if the debtor gave the third person only $500 to be used to pay the $1,000 debt, the third person's oral promise to pay the debt would be enforceable only to that extent.[28]

On similar reasoning, it has been held that the suretyship provision does not bar enforcement of an oral promise by a surety if by their terms the promises of the principal and surety are joint and the resulting duties are neither several nor joint and several.[29] Though the relation between joint promisors is one of suretyship, at common law they were treated as a unit for many purposes, and courts therefore reasoned that the duty undertaken was that of the surety and not that "of another" within the meaning of the statute of frauds. The old common law rules relating to joint promisors have been changed in virtually all states, and in many states statutes convert what would otherwise be joint duties into joint and several ones. In these states, the exception for joint promisors is no longer significant. But in states that retain the distinction between duties that are joint and those that are joint and several, the exception for joint promisors persists.[30]

Not applicable to joint duties

Another situation in which the suretyship provision does not apply to a promise, even though the promisor is a surety, arises if the surety promise is made to the principal rather than to the obligee.[31] Thus if A owes a debt to C and B orally promises A that B will pay that debt to C, B's promise is not within the suretyship provision, even though C can enforce B's promise as an

Not applicable if promise to principal

---

[27] Reid v. Wilson, 34 S.E. 608 (Ga. 1899) ("debt of a partnership is the debt of each of its members, and a new promise by one or more of the partners, made after the dissolution of the firm, to pay a partnership debt, is not, within the meaning of the statute of frauds, a promise to pay the debt of another").

[28] Holmes v. Hughes, *supra* note 26.

[29] Gibbs v. Blanchard, 15 Mich. 292 (1867) ("if the promise . . . be joint, as between them, . . . then neither is collateral to the other; and such joint promise is original as to both"). *See* Restatement Second §113 & cmt. *b*.

[30] At common law, if two or more parties to a contract were under "joint" duties to render the same performance to a promisee, the promisee was under a number of procedural disadvantages. For example, the promisee could not sue one of the joint promisors without joining all other living joint promisors. However, promisees could avoid these disadvantages by having the promisors undertake "joint and several" duties, and statutes in many states now make this formality unnecessary by providing that, though the promises of the parties are in their terms joint, the resulting duties are joint and several. Even in states that do not have such statutes, modern procedural reforms have done away with the rule of compulsory joinder. *See generally* Restatement Second ch. 13.

[31] Stewart v. State Farm Mut. Auto. Ins. Co., 605 So. 2d 1214 (Ala. 1992) (suretyship provision not applicable to "promise made to a debtor whereby the promisor undertakes to discharge the debt"). *See* Restatement Second §123.

intended beneficiary.[32] In the common situation in which B assumes A's duty, it is understood between them that B is the principal and A the surety, so that for this reason the suretyship provision would be inapplicable to B's promise.[33] However, even if B is a surety, it is reasoned that the suretyship provision should not apply because its purpose is limited to requiring reliable evidence when the promise is made to the creditor and therefore the words "of another" should be read to mean someone other than the promisor *or the promisee*, and not merely someone other than the promisor.[34]

Not applicable because of main purpose rule

A particularly important situation in which the suretyship provision does not apply to a promise, even though the promisor is a surety, is the subject of the "main purpose" (or "leading object") rule. Under this rule, the promise does not come within the statute if the surety's actual or apparent main purpose in making the promise is an economic advantage to the surety rather than a benefit to the principal.[35] A modern rationalization is that if the surety's

> main purpose is its own pecuniary or business advantage, the gratuitous or sentimental element often present in suretyship is eliminated, the likelihood of disproportion in the values exchanged between [surety] and obligee is reduced, and the commercial context commonly provides evidentiary safeguards [so that] there is less need for cautionary or evidentiary formality . . . .[36]

The Restatement excludes from the main purpose rule "contracts of guaranty insurance whether or not making such contracts is the [surety's] regular business," noting that "promises of commercial surety companies are practically always in writing."[37]

---

[32] Brad Ragan, Inc. v. Callicutt Enters., 326 S.E.2d 62 (N.C. App. 1985) ("purchaser of property who agrees, in payment of its price, to discharge a debt due by the seller, is not protected by the statute of frauds"). For descriptions of such transactions and of C's right as an intended beneficiary, see the discussions of a promise to pay the promisee's debt in §10.3 and of assumption by a delegate in §11.11 *infra*.

[33] Langman v. Alumni Assn. of Univ. of Va., 442 S.E.2d 669 (Va. 1994) ("grantee who assumes an existing mortgage is not a surety"). The suretyship provision does not apply to such involuntary suretyship for the reason given in the discussion of scope in general *supra*.

[34] It is the obligee and not the principal who is likely to be tempted falsely to claim that a promise was made by the alleged surety, and the risk is not great that the obligee will be able to establish by the obligee's own perjured testimony that the alleged surety made a promise to the principal.

[35] For an early statement of the rule, *see* Nelson v. Boynton, 44 Mass. (3 Met.) 396 (1841) (dictum: "cases are not considered as coming within the statute, when the party promising has for his object a benefit which he did not before enjoy"). *See also* Restatement (Third) of Suretyship and Guaranty §11(3)(c); Restatement Second §116.

[36] Restatement (Third) of Suretyship and Guaranty §11 cmt. *k*.

[37] Restatement (Third) of Suretyship and Guaranty §11(c) cmt. *m*; Restatement Second §116 cmt. *c*.

In applying this rule, it is often easy to see that a surety derives some economic advantage from making a promise, but it is nevertheless difficult to decide whether that advantage was the surety's main purpose in making it. Courts generally agree that the mere fact that the surety may have had a selfish motive in making the promise — that the consideration for the promise was a benefit to the surety, as distinguished from a detriment to the promisee — is not enough to bring it within the rule.[38] Take the common situation in which a stockholder in a corporation makes a promise as a surety for the corporation in order to induce a supplier to continue furnishing goods or services to the corporation on credit. Though the surety's purpose may be to some extent a selfish one, courts have generally held that the surety's *main* purpose is not personal economic advantage but benefit to the corporation.[39] A contrary conclusion has been reached where the surety owns a controlling interest in the corporation.[40] A few courts have even held that a promise by an unsecured creditor that is not a shareholder comes within the main purpose rule.[41] Although in most of the cases in which the rule has been applied the surety's promise has been made on some new or "fresh" consideration after the initial extension of credit to the principal, the rule extends to cases in which the surety's promise is contemporaneous with the extension of credit.[42] But if the promise is contemporaneous with the extension of credit, the fact that the promisor had a motive to obtain a benefit may suggest that the promisor was the one to whom credit was extended and that there is therefore no suretyship relation at all.[43]

> **Selfish purpose not enough**

The Restatement (Third) of Suretyship and Guaranty lists some factors tending to indicate that the surety's main purpose is to advance its own interests.[44] One of these is "forbearance of the obligee to enforce a lien on property in which the [surety] has an interest or which it intends to use." Suppose, for example, that a mortgagee is about to foreclose on property

> **Factors indicating the rule's application**

---

[38] Colpitts v. L.C. Fisher Co., 193 N.E. 833 (Mass. 1935) ("Even consideration which is not only a detriment to the promisee but also a benefit to the promisor, is not enough to take a case out of the statute.").

[39] Luson Intl. Distribs. v. Mitchell, 939 F.2d 493 (7th Cir. 1991) (main purpose rule did not apply when "president, chief executive officer, and principal shareholder" became surety for corporation).

[40] Garland Co. v. Roofco Co., 809 F.2d 546 (8th Cir. 1987) (company's principal shareholder and president "had a unique personal interest" in extensions of credit that allowed company "to continue its operations and to realize money from several jobs").

[41] Ries Biologicals v. Bank of Santa Fe, 780 F.2d 888 (10th Cir. 1986) (bank's promise came within rule where it was owed some $620,000 of which $120,000 was not guaranteed by Small Business Administration).

[42] Jefferson-Travis v. Giant Eagle Markets, 393 F.2d 426 (3d Cir. 1968) (rejecting argument that "rule applies only to promises predicated upon previously existing obligations").

[43] Brindley Constr. Co. v. Byes Plastics, 456 So. 2d 269 (Ala. 1984) (promise may be original if "credit is extended *simultaneously* to both the promisor and the debtor").

[44] Restatement (Third) of Suretyship & Guaranty § 11 cmt. *l*.

in which another person in addition to the mortgagor has an interest subject to the mortgage, and the other person as surety orally promises the mortgagee to pay the mortgage debt if the mortgagee will refrain from foreclosing. It is generally accepted that the surety's oral promise is not within the suretyship provision because the surety's main purpose in making the promise is personal economic advantage in protecting an interest in the property.[45] Another factor listed is "prior default, inability or repudiation of the principal obligor." Suppose, for example, that a subcontractor refuses to continue work because the general contractor has failed to pay for what has been done, and the owner as surety orally promises the subcontractor to pay the general contractor's debt if the subcontractor will go back to work. Courts have held that the owner's oral promise is not within the suretyship provision because the owner's main purpose in making the promise is the owner's own economic advantage in having the work finished.[46] Similar reasoning has been applied in other situations.[47] Two other factors listed are: "equivalence between the value of the benefit and the amount promised; and lack of participation by the principal obligor in the making of the [surety's] promise."

Not applicable in similar situations   There are several other situations in which a surety's promise has been held not to be within the suretyship provision, at least partly because of reasoning like that underlying the main purpose rule. One of these involves a *del credere* agent, an agent that sells goods for the owner on commission and orally promises the owner that the purchasers will pay their accounts. Though the agent is a surety for the debts owed by the purchasers to the owner, courts have concluded for a variety of reasons that the agent's promise is not within the suretyship provision.[48] The most common of these reasons is that the agent's main purpose is the advancement of a personal interest.[49] Another situation involves an assignor that assigns a right against an obligor and orally promises the assignee that the obligor will perform. Again, the most common reason for concluding that the oral promise is not within the suretyship provision, even though the promisor

---

[45] Kahn v. Waldman, 186 N.E. 587 (Mass. 1933) ("controlling purpose" of second mortgagee's promise to pay mortgage debt to first mortgagee was "the prevention, for her own benefit, of the foreclosure of the mortgage").

[46] Treasure Valley Plumbing & Heating v. Earth Resources, 766 P.2d 1254 (Idaho App. 1988) (owner orally promised subcontractor to pay for work and materials).

[47] Contractor's Crane Serv. v. Vermont Whey Abatement Auth., 519 A.2d 1166 (Vt. 1986) (joint venturers' "main purpose in promising to pay for the whey hauling was to enable them to continue disposing of their whey").

[48] Sherwood v. Stone, 14 N.Y. 267 (1856), relying on Couturier v. Hastie, 8 Ex. (W.H. & G.) 40 (1852). *See also* Restatement Second §121(2).

[49] *See* Restatement Second §121(2) & cmt. *a* ("an important inducement for the promise is his desire to advance his own interest"); Restatement (Third) of Suretyship and Guaranty §11(3)(g) & cmt. *q.* ("important inducement for the promise is the agent's desire to advance his or her own interest").

is a surety, is that the surety's main purpose is the advancement of a personal interest.[50]

Contract of executor or administrator

Most states have preserved, along with the suretyship provision, a provision derived from the English Statute applicable to contracts of an executor or administrator to answer for a duty of the decedent.[51] The provision applies when the executor or administrator, in handling the affairs of the decedent's estate, orally promises personally to pay a debt incurred by the decedent before death (e.g., for medical care) or one incurred by the estate after death (e.g., for funeral expenses).[52] More than a century ago, the Supreme Court of Vermont explained that the provision "was enacted to prevent executors or administrators from being fraudulently held for the debts or liabilities of the estates upon which they were called to administer."[53] Like the suretyship provision, it unquestionably performs a cautionary function in addition to this evidentiary one.

Analogy to suretyship provision

Although the suretyship provision may not literally apply to the situation in which a debtor has died before the oral promise to pay the debt is made, the principle underlying the suretyship provision is regarded as applicable. Courts have therefore imposed on it the same limitations and exceptions, including the main purpose rule, as they have to the suretyship provision.[54]

Our inquiry into the statute of frauds now turns to a much more questionable provision, that applicable to contracts not to be performed within a year.

§6.4. Contracts Not to Be Performed Within a Year. The one-year provision covers contracts that are not to be performed within one year of their making. It applies regardless of the subject matter of the contract and may cover a contract that is also covered by some other provision of the statute.[1] In

Scope in general

---

[50] *See* Restatement Second §121(1) & cmt. *a* ("assignor's promise is ordinarily made for a consideration wholly for his own benefit"); Restatement (Third) of Suretyship and Guaranty §11(3)(f) & cmt. *q* (assignor's promise is ordinarily "for a consideration wholly for the assignor's own benefit").

[51] Stat. 29 Car. 2, c.3, §4 (1677) ("whereby to charge any executor or administrator upon any special promise, to answer damages out of his own estate"). *See* Restatement Second §111. Minnesota and Wisconsin have no such provision.

[52] The provision applies only to a promise by an executor or administrator to pay out of the assets of "his own estate" and not to a promise to pay out of the assets of the decedent's estate. Mann v. Rudder, 144 So. 13 (Ala. 1932) (provision inapplicable to promise to account to estate for estate's own funds loaned to another).

[53] Bellows v. Sowles, 169 (Vt. 1884).

[54] Mackin v. Dwyer, 91 N.E. 893 (Mass. 1910) (provision not applicable because executor's main purpose was "his own benefit").

§6.4 [1] See the discussion of requirements as cumulative in §6.2 *supra*. However, statutes in most states that exempt one-year leases from the land contract provision have the effect of exempting such a lease from the one-year provision even though it begins at a future date. See the discussion of leases in §6.5 *infra*. Furthermore, the one-year provision does not prevent specific performance of a land contract if the part-performance exception applies. See the discussion of the land contract provision in §6.9 *infra*. UCC 8-113, which makes the statute inapplicable to a

measuring the period, the two points of reference are the time of the making of the contract and the time when performance is to be completed.[2] Thus a ten-month employment contract is not within the statute if performance is to begin at once, but it is within the statute if performance is not to begin until three months after the contract is made.[3] If any promise of either party cannot be fully performed within the one-year period, the entire contract is within the statute, and it cannot then be enforced against either party unless it is satisfied as to that party.[4]

Difficult to rationalize

Although the one-year provision has been repealed in England, it is law in virtually all of the American states.[5] But of all the provisions of the statute, it is the most difficult to rationalize. It is ill-contrived if it is intended to serve an evidentiary purpose and equally ill-contrived if it is intended to single out significant contracts of long duration.

Does not well serve evidentiary purpose

The one-year provision is ill-contrived if it is based on the tendency of memory to fail and of evidence to go stale with the passage of time. The one-year period does not run from the time that the contract is made to the time for proof that it was made, but from the time that the contract was made to the time for completion of performance. If an oral contract that cannot be performed within a year is broken the day after its making, the provision applies though the terms of the contract are fresh in the minds of the parties. But if an oral contract that can be performed within a year is broken and suit is not brought until nearly six years (the usual statute of limitations for contract actions) after the breach, the provision does not apply, even though the terms of the contract are no longer fresh in the minds of the parties.

Does not single out significant contracts

The one-year provision is equally ill-contrived if it is an attempt to separate significant contracts of long duration, for which writings should be required, from less significant contracts of short duration, for which writings are unnecessary. The one-year period does not run from the time for commencement of performance to the time for completion of performance, but from the time that the contract is made to the time for completion of performance. If an oral contract to work for one day, 13 months from now, is broken, the provision

---

contract for the sale of securities, provides that this is so even if the contract cannot be performed within a year.

[2] Because the time when the offer is made is immaterial, a supplier of services can make a continuing offer to give a discount on all services that a customer orders for a period of, say, three years, and the statute will not apply because each order results in a separate contract to be performed within a year of its making. Nat Nal Serv. Stations v. Wolf, 107 N.E.2d 473 (N.Y. 1952) ("each order and acceptance is a separate contract").

[3] Kass v. Ronnie Jewelry, 371 A.2d 1060 (R.I. 1977) (one-year employment contract was within statute where employee could not have begun work until four days after making).

[4] Broadwell v. Getman, 2 Denio 87 (N.Y. 1846) ("The agreement is entire, and if it cannot be executed fully, on both sides, within the year, I think it is void.").

[5] See Restatement Second §130. The one-year provision has been omitted in North Carolina and Pennsylvania.

applies, even though the duration of performance is only one day.[6] But if an oral contract to work for a year beginning today is broken, the provision does not apply, even though the duration of performance is a full year.[7]

Because of the difficulty in justifying the one-year provision, courts have regarded it with hostility and have limited it in ways not noted for their logic.[8] Most important, most courts have read the words "not to be performed" to mean "not performable." Therefore, if the contract is one of indefinite duration, but performance within a year is possible by its terms, the contract is not within the statute no matter how unlikely it is that it will actually be performed within a year.[9] Thus the Supreme Court of Connecticut held that an oral contract for the "construction of twenty industrial buildings, a 280 room hotel and convention center, and housing for 592 graduate students and professors" at cost of $120 million was not within the statute where the "contract itself does not explicitly negate the possibility of performance within one year." In such a case, Chief Justice Peters explained, "no sound reason of policy commends judicial pursuit of a collateral inquiry into whether, at the time of the making of the contract, it was realistically possible that performance of the contract would be completed within a year."[10] Some courts, however, have been willing to look at what is possible in fact.[11] If the time fixed is a reasonable time, it has been held that the contract is within the statute if a reasonable time is longer than a year.[12]

Inapplicability if performance possible

---

[6] Lund v. E.D. Etnyre & Co., 242 N.E.2d 611 (Ill. App. 1968) (contract to design chipspreading machine was within statute where employee was not to begin work until two years after making).

[7] If the contract is to be performed over the term of a year beginning on the day of the making of the contract, the statute is clearly inapplicable. If the contract is to be performed over the term of a year beginning on the day following the day of the making of the contract, there is disagreement as to the applicability of the statute. Many courts have been willing to disregard fractions of a day and have held the statute to be inapplicable if the employee could have begun work the next day, even if the employee did not. Co-Op Dairy v. Dean, 435 P.2d 470 (Ariz. 1967) (statute did not apply where, although employee waited 14 days before going to work under one-year contract, "there was nothing to prevent [him] from turning over the moving details to his wife and going to work the next day").

[8] Goldstick v. ICM Realty, 788 F.2d 456 (7th Cir. 1986) (Posner, J., citing this treatise: courts "find the one-year limitation irksome" and "Illinois courts evidently share the prevailing distaste for the provision"); C.R. Klewin, Inc. v. Flagship Properties, 600 A.2d 772 (Conn. 1991) (Peters, C.J.: "the one-year provision . . . has caused the greatest puzzlement among commentators," quoting this treatise).

[9] Center State Farms v. Campbell Soup Co., 58 F.3d 1030 (4th Cir. 1995) (contract was not within statute though it was enforceable for a reasonable period in order to allow agribusiness to recoup its investment).

[10] C.R. Klewin, Inc. v. Flagship Properties, *supra* note 8, at 779 (quoting this section).

[11] Dean v. Myers, 466 So. 2d 952 (Ala. 1985) (joint venture agreement to construct condominium complex was within statute where there was no "reasonable possibility of performance within a year").

[12] Mercer v. C.A. Roberts Co., 570 F.2d 1232 (5th Cir. 1978) (reasonable time was more than a year because "parties contemplated that [employee] would develop the Dallas office to maturity, a process that would take three to five years").

If a party's performance can be rendered in two or more ways, the contract is not within the one-year provision if any of the alternatives can be performed within the one-year period.[13]

Performance on occurrence of event

Courts have used similar reasoning to hold that the one-year provision does not apply to a contract that will be fully performed on the happening of an event that may possibly occur within the one-year period. For this reason a promise to insure for more than a year is not within the one-year provision because the event insured against may occur within the one-year period.[14] A typical case involved an agreement under which "a self-described retired industrialist" was to procure for a contractor a contract to construct a chemical plant in Saudi Arabia in return for a fee to be paid on completion of the construction. Although it took the retired industrialist over three years to procure the contract and the contractor another six years to construct the plant, the New York Court of Appeals held that the agreement was not within the one-year provision. "It matters not . . . that it was unlikely or improbable that a $41 million plant would be constructed within one year. The critical test, instead, is whether 'by its terms' the agreement is not to be performed within a year."[15] However, a contract to do something that will take only a year, but is not to begin until something else has been done, is within the one-year provision.[16]

Performance on death

Under a particularly important application of this line of reasoning, a contract that will be performed in the event of the death of a person, whether one of the parties or a third person, is not within the one-year provision since death can occur at any time. Courts have therefore held that the provision does not apply to a contract to make a will.[17] Nor does it apply to the following promises: a promise by A to work for B for the rest of A's life (whether the term is called "lifetime" or "permanent");[18] a promise by A to work for B for the rest of B's life;[19] a promise by A to work for B for five years if A lives that long;[20] and a

---

[13]Frigon v. Whipple, 360 A.2d 69 (Vt. 1976) (where debtor could repay loan at two dates within one-year period, "either alternative, standing alone, is sufficient to take the oral promise out of the statute").

[14]International Ferry Co. v. American Fidelity Co., 101 N.E. 160 (N.Y. 1913) ("a parol contract of insurance may be completely performed within a year upon the happening of a contingency").

[15]Freedman v. Chemical Constr. Corp., 372 N.E.2d 12 (N.Y. 1977).

[16]General Fed. Constr. v. James A. Federline, Inc., 393 A.2d 188 (Md. 1978) (contract to install equipment and to provide maintenance for it for one year after installation).

[17]Appleby v. Noble, 124 A. 717 (Conn. 1924) (part of payment for services to be made by will). Such a contract may, however, be within the land contract provision. See the discussion of the meaning of *contract for sale* in §6.5 *infra*.

[18]Hodge v. Evans Fin. Corp., 823 F.2d 559 (D.C. Cir. 1987) (2-1 decision: "permanent or lifetime employment contract does not fall within the statute because it is capable of full performance within one year if the employee were to die").

[19]Silverman v. Bernot, 239 S.E.2d 118 (Va. 1977) (agreement to remain in employment until employer reached age 62 or died).

[20]Silverman v. Bernot, *supra* note 19.

promise by A to support B for the rest of B's life.[21] Furthermore, it has been held that a promise by A to support B, with no express limitation of the period to B's life, can be performed within a year since such a limitation is implicit in the concept of support.[22] Whether this reasoning also applies to a covenant not to compete is a question on which courts have disagreed, some following the analogy of a contract of support[23] and others rejecting it.[24]

In a few states, notably California and New York, the one-year provision has been supplemented by provisions applicable to contracts not to be performed within a lifetime.[25] A one-year provision supplemented by a lifetime provision would cover all of the examples in the preceding paragraph except for A's promise to work for B for five years if A lives that long.[26]

Lifetime provision

Courts have made a fine and often tenuous distinction between performance on the one hand and excuse on the other. Thus a promise by A to work for B "for five years if A lives that long" is not within the one-year provision because it is by its terms *performed* if A dies within a year. But a promise by A to work for B "for five years" is within the one-year provision because even though A would be *excused* from performing it within a year if A should die within that time, this would not amount to performance. It has been held that excuse is not performance even if the excuse is expressed in the promise. Thus a promise by A to work for B for five years is within the one-year provision even though it states that "A is excused from performance if he dies or is incapacitated."[27]

Excuse distinguished

On similar reasoning, some courts have held that a contract is within the statute even though it provides that one or both parties have the power to terminate the contract within one year of its making.[28] *Termination* is distinguished from *performance*, just as excuse is distinguished from performance.[29]

Termination distinguished

---

[21] Thurston v. Nutter, 134 A. 506 (Me. 1926) ("contract to support one during life is not within the statute").

[22] Duncan v. Clarke, 125 N.E.2d 569 (N.Y. 1955) ("If the child were to die, the agreement would be fully performed, since the purpose is to furnish necessaries to the child, not to purchase services or to accomplish some other objective throughout a term of years.").

[23] A seminal case is Doyle v. Dixon, 97 Mass. 208 (1867) (promise not to go into grocery business in Chicopee for five years was "only a personal engagement to forbear doing certain acts" and "would be fully performed if he died within the year"), followed in Restatement Second §130 illus. 9.

[24] Reagan Outdoor Advertising v. Lundgren, 692 P.2d 776 (Utah 1984) ("agreement not to compete for two years . . . was, by its terms, not to be performed within one year").

[25] Cal. Civ. Code §1624(a)(5); N.Y. Gen. Oblig. Law §5-701(a)(1).

[26] Wior v. Anchor Indus., 669 N.E.2d 172 (Ind. 1996) ("death does not constitute performance in contract involving employment until retirement" when retirement is more than one year off).

[27] Gilliam v. Kouchoucos, 340 S.W.2d 27 (Tex. 1960) ("the addition of the words 'but the agreement shall terminate on the death of the operator', added nothing").

[28] Deevy v. Porter, 95 A.2d 596 (N.J. 1953) (employees "could quit at any time").

[29] See Taylor v. Canteen Corp., 69 F.3d 773 (7th Cir. 1995) (where "promise of employment is cast in terms of lasting as long as the employee wants the job, the promise is capable of performance within one year").

Thus a contract under which A is to work for B and B is to employ A for five years is within the one-year provision, even if either A or B or both can terminate at any time on thirty days' notice.[30] There is a strong contrary view, with a growing number of courts coming to regard a contract as not within the statute if one, or sometimes both, parties can terminate it within a year of its making.[31] The Restatement Second seems in accord.[32] Courts taking this view have, however, disagreed as to whether a power of termination for cause counts as a power of termination for this purpose, some holding that it does[33] and others holding that it does not.[34] Courts have also disagreed as to the effect of a provision under which one party has the power to renew the contract at some time within a year of its making, some courts holding that such a provision takes a contract out of the statute,[35] and others holding that it does not.[36]

Unilateral contracts

Although a promise under a unilateral contract may not be capable of performance within a year of the making of the contract, it would be anomalous to apply the one-year provision to such a contract in any jurisdiction in which full performance within a year satisfies that provision.[37] Even in a jurisdiction in which full performance does not have this effect, the time for performance by the promisee should not bring the contract within the one-year provision, since the performance amounts to the acceptance that creates the contract and is therefore complete at the inception of the one-year period.[38]

We next examine the land contract provision.

History and functions

§6.5. Contracts for the Sale of an Interest in Land. The land contract provision, along with the suretyship provision, is all that remains of the Statute

---

[30] New York has developed an elaborate body of case law on this point, beginning with Blake v. Voight, 31 N.E. 256 (N.Y. 1892), in which the Court of Appeals held that the contract was not within the statute where either party could terminate "by due notice."

[31] A seminal case is Hopper v. Lennen & Mitchell, 146 F.2d 364 (9th Cir. 1944) (one party had right twice a year to terminate on four weeks' notice).

[32] Illustration 6 to §130 takes this position where "either party may terminate the contract by giving 30 days notice at any time."

[33] Foley v. Interactive Data Corp., 765 P.2d 373 (Cal. 1988) ("good-cause termination clause does not render an employment agreement unenforceable under the statute of frauds").

[34] Graham v. Central Fid. Bank, 428 S.E.2d 916 (Va. 1993) ("discharge for cause is not a performance of the contract within the meaning of the statute of frauds, but a termination of the contract by reason of its breach").

[35] Ward v. Hasbrouck, 62 N.E. 434 (N.Y. 1902) (lease for four months with an option for an extension of not more than three years was not a lease for a longer period than a year).

[36] Hand v. Osgood, 64 N.W. 867 (Mich. 1895) (lease for one year "with the privilege of three" was a lease for a longer period than a year).

[37] See Restatement Second §130 cmt. d & illus. 13. See the discussion of the one-year provision in §6.9 infra.

[38] Auerbach's, Inc. v. Kimball, 572 P.2d 376 (Utah 1977) (where employer promised pension for life if employee remained for at least 20 years and until 65, contract was not within statute).

in England[1] and, with the suretyship provision, is the most universally adopted provision of the statute in the United States. Its durability is due in part to the fact that transactions in land are almost always of such significance as to warrant an evidentiary formality[2] and in part to the fact that the provision also performs a channeling function, by furnishing a simple test to mark off unenforceable agreements from enforceable ones.[3]

Although §4 of the English Statute of 1677 spoke of a "contract *or* sale," the formal requirements for a present conveyance of land were governed by other sections of the Statute and §4 was read as applicable only to a "contract *for* sale" and not to a present sale.[4] The land contract provision of American statutes of frauds is generally limited to a contract for the sale of an interest in land; the formal requisites for a conveyance of land (e.g., a deed) are determined by other statutes.[5]

> **Not applicable to conveyance**

If the provision applies to a contract, it applies to all of the promises. It therefore applies to the promise by the purchaser to pay the price, as well as to a promise by the vendor to transfer title.[6]

> **Whole contract within provision**

The remaining problems relating to the statute as it applies to contracts for the sale of an interest in land will be considered under three headings: the meaning of a *contract for sale*; the nature of an *interest*; and the scope of the term *land*.

> **Three problems**

The term *contract for sale* covers any agreement that contains a promise to create or transfer an interest in land.[7] It applies to an agreement between partners or joint venturers for the sale of land from one to another,[8] though not to an agreement between partners or joint venturers to buy or sell

> **Meaning of *contract for sale***

---

§6.5   [1] The land contract provision in §4 of the English Statute of 1677 was replaced by the Law of Property Act, 1925, 15 Geo. 5, c.20, §40(1), which was not affected by the repeal of other parts of the statute in 1954. See the discussion of repeal of the Statute in England in §6.1 *supra*.

[2] Note that, unlike the sale of goods provision, the land contract provision has no minimum dollar amount. See the discussion of the limitation of $500 in §6.6 *infra*.

[3] See the discussion of the functions of the statute in §6.1 *supra*.

[4] Boyd v. Stone, 11 Mass. 342 (1814) ("It is somewhat singular, that a very incorrect phraseology of the statute . . . should have been adopted, both in the provincial act, and in the statute of the commonwealth. No contract *or* sale . . . was probably at first misprinted or miswritten for, no contract *for* the sale . . . .").

[5] *See* Mich. Comp. Laws Ann. §565.1; R.I. Gen. Laws §34-11-1.

[6] Brown v. Gray, 70 S.E. 276 (W. Va. 1911) ("statute was as much designed to protect the purchaser as the seller"). *See* Restatement Second §125 cmt. *d*. A similar point is made as to the one-year provision in §6.4 *supra*.

[7] It has been held, however, that it does not cover a contract to fix a boundary line. Norberg v. Fitzgerald, 453 A.2d 1301 (N.H. 1982) ("agreement affecting a boundary line of adjoining landowners is not a sale of land").

[8] Filippi v. Filippi, 818 A.2d 608 (R.I. 2003) (agreement was for "transfer of land between partners" not for sharing proceeds).

land and divide the profits.[9] It has been held applicable to an option contract,[10] though there is contrary authority.[11] The promised creation or transfer may be by any means, including deed or will, but interests created by operation of law, as distinguished from agreement of the parties, are not included.[12] Nor does it cover a contract to refrain from making a transfer.[13] Since the land contract provision does not apply to present conveyances, it does not cover a unilateral contract under which a purchaser promises to pay the price in return for a present conveyance of land.[14]

Broad scope   Courts have given a very broad scope to the term *contract for sale*. The consideration may be money or something else.[15] The land may be transferred to the person who promises to furnish the consideration or to a third person.[16] The provision covers a contract to procure the transfer of land by a third person,[17] but not an agreement to attempt to arrange a transfer of land on behalf of another as an agent or broker,[18] though such agreements are covered by special provisions in some states.[19] The land contract provision covers an agreement of rescission that will extinguish an interest in land that the purchaser has acquired and revest it in the

---

[9] Malnar v. Carlson, 910 P.2d 455 (Wash. 1996) ("oral agreement of partners for the purpose of buying and selling real estate, whereby lands are purchased and held in the name of one partner for profit and resale, is not within the statute").

[10] Chevron U.S.A. v. Schirmer, 11 F.3d 1473 (9th Cir. 1993) ("Arizona's Statute of Frauds provisions require an option agreement for real property to be in writing.").

[11] Marina Bay Condominiums v. Schlegel, 423 N.W.2d 284 (Mich. App. 1988) (option contract is "collateral to the offer" and "does not create an interest in land").

[12] Collins' Estate v. Dunn, 103 So. 2d 425 (Miss. 1958) ("oral agreement to convey land by will . . . is within the statute of frauds").

[13] Foman v. Davis, *supra* note 12 (contract not to make a will).

[14] *See* Restatement Second §125 cmt. *e* ("once the transfer has been made, the promise to pay the price becomes enforceable, unless the price is land"). A similar point is made with respect to the one-year provision in §6.4 *supra*.

[15] Tsiatsios v. Tsiatsios, 663 A.2d 1335 (N.H. 1995) (dictum: generally "oral contracts to devise real property as compensation for personal services are unenforceable under the statute of frauds").

[16] Outback Contracting v. Stone Southwest, 1 P.3d 469 (Or. App. 2000) (agreement between contractor and manufacturer that manufacturer would purchase timberland located by contractor, and vendor would deed timber to manufacturer and real property to contractor).

[17] De Lucca v. Flamingo Corp., 121 So. 2d 803 (Fla. App. 1960) (where broker acting for buyer obtained owner's promise that he would sell to buyer for stated price, this was "not a promise to pay a commission . . . but a promise to convey").

[18] Roberts v. Ross, 344 F.2d 747 (3d Cir. 1965) (land contract provision has "no application to agreements to compensate agents or brokers in connection with the purchase or sale of real estate").

[19] See the discussion of additional provisions in §6.2 *supra*.

vendor,[20] though it[does not cover the revocation of a revocable offer to sell land.[21]

The term *interest*, within the meaning of this provision, includes "any right, privilege, power or immunity, or combination thereof."[22] The land contract provision covers transfers of both legal and equitable interests and of both present and future interests, including an assignment of the right of a purchaser or vendor under a specifically enforceable contract,[23] a right under an easement,[24] and a right under a restrictive covenant.[25] But the mere fact that a contract relates to land or involves the use of land does not bring it within the land contract provision.[26] Thus the provision does not apply to a right to use land if it is characterized as a mere "license," as opposed to a lease or an easement.[27]

The right of a mortgagee is generally recognized as an interest in land, and the statute must be satisfied with respect to the creation of such an interest.[28] Courts have made an exception, however, with respect to the transfer of such an interest, holding that the[transfer is not within the statute if, as is ordinarily the case, the transfer is only incidental to an assignment of the debt secured by the mortgage.[29]

Nature of interest

Mortgages

---

[20]McCulloch v. Tapp, 2 Ohio Dec. Rep. 678 (1863) ("this equitable title and interest could not be divested except by a written contract, and hence a verbal contract to *rescind* them, would, under the statute, *be void*"). *See* Restatement Second §14 cmt. *c.*

However, most courts have not extended this to executory contracts, even though the contract itself, if enforceable, would create an equitable property interest in the buyer. Solana Land Co. v. National Realty Co., 266 P.2d 739, 267 P.2d 895 (Ariz. 1954) (question is moot "when the contract of rescission has been fully executed"). *See* Restatement Second §148 cmt. *c* & Reporter's Note.

[21]Board of Control of E. Mich. Univ. v. Burgess, 206 N.W.2d 256 (Mich. App. 1973) (offer creates no interest in land and statute "does not require that the revocation of an offer to sell land be in writing").

[22]Restatement Second §127.

[23]Coldwell v. Davidson, 219 S.W. 445 (Ky. 1920) ("equitable estate of the purchaser under such a contract is itself real estate").

[24]Pick v. Bartel, 659 S.W.2d 636 (Tex. 1983) (right of way).

[25]Remilong v. Crolla, 576 P.2d 461 (Wyo. 1978) (it is of "particular importance that such restrictive covenants be classified as interests in land without reference to particular terminology because of their increasing importance and use in our modern-day society").

[26]Scales v. Wiley, 33 A. 771 (Vt. 1895) (agreement to take down barn and rebuild it on other party's land was not within land contract provision).

[27]Burgess v. Swetnam, 77 S.W.2d 385 (Ky. 1934) (right to use gas from well on neighbor's property was an irrevocable license and not within land contract provision).

[28]Sleeth v. Sampson, 142 N.E. 355 (N.Y. 1923) (Cardozo, J.: "the word 'sale' when applied to such a transaction, is inexact and inappropriate").

[29]It is reasoned that the transfer of the mortgagee's interest is one by operation of law. Southern v. Mendum, 5 N.H. 247 (1842) ("The debt is the principal thing. The right of the mortgagee in the land is a mere incident inseparable from the debt."). See the point that the assignment of a right carries with it any security in a footnote to the discussion of a present transfer as required in §11.3 *infra*.

Leases

A contract to make a <u>lease</u> is plainly [one to transfer an interest in land.][30] Statutes of frauds generally make an exception, however, for short-term leases, typically those for one year or less,[31] and most states have held that such statutes have the effect of excepting from the one-year provision a lease for a year to begin in the future.[32]

Scope of *land*

The term *land* is now used instead of the phrase *land, tenements and hereditaments* of the original Statute. It comprises <u>all tangible property other than goods</u>. The law of property generally determines what is land and what is goods for this purpose, and over the centuries courts have developed many learned distinctions to deal with borderline cases.[33] Fortunately, some of the most important rules have now been codified by the Uniform Commercial Code.

Code provisions

Contracts for the <u>sale of products of the soil</u>, such as annual crops, that result from cultivation have generally been regarded as <u>contracts for the sale of goods</u>, even though the products are attached to the soil when the contract is made.[34] The Code preserves this rule by providing that a contract for the sale "of growing crops and other things attached to realty and capable of severance without material harm thereto . . . or of timber to be cut" is one for the sale of goods.[35] However, in the case of a "contract for the sale of minerals or the like (including oil and gas) or a structure or its materials to be removed from realty," the classification depends on who is to sever the property to be sold from the land. If it is the vendor that is to sever it, the contract is one for the sale of goods; if it is the purchaser that is to sever it, the contract is one for the sale of an interest in land.[36] The problem of the mixed contract of sale, involving both land and goods, is discussed in the next section.[37]

---

[30] Cooper v. Aiello, 107 A. 473 (N.J. Sup. 1919) (agreement to make lease was "contract relating to . . . an interest in lands, tenements, and hereditaments").

[31] *See* Cal. Civ. Code §1624(a)(3); N.Y. Gen. Oblig. Law §5-703; Restatement Second §125 cmt. *b*.

[32] Bell v. Vaughn, 53 P.2d 61 (Ariz. 1935) ("a general provision in a statute (all agreements) is controlled by a special one (agreements to lease real property)").

[33] For a representative case, *see* Rosenstein v. Gottfried, 176 N.W. 844 (Minn. 1920) (though there is "much confusion in the decisions as to when a sale of things attached to land, but which are to be removed, is to be considered a sale of land, and when a sale of personal property," a contract giving the purchaser a present interest and a right of removal in "a large and substantial two-story frame dwelling built on a permanent stone foundation, not to be immediately removed . . . is a sale of an interest in land").

[34] This includes fruit on trees as well as wheat, corn, and the like.

[35] UCC 2-107(2). The section states that this rule applies even though the property "forms part of the realty at the time of contracting."

[36] UCC 2-107(1).

[37] See the discussion of interests in real property in §6.6 *infra*. There the question is whether a contract for the sale of both goods and land comes within the provision for goods or the provision for land. Because the provision for land, unlike that for goods, is not limited to sales, there are also cases in which the question is whether a contract to leave both goods and land by will comes within the provision for land or is not within the statute at all.

From contracts for the sale of interests in land, we turn to contracts for the sale of goods.

§6.6.   **Contracts for the Sale of Goods.**   The sale of goods provision has always been regarded as distinct from the other provisions of the statute of frauds. In the English Statute of 1677, it was set out in a separate section.[1] Furthermore, all of its various versions have been unique in expressly permitting satisfaction not only by a memorandum but by part performance as well.[2] A similar provision was contained in the Uniform Sales Act, adopted by most states in the first half of the twentieth century.[3] And the Uniform Commercial Code contains a statute of frauds for contracts that in original Article 2 applied to contracts "for the sale of goods for the price of $500 or more," an amount raised in revised Article 2 to "$5,000 or more."[4] The Code made some significant changes, making it easier to satisfy the statute.[5] These changes relate to the requirements for a memorandum,[6] the possibility of satisfaction by an admission[7] or by a confirmatory memorandum,[8] the effect of part performance,[9] and the exception for specially manufactured goods.[10] In revised Article 2, the term *record* is used in place of *writing*.[11] As has already been explained, there is no requirement of a writing for contracts of international sale governed by the Vienna Convention.[12]

Because UCC 2-201 applies only to "a contract for the sale of goods," its scope is arguably narrower than that of Article 2 in general, which applies to "transactions in goods."[13] Nevertheless, UCC 2-201 applies to both a contract under which ownership of the goods passes immediately to the buyer and also

History

Sale of goods

----

§6.6   [1] See the discussion of the scope of the Statute in §6.1 *supra*. In 1893 the sale of goods provision in England became §4 of the Sale of Goods Act (see the discussion of early statutes on the sale of goods in §1.9 *supra*), where it remained until its repeal in 1954.

[2] See the discussion of the sale of goods provision in §6.9 *infra*.

[3] Uniform Sales Act §4. Prior to the adoption of the Uniform Sales Act, most states had adopted provisions patterned on the original English Statute.

[4] See the discussion of statutes remaining in the United States in §6.1 *supra*.

[5] *See* Metz Beverage Co. v. Wyoming Beverages, 39 P.3d 1051 (Wyo. 2002) ("rigid adherence to the statute of frauds is contrary to the philosophy" of the Code).

[6] See the discussion of the Code's relaxation of the requirement in §6.7 *infra*.

[7] See the discussion of admissions in court proceedings in §6.7 *infra*.

[8] See the discussion of a writing in confirmation under the Code in §6.8 *infra*.

[9] See the discussion of the sale of goods provision in §6.9 *infra*.

[10] See the discussion of reliance under the sale of goods provision in §6.12 *infra*.

[11] See the discussion of revised Article 2 in §1.9 *supra*.

[12] See the discussion of no requirement for international contracts in §6.1 *supra*.

[13] Included in the few cases to recognize this is Continental Can Co. v. Poultry Processing, 649 F. Supp. 570 (D. Me. 1986) (dictum: "specific language in section 2-201 appears to reflect an intention . . . to give the Article Two statute of frauds a more narrow application than the rest of the Article").

to a contract under which ownership is to pass at some future time.[14] Moreover, the provision applies to an agreement of rescission that will revest title to the goods in the seller after the buyer has acquired it.[15] UCC 2-201 applies regardless of whether the goods are in existence at the time the contract is made, even if they are to be specially manufactured by the seller for the buyer.[16] It has been held to cover franchise or distributorship agreements.[17] It does not apply, however, to a contract of agency or brokerage, under which the agent or broker is merely to arrange a sale of goods for another,[18] nor does it apply to leases of goods.[19]

Limitation of $500 raised to $5,000

UCC 2-201 does not apply unless the contract is one "for the price of $500 or more,"[20] raised in revised Article 2 to "$5,000 or more." If the price exceeds the dollar threshhold and the statute is not satisfied, the section does not make the contract enforceable up to the amount of the dollar threshhold; it is unenforceable in its entirety.[21] Since the price need not be payable in money alone, the applicability of the provision may turn on the value of the nonmonetary part.[22] If a number of items are sold, its applicability may turn on whether there is a single contract or several contracts.[23]

Intangible property

Because the definition of goods specifies "all things" that are "moveable,"[24] UCC 2-201 does not apply to intangible property. Nor, in revised Article 2, does

---

[14] UCC 2-106(1) ("'Contract for sale' includes both a present sale of goods and a contract to sell goods at a future time."). This is in contrast to the land contract provision, which does not apply to present sales. See the discussion of its inapplicability to conveyances in §6.5 *supra*.

[15] Padgham v. Wilson Music Co., 88 N.W.2d 679 (Wis. 1958) (sale of goods provision applied to agreement of rescission after "original contract of sale was completely executed").

[16] UCC 2-201(3)(a), which applies to specially manufactured goods, is discussed in §6.12 *infra*.

[17] Omaha World-Herald v. Nielsen, 369 N.W.2d 631 (Neb. 1985) (rejecting argument that "distributorship agreement was primarily for the service of delivering newspapers").

[18] Around the World Merchandisers v. Rayovac Corp., 585 A.2d 437 (N.J. Super. 1990) (UCC 2-201 does not apply "when the distributor or middleman does not obtain title to the goods").

[19] Mueller & Sons v. Northern Ill. Gas Co., 299 N.E.2d 601 (Ill. App. 1973) (UCC 2-201 did not apply to rental of vending machines). This is in contrast to the land contract provision, which covers leases. See the discussion of leases in §6.5 *supra*.

[20] In the English Statute of 1677 the figure was "the price of ten pounds sterling"; in the English Sale of Goods Act it was "the value of ten pounds"; in early American statutes it was usually $50; and in the Uniform Sales Act it was "the value of five hundred dollars."

[21] This is in contrast to former UCC 1-206, deleted in the revision of Article 1, under which if the provision was not satisfied, the contract was not enforceable "*beyond* five thousand dollars in amount or value of remedy."

[22] UCC 2-304(1) ("The price can be made payable in money or otherwise.").

[23] S.L. Munson Co. v. DeVries, 189 N.W. 859 (Mich. 1922) (two orders for goods resulted in separate contracts, though made through same salesperson on same date).

[24] UCC-O 2-105(1); UCC-R 2-103(1)(k). The original English Statute spoke of "goods, wares and merchandizes."

it apply to "information."[25] Under the former version of Article 1, contracts for the sale of other intangibles might be covered by a residual provision that was deleted in the revision.[26]

UCC 2-201 does not apply to sales of interests in real property as distinguished from goods, a distinction that has already been explored.[27] If the contract is a mixed one, involving the sale of both goods and real property, the Code suggests that in some instances it might apply only to the goods,[28] but courts have been reluctant to do this and prefer to classify the contract according to the dominant element.[29]

Interests in real property

A particularly vexing problem of classification, here as under Article 2 generally, arises when the contract is one to supply both goods and services. On the one hand, a contract does not come within the sale of goods provision merely because it incidentally involves the supply of goods, as does a contract to paint a house or to repair a car.[30] On the other hand, a contract is not taken out of the provision merely because it incidentally requires the furnishing of services, as does a contract to deliver and install a furnace or to furnish and service a generator.[31] In doubtful cases courts have usually searched for the "predominant factor" of the contract, as they have done under other provisions of Article 2.[32]

Services

The following sections deal with satisfaction of the statute of frauds, a matter as to which the sale of goods provision differs significantly from the other provisions.

---

[25] UCC-R 2-103(1)(k). See the discussion of revised Article 2 in §1.9 *supra*.

[26] The comment to former UCC 1-206 cmt. said that its purpose is to "fill the gap" left by the Code's other statute of frauds provisions, and that "the principal gap relates to the sale of 'general intangibles' [including] bilateral contracts, royalty rights or the like."

[27] See the discussion of Code provisions in §6.5 *supra*.

[28] UCC 2-304(2) provides that if "all or part of the price is payable in an interest in realty the transfer of the goods . . . [is] subject to this Article, but not the transfer of the interest in realty"). This does not, however, apply to the situation of a seller who transfers both goods and an interest in realty. *See* Dehahn v. Innes, 356 A.2d 711 (Me. 1976) ("severability or entirety of a contract depends on the intent of the parties and in the case of an oral contract is a question of fact for the fact-finder").

[29] Dehahn v. Innes, *supra* note 28 (where "contract is predominantly a contract for the sale and purchase of goods [heavy equipment] and . . . the gravel pit involved represented only about 5% of the total price agreed upon," UCC 2-201(3)(b) on admissions applied to the whole contract). See also the discussion of Code provisions in §6.5 *supra*.

[30] Robertson v. Ceola, 501 S.W.2d 764 (Ark. 1973) (UCC 2-201 did not apply to contract to install tile that cost over $15,000 because "the essence of the agreement is a service contract").

[31] Colorado Carpet Installation v. Palermo, 668 P.2d 1384 (Colo. 1983) (UCC 2-201 applied to contract purchase and installation of carpeting, tile, and other floor covering).

[32] Zayre Corp. v. S.M. & R. Co., 882 F.2d 1145 (7th Cir. 1989) (contract for selection and sale of jewelry was "predominantly" sale of goods). See the discussion of the scope of Article 2 in §1.9 *supra*.

C.   HOW THE STATUTE CAN BE SATISFIED

**Writing is usual
way to satisfy
statute**

§6.7.   Nature and Contents of Writing Required. Section 4 of the English Statute of 1677 required that "the agreement . . . or some memorandum or note thereof . . . be in writing, and signed."[1] Although some provisions of the statute can be satisfied in other ways,[2] the traditional way to satisfy the statute is by a signed writing, commonly called a "memorandum."

**Form of
memorandum**

The memorandum need not take any particular form. It may be made up of several writings, and they may have been made at different times.[3] It need not have been delivered or communicated to the other party.[4] It need not even have been directed to the other party or made for the purpose of satisfying the statute.[5] Among the many kinds of writings that have been held to satisfy the statute are: a letter,[6] an email,[7] a telegram or telex,[8] a receipt,[9] an invoice,[10] a check,[11] a penciled price list,[12] the minutes of a meeting,[13] another contract,[14] and a will.[15] Some courts have held that a tape recording will suffice,[16] though

---

§6.7   [1] Stat. 29, Car. 2, c.3, §4 (1677).

[2] See §6.9 *infra*.

[3] Nebraska Builders Prods. v. Industrial Erectors, 478 N.W.2d 257 (Neb. 1992) (five letters read together to satisfy statute).

[4] D'Angelo v. Schultz, 760 P.2d 866 (Or. 1988) ("delivery is not required"); UCC 2-201 cmt. 6 ("It is not necessary that the writing be delivered to anybody.").

[5] Morris Cohon & Co. v. Russell, 245 N.E.2d 712 (N.Y. 1969) (clause in contract for sale of stock indicated that broker had rendered services). According to Restatement Second §133, an exception is made to this rule in the case of the marriage provision because it "performs a cautionary function." Restatement Second §133 cmt. *a*. However, no exception is said to be made in the case of the suretyship provision, which also performs a cautionary function.

[6] Aragon v. Boyd, 450 P.2d 614 (N.M. 1969) (letters to other party reciting earlier agreement).

[7] Cloud Corp. v. Hasbro, Inc., 314 F.3d 289 (7th Cir. 2002).

[8] Hawley Fuel Coalmart v. Steag Handel GmbH, 796 F.2d 29 (2d Cir. 1986) (telexes); Hansen v. Hill, 340 N.W.2d 8 (Neb. 1983) (telegram).

[9] Goetz v. Hubbell, 266 N.W. 836 (N.D. 1936) (receipt by vendor of building for part payment).

[10] Mid-South Packers v. Shoney's, 761 F.2d 1117 (5th Cir. 1985) (though contract "was initially unenforceable . . . , invoice rendered [it] enforceable").

[11] Clark v. Larkin, 239 P.2d 970 (Kan. 1952) (check for down payment on real estate with notation of terms).

[12] Southwest Engrg. Co. v. Martin Tractor Co., 473 P.2d 18 (Kan. 1970) (penciled list of generator components with prices). *See* UCC 2-201 cmt. 1 ("may be written in lead pencil on a scratch pad").

[13] Conner v. Lavaca Hosp. Dist., 267 F.3d 426 (5th Cir. 2001) ("minutes of a board meeting can satisfy this writing requirement").

[14] Morris Cohon & Co. v. Russell, *supra* note 5 (contract between buyer and seller of stock interest recited broker's right to commission).

[15] Newman v. Huff, 632 N.E.2d 799 (Ind. App. 1994) (revoked will).

[16] Londono v. City of Gainesville, 768 F.2d 1223 (11th Cir. 1985) (fn.4: "tape recording of the City Commission's action at the meeting satisfies the statute").

there is contrary authority.[17] In revised Article 2, the requirement of a "writing" is replaced by the requirement of a "record," defined as "information that is inscribed on a tangible medium or that is stored in an electronic form or other medium and is retrievable in perceivable form."[18] The revised article provides that a record "may not be denied legal effect or enforceability solely because it is in electronic form."[19]

The memorandum may be made either before or after the formation of the contract.[20] An offer, which necessarily precedes the time of formation, should suffice.[21] However, some courts have held that an offer by itself is not sufficient to satisfy the peculiar requirement of UCC 2-201 that the writing show that a contract of sale "has been made,"[22] a conclusion that conflicts with the drafters' intention to relax the requirements of the statute. The statute may be satisfied by a letter written after the time of formation and acknowledging the contract,[23] even if the letter also repudiates the contract.[24] Although statutes of frauds generally provide that "no action shall be brought" without a memorandum, little support remains for the view that the memorandum must have been made before suit is brought,[25] a view that would have special significance in connection with admissions in court proceedings.

Time of memorandum

Courts agree that a writing is not insufficient as a memorandum merely because it has been made in a court proceeding, at least if the writing was made

Admissions in court proceedings

---

[17] Sonders v. Roosevelt, 476 N.E.2d 996 (N.Y. 1985) (tape recording "is not a memorandum in writing subscribed").

[18] UCC-R 2-103(1)(m). See the discussion of revised Article 2 in §1.9 *supra*.

[19] UCC-R 2-211(1). *See* UCC-R 2-211(2) ("contract may not be denied legal effect or enforceability solely because an electronic record was used in its formation"). These subsections are derived from UETA §7(a) & (b). As to the relation of revised Article 2 to UETA and E-Sign, see the discussion of electronic commerce in §1.7 *supra*.

[20] Metz Beverage Co. v. Wyoming Beverages, 39 P.3d 1051 (Wyo. 2002) ("writings need not be made contemporaneously with the initial agreement, especially where . . . agreement was of long duration and the writings occurred during the performance").

[21] First Natl. Bank v. Laperle, 86 A.2d 635 (Vt. 1952) ("written offer accepted by parol may constitute a sufficient memorandum of the contract, provided the person making the offer is the party to be charged").

[22] Micromedia v. Automated Broadcast Controls, 799 F.2d 230 (5th Cir. 1986) (fn.4: observing "that the 'has been made' language finds no counterpart in the wording of the general statute of frauds").

[23] Mid-South Packers v. Shoney's, *supra* note 10; Aragon v. Boyd, *supra* note 6. This rule is not easy to justify where the statute is seen as having a cautionary function, but it has been followed even though the statute says that a contract is "void" unless there is a sufficient memorandum.

If a subsequent promise to perform the unenforceable "moral" obligation is regarded as enforceable in its own right, the statute may be circumvented, as is pointed out in note 33 *infra*.

[24] Sennott v. Cobb's Pedigreed Chicks, 84 N.E.2d 466 (Mass. 1949) (buyer wrote: "please accept my cancellation of all three cars of oats . . . under contract number 6077").

[25] Bird v. Munroe, 66 Me. 337 (1877) (dictum: though "there may be some logic" in contrary view, "the current of decision requires that the writing must exist before action brought"). This was the rule stated in the first Restatement §215. Restatement Second §136 rejects this view "as contrary to the spirit of modern procedural reforms." Restatement Second §136, Reporter's Note.

voluntarily.[26] To the extent that the statute's function is viewed as evidentiary, it is difficult to see why the statute should not be satisfied by a written admission in a pleading, stipulation, or deposition, even though it is in the same action in which the statute is raised as a defense. The Code goes beyond this and gives effect to oral admissions. Under 2-201(3)(b), the statute is satisfied if a party admits in its pleading, testimony or otherwise "that a contract for sale was made," even if the admission is not in a writing or other record.[27] It has been held that the admission may be by an agent.[28] With respect to content, courts have often found admissions sufficient,[29] but also have often found them wanting.[30] In order to meet the requirement as to content, an admission may be read together with writings or other records.[31] Even absent a statutory provision, some courts have held that an oral admission[32] and even an admission by failure to object[33] can satisfy the statute. The ethical aspects of these rules are discussed later in this treatise.[34]

May be lost or destroyed

The memorandum need not still be in existence at the time of the suit. If it has been lost or destroyed, its contents may be shown by other evidence, even if that evidence is not written.[35]

Contents of memorandum

What must the memorandum contain in order to satisfy the statute? In general, the memorandum must do the following with reasonable certainty: (1) identify the parties to the contract and show that a contract has been made by them or offered by the signatory to the other; (2) indicate the nature of the

---

[26] Bower v. Jones, 978 F.2d 1004 (7th Cir. 1992) ("deposition may qualify as a signed writing," quoting following sentence of this treatise).

[27] UCC-O 2-201(3)(b) ("admits in his pleading, testimony or otherwise in court"); UCC-R 2-201(3)(b) ("admits in the party's pleading, or in the party's testimony or otherwise under oath"). UCC 2A-201 contains a comparable provision. For a similar statute applicable to contracts generally, *see* Alaska Stat. §09.25.020(4). In keeping with the Code's emphasis on quantity, UCC 2-201(3)(b) provides that "the contract is not enforceable . . . beyond the quantity of goods admitted."

[28] Roth Steel Prods. v. Sharon Steel Corp., 705 F.2d 134 (6th Cir. 1983).

[29] Quaney v. Tobyne, 689 P.2d 844 (Kan. 1984) ("not necessary that there be an express declaration in which the party admits the making of the oral contract" during testimony and "sufficient if his words or admitted conduct reasonably lead to that conclusion").

[30] Dairyland Fin. Corp. v. Intermediate Credit Bank, 852 F.2d 242 (7th Cir. 1988) (deposition testimony did not describe "circumstances from which a reasonable jury could infer the existence of an agreement between [the parties] for the sale of the loan portfolio").

[31] In re F & S Cent. Mfg. Co., 70 Bankr. 569 (Bankr. E.D.N.Y. 1987) ("combination of the writings and testimony unequivocally lead to the conclusion" that statute is satisfied).

[32] Bentley v. Potter, 694 P.2d 617 (Utah 1984) (party who "admitted at trial that . . . he intended . . . to be a guarantor" could not set up statute). *See* Restatement Second §133 cmt. *d* ("An oral statement before the court is treated in some states as the equivalent of a signed writing.").

[33] Stoetzel v. Continental Textile Corp., 768 F.2d 217 (8th Cir. 1985) (failure to object to admission of evidence establishing oral agreement).

[34] See the discussion of the ethical problem in §6.10 *infra*.

[35] Brooks v. Toperzer, 441 A.2d 1177 (N.H. 1982) (land contract provision satisfied where signed writing was lost).

contract and its subject matter; (3) state the essential terms of the promises to be performed under the contract.[36] In applying these general requirements courts should bear in mind the purposes of the statute of frauds and be more demanding when the statute also serves a cautionary function (as in the case of the suretyship provision) or a channeling function (as in the case of the land contract provision), in addition to an evidentiary one.

Courts have had relatively little difficulty with the first two requirements. The context of the memorandum may help to show that a contract was made, or at least offered,[37] and to identify the parties[38] and the subject matter.[39] Identification of the subject matter is a source of much litigation in connection with the land contract provisions, with many decisions holding that the requirement has been met[40] and many others holding that it has not.[41] If the contract is made by an agent for an unnamed principal, it is enough if the agent is identified.[42]

Subject matter and parties

Courts have had more trouble with the third requirement — that the memorandum state with reasonable certainty the essential terms of the unperformed promises under the contract.[43] One difficulty arises in distinguishing essential terms from details or particulars.[44] This inevitably vague distinction often

Essential terms

[36]Courts have occasionally avoided these requirements by holding that a bare promise to pay money is enforceable on grounds of moral obligation (*see* the discussion of the scope of the exception in §2.8 *supra*). This has been done in the case of a subsequent writing, such as a promissory note, that is not itself a sufficient memorandum, and has particular appeal under special statutes applicable to brokers because restitution is unavailable (*see* the discussion of restitution as contrary to policy in §6.11 *infra*). Muir v. Kane, 104 P. 153 (Wash. 1909) (writing insufficient under brokerage provision).

[37]This requirement is especially troublesome where a writing signed by a seller offers the buyer a choice. *See* Southwest Engrg. Co. v. Martin Tractor Co., *supra* note 12 (writing listing prices of alternative generators afforded "substantial basis for the belief that it rests on a real transaction").

[38]Randazzo v. Kroenke, 127 N.W.2d 880 (Mich. 1964) (writing was sufficient, though it did not identify purchaser of land, where vendor "never seriously contended that plaintiff was not the vendee under the contract which he sought to establish").

[39]James Talcott, Inc. v. Fullerton Cotton Mills, 208 F.2d 81 (5th Cir. 1953) (suretyship provision: identity of principal shown by circumstances).

[40]Clark v. Larkin, *supra* note 11 ("405 East 'A'" was sufficient description of land where it was the only tract owned by vendor or listed with broker that fit description and purchaser personally inspected it).

[41]Martin v. Seigel, 212 P.2d 107 (Wash. 1949) (street address insufficient description since contract for sale of "platted real property must contain, . . . the description of such property by the correct lot number(s), block number, addition, city, county and state").

[42]Looman Realty Corp. v. Broad St. Natl. Bank, 161 A.2d 247 (N.J. 1960) (purchaser was sufficiently identified where purchaser's agents signed writing and stated in it that they were acting for unnamed company that they owned).

[43]*See* Opdyke Inv. Co. v. Norris Grain Co., 320 N.W.2d 836 (Mich. 1982) (rejecting former requirement that "memorandum . . . must be complete in itself, and leave nothing to rest in parol").

[44]*See* Opdyke Inv. Co. v. Norris Grain Co., *supra* note 43 (failure to specify exact construction site not fatal where "parties did not regard the precise construction site . . . as an essential term").

becomes more precise, however, in the context of the particular contract and the precise dispute. The Supreme Court of Connecticut expressed a sound view that is gaining currency when it held that it was error to disallow a memorandum that referred to "the usual provisions found in . . . purchase money mortgage deeds" where, as Ellen Peters put it, "the parties' disputes about performance relate to matters entirely independent of the purchase money mortgage."[45] Aside from the writing, much may depend on the quality of corroborative evidence and on the extent of any forfeiture that will result from a refusal to enforce the contract.[46] Omission of a term is never fatal if the court will supply it by implication.[47]

Consideration as essential term

Must the memorandum set out the consideration for the promise that is sought to be enforced, in addition to the terms of that promise? This question is particularly likely to arise under the suretyship provision. Most courts now agree that the memorandum need not state the consideration if it has already been given,[48] so that even a false recital of such a past event will not affect the sufficiency of the memorandum.[49] Thus if a vendor of land has already been paid, a memorandum is sufficient, even though it does not state the price or states it incorrectly. Most courts insist, however, that the memorandum state the consideration if it has not already been given.[50] Thus if the vendor has not yet been paid, a memorandum signed by the vendor is not sufficient if it does not state the price.

Code relaxes requirement

The Uniform Commercial Code significantly relaxes the requirement that the memorandum state all the essential terms by insisting only that, in addition to indicating "that a contract for sale has been made between the parties," it state the quantity of goods.[51] Other terms need not be stated and, if stated, the statement need not be precise or accurate. The requirement as to quantity is imposed obliquely by the provision that the contract is not enforceable "beyond

---

See also Restatement Second §131 cmt. *g* ("The 'essential' terms of unperformed promises must be stated; 'details or particulars' need not.").

[45] Lynch v. Davis, 435 A.2d 977, 980 (Conn. 1980). Restatement Second §131 cmt. *c*, cited by the court, goes far in this direction: "where only an evidentiary purpose is served, the requirement of a memorandum is read in the light of the dispute which arises and the admissions of the party to be charged; there is no need for evidence on points not in dispute."

[46] This will depend, in turn, on the possibility of recovery based on restitution or reliance, discussed in §§6.11, 6.12 *infra*.

[47] Christophersen v. Blount, 582 A.2d 460 (Conn. 1990) ("because the law implies a reasonable time to perform . . . , this contract did not fail to comply with the statute of frauds").

[48] The contrary view stems from Wain v. Warlters, 102 Eng. Rep. 972 (K.B. 1804), in which it was held that a written promise of suretyship was unenforceable because the writing did not express the fully executed consideration.

[49] See the discussion of no power over the truth §2.17 *supra*.

[50] Houston v. McClure, 425 So. 2d 1114 (Ala. 1983) (writing that acknowledged receipt of $10,000 and referred to "balance" to be paid was not sufficient because of "failure to express the entire consideration").

[51] UCC 2-201(1) (contract not enforceable "beyond the quantity of goods shown").

the quantity of goods shown" in the writing or other record, so that if no quantity is shown the contract is not enforceable at all.[52] As the commentary explains: "The price, time and place of payment or delivery, the general quality of the goods, or any particular warranties may all be omitted." The price of the goods need not be stated since "it can normally be supplied without danger of fraud." In some instances "the parties do not mention the price in express terms, the buyer being bound to pay and the seller to accept a reasonable price"; in other instances "the price is not mentioned since the parties have based their agreement on a price list or catalogue"; and, in any event, "'market' prices . . . that are current in the vicinity constitute a similar check."[53] Furthermore, courts applying UCC 2-201 have been lenient in applying the requirement of a statement of the quantity of goods. For example, a statement of quantity in terms of "output" or "requirements" or of "best efforts" will suffice.[54] If a contract is evidenced by a memorandum that satisfies the statute and is then modified, no new memorandum seems to be required unless the quantity of the goods is changed.[55]

In preparing the memorandum, parties sometimes omit or misstate a term. If the agreement is not integrated, the parol evidence rule will not bar evidence of prior negotiations to show this.[56] If the omission or misstatement was the result of mutual mistake or fraud, the court can reform the memorandum to reflect the agreement, and the statute is then satisfied if the memorandum as reformed is sufficient. Most courts have held that the statute of frauds does not preclude reformation in this situation.[57] However, if reformation is unavailable and the term is essential, the inaccurate memorandum will not satisfy the statute.[58] Under UCC 2-201, the availability of reformation is significant only in connection with the quantity term, since only that term need be stated in the memorandum. The language of that section barring enforcement of the

Erroneous omission or misstatement

---

[52] Simmons Foods v. Hill's Pet Nutrition, 270 F. 3d 723 (8th Cir. 2001) ("fax did not set forth an enforceable contract for the years 1999 and 2000 because it contained no quantities for those years").

[53] UCC 2-201 cmt. 1. There is not even a requirement that the kind of goods be specified.

[54] Nora Beverages v. Perrier Group, 164 F.3d 736 (2d Cir. 1998) ("projected range" of 1/2 to 1 million cases sufficed).

[55] See the discussion of modification and rescission in §6.2 *supra*.

[56] Williams v. Pittsfield Lime & Stone Co., 154 N.E. 572 (Mass. 1927) (where contract was not totally integrated, it could be shown that it omitted term that it was not to be performed within a year and that therefore it did not satisfy the statute). If the contract is only partially integrated, omissions but not misstatements can be shown; if it is totally integrated, neither can be shown. See §7.3 *infra*.

[57] See §7.5 *infra*.

[58] The statute of frauds is not a rule of evidence, and it does not exclude the evidence of the omitted or misstated term in this situation. However, the evidence can be used only to show the defect in the memorandum and not to cure that defect. This result is sometimes described as though the statute had the effect of an exclusionary rule similar to the parol evidence rule.

contract "beyond the quantity of goods shown" in the writing or other record should not be read as precluding reformation of that term.

We look next at satisfaction of the requirement that the writing be signed.

Test of intent to authenticate

§6.8. Requirement of Signature. The statute's requirement that the writing be signed is not applied with rigor. The modern test is whether the other party reasonably believes that the asserted signer's intention is to authenticate the writing as the asserted signer's own.[1] Under the Uniform Commercial Code, "signed" includes the use of "any symbol executed or adopted with present intention to adopt or accept a writing."[2] Under revised Article 2, "sign" means the execution or adoption of "a tangible symbol" or the attachment or logical association with a record of "an electronic sound, symbol, or process" if this is done "with present intent to authenticate or adopt a record"[3] The revised article provides that a signature "may not be denied legal effect or enforceability solely because it is in electronic form."[4] Initials or another symbol will suffice if the test for a signature is met.[5] In the case of an electronic communication a symbol added to authenticate should therefore be sufficient even if there is no digital signature.[6] The requisite intention may be inferred from the fact that the symbol appears at the end of the writing, and it may be proved by other evidence if the symbol appears elsewhere.[7] Though the symbol is usually added after the writing has been made, a party can adopt a symbol that is already on the paper.[8] Thus while it is customary to initial changes in the memorandum

---

§6.8 [1] Hansen v. Hill, 340 N.W.2d 8 (Neb. 1983) (telegram to which name of vendor of land "has been affixed may be considered as having been signed").

[2] UCC-R 2-103(1)(p).

[3] UCC 1-201(37). As to when an electronic signature is attributable to a person, *see* UCC-R 2-212, based on UETA § 9.

[4] UCC-R 2-211(1). This subsections is derived from UETA §7(a). As to the relation of revised Article 2 to UETA and E-Sign, see the discussion of electronic commerce in §1.7 *supra*.

[5] Monetti, S.P.A. v. Anchor Hocking Corp., 931 F.2d 1178 (7th Cir. 1991) ("typed initials are sufficient"). *See* UCC 1-201 cmt. 37 (symbol "may be by initials or by thumbprint").

[6] The mere fact that the communication indicates that it originated in the office of the sender may not suffice. As to emails, *see* Cloud Corp. v. Hasbro, Inc., 314 F.3d 289 (7th Cir. 2002) (sender's name on email satisfied statute); Toghiyany v. Amerigas Propane, 309 F.3d 1088 (8th Cir. 2002) (unsigned emails did not satisfy statute). As to the requirement of a writing in such cases, see the discussion of the form of the memorandum in §6.7 *supra*.

[7] McMillen v. Terrell, 23 Ind. 163 (1864) ("If the signature is placed at the close, at the ordinary place of signature, the inference is that it was so placed as the final execution of the instrument. This inference, however, does not necessarily arise where the name is found at the commencement or in the body."). *See* Southwest Engrg. Co. v. Martin Tractor Co., 473 P.2d 18 (Kan. 1970) (hand-printed name at top sufficed where trial court "found this sufficient").

[8] A common example is that of the letterhead. See the discussion of the means of signature *infra*. Another is that of a signed writing with blanks that are properly filled in later. *See* Restatement Second §134 cmt. *c* ("the prior signature is effectively adopted with reference to the added portion"). *But cf.* Parma Tile Mosaic & Marble Co. v. Estate of Short, 663 N.E.2d 633

that are made after signing, it may be shown that the signer intended to adopt a prior signature to authenticate the changes.[9]

Although the English Statute of 1677 required that the writing be "signed," it did not insist that the signature appear at the end of the writing.[10] The same is true of most American versions,[11] and under these statutes it has been held that the signature may appear anywhere in the writing.[12] Occasionally, however, a statute requires that the writing be "subscribed,"[13] and courts have differed as to whether this should be read merely as a synonym for "signed"[14] or as requiring that the writing be signed at the end.[15]

Location of signature

The symbol may be put in the writing by any means. It may be written in ink or pencil;[16] it may be typed, stamped, printed or put on by photographic process.[17] Even a printed letterhead may serve as a signature as long as the other party reasonably believes that it is used with the intention of authenticating the writing.[18]

Means of signature

The memorandum need not be signed by both parties; it is enough that it be signed by the party against whom enforcement is sought or, as the English Statute of 1677 put it, "the party to be charged."[19] Courts have shown little concern with the lack of mutuality that results when only one party has signed.[20]

Who must sign

(N.Y. 1996) (rejecting contention that requirement was satisfied "because the fax machine had been programmed . . . to identify each page" with name of sender).

[9] Bluck v. Gompertz, 155 Eng. Rep. 1199 (Ex. 1852) ("words introduced into a paper signed by a party, or an alteration in it, may be considered as authenticated by a signature already on the paper, if it is plain that they were meant to be so authenticated"). *See* Restatement Second §134 cmt. *c* ("re-adoption of the prior signature is equally effective").

[10] Stat. 29 Car. 2, c.3, §4 (1677) ("signed" by party to be charged); id. §17 ("signed" by parties to be charged).

[11] *See* UCC 2-201(1) ("signed" by party against which enforcement is sought); N.J. Stat. Ann. §25:1-5 ("signed" by party to be charged).

[12] Southwest Engrg. Co. v. Martin Tractor Co., *supra* note 7 (hand-printed name in upper corner sufficed).

[13] *See* Cal. Civ. Code §1624(a) ("subscribed" by party to be charged); N.Y. Gen. Oblig. Law §5-701(a) (same).

[14] California Canneries Co. v. Scatena, 49 P. 462 (Cal. 1897) (place of signature is immaterial because *subscribe* is used to mean "attest by writing").

[15] 300 West End Ave. Corp. v. Warner, 165 N.E. 271 (N.Y. 1929) (where earlier statute said "signed" and this was changed to "subscribed," the writing must be signed at the end).

[16] Merritt v. Clason, 12 Johns. (N.Y.) 102 (Sup. Ct. 1815), aff'd sub nom. Clason v. Bailey, 14 Johns. (N.Y.) 484 (1817).

[17] Barber & Ross Co. v. Lifetime Doors, 810 F.2d 1276 (4th Cir. 1987) (seller's trademark on sales brochures sufficed).

[18] Merrill, Lynch, Pierce, Fenner & Smith v. Cole, 457 A.2d 656 (Conn. 1983) ("letterhead or billhead satisfies the signature requirement"). *See* UCC 1-201 cmt. 37 (symbol "in appropriate cases may be found in a billhead or letterhead").

[19] Stat. 29 Car. 2, c.3, §4 (1677).

[20] *See* UCC 2-201 cmt. 6 ("Prior to a dispute no one can determine which party's signing of the memorandum may be necessary but from the time of contracting each party should be aware that to him it is signing by the other which is important.").

Agency

A party's signature may be made by an agent.[21] Unless the statute provides otherwise,[22] the agency may be conferred by words, written or oral, or by other conduct.[23] A third person may be the agent of both parties for this purpose,[24] and an auctioneer is generally regarded as having a power to sign for both buyer and seller that is irrevocable for a reasonable time on the day of the sale.[25]

Several writings

If the memorandum consists of several writings, the requirement of a signature must be met with respect to the entire memorandum. This poses no problem if there are several signed writings and their contents show that they relate to the same transaction.[26] Nor is there a problem if there is a signed writing that incorporates or refers to other unsigned writings[27] or that is attached to or enclosed with other unsigned writings.[28] As Cardozo put it, "The memorandum exacted by the statute . . . may be pieced together out of separate writings, connected with one another either expressly or by the internal evidence of subject-matter and occasion."[29]

Example of Crabtree v. Elizabeth Arden

In *Crabtree v. Elizabeth Arden Sales Corp.*, the New York Court of Appeals applied this reasoning to a situation in which a signed writing made no reference to other unsigned writings. There, an employment agreement was evidenced by two payroll cards (which had been signed by the employer after the employment had begun and contained all the essential terms except the duration of the employment), along with the employer's memorandum of her oral offer, which recorded all the essential terms but was unsigned. The court rejected the view

---

[21] J.E. Tarbell Co. v. Grimes, 149 A. 73 (N.H. 1930) (law "does not require that a memorandum under the statute shall show that the signer acted as agent for the party sought to be charged"). Compare the question of the adequacy of the description of the parties. See the discussion of subject matter and parties in §6.7 *supra*.

[22] This is especially common in connection with the land contract provision. Glasgow v. G.R.C. Coal Co., 442 A.2d 249 (Pa. Super. 1981) ("agency agreement for the sale of land must be in writing").

[23] Vickers v. North Am. Land Devs., 607 P.2d 603 (N.M. 1980) ("agency may be created orally even where the contract to be executed by the agent . . . must be in writing").

[24] Dinuba Farmers' Union Packing Co. v. J.M. Anderson Grocer Co., 182 S.W. 1036 (Mo. App. 1916) (when broker "strikes a bargain between the parties and the contract of sale is definitely settled, he becomes the agent of both parties for the purposes of executing the memorandum").

[25] Holston v. Pennington, 304 S.E.2d 287 (Va. 1983) ("auctioneer is the agent both of the buyer and of the seller").

[26] Jennings v. Ruidoso Racing Assn., 441 P.2d 42 (N.M. 1968) (minutes of board of directors of employer corporation and salary check together satisfied statute).

[27] Leach v. Crucible Center Co., 388 F.2d 176 (1st Cir. 1968) (four writings, not all signed by vendor of land, satisfied statute as long as "signed writing refers to the unsigned ones or is physically annexed").

[28] Scholtz v. Philbin, 145 A. 487 (Md. 1929) (auctioneer's memorandum signed by buyer and "copy of the advertisement of the sale affixed to it").

[29] Marks v. Cowdin, 123 N.E. 139, 141 (N.Y. 1919). In that case, the contract was for renewal of an existing employment and the signed writing referred to the employee's existing employment without describing it. Cardozo's point was that the nature of his employment could be pieced together from what the employer had written during the employment.

of some jurisdictions that there must "be a reference, of varying degrees of specificity, in the signed writing to that unsigned." It is enough "that a sufficient connection between the papers is established simply by a reference in them to the same subject matter or transaction . . . , and oral testimony is admitted to show the connection between the documents and to establish the acquiescence of the party to be charged, to the contents of the one unsigned." The court held that, in the light of all the circumstances, including the identity of the terms contained in the writings, "it is apparent, . . . that all three refer on their face to the same transaction" and that oral evidence was admissible to explain a reference in one of the payroll cards to "contractual arrangements" with the employer. The statute was therefore satisfied.[30] The decision has attracted widespread support,[31] with the reservation that if writings are to be connected by extrinsic evidence the evidence must be "clear and convincing" with respect to both the reference to the same transaction and acquiescence to the contents of the unsigned writing.[32] But though the decision exemplifies an enlightened attitude toward the statute, not all courts have been willing to go so far.[33]

Under the Uniform Commercial Code, there is one instance in which a writing or other record may satisfy the statute against a party who has not signed it or any other writing or record. UCC 2-201(2) provides that if both parties to a contract for the sale of goods are merchants,[34] and one sends the other "within a reasonable time[35] a writing or other record in confirmation of the contract and sufficient against the sender,"[36] the party receiving it must give "notice of objection to its contents"[37] in a writing or other record "within

Writing in confirmation under Code

---

[30]110 N.E.2d 551, 553-54 (N.Y. 1953) (Fuld, J.).

[31]Migerobe, Inc. v. Certina USA, 924 F.2d 1330 (5th Cir. 1991) ("signed writing need not refer explicitly to the unsigned writing").

[32]Crabtree v. Elizabeth Arden Sales Corp., *supra* note 30 (if evidence does not "convincingly connect the papers [and] show assent to the unsigned paper," judge may conclude that statute is not satisfied); Restatement Second §132 cmt. *a*.

[33]Owen v. Hendricks, 433 S.W.2d 164 (Tex. 1968) (where "two letters obviously relate to the same subject matter, but there is nothing in the letter signed by [defendant] that even remotely suggests the existence of another writing, . . . the two letters cannot be taken together as constituting the signed memorandum required").

[34]See the discussion of the Code's use of *merchant* in §1.10 *supra*.

[35]As to what is a "reasonable time," *see* Gestetner Corp. v. Case Equip. Co., 815 F.2d 806 (1st Cir. 1987) (where relationship between parties was "continuing one," from spring to September was reasonable).

[36]Thus it must at least be signed by the sender and state the quantity of goods. *See* R.S. Bennett & Co. v. Economy Mechanical Indus., 606 F.2d 182 (7th Cir. 1979) (rejecting the argument "that section 2-201(2) . . . sets forth a less stringent requirement than 2-201(1)").

[37]Courts that have faced the problem have insisted on a denial that the transaction took place and not merely an objection to a term in the confirmation. Simmons Oil Co. v. Bulk Sales Corp., 498 F. Supp. 457 (D.N.J. 1980) (telex that "payment clause is not acceptable" is not a sufficient notice of objection because it "volunteers too much").

10 days after it is received"[38] or the statute will be satisfied in favor of the sender.[39] A seller or buyer may thus send such a confirmation, wait ten days plus twice the time for the mail, and be assured that the statute has been satisfied against the other party. Though it is clear that an acceptance of an offer will not qualify as a confirmation of a contract,[40] it is not clear whether a confirmation must indicate on its face that a binding agreement has already been made.[41] The mere omission or incorrect statement of a term other than the quantity term is not fatal.[42] Even if the statute is satisfied, however, the sender of the confirmation still has the burden of proving the oral agreement that the confirmation purports to confirm.[43]

We turn now to other ways of satisfying the statute.

Satisfaction by part performance exceptional

§6.9. **Satisfaction by Part Performance.** As a general rule, part performance does not of itself make a contract within the statute enforceable. Part performance may, however, give the performing party an argument based on reliance[1] or at any rate a right to restitution.[2] In a few exceptional situations, however, part performance removes the bar of the statute at least to some extent. These exceptions are based on the premise that part performance affords reliable evidence of an agreement. Part performance has therefore no effect under the suretyship provision, which serves a cautionary in addition to an evidentiary function and which would be drastically reduced in scope by such an exception.[3]

---

[38]UCC 2-201(2) requires that the person receiving the writing have "reason to know its contents."

[39]UCC 2A-201 does not contain a similar provision for leases.

[40]R.S. Bennett & Co. v. Economy Mechanical Indus., *supra* note 36 (language of letters, consisting of firm offer and amendment of it, "quite clearly indicates that the writings are offers and are not 'in confirmation of a contract'").

[41]In Harry Rubin & Sons v. Consolidated Pipe Co., 396 Pa. 506, 153 A.2d 472 (1959), the court held that a buyer's letter, asking the seller to enter an "order" pursuant to an earlier telephone conversation, was "in confirmation." The court concluded from a reference in the letter to completion of another "order" that the parties had used the word "order" to refer to an existing agreement.

[42]See the discussion of the Code's relaxation of the writing requirement in §6.7 *supra*.

[43]Howard P. Foley Co. v. Phoenix Engrg. & Supply Co., 819 F.2d 60 (4th Cir. 1987) (UCC 2-201 cmt. 3 "undercuts the claim that an unanswered confirmation is dispositive of both the existence and terms of a contract"). Compare the discussion of the effect of UCC 2-207(2) as incorporating terms by silence in §3.21 *supra*.

§6.9 [1]See §6.12 *infra*.

[2]See §6.11 *infra*.

[3]Brown & Shinitzky Chartered v. Dentinger, 455 N.E.2d 128 (Ill. App. 1983) (exception "would render these provisions totally meaningless" because normally party "does not attempt to enforce a surety contract until after [that party's] performance . . . is complete"). As to the possibility of an exception for full performance of a contract to pay a broker, see the discussion of restitution contrary to policy in §6.11 *infra*.

The oldest exceptions for part performance are those under the sale of goods provision. Section 17 of the English Statute of 1677, which covered contracts for the sale of goods, could be satisfied not only by a writing but also if "the buyer shall accept part of the goods . . . sold, and actually receive the same, or give something . . . in part of payment."[4] A comparable provision was inserted in the Uniform Sales Act.[5] No matter how trivial the part performed, the contract was enforceable in its entirety.[6] The drafters of the Code agreed that "receipt and acceptance either of goods or of the price constitutes an unambiguous overt admission by both parties that a contract actually exists."[7] They cut back the exception, however, by providing that the statute is enforceable only "with respect to goods for which payment has been made and accepted or which have been received and accepted."[8] As the comments explain, consistent with the Code's emphasis on the quantity term, part performance

Sale of goods provision

> can validate the contract only for the goods which have been accepted or for which payment has been made and accepted . . . . If the court can make a just apportionment, therefore, the agreed price of any goods actually delivered can be recovered without a writing or, if the price has been paid, the seller can be forced to deliver an apportionable part of the goods.[9]

If, for example, a contract is made for the sale of 1,000 yards of textiles for $10,000 and the buyer receives and accepts 100 yards, the contract is enforceable against the buyer to the extent of $1,000.[10] Similarly, if the seller accepts part payment of $1,000, the contract is enforceable against the seller to the extent of 100 yards.[11] If the court cannot make a just apportionment, as in the case of acceptance and receipt of some but not all of the parts of a dismantled machine, or partial payment against an indivisible unit of goods, the prevailing

---

[4] Stat. 29 Car. 2, c.3, §17 (1677).

[5] Uniform Sales Act §4.

[6] In one notorious case, the New York Court of Appeals held that the statute was satisfied by the buyer's acceptance of only three small pieces of cloth under an oral contract for the sale of thousands of yards since "the three five-yard pieces were not samples sent for approval but were 'part of the goods' accepted and received by the buyer." Helen Whiting v. Trojan Textile Corp., 121 N.E.2d 367, 370 (N.Y. 1954).

[7] UCC 2-201 cmt. 2. It seems clear from the comment that neither party can then assert UCC 2-201. Mann v. Commissioner, 483 F.2d 673 (8th Cir. 1973) ("the clear majority view is that the partial performance exception renders the contract enforceable by either party").

[8] UCC 2-201(3)(c).

[9] UCC 2-201 cmt. 2. However, since the goods are often not apportionable, the assertion in the commentary as to payment of part of the price is an overstatement.

[10] In re Estate of Nelsen, 311 N.W.2d 508 (Neb. 1981) (to "extent that the contract covers goods in excess of 1,762.68 bushels of soybeans" received and accepted). As to the meaning of *receipt* and *acceptance, see* UCC 2-103(1)(c), 2-606.

[11] Wright Grain Co. v. Augustin Bros. Co., 460 F.2d 376 (8th Cir. 1972) (part payment for corn). *See* UCC 2-201 cmt. 2 ("part payment may be made by money or check").

view is that the contract is enforceable in its entirety.[12] It seems that the Code's exception for part performance also applies to an alleged oral modification of the contract, as long as the performance is consistent with that modification.[13]

Land contract provision

What is often called a "part performance doctrine" is also recognized in connection with the land contract provision. Under this doctrine, a court may grant specific performance of an oral contract to transfer an interest in land if there has been, in Cardozo's words, "performance 'unequivocally referable' to the agreement, performance which alone and without the aid of words of promise is unintelligible or at least extraordinary unless as an incident of ownership."[14] If specific performance is available under this exception to the land-sale provision, the fact that the contract also falls within some other provision of the statute, such as the one-year provision, does not bar relief.[15] The part performance doctrine is more limited in several respects than that applicable to the sale of goods.[16] First, it is generally regarded as making the contract enforceable only in equity and not in an action at law for damages.[17] Second, it has generally been applied only in favor of purchasers and not of vendors.[18] And third, courts have required a measure of reliance that often seems unrelated to any evidentiary function. Thus it is clear that, in contrast to the rule for the sale of goods, mere payment by the purchaser of part or all of the price is not sufficient, since the purchaser is to this extent protected by a right to restitution.[19] The precise contours of the requirement of reliance are uncertain.[20] It has, however, often been held to include acts that are not performance at all. Thus it is generally sufficient if the purchaser has taken possession of the

---

[12]Paloukos v. Intermountain Chevrolet Co., 588 P.2d 939 (Idaho 1978) ($120 payment on pickup truck sold for $3650). *But cf.* Monetti, S.P.A. v. Anchor Hocking Corp., 931 F.2d 1178 (7th Cir. 1991) (Posner, J.: "UCC does not abolish the partial-performance exception," where manufacturer transferred its entire domestic distribution operation, but "merely limits the use of partial delivery as a ground for insisting on the full delivery allegedly required by the oral contract").

[13]See the discussion of modification and rescission in §6.2 *supra.*

[14]Burns v. McCormick, 135 N.E. 273 (N.Y. 1922).

[15]*See* Restatement §129 cmt. *f.*

[16]However, it is also broader in one respect: there is no rule requiring apportionment where it is possible.

[17]Trollope v. Koerner, 470 P.2d 91 (Ariz. 1970) ("notwithstanding the procedural merger of law and equity, the equitable doctrine of part performance is inapplicable in a suit where only *money damages* are sought").

[18]For an exceptional case applying the doctrine in favor of a seller, *see* Walter v. Hoffman, 196 N.E. 291 (N.Y. 1935) (buyer's "possession has been long continued [and] there has been alteration of the property"). *See also* Restatement Second §129 cmt. *e.*

[19]Johnson Farms v. McEnroe, 568 N.W.2d 920 (N.D. 1997) ("partial payment of the purchase price alone will not constitute part performance," though "partial payment considered in connection with other facts such as the making of substantial performance" may do so).

[20]*See* Austin v. Cash, 906 P.2d 669 (Mont. 1995) (purchasers reduction in price of their own home not included because acts "in contemplation of eventual performance are to be distinguished from acts which truly contemplate part performance").

land and made substantial improvements,[21] as long as the improvements are not compensable in money and are such as to evidence a contract to sell (as distinguished, for example, from a landlord-tenant relationship).[22] It has also been held enough if the purchaser has taken possession of the land and paid at least part of the price.[23] The rule as formulated by the Restatement Second goes beyond such cases and states in general terms that the statute does not bar specific performance if the purchaser "has so changed his position that injustice can be avoided only by specific enforcement."[24] A vendor that has conveyed the land to the purchaser can recover the price, but the vendor's right is independent of the part performance doctrine, and recovery is available at law as well as in equity.[25]

Though there is no exception for a party's part performance of a contract within the one-year provision, most courts have held that a party who has fully performed such a contract can enforce it.[26] Part performance on one side does not have this effect.[27] It is difficult to justify the exception for full performance except on the ground of an unstated hostility to the one-year provision.[28] Some courts qualify the exception by requiring that the performance must have taken

One-year provision

---

[21] A seminal case is Seavey v. Drake, 62 N.H. 393 (1882) ("equity protects a parol gift of land equally with a parol agreement to sell it, if accompanied by possession, and the donee has made valuable improvements upon the property").

[22] Kurland v. Stolker, 533 A.2d 1370 (Pa. 1987) (evidence must show "that possession was taken in pursuance of the contract, and, at or immediately after the time it was made, . . . that the change of possession was notorious, . . . that it has been exclusive, continuous and maintained" and that the part performance "could not be compensated in damages, and . . . would make rescission inequitable and unjust").

[23] Shaughnessy v. Eidsmo, 23 N.W.2d 362 (Minn. 1946) ("the acts of taking possession and of making part payment, when they are performed under . . . the oral contract as to be unequivocally referable to the vendor-vendee relationship . . . are sufficient to remove the contract from the statute of frauds").

[24] Restatement Second §129. The commentary adds that, though the evidence is generally required to be "clear and convincing" (cmt. *b*), the part performance need not be unequivocally referable to the oral agreement "if the making of the promise is admitted or clearly proved" (cmt. *d*).

[25] Johnson Farms v. McEnroe, *supra* note 19 ("when a conveyance has been executed and accepted under an oral contract for the sale of land, a party can sue for breach of the promise to pay the contract price, because the statute of frauds is inapplicable to an executed agreement"). *See* Restatement Second §125(3).

[26] Mason v. Anderson, 499 A.2d 783 (Vt. 1985) (overruling earlier decision and following "majority rule"). *See* Restatement Second §130.

[27] Pollman v. Belle Plaine Livestock, 567 N.W.2d 405 (Iowa 1997) (one-year provision "would be meaningless in the employment context if commencement of employment constituted partial performance and barred application of the statute").

[28] For a manifestation of such hostility, *see* Grondin v. Rossington, 690 F. Supp. 200 (S.D.N.Y. 1988) (where full performance is impossible "due to the perpetual nature of the contract," but "both parties . . . perform as though bound for ten years, the likelihood of fraud . . . is scarcely a threat"). See the discussions of the difficulty of rationalizing the provision and its inapplicability if performance is possible in §6.4 *supra*.

place within a year from the time of the making of the contract.[29] A few courts, more logically, reject the exception in its entirety, leaving the party who has performed with any right to restitution that that party may have.[30] Even if the contract is unenforceable, restitution is available in an amount that will often approximate the contract rate.[31] If that is so, the full-performance exception merely avoids any dispute over valuation of the performance rendered.

Brokerage provision

A few courts have held that a brokerage provision of the statute does not prevent enforcement by a broker that has fully performed.[32] It is difficult to reconcile this with the general view that allowing restitution to a broker would circumvent such a provision.[33]

The impact of these limited exceptions can best be judged in connection with the recognition of restitution and reliance as grounds for recovery, matters that are taken up in the sections that follow.

D.　EFFECTS OF FAILURE TO COMPLY

Variations in wording

§6.10.　Effects in General. Statutes of frauds vary in describing the consequences of noncompliance with their provisions. Though the original English Statute and many of its American progeny state that "no action shall be brought whereby to charge" a person as to whom the statute has not been satisfied,[1] statutes sometimes describe noncomplying contracts as "void," "invalid," or "not binding."[2] Courts have not, however, been much influenced by such differences in language, and there is widespread though not complete agreement that, whatever the language of the particular provision, a failure to satisfy the statute as to a party merely precludes enforcement of the agreement against that party.[3]

---

[29] McIntire v. Woodall, 666 A.2d 934 (N.H. 1995) (if agreement is performed by either party within the year, the agreement of the other party is not within the statute though it may be impossible to perform it within the year). Comment *d* to Restatement Second §130 rejects this requirement.

[30] Meyers v. Waverly Fabrics, 479 N.E.2d 236 (N.Y. 1985) ("full performance . . . within a year is insufficient to take the oral contract out of the statute").

[31] See the discussion of the amount of recovery in §6.11 *infra*.

[32] Wyoming Realty Co. v. Cook, 872 P.2d 551 (Wyo. 1994) ("written listing agreement is [not] a prerequisite to recovery of a real estate sales commission, if the contract has been performed by the broker").

[33] See the discussion of restitution contrary to policy in §6.11 *infra*.

§6.10 [1] Stat. 29 Car. 2, c.3, §4. *See* UCC 2-201(1) ("not enforceable by way of action or defense"); N.J. Stat. Ann. §25:1-5 ("no action shall be brought").

[2] *See* Cal. Civ. Code §1624(a) ("invalid"); Ga. Code Ann. §13-5-30 (not "binding"); N.Y. Gen. Oblig. Law §5-701(a) ("void").

[3] Herring v. Volume Merchandise, 106 S.E.2d 197 (N.C. 1958) (*void* "has been regularly interpreted to mean voidable").

As we shall see, the statute does not deprive the agreement of all effect, and it is still appropriate to refer to the agreement as a "contract."[4] Indeed, as we have already seen, a contract that is originally unenforceable because of the statute becomes enforceable if it is later satisfied.[5] And, as already noted, the unenforceable promise of one party is sufficient to bind the other party as long as the statute is satisfied as to that other party.[6]

Not deprived of all effect

What does *unenforceable* mean in this context? If the statute precludes enforcement against a party, the contract cannot be the basis of an action brought against that party. Nor can it be the ground of a claim against that party in an action brought by that party. Nor can it be the basis of a defense to a claim asserted by that party.[7] But if the contract is enforceable by one party and not by the other party and the party that can enforce it seeks to do so, the other party is not precluded from asserting defenses based on the terms of the contract even though that party could not have enforced the contract. Thus if a party that has not signed a memorandum brings an action for breach of contract against a party that has signed, the statute does not preclude the defendant's asserting as a defense the nonoccurrence of a condition of the defendant's duty or a repudiation or other breach by the plaintiff.[8]

Meaning of unenforceable

In addition, procedural rules in most jurisdictions accord some effect to a contract that is unenforceable because of the statute. A court will not raise the statute on its own motion and will enforce the contract unless the party against whom enforcement is sought raises the defense in some proper way.[9] Furthermore, it is generally agreed that the statute cannot be raised for the first time on appeal.[10] In most jurisdictions, the defense of the statute must be specially pleaded and cannot be raised by a general denial.[11] Moreover, courts have traditionally held that, though the plaintiff need not allege facts showing that the statute was satisfied,[12] the complaint is subject to demurrer or motion to dismiss if the complaint shows on its face that the contract is within the statute and that the statute has not been satisfied. Thus the New York Court of

Effects under procedural rules

---

[4] See the discussion of the definition of *contract* in §1.1 *supra. See also* UCC 2-201 cmt. 4 (failure to satisfy section's requirements "merely prevents it from being judicially enforced in favor of a party to the contract.").

[5] See the discussion of the time of the memorandum in §6.7 *supra.*

[6] See the discussion of who must sign in §6.8 *supra.*

[7] *See* Restatement Second §138.

[8] *See* Restatement Second §140.

[9] Forman v. Smith, 135 S.E. 653 (W. Va. 1926) (party "must distinctly call [statute] to the attention of the court . . . or it will be considered waived").

[10] Phillips v. JCM Dev. Corp., 666 P.2d 876 (Utah 1983) ("defense of statute of frauds cannot now be raised [on appeal] to attack the evidence received by the trial court").

[11] Fed. R. Civ. P. 8(c) ("a party shall set forth affirmatively . . . statute of frauds"); Frigon v. Whipple, 360 A.2d 69 (Vt. 1976) (Vermont rules "make the Statute of Frauds an affirmative defense").

[12] Vassault v. Edwards, 43 Cal. 458 (1872) ("averment that the agreement was made is sufficient, without alleging that it was reduced to writing and signed").

Appeals concluded, over a vigorous dissent, that nothing in Code's provision on admissions suggests that a motion to dismiss on grounds of statute "may not be entertained until there has been an opportunity for an admission."[13] A vigorous dissent argued that such a motion amounts to an admission and that denial of the oral agreement "is a *sine qua non*" of reliance on the statute.[14]

Ethical problem   The party relying on the statute as a defense need not deny the making of the alleged contract, and that party has traditionally been allowed to admit the making of the contract for the purpose of argument and yet insist on its unenforceability.[15] A perceptive scholar saw in this an ethical problem in which "the lawyer's conscience may be in conflict . . . with judge-made law, that is all but unanimously adopted, to the effect that the defendant can admit an honest obligation and yet defeat its enforcement by pleading that the agreement was only oral and that there is no written evidence of the obligation as required by the Statute of Frauds."[16] Under a rule like that of UCC 2-201, which makes a contract for the sale of goods enforceable against a party that admits in its pleading, in testimony or otherwise under oath that a contract for sale was made, this ethical problem might be solved by allowing the plaintiff a reasonable opportunity to elicit an admission from the defendant by pretrial discovery procedure or by examination at trial.[17] Since it is generally agreed that an admission before or during trial is effective, even if it is not voluntary,[18] a few courts have abandoned the traditional rule under which the defense of the statute could be raised by demurrer or motion to dismiss and allow the plaintiff such an opportunity.[19]

[13] Boylan v. G.L. Morrow Co., 468 N.E.2d 681, 682 (N.Y. 1984).

[14] 468 N.E.2d at 687.

[15] Durham v. Harbin, 530 So. 2d 208 (Ala. 1988) (apart from Code, Alabama "adheres to the general rule that a defending party may admit in judicial proceedings the substance of a contract and nevertheless assert the Statute").

[16] Stevens, Ethics and the Statute of Frauds, 37 Cornell L.Q. 355 (1952).

[17] Theta Prods. v. Zippo Mfg. Co., 81 F. Supp. 2d 346 (D.R.I. 1999) (because "plaintiff must have an opportunity to obtain an admission," to dismiss complaint "at this juncture would subvert the purpose of the admission exception").

[18] See the discussion of admissions in court proceedings in §6.7 *supra*.

[19] Flight Sys. v. Electronic Data Sys. Corp., 112 F.3d 124 (3d Cir. 1997) (to allow prospective lessee "to dispose of the breach of contract before it has even submitted an answer would enable [it] to use the statute of frauds as a sword, in contravention of the statute's purpose").

There was an impassioned dissenting plea for such a rule in *Boylan*, quoted in part in the discussion of the effects under procedural rules *supra*, arguing that the admission exception "would be meaningless were the defendant permitted by the simple expedient of a motion to dismiss to deprive plaintiff of the opportunity to obtain from defendant either an admission . . . or a sworn denial of the existence of a contract"). 468 N.E.2d at 687.

Even under such a rule, it seems proper to allow the defendant to cut off the plaintiff's opportunity by a sworn denial. DF Activities Corp. v. Brown, 851 F.2d 920 (7th Cir. 1988) (Posner, J.: if "defendant swears in an affidavit that there was no contract, we see no point in keeping the lawsuit alive" for though "defendant *may* blurt out an admission in a deposition, . . . this is hardly likely").

A contract that is unenforceable because of the statute of frauds may have   **Other effects**
other effects than those mentioned. It may be admissible in evidence for any
purpose other than to enforce the contract.[20] It may, if not repudiated, prevent
conduct from being tortious.[21] It may be the basis for an action in tort for misrepresentation.[22] It is effective to bar either party from obtaining restitution[23]
once it has been fully performed on both sides. And it is effective against a third
person who is not a transferee or a successor of a party to it.[24]

The concept of divisibility has had little impact in mitigating the effects of the   **Divisibility**
statute of frauds.[25] In general, if one promise is within the statute, the entire
contract is within the statute, and no part of the contract is enforceable unless
the statute is satisfied. Even if the promises of the parties can be divided into two
exchanges, to one of which the statute does not apply, courts have been reluctant
to employ the concept of divisibility to enforce that part of the exchange, except
where the parties can be said to have made two distinct contracts.[26] According
to the Restatement Second, however, a court may enforce part of a contract
that is not within the statute if performance of the promises that bring the
contract within the statute is exclusively beneficial to one party. By agreeing
to forgo this performance, that party may make the remainder of the contract

[20] *See* Restatement Second §143. In an action seeking restitution, the claimant may use the
unenforceable contract not only to show that the benefit was not conferred officiously but also to
show the amount of the benefit. See the discussion of the amount of recovery in §6.11 *infra*.

[21] For a simple illustration, *see* UCC 2-201 cmt. 4 ("a buyer who takes possession of goods as
provided in an oral contract which the seller has not meanwhile repudiated, is not a trespasser").
See also Restatement Second §142.

[22] Hanson v. American Natl. Bank & Trust Co., 865 S.W.2d 302 (Ky. 1993) ("our statutes do
not abrogate the common law remedy for fraud merely because the fraudulent misrepresentation
is not in writing").

[23] Weld v. Weld, 81 P. 183 (Kan. 1905) (oral contract under which man promised his fiancee
that their marriage would operate as satisfaction of debt she owed him was fully performed when
marriage took place, and statute did not affect discharge of debt). *See* Restatement Second §145.
Contrast the situation of a party that has a right to avoid a contract and get restitution by returning
what has been received, even after the contract has been fully performed on both sides. See the
discussion of remedies on avoidance in §4.15 *supra*.

[24] For a simple illustration, *see* UCC 2-201 cmt. 4 (statute is not "a defense to a third person
who wrongfully induces a party to refuse to perform an oral contract, even though the injured
party cannot maintain an action for damages against the party so refusing to perform").

[25] *See* Hornaday v. Plaza Realty Co., 437 So. 2d 591 (Ala. Civ. App. 1983) ("parts of the contract
are so interwoven that the parties cannot reasonably be considered to have contracted with other
than full performance of the entire agreement in mind").

For an exception under the Uniform Commercial Code, see the discussion of the sale
of goods provision in §6.9 *supra*. Contrast the impact of divisibility, in connection with contracts unenforceable on grounds of public policy (§5.8 *supra*) and with nonperformance (§8.13
infra).

[26] Blanchard v. Calderwood, 260 A.2d 118 (N.H. 1969) (rejecting "argument that the alleged
contract may be considered divisible, and that [land contract provision] should be held not
to bar enforcement of 'that part of the agreement' which relates to the decedent's personal
estate").

enforceable.[27] Thus a party that has made an oral contract for both goods and services can enforce the contract as to the services if the party is willing to give up the right to the goods.[28]

We turn now to the right of a party to restitution of benefits conferred under a contract that the party is precluded from enforcing because of the statute.

Restitution from party in breach

§6.11.   Restitution. Even though the statute of frauds may prevent an injured party from enforcing the contract when the other party unjustifiably refuses to perform, courts generally allow the injured party restitution of any benefit that the injured party has conferred on the other by part performance or otherwise.[1] The injured party's right is similar to that of a party who seeks restitution as a remedy for breach of an enforceable contract, with the difference that here restitution should not be denied on the ground that the injured party has fully performed and all that remains for the party in breach to do is pay money.[2] Though a court will occasionally grant restitution by ordering specific restitution[3] or imposing a constructive trust,[4] the usual relief is a money judgment.

---

[27] Restatement Second §147(1). This explains the cases in which the promise is to render alternative performances, only one of which brings the promise within the statute. Section 147(1) states that "this rule does not apply to a contract to transfer property on the promisor's death." Thus, according to Comment *a*, "the rule is not applied to a promise to make a will covering both real and personal property for a single consideration, even though the entire consideration has been given, presumably because of the policy of the Statute of Wills and because of the availability of the remedy of restitution."

[28] The same section of the Restatement Second also says that if the promises that bring the agreement within the statute have become enforceable or the duty to perform them has been discharged by performance or otherwise, the statute does not then prevent enforcement of the remaining promises. Restatement Second §147(2).

§6.11 [1] Estate of McKellar v. Brown, 404 So. 2d 550 (Miss. 1981) (contract to leave house by will in repayment of loan); Robertus v. Candee, 670 P.2d 540 (Mont. 1983) (contract to lease land to lessees who were to break it and farm it). The contract, though unenforceable, shows that the benefit was not conferred as a gift. Gay v. Mooney, 50 A. 596 (N.J. Sup.), aff'd mem., 52 A. 1131 (N.J. 1901). *See* Restatement Second §375; 2 G. Palmer, Law of Restitution ch. 6 (1978).

If full performance makes the contract enforceable by the injured party, that party will not seek restitution. But if, as is the case under a lifetime provision, full performance does not make the contract enforceable, the injured party should not be denied restitution. *See* Restatement Second §375 cmt. *b*; 2 G. Palmer, Law of Restitution §6.4 (1978).

If the unenforceable contract is one for the benefit of a third person and the promisee has conferred a benefit on the promisor, it is the promisee and not the intended beneficiary who is entitled to restitution. Pickelsimer v. Pickelsimer, 127 S.E.2d 557 (N.C. 1962).

[2] As to the rule denying restitution in that situation under an enforceable contract, see the discussion of the benefit as full performance in §12.20 *infra*.

[3] Dietrich v. Hoefelmeir, 87 N.W. 111 (Mich. 1901) (bailor's action of trover to recover sheep allowed though oral contract of bailment was void under one-year provision).

[4] The classic case is one in which a grantor conveys property to a grantee, who orally promises to hold it in trust for the grantor or for a third person. If the grantee later repudiates the trust, the grantor may seek to subject the property to a constructive trust. Most courts will give such

If the claimant has paid money under an unenforceable contract, recovery **Amount of** is based on the amount paid.[5] If the claimant has rendered services or made **recovery** improvements under an unenforceable contract, recovery is based on the value of the services or improvements to the recipient.[6] To the extent that the injured party has also received a benefit, recovery will be accordingly reduced.[7] In measuring the benefit conferred by the injured party, courts generally allow the more generous measure of recovery based on cost avoided, instead of the less generous measure based on net enrichment.[8] In addition, one who has done something, either by way of performance or pursuant to the other party's request, may recover the reasonable value of what has been done on the ground that it was in the other party's interest, without regard to the extent of the actual benefit.[9] And even though the contract is unenforceable, evidence of its terms is admissible in evidence to show the amount of recovery.[10] There is, however, no recovery for reliance by the injured party that was not bargained for or requested and that has conferred no benefit whatsoever.[11]

In some jurisdictions, courts deny restitution to a claimant if the other party's **Restitution from** failure to perform is justified, either because the performance is not yet due **party not in** under the contract or because the claimant is itself in breach.[12] Of course, in **breach**

---

relief if the grantee used fraud or other improper means to procure the conveyance, if the grantee stands in a fiduciary or other confidential relationship to the grantor, or if the conveyance was for security only. Moses v. Moses, 53 A.2d 805 (N.J. Eq. 1947).

[5] Gilton v. Chapman, 230 S.W.2d 37 (Ark. 1950) (purchaser of land who made part payment entitled to restitution).

[6] Dale v. Fillenworth, 162 N.W.2d 234 (Minn. 1968) (lessee entitled to "reasonable value of the services and materials furnished" in plowing and fertilizing). A party to a land contract may have restitution even though that party's performance is not sufficient under the part performance doctrine to remove the bar of the statute. Wilson v. Le Van, 238 N.E.2d 738 (N.Y. 1968).

[7] Pickelsimer v. Pickelsimer, *supra* note 1 (measure of damages is "reasonable value of the services rendered by the one and accepted by the other, less any benefits received by the one").

[8] Farash v. Sykes Datatronics, 452 N.E.2d 1245 (N.Y. 1983) ("Whether denominated 'acting in reliance' or 'restitution,' . . . a promisee who partially performs . . . at a promisor's request should be allowed to recover the fair and reasonable value of the performance rendered . . . ."). The two measures of benefit are discussed in §2.20 *supra*.

[9] Minsky's Follies v. Sennes, 206 F.2d 1 (5th Cir. 1953) (lessor could recover cost of liquor license, salary of watchman, counsel fees for preparing lease, and similar expenses incurred at request of lessee, though lessee never occupied premises). Such cases are similar to those in which restitution is sought as a remedy for breach of an enforceable contract. See §12.20 *infra*.

[10] Bennett Leasing Co. v. Ellison, 387 P.2d 246 (Utah 1963) (rental fixed in oral agreement to lease car was "at least some evidence of the rental value"). *See* Restatement Second §143 & §130 cmt. *e*.

[11] Bendix v. Ross, 238 N.W. 381 (Wis. 1931) (purchaser of land who made improvement "can recover only to the extent that the building has enriched [vendor], regardless of the cost to the [purchaser] or the reasonable value of the improvement"). Note that what was done in such cases was neither bargained for nor requested by the other party.

[12] Braunger v. Snow, 405 N.W.2d 643 (S.D. 1987) ("nonsigning party to a contract . . . within the statute . . . has [no] right to return of the consideration furnished by him . . . , where the other party . . . stood willing and able to perform").

order to determine whether the other party's failure to perform is justified, the court must receive evidence of the very contract that is unenforceable against that party.[13] However, as explained later in this treatise, an increasing number of jurisdictions allow restitution, subject to some limitations, to a party in breach of an enforceable contract,[14] and in these jurisdictions courts allow restitution, subject to similar limitations, to a party in breach of a contract that is unenforceable because of the statute of frauds.[15] As in the case where the contract is enforceable, recovery is generally determined by the less generous measure, based on net enrichment, rather than the more generous measure, based on cost avoided, and recovery is reduced by any damages for which the claimant is liable because of the breach.[16]

Right to demand memorandum   Suppose that only one party has signed a memorandum. That party may find itself in a predicament if it has begun to perform but has not yet been paid. If it continues to perform, recovery may be limited to restitution as distinguished from the price;[17] if it stops performing, the right to restitution for the benefit already conferred will be reduced by any damages caused by the breach. According to the Restatement Second, a party can extricate itself from this predicament by demanding that the party that can enforce the contract sign a memorandum. If demand is refused, the party making the demand is entitled to suspend performance without being itself in breach and can therefore claim restitution with no deduction for damages caused by the failure to finish performing.[18]

Restitution contrary to policy   Occasionally courts have denied restitution, regardless of which party is in breach, on the ground that to allow it would contravene the policy underlying the applicable provision of the statute. The leading example involves the special provision, enacted by a number of states, that requires a writing for a contract to pay a broker a commission for arranging the sale of real estate or of a business

---

[13]The contract might be enforceable by the other party, however. See the discussion of who must sign in §6.8 *supra*.

[14]See §8.14 *infra*.

[15]Stuesser v. Ebel, 120 N.W.2d 679 (Wis. 1963) (adopting "the more liberal rule" allowing purchaser of land to recover "the down payment in excess of [vendor's] expenses incurred in reliance upon the void contract"), codified in Wis. Stat. §706.04(2). *See* Restatement Second §375.

[16]This assumes that the statute has been satisfied as to the claimant. See the discussion of measurement of recovery in §8.14 *infra*.

[17]This assumes that the party's performance will not remove the bar of the statute. See §6.9 *supra*.

[18]Restatement Second §141. According to Comment *b*, the rule applies "whether or not [the contract] is enforceable against" the claimant. The analogy suggested in Comment *b* to a party's right to demand adequate assurances of performance is imperfect because that right cannot be based on a circumstance (here, that there is no writing to satisfy the statute) that was known to the party when the contract was made. See the discussion of examples of application in §8.23 *infra*. Nevertheless, as the Comment suggests, the other party might give adequate assurance of performance or actually perform instead of signing a memorandum.

opportunity.[19] Were restitution allowed based on the reasonable value of the broker's services, recovery would differ little, if at all, from the amount provided in the unenforceable contract. Courts have therefore denied brokers the right to restitution to prevent the provision from being circumvented.[20]

The following section deals with a less traditional ground for mitigating the effects of the statute of frauds, that of reliance.

§6.12. **Reliance.** Although a party that is precluded from enforcing a contract because of the statute of frauds is generally entitled to restitution, this will often not fully compensate that party for out-of-pocket expenses and other loss sustained in reliance on the contract.[1] To the extent that the reliance has not resulted in a legally recognizable benefit to the other party, restitution will be unavailable.[2] It is hardly surprising, then, that parties who have incurred losses in reliance on contracts unenforceable because of the statute of frauds have often claimed that the other party is "estopped" to assert the statute as a defense. The success of such claims has been responsible for a remarkable erosion of the statute. Although claimants have not hesitated to adorn their prayers for relief with the time-worn exhortation that the statute of frauds should not itself be used as "an instrument of fraud,"[3] their success is better explained as a victory of the fundamental appeal to fairness of recovery based on reliance over the bar of a formality of questionable merit.

Traditionally, a party's reliance estopped the other party from asserting the statute of frauds only if the doctrine of equitable estoppel applied. Since, as we saw earlier, equitable estoppel was based on a misrepresentation,[4] it was available if one party had relied on a misrepresentation by the other that a writing was not necessary, that the other had executed or intended to execute one, or that the other did not intend to rely on the statute.[5] But equitable estoppel was not available if there was no misrepresentation and one party had simply relied on a promise by the other party that came within the statute of

Limits of restitution

Equitable estoppel

---

[19] See the discussion of additional provisions in §6.2 *supra*.

[20] Louisville Trust Co. v. Monsky, 444 S.W.2d 120 (Ky. 1969) (overruling case "which had the effect of nullifying [brokerage provision] of the Statute of Frauds"). *See* Restatement Second §375 (restitution not available if statute's "purpose would be frustrated").

§6.12   [1] As to the extent to which reliance that takes the form of part performance may make the contract enforceable, see §6.9 *supra*.

[2] See the discussion of amount of recovery in §6.11 *supra*.

[3] Loeb v. Gendel, 179 N.E.2d 7 (Ill. 1961) ("courts of equity will not permit the Statute of Frauds . . . to be used where the effect will be to accomplish a fraud").

[4] See the discussion of the derivation of the concept of estoppel in §2.19 *supra*. Despite its name, equitable estoppel is available in actions at law as well as in suits in equity. This is an advantage over the part performance doctrine as applied to reliance under a land contract. See the discussion of the land contract provision in §6.9 *supra*.

[5] Loeb v. Gendel, *supra* note 3 (husband, a lawyer, represented to wife that she did not need . . . independent counsel and that agreement was enforceable, and "promised to confirm the agreement by letter").

frauds. Only promissory estoppel would fit this situation, and courts generally took the view that promissory estoppel was not available where the statute of frauds was raised as a defense.[6]

Reliance under sale of goods provision

A statutory exception to this generalization was made in the case of contracts for specially manufactured goods and is now found in UCC 2-201(3)(a).[7] A contract for goods that "are to be specially manufactured for the buyer and are not suitable for sale to others in the ordinary course of the seller's business" becomes enforceable if the seller makes "either a substantial beginning of their manufacture or commitments for their procurement." Though it is the seller's reliance on the buyer's promise that makes the contract enforceable, this statutory exception has been narrowly construed,[8] and its impact on analogous situations not involving the sale of goods has been negligible. The recognition of reliance has come instead through case law and through the Restatement Second.

Monarco v. Lo Greco

The seminal case is *Monarco v. Lo Greco*, decided by the Supreme Court of California in 1950. When Christie Lo Greco was 18 years old, his mother, Carmela, and his stepfather, Natale, promised him that if he stayed down on the farm and participated in the family venture, they would leave the bulk of their property to him. Christie did as they asked, and the family venture prospered. But when Natale died 20 years later, he left the property to his grandson in breach of his promise to Christie. The Supreme Court of California upheld Christie's claim to the property over the objection that Natale's promise was unenforceable because of the statute of frauds. Roger Traynor rejected the contention that "an estoppel to plead the statute of frauds can only arise when there have been . . . representations going to the requirements of the statute itself," and concluded that an estoppel might also arise when a party relies on "the promise that the contract will be performed . . . when he changes his position."[9] But he carefully circumscribed the court's holding by pointing out that the doctrine of promissory estoppel was appropriate only "where either an unconscionable injury or unjust enrichment would result from refusal to enforce the contract" and by observing that Natale and his devisees "would be

---

[6]McInerney v. Charter Golf, 680 N.E.2d 1347 (Ill. 1997) (equitable estoppel is available only "if one party has relied upon another party's misrepresentation or concealment of a material fact" and "promissory estoppel does not bar the application of the statute of frauds in Illinois").

[7]The antecedent of this provision, in Uniform Sales Act §4, simply made the statute inapplicable to contracts for goods that "are to be manufactured for the buyer and are not suitable for sale to others in the ordinary course of the seller's business." By enlarging the exception to include manufacture by one other than the seller, and by requiring a substantial beginning or a commitment, the drafters of the Code transformed this into an exception based on reliance.

[8]Chambers Steel Engraving Corp. v. Tambrands, Inc., 895 F.2d 858 (1st Cir. 1990) ("designing, developing and manufacturing a prototype did not constitute a substantial beginning to an alleged oral contract to manufacture twenty or thirty embossing machines").

[9]220 P.2d 737, 740, 741 (Cal. 1950). The applicable provision of the statute was California's lifetime provision, cited in the discussion of that topic in §6.4 *supra*.

unjustly enriched if the statute of frauds could be invoked," because the benefit that Christie had conferred on them could not be translated into dollars.[10] As we shall see, Justice Traynor's care in detailing the limits of the holding was to turn *Monarco* from a harbinger of change into a bastion of tradition.

The influence of *Monarco* was soon felt in other cases. It was relied on four years later by the Court of Appeals for the Ninth Circuit in *Alaska Airlines v. Stephenson*. That case upheld, under Alaska law, the claim of an airline pilot against Alaska Airlines for breach of an oral contract under which they promised to give him a two-year written contract as soon as they obtained a certificate to fly between Seattle and Alaska. In reliance on the oral contract, the pilot let his right to return to his previous employer expire. The court quoted Restatement §90 and concluded that the first Restatement evinced "an intention to carry promissory estoppel (or call it what you will) into the statute of frauds if the additional factor of a promise to reduce the contract to writing is present."[11]

Subsequent cases

In response to this line of cases, the Restatement Second added a new section, §139. Its first subsection states:

Restatement Second §139

> A promise which the promisor should reasonably expect to induce action or forbearance on the part of the promisee or a third person and which does induce the action or forbearance is enforceable notwithstanding the Statute of Frauds if injustice can be avoided only by enforcement of the promise. The remedy granted for breach is to be limited as justice requires.

A second subsection lists circumstances that are significant in "determining whether injustice can be avoided only by enforcement of the promise," and one of these is "the availability and adequacy of other remedies, particularly . . . restitution."[12] But neither the section itself nor its commentary carries forward the requirement of *Monarco* that there be some unjust enrichment of the party against whom enforcement is sought for which a money judgment will not make adequate restitution. Nor does either mention the alternative requirement of *Stephenson* that there be a promise to reduce the contract to writing.[13]

---

[10] 220 P.2d at 741, 740. On the difficulty of measuring benefit, see the discussion of the meaning of *measurable* in §2.20 *supra*.

[11] 217 F.2d 295, 298 (9th Cir. 1954). The court cited Comment *f* to the first Restatement §178, which says, analogizing to the case of equitable estoppel, that "a promise to make a memorandum . . . may give rise to an effective promissory estoppel if the Statute would otherwise operate to defraud."

[12] *See* §139 cmt. *c* ("The force of the factors listed varies in different types of cases . . . .").

[13] *Stephenson* is the basis of Illustration 2 to §139, which does recite that the employer promises to give the employee a written contract. Curiously, the Reporter's Note does not cite *Monarco*. That it is misleading to characterize the rule as one of "estoppel," *see* E. Farnsworth, Changing Your Mind ch. 17 (1998).

The grain cases

The impact of §139 was immediate. While that section was still in tentative draft, courts were confronted with a rash of grain cases that grew out of sharp price increases in 1973 and 1974. Farmers who had made oral contracts to sell to grain elevators reneged on their contracts and set up the statute of frauds as a defense. The elevators claimed that they had relied on the farmers' promises by making resale contracts and that the farmers were therefore precluded from setting up the statute of frauds. Some courts rejected the Restatement Second rule and adhered to the traditional position that such reliance did not make the farmers' oral promises enforceable.[14] But others relied on the Restatement Second rule to add a case-law exception. They enforced the farmers' oral promises, even though there was no claim that they had been unjustly enriched and no promise to execute a memorandum.[15] The recognition of reliance as a means of avoiding the defense of the statute of frauds had come a long way since Christie Lo Greco made his claim.

Other cases

Though the grain cases produced much of the discussion of the effect of reliance under the statute of frauds, the division of judicial opinion is reflected in other cases as well. Courts have continued to erode the statute by holding that reliance removes the bar of the statute. Some courts have done this under the sale of goods provision for both contracts[16] and modifications.[17] They have done so in the face of the contention, persuasive for other courts, that the list of exceptions in UCC 2-201(3) is exclusive and an additional judge-made exception is therefore inappropriate.[18] The drafters of revised Article 2 have eliminated the introductory phrase of original UCC 2-201, "Except as otherwise provided in this section," to make clear that the list of esceptions in UCC 2-201(3) is not to be read as excluding the possibility of a further exception for estoppel.[19]

---

[14] Farmland Serv. Coop. v. Klein, 244 N.W.2d 86 (Neb. 1976) (if "mere pleading of reliance on the contract [were] sufficient to permit a party to assert rights and defenses based on a contract barred by the statute of frauds . . . the statute of frauds would be rendered meaningless and nugatory").

[15] Warder & Lee Elevator v. Britten, 274 N.W.2d 339 (Iowa 1979) ("In keeping with the standard in Restatement §[139], we hold that injustice could be avoided only by enforcement of [farmer's] promise.").

[16] Northwest Potato Sales v. Beck, 678 P.2d 1138 (Mont. 1984) (rejecting contention "that estoppel cannot apply to a UCC statute of frauds transaction").

[17] Trad Indus. v. Brogan, 805 P.2d 54 (Mont. 1991) (where seller repeatedly "assured [buyer] that the elk contracted for would be available even if past the cut-off dates" and buyer "justifiably believed it did not need to find replacement elk to fulfill its contracts with third-parties," seller was precluded from asserting statute of frauds as to modification).

[18] C.R. Fedrick, Inc. v. Borg-Warner Corp., 552 F.2d 852 (9th Cir. 1977) (estoppel would "render [UCC 2-201] a nullity"); Lige Dickson Co. v. Union Oil Co., 635 P.2d 103 (Wash. 1981) (joining "other courts which limit the doctrine of promissory estoppel from overcoming a valid defense based on the statute of frauds contained within the Uniform Commercial Code").

[19] *Compare* UCC-R 20201(1) ("A contract . . . is not enforceable . . . ."), *with* UCC-O 2-201(1) ("Except as otherwise provided *in this section*, a contract . . . is not enforceable . . . ." [emphasis added]).

Many courts have held that reliance removes the bar of the statute under other provisions,[20] though there is disagreement as to what amounts to reliance. It is, for example, unclear whether quitting a job to take a different one can count as reliance.[21] Some of the courts that have recognized an exception for reliance have confined the exception by limiting recovery to the reliance interest.[22] And others have confined the exception by adhering to what is now the more traditional view represented by *Monarco*, requiring something in the nature of unjust enrichment.[23] This reasoning has been applied to the situation in which a building contractor whose bid has been accepted seeks to hold a subcontractor furnishing goods to an oral subbid, on the ground that the contractor relied on it in making up the contractor's bid. In spite of the similarity of the situation to that in *Drennan v. Star Paving*,[24] courts that adhere to the reasoning in *Monarco* have distinguished the two situations and held that the contractor's reliance does not preclude the subcontractor from setting up UCC 2-201, because the subcontractor is not unjustly enriched.[25]

Most situations in which reliance has been invoked to avoid the bar of the statute of frauds have involved promises supported by consideration.[26] Some,

Relation to promissory estoppel claims

---

[20]This has been especially true for the much-criticized one-year provision. McIntosh v. Murphy, 469 P.2d 177 (Haw. 1970) (employer was estopped to assert statute where employee had moved from Los Angeles to Hawaii and worked for two and one-half months in reliance on oral agreement). There is, however, contrary authority. Stearns v. Emery-Waterhouse Co., 596 A.2d 72 (Me. 1991) (in employment context it is "too easy for a disgruntled former employee to allege reliance"). See the discussion of the one-year provision in §6.9 *supra*.

Courts have been more reluctant where the suretyship provision has been involved. *Compare* Colonial Ford Truck Sales v. Schneider, 325 S.E.2d 91 (Va. 1985) (recognition of estoppel "would effectually repeal" suretyship provision), *with* Prize Steak Prods. v. Bally's Tom Follery, 717 F.2d 367 (7th Cir. 1983) (in order to avoid taking "most, if not all guarantees outside of the statute of frauds, . . . some additional facts must be clearly proven to create a strong inference of actual reliance"). The same is true of the brokerage provision. *See* Philippe v. Shapell Indus., *supra* note 9 (licensed broker's "reliance on the oral contract was not reasonable in light of the broker's presumed knowledge of the requirements of the statute of frauds").

[21]That it can, *see* Eavenson v. Lewis Means, Inc., 730 P.2d 464 (N.M. 1986) (employee's quitting job could constitute reliance resulting in estoppel). As to the applicability of §90 in such situations, see the discussion of how recovery may be limited in §2.19 *supra*.

[22]Glasscock v. Wilson Constructors, 627 F.2d 1065 (10th Cir. 1980) (employee's damages based on reliance included rights under old employer's profit-sharing plan that he lost in reliance on new employer's oral employment contract).

[23]D & S Coal Co. v. USX Corp., 678 F. Supp. 1318 (E.D. Tenn. 1988) (in Tennessee, "promissory estoppel, if it is to be applied [to statute], must be applied only to avoid the perpetration of a fraud").

[24]Drennan is discussed in §3.25 *supra*.

[25]C.R. Fedrick, Inc. v. Borg-Warner Corp., *supra* note 18 (contractor conceded that supplier of material was not unjustly enriched and court held that there was no unconscionable injury since contractor's only loss was loss of profit).

[26]Humetrix, Inc. v. Gemplus S.C.A., 268 F.3d 910 (9th Cir. 2001) (rejecting argument that damages were limited to amount spent in reliance where equitable estoppel was invoked to bar statute because argument "conflates equitable estoppel with promissory estoppel").

however, have involved promises enforceable because of reliance. In the latter situations, the reliance that makes the promise enforceable may also suffice to remove the bar of the statute, though this will not necessarily be so. Some courts have rejected this possibility entirely and concluded that the statute simply does not apply to claims based on "promissory estoppel."[27]

Reliance on modification agreements

To the extent that an agreement modifying an existing contract is within the statute of frauds,[28] reliance can be expected to have an effect that is similar to that discussed above. Under UCC 2-209, an attempt at modification that does not satisfy the sale of goods provision may nevertheless "operate as a waiver"[29] that can no longer be retracted if "the retraction would be unjust in view of a material change of position in reliance on the waiver."[30] The Restatement Second states a similar rule for contracts in general, under which an oral modification agreement is enforceable if "reinstatement of the original terms would be unjust in view of a material change of position in reliance on the subsequent agreement."[31] The rule also applies if there has been reliance on an oral modification that would otherwise be unenforceable because the parties have erected a kind of private statute of frauds by inserting a no-oral-modification clause in their agreement.[32]

From the enforceability of promises we turn in the three following chapters to the scope and effect of promises.

---

[27] Janke Constr. Co. v. Vulcan Materials Co., 386 F. Supp. 687 (W.D. Wis. 1974) ("Statute of Frauds relates to the enforceability of *contracts*; promissory estoppel relates to *promises* which have no contractual basis"), aff'd, 527 F.2d 772 (7th Cir. 1976).

[28] See the discussion of modification and rescission in §6.2 *supra*.

[29] UCC 2-209(4). That conduct may amount to a waiver, *see* Farmers Elevator Co. v. Anderson, 552 P.2d 63 (Mont. 1976) (by delivering 36 truckloads of wheat, seller "established a course of conduct sufficient to constitute a waiver of his right to assert a defense under the statute").

[30] UCC 2-209(5).

[31] Restatement Second §150.

[32] See the discussion of statutory inroads in §7.6 *infra*.

PART III

Scope and Effect of Promises

Chapter 7

The Law of the Contract:
Interpretation and Omitted Cases

A.   THE LAW OF THE CONTRACT IN GENERAL

§7.1.   Significance of the Law of the Contract Most of what we usually think of as "contract law" consists of a legal framework within which parties may create their own rights and duties by agreement. Up to now our concern has been mainly with this framework and particularly with the enforceability of promises and the mechanics of agreement. Yet many contract disputes relate, not to such matters, but rather to the nature and extent of the rights and duties that the parties themselves have created. These controversies over what is commonly called the "interpretation" or "construction" of the contract can be thought of as disputes over "the law of the contract," as distinguished from disputes over "contract law."

Meaning of law of the contract

413

Practical significance

Disputes over the law of the contract represent a substantial and growing fraction of all contract disputes.[1] Their practical significance stems from the fact that our society confers upon contracting parties wide power to shape their relationships. Although rules of case or statute law may be found to fill the gap in an agreement if the parties are silent on a matter, most of these rules are default rather than mandatory rules and are therefore subject to contrary agreement.[2] In this country more than in most, parties tend to take advantage of their power to define their relationships by written agreements that are detailed and prolix. Those prepared by lawyers often contain what is popularly called "boilerplate," standard clauses lifted from other agreements on file or in form books. Even if a lawyer is not directly involved, the parties may use or incorporate by reference a standard printed form that has been drafted by a lawyer, perhaps for a particular enterprise, perhaps for an association of enterprises, or perhaps for commercial distribution to the general public. This attention to detail is characteristically American and is due to a number of causes, including the standardization of routine transactions, the frequent involvement of lawyers in all stages of exceptional transactions, the inclination to use language tested in previous controversies, and the desire to avoid uncertainty where the law of more than one state may be involved. These factors all contribute to the general disposition of lawyers to provide expressly for the resolution of every dispute that might conceivably arise.[3]

Importance of drafting

It is well to remember that many potential disputes over the law of a contract never arise because the contract is well drafted, and that many actual disputes would not have arisen had the contract been better drafted. Each case involving a dispute over the law of the contract is therefore a lesson for the drafter of other contracts.[4]

Our inquiry into the law of the contract begins with the parol evidence rule, a rule that helps to determine the scope of what is to be interpreted.

B.   DETERMINING THE SUBJECT MATTER TO BE INTERPRETED

Effect of rule

§7.2.   The Rationale of the Parol Evidence Rule. The parties to a contract often reduce to writing part or all of their agreement, following

§7.1   [1] *See* Shepherd, Contracts in a Prosperity Year, 6 Stan. L. Rev. 208, 223, 226 (1954) (classifying a total of 25.8 percent of 500 contracts cases from the National Reporter System in 1951 under either "principles of interpretation and construction" or "parol evidence").

[2] See the discussion of the point that most contract rules are default rules in §1.10 *supra*.

[3] *See* Langbein, Comparative Civil Procedure and the Style of Complex Contracts, 35 Am. J. Comp. L. 381, 384 (1987) (describing as "curious" the American drafter's "propensity for incorporating into a contract numerous well-settled principles of law").

[4] *See* S. Burnham, The Contract Drafting Guidebook (1992); R. Feldman & R. Nimmer, Drafting Effective Contracts (2d ed. looseleaf).

negotiations during which they have given assurances, made promises, and reached understandings. They do this in order to provide trustworthy evidence of the fact and terms of their agreement and to avoid reliance on uncertain memory. However, should litigation ensue, one party may seek to introduce evidence of the earlier negotiations in an effort to show that the terms of the agreement are other than as shown on the face of the writing. The party will be met with a rule known as the "parol evidence rule," which may bar the use of such extrinsic evidence to contradict and perhaps even to supplement the writing.[1]

Gianni v. R. Russel & Co. is a classic example of the rule in operation. Frank Gianni sold tobacco, fruit, candy, and soft drinks in a Pittsburgh office building. When the building was sold, Gianni had discussions with the new owner's rental agent and signed a three-year lease that provided that Gianni could "use the premises only for the sale of fruit, candy [and] soda water" but that he was "not allowed to sell tobacco." Later, when a drugstore leased space in the building and began to sell soft drinks, Gianni sued the owner for breach of an alleged promise that Gianni was to have the exclusive right to sell soft drinks in the building. Gianni sought to show that before he had signed the lease the rental agent had made this promise in return for Gianni's promises not to sell tobacco and to pay an increased rent. This would have, in effect, added a term to the lease. The Supreme Court of Pennsylvania held that it was error to admit testimony to this effect. "As the written lease is the complete contract of the parties and since it embraces the field of the alleged oral contract, evidence of the latter is inadmissible under the parol evidence rule."[2] Even if the agent had in fact made the promise, the rule barred Gianni from using evidence of the negotiations to prove it.

The parol evidence rule is universally recognized and is embodied in the Uniform Commercial Code in a statutory formula applicable to contracts for the sale of goods.[3] If kept within sensible limits, the rule has much to commend it.[4] It has, however, generated its share of criticism,[5] though this criticism often assumes that the purpose of the rule is evidentiary and fails to address the parties' freedom to invoke the rule by a merger clause. The rule has also

Example of Gianni

Rule universally accepted

---

§7.2 [1]The function of the parol evidence rule, which may bar extrinsic evidence if there is a writing, should not be confused with that of the statute of frauds, which may make a contract unenforceable if there is no writing. *See* the discussion of the significance of a writing requirement in §6.1 *supra*.

[2]126 A. 791, 792 (Pa. 1924). As to the effect of the parol evidence rule where the claim is based on promissory estoppel, *see* the discussion of promissory estoppel in §7.3 *infra*.

[3]UCC 2-202.

[4]Olympia Hotels Corp. v. Johnson Wax Dev. Corp., 908 F.2d 1363 (7th Cir. 1990) (Posner, J.: though "rule is maligned in some circles . . . it has stubbornly refused to die" and "serves an important social purpose").

[5]*See* Cobb State Bank v. Nelson, 413 N.W.2d 644 (Wis. 1987) (rule "is an exclusionary rule not favored by the law").

generated its share of confusion. Long ago a scholar, with some hyperbole, wrote that "few things are darker than this or fuller of subtle difficulties."[6] Surely the rule is curiously captioned for, as will be seen, it is not limited to "parol" — in the sense of "oral" — negotiations, nor is it, properly speaking, a rule of "evidence." It may help to avoid confusion if the rule is thought of as applicable to prior negotiations rather than to parol evidence.

Not limited to parol

That the rule is not limited to oral negotiations is clear. A host of cases have applied the so-called parol evidence rule to exclude such writings as letters, telegrams, memoranda, and preliminary drafts exchanged by the parties before execution of a final written agreement.[7]

Not a rule of evidence

That the rule is not one of "evidence" is affirmed by courts and scholars, specialists in the field of evidence, who assure us that the rule is one of "substantive law."[8] Admittedly, the rule is exclusionary, making certain types of evidence inadmissible. But this does not make it a rule of "evidence," for it is not based on the idea that the evidence excluded is "for one or another reason [an] untrustworthy or undesirable means of evidencing some fact to be proved."[9] Rules of evidence, such as the hearsay rule, bar some methods of proof to show a fact but permit that fact to be shown in a different way. In contrast, the parol evidence rule bars a showing of the fact itself — the fact that the terms of the agreement are other than those in the writing.

Contrary view

The view that the rule is evidentiary in purpose once had currency. Several centuries ago, an English judge warned that "it would be inconvenient, that matters in writing made by advice and on consideration, and which finally import the certain truth of the agreement of the parties should be controlled by averment of the parties to be proved by the uncertain testimony of slippery memory."[10] However, since those words were spoken, the law has become more receptive to evidence of oral statements, while the faith in the infallibility of a writing has declined. Now the conceit that the parol evidence rule is rooted in the relative unreliability of testimony based on "slippery memory," in contrast with the "certain truth" afforded by a writing, has fallen from favor. It has not vanished entirely, however, and an authority on evidence has suggested that "usually the one who sets up the spoken against the written word is economically

---

[6]Thayer, The "Parol Evidence" Rule, 6 Harv. L. Rev. 325 (1893), reprinted in J. Thayer, Preliminary Treatise on Evidence at the Common Law 390 (1898).

[7]*See* Hoover Universal v. Brockway Imco, 809 F.2d 1039 (4th Cir. 1987) (representation in seller's handout properly excluded).

[8]First State Bank in Durant v. Honey Creek, 54 P.3d 100 (Okl. 2002) ("parol evidence rule is not a rule of evidence but is instead a rule of substantive law" that fosters "certainty and stability of contracts").

[9]9 J. Wigmore, Evidence §2400 (Chadbourn rev. ed. 1981). Wigmore's treatise devotes some 270 pages to the rule, concluding that "the rule is in no sense a rule of evidence, but a rule of substantive law" (emphasis omitted). *See also* Restatement Second §213 cmt. *a* ("not a rule of evidence but a rule of substantive law").

[10]Countess of Rutland's Case, 77 Eng. Rep. 89, 90 (K.B. 1604).

the underdog," and that jurors would tend to favor the underdog in spite of the unreliability as evidence of spoken words when given months or years later, even by a disinterested witness and particularly by a party itself.[11] Nevertheless, the goal of keeping evidence of the "spoken word" away from the jury is scarcely an adequate justification for a rule that bars evidence of prior negotiations, even if written, while it does not bar evidence of subsequent negotiations, even if oral.[12]

Furthermore, to the extent that courts are required to distinguish between rules that are "evidentiary" and rules that are "substantive," they generally treat the parol evidence rule as "substantive." To take one example, it is usually incumbent on a party in our adversary trial system to make timely objection to the admission of evidence in order to give the trial judge an opportunity to rule on its admissibility. Therefore, under an exclusionary rule of evidence, failure to object at trial ordinarily waives any ground of complaint against admission and the evidence becomes part of the proof in the case. There is, however, sound authority that an objection based on the parol evidence rule is not lost by failure to raise it at trial, so that in this context the parol evidence rule is treated as "substantive" rather than as "evidentiary."[13] To take another example, under the *Erie* doctrine,[14] federal courts sitting in diversity cases are bound to apply state rather than federal law to matters that are "substantive." The cases hold that in such circumstances the court is bound to apply the parol evidence rule of the state in question, thus treating the parol evidence rule as "substantive" rather than as "evidentiary."[15] In sum, the true basis of the parol evidence rule is something other than a desire to keep from the jury an inherently unreliable type of evidence.

Substantive in application

The most satisfactory basis of the rule is that suggested by Corbin:

True basis of rule

> Any contract . . . can be discharged or modified by subsequent agreement of the parties . . . . If the foregoing is true of antecedent contracts that were once

---

[11] McCormick, The Parol Evidence Rule as a Procedural Device for Control of the Jury, 41 Yale L.J. 365, 366 (1932).

[12] *See* Corbin, The Parol Evidence Rule, 53 Yale L.J. 603, 608-09 (1944) (though it "has been very plausibly argued that the 'parol evidence rule' . . . became in time a device for the control of the jury," it should be observed "that parol testimony to prove the variation or contradiction of a written instrument by an oral agreement or understanding made subsequently to the execution of the writing has not been excluded, although the danger of a sympathy-induced verdict may have been equally great.").

[13] In re Estate of Smith, 427 P.2d 443 (Kan. 1967) ("parol evidence rule is one of substantive law and not merely a rule of evidence, and therefore, it must be adhered to, irrespective of whether or not proper objection is interposed at trial").

[14] Erie R.R. v. Tompkins, 304 U.S. 64 (1938).

[15] Betz Laboratories v. Hines, 647 F.2d 402 (3d Cir. 1981) ("parol evidence rule is substantive rather than evidentiary, so we apply state law"). Similarly, the parol evidence rule is not a rule of evidence so as to be determined by the law of the forum under the principles of conflict of laws. *See* Restatement (Second) of Conflict of Laws §140.

legally operative and enforceable, it is equally true of preliminary negotiations that were not themselves mutually agreed upon or enforceable at law. The new agreement is not a discharging contract, since there were no legal relations to be discharged; but the legal relations of the parties are now governed by the terms of the new agreement.[16]

Viewed in this way, the rule simply affirms the primacy of a subsequent agreement over prior negotiations and even over prior agreements.

Utility of rule

In spite of the obloquy that the rule's critics have heaped on it, the rule is amply justified if it is seen as fulfilling this purpose. There are many instances in which the parties, after concluding their negotiations, want to simplify the administration of the resulting contract and to facilitate the resolution of possible disputes by excluding from the scope of their agreement those matters that were raised and dropped or even agreed upon and superseded during the negotiations. It is often useful to be able to replace the negotiations of yesterday with an authoritative agreement of today. It is this purpose that the parol evidence rule ought to serve — giving legal effect to whatever intention the parties may have had to make their writing a complete expression of the agreement that they reached, to the exclusion of all prior negotiations, whether oral or written.[17]

We now turn to the application of the rule.

Integration

§7.3.   The Application of the Parol Evidence Rule. The parol evidence rule is best understood in light of its purpose: to give legal effect to whatever intention the parties may have had to make their writing at least a final and perhaps also a complete expression of their agreement. If the parties had such an intention, the agreement is said to be "integrated,"[1] and the parol evidence rule bars evidence of prior negotiations for at least some purposes. If the parties had no such intention, the agreement is said to be "unintegrated," and the parol evidence rule does not apply.

Degree of integration

If an agreement is integrated, it is considered "partially integrated" or "completely integrated" according to the degree to which the parties intended the writing to express their agreement. If they intended the writing to be a final

---

[16]Corbin, The Parol Evidence Rule, 53 Yale L.J. 603, 607-08 (1944). Restatement Second §213 expresses this thought by stating that the later written agreement "discharges prior agreements."

[17]Patton v. Mid-Continent Sys., 841 F.2d 742 (7th Cir. 1988) (Posner, J.: describing this as a "somewhat more satisfactory explanation of the rule"). Indeed, although it is generally assumed that the integration is written, it is conceivable that an oral agreement might operate as an integration. *See* Restatement Second §209 cmt. *b* ("parties to an oral agreement may choose their words with such explicit precision and completeness that the same legal consequences follow as where there is a completely integrated agreement").

§7.3   [1]Wigmore is credited with the introduction of this term, which he used in his 1899 edition of Greenleaf. *See* 1 S. Greenleaf, Law of Evidence §305b (16th ed. by J. Wigmore 1899) (process of reducing terms to a single memorial may be "termed Integration, i.e. the constitution of the whole in a single document").

expression of the terms it contains, but not a complete expression of all the terms agreed upon — some terms remaining unwritten — the agreement is partially integrated. If the parties intended the writing to be a complete expression of all the terms agreed upon, as well as a final expression of the terms it contains, the agreement is completely integrated.

The legal effect of a determination that the agreement is integrated, according to the Restatement Second, is that "evidence of prior or contemporaneous agreements or negotiations is not admissible to contradict a term of the writing."[2] This preclusion generally does not extend to usage or course of dealing.[3] If the agreement is only partially integrated, however, evidence of prior agreements or negotiations is admissible to supplement the writing though not to contradict it.[4] If the agreement is completely integrated, not even evidence of "a consistent additional term" is admissible to supplement the writing.[5]

Legal effect

In applying the parol evidence rule, therefore, agreements can be classified as unintegrated, partially integrated, or completely integrated. This can be done by asking two questions. First: is the agreement integrated? Second: if it is integrated, is it completely or only partially integrated?

Two questions

Although there is general agreement on this analysis, controversy arises as to its application. "There is scarcely any subject more perplexed," lamented one court, "than in what cases and to what extent parol evidence shall be admitted."[6] Those who favor broad application of the rule have a champion in Williston, and those who favor a narrow application have a champion in Corbin. The trend has favored Corbin's view. The Code reflects this view, and the Restatement Second has been influenced by both Corbin and the Code.

Controversy in application

We turn to the first question: Is the agreement integrated? The answer turns on whether the parties intended the writing as a final expression of the terms it contains, even if the writing was not intended as a complete and exclusive statement of all terms on which agreement was reached.[7] No particular form is

Test of integration

---

[2]Restatement Second §215. The Code language is similar. UCC 2-202 ("may not be contradicted by evidence of any prior agreement").

[3]UCC-R 2-202(1)(a) (agreement may be supplemented by evidence of "course of performance, course of dealing or usage of trade"). The inclusion of course of dealing seems unnecessary since course of dealing is subsequent to the agreement.

[4]Restatement Second §§210(2), 215, 216. *See also* UCC 2-202 cmt. 3 ("consistent additional terms, not reduced to writing, may be proved unless the court finds that the writing was intended by both parties as a complete and exclusive statement of all the terms").

[5]Restatement Second §216(1). The Code language is again similar. UCC-O 2-202 ("explained or supplemented . . . by evidence of conditional additional terms"); UCC-R 2-202 ("supplemented by evidence of . . . consistent additional terms").

[6]Thompson v. M'Clenachan, 17 Serg. & Rawle 110, 113 (Pa. 1827).

[7]Restatement Second §209(1) (a writing "constituting a final expression of one or more terms of an agreement"); UCC 2-202 (a writing or other record "intended by the parties as a final expression of their agreement with respect to such terms as are included therein").

required for an integrated agreement,[8] and the writing need not be signed by either party.[9] Although preliminary written proposals exchanged by the parties are not ordinarily intended as final expressions of the terms they contain, they may later be assented to as such — orally, in writing, or by other conduct.[10] The character of the writing itself is often persuasive as to the intention of the parties. Indeed, it has been held that if a writing appears in view of its thoroughness and specificity to embody a final agreement on the terms that it contains, the agreement is conclusively to be taken as an integrated one with respect to those terms.[11] However, the Restatement Second[12] reflects the prevailing view that other evidence, including evidence of prior negotiations, is still admissible to show that the writing was not intended as a final expression of the terms it contains.[13] Thus the intention of the parties is determined from all the circumstances, including their language and other conduct, just as intention is determined for any other purpose.[14]

Meaning of
consistent

If an agreement is only partially integrated, it must then be determined whether the evidence of prior negotiations sought to be introduced would be "consistent" with the writing and would therefore merely "supplement" it, or whether it would "contradict" a term of the writing.[15] In the former case it is admissible but in the latter it is not.[16] There is no requirement that the writing be ambiguous in order for the evidence to be admitted.[17] As might be

[8]It might even be oral. *See* the discussion of the utility of the rule in §7.2 *supra*.

[9]Tow v. Miners Memorial Hosp. Assn., 305 F.2d 73 (4th Cir. 1962) (party acquiesced in unsigned writing by conduct).

[10]*See* Restatement Second §209 cmt. *b* ("letter, telegram or other informal document written by one party may be orally assented to by the other as a final expression of some or all of the terms of their agreement").

[11]Intershoe v. Bankers Trust Co., 571 N.E.2d 641 (N.Y. 1991) (confirmation slip was partial integration since UCC 2-202 does not require "that there be some express indication in the writing itself or some other evidence that the parties intended it to be the final expression of their agreement").

[12]Restatement Second §209(3) (if "parties reduce an agreement to a writing which in view of its completeness and specificity reasonably appears to be a complete agreement, it is taken to be an integrated agreement unless it is established by other evidence that the writing did not constitute a final expression").

[13]Antonellis v. Northgate Constr. Corp., 291 N.E.2d 626 (Mass. 1973) (whether there was integration was question of intention of "parties on which proof could be received ranging beyond the writing proper.").

[14]Middletown Concrete Prods. v. Black Clawson Co., 802 F. Supp. 1135 (D. Del. 1992) (quoting this section of this treatise). *See* the discussion of the point that a court should look to all circumstances in §7.10 *infra*.

[15]Hatley v. Stafford, 588 P.2d 603 (Or. 1978) (since writing contains nothing on duration of buy out provision. "oral time limitation is 'not inconsistent' with the terms of the writing").

[16]Abercrombie v. Hayden Corp., 883 P.2d 845 (Or. 1994) (quitclaim deeds may not be contradicted "regardless of whether they are partial or complete integrations").

[17]For a case in which there was no ambiguity and no inconsistency, *see* Michael Schiavone & Sons v. Securalloy Co., 312 F. Supp. 801 (D. Conn. 1970) (evidence that parties understood "500

expected, the outcome in borderline cases often depends on whether the court is sympathetic to the parol evidence rule itself.

In *Masterson v. Sine*, a leading California case, a husband and wife conveyed a ranch to his sister and the sister's husband, reserving in the deed an option to repurchase the land. One of the grantors went bankrupt, and his trustee in bankruptcy, together with the other grantor, sought to exercise the option. The grantees sought to show that it had been orally agreed among the grantors and grantees that the option was personal to the grantors, having been designed to keep the property in the family, and could not be exercised by the trustee. The trustee argued that the parol evidence rule precluded such a showing. The Supreme Court of California concluded that the agreement was only partially integrated in the deed. The trustee argued that the evidence was inadmissible nevertheless, because it would contradict a term of the writing that created the option, pointing out that under California law the holder of an option to purchase property has the right to transfer that option unless the option itself restricts transfer. A majority of five judges rejected this argument, however, on the ground that the transferability of the option was read in as a matter of law and not from the language of the option. "The fact that there is a written memorandum . . . does not necessarily preclude parol evidence rebutting a term that the law would otherwise presume."[18] Two judges dissented on the ground that the evidence would "vary or contradict the terms of a written instrument."[19] As is often true in borderline cases, the conflicting views as to the application of the rule reflected conflicting views as to the merits of the rule itself.

We turn now to the second question: Assuming that the agreement is integrated, is it completely, as distinguished from only partially, integrated? The answer depends on whether the parties intended the writing as a complete and exclusive expression of all terms on which agreement was reached, as distinguished from merely a final expression of the terms that it contains.[20] The sharpest disagreement in connection with the parol evidence rule has been over the application of this test. It is one thing to accept that what is written cannot be contradicted. It is quite another to accept that what is written cannot be supplemented even by consistent terms. It is generally agreed that the mere fact that the agreement is integrated does not give rise to a

*Example of
Masterson v. Sine*

**Dispute over
complete
integration**

---

tons" to mean "up to 500 tons" was evidence of a "consistent" additional term under UCC 2-202 because "a term which has a lesser effect is deemed to be a consistent term").

[18] 436 P.2d 561, 565 (Cal. 1968). *See* the discussion of the test in practice *infra*.

[19] 436 P.2d at 571. The dissent also stressed, at 567, that, under the decision, by "the proffered testimony of the bankrupt optionee himself" one of his assets "would be withheld from the trustee in bankruptcy and from the bankrupt's creditors" and kept in the family.

[20] Restatement Second §210(1) ("an integrated agreement adopted by the parties as a complete and exclusive statement of the terms of the agreement"); UCC 2-202 ("intended also as a complete and exclusive statement of all the terms").

presumption that it is completely integrated.[21] The commentary to the Code concurs in rejecting "any assumption that because a writing has been worked out which is final on some matters, it is to be taken as including all the matters agreed upon."[22] The point in dispute is whether the fact that the writing appears on its face to be a complete and exclusive statement of the terms of the agreement establishes conclusively that the agreement is completely integrated.

Williston's view   In Williston's view, it does. "It is generally held that the contract must appear on its face to be incomplete in order to permit parol evidence of additional terms."[23] Many courts, particularly in cases decided in the first half of the twentieth century, agreed that the issue is to be resolved by first inspecting the writing alone. If, on its face, the agreement appears to be completely integrated, the court should simply accept that this is so.[24] Some courts have recognized the futility of trying to tell whether the writing is completely integrated without looking beyond the four corners of the writing and so have softened the test. These courts read the writing in the light of surrounding circumstances — excluding, however, the most vital circumstances of all, the evidence of the prior negotiations themselves.[25]

Corbin's view   The opposing camp, inspired by Corbin, rejects even this exclusion. According to Corbin, account should always be taken of all circumstances, including evidence of prior negotiations, since the completeness and exclusivity of the writing cannot be determined except in the light of those circumstances. "The writing cannot prove its own completeness and accuracy."[26] The trend clearly favors Corbin.[27] The Restatement Second commentary agrees that "a writing

---

[21] For an example of a few loose assertions to the contrary, *see* Lese v. Lamprecht, 89 N.E. 365 (N.Y. 1909) (where subject matter upon which parties contracted "was within the consideration of the parties in making the written contracts . . . it is conclusively presumed that the contracts as written include an accurate and full statement of the intention of the parties").

[22] UCC 2-202 cmt. 1.

[23] 2 S. Williston, Contracts §633 (1st ed. 1920).

[24] J & B Steel Contractors v. C. Iber & Sons, 642 N.E.2d 1215 (Ill. 1994) (adhering to "better view" that writing itself is only criterion of completeness despite "more modern approach"); Gianni v. R. Russel & Co., 126 A. 791 (Pa. 1924) (if writing "appears to be a contract complete within itself, . . . 'it is conclusively presumed'" that the agreement was completely integrated). This view should not be confused with that described in the discussion of the test of integration *supra*, which goes to whether the writing is integrated at all.

[25] Bussard v. College of St. Thomas, 200 N.W.2d 155 (Minn. 1972) ("the writing must be read in light of the situation of the parties, the subject matter and purposes of the transaction, and like attendant circumstances").

[26] Corbin, The Parol Evidence Rule, 53 Yale L.J. 603, 630 (1944). If there seems to be some circularity in examining the very evidence whose admissibility is at stake in order to determine its admissibility, it may help to keep in mind that this examination is made as a matter of law in order to determine whether the evidence shall go to the trier of fact.

[27] Masterson v. Sine, *supra* note 18 ("The requirement that the writing must appear incomplete on its face has been repudiated in many cases [in California].").

cannot of itself prove its own completeness, and wide latitude must be allowed for inquiry into circumstances bearing on the intention of the parties."[28]

Surprisingly little light is shed on the problem by the hundreds of decisions resolving the issue of whether an agreement is completely integrated.[29] Opinions often fail to set out the text of the writing in full, and each case turns on its own peculiar facts. "The focus plainly is on the intention of the parties, not the integration practices of reasonable persons acting reasonably and naturally."[30] The length of the agreement and the detail with which its provisions are set out are, of course, important factors, as is the formality or informality of the setting. Some writings, such as elaborately drafted agreements signed by both parties, suggest complete integration;[31] others, such as informal memoranda, do not.[32] Some writings, such as confirmations sent at the close of a deal, suggest complete integration; others, such as exploratory letters and telegrams, do not.[33] Documents that characteristically embody obligations on only one side, such as deeds and promissory notes, are not usually regarded as complete integrations.[34] But although such a writing alone may not show a completely integrated agreement, it may do so in combination with other writings.[35]

In the face of this uncertainty, the contract drafter is wise to recite that the agreement is completely integrated if it is meant to be so regarded. The drafter can do this by what is commonly known as a "merger clause" (sometimes an "integration" or "entire agreement" clause), which "merges" prior negotiations into the writing. A typical clause includes a recital that the writing "contains the entire agreement of the parties." Because integration depends on the parties' intention, courts have traditionally given effect to such clauses as showing an intention that the agreement be completely integrated,[36] though there has

Test in practice

Merger clauses

---

[28] Restatement Second §210 cmt. *b*. *See* UCC 2-202 cmt. 3 (test is whether "additional terms are such that, if agreed upon, they would certainly have been included in the document").

[29] For an analysis based on the sophistication of the parties, *see* Childres & Spitz, Status in the Law of Contract, 47 N.Y.U. L. Rev. 1 (1972).

[30] Interform Co. v. Mitchell, 575 F.2d 1270, 1277 (9th Cir. 1978).

[31] Gianni v. R. Russel & Co., *supra* note 24 (lessee signed lease after it had been left in his hands and "read over to him by two persons").

[32] Kramer v. Alpine Valley Resort, 321 N.W.2d 293 (Wis. 1982) ("narrowly drawn lease agreement" that "dealt with one minor aspect . . . of a much larger business relationship" was not completely integrated).

[33] Paymaster Oil Mill Co. v. Mitchell, 319 So. 2d 652 (Miss. 1975) (confirmation of sale was not complete integration). In contrast to the questions raised in the discussion of the nature of the problem in §3.8 *supra*, the question here is whether parties that intend to make a contract also intend the preliminary writing to serve as a complete integration of that contract.

[34] Masterson v. Sine, *supra* note 18 ("the difficulty of accommodating the formalized structure of a deed to the insertion of a collateral agreement makes it less likely that all the terms of such an agreement were included").

[35] *See* Restatement Second §209 cmt. *b*.

[36] ADR N. Am. v. Agway, 303 F.3d 653 (6th Cir. 2002) ("integration clause is conclusive evidence that the parties intended the document to be the final and complete expression of their agreement").

been a tendency to deny such clauses conclusive effect.[37] It is difficult to see why their effect should not be conclusive, however, subject to the exceptions discussed here and the grounds that suffice to invalidate any other clause in an agreement.

Collateral agreement rule

The fact that an agreement is completely integrated does not, of course, affect an attempt to show an entirely separate and distinct agreement between the same parties.[38] This truism forms the basis for the "collateral agreement" rule. Under this rule even the finding of a completely integrated agreement does not preclude a showing of a "collateral agreement," as long as it does not contradict the main agreement. Although courts have said that the agreement must be "collateral" in form, they have not insisted that it be supported by consideration distinct from that supporting the main agreement.[39] It is enough if the collateral agreement is one that "in the circumstances might naturally be omitted from the writing."[40]

Example of Mitchill v. Lath

In *Mitchill v. Lath*, the leading collateral agreement case, a purchaser of land under a written contract attempted to show a prior agreement by the vendor to remove an unsightly ice house from a nearby tract. The New York Court of Appeals held that the parol evidence rule precluded such a showing because

> an inspection of this contract shows a full and complete agreement, setting forth in detail the obligations of each party. On reading it, one would conclude that the reciprocal obligations of the parties were fully detailed . . . . Were such an

---

Neither the Vienna Convention nor the UNIDROIT Principles deal with the parol evidence rule as such and the Convention is silent on merger clauses. However, the Principles state without qualification that if there is a merger clause the writing "cannot be contradicted or supplemented by evidence of prior statements or agreements." UNIDROIT Principles 2.17 ("Merger clauses"). In MCC-Marble Ceramic Ctr. v. Ceramica Nuova D'Agostino, 144 F.3d 1384, 1388-90 (11th Cir. 1998), the court noted that the Vienna Convention "contains no express statement on the role of parol evidence" and concluded that reading art. 8(3) as a rejection of the parol evidence rule "is in accordance with the great weight of academic commentary." However, as the court (at 1387) recognized, article 8 deals with interpretation, and the holding may therefore be only that in matters of interpretation that part of the parol evidence rule known as the *plain meaning rule* is rejected. *See* §7.12 *infra*.

[37] Restatement Second §209 cmt. *b*, cautions that "such a declaration may not be conclusive." *See* §216 cmt. *e*. A number of courts have expressed a similar view. Sierra Diesel Injection Serv. v. Burroughs Corp., 874 F.2d 653 (9th Cir. 1989) (merger clause did not "as a matter of law" determine integration when contract was "pre-printed form drawn by a sophisticated seller" and agreement "involved at least four different kinds of writings"). A merger clause may, of course, be held to be unconscionable. Furthermore, even with a merger clause, all of the exceptions to the parol evidence rule apply. See §§7.4, 7.12, 7.13 *infra*.

[38] Belmont Homes v. Law, 841 So. 2d 237 (Ala. 2002) ("merger rule applies only to contracts between the *same* parties").

[39] Aboussie v. Aboussie, 441 F.2d 150 (5th Cir. 1971) ("independent consideration is not necessarily a prerequisite to enforcement of an extrinsic oral agreement").

[40] Restatement Second §216 requires either that there be "separate consideration" or that the term be one that "in the circumstances might naturally be omitted from the writing."

agreement [as to the ice house] made it would seem most natural that the inquirer should find it in the contract.[41]

Other courts, however, have been more flexible in determining whether a term might "naturally" have been omitted from the writing. It has been held, for example, that there was nothing "inherently improbable in the fact that, as a contemporaneous independent contract," the parties to a contract for the conditional sale of automobiles orally agreed that the proceeds of insurance covering missing parts should be paid to the buyer.[42] And it has been held that "it would *not* be expected" that an oral agreement under which a distiller was to give liquor distributors another distributorship would be integrated into the sales contract under which the distiller bought the distributorship.[43] What is in effect decided in such cases, however, is that the agreement is only partially integrated. Analysis in terms of "collateral agreement" obscures the real issue.[44] Only if the writing contained a binding merger clause, precluding argument that the agreement is only partially integrated, would the court have to determine whether there was a true collateral agreement.[45]

Other views

A few courts have avoided the parol evidence rule by holding promises enforceable on grounds of promissory estoppel.[46] If the promise is not fraudulent, it is difficult to justify this result unless the agreement is only partially integrated or the promise is a true collateral agreement.[47]

Promissory estoppel

Who decides whether an agreement is integrated and, if it is, whether it is completely integrated? Since these questions are decided on the basis of what the parties intended, they seem to be questions to be resolved by the trier of fact. However, most courts have favored resolution of these issues by the

Question of fact or law

---

[41] 160 N.E. 646, 647 (N.Y. 1928).

[42] State Fin. Corp. v. Ballestrini, 150 A. 700, 702 (Conn. 1930).

[43] Lee v. Joseph E. Seagram & Sons, 552 F.2d 447, 452 (2d Cir. 1977).

[44] *See* Brown v. Financial Serv. Corp., 489 F.2d 144 (5th Cir. 1974) (considering a cover letter would not violate the parol evidence rule since "the existence of the cover letter and the circumstances surrounding the execution of the stock purchase agreement preclude the conclusion that it was intended by the parties as the final memorial"). Restatement Second §216(2) demonstrates the identity of the two issues by formulating what is in substance the "collateral agreement" rule without using that term, stating merely that, where the rule applies, the "agreement is not completely integrated."

[45] For such a case, *see* Gem Corrugated Box Corp. v. National Kraft Container Corp., 427 F.2d 499 (2d Cir. 1970) (although requirements contract for boxes contained merger clause, evidence as to related stock purchase agreement was not barred because it was a collateral although "vital element of overall transaction").

[46] Ehret Co. v. Eaton, Yale & Towne, 523 F.2d 280 (7th Cir. 1975) (enforcing promise in manufacturer's letter to agent that it would get more on termination than contract provided because unenforceability "would have the fraudulent effect that an estoppel was designed to prevent").

[47] On the possibility of a tort action for fraud, see the discussion of misrepresentation in §7.4 *infra*.

trial judge before the evidence goes to the jury,[48] though some courts have sought the aid of the jury.[49] In this respect at least, the parol evidence rule is still treated as procedural, like exclusionary rules of evidence in general, rather than as substantive.[50]

Limits of rule

In understanding the parol evidence rule, it is as important to know what kinds of evidence it does not exclude as it is to know what kinds it does exclude. First, since it applies only to evidence of prior — and, as is sometimes said, contemporaneous[51] — negotiations, it does not exclude evidence of negotiations that took place after the written agreement was made.[52] Second, since the rule assumes a valid written agreement,[53] it does not exclude evidence to show that there was no agreement or that the agreement was invalid.[54] Third, since the rule excludes evidence only if it contradicts the writing — or, if the integration is complete, only if the evidence contradicts or supplements the writing — the rule does not exclude evidence offered to help interpret the language of the writing.[55] These limitations are dealt with in the following sections.[56]

We turn to the admissibility of evidence to show that there was no valid written agreement.

Must be enforceable agreement

§7.4. Evidence to Show No Valid Written Agreement. If the parol evidence rule rests on the rationale that a later written agreement has supplanted

---

[48] Ozerol v. Howard Univ., 545 A.2d 638 (D.C. 1988) (question is for the trial court to determine as "a question of fact" and finding is to be treated as "presumptively correct" on appeal).

[49] Associated Hardware Supply Co. v. Big Wheel Distrib. Co., 355 F.2d 114 (3d Cir. 1966) ("the intent of the parties that a writing be a final expression of their agreement is normally a question for the jury").

[50] See the discussion of the point that it is not a rule of evidence in §7.2 *supra*.

[51] UCC 2-202 ("may not be contradicted by evidence of any prior agreement or of a contemporaneous oral agreement"); Restatement Second §215 ("evidence of prior or contemporaneous agreements or negotiations is not admissible in evidence to contradict a term of the writing").

[52] Crimson Indus. v. Kirkland, 736 So. 2d 597 (Ala. 1999) (quoting this section of this treatise). See the discussion of oral modifications as valid in §7.6 *infra*.

[53] *But see* Restatement Second §213(3), under which an integrated agreement, even if not binding, may "render inoperative a term which would have been part of the agreement if it had not been integrated." The purport of this is less than clear, but it was evidently designed to support Illustration 6, which speaks of an integrated agreement that is effective to "discharge" an earlier offer.

[54] See §7.4 *infra*.

[55] See §7.12 *infra*. As to course of dealing and usage, *see* §7.13 *infra*.

[56] An additional limitation where reformation is sought is dealt with in the discussion of the parol evidence rule in §7.5 *infra*. It is sometimes suggested that the rule has a further limitation in that it does not apply in favor of or against third parties that are "strangers" to the contract. If the rationale of the rule is that legal effect is to be given to the parties' intention to make their writing a final and complete expression of their agreement, it is difficult to justify such a limitation.

The limitation, however, is supported by statements in many decisions, although they often appear to involve third parties whose rights are simply not determined by the written agreement at all. As to third party beneficiaries, *see* the discussion of the parol evidence rule in §10.3 *infra*.

prior negotiations,[1] it follows that the rule does not come into play until the existence of an enforceable written agreement has been shown.[2] Evidence of the negotiations between the parties should therefore be admissible to show that no agreement was reached or that the agreement reached was invalid. The parol evidence rule does not speak to these questions. Even a merger clause should not preclude such a showing, since the effectiveness of the clause itself depends on its being part of a valid agreement.

Therefore, even though a writing purports to be a complete integration, evidence of negotiations is admissible to show that no enforceable agreement was reached. As Learned Hand reminded, "whatever the formal documentary evidence, the parties to a legal transaction may always show that they understood a purported contract not to bind them."[3] It may still be shown, for example, that the offer was not accepted;[4] that the writing was a forgery, joke, or sham;[5] or that the agreement is unenforceable on grounds of public policy.[6]

Can show no agreement

On similar reasoning, evidence is admissible to show an oral agreement that the written agreement is not to take effect, in the sense that no duty of performance on either side arises, unless a stated condition occurs.[7] In the seminal English case, the buyer of an invention was allowed to show that his written agreement with the inventor was subject to the condition that a named engineer approve of the invention. The court reasoned that, although "evidence to vary the terms of an agreement in writing is not admissible, . . . evidence to shew that there is not an agreement at all is admissible."[8] This qualification

Condition of agreement

§7.4 [1] See the discussion of the true basis of the rule in §7.2 *supra*.

[2] InfoComp, Inc. v. Electra Prods., 109 F.3d 902 (3d Cir. 1997) (merger clause in proposed written agreement that did not become contract was of no effect). *See* the discussion of the limits of the rule in §7.3 *supra*.

[3] In re H. Hicks & Sons, 82 F.2d 277, 279 (2d Cir. 1936) ("it may, for example, be a joke, or a disguise to deceive others").

[4] Sho-Pro of Indiana v. Brown, 585 N.E.2d 1357 (Ind. App. 1992) (parol evidence rule has no application to "whether there was a meeting of the minds"). *See* the discussion of the requirement that the commitment be unconditional in §3.13 *supra*.

[5] Nice Ball Bearing Co. v. Bearing Jobbers, 205 F.2d 841 (7th Cir. 1953) (parties "can show by extrinsic evidence that . . . they did not, at the time of its execution, intend it to be a contract" and that it was a sham to help avoid friction with competitors). For discussion of the effect of an intention not to be bound, see §3.7 *supra*.

[6] Schara v. Thiede, 206 N.W.2d 129 (Wis. 1973) ("parol evidence is admissible to show that a writing valid on its face is a mere cover for an illegal transaction").

[7] Hicks v. Bush, 180 N.E.2d 425 (Kan. 1962) (agreement that contract to merge corporate interests "was not to operate" unless $672,500 in equity expansion funds was first procured). Such cases differ from those in the discussion of the point that one can show no agreement *supra* in that here the existence of a contract is not subject to the volition of the offeree. In cases like *Hicks* it is not correct to say that the agreement does not take effect unless the condition occurs because a party may be liable for a repudiation even before the condition occurs. *See* the discussion of how conditions relate in §8.3 *supra*.

[8] Pym v. Campbell, 119 Eng. Rep. 903, 905 (Q.B. 1856). Restatement Second §217 cmt. *b* says, "If the parties orally agreed that performance of the written agreement was subject to a

of the parol evidence rule has been read into UCC 2-202, even though that section contains no specific language on the point.[9]

Limitations on qualification

There are, however, two limitations on this qualification of the parol evidence rule. The first is that extrinsic evidence is admissible only to show a condition that must occur before any duty of performance arises on either side. Such evidence is not admissible to show that the duty of just one party is conditional, since this would be regarded as an attempt to vary the terms of the writing rather than to show that the written agreement never took effect.[10] This distinction has, however, sometimes been overlooked and the qualification applied where the duty of just one party was conditional,[11] as shown by that party's power to waive the condition.[12] The second limitation is that extrinsic evidence is not admissible even to show a condition to the written agreement taking effect if showing this would contradict a term of the writing.[13] In a sense, of course, every such condition contradicts a seemingly unconditional agreement, but more of a contradiction than this is required if evidence of the condition is to be barred. However, the parol evidence rule has been held to apply, not only where the condition contradicts the language of the writing, but also where it contradicts its implication.[14] It is uncertain whether a court would give effect to

---

condition, either the writing is not an integrated agreement or the agreement is only partially integrated until the condition occurs." This seems an uneasy rationale, however, since — as the following sentence of the Comment admits — even a valid merger clause, which shows complete integration, will not bar extrinsic evidence of the condition. Furthermore, "performance of the written agreement" should be understood as meaning "performance of the written agreement on either side."

[9] Hunt Foods & Indus. v. Doliner, 270 N.Y.S.2d 937 (App. Div. 1966) (agreement that option to buy stock was only to be exercised if stockholder sought other bids; UCC 2-202 assumed to apply to contract to sell stock).

[10] Illustrative is Pitcairn v. Philip Hiss Co., 125 F. 110 (3d Cir. 1903), in which it was held that extrinsic evidence was not admissible to show that a homeowner's duty to pay for decoration was conditional on the satisfaction of his wife. Here the decorator's duty to decorate arose under the written agreement regardless of whether the homeowner's wife was subsequently satisfied with the work. Extrinsic evidence was therefore properly excluded.

[11] For an example, *see* Luther Williams, Jr., Inc. v. Johnson, 229 A.2d 163 (D.C. 1967), in which a homeowner was allowed to show that it was agreed that he would not be bound under a contract for home improvements unless he obtained financing, a condition that he could surely have waived. This may also have been true for Pym v. Campbell, *supra* note 8.

[12] See the discussion of promise as waiver in §8.5 *infra*.

[13] Intercontinental Monetary Corp. v. Performance Guarantees, 705 F. Supp. 144 (S.D.N.Y. 1989) (distinguishing Hicks v. Bush, *supra* note 7, where alleged condition was "inconsistent with the terms of the loan agreement").

[14] Travers-Newton Chautauqua Sys. v. Naab, 196 N.W. 36 (Iowa 1923) (evidence of prior negotiations could not be introduced to show that agreement reading "not valid until signed by 10 or more persons" was not valid until signed by ten or more *financially responsible persons*, including three named ones).

a mere recital that "there are no conditions to the effectiveness of this writing" as part of a boilerplate merger clause.[15]

Just as the parol evidence rule does not exclude evidence showing that no agreement was reached with respect to the writing, the rule does not exclude evidence showing that the agreement is unenforceable for lack of consideration. Even if a completely integrated agreement recites that consideration was given, it may be shown that the recital is untrue.[16] If, however, the consideration is a promise that is expressed as a term of the writing, the parol evidence rule applies to bar evidence offered to contradict or to add to that term.[17]

Lack of consideration

Courts have applied similar reasoning when a party seeks to show that an otherwise effective written agreement is voidable. Thus the parol evidence rule does not exclude evidence to show mistake, misrepresentation, or duress as a ground for avoidance.[18]

Invalidating causes

Of these grounds, misrepresentation has produced the most litigation. It is generally agreed that the parol evidence rule does not bar extrinsic evidence to show fraud as a ground for rescission,[19] a tort action for damages,[20] or reformation.[21] This qualification of the rule has been read into the Code, even though UCC 2-202 contains no specific language on the point.[22] Most courts treat promissory fraud like other types of fraud for this purpose.[23] However, a few courts have held that the parol evidence rule bars extrinsic evidence of promissory fraud, evidently out of fear that to do otherwise would tempt litigants, courts, and juries to transform every broken promise

Misrepresentation

---

[15] See Kryl v. Mechalson, 47 N.W.2d 899 (Wis. 1951) (merger clause did not prevent orchestra leader from showing that "the paper was not to become effective as a contract until the consent of the union . . . had been obtained").

[16] Kay v. Spencer, 213 P. 571 (Wyo. 1923) (recital of "$1.00 in hand paid" for option).

[17] Crooke v. Gilden, 414 S.E.2d 645 (Ga. 1992) ("contract as written contains sufficient . . . consideration"). A false recital will, however, suffice in instances where a recital itself has effect independent of any consideration. See the discussion of option contracts under the Restatement Second in §3.23 supra. As to the impact of the statute of frauds, see the discussion of consideration as an essential term in §6.7 supra.

[18] See Restatement Second §214.

[19] Centronics Fin. Corp. v. El Conquistador Hotel Corp., 573 F.2d 779 (2d Cir. 1978) (rescission of lease of computer equipment).

[20] Curry Motor Co. v. Hasty, 505 So. 2d 347 (Ala. 1987) (tort action against seller of used truck).

[21] See the discussion of the parol evidence rule in §7.5 infra.

[22] City, Dodge v. Gardner, 208 S.E.2d 794 (Ga. 1974) (tort action). UCC 2A-108 cmt. speaks to an instance of misrepresentation that may amount to unconscionability, suggesting that making "a statement to induce the consumer to lease the goods, in the expectation of invoking an integration clause in the lease to exclude the statement's admissibility in a subsequent dispute, may be unconscionable."

[23] Lovejoy Elecs. v. O'Berto, 873 F.2d 1001 (7th Cir. 1989) (Posner, J.: "plenty of cases . . . confirm the unavailability of the parol evidence rule as a defense" to promissory fraud). See the discussion of promissory fraud in §4.14 supra.

into a false promise.[24] Clearly the qualification admitting evidence of fraud does not extend to evidence of express warranty, nor to other nonfraudulent misrepresentations.[25]

Merger clause ineffective

To the extent that evidence of misrepresentation is admissible even if the agreement is completely integrated, it is admissible in the face of the usual merger clause,[26] though, as pointed out elsewhere in this treatise, a few courts have countenanced clauses specifically reciting that there have been no misrepresentations.[27] Indeed, there is very little that the parties can do in their agreement to prevent the use of extrinsic evidence to attack the written agreement on any of the grounds discussed in this section. Such evidence is admissible even if the agreement is completely integrated and the usual merger clause shows no more than that. The only clear exception to this generalization is that extrinsic evidence of a condition to the effectiveness of the written agreement will be barred if the parties have had the foresight to put a sufficiently specific provision in their agreement.[28]

We consider now the impact of the parol evidence rule on the right to reformation.

Reformation for mistake

§7.5. Reformation and the Parol Evidence Rule. Occasionally, an error in reducing negotiations to writing produces a writing that does not accurately express the agreement of the parties. Their erroneous belief that the writing expresses their agreement can be characterized as a mistake as to expression (or a mistake as to integration) — one that goes to the contents or effect of the writing intended to express their agreement.[1] In such a case the court, at the request of a party,[2] may reform the writing to express the agreement

---

[24]*Cf.* Watkins & Son Pet Supplies v. Iams Co., 254 F.3d 607 (6th Cir. 2001) (parol evidence rule applies to promissory fraud unless false promise is independent of or consistent with the writing and bars "promise of future performance that is within the scope of the subject matter of the written contract").

[25]Jordan v. Doonan Truck & Equip., 552 P.2d 881 (Kan. 1976) (though fraud is exception to rule, "trial court erred in admitting the parol evidence of the alleged express warranties").

[26]Smith v. Rosenthal Toyota, 573 A.2d 418 (Md. App. 1990) ("even when there is an integration clause . . . principle of allowing parol evidence . . . is particularly applicable where the written agreement is challenged on grounds of fraud").

[27]See the discussion of the effect of investigation in §4.13 *supra*.

[28]See the discussion of limitations on the qualification *supra*.

§7.5 [1]Such a mistake is a special instance of mutual mistake, a type of mistake that may make the contract voidable if it cannot be corrected by reformation. *See* the discussion of the effect of other relief in §9.3 *infra*. It differs from a misunderstanding that prevents the formation of a contract. *See* the discussion of the actual *Peerless* case §7.9 *infra*.

[2]Reformation may be granted at the request of any party to the contract, including a contract beneficiary or a party's successor in interest. Hunt v. Century Indem. Co., 192 A. 799 (R.I. 1937) (injured contract beneficiary could have automobile liability policy reformed).

actually reached.[3] In contrast to the rules on avoidance for mistake,[4] the party seeking reformation need not show that the mistake resulted in an inequality adversely affecting that party. For example, a party may seek and be granted reformation making its own performance more burdensome because, absent reformation, the agreement would be unenforceable for lack of consideration or would be voidable by the other party.[5] Formerly a suit had to be brought in equity for reformation before an action could be commenced at law to enforce the contract as reformed, but today a party may generally have both reformation and enforcement in the same action.[6]

Bollinger v. Central Pennsylvania Quarry Stripping & Construction Co. shows the role of reformation. The Bollingers signed a written agreement with a construction company working on the Pennsylvania Turnpike that permitted the company to deposit refuse on the Bollingers' property, near their home. The writing failed to state the parties' understanding that the company would first remove the topsoil and then use it to cover the refuse so as to "make a sandwich of its refuse between the bare earth and the topsoil."[7] Both parties mistakenly assumed that the writing contained such a provision, and the Bollingers succeeded in having the writing reformed to include the provision when they discovered later that it had been omitted.

Example of *Bollinger*

The classic case for reformation is a scrivener's or word processor's error. Reformation is available in the case of the omission of a term agreed on,[8] the inclusion of a term not agreed on,[9] or the incorrect reduction of a term to writing.[10] However, reformation is not limited to these situations. If the mistake of the parties relates to the legal effect of the language that they have used, the writing may be reformed so that it will have the intended effect.[11] Reformation

Causes of mistake

---

[3]Wiener v. Eastern Ark. Planting Co., 975 F.2d 1350 (8th Cir. 1992) (remedy was reformation where party contended "that the language actually used in the contract is an inaccurate rendition of what the parties actually meant"). *See* Restatement Second §155.

Reformation is also available to correct writings other than contracts, such as deeds.

[4]See the discussions of material effect in §9.3 *infra* and of the point that the hardship must be unconscionable in §9.4 *infra*.

[5]Perron v. Lebel, 256 A.2d 663 (Me. 1969) (purchaser of land sought reformation to eliminate one lot included by mistake so as to get specific performance). Reformation will not be granted, however, if the effect of the mistake is trivial.

[6]*See* Palmer, Reformation and the Parol Evidence Rule, 65 Mich. L. Rev. 833, 844-48 (1967), reprinted in 3 G. Palmer, Law of Restitution §13.11 (1978).

[7]229 A.2d 741, 742 (Pa. 1967).

[8]Perron v. Lebel, *supra* note 5 (scrivener failed to include provision excluding lot No. 3 from contract to sell "our farm").

[9]Kaiser v. Caroline Life Ins. Co., 65 S.E.2d 865 (S.C. 1951) (insurer failed to delete exception for death by aviation accident from double-indemnity clause).

[10]Board of Trustees v. Insurance Corp. of Ireland, 969 F.2d 329 (7th Cir. 1992) (parties intended "that separate $5,000,000 limits apply to both the stub and one-year periods, and . . . the policy as written does not reflect that intent").

[11]Kelley v. Ward, 60 S.W. 311 (Tex. 1901) (parties misunderstood legal effect of agreement as imposing no personal liability on one of them).

is available even if the effect of the error is to make it appear that the parties never reached an enforceable agreement.[12] [But if there is no mistake as to expression, and the parties have simply made a written agreement that they would not otherwise have made, the court will not reform the writing to reflect the agreement that it thinks they would have made had they not been mistaken] The remedy in that case is avoidance, not reformation.[13]

Must be prior agreement

The function of reformation as a remedy for mistake is limited to making the writing express the agreement that the parties intended to express. Reformation is not appropriate unless the parties reached an agreement and failed to express it correctly in the writing.[14] There must, therefore, have been some agreement prior to the writing.[15] Furthermore, that agreement must be sufficiently definite to enable the court to reform the writing. The agreement need not be complete and certain enough to be a contract, however, and reformation is sometimes granted even if the parties agreed on only part of a prospective agreement yet failed to express that part accurately when they put their agreement in writing.[16]

Reformation for fraud

Reformation is also available when only one party is mistaken as to the contents or effect of a writing if that mistake was induced by the other party's fraudulent misrepresentation.[17] In such a case, reformation is an alternative to the remedy of avoidance based on fraud.[18] Unlike the situation of mutual mistake just discussed, however, here reformation may be granted even though there was no prior agreement.[19] Therefore reformation would have been appropriate in the *Bollinger* case if the construction company had fraudulently misrepresented that the writing contained a provision about the topsoil, even

---

[12] First Am. Title Ins. & Trust Co. v. Cook, 90 Cal. Rptr. 645 (Ct. App. 1970) (promissory note reformed by deleting mistakenly inserted provision that made loan usurious). As to the reverse situation, see the discussion of the point that a party can show no agreement in §7.4 *supra*.

[13] As to the relation between reformation and avoidance for mistake, see the discussion of the effect of other relief in §9.3 *infra*.

[14] Rink v. NPN, 419 N.W.2d 194 (N.D. 1988) (reformation denied where "unilateral mistake . . . arose from [one party's] failure to read the contract").

This is in contrast to situations in which the parties are silent as to a matter and in which the court itself supplies a term. See §7.16 *infra*. Occasionally courts have spoken of granting "reformation" where the parties have simply used language in an unusual way and interpretation would have sufficed.

[15] Hopper Furs v. Emery Air Freight Corp., 749 F.2d 1261 (8th Cir. 1984) (reformation denied where shipper mistakenly entered value of furs in zip code box on air bill).

[16] State ex rel. Palmer v. Unisys Corp., 637 N.W.2d 142 (Iowa 2001) ("written agreement failed to accurately express an actual cost experience capitalization rate intended by the parties").

[17] Webb v. Culver, 509 P.2d 1173 (Or. 1973) (contract to sell land reformed where vendor's construction of fence amounted to fraudulent misrepresentation that fence marked property line). See the discussion of mistake as to a writing in §4.11 *supra*.

[18] See the discussion of other consequences in §4.15 *supra*. However, the fact that one remedy for fraud is available does not mean that the other is. For example, avoidance may be available even though the representation was not sufficiently definite to permit reformation.

[19] Webb v. Culver, *supra* note 17 (no prior agreement mentioned).

if there had not been a prior understanding about topsoil. However, for reformation to be granted, the misrepresentation must be definite enough to guide the court in reforming the writing.

Fraud sometimes takes the form of nondisclosure. If one party is mistaken as to the contents or effect of a writing, and the other is aware of the mistake but does nothing to correct it, the prevailing view is that this nondisclosure amounts to a representation that the writing is as the mistaken party understands it to be. If this view is accepted, the mistaken party is entitled to have the writing reformed to reflect that party's understanding.[20] If the other party is not aware of the mistake, however, there is no fraud and reformation is not available.[21]

Fraud by nondisclosure

When reformation is sought for either mistake or fraud, the party that resists it often argues that the other should be barred from relief for failure to read the writing with sufficient care. Courts have occasionally accepted this argument, at least if nothing has been done to prevent the victim from reading the writing.[22] They have done so more readily if the party resisting reformation is also mistaken than if that party has made a fraudulent misrepresentation.[23] The better view, however, is that a party's mere failure to read the writing does not bar reformation,[24] unless that failure amounts to a failure to act in good faith and in accordance with reasonable standards of fair dealing, and not merely a lack of reasonable care.[25] The Bollingers, for example, were granted relief even

Failure to read writing

---

[20] Belk v. Martin, 39 P.3d 592 (Idaho 2001) (reformation of lease to correct rental provison was proper where lessees had knowledge of lessors' unilateral mistake).

The party seeking reformation can often argue that there was mutual mistake if the other party did not know that the writing did not express their agreement, and that there was fraud if the other party did know.

[21] Miller v. Stanich, 230 N.W. 47 (Wis. 1930) (lessee's lawyer sent alternative sets of leases to lessor's agent, and lessor, unable to read English, inadvertently signed wrong set). Under an objective standard, a party generally takes the risks of such mistakes of expression. See the discussion of the effect of mistake in language in §3.9 *supra*. Reformation has not been allowed for nonfraudulent misrepresentation. *See* Restatement Second §308. On the availability of avoidance for mistake of only one party, see §9.4 *infra*.

[22] Foster v. Gibbons, 33 P.2d 329 (Or. App. 2001) (to bar reformation, conduct "must amount to a degree of inattention that is inexcusable" and vendor's "failure to investigate and resolve any alleged discrepancies in the legal description, and her willingness to proceed with the sale without modifying the legal description, constitutes gross negligence sufficient to bar reformation").

[23] Nevertheless, the rule has also been applied where there is fraud. Knight & Bostwick v. Moore, 234 N.W. 902 (Wis. 1931) (buyer's negligence in failing to read contract precluded his relying on fraud of seller's agent where buyer did not show that "agent committed any act or resorted to any artifice to prevent the [buyer] from reading the contract").

[24] Anderson, Clayton & Co. v. Farmers Natl. Bank, 624 F.2d 105 (10th Cir. 1980) (fraud: "To bar reformation because of negligence would severely limit the application of this remedy."). See the discussion of failure to read a writing in §4.14 *supra*.

[25] Hess v. Ford Motor Co., 41 P.3d 46 (Cal. 2002) ("gross negligence or 'preposterous or irrational' conduct" will preclude reformation). Restatement Second §§157 (mistake) and 172 (fraud) state that fault does not bar a party from reformation unless the fault "amounts to a failure to act in good faith and in accordance with reasonable standards of fair dealing."

though "they had signed the written agreement without reading it because they assumed that the [provision] had been incorporated into the writing."[26]

Significance of writing

Reformation is not an appropriate remedy for either mistake or fraud unless a rule of law makes the writing itself sufficiently significant to justify its reformation. It is appropriate if the writing is an integration under the parol evidence rule or is at least a memorandum that satisfies the statute of frauds. Otherwise the dispute can be resolved under the ordinary contract rules of offer and acceptance, and no special distinction is needed between oral and written parts of the agreement.[27]

Parol evidence rule

The parol evidence rule does not bar evidence of prior negotiations to show either mistake or fraud as a basis for reformation.[28] Such evidence is admissible even though its purpose is to show that the writing does not properly express the agreement that was reached, rather than to show that there is no valid written agreement as a ground for avoidance. But evidence of prior negotiations has been barred when it is sought to show that the parties intentionally omitted a term, though if the evidence does not contradict the writing it can be argued, at least absent a merger clause, that the agreement is only partially integrated so that the parol evidence rule does not bar the evidence.[29] In applying the rule, it is vital to distinguish cases such as *Bollinger*, in which the plaintiff claims that both parties mistakenly believed that the writing contained a term that had been omitted, from cases such as *Gianni*,[30] in which the plaintiff does not claim that either party believed that the writing contained the term in question. In the latter type of case, reformation is not available, and the parol evidence rule applies if the agreement is integrated.

Statute of frauds

Under the modern cases, the fact that the contract is within the statute of frauds does not preclude reformation for either mistake or fraud.[31] The writing may be reformed before it is subjected to the requirements of the statute since

---

[26] 229 A.2d at 742.

[27] For an interesting discussion of the interplay of contract formation and reformation, *see* Palmer, The Effect of Misunderstanding on Contract Formation and Reformation Under the Restatement of Contracts Second, 65 Mich. L. Rev. 33 (1966), reprinted in 3 G. Palmer, Law of Restitution §15.2 (1978).

[28] Patton v. Mid-Continent Sys., 841 F.2d 742 (7th Cir. 1988) (Posner, J.: "parol evidence rule does not prevent the reformation of a contract" if there is "'clear and satisfactory proof' of mutual mistake").

[29] Grombash v. Oerlikon Tool & Arms Corp., 276 F.2d 155 (4th Cir. 1960) (parol evidence rule barred evidence of secret oral agreement that party would not exercise cancellation clause).

[30] See the discussion of the example of *Gianni* in §7.2 *supra*.

[31] World of Sleep v. Seidenfeld, 674 P.2d 1005 (Colo. App. 1983) (if "reformation is sought and is otherwise appropriate, it is not precluded by the fact that the contract is within the statute of frauds" even though reformation "will require proof of the parties' antecedent oral agreement"). Restatement Second §156 "rejects the rule stated in former §509 that reformation of an instrument falling within the Statute of Frauds is not available unless there has been part performance or a written conveyance has been executed." Restatement Second §298, Reporter's Note. See the discussion of an erroneous omission or misstatement in §6.7 *supra*.

careful examination of the evidence is an adequate safeguard against fraud.[32] The court may reform the writing even if the agreement is not integrated.[33] Furthermore, the reformed writing may satisfy the statute even though the error consisted of omitting a material term, rather than stating it incorrectly.[34] However, reformation will not be granted to satisfy the statute of frauds if the parties merely failed, without mutual mistake or fraud, to include a required term in the writing.[35]

Because the origins of the remedy of reformation lie in equity, a court has discretion to withhold reformation, even if it otherwise would be appropriate, on grounds that have traditionally justified courts of equity in withholding relief.[36] The claim of a party to reformation on the ground of either mistake or fraud, therefore, is subject to the rights of good faith purchasers for value and other third parties that have similarly relied on the finality of the agreement.[37]

> Discretionary nature

Experience teaches that mistake and fraud are the exception and not the rule, and courts have been cautious in granting reformation on these grounds. Although each case turns on unique facts and on the credibility of the writing in the light of those facts, courts have often said that the trier of fact must find mistake or fraud by "clear and convincing evidence" before a writing will be reformed.[38]

> Clear and convincing evidence

We now turn to the admissibility of evidence of subsequent, as distinguished from prior, negotiations.

§7.6. Oral Modifications and No-Oral-Modification Clauses.

Because the parol evidence rule applies only to precontractual negotiations,

> Oral modifications valid

---

[32] *See* Palmer, Reformation and the Statute of Frauds, 65 Mich. L. Rev. 421 (1967), reprinted in 3 G. Palmer, Law of Restitution §§13.13-13.15 (1978).

[33] Grappo v. Mauch, 887 P.2d 740 (Nev. 1994) ("statute of frauds does not apply to reformation of a written instrument such as a deed of trust"); Hughes v. Payne [I], 117 N.W. 363 (S.D. 1908) (receipt for payment on contract for sale of land can be reformed).

[34] Brandwein v. Provident Mut. Life Ins. Co., 146 N.E.2d 693 (N.Y. 1957) (statute of frauds does not forbid "reformation of a written contract to include material orally agreed upon but, because of mutual mistake or unilateral mistake plus fraud, not inserted in writing").

[35] Hughes v. Payne [II], 130 N.W. 81 (S.D. 1911) ("Where an instrument is executed according to the intention and understanding of the parties . . . and with full knowledge of the facts, such knowledge and execution will operate to defeat an action to reform, in that it negatives mutual mistake."). The fact that an agreement is not integrated, so that extrinsic evidence is not barred by the parol evidence rule, will not help the party seeking to enforce the agreement to satisfy the statute of frauds. *See* the discussion of an erroneous omission or misstatement in §6.7 *supra*.

[36] See §12.7 *infra*. Thus reformation may be barred by laches. Aken v. Bullard, 68 S.E. 482 (Ga. 1910) ("deed asked to be reformed was executed twenty-three years before the institution of the suit"). As to mistake of the donor, *see supra* note 3.

[37] Mutual Life Ins. Co. v. Metzger, 172 A. 610 (Md. 1934) (reformation granted on condition that contract beneficiary who had relied to extent of $200 be paid that sum).

[38] Patton v. Mid-Continent Sys., *supra* note 28 (Posner, J.: "danger of facile invocations of mutual mistake to get around the parol evidence rule is limited" because "party alleging mutual mistake must convince the judge . . . clearly").

it does not bar evidence of subsequent negotiations to show modification of the contract. Even a completely integrated agreement can therefore be modified or rescinded orally,[1] subject, of course, to the doctrine of consideration[2] and the statute of frauds.[3] In a few states, legislation requires a writing for the modification or rescission of a written agreement.[4]

No-oral-modification clauses

Parties to a written agreement sometimes insert a specific provision precluding modification in an attempt to make their contract immune to oral modification. Such no-oral-modification clauses are particularly common in commercial construction contracts, where they are inserted to protect the owner from claims that the owner's project superintendent orally modified the contract so as to have the builder do extra work.[5] A clause might read: "This contract may be modified or rescinded only by a writing signed by the parties." A party may also attempt to achieve this kind of protection by a clause limiting the authority of representatives to contract on that party's behalf, but the effectiveness of such clauses turns on the law of agency and will not be dealt with here.[6]

Ineffective at common law

Can the parties, by inserting a no-oral-modification clause, effectively permit only written modifications? The traditional common law answer was that they could not.[7] Courts reasoned that any prior agreement, including the no-oral-modification clause itself, can be modified by a later agreement. In the colorful words of one judge: "The most ironclad written contract can always be cut into by the acetylene torch of parol modification supported by adequate proof . . . .

---

§7.6 [1]Hofelt v. Mehling, 658 N.W.2d 783 (S.D. 2003) ("rule does not apply to conduct and statements taking place *after* a contract has been executed," citing this section of this treatise).

[2]Connell v. Diamond T. Truck Co., 188 A. 463 (N.H. 1936) (though parol evidence rule would not apply if alleged oral agreement was made after written contract, it does not follow that alleged agreement was enforceable since "plaintiff gave or promised no valid consideration for the alleged promise of the defendant to rescind"). As to modification, *see* the discussion of the illustration of the rule at §4.21 *supra*. As to rescission, *see* the discussion of an agreement of rescission in §4.24 *supra*.

[3]See the discussion of modification and rescission in §6.2 *supra*.

[4]*See* Mont. Code Ann. §28-2-1602 ("contract in writing may be altered by a contract in writing or by an executed oral agreement, and not otherwise"). This provision is taken from the Field Code. See the discussion of contract law as seen as essentially case law in §1.8 *supra*.

[5]When combined with a merger clause, the result is known as a "zipper clause." *See* Pace v. Honolulu Disposal Serv., 227 F.3d 1150 (9th Cir. 2000) ("so called because the combination of the integration and no-oral-modification clauses is intended to foreclose claims of any representations outside the written contract"). Extra work, agreed on after the contract has been concluded, is often especially profitable. When a contract is awarded by competitive bidding, the contractor may sometimes bid low to obtain the contract, with the hope that later changes will provide for extra work.

[6]*See* Restatement Second of Agency §167.

[7]Autotrol Corp. v. Continental Water Sys. Corp., 918 F.2d 689 (7th Cir. 1990) ("oral modification is enforceable under Texas law even if the contract forbids oral modifications"). The rule is reflected in Restatement Second §283 cmt. *b*.

The hand that pens a writing may not gag the mouths of the assenting parties."[8] In most cases holding such clauses ineffective, however, the party that seeks to escape the effect of the no-oral-modification clause has relied on the oral modification.[9] As the Supreme Court of Pennsylvania concluded in one such case, "when an owner requests a builder to do extra work, promises to pay for it and watches it performed knowing that it is not authorized in writing, he cannot refuse to pay on the ground that there was no written change order."[10] The cases that have proclaimed the ineffectiveness of no-oral-modification clauses more broadly than this, without regard to reliance, fall short of holding that absent reliance an oral modification is enforceable in the face of such a clause, and are contradicted by sound authority.[11]

Furthermore, the common law rule has been subjected to important statu-   **Statutory inroads**
tory inroads. A New York statute gives effect to provisions in written agreements that prohibit oral modification or termination,[12] and the Uniform Commercial Code follows New York in this respect. Under the Code, a signed agreement "which excludes modification or rescission" except by a signed writing or other record "cannot be otherwise modified or rescinded."[13] This provision enables the parties to require a writing even when the statute of frauds (UCC 2-201) does not apply to the modification.[14] While it is sometimes said that such a requirement amounts to a "private statute of frauds," the writing requirement imposed is more exacting than that of the statute of frauds for, as the District

---

[8]Wagner v. Graziano, 136 A.2d 82, 83-84 (Pa. 1957 (Musmanno, J.). For a less florid statement, *see* Beatty v. Guggenheim Exploration Co., 122 N.E. 378 (N.Y. 1919) (Cardozo, J.: "The clause which forbids a change, may be changed like any other.").

[9]Humiston Grain Co. v. Rowley Interstate Transp. Co., 483 N.W.2d 832 (Iowa 1992) ("in certain cases, such as may exist in claims of estoppel, contractual provisions prohibiting oral modification may be invalidated by the courts"). Reliance is often easier to show after modification than after rescission, since modification is ordinarily followed by performance.

[10]Universal Builders v. Moon Motor Lodge, 244 A.2d 10, 16 (Pa. 1968). This case rejected the requirement (suggested in Wagner v. Graziano, *supra* note 8) that there be a separate waiver of the no-oral-modification clause prior to the oral modification itself.

[11]Foster Wheeler Enviresponse v. Franklin County Convention Facilities Auth., 678 N.E.2d 519 (Ohio 1997) (validity of clause in construction contract is "universally recognized").

[12]N.Y. Gen. Oblig. L. §15-301(1) ("written agreement . . . which contains a provision to the effect that it cannot be changed orally, cannot be changed by an executory agreement unless such executory agreement is in writing and signed").

[13]UCC 2-209(2). UCC 2-209(2) takes on special importance in view of the fact that UCC 2-209(1) removes the requirement of consideration for a modification. *See* the discussion of legislative reform in §4.22 *supra*. UCC 2-209(2) goes on to say that, "except as between merchants," if the requirement is on a form supplied by a merchant, it "must be separately signed by the other party."

Both the Vienna Convention and the UNIDROIT Principles provide for the enforceability of no-oral-modification clauses (though neither refers to a *signed* writing). CISG 29(2), UNIDROIT Principles 2.18. Whether the Principles can override a mandatory rule in a jurisdiction where such clauses are not enforceable is open to question.

[14]See the discussion of how the Code relaxes the requirement in §6.7 *supra*.

of Columbia Circuit observed, the Code speaks of a modification "to be made '*by* an instrument in writing,' . . . and not merely memorialized by such a writing."[15] Such a complete reversal of the common law rule would be severely tested in a case in which one party had relied on the oral modification.[16] The drafters therefore softened the reversal by adding in (4) that "an attempt at modification or rescission . . . can operate as a waiver" even though it is not in writing as required by the clause, but providing in (5) that "a waiver affecting an executory portion of the contract" may be retracted "unless the retraction would be unjust in view of a material change of position in reliance on the waiver."[17]

Example of
Wisconsin Knife

The Seventh Circuit interpreted this language in *Wisconsin Knife Works v. National Metal Crafters*, in which a buyer had terminated a contract for 281,000 spade bit blanks after late delivery of the first 144,000. When the seller contended that the contract had been modified after the late deliveries so that they were acceptable, the buyer protested that, because there was no writing as required by the contract, the modification was not binding absent a showing of reliance by the seller. The court, speaking through Richard Posner and over a vigorous dissent by Frank Easterbrook, held for the buyer. It reasoned that subsection (5) did not apply because, the deliveries having been made, the claimed modification was not one "affecting an executory portion of the contract." The question then became whether a reliance requirement would be read into subsection (4). Noting that the language of that subsection says only that an attempted modification "can" operate as a waiver, the court added the substantial gloss that such a modification "is effective as a waiver only if there is reliance."[18] This reasoning overlooks the possibility that the word *waiver* was used, as it is often in contract law, to refer only to the excuse of conditions

---

[15] *See* Marlowe v. Argentine Naval Commn., 808 F.2d 120, 123 (D.C. Cir. 1986). Furthermore, the statute of frauds may be satisfied without a writing. *See* the discussion of satisfaction by part performance as exceptional in §6.9 *supra*.

[16] In applying such statutory provisions, courts have been generous in finding that the requirement of a writing has been satisfied. Monroe v. Jack B. Parson Constr. Co., 604 P.2d 901 (Utah 1979) (alternative holding: buyer's letter was sufficient under Code even though it was written to state engineer rather than to seller). That courts show a similar attitude toward the requirement of a writing under the statute of frauds, *see* the discussion of the form of the memorandum in §6.7 *supra*.

[17] *See* Securities Indus. Automation Corp. v. United Computer Capital Corp., 723 N.Y.S.2d 668 (App. Div. 2001) (lessor's failure for 8 years to enforce notice provision amounted to waiver, and lessor "was obligated to notify [lessee] if it intended to begin enforcing the notice provision").

[18] 781 F.2d 1280, 1287 (7th Cir. 1986) (remanding for a finding as to reliance). For a later variant, *see* Cloud Corp. v. Hasbro, Inc., 314 F.3d 289 (7th Cir. 2002) (Posner, J.: courts require party asserting modification to "show either that it relied on the other party's having waived the requirement of a writing . . . or that the waiver was clear and unequivocal"). The dissent in *Wisconsin Knife* argued that while under subsection (4) "a waiver may be effective," under subsection (5) "a waiver may be effective *prospectively* only if there was also detrimental reliance," while under the majority's reading "there is no difference." *Id.* at 1291.

as distinguished from the discharge of duties.[19] It would have been perfectly consistent with recognized principles of contract law to have applied subsection (4) as written, without the court's gloss, requiring no reliance for a waiver of the condition of the buyer's duty that the seller deliver on the specified dates.[20] This would not have affected the seller's duty to deliver on those dates and would have left the seller liable in damages for its failure to do so.[21]

This concludes our inquiry into the scope of the agreement, and we turn to its interpretation.

C.   INTERPRETATION

§7.7.   The Process of Interpretation. Interpretation is the process by which a court ascertains the meaning that it will give to the language used by the parties in determining the legal effect of the contract.[1] It is not the only technique used by a court to determine the legal effect of a contract, for even in the absence of relevant contract language a court may, by the process of implication, supply a term to govern an omitted case.[2] Furthermore, the interpretation may not even be decisive as to the legal effect of the contract language itself, for a court may refuse to enforce part or all of the contract because of some overriding legal rule.[3]

The word *interpretation* is sometimes used more narrowly to refer to the process by which a court determines the meaning that the parties themselves attached to their language. This enables the court to determine what the Uniform Commercial Code calls the *agreement*, meaning "the bargain of the parties in fact, as found in their language or inferred from other circumstances."[4] The meaning attached by the parties is not necessarily controlling, however, because a court may take account of factors that are unrelated to the parties' intentions. The word *construction* is then used to refer to the process by which a court

Interpretation as a process

Interpretation **and** *construction*

---

[19] See the discussion of the meaning of *waiver* in §8.5 *infra*. *See also* the discussion of reliance on modification agreements in §6.12 *supra*. The otherwise well-reasoned dissent misses this point.

[20] *See* Restatement Second §84, which makes a waiver of a condition binding regardless of reliance unless the waiver comes while there is still time for the promisee to ensure that the condition occurs. (In *Wisconsin Knife* it was too late for the seller to deliver by the specified dates.)

[21] Since any waiver by the buyer as to undelivered goods would presumably be impliedly subject to a requirement that the goods be delivered by a reasonable time, the buyer could still terminate the contract and sue for total breach if the goods were not delivered within that time.

§7.7 [1] *See generally* Farnsworth, "Meaning" in the Law of Contracts, 76 Yale L.J. 939 (1967) (from which this and the next three sections of this treatise are adapted).

[2] See §7.16 *infra*.

[3] A court might do this on grounds of unconscionability (*see* §4.28 *supra*) or public policy (*see* §5.1 *supra*).

[4] UCC 1-201(3).

determines the meaning that will be given to the language of the contract in giving it legal effect. This enables the court to determine what the Code calls the *contract*, meaning "the total legal obligation that results from the parties' agreement as affected by [the Uniform Commercial Code] as supplemented by any other applicable laws."[6] Under this terminology, while the process of interpretation might lead to one meaning (the one that the parties themselves attached to their language), the process of construction might lead to a different one (the one that would be decisive in determining the legal effect of the contract). Although courts have sometimes endorsed this distinction,[7] they have often ignored it by characterizing the process of construction as that of "interpretation" in order to obscure the extent of their control over private agreement. This distinction between interpretation and construction is a difficult one to maintain in practice and will not be stressed here.[8]

Meaning in semantics

The word *meaning* has also been the subject of controversy. Philosophers and semanticists have debated at length its proper use, if any. It is tempting to look to these discussions for help in dealing with contract language. Most of them, however, are wide of the mark because they concentrate on language as it is used in science to describe experience. The concern of the philosopher or semanticist is with the truth of such language. The terms of a contract ("Seller will deliver goods to Buyer at Seller's warehouse") may be similar in form to the laws of science ("Ice will melt at 0 degrees Celsius"), but they are fundamentally different in significance. The language of a contract is directed not at describing experience but at controlling human behavior, ordinarily the behavior of the contracting parties. The concern of a court is not with the truth of this language but with the expectations that it aroused in the parties.[9] It is therefore to these expectations, rather than to the concern of the philosopher or semanticist, that we must turn in the search for the meaning of contract language.

Faith in language

Judges are not of a single mind in approaching this task of determining the expectations of the parties. They differ in their faith in the reliability of language and in the inherent meaning of words.[10] Judges also differ in their

---

[5]Corbin favored this distinction. 3 A. Corbin, Contracts §534 (1960); Corbin, Conditions in the Law of Contract, 28 Yale L.J. 739, 740-41 (1919). Williston similarly defined *construction* as the determination of the legal meaning of the entire contract. 2 S. Williston, Contracts §602 (1st ed. 1920).

[6]UCC 1-201(12).

[7]Berg v. Hudesman, 801 P.2d 222 (Wash. 1990) ("We use the word 'interpretation' in the sense described by Corbin and the Restatement and distinguish it from 'construction.'").

[8]See, however, the discussion of constructive conditions in §8.9 *infra*.

[9]This is not to say that contract law has no concern for truth. If the seller sells wood as "braziletto," a court may be called upon to decide whether it is in fact braziletto or peachum. *See* Seixas v. Woods, 2 Caines 48 (N.Y. 1804). But such questions of fact, which concern truth, arise only after questions of interpretation, which go in part to the expectations of the parties, have been answered: Was the seller bound to deliver braziletto rather than peachum?

[10]See the discussions of the example of *Pacific Gas & Electric* and of criticism in *Trident* in §7.12 *infra*.

tolerance of the inevitable protraction of the judicial process that results from an abandonment of this faith. These differences can be felt in the debate between the objectivists and subjectivists,[11] in the determination of how far language can be stretched,[12] in the controversy over the effect of the parol evidence rule,[13] and in the characterization of interpretation as "law" or "fact."[14]

We look first at those defects in contract language that give rise to disputes over its meaning, and here the work of philosophers and semanticists is helpful.

§7.8.   Vagueness and Ambiguity.   It is a rare contract that needs no interpretation. It has been wisely observed that there is no "lawyer's Paradise [where] all words have a fixed, precisely ascertained meaning, . . . and where, if the writer has been careful, a lawyer, having a document referred to him may sit in his chair, inspect the text, and answer all questions without raising his eyes."[1] As Holmes cautioned, "A word is not a crystal, transparent and unchanged, it is the skin of a living thought and may vary greatly in color and content according to the circumstances and the time in which it is used."[2]   **Imprecision of language**

A particularly perceptive student of language has emphasized a distinction between *vagueness* and *ambiguity* that is also useful in contract interpretation. According to this distinction, a word is vague to the extent that it defines "not a neatly bounded class but a distribution about a central norm." Thus the word *green* is vague as it shades into yellow at the one extreme and into blue at the other, so that its applicability in marginal situations is uncertain. Ambiguity is an entirely distinct concept. A word may have two entirely different connotations, so that it may be at the same time both appropriate and inappropriate. Thus the word *light* is ambiguous when considered in the context of dark feathers.[3]   **Vagueness and ambiguity**

Contract language abounds in examples of vagueness. Parties contract for the removal of "all the dirt" on a tract: may sand from a stratum of subsoil be taken?[4] An American seller and a Swiss buyer agree upon the sale of "chicken": does stewing chicken conform?[5] A contract for the sale of a photography studio provides that the seller will not compete with the buyer for school photography work in any "school" in the county: is such work in a college included?[6]   **Vagueness in contracts**

---

[11] See the discussion of the objectivist solution in §7.9 *infra*.

[12] See the discussion of purpose interpretation in §7.10 *infra*.

[13] See the discussions of the restrictive view and of the liberal view in §7.12 *infra*.

[14] See the discussion of law or fact in §7.14 *infra*.

§7.8   [1] J. Thayer, A Preliminary Treatise on the Law of Evidence 428-29 (1898).

[2] Towne v. Eisner, 245 U.S. 418, 425 (1918). For an indication that Holmes's flexibility as to the meaning of words was not unlimited, however, *see* the discussion of the restrictive view in §7.12 *infra*.

[3] W. Quine, Word and Object 85, 129 (1960).

[4] Highley v. Phillips, 5 A.2d 824 (Md. 1939) (yes).

[5] Frigaliment Importing Co. v. B.N.S. Intl. Sales Corp., 190 F. Supp. 116 (S.D.N.Y. 1960) (yes).

[6] Lawrence v. Cain, 245 N.E.2d 663 (Ind. App. 1969) (no).

Ambiguity in contracts

Contract language also offers examples of ambiguity. A contract states the quantity in "tons": are they to be long or short tons?[7] An insurance policy issued by a Canadian insurer to an American snowmobile manufacturer provides for payment in "dollars": are they to be American or Canadian dollars?[8] A contract for the sale of Surat cotton provides for delivery on board the ship *Peerless*: does this mean the ship *Peerless* that sails in October or the ship of the same name that sails in December?[9] The three examples given all involve ambiguity of term — *ton, dollar,* and *Peerless*. The last of the three — *Peerless* — involves proper-name ambiguity, a special kind of ambiguity of term.[10] Ambiguity of term is relatively rare in contract cases.

Ambiguity of syntax

A far more common cause of contract disputes is ambiguity of syntax.[11] An insurance policy excludes any "disease of organs of the body not common to both sexes"; does it exclude a fibroid tumor (which can occur on any organ) of the uterus?[12] A construction contract provides that "All domestic water piping and rain water piping installed above finished ceilings . . . shall be insulated"; must the contractor insulate domestic water piping installed below finished ceilings?[13] Syntactical ambiguity is often the result of inadequate punctuation or of the dropping of words to make shorthand expressions.[14] A contract for the sale of "approx. 10,000 heaters" adds "all in perfect condition"; is this, as buyer contends, an express warranty ("all *to be* in perfect condition") or, as seller contends, a limitation on the quantity ("all *that are* in perfect condition")?[15]

---

[7] *See* Chemung Iron & Steel Co. v. Mersereau Metal Bed Co., 179 N.Y.S. 577 (Sup. Ct. 1920) ("tons" means short tons). *But see* Higgins v. California Petroleum & Asphalt Co., 52 P. 1080 (Cal. 1898) ("gross ton" means long ton). For an amusing example of ambiguity, *see* Grove v. Charbonneau Buick-Pontiac, 240 N.W.2d 853 (N.D. 1976) (could prize offered to "first entry who shoots a hole-in-one on Hole No. 8" in 18-hole tournament played twice around a nine-hole course be claimed by player who got hole-in-one into cup with flag marked "8" from tee marked "17"?).

[8] Davis v. Outboard Marine Corp., 415 N.W.2d 719 (Minn. App. 1987) (Canadian dollars).

[9] Raffles v. Wichelhaus, 159 Eng. Rep. 375 (Ex. 1864) (neither party bound to other's meaning). *See* the discussion of the example of the *Peerless* in §7.9 *infra*.

[10] *See* Shakespeare's Julius Caesar act 3 scene 3:

> *Cinna:* I am Cinna the poet . . . . I am not Cinna the conspirator.
> *Second Plebeian:* It is no matter, his name's Cinna. Pluck but his name out of his heart, and turn him going.

[11] A classic example is: "And Satan trembles when he sees/The weakest saint upon his knees." The ambiguity is one of pronominal reference and disappears if it is assumed that the saint is female.

[12] Business Men's Assur. Assn. v. Read, 48 S.W.2d 678 (Tex. Civ. App. 1932) (no).

[13] Paul W. Abbott v. Axel Newman Heating & Plumbing Co., 166 N.W.2d 323 (Minn. 1969) (yes).

[14] A classic example is: "Woman, without her man would be a savage." Should the second comma come after *her* or after *man*?

[15] Udell v. Cohen, 122 N.Y.S.2d 552 (App. Div. 1953) (per curiam) (parol evidence admissible to resolve ambiguity).

Particularly hazardous sources of ambiguity are the words _and_ and _or._ Three **And and or** kinds of ambiguity are particularly likely.[16] The first is the ambiguity between _or_ as a disjunctive (P _or else_ Q) and as a coimplicative (P, _that is to say_ Q). The second is the ambiguity between _or_ as an exclusive disjunctive (P _or else_ Q, _but not both_) and as an inclusive disjunctive (P _or else_ Q, _or else both_). The third is the ambiguity between _and_ as a conjunctive (_only both_ P _and_ Q) and as an inclusive disjunctive (P _or else_ Q, _or else both_). A charter party requires the charterer "to load a full and complete cargo of [A] sugar, [B] molasses, and/or [C] other lawful produce"; what may be loaded? (A and B and C), or else (A and B), or else (C)? (A and B and C), or else (A and B)? (A and B)? (A) or (B) or else (C)? (A) or else (A and B) or (A and C)? (A) or (B) or else (C) or any combination of two or three?[17] The word _shall_ is another source of ambiguity. Does it mean _must_ or only express futurity?[18]

A particularly frequent cause of ambiguity in contracts is the use of incon- **Inconsistent** sistent and conflicting language.[19] A buyer agrees to pay "at the rate of $1.25 **language** per M" for all the timber on a designated tract and that "the entire sale and purchase price of said timber is $1,400.00"; how much will the buyer pay if it turns out that there are 4,000 M feet — $5,000 or $1,400?[20] In many cases the conflict is between language in a standard form and language added by the parties for the particular transaction. A printed form for the sale of a house requires the purchaser to give notice of a breach of warranty "within one year from the date of . . . initial occupancy" but also states that "notice of noncon-formity must be delivered no later than January 6, 1957," the date having been inserted by hand. When must the purchaser give notice if the purchaser moves in on May 16, 1955?[21]

Any problem of interpretation can be eliminated by appropriate changes **Reasons for lack** in the contract language. Why, then, do such problems continue to arise? **of clarity** Sometimes it is the fault of the parties.

> Business men habitually adventure large sums of money on contracts which,
> for the purpose of defining legal obligations, are a mere jumble of words. They

---

[16] For an oft-cited case condemning the use of "and/or," _see_ Employers Mut. Liab. Ins. Co. v. Tollefsen, 263 N.W. 376 (Wis. 1935) ("befuddling, nameless thing, . . . Janus-faced verbal monstrosity").

[17] Cuthbert v. Comming, 156 Eng. Rep. 889 (Ex. Ch. 1855) (performed by loading sugar and molasses).

[18] _Compare_ In re Marriage of Ackerley, 775 N.E.2d 1045 (Ill. App. 2002) (where settlement agreement provided that one party "shall" turn over documents to other party, _shall_ connoted "mandatory obligation"), _with_ Home Fed. Sav. & Loan Assn. v. Campney, 357 N.W.2d 613 (Iowa 1984) (_shall_ given "commonly accepted and ordinary meaning of expressing simple futurity").

[19] Klapp v. United Ins. Group Agency, 663 N.W.2d 447 (Mich. 2003) (if two provisions "irreconcilably conflict with each other, the language of the contract is ambiguous").

[20] Hardin v. Dimension Lumber Co., 13 P.2d 602 (Or. 1932) ($1,400).

[21] McNeely v. Claremont Mgt. Co., 27 Cal. Rptr. 87 (Ct. App. 1962) (not later than January 6, 1957). Rules to resolve such conflicts are discussed in §7.11 _infra_.

trust to luck or the good faith of the opposite party with the comfortable assurance that any adverse result of litigation may be attributed to the hairsplitting of lawyers and the uncertainty of the law.[22]

At other times it is the fault — the incompetence, inattention, oversight, or haste — of lawyers that have drafted the contract. The examples just given of inconsistent and conflicting language are cases in point. At times, however, it is difficult for the drafter to foresee the problem at the time of contracting. An insurance contract on a motor vessel covers "collision with any other ship or vessel" but does not state whether an anchored flying boat is such a "ship or vessel."[23] And at times the drafter may have foreseen the problem but deliberately refrained from raising it — the lawyer who "wakes these sleeping dogs" by insisting that it be resolved may cost the client the bargain. An elderly woman enters a home for the aged, and pays a lump sum to be returned to her "if it should be found advisable to discontinue her stay" during a two-month trial period, but the contract does not indicate whether this applies if she dies within that time.[24] Sometimes the drafter foresees the problem but chooses to deal with it only in general terms, delegating to the appropriate forum the resolution of particular controversies on the basis of their special facts. A contract for the sale of wool requires "prompt" shipment from New Zealand to Philadelphia but does not state the exact number of days within which shipment must be made to be "prompt."[25] This kind of intentional vagueness is a useful technique that is also known to drafters of statutes and constitutions.[26] Intentional ambiguity, on the other hand, has no such defensible place in the drafter's repertoire.

Stating the issue   In dealing with problems of contract interpretation, it is useful to state the issue in terms of the contract language. Generally, the issue should be framed so that it can be answered yes or no, as a court must ordinarily do.[27] It should also be framed so that it contains the controlling language of the contract, with such emphasis as is helpful. And it should be framed so that it recognizes that different meanings are attached to words in different contexts. For example:

[22] Lord Atkin in Phoenix Ins. Co. v. De Monchy, 141 L.T.R. 439, 445 (H.L. 1929).

[23] Polpen Shipping Co. v. Commercial Union Assur. Co., [1943] I K.B. 161 (1942) (it is not).

[24] First Natl. Bank v. Methodist Home for the Aged, 309 P.2d 389 (Kan. 1957) (it does).

[25] Kreglinger & Fernau v. Charles J. Webb Sons Co., 162 F. Supp. 695 (E.D. Pa. 1957) (shipment within 52 days was "prompt"), aff'd per curiam, 255 F.2d 680 (3d Cir. 1958).

[26] For examples from the Uniform Commercial Code, see UCC 1-304 ("obligation of good faith"), 2-306(2) ("obligation . . . to use best efforts"), 2-309(1) (time for delivery "shall be a reasonable time"). For examples from the Constitution of the United States, see U.S. Const. amend. XIV ("due process of law," "the equal protection of the laws").

[27] This is because the question most often presented in a contract interpretation case is: has there been a breach of contract? Only in rare situations, as when asked to frame a decree of specific performance or grant declaratory relief, is a court *required* to give a definition of terms. The mere fact that an issue of contract interpretation is stated so as to require a yes or no answer does not mean that the language in question is ambiguous rather than vague, although this form of sharply stating the legal issue sometimes erroneously suggests that ambiguity is involved.

Is a fibroid tumor of the uterus a *"disease* of *organs* of the body *not common to both sexes"* within the insured's policy?[28]

It is also useful to redraft the language twice, staying as faithful to the original as possible, so that it will clearly require a decision first for one party and then for the other. For example:

> *(For insured)* disease of organs of the body that is not common to both sexes.
> *(For insurer)* disease of organs of the body that are not common to both sexes.

Although, as with all such exercises, there are no uniquely "correct" statements of issues or redrafts of language, these techniques of analysis afford a useful basis for decision as well as for advocacy.

How do courts decide such disputes over interpretation?

§7.9. The Choice of Meaning. In a dispute over contract interpretation, each party claims that the language should be given the meaning that that party attaches to it at the time of the dispute. However, the resolution of the dispute begins, not with these meanings, but with the meanings attached by each party at the time the contract was made. Although disputes over the interpretation of contracts have much in common with disputes over the interpretation of statutes, deeds, and wills, there is an important difference. Since these other legal acts involve a declaration by only one party — the legislature, the grantor, or the testator — the search for meaning begins with the meaning attached by that party to its own language; that party needs no other party's assent. Since a contract involves two parties, however, the search for meaning begins with the meaning attached by both parties to the contract language; each needs the other's assent.[1]

Meaning of two parties

The possible combinations of these two meanings can be analyzed through a series of hypotheticals based on the celebrated case of *Raffles v. Wichelhaus*.[2] The parties had agreed upon the sale of cotton to be sent to the buyer on the ship *Peerless* from Bombay. There happened, however, to be two ships named *Peerless* leaving Bombay at different times, one in October, the other in December. The buyer argued that *Peerless* should be interpreted to require

Example of the Peerless

---

[28] See the discussion of ambiguity of syntax *supra*.

§7.9 [1] *See* A. Denning, The Discipline of Law 32 (1979) ("When construing a statute or will, you are considering the intentions of one body only — be it Parliament or a testator. When construing a contract, be it in writing or by word of mouth, you are considering the intentions of two parties — who have agreed together on the terms that shall bind them."). These generalizations need some qualification. Even in the case of a statute, a deed, or a will, the impact of the language on the reader cannot be ignored. Furthermore, since a promise under seal also involves a declaration by only one party, it is more closely analogous to a deed than to an ordinary contract. *See generally* E. Farnsworth, Changing Your Mind ch. 3 (1998).

[2] 159 Eng. Rep. 375 (Ex. 1864).

October shipment, while the seller argued that it should be interpreted to require December shipment.

Same meaning attached

First, a seemingly simple case can be disposed of. Suppose that it is shown that, when the parties made the contract, both had in mind the same ship, say the December *Peerless*.[3] In practice, only rarely can one party show that the meaning that it asserts at the time of the dispute was shared by both parties at the time the contract was made.[4] Nevertheless, should a party not prevail if successful in showing this, perhaps with the aid of documents obtained on pretrial discovery or the testimony of a disaffected former employee? Surely if one party shows that the other party attached the same meaning that the first party did, the other party should not be able to avoid that meaning by showing that a reasonable person would have attached a different one. According to Corbin, "it is certain that the purpose of the court is in all cases the ascertainment of the 'intention of the parties' if they had one in common."[5]

Objectivist solution

This, however, is one of the areas in which judicial attitudes have differed markedly. Here the controversy between the objective and subjective theories of assent flared up again,[6] and the objectivists refused to concede the primacy of a common meaning, shared by both parties. They maintained that an objective standard of reasonableness should always be applied to determine the meaning of *Peerless*. If under that standard the word *Peerless* would have referred to the October *Peerless*, that should be the meaning of *Peerless*, even though both parties had the other ship in mind. In the words of a staunch objectivist, Judge Learned Hand:

> It makes not the least difference whether a promisor actually intends that meaning which the law will impose upon his words. The whole House of Bishops might satisfy us that he had intended something else, and it would make not a particle of difference in his obligation . . . . Indeed, if both parties severally declared that their meaning had been other than the natural meaning, and each declaration was similar, it would be irrelevant, saving some mutual agreement between them to that effect. When the court came to assign the meaning to their words, it would disregard such declarations, because they related only to their state of mind when the contract was made, and that has nothing to do with their obligations.[7]

But this reasoning might point to the October *Peerless*, even though both parties had in mind the December one. The result under Judge Hand's approach would then sacrifice the actual expectations of the contracting parties to a supposed

[3]The reasoning would be similar under the converse assumption that they both had in mind the October *Peerless*.

[4]*But see* General Discount Corp. v. Sadowski, 183 F.2d 542 (6th Cir. 1950) (plaintiff's understanding corroborated by defendant's lawyer, who had drafted contract).

[5]1 A. Corbin, Contracts §106 (1963).

[6]See the discussion of the victory of the objective theory in §3.6 *supra*.

[7]Eustis Mining Co. v. Beer, Sondheimer & Co., 239 F. 976, 984-85 (S.D.N.Y. 1917).

objective meaning. It has been pointed out in defense of this approach that if "the 'actual state of the parties' minds' is relevant, then each litigated case must become an extended factual inquiry into what was 'intended,' 'meant,' 'believed' and so on," while if "we can restrict ourselves to the 'externals' . . . , then the factual inquiry will be much simplified and in time can be dispensed with altogether as the courts accumulate precedents about recurring types of permissible and impermissible 'conduct.' "[8] It is, however, easier to find statements extolling this approach than it is to find instances in which the approach has clearly carried the day. Instead, such authority as there is supports giving effect to a common meaning shared by both parties in preference to an objective meaning.

One of the few cases to raise the point involved a general contractor that agreed with the State of New Hampshire to construct the superstructure of a bridge. The general contractor, which was to receive $12.60 for each square yard of concrete that it laid on the bridge deck, then engaged a subcontractor to do the concrete work at $12.00 per square yard of "concrete surface included in the bridge deck." The subcontractor later claimed that it was entitled to payment for laying concrete over the number of square yards included in all of the outer surfaces of the deck — top, bottom, and sides — for a total of 8,100 square yards. The general contractor refused to pay for more than the 4,184 square yards on the top surface, for which the state had paid. The trial court concluded that at the time of contracting both parties intended that payment be made on the latter basis[9] and held for the general contractor. The Supreme Court of New Hampshire affirmed, adding:

> The rule which precludes the use of the understanding of one party alone is designed to prevent imposition of his private understanding upon the other party to a bilateral transaction . . . . But when it appears that the understanding of one is the understanding of both, no violation of the rule results from determination of the mutual understanding according to that of one alone. Where the understanding is mutual, it ceases to be the 'private' understanding of one party.[10]

Each party used the words "concrete surface included in the bridge deck" to refer only to the top surface of the deck. Since each party attached the same meaning to the language, there was no need to apply an objective standard of reasonableness. In that situation, no logic compels a court to give a contract a meaning that neither party attached to it. As the Restatement Second states: "Where the parties have attached the same meaning to a promise or agreement

Prevailing view

---

[8] G. Gilmore, The Death of Contract 42 (1974).

[9] In concluding that this was the subcontractor's intention, the trial court relied on the negotiations between the parties. Although there was no direct evidence of the general contractor's intention, the trial court concluded from circumstantial evidence that it must have been the same as the subcontractor's.

[10] Berke Moore Co. v. Phoenix Bridge Co., 98 A.2d 150, 156 (N.H. 1953).

or a term thereof, it is interpreted in accordance with that meaning."[11] If
this reasoning were applied to the example in which both parties had in mind
the December *Peerless*, the actual expectations of the parties would prevail,
and *Peerless* would be taken to mean the December *Peerless*, even though
an objective standard might point to the October one. Other decisions are in
accord.[12] In the rare cases of a common meaning shared by both parties, the
subjectivists have had the better of the argument. Though it is generally safe
to say that a party's "secret intention" will not carry the day, this is not a safe
assertion if it happens that both parties shared the same "secret intention."

Different meanings attached

The usual case, however, is not one of a common meaning shared by both
parties, but one of what is best described as a "misunderstanding."[13] Suppose
that, when the contract was made, the buyer had the October *Peerless* in mind
and the seller had the December one in mind. If the subjective theory were
followed here — if a contract really required a "meeting of the minds" — there
would be no contract. Nor would there be a contract in any of the many cases
in which, in spite of apparent assent, ambiguity or vagueness masks hidden
dissent. Unless no contract is to result whenever the parties have attached
different meanings to the contract language, some basis must be found to tip
the scales in favor of one meaning or the other.

Actual knowledge

In some cases, one party (and only one party) actually knows that the other
party has attached another meaning and knows what that meaning is. Suppose,
for example, that the buyer has in mind the October *Peerless* and the seller the
December one, but the buyer knows, perhaps from something that the seller
has said, that the seller has in mind the December one. In that case, any court
would conclude that there is a contract on the seller's terms — for shipment on
the December *Peerless*.[14] The Restatement Second leads to the same result.[15]

---

[11] Restatement Second §201(1), followed in Sprucewood Inv. Corp. v. Alaska Hous. Fin. Corp.,
33 P.3d 1156 (Alaska 2001) ("what any other builder could have understood the contract to mean
is irrelevant" where there was "no dispute that, when the contract was formed, both [parties]
believed that it required complete demolition"). The UNIDROIT Principles agree that where
possible a contract should be interpreted "according to the common intention of the parties."
UNIDROIT Principles 4.1(1).

[12] Sunbury Textile Mills v. Commissioner, 585 F.2d 1190 (3d Cir. 1978) (where both parties
agree as to meaning actually given by them, "their harmonious recital of what these words mean
is conclusive").

[13] This term is used in Restatement Second §20 in preference to *mistake*. According to Restatement Second §151, "A mistake is a belief that is not in accord with the facts." Examples are the
mistake of one party ("unilateral mistake") that makes a contract voidable (§9.4 *infra*), the mistake
of both parties ("mutual mistake") that makes a contract voidable (§9.3 *infra*), and the mistake of
both parties as to expression that justifies reformation (§7.5 *supra*).

[14] Hamann v. Crouch, 508 P.2d 968 (Kan. 1973) ("where one party to a contract knows the
meaning that the other party intended to convey by his words then he is bound by that meaning").

[15] Restatement Second §201(2). When this section says "the other [party] knew the meaning
attached by the first party," it is understood that the first party must actually have attached that
meaning. Sometimes the Restatement Second does not distinguish between knowing that another

Perhaps the most satisfactory rationalization of this result is that a party that makes a contract knowing of a misunderstanding is sufficiently at fault to justify that party's being subjected to the other party's understanding.[16]

And what if neither party had actual knowledge of the misunderstanding, and one party (and only one party) has reason to know that the other party has attached another meaning and to know what that meaning is? Is the first party then sufficiently at fault to justify being subjected to the other party's understanding? Suppose, for example, that the buyer has in mind the October *Peerless* and the seller the December one, and that, although the buyer does not know of the seller's meaning, the buyer does have reason to know of it, perhaps because the buyer knows of both ships and that the later shipment would normally be meant. Here, too, the generally accepted view is that there is a contract on the seller's terms — for shipment on the December *Peerless*.[17] The Restatement Second again leads to the same result.[18] As in the situation in which the buyer actually knows that the seller attaches another meaning, the result can be rationalized on the ground that the buyer is at fault, but here it is a more attenuated kind of fault. The advantages in terms of predictability and certainty of this use of an objective standard are obvious and are much appreciated by courts. In Judge Easterbrook's words, "parties, like Humpty Dumpty, may use words as they please," but the "meaning held by only one party may not be invoked to change the ordinary denotation of a word" since "unilateral intent does not count."[19] Even if there is a contract, however, one party's mistaken belief as to the other's understanding of the contract language involves a mistake as to a fact and

Reason to know

---

party attached a different meaning and knowing what that different meaning is, but this distinction probably has little practical importance.

As to the effect of the Vienna Convention, *see* MCC-Marble Ceramic Ctr. v. Ceramica Nuova D'Agostino, 144 F.3d 1384 (11th Cir. 1998) (Convention "requires an inquiry into a party's subjective intent as long as the other party to the contract was aware of that intent").

[16]Centron DPL Co. v. Tilden Fin. Corp., 965 F.2d 673 (8th Cir. 1992) (quoting this section of this treatise). Compare the reasoning based on fault in the discussion of the alternative of tort liability in §3.9 *supra*.

[17]Emor, Inc. v. Cyprus Mines Corp., 467 F.2d 770 (3d Cir. 1972) ("it is not necessary that the party *actually know* the other party's intent; it is enough that he had 'reason to know' ").

[18]Restatement Second §201(2). However, Restatement Second §153 illus. 6 suggests that in such a case the contract might be voidable by the seller on the ground of unilateral mistake. *See* the discussion of other types of cases in §9.4 *infra*.

The Vienna Convention provides that if the other party "knew or could not have been unaware" of a party's intent, the latter's intent prevails, and that otherwise recourse is to be had to "the understanding that a reasonable person of the same kind as the other party would have had in the same circumstances." CISG 8. The UNIDROIT Principles use a simpler formula under which in the absence of a common intention, a contract "shall be interpreted according to the meaning that reasonable persons of the same kind" would give it in the circumstances. UNIDROIT Principles 4.1(2).

[19]TKO Equip. Co. v. C & G Coal Co., 863 F.2d 541, 545 (7th Cir. 1988).

might, in a proper case, be the basis for avoidance on the ground of unilateral mistake.[20]

Example of *Frigaliment*

A practical illustration of this reasoning is *Frigaliment Importing Co. v. B.N.S. International Sales Corp.*, which involved the meaning of the word *chicken* in a contract of sale by an American exporter to a Swiss importer. When the seller shipped stewing chicken, the buyer, after accepting it, sued on the ground that *chicken* meant a young chicken, suitable for broiling or frying. The seller maintained that the word was used in a broader sense and included stewers. Since *chicken* can have a spectrum of meanings, the problem was one of vagueness. The court assumed that, when the contract was made, each party attached the meaning that it asserted and that therefore a misunderstanding had arisen. It resolved the misunderstanding in favor of the seller. Although the buyer may have attached the narrower meaning to the word *chicken*, it did not appear that the seller had reason to know this. The court reasoned that the buyer had "the burden of showing that 'chicken' was used in the narrower rather than the broader sense, and this it has not sustained."[21]

Actual *Peerless* case

In *Raffles v. Wichelhaus*, the actual case of the ship *Peerless*, neither buyer nor seller had reason to know that there were two ships of the same name, and therefore neither had reason to know of the meaning attached by the other. In a suit by the seller, the buyer had judgment, evidently on the ground that "there was no consensus ad idem, and therefore no binding contract."[22] Although it is sometimes said that the result follows because there was no "meeting of the minds," this rationale is not helpful since that is true in every case of a misunderstanding.[23] The most satisfactory rationale is that offered by the Restatement Second, which states that there is no contract for lack of assent when "the parties attach materially different meanings to their manifestations and . . . neither party knows or has reason to know the meaning attached by the other."[24] In

---

[20] See the discussion of other types of cases in §9.4 *infra*.

[21] 190 F. Supp. 116, 121 (S.D.N.Y. 1960).

[22] 159 Eng. Rep. 375 (Ex. 1864). This, the accepted rationale of the court's per curiam opinion, comes from the prevailing argument of counsel, at 376.

For a modern American case with a similar rationale, *see* Oswald v. Allen, 417 F.2d 43 (2d Cir. 1969) (where buyer reasonably believed he had offered to buy all Swiss coins owned by seller, while seller reasonably understood offer to refer only to those of her Swiss coins belonging to a collection denominated by her the "Swiss Coin Collection," the "law is settled that no contract exists").

That each party is entitled to restitution, *see* Marcangelo v. Boardwalk Regency Corp., 847 F. Supp. 1222 (D.N.J. 1994) (if "no meeting of the minds occurred" between gambler and casino, gambler would have no right to primary progressive jackpot, but "would be entitled to restitution of the amount of money he put into the machine — $1.25 — provided he returned the $1046.31 he received" as the secondary progressive jackpot).

[23] See the discussion of the subjective theory in §3.6 *supra*.

[24] Restatement Second §20, which also disposes of the even rarer case in which there is a standoff because "each party knows or each party has reason to know the meaning attached by the other."

short a party is not bound by a meaning unless that party either knows or has reason to know of it. Even though the parties manifest assent to the same language, their misunderstanding may prevent the formation of a contract. Holmes gave a much narrower reading to the case, limiting it to situations of proper name ambiguity on the ground that "while other words may mean different things, a proper name means one person or thing and no other," so that the problem is one of "different words" and not merely one of different meanings.[25] Another writer has criticized Holmes's formulation as too narrow and the Restatement formulation as too broad, and would confine the application of the rule to cases of "double meaning" or what we have called here "ambiguity."[26]

There may, however, be a simpler explanation than any of these for the result in the case of the ship *Peerless*. For the seller to prevail in a suit against the buyer, it would seem that the seller would have to sustain "the burden" — as the court in *Frigaliment* put it — of showing that the word *Peerless* was used to refer to the ship that sailed in December. This the seller did not do. But if the buyer had sued the seller, it would seem that the buyer would have had to sustain the burden of showing that the word *Peerless* was used to refer to the ship that sailed in October. This, presumably, the buyer could not do. The explanation, then, for the judgment for the seller is not that there is no contract, but that neither party can sustain the burden of showing that its meaning should prevail. This kind of standoff can arise whether the misunderstanding arises out of ambiguity or out of vagueness — whether it is one over *Peerless* or over *chicken*. If the buyer in *Frigaliment* had rejected the chickens and the seller had sued for the price, the same court might have found for the buyer on the ground that the seller had not sustained the burden of showing that *chicken* was used in the broader sense.[27] If this is so, the Restatement Second is right in formulating the rule generally to apply to both types of misunderstanding. The misunderstanding must, however, be a significant one, for the meanings attached by the parties will never be identical in all respects. According to the Restatement Second commentary, "it is enough that there is a core of common meaning sufficient to determine their performances with reasonable certainty or to give a reasonably certain basis for an appropriate legal remedy."[28] As in the analogous situation of the requirement of definiteness, a court must apply

Burden as explanation

---

[25] This analysis, not among Holmes's most trenchant, appears in Holmes, The Theory of Legal Interpretation, 12 Harv. L. Rev. 417, 418 (1899).

[26] Young, Equivocation in the Making of Agreements, 64 Colum. L. Rev. 619, 646-47 (1964).

[27] Under UCC 2-607(4), the buyer has the burden "to establish any breach with respect to the goods accepted." By negative inference, the seller has the burden as to goods rejected. This burden would seem to include showing what the contract means, to the extent that there can be said to be a burden as to interpretation even if the court treats the question of interpretation as one of law. *See* the discussion of judge or jury in §7.14 *infra*.

If the trier of the facts arrives at an interpretation different from that asserted by either party, there seems no reason why relief should not be granted accordingly.

[28] Restatement Second §20 cmt. *b*.

this requirement with an eye to what can be expected in practice and with a view to the extent to which the parties have relied on the agreement.[29]

No meaning attached

In the situations discussed thus far, it has been assumed that each party attached a meaning to the language in question at the time the attached contract was made. In many disputes arising out of contemporary business transactions, however, the parties gave little or no thought to the impact of their words on the case that later arose. Perhaps the contract is embodied in a printed form that neither party prepared; perhaps its clauses have been lifted from a form book; perhaps the deal is a routine one struck by minor functionaries. For these and many other reasons the analysis suggested earlier may be unsuitable. The court will then have no choice but to look solely to a standard of reasonableness. Interpretation cannot turn on meanings that the parties attached if they attached none, but must turn on the meaning that reasonable persons in the positions of the parties would have attached if they had given the matter thought.[30] If the contract is on a widely used standard form, the use of this purely objective test has the advantage of promoting uniform interpretation, without regard to the chance circumstances of the parties.[31]

Intention of the parties

In conclusion, the reader should look with some skepticism on the judicial commonplace that in interpreting a contract the court merely carries out "the intentions of the parties." The court does indeed carry out their intentions in those relatively rare cases in which the parties attached the same meaning to the language in question. But if the parties attached different meanings to that language, the court's task is the more complex one of applying a standard of reasonableness to determine which party's intention is to be carried out at the expense of the other's. And if the parties attached no meaning to that language, its task is to find by a standard of reasonableness a meaning that does not accord with any intention at all.

What principles guide a court in these tasks?

---

[29] See the discussion of sensitivity to the problems of the drafter in §3.28 *supra*. It has been suggested that although "there is much room for interpretation once the parties are inside the framework of a contract, . . . it seems that there is less in the field of offer and acceptance." United States v. Braunstein, 75 F. Supp. 137, 139 (S.D.N.Y. 1947).

[30] Southern Bell Tel. & Tel. Co. v. Florida E.C. Ry., 399 F.2d 854 (5th Cir. 1968) ("If after examining all [extrinsic] sources of information, it is still not possible to determine the intent of the parties, courts can rely on rules of law which purport to determine what, in certain circumstances the parties intended, when, in fact, no one really knows what was intended or that the parties even thought about the matter.").

It is possible that one party attached a meaning to the language and that the other attached none. In that event the first party's meaning will prevail if the other party had reason to know this. Home Fed. Sav. & Loan Assn. v. Campney, 357 N.W.2d 613 (Iowa 1984) (where mortgagee used "shall" to express simple futurity and mortgagors did not read mortgage, mortgagee's meaning prevailed where it was "the commonly accepted and ordinary meaning"). *See* Restatement Second §201.

[31] Where the contract is on such a standard form, there is authority that this purely objective test should be used regardless of the meanings attached by the parties. *See* the discussions of the problem on inequality in §4.26 *supra* and of standardized terms in §7.11 *infra*.

§7.10. **Fundamental Principles of Interpretation.** At the time the
contract was made, a party may have attached a particular meaning to the
language that is later in dispute or may not have considered its meaning. A party that attached a meaning to the language can at least testify
to show this at trial, though the party is likely to have difficulty establishing that the other party should reasonably have been aware of this at the
time of agreement. A party that did not consider the meaning of the language when contracting is likely to have difficulty showing that the meaning
that party asserts at trial was the more reasonable meaning at the time of
agreement. In either case, the court must apply a standard of reasonableness in interpreting the contract language. The same general principles are
applied to a wide variety of contracts,[1] sometimes with variations for contracts of insurance[2] or contracts creating secondary obligations.[3] What are these
principles?

Standard of reasonableness

Judges are fond of asserting that contract interpretation is a matter of "common sense"[4] and that the "'plain and ordinary meaning' doctrine is at the heart
of contract construction."[5] In its search for that meaning, the court is free
to look to all the relevant circumstances surrounding the transaction. This
includes the state of the world, including the state of the law, at the time.[6]
It also includes all writings, oral statements, and other conduct by which the
parties manifested their assent, together with any prior negotiations between
them and any applicable course of dealing, course of performance, or usage.[7]
The entire agreement, including all writings, should be read together in the
light of all the circumstances.[8] Since the purpose of this inquiry is to ascertain

Look to all circumstances

§7.10 [1]CSX v. Chicago & North Western Transp. Co., 62 F.3d 185 (7th Cir. 1995)
(indemnification agreements "are to be construed like any other contract").

[2]See the discussion of standardized agreements in §4.11 *infra*.

[3]Production Credit Assn. v. Schmer, 448 N.W.2d 123 (Neb. 1989) ("Nebraska adheres to the
rule of strict construction of guaranty contracts."). But for a statement that "standards that apply
to interpretation of contracts in general apply to interpretation of contracts creating secondary
obligations," *see* Restatement (Third) of Suretyship and Guaranty §14.

[4]McElroy v. B.F. Goodrich Co., 73 F.3d 722 (7th Cir. 1996) (Posner, C.J.: "body of knowledge
that goes by the name of 'common sense' is part of the context of interpreting most documents").

[5]Appoini v. Sunshine Biscuits, 652 F.2d 643, 647 (6th Cir. 1981).

[6]Maryland-National Capital Park & Planning Commn. v. Lynn, 514 F.2d 829 (D.C. Cir.
1975) (proper to consider federal statute in interpreting contract between state and federal
agencies).

[7]For an illuminating discussion of drafting history, *see* Consolidated Gas Supply Corp. v. Federal Energy Regulatory Commn., 745 F.2d 281 (4th Cir. 1984) (while generally "broad changes in
phraseology signify differences in meaning," it is also possible that "a simple desire to demonstrate
versatility in expressing the same idea — not a variation in intent — may underlie the changes").
As to the admissibility of evidence of prior negotiations, *see* §7.12 *infra*.

[8]Paolella v. Radiologic Leasing Assocs., 769 A.2d 596 (R.I. 2001) (court considers situation
of parties and accompanying circumstances in interpreting unambiguous contracts). See the
discussion of more special rules in §7.11 *infra*.

the meaning to be given to the language, there should be no requirement that the language be ambiguous, vague, or otherwise uncertain before the inquiry is undertaken.

Dictionary definitions

Indeed, it is questionable whether a word has a meaning at all when divorced from the circumstances in which it is used.[9] [Dictionary definitions may be of help in showing the general use of words,[10] but they are not necessarily dispositive.] In Learned Hand's words, "it is one of the surest indexes of a mature and developed jurisprudence not to make a fortress out of the dictionary."[11] A word may be ambiguous, so that the dictionary gives both of the meanings asserted by the parties. Or a word may be vague, so that the application of the dictionary meaning to the particular case is uncertain. Furthermore, parties do not always use words in accordance with their dictionary definitions. Often the meaning attached to a word by the parties must be gleaned from its context, including all the circumstances of the transaction.[12] Sometimes the nature of either the parties or the subject matter shows that the contract was made with reference to a specialized vocabulary of technical terms or other words of art.[13] And sometimes it can be demonstrated that the parties contracted with respect to a usage in their trade or even with respect to a restricted private convention or understanding.[14]

Purpose interpretation

The significance of surrounding circumstances in interpreting contract language is reflected in a judicial emphasis on "purpose interpretation."[15] According to the Restatement Second, "if the principal purpose of the parties is ascertainable it is given great weight."[16] Such purpose interpretation has

---

[9] *See* Farnsworth, "Meaning" in the Law of Contracts, 76 Yale L.J. 939, 940-42 (1967).

[10] Bock v. Computer Assocs. Intl., 257 F.3d 700 (7th Cir. 2001) (interpretation of "incentive compensation" involves "plainly descriptive term that lends itself straightforwardly to dictionary definitions").

[11] Cabell v. Markham, 148 F.2d 737, 739 (2d Cir.), aff'd, 326 U.S. 404 (1945). *See* Giuseppi v. Walling, 144 F.2d 608 (2d Cir. 1944) (L. Hand, J., concurring: "There is no surer way to misread any document than to read it literally."). For an indication that Hand's flexibility as to the meaning of words was not unlimited, however, *see* the discussions of the limits of language *infra* and of the objective theory in §3.6 *supra*.

[12] Iowa Fuel & Minerals v. Iowa State Bd. of Regents, 471 N.W.2d 859 (Iowa 1991) ("while words are to be given their ordinary meaning, particular words and phrases in a contract are not to be interpreted in isolation"). *See* the quotations from Thayer and Holmes in the discussion of the imprecision of language in §7.8 *supra*.

[13] Schneider Leasing v. United States Aviation Underwriters, 555 N.W.2d 838 (Iowa 1996) (appropriate to consider extrinsic evidence of "commercial aviation industry's specialized vocabulary" in determining difference between "rental" and "charter" of airplane).

[14] In re Soper's Estate, 264 N.W. 427 (Minn. 1935) (insured and insurer used *wife* to refer to partner in invalid marriage rather than to legal wife).

[15] New England Structures v. Loranger, 234 N.E.2d 888 (Mass. 1968) (shortness of five-day period for notice "suggests that its purpose is at most to give the defaulting party time" to arrange to stop work and not to cure default).

[16] Restatement Second §202(1).

a secure place in the field of statutory interpretation, where it stems from *Heydon's Case*.[17] The analogy to contracts, however, is less than perfect because, although a legislature may be said in a sense to have but one collective purpose, the two parties to a contract often have different purposes.[18] Nevertheless, each party may have an understanding of the purposes that the other expects the contract to serve. It seems proper to regard one party's assent to the agreement with knowledge of the other party's general purposes as a ground for resolving doubts in favor of a meaning that will further those ends, rather than a meaning that will frustrate them.[19]

Sometimes, if the contract is written, the court need not look outside the writing to discern the parties' purpose. As in the case of a statute, it may find a helpful statement of the purpose set forth in the writing itself in the form of a recital. It is not uncommon for written contracts to begin with a series of such recitals of the surrounding circumstances and of the objectives of the parties. Traditionally prefixed by the word *whereas*, contract recitals are not ordinarily drafted as promises or conditions. Although their proper role in the interpretation of the main body of the contract has sometimes been unclear, it is plain that they are frequently intended to, and often do, shed light on the circumstances the parties wished to have considered in the interpretation of the contract.[20]

Recitals

But even though a court may look at all the circumstances in the process of interpreting contract language, the language itself imposes a limit on how far the court will go in that process. In Corbin's words: "The more bizarre and unusual an asserted interpretation is, the more convincing must be the testimony that supports it. At what point the court should cease listening to testimony that white is black and that a dollar is fifty cents is a matter for sound judicial discretion and common sense."[21] This is another area in which judicial

Limits of language

---

[17] 76 Eng. Rep. 637 (Ex. 1584).

[18] For a case in which the parties to a contract had a collective purpose, *see* Spaulding v. Morse, 76 N.E.2d 137 (Mass. 1947) ("main purpose of the parents of Richard [as parties to the contract] was to arrive at an agreement for his maintenance and education and to provide security therefor").

[19] Corinno Civetta Constr. Corp. v. City of New York, 493 N.E.2d 905 (N.Y. 1986) ("even exculpatory language which purports to preclude [owner's] damages for *all* delays resulting from *any* cause whatsoever are not read literally" since it "can hardly be presumed" that contractor bargained away right to "damages resulting from delays which the parties did not contemplate").

[20] Lord Esher stated three rules for recitals: "If the recitals are clear and the operative part is ambiguous, the recitals govern the construction. If the recitals are ambiguous and the operative part is clear, the operative part must prevail. If both the recitals and the operative part are clear, but they are inconsistent with each other, the operative part is to be preferred." Ex parte Dawes, 17 Q.B.D. 275, 286 (Ct. App. 1886).

Though American courts have often repeated these rules with approval, they have been wary about giving effect to recitals. *See* Grynberg v. FERC, 71 F.3d 413 (D.C. Cir. 1995) ("a Whereas clause, while sometimes useful as an aid to interpretation," cannot create right beyond those arising from terms of document).

[21] Corbin, The Parol Evidence Rule, 53 Yale L.J. 603, 623 (1944).

attitudes differ. Learned Hand suggested somewhat less flexibility when he wrote that "there is a critical breaking point . . . beyond which no language can be forced."[22] Most judges would probably agree with Hand. But just where that critical point comes in an actual case will turn not only on the language of the contract and other relevant facts. It will also depend on the attitude of the particular court toward the authority of words and the sanctity of written language used in the contracting process and toward the protraction of the judicial process that results from entertaining such disputes over the meaning of language. But even though judicial attitudes differ considerably, some generally accepted rules in aid of interpretation can be distilled from the collective attitudes of judges as a body.

We now turn to rules in aid of interpretation.

Habits as to language

§7.11. **Rules in Aid of Interpretation.** When interpreting contract language, courts start with the assumption that the parties have used the language in the way that reasonable persons ordinarily do and in such a way as to avoid absurdity.[1] This assumption covers matters of grammar and syntax as well as the meaning of words. The process of interpretation therefore turns in good part on what the court regards as normal habits in the use of language, habits that would be expected of reasonable persons in the circumstances of the parties. Often an asserted meaning is challenged on the ground that, if the parties had intended this meaning, these habits would have led them to express it in a different way. As the New York Court of Appeals said of an asserted interpretation of a lease, if that had been the parties' intention, "surely no problem of draftsmanship would have stood in the way of its being spelled out."[2]

Rules and maxims

Some of the assumptions that courts make as to normal habits in the use of language are so widely shared and so frequently articulated that they have come to be regarded as rules of contract interpretation.[3] Some of these rules have been encapsulated in Latin maxims that have a special ring of authority, albeit sometimes a hollow one. None of these rules, however, has a validity beyond that of its underlying assumptions. Their use in judicial opinions is often more ceremonial (as being decorative rationalizations of decisions already reached on other grounds) than persuasive (as moving the court toward a decision not yet reached). Judicial opinions on problems of

[22] Eustis Mining Co. v. Beer, Sondheimer & Co., 239 F. 976, 982 (S.D.N.Y. 1917).

§7.11 [1] North German Lloyd v. Guaranty Trust Co., 244 U.S. 12 (1917) (Holmes, J.: "Business contracts must be construed with business sense, as they naturally would be understood by intelligent men of affairs."). See Nelson v. Schellpfeffer, 656 N.W.2d 740 (S.D. 2003) (absurd result is one that "parties, presumed to be rational persons pursuing rational ends, are very unlikely to have agreed upon").

[2] George Backer Mgt. Corp. v. Acme Quilting Co., 385 N.E.2d 1062, 1065 (N.Y. 1978). See the exercise along these lines suggested in the discussion of stating the issue in §7.8 supra.

[3] See Friedman, Law, Rules and the Interpretation of Written Documents, 59 Nw. U. L. Rev. 751 (1965).

contract interpretation sometimes resemble bouquets of such rationalizations, plucked from among many and arranged so as to harmonize with the result. Indeed, a court can often select from among pairs of opposing or counter-vailing rules that seem to conflict,[4] although it should come as no surprise to lawyers that there are situations in which two sound policies argue for opposite results.[5]

Many assumptions as to how words are used are not limited to contract language but apply to language generally. The resulting rules have a univer-sality that fits them for use, for example, in connection with statutes as well as contracts.[6] One illustration is the assumption that when parties list spe-cific items, without any more general or inclusive term, they intend to exclude unlisted items, even though they are similar to those listed. From this assump-tion comes the rule *expressio unius est exclusio alterius* ("the expression of one thing is the exclusion of another"). A court may apply it to read a contract for the sale of a firm together with "cattle and hogs" to exclude the seller's sheep and house-dog.[7] Another illustration is the assumption that when parties list specific items, followed by a more general or inclusive term, they intend to include under the latter only things that are like the specific ones. From this assumption comes the *ejusdem generis* ("of the same kind") rule. A court may apply it to read a contract for the sale of a farm together with "cattle, hogs and other animals" to exclude the seller's house-dog, although it might include a few sheep that the seller was raising for the market.[8] Other rules for interpret-ing contract language can also be derived by analogy to those used in statutory interpretation.[9]

Other assumptions relate more specifically to the way in which reasonable persons ordinarily use language during the agreement process. Illustrative are

General rules

More special rules

---

[4] A list of such pairs of maxims of statutory interpretation appears in K. Llewellyn, The Common Law Tradition — Deciding Appeals 521-35 (1960), adapted from Llewellyn, Remarks on the Theory of Appellate Decision and the Rules or Canons About How Statutes Are to Be Construed, 3 Vand. L. Rev. 395 (1950).

[5] North Gate Corp. v. National Food Stores, 140 N.W.2d 744 (Wis. 1966) (rule of interpretation *contra proferentem* outweighed rule that interpretation that leaves part of language useless or creates surplusage is to be avoided).

[6] *See* Patterson, The Interpretation and Construction of Contracts, 64 Colum. L. Rev. 833 (1964), from which several of the following examples are taken.

[7] Central Hous. Inv. Corp. v. Federal Natl. Mortgage Assn., 248 P.2d 866 (Ariz. 1952) (mortgage covering "all heating, plumbing and lighting fixtures and equipment" did not cover cooling and refrigerating equipment).

[8] State ex rel. Commissioners of Land Office v. Butler, 753 P.2d 1334 (Okl. 1987) ("reservation of an interest in 'oil, gas and other mineral rights'" did not include coal).

[9] An example is the rule that the meaning of a word may be gathered from its accom-panying words. It is embodied in the maxim *noscitur a sociis* ("it is known from its asso-ciates"). Allstate Ins. Co. v. Russo, 641 A.2d 1304 (R.I. 1994) ("meaning of the general term 'misrepresentation' is qualified . . . by its association with the terms 'libel,' 'slander,' and 'defamation'").

those that are made in the common situation of an ambiguity caused by inconsistent and conflicting language.[10] There is, first, the assumption that the parties intend every part of the agreement to mean something, although not necessarily to be legally binding.[11] The agreement is therefore to be read as a whole[12] and an interpretation that gives effect to every part of the agreement is favored over one that makes some part of it mere surplusage.[13] A corollary is that words used repeatedly have a meaning that is the same throughout the contract[14] and that is consistent with the sense of the contract as a whole.[15] A similar assumption is made where two or more related contracts are made and, according to the Eighth Circuit, this is so even though the parties to the contracts differ and the contracts do not refer to each other, "as long as 'the several contracts were known to all the parties and were delivered at the same time to accomplish an agreed purpose.'"[16] If, however, two provisions in a contract so clearly conflict that both cannot be given full effect, it is assumed that the more specific the provision, the more likely it is to reflect the parties' intention. Accordingly, a specific provision controls a general one and may operate as an exception to it.[17] Another assumption to which courts frequently resort is that the greater the attention devoted to negotiating a term and reducing it to writing, the more likely it is to reflect the parties' intention. Accordingly, separately negotiated terms are given greater weight than standardized terms,[18] and generally handwritten terms control typewritten or printed ones, while typewritten terms control printed ones.[19] These rules are usually applied even though their effect

[10] See the discussion of inconsistent language in §7.8 *supra*.

[11] Contracts may, for example, contain recitals and hortatory language. The same assumption lies behind the maxim *ut res magis valeat quam pereat*. See the discussion of interpretation affected by public policy in §5.1 *supra*.

[12] Central Fla. Invs. v. Parkwest Assocs., 40 P.3d 599 (Utah 2002) ("we attempt to harmonize all of the contract's provisions and all of its terms").

[13] Standard Banner Coal Corp. v. Rapoca Energy Co., 576 S.E.2d 435 (Va. 2003) ("parties are presumed not to have included needless words").

[14] Taracorp, Inc. v. NL Indus., 73 F.3d 738 (7th Cir. 1996) ("we assume that the same words have the same meaning . . . and that the choice of substantially different words to address analogous issues signifies a different approach").

[15] Barco Urban Renewal Corp. v. Housing Auth., 674 F.2d 1001 (3d Cir. 1982) ("corollary to the principle that a writing is interpreted as a whole is that an ambiguous subsidiary contractual provision must be given an interpretation consistent with the dominant purpose of the contract").

[16] Dakota Gasification Co. v. Natural Gas Pipeline Co., 964 F.2d 732, 735 (8th Cir. 1992).

[17] Enchanted World Doll Museum v. Buskohl, 398 N.W.2d 149 (S.D. 1986) (specific provision governs if "conflict exists" with general provision). *See* Restatement Second §203(c).

[18] Restatement Second §203(d).

[19] House of Lloyd v. Director of Revenue, 824 S.W.2d 914 (Mo. 1992) (when there is "conflict between the typewritten and preprinted language in a contract, the typewritten will prevail"). *See* Restatement Second §203 cmt. *f*; UCC 3-114 (rule for negotiable instruments).

is to subordinate to the language of the agreement as a whole minor points of grammar[20] or punctuation.[21]

Besides such rules of interpretation, which are designed to ascertain the meaning that the parties might reasonably have attached to their language, there are other rules that have, at least in part, a different purpose. These would be called <u>rules of construction</u>, rather than of interpretation, by those partial to that terminology, because <u>they help to determine the legal effect of language quite independently of the meaning that the parties may have attached to it.</u>[22] An example is the assumption that the bargaining process results in a fair bargain, so that, between an interpretation that would yield such a bargain as a reasonable person would have made and one that would not, the former is preferred.[23] So, reasoned the Second Circuit:

Rules not dependent on meaning attached

> An interpretation which sacrifices a major interest of one of the parties while furthering only a marginal interest of the other should be rejected in favor of an interpretation which sacrifices marginal interests of both parties in order to protect their major concerns.[24]

Courts adhere to this assumption of a fair bargain with even greater tenacity when a lack of fairness on the part of one party is shown, which suggests that courts take into consideration more than just the meaning that the parties attached to the language. Courts have often used this technique to avoid giving effect to an inherently unfair provision of an agreement when a decision based on unconscionability would have been more candid.[25]

An especially common example is the rule that if language supplied by one party is reasonably susceptible to two interpretations, one of which favors each party, the one that is less favorable to the party that supplied the language is preferred.[26] Such interpretation *contra proferentem* ("against the profferer")

Contra proferentem

---

[20]Overhauser v. United States, 45 F.3d 1085 (7th Cir. 1995) (Posner, J.: "actual *practice* of the relevant linguistic community . . . in matters of the placement of commas is notably casual" and "Supreme Court cannot make up its mind whether to be skeptical or credulous about imputing grammatical expertise to drafters of legal documents").

[21]Royal Ins. Co. v. Ideal Mut. Ins. Co., 649 F. Supp. 130 (E.D. Pa.) ("although punctuation is often used as an aid in contract interpretation, it should not be permitted to control a meaning which is evident from a consideration of the [contract] as a whole"), aff'd mem., 806 F.2d 254 (3d Cir. 1986).

[22]See the discussion of *interpretation* and *construction* in §7.7 *supra.*

[23]Frigaliment Importing Co. v. B.N.S. Intl. Sales Corp., 190 F. Supp. 116 (S.D.N.Y. 1960) (market price of chicken at time of contract helped to show that *chicken* did not mean broilers since buyer "must have expected [seller] to make some profit").

[24]Sharon Steel Corp. v. Chase Manhattan Bank, 691 F.2d 1039, 1051 (2d Cir. 1982).

[25]See the discussion of interpretation of terms in §4.26 *supra.*

[26]Intel Corp. v. VIA Techs., 319 F.3d 1357 (Fed. Cir. 2002) (*contra proferentem* applied where one party "alone drafted the agreement" and there "was no negotiation"). *See* Restatement Second §206.

is often rationalized on the ground that the party against whom it operates had the possibility of drafting the language so as to avoid the dispute.[27] Since decisions adopting this rationale place the burden on the drafter, they are distinguishable from decisions based on the evenhanded reasoning that if the parties had intended an asserted meaning, they would have chosen different language. Interpretation *contra proferentem* is much favored in the context of standard form contracts, particularly if adhesive,[28] where it often favors a party that is at a distinct disadvantage in bargaining.[29] The rule is not limited to such cases, however, and may be invoked even if the parties bargained as equals.[30] It should be of interest to lawyers that ambiguities are sometimes resolved against a party on the ground that it has been represented by a lawyer during the drafting process.[31] Although the *contra proferentem* rule may encourage care in the drafting of contracts, it can scarcely be said to be designed to ascertain the meanings attached by the parties. It is not applicable if the language is unambiguous[32] and it is often denigrated as a rule of "last resort."[33]

---

[27]Dardovitch v. Haltzman, 190 F.3d 125 (3d Cir. 1999) (rejecting contention that rule does not apply in favor of one not party to contract because rule is based on idea that party drafting agreement is likely to provide more carefully for his own interests).

Sir Francis Bacon defended the rule as "a schoolmaster of wisdom and diligence in making men watchful in their own business," but conceded that it "is the last to be resorted to." F. Bacon, A Collection of Some Principal Rules and Maximes of the Common Law 3, 16 (1597).

[28]Victoria v. Superior Court, 710 P.2d 833 (Cal. 1985) (if "arbitration clause is adhesive, ambiguities will be subject to stricter construction").

As to compulsory contracts and terms, Restatement Second §206 cmt. *b* says that although the rule "has no direct application to cases where the language is prescribed by law, as is sometimes true with respect to insurance policies, bills of lading and other standardized documents, [sometimes] the statute or regulation adopts language which was previously used without compulsion and was interpreted against the drafting party, and there is normally no intention to change the established meaning, [and furthermore] insurers are more likely than insureds to participate in drafting prescribed forms and to review them carefully before putting them into use."

[29]Mastrobuono v. Shearson Lehman Hutton, 514 U.S. 52 (1995) Stevens, J.: rule protected parties "who did not choose the language from an unintended and unfair result" where it was unlikely that "they had any idea that by signing a standard-form agreement to arbitrate disputes they might be giving up an important substantive right").

[30]Bay State Smelting Co. v. Ferric Indus., 292 F.2d 96 (1st Cir. 1961) (exporter drafted order confirmation in sale of copper to itself from smelting company).

[31]Weiland Tool & Mfg. Co. v. Whitney, 251 N.E.2d 242 (Ill. 1969) ("we have taken into consideration not only that inferences from ambiguous language must be resolved against its author . . . , but also that he is a lawyer with a number of years . . . experience as a legal advisor in commercial transactions").

[32]Federal Deposit Ins. Corp. v. Connecticut Natl. Bank, 916 F.2d 997 (5th Cir. 1990) ("no need to turn to the rule of contra proferentem" where language not ambiguous).

[33]Residential Mktg. Group v. Granite Inv. Group, 933 F.2d 546 (7th Cir. 1991) (Posner, J.: "venerable principle . . . that ambiguities . . . are to be resolved against the draftsman does not bar the use of oral testimony to disambiguate a written contract," but "is a tie-breaker, used to resolve cases in which the written contract remains ambiguous even after oral evidence has been admitted").

Another example is the rule that if the language is reasonably susceptible to two interpretations and only one favors the public interest, this interpretation will be preferred. It can be justified on the grounds that underlie decisions holding a contract or term invalid as contrary to public policy, a justification unrelated to the intentions of the parties. It can also be rationalized as furthering their intentions by giving effect to all of the agreement rather than invalidating some part of it.[34]

Public interest

A particularly interesting example is found in the Restatement Second in connection with the interpretation of standardized agreements: "Such a writing is interpreted whenever reasonable as treating alike all those similarly situated, without regard to their knowledge or understanding of the standard terms of the writing."[35] This rule plainly subordinates the meaning that an individual party may have attached to the contract language to the goal of equality of treatment for parties that are similarly situated. But that equality is attained by asking what a reasonable party in the position of the adhering party would think the language meant, not what a reasonable party in the position of the profferor of the form would think such a reasonable party would think. In recent decades, many courts have gone beyond this and applied to contracts of insurance a "reasonable expectations" test, giving an interpretation that an insured would reasonably expect even if it is contrary to the insurer's expressed intention.[36]

Standardized agreements

The rules discussed in this section have made use of intrinsic aids, derived from the contract itself and not dependent on outside circumstances. To what extent will a court also look to extrinsic aids for guidance in interpreting contract language?

§7.12. Evidence of Prior Negotiations. It has already been pointed out that in interpreting a contract, a court should be free to look to all the relevant circumstances surrounding the transaction.[1] A court may, for instance, consider evidence of prior negotiations, even if it shows that both parties attached to the contract language a meaning different from the one that would ordinarily be given to it.[2] All courts agree that the parol evidence rule permits them to do this, even though the agreement is integrated, as long as the language itself is

Effect of integration

---

[34] See the discussion of interpretation affected by public policy in §5.1 *supra*.

[35] Restatement Second §211(2). *See* the discussions of the situation where no meaning is attached in §7.9 *supra* and of the traditional view in §7.14 *infra*.

[36] Max True Plastering Co. v. United States Fidelity & Guar. Co., 912 P.2d 861 (Okl. 1996) (underlying principle that reasonable expectations should be honored "has been recognized by the majority of jurisdictions which have considered the issue").

The insured's expectations might be based, for example, on the insurer's policy description or marketing practices or on notions of fairness. *See* the discussion of the standard of reasonableness in §7.10 *supra*.

§7.12 [1] See the discussion of the point that a court should look to all circumstances in §7.10 *supra*.

[2] See the discussion of the prevailing view in §7.10 *supra*.

"ambiguous" or "vague."[3] Controversy arises, however, when it is contended that the language is "clear," "plain," and "unambiguous."[4]

Imperfect analogy to statutes

In the field of statutory interpretation, the plain meaning rule, where it persists, bars the use of legislative history to interpret *statutory* language that is "clear on its face." To what extent is there an analogous rule that bars the use of evidence of prior negotiations to interpret *contract* language that is "clear on its face"? To what extent, in other words, is there a plain meaning rule for contracts? Even the rule's opponents would have to admit that it appears to have retained more vitality in the field of contract interpretation than in the area of statutory interpretation. The explanation for this continued vitality may be that the analogy is far from perfect. If legislative history is used in statutory interpretation, it is documentary in form and its evaluation is in the hands of judges, but this is not the case if evidence of prior negotiations is used in contract interpretation. This has two consequences for contract interpretation. First, if evidence of prior negotiations is excluded, disputes can be disposed of more expeditiously: pre-trial discovery can be limited and summary judgment will be more available.[5] A rule that excludes such evidence naturally finds favor with judges conscious of the burdens imposed on them by disputes over contract interpretation.[6] Second, if evidence of prior negotiations is excluded, issues of contract interpretation will more often be left to judges as issues of "law" rather than "fact": issues to be addressed by the trial judge rather than by a jury and to be reviewed on a plenary rather than a clearly erroneous basis. A rule that excludes such evidence has an obvious appeal to appellate judges confident of their own abilities in resolving issues of contract interpretation.[7] In this respect, the rationale for excluding evidence of prior negotiations when it is offered to interpret language may differ from the rationale for excluding such evidence when it is offered to contradict or add to language.[8] In addition, judges may be

---

[3] Hokama v. Relinc Corp., 559 P.2d 279 (Haw. 1977) (all evidence outside writing is to be considered "if there is any doubt or controversy as to the meaning of the language embodying their bargain").

[4] *See generally* Farnsworth, "Meaning" in the Law of Contracts, 76 Yale L.J. 939, 957-65 (1967) (from which this section of this treatise is adapted).

[5] Wards Co. v. Stamford Ridgeway Assocs., 761 F.2d 117 (2d Cir. 1985) (summary judgment is "improper unless the terms of the agreement are 'wholly unambiguous,'" and if moving party cannot show this "a material issue exists concerning the parties' intent, and the non-moving party has a right to present extrinsic evidence").

[6] Federal Deposit Ins. Corp. v. W.R. Grace & Co., 877 F.2d 614 (7th Cir. 1989) (Posner, J.: parties may prefer "to avoid the expense and uncertainty of having a jury resolve a dispute between them").

[7] *See* AM Intl. v. Graphic Mgt. Assocs., 44 F.3d 572 (7th Cir. 1995) (Posner, C.J.: though "the rules do not differentiate between judge and jury," there is no doubt that "suspicion of juries plays a role in the doctrines that limit the admissibility of evidence by which a party seeks to avoid the consequences of his written words"). See also the discussions of judge or jury and of scope of review in §7.14 *infra*.

[8] See the discussion of the true basis of the rule in §7.2 *supra*.

more skeptical of the authenticity of proffered evidence of prior negotiations than of asserted legislative history.

The essence of a plain meaning rule is that there are some instances in which the meaning of language, when taken in context, is so clear that evidence of prior negotiations cannot be used in its interpretation. If this is true, a court must make a preliminary determination that the meaning of the language in dispute falls short of that degree of clarity before admitting such evidence to interpret it. Can the meaning of language ever be that clear? Corbin thought not: "No parol evidence that is offered can be said to vary or contradict a writing until by process of interpretation the meaning of the writing is determined."[9] On this view, the plain meaning rule should be discarded and evidence of prior negotiations freely admitted with no preliminary determination as to clarity.[10] The Supreme Court of Alaska has done just this by abandoning the rule "that resort to extrinsic evidence can take place only after a preliminary finding of ambiguity" on the ground that it is "artificial and unduly cumbersome" and "offers no advantage over one which initially turns to extrinsic evidence for such light as it may shed on the reasonable expectations of the parties."[11] A few other courts have shown sympathy for Corbin's view,[12] but the overwhelming majority of courts retains some kind of plain meaning rule.

Under a plain meaning rule there is a two stage process. In the first stage the court makes a preliminary determination of whether the language in dispute lacks the required degree of clarity before going on to the second stage, that of interpretation. Only if the court determines that the language lacks this required degree of clarity will evidence of prior negotiations be admitted during the second stage for the purpose of interpretation. A question then arises as to whether evidence of prior negotiations is admissible during the first stage to aid the court in its preliminary determination, and it is this question about which controversy has swirled. Can evidence of prior negotiations be used to show whether contract language lacks the required degree of clarity, whether it is "ambiguous" as opposed to "plain"?

---

[9]Corbin, The Parol Evidence Rule, 53 Yale L.J. 603, 622 (1944). The UNIDROIT Principles state flatly that even in the face of a merger clause, prior statements or agreements "may be used to interpret the writing"). UNIDROIT Principles 2.17. The Principles, however, are designed for use primarily in arbitration.

[10]Even on this view, evidence of prior negotiations might be excluded if it *contradicted* the language in question. *See* Taylor v. State Farm Mut. Auto. Ins. Co., 854 P.2d 1134 (Ariz. 1993) ("even under the Corbin view, the court can admit evidence for *interpretation* but must stop short of *contradiction*"). *See* the discussion of the meaning of *consistent* in §7.3 *supra.*

[11]Alyeska Pipeline Serv. Co. v. O'Kelley, 645 P.2d 767, 771 n.1 (Alaska 1982).

[12]Hilton Hotels Corp. v. Butch Lewis Prods., 808 P.2d 919 (Nev. 1991) (approving instruction to jury to consider "all of the circumstances leading to the contract, such as negotiations and statements of the parties"). Cases dealing with circumstances other than prior negotiations are sometimes misleadingly cited in support of Corbin's view on prior negotiations. *See* the discussion of the "four corners" and "context" rules *infra.*

At times it is misleadingly suggested that a plain meaning rule excludes more than evidence of prior negotiations during the first stage. Such a rule, under which the court cannot look to any circumstances outside the writing to determine whether the language lacks the required degree of clarity, is often called a "four corners rule."[13] It is sometimes associated with a distinction, attributed to Sir Francis Bacon, between latent and patent ambiguity[14] or intrinsic and extrinsic ambiguity.[15] But even under a plain meaning rule, evidence of surrounding circumstances, as distinguished from evidence of prior negotiations, should be admitted during the first stage.[16] The Supreme Court of Washington has aptly described this as a "context rule" and has wisely rejected "the theory that ambiguity in the meaning of contract language must exist before evidence of the surrounding circumstances is admissible."[17] But evidence of prior negotiations is a different matter.

Restrictive view   Under the older and more restrictive view, evidence of prior negotiations is inadmissible to show this during the first stage. The determination of whether the language in dispute lacks the required degree of clarity is made by the trial judge on the basis of the language itself, in the light of the surrounding circumstances but without regard to prior negotiations.[18] Evidence of prior

---

[13] Treemont, Inc. v. Hawley, 886 P.2d 589 (Wyo. 1994) (if "provisions are clear and unambiguous, our examination is confined to the 'four corners' of the document").

[14] F. Bacon, A Collection of Some Principal Rules and Maximes of the Common Law 90-91 (1597) ("There be two sorts of ambiguities of words, the one is *ambiguitas patens*, and the other *latens*. *Patens* is that which appears to be ambiguous upon the deed or instrument. *Latens* is that which seemeth certain and without ambiguity, for any thing that appeareth upon the deed or instrument, but there is some collateral matter out of the deed, that breedeth the ambiguity."). *See* Allegheny Intl. v. Allegheny Ludlum Steel Corp., 40 F.3d 1416 (3d Cir. 1994) ("Supreme Court of Pennsylvania has identified two types of ambiguity," patent and latent).

[15] Interim Health Care of No. Ill. v. Interim Health Care, 225 F.3d 876 (7th Cir. 2000) ("Intrinsic ambiguity exists when the agreement itself is unclear, and extrinsic ambiguity exists when a perfectly clear agreement is unclear when applied to the real-world context of the deal.").

[16] Florida East Coast Ry. Co. v. CSX Transp., 42 F.3d 1125 (7th Cir. 1994) (Florida law: "language of a contract cannot be properly understood if it is read without attention to the circumstances"). Restatement (Second) §202 cmt. *a* explains that the rule that language is interpreted "in the light of all the circumstances" does not depend "upon any determination that there is an ambiguity."

[17] Berg v. Hudesman, 801 P.2d 222, 230 (Wash. 1990).

[18] Holmes even argued against the acceptance of evidence of special agreements between the parties as to the meaning of words, sometimes referred to as "private conventions" or "codes," if the language was plain. He rejected the notion that the parties could show "that when they wrote five hundred feet it should mean one hundred inches, or that Bunker Hill Monument should signify Old South Church." Holmes, The Theory of Legal Interpretation, 12 Harv. L. Rev. 417, 420 (1899), adapted from his opinion in Goode v. Riley, 28 N.E. 228 (Mass. 1891).

Some advocates of the restrictive view have shown more tolerance of private conventions or codes than of mere informal understandings. Learned Hand, for example, conceded that the parties' shared meaning might prevail over the "natural meaning" of the words they used if there was "some mutual agreement between them to that effect." See the discussion of the objectivist solution in §7.9 *supra*.

negotiations does not come in until the second stage, that of interpretation, and then only if it has first been determined that the language lacks the required degree of clarity. This view was reflected in the first Restatement[19] and still finds expression in many judicial opinions.[20] Courts following this view have insisted that a party seeking to introduce such extrinsic evidence be specific in pointing to the claimed lack of clarity.[21]

The restrictive view is defended on the grounds that it simplifies the process of interpretation in many cases by eliminating from consideration evidence of prior negotiations and that it gives predictability in the interpretation of commonly used terms. As the Supreme Court of Pennsylvania argued, "the plain meaning approach enhances the extent to which contracts may be relied upon by contributing to the security of belief that the final expression of *consensus ad idem* will not later be construed to import a meaning other than that clearly expressed."[22] And as Judith Kaye wrote for the New York Court of Appeals, the "rule imparts 'stability to commercial transactions,'" a consideration that is "all the more compelling in the context of real property transactions, where commercial certainty is a paramount concern," while an "analysis that begins with consideration of extrinsic evidence of what the parties meant . . . unnecessarily denigrates the contract and unsettles the law."[23]

Advantage of restrictive view

With a decline in judicial reverence for the written word and a growing recognition that the meaning of language may vary greatly according to the circumstances, the restrictive view has come under attack even though it may tend to simplify the process of interpretation. If it is recognized that all language is infected with ambiguity and vagueness and that even language that seems on its face to have only one possible meaning may take on a different meaning when all the circumstances are disclosed, it is difficult to require a court to ask the threshold question: is the language on its face "ambiguous" or "vague" as opposed to "clear" or "plain"?[24] A liberal view has therefore emerged.

Dissatisfaction with restrictive view

---

[19] Restatement §230 & cmt. *a* ("oral statements by the parties of what they intended the written language to mean are excluded, though these statements might show the parties gave their words a meaning that would not otherwise be apparent").

[20] W.W.W. Assocs. v. Giancontieri, 566 N.E.2d 639 (N.Y. 1990) (Kaye, J.: "extrinsic evidence should [not] be considered in order to create an ambiguity in the agreement"). *W.W.W. Assocs.* was followed but modified in Kass v. Kass, 696 N.E.2d 174 (N.Y. 1998) (Kaye, C.J.: ambiguity "is determined by looking within the four corners of the document, not to outside sources," but "in deciding whether an agreement is ambiguous courts 'should . . . consider the relation of the parties and the circumstances under which it was executed' ").

[21] Hunt Ltd. v. Lifschultz Fast Freight, 889 F.2d 1274 (2d Cir. 1989) (language "does not become ambiguous merely because the parties urge different interpretations").

[22] Steuart v. McChesney, 444 A.2d 659, 663 (Pa. 1982).

[23] W.W.W. Assocs. v. Giancontieri, *supra* note 20, at 642, 643.

[24] Hamilton v. Wosepka, 154 N.W.2d 164 (Iowa 1967) (evidence of "antecedent negotiations" admissible because proof of "circumstances may make a meaning plain and clear when in the absence of such proof some other meaning may also have seemed plain and clear"). Indeed, one court has held that a clause that would forbid resort to prior negotiations for the purpose of

Liberal view

It is often said that this liberal view rejects the plain meaning rule, but since there are still two stages it is more accurate to say that it relaxes the rule. Under the liberal view, evidence of prior negotiations is admissible during the first stage for the limited purpose of enabling the trial judge to determine whether the language in dispute lacks the required degree of clarity. Thus the trial judge need not make that determination, as the judge must under the restrictive view, on the basis of the language and the surrounding circumstances alone. This appears to be the position taken by the Restatement Second, which explains in comment that "determination of meaning or ambiguity should only be made in the light of the . . . preliminary negotiations."[25]

Limits of liberal view

Even under this liberal view, evidence of prior negotiations is admissible during the first stage only if it is offered for the purpose of "interpreting" the writing and not to "contradict" it or, in the case of a complete integration, to "add to" it.[26] The question then is: where does "interpretation" end and "contradiction" or "addition" begin? The answer must be that interpretation ends with the resolution of problems that derive from the failure of language, that is to say, with the resolution of ambiguity and vagueness. Accordingly, even under the liberal view, extrinsic evidence is admissible during the first stage only where it is relevant to ambiguity or vagueness rather than inaccuracy or incompleteness. Furthermore, the mere fact that a contract is inartfully worded or clumsily arranged does not necessarily mean that it lacks the required degree of clarity.

Example of *Pacific Gas & Electric*

The liberal view was famously expounded in *Pacific Gas & Electric Co. v. G.W. Thomas Drayage & Rigging Co.* As part of a contract to do work on a steam turbine for a utility power company, the contractor agreed to "indemnify" the utility company "against all loss, damage, expense and liability" resulting from injury to property connected with the work. When, during the work, the turbine cover fell and damaged the rotor, the contractor refused to pay the utility company the amount that the company spent on repairs. The contractor argued that the word *indemnify* referred only to compensation for liability incurred by the utility company as a result of injury to the property of third parties and not to payment for loss to the company's own property. The trial court refused to allow the contractor to introduce evidence of prior negotiations to support this argument, because the "plain language" of the agreement covered loss to

---

interpretation is void as against public policy. Garden State Plaza Corp. v. S.S. Kresge Co., 189 A.2d 448 (N.J. Super. 1963) (clause would have court "wearing judicial blinders"). It may be that this would only be so if the disputed language lacked the required degree of clarity.

[25] Restatement Second §212 cmt. *b*. (The comment's use of the word "meaning" in addition to "ambiguity" leaves some room for doubt.)

[26] HLO Land Ownership v. City of Hartford, 727 A.2d 1260 (Conn. 1999) (agreeing that phrase is ambiguous but concluding that evidence that "would have gone beyond explaining the meaning of the phrase" was "not admissible because it would have varied or contradicted the contract"). See the discussions of legal effect in §7.3 *supra*.

the utility company's property.[27] The Supreme Court of California reversed, Roger Traynor characterizing the "judicial belief in the possibility of perfect verbal expression" as a "remnant of a primitive faith in the inherent potency and inherent meaning of words" and concluding that the test is not whether the writing "appears to the court to be plain and unambiguous on its face, but whether the offered evidence is relevant to prove a meaning to which the language of the instrument is reasonably susceptible." There is, however, still a two-stage process, for "rational interpretation requires at least a preliminary consideration of all credible evidence offered to prove the intention of the parties." Only if the trial judge decides, after considering this evidence during the first stage, "that the language of a contract in the light of all the circumstances, is 'fairly susceptible of either one of the two interpretations contended for' " — that it lacks the required degree of clarity — will the judge admit "extrinsic evidence relevant to prove either of such meanings" during the second stage, that of interpretation.[28] The result would have been the same even under the restrictive view, however, for the court added in a footnote that *indemnify* has a double sense and that therefore the "exclusion of extrinsic evidence in this case would be error even under a rule that excluded such evidence when the instrument appeared to the court to be clear and unambiguous on its face."[29]

Less than a year later, however, the Supreme Court of California was presented with a case that required it to make a clearer choice between the two views. In *Delta Dynamics v. Arioto*, a lock manufacturer sued a distributor for damages caused by the distributor's alleged failure to sell its promised yearly quota of units. The contract was "subject to termination" by the manufacturer in the event of such a failure, and the distributor sought to show that termination, and not damages, was the manufacturer's exclusive remedy. The trial judge excluded evidence, offered by the distributor, of conversations during the negotiations. The Supreme Court held that this was error, since the provision that the contract was "subject to termination" was "reasonably susceptible of the meaning contended for" and there was "nothing in the rest of the contract to preclude that interpretation."[30] Three of seven judges dissented, one lamenting the "serious impediment to the certainty required in commercial transactions," for the "written word, heretofore deemed immutable, is now at all times subject to alteration by self-serving recitals based upon fading memories of antecedent

Subsequent history in California

---

[27] According to the Supreme Court, the contractor's offer of proof included not only admissions of the utility company's agents, presumably relating to the negotiations, but also the contractor's conduct under similar contracts with the utility company. As to the latter, *see* the discussion of course of dealing in §7.13 *infra*. From a brief of the contractor, it appears that the offer of proof included testimony by the drafter of the contract, as an adverse witness, as to what he intended the indemnity provision to cover. Appellant's Opening Brief in District Court of Appeal at 6, citing Record of Trial at 47, 296.

[28] 442 P.2d 641, 644 (Cal. 1968).

[29] 442 P.2d at 646 n.9.

[30] 446 P.2d 785, 787 (1968).

events."[31] The result argued for by the dissenters could more logically have been supported on the ground that the evidence was properly excluded by the trial judge on the ground that it was *not* "relevant to prove a meaning to which the language of the instrument is reasonably susceptible." It was not offered to *interpret* the words "subject to termination" but instead to add a term so that the contract would read "subject to termination *as an exclusive remedy*," and this was prohibited by the parol evidence rule.[32]

Sometimes no difference in result

In three kinds of cases the restrictive and liberal views lead to the same result. First, if what is involved is not interpretation but contradiction or addition, the admissibility of evidence of prior negotiations is not affected by either view.[33] Second, if what is involved is interpretation but the dispute is over the admissibility of evidence of the surrounding circumstances that does not include prior negotiations, the evidence is admissible under both views.[34] Third, if what is involved is interpretation and the dispute is over the admissibility of evidence of prior negotiations but the language in dispute lacks the required degree of clarity without resort to that evidence, the evidence is admissible under both views.[35]

Criticism in Trident

Two decades after the decision in *Pacific Gas & Electric*, the liberal view as expounded in that case was vehemently criticized by the Ninth Circuit, speaking through Judge Alex Kozinski in *Trident Center v. Connecticut General Life Insurance Co.* A promissory note provided that the borrower "shall not have the right to prepay the principal amount hereof in whole or in part before January 1996." Another clause, however, provided that in "the event of a prepayment resulting from a default hereunder . . . prior to January 10, 1996, the prepayment fee will be ten percent (10%)." The borrower contended that this clause gave it the option of prepaying the loan at any time if it was willing to incur the prepayment fee. The court concluded that the first provision, particularly in the light of the contract as a whole, "leaves no room for this construction." Nevertheless, *Pacific Gas & Electric*, "casts a long shadow of uncertainty over all transactions negotiated and executed under the law of California," for "it matters not how clearly a contract is written, nor how completely it is integrated, nor how carefully it is negotiated, nor how squarely it addresses the issue before the court; the contract cannot be rendered impervious to attack by parol evidence." Extrinsic evidence was therefore admissible to show "that the parties had agreed [borrower] could repay at any time within the first 12 years

---

[31] 446 P.2d at 788 (Mosk, J.).

[32] See the discussion of the example of *Gianni* in §7.2 *supra*.

[33] See the discussions of the liberal view and of subsequent history in California *supra*.

[34] See the discussion of the "four corners" and "context" rules *supra*.

[35] See the discussion of the example of *Pacific Gas & Electric supra*.

Under the liberal view evidence of prior negotiations is also admissible to give additional support to a meaning that would otherwise be regarded as sufficiently clear under the restrictive view. This would not, however, give a different result, though there is a possibility that it might make the resolution of the dispute less expeditious.

by tendering the full amount plus a 10 percent prepayment fee."[36] The court did not address *Pacific Gas & Electric's* requirement of a first stage in which the language must be determined to be "reasonably susceptible" of the asserted meaning. Had it done so, it might well have concluded that the evidence was inadmissible even under the liberal view because its purpose was not to give the language such a meaning but rather to contradict it. A few months later the Ninth Circuit cast doubt on the "broad language in *Trident* [that] suggests that under California law courts must always admit extrinsic evidence to determine the meaning of disputed language." Though the "case must proceed beyond the pleadings so that the court may consider the evidence," if the court then "determines that the contract is not reasonably susceptible to the interpretation advanced, the parol evidence rule operates to exclude the evidence" and the court may grant a motion for summary judgment.[37] Richard Posner observed that the doctrine of extrinsic ambiguity "makes it difficult to decide contract cases on the pleadings," but noted that "California decisions since *Trident* have declined to endorse that decision's interpretation of California law."[38] Conflicting currents of opinion on the proper role of evidence of prior negotiations in contract interpretation assure that controversy will continue to swirl about the plain meaning rule.

Having considered the admissibility of extrinsic evidence of prior negotiations, we turn next to the admissibility of other kinds of extrinsic evidence.

§7.13. **Evidence of Course of Dealing, Usage, and Course of Performance.** Sometimes a party to an agreement contends that it is to be read in the light of a prior course of dealing between the parties, a usage current in a trade, vocation, or place involved in the transaction, or a subsequent course of performance between the parties. Such contentions are especially common in disputes over commercial contracts, and the Uniform Commercial Code contains an important provision on course of dealing, usage of trade, and course of performance.[1] Because this section is found in Article 1, General Provisions, it

Importance of Code

---

[36] 847 F.2d 564, 567, 568, 569 (9th Cir. 1988).

[37] A. Kemp Fisheries v. Castle & Cooke, 852 F.2d 493, 496-97 n.2 (9th Cir. 1988).

[38] Bank v. Truck Ins. Exch., 51 F.3d 736, 737, 738 (7th Cir. 1995).

§7.13 [1] UCC 1-303. Both the Vienna Convention and the UNIDROIT Principles contain provisions on practices that the parties have established between themselves and on usages, both requiring that a usage be one that in international trade is "widely known to" and "regularly observed by" parties in the trade concerned. CISG 9(2), UNIDROIT Principles 1.8(2). We are not concerned here with the incorporation by explicit reference of written "usages," "customs," or "trade codes." See note 22 *infra*.

For a suggestion "that the Code's conception of widely known commercial standards and usages that are geographically coextensive with the scope of trade does not correspond to merchant reality but rather is a legal fiction," *see* Bernstein, The Questionable Empirical Basis of Article 2's Incorporation Strategy: A Preliminary Study, 66 U. Chi. L. Rev. 710, 777 (1999).

is not limited to agreements for the sale of goods but applies to all commercial contracts.[2] Its principles extend by analogy to noncommercial contracts as well.

Course of dealing   The Code describes a course of dealing as "a sequence of conduct concerning previous transactions between the parties to a particular transaction that is fairly to be regarded as establishing a common basis of understanding for interpreting their expressions and other conduct."[3] The concept of a course of dealing, therefore, is relevant only when the parties to an agreement have dealt with each other in similar transactions on previous occasions. Under the Code a sequence of conduct by the parties in their earlier transactions "may give particular meaning to specific terms . . . and may supplement or qualify the terms" of their later agreement.[4] The Code does not make it a condition that the language be ambiguous. The words *supplement or qualify* make it clear that conduct may have an effect beyond mere interpretation of those terms. Although the term *course of dealing* has been popularized by the Code, the underlying idea that an agreement is to be read in the light of the parties' previous dealings is not novel and has force even in situations to which the Code is not literally applicable.[5]

Usage or custom   The Code describes a usage of trade as a "practice or method of dealing having such regularity of observance in a place, vocation, or trade as to justify an expectation that it will be observed with respect to the transaction in question."[6] A usage may be limited to a particular geographical area or to a particular kind of activity, or it may be limited in both ways. Under the Code a "usage of trade in the vocation or trade in which [the parties] are engaged or of which they are or should be aware is relevant in ascertaining the meaning of the parties' agreement, may give meaning to specific terms of the agreement, and may supplement or qualify the terms of the agreement."[7] As in the case of course of dealing, the Code does not make it a condition that the language be ambiguous.[8]

---

[2] See the discussion of the scope of Article 2 in §1.9 *supra*.

[3] UCC 1-303(b). A course of dealing should not be confused with the prior negotiations that resulted in the agreement in question, especially because the Code relaxes the parol evidence rule as to course of dealing. *See* the discussion of the effect of a writing *infra*.

[4] UCC 1-303(d).

[5] *See* Restatement Second §223, which states an analogous rule.

[6] UCC 1-303(c). As Comment 6 makes clear, "usages may be either general to trade or particular to a special branch of trade." *See* Williams v. Curtin, 807 F.2d 1046 (D.C. Cir. 1986) (usages of cabbage trade in interstate market rather than in Georgia); Nanakuli Paving & Rock Co. v. Shell Oil Co., 664 F.2d 772 (9th Cir. 1981) (usage of "the asphaltic paving trade in Hawaii, rather than the purchase and sale of asphalt alone").

[7] UCC 1-303(d). Although there is no requirement that the usage be reasonable, it cannot vary a rule of law, such as the statute of frauds, that the parties could not vary by explicit agreement. Rudiger Charolais Ranches v. Van De Graaf Ranches, 994 F.2d 670 (9th Cir. 1993) ("a custom or practice which violates a statute is not a reasonable commercial standard").

[8] C-Thru Container Corp. v. Midland Mfg. Co., 533 N.W.2d 542 (Iowa 1995) (rejecting "argument that evidence of usage of trade is admissible only when the contract is ambiguous").

470

The term *usage of trade* is relatively new and is favored by the Code over the more traditional and narrower term *custom.*⁹ However, the underlying principle, which is that an agreement is to be read in the light of a common practice or method of dealing, is an old one. This principle extends to "usages" generally, even though they may not be "of trade" and therefore not subject to the Code.[10] As in the case of a course of dealing, the Code's use of the words *supplement or qualify* makes clear that more may be involved than mere interpretation of contract language, although many cases involve no more than that.[11]

Reliance on usages to "supplement" the terms of an agreement has sometimes been criticized as an unwarranted encroachment on the general rules of law that would otherwise be used to perform this task. However, the Code, according to its commentary, rejects "those cases which see evidence of 'custom' as representing an effort to displace or negate 'established rules of law'" and asserts that usages "are the framework of common understanding controlling any general rules of law which hold only when there is no such understanding."[12] In a study of the lumber industry in Wisconsin, a noted legal historian found that the "generality in contract concepts . . . was a source of strength, so far as it meant that the legal order could efficiently and smoothly adapt itself to varied circumstances. But there was weakness, so far as contract law achieved this generality by intense devotion to a quite limited range of policies, abstracted from the living context in which they arose." He went on to suggest that by allowing proof of usage to remedy this weakness, "lumber-contract case law made its most distinctive adaptation to the peculiarities of the industry."[13]

Modifying general rules

Whether a usage exists is a matter of fact rather than law. "The existence and scope of . . . a usage," the Code provides, "must be proved as facts."[14] A party commonly shows a usage by producing expert witnesses who are familiar with the activity or place in which the usage is observed.[15] Their testimony must establish that the practice or method of dealing has "such regularity in

Proof of usage

---

[9]For the difference between *usage* and *custom*, see the discussion of proof of usage *infra*. The Code makes a passing reference to custom in UCC 1-103(a)(2) ("to permit the continued expansion of commercial practices through custom, usage, and agreement of the parties").

[10]*See* Restatement Second §§219-222, which state analogous rules.

[11]For a representative Code case involving only interpretation, *see* Williams v. Curtin, *supra* note 6 ("slaw cabbage"). *But see* the cases described in the discussions of a case excluding evidence and of a case admitting evidence *infra*, in which more than interpretation was involved.

[12]UCC 1-303 cmt. 3.

[13]W. Hurst, Law and Economic Growth: The Legal History of the Lumber Industry in Wisconsin 1836-1915 290 (1964).

[14]UCC 1-303(c). The Code does not require the party that seeks to show a usage to plead it, but under UCC 1-303(g) the party offering evidence of a usage must give the other party notice "sufficient to prevent unfair surprise."

[15]For example, *see* Frigaliment Importing Co. v. B.N.S. Intl. Sales Corp., 190 F. Supp. 116 (S.D.N.Y. 1960) (operator of chicken eviscerating plant and employee of publisher of market report on poultry trade testified as to meaning of *chicken*). If the dispute is heard by one or more arbitrators who are themselves experts familiar with usages, such testimony may be unnecessary.

a place, vocation or trade as to justify an expectation that it will be observed with respect to the transaction in question." As the Code commentary points out, however, this is a considerable relaxation of the "ancient English tests for proof of 'custom,'" which required not only that the custom be notorious but also that it "be 'ancient or immemorial,' 'universal' or the like."[16]

Awareness of usage

A party, having proved a usage, must also prove that the other party is chargeable with knowledge of it. The first party may do this by showing that at the time the contract was made the other party either was actually aware of the usage or should have been aware of it. Under the Code, a party that is engaged in the vocation or trade in question is presumed to have the requisite knowledge.[17] A party that enters a vocation or trade, therefore, is subject to usages of which that party may not in fact be aware.[18] It has been suggested that this assumption has "the salutary effect of inducing newcomers to master the language of the trade promptly."[19] But it goes well beyond the rule relating to a course of dealing, as to which a party could not help but be aware, and cases are rare in which a court has charged a party with a usage in a vocation or trade in which the party is not engaged.[20]

Course of performance

Sometimes the conduct of the parties after the contract is made indicates the meaning that they attach to the contract language subsequently in dispute. Such a "course of performance," which consists of conduct subsequent to the agreement, should not be confused with a "course of dealing," which consists of conduct prior to the agreement in question. A course of performance — sometimes called "practical construction — is often influential. As the Supreme Court of Arkansas has said,[21] "a court will accord considerable weight to the construction the parties themselves give to it, evidenced by subsequent statements, acts, and conduct." Conduct bearing on interpretation usually occurs during the course of performance of the contract. The Code defines a "course of performance" as "a sequence of conduct between the parties to a particular transaction that exists if" their agreement "involves repeated occasions for performance by a party" and "the other party, with knowledge of the nature of the performance and opportunity for objection to it, accepts the performance or acquiesces in it without objection."[22] Although

---

[16]UCC 1-303 cmt. 4 ("full recognition is thus available for new usages and for usages currently observed by the great majority of decent dealers, even though dissidents ready to cut corners do not agree").

[17]UCC 1-303(d) ("in the vocation or trade in which they are engaged").

[18]Foxco Indus. v. Fabric World, 595 F.2d 976 (5th Cir. 1979) (buyer bound by usage of trade association as to meaning of "first quality," although it was not a member and "did not know of the industry's usage").

[19]R. Posner, Economic Analysis of Law 98 (6th ed. 2002).

[20]Mieske v. Bartell Drug Co., 593 P.2d 1308 (Wash. 1979) (retail customer of film processor not bound by usages among film processors).

[21]Sturgis v. Skokos, 977 S.W.2d 217, 223 (Ark. 1998).

[22]UCC 1-303(a). Both the Vienna Convention and the UNIDROIT Principles make any subsequent conduct relevant. CISG 8(3), UNIDROIT Principles 4(3)(c).

under the Code's former provision, course of performance was relevant only "to determine the meaning of the agreement,"[23] Article 1 now provides that course of performance may "may supplement or qualify the terms of the agreement."[24]

As in the cases of usage and course of dealing, the Code does not make it a condition that the language be ambiguous.[25] The concept of a course of performance is not limited to the sale of goods and has long been applied to contracts of all kinds.[26] It is sometimes difficult to draw the line between conduct that is the basis for a course of performance, on the one hand, and conduct that is the basis for waiver or modification, on the other.[27] One distinction is that though a single occasion of conduct may result in waiver or modification, a course of performance under the Code is said to require "a sequence of conduct" when there are "repeated occasions for performance."[28] Another is that while it is desirable to confine waiver to conditions, course of performance is not so limited.[29]

Ambiguity not required

It is not easy to explain why subsequent conduct should be relevant to what the parties intended when the contract was made.[30] Perhaps the most satisfactory explanation is that it operates as an admission. If that is so, presumably the reason for requiring more than one occasion of conduct is to justify a court in inferring an admission from the conduct. It would then seem that if the conduct takes the form of a statement (and surely statements must be at least as effective as other conduct in this regard), a single statement from which an inference can clearly be drawn should suffice.

Rationale

To what extent is a party precluded from showing a course of dealing, a usage, or a course of performance by the fact that the agreement in question is a written one? On this important question the Code has two opposing provisions.

Effect of a writing

---

[23] UCC-O 2-208(1); J.W.S. Delavau, Inc. v. Eastern Am. Transp. & Warehousing, 810 A.2d 672 (Pa. Super, 2002) (" 'course of performance' can only be used to interpret, not to supplement").

[24] UCC 1-303(d).

[25] Courts have, however, occasionally imposed such a requirement where the Code provision does not apply. Paradise Restaurant v. Somerset Enters., 671 A.2d 1258 (Vt. 1995) ("principle applies only where there is an ambiguity").

[26] The provision on course of performance, which originally appeared in UCC-O 2-208, was moved to UCC 1-303 in the revision of Article 1. Restatement Second §202(4) presents course of performance as a generally applicable rule. *See* Wurst v. Blue River Bank, 454 N.W.2d 665 (Neb. 1990) (proper to consider "parties' interpretative conduct in relation to performance" of loan agreement).

[27] *See* UCC 1-303(f) ("course of performance shall be relevant to show a waiver or modification of any term inconsistent with such course of performance").

[28] UCC 1-303(a).

[29] See the discussion of the meaning of waiver in § 8.5 *infra*.

[30] On this reasoning course of performance is not accepted in English law. James Miller & Partners v. Whitworth Street Estates, [1970] A.C. 583 (H.L. 1970) (Lord Reid: "Otherwise one might have the result that a contract meant one thing the day it was signed, but by reason of subsequent events meant something different a month or a year later.").

Under the Code's formulation of the parol evidence rule, a writing may be supplemented by evidence of course of dealing, usage of trade, or course of performance even if it is a complete integration.[31] There is no requirement that an ambiguity be demonstrated, and there is no prohibition against showing a meaning different from the one that would otherwise be apparent. Under the Code's provisions, however,

> the express terms of an agreement and any applicable course of performance, course of dealing, or usage of trade must be construed whenever reasonable as consistent with each other.

Code's hierarchy   If such an interpretation is unreasonable, the Code establishes a hierarchy in which express terms prevail over course of dealing, usage, and course of performance, but course of performance prevails over both course of dealing and usage, and course of dealing prevails over usage.[32] Thus evidence will only be admitted to show a course of dealing, usage of trade, or course of performance that is "consistent" with the express terms; otherwise the terms alone will control. The question is then: What is meant by "consistent"? If the evidence is offered merely for the purpose of interpretation, to "give particular meaning to . . . terms of an agreement," the Code commentary suggests that it will be admissible unless the course of dealing or usage of trade is "carefully negated" by the writing.[33] As in the case of a partial integration, there is no requirement that the writing be ambiguous in order for the evidence to be admitted.[34] This, however, merely rejects the plain meaning rule as to such evidence when it is offered for the purpose of interpretation. In contrast to a plain meaning rule, under which evidence is not considered for the purpose of interpretation until there has been an evaluation of the clarity of the written contract, a test of consistency requires a consideration of the evidence of usage in order to determine whether it comports with the language of the written contract.[35] The controversial cases under the Code are those in which evidence is introduced not to interpret but to "supplement or qualify" terms of the agreement. In these cases courts have differed as to whether the evidence is admissible.

Example of Division of Triple-T   In *Division of Triple T Service v. Mobil Oil Corp.*, the operator of an automobile service station sought to restrain an oil company from terminating its franchise agreement, despite a provision that allowed either party to ter-

---

[31] UCC 2-202. *See* C-Thru Container Corp. v. Midland Mfg. Co., *supra* note 8 ("unlike the common law, parol evidence [of trade usage] may be used to supplement a fully integrated agreement governed by the U.C.C.").

[32] UCC 1-303(e).

[33] UCC 2-202 cmt. 2.

[34] See the discussion of the meaning of *consistent* in §7.3 *supra*.

[35] Under the liberal view of the plain meaning rule, however, the difference between that rule and the consistency test is lessened because evidence is considered for the purpose of evaluating the clarity of the written contract. See the discussion of the liberal view in §7.12 *supra*.

minate the agreement at the end of the franchise period by giving 90 days notice. The operator sought to show a "custom of the gasoline-service industry to renew franchise agreements unless the franchisee has failed in a material respect to adhere to the contract provisions." A lower court in New York barred the evidence, however, holding that "the Code itself codifies the well established rule . . . that evidence of custom or usage in the trade is not admissible where inconsistent with the express terms of the contract," and that in the case before it,

> the express terms of the contract cover the entire area of termination and negate plaintiff's argument that the custom or usage in the trade implicitly adds the words "with cause" in the termination clause . . . . Only language *consistent* with the tenor of the otherwise complete agreement is admissible under the guise of "custom and usage" and the Code effects no change in that doctrine.[36]

The Fourth Circuit displayed a far more tolerant attitude toward evidence of usage in a later case, *Columbia Nitrogen Corp. v. Royster Co.*, in which a seller sued a buyer for breach of a contract to sell phosphate with a "Minimum Tonnage Per Year" of 31,000 tons for each of three years. Phosphate prices had dropped sharply, and the buyer had failed to order the stated minimum for the first year. The buyer offered evidence that "because of uncertain crop and weather conditions, farming practices, and government agricultural programs, express price and quantity terms in contracts for materials in the mixed fertilizer industry are mere projections to be adjusted according to market forces," but the trial court excluded this evidence. The Fourth Circuit held that this was error, although it expressly accepted the conclusion of the New York court in *Division of Triple T* that "the Uniform Commercial Code restates the well established rule that evidence of usage of trade and course of dealing should be excluded whenever it cannot be reasonably construed as consistent with the terms of the contract." The court pointed out that the contract did "not expressly state that course of dealing and usage of trade cannot be used to explain or supplement the written contract" but stopped short of saying that such a general provision would have been decisive.[37] The court concluded that because the contract was "silent about adjusting prices and quantities to reflect a declining market," it was "reasonable to construe this evidence as consistent with the express terms of the contract," and therefore the evidence was admissible.[38] Thus, though both the New York court and the Fourth Circuit used a test of consistency, their applications of that test were inconsistent.

Example of Columbia Nitrogen

---

[36]304 N.Y.S.2d 191, 202-03 (Sup. Ct. 1969), aff'd mem., 311 N.Y.S.2d 961 (App. Div. 1970).

[37]*See* A & A Mechanical v. Thermal Equip. Sales, 998 S.W.2d 505 (Ky. 1999) ("even a merger clause, to overcome the UCC's presumption in favor of admissibility of course of dealing, course of performance, and usage of trade, must expressly refer to such evidence").

[38]451 F.2d 3, 9 (4th Cir. 1971).

Faced with this inconsistency, the Ninth Circuit in *Nanakuli Paving & Rock Co. v. Shell Oil Co.*, propounded a "total negation" test. Although usage may be used to "qualify" an agreement, in the sense of to "cut down" express terms, total negation of such terms will not be permitted. An asphaltic paving contractor claimed that the seller had broken a long-term contract to supply the contractor's requirements of asphalt by failing to provide, as usage required, price protection — holding the price on tonnage that the contractor had already committed through contracts to third parties — even though the express price term was seller's "Posted Price at time of delivery." The court concluded that "a reasonable jury could have found that price protection was incorporated into the . . . agreement . . . and that price protection was reasonably consistent with the express term of seller's posted price at delivery."

> A total negation of that term would be that the buyer was to set the price. It is a less than complete negation of the term that an unstated exception exists at times of price increases, at which times the old price is to be charged, for a certain period or for a specified tonnage, on work already committed at the lower price on nonescalating contracts. Such a usage forms a broad and important exception to the express term, but does not swallow it entirely.[39]

Nanakuli is unlikely, however, to be the final word on the troublesome question of when it is reasonable to read as "consistent" express terms and a usage of trade or, by extension, express terms and a course of dealing or course of performance.

What are the respective roles of judge and jury in interpreting contract language?

§7.14.   Question of Law or Fact.   Is interpretation a question of "law" or "fact"? Since interpretation turns on the meanings that the parties actually attached and reasonably ought to have attached to the language of their agreement, it is indisputably a matter of fact, not of law. Nevertheless, courts have often treated it as a matter of law. The characterization may have three possible consequences. First, it may determine whether the question of interpretation is sent to a jury or resolved by the trial judge. Second, it may determine the scope of review by an appellate court. Third, it may determine whether the decision has *stare decisis* effect in a later case. The proper characterization may depend on which of the three consequences is at issue, since the central question is usually which actor in the judicial process is best equipped to deal with the particular issue of interpretation and the answer to this question will be affected by the choice of actors that is presented. We turn to the three consequences in order.

First, if a question of interpretation is characterized as one of "fact," it is for the jury, while if it is characterized as one of "law," it is for the judge. If

---

[39] Supra note 6, at 805.

the agreement is integrated, questions of interpretation traditionally have been withdrawn from the jury and reserved for the judge by characterizing them as questions of "law."[1] In some instances this practice is justified under the court's general power to treat a question of fact as one of "law" if the jury could reasonably find only one way,[2] but the practice is not limited to such cases. This is another area in which judicial attitudes differ, and it is possible to find a wide variety of statements about the proper role of judge and jury in the interpretation process.

The traditional view is that interpretation is generally for the judge. This view was well stated over a century and a half ago by Justice Story, who thought it "certainly true, as a general rule that the interpretation of written instruments properly belongs to the court and not to the jury," although he admitted that there may be **Traditional view**

> cases in which, from the different senses of the words used, or their obscure and indeterminate reference to unexplained circumstances, the true interpretation of the language may be left to the consideration of the jury for the purpose of carrying into effect the real intention of the parties.[3]

The traditional view may reflect a distrust of unsophisticated, uneducated, and at one time illiterate jurors,[4] but it is widely followed by courts when interpreting integrated writings as to which no extrinsic evidence is introduced.[5]

Some courts, however, have shown greater willingness to send questions of interpretation to the jury. As Henry Friendly expressed it, **Another view**

> with the courts' growing appreciation of Professor Corbin's lesson that words are seldom so "plain and clear" as to exclude proof of surrounding circumstances and other extrinsic aids to interpretation . . . the exception bids fair largely to swallow the supposed general rule . . . . Whether determination of meaning be regarded as a question of fact, a question of law, or just itself, reliance on a jury to resolve ambiguities in the light of extrinsic evidence seems quite as it should

---

§7.14 [1] ERA Commander Realty v. Harrigan, 514 So. 2d 1329 (Ala. 1987) (ambiguity is a question of law "and if the parties' intent can be discerned from reading the contract, then that is also a question of law for the trial judge"). Even though a court treats a question of interpretation as one of law, it may nevertheless be proper to treat a party as having a "burden" as to that question. *See* the discussion of burden as an explanation in §7.9 *supra*.

[2] General Cas. Co. v. Hines, 156 N.W.2d 118 (Iowa 1965) (in interpretation, "application of particular facts to a given case normally rests with the trier of the facts, unless they are such no reasonable man could dispute them, in which case a question for the court alone is presented").

[3] Brown & Co. v. M'Gran, 39 U.S. (14 Pet.) 479, 493 (1840).

[4] For a rare exception to the traditional view, *see* Dobson v. Masonite Corp., 359 F.2d 921 (5th Cir. 1966) (interpretation "is always a question of fact," even where "there was no dispute regarding the existence of the oral contract or its terms").

[5] Sharon Steel Corp. v. Chase Manhattan Bank, 601 F.2d 1039 (2d Cir. 1982) ("meaning of boilerplate provisions" is a matter of law).

be, save where the form or subject matter of a particular contract outruns a jury's competence . . . .[6]

Some courts have followed Judge Friendly's lead and taken the position that a mere preliminary determination by the trial judge that language lacks the required degree of clarity is enough to require the judge to defer to the jury.[7]

Intermediate position

The Restatement Second, however, takes the sound intermediate position that the judge should not defer to the jury unless interpretation "depends on the credibility of extrinsic evidence or on a choice among reasonable inferences to be drawn from extrinsic evidence,"[8] and many courts have done the same.[9] The issue differs from that addressed by a plain meaning rule. Under such a rule, even in the case of a jury trial the trial judge must make a preliminary determination during the first stage as to the admissibility of evidence during the second stage, that of interpretation.[10] It is only during this second stage that a question arises as to the roles to be played by the trial judge and the jury. A judge will always defer to the jury if interpretation raises questions concerning the credibility of the evidence or the inferences to be drawn from it.[11] The issue here is: Should they do the same even if there are no such questions? A similar issue arises in connection with evidence relating to surrounding circumstances other than prior negotiations (evidence that is always admissible without a preliminary determination), as long as there is no question as to its credibility or the inferences to be drawn from it. Answering these questions in the affirmative, as Judge Friendly's statement suggests, seems to put too much faith in the jury when there is no real dispute as to the facts.

Scope of review

Second, if a question of interpretation is characterized as one of "fact," the interpretation at the trial court level is reviewable only on a clearly erroneous basis, while if it is characterized as one of "law" it is reviewable on a plenary basis. As the Third Circuit has correctly pointed out, the reasons that determine whether a question of interpretation should go to judge or jury are not identical with those that should control the scope of review. Therefore, "assignment to judge or jury does not of itself determine the standard

[6] Meyers v. Selznick Co., 373 F.2d 218, 222 (2d Cir. 1966).

[7] United States Naval Inst. v. Charter Communications, 875 F.2d 1044 (2d Cir. 1989) (Kearse, J.: "meaning of a contract term that is susceptible to at least two reasonable meanings is generally an issue of fact").

[8] Restatement Second §212(2) (question of interpretation of integrated agreement is one of law unless it "depends on the credibility of extrinsic evidence or on a choice among reasonable inferences to be drawn from extrinsic evidence").

[9] Baker v. America's Mortgage Serv., 58 F.3d 321 (7th Cir. 1995) (Illinois law: if ambiguity "arises only from the particular meaning of terms used in the contract, meaning is question of law" unless interpretation hinges "on an evaluation of disputed extrinsic evidence").

[10] See the discussion of the essence of a plain meaning rule in §7.12 *supra*.

[11] Christopher v. Safeway Stores, 644 F.2d 467 (5th Cir. 1981) (absent ambiguity, "meaning of the contract is a matter of law to be decided by the court," but, if ambiguity exists, "intent of the parties is a question of fact to be decided by the jury").

of review to be applied on appeal." The Third Circuit went on to accept the distinction between "construction" and "interpretation." It reasoned that a question of interpretation is one of fact and the trial court's decision "is reviewable on a clearly erroneous basis, rather than as a plenary one," while a question of construction "is one of law and freely reviewable."[12] The court concluded that the question before it — whether there were two separate agreements — involved determining what "legal consequences" followed and this was one of construction. In a later decision, the Third Circuit followed this analysis in concluding that the question before it — whether the dispute was governed by the arbitration clause in the subcontract or the one in the prime contract — involved "ascertaining the intent of the parties," and this was a question of interpretation reviewable only under the "clearly erroneous standard."[13] According to the Fifth Circuit, however, the clearly erroneous rule applies only

> when extrinsic evidence is used to interpret an *ambiguous* contract, and ambiguity is a question of law . . . . It follows that we must first review the decision that the contract terms are ambiguous. If we find ourselves in agreement with the district court decision we thereafter accord "clearly erroneous" deference to its interpretation of that contract in light of extrinsic evidence.[14]

This seems a sound view if the case is subject to a plain meaning rule, under which ambiguity is the key to admission of extrinsic evidence. But the ultimate criterion should be whether the lower court's interpretation was based on extrinsic evidence — in which case it should be treated as a matter of fact.[15]

Third, if a question of interpretation is characterized as one of "fact," the decision has no effect as *stare decisis,* while if it is characterized as one of "law" it has that effect. The Fifth Circuit has rightly pointed out that a determination of whether an issue of interpretation should go to judge or jury should not be determinative because a decision "does not become imbued with *stare decisis* effect just because a judge made it."[16]

Effect as *stare decisis*

From this discussion of how a court interprets what the parties have said about the case before it, we turn to what a court does when the parties have not spoken to that case.

[12] Ram Constr. Co. v. American States Ins. Co., 749 F.2d 1049, 1053 (3d Cir. 1984).

[13] John F. Harkins Co. v. Waldinger Corp., 796 F.2d 657, 659 (3d Cir. 1986).

[14] Paragon Resources v. National Fuel Gas Distrib. Corp., 695 F.2d 991, 995 (5th Cir. 1983).

[15] Williston Educ. Assn. v. Williston Pub. School Dist., 483 N.W.2d 567 (N.D. 1992) (because "ambiguity resolved by the use of extrinsic evidence is a question of fact for the trial court to decide . . . , we will not set aside a finding of fact unless it is clearly erroneous").

[16] South Hampton Co. v. Stinnes Corp., 733 F.2d 1108, 1115 n.5 (5th Cir. 1984).

D. DECIDING OMITTED CASES

Disputes over omission

§7.15. Reasons for Omission. Up to this point, our concern has been with disputes over the meaning of contract language as applied to particular situations. Courts resolve such disputes over *expression* by interpretation of the relevant contract language. Sometimes, however, disputes arise because there is no contract language that is relevant to the situation that has arisen. The parties have failed to reach the illusory goal of the "perfectly contingent contract" — "a paradigm in which parties . . . are presumed able, at reasonable cost, to allocate explicitly the risks [of] future contingencies."[1] They have written what is sometimes called an "incomplete contract."[2] Courts must resolve such disputes arising from *omission* by some process other than that of interpretation.[3]

Examples of omission

Two examples of omitted cases well illustrate the problems courts face. In the first, an advertising agency in England contracted to fly, during a nine-month period, an airplane towing a streamer that read "Eat Batchelor's Peas." Through oversight, the pilot flew over Manchester on Armistice Day, while crowds were observing two minutes of silence during memorial services, thereby injuring Batchelor's reputation and subjecting it to denunciations such as "You are beneath contempt" and "I will see that your goods never enter my house." The contract contained no term that excluded flying on Armistice Day. Should the advertising agency nevertheless be liable for damages?[4] In the second example, Dr. Lawrence granted Mr. Lambert in 1881 the exclusive commercial use of the secret formula for an antiseptic, in exchange for which Lambert bound himself and his successors to pay royalties to Lawrence and his successors. Royalties on the antiseptic, known as Listerine, rose to $1,500,000 per year, but the formula unavoidably became a matter of public knowledge so that the same antiseptic could be produced by anyone. The contract contained no clause providing for its termination in the event that the formula became a matter of public knowledge. Should the contract nevertheless be terminable by Lambert?[5]

Reasons for omissions

Omissions in contracts occur in two types of situations.[6] Sometimes a potential dispute is foreseen but there is a conscious decision not to deal with it. Sometimes the potential dispute is simply not foreseen. In both types of

---

§7.15 [1]Goetz & Scott, The Limits of Expanded Choice: An Analysis of the Interactions Between Express and Implied Contract Terms, 73 Cal. L. Rev. 261, 267 n.10 (1985).

[2]This is not the same as a contract with open terms, in which the parties intentionally omit matters to be agreed on later. See the discussion of the second premise as possible in §3.7 *supra*.

[3]*See* William B. Tanner Co. v. Sparta-Tomah Broadcasting Co., 716 F.2d 1155 (7th Cir. 1983), described in the discussion of the example of *Tanner* in §7.17 *infra*.

[4]Aerial Advertising Co. v. Batchelor's Peas, [1938] 2 All. E.R. 788 (K.B. 1938) (yes).

[5]Warner-Lambert Pharmaceutical Co. v. John J. Reynolds, Inc., 178 F. Supp. 655 (S.D.N.Y. 1959) (no), aff'd mem., 280 F.2d 197 (2d Cir. 1960).

[6]NEA-Coffeyville v. Unified School Dist., 996 P.2d 821 (Kan. 2000) (omission may come about because parties "have expectations regarding a situation which arises but fail to manifest them" or because parties "entirely fail to foresee the situation which later arises").

situations, courts supply rules that are commonly described as *default* rules, though in situations of the latter type they might more accurately be styled *gap-filling* rules.

In informal agreements much goes without saying. When a consumer buys a can of tuna in a grocery store, the terms of the transaction are left to be supplied by law — the buyer does not demand express warranties nor does the seller disclaim implied warranties. If all terms were expressly agreed to, even the simplest contracts would become intolerably long.

Informality

Even in a complex transaction, a party that foresees a potential dispute may decide not to deal with it if the dispute seems unlikely to arise. Parties tend to expect that the prescribed performances will be rendered. Therefore, "businessmen pay more attention to describing the performance in an exchange than to planning for contingencies or defective performance or to obtaining legal enforceability of their contracts."[7] The law reinforces this tendency by requiring that the parties express their expectations as to performance with considerable definiteness and sometimes in writing.[8] But the law does not require the parties to state what their expectations are in the event of breach and other remote contingencies, and such matters are often omitted from the agreement.

Unlikely to arise

Sometimes conscious omissions can also be explained by a party's reluctance to raise the matter in negotiations. Thus, it has been suggested, "contractual incompleteness" may occur "when one party to a contract knows more than the other" and "strategically decide[s] not to contract around even an inefficient default" because to do so "can reveal information."[9] A party may fear that to raise the point will result in delay or the addition of an unfavorable provision or even the loss of the entire bargain. Recall the case of the elderly woman who enters a home for the aged, paying a lump sum to be returned to her "if it should be found advisable to discontinue her stay" during a probationary period. Must the home refund the money if she dies during that period?[10] It is hard to conceive that the home did not foresee this possibility when it drafted its form, but easy to imagine that it chose not to broach so delicate a subject.

Reluctance to raise matter

When contract language fails to cover a situation because the parties did not foresee it, they may simply have overlooked the obvious through haste or inadvertence. Suppose that parties provide for repayment of a loan on a house, using a formula under which a fixed monthly sum is to be applied first to interest, then to property taxes, and the balance to principal. What are the

Haste or inadvertence

---

[7] Macaulay, Non-Contractual Relations in Business: A Preliminary Study, 28 Am. Soc. Rev. 55, 60 (1963).

[8] See §§3.28, 6.7 *supra.*

[9] Ayres & Gertner, Filling Gaps in Incomplete Contracts: An Economic Theory of Default Rules, 99 Yale L.J. 87, 127 (1989).

[10] First Natl. Bank v. Methodist Home for the Aged, 309 P.2d 389 (Kan. 1957), mentioned in the discussion of reasons for lack of clarity in §7.8 *supra.*

rights of the lender when property taxes rise, so that nothing is left to be applied to principal?[11]

Unforeseeability

At other times when the situation is not foreseen, even the most sibylline drafter would not have anticipated the turn of events.[12] Suppose that a franchisor gives a franchisee the exclusive rights to produce and market a kosher cooking oil for 25 years on a royalty basis. What are the franchisor's rights if, over 15 years later, royalties drop because the franchisee has begun to market its own kosher cooking oil, similar to two new competing products, Spry and Crisco?[13] Not surprisingly, the risk of unforeseen and unforeseeable developments grows as the lifetime of the contract increases.[14]

Mixed reasons in Haines

It is often impossible to know whether the parties failed to provide for a particular situation because they foresaw it but misjudged its significance, or because they did not foresee it at all. Since any agreement involves at least two parties, and each may have several representatives, the omission often results from a combination of reasons. *Haines v. City of New York*[15] involved an agreement between the city and two upstate communities, under which the city promised to assume "all costs of construction and subsequent operation, maintenance and repair" of a sewerage system and to extend the sewer lines as "necessitated by future growth and building construction of the respective communities." The city wanted the agreement to prevent the discharge of untreated sewage into a stream that fed its water supply system but continued to operate the system even after a state environmental control law was enacted prohibiting the discharge of raw sewage into the stream. After half a century, however, the system reached its full capacity and, when the city refused to either enlarge the existing sewage disposal plant or build a new one to meet continued needs, the upstate communities brought suit. The parties must have foreseen that the plant would reach full capacity, yet the agreement was silent as to the city's obligations in this event. Was this because they did not want to delay the negotiations? Because they were uneasy about the provision that might have resulted? Because they preferred to have the matter settled by a later of officials

[11] Miller v. Campello Co-op. Bank, 181 N.E.2d 345 (Mass. 1962) (contract of sale turned into option contract), treated in a footnote to the discussion of anomalous cases in §9.7 *infra*.

[12] Lord Denning expressed the hope that the time "is coming when judges will realize that the people who draft . . . contracts cannot envisage all the things that the future may bring." A. Denning, The Discipline of Law 56 (1979).

[13] Parev Prods. Co. v. I. Rokeach & Sons, 124 F.2d 147 (2d Cir. 1941) (franchisee could sell its own oil "so long as it does not invade" the market of franchisor's oil).

[14] *See* Cadle Co. v. Vargas, 771 N.E.2d 179 (Mass. App. 2002) (when unforeseen situation arises in long-term contractual relationship, "old text should not be applied if common sense tells us that the result would be absurd or unreasonable"). Particularly troublesome problems are posed by the impact of technological breakthroughs on long-term contracts. An example is Greenfield v. Phillies Records, 780 N.E.2d 166 (N.Y. 2002) (transfer of rights to master recordings of musical performances carried with it right to redistribute performances in any technological format).

[15] 364 N.E.2d 820 (N.Y. 1977).

on the basis of the facts of an actual dispute? All of these explanations may have been involved, though the opinion is not enlightening on this.[16]

How do courts deal with such disputes over omission, however they may be caused?

§7.16. The Process by Which a Court Supplies a Term. If the agreement of the parties does not resolve the dispute that has arisen, it is up to the court to supply a term to deal with the omitted case. Terms supplied by courts for such cases have traditionally been called *implied* or occasionally *constructive* terms and the correlative rules are now commonly called *default* rules. Some of the most important instances are reserved for discussion in the next two chapters, in connection with the concept of constructive conditions of exchange and the doctrines of impracticability and frustration.[1] Our present concern is with the process that is involved in dealing with an omitted case.

Court supplies implied term

Interpretation is necessarily the first step in that process, since a court will supply a term only after it has determined that the language of the agreement does not cover the case at hand. It follows that any term that a court would supply can be derogated from by agreement of the parties, either explicitly or by necessary inference.[2] The resulting rule is therefore a default rule rather than a mandatory rule.[3]

Interpretation as first step

In *Haines v. City of New York*, for example, the court first considered interpretations of the contract language offered both by the upstate communities and by the city on the issue of the length of their agreement. Only after the court had rejected the communities' interpretation "that the city is perpetually bound" and the city's interpretation that "the contract is terminable at will because it provides for no express duration,"[4] did it determine that it was faced with an omitted case.

Example of *Haines*

---

[16] In response to the city's argument that the enactment of environmental control laws terminated its obligation, the court did say, at 823, that this circumstance was one that "the parties did not contemplate," but it thought "it reasonable to infer from the circumstances of the 1924 agreement that the parties intended the city to maintain the sewage disposal facility until such time as the city no longer needed or desired the water," and it concluded that the unforeseen enactment of environmental protection laws did not relieve the city of its obligations. The city did not, however, have to extend the sewer lines if this would overload the system.

§7.16 [1] On constructive conditions of exchange, see §8.9 *infra*. On impracticability and frustration, see in §§9.5-9.7 *infra*. For other examples of terms supplied by courts, see §7.17 *infra*.

[2] City of Yonkers v. Otis Elevator Co., 844 F.2d 42 (2d Cir. 1988) (quoting: "court will generally not imply a term in the face of the parties' expressed intent to the contrary").

[3] See the discussion of default and mandatory rules in §1.10 *supra*. For helpful discussion, *see* Ayres & Gertner, Filling Gaps in Incomplete Contracts: An Economic Theory of Default Rules, 99 Yale L.J. 87 (1989).

[4] 364 N.E.2d 820, 822 (N.Y. 1977), described in the discussion of mixed reasons in *Haines* in §7.15 *supra*.

Nature of agreement

The process of interpretation used in determining whether there is an omitted case is essentially the same as that used for vague and ambiguous language. Courts rely on common habits and practices in the use of language in deciding what parties might be expected to say in the circumstances. In rejecting the claim that a party could avoid termination by curing a default within a stated period, one court reasoned, "It would have been natural for the parties to have provided expressly [for this] if that had been the purpose."[5] As might be expected, the more detailed and comprehensive the agreement, the less likely it is that the court will conclude that the case before it was omitted. In the words of one judge, "we are obviously influenced by the fact that this was a carefully negotiated contract in which the parties had the opportunity to spell out their obligations carefully."[6]

Role of foreseeability

In interpreting the agreement, the court will also consider the foreseeability of the situation. If the court is convinced that the parties could not have foreseen it, and therefore could not have intended their agreement to cover it, the court may refuse to apply the contract language, despite its apparent applicability, and may find that the case before it is an omitted one. This result is particularly likely under long-term contracts, where unforeseeability is endemic.[7] In the converse case, in which the court believes that the situation was foreseeable, it may conclude that the parties intended their apparently applicable language to cover the case. In the words of Roger Traynor, "If it was foreseeable there should have been provision for it in the contract, and the absence of such a provision gives rise to the inference that the risk was assumed."[8] The problem with this reasoning is that, as already suggested, a party may have foreseen the situation in question, yet not have intended the contract language to cover it. The party may have intentionally failed to raise it to avoid delay, the breakdown of negotiations, or the inclusion of an unfavorable provision.[9] As the commentary to the Restatement Second notes, "Factors such as the practical difficulty of reaching agreement on the myriad of conceivable terms of a complex agreement may excuse a failure to deal with improbable contingencies."[10] When this is so, the court should recognize that it is faced with an omitted case, even though the dispute was foreseeable.

Implication as second step

Once the court has determined through interpretation that it is faced with an omitted case, it must supply a term to deal with that case. The process by which

[5]New England Structures v. Loranger, 234 N.E.2d 888 (Mass. 1968).

[6]S.M. Wilson & Co. v. Smith Intl., 587 F.2d 1363, 1372 (9th Cir. 1978).

[7]See the discussion of unforeseeability in §7.15 *supra*. On the problems posed by long-term contracts, see the discussion of the limits of traditional analysis in §3.5 *supra*.

[8]Lloyd v. Murphy, 153 P.2d 47, 50 (Cal. 1944). This is a nearly irresistible conclusion if it can be shown that the parties omitted a provision after discussing it. Glidden Co. v. Hellenic Lines, 275 F.2d 253 (2d Cir. 1960) (shipowner had asked for clause excusing it in case Suez Canal was closed, but shipper refused).

[9]See the discussion of reluctance to raise a matter in §7.15 *supra*.

[10]Restatement Second §261 cmt. *c*.

a court supplies a term is commonly called "implication" and the resulting term is called an "implied term."[11] (Such terms are also called "implied-in-law" terms to distinguish them from "implied-in-fact" terms, which are derived from the behavior of the parties and are treated in the same way as "express" terms.[12]) The process of implication may have two bases.

The first basis for implication is the actual expectations of the parties. If the court is persuaded that the parties shared a common expectation with respect to the omitted case, the court will give effect to that expectation, even though the parties did not reduce it to words. However, if the parties' expectations were significantly different or if one party had no expectation, the court will substitute for the subjective test of shared expectation an objective test of whether one party should reasonably have known of the other's expectation.[13] Expectation can sometimes be gleaned from the agreement itself. Thus a recital or a provision dealing with a related case may suggest the parties' intention with respect to the omitted case.[14] Their intention may also be deduced from a course of performance, course of dealing, or usage,[15] or from the negotiations that led up to the agreement if the parol evidence rule permits.[16] In many cases, however, no reliable indication of expectation can be found. The court must then seek some other basis for implication.

Expectation as basis

It is sometimes suggested that if a court cannot determine the actual expectations of the parties, it should implement the expectations that it thinks they would have had if they had considered the matter, thereby remedying "the shortsightedness of individuals, by doing for them what they would have done for themselves if their imagination had anticipated the march of nature."[17] However, even if the parties did not foresee the situation, it is often naive to

Hypothetical expectation

---

[11] The process by which the court derives its conclusion might better be described as "inference," but "implication" is generally used. Restatement Second §204 avoids the use of either term: "a term which is reasonable in the circumstances is supplied by the court." *See* UNIDROIT Principles 4.8 ("Supplying an omitted term"). The process is sometimes also referred to as "gap filling," though it seems preferable to think of the case as "omitted" than to think of the contract as having a "gap."

[12] That the distinction between "implied-in-fact" and "express" terms has no legal significance, see the discussion of no formalities required in §3.10 *supra*. See also the discussions of the meaning of *quasi-contract* and *restitution* in §2.20 *supra* and of implied conditions in §8.2 *infra*.

[13] See the discussion of reason to know in §7.9 *supra*.

[14] *See* Parev Prods. Co. v. I. Rokeach & Sons, 124 F.2d 147, 149 (2d Cir. 1941) ("what we should seek is therefore that which will most nearly preserve the status created and developed by the parties").

[15] Columbia Nitrogen Corp. v. Royster Co., 451 F.2d 3 (4th Cir. 1971) (buyer of phosphate should have been permitted to show usage that buyer was under no duty to accept minimum quantities stated in contract). See also the discussion of awareness of usage in §7.13 *supra*. As explained there, a party may be bound by a usage of which the party is unaware, so that usage may not represent a party's actual intention.

[16] See the discussion of the parol evidence rule *infra*.

[17] J. Bentham, A General View of a Complete Code of Laws, in 3 Works of Jeremy Bentham 191 (J. Bowring ed. 1843).

assume that a court can determine how the parties would have dealt with it had they foreseen it.[18] And even if a court could determine this, it might find that the term the parties would have chosen would be unjust for a court to supply because of the greater bargaining power of one of the parties.[19]

Justice as basis

In such situations, it should not be hypothetical expectations or fictitious intentions, but basic principles of justice that guide a court in extrapolating from the situations for which the parties provided to the one for which they did not. As an English judge observed, "it might seem that the parties themselves have become so far disembodied spirits that their actual persons should be allowed to rest in peace. In their place there rises the figure of the fair and reasonable man, . . . the anthropomorphic conception of justice."[20] Where do courts find these basic principles of justice? Often they look to the idea of fairness in the exchange. In searching for what Lord Mansfield called "the essence of the agreement,"[21] a court seeks a fair bargain — a bargain that an economist would describe as maximizing the expected value of the transaction. A court may, for example, justify the term it supplies on the ground that the term prevents one party from being in a position of "economic servility" and "completely at the mercy" of the other.[22] It may supply a term that is suitable for a particular market or other segment of society or even for society in general.

Off-the-rack default rules

If the situation is a recurring one, the term that a court will imply may be well known and, because it accords with their expectations, the parties may rely on it by remaining silent on the matter when making their agreement. Such "off-the-rack" default rules often find their way into statutes such as the Uniform Commercial Code. It is a commonplace that, in the words of the Tenth Circuit, "unless the contract discloses a contrary intention, an existing statute will be read into it to the same effect as an express provision."[23] But in fashioning off-the-rack rules for recurring situations it is important to be sensitive to the difficulties that courts will have in administering them, a consideration that may yield a rule that is practical and that promotes certainty even though it may not be based on the supposed expectations of the parties. Such a rule may encourage parties not to remain silent on the matter but to derogate from the rule by fashioning their own explicit provision. An example is the rule under which, if one party's

---

[18] For an example, *see* Prudential Ins. Co. v. Gray Mfg. Co., 328 F.2d 438 (2d Cir. 1964) (Friendly, J., after quoting Bentham, *supra* note 17: "clear enough that if Gray had asked for such a condition, either Ditmars would have agreed to it or there would have been no contract," but not so clear "that Gray would have sought a condition of this sort if the possibility of such action had occurred to it").

[19] For an example, *see* Perkins v. Standard Oil Co., 383 P.2d 107 (Or. 1963) (dealership agreement was "a contract of 'adhesion' in the sense that it is a take-it-or-leave-it whole").

[20] Davis Contractors v. Fareham Urban Dist. Council, [1956] A.C. 696, 728 (1956) (Lord Radcliffe).

[21] Kingston v. Preston, 98 Eng. Rep. 606, 608, 99 Eng. Rep. 437, 438 (K.B. 1773).

[22] Perkins v. Standard Oil Co., *supra* note 19, at 112.

[23] United States v. Essley, 284 F.2d 518, 520 (10th Cir. 1960).

performance will take time and the other's will not, the former must go first, a rule that has the advantage of clarity but that, at least in construction contracts, is more often departed from than accepted.[24] The term "penalty default rule" has been coined to describe rules that "are designed to give at least one party to the contract an incentive to contract around the default rule and therefore to choose affirmatively the contract provision they prefer." Such rules, it is argued, "are purposefully set at what the parties would not want — in order to encourage the parties to reveal information to each other or to third parties (especially the courts)."[25] Certainty and practicality are desirable ends for off-the-rack rules since, as the Supreme Court of Pennsylvania has said, "It would obviously be quite unreasonable and wholly undesirable to imply an obligation that would necessarily be vague, uncertain and generally impractical."[26]

An important factor in fashioning off-the-rack default rules is what might be called the "burden of expression." Although the parties can by express provision derogate from any term that the court would supply, doing so is not cost free and the party that would do so bears the burden of having the provision added to the agreement. Thus in the case of a construction contract it is the builder that has the burden of derogating from the off-the-rack rule by providing for progress payments. It has been suggested that "as more complex and refined terms are implied . . . , variation by express agreement becomes more difficult and costly than is commonly realized," and that "the courts' tendency to treat state-created rules as presumptively fair often leads to judicial disapproval of efforts to vary standard implied terms by agreement."[27] A court should consider the realities of the negotiating and drafting processes and supply a term that will put the burden of expression on the party that can better cope with it because of bargaining power and drafting skill.

Burden of expression

The parol evidence rule plays only a limited role in the process by which a court supplies a term to govern an omitted case. Its role as a plain meaning rule in the initial step of interpretation has already been discussed.[28] It may play no role at all in the second step of implication, because it is often unnecessary to resort to extrinsic evidence: the court's solution is based on circumstances that appear on the face of the contract.[29] If it is necessary to resort to extrinsic evidence, the rule should not bar such evidence for the limited purpose of showing the circumstances on which a court must rely in deciding whether to supply a term. Evidence should be admissible for this purpose even if the agreement is

Parol evidence rule

[24] See the discussion of performance requiring time in §8.11 *infra*.

[25] Ayres & Gertner, Filling Gaps in Incomplete Contracts: An Economic Theory of Default Rules, 99 Yale L.J. 87, 91 (1989).

[26] Dickey v. Philadelphia Minit-Man Corp., 105 A.2d 580, 582 (Pa. 1954).

[27] Goetz & Scott, The Limits of Expanded Choice: An Analysis of the Interactions Between Express and Implied Contract Terms, 73 Cal. L. Rev. 261, 263, 264 (1985).

[28] See the discussion of the restrictive view in §7.12 *supra*.

[29] Seashore Performing Arts Center v. Town of Old Orchard Beach, 676 A.2d 482 (Me. 1996) (even integrated contract "may include an unwritten implied term").

completely integrated. Thus it should be admissible to show whether a sum is "substantial" in order to determine if a grant of exclusive rights in return for a percentage of revenues gives rise to a duty of best efforts.[30] And it should be admissible to show whether a seller of goods had reason to know of the buyer's purpose and of the buyer's reliance on the seller to furnish goods suitable for that purpose in order to determine whether the seller warranted their fitness for that purpose.[31] But if the agreement is completely integrated, the parol evidence rule will bar extrinsic evidence for the purpose of showing additional promises or agreements of the parties, even if that evidence would enable the court to avoid having to supply a term.[32]

We now examine some examples of terms that courts supply.

Many kinds of terms supplied

§7.17. **Examples of Terms Supplied by Courts.** Courts have been called upon to supply many different kinds of terms. This section considers three kinds as representative of the process described in the preceding section: terms imposing a duty of good faith, terms imposing a duty of best efforts, and terms providing for termination of the agreement. Other important kinds of terms supplied by courts include those making a party's duties conditional on performance by the other party and those excusing a party on grounds of impracticability or frustration. However, since these are examined in the following chapters, they will not be discussed here.[1] In supplying all of these kinds of terms, a court follows the process described in the preceding section of

---

[30] As to the rule that even a grant of exclusive rights in return for a percentage of revenues does not give rise to a duty of best efforts if there is a "substantial" sum payable in any event, *see* the discussion of the example of a percentage lease in §7.17 *infra*.

[31] Under UCC 2-315, a seller of goods warrants their fitness for a particular purpose if the seller "has reason to know [that purpose] and that the buyer is relying on the seller's skill and judgment to select or furnish suitable goods." A meticulous reading of the Code supports the admissibility of extrinsic evidence to show that these requirements have been met. Under UCC 2-202, the Code's version of the parol evidence rule, even a totally integrated agreement excludes only "terms." A *term* is defined as "a portion of an agreement that relates to a particular matter" (UCC 1-201(40)), and an *agreement* is "the bargain of the parties in fact, as found in their language or inferred from other circumstances" (UCC 1-201(3)). (Contrast the definition of *contract* in UCC 1-201(12).) It can therefore be argued that an implied warranty of fitness is read in by law and "by implication from other circumstances," such as language, and is therefore not a "term" barred by UCC 2-202. *See also* Restatement Second §204 cmt. *e*.

[32] This seems evident from the nature of a completely integrated agreement. See the discussion of the degree of integration in §7.3 *supra*. For example, in Hayden v. Hoadley, 111 A. 343 (Vt. 1920), it was held that the parol evidence rule barred extrinsic evidence for the purpose of showing that repairs were to be finished by a stated date, even though in the absence of an agreement the court had to supply a term requiring that they be done in a reasonable time. The evidence might, however, have been admissible as bearing on what was reasonable in the circumstances.

§7.17   [1] See the discussions of constructive conditions in §8.9 *infra* and of supplying a term in §9.5 *infra*. *See also* E. Farnsworth, Changing Your Mind ch. 10 (1998).

this treatise, resorting if possible to the parties' actual intention and otherwise to its own sense of justice.[2]

Courts have often supplied a term requiring both parties to a contract to exercise what is called "good faith" or sometimes "good faith and fair dealing,"[3] and the Uniform Commercial Code provides that every contract governed by it "imposes an obligation of good faith in its performance."[4] This implied duty is based on fundamental notions of fairness. Under the Code it "may not be disclaimed by agreement," though the "parties, by agreement, may determine the standards by which the performance of [that obligation] is to be measured if those standards are not manifestly unreasonable."[5] A similar restriction has been imposed outside the scope of the Code.[6]

Duty of good faith

The Vienna Convention does not contain a provision imposing a duty of good faith in the performance of an agreement. It does however, state that in the interpretation of the Convention, "regard is to be had to . . . the observance of good faith in international trade."[7] This provision, which falls short of imposing any duty of good faith performance on the *parties*, resolved a stalemate between those representatives, primarily from civil law countries, who favored the imposition of such a duty and those, primarily from common law countries, who opposed the imposition of such a duty. There are three views as to what this compromise means.[8] One view, supported by the drafting history, is that since there was no agreement on imposing such a duty none

International solutions

---

[2] See the discussion of justice as a basis in §7.16 *supra*. Other examples of terms that will be supplied by a court include the implied warranties of merchantability and of fitness for a particular purpose provided for in UCC 2-314, 2-315.

[3] Anthony's Pier Four v. HBC Assocs., 583 N.E.2d 806 (Mass. 1991) ("covenant of good faith and fair dealing is implied" even "in contracts between sophisticated business people"). *See* Restatement Second §205 ("Every contract imposes upon each party a duty of good faith and fair dealing in its performance and its enforcement."). As to good faith and the requirement of definiteness, see the discussion of the role of the drafter in §3.28 *supra*.

"Good faith" has also been used in other connections. It has traditionally been used to set the standard of honesty for good faith purchase, rather than for performance. "Good faith" has also been used in connection with the doctrine of bad faith breach, which grew up in connection with an insurer's liability in settling of a claim. See the discussion of the origins of bad faith breach in §12.8 *infra*.

[4] UCC 1-304. According to Comment 1, "This section sets forth a basic principle running throughout the Uniform Commercial Code." As to the duty of good faith in "enforcement," also imposed by UCC 1-304, *see* Restatement Second §205 cmt. *e*.

[5] UCC 1-302(b).

[6] Carmichael v. Adirondack Bottled Gas Corp., 635 A.2d 1211 (Vt. 1993) (though contract with distributor terminated with his death, supplier still owed "duties with respect to winding down," and "duty of good faith is imposed by law and is not a contractual term that the parties are free to bargain in or out as they see fit").

[7] CISG 7(1).

[8] For legislative history and different views, *see* Commentary on the Uniform Sales Law: The 1980 Vienna Sales Convention 85 (C. Bianca & M. Bonell eds. 1987) (Bonell: "good faith is . . . one of the 'general principles' underlying the Convention as a whole"); J. Honnold, Uniform Law for

was imposed. At the other extreme is the view that the duty of good faith performance is so fundamental that the language of compromise should be tortured to impose it. In between these extremes is the view that though the language of compromise does not impose a duty of good faith performance, such a duty underlies a number of the Convention's specific provisions so that it can be said to be one of "the general principles on which [the Convention] is based" and which are to govern matters not "expressly settled" by the Convention.[9] The UNIDROIT Principles avoid such uncertainty by stating that each party "must act in accordance with good faith and fair dealing in international trade."[10]

Existing agreement
Since a court supplies a term to govern a case that the parties have omitted from their agreement, the implied duty of good faith does not arise, under either the Code or case law, unless an agreement is already in existence. The duty of good faith is therefore not imposed on parties until they have reached agreement and does not bind them during their earlier negotiations.[11] When parties to an existing contract negotiate for its modification, however, they are bound by a duty of good faith imposed by that contract.[12]

Restriction of "no independent duty"
Some courts, concerned lest the doctrine of good faith get out of hand, have imposed a judicially fashioned restriction under which the doctrine does not create "independent" rights separate from those created by the provisions of the contract. According to this view, the duty of good faith must be connected to a duty clearly imposed by the contract itself. As the Third Circuit put it, "courts generally utilize the good faith duty as an interpretive tool to determine 'the parties' justifiable expectations,' and do not enforce an independent

---

International Sales under the 1980 United Nations Convention §94 (3d ed. 1999) ("Convention rejects 'good faith' as a general requirement").

[9]CISG 7(2).

[10]UNIDROIT Principles 1.7(1).

[11]Potlatch Corp. v. Beloit Corp., 979 P.2d 114 (Idaho 1999) ("allegations of bad faith must relate exclusively to the failure to perform the obligations of the contract, not to misrepresentations occurring during the negotiations preceding the contract").

Some interesting qualifications to this generalization can be found in the Restatement Second. The concept of good faith is used in stating that a party is precluded from obtaining relief for mistake or misrepresentation if the party's fault "amounts to a failure to act in good faith." Restatement Second §157 (effect of fault of party seeking relief for mistake), §172 (effect of fault of party seeking relief for misrepresentation). *See also* Restatement Second §161(b) (when nondisclosure amounts to a misrepresentation), §176(1) (when a threat is improper). However, in none of these cases is it appropriate to say that a duty of good faith is imposed on the negotiating parties. It should also be recalled that a duty of good faith may prevent a promise from being illusory and the agreement from being unenforceable. See the discussions of the duty of good faith in §2.13 *supra* and of the Code response in §2.15 *supra*. See also the discussion of good faith in bargaining in §3.26 *supra*.

UNIDROIT Principles art. 2.15(2) takes a different view, imposing liability on a party "who negotiates or breaks off negotiation in bad faith."

[12]See the discussion of legislative reform in §4.22 *supra*.

duty divorced from the specific clauses of the contract."[13] This view has been reinforced by an addition to the Code commentary.[14] However not all courts have felt so constrained. This has been so, for example, where the rights of franchisees have been concerned. The Ninth Circuit ignored the restriction in holding that a franchisor's construction of competing restaurant within a mile and a half of a franchisee's restaurant was breach of duty of good faith even though the franchise was not exclusive.[15]

Contracting parties, similarly concerned lest the doctrine of good faith get out of hand, have invoked the principle, often repeated by courts, that there is no duty of good faith if it would conflict with an express provision of the contract. As the Fourth Circuit put it, the "implied duty of good faith cannot be used to override or modify explicit contractual terms."[16] However, not all courts have been so respectful of the express provisions of the contract. The Supreme Court of New Jersey held that though the implied covenant of good faith and fair dealing could not override a 90 days cancellation clause, the jury could find that a clam buyer "was not 'honest in fact'" as the covenant required because its conduct, including termination, destroyed the clam supplier's "reasonable expectations and right to receive the fruits of the contract."[17] It is sometimes no simple matter to reconcile the mandatory character of the duty of good faith[18] with respect for the autonomy of the parties.

Restriction of no conflict with express terms

What is the scope of the duty of good faith? Article 1 formerly defined *good faith* simply as "honesty in fact."[19] At that time, however, Article 2 contained a special more exacting definition of *good faith* in the case of a merchant that required "the observance of reasonable commercial standards of fair dealing

Scope of duty

---

[13] Duquesne Light Co. v. Westinghouse Elec. Co., 66 F.3d 604, 617 (3d Cir. 1995). Use of the term "independent duty" often occurs in insurance cases in connection with claims of bad faith breach. See the discussion of the origins of bad faith breach in §12.8 *infra*.

[14] In 1994, the Uniform Commercial Code's Permanent Editorial Board muddied the waters by issuing its Commentary No. 10 on its good faith provision. No reasons were given for its issuance. It resulted in the addition of language to the commentary stating that the section "does not support an independent cause of action for failure to perform or enforce in good faith" and seeks to make clear "that the doctrine of good faith merely directs a court towards interpreting contracts within the commercial context in which they are created, performed and enforced, and does not create a separate duty of fairness and reasonableness which can be independently breached." UCC 1-304 cmt. 1.

[15] Vylene Enters. v. Naugles, Inc., 90 F.3d 1472 (9th Cir. 1996) (franchisee "entitled to expect that the franchisor would 'not act to destroy the right of the franchisee to enjoy the fruits of the contract'").

[16] Riggs Natl. Bank of Washington v. Linch, 36 F.3d 370, 373 (4th Cir. 1994).

[17] Sons of Thunder v. Borden, Inc., 690 A.2d 575, 589 (N.J. 1997), qualified in Wade v. Kessler Inst., 798 A.2d 1251 (N.J. 2002) (error to suggest "that in breaching a literal term of the manual, [employer] also could be found separately liable for breaching the implied covenant of good faith and fair dealing").

[18] See the discussion of the duty of good faith *supra*.

[19] Former UCC 1-201(19).

in the trade."[20] When Article 1 was revised, its definition was changed to read "honesty in fact and the observance of reasonable commercial standards of fair dealing," and the special definition for merchants was deleted from revised Article 2.[21] The definition in Article 1 now applies throughout the Code with the exception of Article 5, which retains the old definition of Article 1 for letters of credit.[22] Coupling "honesty in fact" with the "observance of reasonable commercial standards of fair dealing" both makes the requirement more descriptive of performance and suggests an element of objectivity. But the precise scope of the duty of good faith necessarily varies according to the nature of the agreement. Behavior such as subterfuge and evasion clearly violates the duty.[23] The same is true for many other kinds of behavior described as "opportunistic," a term that in the present context generally signifies, in Judge Easterbrook's words, two situations.

> First, an effort to wring some advantage from the fact that the party who performs first sinks costs, which the other party may hold hostage by demanding greater compensation in exchange for its own performance .... Second, there is an effort to take advantage of one's contracting partner "in a way that could not have been contemplated at the time of drafting, and which therefore was not resolved explicitly by the parties."[24]

However, the duty may not only proscribe undesirable conduct, but may require affirmative action as well. A party may thus be under a duty not only to refrain from hindering or preventing the occurrence of conditions of the party's own duty[25] or the performance of the other party's duty,[26] but also to take some affirmative steps to cooperate in achieving these goals. A promisee, as one court put it, "must not only not hinder his promisor's performance, he must do whatever is necessary to enable him to perform."[27] On this reasoning, it has been held that a husband who had agreed to pay part of his earnings to support

---

[20] UCC-O 2-103(1)(b).

[21] See UCC 1-201 cmt. 20 (when "amendments to the Uniform Commercial Code brought the Article 2 merchant concept of good faith (subjective honesty and objective commercial reasonableness) into other Articles," it became "appropriate to move the broader definition of 'good faith' to Article 1."

[22] UCC 5-102(7) ("honesty in fact").

[23] See Restatement Second §231 cmt. d.

[24] Industrial Representatives v. CP Clare Corp., 74 F.3d 128, 129-30 (7th Cir. 1996). The risk that the other party will behave in an opportunistic manner because that party may not suffer the full consequences of its actions is one variety of what is sometimes called "moral hazard," a term that is often used to encompass rational economic behavior that is not perfidious. A contracting party that anticipates such behavior may adjust the price of the contract accordingly.

[25] See the discussion of breach by prevention in §8.6 infra. See also the discussion of a term prohibiting assignment in §11.4 infra.

[26] See the discussion of breach of an implied duty in §8.15 infra.

[27] Kehm Corp. v. United States, 93 F. Supp. 620, 623 (Ct. Cl. 1950).

his ex-wife violated his duty of good faith "when he decided on his own to retire from a successful career while in his mid-fifties and in good health without making some other provision for his former wife's support."[28] Similar reasoning has been applied in a wide variety of situations,[29] some of the most important involving construction contracts,[30] where it has been held, for example, that a party furnishing plans or specifications under such a contract may be held liable for loss due to their inadequacy.[31]

The New York Court of Appeals addressed the scope of the duty of good faith and fair dealing in *Dalton v. Educational Testing Service*, which arose out of the refusal of the Educational Testing Service (ETS) to release the score of Brian Dalton, a high school senior, after he had retaken the Scholasic Aptitude Test for admission to college. ETS justified its refusal on the ground that Dalton's score was dramatically higher than his score when he had first taken the test six months earlier, together with what ETS considered to be discrepant handwriting. Dalton's agreement with ETS gave it the "right to cancel any test score . . . if ETS believes that there is reason to question the score's validity" and gave him an option to provide additional information in that event. Dalton did this, providing evidence that he had been ill when he was first tested and that he had taken a preparatory course after the first test, along with statements from witnesses that he had been in the classroom during the second test and a report from a handwriting expert. ETS nevertheless concluded that someone else had taken the second test for Dalton. After a trial without a jury, the trial court found a breach of the duty of good faith by ETS in failing "to make even rudimentary efforts to evaluate or investigate" this information and ordered ETS to release Dalton's second score. When the case reached the Court of Appeals, that court upheld the trial court's decision as to breach. Writing for the court, Chief Judge Judith Kaye reasoned that when ETS "refuses to exercise its discretion in the first instance by declining even to consider relevant material submitted by the test-taker, the legal question is whether this refusal breached an express or implied term of the contract, not whether it was arbitrary or irrational." She concluded that by its refusal, "ETS failed to comply in good faith with its own test security procedures, thereby breaching its contract with Dalton." The

Example of
Dalton

---

[28] Larson v. Larson, 636 N.E.2d 1365, 1368 (Mass. App. 1994).

[29] Hilton Hotels v. Butch Lewis Prods., 808 P.2d 919 (Nev. 1991) (prizefight promoters had duty to promote events in "fair manner and not to manipulate who would be or who would not be the IBF champion and so advance their own interests in a manner that would compromise [hotel's] benefits under the contract"). See the discussions of breach by inaction in §8.6 *infra* and of breach of an implied duty in §8.15 *infra*.

[30] L.L. Hall Constr. Co. v. United States, 379 F.2d 559 (Ct. Cl. 1966) ("Government is obligated to prevent interference with orderly and reasonable progress of a contractor's work by other contractors over whom the Government has control").

[31] United States v. Spearin, 248 U.S. 132 (1918) (Brandeis, J.: where government furnished contractor plans and specifications for sewer, this "imported a warranty that, if the specifications were complied with, the sewer would be adequate").

**Example of
Market Street
Associates**

appropriate remedy, however, was not to order ETS to release Dalton's score but to order it to give "good-faith consideration" to the material he submitted."[32]

Market Street Associates v. Frey is also graphic. A shopping-center lessee had the right to ask its lessor for financing of improvements and, if turned down, to exercise an option to purchase the property. It requested financing, making no reference to the option provision in the lease, and, when the lessor refused the request, the lessee exercised the option and sued for specific performance when the lessor refused to convey. The trial court found that the lessee did not want financing, but "just wanted an opportunity to buy the property at a bargain price and hoped that the [lessor] wouldn't realize the implications of turning down the request for financing." On appeal, the Court of Appeals for the Seventh Circuit, through Richard Posner, held that, on these facts, there would have been a breach of the lessee's duty of good faith: "it is one thing to say that you can exploit your superior knowledge of the market," but "another thing to say that you can take deliberate advantage of an oversight by your contract partner concerning his rights under the contract."[33]

**Significance of
discretion**

Courts have often supplied a term requiring a party to exercise good faith when that party has been given a discretionary power over one of the terms of the contract. When a seller or a buyer is empowered to fix the price, UCC 2-305(2) imposes a requirement that the price be fixed "in good faith."[34] It is said more generally that a "duty of good faith and fair dealing applies when one party has discretionary authority to determine certain terms of the contract, such as quantity, price, or time."[35] In such situations the party with the discretionary power must exercise "a good faith business judgment,"[36] which suggests that the judgment may be to some extent in one's self-interest and that far less is expected than is expected of fiduciaries.[37] Output and requirements contracts are leading instances in which a requirement of good faith is implicit.

[32] 663 N.E.2d 289, 293, 294 (N.Y. 1995).

[33] 941 F.2d 588, 592, 594 (7th Cir. 1991) (error to grant summary judgment), followed after remand, 21 F.3d 782 (7th Cir. 1994).

[34] As to the meaning of good faith in this connection, *see* Mathis v. Exxon Corp., 302 F.3d 448 (5th Cir. 2002) (in fixing a price under UCC 2-305, requirement of good faith "embraces both the objective . . . and subjective senses of good faith," though "objective good faith is satisfied by a 'price in effect' as long as there is honesty in fact").

[35] Amoco Oil Co. v. Ervin, 908 P.2d 493, 498 (Colo. 1995).

[36] Zilg v. Prentice Hall, 717 F.2d 671, 680 (2d Cir. 1983) (publisher that allegedly "privished" [the opposite of "published"] book by insufficient promotion had only such a duty after initial period). See the discussion of the nature of *satisfaction* in §8.4 *infra*.

[37] Original Great Am. Chocolate Chip Cookie Co. v. River Valley Cookies, 970 F.2d 273 (7th Cir. 1992) (Posner, J.: contract law "does not require parties to behave altruistically toward each other" or "proceed on the philosophy that I am my brother's keeper," a philosophy that "may animate the law of fiduciaries"), distinguished in Interim Health Care of No. Ill. v. Interim Health Care, 225 F.3d 876 (7th Cir. 2000) ("seems the paradigmatic case of a contract party invoking a reasonable contract term . . . dishonestly to achieve a purpose 'contrary to that for which the contract had been made.'"). See the discussion of the exception in §12.20 *infra*.

Under an output contract, the seller's duty to deliver is determined by its output, as to which the seller has some discretion; and under a requirements contract, the buyer's duty to purchase is determined by its requirements, as to which the buyer has some discretion. Unless the parties have provided otherwise, the court will define the obligation to maintain output or requirements in terms of good faith. Any reduction in output or requirements, including the extreme case of complete cessation on going out of business, must be in good faith.[38] Any increase must also be in good faith, so that, for example, a buyer under a requirements contract has no right to goods for the purpose of stockpiling or speculation.[39] However, this limitation on increases is usually less significant than that on reductions because an estimate, prior dealings, or other factors usually fix a ceiling on increases.[40]

Output and requirements

Another term that courts often supply is one imposing a duty of "best" or "reasonable" efforts. Such a duty requires a party to make such efforts as are reasonable in the light of that party's ability and the means at its disposal and of the other party's justifiable expectations.[41] Although the scope of this duty is no better defined than is the scope of the duty of good faith, it is clear that the duty of best efforts is more onerous than that of good faith.[42]

Duty of best efforts

[38]UCC 2-306(1) ("such actual output or requirements as may occur in good faith"). According to UCC 2-306 cmt. 2, "A shut-down by a requirements buyer for lack of orders might be permissible when a shut-down merely to curtail losses would not."

[39]Empire Gas Corp. v. American Bakeries Co., 840 F.2d 1333 (7th Cir. 1988) (Posner, J.: good faith "requires at a minimum that the reduction of requirements not have been motivated solely by a reassessment of the balance of advantages and disadvantages under the contract to the buyer," as, for example, where the buyer decides "that its capital would be better employed in some other investment").

[40]For such a case, *see* Orange & Rockland Util. v. Amerada Hess Corp., 397 N.Y.S.2d 814 (App. Div. 1977) (although buyer's demands for oil under requirements contract may have been in good faith after first year, they were unreasonably disproportionate to stated estimates). For the Code's rules on output and requirements contracts, *see* the discussion of the Code response in §2.15 *supra*.

[41]Absent agreement, this is the usual duty of a person engaged in a trade or profession. Milau Assoc. v. North Ave. Dev. Corp., 368 N.E.2d 1247 (N.Y. 1977) (contract to design and install sprinkler system: "those who hire experts for the predominant purpose of rendering services . . . cannot expect infallibility [and] reasonable care and competence owed generally by practitioners in the particular trade or profession defines the limits of an injured party's justifiable demands").

As to the relation of the duty of best efforts to the doctrine of impracticability, see the discussion of examples of qualified duties in §9.1 *infra*.

[42]T.S.I. Holdings v. Jenkins, 924 P.2d 1239 (Kan. 1996) (quoting this section of the treatise: best efforts provision created standard of conduct "above and beyond the implied obligation of good faith").

As to what amounts to performance under an express provision requiring "best efforts," *see* Bloor v. Falstaff Brewing Corp., 454 F. Supp. 259 (S.D.N.Y. 1978) (although as exclusive distributor of beer, "Falstaff did not contract to promote Ballantine [as] Anheuser-Busch or Schlitz might have done, [it did] contract to merchandise Ballantine . . . to the extent of its own total capabilities"), aff'd, 601 F.2d 609 (2d Cir. 1979) (though Falstaff was not required "to spend itself into bankruptcy," it could not apply "philosophy emphasizing profit *über alles* without fair

Exclusive agreements and *Wood v. Lucy*

Courts have often supplied a term calling for best efforts under exclusive dealing agreements. The classic opinion is that of Cardozo speaking for the New York Court of Appeals in *Wood v. Lucy, Lady Duff-Gordon*, discussed earlier.[43] There the rights given Wood were exclusive, disabling Lady Duff-Gordon from further activity and from granting rights to others. Since her remuneration depended entirely on his efforts, the court supplied a term requiring that Wood use his best efforts to sell her fashions. Courts have supplied terms requiring best efforts by parties with exclusive rights under various kinds of exclusive dealing agreements, including contracts for the sale of goods[44] and contracts of real estate brokerage.[45] The court will not supply such a term, however, if the rights given are not exclusive, since in that case the grantor of the rights does not disable itself from further activity or from granting rights to others.[46] Furthermore, even if the rights given are exclusive, a court will not supply a term requiring best efforts if the grantor's remuneration is a fixed sum.[47]

Example of percentage lease

Courts also supply terms requiring best efforts under percentage leases. In such a lease the lessor typically gives the lessee an inherently exclusive right to land in return for a stated percentage of the lessee's gross receipts, rather than for a fixed rental. If the lease is silent on the matter, the court will supply a term requiring the lessee to use best efforts, in addition to the normal obligation of good faith.[48] Many percentage leases, however, provide not only for some fraction of receipts but also for a fixed minimum rental. If the minimum

---

consideration" of effect on volume). As to best efforts and the requirement of definiteness, *see* the discussion of the role of the drafter in §3.28 *supra*.

According to UNIDROIT Principles 5.4(2), a duty of best efforts requires a party to "make such efforts as would be made by a reasonable person of the same kind in the same circumstances."

[43] 118 N.E. 214 (N.Y. 1917), described in the discussion of the duty of reasonable efforts in §2.13 *supra*. The suit was brought by Wood, and Lady Duff-Gordon's defense was that there was no consideration for her promise because he had made no promise in return.

[44] UCC 2-306(2).

Curiously, the Code states that both seller and buyer have a duty of best efforts under an agreement for exclusive dealing in goods, a statement followed in Thermal Sys. v. Sigafoose, 533 So. 2d 567 (Ala. 1988). But this is questionable because an output contract, for example, can be viewed as an agreement under which the buyer gets exclusive rights and yet it imposes on the *seller* merely a duty of good faith and not one of best efforts. (The duty of the *buyer* under such a contract is expressly made absolute — to take all the seller's output — not merely to use best efforts.)

[45] See the discussion of a real estate brokerage transaction in §3.24 *supra*.

[46] Zehyer v. S.S. & S. Mfg. Co., 319 F.2d 606 (7th Cir. 1963) (salesperson "did not have an exclusive agency").

[47] Cases are scarce because the failure to use best efforts in this situation usually causes the grantor no loss.

[48] Seggebruch v. Stosor, 33 N.E.2d 159 (Ill. App. 1941) (where lessor leased gas station for rent of 1.25 cents per gallon of gas sold, "it was clearly implied that [lessee] would use reasonable diligence in operating the gas station"). Such an arrangement plainly invites tension between the lessor, which is interested in high gross receipts, and the lessee, which is interested in high net profits.

is substantial, the court will not impose on the lessee a duty of best efforts, even though the rental also is in part dependent on the lessee's efforts.[49] The explanation is that the substantial minimum, coupled with the normal obligation of good faith,[50] is considered fair compensation for the grantor of the right. To impose a duty of best efforts, the grantor must then add an express provision to the agreement.[51] The same principle has been applied to other types of exclusive dealing agreements.[52]

A third type of term that courts supply relates to termination of the agreement. A party that seeks to terminate an agreement that is silent with respect to duration or termination will argue that since nothing is said about duration, the agreement is terminable at will. The other party will claim that since the agreement says nothing about termination, it admits of no termination. Despite the superficial appeal of such arguments, courts may reject both and fashion a term appropriate to the omitted case.

Termination

An example is *William B. Tanner Co. v. Sparta-Tomah Broadcasting Co.*, in which the contract provided that a radio station would, in exchange for promotional material, provide Tanner, a "distributor" of air time, with commercial air spots that were, in what the court called "words of somewhat astonishing imprecision . . . to be 'valid until used.'" The Seventh Circuit, after noting that this provision "has turned out to be a significant boon to the legal profession" by having "prompted a raft of cases across the country where courts have struggled to discern exactly what was intended," went on to hold that it was error to read the language so as to give Tanner a right to the spots without any time limitation. After criticizing the analysis of courts that "do not appear to have adequately distinguished between disputes over *expression* as opposed to disputes arising from *omission*," the court concluded that the words "valid until used" were not ambiguous but did not cover the case before it, and that the contract "is incomplete with respect to the duration of the validity of the spots." It therefore remanded the case to the trial court "to determine what is a 'reasonable time' to imply as to duration of validity."[53] Many other courts have used a similar

**Example of
*Tanner***

---

[49] Dickey v. Philadelphia Minit-Man Corp., 105 A.2d 580 (Pa. 1954) (lessee under no obligation of best efforts "where a substantial minimum rental is provided the obvious purpose of which is to protect the lessor from any unfavorable circumstances that might subsequently arise whether caused by voluntary conduct of the lessee or by events beyond his control").

As to the effect of the parol evidence rule on the use of extrinsic evidence to show what is "substantial," see the discussion of the parol evidence rule in §7.16 *supra*.

[50] For a case in which it was held that there was no breach of the duty of good faith when the lessee, a retail store, moved its fur department from the floor on which it paid a percentage of profits to a floor on which it did not, *see* Mutual Life Ins. Co. v. Tailored Woman, 128 N.E.2d 401 (N.Y. 1955).

[51] For a case in which this was done, *see* Bloor v. Falstaff Brewing Corp., *supra* note 42.

[52] HML Corp. v. General Foods Corp., 365 F.2d 77 (3d Cir. 1966) (no duty of best efforts where exclusive right to use salad dressing sold for $250,000 plus a percentage of profits).

[53] 716 F.2d 1155, 1157, 1158-59 (7th Cir. 1983).

Franchise cases

approach to find a solution between the two extremes of termination at will and perpetual duration,[54] though not all courts have been willing to do so.[55]

Courts have traditionally applied the rule of termination at will to exclusive agency, distributorship, and franchise agreements (collectively referred to here as "franchise agreements") on the ground that "parties ordinarily do not intend to maintain their business relationships forever" and should not be "required to remain in the business relationship after it has soured."[56] However, courts in growing numbers have recognized the hardship that this rule may impose on franchisees and offered them some protection.[57] Sometimes courts have done this through the process of interpretation.[58] More often they have done so by holding, following the Uniform Commercial Code,[59] that the obligation of good faith and fair dealing requires that the francisor give reasonable notice of termination,[60] unless there is a contrary provision in the form of either specific at-will language[61] or a fixed notice period.[62] The length of the notice is often tailored to give the franchisee time to make alternative arrangements.[63] Some courts have instead required that the franchisee be given a reasonable time after beginning activity to recoup its original investment.[64] Both courts

---

[54] Haines v. City of New York, 364 N.E.2d 820 (N.Y. 1977), described in the discussion of mixed reasons in *Haines* in §7.15 *supra* ("reasonable to infer from circumstances "that the parties intended the city to maintain the sewage disposal facility until such time as the city no longer needed or desired the water" from reservoir).

[55] Warner-Lambert Pharmaceutical v. John J. Reynolds, 178 F. Supp. 655 (S.D.N.Y. 1959) (licensee of secret formula for antiseptic Listerine still obligated to pay royalties even after formula became matter of public knowledge), aff'd per curiam, 280 F.2d 197 (2d Cir. 1960).

[56] Delta Servs. & Equip. v. Ryko Mfg. Co., 908 F.2d 7, 11 (5th Cir. 1990) ("termination clause permitting [manufacturer] to immediately terminate the contract if [distributor] did not meet its sales quota is [not] sufficient to rebut the presumption that the contract was terminable at will," though reasonable notice was required).

[57] A few aberrational cases have gone so far as to base liability on breach of a supposed fiduciary duty. *See* Arnott v. American Oil Co., 609 F.2d 873 (8th Cir. 1979) (fiduciary duty is "inherent" in franchise relationship).

[58] City of Homestead v. Beard, 600 So. 2d 450 (Fla. 1992) (nature and circumstances of agreement distinguished it "from agreements which, by their inherent nature, imply the parties intended to terminate the agreement at will").

[59] UCC 2-309(3) (requiring "reasonable notification").

[60] Jen-Rath Co. v. KIT Mfg. Co., 48 P.3d 659 (Idaho 2002) ("jury could reasonably conclude that the notice . . . was unreasonable [under Code] in the light of the time it would take [dealer] to liquidate its remaining inventory and to fully transition to using a new manufacturer").

[61] Taylor Equip. v. John Deere Co., 98 F.3d 1028 (8th Cir. 1996) (covenant does not "limit a clear contractual provision allowing termination . . . without cause").

[62] Cloverdale Equip. Co. v. Simon Aerials, 869 F.2d 934 (6th Cir. 1989) (provision for 60 days notice "not ambiguous").

[63] UCC 2-309 cmt. 8 ("principles of good faith and sound commercial practice normally call for such notification of the termination of a going contract relationship as will give the other party reasonable time to seek a substitute arrangement").

[64] Cambee's Furniture v. Doughboy Recreational, 825 F.2d 167 (8th Cir. 1987) ("a distributor is entitled to a reasonable period to recoup its investment, during which the agreement may not be terminated without good cause").

and legisatures have sometimes protected franchisees with mandatory rules that are not subject to contrary agreement, measures that go beyond merely supplying a term to deal with an omitted case and raise questions of public policy that are dealt with elsewhere in this treatise.[65]

The judicial preference for termination at will was historically strongest where employment contracts were concerned. Under what is known as "Wood's rule," an employer is free to discharge an employee for any reason or for no reason at all.[66] Although federal and state legislation has contributed to the reduction of this freedom, the emphasis here is on case law[67] and, in any event, relief under a statute may not be exclusive.[68] Wood's rule is, of course, subject to contrary agreement, as in the case of unionized employees covered by a collective bargaining agreement. For decades, however, most courts resolutely ignored such contrary indicia as a promise of "permanent employment" in safeguarding the employer's freedom.[69] Two important judicial developments, however, have now dramatically expanded the rights of employees and contributed to the burgeoning field of employment law. The first is the recognition of claims by employees that the employer's freedom has been limited by implied-in-fact agreements based on handbooks distributed to employees, a development discussed elsewhere in this treatise.[70] The second is the qualification of the employer's unrestrained power of terminate under at-will employment, the result of a judicial revolution that began in the mid-1970s.[71]

Employment cases

This revolution began with the recognition that a plainly opportunistic discharge is actionable. Thus if an employee is discharged without good cause "the obligation of good faith and fair dealing imposed on an employer requires that the employer be liable for the loss of compensation that is . . . clearly related

Public policy exception

---

[65] See the discussions of unconscionability as not limited to consumer contracts in §4.28 *supra* and of legislation as common in §4.29 *supra*.

[66] Horace Gray Wood gained a modest immortality by writing in his treatise in 1877 that "the rule is inflexible, that a general or indefinite hiring is *prima facie* a hiring at will," and the burden is on the employee to show otherwise. H. Wood, Master and Servant §134 (1877).

It might be better to think of at-will employment as involving an "agreement" rather than a "contract."

[67] See Yeitrakis v. Schering-Plough Corp., 804 F. Supp. 238 (D.N.M. 1992) (lawmakers "have made significant modifications to the rule," citing examples); Rose v. Allied Dev. Co., 719 P.2d 83 (Utah 1986) (employer's absolute right "has been somewhat limited by subsequent federal and state legislation," citing examples).

[68] Collins v. Rizkana, 652 N.E.2d 653 (Ohio 1995) (rejecting contention that availability of statutory remedies defeats sexual harassment tort claim).

[69] Friedman v. BRW, 40 F.3d 293 (8th Cir. 1994) ("general rule is that an employer's offer of 'permanent employment' . . . does not change an at-will contract into one of 'discharge-for-cause-only' or create an implied covenant of discharge only in good faith"). *See* the discussion of special contracts in §3.14a *supra*.

[70] The handbook cases are described in the discussion of cases where performance is sought in §3.12 *supra*.

[71] The seminal case was Monge v. Beebe Rubber Co., 316 A.2d 549 (N.H. 1974) (worker fired because she resisted foreman's sexual advances).

to an employee's past service,"[72] such as commissions earned by past service.[73] Courts also granted relief to employees discharged for filing workers' compensation claims.[74] Many courts then went beyond this and held, as Ellen Peters put it for the Supreme Court of Connecticut, "that the employer [is] responsible in damages if the former employee can prove a demonstrably *improper* reason for dismissal, a reason whose impropriety is derived from some important violation of public policy."[75] Few courts have gone so far as to hold that a duty of good faith and fair dealing imposes liability on an employer merely for termination without good cause. Thus in *Foley v. Interactive Data Corp.*, the Supreme Court of California declined to extend the doctrine of "bad faith breach," discussed elsewhere in this treatise,[76] to the relation between employer and employee, reasoning that "a breach in the employment context does not place the employee in the same economic dilemma that an insured faces when an insurer in bad faith refuses to pay a claim or accept a settlement offer within policy limits."[77]

[72] Gram v. Liberty Mut. Ins. Co., 429 N.E.2d 21, 29 (Mass. 1981), with a later appeal as to damages after remand in 461 N.E.2d 796 (Mass. 1984).

[73] Wakefield v. Northern Telecom, 769 F.2d 109 (2d Cir. 1985) (though salesperson could not "recover for his termination *per se* . . . , the contract for payment of commissions creates rights distinct from the employment relation").

[74] Jackson v. Morris Communications Corp., 657 N.W.2d 634 (Neb. 2002) (recognizing public policy exception "when an employee has been discharged for filing a workers' compensation claim").

[75] Sheets v. Teddy's Frosted Foods, 427 A.2d 385, 386-87 (Conn. 1980) (discharge for insistence that employer comply with state Food, Drug and Cosmetics Act).

[76] See the discussion of the fall of bad faith breach in §12.8 *infra*.

[77] 765 P.2d 373, 396 (Cal. 1988).

Chapter 8

Performance and Nonperformance

A.   PERFORMANCE IN GENERAL

§8.1.   Goals and concepts. This chapter deals with the performance stage of contracts. When parties negotiate agreements, they usually assume that they will perform their obligations. Therefore they devote more attention to spelling out the required performances than to detailing what is to happen if those performances are not forthcoming. As Melvin Eisenberg has explained it:

Focus on nonperformance

> Contracting parties will normally find it relatively easy to evaluate proposed performance terms, such as subject matter, quantity, and price. In contrast, at the

time the contract is made it is often impracticable, if not impossible, to imagine all the scenarios of breach.[1]

Frequently, then, it is left to the courts to determine the consequences of any nonperformance. Our focus here is on the rules courts fashion to deal with the nonperformance of bilateral contracts.[2]

Goal of rules

When parties make a bilateral contract, they exchange promises in the expectation of a subsequent exchange of performances. Although the consideration for each party's promise is the other party's return promise, each party enters into the transaction only because of the expectation that the return promise will be performed. The principal goal of the rules applicable to the performance stage of such contracts is to protect that expectation against a possible failure of the other party to perform.[3] It would be possible, of course, to leave a party who has not received the expected performance to pursue a claim for damages. But the injured party bargained for performance rather than for a lawsuit. Therefore courts have developed rules to afford the injured party, in addition to any claim for damages, a variety of types of self-help, the most important of which is the right to suspend its own performance and ultimately to refuse to perform if the other party fails to perform.[4]

Conditions

In developing these rules, courts have relied on the concept of a *condition*, an event that must occur before performance of a contractual duty becomes due. In general, a party whose duty is conditioned on such an event is not required to perform unless the event has occurred.[5] Suppose that the owner of a house pays $1,000 to an insurance company in return for the company's promise to pay the owner $100,000 if the house is destroyed by fire. The burning of the house is a condition of the company's duty to pay. If the house burns, payment becomes due; if it does not burn, payment does not become due.

Constructive conditions of exchange

By analogy to conditions, courts developed a concept of constructive (i.e., implied) conditions of exchange. To the extent practicable, a court will supply terms under which a party's duties are conditioned on the performance to be

---

§8.1   [1]Eisenberg, The Limits of Cognition and the Limits of Contract, 47 Stan. L. Rev. 211, 227 (1995). This tendency is reinforced by the requirement of definiteness, which is more exacting with respect to the performance required than with respect to the consequences of nonperformance. See the discussion of Restatement and Code requirements in §3.27 *supra*.

[2]Our concentration on bilateral contracts is only partly due to the fact that they are economically more significant than unilateral contracts. See the discussion of a promise as consideration — bilateral contract in §2.3 *supra*. Under the typical unilateral contract, the rules of offer and acceptance give the offeror the kind of security that must be achieved in a more complex way under a bilateral contract, and the offeree cannot avoid the risk inherent in performing first.

[3]As to opportunistic behavior intended to frustrate that expectation, see the discussion of the scope of the duty in §7.17 *supra*.

[4]The terms *failure to perform* and *nonperformance* are used interchangeably in this treatise. They include a defective performance as well as an absence of performance. *See generally* Taylor, Self-Help in Contract Law: An Exploration and Proposal, 33 Wake Forest L. Rev. 839 (1998).

[5]See the discussion of performance not due in §8.3 *infra*.

given in return. A party whose duty is in this way impliedly conditional on the other party's performance is afforded the security of not having to perform unless the other party has performed.[6] Suppose that a house painter promises to paint a house in return for the owner's promise to pay $1,000. Even though the language of the contract does not make the owner's promise to pay conditional on the painter's performance, it is impliedly conditional on that performance. If the painter paints the house, payment becomes due; if the painter does not paint it, payment does not become due.

Although the problems dealt with in this chapter most often arise if the failure of performance amounts to a breach, they may also arise if the failure is justified on a ground such as impracticability or frustration. A buyer is no less reluctant to pay for goods that the seller has failed to deliver if delivery was impracticable than if the failure was a breach. In both situations, the buyer is usually entitled to refuse to pay for goods that have not been delivered. However, the buyer has a right to recover damages from the seller only if the failure is a breach and not if it is justified.

We begin with the concept of a condition.

> **Not limited to breach**

B. CONDITIONS

§8.2. The Meaning of *Condition*. Promises and the duties they generate can be either unconditional ("I promise to pay you $100,000") or conditional ("I promise to pay you $100,000 if your house burns down"). Lawyers use *condition* in several senses. Sometimes they use it to refer to the term in the agreement that makes the promise conditional.[1] If the word is used in this sense, it can be said that promises, which impose duties, and conditions, which make duties conditional, are the main components of agreements. However, lawyers also use *condition* to refer to an operative fact rather than to a term. According to the Restatement Second a condition is "an event, not certain to occur, which must occur, unless occurrence is excused, before performance under a contract becomes due."[2] This use of the word has the support of leading

> **Condition as term or event**

---

[6] See the discussion of the need for security in §8.9 *infra*.

§8.2 [1] Sometimes lawyers use *condition* in an even broader sense to refer to any term in an agreement (e.g., "standard conditions of sale").

[2] Restatement Second §224. In rare cases, the event that is the condition may have occurred before the contract was made, as where a marine insurance policy insures against a loss that may already have occurred. For a less precise definition based on The Cat in the Hat by Dr. Seuss, *see* Northern Heel Corp. v. Compo Indus., 851 F.2d 456 (1st Cir. 1988) (defining condition as "something (Thing One) which, by its terms, is made a condition to the performance of some corresponding obligation (Thing Two) by the other party, as where the latter agrees to do Thing Two if the former shall carry out Thing One").

writers.[3] Although the use of *condition* to refer to a term is perfectly acceptable and occasionally difficult to avoid, its use to refer to an event is more helpful analytically. To reduce confusion, the word will be used here in accordance with the Restatement Second definition.

Nature of event   Almost any event may be made a condition. The event may be largely within the control of the obligor, as when the owner of a house conditions the duty to pay for painting the house on the owner's "honest satisfaction" with the job. It may be largely within the control of the obligee, as when an insurer conditions its duty to pay for loss due to fire on the insured's furnishing proof of loss within 60 days of the loss. It may be largely within the control of a third person, as when a purchaser of a house conditions the promise to go through with the deal on a bank's approval of a mortgage application. Or it may be largely beyond the control of anyone, as when an insurer conditions its duty to pay under a fire insurance policy on damage as a result of fire. Each obligor comes under a duty as soon as the contract is made, but that duty is conditional. The obligor need not render performance until the occurrence of the event on which the obligor's duty is conditioned — the homeowner's honest satisfaction with the paint job, the insured's furnishing of proof of loss, the bank's approval of the mortgage application, or damage as a result of fire.[4]

Need not be material   Although a condition is usually an event of significance to the obligor, this need not be the case. In exercising their freedom of contract the parties are not fettered by any test of materiality or reasonableness. If they agree, they can make even an apparently insignificant event a condition.[5] Their freedom is subject only to the doctrine of unconscionability[6] and a few other constraints discussed in the sections that follow.

Express conditions   Conditions that are agreed to by the parties, as in the examples given above, are commonly referred to as "express conditions." Parties often use language such as "if," "on condition that," "provided that," "in the event that," and "subject to" to make an event a condition, but other words may suffice.[7] For example, a party may condition a duty to pay on the sufficiency of a particular fund or

---

[3] Corbin was especially vehement on the point. Using the word to refer to a term "performs no useful service; instead it affords one more opportunity for slovenly thinking. In its proper sense the word *'condition' means some operative fact* . . . ." Corbin, Conditions in the Law of Contracts, 28 Yale L.J. 739, 743 (1919).

[4] Harris v. North British & Mercantile Ins. Co., 30 F.2d 94 (5th Cir. 1929) (requirement that "'insured shall . . . within sixty days after the fire' make sworn proof of loss" was "a condition precedent to the right of the insured to maintain suit").

[5] Jungmann & Co. v. Atterbury Bros., 163 N.E. 123 (N.Y. 1928) (where seller failed to give required notice to buyer, court "may not weigh the benefit it might receive from other notice").

[6] See §4.28 *supra*.

[7] Stacy v. Williams, 834 S.W.2d 156 (Ark. App. 1992) ("fact that a clause fails to employ the usual words denoting a condition such as 'subject to' or 'if,' is not controlling").

source, by providing that payment is to be made only from that fund or source.[8] A court determines whether an agreement makes an event a condition by the process of interpretation.

Even if the agreement does not make an event a condition, the court may supply a term that does so. Thus if an obligor's duty cannot be performed without some act by the obligee, such as giving notice to the obligor, the court will supply a term making that act a condition of the obligor's duty.[9] Such conditions are often referred to as "implied" conditions, since a court uses the process of implication to determine whether to supply a term that makes an event a condition and what term to supply.[10] The distinction between an express and an implied condition is ingrained in the thinking of lawyers and is rooted in a faith in freedom of contract. It is of practical importance because the rule of strict compliance is limited to express conditions.[11]

Implied conditions

Our present concern is with express conditions. Why does an obligor qualify its duty by making the duty conditional on the occurrence of an event? The most common reason is to shift to the obligee the risk of nonoccurrence of the event. This may be the reason, whether the event is largely within the control of the obligor (the homeowner's honest satisfaction with the paint job), the obligee (the insured's furnishing proof of loss), or a third person (the bank's approval of the mortgage application), or is largely beyond the control of anyone (damage as a result of fire). If the event is within the control of the obligee, the obligor may also have made it a condition in order to induce the obligee to cause that event to occur. Of course the obligor might have tried instead to obtain the obligee's promise that the event would occur,[12] but the obligee might not have been willing to make such a promise. And, even if the obligee did make a promise, damages for its breach might not be a satisfactory remedy. Therefore, the obligor may prefer to make the event a condition.

Reasons for conditions

---

[8] Hood v. Gordy Homes, 267 F.2d 882 (4th Cir. 1959) (promise to pay one-half of "all monies received [from collaboration] such as dividends or profits" was conditional on receipt of money).

[9] Wal-Noon Corp. v. Hill, 119 Cal. Rptr. 646 (Ct. App. 1975) (notice by tenant was a condition of landlord's duty under covenant to repair, since it could be "inferred from the writing" and "is not only clearly apparent from the terms of the written lease, [but] is indispensable to effectuate the intention of the parties"). For a more important example, see the discussion of dependency through conditions in §8.9 *infra*.

[10] See §§7.16, 7.17 *supra*.

[11] See the discussion of strict compliance in §8.3 *infra*. A further distinction is sometimes made between an implied-in-law condition and an implied-in-fact condition. See the discussion of implication as a second step in §7.16 *supra*. However, this distinction is of little practical importance. Although in principle an implied-in-fact condition is subject to the rule of strict compliance, the consequences are easily avoided if the court that infers that an event, such as giving notice, is a condition uses a standard of reasonableness in doing so.

[12] As we shall see later, the court would then regard the obligee's performance of that promise as a constructive (i.e., an implied) condition of the obligor's duty to perform. However, the impact of this is softened by the doctrine of substantial performance. See the discussion of the need for mitigation in §8.12 *infra*.

Other events distinguished

Although almost any event can be a condition, there are a few exceptions. The Restatement Second definition excludes three important kinds of events: (1) events that must occur before a contract comes into existence; (2) events that are certain to occur; and (3) events that extinguish a duty after its performance has become due.

Precontractual events

The Restatement Second uses *condition* in the context of a contract that already exists. This excludes events, such as the acceptance of an offer, that must occur before a contract is made. For example, if an offeror makes a promise in the form of an offer "to sell this cotton to you on condition that you pay me $1,000," the payment is regarded as acceptance of the offer but not as a condition of the promise. Although formation of the contract could be said to be conditional on payment of the $1,000, no contract exists until payment is made. Under the Restatement Second definition, the making of the contract marks the border between the law of offer and acceptance, which relates to the formation stage, and the law of conditions, which relates to the performance stage.[13] The line is a fine one, however. If parties make a contract under which neither has a duty to perform until the occurrence of some event, such as the raising of a stated amount of capital or the approval of a third person, that event is a condition of the duty of each party.[14] Both parties are bound by the contract, although neither will have to perform if the event does not occur. Similarly, if an offer is coupled with an option contract, acceptance of that offer is a condition of the offeror's duty under the option contract.[15] The grantor is bound by the option contract though the grantor will not have to perform if the option is not exercised.

Events certain to occur

The Restatement Second further limits *condition* to an event not certain to occur. It excludes events, such as the passage of time, that are certain to occur.[16] A promise "to pay $1,000 on condition that 30 days shall have passed" is an unconditional promise in this sense. The justification for this limitation is

---

[13]Comment *c* to Restatement Second §224 says that such events as offer and acceptance, for the most part, "are required by law and may not be dispensed with by the parties, while conditions are the result of, or at least subject to, agreement." An even more important aspect of the distinction is that the law of conditions includes the concept of waiver, while that of offer and acceptance does not. See §8.5 *infra*. Other examples of the distinction include the rules treated in the discussions of breach by repudiation in §8.6 *infra* and of impracticability as an excuse and of disproportionate forfeiture in §8.7 *infra*.

[14]Omaha Pub. Power Dist. v. Employers' Fire Ins. Co., 327 F.2d 912 (8th Cir. 1964) (surety not bound on performance bond because, though obtaining insurance "was not a condition precedent to the existence of the contract, it was a condition precedent to performance of the work"). See the discussion of condition of agreement in §7.4 *supra*.

[15]As to conditions under option contracts, see the discussions of the point that a condition must be minor in §8.5 *infra* and of the effect on option contracts in §8.7 *infra*.

[16]The only example given of such an event is the passage of time, and other examples are not obvious. Such inevitable events as dawn and death can be regarded merely as marking the passage of time (a day and a lifetime). *See* Restatement Second §224 cmt. *b* & illus. 2.

that conditionality presupposes some degree of risk arising out of uncertainty as to whether the event will occur.[17]

The Restatement Second also limits *condition* to an event that must occur before a duty of performance arises. This excludes events that extinguish either a duty after performance has become due or a duty to pay damages for breach. Suppose an insurance policy provides that after the insurer has come under a duty to pay, its duty "is discharged if the insured fails to commence an action against the insurer within twelve months." The insured's commencing an action is not a condition, because it need not occur before payment by the insurer becomes due. Instead, its failure to occur terminates the insurer's duty to pay after it has become due.[18]

Although an event that extinguishes a duty that has already arisen is excluded from the Restatement Second definition of *condition*, such an event has traditionally been called a "condition subsequent."[19] In this terminology, what we have been calling a "condition" has been called a "condition precedent."[20] The main impact of this distinction between conditions precedent and subsequent has come, not in the law of contracts as such, but in the law of procedure. There it was accepted that the plaintiff had the burden of pleading and proof as to a condition precedent to the defendant's duty,[21] but the defendant had the burden as to a condition subsequent.[22]

Although it is unusual to encounter a true condition subsequent apart from examples of the sort just given, it is not unusual to encounter a condition precedent cast in the form of a condition subsequent.[23] Compare a provision that an insurer is "under no duty to pay for a fire loss unless the insured furnishes proof of loss within 60 days" with a provision that the insurer's "duty to pay for

Events that terminate duty

Condition subsequent

Form and substance

[17] However, an event that is not certain to occur is not necessarily a condition. Sometimes it is referred to merely as a convenient means of measuring the time after which the obligor is under a duty to perform. See the discussion of condition or time period in §8.4 *infra*.

[18] Sometimes the parties are restricted in their power to reduce, in effect, the period of limitations provided by statute. *See* UCC 2-725(1) (parties may reduce four-year period to not less than one year).

[19] Northwestern Natl. Life Ins. Co. v. Ward, 155 P. 524 (Okl. 1916) (provision "that an action could not be brought to recover on the policy after one year from the actual date of death of the insured . . . was in the nature of a condition subsequent").

[20] Pronounced *pre-CEE-dent*.

[21] On proof, *see* Henschel v. Hawkeye-Security Ins. Co., 178 N.W.2d 409 (Iowa 1970) (under provision in insurance contract making timely notice of loss "a condition precedent," burden was on insureds to prove timely notice). The distinction retains its vigor as to burden of proof.

[22] Gray v. Gardner, 17 Mass. 188 (1821) (where promise "was to be defeated by the happening of an event . . . the burden of proof is upon" the promisor).

[23] A classic illustration is the penal bond. A standard performance bond for a building contract states the surety's obligation thus: "Now, therefore, the condition of the obligation is such that if Contractor shall promptly and faithfully perform said Contract, then this obligation shall be null and void. . . . " What this means is that a breach by the contractor is a condition of the surety's duty to pay. Stewart v. Griffith, 217 U.S. 323 (1910).

a fire loss is discharged if the insured does not furnish proof of loss within 60 days." The substance is the same. In each case, the insured's furnishing proof of loss within 60 days is analytically a condition precedent to the insurer's duty to pay, since payment is not due until proof of loss has been furnished. Courts often conclude, however, that because of the form of expression, a provision of the first kind imposes a condition precedent, putting the burden of pleading and proof on the insured, while a provision of the second kind imposes a condition subsequent, putting the burden on the insurer.[24] It is surely preferable to allocate procedural burdens according to factors that are relevant to the policies that underlie them. If the owner of a house conditions the duty to pay for painting the house on the owner's "satisfaction" with the job,[25] it may make more sense to put the burden of proving that the owner is not satisfied on the owner than to put the burden of proving that the owner is satisfied on the painter, since the relevant facts are peculiarly within the knowledge of the owner. Some courts have done this, ignoring both the form of expression of the provision and the analytical distinction drawn in contract law.[26] But the terms *precedent* and *subsequent* have not proved well suited to this end.

Restatement Second terminology

The Restatement Second has abandoned the term *condition subsequent* and refers more fully to an event that "terminate[s] an obligor's duty of immediate performance or one to pay damages for breach."[27] What has been called a *condition precedent* is called simply a *condition*. The Reporter's Note recognizes that the traditional terminology "has long been criticized and has caused confusion when used in an attempt to answer questions relating to the burdens of pleading and proof."[28] It is too early to tell whether the new terminology will help to clear up the confusion by divorcing those questions from substantive contract law.

What happens if a condition does not occur?

Two effects

§8.3.　Effects of Nonoccurrence of a Condition.　The nonoccurrence of a condition of an obligor's duty may have two distinct effects.[1] First, the

---

[24] A leading case following this approach is Gray v. Gardner, *supra* note 22. There a promise to pay was made "on the condition that if a greater quantity of sperm oil should arrive in whaling vessels" during a stated period than in the previous year, "then this obligation to be void." The court concluded that the burden of proof was on the promisor. "The very words of the contract show that there was a promise to pay, which was to be defeated by the happening of an event. . . . " If the form of the provision is disregarded, however, arrival of no greater quantity of oil during the stated period was a condition precedent of the duty to pay, since no duty to pay arose until that event occurred.

[25] See the discussion of the nature of *satisfaction* in §8.4 *infra*.

[26] Buick Motor Co. v. Thompson, 75 S.E. 354 (Ga. 1912) (where seller promised to supply cars "conditions permitting," this was a condition subsequent because otherwise buyer would have an "impossible burden" in suit for breach of seller's duty).

[27] Restatement Second §230.

[28] Restatement Second §224, Reporter's Note.

§8.3　[1] *See* Restatement Second §225.

obligor is entitled to suspend performance on the ground that the performance is not due as long as the condition has not occurred. Second, if a time comes when it is too late for the condition to occur, the obligor is entitled to treat its duty as discharged and the contract as terminated.

Allowing the obligor to suspend performance follows from the very definition of a condition. If a home purchaser conditions the duty to close the deal on the bank's approval of the purchaser's mortgage application, the purchaser is under no duty to take the deed and pay for the house if the bank has not approved the application. The purchaser may choose to suspend performance on the ground that the condition has not occurred.[2]

Performance not due

Allowing the obligor to treat its duty as discharged follows because ordinarily the suspension cannot last indefinitely. There is usually some period of time within which the condition must occur if it is to occur at all. This may be stated in a provision of the agreement or it may be a reasonable time under an implied term. Once the period has passed, it is too late for the condition to occur, and the party whose duty was originally conditional may choose to treat that duty as discharged — as no longer enforceable. If the bank does not approve the purchaser's mortgage application within the appropriate period of time, the purchaser may treat the duty to take the deed and pay for the house as discharged.[3] If the purchaser does so, the home owner's duty to tender a deed to the house is also discharged.[4] The purchaser is entitled to restitution of any down payment or part payment.[5]

Duty discharged

These effects do not follow, however, if the condition has been excused. Even if a duty is conditional at the time the contract is made, subsequent events may cause the performance to become due, even though the condition has not occurred at all or has not occurred within the required time. The occurrence of the condition, or its occurrence within the required time, is then said to be "excused." A condition may be excused by waiver, by breach, or by a court acting to avoid forfeiture.[6] Since the excuse of a condition ordinarily deprives the obligor of an advantage without compensating the obligor if the event does

Possibility of excuse

---

[2] Luttinger v. Rosen, 316 A.2d 757 (Conn. 1972) (contract conditional on purchasers' obtaining mortgage for $45,000 for at least 20 years at not more than 8 1/2 percent). If the sale is not consummated for this reason, the broker is not entitled to a commission.

As to practices relating to such conditions, *see* Raushenbush, Problems and Practices with Financing Conditions in Real Estate Purchase Contracts, 1963 Wis. L. Rev. 566.

[3] Palmer v. Gulliow, 112 N.E. 493 (Mass. 1916) (borrower's duty to pay if there were dividends from his venture was discharged when, after six years of effort, he died without having been successful).

[4] This follows from the concept of constructive conditions of exchange. See §8.9 *infra*.

[5] Lach v. Cahill, 85 A.2d 481 (Conn. 1951) (purchaser recovered deposit when he was unable to obtain mortgage on which his duty to pay was conditioned).

[6] See §§8.5 (waiver), 8.6 (breach), 8.7 (forfeiture) *infra*. The phrase *excuse of a condition* is commonly used, felicitously if elliptically, in place of the more precise phrase *excuse of the nonoccurrence of a condition*.

not occur, a condition will not usually be excused unless it is a relatively minor part of the bargain.[7]

Strict compliance   If the occurrence of a condition is required by the agreement of the parties, rather than as a matter of law, a rule of strict compliance traditionally applies. As the Supreme Court of New Hampshire explained, "when the parties expressly condition their performance upon the occurrence or non-occurrence of an event, rather than simply including the event as one of the general terms of the contract, the parties' bargained-for expectation of strict compliance should be given effect."[8] Just as the event that is made a condition need not be of great moment,[9] the respect in which the event has failed to occur need not be of great moment. If the purchaser's duty to close the deal is conditioned on the bank's approval of an eight and one-half percent mortgage, the condition has not occurred if the bank approves an eight and three-quarters percent mortgage.[10] Courts have the occasion to apply this rule of strict compliance more often to suspension of performance than to discharge of duty, because agreements are usually more specific about the nature of the condition than the time by which it must occur. If the agreement is specific as to the time, however, the rule of strict compliance is as applicable to discharge as it is to suspension. If the purchaser's duty is conditioned on approval of a mortgage application "on or before June 30," the purchaser can claim discharge if approval does not come until July 1.[11]

Example of *Inman* case   *Inman v. Clyde Hall Drilling Co.* illustrates the rule. Inman sued his employer for firing him without justification. His employment contract made his giving written notice of any claim within 30 days after it arose a condition of the employer's liability, and it provided that he was not to file suit earlier than six months or later than one year from the time of notice. Inman did not give written notice, but did file suit within 30 days after being fired. Summary judgment for the employer was upheld. To hold "that the commencement of an action and service of the complaint was . . . an effective substitute for the kind of notice called for by the agreement . . . would be to simply ignore an explicit provision of the contract and say that it had no meaning."[12] Since timely notice

---

[7]Promissory conditions are exceptions to this general rule. See the discussion of the effect of condition and duty *infra*.

[8]Renovest Co. v. Hodges Dev. Corp., 600 A.2d 448, 452-53 (N.H. 1991) (quoting this section of this treatise).

[9]See the discussion of the point that a condition need not be material in §8.2 *supra*.

[10]Luttinger v. Rosen, *supra* note 2 (purchasers could reject vendor's offer to fund the difference in interest payments). (If a bank will not give a mortgage on the stated terms, the vendor, in order to save the deal, occasionally offers the purchaser a purchase money mortgage on the same terms.)

[11]Internatio-Rotterdam v. River Brand Rice Mills, 259 F.2d 137 (2d Cir. 1958) (where buyer's giving "shipping instructions on or before December 17" was a condition of seller's duty to ship, "the nonoccurrence of that condition" during the time allowed entitled seller on December 18 "to treat its contractual obligations as discharged").

[12]369 P.2d 498, 501 (Alaska 1962).

was no longer possible, the employer was discharged. Courts have seized on several grounds to avoid this rule of strict compliance, as we shall see in later sections.[13]

In much the same spirit as the rule of strict compliance is the rule that the obligor's ignorance is immaterial. If the nonoccurrence of a condition entitles an obligor to suspend its performance or treat its duty as discharged, the obligor is entitled to do so even though unaware that the condition has not occurred.[14] The purchaser that mistakenly believes that the mortgage application has been approved is as justified in refusing to close the deal as is the purchaser that knows that it has not been approved.

Ignorance immaterial

Controversy has arisen over whether this reasoning permits an employer, whose right to discharge an employee is conditional on cause, to use evidence of misconduct discovered after discharge to justify a discharge. In 1995 the Supreme Court of the United States held that the after-acquired-evidence defense did not immunize from liability an employer that discharged an employee in violation of the federal age discrimination law because the statutory objectives "are furthered when even a single employee establishes that an employer has discriminated."[15] It is unclear, however, that the same result should follow if no statute is involved and an employer whose right to discharge an employee is conditional on cause seeks to use after-acquired evidence to show cause.[16]

Employer's use of after-acquired evidence

A single duty may be subject to a number of conditions. They may be alternative, so that performance becomes due if any one of them occurs.[17] Or they may be cumulative, so that performance does not become due unless all of them occur.[18] Or some may be alternative and some cumulative. And the same condition may qualify the duties of both parties if, for example,

How conditions relate

---

[13]See §§8.4 to 8.7 *infra*. This is particularly true where the liability of an insurer is involved. *See* Great Am. Ins. Co. v. C.G. Tate Constr. Co., 279 S.E.2d 769 (N.C. 1981) (rejecting "the strict contractual approach to construction of notice provisions" and holding that though it was a condition under liability insurance policy that insured give notice "as soon as practicable," insurer should not be excused "if the delay in giving notice has not materially prejudiced the ability of the insurer to defend the claim").

[14]Bertrand v. Jones, 156 A.2d 161 (N.J. Super. 1959) (purchasers of land refused to settle without knowing of defect in title). *See* Restatement Second §225 cmt. *e* & illus. 9.

[15]McKennon v. Nashville Banner Publishing Co., 513 U.S. 352, 358 (1995) (Kennedy, J.).

[16]Schuessler v. Benchmark Marketing & Consulting, 500 N.W.2d 529 (Neb. 1993) ("if post-termination evidence would justify termination, the employee may not recover any damages for the period following the actual discharge").

[17]Wortman v. Jessen, 159 N.W.2d 564 (Neb. 1968) (three listed events were alternative conditions). See the discussion of the nature of *satisfaction* in §8.4 *infra*.

[18]Youssoupoff v. Widener, 158 N.E. 64 (N.Y. 1927) (seller's tender of amount buyer paid for Rembrandts and seller being in financial position to keep and enjoy them were cumulative conditions of buyer's duty to resell them). There is often a time sequence in cumulative conditions, as where performance becomes due only if a stated event first occurs and one of the parties then gives notice to the other.

neither is required to go through with a deal unless a stated amount of capital is raised or a third party gives approval.[19] In that case there is a binding agreement so that a party may be liable for a repudiation even before the condition occurs.[20]

Condition and *duty* distinguished

In analyzing the effects of the nonoccurrence of a condition, it is important to distinguish between an event that is a condition of a duty and an event that is the subject of a duty. An obligor who wants to induce the other party to cause an event to occur can do so in one of three ways.[21] First, the obligor may make the event a condition of the obligor's own duty, so that the other party will have to see that the event occurs in order to have a right to the obligor's performance. Second, the obligor may have the other party undertake a duty to see that the event occurs, so that the other party will have to see that the event occurs in order to avoid liability in damages. Third, the obligor may combine the approaches of the carrot and the stick by both making the event a condition of the obligor's own duty and having the other party undertake a duty to see that the event occurs.[22] Such an event, that is both a condition and the subject of a promise, is sometimes called a "promissory condition."[23] Although the obligor's objective may be the same under all three approaches, the effects of the approaches are fundamentally different.[24]

Example of *Constable v. Cloberie*

The differences in the effects of these approaches can be illustrated by using a variation on the facts of the venerable English case of *Constable v. Cloberie*,[25] in which a shipowner promised to carry cargo from England to Cadiz in return

---

[19]Standefer v. Thompson, 939 F.2d 161 (4th Cir. 1991) (even in absence of traditional words such as "if," provision stating objective as forming corporation to carry out duties "under the joint venture" made establishment of joint venture a condition).

[20]As to the effect of such conditions under the parol evidence rule, see the discussion of condition of agreement in §7.4 *supra*.

[21]If the obligor chooses not to use a bilateral contract, the obligor can do so in a fourth way by using a unilateral contract ("I offer to deliver this cotton to you if you pay me $1,000 now"). This does not involve a condition for the reasons given in the discussion of precontractual events in §8.2 *supra*.

[22]A term that makes an event a condition of one party's duty does not of itself impose a duty on the other party that the event occur, and the nonoccurrence of a condition is therefore not of itself a breach of contract by that other party. United States v. O'Brien, 220 U.S. 321 (1911) (although contractor's right to continue dredging was conditional on satisfaction of government's engineer, failure to satisfy engineer was not breach). A party may, however, be under a duty to cooperate in bringing about a condition of the party's duty. See the discussion of breach by inaction in §8.6 *infra*.

[23]The term is Corbin's. *See* Corbin, Conditions in the Law of Contract, 28 Yale L.J. 739, 745 (1919) ("Such a condition might be described as a promissory condition.").

[24]Ross v. Harding, 391 P.2d 526 (Wash. 1964) ("breach of a 'promise' subjects the promisor to liability in damages, but does not necessarily excuse performance on the other side [while] nonoccurrence of a 'condition' prevents the promisee from acquiring a right . . . but subjects him to no liability").

[25]81 Eng. Rep. 1141 (K.B. 1626) (sailing with the next wind, although promised by the shipowner, was not a condition of the cargo owner's duty to pay freight).

for the cargo owner's promise to pay freight. Suppose that the normal freight for such a voyage consists of a base amount plus a premium and that the cargo owner wants the shipowner to sail with the next wind. The cargo owner can seek to induce the shipowner to do so in several ways: first, by making sailing with the next wind a condition of the cargo owner's duty to pay the premium; second, by having the shipowner undertake a duty to sail with the next wind; or third, by doing both.

The cargo owner might try the first way with the language "premium is to be payable only on condition that shipowner sails with the next wind." Under this language, if the shipowner carries the cargo to Cadiz but delays sailing beyond the next wind, the cargo owner will not have to pay the premium but will have no right to any damages caused by the delay.[26]

Effect of condition

The cargo owner might try the second way with the language "shipowner promises to sail with the next wind." Under this language, if the shipowner carries the cargo to Cadiz but delays sailing beyond the next wind, the cargo owner will have a right to any damages caused by the delay but will not be relieved of the duty to pay the premium.[27]

Effect of duty

The cargo owner might try the third way with the language "shipowner promises to sail with the next wind and the premium is to be payable only on condition that shipowner does so." Under this language, sailing with the next wind is a promissory condition because not only is the cargo owner's duty to pay the premium conditional on that event but the shipowner is under a duty to cause the event to occur.[28] Thus if the shipowner carries the cargo to Cadiz but delays sailing beyond the next wind, the cargo owner will have a right to any damages caused by the delay in addition to not having to pay the premium. Since the excuse of such a condition still leaves the obligor with a claim for damages if the event does not occur, such a condition may be excused even if it is not a relatively minor part of the bargain.

Effect of condition and duty

Because a determination of which of these three approaches has been used raises questions of interpretation, we now turn to those questions.

§8.4.   **Interpretation and Conditions.** If a party to an agreement asserts that it was not required to perform a duty because a condition of that duty did not occur, two questions of interpretation arise. First, was that party's duty conditional or not? Second, if the duty was conditional, what is the event on which it was conditioned? (Whether the condition was a promissory condition,

Two questions

---

[26] Merritt Hill Vineyards v. Windy Heights Vineyard, 460 N.E.2d 1077 (N.Y. 1984) (while "failure to fulfill a condition excuses performance by the other party" it is not "a breach of contract"). The impact of excuse to avoid forfeiture is considered in §8.7 *infra*.

[27] The impact of the concept of constructive conditions of exchange is considered in §8.9 *infra*.

[28] This treatment of promissory conditions has an important consequence in connection with constructive conditions of exchange. See the discussion of the effect of waiver in §8.19 *infra*.

so that the other party was under a duty to cause the event to occur, is yet a third question.[1])

Same process

The process of interpretation by which these questions are resolved is essentially the same as that by which other questions of interpretation are resolved.[2] The same emphasis is put on purpose,[3] maxims,[4] prior negotiations,[5] usage of trade, course of dealing, and course of performance.[6]

Example of financing

Suppose that a contract for the sale of a house provides, "This contract is conditional on approval of the purchaser's pending mortgage application." Is approval a condition of the vendor's duty as well as the purchaser's? Can the vendor refuse to go through with the deal if approval is not forthcoming, or can only the purchaser refuse? In concluding that approval was a condition only of the purchaser's duty, the Supreme Judicial Court of Massachusetts considered the purpose of the provision:

> The buyer was dependent upon financial assistance in order to fulfill his obligations under the contract. It was obviously to the buyer's advantage that he be released from his obligation in the event he should be unable to procure financial assistance. It would be of no importance to the [sellers] whether the buyer was offered a . . . loan if the buyer was still able to tender the full purchase price.[7]

Two preferences

Although courts apply traditional techniques of interpretation in such cases, they have displayed two preferences in interpretation that merit special attention.[8] One preference is for an interpretation that imposes on a party a duty to see that an event occurs, rather than one that makes the other party's duty conditional on occurrence of the event. The other preference is for an interpretation that will reduce an obligee's risk of forfeiture if the event does not occur.

---

§8.4   [1] Stewart v. Griffith, 217 U.S. 323 (1910) (promise by purchaser to pay balance of price for land inferred from provision making payment a condition of vendor's duty to convey land).

[2] See Della Ratta, Inc. v. American Better Community Developers, 380 A.2d 627 (Md. App. 1977) (in determining meaning of *building permits*, recourse may be had to "the negotiations of the parties, the circumstances surrounding execution of the contract, the parties' own construction of the contract and the conduct of the parties" as well as "the ordinary and customary use of those words in the construction industry").

[3] See the discussion of purpose interpretation in §7.10 *supra*.

[4] See the discussion of rules and maxims in §7.11 *supra*.

[5] See §7.12 *supra*.

[6] See §7.13 *supra*.

[7] De Freitas v. Cote, 174 N.E.2d 371, 373-74 (Mass. 1961) ("sale is subject to G.I. Loan" in stated amount).

[8] One preference that does not merit attention was set out in the first Restatement §260. If the words to be interpreted purport to be those of a party that is to do the act, there was said to be a preference for imposing a duty on that party to perform the act. If they purport to be those of a party that is not to do the act, there was said to be a preference for making the act a condition of that party's duty. This unhelpful rule is not carried over in Restatement Second §227.

Courts manifest the first preference when an agreement refers to an event within the control of one of the parties but does not make clear if that party is under a duty to see that the event occurs or if, instead, the event is a condition of the other party's duty.[9] As we shall learn, if the court holds that the obligee is under a duty to see that the event occurs, the event will still be a condition of the obligor's duty because of the concept of constructive conditions of exchange,[10] but the doctrine of substantial performance will apply.[11] If the court holds that the agreement makes the event a condition of the obligor's duty, however, then the rule of strict compliance will apply. If the agreement is ambiguous, the court will lean toward the former interpretation. Courts prefer the flexible doctrine of substantial performance, which is the product of judicial decision, to the draconian rule of strict compliance, which can be justified only by freedom of contract.[12]

Preference for finding duty

Suppose that a contract for the sale of goods contains the clause, "Selection by the buyer to be made before September 1," but the buyer does not make a selection until September 10. Does the agreement make the seller's duty conditional on selection by the buyer before September 1? If so, the seller's duty is discharged, because it is now too late for the condition to occur. If selection before September 1 is not a condition, the obvious alternative[13] is that it imposes a duty on the buyer to make a selection by September 1. A failure to do so before September 1 would be a breach of that duty for which the buyer would be liable in damages. As we shall learn, under the concept of constructive conditions of exchange, the buyer's substantial performance of that duty would also be a condition of the seller's duty. The buyer's short delay would not necessarily discharge the seller, however, because of the flexible rules applicable to such conditions.[14] This is the preferred result.[15]

Example of buyer's selection

---

[9] Since we are interested here in conditions and not duties, we shall not discuss situations in which it is clear that the event is a condition of the obligor's duty but unclear whether the obligee is also under a duty to see that it occur (i.e., whether it is a "promissory condition"). See the discussion of a *condition* and a *duty* distinguished in §8.3 *supra*.

Nor shall we discuss situations in which it is clear that the obligee is under a duty to see that the event occurs but unclear if the event is also a condition of the obligor's duty. Under the concept of constructive conditions of exchange, substantial performance of the obligee's duty would be a condition of the obligor's duty anyway, and a court will be reluctant to hold that the agreement makes it a condition, because the doctrine of strict compliance would then be applicable. See the discussion of substantial performance in §8.12 *infra*.

[10] See §8.9 *infra*.

[11] See the discussion of substantial performance in §8.12 *infra*.

[12] Castle v. Cohen, 840 F.2d 173 (3d Cir. 1988) (trustees' valuation "should . . . be considered a promise rather than a condition precedent").

[13] Unless an alternative interpretation is found, the clause will be denied effect and reduced to surplusage. See the discussion of more special rules in §7.11 *supra*.

[14] See §8.12 *infra*.

[15] Landscape Design & Constr. v. Harold Thomas Excavating, 604 S.W.2d 374 (Tex. Civ. App. 1980) (provision that subcontractor "agrees to complete the work . . . within 10 working

**Exceptions to
preference**

This preference in the interpretation of the agreement may yield to contrary arguments, however. For example, the impracticality of compensation in damages may favor the conclusion that the event is a condition.[16] The fact that the event is not within the control of the party that would be under the duty may suggest the same conclusion. If a construction contract calling for monthly progress payments contains the clause "monthly certificates to be issued by architect indicating satisfaction as work progresses," it will not be read as imposing on the contractor a duty to obtain monthly certificates for the breach of which the contractor would be liable in damages. Since issuance of the certificates is not within the contractor's control, the clause will probably be read to make issuance of the certificates a condition of the owner's duty to make monthly payments.[17] Similarly, the preference does not apply if the contract is of a type under which usually only one party undertakes duties. If a fire insurance policy contains the clause "other insurance is prohibited," it will not be read as imposing on the insured a duty to refrain from procuring other fire insurance for the breach of which the insured would be liable in damages. Even though procuring other insurance is within the control of the insured, an insurance policy is a contract under which usually only the insurer undertakes duties.[18]

**Preference
against forfeiture**

Courts manifest the second preference — for an interpretation that will reduce an obligee's risk of forfeiture — when the event in question is not likely to occur until the obligee has relied on the expected exchange by, for example, performing or preparing to perform.[19] In that situation, nonoccurrence of the condition results in the obligee's loss of its reliance interest when the obligee loses the right to that exchange. This loss of reliance interest is often described

---

days" was promise that "work will be completed within ten days" but not "condition precedent to [subcontractor's] right to payment").

[16] Globe Am. Corp. v. Miller Hatcheries, 110 S.W.2d 393 (Mo. App. 1937) (provision in compromise agreement that it was "agreed that the Globe American will drop the suit now pending" made this a condition because "how the breach of the alleged covenant . . . could be compensated in damages . . . is difficult . . . to understand").

[17] *Cf.* United States v. O'Brien, 220 U.S. 321 (1911) (Holmes, J.: "it would be a very severe construction of the contract . . . to read the reservation of a right to annul, for want of diligence not otherwise promised, as importing a promise to use such diligence as should satisfy the judgment of the engineer").

[18] Graham v. American Eagle Fire Ins. Co., 182 F.2d 500 (4th Cir. 1950) ("provision forbidding . . . additional insurance is clearly intended not as prescribing something to be done by the insured but as expressing a condition"). Furthermore, in most such cases, even if the insured were regarded as being under a duty to cause the event to occur, the insurer would have difficulty proving its damages.

[19] The reliance may consist of performance or preparation for performance (essential reliance) or of some other act (incidental reliance). For the distinction between essential and incidental reliance, see the discussion of the reliance interest in §12.1 *infra*.

as "forfeiture."[20] If the obligee's reliance has conferred a benefit on the obligor, the reliance interest will include a restitution interest, so that forfeiture will also result in unjust enrichment unless restitution is granted. In contrast, if the obligee has not yet relied on the expected exchange at the time of the nonoccurrence of the condition, the obligee loses only the right to that exchange. The owner of the house who has not yet relied on receiving the price for the house loses only the expectation interest if the purchaser's mortgage application is disapproved.[21] As the term *forfeiture* suggests, the obligee's loss of the reliance interest is regarded as more serious than is the obligee's loss of the expectation interest.[22]

To be sure, freedom of contract generally requires that the parties' agreement be honored even if forfeiture results.[23] Often it is clear from the agreement or from surrounding circumstances that the obligee has assumed the risk of forfeiture. If this is not clear, however, an interpretation that reduces that risk is preferred.[24]

Primacy of agreement

To understand the judicial aversion to forfeiture, it will be helpful to focus on two situations that have frequently produced litigation. One situation involves provisions relating to the time for payment; the other involves provisions making a party's satisfaction a condition of that party's duty.

Two situations

In the first situation, the question is: was a party's duty conditional or not? Agreements sometimes ambiguously provide that payment is due "when" or "not until" a stated event occurs. Is the event a condition or merely a means of measuring time? If a debtor borrows money at interest, promising to repay it "as soon as I sell my timber," is the debtor bound to repay the debt after a reasonable time has passed, even if the debtor has not sold the timber? A court

Condition or time period

---

[20] *See* Sturges v. System Parking, 834 S.W.2d 472 (Tex. App. 1992) (promise to pay broker half "of all management fee amounts retained or paid" was "not conditioned on what [promisor] actually retains or pays" but on what it "is entitled to be retained or paid" since "forfeiture . . . is to be avoided when another reasonable reading of the contract is possible.").

[21] The owner may have relied by taking the property off the market. However, courts have not been receptive to claims for damages based on possible lost opportunities. See §12.1 *infra*.

[22] Sometimes courts also manifest a preference against forfeiture in deciding whether the agreement imposes on a party a duty to see that an event occurs or makes the other party's duty conditional on the event's occurrence. Their inclination toward the former interpretation may be partly to avoid forfeiture. This does not, however, explain their inclination toward the former interpretation in the case of executory contracts.

[23] Wemhoff v. Investors Mgt. Corp., 528 A.2d 1205 (D.C. 1987) (though "reluctant to interpret the servicing aspect of the agreement as a condition precedent, as that would in effect work a forfeiture," court is "unable to reach any other conclusion"). Some limits of this requirement are explored in §8.7 *infra*.

[24] Restatement Second §227(1) says that "an interpretation is preferred that will reduce the obligee's risk of forfeiture, unless the event is within the obligee's control or the circumstances indicate that he has assumed that risk." It might be asked whether such an interpretation is not also to be preferred, although less strongly, even if the event is within the obligee's control.

Example of subcontractor

would probably hold that the debtor is bound.[25] It is unlikely that the creditor assumed the risk of losing the money if the debtor did not sell the timber. This suggests that the event of selling the timber was not a condition, but merely a means of measuring the time after which the debt was to be repaid.[26] The creditor's case would be even stronger if the loan had already come due and the parties had then agreed to an extension on the debtor's promise to repay it "when I sell my timber."[27]

Most of the litigation in this area has involved claims for payment for services rendered. The most common case involves a subcontractor that has made a contract under which the subcontractor is to be paid by the general contractor "when" (or is not to be paid "until") the general contractor is paid by the owner for the work. Is the general contractor liable to the subcontractor for work that the subcontractor has done if the owner, because of insolvency or for some other reason, does not pay the general contractor?[28] Does the language mean "if" (or "not unless") or does it mean "at such time as" (or "not before such time as"), but, in any case, within a reasonable time? If it means the former, payment by the owner is a condition, and the risk of the owner's nonpayment, commonly occasioned by bankruptcy, is on the subcontractor.[29] If it means the latter, payment by the owner is not a condition, and the risk of the owner's nonpayment is on the general contractor. (Such a provision is often called a *pay-when-paid* provision or, if payment is a condition, sometimes a *pay-if-paid* provision.) Almost invariably, courts hold that payment by the owner is merely a convenient means for measuring the time after which the general

---

[25] Ewell v. Landing, 85 A.2d 475 (Md. 1952) ("there can be no doubt that there was absolute liability, and that payment was merely postponed until timber could be sold").

[26] A somewhat similar controversy has arisen over a promise to repay a debt "on demand." It has been held that, since the purpose of the term is to fix the time after which interest at the legal rate is payable, a demand is not a condition of the debtor's duty and that the creditor's suit should not be dismissed merely because the creditor did not demand payment. Farmers' Natl. Bank v. Venner, 78 N.E. 540 (Mass. 1906) (where note is payable on demand, "no demand . . . is necessary in order to entitle the holder to maintain an action"). As to the statute of limitations, *see* UCC 3-118(b).

[27] Mularz v. Greater Park City Co., 623 F.2d 139 (10th Cir. 1980) (where "debt constitutes an absolute rather than a contingent liability, and payment was agreed to be made on the occurrence of an event which does not occur, payment must be made within a reasonable time").

[28] A reason other than the owner's insolvency was suggested in Midland Engrg. Co. v. John A. Hall Constr. Co., 398 F. Supp. 981 (N.D. Ind. 1975) (since percentage retained by general contractor under subcontract often exceeds percentage retained by owner under prime contract, "a malefic general contractor might intentionally maintain a dispute with the owner which would cause the owner to refuse to make payment [so that] the general contractor could thereby avail himself for several years of funds to which he has no right").

[29] That such a provision may be against public policy, *see* Wm. R. Clarke Corp. v. Safeco Ins. Co., 938 P.2d 372 (Cal. 1997) ("pay-*if*-paid" provision that applied "regardless of the reason for Owner's nonpayment," even if due to fault of owner, contractor or subcontractor, was unenforceable as contrary to public policy underlying constitutional right to mechanic's lien).

contractor must pay the subcontractor.[30] They regard the provision as designed to help the general contractor with its "cash flow," but not as intended to shift to the subcontractor the owner's credit risk. As the Supreme Court of Florida explained, "small subcontractors, who must have payment for their work in order to remain in business, will not ordinarily assume the risk of the owner's failure to pay the general contractor."[31] In a later case the same court added that in "purported risk-shifting provisions between a contractor and subcontractor, the burden of clear expression is on the general contractor," but the court found that the burden had been met.[32] The general contractor can more easily check the owner's credit and can use other devices for protection against the owner's insolvency,[33] but courts seem motivated primarily by their aversion to the risk of forfeiture, particularly since the subcontractor cannot control the occurrence of the condition. This conclusion is supported by a similar interpretation that favors a party that has supplied services, even when the other party has none of the protective devices that are available to the general contractor.[34]

Since the problem is one of interpretation, each case turns on its own facts, including the language of the particular agreement and any other circumstances that suggest whether the risk of forfeiture has been assumed.[35] One such circumstance is apparent in the case of a real estate broker that, having found a purchaser for a landowner, contracts with the landowner for a commission to be paid "on the passing of title." The risk of forfeiture in the event that the deal falls through would be more readily assumed by the broker, which deals exclusively in services and which characteristically hazards energies in projects where the outcome is doubtful.[36] Therefore, courts tend to conclude that the

Exceptional case

---

[30] Peacock Constr. Co. v. Modern Air Conditioning, 353 So. 2d 840 (Fla. 1977) (payment due "within 30 days after . . . full payment" by owner).

[31] Peacock Constr. Co. v. Modern Air Conditioning, *supra* note 30, at 842.

[32] DEC Elec. v. Raphael Constr. Corp., 558 So. 2d 427, 429 (Fla. 1990) (distinguishing *Peacock* where contract provided: "No funds will be owed to the subcontractor unless the General Contractor is paid by the owner. . . . ").

[33] The general contractor can, for example, provide for progress payments from the owner and is probably secured by a mechanic's lien.

[34] North Am. Graphite Corp. v. Allan, 184 F.2d 387 (D.C. Cir. 1950) ("The successful operation of the mine was known by all the parties concerned to be a speculative undertaking and had they intended a contingent fee contract we believe clearer language would have been used to convey that meaning."). This is not to say that this interpretation is justified only where there is the risk of forfeiture.

[35] Zane v. Mavrides, 394 So. 2d 197 (Fla. App. 1981) (loan repayable "as soon as able," as compared with another repayable "as soon as possible," was conditioned on debtor's ability to pay and not repayable within reasonable time regardless of ability).

[36] A court may be less willing to shift to the broker the risk of a contingency that is not one of the ordinary risks of the brokerage business. DeWolfe v. French, 51 Me. 420 (1864) (shipowner's duty to pay broker commission for obtaining cargo for vessel was not conditional on return of vessel that was lost at sea).

passing of title is a condition of the broker's right to a commission and is not merely a means for measuring time.[37]

Nature of satisfaction

In the second situation, the question is: What is the event on which a party's duty was conditioned? Some agreements condition one party's duty to pay or otherwise to perform on that party's satisfaction with the obligee's performance or with something else, such as the propitiousness of circumstances for the enterprise.[38] Such agreements often speak simply of "satisfaction" (or "approval"). It is clear that the event of satisfaction is a condition, but is "honest" (subjective) satisfaction required, or is "reasonable" (objective) satisfaction enough? (More precisely, the question is whether honest satisfaction is the *sole* condition, or whether honest satisfaction and reasonable satisfaction are *alternative* conditions, so that the occurrence of either makes the duty to pay unconditional.[39]) In other words, is the obligor relieved of the duty if actually not satisfied, even though the obligor reasonably ought to be satisfied?[40] Of course, the language of the agreement may be so clear as to be decisive,[41] but the judicial aversion to forfeiture is such that a court will make reasonable satisfaction the condition if presented with a choice in which forfeiture may result.[42] Therefore, the trier of fact may have to decide whether the obligor reasonably ought to have been satisfied, even if it is clear that the obligor was not actually satisfied.

Example of contractor

Suppose that a contractor agrees to do work for which the owner is to pay only on condition that the owner is "satisfied" with the work. If the contract is interpreted to require actual satisfaction, the contractor is not entirely at

---

[37] Amies v. Wesnofske, 174 N.E. 436 (N.Y. 1931) (promise to pay broker "on the closing of title" was "a promise to pay . . . upon a condition").

[38] Mattei v. Hopper, 330 P.2d 625 (Cal. 1958) (duty of purchaser of land for shopping center subject to arrangement of leases for shopping center that were "satisfactory" to him); Western Hills v. Pfau, 508 P.2d 201 (Or. 1973) (closing of land sale "subject to ability of purchaser to negotiate with City of McMinnville as to a planned development satisfactory to both . . . parties").

[39] See the discussion of how conditions relate in §8.3 *supra*.

[40] That the unreasonableness of the dissatisfaction may be relevant even under a subjective test, *see* Grobarchik v. Nasa Mortgage & Inv. Co., 186 A. 433 (N.J. Sup. 1936) (although unreasonable dissatisfaction "does not . . . afford the basis for a conclusive inference of bad faith," evidence of strict performance "justifies an inference that the owner's rejection was arbitrary, and in bad faith").

[41] Words such as *personal* or *entire* satisfaction and *sole judgment* help to show that honest satisfaction was intended. Kohler v. Leslie Hindman, Inc., 80 F.3d 1181 (7th Cir. 1996) (consignment agreement allowing auction house to rescind sale of painting in its "sole discretion" was analogous to satisfaction agreement); Gibson v. Cranage, 39 Mich. 49 (1878) ("perfectly satisfactory").

[42] Willig v. Dowell, 625 N.E.2d 476 (Ind. App. 1993) (developer was to pay balance on "satisfactory completion" of house).

the owner's mercy.[43] The owner cannot avoid liability merely by expressing dissatisfaction; the owner's discretion must be exercised in good faith.[44] "The promisor may in fact be satisfied with the performance, but not with the bargain,"[45] as Learned Hand noted, and the promisor's dissatisfaction must not be with the bargain itself.[46] And the dissatisfaction must not be based on matters of which the owner was aware when the contract was made.[47] Nevertheless, the contractor runs a risk of losing the right to payment. As Holmes said in the context of a promise to pay for a heating system on "satisfactory completion,"

> when the consideration furnished is of such a nature that its value will be lost to the plaintiff, either wholly or in great part, unless paid for, a just hesitation must be felt and clear language required, before deciding that payment is left to the will, or even to the idiosyncrasies, of the interested party.[48]

In construction contract cases, this preference for an interpretation that will reduce the risk of forfeiture is reinforced because denial of recovery will result in the enrichment of the owner as well as forfeiture by the contractor. This leads to what Richard Posner, writing for the Seventh Circuit, described as "the presumption that the performing party would not have wanted to put himself at the mercy of the paying party's whim."[49] Courts have been somewhat less reluctant to apply a test of honest satisfaction if, although forfeiture results, no benefit is conferred. For example, when a buyer can reject goods if dissatisfied, a subjective test is sometimes applied, even though the goods were specially manufactured so that they cannot be sold to others.[50] And courts have been quite willing to apply a test of honest satisfaction if no forfeiture results and no benefit is conferred. A subjective test is commonly applied, for example, when

Significance of forfeiture and enrichment

---

[43] Such a contract is therefore not illusory. Mattei v. Hopper, *supra* note 38 ("the promisor's duty, to exercise his judgment in good faith is an adequate consideration to support the contract"). See the discussion of the duty of good faith in §2.13 *supra*.

[44] Greenwood v. Koven, 880 F. Supp. 186 (S.D.N.Y. 1995) ("requirement that [auctioneer] honestly believe it might be subject to litigation . . . is undoubtedly not the level of protection [seller of painting] might like, but it is significant protection in assuring that [auctioneer] not use its broad power with indifference to [seller's] interest," quoting this section of this treatise).

[45] Thompson-Starrett Co. v. La Belle Iron Works, 17 F.2d 536, 541 (2d Cir. 1927).

[46] Devoine Co. v. International Co., 136 A. 37 (Md. 1927) (buyer who contracted to buy cherries "quality satisfactory" wrote letter expressing satisfaction and explained refusal to take cherries at first on ground that business had slackened and later on ground that buyer decided to use own supply).

[47] Western Hills v. Pfau, *supra* note 38 (purchasers who contracted to buy land if negotiations with city as to development were "satisfactory" claimed dissatisfaction for reasons known at time contract was made).

[48] Hawkins v. Graham, 21 N.E. 312, 313 (Mass. 1889).

[49] Morin Bldg. Prods. Co. v. Baystone Constr., 717 F.2d 413, 415 (7th Cir. 1983).

[50] Brown v. Foster, 113 Mass. 136 (1873) (contract to make suit of clothes); Gibson v. Cranage, *supra* note 41 (contract to make portrait from photograph). See the discussions of the example of *Dalton* and the significance of discretion in §7.17 *supra*.

a purchaser of land can refuse to go through with the transaction if dissatisfied with some circumstance, such as arrangements for financing or changes in zoning.[51] The same is true if a continuing arrangement with an employee or independent contractor is subject to termination if the party receiving the services is not satisfied with them.[52]

Significance of impracticality

The impracticality of applying an objective test is another factor that may influence a court in deciding which test of satisfaction to apply. Some contracts involve "fancy, taste, sensibility, or judgment" — for example, contracts for "the making of a garment, the giving of a course of instruction, the services of an orchestra, the making of recordings by a singer, and the painting of a portrait."[53] If it is impractical to apply a test of reasonable satisfaction to such a contract, a court may resign itself to one of honest satisfaction even if that will increase the obligee's risk of forfeiture.[54]

Third-party satisfaction

The risk to the contractor in conditioning the owner's duty to pay on even reasonable satisfaction can be avoided by making the condition the satisfaction of an independent third person. When this is done, courts have generally been willing to read "satisfaction" to mean "honest satisfaction."[55] In construction contracts, the owner's duty to pay as the work progresses is often conditioned on the satisfaction of the architect, evidenced by issuance of architects' certificates.[56] If a certificate is refused, the fact that the architect's dissatisfaction may be unreasonable does not give the contractor a claim to payment as long

---

[51] Mattei v. Hopper, *supra* note 38; Western Hills v. Pfau, *supra* note 38.

[52] Tow v. Miners Memorial Hosp. Assn., 305 F.2d 73 (4th Cir. 1962) (contract to employ pediatrician for "as long as you render satisfactory service").

[53] Gibson v. Cranage, *supra* note 41 ("Artists or third parties might consider a portrait an excellent one, and yet it prove very unsatisfactory to the person who had ordered it. . . .").

[54] Doing satisfactory work is largely within the contractor's control, to be sure, but the owner's honest satisfaction is not.

[55] Brant Constr. v. Metropolitan Water Reclamation Dist., 967 F.2d 244 (7th Cir. 1992) ("jury is not the appropriate arbiter of soil suitability where the contract explicitly delegates that task to the . . . chief engineer"). Since the result is subject to the agreement of the parties, the language of the agreement may be controlling. The widely used standard forms of the American Institute of Architects contain such language.

New York persists in applying an objective test if forfeiture would otherwise result. Nolan v. Whitney, 88 N.Y. 648 (1882) ("an unreasonable refusal on the part of an architect . . . to give the certificate dispenses with its necessity").

[56] Laurel Race Course v. Regal Constr. Co., 333 A.2d 319 (Md. 1975) ("where payments under a contract are due only when the certificate of an architect or engineer is issued, production of the certificate becomes a condition precedent to liability of the owner . . . in the absence of fraud or bad faith"). We are not here concerned with whether the issuance of a certificate is *conclusive* as to the *owner*.

An architect, even though retained by the owner, is assumed to be sufficiently independent, and the same is true of an outside engineer retained by the owner for the particular job. Furthermore, courts have indulged in the same assumption when the owner's duty to pay is conditioned on approval by an engineer who, as a salaried employee of the owner, may be considerably less independent.

as the dissatisfaction is honest. However, the requirement of a certificate will be dispensed with if the refusal can be characterized as "not in good faith" or as "dishonest" or "fraudulent."[57] If the third party's dissatisfaction is unreasonable in the extreme, courts have sometimes dispensed with the requirement by using justifications that include characterizing the refusal as "constructive fraud."[58]

Interpretation is only one of the devices used by courts to avoid forfeiture when a condition fails to occur. The next three sections discuss another device — excuse of condition.

§8.5. Excuse of Condition by Waiver. We have already seen that, even if a duty is conditional at the time a contract is made, subsequent events may excuse the condition, causing performance to become due even though the condition has not occurred at all or even though it has not occurred within the required time.[1] A common ground for excuse of a condition is that, after the contract was made, the obligor promised to perform despite the nonoccurrence of the condition or despite a delay in its occurrence. Such a promise is known as a *waiver*. If an owner whose duty to make progress payments is conditional on the contractor's furnishing architect's certificates excuses that condition by promising to make payments without certificates, the owner is said to waive the condition. The promise may be made either before or after expiration of the time during which the condition must occur. The obligor's promise to perform is not effective unless the obligor knows or at least has reason to know of the essential facts, but the obligor's knowledge of its legal situation and of the legal effect of the promise is immaterial.[2] A party can waive a condition only if the condition is for that party's own benefit, i.e., only if that party is the obligor that owes the duty that is subject to the condition.[3] If the duty of the purchaser of a house is conditional on the purchaser's obtaining a mortgage, that condition can be waived by the purchaser, but not by the vendor. And in the unusual situation in which the condition is a condition of the duties of both parties, it cannot be waived by one party alone.[4]

Promise as waiver

---

[57]RaDec Constr. v. School Dist. No. 17, 535 N.W. 408 (Neb. 1995) (architect's determination of cost solely on basis of subcontractor's figures "without attempting to verify whether those figures bore a reasonable relationship to actual costs . . . constituted a gross mistake, . . . was patently erroneous and therefore legally equivalent to bad faith").

[58]Terminal Constr. Corp. v. Bergen County, 113 A.2d 787 (N.J. 1955) ("'arbitrary action' or 'gross mistake' . . . come within the definition . . . of constructive fraud"). *See* Illustration 8 to Restatement Second §227, which rationalizes this result on the ground that because "the parties have omitted an essential term to cover this situation, the court will supply a term."

§8.5 [1]See the discussion of the possibility of excuse in §8.3 *supra*.

[2]According to Restatement Second §93, though the promisor must know or have reason to know the essential facts, "his knowledge of the legal effect of the facts is immaterial."

[3]Francis v. Buttonwood Realty Co., 765 A.2d 437 (R.I. 2001) (purchaser could waive condition that vendor procure tax abatements because it was "included for the benefit of the waiving party").

[4]See the discussion of how conditions relate in §8.3 *supra*.

Meaning of
waiver

    The meaning of *waiver* has provoked much discussion. Although it has often been said that a waiver is "the intentional relinquishment of a known right,"[5] this is a misleading definition. What is involved is not the relinquishment of a right and the termination of the reciprocal duty but the excuse of the nonoccurrence of or a delay in the occurrence of a condition of a duty.[6] The owner that leads the builder to believe that progress payments will be made without architect's certificates "waives" the condition, since the owner's duty to pay is no longer conditional on certificates. But the creditor that discharges a debt by release or renunciation does not "waive" the debt in the sense in which that term is used here.[7] It is desirable to confine the use of *waiver* in this way to avoid confusion. "Waiver is then properly described," I have written elsewhere, "as consent to have up a condition of one's duty, and when one gives such consent one can be said to waive the condtion."[8] Yet as Corbin put it, the word is one "of indefinite connotation" that, "like a cloak, covers a multitude of sins."[9] What explains the fondness courts have shown for this cloak?

Advantages of
concept

    The explanation seems to be that the rules applicable to waiver permit more flexibility in dealing with the conduct of the parties at the performance stage than would the rules applicable to either course of performance or modification.[10] An argument based on waiver has an advantage over one based on course of performance since the latter is confined to interpretation. And it has an advantage over an argument based on modification because it avoids three requirements for a modification. By characterizing conduct as a "waiver" rather than a "modification," a court may avoid the requirement of assent, the requirement of a writing under the statute of frauds, and the requirement of consideration or of detrimental reliance.

Requirement of
assent

    First, if a court asks whether the conduct of the parties amounted to a "modification," it will determine whether there was assent by applying the usual rules for the formation of contracts; if the court asks whether the conduct amounted to a "waiver," it may give effect to more dubious manifestations of assent. The promise that is the basis of a waiver may be expressed in words,[11] but often it is inferred. Conduct such as continuing performance with knowledge that the

---

    [5]Clark v. West, 86 N.E. 1 (N.Y. 1908) ("A waiver has been defined to be the intentional relinquishment of a known right.").

    [6]The quoted definition is also misleading in that the word *known* must be read as going only to the facts and not to their legal effect.

    [7]The title to UCC 1-306 uses the word *waiver* as equivalent to a renunciation, but Restatement Second §277(1), which is based on the Code in substance, does not.

    [8]*See* E. Farnsworth, Changing Your Mind ch. 16 at 155 (1998).

    [9]Corbin, Conditions in the Law of Contracts, 28 Yale L.J. 739, 754 (1919).

    [10]International Bus. Lists v. American Tel. & Tel. Co., 147 F.3d 636 (7th Cir. 1998) ("valid modification must satisfy all the criteria essential for a valid contract: offer, acceptance, and consideration").

    [11]Clark v. West, *supra* note 5 (author's abstinence from liquor while writing book as condition of publisher's duty to pay additional sum was waived when publisher with "full knowledge of

condition has not occurred might be questionable as the manifestation needed for a modification but sufficient for waiver.[12] An owner that repeatedly makes progress payments without demanding the architect's certificates on which the duty to pay is conditioned may find that the condition has been waived.[13] When a party under a conditional duty that calls for repeated performance performs without insisting on the condition, it is often difficult to determine whether that party is assenting to continue to do so in the future.[14] Characterizing the question as one of "waiver" rather than one of "modification" facilitates a finding of assent.

Second, if a court concludes that the conduct of the parties amounted to a "modification," it must then determine whether the contract as modified comes within the statute of frauds and, if it does, whether the statute is satisfied;[15] if the court concludes that the conduct amounted to a "waiver," the statute is not relevant.[16] Thus, by characterizing the conduct as a "waiver," a court may avoid any requirement of a writing and give effect to oral assent. The concept of waiver may be similarly effective against a no-oral-modification clause, by which the parties have erected their own private writing requirement as to future modification.[17]

Requirement of a writing

Third, if a court characterizes the conduct of the parties as a "modification," it must then, to the extent that the pre-existing duty rule retains its vigor,[18] ask whether the modification is supported by consideration or at least detrimental reliance; if the court characterizes the conduct as a "waiver," it begins with the proposition that a waiver is effective though not supported by consideration or detrimental reliance.[19] However, even if effective, a waiver may be subject to retraction.

Requirement of consideration

---

the . . . non-observance of that stipulation . . . not only accepted the completed manuscript without objection but 'repeatedly avowed and represented . . . that he . . . would receive said royalty payments' ").

[12] Schultz v. Los Angeles Dons, 238 P.2d 73 (Cal. App. 1951) (professional football player's failure to give written notice of injury as condition of club's duty to pay full season's salary was waived when head coach and trainer supervised examination and treatment after oral notice).

[13] McKenna v. Vernon, 101 A. 919 (Pa. 1917) ("with a single exception each of the seven payments made as the work progressed was made without a certificate being asked for").

[14] In such situations it is often difficult to draw the line between waiver and course of performance or practical construction. See the discussion of course of performance in §7.13 *supra.* The practical importance is that a party may be able to retract a waiver but cannot wipe out a course of performance or practical construction.

[15] See the discussion of modification and rescission in §6.2 *supra.*

[16] North v. Simonini, 457 A.2d 285 (Vt. 1983) ("waiver and estoppel operate independently of the statute"). *See* UCC 2-209(4) (attempt at modification or rescission that does not satisfy requirements of statute of frauds "can operate as a waiver").

[17] See the discussion of statutory inroads in §7.6 *supra.*

[18] See §§4.21, 4.22 *supra.*

[19] Wachovia Bank & Trust Co. v. Rubish, 293 S.E.2d 749 (N.C. 1982) ("waiver is valid even if not supported by consideration or estoppel").

Retraction of waiver

A party that, without consideration, has waived a condition that is within the other party's control *before* the time for occurrence of the condition has expired, can retract the waiver and reinstate the condition unless the other party has relied to such an extent that retraction would be unjust.[20] The retracting party must either give notice while there is still a reasonable time to permit the other party to cause the condition to occur or must give an extension of time. The owner that has waived the condition that the contractor furnish architect's certificates can retract the waiver and reinstate the condition as to future payments if the owner allows the contractor a reasonable time to obtain the certificates and if the contractor has not detrimentally relied on the waiver.[21] However, a party that has waived a condition *after* the time for occurrence of the condition has expired is subject to a dramatically different rule, one that has been influenced by the concept of election.[22]

Concept of election

The word *election* signifies a choice, one that is often binding on the party that makes it.[23] Holmes called election "a choice, shown by an overt act, between two inconsistent rights, either of which may be asserted at the will of the chooser alone."[24] The Romans fixed the concept in a maxim: *Quod semel placuit in electione, amplius displicere non potest* (If a man once determines his election, it shall be determined forever).[25] When the time for occurrence of a condition has expired, the party whose duty is conditional has such a choice. That party can take advantage of the nonoccurrence of the condition and treat the duty as discharged or can disregard the nonoccurrence of the condition and treat the

---

[20] UCC 2-209(5) (party "may retract the waiver by reasonable notification . . . unless the retraction would be unjust in view of a material change of position in reliance on the waiver"); Restatement Second §84(2) ("promisor can make his duty again subject to the condition" by notice if "reinstatement of the requirement of the condition is not unjust because of a material change of position").

As to the importance of convincing proof of waiver, *see* Cole Taylor Bank v. Truck Ins. Exch., 51 F.3d 736 (7th Cir. 1995) (Posner, C.J.: "courts have not been indifferent to the danger of self-serving testimony that the other party to the contract waived a right").

[21] Restatement Second §84(2)(a) (enough if there is "a reasonable time to cause the condition to occur under . . . an extension given by the promisor").

[22] Under Restatement Second §84, this is also true if the condition is not within the control of the party asserting the waiver, even if the time for occurrence of the condition has not expired. *See* E. Farnsworth, Changing Your Mind ch. 16 at 158-62 (1998) (criticizing the Restatement Second's treatment of "promissory waiver" as distinguished from "true waiver").

[23] *See* E. Farnsworth, Changing Your Mind ch. 19 (1998).

[24] Wm. W. Bierce, Ltd. v. Hutchins, 205 U.S. 340, 346 (1907) (Holmes, J.).

[25] *See* Longfellow, Masque of Pandora, Tower of Prometheus on Mount Caucasus (1895) (Hermes to Pandora):

> Decide not rashly. The decision made
> Can never be recalled. The Gods implore not,
> Plead not, solicit not; they only offer
> Choice and occasion, which once being passed
> Return no more.

duty as unconditional.[26] Courts often hold that a party that chooses to disregard the nonoccurrence of a condition is bound by an election to treat the duty as unconditional; that party cannot reinstate the condition even if the other party has not relied on this choice.[27] The parties that have most often been bound by election waivers are insurers. The insurer that chooses to engage in settlement negotiations despite the insured's failure to give timely notice of loss is likely to be precluded by its election from later resisting the claim on that ground, even if the insured in no way relied on the election.[28]

The concept of waiver — including both ordinary and election waiver — has been responsible for substantial erosion of the rule of strict compliance generally applicable to conditions. To keep this erosion in check, the concept of waiver is restricted to conditions that are relatively minor.[29] A vendor that has made an offer coupled with an option contract to sell land on condition that the purchaser pay $100,000 cannot waive this condition. Nor can an obligor waive a condition that is material to the likelihood of the obligor's having to render its own performance. An insurance company that has promised to pay the owner of a house $100,000 on condition that the house is destroyed by fire cannot waive that condition.[30] Parties can most easily waive conditions that are essentially procedural or technical, as in the example given above involving the furnishing of architect's certificates as a condition of the duty to make progress payments. Waiver is often invoked to excuse delay in the occurrence of a condition, and courts have been especially receptive to claims that an insurer has waived the insured's delay in giving notice of loss.[31]

Condition must be minor

An obligor may excuse a condition of its duty by breach as well as by waiver.

§8.6.   Excuse of Condition by Breach. An obligor may excuse a condition of its duty by committing a breach that causes the nonoccurrence of the condition. When the condition is excused, the obligor's duty becomes absolute.[1]

Nature of breach

[26] See the discussion of duty discharged in §8.3 *supra*.

[27] Restatement Second §84.

[28] United States Fidelity & Guar. Co. v. Bimco Iron & Metal Corp., 464 S.W.2d 353 (Tex. 1971) (when burglary insurer admitted partial liability, the case was "one of waiver" and need not have been "based upon an estoppel").

[29] Restatement Second §84(1)(a) (occurrence of the condition must not be "a material part of the agreed exchange for the performance of the duty"); Cole Taylor Bank v. Truck Ins. Exch., *supra* note 20 (Posner, C.J., citing this section of the treatise: waiver is limited to a minor condition, otherwise "why would someone give it up in exchange for nothing?"). However, if the condition is a promissory condition, the requirement of immateriality does not apply. See the discussion of the effect of a condition and a duty in §8.3 *supra*.

[30] *Cf.* National Util. Serv. v. Whirlpool Corp., 325 F.2d 779 (2d Cir. 1963) (party "cannot by waiver of a condition precedent to his own liability create obligation in himself where none previously existed").

[31] *See* United States Fidelity & Guar. Co. v. Bimco Iron & Metal Corp., *supra* note 28.

§8.6   [1] There are two possible rationales for the result. One is that the obligor is liable for breach of an ancillary duty not to cause the nonoccurrence of the condition. Another is that the

Breach by prevention

The breach may take the form of nonperformance, either by prevention or by failure to cooperate, or it may take the form of a repudiation.[2]

The duty of good faith and fair dealing that is usually imposed requires at least that a party do nothing to prevent the occurrence of a condition of that party's duty.[3] Thus if a party has conditioned a duty to pay on honest satisfaction with the other party's performance, the condition is excused if the party to be satisfied refuses to look at the performance.[4] Such a refusal would amount to a breach that would excuse the condition and make the duty of pay unconditional. For the same reason, the owner that conditions a duty to make progress payments on the architect's issuance of a certificate may not refuse to pay on the ground that no certificate has been issued if the owner improperly induced the architect not to issue it. Such improper action would amount to a breach that would excuse the condition and make the duty to pay unconditional.[5]

Breach by inaction

A party may be required to do more than refrain from action that will prevent the occurrence of the condition, however. A party is often expected to take affirmative steps to see that the condition occurs. The purchaser that conditions the duty to close on obtaining a mortgage is expected to take suitable steps to obtain one.[6] The purchaser is not, however, under an absolute duty to see that the condition occur, but only under a duty to try to do so. As long as the purchaser has taken suitable steps, the purchaser's failure to obtain a mortgage is not a breach, and the condition is not excused.[7] Although the purchaser's duty in this situation is often described as one of "good faith," it is more accurate to call it a duty to use "best efforts."[8]

Risk assumed by obligee

Not every obligor undertakes such a duty. Courts frequently have refused to burden the obligor with a duty to use best efforts, on the ground that the obligee has assumed the risk that the obligor would not exert itself to that

---

condition has been excused and the obligor is liable for breach of the main duty that then became unconditional. There seems to be no practical difference between these rationales.

[2] *See* Restatement Second §§245, 255.

[3] Bradford Dyeing Assn. v. J. Stog Tech GmbH, 765 A.2d 1226 (R.I. 2001) (where parties make performance conditional on event, "the contract imposes upon the party required to bring about the happening of that [event] an implied promise to use good faith, diligence and best efforts" to bring it about and if that party prevents the happening of the event, "that action eliminates the condition").

[4] See the discussion of the nature of *satisfaction* in §8.4 *supra*.

[5] Fay v. Moore, 104 A. 686 (Pa. 1918) (architect did not act "upon his own impartial judgment . . . but at the dictation . . . of the owner"). See the discussion of third-party satisfaction in §8.4 *supra*.

[6] Lach v. Cahill, 85 A.2d 481 (Conn. 1951) (dictum: where contract for sale of house was "contingent upon buyer being able to obtain mortgage," the "condition in the contract implied a promise by the plaintiff that he would make reasonable efforts to secure a suitable mortgage").

[7] Lach v. Cahill, *supra* note 6.

[8] Lach v. Cahill, *supra* note 6 ("reasonable efforts").

extent.[9] Although the seller's duty under an output contract can be considered conditional on output, the buyer is usually understood to have assumed the risk that the seller may not use best efforts. The buyer will not, however, be found to have assumed the risk that the seller will fail to act in good faith.[10]

Much of the litigation over the scope of the obligor's duty to cooperate has involved real estate brokers. Suppose that the owner of a house makes a contract with a real estate broker under which the duty to pay the broker a commission is conditioned on the passing of title. It is clear that if the owner wrongfully prevents title from passing, the owner is in breach of the contract with the broker and the condition is excused.[11] On the other hand, if the purchaser reneges, the owner is under no duty to take affirmative action to sue the purchaser for specific performance in order to cause title to pass.[12] The owner's duty is only one of good faith; the broker assumes the risk that the owner may not use best efforts to consummate the sale. There is some authority that the owner can negate even the duty of good faith, so that the broker would assume the risk that the owner might choose not to go through with the sale for any reason whatever.[13]

Real estate brokers

The breach that excuses a condition may be a repudiation of a duty instead of nonperformance of the duty. If the condition is at least partly within the control of one party and the other repudiates by stating that it will not perform even if the condition occurs, the first party can take the other's word and do nothing further to see that the condition occurs. Suppose that an owner's duty to pay is conditional on the contractor's furnishing an architect's certificate. If the owner repudiates by stating that no payment will be made, even if a certificate is furnished, the condition is excused if the contractor relies on the statement and fails to obtain a certificate.[14]

Breach by repudiation

[9] District-Realty Title Ins. Corp. v. Ensmann, 767 F.2d 1018 (D.C. Cir. 1985) ("by stating that the funds were to be returned to [financial broker] if settlement did not occur 'for any reason,' the contract allocates to [developer] the risk of nonsettlement, regardless of cause").

[10] The same can be said of the buyer's promise under a requirements contract. For discussion of both types of contracts, see the discussion of output and requirements contracts in §7.17 *supra*.

[11] Shear v. National Rifle Assn., 606 F.2d 1251 (D.C. Cir. 1979) (condition was excused when new management of owner prevented approval by its board of directors).

[12] Beattie-Firth v. Colebank, 105 S.E.2d 5 (W. Va. 1958) (where contract provided for commission if sale was consummated "or if it be not consummated by reason of any default of seller," seller was under no duty to sue for specific performance when buyer refused to consummate sale).

[13] Dixon v. Bernstein, 182 F.2d 104 (D.C. Cir. 1950) (where contract of sale gave vendor right to withdraw "for any reason whatsoever," issue of good faith was "irrelevant" to broker's claim to commission on consummation of sale).

[14] Craddock v. Greenhut Constr. Co., 423 F.2d 111 (5th Cir. 1970) (where contractor told subcontractor that it was unnecessary to furnish bond because contractor was getting another subcontractor, furnishing bond "was a useless gesture" and was excused). See the discussion of precontractual events in §8.2 *supra*.

Causal connection   However, the breach that excuses a condition must be causally connected to its nonoccurrence. Courts have not made clear the precise nature of this requirement, but the Restatement Second has abandoned the first Restatement's requirement of a "but-for" cause[15] and says that it is enough if the breach "contributes materially" to the nonoccurrence of the condition.[16] One court, endorsing this relaxation, pointed out that "almost all cases in which prevention is alleged will involve speculation as to what would have happened had the defendant's conduct not taken place."[17]

However, the breach that excuses a condition must be causally connected to its nonoccurrence. We now look at the prevention of forfeiture, a ground for excuse that does not turn on any act by the obligor.

Two exceptional situations   **§8.7. Excuse of Condition to Avoid Forfeiture.** Suppose that the nonoccurrence of a condition will cause forfeiture,[1] but the facts do not lend themselves to relief by interpretation, and the condition has not been excused by waiver or breach. Has a court the power to avoid the harsh effects of the nonoccurrence of the condition nevertheless? Courts have found the means to avoid those harsh effects in two exceptional kinds of situations.

1. Impracticability as excuse   In one situation, courts have excused a condition when its occurrence becomes impossible, or at least impracticable, and forfeiture would result if it were not excused.[2] Suppose that an owner's duty to make progress payments is conditional on the contractor's furnishing architect's certificates, and, though the work is properly done, the architect dies before giving a certificate. Excuse of the condition seems fair to avoid forfeiture.[3] Most controversy has centered around situations in which an insured has claimed that, because of disability, the condition of timely notice to the insurer has been excused. Some courts have found for the insured in order to avoid forfeiture, an approach that has special

---

[15]Restatement §295 ("the condition would have occurred . . . except for such prevention or hindrance").

[16]Restatement Second §245 ("breach by non-performance contributes materially to the non-occurrence of a condition"), §255 ("repudiation contributes materially to the non-occurrence of a condition").

[17]Shear v. National Rifle Assn., *supra* note 11, at 1257. See the discussion of causation and expectation in §12.1 *infra*.

§8.7 [1]For the sense in which *forfeiture* is used here, see the discussion of the preference against forfeiture in §8.4 *supra*.

[2]*See* Restatement Second §271. The meaning of *impracticability* here is the same as that in the discussion of performance as impracticable in §9.6 *infra*. This is a distinction between the law of offer and acceptance and the law of conditions (see the discussion of precontractual events in §8.2 *supra*), since "impossibility preventing the acceptance of an offer can not result in a contract, but in some cases impossibility may excuse the performance of a condition." Compare also the cases where a change of circumstances prevents the operation of a price term, resulting in termination of the contract. See the discussion of anomalous cases in §9.7 *infra*.

[3]*See* Restatement Second §271 illus. 1.

appeal when the policy itself covers just such disability.[4] However, other courts have reasoned that the insurer is entitled to limit its risk by such a provision and have applied the provision as it is written.[5] Most courts agree that the condition is not excused if it is a material part of the exchange, as when a life insurance policy makes it a condition that premiums be paid within a prescribed time.[6]

In the other situation, courts have excused a condition when extreme forfeiture would result if it were not excused. According to the Restatement Second, a court may excuse a condition to the extent that its nonoccurrence would cause "disproportionate forfeiture."[7] The commentary explains that, "In determining whether the forfeiture is 'disproportionate,' a court must weigh the extent of the forfeiture by the obligee against the importance to the obligor of the risk from which he sought to be protected and the degree to which that protection will be lost if the non-occurrence of the condition is excused to the extent required to prevent forfeiture."[8] Thus the concept of disproportionality requires a balancing between the forfeiture that one party would suffer and the interests that the other sought to protect. In estimating the forfeiture that a party would suffer, a court will take account of any restitution to which the party would be entitled. As in the case of excuse on other grounds, a court will excuse only a relatively minor condition to avoid disproportionate forfeiture; it will not excuse a condition if "its occurrence was a material part of the agreed exchange."[9]

The concept of disproportionate forfeiture is necessarily a flexible one, to be used by a court in its sound discretion as a last resort. It is similar in this respect to the doctrine of unconscionability, but it is designed to reach a different type of situation. The doctrine of unconscionability is directed at unfairness in the

2. Disproportion-ate forfeiture

Nature of rule

---

[4]Mutual Life Ins. Co. v. Johnson, 293 U.S. 335 (1934) (Cardozo, J.: where life insurer's duty to make monthly payments was conditional on receipt of proof of disability by age 60, condition "was excused by the physical and mental incapacity to give it").

[5]Sherman v. Metropolitan Life Ins. Co., 8 N.E.2d 892 (Mass. 1937) (to hold otherwise "would render uncertain the obligation of an insurer upon a supposedly lapsed policy or upon a policy upon which premiums are being paid and no claim has been made").

[6]The leading cases arose under life insurance policies held in the South during the Civil War. Klein v. Insurance Co., 104 U.S. 88 (1881) ("stipulation for the release of the company from liability in default of punctual payment" of life insurance premiums is "of the essence of the contract").

[7]Restatement Second §229. This is a significant distinction between the law of offer and acceptance and the law of conditions. See the discussion of precontractual events in §8.2 *supra*.

[8]Restatement Second §229 cmt. *b*.

[9]The commentary suggests, however, that even if it is made a condition that a material part of the performance be done by a stated time, a short delay in performance can still be excused to prevent disproportionate forfeiture on the rationale that the time aspect can be regarded as a separate condition that is not a material part of the agreed exchange. *See* Restatement Second §229 ills. 3 & 4. Illustration 4 is based on the *Holiday Inns* case. See the discussion of that case *infra*. However, in the case of a promissory condition, there seems to be no reason for such a requirement of immateriality. *See* the discussion of the effect of a condition and a duty in §8.3 *supra*.

contract "at the time it was made,"[10] while the rule on excuse of conditions is directed at unfairness that would occur at some later time if the condition were not excused. The Restatement Second commentary explains, "It is intended to deal with a term that does not appear to be unconscionable at the time the contract is made but that would, because of ensuing events, cause forfeiture."[11]

Support for rule

Many courts have used such subterfuges as strong-arm interpretation and liberal use of waiver to reach results consistent with this rule of last resort.[12] A few courts have relied explicitly on the concept of disproportionate forfeiture.[13]

Effect on option contracts

Among the most troublesome cases dealing with excuse of a condition to avoid forfeiture are those involving option contracts. In the typical case, a prospective purchaser has bought an option contract on land, the option to be exercised by a stated date. Courts have held that the right under the option is conditional on the purchaser exercising the option by that date and the right is lost if the purchaser does not do so. Any delay is fatal, regardless of whether it causes harm to the owner.[14] The justification for the severity of this rule is that the option holder has paid for an option that is good for a stated period, during which the holder has the opportunity to speculate on market changes at the expense of the owner; it would be unfair to allow the holder to prolong this period by delay.[15] The severity may be heightened because, since the mailbox rule does not apply, a communication exercising the option is not usually effective until receipt.[16] The situation of the option holder is distinguishable from that of a purchaser that has contracted to buy land, the price to be paid by a stated date. The purchaser's right under the contract of sale is not necessarily conditional on payment by the stated date, and a delay may not be fatal.[17] The purchaser's delay does not affect the owner's risk, since the purchaser is legally bound to pay and the owner can resort to remedies for breach in the case of nonpayment.

---

[10] UCC 2-302, discussed in §4.28 *supra*.

[11] Restatement Second §229 cmt. *a*.

[12] See §§8.4, 8.5 *supra*. For a case refusing to resort to subterfuges in spite of a harsh result, *see* Inman v. Clyde Hall Drilling Co., 369 P.2d 498 (Alaska 1962), discussed in §8.3 *supra*. For an exaggerated description of the impact of these subterfuges, *see* Childres, Conditions in the Law of Contracts, 45 N.Y.U. L. Rev. 33 (1970).

[13] Alcazar v. Hayes, 982 S.W.2d 845 (Tenn. 1998) (applying principle of §229, "we find that the notice requirement is immaterial to the insurance contract in the event that the insurer is not prejudiced").

[14] Livesey v. Copps Corp., 280 N.W.2d 339 (Wis. 1979) (where option expired on November 15 and letter exercising it was not received until November 16, exercise was "not effective" because "time is ordinarily of the essence of an option").

[15] See the discussion of the risk of speculation in §3.2 *supra*.

[16] See the discussion of other applications of the rule in §3.22 *supra*.

[17] Ledford v. Atkins, 413 S.W.2d 68 (Ky. 1967) ("equity should not permit the forfeiture of an oil lease because of a delay of 13 days in making payments, where the facts show that the lessee was severely ill and comatose for a period of 23 days, at a critical time when payments came due under the lease"). See the discussion of time of the essence in §8.18 *infra*.

The harsh rule for option contracts is not well adapted to a lessee's option to renew a lease. The lessee's reliance while on the premises gives the lessee an argument based on forfeiture, and the delay, if it results from inadvertence, usually affords the lessee no significant opportunity for speculation at the expense of the lessor.[18] A growing number of courts have succumbed to this argument and have excused the delay as long as it has been slight, inadvertent, and has caused no loss to the lessor.[19]

Exceptions to option rule

A leading case on options is *Holiday Inns of America v. Knight*, decided by the Supreme Court of California in 1969. Holiday Inns held an option to purchase, for some $200,000, land owned by the Knights. The option, acquired in 1963 for an initial payment of $10,000, could be kept alive by a $10,000 payment on July 1 of each succeeding year and was to be exercised no later than April 1, 1968. Holiday Inns developed a major residential and commercial center on land adjacent to the Knights's property, causing the option property to increase substantially in value. Holiday Inns made annual payments in 1964 and 1965 and in 1966 mailed a check dated June 30 that was received on July 2. When the Knights refused to accept it, "stating that the option contract was cancelled," Holiday Inns sought a declaratory judgment that the contract was still in force, and the Supreme Court directed summary judgment for Holiday Inns. Roger Traynor discussed the court's aversion to forfeiture but found no forfeiture resulting from Holiday Inns' work on the adjacent land. He concluded instead that part of the $30,000 Holiday Inns had already paid was "for the right to exercise the option during the last two years" and that under the judgment appealed from, Holiday Inns would "suffer a forfeiture of that part." Admittedly, extending the time for exercise of the option beyond that given in the contract would give Holiday Inns a more extensive option than the one bargained for. But the July 1 deadline for payment of the $10,000 was distinguishable from the April 1 deadline for the $200,000 commitment and Holiday Inns was "not seeking to extend the period during which the option can be exercised but only to secure relief from the provision making time of the essence in tendering the annual payments."[20]

Example of *Holiday Inns*

The distinction is less clear than the court suggests. Holiday Inns was under no duty to make the annual payments; had it failed to make the 1966 payment,

Rationale of decision

[18]Compare the lease cases mentioned in the discussion of reluctance to extend the premise in §3.29 *supra*, where reliance may encourage a court to uphold an option to renew against a claim of indefiniteness.

[19]J.N.A. Realty Corp. v. Cross Bay Chelsea, 366 N.E.2d 1313 (N.Y. 1977) (4-3 decision: lessee that inadvertently exercised option four and one-half months late, but had made "considerable investment in improvements on the premises," would be entitled to equitable relief if there was "no prejudice to the landlord").

[20]450 P.2d 42, 44-45 (Cal. 1969). Although California has a statutory provision on forfeiture taken from the Field Code (see the discussion of contract law seen as essentially case law in §1.8 *supra*), the court's reasoning would not necessarily be different in a jurisdiction without such a provision.

the Knights would have had no recourse.[21] By giving additional time for the 1966 payment, the court extended the time within which Holiday Inns could decide whether to keep the option alive. This extended the time during which the Knights were subject to speculation by Holiday Inns, just as if the court had extended beyond April 1, 1968, the time for exercise of the option itself. Perhaps a different thought underlies the court's decision. On July 1, 1966, Holiday Inns was risking payment of only $10,000, to keep open an option on property worth 20 times that amount and it was unlikely that Holiday Inns would speculate by withholding this relatively small sum for a few days when so much was at stake.[22] The importance to the Knights of strict observance of the July 1 deadline, to keep Holiday Inns from speculating, was therefore not great. In contrast, the forfeiture that Holiday Inns would suffer if strict observance were required could be characterized as disproportionately large. However, the April 1 deadline was distinguishable because extending that deadline for even a few days would invite Holiday Inns to speculate by withholding the entire $200,000 commitment for a longer period than agreed to by the Knights. On this ground, the court's distinction between the two deadlines can be rationalized.

The following sections to problems of nonperformance what we have learned in the preceding sections about the law of conditions.

C.   NONPERFORMANCE

Performance is discharge

§8.8.   Performance as Discharge and Nonperformance as Breach. If a duty is fully performed, it is discharged.[1] A builder's duty to build a house is discharged when the house has been built; the owner's duty to pay the price is discharged when the builder has been paid. If the scope of the duty is unclear (as when the specifications are vague, ambiguous, or incomplete), a question may arise as to exactly what performance is required. Questions of this kind are answered by the processes of interpretation and implication discussed in the preceding chapter.[2] If an obligor owes more than one duty (as when the owner owes the builder for several houses and sends one check in part payment), it may be unclear which of the duties is being performed. Questions of this kind are resolved by rules relating to how payments and other performances are to

---

[21]The agreement provided that "failure to make payment on or before the prescribed date will automatically cancel the option."

[22]This can be seen more clearly by supposing a case in which the annual payments are, say, $10 rather than $10,000.

§8.8 [1]Performance is only one of many possible grounds for the discharge of a contract duty. For examples of other grounds, *see* §§4.24, 4.25 (agreement) *supra* and §§9.6, 9.7 (impracticability and frustration) *infra*.

[2]See §§7.7, 7.16 *supra*.

be applied; they will not be dealt with in this treatise.[3] Such questions aside, the principle is clear that full performance operates as a discharge.

The converse is equally clear. Nothing less than full performance operates as a discharge. The builder that fails in any respect to perform has not earned a discharge. This is true even if the defect is insubstantial, even if it is neither willful nor negligent, and even if the builder is unaware of it. Courts occasionally ignore trifling defects under the principle *de minimis non curat lex* ("the law does not concern itself with trifles"). Even so, courts usually render lip service to the requirement of full performance by concluding that, properly read, the contract itself tolerates such trifling defects.[4] A court may rest a decision that the builder has performed despite apparent defects on the ground that the variance was within the range allowed by the specifications.[5]

Nonperformance is not discharge

However, nonperformance does not always amount to a breach. Full performance may not yet be due, either because a required period of time has not yet passed or a condition has not yet occurred.[6] Or the duty may already have been discharged, on a ground such as impracticability of performance or frustration of purpose.[7] In these situations, the nonperformance is said to be "justified." The builder's nonperformance is justified if the owner has failed to provide the plans on which the duty to begin work was conditioned.

May not be breach

When performance is due, however, any failure to render it is a breach. The builder that fails in any respect to perform when performance is due has not only failed to earn a discharge but has also become liable for breach of contract.[8] This is true even if the defect is insubstantial, even if it is neither willful nor negligent, and even if the builder is unaware of it.[9]

When it is breach

A party's nonperformance may have even more dramatic consequences than that of making that party liable for breach of contract. We turn to those next.

§8.9. Constructive Conditions of Exchange. If the only consequence of a party's nonperformance were liability for breach of contract, a party to a

Need for security

---

[3] These rules are set out in Restatement Second §§258-260.

[4] Van Clief v. Van Vechten, 29 N.E. 1017 (N.Y. 1892) (dictum: "slight and insignificant imperfections or deviations may be overlooked on the principle of *de minimis non curat lex*").

[5] *Cf.* Intermeat v. American Poultry, 575 F.2d 1017 (2d Cir. 1978) (seller performed by delivery of meats marked "Tasmeats" though contract called for "Richardson Production," since it was common knowledge in the trade that they were equivalent).

[6] See the discussion of performance as not due in §8.3 *supra*.

[7] See §§9.6, 9.7 *infra*. A purist might argue that, since the duty has been discharged, this is not even a case of nonperformance.

[8] This is so whether the duty is imposed by the language of the agreement itself or by implication, as is the duty of good faith.

[9] If at the time of nonperformance the contract is unenforceable because of the statute of frauds, the nonperformance can be a breach if the statute is subsequently satisfied. A claim for damages is then one for a breach that occurred previously, at the time of the actual nonperformance, and not for one that occurred at the time of the later satisfaction of the statute. See the discussion of the agreement as not deprived of all effect in §6.10 *supra*.

bilateral contract would have little assurance of receiving the promised return performance.[1] If the other party failed to perform, the injured party would still be bound to perform. If the builder failed to build the house, the owner would still be bound to pay the price. The injured party would have a remedy for breach, but this remedy might be no more than a claim for damages, collectible only after much delay. Were the injured party to refuse to perform in response to the other party's breach, the injured party would be exposed to a claim for damages that might exceed the injured party's own claim.[2]

Early English response

This problem did not arise in English law until the end of the sixteenth century, when the development of the action of assumpsit made it clear that a wholly executory bilateral contract was enforceable.[3] Prior to that time, the builder had been confined to the action of debt, and the requirement of a *quid pro quo* precluded any claim until the builder had actually conferred a benefit on the owner by performing.[4] An analogous problem had arisen as early as 1500 out of an exchange of promises under seal. However, it was then said: "If one covenant with me to serve me for a year and I covenant with him to give him £20, if I do not say 'for the said cause,' he shall have action for the £20 even though he has not served me. It is otherwise if I say that he shall have the £20 'for the same cause.' "[5] Absent some such qualifying words making the employer's duty conditional on performance by the employee, the employee's right to enforce the employer's promise did not depend on the employee's own performance. This literalism was carried over from actions on sealed promises to actions in assumpsit on bilateral contracts in 1615, shortly after the expansion of the action of assumpsit was complete. In an action by the seller on a bilateral contract for the sale of a cow, the Court of King's Bench held in *Nichols v. Raynbred* "that the plaintiff need not aver the delivery of the cow, because it is promise for promise."[6] If the seller did not deliver the cow, the buyer's recourse was presumably a cross-action in assumpsit against the seller. The cases that applied this literalistic solution were later said by an English judge to "outrage common sense,"[7] but English courts applied it for over a century and a half,[8]

---

§8.9   [1]As pointed out in the discussion of the focus on nonperformance in §8.1 *supra*, our concern is with bilateral contracts.

[2]This will not often be the case, however, since a party usually does not break a contract that is advantageous to that party.

[3]See the discussion of the supplanting of debt by *indebitatus assumpsit* in §1.6 *supra*.

[4]See the discussion of the unsuitability of the action of debt as a general basis in §1.5 *supra*.

[5]Anon., Y.B. 15 Hen. VII, fo. 10b, pl. 17 (1500) (Fineux, C.J.).

[6]80 Eng. Rep. 238 (K.B. 1615).

[7]Lord Kenyon in Goodisson v. Nunn, 100 Eng. Rep. 1288, 1289 (K.B. 1792).

[8]For a notorious case in which literalism prevailed, *see* Pordage v. Cole, 85 Eng. Rep. 449 (K.B. 1669).

sometimes softening it by finding that the parties had expressed a condition in their agreement.[9]

It was left to Lord Mansfield to set the law right in the great case of *Kingston v. Preston*, decided by the Court of King's Bench in 1773. A silk mercer had made a contract with his apprentice, under which, after a year and a quarter, the mercer was to convey his business, including his stock in trade, to the apprentice and a partner. In return, the apprentice was to pay for his share of the business in monthly installments and, to assure these payments, was to give "good and sufficient security" before the conveyance of the business to him. The apprentice sued the mercer for damages for failure to convey the business, and the mercer defended on the ground that the apprentice had not given the required security. It was argued for the apprentice that the mercer's promise to convey the business was "independent" of the apprentice's promise to give security, and that the defendant might have his remedy for the plaintiff's breach in a separate action. Mansfield rejected this argument and the defendant prevailed.

Kingston v. Preston

Mansfield admitted that there were instances in which one promise under a bilateral contract was "independent" of a return promise, in the sense of its not being conditional on the performance of the return promise. In such cases non-performance of the return promise was no excuse for nonperformance of the first promise, even if the nonperformance of the return promise were actionable as a breach. But, Mansfield said, there were also instances in which one promise under a bilateral contract was "dependent" on a return promise in the sense of being conditional on the return performance, and in such cases nonperformance of the return promise, in addition to being actionable as a breach, was an excuse for the nonperformance of the first promise. Whether a promise was independent or dependent on a return promise "was to be collected from the evident sense and meaning of the parties."[10] Even though the agreement contained no language making the mercer's duty to convey the business conditional on the apprentice's giving the required security, Mansfield reasoned:

Mansfield's reasoning

> It would be the most monstrous case in the world, if the argument [of the plaintiff] was to prevail. It's of the very essence of the agreement, that the defendant will not trust the personal security of the plaintiff. A Court of Justice is to say, that by operation of law he shall, against his teeth. He is to let him into his house to squander every thing there, without anything to rely on but what he has absolutely refused to trust. This payment, therefore, was a precedent condition

[9] Peeters v. Opie, 85 Eng. Rep. 1144 (K.B. 1671) (where builder was to be paid "for his work," the word *for* made work a condition).

[10] 99 Eng. Rep. 437, 438 (K.B. 1773). The report of this case that is commonly relied on appears in the argument of counsel in Jones v. Barkley, 99 Eng. Rep. 434 (K.B. 1781). Another version appears in 98 Eng. Rep. 606.

before the covenant of putting into possession was to be performed on the part of the defendant.[11]

Dependency through conditions

In the scheme that Mansfield devised in *Kingston v. Preston*, the court itself determines whether one party's promise is dependent upon the other party's return promise. If it is, the court supplies a term making the first party's promise conditional on performance of the return promise. If an agreement provides that a builder is first to build and the owner is then to pay, the court will supply a term making the builder's performance a condition of the owner's duty to pay. Two conclusions follow from Mansfield's scheme. First, the owner is under no duty to pay until the builder performs. Second, after the time for performance has passed, the owner may treat the duty to pay as discharged by the delay and therefore may terminate the contract.[12]

Constructive conditions

Mansfield was dealing with an omitted case.[13] Speaking in the eighteenth century, he rested his decision on "the evident sense and meaning of the parties" and on "the essence of the agreement." Today we would describe the process that he used as that of implication and the term he supplied as implied or constructive. In Corbin's words, a fact that operates as a condition "because the court believes that the parties would have intended it to operate as such if they had thought about it at all, or because the court believes that by reason of the *mores* of the time justice requires that it should so operate, . . . may . . . be described as a condition implied by law, or better as a *constructive condition*."[14] Since a bilateral contract involves an exchange of promises and the performance of each is made a condition of the duty to perform the other, such implied conditions are often called *constructive conditions of exchange*.

Preference for dependent promises

Constructive conditions of exchange play an essential role in assuring the parties to a bilateral contract that they will actually receive the performance that they have been promised. In the centuries since *Kingston v. Preston*, courts have sensibly imposed such conditions whenever possible.[15] Courts occasionally still revert to the notion of independence of promises when it would be less

---

[11] 99 Eng. Rep. at 608. The other report of this case has a less colorful version of this passage. 98 Eng. Rep. at 438.

[12] As to suspension and termination, see §8.15 *infra*.

[13] See §§7.15, 7.16 *supra*.

[14] Corbin, Conditions in the Law of Contracts, 28 Yale L.J. 739, 743-44 (1919). The Restatement Second uses this terminology and "avoids as misleading, as did the former Restatement, any classification of promises as either 'dependent' or 'independent.'" The Restatement Second rules do not treat individual promises as dependent or independent, but apply "to all of the performances to be rendered by each party taken collectively." Restatement Second §232 cmt. *b*.

[15] Conley v. Pitney Bowes, 34 F.3d 714 (8th Cir. 1994) (where employer was required to inform employee at the time it denied him benefits, employer's "performance had necessarily to precede" and was therefore constructive condition of employee's exhaustion of remedies).

According to Restatement Second §232, under a bilateral contract all the performances that each party is to render "taken collectively are treated as performances to be exchanged under an exchange of promises unless a contrary intention is clearly manifested."

confusing to treat all promises as dependent and base the result on the immateriality of the breach.[16] As one scholar put it, "a decision that the promises are
independent is frequently a means of rejecting a defense because the breach
is not regarded as sufficient to justify excusing the innocent party from his
obligations under the contract."[17] By and large, however, only by the clearest
language can the parties make a promise to which the concept of constructive
conditions does not apply.[18] Of course if the parties have made two separate
contracts, a court will not go so far as to hold that one party's duty under one
contract is constructively conditioned on the other party's performance under
the other contract.[19] But if there is a choice, the judicial preference for constructive conditions of exchange and the self-help remedies that they afford the
injured party is overwhelming.[20]

A major exception has been made for leases.[21] Because a lease has tradition-   **Applicability to**
ally been regarded, not as a contract between landlord and tenant, but as a con-   **leases**
veyance by the landlord of an interest in land for which the tenant has agreed to
pay rent, courts have held that the tenant's promise is independent of any duties
that the landlord may have to make repairs or provide services.[22] However,
many courts have begun to apply the concept of constructive conditions
to leases.[23] The traditional view of leases has not prevented courts from holding
that a lessee's right to renew a lease is conditional on the lessee's performance
during the term of the lease, so that nonpayment of rent bars the lessee from
demanding a right of first refusal or exercising an option to renew.[24]

---

[16] See the discussion of first material breach in §8.15 *infra*.

[17] 1 G. Palmer, Law of Restitution §45 at 415 (1978).

[18] Orkin Exterminating Co. v. Harris, 164 S.E.2d 727 (Ga. 1968) (employer's breach in firing
employee did not discharge employee's duty under covenant not to compete where agreement
provided that covenant was "independent").

[19] Rudman v. Cowles Communications, 280 N.E.2d 867 (N.Y. 1972) (upholding as "a question of fact" the trial court's finding "that each agreement was a 'separate and independent
transaction'").

[20] Courts make important exceptions so that a party in breach can nevertheless enforce a choice
of forum clause or an arbitration clause. *See* Marra v. Papandreou, 216 F.3d 1119 (D.C. Cir. 2000)
(choice of forum), following Kulukundis Shipping Co. v. Amtorg Trading Corp., 126 F.2d 978 (2d
Cir. 1942) (arbitration).

[21] It is sometimes supposed that there is an exception for aleatory contracts. See the discussion
of choice by inaction in §8.19 *infra*.

[22] Rock County Sav. & Trust Co. v. Yost's, 153 N.W.2d 594 (Wis. 1967) ("In a lease which
amounts to a conveyance as does the instant lease . . . the covenants are independent unless
expressly made dependent.").

[23] *See* Restatement (Second) of Property (Landlord & Tenant) §7.1, Reporter's Note ("rule of
this section, in its adoption of the dependence-of-obligations doctrine with respect to the landlord's
promise, is based on a logical extension of the position taken by a significant number of judicial
decisions which have applied the doctrine in connection with the failure of the landlord to fulfill
his obligations in regard to the condition of the leased property").

[24] Hieb v. Jelinek, 497 N.W.2d 88 (N.D. 1993) (commonly held that the right to renew "is
implicitly dependent" on performance).

Applies even if no breach

The concept of constructive conditions of exchange is most often called into play when one party seeks to justify its own refusal to perform on the ground that the other party has committed a breach of contract. The concept is not restricted to that situation, however, and may justify such a refusal whenever the other party fails to perform, even if that failure does not amount to a breach.[25] Indeed, courts sometimes speak confusingly in such cases of "failure of consideration" when what is meant is failure of performance.[26] If the purchaser of a house makes a promise to close the deal conditional on a bank's approval of a mortgage application and then justifiably refuses to proceed when approval is refused, the purchaser's failure of performance justifies the vendor in refusing to convey the house. Even though the purchaser's failure to perform does not amount to a breach, it justifies the vendor's refusal to convey.[27] But for the sake of clarity the discussion in the remainder of this chapter will be confined to the situation where the nonperformance is a breach.

Limits of dependence

The timing of the parties' performances imposes some limits on the use of constructive conditions. One party's duty to perform can be conditioned or dependent on the other party's rendering a performance that is due at an earlier time. But one party's duty to perform cannot be conditioned or dependent on the other party's rendering performance that is to come at a later time.[28] If the builder is to build first and the owner is to pay later, the law can afford the owner security by conditioning the duty to pay on the house being built first, but it cannot afford the builder comparable security. If the owner is to make payments as the work progresses, the owner gives up some security with each payment.[29] Thus the order in which parties are to perform under a bilateral contract takes on an enhanced importance because of its relation to constructive conditions of exchange. The security afforded by the concept of constructive conditions cannot easily be extended to protect the party whose duty it is to go first.[30]

---

[25] For some minor exceptions, see the discussion of the effect on the other party in §9.9 *infra*.

[26] First Natl. Bank v. Burich, 367 N.W.2d 148 (N.D. 1985) (fn.3: "'failure of consideration' . . . is potentially misleading" and its use "should be discouraged").

[27] See the discussion of how nonperformance may not be a breach in §8.8 *supra*. The same is true if the other party's duty has been discharged as a result of impracticability and frustration. As to the impact of the concept of constructive conditions of exchange in those cases, see the discussion of the effect on the other party in §9.9 *infra*.

[28] Price v. Van Lint, 120 P.2d 611 (N.M. 1941) (since "the parties must have known that the day for performance by [lender] might arrive before the [borrower] would be in a position to give the promised mortgage following delivery of his deed upon its return from abroad," lender's duty to make loan was not conditioned on borrower's giving mortgage).

[29] For more on progress payments, see the discussion of the time for performance distinguished in §8.13 *infra*.

[30] However, even the promise to perform earlier is dependent on the promise to perform later, in the sense that the duty to perform earlier may be discharged by anticipatory repudiation of the promise to perform later. *See* the discussion of how such a repudiation discharges duties in §8.20 *infra*. As to the situation in which the performance of the party that is to go first is delayed until

We look now to the problems that arise when the parties are to perform at
the same time.

§8.10. **Concurrent Conditions.** The situation in which the parties are   **Performance at**
to perform at the same time, rather than one after the other, calls for special   **same time**
attention. In *Kingston v. Preston*, Mansfield spoke of promises

> which are mutual conditions to be performed at the same time; and, in these, if
> one party was ready, and offered, to perform his part, and the other neglected, or
> refused, to perform his, he who was ready, and offered, has fulfilled his engage-
> ment, and may maintain an action for the default of the other; though it is not
> certain that either is obliged to do the first act.[1]

The Court of King's Bench applied this analysis in *Morton v. Lamb* in   *Morton v. Lamb*
1797, several years after Mansfield's death. A buyer of grain alleged that
the seller had failed to deliver the grain at the time and place agreed upon,
although the buyer was ready and willing to receive it. The court upheld
the seller's objection that the buyer had failed to allege that he was ready
to pay for the grain, explaining "that where two concurrent acts are to be
done, the party who sues the other for non-performance must aver that he
has performed, or was ready to perform, his part of the contract."[2] Performance of the promise to deliver and performance of the promise to pay
were, in Mansfield's terms, "mutual conditions to be performed at the same
time."

Courts still apply the rule laid down in *Morton v. Lamb* to contracts for   **Concurrent**
the sale of goods in which there is no provision for credit or other means of   **conditions**
payment.[3] Courts express the mutual dependence of the parties' promises by
saying that tender of the goods by the seller and tender of the price by the buyer
are "concurrent conditions."[4] As the Uniform Commercial Code makes clear,

---

the time for the other party to perform, see the discussion of simultaneous performances possible
later in §8.11 *infra*.

§8.10 [1] 9 Eng. Rep. 437, 438 (K.B. 1773). *See* the discussion of *Kingston v. Preston* in §8.9
supra.

[2] 101 Eng. Rep. 890, 892 (K.B. 1797).

[3] UCC 2-507(1), 2-511(1). It will be recalled that this was apparently the situation in Nichols v.
Raynbred, described in the discussion of the early English response in §8.9 *supra*. In commercial
sales, where the transaction is not to be face-to-face, the parties often agree on payment against
a bill of lading covering the goods, rather than against the goods themselves. Such arrangements
are beyond the scope of this treatise.

[4] Of course, as the quotation from Morton v. Lamb indicates, actual performance, rather than
mere tender of performance, will suffice.

tender of the goods is a condition of the buyer's duty to pay,[5] and tender of the price is a condition of the seller's duty to deliver.[6]

Meaning of *tender*   Strictly speaking, what is required on either side is not quite a tender, because tender requires that the subject matter be produced. The commentary to the Restatement Second explains that a party need not actually hold out what that party is to deliver; it is enough if there is an "offer of performance . . . accompanied with manifested present ability to make it good."[7] But for the sake of simplicity, *tender* will generally be used in this treatise to include an offer of performance that is not a strict tender. The mechanics by which a party can offer performance depends on the circumstances. The comments to the Uniform Commercial Code explain that, in the present context, "'due tender' . . . contemplates an offer coupled with a present ability to fulfill all the conditions resting on the tendering party."[8] The Code requires only that a seller "put and hold conforming goods at the buyer's disposition and give the buyer any notification reasonably necessary" to enable the buyer to take delivery,"[9] subject to any right that the buyer may have to inspect the goods before paying.[10]

Effect of failure   Even a party that requires concurrent performance by the other party must still have made an offer to perform before bringing an action for breach, for otherwise, in Williston's words, "both parties might be ready and willing and each stay at home waiting for the other to come forward."[11] Should each party "stay at home" too long, failing to make even a conditional offer to perform within the appropriate time, their mutual abandonment will be considered an agreement of rescission, after which neither can put the other in default and acquire a cause of action.[12] Although one party's offer to perform will suffice to

---

[5]UCC 2-507(1) (tender of delivery "is a condition to the buyer's duty to accept the goods" and, unless otherwise agreed, to the duty to pay for them). As to the place of the seller's tender, *see* UCC 2-308(a) (unless otherwise agreed "the place for delivery of goods is the seller's place of business" or if the seller has none then its residence).

[6]UCC 2-511(1) (unless otherwise agreed "tender of payment is a condition to the seller's duty to tender and complete any delivery"). As to the place, *see* UCC 2-310(a) (unless otherwise agreed "payment is due at the time and place at which the buyer is to receive the goods"). Under UCC 2-511(2), the condition is tender by the buyer of legal tender, but tender of payment "by any means or in any manner current in the ordinary course of business" is sufficient if the seller does not demand payment in legal tender. By failing to make a demand, the seller waives the condition. See the discussion of how a condition must be minor in §8.6 *supra*.

[7]Restatement Second §263 cmt. *b*.

[8]UCC 2-503 cmt. 1.

[9]UCC 2-503(1).

[10]On the buyer's right to inspect, *see* UCC 2-513.

[11]3 S. Williston, Contracts §832 (1st ed. 1920).

[12]Guillory Corp. v. Dussin Inv. Co., 536 P.2d 501 (Or. 1975) ("agreement expired by its own terms" where "neither party . . . either demanded performance by the other or claimed any excuse" by expiration date). UCC 2-309 cmt. 5 suggests that mutual postponement may precede mutual abandonment: "When both parties let an originally reasonable time go by in silence, the

put the other party under a duty to perform, the offer alone does not discharge the first party's duty to perform.[13]

Real estate transactions

The concept of concurrent conditions plays an especially significant role in real estate transactions, where the parties commonly expect that the vendor will deliver a deed and simultaneously the purchaser will pay part or all of the price.[14] This is often done at a "closing," held at a time and place specified in the agreement.[15] Each party is expected to be at the appointed place at the time specified and to tender performance.[16] A party that does not do this has no right against the other party, even if the other party could not have performed, unless the other party's prospective inability to perform was such as to excuse the first party from even tendering performance.[17]

Three-cornered settlements

Tender of a deed by the vendor becomes more complex if the real estate is subject to a mortgage and the vendor has promised to convey it free of encumbrances. Usually the vendor plans to pay off the mortgage with part of the price to be paid by the purchaser. It has been held that the vendor has the right to do this at a "three-cornered settlement," with vendor, purchaser, and mortgagee present, even though the concept of concurrent conditions requires simultaneous performance. "The process of closing is, for this purpose, an integral transaction, though it may take hours or even days to complete."[18]

Inapplicable to specific performance

The requirement of tender is obviated if the action is one for specific performance, as is often the case in real estate transactions. If a court grants specific performance, it can condition its order on simultaneous performance by the injured party, the exchange taking place under the supervision of the court.[19]

The next section deals with the order in which the parties are to perform.

---

course of conduct under the contract may be viewed as enlarging the reasonable time for tender or demand of performance. The contract may be terminated by abandonment." See the discussion of agreement of rescission in §4.24 *supra*.

[13] Pelletier v. Dwyer, 334 A.2d 867 (Me. 1975) (vendor could not claim forfeiture of purchaser's deposit without tender).

[14] Kane v. Hood, 30 Mass. (13 Pick.) 281 (1832) (where purchaser was to pay in three installments, "the deed to be executed at the completing of the last payment," payment of the last installment and delivery of the deed were concurrent conditions). See the discussion of simultaneous performances in §8.11 *infra*.

[15] In parts of the United States, a process known as an escrow closing is used, in which the parties do not meet face to face; instead the vendor deposits a deed and the purchaser deposits the price "in escrow" with an escrow agent who consummates the transaction for them.

[16] Hellrung v. Hoechst, 384 S.W.2d 561 (Mo. 1964) (not sufficient where purchaser of land said "I will give you the money if you give me a clear title," but did not have the money with him).

[17] See the discussion of repudiation by conduct in §8.21 *infra*.

[18] Robeson-Marion Dev. Co. v. Powers Co., 183 S.E.2d 454 (S.C. 1971).

[19] Love v. Givens, 331 P.2d 585 (Kan. 1958) (equity court "is amply able to safeguard the rights of the defendant and to provide that plaintiffs shall convey the interest in the property to defendant in exchange for the purchase price"). *See* the discussion of insecurity in §12.7 *infra*.

Significance of order

§8.11. Order of Performance. Courts developed the concept of constructive conditions of exchange in an effort to give both parties to a bilateral contract as much security as the order of their performances will permit. This result is achieved by making each party's duty to perform conditional on the other party's rendering any performance due at an earlier time and tendering any performance due at the same time. In *Kingston v. Preston*, Lord Mansfield said that the "precedency [of promises] must depend on the order of time in which the intent of the transaction requires their performance."[1] This order is therefore critical in determining the amount of security that the concept of constructive conditions of exchange can afford.

How order is determined

Sometimes the parties themselves fix the order of performance by the language of their agreement. If they do not, the situation may dictate that order.[2] And over the years courts have developed some fairly simple rules to determine the order of performance under a bilateral contract if neither language nor circumstances indicates the order.

Simultaneous performances

One of the most important of these rules is that, insofar as the agreement permits return performances to be rendered simultaneously, they are due simultaneously. This rule applies not only if no time is fixed for performance of either party, but also if a time is fixed for the performance of only one of the parties, or if one period is fixed within which both parties are to perform.[3] It applies whether the performances that can be rendered simultaneously are whole or part performances. Thus, the law favors an order of performances that results in concurrent conditions of exchange.[4] The Uniform Commercial Code reflects this preference in its general rule that delivery of the goods and payment of the price are to be simultaneous, so that tender of performance by each party is a condition of the other party's duty to perform.[5] The general rule for sales of land is the same.[6] In addition to giving the parties symmetrical security, the rule avoids placing on either party the burden of financing the other party before the other has performed.

---

§8.11 [1] 99 Eng. Rep. 437, 438 (K.B. 1773). See the discussion of this case in §8.9 *supra*.

[2] Clark v. Gulesian, 84 N.E. 94 (Mass. 1908) (owner's posting of bond was to precede builder's commencement of work since "the giving of security for the payment of the price was intended to be a precedent condition, before performance by the [builder] could be demanded").

[3] Morton v. Lamb, 101 Eng. Rep. 890 (K.B. 1797) (where seller agreed to deliver grain within a month from the time of the sale, "there can be no doubt but that the parties intended that the payment should be made at the time of the delivery"). See the discussion of this case in §8.10 *supra*. The rule does not apply where different periods of time are fixed within which each party is to perform, since the parties have indicated a contrary intention. *See* Restatement Second §234 cmt. *b*.

[4] *See* Restatement Second §234(1).

[5] See the discussion of concurrent conditions in §8.10 *supra*.

[6] Rushton v. Campbell, 142 N.W. 902 (Neb. 1913) (where agreement fixed a time for payment but not for delivery of deed, "the payment of the price and the delivery of the deed are concurrent acts").

This preference for simultaneous performances prevails when performance at the same time becomes possible as a result of later events, even though it was not possible at the time the contract was made. For example, if the agreement fixes different times or periods for the parties' performances, the party that is to perform first may delay until the time for the return performance. If the delay amounts to a total breach, the party that is to render the return performance may treat it as such, and then neither party is expected to perform.[7] But if the delay amounts to only a partial breach or the injured party treats it as such, the party in breach can insist on simultaneous performances. A party thereby acquires greater security than the agreement gave, though that party is liable in damages for the breach. In one case, a purchaser of land who contracted to pay the price in five installments, the last installment to be paid at the time of delivery of the deed, delayed paying anything until the last installment was due. The court held that the vendor, "having elected to wait until the fifth and last installment became due . . . , cannot now sustain his action for [any] installments, without proof of performance or readiness to perform on his part. . . . The truth is, the parties, by lapse of time, are in the same situation as if the purchase money was all payable at one time."[8] In unusual circumstances, however, the court may preserve the order of performance provided in the agreement, as when it is understood that a buyer will need the time specified between delivery and payment to resell the goods in order to raise the money to pay the price.

Simultaneous performances possible later

The judicial preference for simultaneous performances yields to the intention of the parties, as shown by their agreement or other circumstances.[9] A common example of an agreement under which performances are not to be simultaneous is a contract for delivery of goods to the buyer on credit. In agreeing to such terms, the buyer loses none of the security that the buyer would have had under a simultaneous exchange, since the buyer's duty to pay is conditional on the seller's delivery of the goods. The seller, in contrast, loses the security that the seller would have had, since the seller's duty to deliver the goods is no longer conditional on the buyer's tender of the price.[10] A seller on credit that is unwilling to run this risk may take a security interest in the goods sold, but such transactions are beyond the scope of this discussion.[11]

Derogation from rule

Often it is impossible for the parties to perform simultaneously. Sometimes, as in the case of a construction contract, the performance of one party will

Performance requiring time

---

[7] See the discussion of time as of the essence in §8.18 *infra*.

[8] Beecher v. Conradt, 13 N.Y. 108, 110-11 (1855).

[9] Rubin v. Fuchs, 459 P.2d 925 (Cal. 1969) (vendor's recordation of tract map was to precede purchaser's execution of deed of trust).

[10] Similarly, if the buyer prepays the price, the buyer loses the security that the buyer had. E.E.E., Inc. v. Hanson, 318 N.W.2d 101 (N.D. 1982) (purchaser's "promise to pay the first two installments [was] independent of any performance by the seller" because parties "required the second installment to be paid before delivery of the abstract").

[11] Secured transactions are governed by Article 9 of the Uniform Commercial Code.

take time and that of the other will not.[12] One of the parties must go first, forgoing the security that simultaneous performance would afford and bearing the burden of financing the transaction until the other party performs. Centuries ago the rule evolved that if one party is to do work and the other party is to pay, the performance of the work is to precede payment or, as the New York Court of Appeals expressed it, "When the performance of a contract consists of doing (*faciendo*) on one side, and in giving (*dando*) on the other side, the doing must take place before the giving."[13] The rule had its greatest impact on contracts of service, such as employment and construction contracts,[14] but it also affected contracts to supply goods over a period of time.[15] It has been suggested that the rule grew up in connection with employment contracts "and reflects a conviction that employers as a class are more likely to be responsible than are workmen paid in advance."[16]

Lessening of effect

Whether or not the rule originated in connection with employment contracts, its effect on such contracts has been significantly diminished by the widespread enactment of statutes that give the employee a right to frequent periodic payment of wages.[17] Furthermore, its effect on construction contracts has been reduced by express provisions that progress payments are to be made at stated intervals as work proceeds, with only a relatively small retainage by the owner as the final payment. The rule remains as a residual one from which the parties can depart if they choose. After all, it would not be feasible for courts to devise rules for progress payments in the wide variety of cases in which the parties have failed to do so, and the established rule is at least as fair as the opposite one would be.

Performance at one time

Another judicial preference that affects a court's determination of the order of performance is a preference for performance at one time rather than over a period of time. If a party's whole performance can be given at one time, it is due at one time.[18] The Uniform Commercial Code applies this rule to the sale of goods: "Unless otherwise agreed all goods called for by a contract

---

[12]Occasionally, simultaneous performance is impossible even though both parties can perform instantaneously. Distance and lack of adequate communications may make it impossible to ensure that performance is taking place simultaneously. But the mere fact that one party's performance cannot be literally instantaneous, as in the case of delivery of a large quantity of bulky goods, does not prevent the application of the rule requiring simultaneous performances.

[13]Coletti v. Knox Hat Co., 169 N.E. 648, 649 (N.Y. 1930). A contemporary statement of the rule can be found in UNIDROIT Principles 6.1.4(2).

[14]Stewart v. Newbury, 115 N.E. 984 (N.Y. 1917) (construction contract).

[15]Kelly Constr. Co. v. Hackensack Brick Co., 103 A. 417 (N.J. 1918) (sale of all brick required for a school "to be delivered as required by us").

[16]Restatement Second §234 cmt. *e.*

[17]*See* Cal. Lab. Code §204; N.Y. Lab. L. §191.

[18]This is true even though the performance cannot be literally instantaneous, as in the case of delivery of a large quantity of bulky goods. See note 12 *supra.*

for sale must be tendered in a single delivery and payment is due only on such tender. . . ."[19] This reluctance to break performance into parts probably reflects the usual understanding of the parties and stems from the unfairness of imposing the burden of performing or of receiving performance in installments on a party that has not assented to it. Under a contract for the sale of goods, such assent might be found in a provision for delivery of the goods in installments, from usage of trade or course of dealing, or from special circumstances that indicate that this was the parties' understanding.[20]

The law's reluctance to break performance into parts yields, however, to its preference for the symmetrical protection afforded by simultaneous performances. If the parties have agreed that one party's performance is due in installments, and the other party's return performance can be apportioned so that a comparable part can be given simultaneously, that part will be due simultaneously.[21] Typically, the return performance is payment of the price, and the question is whether the price can be apportioned. Under the Uniform Commercial Code, "where the circumstances give either party the right to make or demand delivery in lots the price [of it] if it can be apportioned may be demanded for each lot."[22]

> **Rule for installment contracts**

We now turn to three means that courts have used to avoid the forfeiture that might otherwise result from the concept of constructive conditions of exchange: the doctrine of substantial performance, the concept of divisibility, and the remedy of restitution.

§8.12. **Substantial Performance as a Means of Avoiding Forfeiture.** No sooner had Lord Mansfield conceived of what we now call constructive conditions of exchange than the need arose to [mitigate the harsh effects of the rules traditionally applied to express conditions.] By invoking the concept of a condition to secure the expectations of one party, he exposed the other party to the risk of forfeiture. If strict performance by a builder were regarded as a condition of the owner's duty to pay, the slightest breach by the builder[1] would deprive the builder of any right to payment under the contract.[2] King's

> **Need for mitigation**

---

[19] UCC 2-307. *See* UNIDROIT Principles 6.1.4(1).

[20] *See* UCC 2-307 cmt. 3.

[21] Restatement Second §233(2).

[22] UCC 2-307. *See* Restatement Second §233(2). The Reporter's Note says that Illustration 3 rejects the reasoning in Kelly Constr. Co. v. Hackensack Brick Co., *supra* note 15 (no right to payment for each delivery of brick although delivery in installments was necessary).

§8.12 [1] As noted earlier, for the sake of clarity this discussion is limited to a failure of performance that is a breach. However, the rules governing constructive conditions of exchange apply generally to any failure of performance. See the discussion of the point that the concept applies even if no breach in §8.9 *supra*.

[2] However, the fact that the builder's performance is a condition of the owner's duty to pay does not affect the builder's right to retain any progress payments already received. See the discussion of the limits of dependence in §8.9 *supra*.

Bench faced this problem in *Boone v. Eyre* only four years after it had decided *Kingston v. Preston*.[3]

Boone v. Eyre

Boone v. Eyre arose from a contract for the sale of an interest in a West Indies plantation. When the vendor sued for the price, the purchaser defended on the ground that the vendor did not legally possess all of the slaves on the plantation. Lord Mansfield rejected the purchaser's plea, saying that "where mutual covenants . . . go only to a part [of the consideration on both sides], where a breach may be paid for in damages, there the defendant has a remedy on his covenant, and shall not plead it as a condition precedent. If this plea were to be allowed, any one negro not being the property of the plaintiff would bar the action."[4] The logic is plain: the purchaser should not be allowed to resist paying the price merely on the ground of an insubstantial breach by the vendor.[5]

Substantial performance

From this and later cases the doctrine evolved that if one party's performance is a constructive condition of the other party's duty, only "substantial" performance is required of the first party before that party can recover under the contract. This flexible requirement of substantial performance stands in sharp contrast to the requirement of strict compliance that protects a party that has taken the precaution of making its duty expressly conditional.[6] Courts have applied the doctrine mainly to contracts for services, particularly construction contracts.[7]

Building contracts

If a builder can meet the test of substantial performance, the builder can recover on the contract the full price, less any damages to which the owner is entitled because of the breach. These damages are based sometimes on the loss in value to the owner and sometimes on the cost to the owner to remedy the defect.[8] Most courts have put on the owner the burden of showing the amount of these damages.[9]

---

[3] See the discussion of this case in §8.9 *supra*.

[4] 126 Eng. Rep. 160(a) (K.B. 1777). For Mansfield's views on slave-holding, *see* Biographical Appendix.

[5] For a discussion of the effect of retention of property by a buyer, see the discussion of choice by conduct in §8.19 *infra*.

[6] See the discussion of strict compliance in §8.3 *supra*. See also the discussions of substantial performance compared and of significant circumstances in §8.16 *infra*.

[7] *See* Shaeffer v. Kelton, 619 P.2d 1226 (N.M. 1980) ("contract included both an agreement to construct a building and a promise to convey property" and doctrine of substantial performance applied to former).

[8] Jacob & Youngs v. Kent, 129 N.E. 889 (N.Y. 1921) (damages for use of some pipe of Cohoes rather than Reading manufacture, as required by contract to build country home, held based on "the difference in value, which would be either nominal or nothing."). See the discussion of the example of *Jacob & Youngs* in §12.13 *infra*.

[9] Nepstad Custom Homes Co. v. Krull, 527 N.W.2d 402 (Iowa App. 1994) (after "contractor has met its burden to show substantial performance, the homeowner has the burden to show any defects or incompletions which may be deducted").

Plainly a test as flexible as substantial performance sacrifices predictability to achieve justice. Whether performance is "substantial" is a question of fact that depends on the particular circumstances of the case. In Cardozo's words, "Where the line is to be drawn between the important and the trivial cannot be settled by a formula. . . . The question is one of degree, to be answered, if there is doubt, by the triers of the facts. . . ."[10] The situation of each party is relevant to a determination of whether performance is substantial.

The main focus, of course, is on the injured party. How much of the benefit that the injured party reasonably expected from the exchange has been received? To answer this question the court must ask why the injured party made the contract.[11] In a case arising from a contract to repair a roof, the court concluded that "the purpose to be served, the desire to be gratified, was not merely to have a serviceable roof installed but to have one of a uniform color installed. It refused to concede that "a roof which so lacks uniformity in color as to give the appearance of a patch job serves essentially the same purpose as a roof of uniform color which has the appearance of being a new roof."[12] If the contract is one to construct a building, it is often said that there can be no substantial performance if the defects are such as to be characterized as "structural," in the sense of affecting the solidity of the building.[13] On the other hand, courts have sometimes been generous in finding substantial performance in building contracts, despite significant variations from plans, when the plans and other circumstances indicate that details are not essential.[14] Courts have occasionally expressed the degree of substantiality in terms of a numerical ratio between the supposed cost or value of the work done and the cost of complete performance or the contract price.[15] No

Question of fact

Look at injured party

---

[10]Jacob & Youngs v. Kent, *supra* note 8, at 891.

[11]For an interesting application of such a test, *see* Kreyer v. Driscoll, 159 N.W.2d 680 (Wis. 1968) (since price paid by owner "pays for the relief from trouble and personal effort on the part of the owner in respect to building . . . a dispensation in favor of the contractor on the theory of substantial performance should be granted in cases of incompleteness only when such details are inconsiderable and not the fault of the contractor"). Courts have not required that the party in breach know of the reason the injured party made the contract. Contrast the rule on foreseeability of damages. See §12.14 *infra*.

[12]O.W. Grun Roofing & Constr. Co. v. Cope, 529 S.W.2d 258, 263 (Tex. Civ. App. 1975).

[13]Spence v. Ham, 57 N.E. 412 (N.Y. 1900) ("the 'failure to have girders of certain length and properly placed' and 'the failure to place wooden partition on a brick wall in basement' . . . were structural defects which affected the solidity of the building").

[14]Plante v. Jacobs, 103 N.W.2d 296 (Wis. 1960) (misplacing of wall, which narrowed living room by more than a foot, did not preclude finding of substantial performance where absence of blueprints and use of "stock floor plan" that did not show detailed construction indicated that details were not of the essence).

[15]Ervin Constr. Co. v. Van Orden, 874 P.2d 506 (Idaho 1993) ("breach did not destroy the entire purpose of the contract" where on completion builder would have been entitled to only $6,000 more, out of a total of $41,000).

such simple rule can be relied on, however, and all circumstances must be considered.[16]

Possibility of compensation

A factor of special importance in assessing the impact of a breach on the injured party's expectations is the extent to which that party can be compensated adequately in damages. A court is more likely to find that there has been substantial performance if, as Mansfield said in *Boone v. Eyre*, the "breach may be paid for in damages."[17] Any difficulty that the injured party may have in proving loss with sufficient certainty to be fully compensated in damages will diminish the adequacy of the damage claim and will make a finding of substantial performance less appealing.[18] A court is likely to find substantial performance if the owner can easily get another builder to correct the defects and can withhold the cost of correction from the price owed the first builder.[19] But a court is unlikely to find substantial performance if the defect is serious and damages would be uncertain in amount or insufficient to pay for the correction.

Look at party in breach

In addition to looking at the extent to which the injured party has received the benefit that it expected from the bargain, a court will also look at the party in breach. Since the concept of substantial, as opposed to strict, performance evolved in response to the risk of forfeiture, the extent of forfeiture that the party in breach will suffer is relevant in determining whether performance has been substantial. Thus, if the performance can be returned to and salvaged by the party in breach, performance is less likely to be regarded as substantial. The importance of the concept of substantial performance in the building contract cases stems largely from the fact that the builder's performance cannot usually be returned to the builder. However, the extent of forfeiture will be reduced if the builder has already received progress payments under a provision in the contract[20] or if the builder has a claim in restitution against the owner for the benefit conferred.[21] In such a case, the impact of denying the builder the right to enforce the contract will be less severe.

Role of willfulness

Courts have often said that if a party's breach is "willful," that party's performance cannot be substantial, regardless of the impact of denying the right to

---

[16]Plante v. Jacobs, *supra* note 14 ("No mathematical rule relating to the percentage of the price, of cost of completion, or of completeness can be laid down to determine substantial performance of a building contract.").

[17]See the discussion of *Boone v. Eyre supra.*

[18]This is especially true where the party in breach seeks specific performance. That party's right to such relief will turn on whether damages can adequately compensate the injured party for the failure of performance. *See* §12.6 *infra.*

[19]Ahlers Bldg. Supply v. Larsen, 535 N.W.2d 431 (S.D. 1995) (homeowners "corrected the defects by hiring others to repair [contractor's] mistakes and finish the job" and except for "difference in room levels, every other defect could be recompensed with money").

[20]See the discussion of the limits of dependence in §8.9 *supra.*

[21]See §8.14 *infra.*

enforce the contract.[22] In spite of the general disregard of "willfulness" in contract law and of the difficulty of defining *willful* with precision, it is clear that a party that not only has failed strictly to perform, but also failed to observe standards of good faith, will have difficulty establishing substantial performance.[23] By ignoring bad faith, a court risks letting one party force the other to take a deficient performance together with damages. But courts are beginning to realize that a party's failure to observe standards of good faith should not by itself preclude a finding of substantial performance. As the Supreme Court of Connecticut put it, the "contemporary view . . . is that even a conscious and intentional departure from the contract specifications will not necessarily defeat recovery, but may be considered as one of the several factors involved in deciding whether there has been full performance."[24]

Strict performance for sales of goods

The doctrine of substantial performance has not found universal favor. Courts generally have not applied it to a seller's claim against a buyer that has rejected either real or personal property under a contract of sale. In this situation, the seller can often avoid forfeiture by selling the rejected property elsewhere at a reasonable price. In cases of contracts for the sale of real property where there is a deficiency in the acreage and the buyer refuses to perform, courts have held the seller to strict performance if the seller seeks damages in an action at law[25] but have been more indulgent if the seller sues in equity, allowing specific performance with an abatement of part of the price.[26] The standard of strict performance traditionally applied to contracts for the sale of goods has been particularly exacting.

Perfect tender rule

During the nineteenth century a rule developed that a buyer was entitled to reject goods unless the seller made a "perfect tender." The requirement of perfection covered not only the quantity and quality of the goods but also the details of shipment.[27] In the words of Learned Hand, "There is no room

[22] In a noted dictum, Cardozo wrote: "The willful transgressor must accept the penalty of his transgression." Jacob & Youngs v. Kent, *supra* note 8, at 891 (wrong brand of pipe used as result of oversight of builder's subcontractor).

[23] *See* Restatement Second §241 (among the circumstances that are "significant" is "the extent to which the behavior of the party failing to perform or to offer to perform comports with standards of good faith and fair dealing").

[24] Vincenzi v. Cerro, 442 A.2d 1352, 1354 (Conn. 1982).

[25] Smyth v. Sturges, 15 N.E. 544 (N.Y. 1888) (in action at law for damages a vendor of land "must be held strictly to the very terms of his engagement," although if vendor had sued for specific performance "it is not improbable that he would have succeeded").

[26] Reigart v. Fisher, 131 A. 568 (Md. 1925) (rule that vendor may not insist on performance with abatement "where the part is a considerable portion of the entire subject-matter, or is material to the enjoyment of the other part" was not applicable where contract for sale of country home called for "about seven acres, more or less" and vendor tendered under 4.8 acres).

[27] In this country, the rule was announced in Norrington v. Wright, 115 U.S. 188 (1885) (seller of 5,000 tons of iron rails to be shipped "at the rate of about one thousand (1,000) tons per month" made monthly shipments of 400, 885, 1571, 850, 1000, and 300 tons).

in commercial contracts for the doctrine of substantial performance."[28] This rule of strict performance remained unchallenged during the first half of the twentieth century. In its terms, it applied even though it was not practical for the seller to resell the rejected goods as, for example, if the goods were perishable[29] or specially manufactured.[30] Because the buyer's right to reject did not depend on the buyer's having been harmed by the breach, the rule offered an inviting pretext for buyers that sought to escape their contract obligations on discovering that they no longer needed the goods or that the market price had fallen.[31] The shortcomings of the rule did not escape criticism.[32]

Code rules

Nevertheless, the Code adopts the perfect tender rule. The buyer can reject "if the goods or the tender of delivery fail in any respect to conform to the contract."[33] However, the rule has been eroded by a number of related sections that soften its impact.[34] Among the most significant are those that subject a buyer that has accepted goods to a standard of substantial performance if the buyer chooses to revoke the acceptance,[35] that subject a buyer under an installment contract to a similar standard if the buyer chooses to reject an installment,[36] and that grant a seller the right to "cure" after the buyer has rejected the goods.[37] These matters are dealt with later in this chapter.

Vienna Convention rule

The Vienna Convention rejects the perfect tender rule in favor of a test of "fundamental breach."[38] A breach is not fundamental unless it "results in such

---

[28] Mitsubishi Goshi Kaisha v. J. Aron & Co., 16 F.2d 185, 186 (2d Cir. 1926) (seller of soy bean oil, to be shipped "f.o.b. . . . Pacific Coast" and paid for against documents, presented documents showing shipment from Dallas).

[29] Parties to a contract for perishables may dispense with the perfect tender rule, however, by contracting under regulations promulgated by the Secretary of Agriculture pursuant to the Perishable Agricultural Commodities Act of 1930, 7 U.S.C.A. ch. 20A.

[30] Ellison Furniture & Carpet Co. v. Langever, 113 S.W. 178 (Tex. Civ. App. 1908) (specially constructed electric sign).

[31] For a case in which a buyer for resale rejected after its purchaser repudiated, *see* Mitsubishi Goshi Kaisha v. J. Aron & Co., *supra* note 28. For an analogous situation in which a party uses the "mirror-image" rule to get out of a disadvantageous contract, *see* the discussion of two types of disputes in §3.21 *supra*.

[32] *See* Honnold, Buyer's Right of Rejection, 97 U. Pa. L. Rev. 457 (1949).

[33] UCC 2-601. (The Code slightly limits the perfect tender rule as to details of shipment in UCC 2-504.)

[34] In addition to the rules mentioned here, *see* those involving waiver by failure to particularize in the discussion of exceptional cases in §8.19 *infra*.

[35] UCC 2-608(1) (buyer can revoke acceptance only if non-conformity "substantially impairs" the value of the goods to buyer).

[36] UCC 2-612(2) (buyer can reject installment only "if the non-conformity substantially impairs the value of that installment," unless the defect is in the required documents).

[37] UCC 2-508, treated in the discussion of cure under the Code in §8.17 *infra*.

[38] Under CISG 49(1)(a) and 64(1)(a), a party may "avoid" the contract and thus become free from further contract duties (to take and pay for the goods or to deliver them) if the other party commits a breach that is "fundamental." *See also* UNIDROIT Principles 7.3.1(1) (party may terminate contract where other party's failure "amounts to a fundamental non-performance").

detriment to the other party as substantially deprives him of what he is entitled to expect under the contract."[39]

We turn first to use of the concept of divisibility as another means of avoiding forfeiture.

§8.13.   Divisibility as a Means of Avoiding Forfeiture. Even if a party's performance falls short of that required by the doctrine of substantial performance, a court can avoid forfeiture and allow recovery on the contract by holding that the contract is *divisible* (or severable) rather than entire. It will then allow pro rata recovery based on the contract price for the proportion of the performance rendered.[1] A contract is said to be divisible if the performances to be exchanged can be divided into corresponding pairs of part performances in such a way that a court will treat the parts of each pair as if the parties had agreed that they were equivalents.

> **Meaning of divisible**

Many of the early divisibility cases involved employment contracts, and the concept enabled the employee to recover unpaid wages for work done before the employee's breach of contract.[2] Two developments reduced the significance of divisibility in such cases. First, state statutes requiring periodic payment of wages have reduced the frequency of substantial claims for unpaid wages. Second, the courts' tendency to hold that employment agreements are terminable at will has reduced the frequency of cases in which the employee is in breach.[3] However, the concept of divisibility remains significant in connection with contracts of other kinds.

> **Early cases**

Suppose, for example, that a builder has made a contract to build three houses at $100,000 each for a total price of $300,000. The builder breaks the contract by building only one of the houses and claims its price of $100,000. Will a court allow the builder to recover on the contract to build three houses, even though the builder has not substantially performed it? It will, if it regards the contract as divisible into three pairs of part performances, each pair consisting of the building of a house and the payment of $100,000. The builder is then entitled to recover $100,000 on the contract for the house that was built, less such damages as the owner can prove were suffered by the builder's breach in not

> **Example of divisibility**

---

[39]CISG 25. Even then, however, the breach is not fundamental if "the party in breach did not foresee, and a reasonable person of the same kind in the same circumstances would not have foreseen, such a result." For a similar formulation, *see* UNIDROIT Principles 7.3.1(2)(a). See the discussion of significant circumstances in §8.16 *infra*.

§8.13   [1]*See* Stone Forest Indus. v. United States, 973 F.2d 1548 (Fed. Cir. 1992) ("only in exceptional circumstances will equity require the non-breaching party to continue to perform the remainder of the contract").

[2]For a typical case, *see* Matthews v. Jenkins, 80 Va. 463 (1885) ("two hundred dollars ($200) per month for one year").

[3]See the discussion of the employment cases in §7.17 *supra*.

building the other two.[4] Indeed, if the contract is divisible, the builder is entitled to recover on the contract for building the first house even if performance of that part of the contract is only substantial. The builder's recovery will then be reduced by damages resulting from the defects in the first house as well as from the failure to build the other two houses.[5]

Two requirements　　How does a court decide whether a contract is divisible? The Supreme Court of Colorado warned that "there is no set formula which furnishes a foolproof method for determining in a given case just which contracts are severable and which are entire."[6] The Restatement Second lays down two requirements: it must be possible to apportion the parties' performances into corresponding pairs of part performances; and it must be proper to regard the parts of each pair as agreed equivalents.[7]

First: apportionment　　The requirement that apportionment be possible is met if the price for parts of the performance can be determined. It is enough if the agreement states separate prices for different parts of the work or for units of work, or if a price list, on which the agreement was based, states separate prices for various items.[8] It should also be enough if a reliable calculation can be made from a total price that is an obvious multiple of a price for a number of identical items.[9]

Second: agreed equivalents　　Even if apportionment is possible, a court will not treat a contract as divisible unless it thinks it proper to regard the parts of each pair of performances as agreed equivalents. If the parties indicated in their agreement or by their subsequent conduct that they so regarded them, the court will give effect to their intention.[10] Usually the parties had no intention on the point, however, so the propriety of regarding the part performances as agreed equivalents depends on considerations of fairness like those that guide a court in determining whether to supply a term.[11] The fundamental question is whether the part performances are of roughly equivalent value to the injured party when viewed against the background of that party's expectations as to the agreement as a whole.[12]

---

[4]Carrig v. Gilbert-Varker Corp., 50 N.E.2d 59 (Mass. 1943) (contractor who had agreed to build 35 houses recovered for 20 although he refused to build remaining 15).

[5]Lowy v. United Pac. Ins. Co., 429 P.2d 577 (Cal. 1967) (contractor "completed 98 percent of the work under the first phase").

[6]John v. United Advertising, 439 P.2d 53, 56 (Colo. 1968).

[7]*See* Restatement Second §240.

[8]Lowy v. United Pac. Ins. Co., *supra* note 5 (agreement stated prices separately for excavation and grading and for street improvement). A classic case is Gill v. Johnstown Lumber Co., discussed in note 13 *infra*.

[9]British Films Do Brasil v. London Film Prods., 166 N.Y.S.2d 703 (Sup. Ct. 1957) ("since there were 23 pictures involved, and royalty payment of $23,000 made, it seems that the rate was $1,000 each").

[10]Goodman v. Newzona Inv. Co., 421 P.2d 318 (Ariz. 1966) (entire by agreement).

[11]See the discussion of reasons for omission in §7.16 *supra*.

[12]Lowy v. United Pac. Ins. Co., *supra* note 5 (by arranging for separate surety bonds "the parties treated the contract as a divisible one").

Fairness requires that a party that has received only a fraction of what that party expected under a contract should not be asked to pay an identical fraction of the contract price unless it appears that the value to that party of what was received is roughly that same fraction of the value to that party of full performance.

A good example is *Gill v. Johnstown Lumber Co.*, which arose out of the great Johnstown flood. Gill had contracted with a lumber company to drive logs down river, but after he had driven some of them to the specified destination the flood carried the rest away. The Supreme Court of Pennsylvania held that the contract was divisible so that Gill could recover according to the unit prices for the logs driven, but that "there is neither reason nor authority for the claim for compensation in respect to logs that were swept away by the flood [even though] they had been driven part of the way."[13] The value to the lumber company of a log driven part way would have been far less than the appropriate fraction of the price for a log driven the entire way. On similar reasoning, a provision for progress payments, intended to finance construction, does not make the contract divisible, because the payments do not fairly represent the extent to which the owner's interests have been advanced, and the builder cannot claim such payments if in breach.[14] The fact that prices are stated separately or for units of work will not make a contract divisible if the injured party cannot make full use of the part received without the rest. Thus a buyer will not be expected to pay for a machine received if deprived of an attachment that is necessary for its use.[15] However, a court will take account of the availability of the rest of the performance elsewhere, as when the attachment can be bought on the market.

The divisibility of a contract is not necessarily determined by whether the performance of either party is to be rendered at one time or in installments. A contract may be divisible even though the price is payable at one time on completion of the work.[16] On the other hand, a contract may be entire even though the price is to be paid as the work progresses, as in the example given above of a construction contract with a provision for progress payments.

Examples

Time for performance distinguished

---

[13]25 A. 120, 120 (Pa. 1892). Cases in which this second test was met are cited in the discussion of apportionment *supra*.

[14]Kirkland v. Archbold, 113 N.E.2d 496 (Ohio App. 1953) ("fact that a schedule of payments was set up based on the progress of the work does not change the character of the agreement").

[15]*Cf.* Pennsylvania Exch. Bank v. United States, 170 F. Supp. 629 (Ct. Cl. 1959) (though government contractor was to be paid after each of first three steps of project and had completed each of these steps, enabling it in fourth step to stand by to produce "magic tees" in volume in case of war, government sought "all four steps as an entire, indivisible undertaking").

[16]Gill v. Johnstown Lumber Co., *supra* note 13. If the price is not payable until completion of the work, full performance is a condition of the other party's duty of payment. For this reason, it is not correct to say that one party's part performance is a condition of the other party's duty of part performance simply because the contract is divisible. A right to part payment only arises if, after part performance, it appears that no further performance will be forthcoming.

Indeed, a contract for the sale of goods may be entire even though both the goods and the price are due in installments.[17]

Separate contract distinguished

The fact that a contract is divisible does not mean that it will be treated like two or more separate contracts in all respects. If there are two separate contracts, repudiation of one has no direct effect on the rights and duties under the other.[18] But if a contract is divisible, a repudiation as to one part affects rights and duties as to all parts.

Importance of context

Because the concept of divisibility is used for a variety of purposes, the fact that a contract is divisible or entire in one context, say the context under consideration here, does not necessarily mean that it is divisible or entire in another, say the context of unenforceability on grounds of public policy.[19] Therefore, a resolution of the issue of divisibility, for the purpose of determining whether the party in breach can recover for part performance, does not control if the issue is whether the injured party[20] or one whose remaining performance has become impracticable[21] can recover for part performance or whether a party can salvage part of a contract if the balance is unenforceable on the ground of indefiniteness.[22]

Another means of avoiding forfeiture is restitution in favor of the party in breach.

Restitution as means of mitigation

§8.14.   Restitution as a Means of Avoiding Forfeiture.   In recent decades, courts have tended to grant restitution to the party in breach. Thus, a party that is precluded from recovering on the contract because of not having substantially performed can at least recover for any benefit conferred, less damages for which that party is liable because of breach.[1] Granting restitution has become one of the principal means of mitigating the potentially harsh results of the concept of constructive conditions of exchange. In this respect, restitution plays a role similar to that of the doctrine of substantial performance[2] and the concept of divisibility.[3]

Traditional view

Traditionally, courts denied restitution to the party in breach. In 1824 the Supreme Judicial Court of Massachusetts proclaimed, "It will not admit of the

---

[17] See Johnson v. Walker, 824 S.W.2d 184 (Tex. App. 1991) (agency contract for marketing insurance policies "contemplated agreement to the entire bundle of rights and duties" and was not divisible though "employee receives commission for each sale").

[18] See the discussion of repudiation in general in §8.21 *infra*.

[19] See §5.8 *supra*. For contexts other than those mentioned in this paragraph of the text in which divisibility is relevant, see the discussions of the principle of revocability in §3.17 *supra*, of interpretation of an offer as divisible in §3.24 *supra*, and of divisibility in §6.10 *supra*.

[20] See the discussion of divisibility in §12.20 *infra*.

[21] See the discussion of divisibility in §9.9 *infra*.

[22] See the discussion of relief based on the terms of the agreement in §3.30 *supra*.

§8.14   [1] The Reporter's Note to Restatement Second §374 states that it "is more liberal in allowing recovery" than first Restatement §357.

[2] See §8.12 *supra*.

[3] See §8.13 *supra*.

monstrous absurdity, that a man may voluntarily and without cause violate his agreement, and make the very breach of that agreement the foundation of an action which he could not maintain under it."[4] Courts also opposed restitution because it would impose on the injured party both an obligation different from the one for which that party had bargained and the burden of proving damages resulting from the breach.[5] They preferred to deny to the defaulting employee recovery for the benefit conferred on the injured employer by part performance[6] and to deny the defaulting purchaser recovery for the benefit conferred on the injured vendor by part payment.[7]

In 1834 the Supreme Court of New Hampshire forcefully stated the opposite view in *Britton v. Turner*. Britton, who had agreed to work for Turner for a year for $120, left his service without cause after less than ten months and sued for the value of the work done. The court pointed out that, under the traditional view, the forfeiture a party suffers on its breach increases as the party's performance continues, so that "the party who attempts performance may be placed in a much worse position than he who wholly disregards his contract." In addition, the injured party might receive a windfall since that party "may receive much more, by the breach of the contract, than the injury which he has sustained by such breach." The court concluded that if "a party actually receives labor, or materials, and thereby derives a benefit and advantage, over and above the damage which has resulted from the breach of the contract by the other party, . . . the law thereupon raises a promise to pay to the extent of the reasonable worth of such excess."[8] Since then, this liberal view has become widely though not universally accepted.[9]

Britton v. Turner

The rule in *Britton v. Turner* was readily applied to contracts for services in which claimants, like Britton, would otherwise lose any right to recover for

Party furnishing services

[4] Stark v. Parker, 19 Mass. (2 Pick.) 267, 275 (1824).

[5] Patterson, Restitution for Benefits Conferred by Party in Default Under Contract, 1952 Report of N.Y. Law Revision Commn. 93 (N.Y. Leg. Doc. No. 65, 1952).

[6] Stark v. Parker, *supra* note 4 (employee who agreed to work for a year for $120 left before the end of the year).

[7] Lawrence v. Miller, 86 N.Y. 131 (1881) (purchaser of land denied restitution of $2,000 down payment since "to declare that a party may violate his agreement, and make an infraction of it by himself a cause of action . . . would be ill doctrine").

[8] 6 N.H. 481, 487, 492 (1834). In an attempt to fit the theory of recovery into a contractual rather than a restitutionary framework, the court, in the omitted part of the quotation, explained that "the labor actually done, and the value received, furnish a new consideration" for the promise raised by the law, and added that "this may be considered as making a new case, one not within the original agreement."

[9] *See* Dawson, Restitution Without Enrichment, 61 B.U. L. Rev. 563, 601 (1981) ("courts have been unable to maintain this posture of stern denial," resulting in "an exceptional degree of incoherence"). *But see* 1 G. Palmer, Law of Restitution §5.13 (1978) (stating that Britton v. Turner "remains a minority position" for personal service contracts).

their labor.[10] But its significance for employment contracts has diminished as a result of the enactment of state statutes requiring periodic payment of wages, the tendency of courts to hold that employment agreements are terminable at will, and the application of the concept of divisibility.[11] Courts also applied the rule of *Britton v. Turner* to allow restitution to defaulting builders under construction contracts, so that the builder that had not substantially performed was not barred from all recovery.[12]

Buyer of goods

Courts were less receptive to the rule if the party in default had paid money rather than rendered services. Thus a court would deny restitution to a buyer of goods that defaulted after making a down payment or part payment, even though the amount of the payment exceeded what the court would have allowed had the contract merely stipulated that sum as damages recoverable by the seller. But the Uniform Commercial Code reformed the law, giving the buyer a limited right to restitution. Even under the Code, however, the seller may retain the amount of its damages,[13] including liquidated damages.[14] And, under a provision eliminated by revised Article 2, the seller might, without proving damages, retain as a statutory minimum the lesser of $500 or 20 percent of the contract price, unless the contract provides for liquidated damages in a smaller amount.[15]

Purchaser of land

Courts also denied restitution to a purchaser of land that defaulted after making a down payment or part payment.[16] Now, however, the Code rule on contracts for the sale of goods has encouraged courts to extend the rule of *Britton v. Turner* to contracts for the sale of land as well.[17] When a purchaser pays money in advance, it is sometimes provided, or at least understood, that the sum is to be retained by the vendor if the purchaser defaults. Parties often

---

[10] Burke v. McKee, 304 P.2d 307 (Okl. 1956) (clearing timber).

That a party can contract away the right to restitution, see the discussion of restitution in §9.9 *infra*.

[11] See the discussion of early cases in §8.13 *supra*.

[12] PDM Mechanical Contractors v. Suffolk Constr. Co., 618 N.E.2d 72 (Mass. App. 1993) (restitution "is particularly applicable in actions involving building contracts in order to avoid the harsh result of the long established rule that there can be no recovery on a building contract in the absence of complete performance").

[13] UCC 2-718(3). Any benefit received by the buyer is included, along with damages, in the seller's offset.

[14] UCC 2-718(2). On liquidated damages, see §12.18 *infra*.

[15] UCC-O 2-718(2).

[16] Lawrence v. Miller, *supra* note 7, followed with a qualification in Maxton Builders v. Lo Galbo, 502 N.E.2d 184 (N.Y. 1986) ("rule permitting a party in default to seek restitution for part performance has much to commend it in its general applications" but "as applied to real estate down payments approximating 10% it does not appear to offer a better or more workable rule than the long-established 'usage' in this State with respect to the seller's right to retain a down payment upon default").

[17] Maxey v. Glindmeyer, 379 So. 2d 297 (Miss. 1980) (vendor should not be entitled to retain down payment "beyond a sum reasonably necessary to cover her actual damages"; court was "influenced by the logic and reason" of UCC 2-718).

indicate this understanding by describing the sum as "earnest money." If the sum is a reasonable one that would be sustained as liquidated damages had the parties stipulated it, the vendor is entitled to retain it.[18] Otherwise the purchaser is entitled to restitution if the rule in *Britton v. Turner* is applied.[19] The inconsistency of treatment between a sum of money paid in advance and a sum stipulated as damages is thus eliminated.

Some courts have denied restitution to the party in breach on the ground **Effect of** that the breach was "willful," rather than accidental or negligent.[20] Others **willfulness** have declined the difficult task of determining the quality of the breach and have granted restitution regardless of willfulness.[21] The argument for taking account of the quality of the breach is stronger when the claim is for payment of the value of some benefit conferred by the party in breach than when it is for the return of money paid. Allowing restitution in the former case imposes on the injured party both an obligation different from the one for which that party bargained and the burden of proving damages resulting from the breach. The Restatement Second rejects the idea that "willfulness" is an absolute bar to restitution.[22] Nevertheless, according to the commentary, "A party who intentionally furnishes services or builds a building that is materially different from what he promised is properly regarded as having acted officiously and not in part performance of his promise and will be denied recovery on that ground even if his performance was of some benefit to the other party."[23] The argument against recovery is particularly strong if the party has broken the contract for its own convenience or financial advantage.

If restitution is allowed, how is the recovery measured? If the party in breach **Measurement of** seeks the return of money paid, the value of the benefit conferred is clear.[24] **recovery** But if the party in breach seeks to recover the value of the benefit conferred by a performance of some other kind, measurement of that value may pose

---

[18]Vines v. Orchard Hills, 435 A.2d 1022 (Conn. 1980) (Peters, J.: "liquidated damages clause allowing the seller to retain 10 percent of the contract price as earnest money is presumptively a reasonable allocation of the risks associated with default"). On liquidated damages, see §12.18 *infra*.

[19]Caplan v. Schroeder, 364 P.2d 321 (Cal. 1961) (purchaser was entitled to restitution where vendors did not seek to show that $15,000 down payment was liquidated damages).

[20]Harris v. The Cecil N. Bean, 197 F.2d 919 (2d Cir. 1952) (cleaning hold of ship).

[21]Begovich v. Murphy, 101 N.W.2d 278 (Mich. 1960) (claim for restitution of sum paid to attorney by client whose suicide "we must presume . . . represented a wilful breach").

[22]Restatement Second §374 has dropped the requirement of first Restatement §357 that the breach be "not wilful and deliberate."

[23]Restatement Second §374 cmt. *b*.

[24]Recovery is, however, reduced by the injured party's damages, and courts have denied restitution where the party in breach has failed to sustain the burden of showing those damages. Honey v. Henry's Franchise Leasing Corp., 415 P.2d 833 (Cal. 1966) ("On retrial the burden will be on [buyer] to prove the excess, if any, of his payments over the amount necessary to give [seller] the benefit of his bargain."). Compare the burden in the case of substantial performance, mentioned in the discussion of building contracts in §8.12 *supra*.

a difficult problem. Since it is the party seeking restitution that is responsible for the problem, courts resolve doubts against that party and generally limit recovery to net enrichment and do not allow cost avoided.[25] In contrast to claims based on substantial performance or divisibility, where recovery is on the contract, here the contract price is not conclusive. Still, it is often taken as evidence of the value of the benefit had the contract been performed. Recovery will then equal the contract price, minus the diminution in value resulting from the breach. The result is as generous as if recovery were allowed on the contract on the ground that performance was substantial.[26] When courts can determine a ratable portion of the contract price, they have sometimes allowed recovery of that amount. Then the result is as generous as if recovery were allowed on the contract on the ground that the contract was divisible.[27] But unlike the situation in which the injured party seeks restitution, a court will not allow recovery to exceed the ratable portion of the price.[28]

We now turn to more complex situations of breach by nonperformance.

D.   RESPONSES TO BREACH BY NONPERFORMANCE

Nature of dispute   **§8.15.   Power to Suspend Performance and to Terminate the Contract.** Courts developed the doctrine of substantial performance to deal with the relatively simple case in which the party in breach had finished performing and the injured party refused to pay the price because the performance was defective or incomplete. Often the dispute arises at a much earlier stage of performance, however, and the question is whether a breach justifies the injured party in exercising a right to self-help by terminating the contract and refusing either to render any remaining performance or to accept any further performance by the party in breach. The injured party may be the defendant, seeking merely to justify its nonperformance in an action that has been brought by the other party. Or the injured party may be the plaintiff, seeking to justify

---

[25]H.W. Jaeger & Assocs. v. Slovak Am. Charitable Assn., 507 N.E.2d 863 (Ill. App. 1987) (recovery denied where builder based "estimates of benefit received solely on the estimated cost of construction"). On the two measures, see the discussion of net enrichment or loss avoided in §2.20 *supra*.

[26]Ducolon Mechanical v. Shinstine/Forness, 893 P.2d 1127 (Wash. App. 1995) (Restatement Second permits subcontractor "to recover an amount equal to its alleged actual costs if its actual costs are equal to the benefit it conferred" on contractor with offset for "contractor's cost to complete and repair").

[27]Britton v. Turner, discussed *supra* (employee recovered $95 for about nine and one-half months' work at $120 per year).

[28]Ducolon Mechanical v. Shinstine/Forness, *supra* note 26 (subcontractor that made a bid error may not recover "an amount in excess of the contract price"). Compare the discussion of the contract rate as no limit in §12.20 *infra*.

its nonperformance in an action that it has brought against the other party for damages for total breach.[1]

Suppose that in breach of a construction contract the owner has delayed making a required progress payment, and the builder, after first refusing to go forward with the work, has finally terminated the contract,[2] leaving the building unfinished. Has the builder a defense if sued by the owner? Has the builder a claim against the owner for damages for total breach? Under the concept of constructive conditions of exchange, the owner's payment of progress payments is an implied condition of the builder's duty to continue to work. Therefore, the owner's breach in failing to make a progress payment may have two effects on the builder's duty.[3] First, further performance will not become due, so the builder will be justified in exercising a right to self-help by suspending performance.[4] Second, after an appropriate period of time, the builder can choose to treat its remaining duties of performance under the contract as discharged and can exercise a right to self-help by terminating the contract.[5] Two distinct issues are therefore raised. First, was the owner's breach in failing to make the progress payments significant enough to justify the builder's suspending performance? Second, did the owner's breach continue long enough to justify the builder's terminating the contract? If the answer to both questions is yes, the builder was entitled to terminate the contract and claim damages for total breach against the owner. But if the answer to either is no, the builder's action was precipitous and unjustified, itself amounting to a breach that gave the owner a right to terminate and claim damages for total breach against the builder.

Example of construction contract

---

§8.15 [1] For the sake of clarity, this discussion is confined to claims for damages. However, a party that has a claim for damages for total breach may, as an alternative, have a claim for restitution based on the benefit conferred by that party's own performance. See §12.20 *infra*. What is said here applies to both types of claims. Somewhat different rules may apply to actions for specific performance. See note 29 *infra* and the discussions of tender as inapplicable to specific performance in §8.10 *supra* and of time of the essence in §8.18 *infra*.

[2] Although UCC 2-106 defines *cancellation* to refer to a party's act in putting "an end to the contract for breach by the other" and *termination* to refer to a party's act in putting "an end to the contract otherwise than for its breach," the word *termination* is used broadly in this treatise to refer to both kinds of acts. Courts sometimes use *rescission* instead of termination, but this usage is undesirable because it suggests avoidance of the contract, which would leave the injured party with no remedy other than restitution.

[3] See the discussion of two effects in §8.3 *supra*. As noted earlier, for the sake of clarity this discussion is limited to a failure of performance that is a breach. However, the rules governing constructive conditions of exchange apply generally to any failure of performance. See the discussion of the point that the concept applies if there is no breach in §8.9 *supra*.

[4] Magnet Resources v. Summit MRI, 723 A.2d 976 (N.J. Super. 1998) (maintenance and repair services supplier's "suspension of performance . . . did not materially breach [its] contractual obligations," because of other party's prior material breach).

[5] See the discussion of termination after some time in §8.18 *infra*.

Keeping the deal together

This sensible two-step analysis is carefully articulated in the Restatement Second.[6] It is in society's interest to accord each party to a contract reasonable security for the protection of that party's justified expectations. But it is not in society's interest to permit a party to abuse this protection by using an insignificant breach as a pretext for evading its contractual obligations.[7] If the other party relied on the agreement, by performance or otherwise, "keeping the deal together" avoids the risk of forfeiture. Courts encourage this course as long as it will not seriously disappoint justified expectations.[8] They do this by allowing the injured party to suspend performance only if the breach is *material*, that is, sufficiently serious to warrant this response. They curb abuse of this power to suspend by denying the injured party the power to exercise it if the breach is immaterial, so that minor breaches will not disrupt performance. Courts also encourage the parties to keep the deal together by allowing the injured party to terminate the contract only after an appropriate length of time has passed. They restrain abuse of this power to terminate by denying the injured party the power to exercise it hastily, so that not all delays will bring the contract to an end, and the party in breach will be afforded some time to cure its breach.[9] An injured party that chooses to exercise a right of self-help either by suspending or by electing to terminate takes the risk that a court may later regard the exercise as precipitous. According to the Supreme Court of Michigan, that party's decision "is fraught with peril, for should such determination, as viewed by a later court in the calm of its contemplation, be unwarranted, the repudiator himself will have been guilty of material breach and himself have become the aggressor, not an innocent victim."[10] The injured party can, to be sure, avoid this risk simply by deciding not to suspend or terminate, choosing instead to continue performance and claim damages for partial breach. But even this course is not entirely free of risk.[11]

Damages for total breach

If the injured party chooses to terminate the contract, it is said to treat the breach as *total*. The injured party's claim for damages for total breach takes

---

[6]*See* Restatement Second §237 & cmt. *a*. In older terminology it was said that the injured party could terminate if the breach was material. No special term existed to describe a breach that justified suspension. *See* Cary Oil Co. v. MG Ref. & Mktg., 90 F. Supp. 2d 401 (S.D.N.Y. 2000) (applying the analysis in this treatise).

[7]RW Power Partners v. Virginia Elec. & Power Co., 899 F. Supp. 1490 (E.D. Va. 1995) (quoting this section of this treatise).

[8]*See* Hillman, Keeping the Deal Together After Material Breach — Common Law Mitigation Rules, the UCC, and the Restatement (Second) of Contracts, 47 U. Colo. L. Rev. 553, 594-97 (1976) (the drafters of the Restatement Second "have attempted to lessen the impact of the material breach doctrine" by restricting the injured party "to suspending performance until it is too late for the breaching party to cure the default").

[9]On cure, see §8.17 *infra*. For approval of the analysis in the text, *see* Stanley Gudyka Sales Co. v. Lacy Forest Prods. Co., 915 F.2d 273 (7th Cir. 1990) (characterizing power to terminate as "self-help remedy").

[10]Walker & Co. v. Harrison, 81 N.W.2d 352, 355 (Mich. 1957).

[11]See the discussion of election in §8.19 *infra*.

the place of its remaining substantive rights under the contract.[12] Damages are calculated on the assumption that neither party will render any remaining performance. They therefore compensate the injured party for the loss that it will suffer as a result of being deprived of the balance of the other party's performance, minus the amount of any saving that resulted from the injured party not having to render any remaining performance of its own.[13] In the case of a long term contract, calculation of damages on this basis may make it necessary to forecast events far into the future.[14] For example, the Supreme Court of New Jersey held that recovery for breach of a promise of support would be "a lump-sum payment to the promisee representing the present value of reasonable future support calculated . . . on the basis of the promisee's life expectancy."[15] The difficulties of making such a forecast may have important effects on the availability both of damages and of specific performance.[16]

If the injured party does not terminate the contract, either because that party has no right to or does not choose to, the injured party is said to treat the breach as *partial*. The injured party has a claim for damages for partial breach, in addition to its remaining substantive rights under the contract.[17] Damages are calculated on the assumption that both parties will continue to perform in spite of the breach. They therefore compensate the injured party only for the loss it suffered as the result of the delay or other defect in performance that constituted the breach, not for the loss of the balance of the return performance. Since the injured party is not relieved from performing, there is no saving to it to be subtracted.[18] The Uniform Commercial Code gives a buyer the right, on notifying the seller, to deduct damages for partial

Damages for partial breach

---

[12] *See* Restatement Second §236(1) ("A claim for damages for total breach is one for damages based on all of the injured party's remaining rights to performance."). However, according to Comment *e* to §237, "only duties to render performance are affected" and a "claim for damages that has already arisen as a result of a claim for partial breach is not discharged."

[13] See the discussions of cost avoided and of loss avoided in §12.9 *infra*.

[14] See the discussions of causation and expectation in §12.1 *infra*, of termination after some time in §8.18 *infra*, and of treating the contract as terminated in §8.22 *infra*.

[15] *See* In re Estate of Roccamonte, 808 A.2d 838, 847 (N.J. 2002).

[16] As to damages, see the discussion of the origin of the requirement in §12.15 *infra*, and as to specific performance, see the discussion of uncertainty of damages in §12.6 *infra*.

[17] Dr. Franklin Perkins School v. Freeman, 741 F.2d 1503 (7th Cir. 1984) (though school's failure to apply for tuition reimbursement "was not a material breach, [parent] still may recover . . . damages"). *See* Restatement Second §236(2) ("A claim for damages for partial breach is one for damages based on only part of the injured party's remaining rights to performance."). See also the discussion of damages for partial and total breach in §12.9 *infra*.

[18] See the discussion of damages for partial and total breach in §12.9 *infra*.

breach from the balance due on the price.[19] This was not the traditional rule,[20] and whether courts will extend it to cases not involving the sale of goods is unclear.[21]

Example of construction contract

Suppose that the builder under a construction contract is in breach because of delay. If the breach is immaterial, the owner has no choice but to treat it as partial and continue to perform. The owner's only remedy is to claim damages for partial breach as compensation for the loss caused by the delay. Similarly, if the breach is material, but the builder has cured it in time, the owner must continue to perform and claim damages for partial breach. If the breach is material and an appropriate length of time has passed, however, the owner can treat the breach as total and terminate the contract. The duties of both parties to perform are discharged,[22] and the owner has a claim for damages for total breach in place of its substantive rights under the contract. In calculating the amount of this claim, the court will subtract the amount the owner saved by not having to pay the balance of the price from the owner's loss resulting from the builder's failure to complete the building.[23]

Risk of splitting claim

The injured party that sues immediately for damages for partial breach runs some risk of later being regarded as having "split" its claim. Under the general rules governing the effects of a judgment, when a claimant gets a judgment in an action, its claim is extinguished and is merged in the judgment, so that it is precluded from maintaining a second action on the same claim. To allow the claimant to split its claim and prevail in the second action would offend the interest of the defendant and the courts in bringing litigation to a close. But it is difficult to define *claim* for this purpose.[24] Williston suggested that a party that gets a judgment for damages for partial breach, when it could not treat the breach as total, is thereafter precluded from recovering additional damages for total breach should the breach continue because the claim is the same as that in

---

[19]UCC 2-717.

[20]*See* 2 S. Williston, Contracts §859 (1st ed. 1920) (admitting that a "contrary conception undoubtedly is popular").

[21]In support of extending the right to withhold, *see* Stanley Gudyka Sales Co. v. Lacy Forest Prods. Co., *supra* note 9 (dealer had "self-help remedy of deducting . . . the amount owed . . . from a commission check"); Note, 62 Fordham L. Rev. 163 (1993). *Contra:* ARP Films v. Marvel Entertainment Group, 952 F.2d 643 (2d Cir. 1991) (rejecting contention "that withholding the payments and reports was a self-help measure designed to force [other party] to repent from its repudiation, and did not amount to a material breach").

[22]Lease-It v. Massachusetts Port Auth., 600 N.E.2d 599 (Mass. App. 1992) (on being "relieved from performance, the injured party is not liable for further damages incurred by the party in material breach").

[23]See the discussion of the example of a construction contract in §12.11 *infra*.

[24]Restatement (Second) of Judgments §24 (1982) (what constitutes a *claim* is "to be determined pragmatically"). For the peculiar California approach, *see* Mycogen Corp. v. Monsanto Co., 51 P.3d 297 (Cal. 2002) (discussing "primary right theory").

the earlier action.[25] However, this seems too severe a penalty to impose on the injured party for its failure to wait until the full extent of the breach is clear.[26]

Sometimes, when a dispute arises during the course of performance of a contract, both parties stop performing, and each claims that it was justified in terminating the contract because of the other's breach. The builder that has not received a progress payment may suspend and later terminate on the ground of nonpayment. On the other hand, the owner that has failed to pay may contend that the nonpayment was not a breach because the builder had already committed a material breach by failing to follow specifications, and the owner may terminate on that ground. In resolving such disputes, courts apply the principles discussed in this section. Often these principles lead a court to impose liability on the party that committed the *first material breach*. If the owner is correct in asserting that the builder committed the first material breach, that breach justified suspension by the owner, and the builder is liable for damages for total breach for wrongful termination.[27] Indeed, even if the owner had terminated and ordered the builder off the site because of the builder's breach in not following specifications, the builder might be liable in damages for total breach if the owner had waited an appropriate time for the builder to cure its breach.[28] But if the owner had not waited long enough before ordering the builder off the site, the owner's precipitous action would render the owner liable to the builder in damages for total breach of contract. This would be the result even though the builder was the first to commit a material breach.[29]

A similar problem may arise if there are concurrent conditions under an agreement, so that tender by each party is a constructive condition of the other party's duty to perform.[30] Each party may claim that it was justified in terminating the contract because of the other party's breach. The seller of goods may

First material breach

Concurrent conditions

---

[25]3 S. Williston, Contracts §1291 (1st ed. 1920) (even if it later appears that defendant will not perform, if plaintiff has "already recovered, in an action on the same breach of promise, damages based on the assumption that the contract is to be carried out in the future he can bring no further action").

[26]*See* first Restatement of Judgments §62 cmt. *h* (1982).

[27]K & G Constr. Co. v. Harris, 164 A.2d 451 (Md. 1960) (subcontractor's discontinuance of work was not justified because contractor was entitled to suspend progress payments on subcontractor's breach).

It is said that the owner's suspension would be justified even if the owner did not know of the breach when suspending performance. Restatement Second §237 cmt. *c* ("one party's material failure of performance has the effect of the nonoccurrence of a condition of the other party's remaining duties . . . even though that other party does not know of the failure"). For similar rules, *see* the discussions of ignorance immaterial in §8.3 *supra*, of termination after some time in §8.18 *infra*, and of giving an insufficient reason in §8.19 *infra*.

[28]Wasserburger v. American Scientific Chem., 514 P.2d 1097 (Or. 1973) (employer justified in terminating).

[29]Walker & Co. v. Harrison, *supra* note 10 (lessee of sign liable for termination).

[30]See §8.10 *supra*. See also the discussion of time as of the essence in §8.18 *infra*.

claim that it terminated on the ground that the buyer did not pay, and the buyer may claim that it terminated on the ground that the seller did not deliver the goods. In this situation, a party must tender its own performance in order to put the other party in breach.[31] If the seller tenders the goods and the buyer does not pay, the seller has the right to terminate after an appropriate time. If the buyer tenders the price and the seller does not deliver the goods, the buyer has the right to terminate after an appropriate time. On termination, the injured party is excused from performing and has a claim for damages for total breach.[32]

Breach of implied duty

The breach on which an injured party relies in cases like these need not be of a duty that is stated in the agreement itself. Often the duty is an implied one, such as the duty of good faith that is generally imposed on a party to a contract.[33] A party whose performance is hindered or prevented by the other party in violation of the duty of good faith may not be limited to a claim for damages for the other party's breach. If the breach is material, the injured party can suspend its performance and, should the breach continue too long, can terminate.[34] The same results may follow from a breach of an implied duty to take affirmative steps to cooperate.[35]

How significant must a breach be in order to justify suspension?

Material breach required

§8.16. Material Breach and Suspension. In order for a breach to justify the injured party's suspension of performance, the breach must be significant enough to amount to the nonoccurrence of a constructive condition of exchange. Such a breach is termed "material."[1] (The word *total* is sometimes used instead of *material* to describe a breach that justifies suspension of performance, but it seems preferable to use *material* for this purpose and to reserve *total* to describe a breach that justifies termination

---

[31] *See* 2 S. Williston, Contracts §832 (1st ed. 1920) ("while the situation is possible of each of two parties having a right to specific performance against the other, it is not possible that each shall have a right to damages for a total breach of the contract").

[32] Canda v. Wick, 2 N.E. 381 (N.Y. 1885) (when buyer refused to accept cargo, sellers "were at liberty to treat the contract as broken, and were not bound to make an actual tender of the remainder of the brick").

[33] See the discussion of the duty of good faith in §7.17 *supra*.

[34] Patterson v. Meyerhofer, 97 N.E. 472 (N.Y. 1912) (purchaser prevented vendor from acquiring land by outbidding him at auction).

[35] Gatoil (U.S.A.) v. Washington Metro. Area Transit Auth., 801 F.2d 451 (D.C. Cir. 1986) (seller failed "to make a good-faith effort to obtain a performance bond"). Note the analogy to excuse of an express condition in the discussions of breach by prevention and by inaction in §8.6 *supra*.

§8.16 [1] Liddle v. Petty, 816 P.2d 1066 (Mont. 1991) (if party "materially breaches the contract, the injured party is entitled to suspend his performance," and farm purchaser's failure to make payments was material breach).

of the contract.[2]) The injured party need not suspend, however, but instead may continue to perform and claim damages for partial breach. An immaterial breach does not amount to the nonoccurrence of a constructive condition of exchange, so the injured party is not entitled to suspend, though it may claim damages for partial breach. If the injured party disrupts performance by suspending in response to an immaterial breach, that party commits a breach itself.

The doctrine of material breach is simply the converse of the doctrine of substantial performance. Substantial performance is performance without a material breach, and a material breach results in performance that is not substantial.[3] The substantiality of a party's performance is questioned when that party, despite its breach, claims that it is entitled under the contract to the value of the return performance. The materiality of a party's breach is questioned when the injured party seeks to use that breach to justify its own refusal to proceed with performance.

Substantial performance compared

The time for determining materiality is the time of the breach and not the time that the contract was made.[4] Whether a breach is material is a question of fact,[5] with the answer depending on circumstances similar to those used to determine whether a performance has been substantial. The Restatement Second looks to the injured party and asks to what extent that party will be deprived of the benefit it reasonably expected, account being taken of the possibility of adequate compensation for that part. It also looks to the other party — to the possibility that it will suffer forfeiture, to the likelihood that it will cure its failure, and to the degree that its behavior comported with standards of good faith and fair dealing.[6] Most significant is the extent to which the

Significant circumstances

---

[2]*See* Restatement Second §237 ("material" failure of performance justifies suspension). For the suggested use of *total*, see the discussion of termination after some time in §8.18 *infra*.

[3]First Sec. Bank v. Murphy, 964 P.2d 654 (Idaho 1998) ("breach of contract is not material if substantial performance has been rendered"). Although usage is not uniform, there is a commendable tendency among courts and scholars to use *substantial* in the sense of "almost complete" and *material* in the sense of "more than just a little."

[4]*Cf.* UCC 2-608 cmt. 2 (in applying test of substantial impairment where buyer revokes acceptance, "the test is not what the seller had reason to know at the time of contracting" and it makes no difference that "the seller had no advance knowledge as to the buyer's particular circumstances"). Contrast the rule for determining foreseeability of damages. See the discussion of the meaning of *foreseeability* in §12.14 *infra*.

[5]McLean v. Buffalo Bills Football Club, 301 N.Y.S.2d 872 (App. Div. 1969).

[6]Restatement Second §241. For list of factors in determining "fundamental non-performance," *see* UNIDROIT Principles 7.3.1(2). See the discussion of the Vienna Convention rule in §8.12 *supra*. The Principles, following CISG 25, require that the magnitude of the impact on the aggrieved party must have been foreseeable by the party in breach, a requirement not found in American formulations.

breach will deprive the injured party of the benefit that it justifiably expected,[7] a factor that is often decisive in determining whether a breach is material[8] or not.[9] This may depend in turn on the adequacy of damages. A court is less likely to characterize a breach as material where, in Mansfield's words, the "breach may be paid for in damages."[10] Both the Vienna Convention and the UNIDROIT Principles add a factor unknown to the common law by making foreseeability by the party in breach of the impact on the injured party a factor in determining whether a breach is "fundamental," their counterpart of material.[11]

Example of progress payment

For example, an owner's failure to make a single progress payment is generally held to justify the builder in suspending performance.[12] The breach deprives the builder of the benefit that it had expected from such payments — relief from having to finance the work in some other fashion — and may put the builder under great financial strain.[13] Furthermore, it is unlikely that a court would award damages to compensate the builder for this burden.[14] According to the Supreme Court of Pennsylvania, "the builder could undoubtedly have ceased operations temporarily if overdue demands remained unsatisfied." But to say that the injured party can suspend its performance is not to say that it can terminate the contract. The same court concluded that

---

[7] Gibson v. City of Cranston, 37 F.2d 731 (1st Cir. 1994) (though "material breach of an employment contract need not completely frustrate the entire purpose of the contract, it must be so important that it makes continued performance by the [employee] virtually pointless").

[8] Bernstein v. Nemeyer, 570 A.2d 164 (Conn. 1990) (Peters, C.J.: one of most important factors was that "breach deprived the plaintiffs of a substantial benefit for which they had clearly bargained").

[9] Cady v. Burton, 851 P.2d 1047 (Mont. 1993) ("contract provisions requiring the earnest money to be held on deposit [by vendor] were only incidental to the purpose of the contracts" so that vendor's breach would not be material since it did not defeat "primary purpose of the contract").

[10] Boone v. Eyre, 126 Eng. Rep. 160(a) (K.B. 1777), discussed in §8.12 *supra*.

[11] See the discussion of the Vienna Convention rule in §8.12 *supra*. Since it is foreseeability at the time of the breach that is in question, this is inconsistent with the rationale behind the rule in Hadley v. Baxendale, under which it is foreseeability at the time of the making of the contract that is relevant. *See* the discussion of the meaning of *foreseeability* in §12.14 *infra*.

[12] Aiello Constr. v. Nationwide Tractor Trailer Training & Placement Corp., 413 A.2d 85 (R.I. 1980) ("failure to pay installments . . . is a breach that would excuse further performance").

[13] It is useful to compare the situation of the builder to that of the seller that is to deliver goods under an installment sale in separate lots to be separately paid for. If the buyer's failure to pay an installment gives the seller reasonable grounds for insecurity with respect to the buyer's performance, the seller can demand adequate assurance of performance and "may if commercially reasonable suspend any performance" for which the seller "has not already received the agreed return." UCC 2-609(1). As to the builder's right to such assurances, see §8.23 *infra*. Even if the builder has such a right, the builder's need for cash may be such that it cannot be met by mere assurances.

[14] On the difficulty of recovering damages for breach of a promise to lend money, see the discussion of a promise of money or credit in §12.14 *infra*.

"it cannot be said that the abandonment of a contract of the magnitude here shown, within a few hours of a large payment, was justifiable."[15]

When can a party cure a breach and what are the legal effects of cure?

§8.17. Cure. Even though a breach is serious enough to justify the injured party's suspending performance, the party in breach often can "cure" the breach by correcting the deficiency in performance.[1] A buyer of goods that has failed to furnish means for shipping on time may do so after a delay. An owner of land that has failed to make a progress payment on construction when due may make a late payment. A vendor of land that has tendered a defective title may correct the defects. In such cases, courts have often been willing to allow the party in breach some period of time to cure its breach.[2] It would therefore seem that if cure is possible, notice of suspension, and perhaps of the breach relied on to justify it, ought to be required if the party in breach would not otherwise be aware of them.[3]

Examples of cure

Although the concept of cure was known before the Uniform Commercial Code, the Code must be credited with giving a seller of goods a clear right to cure[4] and with popularizing the word *cure* in this context. The Code provisions on cure apply only to contracts for the sale of goods, but they may be applied by analogy to other contracts.[5] However, the right to cure is more important in some situations than in others. For example, it is more important to a seller of goods, which is subject to the perfect tender rule, than it is to a builder under a construction contract, which already has the benefit of the doctrine of substantial performance.

Significance of cure under Code

The Code allows cure in two situations. The more obvious arises when the "time for performance has not yet expired."[6] The seller then has the right, on notifying the buyer, to make a conforming tender within that time. The second and less obvious situation arises when the time for performance has expired. In limited circumstances, when cure is appropriate despite the expiration of that time, the Code gives a seller that has performed in good faith an opportunity,

Cure under Code

---

[15]Turner Concrete Steel Co. v. Chester Constr. & Contracting Co., 114 A. 780, 782 (Pa. 1921). See the discussion of termination after some time in §8.18 *infra*.

§8.17 [1]Cure is not always possible, as in the case of a singer who fails to show up on the night of the opera.

[2]Stanley Gudyka Sales Co. v. Lacy Forest Prods. Co., 915 F.2d 273 (7th Cir. 1990) (requirement of "notice and an opportunity to cure . . . comports with general contract theory"). See the discussion of the example of a progress payment in §8.16 *supra*.

[3]That notice of suspension is not required, however, *see* Howard S. Lease Constr. Co. v. Holly, 725 P.2d 712 (Alaska 1986) (following *K & G*). See the discussion of exceptional cases in §8.19 *infra* for the Code's requirement that a rejecting buyer state the defect relied on if the seller could have cured.

[4]Before the Code, it was unclear whether a seller who had made a defective delivery could cure, even though the time for delivery had not expired.

[5]*See* Reporter's Note to Restatement Second §237, which relies on the Code in adopting the term *cure* for contracts in general.

[6]UCC 2-508(1).

on notifying the buyer, to cure.[7] Original Article 2 provides for cure only in the case where the buyer rejects, leaving it unclear whether the seller can cure where the buyer revokes acceptance.[8] Revised Article 2 extends the right to cure to the case where the buyer revokes acceptance, but this extension does not apply under a consumer contract.[9] The Code is silent on when, over the buyer's objection, cure may consist of repair of the rejected goods,[10] and when it must consist of tender of replacement goods.[11]

What cure is not   The right of cure should not be mistaken for what it is not. Strictly speaking, it is a power of the seller, whose performance or tender is a constructive condition of the buyer's duty to perform, to nullify the effect of a nonoccurrence of that condition.[12] The effect of the seller's cure is that the buyer must perform when it would otherwise have been excused by the seller's breach. In this respect the seller's power to cure goes beyond the mere power to make an offer of an appropriate substitute that may reduce the buyer's damages under the limitation of avoidability.[13] The seller's cure does not wipe out its liability for its breach; once the seller has broken the contract and become liable in damages, the seller cannot unilaterally discharge that liability by replacing or repairing defective goods.[14] Revised Article 2 makes it clear that a seller that exercises its right to

---

[7]Original Article 2 allows cure after the time for performance has expired if the "seller had reasonable grounds to believe [the non-conforming tender] would be acceptable with or without money allowance"). UCC-O 2-508(2). *See* UCC 2-508 cmt. 2 (seller's reasonable grounds for belief "can lie in prior course of dealing, course of performance or usage of trade as well as in the particular circumstances surrounding the making of the contract"). Revised Article 2 allows cure after that time if the seller "performed in good faith" and "if cure is appropriate and timely under the circumstances." UCC-R 2-508(2).

[8]*Compare* Jensen v. Seigel Mobile Homes Group, 668 P.2d 65 (Idaho 1983) ("Code does not allow a seller the right to cure defects following a buyer's acceptance of the goods"), *with* Ayanru v. General Motors Acceptance Corp., 495 N.Y.S.2d 1018 (N.Y.C. Civ. Ct. 1985) (if revocation is effective, seller has right to cure).

[9]UCC-R 2-508(1), (2) (no right to cure after revocation of acceptance under consumer contract). Furthermore, the seller has no second chance to cure under a nonconsumer contract if the buyer has revoked acceptance on the assumption that the seller would cure and the seller has already failed to cure (UCC 2-608(1)(a)).

[10]Wilson v. Scampoli, 228 A.2d 848 (D.C. 1967) (seller entitled to repair new color television set, though buyer wanted replacement set).

[11]Zabriskie Chevrolet v. Smith, 240 A.2d 195 (N.J. Super. 1968) ("For a majority of people the purchase of a new car is a major investment, rationalized by the peace of mind that flows from its dependability and safety. Once their faith is shaken, the vehicle loses not only its real value in their eyes, but becomes an instrument whose integrity is substantially impaired and whose operation is fraught with apprehension.").

[12]See Hohfeld's definition of *power* in a footnote to the discussion of the meaning of *bilateral* and *unilateral* in §3.4 *supra*.

[13]See the discussion of what is an appropriate substitute in §12.12 *infra*.

[14]*See* Jensen v. Seigel Mobile Homes Group, *supra* note 8. It is, of course, always open to the seller to get the buyer to agree to a compromise under which the buyer will accept replacement or repair instead of damages. However, such an agreement does not involve cure, which is the unilateral exercise of a power by the seller.

cure is liable to the buyer for reasonable expenses caused by both breach and by cure.[15] The Code does not give the buyer a right to require the seller to cure a breach; the buyer's only right to require the seller to remedy the defects in its performance is the very limited right to specific performance.[16]

If the party in breach does not cure within an appropriate time, the injured party may terminate the contract. The next section discusses how courts determine what length of time is appropriate.

§8.18. Total Breach and Termination. Although a material breach justifies the injured party in exercising a right to self-help by suspending performance, it does not necessarily justify the injured party in exercising such a right by terminating the contract. Fairness ordinarily dictates that the party in breach be allowed a period of time — even if only a short one — to cure the breach if it can. If the party in breach does cure within that period, the injured party is not justified in further suspension of its performance and both parties are still bound to complete their performances. This follows from the fact that the breach is treated as the nonoccurrence of a condition.[1]

The injured party need not suspend performance indefinitely, however. After some period of time, the injured party can put an end to the contract by terminating it. For example, after some period of time, the builder that has suspended its performance in response to the owner's failure to make a progress payment can treat the breach as total if the owner has not cured.[2] The builder will then have both a valid defense for its abandonment of the work (if the builder is sued by the owner) and a claim for damages for total breach (if the builder sues the owner). A claim for damages for total breach does not rest on the premise that the contract has been avoided but rather on the premise that the injured party is entitled to compensation for the performance that has not been rendered.[3] To recover such damages the injured party must show that, had there been no breach, it could have performed or tendered performance as required under the contract. For example, the builder must show that the building could have

Time for cure

Termination after some time

---

[15]UCC-R 2-508(1), (2).

[16]See §12.6 *infra*. However, the Vienna Convention gives a buyer, in some circumstances where goods are nonconforming, a right to "require delivery of substitute goods" (CISG 46(2)) or a right "to require the seller to remedy the lack of conformity by repair" (CISG 46(3)).

§8.18 [1]This analogy is stressed in Restatement Second §237 cmt. *a*. For an illustration, see the discussion of the example of a construction contract in §8.15 *supra*.

[2]Zulla Steel v. A & M Gregos, 415 A.2d 1183 (N.J. Super. 1980) (though not "every delay in payment will justify a contractor in terminating performances . . . , here there was a substantial underpayment for a prolonged period of time"). See the discussion of the example of a progress payment in §8.16 *supra*.

[3]See the discussions of four possible effects if total in §12.9 *infra* and of the basic requirements in §12.19 *infra*.

been finished.[4] If an injured party terminates, a court will not ask whether the injured party was actually motivated by the other party's breach or even whether the injured party knew of the breach.[5] But an injured party that acts precipitously and terminates before it is entitled to do so loses its defense, as well as the possibility of claiming for damages for total breach, and will itself be liable for damages for total breach.[6]

Significant circumstances   How long must the injured party wait before terminating the contract? Whether a material breach has remained uncured for long enough to justify termination is a question of fact, much like the question whether the breach is material in the first place. Similar circumstances are significant, including the extent to which further delay will deprive the injured party of the benefit that it justifiably expected from the exchange and the extent to which it will otherwise cause the injured party loss. Also significant is the degree to which the injured party can be compensated adequately in damages for that loss.[7]

Risk of forfeiture   The situation of the party in breach may be significant too. Termination involves a risk of forfeiture that is not present in the case of suspension because, after termination, it is too late for the party in breach to avoid forfeiture by curing its breach. For this reason, courts generally tolerate more delay by the party in breach when the breach comes after that party has relied on the contract by performance or otherwise than when the breach comes before that party has relied.[8] For the same reason, courts generally tolerate more delay on the part of a seller of specially manufactured goods, not suitable for sale to others, than on the part of a seller of readily resaleable commodities.[9]

Likelihood of cure   Since the purpose of requiring a period of time before termination is to give the party in breach an opportunity to cure, the likelihood that the party will do so is particularly important in determining how long the injured party must wait before treating the breach as total. Facts that indicate inability or unwillingness

---

[4]See the discussion of damages for total breach in §8.15 *supra*. For an analogous burden in the case of express conditions, see the discussion of a causal connection in §8.6 *supra* and for a similar rule in the case of a repudiation, see the discussion of treating the contract as terminated in §8.22 *infra*.

[5]See First Commodity Traders v. Heinold Commodities, 766 F.2d 1007 (7th Cir. 1985) (where clause allowed party to terminate on breach, party could rely on breach "even though he was unaware that the excuse existed at the time he terminated"). For similar rules, *see* the discussions of ignorance immaterial in §8.3 *supra* and of giving an insufficient reason in §8.19 *infra*.

[6]Walker & Co. v. Harrison, 81 N.W.2d 352 (Mich. 1957) (lessee of sign liable for terminating on ground that lessor had failed to maintain it).

[7]See the list of significant circumstances in Restatement Second §242.

[8]Leazzo v. Dunham, 420 N.E.2d 851 (Ill. App. 1981) (where "failure is at the outset, a very slight failure is often sufficient"). Such a breach is sometimes called a breach *in limine* (at the outset).

[9]Bradford Novelty Co. v. Technomatic, 112 A.2d 214 (Conn. 1955) ("Where the contract calls for the manufacture and sale of an article as yet nonexistent, the time specified for delivery is less likely to be considered of the essence.").

to cure strongly suggest that the injured party is justified in terminating.[10] A lack of good faith or a failure to observe reasonable standards of fair dealing may indicate that cure is unlikely.[11] If the breach is accompanied or followed by a repudiation, the injured party can treat the breach as total, even though the breach would otherwise be only partial.[12]

Courts also base their determination of the required length of time on the nature of the contract. In doing so, they have distinguished contracts for the sale of goods from contracts for the sale of land or for services. Time will be important to the seller of goods that has contracted to obtain the goods from a third person or that must make arrangements with forwarding agents and carriers to ship them; time will be important to the buyer of goods that must make arrangements through banking channels to pay for the goods or that has contracted to resell them to a third person. Furthermore, the market for goods is often subject to rapid fluctuation, so even a short delay before termination may result in a disadvantageous cover or resale contract and impose on the injured party a financial burden that it must bear until it is compensated in damages for its loss. Therefore courts have often held that "time is of the essence" under a contract for the sale of goods,[13] though even under such a contract the injured party may not be allowed to terminate immediately on breach without giving a chance for cure.[14] Courts have not routinely required prompt performance of other types of contracts, absent a showing of a contrary intent,[15] and have been especially tolerant in actions for specific performance.[16]

Time of the essence

Contracts often contain language making one party's performance by a specified date a condition of the other party's duty, and courts will usually honor

Contractual provisions

---

[10] Sackett v. Spindler, 56 Cal. Rptr. 435 (Ct. App. 1967) (seller of stock justified in terminating where "it was extremely uncertain" whether buyer intended to perform).

[11] Sackett v. Spindler, *supra* note 10 (buyer's "failure to pay could certainly not be characterized as innocent").

[12] Riess v. Murchison, 329 F.2d 635 (9th Cir. 1964) ("A breach of contract which, by itself, would be considered partial may be total if it is accompanied by an unequivocal repudiation of the whole contract. . . ."). *See* Restatement Second §243(2). *But see* the discussion of a duty to pay money in installments *infra*. As to what constitutes a repudiation, see §8.21 *infra*.

[13] Norrington v. Wright, 115 U.S. 188 (1885) ("In the contracts of merchants, time is of the essence. The time of shipment is the usual and convenient means of fixing the probable time of arrival, with a view of providing funds to pay for the goods, or of fulfilling contracts with third persons."). For comparison, see the discussion of the perfect tender rule in §8.12 *supra*.

[14] Courts have been more tolerant with buyers than with sellers. Fitz v. Coutinho, 622 A.2d 1220 (N.H. 1993) ("Time [for payment] is generally not of the essence . . . , unless the contract specifically so states, even if a particular time schedule is specified").

[15] Kakalik v. Bernardo, 439 A.2d 1016 (Conn. 1981) (Peters, J.: "In real estate contracts 'the fact that a specific tiem is fixed . . . does not make performance at the *specified* time of the essence' ").

[16] McFadden v. Walker, 488 P.2d 1353 (Cal. 1971) (willful delay in payment of installments for over two years was "at worst . . . the petulant reaction of an elderly lady to an apparent theft of timber from her property").

such language if it is clear.[17] Courts will occasionally find such a condition by inference from language that is less than clear.[18] Still, one may question the wisdom of the court that concluded that a contract providing for the delivery of goods "*at* a specified date, followed by specification of a date, requires delivery upon that date and none other."[19] And although courts have sometimes given a similar effect to the stock phrase "time is of the essence,"[20] such language should be considered along with other circumstances.[21]

Installment contracts

Courts are often faced with claims of total breach under installment contracts for the sale of goods in which a seller is to deliver separate lots to be separately paid for. According to the Uniform Commercial Code, "Whenever nonconformity or default with respect to one or more installments substantially impairs the value of the whole contract there is a breach of the whole."[22] Therefore the mere fact that the buyer is entitled to reject one installment does not necessarily justify the buyer's terminating the contract. Nor does the buyer's failure to pay for one installment necessarily justify the seller's terminating the contract. Whether a seller can treat a buyer's failure to pay for an installment as a total breach is a question much like whether a builder can so treat an owner's failure to make a progress payment.[23] In Cardozo's words:

> If the default is the result of accident or misfortune, if there is a reasonable assurance that it will be promptly repaired, and if immediate payment is not necessary to enable the vendor to proceed with performance, there may be one conclusion. If the breach is willful, if there is no just ground to look for prompt reparation, if the delay has been substantial, or if the needs of the vendor are urgent so that continued performance is imperilled, in these and other circumstances, there may be another conclusion.[24]

---

[17] Mailloux v. Dickey, 523 A.2d 66 (N.H. 1986) (provision that vendor could terminate land-sale contract if purchaser did not pay balance of price within time provided "was even more specific than 'time is of the essence'"). See the discussion of strict compliance in §8.3 *supra*.

[18] C & M Realty Trust v. Wiedenkeller, 578 A.2d 354 (N.H. 1990) (reasonable to conclude that time was of the essence from "letters' express references to the date of closing, together with the practical interpretation by the parties").

[19] Oshinsky v. Lorraine Mfg. Co., 157 F.121 (2d Cir. 1911).

[20] Corbray v. Stevenson, 656 P.2d 473 (Wash. 1982) (words "time is of the essence" were "plain, direct, and unambiguous").

[21] Kaiman Realty v. Carmichael, 655 P.2d 872 (Haw. 1982) ("a 'time is of the essence' clause . . . will not foreclose equitable relief where . . . forfeiture would be harsh and unreasonable"). *See* Restatement Second §242 cmt. *d*.

[22] UCC 2-612(3).

[23] If the seller cannot or does not choose to treat the buyer's breach as total and recovers damages for partial breach, the doctrine of merger should not preclude the seller from suing for damages for total breach if there is a subsequent failure by the buyer to pay a later installment. *See* the discussion of the risk of splitting a claim in §8.15 *supra*.

[24] Helgar Corp. v. Warner's Features, 119 N.E. 113, 114 (N.Y. 1918).

Prior to the Code, courts had shown a tendency to be tolerant of the buyer,[25] and the Code commentary encourages this tendency.[26]

There is an important exception to the general rule that a breach by nonperformance, if sufficiently serious, gives the injured party a claim for damages for total breach. If, at the time of the breach, the injured party has fully performed and the only remaining duty of performance of the party in breach is to pay money in independent installments, the failure to pay one or more installments does not amount to a total breach that will accelerate the time for payment of the balance of the debt.[27] The injured party may maintain successive actions for partial breach as successive installments fall due.[28] The rule applies both to unilateral contracts and to bilateral contracts under which the injured party has fully performed. It applies even if the breach is accompanied or followed by a repudiation.[29] To avoid the effect of this rule, creditors often include acceleration clauses in their agreements. Under such a clause, if the debtor is in breach as to one installment, all the remaining installments become due, either automatically or at the option of the creditor.

Duty to pay money in installments

In the section that follows, we consider the impact of the doctrine of waiver in excusing constructive conditions of exchange.

§8.19.   Waiver and Election. We have already seen how an express condition may be excused by waiver.[1] Analogous rules may excuse a constructive condition by waiver. If it is a constructive condition of one party's duty that the

Effect of waiver

---

[25] Helgar Corp. v. Warner's Features, *supra* note 24 (seller was not "justified in its precipitate election to declare the contract at an end").

[26] UCC 2-612 cmt. 6 ("If only the seller's security in regard to future installments is impaired, he has the right to demand adequate assurances of proper future performance but has not an immediate right to cancel the entire contract.").

[27] Quick v. American Steel & Pump Corp., 397 F.2d 561 (2d Cir. 1968) (in suit by retired president of company for breach of pension plan, "we see no reason not to apply the usual rule that contracts to pay money in installments are breached one installment at a time"). *See* Restatement Second §243(3). According to Comment *c*: "Whether there is a relationship between installments or other acts depends on the extent to which, in the circumstances, a breach as to less than the whole of such installments or acts can substantially affect the injured party's expectation under the contract."

[28] The doctrine of merger does not bar later actions. Goodwin v. Cabot Amusement Co., 149 A. 574 (Me. 1930) (if "agreement provides for the payment of installments of money, suit may be brought for successive installments, . . . and a judgment recovered in the first suit is no bar to the second suit"). On the doctrine of merger, see the discussion of the risk of splitting a claim in §8.15 *supra*. On the possibility of an installment judgment, see the discussion of other types of relief in §8.20 *infra*.

[29] John Hancock Mut. Life Ins. Co. v. Cohen, 254 F.2d 417 (9th Cir. 1958) (15-year endowment policy under which, after death of insured, insurer was "to pay definite sums of money at specified future dates"). This aspect of the rule is discussed in §8.20 *infra*.

§8.19   [1] See §8.5 *supra*.

other party render a return performance, the first party can waive that condition by promising to perform despite its nonoccurrence. That party will then be under a duty to perform, even if there is a breach by the other party in rendering the return performance; the injured party cannot treat the breach as a ground for termination. Nevertheless, the injured party can recover damages for partial breach, so that party will be compensated for the breach even though it does not justify it in refusing to perform.[2]

Similarity to express conditions
For the most part, the rules governing waiver of constructive conditions are similar to those governing express conditions. A constructive condition can be waived either before or after the time for its occurrence. The waiver is not effective unless the injured party knows, or at least has reason to know, of the relevant facts, though that party's knowledge of its legal situation and of the legal effect of its promise is immaterial.[3] In contrast to the rule governing express conditions, however, a constructive condition of exchange can be waived, even if it is a material part of the agreed exchange, since the injured party will still be compensated for the breach.[4] Thus an owner can waive the constructive condition of substantial performance under a building contract by promising to pay despite material defects and still retain a claim for damages for partial breach.[5]

Example of delay
Many of the cases dealing with waiver of constructive conditions involve delay in performance. A party that is late in performing often invokes the concept of waiver as an excuse. If the other party has indicated that it will tolerate the delay, it cannot later seize on the delay as a ground for termination, though that party is entitled to damages for any loss the delay may have caused.[6] Thus a vendor of real property that has indicated that it will perform, despite

---

[2] Towery v. Carolina Dairy, 75 S.E.2d 534 (N.C. 1953) ("the party not in fault may elect to waive the breach and continue performance regardless of the breach"). It is possible, of course, for the injured party to give up its claim for damages for partial breach, but it is preferable not to describe this as a "waiver." *See* the discussion of the meaning of *waiver* in §8.5 *supra*.

[3] Bertrand v. Jones, 156 A.2d 161 (N.J. Super. 1959) (purchasers of land "could not have waived the right to raise a defense about which they knew nothing"). Under UCC 2-608(1), a buyer can revoke acceptance of goods that the buyer accepted without discovery of the non-conformity if the buyer's "acceptance was reasonably induced . . . by the difficulty of discovery before acceptance." However, the buyer must also show that the nonconformity "substantially impairs" the value of the goods to the buyer and cannot rely on the perfect tender rule. See the discussion of the perfect tender rule in §8.12 *supra*.

[4] This is not true when one waives an express condition, except in the unusual case where the condition is promissory. *See* Restatement Second §84(1) (condition cannot be waived if "occurrence of the condition was a material part of the agreed exchange . . . and the promisee was under no duty that it occur").

[5] *See* Restatement Second §246 illus. 7.

[6] Fracassa v. Doris, 814 A.2d 357 (R.I. 2003) ("like any other provision . . . , time is of the essence may be waived by express agreement or impliedly by conduct that contributes to the delay in performance").

a delay that would justify the termination, may itself be held for damages for total breach if it refuses to go through with the sale on the ground of such a delay.[7]

A particularly troublesome question arises if an injured party that is fully aware of a breach indicates that it will treat the breach as partial, rather than total, and then reconsiders and seeks to treat it as total. Once a material breach has continued long enough to be total, the injured party can choose either to terminate the contract and claim damages for total breach, or not to terminate the contract and claim damages for only partial breach. This power to choose is analogous to that of a party whose duty is expressly conditional. Such a party can also choose whether to treat its duty as discharged, once it is too late for the condition to occur. That party's choice is designated an "election" and is binding even if it has not been relied on.[8] Courts often reason by analogy that the injured party that waives a constructive condition is similarly bound by an election, even in the absence of reliance.[9] Under this reasoning, the injured party cannot later reconsider, terminate, and recover damages for total breach unless the party in breach should commit a further breach, subsequent to the election, that would give the injured party a second chance to terminate.[10] It is not easy to justify this rule of election. The analogy to the election cases involving express conditions is weak. Virtually all of those cases involve insurance policies, and the doctrine of election is confined to relatively minor conditions.[11] Nevertheless, extending the doctrine to constructive conditions of exchange gives to decisions made in response to breach a finality that may be desirable. Furthermore, if the transaction is an ongoing one, as in the case of a breach by a builder in the course of construction, the doctrine helps to keep the deal together.[12]

Election

---

[7] Dreier v. Sherwood, 238 P. 38 (Colo. 1925) (purchasers of land relied on vendor's statement that time for payment would be extended).

[8] See the discussion of the concept of election in §8.5 *supra*. Similarly, under UCC 2-612(3), an "aggrieved party reinstates the contract" if the party "brings an action with respect only to past installments."

[9] Wheeler v. Wheeler, 263 S.E.2d 763 (N.C. 1980) ("a party may waive the breach . . . without consideration or estoppel"). *See generally* E. Farnsworth, Changing Your Mind ch. 19 (1998).

Under the Uniform Commercial Code, a buyer that has chosen to treat a breach as partial and has accepted the goods with knowledge of their nonconformity is generally precluded from revoking acceptance. UCC 2-608(1).

[10] K & G Constr. Co. v. Harris, 164 A.2d 451 (Md. 1960) (though contractor "treated the breach by the subcontractor as a partial one . . . the subcontractor again breached the contract when he "discontinued work on the project, which rendered him liable" for damages for total breach).

If the injured party has already recovered damages for partial breach, the doctrine of merger should not preclude that party's suing for damages for total breach in this situation. See the discussion of the risk of splitting a claim in §8.15 *supra*.

[11] See the discussion of the point that a condition must be minor in §8.5 *supra*.

[12] For a critical discussion of the doctrine, *see* Cities Serv. Helex v. United States, 543 F.2d 1306, 1313-17 (Ct. Cl. 1976).

Choice by conduct   A party's choice to treat a breach as only partial is often inferred from that party's conduct.[13] A court usually concludes that a party has made such a choice if that party accepts the other's performance or retains it for more than a reasonable time.[14] Thus, if a buyer of goods accepts them, knowing that they have defects that would justify rejection, the buyer must pay their price,[15] though the buyer may have a damage claim for the defects.[16] The buyer's conduct operates as a promise to perform its duty to pay the price, despite nonoccurrence of a constructive condition of that duty. The buyer's conduct has the same effect when it accepts or retains only a part performance.[17] Thus the buyer's acceptance of one installment waives defects in that installment and in prior installments, just as acceptance of the whole would have waived them.[18] Furthermore, since a party that receives a whole performance usually has no right to accept part and reject part, the buyer's acceptance of part may waive defects in the whole.[19] But if a party accepts a conforming part of the other party's performance with no reason to know that the other party will subsequently commit a breach, the first party does not lose the right to assert the subsequent breach to justify its refusal to perform.[20]

Effect on later breaches   In some circumstances the obligor's acceptance of part of the obligee's performance may waive subsequent breaches as well as existing ones.[21] But it has

---

[13] Longenecker v. Brommer, 368 P.2d 900 (Wash. 1962) (right to terminate was waived by party that "continued to accept the benefit of [other party's] performance and did not assert the breach as a ground for rescission of the contract until this action was instituted").

[14] Lindsay Mfg. Co. v. Universal Sur. Co., 519 N.W.2d 530 (Neb. 1994) ("express or implied acceptance of work as in compliance with a building contract operates as a waiver of defective performance" where acceptance was not "under protest or induced by fraud" and defects were not "latent and unknown to the owner"). *See* Restatement Second §246(1).

[15] UCC 2-709(1)(a). There is an exception if the buyer accepted the goods on the reasonable assumption that the defects would be cured. UCC 2-607(2), 2-608(1)(a).

[16] UCC 2-714. As to the possibility that the buyer may lose the right to damages by failing to give the seller timely notice of breach, *see* UCC 2-607(3)(a). Under revised Article 2, however, failure to give timely notice bars the buyer "only to the extent that the seller is prejudiced by the failure." UCC-R 2-607(3)(a).

[17] *See* Restatement Second §246 cmt. *c*.

[18] UCC 2-612(3).

[19] *See* Restatement Second §246 cmt. *c*. Under the Code, however, the buyer can "accept any commercial unit or units and reject the rest" (UCC 2-601(c)), but "must pay at the contract rate for any goods accepted" (UCC 2-607(1)).

[20] Norrington v. Wright, 115 U.S. 188 (1885) ("previous acceptance of the single cargo of 400 tons shipped in February was no waiver of this right, because it took place without notice or means of knowledge, that the stipulated quantity had not been shipped in February"). This is not true, however, if the injured party retains the accepted part for more than a reasonable time after it knows or has reason to know of the breach. *See* Restatement Second §246 cmt. *c*; UCC 2-608(2).

[21] Heinzman v. Howard, 348 N.W.2d 147 (S.D. 1984) (vendor's acceptance of late payments "waived the contract provision that time of payment was essential"). *See* Restatement Second §247.

this effect only if it justifies the obligee in believing that subsequent performances will also be accepted despite similar defects. For example, if a buyer has accepted several defective installments in succession, the seller may be justified in believing that the buyer will continue to accept similarly defective installments.[22] And if a seller has accepted several late installment payments in succession, the buyer may be justified in believing that the seller will continue to accept late payment.[23] However, it is clear that a party can revoke its waiver as to subsequent breaches if the party in breach has not relied on the waiver to such an extent that revocation would be unjust.[24]

Exception to principle

There is an important exception to the principle that a party's acceptance or retention of a defective performance operates as a choice to treat the breach as only partial. The exception is made when the defective performance is so attached to the recipient's property that removal of it would cause material loss.[25] If a builder has not substantially performed a contract to construct a house for a landowner, the owner does not waive the condition of substantial performance by failing to have the house removed from the land or even by moving into it. As the New York Court of Appeals said: "This is not a case of the sale of goods. . . . The house was built upon the defendants' property. They could move into it, live in it and in this sense accept it without waiving any defects in construction."[26] But if the recipient goes beyond mere acceptance and retention of the performance and manifests assent to be bound despite nonoccurrence of a constructive condition, the recipient will be regarded as having waived that condition.[27] The assent waives the condition even though the recipient reserves a right to claim damages for partial breach.

Choice by inaction

In rare situations, the injured party's inaction may amount to an election to treat a breach as merely partial.[28] Suppose that an insurance company issues a policy of fire insurance for a year beginning January 1, in return for the insured's promise to pay the premium on the following July 1. If the insured fails to pay and the house burns on December 31, can the insured recover under

---

[22] *See* Restatement Second §247 cmt. *a*.

[23] Westinghouse Credit Corp. v. Shelton, 645 F.2d 869 (10th Cir. 1981) (summary judgment precluded by question whether creditor waived "its right to strictly enforce the contract's terms, of which the 'anti-waiver' clause is one, by accepting . . . late payments").

[24] Sethness-Greenleaf, Inc. v. Green River Corp., 65 F.3d 64 (7th Cir. 1995) (Easterbrook, J.: "vendor who cuts the buyer some slack — even 14 months worth of slack — does not thereby 'agree' to forbear indefinitely").

[25] *See* Restatement Second §246(2).

[26] Cawley v. Weiner, 140 N.E. 724, 725 (N.Y. 1923).

The owner's taking possession has, however, been held to waive the condition of an architect's certificate, though the contractor is still liable for defects. Creith Lumber v. Cummins, 126 N.E.2d 323 (Ohio 1955) (contractor is "entitled to recover the amount due . . . less deductions for deficiencies").

[27] *See* Restatement Second §246 illus. 7.

[28] These should not be confused with the situation, mentioned *supra* note 16, in which inaction may bar a buyer's claim for damages for partial breach under UCC 2-607(3)(a).

the policy despite the breach? If there had been no fire before the end of the year, the insurer could have recovered the overdue premium from the insured. If the insurer can terminate and resist payment when a fire occurs, it is in the position, when the default occurs, of being able to wait out the year and either sue for the overdue premium or resist payment under the policy, depending on whether there has been a fire. The unfairness of this is apparent.[29] Therefore, the Restatement Second provides that, in the case of an aleatory contract, the injured party cannot terminate unless it does so before any adverse change in its situation "resulting from the occurrence of [the fortuitous] event or a material change in the probability of its occurrence."[30] If the insurer has not terminated before the fire, it is taken to have elected not to treat the breach as total.[31]

Giving insufficient reason

A different problem involving waiver arises when a party gives an insufficient reason for rejecting a defective performance or offer of performance. Ordinarily, a party need not give any reason for rejection. A party may even justify rejection on a ground of which the party was unaware at the time it rejected.[32] However, if a party gives an insufficient reason for rejecting, and the party in breach reasonably understands that to be the exclusive reason, the court will treat the giving of that reason as a promise not to assert other reasons.[33] Thus the builder that receives from the owner a list of asserted defects in construction may reasonably understand this as a promise not to assert other defects. No election is involved in this case; the owner that has rejected does not choose to treat the breach differently by asserting other defects. Therefore the owner will be allowed to assert them as long as the builder has not relied on the list.[34]

Exceptional cases

There are exceptions to the rule that a party need not give any reason for rejection. One exception is made when a party rejects the payment or tender of money that is a condition of that party's duty. Because money claims are so

---

[29]The first Restatement avoided this result by a complicated scheme. The rules on constructive conditions were said not to apply to such aleatory contracts, so that payment under the policy by the insurer was not conditional on payment of the premium by the insured, but the insurer could rescind if the occurrence of the event had not become more probable. Restatement §293.

[30]Restatement Second §379. For a definition of *aleatory*, see the discussion of risk affecting imbalance in §2.11 *supra*.

[31]Dwelling-House Ins. Co. v. Hardie, 16 P. 92 (Kan. 1887) (instead of "declaring the policy at an end when default was made, [insurer] allowed the note to run").

[32]Bertrand v. Jones, *supra* note 3 (purchasers of land were ignorant of encumbrance when they refused to settle). For similar rules, see the discussions of ignorance immaterial in §8.3 *supra* and of termination after some time in §8.18 *supra*.

[33]*See* Restatement Second §248. Under that section, the resulting promise operates as a waiver only if the rejecting party knew or had reason to know of the nonoccurrence of the condition "and then only to the extent that the giving of an insufficient reason substantially contributes to a failure by the other party to cure." *See* the discussion of the similarity to express conditions *supra*.

[34]New England Structures v. Loranger, 234 N.E.2d 888 (Mass. 1968) (jury should have been instructed that they might consider grounds not stated by general contractor in telegram "unless they found as a fact that [subcontractor] had relied to its detriment upon the fact that only one particular ground for termination was mentioned in the telegram").

commonly paid by check or other means that are not legal tender, payment in any manner current in the ordinary course of business will suffice, unless the creditor demands payment in legal tender and gives any extension of time reasonably necessary to procure it.[35] The Uniform Commercial Code makes two other exceptions. First, a buyer is precluded from relying on an unstated defect if the seller could have cured had the buyer stated the defect. Second, in a transaction between merchants, a buyer is precluded from relying on an unstated defect if the seller has made a request in a writing or other record "for a full and final" statement of all defects.[36]

We turn now from nonperformance to prospective nonperformance.

E.   PROSPECTIVE NONPERFORMANCE

§8.20.   Anticipatory Repudiation as a Breach. We have thus far been concerned with the effects of a party's breach of its duty by nonperformance when the time for performance has arrived. We have seen that if a repudiation accompanies a breach by nonperformance, the injured party can treat the breach as total, even if the breach would otherwise have been only partial.[1] We now turn to the effects of a party's repudiation of its duty before the time for performance has arrived. Such a repudiation, occurring before there has been any breach by nonperformance, is called an "anticipatory breach" or, more precisely, an "anticipatory repudiation."[2]

Anticipatory repudiation

It has long been accepted that an anticipatory repudiation discharges any remaining duties of performance of the injured party.[3] In other words, the repudiation has the same effect as the nonoccurrence of a condition of those remaining duties. Once there has been a repudiation, the injured party is no longer expected to hold itself ready to perform; that party is free to make such substitute arrangements as may be appropriate. It was less clear, however, that the repudiation gave the injured party an immediate action for damages for total

Discharges duties

---

[35] UCC 2-511(2); Restatement Second §249.

[36] UCC 2-605. UCC-R 2-605(1) extends these rules to revocation of acceptance, consistent with UCC-R 2-508's extension of the right to cure to revocation of acceptance. See the discussion of cure under the Code in §8.17 *supra.*

§8.20   [1] See the discussion of the likelihood of cure in §8.18 *supra.*

[2] The term *anticipatory breach* is elliptical, for what is meant is "breach by anticipatory repudiation."

[3] Thus the injured party can always sue for damages once the time for performance has come, even if that party has already made substitute arrangements. Cort & Gee v. Ambergate, N. & B. & E.J. Ry., 117 Eng. Rep. 1229 (Q.B. 1851). It is also clear that an anticipatory repudiation gives the injured party an immediate claim to restitution. (The discussion here assumes that the promises are not independent. See the discussion of the preference for dependent promises in §8.9 *supra.*)

breach, so that that party would not have to await the time for performance to sue for damages.[4]

Hochster v. De la Tour

In 1853 the Court of Queen's Bench allowed such an action in the celebrated case of *Hochster v. De la Tour*. On April 12 of the preceding year, Hochster and De la Tour had made a contract under which Hochster was to serve as a courier for De la Tour during his travels in Europe for three months, beginning on June 1. On May 11, De la Tour wrote Hochster that he had changed his mind and that Hochster was discharged. On May 22, Hochster brought suit for damages. De la Tour's counsel argued that the suit was brought prematurely, since there could be no breach of contract before June 1, when performance was to begin. To the sensible premise that Hochster should be "at liberty to consider himself absolved from any future performance," the opinion adds this non sequitur: "If the plaintiff has no remedy for breach of the contract unless he treats the contract as in force, and acts upon it down to the 1st June 1852, it follows that, till then, he must enter into no employment which will interfere with his promise . . . ."[5] On this reasoning it was concluded that Hochster's action was not premature. This doctrine of anticipatory repudiation soon became the center of controversy.

Criticism of doctrine

Critics of the doctrine were quick to point out the illogic of the argument in *Hochster*.[6] The court could have decided that, although De la Tour's repudiation immediately freed Hochster to take other employment, a conclusion consonant with the concept of avoidability as a limitation on damages, Hochster had no cause of action for breach until the time for performance came. Although it was important to Hochster to know whether he was free to take other jobs, he was not helped in this by being allowed to sue before the time for performance. For this purpose it would have sufficed to regard the repudiation as the nonoccurrence of a condition of Hochster's remaining duties, which discharged those duties but did not operate as a breach. Critics of the doctrine also objected that mere words could not amount to a breach of a duty the performance of which was not yet due. As one writer protested, "There can be no fine-spun reasoning which will successfully make that a breach of promise which, in fact, is not a breach

---

[4] As to the injured party's right to sue for specific performance before the time for performance has come, see the discussion of specific performance in §12.5 *infra*.

That a party in breach because of a repudiation can nevertheless enforce a choice of forum clause or an arbitration clause, *see* Marra v. Papandreou, 216 F.3d 1119 (D.C. Cir. 2000) (choice of forum), following Kulukundis Shipping Co. v. Amtorg Trading Corp., 126 F.2d 978 (2d Cir. 1942) (arbitration).

[5] 118 Eng. Rep. 922, 926 (Q.B. 1853).

[6] Williston strongly criticized the doctrine of Hochster v. De la Tour. Williston, Repudiation of Contracts (pt. 2), 14 Harv. L. Rev. 421, 432 (1901), surmising that, "apparently misled by the argument of counsel, Lord Campbell drew the conclusion that the plaintiff must have an immediate right of action." Corbin thought that De la Tour's barrister contributed to the non sequitur of an aged Lord Campbell by making a "defective argument" in which he "claimed too much for his client in asserting that the repudiation was an offer to rescind the contract." 4 A. Corbin, Contracts §960 (1951).

of promise. . . . To say that [a promise] may be broken by anticipation is to say that which, in the nature of things, cannot be so." Furthermore, attempting to estimate damages in an action brought before the time for performance would be a "matter of pure speculation and guesswork."[7]

Supporters of the doctrine replied that a contracting party has the right to expect not only that the other party will perform when the time comes, but that it will do nothing substantially to impair that expectation before the time comes. In Learned Hand's words:

Support of doctrine

> a promise to perform in the future by implication includes an engagement not deliberately to compromise the probability of performance. . . . Such intermediate uncertainties as arise from the vicissitudes of the promisor's affairs are, of course, a part of the risk, but it is hard to see how, except by mere verbalism, it can be supposed that the promisor may within the terms of his undertaking gratuitously add to those uncertainties by announcing his purpose to default.[8]

Supporters of the doctrine carried the day, and the doctrine of anticipatory repudiation gained widespread acceptance.[9] With the notable exception of Massachusetts,[10] courts have accepted the general rule that an anticipatory repudiation gives the injured party an immediate claim to damages for total breach, in addition to discharging that party's remaining duties of performance. The problems in estimating these damages do not differ significantly from those posed when a party claims damages for future loss caused by a total breach by nonperformance. Furthermore, in many cases delay in coming to trial eliminates the difficulty. As Learned Hand observed, though it is "one of the consequences of the doctrine of anticipatory breach that, if damages are assessed before the time of performance has expired, the court must take the chance of forecasting the future as best it can," this "does not mean that it will ignore what has happened, when the period of performance has already

Acceptance of doctrine

---

[7]Terry, Book Review, 34 Harv. L. Rev. 891, 894 (1921).

[8]Equitable Trust Co. v. Western Pac. Ry., 244 F. 485, 502 (S.D.N.Y. 1917), aff'd, 250 F. 327 (2d Cir.). See UCC 2-609(1) ("contract for sale imposes an obligation on each party that the other's expectation of receiving due performance will not be impaired"). Today, Hand's point might be paraphrased by saying that a repudiation is a breach of the duty of good faith.

[9]Roussalis v. Wyoming Med. Ctr., 4 P.3d 209 (Wyo. 2000) (quoting this section of this treatise). See Restatement Second §253(1); UCC 2-610, 2-611. For the doctrine as it appears in the Vienna Convention, see CISG 72(1) (if before time for performance "it is clear" that a party will commit a fundamental breach of contract, the other party may declare the contract avoided). A similar provision is contained in UNIDROIT Principles 7.3.3.

[10]Daniels v. Newton, 114 Mass. 530 (1874) (though "renunciation of the agreement, . . . may . . . relieve [the other party] from the necessity of offering performance in order to enforce his rights, . . . we are unable to see how it can, of itself, constitute a present violation of any legal rights of the other party, or confer upon him a present right of action").

expired."[11] And while the injured party must prove that it could have performed absent the repudiation,[12] the difficulty of doing this is not unlike that faced by a party injured by a present breach in proving that it could have performed absent the breach.[13]

Exception to doctrine

The critics of the doctrine, however, appear to have been responsible for a significant exception to it.[14] Repudiation of a duty does not operate as a breach if it occurs after the repudiating party has received all of the agreed exchange for that duty. The injured party must then await the time for performance to sue for damages.[15] Thus courts have refused to apply the doctrine when a party repudiates either a unilateral contract[16] or a bilateral contract that has been fully performed by the injured party.[17] It is difficult to explain the development of this exception, except as the result of a grudging acceptance of the doctrine itself.[18] Parties, especially to loan agreements, have often avoided the exception by including an acceleration clause under which the balance of the performance becomes due, or can be declared due, on default.[19]

Avoidance of exception

Courts have often avoided the exception by finding that some part of the agreed exchange has not been rendered. Thus, when a corporation repudiated a contract under which a railroad had given it the right to install and use a pipeline along the railroad's right-of-way in return for annual payments, the court held that the railroad had an action for anticipatory breach. Even though the corporation had not availed itself of its right, the railroad was "obligated to

---

[11] New York Trust Co. v. Island Oil & Transp. Corp., 34 F.2d 653, 654 (2d Cir. 1929). *See* the discussion of loss avoided in §12.9 *infra.*

[12] Kanavos v. Hancock Bank & Trust Co., 479 N.E.2d 168 (Mass. 1985) (holder of right of first refusal could not recover if holder could not perform even if other party repudiated).

[13] See the discussions of damages for total breach in §8.15 *supra* and of termination after some time in §8.18 *supra.*

[14] Equitable Trust Co. v. Western Pac. Ry., *supra* note 8 (if "doctrine has any limits, . . . they result because the eventual victory of the doctrine over vigorous attack . . . has not left it scathless").

[15] Texas rejects this exception. Pitts v. Wetzel, 498 S.W.2d 27 (Tex. Civ. App. 1973) ("doctrine of anticipatory breach is to be applied without distinction to contracts still to be performed by both parties and to those fully executed by one party").

[16] Rosenfeld v. City Paper Co., 527 So. 2d 704 (Ala. 1988) (collecting authorities: "majority of jurisdictions . . . have not allowed the 'anticipatory breach' doctrine to apply to unilateral contracts, particularly for the payment of money only").

[17] Phelps v. Herro, 137 A.2d 159 (Md. 1957) ("doctrine of anticipatory breach . . . has no application to money contracts, pure and simple, where one party has fully performed his undertaking, and all that remains for the opposite party to do is to pay a certain sum of money . . . , and . . . this is as far as we need to rule").

[18] See Central States, S.E. & S.W. Areas Pension Fund v. Basic Am. Indus., 252 F.3d 911 (7th Cir. 2001) (Posner, J. [dictum]: "Why the doctrine . . . should be so limited eludes our understanding. Announcement by the other party that he has no intention of paying should entitle the prospective victim of the payor's breach to take immediate steps to protect his interest, as by suing.").

[19] Rosenfeld v. City Paper Co., *supra* note 16 (use of acceleration clause "is in recognition of the nonapplicability of the anticipatory breach doctrine in installment payment contracts").

future performance" because it had to remain in a "condition to perform" and was under a duty not to abandon the property or dispose of it to one whose use would prevent the construction of the pipeline.[20]

Furthermore, even if the injured party was under no duty to render any performance, courts have applied the doctrine if some performance by that party was a condition of the repudiated duty and was in this sense part of the agreed exchange. Thus the doctrine applies if the injured party is the holder of an option to purchase land and the vendor repudiates before the option is exercised. Although the holder of the option is under no duty to pay the price of the land, payment of the price is a condition of the vendor's repudiated duty.[21] Similarly, courts have allowed such suits for anticipatory repudiation against life insurers that have repudiated. Although the insured is under no duty to pay premiums, the insured's payment of premiums is a condition of the insurer's repudiated duty.[22]

Performance as condition

The doctrine of anticipatory repudiation is especially troublesome in its application to policies of disability insurance. In contrast to cases involving life insurance, in which damages are based on tables of life expectancy, cases involving repudiation of disability insurance policies often involve damage claims based on highly uncertain predictions of the extent and duration of the disability. The difficulty is eased in practice because cases involving repudiation of disability policies virtually always arise in connection with the insurer's failure to make a payment for a claimed disability. They are not cases of anticipatory repudiation at all, therefore, but cases of a breach by nonperformance accompanied by a repudiation. Unfortunately, courts and writers have often overlooked this distinction and, as a result, their analyses have added to the confusion already surrounding the doctrine of anticipatory repudiation.[23] Foreseeing the difficulty of calculating damages in these cases, courts have often struggled to find some pretext to deny recovery of damages for total breach.[24] Since the insured must usually furnish proof of continued disability as a condition of the insurer's repudiated duty, however, the exception to the doctrine of anticipatory repudiation

Disability insurance

---

[20] Long Island R.R. v. Northville Indus. Corp., 362 N.E.2d 558, 565 (N.Y. 1977).

[21] Space Center v. 451 Corp., 298 N.W.2d 443 (Minn. 1980) ("option contract, like other contracts, can be anticipatorily breached"). *See* Restatement Second §253 illus. 3.

[22] American Ins. Union v. Woodward, 247 P. 398 (Okl. 1926) (rule "authorizing the assured to maintain an action on the contract for damages for its breach immediately after being notified of the wrongful forfeiture, is . . . supported by the decided weight of authority").

[23] For such a case, *see* Greguhn v. Mutual of Omaha Ins. Co., 461 P.2d 285 (Utah 1969) (characterization as "anticipatory breach" criticized in dissent). In New York Life Ins. Co. v. Viglas, 297 U.S. 672 (1936), a disability insurance case, Cardozo said that to "blur" the line between "an anticipatory breach and others . . . is prejudicial to accuracy of thought as well as precision of terminology."

[24] See the discussion of the example of *Viglas* in §8.21 *infra*.

seems not to apply.[25] The most satisfactory solution may well be that suggested by Corbin, who argued that, though there was a total breach by the insurer:

> it does not follow necessarily that the injured party should be given a judgment for the present value of that uncertain number of future instalments that will fall due while the insured lives and remains disabled. . . . It may therefore be desirable, while recognizing the insured's common law right to full damages, to limit the execution to the amount of overdue instalments with interest, and at the same time decree specific performance by the insurer with respect to future instalments as they become due.[26]

Other types of relief

The availability of relief, other than a lump-sum damage award, affects the practical importance of the scope of the doctrine of anticipatory repudiation. Courts have not been generally empowered to grant installment judgments,[27] but a declaratory judgment may have much the same effect on the insurer, and such judgments have become increasingly available.[28] And in any event, the injured party may at least have restitution when the other party has repudiated.[29]

What constitutes a repudiation?

Repudiation in general

§8.21. What Constitutes a Repudiation. A repudiation is a manifestation by one party to the other that the first cannot or will not perform at least some of its obligations under the contract.[1] It may be by words or other conduct. Revised Article 2 adds a provision that:

---

[25]*But see* Cobb v. Pacific Mut. Life Ins. Co., 51 P.2d 84 (Cal. 1935) ("fact that he was required . . . to submit to reasonable future medical examinations or furnish an occasional health report is too trivial and inconsequential to be regarded as an unperformed obligation"). In any case it would seem that there are grounds to regard the breach as total, even if the case is regarded as one of a partial breach accompanied by a repudiation. Though the only remaining duty is the insurer's duty to pay money in installments, these installments can be regarded as related to one another because they are all to be made only on condition that the insured's disability continues. See the discussion of a duty to pay money in installments in §8.18 *supra*.

[26]4 A. Corbin, Contracts §969 (1951).

[27]For a leading case granting an installment judgment, *see* Caporali v. Washington Natl. Ins. Co., 307 N.W.2d 218 (Wis. 1981) ("award of future payments . . . in installments as they become due, is the proper reconciliation of the competing interests" under disability policy).

[28]*See* First State Bank of Floodwood v. Jubie, 86 F.3d 755 (8th Cir. 1996) (refusing to uphold award of future damages for breach of contract to make monthly retirement payments but noting that "any risk of multiple lawsuits can be reduced, if not eliminated, by a judgment that declares valid, or even specifically enforces, future installment obligations").

[29]See the discussions of restitution as a means of mitigation in §8.14 *supra* and of the general principle in §12.20 *infra*. For a case allowing restitution on anticipatory repudiation, *see* Martin v. Kavanewsky, 255 A.2d 619 (Conn. 1969) (builder entitled to restitution on owner's repudiation).

§8.21 [1]Congress Life Ins. Co. v. Barstow, 799 So. 2d 931 (Ala. 2001) (quoting this section of this treatise).

Repudiation includes language that a reasonable person would interpret to mean that the other party will not or cannot make a performance still due under the contract or voluntary affirmative conduct that would appear to a reasonable person to make a future performance by the other party impossible.[2]

A repudiation of one contract, however, does not amount to a repudiation of a different contract.[3] For a repudiation to have legal effect, courts have generally required that the threatened breach be serious.[4] According to the Restatement Second, it must be serious enough that the injured party could treat it as total if it occurred[5] and under the Code it must "substantially impair the value of the contract."[6]

Usually a repudiation consists of a statement that the repudiating party cannot or will not perform.[7] The statement must be sufficiently positive to be reasonably understood as meaning that the breach will actually occur.[8] A party's expressions of doubt as to its willingness or ability to perform do not constitute a repudiation.[9] In addition, the intention not to perform must be communicated and must be made to a party to the contract, not to a mere stranger to it.[10]

Repudiation by words

An especially troublesome situation arises when a party's statement results from an honest but mistaken understanding of its rights under the contract. The traditional view is that the party's good faith will not prevent the statement from amounting to a repudiation. A party therefore acts at its peril if that party, insisting on what it mistakenly believes to be its rights, refuses to perform

Good faith irrelevant

---

[2]UCC-R 2-610(2).

[3]UMIC Govt. Sec. v. Pioneer Mortgage Co., 707 F.2d 251 (6th Cir. 1983) (attempt to modify May contracts was not repudiation of June contract). But a repudiation of a different contract may give grounds for a demand for assurances. See the discussion of examples of application in §8.23 *infra.*

[4]Blue Creek Farm v. Aurora Coop. Elevator Co., 614 N.W.2d 310 (Neb. 2000) (letter did note evince intention not to perform but rather that "performance will be delayed by up to 30 days").

[5]Restatement Second §250 (statement "indicating that the obligor will commit a breach that would of itself give the obligee a claim for damages for total breach").

[6]UCC 2-610 (must be repudiation as to "a performance . . . the loss of which will substantially impair the value of the contract to the other"). Strictly speaking, a statement that threatens only a minor breach is not a repudiation under the Restatement Second, and it is a repudiation that has no legal consequence under the Code.

[7]Petrangelo v. Pollard, 255 N.E.2d 342 (Mass. 1970) (owner told builder "that there would be no money available for him on December 15 . . . after many requests by him for payments, and many statements by the defendants of inability, to pay").

[8]Wallace Real Estate Inv. v. Groves, 881 P.2d 1010 (Wash. 1994) ("party's intent not to perform may not be implied from doubtful and indefinite statements that performance may or may not take place," but purchaser's "letter stated that he could not perform on December 17 and requested a new agreement").

[9]Lantec, Inc. v. Novell, Inc., 306 F.3d 1003 (10th Cir. 2002) ("message only states two [corporate] executives *wanted* to terminate" the relationship, not that corporation "would not perform its duties").

[10]An intended beneficiary or an assignee is a party for this purpose. Marshall v. Franklin Fire Ins. Co., 35 A. 204 (Pa. 1896) (assignee).

its duty.[11] As the commentary to the Uniform Commercial Code puts it, "a statement of the intention not to perform except on conditions which go beyond the contract" is a repudiation.[12] Furthermore, if a party wrongfully states that it will not perform unless the other party consents to a modification of the contract, the statement is a repudiation; although the concession that the first party seeks may be a minor one, the breach that it threatens in order to exact it is not.[13] A proposal of or a demand for performance on terms that go beyond the contract is not a repudiation, however, unless it is coupled with a threat of nonperformance if those terms are not accepted.[14]

Example of *Viglas*   Courts have occasionally suggested that good faith will prevent a statement from being a repudiation. The most noted suggestion was made by Cardozo in *New York Life Insurance Co. v. Viglas*, a case in which a disability insurer had refused to make periodic payments to an insured because of an erroneous determination of his disability. Cardozo was plainly reluctant to hold that the insurer's refusal was a repudiation, for that would have given the insured a claim for damages for total breach and would have necessitated a forecast of the continuance of the disability over the insured's lifetime. If refusal were not a repudiation, the insured would be limited to the payments already due, with the possibility of subsequent suits for later payments. This would save the insurer "from a heavy, perhaps a crushing liability as the consequence of a claim of right not charged to have been made as a disingenuous pretense." Cardozo reached this result by finding that the refusal was not a repudiation because there was "nothing to show that the insurer was not acting in good faith."[15] The outcome may be appealing in this particular case. However, to abandon the traditional view and take account of good faith in all cases would probably be unworkable and has been firmly rejected by most courts.[16] Moreover, the insurer can often

---

[11] Chamberlin v. Puckett Constr., 921 P.2d 1237 (Mont. 1996) (demand for performance of term not in contract "accompanied by an unequivocal statement that the demanding party will not perform unless the additional term is met, constitutes an anticipatory breach"). This is an illustration of the point that a party may commit a breach even though not aware of it. See the discussion of when a failure is a breach in §8.8 *supra*. Conversely, a party that thinks its statement is a repudiation may discover that the statement was justified and therefore not a breach.

[12] UCC 2-610 cmt. 2.

[13] Peter Kiewit Sons' Co. v. Summit Constr. Co., 422 F.2d 242 (8th Cir. 1969) (general contractor's "meager offer of $143,000 . . . as compensation for all the extra backfill work is so lacking in good faith as to constitute a repudiation of the Subcontract").

[14] P & L Contractors v. American Norit Co., 5 F.3d 133 (5th Cir. 1993) (to be a repudiation, a demand for more than is due "must be accompanied by a clear manifestation of intention not to perform in accordance with any other interpretation").

[15] 297 U.S. 672, 676, 678 (1936). As to the effect of a repudiation when coupled with a present breach of such a contract, see the discussion of a duty to pay money in installments in §8.18 *supra*.

[16] Snow v. Western Sav. & Loan Assn., 730 P.2d 204 (Ariz. 1987) ("repudiator's state of mind is irrelevant; the adverse effects of a dispute over the meaning of a contract should be borne by the mistaken party, even if acting in good faith").

avoid the harsh results of the traditional view in cases like *Viglas* by seeking a declaratory judgment.

A party may repudiate by conduct as well as by words. A promisor's voluntary affirmative act that renders the promisor actually or apparently unable to perform without a breach is a repudiation. A vendor of land, by conveying the deed to a third person, may indicate as clearly as by words that the vendor cannot perform.[17] Since the conduct must be an affirmative act, mere delay in performing is not a repudiation. Since the act must be voluntary, inability to perform due to incompetence or financial difficulties is not a repudiation.[18] Furthermore, courts have required that the act make the promisor's performance impossible, so that conduct that indicates mere unwillingness is not enough.[19]

Repudiation by conduct

If a party to a contract goes into bankruptcy, the trustee that represents the estate may reject the contract. Such a rejection has the effect of a repudiation, but this is a matter of bankruptcy law and is not dealt with here.[20]

Effect of bankruptcy

We turn next to the possible responses to a repudiation.

§8.22.   Responses to Repudiation. If a party repudiates before the time for its performance has arrived, the injured party might respond in one of several ways.[1] First, the injured party might treat the contract as terminated and claim damages. Second, the injured party might attempt to save the deal by insisting that the other party perform or by urging it to retract its repudiation. Third, the injured party might ignore the repudiation and await the time for performance.

Three responses

As to the first response, we have already seen that the injured party generally is entitled to treat its remaining duties to render performance as discharged and to bring suit immediately for damages for total breach.[2] That party need

First: treat contract as terminated

---

[17]Pappas v. Crist, 25 S.E.2d 850 (N.C. 1943) (where owner leased premises to another lessee, this was an "unequivocal and absolute renunciation of the entire agreement to make the lease to the plaintiff").

[18]Ringel & Meyer v. Falstaff Brewing Corp., 511 F.2d 659 (5th Cir. 1975) ("So far as we know, no court . . . has yet held that obvious incapability of performance due to financial difficulties constitutes anticipatory breach.").

[19]Taylor v. Johnston, 539 P.2d 425 (Cal. 1975) ("there is no implied repudiation, i.e., by conduct equivalent to unequivocal refusal to perform, unless 'the promisor *puts it out of his power to perform*'"). The commentary to the Code, however, suggests that conduct indicating unwillingness may be enough. *See* UCC 2-610 cmt. 2 (repudiation can result from action that "reasonably indicates a rejection of the continuing obligation"). As to the consequences of conduct that gives grounds for insecurity but does not amount to a repudiation, see §8.23 *infra*.

[20]11 U.S.C. (Bankruptcy Code) §365 (trustee "may assume or reject any executory contract"). *See* 1 D. Epstein, S. Nickles & W. White, Bankruptcy §5-7 (1992). Insolvency does not amount to repudiation, though it may allow the other party to suspend performance.

§8.22   [1]This discussion does not consider the availability of specific performance to the injured party. That specific performance is as available for repudiation as it is for nonperformance, see the discussion of specific performance in §12.5 *infra*.

[2]See the discussion of how an anticipatory repudiation discharges duties in §8.20 *supra*.

not demand performance or take any other action before doing so.[3] Just as the repudiation may excuse express conditions of the repudiating party's duty, it also excuses constructive conditions of that duty.[4] Therefore, if it was a constructive condition of the repudiated promise that the injured party perform or tender performance, that condition is excused, and the injured party can recover damages for total breach without performance or a tender. If the owner of a building under construction repudiates, the builder need not finish the building in order to recover damages for total breach. If a purchaser of land repudiates, the vendor need not tender a deed in order to recover damages for total breach.[5] But, to recover damages, the injured party must show that, had there been no repudiation, that party could have performed or tendered performance as required under the contract:[6] the builder must show that the building could have been finished; the vendor must show that the deed could have been tendered.[7] Nevertheless, the injured party is free to salvage and reallocate any resources that it had committed to the contract.

Avoidable loss   In calculating damages, a court will take into account any cost the injured party has avoided as a result of not having to render any further performance and any loss that party has avoided by reallocating any resources that were salvageable.[8] Indeed, the injured party is expected to take appropriate steps to avoid such loss.[9] For example, if the injured party can arrange a substitute transaction promptly after repudiation, but waits until the time for performance to do so, that party may be barred from recovering for any loss that it could have avoided by such prompt action.[10]

---

[3]That the injured party must, however, comply with any notice provisions in the contract, *see* Bausch & Lomb Inc. v. Bressler, 977 F.2d 720 (2d Cir. 1992) (cases in which "repudiating party expressly disavowed any further duties under the contract . . . , in effect declaring the contract at an end," are inapplicable).

[4]Excuse of a condition on the ground of repudiation is discussed in §8.6 *supra*.

[5]Midwest Engrg. & Constr. Co. v. Electric Regulator Corp., 435 P.2d 89 (Okl. 1967) (seller of electrical equipment did not have to tender delivery or deliver after repudiation by buyer).

[6]Income Properties/Equity Trust v. Wal-Mart Stores, 33 F.3d 987 (8th Cir. 1994) (fn.2: "to recover damages for anticipatory repudiation, the promisee must prove that all conditions precedent to performance would have been performed"). See the discussions of termination after some time in §8.18 *supra*, of damages for total breach in §8.15 *supra*, and of acceptance of the doctrine in §8.20 *supra*.

[7]Caporale v. Rubine, 105 A. 226 (N.J. 1918) (where parties contracted to exchange tracts of land, but one repudiated by conveying his tract to a third person, the other was relieved from making tender but could not recover damages without showing that he could have conveyed good title to his tract).

[8]See the discussions of cost avoided and loss avoided in §12.9 *infra*.

[9]See §12.12 *infra*.

[10]See the discussion of market price formulas in §12.12 *infra*. A party claiming damages for anticipatory repudiation must prove them with the certainty that is required for other damage claims. The problems in doing this may be considerably lessened if, as is often the case, delays postpone the time of the trial at which proof is to be made until after the time for performance. These and related matters are dealt with later in connection with damages. See §12.15 *infra*.

The repudiating party can prevent the injured party from treating the contract as terminated by retracting the repudiation before the injured party has acted in response to it. If the repudiation consists of a statement, the repudiating party can nullify it by giving notice of retraction to the injured party.[11] If the repudiation consists of an act other than a statement, the repudiating party can nullify it by correcting the situation that amounted to a repudiation.[12] However, the injured party does not have to "accept" the repudiation or notify the repudiating party that the contract is terminated in order to cut off this power of retraction.[13] As soon as the injured party has materially changed its position in reliance on the repudiation, however, it is too late for the repudiating party to retract.[14] Since a rule based on reliance alone would sometimes leave the injured party uncertain as to its rights, the rule is often modified to allow the injured party to terminate the power of retraction by indicating to the repudiating party that the injured party considers the repudiation final.[15] The injured party need not do this, though, if it can show reliance.

Retraction of repudiation

With regard to retraction, a breach by repudiation may differ from a breach by nonperformance. It is clear that a breach by nonperformance cannot be nullified by retraction, so that the injured party should be allowed damages for any delay even if the breach is cured.[16] On the other hand, it is commonly said that an effective retraction nullifies a repudiation, with no mention of damages

Effect of retraction

---

[11]Sachs v. Precision Prods. Co., 476 P.2d 199 (Or. 1970) (any repudiation "was not effective . . . because it was not accepted or acted upon" before withdrawal).

[12]In re Vaughan's Estate, 282 N.Y.S. 214 (Surr. Ct.) (seller who had conveyed lots to third person reacquired them before change of position by injured party), aff'd mem., 289 N.Y.S. 825 (App. Div. 1935).

[13]William B. Tanner Co. v. WIOO, Inc., 528 F.2d 262 (3d Cir. 1975) ("acceptance is no longer required by Pennsylvania law to give rise to an anticipatory breach").

[14]Freedman v. Rector of St. Matthias Parish, 230 P.2d 629 (Cal. 1951) (Traynor, J.: though purchaser of land "made various oral proposals to continue with the purchase on terms other than those provided in the contract, he did not unconditionally withdraw his repudiation until after [vendor], in reliance thereon, had sold the property to another").

[15]United States v. Seacoast Gas Co., 204 F.2d 709 (5th Cir. 1953) ("All that is required to close the door to repentance is definite action indicating that the anticipatory breach has been accepted as final, and this requisite can be supplied either by the filing of a suit or a firm declaration, as here, that unless within a fixed time the breach is repudiated, it will be accepted."). *See* UCC 2-611(1) (power of retraction cut off if injured party has "cancelled or materially changed" its position or otherwise indicated that the repudiation is "final"); Restatement Second §256 (power of retraction cut off if injured party "materially changes his position in reliance on the repudiation or indicates to the other party that he considers the repudiation to be final").

Comment *c* to §256 explains that "it is undesirable to make the injured party's rights turn exclusively on such a vague criterion" as material reliance. *See* E. Farnsworth, Changing Your Mind ch. 6 (1998).

[16]See the discussion of what cure is not in §8.17 *supra.*

for delay.[17] However, the Code wisely provides that a retraction "reinstates the repudiating party's rights under the contract with due excuse and allowance to the aggrieved party for any delay occasioned by the repudiation."[18]

Second: urge retraction

In practice, the injured party often chooses the second response, preferring to save the deal rather than to treat the contract as terminated. The injured party will insist that the repudiating party perform or urge that party to retract its repudiation. If the repudiating party responds by retracting, the contract remains in force and the injured party has no claim to damages other than for any delay caused by the repudiation. If the repudiating party fails to retract, the injured party can still treat the contract as terminated and claim damages, just as if the injured party had not urged retraction. Under the prevailing view, the injured party's response in trying to save the deal does not amount to an election;[19] that party is not precluded from reconsidering at any time before retraction and treating the contract as terminated.[20] Thus the injured party can cut off the repudiating party's power to retract just as if the injured party had never insisted on performance or urged retraction. An injured party that continues to insist on performance or urge retraction for more than a reasonable time, however, risks the perils of the third response.

Third: ignore repudiation

The third response is the least satisfactory. An injured party that ignores the repudiation and awaits the time for the return performance remains in a state of vulnerability. In that situation, as we have seen, the repudiating party can at any time retract the repudiation on deciding that it is in its interest to do so. The seller that repudiated when the market rose may retract its repudiation if the market falls.[21] If the repudiation is not retracted before the time for performance comes, a failure to perform at that time will amount to a breach by nonperformance, which cannot be retracted. In this situation, however, the law of damages may put the injured party in a very unfavorable position. If, while awaiting the return performance, the injured party continued to perform, that party's damages will not include the cost of its performance because of the limitation of avoidability.[22] Furthermore, if the injured party could have arranged a substitute transaction promptly after repudiation, that party may be denied

---

[17] *See* Restatement Second §256(1) ("effect . . . is nullified by a retraction").

[18] UCC 2-611(3).

[19] United Cal. Bank v. Prudential Ins. Co., 681 P.2d 390 (Ariz. App. 1983) ("modern rule" is that "innocent party . . . may continue to treat the contract as operable and urge performance by the repudiating party without waiving any right to sue for that repudiation").

[20] UCC 2-610 (aggrieved party may "resort to any remedy for breach" even though aggrieved party has notified repudiating party that aggrieved party "would await . . . performance and has urged retraction"); Restatement Second §257 ("injured party does not change the effect of a repudiation by urging the repudiator to perform . . . or to retract his repudiation").

[21] Long Inv. Co. v. O'Donnel, 88 N.W.2d 674 (Wis. 1958) (injured party "has an election to treat [repudiation] as an anticipatory breach, but if [injured party] fails to do so, then such repudiation is immaterial in an action thereafter brought to enforce the contract").

[22] See the discussion of stopping performance in §12.12 *infra.*

recovery for any loss that it could have avoided by arranging it.[23] The same principles apply to the situation in which the repudiation is not anticipatory, but is accompanied by a present breach.

There is an important difference, therefore, between the situation in which there has been a repudiation, whether or not anticipatory, and that in which there has been a total breach without a repudiation. In the latter situation the injured party can safely treat the breach as partial only and await the return performance.[24] Where there has been a repudiation, however, the injured party cannot safely do this. The injured party may without risk insist for a reasonable time on performance or retraction. But when that time is past, the injured party has no choice but to treat any remaining duties as discharged; that party ignores the repudiation at its peril. And if, while awaiting performance, the injured party sues and is awarded damages for partial breach, that party will be barred from claiming further damages on the ground that the only cause of action was for damages for total breach and it could not be split up.[25]

Cannot treat as partial

What are the consequences of prospective inability to perform that falls short of repudiation?

§8.23. Effect of Insecurity as to Return Performance. Mere doubts by one party that the other party will perform when performance is due will not excuse the first party from performing.[1] For example, a purchaser of land is not excused on discovering a remediable defect in the vendor's title to the land; the vendor has until the time when it is to tender the deed to perfect the title.[2] Furthermore, a party traditionally had no right to require reassurance that the other party would perform, and the other party could ignore a request for such reassurance with impunity.[3]

Doubts not enough

---

[23] See the discussion of the time for a substitute in §12.12 *infra*.

[24] See the discussion of keeping the deal together in §8.15 *supra*.

[25] Jameson v. Board of Educ., 89 S.E. 255 (W. Va. 1916) (when employer repudiated nine-month contract, employee who recovered damages for first two months was barred from recovery of damages for later months).

§8.23 [1] Mor-Cor Packaging Prods. v. Innovative Packaging Corp., 328 F.3d 331 (7th Cir. 2002) (dictum: "merely planning to engage in a transaction that if consummated would create a conflict of interest justifying termination is not itself a breach"); Koppelon v. W.M. Ritter Flooring Corp., 116 A. 491 (N.J. 1922) ("mere doubts of the solvency of a party to a contract or mere belief that he will be unable to perform when the time for his performance comes, will not excuse performance by the other party"). See the discussion of repudiation by conduct in §8.21 *supra*.

[2] Hellrung v. Hoechst, 384 S.W.2d 561 (Mo. 1964) ("before the vendee may rely on a defect in title or an anticipatory breach of the contract thereby excusing tender the vendors must have openly and unconditionally refused to perform or the defect in title must have been irremediable"). But see the discussion of repudiation by conduct in §8.21 *supra*.

[3] McCloskey & Co. v. Minweld Steel Co., 220 F.2d 101 (3d Cir. 1955) (subcontractor's letter saying "we cannot give you any positive promise as to our ability to obtain the steel or delivery dates" was not a repudiation where there was "nothing in the contracts which authorized [contractor] to demand or receive such assurances").

Rights on insolvency

The common law recognized a limited exception when the other party became insolvent. We have seen that the other party's insolvency is not a repudiation and is not a ground for termination of the contract.[4] But it may give the first party reason to believe that the insolvent party will commit a breach.[5] If it does, the first party is entitled to exercise a right to self-help by suspending any performance for which that party has not already received the agreed exchange until that party receives the remaining performance or an offer of adequate security for that performance.[6] In a typical case, a seller that has contracted to deliver goods on credit discovers that the buyer is insolvent.[7] According to the Uniform Commercial Code, the seller "may refuse delivery except for cash including payment for all goods theretofore delivered under the contract."[8] Mere doubts as to the other party's solvency, however, do not give the first party the right to suspend performance.[9]

Right to assurance under Code

A broader exception to the traditional rule that a party has no right to assurance of performance was introduced by the Uniform Commercial Code. Under UCC 2-609, when "reasonable grounds for insecurity arise with respect to the performance of either party," the other party may "demand adequate assurance of due performance" and until receiving such assurance the other party "may if commercially reasonable suspend any performance" for which it has not received the agreed return. "After receipt of a justified demand failure to provide within a reasonable time not exceeding thirty days such assurance of due performance as is adequate under the circumstances of the particular case is a repudiation of the contract."[10] In contrast to the Code's rule on insolvency,

---

[4]See the discussions of repudiation by conduct and the effect of bankruptcy in §8.21 *supra*.

[5]As in the case of a repudiation, the prospective breach must be more than a minor one. See the discussion of repudiation in general in §8.21 *supra*.

[6]*See* Restatement Second §252. According to Comment *a*, this rule "only empowers the obligee to suspend his own performance." If the obligee wishes to hold the obligor for breach of contract, the obligee must first demand assurance and then treat the obligor's failure to furnish them as a repudiation.

[7]Rock-Ola Mfg. Corp. v. Leopold, 98 F.2d 196 (5th Cir. 1938) ("seller of goods on credit, on learning of his buyer's insolvency, may refuse to deliver except for cash").

[8]UCC 2-702(1). Unlike the Restatement Second, the Code does not appear to accord the buyer a right to require delivery of the goods by giving security rather than paying cash. As to the significance of delivery, *see* E. Farnsworth, Changing Your Mind ch. 12 (1998).

[9]*Insolvency* is broadly defined. UCC 1-201(23) provides that *insolvent* means "having generally ceased to pay debts in the ordinary course of business . . . , being unable to pay debts as they become due, or . . . being insolvent within the meaning of federal bankruptcy law." Restatement Second §252(2) is virtually identical. A party may, of course, explicitly provide for rights when it deems itself insecure. *See* UCC 1-309.

[10]For a similar provision applicable to leases, *see* UCC 2A-401. Under the Vienna Convention, a party may suspend performance where, "after the conclusion of the contract, it becomes apparent that the other party will not perform a substantial part of his obligations," but must continue performance "if the other party provides adequate assurance of his performnce." CISG 71. For a comparable provision, *see* UNIDROIT Principles 7.3.4 (giving party that "reasonably believes

this rule can be invoked by buyers as well as sellers.[11] The section itself states that the basis for the rule is each party's obligation "that the other's expectation of receiving due performance will not be impaired," an obligation akin to that of good faith and fair dealing.[12]

Even without the benefit of the rule of UCC 2-609, a party that believes that the other party will not perform is free to act on that belief. If the belief turns out to be correct, the party is shielded from liability, even if it failed to render a performance of its own that was due at an earlier time.[13] If the belief turns out to be wrong, however, the party's own failure to perform may subject it to liability for damages for total breach.[14] The Code spares a party this dilemma by empowering it to demand assurance that performance will be forthcoming, allowing it thereby to avoid the risk that it would otherwise run in acting on its belief. As Ellen Peters has counselled, "If there is reasonable doubt about whether the buyer's default is substantial, the seller may be well advised to temporize by suspending future performance until it can ascertain whether the buyer is able to offer adequate assurance of further payments."[15] If it is reasonable for a party to suspend its own performance while it awaits assurance, it may do so. And a failure by the other party to give adequate assurance will be a repudiation.

Whether a party has "reasonable grounds for insecurity" is a question of fact.[16] It is clear that the insecurity of the party demanding assurance must be based on circumstances that were not known to that party when the contract was made[17] and as to which that party did not assume the risk.[18] According to the Code commentary, the circumstances may impugn "either the willingness or the ability of [the other] party to perform."[19] They may involve defaults by the

Significance of right

Examples of application

---

that there will be a fundamental non-performance by the other party" a right to "demand adequate assurance of due performance").

[11] Therefore, a seller may invoke either UCC 2-702(1) or UCC 2-609 if the buyer's insolvency gives the seller grounds for insecurity.

[12] UCC 2-609(1). See the discussion of the duty of good faith in §7.17 *supra*.

[13] See the discussions of termination after some time in §8.18 *supra* and of treating the contract as terminated in §8.22 *supra*.

[14] Ross Cattle Co. v. Lewis, 415 So. 2d 1029 (Miss. 1982) (seller broke contract when, on feeling insecure, "he elected to treat the contract as broken" by buyer and sold cattle to third party).

[15] Cherwell-Ralli v. Rytman Grain Co., 433 A.2d 984, 987 (Conn. 1980).

[16] AMF v. McDonald's Corp., 536 F.2d 1167 (7th Cir. 1976) (whether "buyer has reasonable grounds for insecurity is a question of fact," and on the record operator of restaurants was entitled to demand assurance as a result of seller's failures in attempting to provide workable prototype for computerized cash register system).

[17] Field v. Golden Triangle Broadcasting, 305 A.2d 689 (Pa. 1973) ("where adequate assurance of performance is already present, and there has been no change in circumstances to give rise to reasonable ground for insecurity, a demand for additional security . . . is not justified").

[18] UCC 2-609 cmt. 3 ("when the buyer has assumed the risk of payment before inspection of the goods, . . . that risk is not to be evaded by a demand for assurance").

[19] UCC 2-609 cmt. 1.

other party on other contracts with other buyers or sellers.[20] Thus a repudiation of a separate contract may justify a demand for assurance, even though the repudiation would not justify outright termination.[21] But, though uncertainty remains as to the limits of UCC 2-609, it seems unlikely that courts will sanction questionable demands for assurance and thereby encourage parties to harass each other.[22]

Adequate assurance

According to the Code commentary, what constitutes "adequate" assurance of due performance is a question of fact.[23] Sometimes an explanation by the party itself or a report or opinion by a third party will suffice. If the buyer "can make use of a defective delivery, a mere promise by a seller of good repute that he is giving the matter his attention and that the defect will not be repeated, is normally sufficient." But "a similar statement by a known corner-cutter might well be considered insufficient without the posting of a guaranty or, if so demanded by the buyer, a speedy replacement of the delivery involved." And if the defects, "though easily curable, . . . interfere with easy use by the buyer, no verbal assurance can be deemed adequate which is not accompanied by replacement, repair, money allowance, or other commercially reasonable cure."[24] In some circumstances security, such as a guarantee by a third party, may be required. A party that has rightfully demanded assurance of due performance may thus be entitled to greater security than was provided for in the contract.

Non-sales contracts

Whether there is a right to assurance under contracts other than those for the sale of goods is still unclear, some courts extending UCC 2-609 by analogy[25] and others declining to do so.[26] The New York Court of Appeals took a cautious approach, concluding that "the policies underlying the UCC 2-609 counterpart should apply with similar cogency" to a controversy involving a "long-term commercial contract [for supply of electricity] between corporate entities . . . , which is complex and not reasonably susceptible of all security features being

---

[20]UCC 2-609 cmt. 3 ("Thus a buyer who falls behind in 'his account' with the seller, even though the items involved have to do with separate and legally distinct contracts, impairs the seller's expectation of due performance. Again, under the same test, a buyer who requires precision parts which he intends to use immediately upon delivery, may have reasonable grounds for insecurity if he discovers that his seller is making defective deliveries of such parts to other buyers with similar needs.").

[21]See the discussion of repudiation in general in §8.21 *supra*.

[22]BAII Banking Group v. UPG, 985 F.2d 685 (2d Cir. 1993) ("party does not contract for oral assurances of performance, but for performance of the contract").

[23]S.J. Groves & Sons v. Warner Co., 576 F.2d 524 (3d Cir. 1978) ("element of erratic deliveries . . . would not necessarily be cured" by mere promise).

[24]UCC 2-609 cmt 4.

[25]Conference Ctr. Ltd. v. TRC-The Research Corp., 455 A.2d 857 (Conn. 1983) (Peters, J.: UCC 2-609, "although not in terms applicable to real property cases, provides by analogy a useful resource").

[26]Ranger Constr. Co. v. Dixie Floor Co., 433 F. Supp. 442 (D.S.C. 1977) (UCC 2-609 not applicable to contract to install flooring).

anticipated," but the "Court needs to go no further" in the case before it.[27] The Restatement Second states a broader rule inspired by and similar to the Code rule, applicable to contracts of all kinds.[28] It departs from UCC 2-609 in several respects, sometimes because the detail of the Code section is more suited to a statute than to a restatement[29] and sometimes in an attempt at improvement.[30] Still, the essence of that section is unequivocally endorsed for application to contracts in general.

In the next chapter we consider when a party is excused from performance because of the failure of a basic assumption on which the contract was made.

---

[27] Norcon Power Partners v. Niagara Mohawk Power Corp., 705 N.E.2d 656, 662 (N.Y. 1998).

[28] Restatement Second §251 ("where reasonable grounds arise to believe that the obligor will commit a breach by non-performance that would of itself give the obligee a claim for damages for total breach . . . , the obligee may demand adequate assurance of due performance. . . .").

[29] The Restatement Second does not require that the demand for assurance be in writing and does not impose a 30-day limit on the reasonable time for furnishing assurance. With respect to the requirement of a writing, *see* AMF v. McDonald's Corp., *supra* note 16 (buyer's "failure to make a written demand was excusable because [of seller's] clear understanding that [buyer] had suspended performance until it should receive adequate assurance of the performance").

[30] Under the Restatement Second the obligee is given a choice as to whether to treat the failure to provide assurance as a repudiation. But the Restatement Second gives the obligee the right to demand assurance only where the prospective failure of performance would amount to a total breach. If the prospective failure is one that would be excusable on the ground of impracticability, for example, the obligee would have no right to demand assurance under this rule. UCC 2-609 does not contain such a limitation, but it would make no sense to treat a refusal to furnish assurance in such a situation as a repudiation.

Chapter 9

Failure of a Basic Assumption: Mistake, Impracticability and Frustration

A.   INTRODUCTION

§9.1.   Nature of the Problem. One who is considering whether to make a contract ordinarily makes a number of assumptions in assessing the benefits to be received and the burdens to be shouldered under the proposed exchange of performances. Some assumptions relate to facts that exist at the time the contract is made. A builder may base the estimated cost of excavation on such assumptions regarding subsoil conditions. Other assumptions relate to events that are expected to occur or circumstances that are expected to exist at some later time. A builder may base the estimated cost of construction on such assumptions regarding weather, the price of labor, and the availability of materials. This chapter is concerned with the problems that arise when one of the parties seeks to be excused from performing on the ground that one of that party's assumptions has turned out to be incorrect.

Basic assumptions

One who seeks to be excused on this ground must contend, at the outset, with the general rule that duties imposed by contract are absolute. The idea that finality is desirable in consensual transactions, lest justifiable expectations be disappointed, is expressed in the maxim, *pacta sunt servanda* ("agreements are to be observed"), rendered by the Seventh Circuit as "a deal's a deal."[1] Well

Duties generally absolute

§9.1 [1]*See* UNIDROIT Principles 6.2.1 ("Contract to be observed"); Waukesha Foundry v. Industrial Engrg., 91 F.3d 1002 (7th Cir. 1996) (*"Pacta sunt servanda*, or 'a deal's a deal.' ").

599

over a century ago, the Supreme Court of Minnesota stated the general rule sternly in refusing to excuse a builder after his partly completed building had, for a second time, collapsed due to quicksand:

> If a man bind himself, by a positive, express contract, to do an act in itself possible, he must perform his engagement, unless prevented by the act of God, the law, or the other party to the contract. No hardship, no unforeseen hindrance, no difficulty short of absolute impossibility, will excuse him from doing what he has expressly agreed to do. This doctrine may sometimes seem to bear heavily upon contractors; but, in such cases, the hardship is attributable, not to the law, but to the contractor himself, who has improvidently assumed an absolute, when he might have undertaken only a qualified, liability.[2]

This severe formulation must be understood, to be sure, in the light of the circumstance that in most cases a court will not require the promisor to perform but only to pay damages for nonperformance.[3]

Examples of qualified duties

Furthermore, as might be expected, parties faced with this strict rule have devised a variety of ways to qualify their contractual obligations. Indeed, a party to a contract may undertake no obligation at all, as in the case of one who has the benefit of an option contract.[4] In other cases a party may undertake an obligation only to use best efforts.[5] Or a party may obligate itself only to the extent of its output or its requirements.[6] Or a party may protect itself by a cancellation clause, giving it a general power of termination;[7] a *force majeure* clause, excusing it on the occurrence of specified types of events;[8] a limitation of remedy clause, restricting its liability for breach;[9] or a flexible pricing clause, allowing it to pass on additional costs to the other party.[10] A party that has not qualified its duty in some way such as these, however, must bring itself within a limited number of judicially created doctrines if it would be excused on the ground that one of its basic assumptions has proved to be wrong.

[2] Stees v. Leonard, 20 Minn. 494, 503 (1874) (claim limited to return of money paid, loss of use of lot, and damage to adjacent lot; no claim for lost profits). This view appears to be peculiar to common law legal systems. *See* B. Nicholas, French Law of Contract 50 (2d ed. 1992) ("French law . . . traditionally bases contractual liability . . . on fault, whereas the Common law has traditionally thought of contractual obligations as in principle absolute").

[3] *See* Holmes, The Path of the Law, 10 Harv. L. Rev. 457, 462 (1897), reprinted in O. Holmes, Collected Legal Papers 175 (1920) ("The duty to keep a contract at common law means a prediction that you must pay damages if you do not keep it — and nothing else.").

[4] See §3.23 *supra*.

[5] That this relieves a party of the need to show impracticability as an excuse, *see* T.S.I. Holdings v. Jenkins, 924 P.2d 1239 (Kan. 1996) (doctrine of impracticability not applicable to party whose duty was only one of best efforts). See the discussion of the duty of best efforts in §7.17 *supra*.

[6] See the discussion of output and requirements in §7.17 *supra*.

[7] See §2.14 *supra*.

[8] See the discussion of the Code synthesis in §9.6 *infra*.

[9] See the discussion of clauses limiting remedies in §4.28 *supra*.

[10] See the discussion of the role of the drafter in §3.28 *supra*.

Conventional treatments of the law of contracts have conceptualized the question of excuse under two distinct headings: mistake, which deals with assumptions concerning facts that exist at the time the contract is made; and impracticability and frustration, which deal largely with assumptions concerning circumstances that are expected to exist, including events that are expected to occur, after the contract is made. This conceptual division reflects a sense that the allocation of the risk of error in an assumption should depend on whether the assumption concerns the state of affairs at the time of agreement or at some later time. Nevertheless, since the problems that arise in cases of mistake are similar to those that arise in cases of impracticability and frustration, it will be helpful to deal with these subjects in the same chapter.[11]

We turn now to mistake.

Mistake, impracticability and frustration

B. MISTAKE

§9.2. Types of Mistake. The word *mistake* is generally used in the law of contracts to refer to an erroneous perception — what the Restatement Second calls "a belief that is not in accord with the facts."[1] To avoid confusion, it should not be used, as it sometimes is in common speech, to refer to an improvident act, such as the making of a contract, which results from such a perception. Nor should it be used, as it sometimes is by courts and writers, to refer to what is more properly called a misunderstanding, a situation in which two parties attach different meanings to their language.[2] Although contract law does not on its face accept ignorance as an alternative to mistake as ground for relief, courts often sweep ignorance into the category of mistake by the covert conceit of inferring mistake from simple ignorance.[3]

Meaning of mistake

Sometimes a contracting party has an erroneous perception about a statute, regulation, or judicial decision, or about the legal consequences of its acts. Some courts have denied relief in such cases on the ground that the mistake is one of "law" rather than "fact," and since everyone is supposed to know the law *ignorantia legis neminem excusat* ("ignorance of the law excuses no one").[4]

Facts include law

---

[11] For further comparison of the two subjects, see the discussion of relationship to mistake in §9.8 *infra*. For types of decisions, including *uninformed*, *improvident*, and *obsolete* decisions, that occasion regret on the part of the promisor, *see* E. Farnsworth, Changing Your Mind ch. 2 (1998).

§9.2 [1] Restatement Second §151.

[2] See the discussion of different meanings attached in §7.9 *supra*.

[3] An example is Wilkin v. 1st Source Bank, 548 N.E.2d 170, 172 (Ind. App. 1990) (estate of widow of artist, dead for over two decades, which contracted to give "clutter" in house to purchasers if they would clean it up, could avoid contract for mistake when valuable works by artist, which neither party "suspected" remained on premises, were found in "clutter," because though the parties were ignorant they "shared a common presupposition" implicit in their ignorance).

[4] Webb v. Webb, 301 S.E.2d 570 (W. Va. 1983) (relief denied for long-term Florida resident's mistake as to West Virginia law).

Prediction excluded

However, the modern view is that the existing law is part of the state of facts at the time of agreement. Therefore, most courts will grant relief for such a mistake, as they would for any other mistake of fact.[5]

An erroneous perception is not a mistake unless it relates to the facts as they exist at the time the contract is made. A misprediction — a poor prediction of events that are expected to occur or circumstances that are expected to exist after the contract is made — is not a mistake. The law of mistake deals only with the risk of error relating to the factual basis of agreement — the state of affairs at the time of agreement. It does not deal with the risk of error as to future matters. Such mispredictions are dealt with by the doctrines of impracticability and frustration, which are thought to be more suited to adjusting the relationship between the parties under their agreement.[6] Thus an erroneous perception as to the existence of specific goods that are the subject of a contract for sale is plainly a mistake as to an existing fact; an erroneous belief that the goods will remain in existence until the time for delivery is just as plainly a misprediction as to the future.

Sometimes difficult to draw line

In some cases, however, this line between a mistake as to an existing fact and a misprediction as to a future event is less clear. A buyer contracts to buy railroad ties as they stand on the seller's property, with the risk of loss to pass to the buyer immediately. At the time of agreement, neither party knows that many underground fires are burning nearby and will soon consume the ties. Mistake as to existing fact or misprediction as to the future?[7] A buyer contracts to buy land for a tennis and swim club, a use then permitted by the zoning laws. At the time of agreement, neither party knows that a few days earlier the town planning board published a notice of a proposed zoning change that will soon prohibit the intended use. Mistake as to existing fact or misprediction as to the future?[8]

Example of *Leasco v. Taussig*

The line between a mistake as to an existing fact and a misprediction as to the future is especially hard to draw when the parties have extrapolated from existing facts to set their expectations as to the future. *Leasco v. Taussig* is an example. In February 1971, Taussig, who had been an officer of Leasco's

[5] Dover Pool & Racquet Club v. Brooking, 322 N.E.2d 168 (Mass. 1975) (mistake as to zoning laws).

[6] Dairyland Power Coop. v. United States, 16 F.3d 1197 (Fed. Cir. 1994) ("mutual mistake of fact cannot lie against a future event" and "availability of commercial reprocessing in the future cannot constitute an existing fact"). See §§9.5, 9.7 *infra*.

[7] Richardson Lumber Co. v. Hoey, 189 N.W. 923 (Mich. 1922) ("not a case of accident or something happening after the contract which destroyed the thing contracted for . . . but rather an existing fact which continued until the property was destroyed"). *Accord:* Lenawee County Bd. of Health v. Messerly, 331 N.W.2d 203 (Mich. 1982) (mistake where defective septic system subsequently affected income-producing capacity of property).

[8] Dover Pool & Racquet Club v. Brooking, *supra* note 5 (when "contract was made both parties made the [mistaken] assumption that the zoning by-laws interposed no obstacle to the use of the premises").

subsidiary MKI, made a contract with Leasco to buy MKI. In May, however, he refused a tender of MKI's stock and sought to avoid the contract on the ground that the parties had erred in estimating MKI's pre-tax earnings for the period ending with September 1971 as $200,000. In fact the company lost $12,000, and Taussig argued that the parties had shared a mistake as to the existing fact "that they were dealing with a company which would earn $200,000 in the fiscal year ending September 30, 1971." The court, however, held that this was merely a misprediction as to a future event. "Both Taussig and Leasco may have hoped, but surely could not have been certain, that MKI would earn $200,000 in fiscal 1971." The court concluded that earnings for the fiscal year 1971 were not part of the state of affairs at the time of agreement but were future matters that came within the scope of the contract. Therefore, each party bore a risk that the earnings might not be as estimated, and each was bound even though, "as it turned out, one party got a better bargain than anticipated. . . . Neither party could safely assume that the projected earnings would be realized."[9]

Aluminum Co. of America v. Essex Group presented a similar issue, but the court reached a different result. Under a 16-year contract made in 1967, ALCOA was to convert alumina supplied by Essex into molten aluminum. Essex had an option to renew for an additional five years. The contract price provisions contained an escalation formula, one portion of which was based on the Wholesale Price Index — Industrial Commodities (WPI). By 1979, it had become apparent that the WPI was not keeping pace with the sharp rise in the cost of energy to ALCOA, and the company stood to lose some $60 million over the balance of the contract term. ALCOA sought relief for mutual mistake. The trial court found that the parties had chosen the WPI to reflect changes in ALCOA's nonlabor costs after a careful investigation showed that the WPI had, over a period of years, tracked ALCOA's actual nonlabor cost fluctuations without marked deviations. In doing this, the judge concluded, the parties had made an error "of fact rather than one of simple prediction of future events. . . . This mistaken assumption was essentially a present actuarial error." He distinguished the *Taussig* case on the ground that there the "parties bottomed their agreement on a naked prediction," while in *ALCOA* the capacity of the WPI "to work as the parties expected it to work was a matter of fact, existing at the time they made the contract." The judge felt that justice required him to find a mistake of fact. "At stake in this suit is the future of a commercially important device — the long term contract. . . . If the law refused an appropriate remedy when a prudently drafted long term contract goes badly awry, . . . [p]rudent business people would avoid using this sensible business

Example of ALCOA

---

[9]473 F.2d 777, 781 (2d Cir. 1972). The court also concluded that Taussig, who "probably knew more about the business of MKI than anyone else at Leasco, . . . assumed 'as one of the elements of the bargain' the risk that a considerably lesser amount would be realized," and it pointed out that in the purchase agreement Leasco had "specifically disclaimed any warranties or representations concerning MKI's financial condition." Id. at 781-82, 783.

Example of personal injury release

tool."[10] This contract had gone "awry." ALCOA stood to lose $60 million over the contract term, and Essex stood to gain by the same amount.

The difficulty of drawing a line between mistakes and mispredictions is illustrated by the personal injury cases. When an injured party has executed a release of all claims against the other party and then discovers that the injuries are much worse than either party had realized, the injured party often seeks to avoid the release on the ground of mistake. In attempting to draw the line between a mistake and a misprediction, many courts have relied on a distinction between an incorrect *prognosis* and an incorrect *diagnosis*. An incorrect prognosis — a misprediction as to the future consequences of that injury — is not a mistake and will not justify relief. As the Supreme Court of New Hampshire said, an incorrect prognosis is "a 'mistake in prophecy,' relating to future and not existing facts" and "of itself constitutes no ground for cancellation."[11] On the other hand, an incorrect diagnosis — a flawed perception as to the very nature of the injury — is a mistake and may justify relief. The victim who signs a release, said a federal Court of Appeals, "may have to take his chances that a properly diagnosed condition was the subject of an overly optimistic prognosis and that his injuries may be more serious and extensive than originally thought" but "the law does not require him to take his chances when the diagnosis is itself erroneous."[12] As might be expected, courts that employ the distinction often seem to manipulate it to reach results that they regard as just.[13]

Unilateral and mutual mistake

Once the party seeking relief has convinced the court that a mistake and not a misrprediction is involved, the party must also convince the court that the mistake justifies relief. As to this, the law differs according to whether the mistake is "mutual" or "unilateral." If one party's mistaken assumption is shared by the other party, the mistake is mutual. If one party's mistaken assumption is not shared by the other party, the mistake is unilateral. Within these two broad categories, however, are situations of almost infinite variety. Because the law of mistake was shaped largely in equity, courts have considerable discretion in applying it to these situations, as we shall see in the next two sections.[14]

---

[10] 499 F. Supp. 53, 63, 64, 89 (W.D. Pa. 1980).

[11] Bee v. Chicopee Manufacturing Corp., 55 A.2d 897, 899 (N.H. 1947).

[12] Robertson v. Douglas Steamship Co., 510 F.2d 829, 836 (5th Cir. 1975), followed in Gleason v. Guzman, 623 P.2d 378 (Colo. 1981) (assumption underlying distinction is that "mistake for legal purposes must relate to a past or present fact rather than an opinion or prophecy about the future").

[13] *See* Poti v. New England Road Mach. Co., 40 A. 587 (N.H. 1928) (mistake justified avoidance when victim's bruise "was severe rather than mild" because at the time of the signing of the release "the deep-seated nature of the bruise was an existing fact, whereas the parties acted in dependence upon a bruise of minor consequence"). For more on this problem, see the discussion of awareness of limited knowledge in §9.3 *infra*.

[14] Mistakes as to expression — those that go to the contents or effect of the writing that is intended to express the agreement — are a special kind of mutual mistake and are discussed in §7.5 *supra*. As to the effect of mistake on the availability of specific performance, see the discussion of unfairness in §12.7 *infra*.

604

We begin with mutual mistake.

§9.3. Mutual Mistake. A mutual mistake occurs when both parties are under substantially the same erroneous perception as to the facts. (If both parties are mistaken, but their mistakes are materially different, the case is one of unilateral mistake.[1] The cases in which an adversely affected party has been allowed to avoid the contract on this ground are not marked by their consistency in either reasoning or result.

Cases not consistent

A landmark case on mutual mistake is *Sherwood v. Walker*, which arose out of a contract for the sale of a cow known as "Rose 2d of Aberlone." According to the seller, both he and the buyer believed that Rose could not breed and therefore the price was fixed at $80, about one-tenth of what the cow would otherwise have been worth. When the seller discovered that Rose was in fact with calf, he attempted to avoid the contract and refused to deliver the cow to the buyer. The Supreme Court of Michigan held that the seller was entitled to avoid if "the cow was sold, or contracted to be sold, upon the understanding of both parties that she was barren, and useless for the purpose of breeding, and that in fact she was not barren, but capable of breeding."[2]

Example of Sherwood v. Walker

Because courts have had great difficulty in formulating rules for mutual mistake cases, it will be helpful to look at the three requirements established by the Restatement Second for avoidance on this ground. The party adversely affected must show that: (1) the mistake goes to a basic assumption on which the contract was made; (2) the mistake has a material effect on the agreed exchange of performances; and (3) the mistake is not one of which that party bears the risk.[3]

Three requirements

Under the first requirement, a contract is not voidable on the ground of mutual mistake unless it is a mistake as to a basic assumption on which both parties made the contract. The term *basic assumption* comes from the Uniform Commercial Code section on impracticability and will be discussed again later in that connection.[4] A party may have such an assumption even though not conscious of alternatives. A person walking into a room may, in this sense, assume that the room has a floor without thinking about it. As the commentary to the Restatement Second explains, if "a party purchases an annuity on the life of another person, it can be said that it was a basic assumption that the other person was alive at the time, even though the parties never consciously addressed themselves to the possibility that he was dead." The term *basic* is apparently intended to exclude mistakes relating to such collateral or peripheral

1. Basic assumption

---

§9.3 [1] Alden Auto Parts Warehouse v. Dolphin Equip. Leasing Corp., 682 F.2d 330 (2d Cir. 1982) (each party was deceived by third person's fraud, "but each was in error as to a different fact"); Page v. Higgins, 22 N.E. 63 (Mass. 1889) (parties made "two different and separate mistakes"). See the discussion of the traditional view in §9.4 *infra*.

[2] 33 N.W. 919, 924 (Mich. 1887).

[3] Restatement Second §152.

[4] See the discussion of basic assumption in §9.6 *infra*.

matters as "market conditions or financial ability."[5] However, a wide variety of assumptions, such as those concerning the existence, identity, quantity, or quality of the subject matter, would seem to be "basic" in the sense that they are regarded as vitiating the judgment of a contracting party, entitling that party to reverse the transaction.[6] It will be helpful to examine this concept of basic assumption in connection with a common kind of case.

Land sale cases   When parties contract to sell a tract of land, they may do so either "in gross" — for a fixed price — or "by the acre" — on the basis of a price for each unit of measurement. Courts have enforced contracts selling land "by the acre" despite mistakes as to the total amount of land. If, for instance, there is a deficiency in the amount, the contract is simply enforced at a price based on the unit price, and a purchaser that has overpaid is entitled to restitution of the overpayment.[7] The situation is different for a sale "in gross." Did the parties share a basic assumption as to the acreage? If so, the purchaser will be granted relief.[8] But even when the parties stated the acreage in the contract, courts have sometimes doubted that it was a basic assumption and have concluded that, given the circumstances, the acreage was merely descriptive and peripheral.[9] If the purchase price is a multiple of the stated number of acres or the number of acres is based on a survey, a court has a basis for finding that the acreage was a basic assumption; if the tract is described by its familiar name or by metes and bounds, however, a court is more likely to find that the contrary was true.[10]

2. Material effect   Under the second of the Restatement Second's requirements, the adversely affected party must show that the mistake had a material effect on the agreed exchange of performances. To do this, that party must show more than a mere loss of advantage from the contract or that the party would not have entered into the contract had there been no mistake. "He must show that the resulting imbalance in the agreed exchange is so severe that he can not fairly be required to carry it out."[11] Although it has been suggested that avoidance for mistake "should depend on the requirement of unjust impoverishment on the

---

[5] Restatement Second §152 cmt. *b*.

[6] Dover Pool & Racquet Club v. Brooking, 322 N.E.2d 168 (Mass. 1975) (parties who contracted to sell land that buyer intended to use for club "made the assumption that the zoning by-laws interposed no obstacle to the use of the premises for a nonprofit tennis and swim club").

[7] Smith v. Osborn, 223 N.W.2d 913 (Wis. 913) (reduction in price where 23.4% less acreage than parties believed in sale by acre). Relief may be given, however, if there is hardship on the purchaser because the tract is markedly smaller than supposed and the purchaser cannot use it for the intended purpose. Slingluff v. Dugan, 56 A. 837, 839 (Md. 1904) (deficiency in dimensions of unimproved lots made "material difference" in their value as building lots).

[8] Moonves v. Hill, 360 A.2d 59 (Vt. 1976) (rescission appropriate where size of tract turned out to be 41.7 rather than 60 acres).

[9] Speedway Enters. v. Hartsell, 251 P.2d 641 (Ariz. 1952) (purchaser could not avoid though contract for sale of ranch stated "approximately 915 acres" and was 80 acres short).

[10] For a discussion of relevant circumstances, *see* Speedway Enters. v. Hartsell, *supra* note 9.

[11] Restatement Second §152 cmt. *c*.

one hand and enrichment on the other,"[12] the commentary to the Restatement Second rejects this suggestion and posits that, at least in "exceptional cases, the adversely affected party may be able to show that the effect on the agreed exchange has been material simply on the ground that the exchange has become less desirable for him, even though there has been no effect on the other party."[13] Case law supports this view that hardship for one party is a sufficient basis for avoidance for mistake.[14] A party who suffers hardship as a result of existing facts may, to be sure, seek relief under the doctrine of frustration as well as mistake, though it is more likely that a party will be regarded as having borne the risk of mistake than the risk of existing frustration.[15]

Ordinarily the mistake affects the agreed exchange by making it both less advantageous for the party adversely affected and more advantageous for the other party. In *Sherwood v. Walker*, for example, when the cow turned out to be more valuable than the parties had supposed, the exchange became both less advantageous to the seller and more advantageous to the buyer.[16] Conversely, if parties contract for the sale of land for a lump sum,[17] mistakenly believing the acreage to be greater than it is, the exchange will turn out to be both more advantageous to the seller and less advantageous to the purchaser. The party adversely affected has a better chance of showing that the effect on the agreed exchange is material if, as in these examples, the mistake also has an impact on the other party. Courts have been reluctant to allow avoidance if the mistake merely makes the exchange less desirable for one party, as is the case if the parties mistakenly suppose that goods sold are suitable for some special

Showing materiality

---

[12]Thayer, Unilateral Mistake and Unjust Enrichment as a Ground for the Avoidance of Legal Transactions, in Harvard Legal Essays 467, 487 (1934).

[13]§152 cmt. *c*.

[14]Dover Pool & Racquet Club v. Brooking, *supra* note 6 (although it "could not yet be said that the purchaser's principal purpose had been frustrated" by proposed zoning change, "as a result of the mistake enforcement of the contract would be materially more onerous to the purchaser").

[15]See the discussion of greater obligation not assumed in §9.7 *infra*.

[16]In the reverse situation, where the goods turn out to be less valuable than the parties had supposed, the buyer usually finds it to its advantage to assert a breach of warranty, not a mutual mistake. Because of the broad scope of a seller's warranties, the buyer will more often be entitled to relief. In addition, recovery for breach of warranty is generally based on the value that the property would have had if it had been as warranted, whereas recovery on avoidance for mistake is limited to restitution. The two remedies are not, however, mutually exclusive, and the buyer may choose between them. Furthermore, a buyer that has no claim for breach of warranty may be entitled to avoidance for mistake. *Cf.* Smith v. Zimbalist, 38 P.2d 170 (Cal. App. 1934) (trial court held for buyer on ground of "a mutual mistake" that violins were made by Guarnerius and Stradivarius; appellate court affirmed, but on the ground that seller warranted that this was so).

[17]If the price is calculated by the acre, however, so that it can be adjusted to take account of the mistake, the effect on the exchange will probably not be enough to justify avoidance. Smith v. Osborn, 223 N.W.2d 913 (Wis. 1974) (purchaser of land entitled to reformation of contract to reflect reduced purchase price when land sold per acre was discovered to contain only 53.59 acres instead of 70).

Effect of other relief

purpose of the buyer.[18] Such cases of hardship are ordinarily left to be dealt with under the rules on impracticability and frustration.[19]

In determining whether the mistake has a material effect on the agreed exchange, a court will also consider whether relief other than avoidance is available to the party adversely affected. If, for example, the mistake concerns the contents or effect of a writing and the party adversely affected can have it rectified by reformation, avoidance is not available as an alternative.[20] A court will also take account of any other relief granted to the other party. For this reason the party that is advantaged by a mistake may seek to have a writing reformed, even though reformation makes that party's own performance more burdensome, in order to prevent the party adversely affected from avoiding the contract for mistake.[21]

Example of *Wood v. Boynton*

In many cases, courts have held that an adversely affected party was not entitled to avoid for mutual mistake, even though that party has met both of the requirements just described. An example is *Wood v. Boynton*,[22] decided by the Supreme Court of Wisconsin two years before *Sherwood v. Walker*. The owner of a small stone sold it to jewelers for $1. Unknown to the parties, who supposed that the stone might be a topaz, it was in fact a rough diamond, worth about $700. When this was discovered, the seller attempted to avoid on the ground of mutual mistake and sought to have the stone returned. The court denied her relief, although it seems clear that, in Restatement Second terms, the mistake involved a basic assumption on which the contract was made and had a material effect of the agreed exchange of performances. How, then, is the case to be reconciled with *Sherwood v. Walker*?

"Identity" or "attributes"

Courts have often sought to reconcile cases such as these by explaining that avoidance is allowed only for mistakes that go to the "identity" or "existence" of the subject matter, not for those that go merely to its "attributes," "quality," or "value."[23] The premise seems to be that relief will be granted only if there was no intention to make the contract in question, even though courts regularly

---

[18]*But see* Dover Pool & Racquet Club v. Brooking, *supra* note 6 ("as a result of the mistake enforcement of the contract would be materially more onerous to the purchaser").

[19]In re Westinghouse Elec. Corp., 517 F. Supp. 440 (E.D. Va. 1981) (refusing relief on ground of mistake and distinguishing *ALCOA*, discussed in §9.2 *supra*: to "extent that *Alcoa* was disadvantaged by the mistake, Essex was enriched," whereas in instant case, "while the unavailability of reprocessing has the effect of making performance by Westinghouse more expensive, it in no way enriches [utility] or gives [utility] any benefit it did not bargain for").

[20]Henn v. McGinnis, 165 N.W. 406 (Iowa 1917) (where vendor sold land on per acre basis, parties mistakenly supposing that tract contained 32.44 acres, whereas it contained 42, vendor "could not have demanded a rescission" and a correction of the computation was "the only relief to which she was entitled").

[21]See the discussion of reformation for mistake in §7.5 *supra*.

[22]25 N.W. 42 (1885).

[23]Costello v. Sykes, 172 N.W. 907 (Minn. 1919) (where parties to sale of bank stock did not know that defalcations by bank employees had reduced its value from $136 to $60 a share, there was no mistake as to stock's "identity or existence" but only as to its "attributes, quality or value").

grant relief when it is clear that in fact both parties had just that intention. In *Sherwood v. Walker,* for example, though the court reasoned that "the mistake was not of the mere quality of the animal, but went to the very nature of the thing" and that a "barren cow is substantially a different creature than a breeding one,"[24] both parties plainly intended to make a contract to sell Rose 2d of Aberlone. Relief is granted in such cases because the mistake vitiates judgment, but this is no less so for the stone in *Wood v. Boynton* than for the cow in *Sherwood v. Walker*. If the cases are to be reconciled, some basis other than this specious and artificial reasoning must be found.

The Restatement Second attempts to reconcile such cases by its third requirement, which is that the party adversely affected must not bear the risk of the mistake.[25] In Restatement Second terms, the seller of the stone bore the risk of the mistake while the seller of the cow did not. But how is it to be determined whether the party adversely affected bears the risk of a mistake? The Restatement Second lists three situations in which a party bears that risk.

3. Must not bear risk

The most obvious situation in which a party bears the risk of a mistake occurs when the agreement itself provides that a party bears the risk of the mistake. Because contracting parties rarely focus on the possibility of mistake, provisions countering claims of mistake often take the form of standard "boilerplate" provisions routinely inserted in a variety of common agreements. "As is" terms in contracts for sale may fend off a disappointed buyer's claim of mistake since, as one court said, it "suggests that . . . the risk should be allocated to the purchasers"[26] and as another court put it, it characterizes the transaction as "on a 'grab bag' basis."[27] "Lost or not lost" terms in policies of property insurance

Agreement to bear risk

---

[24]33 N.W. at 923. *But see* Lenawee County Bd. of Health v. Messerly, 331 N.W.2d 203 (Mich. 1982) (citing court's earlier opinion in Sherwood v. Walker but concluding that "inexact and confusing distinction between contractual mistakes running to value and those touching the substance of the consideration serves only as an impediment to a clear and helpful analysis").

[25]Restatement Second §154.

[26]Lenawee County Bd. of Health v. Messerly, *supra* note 24, at 209, 210 (purchasers of apartment house assumed risk of inadequate sewage system under "as is" clause).

[27]United States v. Hathaway, 242 F.2d 897, 901 (9th Cir. 1957) (government sale of submerged scrap steel, much of which could not be removed). As to whether a quitclaim deed has a similar effect when the vendor lacks title, *see* 2 George E. Palmer, The Law of Restitution § 12.14 (1978).

Courts have not always honored such provisions. Shore Builders v. Dogwood, Inc., 616 F. Supp. 1004 (D. Del. 1985) ("no-reliance" clause denied effect where it was "boilerplate"); S Dev. Co. v. Pima Capital Mgt. Co., 31 P.3d 123 (Ariz. App. 2001) ("in the face of an 'as is' sale," vendor that "fails to disclose a known latent defect or fails to give appropriate opportunity to discover latent defects" will be liable in tort for nondisclosure); C. Lambert & Assocs. v. Horizon Corp., 748 P.2d 504 (N.M. 1988) (" 'as is' clause provides absolute protection" to vendor that fails to disclose that movement of road boundary has diminished acreage "only when the buyer and seller possess equal knowledge of the property"); Grube v. Daun, 496 N.W.2d 106 (Wis. App. 1992) ("as is" clause protects seller "from claims premised on nondisclosure," but "once the seller or his agent has made an affirmative representation about some aspect of the property, the buyer is entitled to rely upon that statement and expect full and fair disclosure of all material facts"). As

609

may preclude the insurer from claiming relief based on mistake where the property was destroyed before the policy was issued.[28] "More or less" language in contracts for the sale of land may encourage a court to reject a claim by either party based on mistake as to acreage.[29] That language disclaiming mistake is not sure of success is shown by the mixed reception received by wording, common in personal injury releases, that purports to cover "unknown and unforeseeable" injuries.[30] In one case, the Supreme Court of Minnesota held that "even though a release expressly covers unknown injuries, it is not a bar to an action for such unknown injuries if it can be shown that such unknown injuries were not within the contemplation of the parties."[31] However, it is difficult to see why, absent inequality of bargaining power, parties should not be able to make a settlement covering unknown as well as known injuries. As the New York Court of Appeals explained, "there are many reasons, including doubtful liability, the willingness to take a calculated risk, the desire to obtain an earlier rather than a later settlement, and perhaps others, why releasors may wish to effect a settlement and intend to give the releasee a discharge of liability for any unknown injuries — in short to bargain for general peace." And if "general peace is the consideration there can be no mutual mistake as to the extent of the injuries, known or unknown."[32]

Awareness of limited knowledge   The second situation in which a party bears the risk of a mistake is one in which a party makes a contract with only limited knowledge of the facts to which the mistake relates. If the party is aware that its knowledge is limited, it bears the risk of the mistake. As the court explained in *Wood v. Boynton*, if the seller, who "had the stone in her possession for a long time, and . . . had made some inquiry as to its nature and qualities . . . chose to sell it without further investigation as to its intrinsic value . . . , she cannot repudiate the sale because it is afterwards ascertained that she made a bad bargain."[33] In such cases it is sometimes said that there was no mistake, but rather "conscious

---

to the effect of such provisions where a misrepresentation is claimed, see the discussion of the effect of investigation in §4.13 *supra*.

[28] *See* Leslie J. Buglass, Marine Insurance and General Average in the United States 558 (2d ed. 1981) (quoting Marine Insurance Act, 1906 §6(1): "where the subject matter is insured 'lost or not lost,' the assured may recover although he may not have acquired his interest until after the loss").

[29] Bowling v. Poole, 756 N.E.2d 983 (Ind. App. 2001) ("description of '3 Ac. more or less' had to be considered" where sale was "in gross" not "per acre").

[30] *See* Dobbs, Conclusiveness of Personal Injury Settlements: Basic Problems, 41 N.C. L. Rev. 665, 706 (1963) (risk of "unknown and unforeseeable" injuries is usually expressly assumed).

[31] Aronovich v. Levy, 56 N.W.2d 570, 576 (Minn. 1953). *See* Reynolds v. Merrill, 460 P.2d 323, 326 (Utah 1969) (observing that releases are "invariably . . . broad enough" to encompass unknown injuries and disregarding, over strong dissents, language covering "all known and unknown" injuries).

[32] Mangini v. McClurg, 249 N.E.2d 386, 392 (N.Y. 1969).

[33] 25 N.W. at 44.

ignorance."[34] The boundaries of "conscious ignorance" are often tested when injured persons seek to avoid settlements on the ground of mistakes as to the extent of their injuries, since such settlements are made for the specific purpose of settling known uncertainties as to those injuries. Even if the injured person can overcome the argument that the release was based on a misprediction rather than a mistake,[35] the injured person must contend with the doctrine of conscious ignorance. Many courts have applied the doctrine if relief is sought for unknown consequences of *known injuries*, as to which one is assumed to be aware of one's ignorance, while courts have been more willing to grant relief for unknown consequences of *unknown injuries*, as to which there is no such assumption.[36] A court may compare the amount received in settlement with the fair value of the claim at the time of settlement.[37] If the amount received is considerably in excess of the fair value, this suggests that the parties took into account the possibility of other injuries,[38] but if the amount received is close to the fair value, this suggests an assumption that all injuries were known.[39] The case for avoidance is particularly strong if the known and unknown injuries are of a different nature, as is plainly the case where the known ones are to property while the unknown ones are to the person.[40] Courts have had more difficulty in deciding whether the injuries are of a different nature when both the known and the unknown ones are to the person.[41] It is difficult to find a consistent approach in these cases.[42] Courts have often been torn between sympathy for

[34] Harbor Ins. Co. v. Stokes, 45 F.3d 499 (D.C. Cir. 1995) (party to settlement agreement made in ignorance that appeal had been decided in party's favor on day before proceeded in what "Restatement has quite logically" termed "conscious ignorance").

[35] See the discussion of prediction excluded in §9.2 *supra*. For a case rejecting the claim that the mistake was mutual, *see* Indiana Bell Tel. Co. v. Mygrant, 471 N.E.2d 660 (Ind. 1984) (no evidence "that, at the time the release was executed, Indiana Bell's representative harbored any belief whatsoever regarding Mygrant's injuries").

[36] For a different view, *see* Witt v. Watkins, 579 P.2d 1065 (Alaska 1978) (rejecting "artificial distinction between cases of a known injury which proves to be much more serious than believed, and an injury different in type from that originally known").

[37] The fair value will depend on the magnitude of the known injuries and the probability of recovery.

[38] Myers v. Fecker Co., 252 N.W.2d 595 (Minn. 1977) (not shown that "parties neither had an understanding nor intended to give final releases with respect to known as well as unknown injuries").

[39] Reed v. Treat, 210 N.E.2d 833 (Ill. App. 1965) ("settlement was negotiated substantially on the basis of the plaintiff's out of pocket expense" and trial judge "could fairly conclude that the defendant was not actually paying any sum for future unforeseen consequences of the injury").

[40] Williams v. Glash, 789 S.W.2d 261 (Tex. 1990) (claimant "had no knowledge of the [personal injury] claim at the time of signing the release," and amount received "was the exact amount of the property damage to her car").

[41] Mitzel v. Schatz, 175 N.W.2d 659 (victim of auto accident could avoid release by showing that while parties believed he had only a black eye, he had a clot on brain).

[42] *See generally* Dobbs, Conclusiveness of Personal Injury Settlements: Basic Problems, 41 N.C. L. Rev. 665, 702-30 (1963).

the injured party and the policy favoring compromise as a means of settling claims, and they have been swayed by many factors, such as unfairness, that are not germane to the issue of avoidance for mutual mistake.[43]

Judicial allocation   The third situation in which a party bears the risk of a mistake occurs when "the risk is allocated to him by the court on the ground that it is reasonable in the circumstances to do so."[44] This is the most common of the three situations. In what kinds of cases will a court find it reasonable to put the risk of a mistake on the party adversely affected by it? Suppose an owner of farm land discovers, after making a contract for its sale, that the land contains mineral deposits that make it much more valuable than either party has supposed. As a general rule, the owner cannot avoid the contract on the ground that both parties were mistaken in assuming, when they fixed the sale price, that the land was suitable only for farming.[45] Suppose a builder discovers, after making a contract to construct a building, that the land contains rock that makes the construction much more expensive than either party had supposed. As a general rule, the builder cannot avoid the contract on the ground that both parties were mistaken in assuming, when they fixed the contract price, that the subsoil conditions were normal.[46] Yet in both examples the mistake clearly involves a basic assumption on which the contract was made and has a material effect on the agreed exchange of performances. However, it is thought more reasonable for the landowner to bear the risk of the mistake as to the presence of minerals than to pass this risk on to the purchaser, particularly in view of the policy favoring the finality of real estate transactions. It is also thought more reasonable for the builder to bear the risk of the mistake as to the presence of rock than to pass this risk on to the owner, especially in the light of the builder's generally greater expertise in judging subsoil conditions. In situations where, unlike the two examples just given, no precedents exist, a court will have to rely on its own perception of the

---

[43] *See* Wheeler v. White Rock Bottling Co., 366 P.2d 527 (Or. 1961) ("while we are mindful of the trend elsewhere toward treating releases as binding only when they do not result in hardship, we believe that our . . . previous choices of competing policy considerations require us to reject mere improvidence as a plausible ground for setting aside otherwise unimpeachable contracts").

Mistake is only one of many grounds on which a release can be attacked. Other common grounds include strict interpretation of the release (see the discussion of interpretation of terms in §4.26 *supra*), reformation on the ground that it does not correctly express the prior agreement (see the discussion of reformation for mistake in §7.5 *supra*), avoidability on the ground of misrepresentation, duress, or undue influence (see §§4.10, 4.16, 4.20 *supra*), and unenforceability on the ground of unconscionability (see §4.28 *supra*).

[44] Restatement Second §154(c).

[45] Tetenman v. Epstein, 226 P. 966 (Cal. App. 1924) ("if the mere ignorance as to the true value of property by one who sells it, where the sale is for a sum considerably less than its value, were a ground to set aside a deed, no transaction would be final until the validity thereof had been determined by a suit to quiet title").

[46] Watkins & Son v. Carrig, 21 A.2d 591 (N.H. 1941) (where "no understanding existed between the parties that no rock would be found in the excavating, . . . a defence of mutual mistake is not available").

purposes of the parties and its own knowledge of human behavior, much as it does in the analogous case of supplying a term by the process of implication.[47] A good deal of common sense underlies this analysis. Most courts would probably agree, for instance, with the cases put by one writer on the subject: "If A buys an annuity on C's life, he takes the risk that C may die soon after the annuity is issued. . . . But if C was already dead when the annuity was issued A could rescind the sale of the annuity because ordinarily A would not have assumed this latter risk."[48] Such analysis in terms of risk candidly acknowledges the considerable discretion exercised by courts in mistake cases, and it is more likely to lead to sensible results than is the specious and artificial reasoning based on such criteria as "identity" or "attributes."

A mistaken party is not barred from relief merely because that party could have avoided the mistake by the exercise of reasonable care.[49] If the law were otherwise, the availability of relief for mistake would be greatly limited. However, in rare cases the mistaken party's fault may be so extreme as to bar the party from relief for the mistake. The critical degree of fault is sometimes described as "gross" or "culpable" negligence,[50] although the use of such terms in the law of torts has met with criticism. The Restatement Second states that relief for mistake is not precluded by the mistaken party's fault unless it "amounts to a failure to act in good faith and in accordance with reasonable standards of fair dealing."[51]

Fault of mistaken party

The disadvantaged party's remedy for mutual mistake is avoidance.[52] As in the case of misrepresentation,[53] the party entitled to avoid for mistake may be barred by failing to act within a reasonable length of time after that party is or ought to be aware of the facts.[54] On avoidance, both parties are entitled to

Avoidance as remedy

---

[47] Sheng v. Sharkey Labs., 117 F.3d 1081 (8th Cir. 1997) (following Restatement Second instruction "to examine 'the purposes of the parties'" and use "'general knowledge of human behavior in bargain transactions' to allocate risk" in finding that employer "chose the certainty of settlement rather than the gamble of ruling on its motion"). As to the process of implication, see §7.16 *supra.*

[48] Rabin, A Proposed Black-Letter Rule Concerning Mistaken Assumptions in Bargain Transactions, 45 Tex. L. Rev. 1273, 1292-93 (1967).

[49] Vermette v. Andersen, 558 P.2d 258 (Wash. App. 1976) (buyers were not "culpably negligent for failing to discover the slope instability present on the land"). As has just been seen, however, a party's lack of care in making a contract while aware of its limited knowledge of the facts may bar it from relief.

[50] Vermette v. Andersen, *supra* note 49.

[51] Restatement Second §157.

[52] That in general the mistaken party must avoid the entire agreement, *see* Leavitt v. Stanley, 571 A.2d 269 (N.H. 1990). The disadvantaged party can, of course, also enforce the contract. Cady v. Gale, 5 W. Va. 547 (1871) ("where a vendor contracts to sell a larger interest in the real estate than he has title to, a court of equity will compel him, at the suit of his vendee, to convey to the latter, such an estate or interest as the former may have . . . contracted to be sold").

[53] See the discussion of avoidance and ratification in §4.15 *supra.*

[54] Grymes v. Sanders, 93 U.S. 55 (1876) (party who "desires to rescind upon the ground of mistake . . . must, upon the discovery of the facts, at once announce his purpose").

restitution.[55] Occasionally, courts have fashioned more imaginative solutions on the ground that restitution will not do justice.[56]

We move now from mutual to unilateral mistake.

Traditional view

§9.4.   Unilateral Mistake. A [unilateral mistake] occurs when only one party has an erroneous perception as to the facts. (In a sense, of course, even in a case of unilateral mistake, both parties are mistaken: one is mistaken as to some fact and the other is mistaken in thinking that the first party is not mistaken.) In general, courts have been reluctant to allow a party to avoid a contract for a mistake that was not shared by the other party. The Supreme Court of Illinois expressed this reluctance in denying avoidance to sellers of lumber who had made a mistake in adding the prices of a list of items:

> If it can be set aside on account of the error in adding up the amounts representing the selling price, it could be set aside for a mistake in computing the percentage of profits which [sellers] intended to make . . . or any other miscalculation on their part. If equity would relieve on account of such a mistake, there would be no stability in contracts. . . .[1]

Many courts, however, have abandoned this strict view and recognized a limited right of avoidance for unilateral mistake.[2]

Mistaken bid cases

Most of the cases in which avoidance has been granted for unilateral mistake have involved errors in the calculation of bids by general contractors on construction contracts. Subcontractors sometimes try to prevent preaward bid shopping by general contractors by waiting until the last moment to submit their bids.[3] The resulting haste with which a general contractor must prepare

---

[55] Renner v. Kehl, 722 P.2d 262 (Ariz. 1986) (purchasers of land had to pay vendors "the fair rental value of the land for the duration of their occupancy" and vendors had to pay purchasers "sum equal to the amount by which their property has been enhanced in value by the [purchasers'] efforts"). *See* Restatement Second §§158(1), 376; Dawson, Restitution Without Enrichment, 61 B.U. L. Rev. 563, 592-600 (1981).

[56] *See* Restatement Second §158(2) (if rules stated "will not avoid injustice, the court may . . . supply a term that is reasonable in the circumstances"). For examples, *see* National Presto Indus. v. United States, 338 F.2d 99 (Ct. Cl. 1964) (court ordered a determination of the unexpected costs attributable to the mistake and directed that the supplier recover half of them, so that it and the government would bear the loss equally); Aluminum Co. of Am. v. Essex Group, 499 F. Supp. 53 (W.D. Pa. 1980) (discussed in §9.2 *supra*; court reformed contract to give expected profit when escalator clause failed to take account of energy costs); Thieme v. Worst, 745 P.2d 1076 (Idaho App. 1987) (where parties were mistaken as to availability of irrigation water, requiring vendors to furnish irrigation system reshaped contract "to achieve a just result").

§9.4 [1] Steinmeyer v. Schroeppel, 80 N.E. 564, 566 (Ill. 1907).

[2] *See* Restatement Second §153.

[3] This practice is described in §3.25 *supra*.

its own bid is conducive to error.[4] The general contractor often checks its calculations only on finding out that its bid is the lowest and only then discovers the mistake. If the bid is revocable, the general contractor may still have time to revoke it, although the general contractor may lose its bid deposit if there is one.[5] However, the bid may already have been accepted, or it may be irrevocable, as is usually the case for bids under government contracts.[6] Nevertheless, courts have granted bidders relief for unilateral mistakes in the calculation of bids in a growing list of jurisdictions. The bidder must show, as in a case of mutual mistake, that the mistake went to a basic assumption on which the contract was made and that it had a material effect on the agreed exchange of performances. Furthermore, the bidder must show that performance would be unduly burdensome and that the other party has not relied on the bid.[8] The bidder that can meet these requirements can avoid even after the bid has been accepted,[9] and presumably even after a formal contract has been entered into.[10]

The requirement that the bidder seek to avoid before any significant reliance by the other party is imposed so that avoidance will cost the other party only its expectation.[11] For this reason, the general contractor's use of the subcontractor's bid when the general contractor prepares its own bid is considered sufficient reliance to preclude avoidance by the subcontractor.[12] If it is a general

Absence of reliance

---

[4] *See* Elsinore Union Elementary School Dist. v. Kastorff, 353 P.2d 713 (Cal. 1960) (general contractor testified that there was "a custom among subcontractors . . . to delay giving . . . their bids until the very last moment").

[5] See the discussion of the effect of a deposit in §3.17 *supra*.

[6] See the discussion of the rule of revocability in §3.17 *supra*.

[7] Elsinore Union Elementary School Dist. v. Kastorff, *supra* note 4 (general contractor subtracted amount of another plumbing sub-bid that he mistakenly thought he had included in his total); Boise Junior College Dist. v. Mattefs Constr. Co., 450 P.2d 604 (Idaho 1969) (general contractor mistakenly failed to include sub-bid for glass).

[8] The requirements for mutual mistake are discussed in §9.3 *supra*. Courts have had no difficulty in the mistaken bid cases in finding a mistake as to a basic assumption nor in finding materiality. The problem of whether the bidder bears the risk of the mistake is discussed later in this section.

[9] James T. Taylor & Son v. Arlington Indep. School Dist., 335 S.W.2d 371 (Tex. 1960) (bidder may avoid "even after acceptance of a bid, but before the execution of the contract").

[10] S.T.S. Transp. Serv. v. Volvo White Truck Corp., 766 F.2d 1089 (7th Cir. 1985) (seller of trucks who erred in calculating price entitled to rescind contract). The dearth of cases on this point involving bids may be due to the fact that if the mistake is not discovered at an earlier stage, it is usually not discovered before relief is precluded by reliance. Where the other party knows or has reason to know of the mistake, relief may be granted at a later stage because, as is pointed out later in this section, it is not precluded by reliance.

[11] Boise Junior College Dist. v. Mattefs Constr. Co., *supra* note 7 ("the party to whom the bid is submitted will not be prejudiced except by the loss of his bargain").

[12] Drennan v. Star Paving Co., 333 P.2d 757 (Cal. 1958) ("As between the subcontractor who made the bid and the general contractor who reasonably relied on it, the loss resulting from the mistake should fall on the party who caused it.").

contractor that has made the mistaken bid, however, the owner's reliance may consist only of release of other bidders, and this reliance will not preclude avoidance if the owner can be compensated for it by an allowance for the cost of readvertising for bids.[13]

Must be unconscionable

The other requirement that the bidder must meet in order to avoid is to show that holding the bidder to the bid would result in a degree of hardship that courts have often characterized as "unconscionable."[14] The extent of hardship depends not only on the magnitude of the error, in comparison with the size of the bid, but also on the profit that the bidder will make or the loss that the bidder will sustain if required to perform.[15] Unconscionability therefore differs from materiality, as the Supreme Court of Idaho has explained:

> An error in the computation of a bid may be material, representing a large percentage of the total bid submitted, and yet requiring compliance with the bid may not be unconscionable. Thus, omission of a $25,000 item in a $100,000 bid would be material, but if the $100,000 bid included $50,000 in profit, no hardship would be created by requiring the contractor to comply with the terms of his bid.[16]

Risk as to judgment

Even if these requirements are met, relief for unilateral mistake, like that for mutual mistake, is not available if the party seeking relief bears the risk of the mistake.[17] For example, if a bidder's mistake is one of "judgment," the bidder bears the risk and cannot avoid.[18] Courts, conscious of what the

---

[13] Board of Regents of Murray State Normal School v. Cole, 273 S.W. 508 (Ky. 1925) (on bidder's payment of cost of advertising for bids a second time, "the parties may be placed in statu quo").

[14] Boise Junior College Dist. v. Mattefs Constr. Co., *supra* note 7 ("enforcement of a contract pursuant to the terms of the erroneous bid would be unconscionable").

[15] Crenshaw County Hosp. Bd. v. St. Paul Fire & Marine Ins. Co., 411 F.2d 213 (5th Cir. 1969) (where general contractor, who made $35,000 mistake on $285,837 bid, "had figured $25,000 profit in the job and . . . some of the subcontractors had offered to cut their prices to help him out of his difficulty . . . to enforce the contract as made was not unconscionable").

[16] Boise Junior College Dist. v. Mattefs Constr. Co., *supra* note 7, at 606.

[17] Anderson Bros. Corp. v. O'Meara, 306 F.2d 672 (5th Cir. 1962) (buyer of dredge who "chose to act on assumption rather than upon inquiry or information obtained by investigation" will not be "released from the resulting consequences on the ground that, because of his mistaken assumption, it would be unconscionable to allow the sale to stand"). This is the best explanation for Kiahtipes v. Mills, 649 P.2d 9 (Utah 1982) (relief denied where vendors were mistaken as to legal effect of mortgage on sales agreement). *See* In re Allegheny Intl., 954 F.2d 167 (3d Cir. 1992) (fn.12: employer "could not succeed on the basis of unilateral mistake if it knew, or should have realized, that it could not determine without further investigation whether [employee] was being honest and forthright about the accounting problems" at subsidiaries).

[18] Tony Down Food Co. v. United States, 530 F.2d 367 (Ct. Cl. 1976) (mistake in bid "resulted not from any clear cut clerical, arithmetical or specification misreading error [but from] mistaken judgment as to economic conditions, and the continued existence of the price freeze"). *See* Restatement Second §154 illus. 6 (no relief for "mistaken estimate as to the amount of labor required to do the work").

Supreme Court of Illinois in the quotation at the beginning of this section called "stability in contracts," will not grant relief for mistakes such as those "in computing the percentage of profits." As an Illinois intermediate appellate court later noted, there is a distinction between "clerical or arithmetic error" and error of "business judgment."[19] Mistakes in reading the other party's specifications have been treated as "clerical" errors rather than as errors in "judgment."[20]

A bidder is not barred from relief for mistake merely because the bidder could have avoided it by the exercise of reasonable care.[21] However, there is a degree of carelessness beyond which the bidder will not be protected.[22]

Effect of bidder's lack of care

If the mistake in the bid is known to the other party, it is clear that the bidder is not bound to perform. "One cannot snap up an offer or bid knowing that it was made in mistake."[23] Moreover, even the most traditional courts agree that the bidder can avoid on the ground of mistake if the other party merely had reason to know of the mistake.[24] A general contractor may be able to show this if the bid was so low — in comparison with other bids, with a reasonable price,

Effect of other party's knowledge

---

[19]People ex rel. Dept. of Pub. Works & Bldgs. v. South East Natl. Bank, 266 N.W.2d 778 (Ill. App. 1971) (general contractor who mistakenly entered sub-bid of $26,170 as $2,617 could avoid). It has even been held that a provision in the invitation for bids that the bidder "will not be released on account of errors" does not suffice to put the risk of a clerical error on the builder. M.F. Kemper Constr. Co. v. City of Los Angeles, 235 P.2d 7 (Cal. 1951) (clause related "to errors of judgment as distinguished from clerical mistakes").

[20]WilFred's v. Metropolitan Sanitary Dist., 372 N.E.2d 946 (Ill. App. 1978) ("incorrect assumption that heavy trucks could be driven into the sand drying beds and onto the plastic pipes").

[21]M.F. Kemper Constr. Co. v. City of Los Angeles, *supra* note 19 ("type of error here involved is one which will sometimes occur in the conduct of reasonable and cautious businessmen"). *See* Restatement Second §157 (fault does not bar relief unless it amounts to "a failure to act in good faith and in accordance with reasonable standards of fair dealing").

Even a bidder that fails to find a mistake on being asked to check the bid may meet this standard. Elsinore Union Elementary School Dist. v. Kastorff, *supra* note 4 (bidder should not be "denied relief from an unfair, inequitable, and unintended bargain simply because, in response to inquiry from board when his bid was discovered to be much the lowest submitted, he informed board, after checking with his clerical assistant, that the bid was correct"). *See* M.F. Kemper Constr. Co. v. City of Los Angeles, *supra* note 19 (dissenting opinion: "There is no reason why he cannot have his arithmetic correct. School boys have been disciplined for stupidity in that field.").

[22]Few cases have found that the degree was exceeded. *See* Zapatero v. Canales, 730 S.W.2d 111 (Tex. App. 1987) ("party is charged with knowledge of all limitations to his title found through the deed records"). A party may, however, be held to have assumed the risk because of "conscious ignorance." Anderson Bros. Corp. v. O'Meara, *supra* note 17 (although buyer of dredge "was conscious of his own lack of knowledge concerning dredges, he took no steps prior to purchase to learn if the dredge . . . was suited to his purpose"). See the discussion of fault of the mistaken party in §9.3 *supra*.

[23]Tyra v. Cheney, 152 N.W. 835, 835 (Minn. 1915).

[24]Geremia v. Boyarsky, 140 A. 749 (Conn. 1928) (owner "had good reason to know" of builder's mistake).

or with the owner's estimate — as to make the mistake palpable.[25] If the other party knew or had reason to know of the mistake, the bidder can avoid even if the other party has relied,[26] presumably without regard to unconscionability.[27] Courts have reached similar results in cases in which the other party's fault was responsible for the mistake, though that party had no reason to know of it.[28]

Other types of cases

Not all of the cases allowing relief for unilateral mistake have involved mistaken bids. The Supreme Court of California, while recognizing that "the most common types of mistakes falling within this category" of unilateral mistake "occur in bids on construction contracts," noted that Restatement Second § 153 "is not limited to such cases" and granted relief to an automobile dealer that had mistakenly offered a more expensive Jaguar for $25,995.[29] Other courts have reached a similar conclusion, granting relief to a purchaser that contracts to buy a tract of land under a unilateral mistake as to the identity of the tract or as to its boundaries[30] and to a holder of a patent that settles a patent infringement claim under a unilateral mistake as to whether the patent would withstand challenge.[31] There is even authority that a party to a contract that has arisen in spite of a misunderstanding may, in some circumstances, be able to avoid it on the ground of a unilateral mistake.[32] The general principles applicable to the mistaken bid cases apply to such cases as well.

Mistake as to identity

Although a mistake as to the identity of the other party has sometimes been treated differently from other unilateral mistakes, the modern trend is not to do so.[33] Such a mistake is, by its nature, a mistake of only one party. The identity

[25] Chernick v. United States, 372 F.2d 492 (Ct. Cl. 1967) ("Any instance of a monetary figure one-tenth or ten times what it might naturally be expected to be, is a warning flag."). See the discussion of no-oral-modification clauses in §7.6 *supra*.

[26] Furthermore, such cases often involve bids by subcontractors that are only irrevocable if there has been reliance, as explained in §3.25 *supra*. Drennan v. Star Paving Co., *supra* note 12 (dictum: if general contractor "had reason to believe that [subcontractor's] bid was in error, he could not justifiably rely on it").

[27] However, if the bid is so low that the other party has reason to know of the mistake, the bidder should have little difficulty in showing unconscionability.

[28] Centex Constr. Co. v. James, 374 F.2d 921 (8th Cir. 1967) (subcontractor was misled by specifications furnished by general contractor).

[29] Donovan v. RRL Corp., 27 P.3d 702, 716 (Cal. 2001).

[30] Beatty v. Depue, 103 N.W.2d 187 (S.D. 1960) (purchaser mistakenly thought land included Forest Service land enclosed by same fence).

[31] Gamewell Mfg. v. HVAC Supply, 715 F.2d 112 (4th Cir. 1983) (independent testing laboratory made errors in tests that precipitated settlement).

[32] *See* Restatement Second §153 illus. 6 and the discussion of reason to know in §7.9 *supra*.

[33] *See* Restatement Second §153 cmt g. One who knows that an offer is not meant for oneself is not an offeree and cannot accept. *See* the discussion of the point that only the offeree can accept in §3.11 *supra*.

of the other party, as distinguished from that party's financial standing,[34] for example, is ordinarily a basic assumption on which the contract is made. Under the modern view, the contract is voidable if the other party had reason to know of the mistake or caused it.[35] Otherwise it is only voidable if its enforcement would be unconscionable. This might be true in the case of a seller that has contracted to sell goods on credit and can show that it would be unconscionable to require delivery of the goods to a party other than the one with which the seller believed it had dealt.[36]

The mistaken party's remedy for unilateral mistake is avoidance, although if the other party actually knew of the mistake it would seem that no contract was formed at all.[37] This power of avoidance is subject to the restrictions applicable to avoidance for mutual mistake,[38] including the requirement of restitution of anything received from the other party.[39] In return, the party seeking avoidance is entitled to restitution for any benefit conferred on the other party.[40] Occasionally, as in the case of mutual mistake, courts have been impelled to shape more inventive solutions.[41] **Avoidance**

From mistake we turn to impracticability and frustration.

C. IMPRACTICABILITY AND FRUSTRATION

§9.5. Growth of Impossibility as an Excuse. The common law was slow to give effect to the maxim *impossibilium nulla obligatio est* ("there is no obligation to do the impossible"). Courts were less receptive to claims of excuse based on events occurring after the making of the contract than they were to claims of excuse based on facts that existed at the time of the agreement. In a seventeenth-century dictum that was to gain wide acceptance, the Court of King's Bench declared that: **Strict view**

---

[34] See the discussion of basic assumption in §9.3 *supra*.

[35] Potucek v. Cordeleria Lourdes, 310 F.2d 527 (10th Cir. 1962) (buyer "either knew or should have known" that seller was mistaken as to its identity).

[36] Moore v. Furstenwerth-Uhl Jewelry Co., 87 S.E. 1097 (Ga. App. 1916) (seller shipped goods on credit to insolvent buyer, mistakenly believing him to be person of good financial standing).

[37] Tyra v. Cheney, *supra* note 23 ("There was a failure to enter a binding contract.").

[38] See the discussion of three requirements in §9.3 *supra*.

[39] Goodrich v. Lathrop, 29 P. 329 (Cal. 1892) ("the fact that the market value of the property [returned by the vendee] may have depreciated while out of the possession of the vendor" does not prevent avoidance by the vendee).

[40] For example, in the case where the bidder has performed under a mistaken bid, restitution is allowed, subject to a limit imposed by the next lowest bid. Tyra v. Cheney, *supra* note 23 (bidder received reasonable value of repairs done).

[41] Chernick v. United States, *supra* note 25 (bidder could not avoid since the "eggs could not be unscrambled," but was entitled to a price based on "conjecture" as to what bidder would have received had there been no mistake).

when the party by his own contract creates a duty or charge upon himself, he is bound to make it good, if he may, notwithstanding any accident by inevitable necessity, because he might have provided against it by his contract. And therefore if the lessee covenant to repair a house, though it be burnt by lightning, or thrown down by enemies, yet he ought to repair it.[1]

The same court, however, had already admitted three important exceptions to this strict view that impossibility is no excuse.

Supervening illegality

The first of these exceptions can be traced back to an even earlier case, in which the Court of King's Bench said that if a seller undertakes to deliver wheat by a stated day in a foreign country and before that day performance is made illegal by statute, the seller's duty is discharged.[2] It subsequently became established that if supervening governmental action prevents a party's performance by prohibiting it or imposing requirements that make it impossible, that party is excused.[3] The supervening governmental action need not be a statute; it may, for example, be an administrative or judicial order.[4] The fact that the party can still perform if willing to break the law and take the consequences does not prevent discharge, nor does the fact that the governmental action may prove to be invalid, as long as the party that claims discharge acts in good faith.[5] The action must, however, directly affect that party's performance, so that the party cannot both comply with it and perform. It is not enough for the action merely to make performance somewhat more difficult by, for example, aggravating a shortage of supply.[6]

Supervening death or disability

The second exception to the strict view that impossibility is no excuse was announced by Queen's Bench in the sixteenth century. In dictum, that court stated that if a contract requires performance by the promisor, no action will lie for its breach if the promisor dies before performing.[7] It later became accepted that if a particular person's existence is necessary for performance of a duty, and performance is prevented by that person's death or disability, the duty is

§9.5   [1] Paradine v. Jane, 82 Eng. Rep. 897, 897 (K.B. 1647). That case arose, the court said, when a lessee sought to be excused from paying rent because a "German prince, by name Prince Rupert, an alien born, enemy to the King and kingdom," ousted him from the land, so that he could not take income from it, but it did not involve impossibility because he could still have paid the rent. See the discussion of impracticability distinguished in §9.7 *infra*.

[2] Abbot of Westminster v. Clerke, 73 Eng. Rep. 59, 63 (K.B. 1536).

[3] Louisville & N.R.R. v. Mottley, 219 U.S. 467 (1911) (railroad's duty to issue passes discharged when federal law prohibited common carriers from doing so). *See* Restatement Second §264.

[4] Kuhl v. School Dist. No. 76, 51 N.W.2d 746 (Neb. 1952) (school district's duty to employ teachers discharged when court injunction closed school).

[5] UCC 2-615(a) ("compliance in good faith with any applicable foreign or domestic governmental regulation or order whether or not it later proves to be invalid").

[6] City of Starkville v. 4-County Elec. Power Assn., 819 So. 2d 1216 (Miss. 2002) (legislature's revocation of unqualified power of eminent domain over public utilities did not make city's performance impracticable). See the discussion of the focus on increased burden in §9.6 *infra*.

[7] Hyde v. Dean of Windsor, 78 Eng. Rep. 798 (Q.B. 1597).

discharged.[8] The person in question is usually the one who owes the duty but may also be the one to whom the duty is owed or a third person. However, the typical bilateral contract does not require the existence of the party that is to receive the performance. "The promise of a painter to paint a landscape is discharged by his physical inability to paint, but the death or illness of one who has contracted to buy the painting will not free his estate from liability."[9] Whether the existence of a particular person is necessary for performance may be determined by the agreement itself; it may, for instance, expressly call for a personal service. If, as often happens, the agreement is silent, a court must resort to the circumstances to determine whether performance, as understood by the parties at the time of agreement, involves enough personal service or discretion to require the existence of a particular person.[10] The services of a portrait painter are clearly personal, and the portrait painter is therefore excused if prevented by illness or death from painting the portrait. The services of a house painter, on the other hand, are usually not personal, and the house painter is therefore not excused by illness or death. If a party can delegate a duty to perform to another, the party's own death or incapacity will not be an excuse.[11]

Supervening destruction

The third exception to the strict rule that impossibility is no excuse was laid down by King's Bench in the seventeenth century. The court held that a bailee's duty to return a horse was discharged when, without the bailee's fault, the horse died, because "that is become impossible by the act of God."[12] The rule came to be that if the existence of a particular thing is necessary for a party's performance, the party is excused if the destruction or deterioration of that thing prevents performance.[13] This rule was confirmed and elaborated in the celebrated case of *Taylor v. Caldwell*, the fountainhead of the modern law of impossibility.

Taylor v. Caldwell

That case arose out of a contract under which Taylor was to have the use of Caldwell's music hall for performances on four days, in return for payment of £100 at the close of each day. When the hall was accidentally destroyed by fire less than a week before the first performance, Taylor sued Caldwell

---

[8] Mullen v. Wafer, 480 S.W.2d 332 (Ark. 1972) (duty of seller of accounting business to assist buyer for two years was discharged when seller died). *See* Restatement Second §262.

[9] 3 S. Williston, Contracts §1941 (1st ed. 1920).

[10] *See* Cazares v. Saenz, 256 Cal. Rptr. 209 (Ct. App. 1989) (rule "not limited to the death or incapacity of a *party* to the contract").

[11] As to whether a duty is delegable, see the discussion of test of delegability in §11.10 *infra*. Compare the discussion of lost volume in §12.10 *infra*.

[12] Williams v. Lloyd, 82 Eng. Rep. 95 (K.B. 1629) ("ceo est deveigne impossible per act de Dieu").

[13] *See* Restatement Second §263. The result is the same if the thing does not come into existence, as in the crop failure cases discussed later in this section. As to the possibility that the lessor of a building may be under a duty to the lessee to rebuild after a fire, *see* Marcovich Land Corp. v. J.J. Newberry Co., 413 N.E.2d 935 (Ind. App. 1980) (25-year lease to variety store).

for breach of contract, claiming as damages the expenses he had incurred in preparing for the performances. The Court of King's Bench held, however, that Caldwell was excused because, "looking at the whole contract, we find that the parties contracted on the basis of the continued existence of the Music Hall at the time when the concerts were to be given; that being essential to their performance."[14] Whether a particular thing is necessary for performance is a question much like whether a particular person is necessary for performance, and the answer depends on all the circumstances. A clear case is dealt with in the Uniform Commercial Code, which excuses the seller from its duty to deliver if "the contract requires for its performance goods identified before the contract is made, and the goods suffer casualty without fault of either party before the risk of loss passes to the buyer."[15] More interesting questions are raised by the repair cases and the crop-failure cases.

Repair cases   In the typical repair case, a contractor claims to be excused from completing the repairs on a building because it has been destroyed. Under the general rule, a builder that promises to erect a building is still bound to do so, even though the nearly completed structure has been destroyed by forces beyond the builder's control.[16] The builder that does not pursue performance to completion is liable not only for the progress payments received but also for any damages that the owner can prove for loss of expectation.[17] However, if the builder is not to erect a new building, but is to do repairs or other work on an existing building, the result is different. In this situation, the existence of the building is regarded as necessary for performance — "the agreement on both sides is upon the implied condition that the . . . building shall continue in existence, and the destruction

---

[14]122 Eng. Rep. 309, 314 (K.B. 1863).

[15]UCC 2-613. Once the risk of loss passes to the buyer, the buyer must pay the price, even though the goods have been destroyed. UCC 2-709(1)(a). Consequently, if goods are identified when the contract is made and are destroyed before risk passes, the seller is not liable in damages for breach of contract because excused, but the seller cannot recover the price; if the goods are destroyed after risk passes, the seller is not liable in damages because of having performed, and the seller can recover the price. Risk passes at a time determined by UCC 2-509, 2-510, most commonly at the receipt of the goods by the buyer.

Similar consequences follow from the passage of risk of loss under a contract for the sale of land, where the traditional rule is that risk passes to the purchaser, as the equitable owner, when the contract is made.

[16]Hartford Fire Ins. Co. v. Riefolo Constr. Co., 410 A.2d 658 (N.J. 1980) (by placing risk on builder until building was "accepted" by school board, parties adopted general rule that "risk of loss during construction rests with the builder, assuming the owner to be free from fault").

[17]The apparent harshness of the result is mitigated in practice by the use of insurance covering the builder's interest. *See* Baker v. Aetna Ins. Co., 262 S.E.2d 417 (S.C. 1980) (builder's insurer not liable to builder where risk had passed to owner on completion). *See also* R. Posner, Economic Analysis of Law 108 (6th ed. 2003) ("contractor is generally better placed for fire protection than the owner, because he controls the premises and is knowledgeable about the fire hazards of the buildings under construction [and] is probably the cheaper insurer as well, being in a better position than the owner to estimate the likelihood and consequences of fire at the various stages of the construction"). This probably explains the dearth of such cases since the nineteenth century.

of it without the fault of either of the parties will excuse performance of the contract."[18] The destruction of the building discharges the builder's duty, under the principle of *Taylor v. Caldwell*. This reasoning in the repair cases has been extended to the situation in which the owner is to furnish some of the materials and labor for a new building to be erected[19] and to the common situation in which the owner or a general contractor engages a specialized contractor to work on a building in the course of its construction.[20]

In the typical crop-failure case, a farmer claims to be excused from delivering a stated quantity of, say, grain because the farmer's crop has failed. A farmer that undertook to deliver a stated quantity of grain without regard to where it was grown is not excused; such a farmer is expected to procure the grain elsewhere.[21] But a farmer that undertook to deliver a stated quantity of grain from the farmer's own land is excused; such a farmer's duty is discharged under the principle of *Taylor v. Caldwell*.[22] However, it is often difficult for a court to tell whether a farmer's undertaking is limited to the farmer's own crop. Sometimes courts have relied on the absolute language of the agreement and have refused to excuse the farmer.[23] Sometimes they have looked to such circumstances as the buyer's inspection of the seller's farm before the making of the contract and have excused the farmer.[24] It has been suggested that a court is less likely to excuse a seller that is not a farmer but a dealer and that therefore is "in a position to spread the risk of a single crop failure among his customers."[25]

Crop-failure cases

When a court excuses a party on the ground of impossibility, it is supplying a term to deal with an omitted case, to fill a gap. But because the language of the promise in question is absolute and admits of no excuse, it is far from obvious that anything has been omitted, that there is any gap to fill. For this reason, courts have often rationalized excuse on grounds of impossibility by saying that

Supplying a term

---

[18] Butterfield v. Byron, 27 N.E. 667, 667 (Mass. 1891).

[19] Butterfield v. Byron, *supra* note 18.

[20] Acme Plumbing & Heating Co. v. Hirsch, 236 N.W. 137 (Neb. 1931) (plumbing contractor excused when building burned).

[21] Conagra v. Bartlett Partnership, 540 N.W.2d 333 (Neb. 1995) (farming operation not excused by hailstorm damage to corn where "contracts did not identify the corn in any other than by kind and amount" or "make any reference to corn grown or to be grown . . . on any identified acreage").

[22] The farmer can avoid the problem entirely by making an output contract, undertaking to sell the crop actually grown on the farmer's land, perhaps with a recital of its estimated size. See the discussion of examples of qualified duties in §9.1 *supra*. Whether the farmer has done so may be a question of interpretation.

[23] Bunge Corp. v. Recker, 519 F.2d 449 (8th Cir. 1975) ("attempt to show that the 10,000 bushels of beans were to be produced on an identified acreage flies in the face of the agreement," which warranted that the beans would be grown within the continental United States).

[24] Unke v. Thorpe, 59 N.W.2d 419 (S.D. 1953) (where contract was made after buyer visited seller's ranch and watched threshing, "the parties contracted for the delivery of 600 to 800 bushels of a specific crop of alfalfa").

[25] Note, 53 Colum. L. Rev. 94, 102 (1953).

it is an "implied condition" of the duty that performance remain possible. Thus, in *Taylor v. Caldwell*, the court spoke of "an implied condition that the parties shall be excused in case, before breach, performance becomes impossible from the perishing of the thing," which would "further the great object of making the legal construction such as to fulfil the intention of those who entered into the contract."[26] However, basing an implied condition on imputed intention is difficult to justify. As a Scottish judge commented much later, "It does seem to me somewhat far-fetched to hold that the non-occurrence of some event, which was not within the contemplation or even the imagination of the parties, was an implied term of the contract."[27] It would be more candid for courts to admit that the resolution of a claim of excuse on the ground of impossibility involves the same two-step process that is employed whenever a court is asked to supply a term to deal with a case that is allegedly not covered by the agreement. The first step is that of interpretation to determine whether the absolute language of the undertaking covers the exceptional case at hand; and if it is determined that it does not, the second step is that of implication to supply a term to govern the case.[28]

We now look at a modern synthesis of the law of impossibility.

Code synthesis   · **§9.6.   A New Synthesis: The Doctrine of Impracticability.** The common law development just described is synthesized in UCC 2-615, Excuse by Failure of Presupposed Conditions. Under that section, except so far as a seller has assumed a greater obligation, delay in performance, in whole or in part, is not a breach of the seller's duty

> if performance as agreed has been made impracticable by the occurrence of a contingency the non-occurrence of which was a basic assumption on which the contract was made.[1]

Despite the possible negative inference that might be drawn from the first dozen words, this is a default rule and is often changed by an express provision — commonly called a *force majeure* clause — excusing the seller in situations not covered by the Code.[2] Nevertheless, the Code's synthesis,

---

[26] 122 Eng. Rep. at 312.

[27] Lord Sands in Scott & Sons v. Del Sel, [1922] Sess. Cas. 592, 596-97 (1922) (Scot.), aff'd, [1923] Sess. Cas. 37 (H.L. 1923).

[28] See §7.16 *supra*.

§9.6   [1] This section of the Code is one of four on impracticability. The others deal with casualty to identified goods (UCC 2-613), substituted performance (UCC 2-614), and procedure on notice claiming excuse (UCC 2-616).

[2] There is no doubt that the parties can enlarge on the excuses provided for in UCC 2-615. Eastern Air Lines v. McDonnell Douglas Corp., 532 F.2d 957 (5th Cir. 1976) (concern about this "is ill-founded," though [fn.96] "there is a point beyond which any such agreement may not go").

designed for the sale of goods, has already had a substantial influence on the law of contract generally and has been adapted by the Restatement Second.[3]

The basis of the new synthesis is far removed from the reasoning in *Taylor v. Caldwell*.[4] As a federal judge pointed out, "The doctrine of impossibility of performance has gradually been freed from the earlier fictional and unrealistic strictures of such tests as the 'implied term' and the parties' 'contemplation.' "[5] The new synthesis candidly recognizes that the judicial function is to determine whether, in the light of exceptional circumstances, justice requires a departure from the general rule that a promisor bears the risk of increased difficulty of performance. However, the Code formulation does not include the word *risk*, and Judge Henry Friendly faulted its language as a "somewhat complicated way of putting [the] question of how much risk the promisor assumed."[6] Nevertheless, the Code formulation is preferable to the alternative, suggested facetiously, of praying for the "wisdom of Solomon."[7]

Basis of synthesis

Under the new synthesis, the party that claims that a supervening event or "contingency" prevented performance must meet four requirements.[8] First, the event must have made "performance as agreed . . . impracticable." Second, the nonoccurrence of the event must have been "a basic assumption on which the contract was made." Third, the impracticability must have resulted without the fault of the party seeking to be excused.[9] Fourth, that party must not have assumed a greater obligation than the law imposes.[10] Although these

Four requirements

---

[3]Restatement Second §261.

[4]122 Eng. Rep. 309 (K.B. 1863), discussed in §9.5 *supra*.

[5]Transatlantic Fin. Corp. v. United States, 363 F.2d 312, 315 (D.C. Cir. 1966) (Skelly Wright, J.).

[6]United States v. Wegematic Corp., 360 F.2d 674, 676 (2d Cir. 1966).

[7]American Trading & Prod. Corp. v. Shell Intl. Marine, 453 F.2d 939, 944 (2d Cir. 1972) (quoting Corbin).

[8]Comment 4 to UCC 2-615, quoted later in this section, suggests that the seller must be able to point to a particular "contingency" that has caused the impracticability. Restatement Second §261 speaks of an "event," while UCC 2-615 speaks of a "contingency," but no difference in meaning seems to have been intended. No event is required for existing, as distinguished from supervening, impracticability. See the discussion of an event existing at the time of agreement in §9.8 *infra*.

[9]This rather obvious requirement appears in Restatement Second §261 but not in UCC 2-615, although presumably it should be read in. It appears in UCC 2-613, which requires that "the goods suffer casualty without fault of either party." *But cf.* United States v. Winstar Corp., 518 U.S. 839 (1996) (Souter, J., plurality opinion: describing sovereign act doctrine, which excuses federal government if it makes its own performance of a contract impracticable by legislation that is "public and general," as exception to principle that excuse "is traditionally unavailable where the barrier to performance arises from the act of the party seeking the discharge").

[10]Restatement Second §261 expresses this with the phrase "unless the language or the circumstances indicate the contrary."

1. Performance impracticable

requirements involve questions of fact, courts have sometimes been reluctant to entrust the granting of excuse on this ground to a jury.[11]

The first requirement for excuse is that the occurrence of the event must have made "performance as agreed . . . impracticable." It is important to bear in mind that since it is a party's "performance as agreed" that must become impracticable before the party will be excused, the first step is to determine what is the agreed performance.[12] If the agreement gives a party a choice between alternative ways of performing, the fact that one of these alternatives becomes impracticable will not excuse the party if another remains open, because the agreed performance has not become impracticable.[13] This was, for example, the courts' conclusion in the Suez cases, in which ocean carriers argued that they were excused by the closing of the Suez Canal, which forced them to use the longer and more costly route around the Cape of Good Hope. Courts reasoned that carriage through the Suez Canal and carriage around the Cape of Good Hope were alternative ways of performing.[14] However, courts do not apply this principle if a party is given an alternative that is not "performance." For example, a party that undertakes to perform or pay liquidated damages is not regarded as having a choice between alternative performances.[15] Courts have also been reluctant to excuse a party when, in the language of the Code commentary, the "impossibility of performance arises in connection with an incidental matter [and does not go] to the very heart of the agreement."[16] In such a case, a party is usually expected to take

[11] See Restatement Second, Introductory Note to Chapter 11 ("question is generally considered to be one of law rather than fact") and the discussion of the Restatement Second synthesis in §9.7 infra. Contra: Opera Co. v. Wolf Trap Found., 817 F.2d 1094 (4th Cir. 1987) (whether event was so likely that "obligor should have guarded against it or provided for non-liability" was "question to be resolved by the trial judge"); Mishara Constr. Co. v. Transit-Mixed Concrete Corp., 310 N.E.2d 363 (Mass. 1974) (questions of impracticability and basic assumption were for jury).

[12] Florida Power & Light Co. v. Westinghouse Elec. Corp., 826 F.2d 239 (4th Cir. 1987) (first step is to ascertain "exact act or thing" promised and "means whereby the parties contemplated performance").

[13] In the crop-failure cases, for example, if the court concludes that the crop from a particular farm was not contemplated, delivery of other goods is an alternative performance. See the discussion of the crop-failure cases in §9.5 supra. But see International Paper Co. v. Rockefeller, 146 N.Y.S. 371 (App. Div. 1914) (seller excused where "source from which the parties contemplated the wood should be furnished" was destroyed by fire, and court "need not say that [he] could not have furnished live wood of equal quality from other lands"). This case is cited in the discussion of anomalous cases in §9.7 infra.

[14] American Trading & Prod. Corp. v. Shell Intl. Marine, supra note 7 (court refused to find "that the parties contemplated or agreed that the Suez passage was to be the exclusive method of performance" although freight rate was based on passage through Suez Canal); Transatlantic Fin. Corp. v. United States, supra note 5 ("the Cape route is generally regarded as an alternative means of performance").

[15] See the discussions of alternative performances and premiums in §12.18 infra.

[16] UCC 2-614 cmt. 1.

advantage of whatever substitute arrangements are available for performance by, for example, finding other means for loading, carrying, or delivering the goods.[17]

In contrast to the rules for mutual mistake, which invite a court to consider the effect on both parties to the exchange, <u>here the focus is on the increased burden on the party that is to perform</u>.[18] The use of *impracticable*, rather than *impossible*, to describe that burden is not an innovation of the Code; courts did not insist on strict impossibility even under the traditional analysis.[19] They recognized, for example, that one's mere apprehension of illness, unaccompanied by actual disability, might excuse one from rendering personal services,[20] and that one's fear of exposing other persons or property to danger might excuse one from performing.[21] Of course, one is expected to exert reasonable efforts to eliminate the impediment to one's performance.[22]

Focus on increased burden

Does this mean that a court may excuse a party merely because its performance has become more expensive? The Code commentary gives an ambivalent answer:

Additional expense

> Increased cost alone does <u>not</u> excuse performance unless the rise in cost is due to some unforeseen contingency which alters the essential nature of the performance. Neither is a rise or a collapse in the market in itself a justification, for that is exactly the type of business risk which business contracts made at fixed prices are intended to cover. But a severe shortage of raw materials or of supplies due to a contingency such as war, embargo, local crop failure, unforeseen shutdown of major sources of supply or the like, which either causes a marked increase in cost or altogether prevents the seller from securing supplies necessary to his performance, is within the contemplation of this section.[23]

---

[17]UCC 2-614(1) (if "the agreed berthing, loading or unloading facilities fail or an agreed type of carrier becomes unavailable or the agreed manner of delivery otherwise becomes commercially impracticable but a commercially reasonable substitute is available, such substitute performance must be tendered and accepted").

[18]See the discussion of showing materiality in §9.3 *supra.*

[19]Impracticability was used in the first Restatement §454 ("impossibility means not only strict impossibility but impracticability"). Williston used it in his first edition. 3 S. Williston, Contracts §1963 (1st ed. 1920) ("not obtainable except by means and with an expense impracticable in a business sense").

[20]Wasserman Theatrical Enter. v. Harris, 77 A.2d 329 (Conn. 1950) (actor's "apprehension that he could not go on with the show" because of tickling in and tightening of throat "was reasonable and reasonably justified [him] in cancelling the performance").

[21]The Kronprinzessin Cecilie, 244 U.S. 12 (1917) (owner of German steamship excused from completing voyage from United States to England by apprehension on eve of World War I that she would be seized as prize).

[22]Pennsylvania State Shopping Plazas v. Olive, 120 S.E.2d 372 (Va. 1961) (developer failed to file formal application for building permit or zoning variance).

[23]UCC 2-615 cmt. 4. *See* Restatement Second §261 cmt. *d.*

Thus far, courts have only occasionally held that a duty is discharged on the ground of mere increase in the expense of performing it.[24] They have generally concluded that the additional expense, even if traceable to an identifiable supervening event, does not rise to the level of impracticability.[25]

Examples of additional expense

For example, in a series of cases in the federal courts, manufacturers that have contracted with the government to produce a product by means of a technological breakthrough have been unsuccessful in arguing that they are excused when technological difficulties have resulted in unexpectedly heavy costs. The federal courts have repeatedly held that the additional expense does not make performance impracticable.[26] Similarly, in the Suez cases, ocean carriers were unsuccessful in arguing that they were excused by the additional expense of going around the Cape of Good Hope. Courts consistently concluded that this expense did not make performance impracticable.[27]

2. Basic assumption

The second requirement for excuse is that the nonoccurrence of the event must have been "a basic assumption on which the contract was made." The commentary to the Restatement Second amplifies this:

> Determining whether the non-occurrence of a particular event was or was not a basic assumption involves a judgment as to which party assumed the risk of its occurrence. In contracting for the manufacture and delivery of goods at a price fixed in the contract, for example, the seller assumes the risk of increased costs within the normal range. If, however, a disaster results in an abrupt tenfold increase in cost to the seller, a court might determine that the seller did not assume this risk by concluding that the non-occurrence of the disaster was a "basic assumption" on which the contract was made.[28]

---

[24]Florida Power & Light Co. Westinghouse Elec. Corp., *supra* note 12 (difference in cost of disposing of spent fuel is "percentages in the hundreds range" and use of alternative method would not only "wipe out the expected profit but [result] in a loss some four or five times the expected profit"). See the discussion of subjective and objective impracticability *infra*.

[25]Karl Wendt Farm Equip. Co. v. International Harvester Co., 931 F.2d 1112 (6th Cir. 1991) ("fact that [manufacturer] experienced a dramatic downturn in the farm equipment market and decided to go out of the business does not excuse its unilateral termination of its dealership agreements due to impracticability").

[26]United States v. Wegematic Corp., *supra* note 6 ("evidence of true impracticability was far from compelling [since expense] must be appraised in relation not to the single computer ordered by the [government], evidently for a bargain price, but to the entire . . . program as originally contemplated"). See the discussions of a greater obligation not assumed *infra* and of the technological breakthrough cases in §9.8 *infra*.

[27]American Trading & Prod. Corp. v. Shell Intl. Marine, *supra* note 7 ("increase of less than one third" over agreed price "is not sufficient to constitute commercial impracticability, under either American or English authority"); Transatlantic Fin. Corp. v. United States, *supra* note 5 ("While it may be an overstatement to say that increased cost and difficulty of performance never constitute impracticability, to justify relief there must be more of a variation . . . than is present in this case . . . ," i.e., under 15 percent of the contract price).

[28]Restatement Second, Chapter 11, Introductory Note.

The assumption may be tacit; a party may be said to have an assumption even though the party is not conscious of alternatives, as one who walks into a room may assume that it has a floor without giving thought to the matter.[29] But the assumption must be shared by both parties; no account is taken of one party's purely private assumptions.

Cases in which courts have traditionally excused promisors on grounds of impossibility can be grouped into three categories according to the basic assumptions involved.[30] First, parties ordinarily assume that the government will not directly intervene and prevent performance. Second, they ordinarily assume that a person who is necessary for performance will neither die nor be deprived of the necessary capacity before the time for performance.[31] Third, they ordinarily assume that a thing that is necessary for performance will remain in existence and in such condition that performance can take place. Nearly all of the cases of impracticability that have arisen can be placed in one of these three traditional categories. However, other assumptions may also be considered "basic," in line with the tendency toward liberality in excusing promisors on the occurrence of extraordinary events.[32]

Examples of basic assumption

In determining what assumptions the parties made, a court should look at all relevant circumstances. Some courts have held that if the agreement is completely integrated, the parol evidence rule bars extrinsic evidence to show the assumptions of the parties.[33] However, as already noted, there is no reason why such evidence should not be admitted for the limited purpose of showing circumstances that would justify the court in supplying a term.[34] The better view allows such evidence to show, for example, an assumption that a particular source of supply would be in existence at the time for performance.[35]

Parol evidence rule

---

[29] Hillside Assocs. of Hollis v. Maine Bonding & Cas. Co., 605 A.2d 1026 (N.H. 1992) ("the more basic the assumption, the less likely it is that the assumption will be articulated").

[30] See the discussions of supervening illegality, of supervening death or disability, and of supervening destruction in §9.5 *supra*. In the Restatement Second, a general statement of the rule on impracticability (§261) is followed by sections on each of these three categories (§§262, 263, 264).

[31] As to confiscation by the government, *see* Jones, Confiscation: A Rationale of the Law of Takings, 24 Hofstra L. Rev. 1, 26 (1995) (no taking occurs when "contracting parties are presumed to be aware of [doctrines of impracticability and frustration] and proceed with forewarning that contractual expectations may be disappointed if the actions of the government intervene").

[32] The situation in which a labor dispute makes performance impracticable is one in which the basic assumption does not seem to fit within any of the three categories. See *infra* note 49.

[33] Bunge Corp. v. Recker, 519 F.2d 449 (8th Cir. 1975) ("To permit the introduction of parol evidence to show that the beans were to be grown on a particular acreage would completely circumvent" UCC 2-202).

[34] See the discussion of the parol evidence rule in §7.16 *supra*. See also the discussions of supervening death or disability and of the crop-failure cases in §9.5 *supra*.

[35] Campbell v. Hostetter Farms, 380 A.2d 463 (Pa. Super. 1977) (in interpreting memoranda to determine whether they called for yield from specific farms, "it is not a prerequisite to the admissibility of testimony under [UCC 2-202] that the wording of the contracts be ambiguous").

3. Not fault of promisor

The third requirement for excuse is that the impracticability must have resulted without the fault of the party seeking to be excused.[36] For example, a seller that is unable to deliver goods because they have been destroyed due to the seller's negligence is not excused.[37] Neither is a party excused if unable to perform personal services because of a disability resulting from the party's own misconduct.[38] However, since it is often difficult to foresee the effect of a party's conduct on the ability to perform, the fault must be clear if it is to prevent excuse.[39]

4. Greater obligation not assumed

The fourth requirement for excuse is that the party must not have assumed a greater obligation than the law imposes. If a party expressly undertakes to perform, even though performance becomes impracticable, impracticability will not be an excuse, and the party will be liable for damages for nonperformance.[40] Even absent an express assumption of a greater obligation, a court may find, by negative implication from a clause excusing a party on the occurrence of some specified events, that the party assumed the risk of some other event.[41] Furthermore, the surrounding circumstances will sometimes justify an inference that a party assumed the risk of impracticability.[42] For example, a manufacturer that has contracted with the government to produce a product by means of a technological breakthrough has generally been held to have assumed the risk that achieving it may be impracticable.[43] If a product is to be manufactured in accordance with specifications furnished by the government, however, courts

[36]Taylor-Edwards Warehouse & Transfer Co. v. Burlington Northern, 715 F.2d 1330 (9th Cir. 1983) ("particularly chary of applying the defense of impossibility to relieve [railroad] of its obligation here, where the expense inherent in performance primarily resulted from [its] own decision to abandon the main rail line").

[37]UCC 2-613 & cmt. 1 ("'Fault' is intended to include negligence and not merely wilful wrong.").

[38]Handicapped Children's Educ. Bd. v. Lukaszewski, 332 N.W.2d 774 (Wis. 1983) ("any health danger associated with performance of the employment contract was the fault of [teacher], not the Board").

[39]CNA Intl. Reins. Co. v. Phoenix, 678 So. 2d 378 (Fla. App. 1996) (to hold that death of actor River Phoenix did not have effect of excuse because apparently drug-related "would create another case by case and hard to interpret rule of law").

[40]Gulf Oil Corp. v. F.P.C., 563 F.2d 588 (3d Cir. 1977) ("By warranting, rather than merely promising, the availability of sufficient quantities of gas, Gulf assumed for itself the entire risk that future conditions would raise the cost of gas.").

[41]Missouri Pub. Serv. Co. v. Peabody Coal Co., 583 S.W.2d 721 (Mo. App. 1979) (seller not excused by increased cost where contract contained escalator clause).

[42]Harper & Assocs. v. Printers, Inc., 730 P.2d 733 (Wash. App. 1986) ("potential problem was known and was discussed prior to the contract being made" and difficulties "were knowingly assumed"). The expertise of the party who seeks to be excused may be an important circumstance. Wills v. Shockley, 157 A.2d 252 (Del. 1960) (salvagor who "had many years of experience in the field of salvage" not excused).

[43]United States v. Wegematic Corp., *supra* note 6 ("no basis for thinking that when an electronics system is promoted by its manufacturer as a revolutionary breakthrough, the risk of the revolution's occurrence falls on the purchaser; the reasonable supposition is that it has already occurred or, at least, that the manufacturer is assuring the purchaser that it will be found to have

usually hold the government to an implied warranty that a satisfactory product will result if the specifications are followed. In that case the manufacturer is not liable if its failure is caused by a shortcoming in the specifications.[44]

It is sometimes said that if an event is foreseeable, a party that makes an unqualified promise to perform necessarily assumes an obligation to perform, even if the occurrence of the event makes performance impracticable.[45] Admittedly there are cases, as the Code commentary explains, "when the contingency in question is sufficiently foreshadowed at the time of contracting to be included among the business risks which are fairly to be regarded as part of the dickered terms."[46] For example, if governmental approval is required for a party's performance, the party may be taken to assume the risk that approval will be denied if there is no provision excusing the party in that event.[47] As Ellen Peters wrote for the Supreme Court of Connecticut in holding that a developer was not excused by a failure to obtain necessary financing, where "sophisticated contracting parties have negotiated termination provisions, courts should be slow to invent additional ways to excuse performance."[48] This reasoning may also explain why courts hesitate to excuse a party for impracticability resulting from labor disputes in the absence of an express provision to that effect.[49] But, as already suggested, a party may fail to provide for a risk, even though it is foreseeable, because the party does not consider it to be significant enough to make it a subject of bargaining or because the party regards its bargaining position as too weak to risk broaching the subject.[50] And the fact that a party foresees harm does not mean that that party has a superior capacity to avoid it. Although the foreseeability of the event will often be a factor that suggests that a promisor assumed the risk of its occurrence, it should not be conclusive

Effect of foreseeability

---

when the machine is assembled"). See *supra* note 26 and the discussion of the technological breakthrough cases in §9.8 *infra*.

[44] See the discussion of the scope of the duty in §7.17 *supra*.

[45] Rockland Indus. v. E+E (US) Inc., 991 F. Supp. 468 (D. Md.) (foreseeability is "key in commercial impracticality [sic] cases"), on reconsideration, 1 F. Supp. 528 (D. Md. 1998) (when "it is foreseeable that [agreed] sole source may fail, the risk of nondelivery is on the seller unless the seller includes exculpatory language").

[46] UCC 2-615 cmt. 8.

[47] Nebaco v. Riverview Realty Co., 482 P.2d 305 (Nev. 1971) (lessee, who knew banking administrator's permission was needed to make agreed investment in premises, took risk that administrator would not approve).

[48] Dills v. Town of Enfield, 557 A.2d 517, 525 (Conn. 1989).

[49] See Mishara Constr. Co. v. Transit-Mixed Concrete Corp., *supra* note 11 ("Certainly, in general, labor disputes cannot be considered extraordinary in the course of modern commerce. . . . Much must depend on the facts known to the parties at the time of contracting. . . . Where the probability of a labor dispute appears to be practically nil, and where the occurrence of such a dispute provides unusual difficulty, the excuse of impracticability might well be applicable.").

[50] L.N. Jackson & Co. v. Royal Norwegian Govt., 177 F.2d 694 (2d Cir. 1949) (court called attention to "the informal and incomplete form of the 'booking' agreement itself [which] obviously does not assume to set forth the obligations of the parties").

on that issue.[51] As the Fourth Circuit wisely concluded, it is not "the modern rule" that excuse is necessarily precluded "if the contingency that occurred was one that could have been foreseen." Instead, foreseeability

> is at best one fact to be considered in resolving first how likely the occurrence of the event in question was and, second, whether its occurrence, based on past experience, was of such reasonable likelihood that the obligor should not merely foresee the risk but, because of the degree of its likelihood, the obligor should have guarded against it or provided for non-liability against the risk.[52]

To put it differently, foreseeability is but one factor to be taken account of in determining the basic assumptions on which the contract was made.

Risks within party's control   A court may deduce, from the general principle that parties should be responsible for risks that are within their control, that a party should bear the risk of the occurrence of an event if the party could have shifted this risk to a third party by contract. On this reasoning, one may be held to have assumed a risk against which one could readily have protected oneself by procuring insurance. For a more complex example, consider a wholesaler that contracts to sell goods obtained from a particular supplier. The wholesaler can easily make a second contract with that supplier to obtain the goods. This will not shift to the supplier the risk of a loss of production because of fire or some other disaster, since, under any ordinary contract between the wholesaler and the supplier, the supplier would be excused on the ground of impracticability. Therefore, in the event of such a loss the wholesaler should be excused from delivering, whether it has made a contract with the supplier or not.[53] This reasoning does not apply in the case of a cut in production by the supplier, however, since that risk can ordinarily be shifted by the wholesaler's contract with the supplier. In this event, then, it would seem that the wholesaler should not be excused.[54] Nevertheless, the commentary to UCC 2-615 suggests that in "case of failure of production by an agreed source for causes beyond the seller's control, the seller should, if possible, be excused" on the condition that the seller turn over to the buyer "his rights against the defaulting source of supply to the extent of the buyer's contract in relation to which excuse is being claimed."[55]

Subjective and objective impracticability   It is sometimes said that, while a party may be excused on the ground of "objective" impossibility ("the thing cannot be done"), the party will not be

[51] See the discussion of the effect of foreseeability in §9.7 *infra*.

[52] Opera Co. v. Wolf Trap Found., *supra* note 11, at 1102-03.

[53] UCC 2-615 cmt. 5 speaks of excuse when "a particular source of supply is exclusive . . . and fails through *casualty*," adding that excuse is conditional on the seller having "employed all due measures to assure himself that his source will not fail."

[54] Lambert v. City of Columbus, 496 N.W.2d 540 (Neb. 1993) ("partial failure of a seller's source of supply has generally 'been treated as a foreseeable contingency, the risk of which is allocated to the seller absent a specific provision to the contrary in the contract' ").

[55] UCC 2-615 cmt. 5.

excused on the ground of "subjective" impossibility ("I cannot do it").[56] Financial inability is commonly cited as an example of subjective impossibility.[57] Under the new synthesis, however, it seems preferable to say that such risks as these are generally considered to be sufficiently within the control of one party that they are assumed by that party.[58]

Transactions that fall under the Vienna Convention are governed not by UCC 2-615 but by article 79 of the Convention, which appears under the heading "exemptions." According to the first paragraph of that article:

Vienna Convention

> A party is not liable for a failure to perform any of his obligations if he proves that the failure was due to an impediment beyond his control and that he could not reasonably be expected to have taken the impediment into account at the time of the conclusion of the contract or to have avoided or overcome it or its consequences.

The article goes on to state a rule for excuse in cases of a party's failure to perform due to "failure to perform by a third person whom he has engaged to perform the whole or part of the contract."[59] It lays down rules for notification. And it concludes by stating that it does not prevent "either party from exercising any right other than to claim damages," such as a right to restitution.[60] It has been suggested that the article, an awkward compromise between common law and civil law views, exhibits a "superficial harmony which merely mutes a deeper discord."[61] Nevertheless, the comparable provision of the UNIDROIT Principles incorporates much of its language.[62]

From impracticability of performance we turn to the closely related subject of frustration of purpose.

---

[56] B's Co. v. B.P. Barber & Assocs., 391 F.2d 130 (4th Cir. 1968) ("subjective impossibility, that is, impossibility which is personal to the promisor and does not inhere in the nature of the act to be performed, does not excuse nonperformance").

[57] Christy v. Pilkinton, 273 S.W.2d 533 (Ark. 1954) ("subjective impossibility — 'I cannot do it' . . . is well illustrated by a promisor's financial inability to pay"). *See* Restatement Second §261 cmt. *b* ("continuation of existing market conditions and of the financial situation of the parties are ordinarily not [basic] assumptions, so that mere market shifts or financial inability do not usually effect discharge").

[58] *See* Restatement Second §261 cmt. *e* (Restatement Second does not use the terms *objective* and *subjective*, but relies on rationale "that a party generally assumes the risk of his own inability to perform his duty").

[59] It has been suggested that, because of its legislative history, this provision should be given a "narrow scope" to exclude general suppliers as distinguished from subcontractors. *See* J. Honnold, Uniform Law for International Sales Under the 1980 U.N. Convention §434 (3d ed. 1999). The UNIDROIT Principles contain no comparable provision.

[60] Under article 81(2) each party is entitled to restitution of whatever it "has supplied or paid under the contract."

[61] Nicholas, *Force Majeure* and Frustration, 27 Am. J. Comp. L. 231, 231 (1979).

[62] UNIDROIT Principles art. 7.1.7.

§9.7.   Frustration of Purpose. The fountainhead of the doctrine of frustration of purpose is the English case of *Krell v. Henry*.[1] In 1902, when King Edward VII succeeded Queen Victoria, Britons awaited their first coronation in more than 60 years. Henry saw in the window of Krell's flat an announcement of windows to be let to view the coronation processions. He arranged with Krell's housekeeper to take the suite for the daytime of June 26 and 27 for £75, of which £25 was paid in advance. On June 22, the House of Commons was informed that the King had been required to undergo an operation for appendicitis, and the coronation was indefinitely postponed. Henry refused to pay the balance of £50, and Krell sued in what became the most noted of the coronation cases.[2] The Court of Appeal held for Henry on the ground that his duty to pay had been discharged because "the coronation procession was the foundation of this contract, and . . . the object of the contract was frustrated by the non-happening of the coronation and its procession on the days proclaimed."[3]

The doctrine announced in *Krell v. Henry* has come to be known as that of frustration of purpose. Cancellation of the procession did not make performance by either party impracticable; it did not prevent Krell from letting Henry use his rooms or Henry from paying Krell the £50. Rather, its effect was to deprive one party entirely of the benefit he expected from the other's performance, since it made the use of Krell's rooms during the period for which they were let virtually worthless to Henry. In general, the doctrine of impracticability of performance operates to the advantage of parties that are bound to furnish goods, land, services, or some similar performance, while the doctrine of frustration of purpose operates to the advantage of parties that are to pay money in return for those performances.[4]

The doctrine of frustration has been generally accepted by American courts.[5] Although the doctrine is not explicitly recognized by the Uniform Commercial

---

§9.7   [1][1903] 2 K.B. 740 (C.A.).

[2]Other noted coronation cases that arose out of the hiring of rooms are Chandler v. Webster, [1904] 1 K.B. 493, and Griffith v. Brymer, 19 T.L.R. 434 (K.B. 1903), treated in the discussion of existing frustration in §9.8 *infra*. For an argument that the circumstance that "the coronation events were only postponed, not cancelled, completely changed the complexion of the coronation cases," *see* Wladis, Common Law and Uncommon Events: The Development of the Doctrine of Impossibility of Performance in English Contract Law, 75 Geo. L.J. 1575, 1619 (1987).

[3][1903] 2 K.B. at 751, 754.

[4]This is in part because the doctrine of impracticability does not operate to discharge a duty to pay money merely because its performance has become impracticable. *See* the discussion of subjective and objective impracticability in §9.6 *supra*. In English law, impossibility is regarded as one example of a more broadly defined doctrine of frustration. *See generally* G. Treitel, Frustration and Force Majeure (1994).

[5]Chase Precast Corp. v. John J. Paonessa Co., 566 N.E.2d 603 (Mass. 1991) (general contractor excused under contract with subcontractor that was to provide median barriers when highway department decided not to install barriers). As to existing as distinguished from supervening frustration, see the discussion of existing frustration in §9.8 *infra*.

Code, there is little doubt that it is applicable to contracts for the sale of goods.[6] It has been incorporated in both the first and second Restatements.[7] It appears to be recognized by the exemption provision of the Vienna Convention, which applies to either party.[8]

The Restatement Second synthesis of the doctrine of frustration of purpose is strikingly similar to that of the doctrine of impracticability of performance.[9] The party that claims that a supervening event frustrated its purpose must meet four requirements, only the first of which is different from those for impracticability. First, the event must have "substantially frustrated" that party's "principal purpose." Second, it must have been "a basic assumption on which the contract was made" that the event would not occur.[10] Third, the frustration must have resulted without the fault of the party seeking to be excused.[11] Fourth, that party must not have assumed a greater obligation than the law imposes.[12] In applying the doctrine of frustration, as in applying that of impossibility, courts have sometimes been reluctant to entrust the granting of excuse on this ground to a jury.[13] Furthermore, despite the similarity of the requirements for the two doctrines, courts have been much more reluctant to hold that a party has been excused on the ground of frustration than on the ground of impracticability. Parties seeking excuse on this ground have found the first and

Restatement Second synthesis

---

[6]UCC 1-103(b) (unless displaced by the Code's particular provisions, "the principles of law and equity . . . supplement its provisions"). *See* Northern Ind. Pub. Serv. Co. v. Carbon County Coal Co., 799 F.2d 265 (7th Cir. 1986) (dictum: UCC 1-103 "is the basis on which [buyer] is able to plead frustration").

A number of courts have relied on a reference to buyers in UCC 2-615 cmt. 9 in concluding that the section applies to buyers, in spite of the fact that by its terms its text applies only to "a seller." This view may make it easier for buyers to meet the requirements for excuse than would the view that the Code is supplemented by the common law doctrine of frustration. It is, however, questionable as a matter of statutory interpretation in view of the use of "seller" in UCC 2-615, repeated in UCC-R 2-615 as a result of gender neutering.

[7]Restatement §288; Restatement Second §265. *See* Washington State Hop Producers v. Goschie Farms, 773 P.2d 70 (Wash. 1989) (adopting "Restatement (Second) . . . doctrine of supervening frustration").

[8]See the excerpt quoted in the discussion of the Vienna Convention in §9.6 *supra*.

[9]Compare Restatement Second §265 *with* §261. See the discussion of the four requirements in §9.6 *supra*.

[10]Groseth Intl. v. Tenneco, 410 N.W.2d 159 (S.D. 1987) ("continuation of existing market conditions and the financial situation of the parties are not ordinarily basic assumptions"), followed in Karl Wendt Farm Equip. Co. v. International Harvester Co., 931 F.2d 1112 (6th Cir. 1991) ("dramatic downturn in the farm equipment market resulting in reduced profitability did not frustrate the primary purpose of the agreement").

[11]Groseth Intl. v. Tenneco, *supra* note 10 (no excuse where "frustrating event was [franchisor's] decision to sell off its division assets and withdraw from the market"), followed in Karl Wendt Farm Equip. Co. v. International Harvester Co., *supra* note 10.

[12]Restatement Second §265 expresses this by the phrase "unless the language or the circumstances indicate the contrary."

[13]Groseth Intl. v. Tenneco, *supra* note 10 (frustration is "question of law, to be determined by the court"). As to impracticability, see the discussion of the four requirements in §9.6 *supra*.

fourth requirements particularly troublesome, and we shall consider these two in detail.

Frustration must be substantial

Under the first requirement, a party must show that its principal purpose in contracting has been substantially frustrated. Courts have raised two obstacles to a party's doing so. First, they have viewed the affected party's principal purpose in broad terms. The mere fact that some exceptional event has prevented a party from taking advantage of the transaction in the particular way expected may not suffice to satisfy the requirement of substantial frustration if the party can turn the bargain to its advantage in some other way. Second, courts have insisted that the frustration be nearly total. The mere fact that what was expected to be a profitable transaction has turned out to be a losing one is not enough.[14]

Example of *Swift Canadian v. Banet*

These two obstacles are illustrated by a Third Circuit case in which an American buyer of lamb pelts that were to be delivered in Toronto by a Canadian seller unsuccessfully urged frustration as an excuse when his planned importation of the pelts into the United States was prevented by the issuance of stricter import regulations. Although the contract itself indicated the buyer's intention to ship the pelts to Philadelphia, the court viewed the purpose of the agreement in much broader terms. According to Judge Goodrich, "the rest of the world was free to the buyer, so far as we know, as destination for the shipment."[15] Viewing the buyer's purpose as that of making any commercial disposition of the pelts, the court concluded that this purpose was not substantially frustrated, even though the buyer's "expectation of a profitable transaction was disappointed."[16]

Greater obligation not assumed

Under the fourth requirement, the party seeking to be excused on the ground of frustration must not have assumed a greater obligation than the law would impose. Even if a party can show that its principal purpose has been frustrated, a court may refuse to excuse the party on the ground that the party assumed the risk of the occurrence of the frustrating event. Sometimes a court does this on the basis of contract language. As Richard Posner put it for the Seventh Circuit, "a fixed-price contract is an explicit assignment of the risk of market price increases to the seller and the risk of market price decreases to the buyer, and the assignment of the latter risk to the buyer is even clearer where, as in this case, the contract places a floor under price but allows for escalation."[17] Furthermore, just as a wholesaler is not

---

[14]For a rare suggestion to the contrary, *see* Aluminum Co. of Am. v. Essex Group, 499 F. Supp. 53 (W.D. Pa. 1980), in which the court found frustration of "ALCOA's 'principal purpose' in making the contract," which was "to earn money." 499 F. Supp. at 76. The main ground of that decision, however, was mistake. See the discussion of the example of *ALCOA* in §9.2 *supra*.

[15]Swift Canadian Co. v. Banet, 224 F.2d 36, 38 (3d Cir. 1955).

[16]224 F.2d at 38. Refusal to excuse a party on grounds of frustration may result in a windfall for the other party if the other party's performance becomes less burdensome.

[17]Northern Ind. Pub. Serv. v. Carbon County Coal Co., *supra* note 6, at 278.

ordinarily excused by impracticability if its supplier defaults, that risk having been assumed by the wholesaler, a wholesaler is not excused by impracticability if its resale buyer defaults, that risk also having been assumed by the wholesaler.[18]

Sometimes a court concludes that a party assumed the risk of the occurrence of the frustrating event merely because the event was foreseeable. In one case, an elderly man who lived in a home for the aged on a trial basis paid a lump sum of $8,500 to be accepted as a permanent resident. When he died only three days later, before his permanent status had begun, his executors unsuccessfully sought return of the payment on the ground of frustration. "Frustration is no defense if it was reasonably foreseeable. . . . That death may at any unexpected time overcome a man of decedent's age, 84 years, is by common observation readily classified as 'reasonably foreseeable.'"[19] For the reasons advanced in the preceding section, however, it seems preferable to be less arbitrary than this court was.[20] As the Supreme Court of Washington put it,

> foreseeability of a possible frustrating event is meaningful only where the party seeking relief could have controlled the language of the contract to the extent of allocating the risk. Here exclusive control of the contract langauge was in the hands of the [other party] . . . .[21]

The judicial reluctance to excuse on the ground of frustration is most evident in cases where lessees have sought to be excused on this ground. In the most noted example, *Lloyd v. Murphy*, an automobile dealer had leased premises, shortly before the entry of the United States into the Second World War, for a term of five years. The lease restricted the lessee's use to selling new cars and operating a gas station and prohibited subleasing without the landlord's consent. When the government imposed wartime restrictions on the sale of new cars, the lessee vacated the premises, even though the lessor waived the restrictions in the lease and offered to lower the rent if the lessee could not otherwise operate profitably. Roger Traynor, writing for the Supreme Court of California, rejected the lessee's claim of frustration. The court observed that traditionally the lessee as the owner of the leasehold estate must bear the risk and the defense of frustration would never be available to a lessee.[22] The court rejected that reasoning, however, and adopted the view that, in a proper case, the doctrine of frustration is available to a lessee. It concluded, however, that this case was not one to which the doctrine applied. The court conceived of the

Effect of foreseeability

Example of *Lloyd v. Murphy*

[18] See the discussion of risks within a party's control in §9.6 *supra.*
[19] Gold v. Salem Lutheran Home Assn., 347 P.2d 687, 689 (Cal. 1959).
[20] See the discussion of the effect of foreseeability in §9.6 *supra.*
[21] Washington State Hop Producers v. Goschie Farms, *supra* note 7, at 77-78.
[22] In Krell v. Henry, *supra* note 1, the court pointed out that the arrangement was a mere license to use the rooms, so the peculiar rule for leases was not applicable.

lessee's purpose broadly, emphasizing that the lessor had waived the restrictions on the use of the land, which enabled the lessee "to use the premises for any legitimate purpose and to sublease them to any responsible tenant. This waiver," said the court, "is significant in view of the location of the premises on a main traffic artery in Los Angeles County and their adaptability for many commercial purposes."[23] The court also required nearly total frustration:

> The doctrine of frustration has been limited to cases of extreme hardship so that businessmen, who must make their arrangements in advance, can rely with certainty on their contracts. . . . The sale of automobiles was . . . merely restricted and if governmental regulation does not entirely prohibit the business to be carried on in the leased premises but only limits or restricts it, thereby making it less profitable and more difficult to continue, the lease is not terminated or the lessee excused from further performance.[24]

Furthermore, the court concluded that the lessee had assumed the risk of wartime regulations. "Automobile sales were soaring [at the time of agreement] because the public anticipated that production would soon be restricted . . . and it cannot be said that the risk of war and its consequences . . . was so remote a contingency that its risk could not be foreseen by . . . an experienced automobile dealer."[25]

Other lease cases   Although most of the other lease cases have also recognized that the doctrine of frustration applies to leases,[26] lessees have had little success in bringing themselves within the doctrine's requirements. Sometimes the lessee has failed to show frustration of its principal purpose.[27] Sometimes the lessee has been held to have assumed the risk on the ground that it was foreseeable.[28] Only rarely has a lessee actually been excused on this ground.[29]

Anomalous cases   Situations occasionally occur in which a failure of a basic assumption interferes with the expected operation of the agreement or some part of it but does not give grounds for relief on the traditional grounds of impracticability or frustration. Most of these anomalous cases involve the operation of the

---

[23] 153 P.2d 47, 52 (Cal. 1944).

[24] 153 P.2d at 50-51. The trial court had found that the lessee "continues to carry on the business of selling and servicing automobiles at two other places." Id. at 49.

[25] 153 P.2d at 51.

[26] Perry v. Champlain Oil Co., 134 A.2d 65 (N.H. 1957) ("The majority of jurisdictions have held that the doctrine of frustration is applicable to leases but have indicated that there must be complete or nearly complete frustration.").

[27] Mel Frank Tool & Supply v. Di-Chem Co., 580 N.W.2d 802 (Iowa 1998) ("fact that the use is less valuable or less profitable or even unprofitable does not mean that [it] has been substantially frustrated").

[28] Essex-Lincoln Garage v. City of Boston, 175 N.E.2d 466 (Mass. 1961) (lessee of parking facility not excused when change in direction of traffic on streets diminished its business because it is "well known that traffic regulations are subject to change").

[29] Garner v. Ellingson, 501 P.2d 22 (Ariz. App. 1972) (lessee of premises for movie theater and bookstore excused when permits to remodel were denied).

price term. For example, parties to a long-term contract for the sale of goods sometimes fix the price by reference to some agreed market or similar standard or in terms of an amount set by an appraiser or other third person. What happens if the price cannot be fixed in this way because, for example, the market posts no prices or the appraiser becomes unavailable? Courts have generally held that the contract is terminated and both parties are excused from further performance.[30] Under the Uniform Commercial Code, however, this result does not follow unless "the parties intend not to be bound unless the price be fixed or agreed."[31] As the commentary explains, in the case of a price to be set by a third party, the result follows only if the "particular person's judgment is not chosen merely as a barometer or index of a fair price but is an essential condition to the parties' intent to make a contract."[32] Furthermore, if the seller has already performed, and the goods cannot be returned, some means must be found to fix a price in order to avoid forfeiture by the seller.[33] Analogous problems may arise involving terms other than the price term.[34]

In *Oglebay Norton Co. v. Armco*, the Supreme Court of Ohio approved a particularly innovative solution on the failure of a flexible pricing formula providing for shipping rates based on rates "recognized by the leading iron ore shippers." The contract provided that, in the absence of such a rate, the parties "shall mutually agree upon a rate . . . , taking into consideration the contract rate being charged for similar transportation," and the Supreme Court held

Example of
Oglebay Norton

---

[30]Interstate Plywood Sales Co. v. Interstate Container Corp., 331 F.2d 449 (9th Cir. 1964) ("When the five-mill formula, intended here as the only binding method of fixing price, became indeterminable [because some of mills went out of business or stopped publishing prices], the contract became unenforceable.").

[31]UCC 2-305(4). See the discussion of the Code solution in §3.29 *supra*.

[32]UCC 2-305 cmt 4. *See* North Cent. Airlines v. Continental Oil Co., 574 F.2d 582 (D.C. Cir. 1978) (where pricing mechanism based on "posted prices" could no longer be used because of change in way prices were posted, a "reasonable price" was substituted).

[33]UCC 2-305(4) (if unable to return goods, buyer "must pay their reasonable value at the time of delivery"). See the discussion of relief based on restitution in §3.30 *supra*.

For an interesting and innovative judicial solution where a payment term failed to work, *see* Miller v. Campello Co-op. Bank, 181 N.E.2d 345 (Mass. 1962) (where buyer had occupied house under installment contract for quarter century, during which taxes and other charges against payments had increased so that payments would never satisfy unpaid balance, court turned agreement into 30-day option contract).

[34]In International Paper Co. v. Rockefeller, 146 N.Y.S. 371 (App. Div. 1914), cited in the discussion of performance as impracticable in §9.6 *supra*, the court excused the seller when his timber was burned. However, it added, "We need not say that the [seller] could not have furnished like wood of equal quality from other lands, but the contract . . . shows the source from which the parties contemplated the wood should be furnished, and when the source is destroyed the [seller] is excused from further performance." This would lead to the extraordinary conclusion that a seller in such a situation might be excused on the ground that there had been a failure of a basic assumption that interfered with the expected operation of the contract, even absent a showing of impracticability.

that it was proper for the trial court to order the parties to negotiate a rate.[35] Not all courts, however, would go this far.[36]

In the next section we consider in more detail the rights of both parties when one of them is excused by either impracticability or frustration.

Event existing at time of agreement

§9.8.   **Existing Impracticability and Frustration.**   The examples discussed in the preceding sections involve impracticability or frustration resulting from an event that occurs after the time of agreement. However, there is no reason why a party should not also be excused on the ground of impracticability or frustration existing at the time of the agreement.

Existing impracticability

Excuse on the ground of existing, as opposed to supervening, impracticability, is well recognized.[1] For example, as the commentary to the Code explains, the rule that excuses the seller in the case of casualty to identified goods "applies whether the goods were already destroyed at the time of contracting without the knowledge of either party, or whether they are destroyed subsequently."[2] In order to be excused on the ground of existing impracticability, a party must meet the four requirements that are imposed in cases of supervening impracticability.[3] In addition the party must show that it neither knew nor had reason to know of the facts that made performance impracticable.[4]

Existing frustration

The excuse of existing frustration was recognized in one of the coronation cases that first dealt with the doctrine of frustration.[5] A contract to hire a room to view the coronation procession was made an hour after the decision to operate on the king made the procession impossible. Since "neither party was aware of this fact when the agreement was entered into," it was held that the contract was "void" because of "a missupposition of the state of facts which went to the whole root of the matter."[6]

Relationship to supervening excuse

It occasionally is difficult to draw the line between existing and supervening impracticability or frustration.[7] However, since the rules governing excuse on

---

[35] 556 N.E.2d 515 (Ohio 1990).

[36] For a more traditional approach, *see* Hennen v. Omega Enters., 872 P.2d 797 (Mont. 1994) (covenant "requiring that the agreement be renegotiated upon a thirty-day notice did not render the contract vague or indefinite" but "when attempts at renegotiation failed, the contract's life was extinguished").

§9.8   [1] Partridge v. Presley, 189 F.2d 645 (D.C. Cir. 1951) (impossible to procure required permit to convert building because of zoning ordinance). *See* Restatement Second §266(1).

[2] UCC 2-613 cmt. 2.

[3] See §9.6 *supra.*

[4] Twombly v. Association of Farmworker Opportunity Programs, 212 F.3d 80 (1st Cir. 2000) ("an organization of national scope and the drafter of the form contract, cannot be said to be 'without fault,' or not to have reason to know of the definition of 'participant'" in federal statute).

[5] See §9.7 *supra.*

[6] Griffith v. Brymer, 19 T.L.R. 434 (K.B. 1903). *See* Restatement Second §266(2).

[7] *See* Northern Corp. v. Chugach Elec. Assn., 518 P.2d 76 (Alaska), modified on rehearing, 523 P.2d 1243 (Alaska 1974) (ice not thick enough to permit rock to be transported across lake).

these grounds are substantially the same in either case, the distinction is rarely of practical significance.[8] The relationship between existing impracticability or frustration and mistake is more troublesome.

A party that claims excuse on the ground of existing impracticability or frustration may also claim excuse on the ground of mistake. For example, in the coronation case mentioned above, the party who hired the room in ignorance of the decision to operate on the king could have argued that he was excused, not only on the ground that his purpose was already frustrated at the time the contract was made, but also on the ground that both parties were mistaken as to the facts at that time.[9] A party that relies on the ground of impracticability or frustration must show that it was impracticable for the party to perform or that the party's purpose was substantially frustrated.[10] By contrast, a party that relies on the ground of mistake need show only that the mistake had a material effect on the agreed exchange of performances.[11] In order to succeed on the ground of mistake, however, a party must show that there was a mistake as to an existing fact, not merely an erroneous prediction as to the future.[12] Furthermore, it is more likely that a party will be regarded as having borne the risk in the case of mistake than in the case of impracticability or frustration.[13]

Relationship to mistake

The advantage of mistake is illustrated by the cases in which a party that must achieve a technological breakthrough in order to perform claims to be excused on failing to achieve the breakthrough.[14] Such a party has two possible grounds for excuse — mistake of both parties and impracticability. In order to succeed on the ground of mistake, however, the party must convince the court that there was a mistake as to an existing fact (the "state of the art"), and not

Technological breakthrough cases

Another example occurs when a court hands down a decision after the time that the contract was made, giving an unanticipated interpretation to a statute enacted before the contract was made. *See* Restatement Second §266 cmt *a*. Compare the similar problem of distinguishing between a mistake as to an existing fact and an erroneous prediction as to the future in the discussion of the point that it is sometimes difficult to draw a line in §9.2 *supra*.

[8] For one difference, concerning knowledge of the facts that made performance impracticable, see the discussion of existing impracticability *supra*. Furthermore, the requirement of an "event" or "contingency" is inapplicable to existing impracticability or frustration, though Restatement Second §266 requires a "fact." See §9.6 *supra*. As to the difference in the effect on the excused party of existing, as distinguished from supervening, impracticability and frustration, see the discussion of the effect on the excused party in §9.9 *infra*.

[9] Indeed, although the court said that the contract was "void," suggesting frustration, the part of the opinion quoted above suggests that the rationale may have been mistake. In contrast to the result reached in Krell v. Henry, [1903] 2 K.B. 740 (1903 C.A.), discussed in §9.7 *supra*, Griffith was allowed to recover the £100 he had paid when the contract was made.

[10] See §§9.6, 9.7 *supra*.

[11] See §9.3 *supra*.

[12] See §9.2 *supra*.

[13] Compare the discussion of must not bear risk in §9.3 *supra* with the discussions of a greater obligation not assumed in §9.6 *supra* and in §9.7 *supra*.

[14] See §9.6 *supra*.

merely an erroneous prediction as to the future (that a breakthrough would be achieved).[15] The advantage in attempting to do this is that, if the party succeeds, it need only show that the mistake as to the "state of the art" had a material effect on the agreed exchange of performances, not that performance was impracticable.[16]

In the next section we consider the effects that follow from excuse on the ground of impracticability or frustration.

Effect on excused party

§9.9.   **Effects of Impracticability and Frustration.**   The effect of *supervening* impracticability or frustration on the excused party is usually to discharge that party's remaining duties of performance.[1] The effect of *existing* impracticability or frustration on the excused party is usually to prevent any duty of performance on that party's side from arising.

Effect on other party

The excused party's failure to perform because of impracticability or frustration affects the other party's duties of performance in the same way as if the excused party had broken the contract.[2] If the failure is material, the other party can suspend performance.[3] If an appropriate time for the excused party to cure has passed, the other party can terminate the contract.[4] Whether the other party is justified in suspending and in terminating is determined in a manner similar to that used when the nonperformance amounts to a breach. However, in determining whether a delay in performance justifies the other party in terminating, account should be taken of the fact that, since that party

---

[15]The disposition of this contention will turn on the considerations discussed in §9.1 *supra*.

[16]For a case in which a government contractor argued successfully that it was excused on the ground of mistake, *see* National Presto Indus. v. United States, 338 F.2d 99 (Ct. Cl. 1964) (parties mistakenly believed that "hot cup-cold draw" process could be used in making artillery shells; court concluded that the contractor did not assume the whole risk of this mistake). For cases in which government contractors argued unsuccessfully that they were excused on the ground of impractibility, see the discussions of examples of additional expense and of a greater obligation not assumed in §9.6 *supra*.

§9.9   [1]On the buyer's duty to notify under UCC 2-615(c), *see* Red River Commodities v. Eidsness, 459 N.W.2d 805 (N.D. 1990) (if seller "seasonably notified [buyer's] agent, who reported that fact to his principal, any breach from failure to notify in a particular way [required by contract] was insubstantial").

[2]Shaw v. Mobil Oil Corp., 535 P.2d 756 (Or. 1975) ("party has no obligation to perform a promise that is conditioned upon the other party's performance when the other party failed to perform even though the other party's failure to perform is excused").

On rare occasions a party will assume the risk that it will have to carry out its side of the exchange, even though the other party is excused from carrying out its side. For example, the traditional rule is that risk of loss under a contract for sale of real property passes as soon as the agreement is made. The rule is treated in a footnote to the discussion of *Taylor v. Caldwell* in §9.5 *supra*. The effect of this is that the buyer of a house assumes the risk of having to pay for the house even though the house has burned and the seller cannot convey it.

[3]See §8.16 *supra*.

[4]See §8.18 *supra*.

has no claim for damages for partial breach, termination is that party's only relief for delay.[5]

A prospective failure of performance due to impracticability or frustration has a similar effect. The fact that one party's anticipated failure to perform will be excused on the ground of impracticability or frustration does not prevent the other party from justifiably suspending performance and from terminating the contract. But the other party cannot recover damages for breach. As in the case of a prospective breach, if the other party acts on the assumption that performance will not be forthcoming, that party takes the risk that there may be no actual failure when the time for performance comes.[6] The other party is discharged, however, and is free to make other arrangements if that party has been told that performance will not be forthcoming because of impracticability or frustration — just as that party would be discharged if there were a repudiation by the party claiming excuse.[7] If the other party has the right to demand assurance of performance, that party may do so and, if adequate assurance is not received, treat this as a statement that performance will not be forthcoming.[8]

Prospective failure

Difficult questions arise when it is clear that the impracticability or frustration will be only temporary. First, when is the other party justified in terminating the contract? Second, if the other party does not terminate the contract, when is the excused party justified in refusing to perform after the impracticability or frustration has ceased?

Temporary impracticability or frustration

Two cases involving singers in nineteenth-century London opera houses illustrate the difficulties raised by the first question. In one case, an impresario had engaged a Mr. Bettini to come to London for 15 weeks of operas and concerts and "to be in London without fail at least six days before the commencement of his engagement for the purpose of rehearsals." The impresario terminated the contract when Bettini was delayed because of illness and arrived only two days before the commencement of his engagement. The court held that this termination was unjustified since the failure "does not go to the root of the matter." It reasoned that "the failure to attend at rehearsals during the six days . . . could only affect . . . the first week or fortnight of this engagement."[9] In the other case, an impresario had employed a Mme. Poussard to sing a leading role in a new opera for three months. When Poussard became ill during rehearsals, the impresario obtained a substitute singer under a contract that gave him a

Termination for delay

---

[5]See §8.18 *supra*.

[6]See §8.23 *supra*.

[7]*See* Restatement Second §268 and the discussion of Poussard v. Spiers & Pond *infra*.

[8]See the discussion of doubts not being enough in §8.23 *supra*. Under UCC 2-609(4), failure to provide adequate assurance "is a repudiation of the contract." This is an inappropriate result if the prospective nonperformance would be excused; it is avoided in the formulation of these rules in the Restatement Second. *See* Restatement Second §268 cmt. *c* & illus. 2.

[9]Bettini v. Gye, 1 Q.B.D. 183, 189 (1876).

right of termination until opening night. When Poussard did not recover by that time, the impresario had the substitute sing on opening night and terminated Poussard's contract. The court held that the termination was justified, even though Poussard recovered less than a week later, since "the illness here was a serious one, of uncertain duration. . . . [I]f no substitute capable of performing the part adequately could be obtained, except on the terms that she should be permanently engaged . . . , in our opinion it follows, as a matter of law, that the failure . . . went to the root of the matter and discharged the [impresario]."[10] The cases can be reconciled on the ground that, while Bettini's and Poussard's illnesses were both short, this fact was known to the impresario at the time he decided to terminate Bettini's contract, but it was not known to the impresario at the time he decided to terminate Poussard's contract. Furthermore, the nature of the production in which Poussard was involved and the range of alternatives available to the impresario left him no reasonable opportunity to delay his decision.

Termination by excused party

If the other party does not terminate, but only suspends its performance, the excused party may be happy, as Bettini and Poussard would have been, to perform as soon as the temporary impracticability or frustration has ceased.[11] But what if circumstances have so changed that the excused party is unwilling to perform at any time? Courts are often sympathetic to the excused party in this event. A movie actor who was unable to perform his contract with his studio because he had gone into the army during World War II was excused when the war was over from performing at his pre-war salary.[12] Similarly, a contractor that was prevented from performing a building contract because of wartime governmental regulations was excused when the regulations were lifted from performing at the pre-war price.[13] It was, to be sure, no longer impracticable for the actor or the contractor to perform. Nevertheless, the temporarily excused party will be permanently excused if that party can show that performance at the later time would be materially more burdensome than the performance to which that party originally agreed.[14]

---

[10]Poussard v. Spiers & Pond, 1 Q.B.D. 410, 415 (1876).

[11]*See* Hall v. Wright, 120 Eng. Rep. 688, 693 (Q.B. 1858) (translated from Rolle's Abridgment of 1668: "if a man covenant to build a house before a certain day, and the plague breaks out . . . before the day, and continues until after the day, the covenantor is excused from the performance of his covenant at the day; for the law will not compel him to venture his life for it, but he may do it after.").

[12]Autry v. Republic Prods., 180 P.2d 888 (Cal. 1947) (actor Gene Autry excused under terms of agreement with studio from resuming performance after military service since "temporary impossibility . . . operates as a permanent discharge if performance after the impossibility ceases would impose a substantially greater burden upon the promisor").

[13]Village of Minneota v. Fairbanks, Morse & Co., 31 N.W.2d 920 (Minn. 1948) (contractor excused from resuming performance).

[14]Village of Minneota v. Fairbanks, Morse & Co., *supra* note 13 ("after the cessation of this excusable temporary impossibility in October 1945 [contractor] would have been compelled to

Sometimes, even though the excused party has not yet rendered any perfor- **Partial**
mance, only part of that party's performance has become impracticable. In that **impracticability**
event, it may be possible to salvage the remainder of the agreement by requiring
the excused party to perform what it can. Difficulty is likely to arise, however,
in determining what proportion of the original compensation the excused party
is still entitled to receive. This difficulty can be resolved if the other party is
willing to render its own performance in full, even though it receives less than
expected. If the other party assures the excused party within a reasonable time
that the other party will perform in full, apportionment should be unnecessary
and the excused party ought to perform what it can.[15] Even absent such assurance, if the excused party can render substantially all its performance, taking
account of any substitute performance that that party can render, courts have
held that apportionment is again unnecessary, and the excused party must perform what it can.[16] Courts have sometimes gone even further than this and have
salvaged part of the agreement by apportioning the performances on both sides,
though the agreement is wholly or partially executory on both sides.[17] Under
UCC 2-615(b), if the impracticability affects "only part of a seller's capacity to
perform," the seller must allocate production and deliveries among the seller's
customers" in a "manner which is fair and reasonable," presumably for a price
that is apportioned.[18]

If the excused party has rendered part of its performance before the remain- **Divisibility**
der has become impracticable, the pressure to apportion the performance is
greater than in the situation just described, because the excused party will suffer forfeiture if that party is allowed to recover nothing and the other party may
be unjustly enriched. If the contract is divisible, the return performance will
be apportioned, and the excused party will recover accordingly.[19] The same is
true when a frustrating event occurs after the excused party has rendered part
of its performance.[20] The test of divisibility in cases of impracticability or frustration is similar to the one used when the failure to render full performance

---

render performance substantially different from what it contracted for in August 1940, because
of changing costs"). *See* Restatement Second §269 ("would be materially more burdensome").

[15] *See* Restatement Second §270(2) & illus. 4, the facts of which are said in the Reporter's Note
to have been suggested by *Van Dusen Aircraft Supplies, infra* note 17.

[16] Meyer v. Sullivan, 181 P. 847 (Cal. App. 1919) (sellers not excused under contract to deliver
on "Kosmos steamer" when such steamer became unavailable due to war, since substitute was
available at no additional expense to sellers). *See* UCC 2-614 cmt. 1.

[17] Van Dusen Aircraft Supplies v. Massachusetts Port Auth., 279 N.E.2d 717 (Mass. 1972)
(though statute subsequently made small part of lease illegal, rest of it was enforce- able).

[18] Roth Steel Prods. v. Sharon Steel Corp., 705 F.2d 134 (6th Cir. 1983) ("allocation system which includes participants other than customers under contract and regular customers is
unreasonable").

[19] A noted if hoary case is Gill v. Johnstown Lumber Co., 25 A. 120 (Pa. 1892) (lumber company
liable for logs driven to destination before Great Johnstown Flood).

[20] For an imaginative use of the concept of divisibility, *see* Patch v. Solar Corp., 149 F.2d
558 (7th Cir. 1945) (since wartime prohibition of manufacture of washing machines was only

is a breach of contract, although it can be expected that when a court applies the test in favor of an excused party, it will be more generous than if the party were in breach.[21]

Restitution   If the excused party has rendered part of its own performance before the remainder has become impracticable and the contract is not divisible, the excused party is entitled to restitution of any benefit that it has conferred,[22] absent an agreement to the contrary.[23] A generous measure of benefit is often used in such cases, using the test of cost avoided, rather than that of net enrichment.[24] For example, in the case of a builder that is repairing a house when it is destroyed by fire, the owner's benefit is measured in terms of what it would have cost the owner to procure similar labor and materials, even though nothing remains of the building.[25] This result may often be justified on the ground that the owner benefits from the repairs through a greater recovery under the owner's insurance policy, but it is not confined to cases in which this rationale applies.[26] The other party is also entitled to restitution for any benefit conferred upon the excused party, by payment or otherwise.[27] The parties have similar rights to restitution when the excuse is on the ground of frustration.[28] Under the Vienna Convention, if a buyer accepts and retains goods with a nonconformity for which the seller is not liable, the seller is entitled to the price with a proportional reduction rather than being entitled to restitution.[29]

---

temporary, agreement licensing patented transmission remained binding for life of patent with period of ban "carved out").

[21] See §8.13 *supra.*

[22] Buccini v. Paterno Constr. Co. 170 N.E. 910 (N.Y. 1930) (Cardozo, C.J.: estate of painter who died before finishing mural entitled to "the benefit to the owner in advancement of the ends to be promoted by the contract").

[23] For a case suggesting that a party can contract away his right to restitution, *see* Cutter v. Powell, 101 Eng. Rep. 573 (K.B. 1795) (second mate "would have received nearly four times as much" as usual rate if he completed voyage "and nothing unless the whole of that duty were performed").

[24] On the difference between the two tests, see the discussion of net enrichment or cost avoided in §2.20 *supra.*

[25] Young v. City of Chicopee, 72 N.E. 63 (Mass. 1904) ("the liability of the owner . . . should be measured by the amount of contract work done which at the time of the destruction of the structure had become so far identified with it as that, but for the destruction, it would have inured to him as contemplated by the contract").

[26] Angus v. Scully, 57 N.E. 674 (Mass. 1900) (party who had contracted to move building entitled to "recover for what he has done" when building burned after having been moved about halfway).

[27] Butterfield v. Byron, 27 N.E. 667 (Mass. 1891) (owner "is to be allowed for all his payments," against which builder could offset his claim).

[28] West v. Peoples First Natl. Bank & Trust Co., 106 A.2d 427 (Pa. 1954) (party entitled to restitution when "the original purpose of the joint adventure agreement could not be carried out"). *See* Restatement Second §377.

[29] CISG 50 ("buyer may reduce the price in the same proportion as the value that the goods actually delivered had at the time of the delivery bears to the value that conforming goods would

Even a generous measure of restitution may not suffice to prevent forfeiture, however. In the repair cases, for example, materials not yet worked into the building or scaffolding erected to aid in the work may be destroyed along with the building, and for these items restitution is not available.[30] Indeed, there is not even authority allowing the contractor to offset such expenses against the owner's claim for restitution of payments made.[31]

Scholarly writers, dissatisfied with the inflexibility of these rules, have suggested that courts take into account the excused party's reliance interest.[32] The Restatement Second states a rule that gives a court the power to "grant relief on such terms as justice requires, including protection of the parties' reliance interests," if this is necessary to "avoid injustice."[33] It has even been suggested that judges should assume a power of "price adjustment" or impose on the parties a duty of good faith modification in connection with long-term contracts.[34] However, courts have expressed their reluctance to do more than allow a generous measure of restitution,[35] and few courts have allowed recovery for reliance expenditures[36] or fashioned more imaginative solutions.[37] A party that wants to be assured of more than restitution would be well advised to insist on an explicit provision.

We next look at some practical aspects of drafting clauses to deal with changed circumstances.

No recovery for reliance

Equitable adjustment

---

have had at that time"). For more on this civil-law concept of price reduction, see the discussion of the effect if partial in §12.9 *infra*.

[30] Young v. City of Chicopee, *supra* note 25 (no recovery for lumber near bridge that had not been "wrought into the bridge" at the time of the fire).

[31] Wallace Studios v. Brochstein's, Inc., 297 S.W.2d 218 (Tex. Civ. App. 1956) (if performance of contract to manufacture and install fixtures became impracticable after their manufacture, buyer could recover part payment, but manufacturer's "right to recover anything . . . depends on whether any goods have been delivered . . . or accepted").

[32] Fuller & Perdue, The Reliance Interest in Contract Damages (pt. 2), 46 Yale L.J. 373, 379-82 (1936) (although "it would seem that the reliance interest should also play an important role, . . . there are, apparently, no American or English cases expressly recognizing a recovery measured by the reliance interest as the means of accomplishing a desirable compromise between the extreme demands of no liability and liability, for the full expectation interest").

[33] Restatement Second §272.

[34] Hillman, Court Adjustment of Long-Term Contracts: An Analysis Under Modern Contract Law, 1987 Duke L.J. 1, 4-17.

For a case that inspired much of this commentary, see the discussion of the example of *ALCOA* in §9.2 *supra*. In that case, after the court concluded that there had been a mutual mistake as to an escalator clause that failed to take account of energy costs, it reformed the contract to give the expected profit.

[35] Iowa Elec. Light & Power Co. v. Atlas Corp., 467 F. Supp. 129 (N.D. Iowa 1978) ("court will not adjust price"), rev'd on other grounds, 603 F.2d 1301 (8th Cir. 1979).

[36] See Albre Marble & Tile Co. v. John Bowen Co., 155 N.E.2d 437 (Mass. 1959) (general contractor liable to subcontractor for fair value of work and labor in preparation for tile and marble work in hospital, though no work was incorporated into hospital, after hospital contract was cancelled because general contractor had not complied with statutory bidding requirements).

[37] For examples of such solutions, see the discussions of anomalous cases and of the example of *Oglebay Norton* in §9.7 *supra*.

PART IV

RIGHTS OF THIRD PARTIES

Chapter 10

Contract Beneficiaries

A.   INTRODUCTION

§10.1.   Nature of the Problem. Owners of land located downstream
from a chicken processing plant seek damages caused them by the plant's over-
saturation of their city's sewer system.[1] A woman to whom a testator intended to
leave the bulk of his estate under his will claims damages from the lawyer whose
negligence in having the woman witness the will resulted in her taking nothing
under it.[2] African-American personnel at an Air Force base bring a class action
seeking relief from a local school board's refusal to admit their children to its
integrated public schools.[3] A tenant brings an action against a power company
for injuries sustained in a fall on a dark walkway.[4] An elderly passenger who fell
while exiting a van sues the daycare center that operated the van.[5] What have
these cases in common? Each arose out of a contract: between the city and the
chicken processing plant, limiting the wastes that it was permitted to deposit
in the city's sewer system; between the testator and his lawyer, requiring the
lawyer to use professional skill in carrying out his client's desires; between the

*Wide variety of
situations*

---

§10.1   [1] Ratzlaff v. Franz Foods, 468 S.W.2d 239 (Ark. 1971).
   [2] Guy v. Liederbach, 459 A.2d 744 (Pa. 1983). See the discussion of the question of to whom
performance is to go in §10.3 *infra*.
   [3] Bossier Parish School Bd. v. Lemon, 370 F.2d 847 (5th Cir. 1967) (alternative ground).
   [4] Vick v. H.S.I. Mgt., 507 So. 2d 433 (Ala. 1987).
   [5] Stewart v. City of Jackson, 804 So. 2d 1041 (Miss. 2002). For cases reaching a different result,
see note 7 *infra*.

United States and the school district, requiring it in return for financial aid to admit children of base personnel to schools in accordance with state law; between the tenant's landlord and the power company, requiring it to install and maintain outdoor lights; between the city and the daycare center, requiring it to provide van service. Each involved an attempt by a person other than one of the parties who had made the contract to enforce it. And in each case the attempt succeeded — it was held that the claimant had the right to enforce the contract. These examples suggest the wide variety of situations in which such contract beneficiaries have prevailed.[6]

Examples of persons who cannot enforce

The performance of a contract usually benefits persons other than the parties who made it, but they cannot ordinarily enforce it.[7] The prompt construction of an office building will benefit prospective tenants by allowing them to move in on schedule, but they cannot recover damages from the builder that wrongfully fails to complete performance on time.[8] A labor union's performance of a collective bargaining agreement with a transit system will benefit riders of the system by making transportation available, but the riders cannot recover damages from the union if it wrongfully calls a strike that paralyzes the system.[9] It is sometimes said that such persons cannot enforce the contract because they are not in "privity" with the promisor, but this begs the question: When does the duty of a promisor extend to one other than the promisee? This troublesome question is raised in what has become a small flood of cases.

Analogous questions

Analogous questions arise in other areas of the law. When does the duty of a seller of goods with respect to the quality of the goods extend to persons with whom the seller did not deal?[10] When does the duty of a person not to misrepresent the facts extend to persons whose reliance on the misrepresentation was not foreseeable?[11] When does the duty of a person to use due care extend to

---

[6] For a suggestion of the wide variety of uses to which contract beneficiary doctrine has been put, see the analysis of Wisconsin cases from the early part of the twentieth century in L. Friedman, Contract Law in America 121 (1965) (third-party beneficiary doctrine, "which began as a handmaiden of abstraction, ended up as a conceptual tool of the court, the uses of which were not necessarily related to abstraction at all").

[7] Mississippi High School Activities Assn. v. Farris, 501 So. 2d 393 (Miss. 1987) (members of high school baseball team could not enforce contract between high school and interscholastic athletic association).

[8] McDonald Constr. Co. v. Murray, 485 P.2d 626 (Wash. App. 1971) (prospective tenant denied recovery though builder was aware it was to occupy building).

[9] Burke & Thomas v. International Org. of Masters, Mates & Pilots, 600 P.2d 1282 (Wash. 1979) (owners of island resorts could not recover damages for labor union's strike of ferry system in breach of its collective bargaining agreement with Washington Toll Bridge Authority).

[10] Such problems may arise whether liability is based on warranty or on strict product liability. Compare UCC-O 2-318 and UCC-R 2-318 (which offer three alternative provisions for liability in warranty) with Restatement (Second) of Torts §402A (strict product liability).

[11] A leading case is Ultramares Corp. v. Touche, Niven & Co., 174 N.E. 441 (N.Y. 1931). See Restatement (Second) of Torts §552 (liability for loss caused by information negligently supplied for the information of others by one not under a public duty to supply it "is limited to the loss

persons to whom injury was not foreseeable?[12] All of these questions concern the extent of the risk assumed by one who owes a duty of some kind.

This chapter addresses one aspect of the extent of risk undertaken by a contracting party. In resisting claims for breach of contract brought by affected third persons, defendants have often evoked the specter of excessive liability, much as defendants have done in resisting similar tort claims.[13] Occasionally the requirement of foreseeability imposed by the law of damages affords protection to a defendant.[14] But often the court cannot avoid difficult questions of the extent of risk assumed by a promisor when the court defines the outer limits of liability to third persons.[15]

Aspect of extent of risk

But before we see how courts now deal with these questions, we consider the doctrinal difficulties that such contract beneficiaries have had to overcome.

B. INTENDED AND INCIDENTAL BENEFICIARIES

§10.2. Historical Development. The right of a third person (C) to sue as a beneficiary of a contract to which that person was not a party — a contract between a promisor (A) and a promisee (B) — was upheld as early as 1677 by the King's Bench in *Dutton v. Poole*.[1] A father (B) planned to sell wood to raise a dowry for his daughter (C). The eldest son (A), who wanted to inherit the wood, promised the father to pay the daughter £1,000 if the father would not sell it. When the son failed to pay the £1,000, the daughter sued him. It was argued for the son that "the action ought not to be brought by the daughter but by the father . . . for the promise was made to the father, and the daughter is neither privy nor interested in the consideration." The court rejected the argument,

Dutton v. Poole

---

suffered . . . by the person or one of a limited group of persons for whose benefit and guidance he intends to supply the information or knows that the recipient intends to supply it"). *See also* Restatement (Second) of Torts §531 (fraudulent misrepresentation).

[12] The classic case is Palsgraf v. Long Island R.R., 162 N.E. 99 (N.Y. 1928). *See* Restatement (Second) of Torts §281 cmt. *c* ("If the actor's conduct creates . . . a recognizable risk of harm only to a particular class of persons, the fact that it in fact causes harm to a person of a different class, to whom the actor could not reasonably have anticipated injury, does not make the actor liable to the person so injured.").

[13] *See* County of Suffolk v. Long Island Lighting Co., 728 F.2d 52 (2d Cir. 1984) (to hold that customers of utility company had claims as intended beneficiaries against company's suppliers under "its numerous supply and construction contracts" would "expose contracting parties to countless unforeseeable lawsuits").

[14] See §12.14 *infra*.

[15] For example, does a department store that leases space in a shopping center risk contract liability to other lessees whose business will be adversely affected if the department store breaks its lease and moves out? *See* Fourth & Main Co. v. Joslin Dry Goods Co., 648 P.2d 178 (Colo. App. 1982) (no).

§10.2 [1] Throughout this chapter, to facilitate comparison, the promisor of the promise sought to be enforced is often designated parenthetically as A, the promisee as B, and the third party that seeks to enforce the promise as C.

noting that "there was such apparent consideration of affection from the father to his children, for whom nature obliges him to provide, that the consideration and promise to the father may well extend to the children."[2] Later English cases approved of *Dutton v. Poole*.[3]

Rule of *Dutton v. Poole* repudiated

In 1861, however, this line of cases was repudiated in *Tweddle v. Atkinson*. Its rejection was explained on the ground that "the law was not settled, as it now is, that natural love and affection is not a sufficient consideration for a promise upon which an action may be maintained; nor was it settled that the promisee cannot bring an action unless the consideration moved from him."[4] In 1915, the House of Lords denied recovery to a contract beneficiary in *Dunlop Pneumatic Tyre Co. v. Selfridge & Co.* One of the Lords declared that "in the law of England certain principles are fundamental. One is that only a person who is a party to a contract can sue on it."[5]

Failure of reform

In 1937, the English Law Reform Committee recommended that "where a contract by its express terms purports to confer a benefit directly on a third party, it shall be enforceable by the third party in his own name subject to any defenses that would have been valid between the contracting parties."[6] However, no action was taken on this recommendation, and, when the issue came before the House of Lords again in 1968, it indicated continued adherence to the rule of *Tweddle v. Atkinson*. One of the lords expressed some doubts on the merits, concluding that "if legislation is probable at an early date I would not deal with [the matter] in a case where that is not essential."[7] English courts succeeded in mitigating the rigor of the rule barring suit by contract beneficiaries by making free, though artificial, use of the concept of trust.[8] Furthermore, statutes conferred rights on beneficiaries under insurance policies.[9] Finally, in 1999, Parliament conferred rights on contract beneficiaries generally.[10]

---

[2]83 Eng. Rep. 523, 523, 524 (K.B. 1677). The court added that "the son hath the benefit by having of the wood and the daughter hath lost her portion by this means."

[3]A century later, Lord Mansfield remarked, "As to the case of Dutton v. Poole, it is a matter of surprise how doubt could have arisen in that case." Martyn v. Hind, 98 Eng. Rep. 1174, 1177 (K.B. 1776).

[4]121 Eng. Rep. 762, 764 (Q.B. 1861) (Crompton, J.).

[5][1915] App. Cas. 847, 853 (H.L. 1915) (Lord Haldane).

[6]Report of the [English] Law Revision Committee on the Statute of Frauds and the Doctrine of Consideration 31-32 (Sixth Interim Report, Cmd. 5449 (1937)), reprinted in 15 Can. B. Rev. 585 (1937).

[7]Beswick v. Beswick, [1968] App. Cas. 58, 72 (H.L. 1867) (Lord Reid).

[8]If A promises B to pay C $100, B, the promisee may be regarded as holding the claim against A, the promisor, as "trustee" for C, the beneficiary.

[9]*See* G. Treitel, Law of Contract 614-16 (10th ed. 1999). Decisions involving beneficiaries of insurance policies have often been treated as in a class by themselves in the United States. See the discussion of the first Restatment's view as to donees in §10.8 *infra*.

[10]Contract (Rights of Third Parties) Act 1999. *See* G. Treitel, Law of Contract 600-14 (10th ed. 1999).

Contract beneficiaries fared better on this side of the Atlantic. The New York Court of Appeals led the way in *Lawrence v. Fox*, decided in 1859, just two years before *Tweddle v. Atkinson*. Holly (B) owed Lawrence (C) $300. Holly then lent Fox (A) $300, in return for which Fox promised Holly to pay Holly's debt to Lawrence. When Fox did not do so, Lawrence sued him. The Court of Appeals noted that if Fox had made his promise to Lawrence instead of to, or in addition to, Holly, there would have been a clear precedent for recovery by Lawrence against Fox.[11] Since the consideration for a promise need not move from the promisee to the promisor,[12] the loan by Holly to Fox would have been consideration for Fox's promise to Lawrence. But Fox's promise had not been made to Lawrence. Nevertheless, the court allowed him to recover directly against Fox.[13] It applied a principle from the law of trusts to the effect that, in the case of "a promise made to one for the benefit of another, he for whose benefit it is made may bring an action for its breach."[14] Because the beneficiary, Lawrence, was a creditor to whom the promisee, Holly, sought to have his debt paid, claimants in the position of Lawrence came to be called "creditor beneficiaries."[15]

Lawrence v. Fox

Claims of such creditor beneficiaries were promptly recognized in analogous circumstances in New York. A particularly important situation was that of the mortgage assumption. When a purchaser buys land from a vendor that has mortgaged it, it is common for the vendor to ask the purchaser to "assume" the mortgage by promising the vendor to make the mortgage payments to the mortgagee. This promise by the purchaser (A) to the vendor (B) to pay the mortgagee (C) was held to be enforceable by the mortgagee as a creditor beneficiary under *Lawrence v. Fox*.[16]

Mortgage assumption cases

Nearly 60 years after *Lawrence v. Fox*, the New York Court of Appeals handed down another influential case involving a contract beneficiary. In *Seaver v. Ransom*, Mrs. Beman (B) had a favorite niece, Marion Seaver (C), to whom she wanted to leave her house. Mrs. Beman was near death and her husband, Judge Beman (A), had already written a will for her signature that left the house to him. Since Mrs. Beman was failing, they decided not to change the will. Instead, Judge Beman promised Mrs. Beman that

Seaver v. Ransom

[11]This would have been so under Farley v. Cleveland, 4 Cow. 432 (N.Y. 1825), aff'd, 9 Cow. 639 (N.Y. 1827). Two of the six judges who concurred in the majority opinion were of the opinion that the promise could be treated as made to Lawrence.

[12]See the discussion of the point that the consideration need not move from promisee to promisor in §2.3 *supra*.

[13]Since Holly's debt to Lawrence had not been paid, Lawrence clearly had an action against Holly.

[14]20 N.Y. 268, 274 (1859) (6-2 decision).

[15]In some of the early cases, courts were hesitant to allow the promisor to be sued by both the promisee and the beneficiary. As to how the promisor is protected, see the discussion of a promise to pay the promisee's debt in §10.7 *infra*.

[16]Burr v. Beers, 24 N.Y. 178 (1861) (the point was "definitely settled" by Lawrence v. Fox).

he would leave Seaver enough in his will to make up the difference, in return for which Mrs. Beman signed the will before she died. When Judge Beman died, it was found that he had not kept his promise. Seaver sued his executors. The Court of Appeals allowed recovery, citing "cases where the contract is made for the benefit of the wife . . . , affianced wife . . . , or child . . . of a party to the contract. . . . The desire of the childless aunt to make provision for a beloved and favorite niece differs imperceptibly in law or in equity from the moral duty of the parent to make testamentary provision for a child." It approved the lower court's dictum: "The doctrine of *Lawrence v. Fox* is progressive, not retrograde. The course of the late decisions is to enlarge, not to limit the effect of that case."[17] Because the beneficiary, Seaver, was a person to whom Mrs. Beman, the promisee, sought to have a gift made, claimants in the position of Seaver came to be called "donee beneficiaries."

First Restatement   The first Restatement classified beneficiaries that could recover as either donee or creditor beneficiaries. One could enforce a contract as a donee beneficiary if it appeared that "the purpose of the promisee in obtaining the promise" was "to make a gift to the beneficiary or to confer upon him a right against the promisor to some performance neither due nor supposed or asserted to be due from the promisor to the beneficiary." One could enforce a contract as a creditor beneficiary if "no purpose to make a gift" appeared and performance of the promise would "satisfy an actual or supposed or asserted duty of the promisee to the beneficiary."[18] A beneficiary that came within neither of these categories was called an "incidental" beneficiary and could not enforce the contract.[19] This was generally representative of the law at the time with a few notable exceptions. Corbin was an influential advocate of the recognition of the rights of contract beneficiaries.[20] Nevertheless, Massachusetts generally refused to countenance recovery by contract beneficiaries as such until 1979.[21] And it was not until 1985 that New York's highest court overtly abandoned the requirement of

---

[17] 120 N.E. 639, 640-41 (N.Y. 1918). For an appreciation of the significance of this, it is helpful to know that in 1877 contract beneficiaries suffered a serious setback at the hands of the Court of Appeals, which declared that "courts are not inclined to extend the doctrine of Lawrence v. Fox." Vrooman v. Turner, 69 N.Y. 280, 284 (1877).

[18] Restatement §133(1)(a) & (b). One may be a creditor beneficiary even though one's underlying claim as a creditor "has been barred by the Statute of Limitations or by a discharge in bankruptcy, or . . . is unenforceable because of the Statute of Frauds." The right extends to promises under seal. *See* Restatement §134. *See also* Restatement Second §303.

[19] Restatement §133(1)(c). A person may, of course, have a right to enforce some, but not all, of a promisor's duties under a contract.

[20] Corbin's influence today is reflected in Choate, Hall & Stewart v. SCA Serv., 392 N.E.2d 1045 (Mass. 1979).

[21] Choate, Hall & Stewart v. SCA Serv., note 20 *supra* ("we make a long anticipated but relatively minor change in the law of the Commonwealth").

a family relationship of some kind between a donee beneficiary and the promisee.[22] In a number of states statutes bear on the rights of contract beneficiaries.[23]

We look now at the present state of the law.

§10.3. A Modern Rule. The Restatement Second departs from the traditional terminology of contract beneficiaries in a formulation that has had a substantial influence on courts in many jurisdictions.[1] While retaining the term *incidental beneficiary* to describe one that does not acquire rights under a contract,[2] it adopts a new term, *intended beneficiary*, to describe one that does acquire rights under a contract.[3] It abandons the familiar dichotomy of donee and creditor beneficiary[4] because, according to the commentary, the terms "carry overtones of obsolete doctrinal difficulties."[5] Any beneficiary that acquires rights under a contract, whether a donee or a creditor beneficiary according to the first Restatement, is an intended beneficiary according to the Restatement Second.

In order to qualify as an intended beneficiary, one must meet two requirements. First, one must show that "recognition of a right to performance in the beneficiary is appropriate to effectuate the intention of the parties." Second, one must show that either:

Restatement Second classification

Requirements for intended beneficiary

---

[22]Fourth Ocean Putnam Corp. v. Interstate Wrecking Co., 485 N.E.2d 208 (N.Y. 1985) (approving the Restatement Second formulations and characterizing them, somewhat disingenuously, as stating "the essence of the prior holdings of this court").

[23]A few states have general provisions derived from the Field civil code (see the discussion of contract law as seen as essentially case law in §1.8 *supra*).

§10.3 [1]Striking examples are Choate, Hall & Stewart v. SCA Serv., 392 N.E.2d 1045 (Mass. 1979) (citing Restatement Second rule in overruling prior case law and recognizing right of beneficiaries to sue), and Guy v. Liederbach, 459 A.2d 744 (Pa. 1983) (quoting and relying on Restatement Second rule in disapproving Spires v. Hanover Fire Ins. Co., 70 A.2d 828 (Pa. 1950)). *Choate* was followed in Rae v. Air-Speed, 435 N.E.2d 628 (Mass. 1982).

See generally Eisenberg, Third-Party Beneficiaries, 92 Colum. L. Rev. 1358 (1992); Waters, The Property in the Promise: A Study of the Third Party Beneficiary Rule, 98 Harv. L. Rev. 1109 (1985).

[2]Restatement Second §315.

[3]Restatement Second §302.

[4]Under the first Restatement, the most significant difference in the rules applicable to donee and creditor beneficiaries relates to the time when the beneficiary's rights are vested. The Restatement Second rejects this difference. See the discussion of the Restatement Second's view in §10.8 *infra*.

[5]Restatement Second ch. 14, Introductory Note. *See also* Restatement Second §302, Reporter's Note ("the word 'donee' was not entirely appropriate to the beneficiary of an executory gift promise; it was sometimes entirely inappropriate where the 'purpose of the promisee' under . . . former §133 was not 'to make a gift' but 'to confer a right'"). Furthermore, the requirement that a gift be delivered was not applicable to a donee beneficiary. On delivery of gifts, see the discussion of the analogy to gift of a chattel in §11.6 *infra*.

(a) the performance of the promise will satisfy an obligation of the promisee to pay money to the beneficiary; or

(b) the circumstances indicate that the promisee intends to give the beneficiary the benefit of the promised performance.[6]

The commentary refers to a promise that comes under subparagraph (a) as a "promise to pay the promisee's debt" and one that comes under subparagraph (b) as a "gift promise."[7] Despite the surprising similarity between these descriptions and the discarded categories of donee and creditor beneficiaries, there are some significant differences. Because the category of beneficiaries of gift promises serves as a catchall for any intended beneficiary as long as the promise is *not* one to pay a debt of the promisee, we begin with this general category of beneficiaries of gift promises.

Gift promises

In order to be an intended beneficiary of a gift promise, one must show both that this is "appropriate to effectuate the intention of the parties" and that "the circumstances indicate that the promisee intended to give the beneficiary the benefit of the promised performance." Prior to the Restatement Second, most authorities agreed that the test was one of intention to benefit the third person,[8] but there was some disagreement over whose intention was controlling. The more common view was reflected in the first Restatement, according to which it was enough if the *promisee's* purpose was "to make a gift to the beneficiary or to confer upon him a right against the promisor to some performance."[9] There was another view, however, according to which, as the Supreme Court of Pennsylvania put it, "it is not enough that it be intended by *one* of the parties [that the third person should be a beneficiary], but *both* parties must so intend."[10]

Test of intention to benefit

In applying the test of intention to benefit, courts have not required that the person to be benefited be identified at the time the promise is made.[11] It is enough that a beneficiary's identity can be determined at the time the promise is

---

[6]Restatement Second §302(1).

[7]In general, this treatise uses the terms *gift promise* and *promise to pay the promisee's debt*, the terminology of the Restatement Second commentary. But it uses the terms *donee beneficiary* and *creditor beneficiary* in discussing cases decided when these terms were in vogue.

[8]Some courts, however, have looked not for an intention to benefit the third party, but for an intention to confer a direct obligation to the third party. Lonsdale v. Chesterfield, 662 P.2d 385 (Wash. 1983) (question was "whether the parties . . . intended that [promisor] assume a direct obligation" to third party).

[9]Restatement §133(1)(a). In order to make the two categories of beneficiaries mutually exclusive, this provision applies only if the right was to a "performance neither due nor supposed or asserted to be due from the promisee to the beneficiary."

[10]Spires v. Hanover Fire Ins. Co., *supra* note 1 ("in other words, a promisor cannot be held liable to an alleged beneficiary . . . unless the latter was within his contemplation at the time the contract was entered into and such liability was intentionally assumed by him").

[11]Commercial Ins. Co. v. Pacific-Peru Constr. Corp., 558 F.2d 948 (9th Cir. 1977) (reinsurer not "deprived of its third-party beneficiary status because its identity as reinsurer was unknown

to be performed,[12] though the failure of the contract to identify the beneficiary may suggest that the beneficiary is only incidental.[13] Nor have courts required that the promisee be inspired in whole or even in part by altruism.[14] The test of intention to benefit may be met even though the promisee's motives were mixed. Since the primary purpose of contracting parties is commonly to benefit themselves, "the promisee need not be motivated solely by its desire to bestow a benefit upon the third party."[15]

When faced with such difficult cases, some courts have asked whether the promisor (A) was to render the promised performance to the beneficiary (C), rather than to the promisee (B).[16] This circumstance has sometimes tipped the scales in favor of the beneficiary,[17] but it is by no means essential to a finding of an intention to benefit. Thus there are many cases in which a beneficiary has been allowed to enforce a promise to forbear, even though it could not be said that the forbearance was to be rendered "directly to" the beneficiary.[18] Furthermore, there are some cases in which a beneficiary has been allowed to enforce a promise to do an act, even though the act was to be done "directly to" the promisee. For example, a number of courts have held that a person who fails to get what a decedent intended under a will has a claim against the lawyer who drafted the will as an intended beneficiary of the contract between the decedent and the lawyer even though the lawyer's performance was rendered to the decedent.[19] Courts have, however, voiced concern over extending malpractice

Question to whom performance is to go

---

at the time the . . . agreement was executed [as] long as [it] was identifiable as a third-party beneficiary at the time of performance of the . . . agreement").

[12] But until the third person is identified, the parties to the contract are presumably free to modify or rescind it, regardless of the rule as to when a beneficiary's right becomes vested. On the vesting of a beneficiary's rights, see §10.8 *infra*.

[13] *See* Restatement Second §308 cmt. *a*.

[14] Vikingstad v. Baggott, 282 P.2d 824 (Wash. 1955) (benefit need not "be of an altruistic nature and completely without thought of any gain to the party extracting the promise").

[15] Beverly v. Macy, 702 F.2d 931, 941 (11th Cir. 1983).

[16] For a case giving this as a reason for denying recovery, *see* Buchman Plumbing Co. v. Regents of Univ., 215 N.W.2d 479 (Minn. 1974) ("If, by the terms of the contract, performance is directly rendered to a third party, he is intended by the promisee to be benefited. Otherwise, if the performance is directly rendered to the promisee, the third party who also may be benefited is an incidental beneficiary with no right of action.").

[17] Lonsdale v. Chesterfield, *supra* note 8 (because developer "could not fully perform its promise . . . without directly benefitting the petitioners as deeded owners of the lots," they "were thus intended . . . beneficiaries"). When a court speaks of a "direct benefit" to a third person, it is not always clear whether the court is referring to the test of direct performance or merely using "direct" in contrast to "incidental."

[18] Ratzlaff v. Franz Foods, 468 S.W.2d 239 (Ark. 1971) (downstream landowner was intended beneficiary of chicken processor's agreement with city not to oversaturate city's sewage treatment facilities).

[19] Lucas v. Hamm, 364 P.2d 685 (Cal. 1961) ("It is true that under a contract for the benefit of a third person performance is usually to be rendered directly to the beneficiary, but this is not necessarily the case"); Stowe v. Smith, 441 A.2d 81 (Conn. 1981) (rejecting argument that "as a

liability to others than clients where what is involved is other than the drafting of a will.[20] Thus while it may be significant that the performance is to be rendered to the beneficiary, this circumstance is neither necessary nor sufficient for a conclusion that a third person can enforce the contract.

Liability insurance cases

Prominent among the cases holding it not to be necessary are those involving promises to procure liability insurance, under which an insurer promises to discharge the liability of the insured in the event that the insured becomes liable to a third person.[21] In one of these cases, the Supreme Court of Wisconsin held that an owner (C) of equipment in a restaurant was an intended beneficiary of an insurance agency's (A's) oral agreement with the operator (B) of the restaurant to procure liability insurance.[22] The owner of the equipment could therefore recover damages from the agency for its failure to do so, even though the agency's performance was not to have been rendered to the owner of the equipment.

Interpretation and omitted cases

The difficulties that courts have experienced in this area cannot be resolved by so simple a test as that of asking to whom the performance is to be rendered. They are, in reality, the same sorts of difficulties that courts have experienced in other cases of interpretation and dealing with omitted cases. If the parties have provided either that the third party has the right to enforce the agreement[23] or that the third party does not have that right,[24] the court will give effect to that provision. If they have included a provision that is not clear, the court's function is that of interpretation. If they have said nothing, the court's function is that of supplying a term to deal with an omitted case. In discharging these functions courts have experienced the same conflict between the subjective and objective theories as in other instances of interpretation.[25] They have faced the same problems of treating questions as being of law or fact.[26] And they have had the same difficulties in applying the parol evidence rule.

---

matter of law a promisor cannot intend to assume a direct obligation to a third party unless the promisor's performance is to be rendered directly to that party").

[20] Spinner v. Nutt, 631 N.E.2d 542 (Mass. 1994) (trust beneficiaries were not intended beneficiaries of contract between trustees and trustees' lawyers).

[21] Cases in which third persons have claimed rights as beneficiaries of liability policies themselves are not discussed here because of the complexities introduced by policy provisions and legislation.

[22] Pappas v. Jack O.A. Nelsen Agency, 260 N.W.2d 721 (Wis. 1978).

[23] Cobert v. Home Owners Warranty Corp., 391 S.E.2d 263 (Va. 1990) (statement that purchaser "is a beneficiary" showed "clear and definite intention" to confer a benefit).

[24] Mississippi High School Activities Assn. v. Farris, 501 So. 2d 393 (Miss. 1987) (statement of purpose in handbook that was part of contract showed no intention to benefit).

[25] Fasse v. Lower Heating & Air Conditioning, 736 P.2d 930 (Kan. 1987) ("court must apply the general rules for construction of contracts").

[26] See Postlewait Constr. v. Great Am. Ins. Cos., 720 P.2d 805 (Wash. 1986) (where "there are no disputed material facts, the contract will be construed by the court as a matter of law").

Although it has been argued that the parol evidence rule should not bar the use of evidence of prior negotiations to show an intention to benefit, courts have been reluctant to go this far.[27] At the other extreme, it has sometimes been said that intention to benefit must be found in the contract itself,[28] or at least in the contract together with surrounding circumstances[29] and basic notions of justice.[30] A more balanced view would treat admissibility of evidence of prior negotiations to show intent to benefit in the same way that it is treated in other cases. Thus if a completely integrated agreement is silent as to intention to benefit, evidence of prior negotiations to show such an intention should not be admitted because it would, in effect, be used to add a term.[31] If the agreement is only partially integrated, however, the evidence should probably be admitted on the ground that the additional term would be consistent.[32] If the agreement is not integrated, there is no reason to refuse to admit the evidence.[33] And if the evidence is to be used for the purpose of interpretation, it should be admitted

Parol evidence rule

[27] Hylte Bruks Aktiebolag v. Babcock & Wilcox Co., 399 F.2d 289 (2d Cir. 1968) (fn.6: Corbin appears more liberal than New York courts for he appears "willing to allow a party to establish his status . . . by evidence wholly extrinsic to the written contract"). For Corbin on the parol evidence rule, see the discussions of Corbin's view in §7.3 and of the essence of a plain meaning rule in §7.12 *supra*. As to his views on beneficiaries, see the discussion of the first Restatement in §10.2 *supra*.

[28] Georgia R.R. Bank & Trust Co. v. Federal Deposit Ins. Corp., 758 F.2d 1548 (11th Cir. 1985) (Georgia law: "person cannot be deemed a third-party beneficiary unless it clearly appears from the contract that the contract was intended for the benefit of the third person").

[29] Trans-Orient Marine Corp. v. Star Trading & Marine, 925 F.2d 566 (2d Cir. 1991) ("In determining third party beneficiary status [under New York law] it is permissible for the court to look at the surrounding circumstances as well as the agreement.").

Courts have looked to surrounding circumstances not only to show that there was an intention to benefit, but also to show that there was no such intention. Sisters of Saint Joseph v. Russell, 867 P.2d 1377 (Or. 1994) ("jury could consider, not only the terms of the contract, but also the circumstances under which the contract was made").

[30] For a case taking account of basic notions of justice, *see* Pstragowski v. Metropolitan Life Ins. Co., 553 F.2d 1 (1st Cir. 1977) (court justified holding that wife was only incidental beneficiary of her husband's employment contract on the ground that "enforcement [by her] would not produce the result intended by [him] at the least cost to society"). *See also* Restatement Second §304 cmt. *e* ("In cases of doubt, the question whether such an intention is to be attributed to the promisee may be influenced by the likelihood that recognition of the right will further the legitimate expectations of the promisee, make available a simple and convenient procedure for enforcement, or protect the beneficiary in his reasonable reliance on the promise").

[31] Hylte Bruks Aktiebolag v. Babcock & Wilcox Co., *supra* note 27 (merger clause "in effect excludes the use of extrinsic evidence").

[32] It is unlikely that evidence of prior negotiations would "contradict" the terms of the writing. See the discussion of the meaning of *consistent* in §7.3 *supra*.

[33] Valdez v. Cillessen & Son, *supra* note 25 (where intentions are unclear, "other evidence may be considered to . . . determine what the parties intended").

**Intention of
promisee**

unless the jurisdiction adheres to a plain meaning rule that would preclude admission.[34]

In view of the Restatement Second's requirement that a right in the beneficiary be "appropriate to effectuate the intention of the *parties*," its additional requirement that the *promisee* have an intention to benefit the third person seems curious at first. No such additional requirement is imposed in other situations in which a court is asked to supply a term. Nevertheless, it makes sense if it is regarded as a factor in determining the intention of the parties, for, compared with such other situations, cases involving claims of beneficiaries are singular in an important respect. If the parties bargain freely before they make their contract, every additional term must be paid for in some way.[35] Thus, whether the term that one of the parties wants included would, for example, impose a duty of best efforts on the other or make the other liable to a third person, the other party will want some concession — perhaps an increase in what is to be paid, perhaps the inclusion of some favorable term. If nothing has been said about best efforts and a court is asked to supply a term requiring the other party to use best efforts,[36] it may take no stretch of the imagination to suppose that the parties bargained on the assumption that such efforts would be exerted and that this was reflected in the price. Certainly there would be every reason for one party to be willing to pay something in order to have the other party undertake such an obligation. But if nothing is said about liability to a third person and a court is asked to supply a term making the other party liable to a third person, the matter is not so simple. A party ordinarily contracts for itself.[37] Why would one party have been willing to pay anything at all in order to have the other party undertake such an obligation? The requirement of the Restatement Second that there be an indication "that the promisee intends to give the beneficiary the benefit of the promised performance" seems designed to deal with this question. It might be paraphrased to require an indication "that the promisee would have been willing to pay the fair value for the promisor's undertaking a duty to the beneficiary." Surely if the contrary appears there is no reason to impose such a duty on the promisor.[38]

---

[34]For a case decided under a plain meaning rule, *see* Oxford Commercial Corp. v. Landau, 190 N.E.2d 230 (N.Y. 1963) (language was "too clear and precise to admit of evidence").

[35]An "additional term" is one that would not be read into the contract anyway. (Even if a term would be read in, a party may have to pay to have it made explicit.)

[36]On supplying a term requiring best efforts, see the discussion of the duty of best efforts in §7.17 *supra*.

[37]Little Rock Wastewater Util. v. Larry Moyer Trucking, 902 S.W.2d 760 (Ark. 1995) ("presumption is that parties contract only for themselves").

[38]Grigerik v. Sharpe, 721 A.2d 526 (Conn. 1998) (looking to intention of both rather than just one of the parties, is "sensible way of minimizing the risk that a contracting party will be held liable to one whom he neither knew, nor legitimately could be held to know, would ultimately be his contract obligee"). For an illustration, see the cases involving suits against architects cited in the discussion of the example of a construction contract — "horizontal" in §10.4 *infra*.

Just as a donee of a gift can refuse the gift, the beneficiary of a gift promise that has not already assented to a contract for its benefit may render any duty to itself inoperative from the beginning by disclaiming it within a reasonable time after learning of the contract.[39]

Disclaimer by beneficiary

The Restatement Second's treatment of gift promises is of heightened importance because this category now includes many of the promises in what were traditionally considered creditor beneficiary situations. According to the first Restatement, a person is a creditor beneficiary if "performance of the promise will satisfy an actual or supposed or asserted duty of the promisee to the beneficiary."[40] The Restatement Second's category of promises to pay the promisee's debt still includes the classic creditor beneficiary situation of *Lawrence v. Fox*.[41] But the Restatement Second's requirements for this category are more exacting than the first Restatement's requirements for creditor beneficiaries in two respects. First, the Restatement Second excludes situations in which the duty that the promisee (B) owes the beneficiary (C) is a duty to do something other than pay money.[42] Second, it excludes situations in which the duty that the promisee owes the beneficiary is a "supposed or asserted duty" rather than an "actual" one.[43] But a beneficiary whose situation is excluded on one of these grounds is not necessarily an incidental beneficiary, for the beneficiary may be an intended beneficiary of a gift promise.[44]

Promise to pay promisee's debt

The law of contract beneficiaries has not been unaffected by the increasing role played by reliance in contract law. The Restatement Second commentary asserts that "if the beneficiary would be reasonable in relying on the promise as manifesting an intention to confer a right upon him, he is an intended beneficiary."[45] Furthermore, the Restatement Second's revised version of §90 speaks of reliance by "action or forbearance on the part of the promisee or a third person."[46] Thus, even though a third person is not an intended beneficiary of

Effect of reliance by beneficiary

---

[39] *See* Restatement Second §306. Compare the right of disclaimer of a donee under a gratuitous assignment in §327(2). See the discussion of gratuitous assignments as generally revocable in §11.6 *infra*.

[40] Restatement §133(1)(b). In order to make the two categories of beneficiaries mutually exclusive, this provision only applies "if no purpose to make a gift appears."

[41] 20 N.Y. 268 (1859) (discussed in §10.2 *supra*).

[42] *But see* Restatement Second §302 cmt. *b* ("Promise of a performance other than the payment of money may be governed by the same principle if the promisee's obligation is regarded as easily convertible into money, as in cases of obligations to deliver commodities or securities which are actively traded in organized markets.").

[43] *See* Restatement Second §302 cmt. *b* (subparagraph (a) does not apply "if the promisee has never been under any duty to the beneficiary"). But subparagraph (a) applies, as did the creditor beneficiary provision of the first Restatement, though the duty "is voidable or is unenforceable by reason of the statute of limitations, the Statute of Frauds, or a discharge in bankruptcy." Id.

[44] *See* Rae v. Air-Speed, *supra* note 1.

[45] Restatement Second §302 cmt. *d*. The comment does not speak of actual reliance, but Illustrations 11 and 12 involve reliance.

[46] See the quotation in the discussion of Restatement §90 in §2.19 *supra*.

a promise, that person's reliance on the promise may give rise to a right against the promisor.[47]

In the following sections we consider some recurring situations involving contract beneficiaries.

Example of construction contract— "horizontal"

§10.4. **Construction Contracts.** Two particularly important recurring situations arise out of construction contracts.[1] In the first, two contractors (A and C) have contracted directly with an owner (B). One contractor (C) makes a claim "horizontally" against the other contractor (A), alleging that the other's delay in performing its contract with the owner hindered the complaining contractor. The older cases generally denied recovery, holding that the owner did not intend to benefit the complaining contractor when making the contract with the other.[2] Courts have been particularly firm on this point when the suit is against the owner's architect.[3] More recently, however, some courts have allowed the complaining contractor to recover as an intended beneficiary, especially where the owner, in order to avoid using a general contractor, has made a number of similar contracts directly with "multi-prime" contractors, each contractor recognizing the other contractor's rights to performance.[4]

Example of construction contract— "vertical"

In the other situation, an owner (C) has contracted with a general contractor (B) who has contracted with a subcontractor (A). The owner makes a claim "vertically" against the subcontractor for damages due to the subcontractor's delayed or defective performance. Here, too, the older cases generally denied

---

[47] Ravelo v. County of Hawaii, 658 P.2d 883 (Haw. 1983) ("the revised [Restatement Second] section provides a sounder legal foundation").

This situation should not be confused with that in which a promisee relies on a gratuitous promise and a third party seeks to enforce the promise. *See* Overlock v. Central Vt. Pub. Serv. Corp., 237 A.2d 356 (Vt. 1967) ("the essential detrimental reliance" was lacking where employer allegedly told local residents that it would take care of injured lineman for rest of his life and they gave up plans to take up a collection for him). *Overlock* is discussed in E. Farnsworth, Changing Your Mind ch. 9 (1998), revised from Farnsworth, Decisions, Decisions: Some Binding, Some Not, 28 Suffolk U. L. Rev. 17 (1994).

§10.4 [1] *See generally* Eisenberg, Third-Party Beneficiaries, 92 Colum. L. Rev. 1358, 1396-1406 (1992); Jones, Economic Losses Caused by Construction Deficiencies: The Competing Regimes of Contract and Tort, 59 U. Cin. L. Rev. 1051, 1083-1101 (1991).

[2] Buchman Plumbing Co. v. Regents of Univ., 215 N.W.2d 479 (Minn. 1974) (mechanical contractor who contracted directly with university was only incidental beneficiary of contract between university and general contractor).

[3] Valley Landscape Co. v. Rolland, 237 S.E.2d 120 (Va. 1977) (landscaping contractor could not recover from landscape architect as beneficiary of latter's contract with owner since, though "any contract for construction is usually of incidental benefit to numerous persons," it is not the benefit to the contractor "that is primarily envisioned by the architect and the owner [since the] owner employs an architect, to a degree, to protect himself from the contractor").

[4] Moore Constr. Co. v. Clarksville Dept. of Elec., 707 S.W.2d 1 (Tenn. App. 1985) (unless contracts "clearly provide otherwise," multiple prime contractors "will be considered to be intended . . . beneficiaries"), aff'd mem., 707 S.W.2d 1 (Tenn. 1986).

recovery.[5] Again, however, some have allowed the owner to recover as a creditor beneficiary despite the fact that the subcontractor's performance is not performance of the general contractor's duty to the owner to furnish a completed building.[6] To the extent that such an owner is in a better position to insist on a contract clause to support its claim than is a contractor in a "multi-prime" situation, the owner who has not done so may be in a weaker position to seek judicial relief.

In the next section we look at another recurring situation.

§10.5. **Payment Bonds.** Another recurring situation involves claims by laborers or suppliers against sureties on payment bonds. A contractor who undertakes a substantial construction project is usually required to furnish such a bond. Payment bonds are required for public works by statutes and ordinances at all levels of government;[1] they are required for private construction jobs by the construction contract itself. Such a bond involves three parties: the contractor (as principal, i.e., principal *obligor*), a bonding company (as *surety*), and the owner (as *obligee*).[2] It embodies promises by two parties, one by the contractor to the owner and one by the surety to the owner, that all debts incurred by the contractor for labor and materials will be paid.[3] The surety charges the contractor a premium for the bond, and the contractor passes this on to the owner as part of its costs. The problem arises if the contractor encounters financial difficulties in the course of performance and fails to pay laborers and suppliers. Do they have claims against the surety as beneficiaries of its promise under the bond?

Payment bonds described

In answering this question, it is useful to ask why the owner requires a payment bond, since any additional cost due to the surety's liability to third persons will be passed on to the owner.[4] The most obvious answer is that the owner has done it to keep the property free of mechanics' liens. State statutes protect laborers and suppliers that make improvements on real property by giving them a lien (i.e., a security interest) on that property to

Owner's reason for bond

---

[5]United States ex rel. Control Sys. v. Arundel Corp., 896 F.2d 143 (5th Cir. 1990) ("mere fact that [general] was to benefit from the [sub]contract . . . does not give [general] the right to maintain a contract action" against subcontractor's supplier).

[6]A leading case is Syndoulos Lutheran Church v. A.R.C. Indus., 662 P.2d 109 (Alaska 1983) (subcontract "was obviously intended to benefit the owner").

§10.5 [1]For example, on contracts with the federal government for public works, a payment bond is required by the Miller Act, 40 U.S.C.A. §§270a-270d. A payment bond should not be confused with a performance bond, which involves the same three parties. A performance bond embodies promises to the owner by both the contractor and a surety that the contractor will perform.

[2]Sometimes a payment bond is furnished by a subcontractor (as principal) and a bonding company (as surety) in favor of a general contractor (as obligee).

[3]If the principal does not perform its promise and the surety does, the principal must reimburse the surety.

[4]See the discussion of the intention of the promisee in §10.3 *supra*.

secure payment for those improvements.[5] By requiring a payment bond, the owner is assured that if such persons are not paid, the owner will be reimbursed by the surety for any payments made to avoid encumbrances on the property.

Government as owner

If the contract is one for public works, however, this cannot be the explanation, since public property is generally exempt from mechanics' liens. When laborers or suppliers have sued as beneficiaries of payment bonds on government contracts, therefore, courts have allowed recovery on the ground that the government must have intended to give them the benefit of the surety's promised payment, perhaps in place of the lien that they would otherwise have, because the government had no need to require such a promise for its own protection.[6] Sometimes the legislation that requires the bond mandates this result.[7]

Private owner

If the owner is private, this reasoning does not apply. It can therefore be argued that the private owner had no intent to benefit laborers and suppliers, but only the selfish motive of protecting the owner's property from liens.[8] The laborer's or supplier's only remedy would then be that afforded by a mechanics' lien. However, courts have overwhelmingly rejected this argument and allowed laborers and suppliers to recover as beneficiaries of payment bonds, even though the owner is private.[9] The laborer or supplier that has failed to take advantage of a mechanics' lien then has a claim against the surety. Sometimes courts have reasoned that the owner is advantaged in attracting laborers and suppliers of good quality by assuring them of payment.[10] Often courts have stressed the supposed

[5]See the discussion of compensation expected from another source in §2.20 *supra*.

[6]Robertson Co. v. Globe Indem. Co., 112 A. 50 (Pa. 1920) (legislature intended "to protect persons furnishing work and materials").

[7]*See* Miller Act, 40 U.S.C.A. §270b.

[8]This argument was at first accepted by the Supreme Court of Alabama, in an opinion that was later set aside on rehearing, in Fidelity & Deposit Co. v. Rainer, 125 So. 55 (Ala. 1929) (in case of a private contract, "all know that the owner has sought to be and is thereby protected from liens and claims of materialmen and others, and therefore that he is the one directly and immediately intended to be protected, and that the protection to the materialmen and others is only incidental").

[9]La Salle Iron Works v. Largen, 410 S.W.2d 87 (Mo. 1967) (noting "a substantial weight of authority" in favor of recovery).

There has been uncertainty as to whether the beneficiary is a donee or a creditor. The first Restatement treated the beneficiary as a donee in §133 illus. 4, but the Restatement Second avoids the question, placing the illustration under the heading "Other Intended Beneficiaries" in §302 illus. 12.

[10]Fidelity & Deposit Co. v. Rainer, *supra* note 8 (payment bond was standard form of American Institute of Architects, and architects' concern is to arrange for owner such protection "as assures the construction of the building as agreed [and] not only indemnifies the owner, but tends to save him from harassing litigation, and to prevent delays to the annoyance of both owner and architect").

meaning of the general language of the bond.[11] The same result has also been reached in cases of claims by laborers or suppliers under bonds furnished by subcontractors in favor of general contractors.[12] Many payment bonds now include provisions giving laborers and suppliers a right against the surety.[13]

We now look at yet another recurring situation.

§10.6.   Government Contracts.   A recurring situation of great and increasing importance arises in connection with government contracts to perform public services. Although such contracts often benefit individual members of the public, courts have been reluctant to accord such persons rights as beneficiaries unless the contract makes it clear that this was intended.[1] While reaffirming that such contracts are subject to the general rules on third-party beneficiaries,[2] judges have been sensitive to such special problems as the possibility of excessive financial burden, the risk of a multitude of claims, and the likelihood of impairment of services,[3] as well as the difficulty in determining the intent of the government.[4]

A classic case is *H.R. Moch Co. v. Rensselaer Water Co.*, decided by the New York Court of Appeals in 1928. A water company had contracted with the City of Rensselaer to furnish water at hydrants. Moch's warehouse burned down because the water company failed to maintain adequate pressure, and he sued the company as a beneficiary of the contract. The court, speaking through Cardozo, rejected the claim. "In a broad sense it is true that every city

Importance of problem

Example of Moch v. Rensselaer Water Co.

---

[11] Fidelity & Deposit Co. v. Rainer, *supra* note 8 (surety's undertaking that contractor shall "pay all persons who have contracts" with it would be "meaningless" unless intended for the benefit of laborers and suppliers).

[12] Daniel-Morris Co. v. Glens Falls Indem. Co., 126 N.E.2d 750 (N.Y. 1955) (payment bond furnished by subcontractor to general contractors was "intended to benefit unpaid materialmen").

[13] Such provisions have themselves proved a source of disputes over interpretation. *See* Moore Constr. Co. v. Clarksville Dept. of Elec., 707 S.W.2d 1 (Tenn. App. 1985) (coprime contractor not intended beneficiary of payment bond because not one of specified claimants), aff'd mem. (1986).

§10.6   [1] Price v. Pierce, 823 F.2d 1114 (7th Cir. 1987) (prospective lower-income tenants were not intended beneficiaries of contract with housing authorities to make apartments available).

[2] La Mourea v. Rhude, 295 N.W. 304 (Minn. 1940) (approving "the obvious conclusion that [this] is but a special application of the principles . . . concerning the rights of donee and creditor beneficiaries"). *See* Restatement Second §313 (general rules apply "except to the extent that application would contravene the policy of the law authorizing the contract or prescribing remedies for its breach").

[3] *See* Restatement Second §313 cmt. *a* ("Among factors which may make inappropriate a direct action against the promisor are arrangements for governmental control over the litigation and settlement of claims, the likelihood of impairment of service or of excessive financial burden, and the availability of alternatives such as insurance.").

[4] Clearwater Constructors Co. v. Gutierrez, 626 S.W.2d 789 (Tex. Civ. App. 1981) ("difficulties in applying the intent test are aggravated" since relevant intent is "that of an amalgam of legislative bodies, administrative agencies and government officials").

contract . . . is for the benefit of the public. More than this, however, must be shown to give a right of action to a member of the public not formally a party." Cardozo noted that the city was under no legal duty to furnish its inhabitants with fire protection, and he expressed the fear that if recovery were to be allowed, the water company's "field of obligation would be expanded beyond reasonable limits."[5]

Similar claims rejected

Other courts, conscious of the extent of the risk that would be placed on water companies and of the availability of insurance against fire,[6] have reached the same result.[7] Similar claims by injured drivers against persons who have contracted with the government to repair or maintain highways have also been unsuccessful.[8] But if consequential damages are not involved, so that the promisor's risk is more limited, as when the contract merely fixes a maximum rate for a utility company, courts have permitted enforcement by third persons.[9]

Government under duty

Furthermore, if the contract is one to perform a duty that the government owes to members of the public, courts have generally allowed recovery by individual members on the theory that they are creditor beneficiaries. On this reasoning, if a city owes a duty to the public to keep its streets in repair, one who contracts to perform this duty will be liable to a member of the public for breach of that contract.[10] But under the general rules of the Restatement Second, the promise would be characterized as a gift promise because it is not one to pay a debt of the promisee,[11] though the Restatement Second sets out some special rules for government contracts.[12]

Provision in contract

Government contracts sometimes by their terms indicate an intention that beneficiaries have a right of enforcement, and courts give effect to such terms.

---

[5] 159 N.E. 896, 897 (N.Y. 1928).

[6] If Moch had been insured for fire, his insurer, on paying him, would have been subrogated to any rights that Moch had against the water company.

[7] Earl E. Roher Transfer & Storage Co. v. Hutchinson Water Co., 322 P.2d 810 (Kan. 1958) ("Kansas has followed the majority rule").

[8] Davis v. Nelson-Deppe, Inc., 424 P.2d 733 (Idaho 1967) (owner of truck was only incidental beneficiary of contract for resurfacing of highway).

[9] Bush v. Upper Valley Telecable Co., 524 P.2d 1055 (Idaho 1974) (resident of city, who subscribed to cable television, was intended beneficiary of contract between city and cable service fixing rates). Restatement Second §313(2), which speaks of "liability to a member of the public for consequential damages," does not cover these cases. See the discussion of the aspect of extent of risk in §10.1 *supra*.

[10] Fowler v. Chicago Rys. Co., 120 N.E. 635 (Ill. 1918) (where a street railway "has agreed with the city [to perform its duty] to keep the street in repair, any person sustaining damage" may maintain suit directly against railway). Whether a government owes a duty to the public in the absence of contract is beyond the scope of this treatise.

[11] See the discussion of gift promises in §10.3 *supra*.

[12] *See* Restatement Second §313 (promisor "not subject to contractual liability to a member of the public for consequential damages . . . unless (a) the terms of the promise provide for such liability; or (b) the promisee is subject to liability to the member of the public and a direct action against the promisor is consistent with the terms of the contract and with the policy of the law").

Thus contracts for public works often provide that the contractor will pay for harm that the contractor's activities cause to members of the public and their property. The contractor's undertaking may, of course, be narrowly read, so that the contractor is liable only to indemnify the government if it is required to pay damages to a member of the public. In that case, the contractor is not directly liable to the individual harmed.[13] It has been held, however, that where language made the contractor "liable for any damages done to . . . private property and injuries sustained by persons," the contractor's liability was not to the government, but to the individuals harmed. On this interpretation of the language, it is clear that the individuals were intended beneficiaries, and it has been so held.[14]

Recent decades have seen a spate of cases involving third-party beneficiary claims under contracts with agencies of the federal government.[15] In *Bossier Parish School Board v. Lemon*,[16] a seminal case, the Fifth Circuit held that African-American personnel at an Air Force base were intended beneficiaries of a funding contract between the United States and the local school district, requiring it in return for financial aid to admit children of base personnel to schools in accordance with state law. The claim in *Bossier* had particular appeal because, had it been denied, the school board would have been left with funds for which it had not rendered its promised performance. This appeal was articulated in a later California case holding tenants in a building financed by a federally insured mortgage to be intended beneficiaries of a provision of the financing agreement under which the landlord was required to charge no more rent than a federally approved schedule allowed.

> Surely it would be unconscionable if a builder could secure the benefits of a government guaranteed loan upon his promise to charge no more than a schedule of rents he had agreed to and then find there is no remedy by which the builder can be forced to disgorge rents he had collected in excess of his agreement simply because the Government had failed to act.[17]

---

[13] Ronnau v. Caravan Intl. Corp., 468 P.2d 118 (Kan. 1970) (third person had no right under contract to indemnity).

[14] La Mourea v. Rhude, *supra* note 2.

[15] As to whether federal common law or state law is to be applied, *see* Price v. Pierce, *supra* note 1 ("issue is potentially so important to the success of the [federal] program . . . that we believe that Congress . . . would have wanted the question to be decided by federal courts applying a uniform principle"). *But see* Zigas v. Superior Court, 174 Cal. Rptr. 806 (Ct. App. 1981) ("though the operations of HUD are of considerable magnitude, there is no reason to conclude that the operations of the department would be unduly burdened or subjected to uncertainty by variant state law interpretations"). To the extent that courts follow the Restatement Second, this question has diminished importance.

[16] 370 F.2d 847 (5th Cir. 1967) (alternative ground).

[17] Zigas v. Superior Court, *supra* note 15, at 813.

It is not, however, necessary to find an element of unjust enrichment in order to make out a claim in such a case.[18] Nor does the presence of such an element assure success, at least if it is not viewed as accruing to the promisor at the expense of the claimant.[19]

Relation to private actions

A particularly troublesome group of cases raises the question of the relationship of third-party beneficiary claims under federal contracts to private right of action claims under federal statutes. The test for the latter laid down by the United States Supreme Court in 1975 asks, among other things, whether the plaintiff is a member of a class for "whose *especial* benefit the statute was enacted" and whether there is "any indication of legislative intent . . . to create such a remedy."[20] As this test has come to be applied with increasing strictness, plaintiffs have resorted to claims as third-party beneficiaries. The obvious difficulty is that the third-party beneficiary test bears such similarity to the private right of action test that a plaintiff who fails to satisfy the latter is likely to fare no better under the former. As a federal district court has put it, while the two kinds of claims are "conceptually distinct," in practice "the considerations determining the validity of the former overlap to a substantial extent those determining the validity of the latter." That court went on to reject both claims.[21]

If a third person qualifies as an intended beneficiary, what are the third person's rights and how do they relate to those of the promisee?

C.   RIGHTS OF PARTIES

Questions raised

§10.7.   Relative Rights of Beneficiary and Promisee. Questions of the relative rights of the parties under a contract for the benefit of a third party are complicated because three parties, rather than the usual two, are involved. We begin with the rights of the beneficiary (C), first against the promisor (A) and, second, against the promisee (B). Then we turn to the rights of the promisee against the promisor.

Beneficiary against promisor

Once it is decided that a third party is an intended beneficiary, it follows that the party has a right against the promisor. The beneficiary can enforce that right without joining the promisee in an action against the promisor for damages or specific performance.[1] The beneficiary's vulnerability to an agreement between

---

[18]Holbrook v. Pitt, 643 F.2d 1261 (7th Cir. 1981) (tenants of housing projects were intended beneficiaries of project owners' contracts with federal agency under which agency was to make rental payments on tenants' behalf).

[19]Price v. Pierce, *supra* note 1 (prospective tenants were not intended beneficiaries of contract between developers and state agency as "agent" of federal agency where, though developers got no rent subsidy from those tenants, "they still had the benefit of . . . mortgage subsidies").

[20]Cort v. Ash, 422 U.S. 66, 78 (1975).

[21]Chaplin v. Consolidated Edison Co., 579 F. Supp. 1470, 1473 (S.D.N.Y. 1984).

§10.7 [1]Baurer v. Devenes, 121 A. 566 (Conn. 1923) (specific performance). *See* Restatement Second §304.

the promisor and the promisee to discharge or modify the promisor's duty and to defenses or claims of the promisor against the promisee are discussed later.[2] The beneficiary ordinarily has no right to restitution from the promisor since any benefit the promisor has received was conferred by the promisee, not by the beneficiary.[3]

In addition to a newly acquired right against the promisor, the beneficiary retains any right that the beneficiary had against the promisee before the contract between the promisor and promisee. In other words, if the promisee already owed a duty to the beneficiary, neither the making of the contract nor the beneficiary's acceptance of it operates to discharge that duty (i.e., there is no novation).[4] Instead, there are now two duties owed to the beneficiary — one owed by the promisor and one by the promisee — and the beneficiary can get judgment against both, though the beneficiary is entitled to "only one complete satisfaction."[5]

Beneficiary against promisee

Take the case of a mortgagor (B) that is under a duty to a mortgagee (C). If the mortgagor transfers the land to a grantee (A) that assumes the mortgage by promising the mortgagor to pay it, the grantee is now also under a duty to the mortgagee as an intended beneficiary. Now two parties — the assuming grantee and the mortgagor — owe overlapping duties to render the same performance to the mortgagee. But the mortgagee is entitled to only one performance, so that payments by either the assuming grantee or the mortgagor discharge the other obligor as well. Since, as between the two obligors, it is the one that assumed who should pay, the assuming grantee is a principal and the mortgagor is a surety.[6] All of the incidents of suretyship apply to the overlapping duties from the time that the mortgagee learns of the relationship. Thus if the mortgagee

Example of mortgage assumption

---

[2]See §§10.8 (discharge and modification), 10.9 (defenses and claims) *infra*.

[3]*See* first Restatement §356 cmt. *d* (usually "third party for whose benefit a contract is made does not himself render any performance that is received by the promisor"). That the beneficiary may have a right to restitution in the unusual situation in which the beneficiary has itself rendered a performance that is received by the promisor, *see* first Restatement §356.

[4]Copeland v. Beard, 115 So. 389 (Ala. 1928) (rejecting the view that "upon election to accept the benefits of the contract, [the creditor] releases the original debtor" and adopting "the doctrine that by acceptance of the promise made for his benefit, and action thereon, the creditor does not release the original debtor, unless so stipulated in the contract and made known to the creditor").

[5]Erickson v. Grande Ronde Lumber Co., 94 P.2d 139, 143 (Or. 1939) (creditor beneficiary "was entitled to maintain this action against the promisor . . . as well as against his original debtor [and] was entitled to judgment against both; however to only one complete satisfaction"). If the two duties are to render the same performance, the promisor will be a principal and the promisee a surety. See the discussion of suretyship described in §6.3 *supra*. But the performance to be rendered by the two parties is not always the same. See the discussion of the example of a construction contract — "vertical" in §10.4 *supra*.

[6]See the discussion of suretyship described in §6.3 *supra*.

grants to the assuming grantee an extension of the time to pay, the mortgagor is discharged under the law of suretyship.[7]

Promisee against promisor

The promisee (B), as well as the beneficiary (C), has a right against the promisor (A). In principle, that right is also enforceable by an action for damages or specific performance to the same extent as are other contract rights.[8] In addition, the promisee may have a claim to restitution of a benefit conferred on the promisor.[9] In practice, however, the availability of damages and specific performance depends to a considerable extent on whether the right of the beneficiary rests on a gift promise or on a promise to pay the promisee's debt.

Gift promise

If the promisee's intention was to make a gift of the promised performance to the beneficiary, the promisee will usually suffer no economic loss if the promisor does not perform.[10] Were the promisee to sue for damages, the promisee would recover only nominal damages. Courts have therefore considered the damage remedy inadequate and have granted specific performance if the other conditions for that remedy are met.[11]

Promise to pay promisee's debt

If the promised performance will satisfy a duty of the promisee to pay money to the beneficiary, the promisee will usually have no difficulty in proving substantial damages.[12] Therefore, the apparent solution is to award those damages and refuse specific performance on the ground that the damage remedy is adequate. But this poses a risk of double liability. For though a single payment by the promisor would have discharged both its duty to the promisee and its duty to the beneficiary, the promisor may now be held liable in full to both. This risk is avoided if the promisee, instead of seeking damages, seeks specific performance of a right as surety to exoneration by the principal (the promisor) — a right under suretyship law to compel the principal to pay the creditor.[13] If the

---

[7]Union Mut. Ins. Co. v. Hanford, 143 U.S. 187 (1892) ("subsequent agreement of the mortgagee with the [assuming] grantee, without the assent of the grantor, extending the time of the mortgage debt, discharges the grantor from all personal liability for that debt"). *See* Restatement Second §314.

[8]*See* Restatement Second §307 (specific performance).

[9]*See* Restatement Second §370 cmt. *a* (if "contract is for the benefit of a third person, the promisee is entitled to restitution unless the duty to the beneficiary cannot be varied under the rule stated in §311").

[10]In re Marriage of Smith & Maescher, 26 Cal. Rptr. 2d 133 (Ct. App. 1993) (ex-wife could not recover as promisee of ex-husband's promise to pay college expenses of donee-beneficiary son). As to the possibility of mixed motives, see the discussion of the test of intention to benefit in §10.3 *supra*.

[11]Drewen v. Bank of Manhattan Co., 155 A.2d 529 (N.J. 1959) (promisee of a contract to make will for benefit of third party "may also invoke the aid of a court of equity, for the general reason that his remedy at law is inadequate"). *See* Restatement Second §307.

[12]Heins v. Byers, 219 N.W. 287 (Minn. 1928) ("the measure of his damages is the amount of the debt").

[13]McKey-Fansher Co. v. Rowen, 5 N.W.2d 911 (Iowa 1942) (because of relation of principal and surety, "action to compel payment . . . was properly brought in equity"). *See* Restatement Second §307 cmt. *c*. On the surety's right to exoneration, *see* Restatement (Third) of Suretyship and Guaranty §21(2) (1996).

promisee seeks damages instead from the promisor, some courts have refused to allow recovery unless the promisee has already paid the creditor.[14] Others have allowed recovery with safeguards to ensure that what the promisee is awarded will be used to pay the creditor.[15]

Our next concern is the vulnerability of the beneficiary to an agreement between the promisor and the promisee to discharge or modify the promisor's duty.

§10.8.   Vulnerability of Beneficiary to Discharge or Modification.

Vesting of beneficiary's right

If the beneficiary (C) consents, the promisor (A) and promisee (B) are generally free to make a subsequent agreement that will discharge or modify the promisor's duty to the beneficiary.[1] All courts agree, however, that a time may come after which a beneficiary that does not consent is no longer vulnerable to such an agreement. At that time the beneficiary's right is said to be "vested." Courts have disagreed, however, over when vesting occurs, and three different views have emerged.

One view is that the beneficiary's right vests as soon as the contract is made, even though the beneficiary may not learn of the contract until later.[2] A second view is that the right vests when, having learned of the contract, the beneficiary assents to it.[3] A third view is that the right does not vest until, having learned of the contract, the beneficiary relies on it.[4]

Three possible views

---

[14]White v. Upton, 74 S.W.2d 924 (Ky. 1934) (promisee must "have paid or otherwise discharged the debt before he may maintain suit").

[15]John Julian Constr. Co. v. Monarch Builders, 306 A.2d 29 (Del. Super. 1973) ("the unjust enrichment that might accrue to the breaching promisor outweighs the risk of multiple liability being imposed upon the promisor"), aff'd, 324 A.2d 208 (Del. 1974).

§10.8   [1]This freedom is not unlimited. Since a promise for the benefit of a creditor of the promisee is an asset of the promisee, a release of the promisor may be ineffective if it is a fraud on other creditors of the promisee. Such problems are beyond the scope of this treatise.

[2]Tweeddale v. Tweeddale, 93 N.W. 440 (Wis. 1903) (donee: "regardless of whether [beneficiary] has any knowledge of the transaction . . . , neither one nor both [of the parties to the contract] can thereafter change the situation as regards the third person without his consent"). Even under this view, a beneficiary of a gift promise could by a subsequent disclaimer render the duty to it inoperative from the beginning. See the discussion of disclaimer by the beneficiary in §10.3 *supra*.

[3]Copeland v. Beard, 115 So. 389 (Ala. 1928) (contract is "offer to the creditor [beneficiary, whose] assent while the offer is open is all that is required").

If the beneficiary is a minor, without legal capacity to assent, courts holding this view have sometimes presumed assent. Restatement Second §311 cmt. *d* rejects this notion of "presumed" assent, saying that the revocability of the right of a beneficiary who is a minor "rests not on fictitious assent but on the manifested intention of the original parties."

[4]Morstain v. Kircher, 250 N.W. 727 (Minn. 1933) (where mortgagee had not "in reliance on the assumption contract placed herself in a position from which she could not retreat from loss," her right as beneficiary was lost when mortgagor released assuming grantee). This was the rule for creditor beneficiaries under first Restatement §143.

Restatement Second's view

There is much to be said for the third view, since it is difficult to deny to the parties who created the beneficiary's right the power to change it, when the beneficiary has done nothing in reliance on it. But reliance is often difficult to prove and, as in the case of contract formation, there is merit in allowing one to protect one's expectations by the simple act of manifesting one's assent. The Restatement Second takes this view, stating that the promisor and promisee have the power to discharge or modify the duty until "the beneficiary, before he receives notification of the discharge or modification, materially changes his position in justifiable reliance on the promise or brings suit on it or manifests assent to it at the request of the promisor or promisee."[5] This view has support in the cases.[6]

First Restatement's view as to donees

The first Restatement, however, distinguished between a donee and a creditor beneficiary and took the first view as to a donee, stating that the donee's right vested as soon as the contract was made.[7] This choice may have been due in part to a supposed analogy between the law of gifts, as to which irrevocability is essential, and the law as to "gift promises."[8] The authority for it consisted, in good part, of old cases involving the vesting of the rights of beneficiaries under life insurance policies.[9] Most courts have not followed the first Restatement either in distinguishing between donees and creditors with respect to vesting or in adhering to the first view.[10] Even if the first

---

[5] Restatement Second §311(3). Comment *h* gives a rationale for the alternative of assent, explaining that the "rule rests in part on an analogy to the law of offer and acceptance and in part on the probability that the beneficiary will rely in ways difficult or impossible to prove." See the discussion of the rationale for protecting expectation in §1.6 *supra. See also* E. Farnsworth, Changing Your Mind ch. 6 (1998).

[6] Olson v. Etheridge, 686 N.E.2d 563 (Ill. 1997) ("we adopt the vesting rule set forth in section 311").

[7] Restatement §142. As to the rule for a creditor beneficiary, see note 4 *supra*.

[8] *See* 1 S. Williston, Contracts §396 (1st ed. 1920) ("question is analogous to that arising upon a gift of property").

[9] Ford v. Mutual Life Ins. Co., 283 Ill. App. 325 (1936) ("beneficiary, the wife of the insured, had a vested right in the policy when the contract of insurance took effect"). Many of the life insurance cases involved, as did the *Ford* case, husbands who had named their wives as beneficiaries. The policy favoring the wife, especially if it was assumed that her efforts had contributed to the premiums, was obvious. Such cases now rarely arise because most policies reserve to the insured the power to change the beneficiary. Restatement Second §311 cmt. *c* says that the rule that protected the beneficiary of a life insurance policy "was not applied to fraternal benefit insurance, partly . . . because of statutes and partly because of charter and by-law provisions." For cases holding that a donee beneficiary's rights were immediately vested though life insurance was not involved, see notes 2 & 4 *supra*.

[10] McCulloch v. Canadian Pac. Ry., 53 F. Supp. 534 (D. Minn. 1943) (rule of first Restatement §142 "is not followed by the majority of the courts"). *See* Restatement Second §311, Reporter's Note ("weight of authority is opposed to a distinction between donee beneficiaries and creditor beneficiaries").

Restatement's rule for donees is rejected, the parties to a contract can give a donee an immediately vested right by the simple expedient of making the donee a promisee.[11]

Whatever view a court takes as to the time of vesting, the rule can be varied expressly or implicitly by the original contract between the promisor and the promisee. Thus the contract may provide that the beneficiary's right is vested when it would not otherwise be, or that it is not vested when it would otherwise be.[12] It is common in life insurance policies, for example, to reserve to the insured (B) a power to discharge the insurer's (A's) duty to the beneficiary (C) by substituting another beneficiary (D).[13]

Variation in contract effective

In addition, the promisor and promisee are not barred from making a subsequent agreement if the promisor's duty to the beneficiary has already been discharged. Thus, if the promisor has justifiably terminated the contract for a breach by the promisee, the promisor and promisee are free to make a new contract.[14]

Effect of breach

We look now at the related question of the vulnerability of a beneficiary to defenses and claims.

§10.9. Vulnerability of Beneficiary to Defenses and Claims. Since an intended beneficiary's (C's) right is based on the contract between the promisor (A) and the promisee (B), it is measured by the terms of that contract[1] and is generally subject to any defenses and claims of the promisor against the promisee arising out of that contract.[2] With the notable exception of a beneficiary under a collective bargaining agreement, which has been described by

Beneficiary is subject to defenses

---

[11] See the discussion of *Lawrence v. Fox* in §10.2 *supra*.

[12] The former is stated in Restatement Second §311(1). The latter follows from the principle that the beneficiary's right is based on the contract.

[13] New York Life Ins. Co. v. Cook, 211 N.W. 648 (Mich. 1927) (where policy provided that insured could change beneficiary, wife as beneficiary had "no vested interest"). Policies similarly empower the insured to surrender the policy for cash, to borrow against it, and to assign it. Occasionally, for estate tax reasons, the insured does not reserve the power to change the beneficiary.

[14] Oman v. Yates, 422 P.2d 489 (Wash. 1967) (after promisee defaulted by failing to pay, promisor could settle with promisee). *But see* Restatement Second §309 cmt. *b* ("there may be an implicit limitation on the extent to which such variation can be effected by the act or neglect of the promisee").

§10.9 [1] Osmond State Bank v. Uecker Grain, 419 N.W.2d 518 (Neb. 1988) (contract limited payment "to proceeds of the sale [of goods] located on [debtor's] farm").

[2] Hampton v. Federal Express Corp., 917 F.2d 1119 (8th Cir. 1990) (beneficiary's right against shipper of blood samples was subject to express $100 limitation under "released value doctrine"). *See* Restatement Second §309. The beneficiary's right against the promisor is also subject to any defenses and claims arising from the beneficiary's own conduct, as when the beneficiary makes a later agreement with the promisor.

the United States Supreme Court as "not a typical third-party beneficiary contract,"[3] the beneficiary's right under the contract rises no higher than the right of the promisee.[4] Of course, the beneficiary (C) is still free to pursue any right against the promisee (B).

Typical defenses and claims

Thus the beneficiary is vulnerable to defenses of the promisor that affect the enforceability of the promisor's agreement with the promisee. These include lack of consideration[5] and unenforceability on grounds of public policy[6] or for failure to satisfy the statute of frauds.[7] They also include voidability on grounds such as incapacity, mistake, misrepresentation, or duress.[8] Since the beneficiary is subject to all of the terms of the contract between the promisor and the promisee, the beneficiary is also vulnerable to defenses of the promisor that arise under those terms during the performance of the agreement.[9] These include nonoccurrence of a condition and failure of performance, whether the failure is a breach or is justifiable.[10] In addition, the beneficiary is subject to recoupment of any claims of the promisor for damages for breach of contract by the promisee.[11] The claim is only good against the beneficiary to the extent that it extinguishes the beneficiary's claim; it cannot be used to impose liability on the beneficiary.[12]

---

[3] Lewis v. Benedict Coal Corp., 361 U.S. 459, 468 (1960) (right of pension fund (C) to royalties was not subject to reduction by amount of employer's (A's) damages due to union's (B's) strikes and work stoppages in breach of contract).

[4] Johnson v. Pennsylvania Natl. Ins. Cos., 594 A.2d 296 (Pa. 1991) (injured person claiming uninsured motorist benefits as beneficiary was bound by arbitration clause in contract).

[5] Lawhead v. Booth, 177 S.E. 283 (W. Va. 1934) (promisor could set up against beneficiary defense that contract lacked consideration).

[6] Naimo v. La Fianza, 369 A.2d 987 (N.J. Super. 1976) (child as beneficiary could not enforce agreement between unwed parents because "illegality of the consideration arising from the illicit act of intercourse and adultery . . . goes to the very heart of the agreement").

[7] Holt v. First Natl. Bank, 418 So. 2d 77 (Ala. 1982) (daughter's "count alleging that she was a third-party beneficiary to [father's and step-mother's] pre-nuptial agreement is defeated on its face by the Statute of Frauds").

[8] Rouse v. United States, 215 F.2d 872 (D.C. Cir. 1954) (beneficiary is subject to promisor's defense based on promisee's fraud).

[9] Camelot Excavating Co. v. St. Paul Fire & Marine Ins. Co., 301 N.W.2d 275 (Mich. 1981) (right of subcontractor as intended beneficiary of payment bond "was subject to the stated conditions of the contract, including the provision that limited the time to bring suit to one year from the date the principal ceased work on the project").

[10] Alexander H. Revell & Co. v. C.H. Morgan Grocery Co., 214 Ill. App. 526 (1919) (it would be "strange rule of law" that would allow beneficiary to recover where promisee failed to render performance).

[11] United States v. Industrial Crane & Mfg. Co., 492 F.2d 772 (5th Cir. 1974) (beneficiary "stood in [promisee's] shoes" and was thus subject to offset of any damages that promisor could have recovered from promisee for breach of covenant not to compete made as part of same transaction).

[12] Indeed, there is authority that a promisor who has already performed and thus conferred a benefit on a beneficiary has no right to restitution. Chrysler Corp. v. Airtemp Corp., 426 A.2d

A troublesome example of the principle that the beneficiary's right is limited by the terms of the contract arises when the promisee that mistakenly believes it owes a duty to the beneficiary exacts a promise from the promisor to discharge that duty. What are the terms of the promisor's undertaking? Is it an undertaking to perform the supposed duty whether or not the duty exists? Or is it only an undertaking to perform the supposed duty to the extent that the duty exists? In a noted case, the promisor (A) bought the promisee's (B's) house and assumed the promisee's supposed duty to pay a contractor (C) for a heating plant installed by the contractor. The promisor refused to pay on the ground that the contractor had not installed the plant properly and therefore the promisee was not under a duty to pay $850, as the promisor had supposed at the time of the assumption. The court rejected this contention, stating that if the promise is to pay a specific debt, the usual interpretation is that it is a promise to pay the debt whether or not it exists.[13] Courts have also held that one assuming a debt cannot raise the defense that the debt is unenforceable on grounds of public policy.[14]

Example of assumption

The principle that the beneficiary's right rises no higher than that of the promisee is subject to contrary agreement. Sometimes the contract itself provides that the beneficiary's right will not be subject to defenses that the promisor might have against the promisee. A common example is the "standard mortgage clause" in a fire insurance policy on mortgaged property, under which the insurer (A) and the mortgagor as insured (B) agree that the mortgagee (C) may recover despite "any act or neglect" of the mortgagor. Courts have allowed the mortgagee to recover under such a clause free of the insurer's defense of nonpayment of premiums or even fraud by the insured.[15] Such a rationale was in part the basis for the United States Supreme Court's decision that a union's pension fund (C) could recover royalty payments that the employer (A) was to make to the fund on coal mined under a collective bargaining agreement, free of the employer's damages caused by the union's strikes and work stoppages in breach of the agreement. The court interpreted the agreement as making the employer's (A's) duty to make payments to the fund as "independent of the union's performance" in this regard.[16] Even though the contract does not preclude the promisor from asserting against the beneficiary those defenses that the beneficiary has against the promisee, the subsequent conduct of the

Exceptions by agreement or estoppel

---

845 (Del. Super. 1980). *See* Restatement of Restitution §110 (1937). As to the analogous situation involving an assignee, see the discussion of typical claims in §11.8 *infra*.

[13] Rouse v. United States, *supra* note 6 (promise to pay specific debt will generally be interpreted as promise to pay that sum of money regardless of "whether the promisee is actually indebted to that amount or at all").

[14] Oppenheimer Indus. v. Firestone, 569 P.2d 334 (Colo. App. 1977) (defense of illegality cannot generally be invoked by third persons).

[15] Goldstein v. National Liberty Ins. Co., 175 N.E. 359 (N.Y. 1931) ("a policy of fire insurance in the standard form, which is void as to the owner, because of his breach of warranty as to ownership and occupancy, may, under the standard mortgagee clause, be valid as to a mortgagee").

[16] Lewis v. Benedict Coal Corp., *supra* note 3, 361 U.S. at 466.

promisor with respect to the beneficiary may estop the promisor from asserting them.[17]

Claims not arising out of agreement distinguished

Whether the beneficiary's (C's) right is subject to claims by the promisor (A) arising out of separate transactions with the promisee (B) is a different question from whether that right is subject to defenses and claims arising out of the contract itself.[18] The better view is that the beneficiary takes free of such claims unless the contract provides otherwise.[19]

In the next chapter we take up the rights of third persons whose connection with the contract arises not at the time of its making, but later by assignment or delegation.

---

[17] Levy v. Empire Ins. Co., 379 F.2d 860 (5th Cir. 1967) (insurer of debentures that failed to provide for conditions in written contract "effectively estopped itself from contending that it did not have a binding insurance contract," because of nonoccurrence of conditions, with beneficiary who relied on written contract).

[18] As to the analogous question involving an assignment, see the discussion of claims not arising out of agreement distinguished in §11.8 *infra*.

[19] Restatement Second §309 cmt. *c* ("the beneficiary's right is direct, not merely derivative, and claims and defenses of the promisor against the promisee arising out of separate transactions do not affect the right of the beneficiary except in accordance with the terms of the contract").

Chapter 11

Assignment and Delegation

A.   INTRODUCTION

§11.1.   Terminology and Practical Background. This chapter deals with the law governing the transfer of contract rights and duties.[1] Since a contract right is one kind of property, many of the rules governing the transfer of such a right are similar to the rules of property law governing the alienation of land and chattels.[2] However, unlike land and chattels, a contract right is a type of intangible property. Historically, it was classified as a *chose in action* ("thing in action") along with a wide variety of other intangibles, including claims to

Aspect of property law

---

§11.1   [1] It does not, however, deal in detail with negotiable instruments, documents of title, or investment securities, all of which are the subject of elaborate provisions in the Uniform Commercial Code. Nor does it deal with covenants in conveyances or leases, which are covered in works on the law of real property.

[2] Portuguese-American Bank v. Welles, 242 U.S. 7 (1916) (Holmes, J.: "When a man sells a horse, what he does, from the point of view of the law, is to transfer a right, and a right being regarded by the law as a thing, even though a *res incorporalis*, it is not illogical to apply the same rule to a debt that would be applied to a horse."). See the discussions of equitable liens and assignments in §11.5 *infra* and of the comparison with delivery of a chattel in §11.6 *infra*.

damages in tort.[3] Its transfer is the subject of many special rules that do not apply to other kinds of property. But, before we turn to the rules governing the transfer of contract rights, some terminology and practical background will be helpful.

Terminology

At the outset, it is vital to distinguish the *assignment of rights* from the *delegation of performance of duties*.[4] An obligee's transfer of a contract right is known as an *assignment* of the right. By an assignment, the obligee as *assignor* (B) transfers to an *assignee* (C) a right that the assignor has against an *obligor* (A). An obligor's empowering of another to perform the obligor's duty is known as a *delegation* of the performance of that duty. By a delegation, the obligor as *delegating party* (B) empowers a *delegate* (C) to perform a duty that the delegating party owes to an *obligee* (A).[5] A party to a contract that both assigns rights and delegates performance to another person will be referred to as a *transferor* (B); the other person will be referred to as a *transferee* (C); and the transaction will be called a *transfer* of the contract. It will be useful to apply this terminology to five common situations.[6]

Gift

The first situation is that of a prospective donor that wants to make a gift. If the prospective donor (B) wants to give $1,000 to a favorite grandchild (C), the prospective donor might, of course, simply give the child cash. However, if the prospective donor is short of cash but is owed $1,000 by a debtor (A), the prospective donor may instead assign the right to payment to the grandchild as a gift. As assignee, the grandchild will then own the right that the donor previously had against the debtor and will collect the $1,000 from the debtor.

Consumer sale

The second situation is that of a retailer that sells to consumers on credit. If the retailer has sold a $1,000 stereo on credit to a consumer (A), the retailer may need cash to finance the business until the $1,000 has been paid. The retailer (B) may therefore assign the right to payment to a financial institution (C) in

---

[3] Borrowing the French word for *thing*, the common law distinguished a "chose in action" from a "chose in possession." Modern usage, reflected in the Uniform Commercial Code, favors the term *intangible*. *See* the definition of "general intangibles" in UCC 9-102(42) as "including things in action."

[4] The term *assignment of a contract* is sometimes used to refer to a transaction in which both rights are assigned and duties are delegated. See the discussion of the language of delegation in §11.10 *infra*. It is also used to refer to a transaction in which only rights are assigned. To avoid confusion, this term is not used in this treatise.

[5] The terms *delegating party* and *delegate* are not as well established as *assignor* and *assignee*. *See* UCC-O 2-210 (using *party delegating* and *delegate*) and UCC-R 2-210 (using *delegating party* and *delegate*); Restatement Second §318(3) (using *delegating obligor* and *person delegated*). As to the delegation of the performance of *conditions*, see the discussion of performance that is a condition in §11.10 *infra*.

[6] Throughout this chapter, to facilitate comparison, the obligor of the right that is assigned or the obligee of the duty the performance of which is delegated is often designated parenthetically as A, the assignor or delegating party as B, and the assignee or delegate as C. An analogous designation is used for the parties to similar transactions, even though they do not actually involve the assignment of a right or the delegation of performance of a duty.

return for the immediate payment by it of $1,000, less a discount to compensate the financial institution for the loss of the use of the $1,000 until it can collect the money from the consumer.[7] The financial institution will then own the right that the retailer previously had against the consumer and will collect the $1,000 from the consumer.

The third situation is that of a wholesaler that sells to retailers on credit. If the wholesaler (B) has sold $10,000 worth of carpets on credit to a retailer (A), the wholesaler may need cash to finance the business until the $10,000 has been paid. The wholesaler may therefore assign the right to payment, which is known as an "account receivable," to a financial institution (C). However, in contrast to the situation just described in which a retailer assigns a consumer debt, the wholesaler engages in what is known as "accounts receivable financing" and assigns accounts in bulk, rather than individually, so that the total of all accounts assigned might be, say, $1,000,000. Furthermore, the wholesaler does not assign them outright but only as security for a loan for, say, $800,000 (somewhat less than the value of the collateral). In what is called "non-notification financing," it is understood that the wholesaler, not the financial institution, will collect from the retailer and that the wholesaler will repay the loan out of the proceeds when the retailer has paid for the goods.[8] The financial institution's compensation is the interest on the secured loan.

Commercial sale

The fourth situation is that of a builder that makes construction contracts. If the builder (B) has contracted with an owner (A) to build a building for $10,000,000, payable as the work progresses, the builder may need funds immediately to begin work. The builder may therefore assign the right to payment from the owner to a financial institution (C) in return for a loan to help finance the construction. Here, in contrast to the wholesaler's account receivable in the situation just described, the builder's right to payment has not yet been earned, since it is constructively conditioned on performance of the contract. As the builder performs and the progress payments become due, they are collected and used to repay the loan.[9]

Assignment of builder's right

---

[7]The financial institution in this situation is usually a bank or finance company. The amount of the discount will also include the risk of nonpayment and transaction costs. Since the financial institution has recourse against the retailer if the consumer defaults, the institution's risk of not being paid is slight.

[8]The financial institution in this situation is usually a bank or finance company. In contrast to the situation described in the text, the financial institution often does not require the wholesaler to repay the loan as the proceeds are collected, but relies on the assignment of future accounts to secure the loan in the original amount. See the discussion of the floating lien under the Code in §11.5 *infra*. There is an alternative to the transaction described in the text in which the financial institution (sometimes called a "factor") purchases the account outright, notifies the obligor, and collects the debt.

[9]The financial institution in this situation is usually a bank.

Sale of business   The fifth and most complex situation is that of an owner of a business that furnishes goods or services to other businesses. If the owner (B) wants to transfer the business as a going concern to a buyer (C) by a sale of the assets of the business,[10] the parties may also plan to transfer long-term contracts with, say, a supplier (A) and a customer (A'). With respect to both the supplier and the customer, such a transfer involves not only assignment but delegation. The seller wants both to assign to the buyer the seller's rights against the supplier and the customer, and also to delegate to the buyer the performances that the seller owes them. There are, therefore, two significant problems not present in the four earlier situations. The first is that, with respect to the supplier, the right that the seller wishes to assign is a right to a performance other than the payment of money. The second is that, with respect to both the supplier and the customer, the seller wishes not only to assign rights but also to delegate performance of duties — the duty of paying the supplier for what is supplied and the duty of furnishing the customer with goods or services. If the seller can overcome these problems and transfer these contracts, the buyer will have both a right to be supplied by the supplier in return for payment and a right to be paid by the customer in return for furnishing goods or services.[11]

We examine first the law of assignment and then that of delegation.

B.   ASSIGNMENT

Modern role of free assignability   **§11.2.   Historical Background and Code Provisions.** Today most contract rights are freely transferable. If the law were otherwise, our modern credit economy could not exist.[1] Recall the seller that assigns the right to the price of goods sold on credit.[2] The seller might occasionally have the means to grant credit, even if the resulting right to future payment were not transferable, but the seller would have to rely on its own resources to do so. Once the right to future payment becomes transferable, however, the seller can enlist the resources of a financial institution, either by selling to it the right to future payment in return for a price payable immediately, or by transferring to it that

---

[10] If the business is incorporated, such a transfer may also be accomplished by a sale of its stock. Because the corporate entity remains after the stock is sold, a transaction of this kind does not raise the questions discussed in this chapter.

[11] Ordinarily, the buyer will, pursuant to the buyer's contract with the seller, undertake to perform the seller's duties under the seller's contracts with both the supplier and the customer. See the discussion of the example of a sale of a business in §11.11 *infra*.

§11.2 [1] *See* 1 H. Macleod, Principles of Economical Philosophy 481 (2d ed. 1872) ("If we were asked — Who made the discovery which has most deeply affected the fortunes of the human race? We think, after full consideration, we might safely answer — The man who first discovered that a Debt is a Saleable Commodity.").

[2] See the discussions of a consumer sale and of a commercial sale in §11.1 *supra*.

right in return for a loan payable immediately. In effect, the financial institution, not the seller, gives the buyer credit. If the seller's right to payment were not transferable to the financial institution, the buyer would have little chance to buy from the seller on credit.[3]

It may therefore seem surprising that the common law began with the rule that choses in action, including contract rights, were not transferable. A rule that a debt was "personal" to the creditor was defensible in a society where sanctions against a defaulting debtor were severe and credit played only a minor role. For the atypical situation in which the transfer of choses in action was important to facilitate credit, special commercial courts were available.[4] As long as common law recognition of the transfer of contract rights served no apparent function, common law judges inevitably viewed such transfers with suspicion.[5] An attempted assignment of a contract right came to be regarded as maintenance — as tending to encourage litigation — much as we still view an attempted assignment of a claim for slander or some other tort. In Lord Coke's opinion, to allow the assignment of contract rights "would be the occasion of multiplying contentions and suits."[6]

Reasons for common law rule

But by the start of the seventeenth century, when the action of general assumpsit had fully developed,[7] the common law courts had made a first grudging concession to the growing importance of credit. Although an assignor's (B) attempt to assign to an assignee (C) a contract right against an obligor (A) was still not effective as an assignment, the courts viewed it as giving the assignee a power of attorney to sue the obligor in the name of the assignor.[8] At first this concession was made only if the assignor's purported assignment

Concept of power of attorney

---

[3]Of course the buyer may be able to get a loan directly from a financing institution and pay the seller with the proceeds of the loan. Such a direct loan is an alternative to the transaction described in the text.

[4]See the discussion of the influence of the law merchant in §1.9 *supra.*

[5]It has also been suggested that the common law mind had difficulty thinking in abstractions and could not conceive of the transfer of an intangible contract right from one person to another. However, it has also been pointed out that "the incapacity of early lawyers to corporealize the incorporeal has been greatly over-stressed by modern writers. Medieval lawyers were perfectly capable of visualizing ownership of disembodied interests — ownership of an office, the right to appoint a parson to a particular church, rights to labor [or] services in homes or in fields, rights to be paid annuities, to collect tolls from passersby, or to occupy a front seat at the King's coronation." J. Dawson, W. Harvey & S. Henderson, Contracts: Cases and Comment 905 (8th ed. 2003).

[6]Lampet's Case, 77 Eng. Rep. 994, 997 (K.B. 1613). *See* J. Dawson, W. Harvey & S. Henderson, Contracts: Cases and Comment 891 (8th ed. 2003) ("[O]ne must imagine a society in which central governments were weak and power was dispersed through an aristocracy that was often turbulent. The favor and support of powerful persons and their armed retainers were much sought after, especially by those who quarrelled with their neighbors. Maintenance . . . was a constant threat to the administration of justice, especially during the civil wars of the fifteenth century.").

[7]See the discussion of the supplanting of debt by *indebitatus assumpsit* in §1.6 *supra.*

[8]A parallel development had taken place in Roman law. *See* W. Buckland & A. McNair, Roman Law and Common Law 307-10 (F. Lawson 2d ed. 1952); M. Radin, Roman Law 53, 290-92 (1927).

was to pay a debt that the assignor owed the assignee.[9] If the assignor simply sold the claim to the assignee, this was still considered maintenance until the end of the seventeenth century, when the courts finally allowed the assignee to sue in the assignor's name. However, the assignee's right was a fragile one, since the assignor's revocation, death, or bankruptcy would destroy it.[10] These infirmities were eliminated at law largely through the competition of equity.[11]

Recognition in equity

During the seventeenth century, assignees began to forsake the courts of common law for chancery in their efforts to enforce their claims. Chancery did not share the antipathy of the common law courts toward assignment and afforded the assignee broad protection, treating the assignee as the owner of the claim, not merely as the assignor's agent. Thus, in equity, the right of an assignee that had given value was not defeated by the assignor's revocation, death, or bankruptcy.[12]

Recognition at law

The common law judges were not insensitive to this threat to their business. Near the end of the eighteenth century, the Court of King's Bench held that an assignee whose assignor had become bankrupt was entitled to the assigned right as against the assignor's trustees in bankruptcy.[13] One of the judges wryly observed that it had "been found productive of great expense to send the parties to the other side of the Hall," meaning to chancery, and concluded that while it was "certainly true that a chose in action cannot strictly be assigned," the common law courts could nevertheless "take notice" of the assignee's right in equity by according to the assignee the same rights that the assignee would have had by going "to the other side of the Hall."[14] Henceforth, the common law courts also would treat the assignee as the owner of the claim though, true to

---

[9] Harvey v. Bateman, 74 Eng. Rep. 1020 (1600) ("if a man assign an obligation to another for a precedent debt due by him to the assignee . . . , that is not maintenance; but if he assign it for a consideration then given by way of contract, that is maintenance").

[10] Litcott, 84 Eng. Rep. 206 (K.B. 1669) (bankruptcy); Potter v. Turner, 124 Eng. Rep. 7 (K.B. 1622) (revocation).

[11] Another factor was the absorption into the common law of the rules of the law merchant during the seventeenth century. See the discussion of the influence of the law merchant in §1.9 *supra*. The law merchant recognized free transferability of contract rights that were embodied in bills of exchange, and the Statute of Anne extended this recognition to promissory notes in 1704. (These kinds of negotiable instruments are described in a footnote to the discussion of an order as an assignment in §11.3 *infra*.) These developments made it increasingly awkward for the common law courts to maintain that an ordinary contract right, especially a right to money, was not transferable.

[12] Peters v. Soame, 23 Eng. Rep. 874 (Ch. 1701) (bankruptcy); Fashon v. Atwood, 22 Eng. Rep. 819, 835 (Ch. 1679, 1680) (death).

[13] Winch v. Keely, 99 Eng. Rep. 1284 (K.B. 1787).

[14] 99 Eng. Rep. at 1286 (Ashhurst, J.). *See* 1 G. Gilmore, Security Interests in Personal Property §7.3 (1965) ("by the typically muddle-headed process of thinking known as the genius of the common law, assignments of intangibles were made effective in fact while basic theory still proclaimed them to be legal impossibilities").

the rhetoric of this decision, the assignee would have to observe the formality of suing in the name of the assignor.

The American states received the English law of assignments as part of the common law. Included were both seventeenth-century precedents, introducing the device of power of attorney, and eighteenth-century precedents, making it a mere formality. The anachronistic requirement that the assignor sue in the name of the assignee was finally abolished in most states in the nineteenth century with the advent of code pleading. Statutes or rules of court that were directed against the institution of nominal or fictitious plaintiffs required that suits be brought in the name of the "real party in interest."[15] The triumph of free assignability was complete.[16]

Triumph of free assignability

An understanding of how the common law courts came to reverse themselves is of historical interest and is of value in reading older cases; it is also helpful for an appreciation of a few contemporary rules relating to assignments.[17] Indeed, some writers have thought it still desirable to describe the assignee's rights as essentially "equitable."[18] However, it is difficult to find instances in which this qualification is an aid to an analysis of the assignee's rights, and it has not found its way into either the Restatement Second or the Uniform Commercial Code.[19]

Significance of history

A major development in the law of assignments came with the enactment of the Uniform Commercial Code. The impact of the Code on the law of assignments is much greater than might at first be supposed, because rules on assignment are found in Article 9 as well as in Article 2. Though Article 9 is concerned primarily with secured transactions, it governs many outright sales of contract rights as well. The commentary explains that the distinction "between transactions in which a receivable secures an obligation and those in which the receivable has been sold outright" is often "blurred" and the approach of covering both types of transactions "has generally been successful in avoiding difficult problems of distinguishing" between the two.[20] The drafters accomplished this in a manner worthy of the common law — by defining a security

Assignments and the Code

---

[15] See Fed. R. Civ. P. 17(a) ("Every action shall be prosecuted in the name of the real party in interest.").

[16] Under UCC-O 2-210(2) and UCC-R 2-210(1)(a) all rights of either seller or buyer can be assigned, subject to exceptions. See UCC 9-406(d) (term restricting assignment of account is ineffective, subject to exceptions). For present-day limitations on free assignability, see §§11.4, 11.5 infra.

[17] See the discussions of gratuitous assignments as generally revocable in §11.6 infra and of typical defenses in §11.8 infra.

[18] Williston took this view. See Williston, Is the Right of an Assignee of a Chose in Action Legal or Equitable?, 30 Harv. L. Rev. 97 (1916).

[19] Farrell v. Passaic Water Co., 88 A. 627 (N.J. Ch. 1913) ("when our legislature in 1797 . . . enacted that the 'assignment . . . shall be good and effectual in law, and an assignee . . . may thereupon maintain an action . . . in his own name,' the only excuse for calling the assignee's title equitable vanished").

[20] UCC 9-109 cmt. 4.

interest to include the interest of an outright purchaser.[21] In this way they ensured that the great bulk of commercially significant assignments would be subject to rules that are far more than a mere codification of the common law. Unlike Article 2, Article 9 is not limited to the assignment of rights arising out of contracts for the sale of goods. It applies generally to transfers for value of "accounts," a term that refers broadly to most rights "to payment of a monetary obligation," including one for goods or services, "whether or not earned by performance."[22] However, Article 9 applies only to the transfer of rights to payment and not to the transfer of rights to goods or services. Nor does it apply at all to the transfer of rights arising out of contracts for the sale of land.

Exclusions from Article 9

In addition, a few kinds of assignments are excluded from the scope of Article 9 and are left to the common law and perhaps to other statutes.[23] Among the assignments excluded are those of wage claims,[24] those that are "for the purpose of collection only,"[25] and those that are made "as part of a sale of the business out of which they arose,"[26] as well as "an assignment of a right to payment under a contract to an assignee that is also obligated to perform under the contract"[27] and an "assignment of a single account . . . to an assignee in full or partial satisfaction of a preexisting indebtedness."[28] Despite these exceptions, the Code leaves relatively little to the common law, and even there it can be expected to have an impact by analogy.[29]

In the following sections we examine some contemporary problems in the law of assignments under the common law and the Code.

Meaning of assignment

§11.3. Effectiveness of an Assignment. The word *assignment* here refers to the act by which an assignor transfers a contract right to an assignee.[1] Such an act will sometimes also be referred to as an *effective assignment*, as

---

[21] UCC 1-201 (35) (*security interest* includes "any interest of . . . a buyer of accounts . . . that is subject to Article 9."); UCC 9-109(a) (with stated exceptions, "this article applies to . . . a sale of accounts").

[22] UCC 9-102(a)(2). The obligor is called an *account debtor.* UCC 9-102(a)(3).

[23] See the discussion of assignments against public policy in §11.4 *infra*.

[24] UCC 9-109(d)(3).

[25] UCC 9-109(d)(5).

[26] UCC 9-109(d)(4).

[27] UCC 9-109(d)(5).

[28] UCC 9-109(d)(7).

[29] In 2001 the United Nations General Assembly adopted a Convention on Assignment of Receivables in International Trade prepared by the United Nations Commission on International Trade Law (UNCITRAL).

§11.3 [1] The Restatement Second uses it in this sense. *See* Restatement Second §317(1) ("assignment of a right is a manifestation of the assignor's intention to transfer it by virtue of which the assignor's right" is transferred). The word is sometimes also used to refer to the transfer itself or to a writing evidencing the transfer.

distinguished from an *attempted* or *purported assignment*. What is necessary for an effective assignment?[2]

To make an effective assignment of a contract right, the owner of that right must manifest an intention to make a present transfer of the right without further action by the owner or by the obligor. The owner may manifest this intention directly to the assignee or to a third person. No words of art are required; the assignor need not even use the word *assign*.[3] Whether the owner of a right has manifested an intention to transfer it is a question of interpretation to be answered from all the circumstances, including words and other conduct.[4] To transfer a contract right is, in essence, to take from the assignor (B) and to give to the assignee (C) the right to performance by the obligor (A).[5] Put in another way, the transfer of a contract right extinguishes the assignor's right to performance by the obligor and gives the assignee a right to that performance.[6] It is important not to confuse an assignment, which is a present transfer, with a contract, which is a promise of future performance. At this point, it will be useful to distinguish several common transactions that, despite some similarities, are not assignments.[7]

Present transfer required

---

[2]The discussion here does not cover the transfer of contract rights by operation of law, as when an executor or administrator is empowered to act for an estate or a trustee for a bankrupt. Nor does it cover the related equitable remedy of subrogation.

[3]Leon v. Martinez, 638 N.E.2d 511 (N.Y. 1994) ("I give" sufficient because "[no] particular words are necessary").

[4]Baker v. Eufaula Concrete Co., 557 So. 2d 1228 (Ala. 1990) ("no requirement that magical words be used").

[5]Furthermore, absent a contrary indication, the assignment of a right carries with it any security and other benefits incidental to it. Kintzel v. Wheatland Mut. Ins. Assn., 203 N.W.2d 799 (Iowa 1973) (seller's assignment of rights under contract for sale of real property that required buyer to insure property transferred seller's right to insurance proceeds). Thus an assignee of a debt secured by a mortgage acquires the assignor's rights under the mortgage as well. See the discussion of mortgages in §6.5 *supra*. An assignee also has the same right as the assignor did to priority in the event of the obligor's insolvency. *See* Restatement Second §340(1). That an assignee succeeds to the assignor's right to arbitrate disputes with the obligor, *see* Green Tree Fin. Corp. v. Channel, 825 So. 2d 90 (Ala. 2002) (assignee under installment agreement "is entitled to enforce the arbitration clause" in the agreement).

[6]It is sometimes said that the test of an assignment is whether the obligor would be justified in paying the third person. Donovan v. Middlebrook, 88 N.Y.S. 607 (App. Div. 1904). This is misleading, because an order from the obligee (B) to the obligor (A) may justify the obligor in paying a third person (C) but may not be an assignment. See the discussion of an order as an assignment *infra*.

Statements can also be found to the effect that there can be no effective assignment "where an assignor retains control over the fund or any authority to collect or any power to revoke." These statements confuse the effectiveness of an assignment with its revocability. See the discussion of the nature of revocation in §11.6 *infra*. As to the effect of an assignment as security on the assignor's rights, see note 19 *infra*.

[7]Although for the sake of simplicity it is assumed in these examples that the performance owed by the obligor is simply the payment of money, the results would be the same if it were a performance of some other kind.

Promise to collect and pay

Sometimes an obligee (B) promises to collect money owed to the obligee by an obligor (A) and to pay it to a promisee (C). Though the obligee's promise may be enforceable as a contract, there is no assignment.[8] The obligee's promise does not result in a present transfer of the obligee's right against the obligor — the obligee retains the right to collect the money, and the promisee's only right is against the obligee, not against the obligor.[9]

Promise to assign

Sometimes an obligee (B) promises to make an assignment to a promisee (C), at some future time, of the obligee's right to payment from the obligor (A). Again, although the obligee's promise may be a contract, it is not an assignment.[10] The obligee has not manifested an intention to transfer the obligee's right against the obligor — the obligee retains the right against the obligor to collect the money, and the promisee acquires no legal right to collect the money from the obligor by virtue of the obligee's promise. However, courts have accorded the promisee rights similar to an assignee's, under what is known as an "equitable assignment," if the obligee's promise is one for which specific performance will be granted.[11]

Order as assignment

Sometimes an obligee (B) orders the obligor (A) to pay a debt to a third person (C), rather than to the obligee. If the order is given directly to the obligor, courts have had little difficulty in concluding that the obligee did not intend to make an assignment: although the obligor's duty to the obligee may be discharged if the obligor pays the third person, the third person gains no right to require the obligor to do so.[12] However, if the obligee delivers a written order to the third person for the third person to present to the obligor, the obligee's intention is less clear.[13] In the most common case, the obligee (B) is the drawer of a check, the obligor (A) is the drawee bank, and the third

---

[8] The leading case is Donovan v. Middlebrook, *supra* note 6 (obligee's (B's) statement that third person (C) "is entitled to one-half the commission" due from the obligor (A) was not assignment).

[9] However, the fact that an assignor agrees to act as the assignee's agent in collecting the money does not prevent an assignment. Cogan v. Conover Mfg. Co., 64 A. 973 (N.J. 1906).

[10] Skandinavia, Inc. v. Cormier, 514 A.2d 1250 (N.H. 1986) (statement "that a party *shall* assign its liability in the future only sets the stage for an assignment; it does not operate as one").

[11] Wilmurth v. National Liberty Ins. Co., 206 S.W.2d 730 (Mo. App. 1947) (promise to assign right to buy land gave promisee "an equitable interest and he could, by a suit for specific performance, compel [promisor] to make the assignment"). See the discussion of equitable liens and assignments in §11.5 *infra*.

[12] Edmund Wright Ginsburg Corp. v. C.D. Kepner Leather Co., 59 N.E.2d 253 (Mass. 1945) (where obligee's letter to obligor was not delivered to third person, even if "letter was more than a mere authority, or direction to pay [third person], it did not operate as an assignment in the absence of a delivery or something equivalent to a delivery to" third person).

[13] Robert S. Pinzur, Ltd. v. The Hartford, 511 N.E.2d 1281 (Ill. App. 1987) (hospital patient's "direct payment [by insurer] clause was couched in the language of authorization" and was not an assignment).

person (C) is the payee of the check.[14] The Uniform Commercial Code makes it clear that a check is not, at least by itself, an assignment.[15] Since a check is regarded as an order to the bank to pay whether or not the drawer has enough in the account to cover it,[16] it makes some sense to conclude that the drawer's intention is not to transfer to the payee any part of what the bank owes the drawer (B).[17] Sometimes, however, the written order is conditional on the existence of a duty of the obligor to the obligee, as in the case of an order to pay only out of a designated fund. The Uniform Commercial Code does not govern such cases,[18] and there is authority that an order of this kind is an assignment.[19]

An assignment may be limited in its effect.[20] It may, for example, be void-able by the assignor on a ground such as misrepresentation or duress, or it may be conditional, taking effect only if the event that is the condition occurs. An assignment can be made as security for the payment of money or for the performance of some other obligation. Just as in the case of the transfer of other kinds of property as security, the transferee thereby acquires a limited interest, called a "security interest," rather than outright ownership of the right.[21] **Assignments with limited effect**

An assignment can also be made of a part of a contract right. At com-mon law, partial assignments were not recognized over the objection of the **Partial assignment**

---

[14]Negotiable instruments are of two main kinds: drafts and notes. A *draft* (traditionally a "bill of exchange") typically involves three parties and embodies an order by the *drawer* (B), directed to the *drawee* (A), ordering the drawee to pay to a *payee* (C) or to the payee's order. A *check* is a special type of draft — one drawn on a bank as drawee and payable on demand. A *note* (traditionally a "promissory note") typically involves only two parties and embodies a promise by the *maker* of the note to pay to the *payee* or the payee's order.

[15]UCC 3-408 ("check or other draft does not of itself operate as an assignment of funds in the hands of the drawee available for its payment").

[16]For a check to be negotiable, the drawer's (B's) order to the drawee bank (A) must be "unconditional." UCC 3-104(a).

[17]There are practical reasons for this also, since banks would have difficulty observing the rules relating to notice if checks were assignments. See the discussion of the effect of notification in §11.7 *infra*.

[18]Such an instrument is not negotiable (see *supra* note 16), and Article 3 does not apply to it.

[19]Herzog v. Irace, 594 A.2d 1106 (Me. 1991) (written "request" delivered by patient to doctor asking that defendant in unrelated personal injury action pay doctor was assignment). This view is endorsed by Restatement Second §325(1) ("written order drawn upon an obligor and signed and delivered to another person by the obligee is an assignment if it is conditional on the existence of a duty of the drawee to the drawer . . . and the drawer manifests an intention that a person other than the drawer is to retain the performance").

[20]*See* Restatement Second §331.

[21]Ralston Purina Co. v. Como Feed & Milling Co., 325 F.2d 844 (5th Cir. 1963) (where assignee of accounts receivable assigned as security recovered judgment against assignor, assignee could reach assignor's remaining interest in accounts by garnishment of obligors). Note, however, that Article 9 of the Code applies to transfers of outright ownership as well as to transfers of a security interest. See the discussion of assignments and the Code in §11.2 *supra*.

obligor.[22] Transfer of only part of a contract right might, of course, inconvenience the obligor by requiring the obligor to split its performance, but the common law's objection was more fundamental than this. The common law courts did not allow suits with more than two adverse parties; therefore, if an obligee could make partial assignments, the obligee could subject the obligor to the risk of multiple suits.[23] But partial assignments were allowed in equity, where these procedural constraints were unknown.[24] Today, with modern procedural codes permitting the joinder of all parties in a single suit without distinguishing between law and equity, there is no reason why the equity rule should not become the general rule.[25] The Restatement Second endorses this solution, stating that "no legal proceeding can be maintained by the assignor or assignee against the obligor over his objection, unless all the persons entitled to the promised performance are joined in the proceeding, or unless joinder is not feasible and it is equitable to proceed without joinder."[26]

Statute of frauds   Absent a statute to the contrary, no writing is necessary for an effective assignment.[27] However, the land contract provision of the statute of frauds

---

[22]Courts sometimes seemed eager to evade the rule by finding assent by the obligor. Cross v. Page & Hill Co., 133 N.W. 178 (Minn. 1911) (rule barring partial assignment "has no application where the debtor has notice of the assignment and makes no objection"). The rule could also be restricted by narrowly defining "partial" assignment. Timmons v. Citizens' Bank, 74 S.E. 798 (Ga. App. 1912) (assignment of single monthly progress payment under construction contract not treated as partial).

[23]First Natl. Bank v. Gross Real Estate Co., 75 N.W.2d 704 (Neb. 1956) (partial assignment is not enforceable at law and even after merger of law and equity, "an equitable right may not properly be asserted in an action unless all of the necessary parties have been made parties to the action").

[24]For a statement of the reason for the equity rule, *see* National Exch. Bank v. McLoon, 73 Me. 498 (1882) ("If [the debtor's] liability can be legally divided at all without his consent, it can be divided and subdivided indefinitely. He would have the risk of ascertaining the relative shares and rights of the substituted creditors. . . . A partial assignment would impose on him burdens which his contract does not compel him to bear. . . . In a court of equity, however, the objections to a partial assignment . . . disappear. In equity, the interests of all parties can be determined in a single suit. The debtor can bring the entire fund into court, and run no risks as to its proper distribution. . . . If he be put to extra trouble in keeping separate accounts, he can, if it is reasonable, be compensated for it.").

[25]In re Fine Paper Litig., 632 F.2d 1081 (3d Cir. 1980) ("partial assignments are recognized, but the rights of the obligor to be free of successive and repeated suits . . . are also protected by the prudent use of joinder rules"). Courts have occasionally held partial assignments not enforceable when they were regarded as burdensome to the obligor. Orr Cotton Mills v. St. Mary's Hosp., 26 S.E.2d 408 (S.C. 1943) (partial wage assignments by 15 employees to pay hospital were unenforceable where compliance by employer would add an hour per week of clerical work). However, the obligor might be compensated for the extra cost of complying with the assignments, as suggested in National Exch. Bank v. McLoon, *supra* note 24.

[26]Restatement Second §326(2).

[27]Anaconda Aluminum Co. v. Sharp, 136 So. 2d 585 (Miss. 1962) (assignment of accounts receivable).

may require a writing if what is assigned is a right under such a contract.[28] Furthermore, an assignment that comes within the scope of Article 9 of the Uniform Commercial Code is not enforceable unless the assignor has authenticated an agreement describing the contract rights assigned.[29]

We now ask what kinds of contract rights cannot be effectively assigned.

§11.4. Limitations on Assignability. Despite the overthrow of the common law prohibition against assignment, the rule that contract rights are freely assignable is not without exception. For example, a court may hold that a purported assignment is not effective on grounds of public policy, just as it may hold that a purported contract is not enforceable on such grounds.[1] Thus a purported assignment by a public officer has been held ineffective to transfer the right to unearned salary because it is thought that allowing a public officer to assign future earnings would impair the officer's service.[2] Furthermore, statutes often impose restrictions on assignments in the public interest. Virtually all states restrict by statute the assignment of wages by employees,[3] and the federal government and some states so restrict the assignment of rights to payment under public contracts.[4]

A court will also find a purported assignment ineffective, even when no public policy is involved, on the ground that transfer of the right would adversely affect the obligor. The Uniform Commercial Code provides that a purported

Assignments against public policy

Adverse effect on obligor

---

[28] See the discussion of the nature of *interest* in §6.5 *supra*.

[29] UCC 9-203(b) ("a security interest is enforceable against the debtor and third parties" only if, with some exceptions, "the debtor has authenticated a security agreement that provides a description of the collateral"). This provision differs from a traditional statute of frauds, which does not require the agreement itself to be in writing. See the discussion of the time of the memorandum in §6.7 *supra*. As noted earlier, Article 9 applies to outright sales of accounts as well as to transfers of accounts for security. See the discussion of assignments and the Code in §11.2 *supra*.

§11.4 [1] See the discussion of the great variety of policies in §5.2 *supra*. Thus a court may prohibit the assignment of a legal malpractice claim. Kommavongsa v. Haskell, 67 P.3d 1068 (Wash. 2003) (following "some 18 jurisdictions [that] have held that public policy considerations dictate" nonassignability of such claims).

[2] Byers v. Comer, 68 P.2d 671 (Ariz.), quoting with approval the explanation that, after such an assignment, officer "would no doubt be in the position of one, as per common parlance, 'paying for a dead horse'"), modified, 70 P.2d 330 (Ariz. 1937).

[3] One object of these statutes is to protect the wage earner and sometimes the spouse against their own improvidence. In re Nance, 556 F.2d 602 (1st Cir. 1977) (restriction "serves the clear purpose of protecting the assignor and his family from deprivation, suffering or a 'hopeless condition of quasi-slavery' caused by one unwise assignment"). Such statutes may also seek to protect the employer against conflicting and uncertain claims and against loss of incentive on the part of the employee. In addition, they often require recordation for the protection of the employee's creditors.

[4] Federal statutes forbid the assignment of claims against the United States before the issuance of a warrant for payment and the assignment of any public contract or order. *See* 31 U.S.C.A. §3727; 41 U.S.C.A. §15. An exception is made to allow a government contractor to make, subject to some limitations, a single assignment to a financial institution.

assignment of rights under a contract for the sale of goods is ineffective if it would: (1) "materially change" the duty of the other party, (2) "increase materially the burden or risk imposed on that party by the contract," or (3) "impair materially that party's chance of obtaining return performance."[5] Such an assignment confers no rights on the purported assignee.[6]

Restriction for benefit of obligor

This restriction on assignability rests, not on any antipathy toward assignment as such, but on a concern for the justifiable expectations of the obligor when making the contract.[7] Because the restriction protects the obligor, the obligor can dispense with it. Even if the assignment affects the obligor adversely, it will be effective if the obligor either agreed in the original contract that the obligee's rights would be assignable[8] or later consented to the assignment.[9]

Material change in obligor's duty

Every assignment of a contract right, even a right to money, goods, or land, changes the obligor's duty to some extent. The obligor must now render the performance to a different person, the assignee, and that person may be less lenient than the assignor. But courts have not regarded these slight burdens as sufficient to outweigh the arguments favoring free assignability.[10] Indeed, in such cases courts have even disregarded the claim that the obligor would not have done business with the assignee.[11] There are, however, situations in which the identity of the obligee is of sufficient importance to the obligor when the bargain was made that the obligor's duty should be considered nonassignable — the obligor should not be required to render performance to anyone except the obligee. If, for example, the obligor's duty depends on the obligee's personal discretion, substitution of an assignee for the obligee may result in a material

---

[5]UCC-O 2-210(2); UCC-R 2-210(1)(a). *See* Restatement Second §317.

It is worth remembering in this context that when a party makes an offer, only the offeree can accept (see the discussion of this point in §3.11 *supra*), and that a party that is mistaken as to the identity of the other party may be able to avoid the contract (see the discussion of mistake as to identity in §9.4 *supra*). Once a party has made a contract, however, that party's right to refuse to deal with a person other than the one with whom that party contracted is more limited. See the discussion of the significance of delegation in §11.10 *infra*.

[6]The warranties of an assignor listed in Restatement Second §333 do not include a warranty of assignability.

[7]State Farm Fire & Cas. Ins. Co. v. Farmers Ins. Exch., 489 P.2d 480 (Okl. 1971) (tort claim).

[8]Washington Capitols Basketball Club v. Barry, 304 F. Supp. 1193 (N.D. Cal.) (provision in contract between basketball club and player providing that club could assign contract is not "contrary to public policy"), aff'd, 419 F.2d 472 (9th Cir. 1969). An attempt to revoke such an agreement would be ineffective.

[9]Pulaski Stave Co. v. Miller's Creek Lumber Co., 128 S.W. 96 (Ky. 1910) ("the nonassignability of a contract, arising by inference from a relation of personal confidence, may be waived by the consent of the parties"). Absent reliance, however, it would seem that the obligor could withdraw its consent.

[10]See the discussion of the triumph of free assignability in §11.2 *supra*.

[11]C.H. Little Co. v. Cadwell Transit Co., 163 N.W. 952 (Mich. 1917) (inland carrier "sought to show that it would not have entered into such a contract" with the assignee).

change in the obligor's duty.[12] Courts have so held if the obligor's duty is to perform services under the personal supervision of the other party to the contract,[13] and some courts have refused to allow assignment though the duty is merely that of a former employee to refrain from competition and the assignment is incident to a sale of the business.[14] Covenants not to compete made in connection with the sale of a business, however, have generally been held to be assignable on the buyer's resale of the business.[15] Before the adoption of the Uniform Commercial Code, courts often held that a buyer's right to goods under a requirements contract was nonassignable, since the assignee's requirements might be very different from the assignor's.[16] The Code, in removing "most of the 'personal discretion' element by substituting the reasonably objective standard of good faith operation of the plant or business to be supplied," has at least made this result less inevitable.[17] In such cases much depends on the circumstances of the assignment: a court will react differently to an assignment to a similar operator taking over the assignor's business[18] than to an assignment to a large corporation adding that business to its own.[19] If the assignee is merely a reorganized reincarnation of the assignor, the case for assignability is particularly strong.[20] Of course, a right to damages for breach of

[12] Finance America Private Brands v. Harvey E. Hall, Inc., 380 A.2d 1377 (Del. Super. Ct. 1977) (right of obligee under guaranty that was "special," i.e., addressed to specific named obligees, was not assignable).

[13] Globe & Rutgers Fire-Ins. Co. v. Jones, 89 N.W. 580 (Mich. 1902) (it is not true that "because one has contracted to render personal service [as insurance agent] for one corporation . . . , his contract of personal service may pass to a new corporation . . . by virtue of . . . merger . . . [since] insurance companies, like individuals, differ in reputation and methods of doing business").

[14] Hess v. Gebhard & Co., 808 A.2d 912 (Pa. 2002) ("covenant not to compete in an employment contract is not assignable . . . to a purchaser of the assets of the employer's business").

[15] Herring Gas Co. v. Whiddon, 616 So. 2d 892 (Miss. 1993) (right of buyer of business under seller's promise not to compete was assignable on buyer's resale of business).

[16] Crane Ice Cream Co. v. Terminal Freezing & Heating Co., 128 A. 280 (Md. 1925) (where small ice cream manufacturer made requirements contract for ice with fixed maximum, its right was not assignable when business was sold to large ice cream manufacturer with plants in two states).

[17] UCC 2-210 cmt. 4. Under UCC 2-306(1) the use of a "stated estimate" or the existence of "normal or otherwise comparable prior output or requirements" may further limit discretion. For more on output and requirements contracts, see §2.15 and the discussion of output and requirements in §7.17 *supra*.

[18] Tolhurst v. Associated Portland Cement Mfrs., [1903] App. Cas. 414 (H.L. 1903) (where cement manufacturer made requirements contract for chalk, its right was assignable to company to which it sold business).

[19] Crane Ice Cream Co. v. Terminal Freezing & Heating Co., *supra* note 16.

[20] Munchak Corp. v. Cunningham, 457 F.2d 721 (4th Cir. 1972) ("it is inconceivable that the rendition of services by a professional basketball player to a professional basketball club could be affected by the personalities of successive corporate owners"). For a similar point relating to delegability, see the discussion of the degree of control retained in §11.10 *infra*.

contract may be assignable even if the right to performance under the contract is not.[21]

Material increase in burden or risk

Occasionally the assignment of a contract right causes a material increase in the obligor's burden or risk, even though it does not result in a material change in the obligor's duty. The standard example is that of a fire insurance policy. Suppose that an owner (B) of a building that is insured against fire by an insurance company (A) sells the building to a purchaser (C) and assigns the owner's rights under the insurance policy to the purchaser. Since the insurance company, at least in theory, took account of the character of the original owner in deciding to issue the policy and in fixing the premium, a shift in ownership to the purchaser will change, to some extent, the insurance company's risk.[22] At least if that change results in a material increase in risk, the assignment is not effective.[23]

Material impairment as to return performance

An assignment of a contract right often slightly impairs the obligor's chances of obtaining the promised return performance. Suppose that a seller contracts to sell a buyer apples in return for the buyer's promise to pay $1,000 to an assignee. The seller's incentive to perform may be somewhat impaired. But courts have not thought such slight impairment sufficient enough to outweigh the arguments favoring free assignability.[24] In rare situations, in which it is important to maintain the assignor's incentive to render the return performance, a different result may be justified.[25] Any security that the obligor may have is relevant in judging the extent to which the assignment impairs the obligor's chances of obtaining return performance.[26]

Term prohibiting assignment

Sometimes parties include in their contract a term prohibiting assignment. Absent statute, most courts have upheld such terms as precluding effective assignment, favoring freedom of contract over free assignability.[27] However,

---

[21] Liberty v. Pooler, 182 A. 216 (Me. 1936) ("contract which was too personal for assignment may on its breach give rise to an assignable action for damages").

[22] Central Union Bank v. New York Underwriters' Ins. Co., 52 F.2d 823 (4th Cir. 1931) (dictum: right of property owner under fire insurance policy is not assignable "because of the confidence reposed by the insurer in the owner," although an assignment of owner's rights, "as security for a debt, is held valid [since it] does not affect the personal relationship . . . upon the faith of which the policy has been issued"). In that case, however, the court held that a mortgagee whose interest was covered by a standard mortgage clause in the policy could assign its right against the insurer along with the mortgage debt.

[23] See the discussion of an adverse effect on the obligor *supra*.

[24] See the discussion of a material change in the obligor's duty *supra*.

[25] See the point concerning assignment by a public officer in the discussion of assignments against public policy *supra*.

[26] The Code gives the obligor a right to demand assurance from a delegating assignor. UCC-O 2-210(5); UCC-R 2-210(2) (c). However, this should not be read to preclude the obligor from having such a right against the assignor in other cases. This right should be considered in judging the extent to which the assignment impairs the obligor's chances of obtaining return performance.

[27] A leading pre-Code case involving an account is Allhusen v. Caristo Constr. Corp., 103 N.E.2d 891 (N.Y. 1952) (provision that any assignment by subcontractor of right to money due or

such anti-assignment clauses have been narrowly construed where possible.[28] Thus they are often read as imposing a duty on the assignor not to assign, but are not read as making an assignment invalid.[29] In the case of accounts, which include most rights to payment of a money whether or not earned,[30] the Code simply makes anti-assignment clauses ineffective.[31] And absent a contrary indication, a prohibition of an assignment of "the contract" is to be interpreted as barring only the delegation of duties, not the assignment of rights.[32] To the extent that an anti-assignment clause is still effective, it will ordinarily be interpreted as being for the obligor's benefit only[33] so that the obligor's consent may deprive it of the protection of the clause, even if the clause is silent on this point.[34] In addition there is a growing tendency to interpret provisions that require the obligor's consent as not barring assignment if consent is withheld unreasonably or in bad faith.[35]

We now consider limitations on the assignability of future rights.

---

to become due under contract "shall be void" was "a valid and effective restriction of the right to assign"). *Allhusen* has been characterized as "a monument to the purest type of conceptualism, untainted by a breath of the workaday world." Gilmore, The Commercial Doctrine of Good Faith Purchase, 63 Yale L.J. 1057, 1119 (1954).

[28] Munchak Corp. v. Cunningham, *supra* note 20 (contract of professional basketball player that prohibited club from assigning its rights to another "club" without his consent did not prevent "its assignment to another owner of the same club").

[29] Manchester v. Kendall, 51 N.Y. Super. (19 Jones & Sp.) 460 (1885) (words "This contract not to be assigned . . . " interpreted as a promise not to assign for breach of which damages would lie, but "would not make the assignment void"), aff'd mem., 103 N.Y. 638 (1886).

[30] UCC 9-102(a)(2).

[31] UCC 9-406(d) (term restricting assignment of account is ineffective, subject to exceptions); Mississippi Bank v. Nickles & Wells Constr. Co., 421 So. 2d 1056 (1982) ("contract which prohibits the assignment of money due or to become due thereunder is ineffective" under Article 9). There are, however, some assignments of the right to payment of money to which Article 9 does not apply (e.g., of accounts as part of a sale of the business out of which they arose and of a right to payment to an assignee that is also to do the performance), and in these situations the old common law rule giving effect to the clause may prevail. See the discussion of exclusions from Article 9 in §11.2 *supra*.

[32] UCC-O 2-210(3); UCC-R 2-210(4).

[33] Fox-Greenwald Sheet Metal Co. v. Markowitz Bros., 452 F.2d 1346 (D.C. Cir. 1971) ("absent manifestation of a broader purpose, such a clause will be construed as protection for the obligor only").

[34] Silman v. Twentieth Century-Fox Film Corp., 144 N.E.2d 387 (N.Y. 1957) ("prohibition against assignment . . . may be waived"). Of course, the typical anti-assignment clause explicitly prohibits only assignment without consent.

[35] Kendall v. Ernest Pestana, Inc., 709 P.2d 837 (Cal. 1985) ("consent may be withheld only where the lessor has a commercially reasonable objection to the assignee or the proposed use").

Cases in accord with *Kendall* appear to admit of a provision to the contrary, as long as it is clear. Carma Developers v. Marathon Dev. Cal., 826 P.2d 710 (Cal. 1992) (lessor's termination under recapture clause "in order to claim for itself appreciated rental value of the premises was expressly permitted by the lease and . . . such conduct can never violate an implied covenant of good faith and fair dealing").

Scope of problem

§11.5. Limitations on Assignability of Future or After-Acquired Rights. Courts have long had both conceptual and practical difficulties regarding the transfer of property that the transferor does not yet own. Our immediate concern is with the effect of a purported assignment of a right not in existence at the time of the assignment. Such a right may at that time be called a "future" right and later, if it comes into existence, an "after-acquired" right. At the outset, it is essential to understand the limited scope of the problem.

Conditional rights distinguished

We are not here concerned with the assignment of rights that are existing but conditional. Whatever the impediments to the assignment of future rights, they do not apply to an obligee's assignment of a right under an existing contract that has not yet ripened into a right to demand performance because of a condition that has not yet occurred.[1] This is true even if the condition that has not occurred is the obligee's own performance, as in the case of a constructive condition of exchange.[2] Such a right, although conditional, is an existing one.[3] To return to the situation of the builder that has made a construction contract,[4] the right to payment that the builder assigns, though constructively conditioned on the builder's finishing the building, is a right under an existing contract. The fact that the builder's right is thus conditional creates no bar to its assignment.

Example of future or after-acquired right

However, if the builder attempts to assign the right to payment under a contract that the builder hopes to make with the owner, but has not yet made, a different problem arises. Here no right at all exists at the time of the purported assignment. What the assignor purports to assign will become an after-acquired right only if the contract is made.

Borderline cases of relationship

Courts have sometimes overlooked this problem in borderline cases; they have treated after-acquired rights as existing at the time of the assignment if they grew out of a continuing relationship that existed at that time. The example of the assignment of a right to wages is the classic one, though its practical importance has been diminished by statutes restricting the assignment of wage claims.[5] Courts have treated such an assignment as a transfer of an existing right, though the employment is indefinite in duration and therefore terminable at will.[6] They have even so treated it when the right arose under a subsequent contract, as long as the employment relationship existed at the

---

§11.5 [1] Nor are we concerned with an *assignment* that is conditional on some event that has not yet occurred. See the discussion of assignments with limited effect in §11.3 *supra*.

[2] See the discussion of constructive conditions in §8.9 *supra*.

[3] Rockmore v. Lehman, 129 F.2d 892 (2d Cir. 1942) (A. Hand, J.: assignment of right to payment under contract to furnish advertising signs was assignment "of existing contracts [and not merely of] rights that have not yet come into being, even as interests contingent upon counter-performance").

[4] See the discussion of the assignment of a builder's right in §11.1 *supra*.

[5] See the discussion of assignments against public policy in §11.4 *supra*.

[6] Citizens Loan Assn. v. Boston & Me. R.R., 182 N.E. 696 (Mass. 1907) ("assignment of future earnings, which may accrue under an existing employment" is effective, though the employment is "indefinite as to time and compensation and terminable at will").

time of assignment.[7] The Restatement Second encourages the extension of this reasoning to other relationships.[8] However, except in these borderline cases, courts have had the same conceptual difficulty and the same practical concern that they have had with respect to the purported transfer of an interest in after-acquired property of other kinds.

The conceptual difficulty is simply stated: how can one make a present transfer of something that one does not yet own? The common law's answer was epitomized in the maxim: *nemo dat qui non habet* ("one who does not have cannot give").[9] For example, how can one mortgage goods that one does not yet own, since a mortgage, like an assignment, is a present transfer of property? To this question the common law gave the same answer for all kinds of property: one cannot do so.

Conceptual difficulty

In the middle of the nineteenth century, however, the rule as to mortgages was overturned on both sides of the Atlantic — on this side in 1842 by *Mitchell v. Winslow*, with a landmark opinion by Story,[10] and on the other side 20 years later by the celebrated English case of *Holroyd v. Marshall*.[11] These cases recognized an "equitable lien," with this line of reasoning: (1) since the mortgagor should not be taken to have done a useless act, the ineffective attempted mortgage should be regarded as a promise to make a mortgage on acquiring the property;[12] (2) such a promise would be enforceable in equity when the mortgagor acquired the property, because the mortgagee's remedy of damages at law would not be adequate;[13] (3) since "equity looks upon that as done which ought to have been done," equity will consider the mortgagor to have mortgaged the property as soon as the mortgagor acquired it.[14] Thus the mortgagee acquired an "equitable lien" on

Equitable liens and assignments

---

[7] Holt v. American Woolen Co., 150 A. 382 (Me. 1930) (assignment of wages was effective in equity, as to wages earned under new contract after assignor was discharged and rehired by same employer).

[8] Restatement Second §321(1) ("Except as otherwise provided by statute, an assignment of a right to payment expected to arise out of an existing employment or other continuing business relationship is effective in the same way as an assignment of an existing right.").

[9] O'Niel v. Wm. B.H. Kerr Co., 102 N.W. 573 (Wis. 1905) (since "a man cannot grant or charge that which he hath not," attempted assignment of right to payment for future delivery of milk was not effective where purported assignor "was under no obligation to deliver milk").

[10] 17 F. Cas. No. 9673 (C.C.D. Me. 1843) ("wherever the parties, by their contract, intended to create a positive lien or charge . . . , it attaches in equity . . . as soon as the assignor or contractor acquired a title thereto").

[11] 11 Eng. Rep. 999 (H.L. 1862) (equitable lien attached "immediately on the new machinery and effects being fixed or placed in the mill").

[12] See the discussion of more special rules in §7.11 *supra*.

[13] On the adequacy test, see §12.6 *infra*. Where an attempted transfer is intended to add security to the obligor's personal obligation, it follows that an award of damages (for which the obligor would be merely personally obligated) would not be adequate.

[14] *See* Cohen & Gerber, The After-Acquired Property Clause, 87 U. Pa. L. Rev. 635 (1939); Williston, Transfer of After-Acquired Personal Property, 19 Harv. L. Rev. 557 (1906). For a

the property as soon as the mortgagor acquired the property. By a similar process, it could be reasoned that a purported assignment of a right under a contract not yet in existence operated to give the assignee an "equitable assignment" as soon as the assignor made the contract.[15] Although not all courts followed this reasoning,[16] those that did so overcame the conceptual difficulties.[17]

Practical concern

      The practical concern, however, remained. To allow a person to assign a right under a contract not yet in existence enabled that person to assign all the contract rights that might be acquired at any time in the future. Courts understandably had reservations about the wisdom of encouraging improvidence by allowing people to sell or pledge their future in this way.[18] Furthermore, if one could put one's future beyond the reach of one's creditors, there was fear of fraud.[19]

Vulnerability of equitable assignment

      The courts that recognized equitable assignments found an answer to these practical difficulties in the solution they devised for their conceptual difficulties. They held that, though an equitable assignment of a future contract right might be effective as against the assignor and the obligor, it was not effective as against a good faith purchaser that acquired a legal interest in the same right by means of a subsequent assignment from the same assignor after the contract was made.[20] Furthermore, some courts concluded that such an assignment was not good as against an attaching creditor of the assignor, which meant that an

---

suggestion (after Voltaire) that "if the equitable lien . . . had not existed, it would have been necessary to invent it," *see* 1 G. Gilmore, Security Interests in Personal Property §11.1 (1965).

[15]The reasoning of Holroyd v. Marshall was applied to an assignment of future accounts receivable in Tailby v. Izon, 13 App. Cas. 523 (H.L. 1888). Some courts have a lamentable tendency to use the term "equitable assignment" to refer to present transfers that merely lack explicit language of assignment and therefore depend on implication.

[16]In re Nelson's Estate, 233 N.W. 115 (Iowa 1930) (assignment of accounts receivable as security for loan was void as to future accounts); Taylor v. Barton Child Co., 117 N.E. 43 (Mass. 1917) (rejecting reasoning of Holroyd v. Marshall as to accounts receivable).

[17]Speelman v. Pascal, 178 N.E.2d 723 (N.Y. 1961) (partial assignment of right to profits under contract not yet in existence to make musical based on Shaw's *Pygmalion* was effective as between assignee and assignor's estate). Such courts have not always been careful to ask whether the implied promise to assign is specifically enforceable, as is usually the case if the assignment is for security of a right under a land contract. *See* Restatement Second §321 cmt. *d*.

[18]Orkow v. Orkow, 23 P.2d 781 (Cal. App. 1933) (assignment by husband to wife of one-third of what he received from "all plays, novels, motion picture scenarios and stories now and hereafter written by me" was void as to rights under future contracts).

[19]Taylor v. Barton Child Co., *supra* note 16 (subjecting after-acquired accounts receivable to an equitable lien would open a "door . . . for the accomplishment of fraud in business").

[20]State Factors Corp. v. Sales Factors Corp., 12 N.Y.S.2d 12 (App. Div. 1939) (where assignor, after assigning future accounts to first assignee, assigned some accounts to second assignee when they were in existence, second assignee "occupied the position of a purchaser for value without notice, whose legal title is superior . . . to the [first assignee's] earlier equitable rights").

unsecured creditor could reach the right as soon as the contract was made.[21]
It also meant that the assignment was vulnerable to the assignor's trustee if the
assignor went into bankruptcy.[22] This helped the assignor that had assigned
future contract rights to obtain unsecured credit, since creditors' attachments
and claims in bankruptcy would be unaffected by the assignor's prior equitable
assignment.

It did not, however, serve the interests of either assignees or assignors. **Need for a**
Recall the example of a wholesaler that has sold to retailers on credit and **floating lien**
assigned the accounts receivable as security for an $800,000 loan from a financ-
ing institution.[23] As each retailer (A) pays an account to the wholesaler (B), the
collateral securing the loan is reduced. To maintain the collateral at the level of
$1,000,000, in order to provide the financial institution (C) with adequate secu-
rity, additional accounts must be assigned. It would be possible, to be sure, for
the wholesaler to assign additional accounts periodically as new contracts were
made, but it would make it easier for both wholesaler and financial institution
if, when the loan was first made, the wholesaler could simply assign as security
all the accounts — existing and future — so that further periodic assignments
would be unnecessary. What the wholesaler and the financial insitution wanted
to create when the loan was made was a "floating lien" on the entire mass of
existing accounts over time — with new accounts replacing old ones as the old
ones were paid and with the security interest automatically carrying over to
each new account as it arose. But as long as the floating lien was vulnerable to
third parties, particularly the wholesaler's trustee in bankruptcy, it offered no
real security to the financial institution.[24]

All this was changed by the Uniform Commercial Code, which "adopts the **Floating lien**
principle of a 'continuing general lien' or 'floating lien'" on collateral of all **under Code**
kinds, including accounts.[25] Article 9 provides generally that "a security agreement may create or provide for a security interest in after-acquired collateral."[26]
During the nineteenth century there had been a prejudice against the floating
lien based on a feeling that a commercial borrower should not be permitted to encumber all its present and future assets, and that a cushion of free
assets should be preserved for the protection not only of the borrower but of
the borrower's other creditors. The Code abandoned restrictions on the creation of a floating lien on the ground that those restrictions were ineffective.

---

[21] Harold Moorstein & Co. v. Excelsior Ins. Co., 254 N.E.2d 766 (N.Y. 1969) (dictum: "the
assignment . . . of a future right . . . does not give the assignee priority over lienors who have
attached before the proceeds have come into existence").

[22] Manchester Natl. Bank v. Roche, 186 F.2d 827 (1st Cir. 1951) (alternative holding: "present
assignment of future accounts receivable is not effective automatically . . . to create a valid lien"
in bankruptcy).

[23] See the discussion of a commercial sale in §11.1 *supra*.

[24] *See* 1 G. Gilmore, Security Interests in Personal Property §7.11 (1965).

[25] UCC 9-204 cmt. 2.

[26] UCC 9-204(1).

Under the Code an effective assignment of future accounts can be made by an "after-acquired property" clause in the security agreement.[27] Assignments of rights that do not come within the scope of Article 9, of course, continue to be governed by common law rules.[28]

We turn to the subject of gifts of contract rights.

Nature of revocation

§11.6. Revocability of a Gratuitous Assignment. Even though an assignment is *effective*, it may be *revocable*. If it is, the assignee's right is terminated if the assignor revokes the assignment, becomes incapacitated, or dies. The assignor (B) may revoke a revocable assignment by notifying either the obligor (A) or the assignee (C), by getting performance from the obligor, or by assigning the same right to another assignee (D).[1]

Gratuitous assignments generally revocable

In general, gratuitous assignments are revocable.[2] An example is the $1,000 gift assignment made by the donor (B) to a favorite grandchild (C).[3] If the donor revoked, became incapacitated, or died, the grandchild's right against the debtor (A) would be terminated, absent some exception to the general rule.[4] It is also open to the assignee to reject the gift by disclaimer.[5]

Historical origins

Some historical background may be helpful here. Recall that when the common law first recognized assignment, an assignee acquired only a power of attorney, revocable by the assignor.[6] Even equity, which generally accorded full protection to the assignee, made an exception for gratuitous assignees. A gratuitous assignment was revocable by the assignor because of the policy embodied in the maxim "equity will not aid a volunteer."[7] Thus when, near the end of the seventeenth century, the common law courts received the equity rule, they also received the exception for gratuitous assignments. At law, as in equity, a gratuitous assignment was revocable.

Analogy to gift of chattel

Courts have sometimes departed from this rule by analogizing to the gift of a chattel. A gift of a chattel could traditionally be made either by delivery of

---

[27] As explained later, the assignee must generally file a financing statement to perfect the assignee's interest against third parties. See the discussion of the first-to-file rule of Article 9 in §11.9 *infra*.

[28] See the discussion of exclusions from Article 9 in §11.2 *supra*.

§11.6 [1] *See* Restatement Second §332(2) (notice must be received).

[2] Adams v. Merced Stone Co., 178 P. 498 (Cal. 1917) (gift of book account by oral assignment was revocable where "no means whatever were delivered by the donor to the donee by which the latter could obtain payment of the indebtedness").

[3] See the discussion of a gift in §11.1 *supra*.

[4] A gift may be *inter vivos* ("between the living") or *causa mortis* ("motivated by death"). A gift *causa mortis* is one made in the expectation of approaching death and is automatically revoked if the donor survives the anticipated peril. However, the distinction between the two kinds of gifts is not significant for the purposes of this discussion.

[5] *See* Restatement Second §327(2).

[6] See the discussion of the concept of a power of attorney in §11.2 *supra*.

[7] For other equitable maxims, see the discussion of discretionary limitations in §12.4 *infra*.

the chattel itself or by delivery of a sealed deed to the chattel.[8] However, this analogy is difficult to apply to a gift of a contract right.

The comparison with the delivery of a chattel is troublesome because a contract right, as an intangible, cannot be delivered. Nevertheless, some contract rights are evidenced by writings that symbolize the right, in the sense that they are required to enforce it, and delivery of such symbolic writings has the same effect as the delivery of a chattel. The classic example is the savings bank passbook, presentation of which is required for a withdrawal.[9] If the donor (B) wishes to make an irrevocable gift of a $1,000 debt owed the donor by a savings bank (A), the donor can do so simply by delivering the passbook to the donee (C). Courts have applied this reasoning to other symbolic writings, such as negotiable instruments and documents of title, insurance policies, bonds, and shares of stock.[10] The Restatement Second extends this reasoning by stating that it applies to any "writing of a type customarily accepted as . . . evidence of the right assigned," such a writing evidencing an integrated contract, even though it is not symbolic in the sense of being required to enforce the right.[11] There is some support for this in the cases.[12] The requirements for the delivery of a writing have been adumbrated by many courts, but these requirements are essentially the same as for the delivery of chattels.[13]

> **Comparison with delivery of chattel**

The comparison with the delivery of a sealed deed to a chattel has been undercut by the abolition of the seal. Of course, a donor can make an irrevocable gift of a contract right by a deed under seal in any state where the seal retains its effect.[14] Furthermore, in some of the remaining states, by virtue of statute[15] or decision,[16] a donor can make an irrevocable gift assignment by delivery of a signed, written assignment, and the Restatement Second states this as the

> **Comparison with delivery of deed**

---

[8] See the discussion of the rule for a completed gift contrasted in §2.5 *supra*. On gifts of chattels, *see* R. Brown, Law of Personal Property ch. 7 (3d ed. 1975).

[9] Hileman v. Hulver, 221 A.2d 693 (Md. 1966) (irrevocable gift of deposit in credit union by oral assignment and delivery of passbook).

[10] First Natl. Bank v. Thomas, 134 A. 210 (Md. 1926) (irrevocable gift of life insurance policy by oral assignment and delivery of policy).

[11] Restatement Second §332(l)(b). If the donee is also the obligor, the question is one of discharge rather than assignment. *See* Restatement Second §274 & cmt. *a*. See also the discussion of delivery of a writing in §4.25 *supra*.

[12] For a case stating the general rule, *see* In re Estate of Bolton, 444 N.W.2d 482 (Iowa 1989) ("authorities seem nearly unanimous" that check must be paid prior to donor's death for gift to be valid).

[13] Jackman v. Jackman, 260 N.W. 769 (Mich. 1935) (there was delivery of notes and mortgage by father to son, although son later left them in safe-deposit box that he rented jointly with father).

[14] O'Gasapian v. Danielson, 187 N.E. 107 (Mass. 1933) (gift by assignment under seal of note and mortgage was irrevocable, even though note was not indorsed or delivered). On the seal, see the discussion of the decline of the seal in §2.16 *supra*.

[15] See N.Y. Gen. Oblig. L. §5-1107, applied in Speelman v. Pascal, 178 N.E.2d 723 (N.Y. 1961) (gift of 5 percent of profits from production of musical based on Shaw's *Pygmalion*).

[16] Thatcher v. Merriam, 240 P.2d 266 (Utah 1952) (irrevocable gift by written and signed assignment of part interest in negotiable promissory note).

law.[17] Thus, a donor (B), that wishes to make an irrevocable gift of a $1,000 debt that is owed by an obligor (A), can do so in some jurisdictions by delivering a signed, written assignment to the donee (C). Such an assignment has been held to be irrevocable, even when the donor could have delivered a symbolic writing but did not do so.[18] The rules governing delivery of the writing are analogous to those governing delivery of a deed to a chattel.[19]

Consummation of gift or reliance

Even if an assignor has the power to terminate a gratuitous assignment when it is made, the assignor may lose that power as the result of the assignee's subsequent acts. Most important, an effective assignment, even if gratuitous, authorizes the assignee to consummate the gift by obtaining performance from the obligor. If the assignee does so, the assignor's power of revocation terminates, and the assignee can retain what has been received.[20] Thus, if the donee (C), that has received from a donor (B) an effective but gratuitous assignment of a contract right to $1,000 from an obligor (A), later collects the $1,000 from the obligor, the donor's power of revocation is terminated, and the donee is entitled to keep the $1,000. The same result follows if, instead of obtaining satisfaction from the obligor, the assignee gets judgments against the obligor or makes a new contract with the obligor by a novation.[21] Furthermore, if, before consummation of the gift, the assignee relies on the assignment, the assignor will be estopped to revoke it, at least to the extent that it would be unjust for the assignor to do so.[22]

What assignments are gratuitous

If an assignee gives value for the assignment, it is not gratuitous and is therefore not revocable. It is important to remember that an assignment is a transfer, not a contract (a promise), and to understand that whether a *transferee* has given *value* is not the same question as whether a *promisee* has given *consideration*. From the several possible definitions of *value*, the Restatement Second chooses the one that accords with the general definition in the Uniform Commercial Code.[23] An assignee gives value by taking the assignment either in exchange for something that would be consideration for a promise, or as security for or in total or partial satisfaction of a preexisting obligation.[24]

---

[17] Restatement Second §332(1)(a). If the donee is also the obligor, however, the question is one of discharge rather than assignment, as in the situation in note 11 *supra. See* Restatement Second §277. See also the discussion of delivery of a writing in §4.25 *supra*.

[18] Petty v. Mutual Benefit Life Ins. Co., 15 N.W.2d 613 (Iowa 1944) (gift of life insurance policy by written assignment was irrevocable, regardless of whether donor delivered policy).

[19] Biehl v. Biehl's Admx., 93 S.W.2d 836 (Ky. 1936) (gift of stock certificate was revocable where owner left it in his pocket after indorsing it).

[20] This result followed even when the assignee was regarded as having only a power of attorney. See the discussion of the concept of a power of attorney in §11.2 *supra*.

[21] Restatement Second §332(3).

[22] Restatement Second §332(4). This seems a reasonable rule, though the Reporter's Note gives no authority for it.

[23] UCC 1-204. For a narrower definition of *value* in the Code, applicable to negotiable instruments, *see* UCC 3-303(a).

[24] Restatement Second §332(5).

We next look into the vulnerability of an assignee to a defense by the obligor that the duty has been discharged or modified by the obligor's dealings with the assignor after the assignment.

§11.7.   Vulnerability of Assignee to Discharge or Modification. Suppose that, after an irrevocable assignment of a debt, the obligor (A) pays the assignor (B) instead of the assignee (C). Does the obligor's payment discharge the debt and give the obligor a defense against the assignee, or is the obligor bound to pay a second time? If the obligor pays the assignor without knowing of the assignment, it would plainly be unfair to require the obligor to pay again. Therefore, if the obligor pays before being notified of the assignment, the debt is discharged.[1] But if the obligor pays after having been notified of the assignment, the debt is not discharged; the obligor's payment is not a defense against the assignee.[2] Notification has the same effect when the obligor's duty is to render a performance other than the payment of money — once the assignee gives notice, the assignee is no longer vulnerable to performance by the obligor to the assignor.[3] These rules do not apply, however, if the right assigned is evidenced by a symbolic writing. In that situation the right is regarded as intimately connected with the writing, and performance rendered to a party that does not produce the writing is rendered at the obligor's peril, regardless of the lack of notification.[4]

In applying the notification requirement, courts have sometimes seemed insufficiently sympathetic to the position of the obligor.[5] Article 9 of the Code contains some useful rules on the sufficiency of the notification that are, for the most part, designed for the obligor's protection. The notification must actually

Effect of notification

What amounts to notification

---

§11.7   [1]Taylor v. Roeder, 360 S.E.2d 191 (Va. 1987) (contrasting "general law of contracts" with "law of negotiable instruments" under which "makers are bound by their contract to make payment to the *holder*").

[2]UCC 9-406(a) (account debtor "may discharge its obligation by paying the assignor until, but not after, the account debtor receives a notification"). Notification usually comes from the assignee, but may also come from the assignor.

[3]*See* Restatement Second §338(1) ("assignor retains the power to discharge the duty of the obligor . . . until but not after the obligor receives notification"). Of course, if the assignment is revocable, the assignor's collection of the debt will revoke the assignment. See the discussion of the nature of revocation in §11.6 *supra*.

[4]*See* Restatement Second §338. Comment *h* explains: "Aside from statute, an obligor who renders performance without requiring production of . . . a symbolic writing takes the risk that the person receiving performance does not have possession of the writing either because he has assigned it or because his right is defective . . . . In addition, the obligor who performs without surrender or cancellation of or appropriate notation on the writing takes the risk of further obligation to an assignee who takes possession of the writing as a bona fide purchaser." *See* UCC 3-601(b), 3-602(b).

[5]Robert Parker's Truck & Trailer Repair v. Speer, 722 S.W.2d 45 (Tex. App. 1986) (obligor had notice where "agents possessed enough information to cause them to make a reasonable inquiry into the existence of an assignment").

be received by the obligor;[6] it must indicate "that the amount due or to become due has been assigned and that payment is to be made to the assignee";[7] and it must "reasonably identify the rights assigned."[8] Furthermore, if requested by the obligor, the assignee "must seasonably furnish reasonable proof that the assignment has been made"; and if the assignee fails to do so, the obligor may pay the assignor.[9] It seems likely that courts will apply these rules by analogy, even when Article 9 does not literally apply.

Liability of assignor

If, in the example given, the obligor pays the assignor rather than the assignee, the assignee may be able to hold the assignor liable for breach of warranty. If one assigns a right under seal or for value, one impliedly warrants that one will do nothing to defeat or impair the value of the assignment, and, if one subsequently obtains performance, one is liable for breach of that warranty.[10] The assignee thus has recourse against the assignor if the obligor is not liable.[11] But there is no implied warranty if a contrary intention is manifested, as often happens when the assignment is for security. For example, in the situation described earlier, of the wholesaler (B) that has sold to a retailer (A) on credit and assigned the resulting account receivable as security for a loan from a financial insitution (C), it is usually understood between the wholesaler and the financial institution that the retailer will not be notified of the assignment and that the wholesaler will collect the account itself.[12] Its doing so is then, of course, not a breach of warranty.

Modification after assignment

If an obligor with notice of an assignment cannot discharge the duty by dealing with the obligee, it might seem logical that the obligor would also be unable to modify the duty by dealing with the obligee.[13] The law was confused, but some courts used this logic to reach the result that, after notification to the

---

[6] UCC 1-202.

[7] UCC 9-406(a).

[8] UCC 9-406(b)(1).

[9] UCC 9-406(c).

[10] Restatement Second §333 sets out the implied warranties of an assignor for value. In some respects they resemble those of a seller of goods. For example, the assignor warrants "that the right, as assigned, actually exists and is subject to no limitations or defenses good against the assignor other than those stated or apparent at the time of the assignment." But the liability goes beyond this, for the assignor also warrants "that he will do nothing to defeat or impair the value of the assignment and has no knowledge of any fact which would do so." The assignment does not of itself, however, "operate as a warranty that the obligor is solvent or that he will perform his obligation."

[11] However, Restatement Second §333 illus. 1 suggests that the assignee's damages for the breach of warranty may depend on whether the assignee can hold the obligor.

[12] *Cf.* St. Paul Fire & Marine Ins. Co. v. James I. Barnes Constr. Co., 381 P.2d 932 (Cal. 1963) (alternative holding: when an assignment is for security, and the debtor pays the assignor after notice, "the assignee can recover from the debtor . . . only if its security has been adversely affected, that is, only if it has suffered a loss"). On non-notification financing, see the discussion of a commercial sale in §11.1 *supra*.

[13] That the obligor can modify its duty in this way before notification, *see* LePorin v. State Exch. Bank, 213 P. 650 (Kan. 1923).

obligor, the assignee was not vulnerable to modification without the assignee's assent.[14] This result caused trouble in practice. Reconsider the situation of the builder (B) that has made a construction contract and assigned the right to payment by the owner (A) as a security for a loan from a financial institution (C).[15] If, after notification and as the work progressed, the builder and the owner wished to modify their contract, a rule under which the financial institution was not vulnerable to modification without its consent would stand in their way.

The desired modification often took the form of an advance of funds to the builder, in order to enable the builder to meet its payroll, buy materials, and thus continue work. Even though an advance after modification might seem perilously close to a payment after notification, some courts distinguished the two situations and gave the owner priority over the financial institution if the owner's advance was "necessary to enable the assignor to perform his contract" and was so used.[16]

Necessary advances

Article 9 of the Code goes beyond these cases and lays down a general rule that a modification of "an assigned contract is effective against an assignee if made in good faith."[17] Within these limits, the builder and the owner can modify the contract and change the right that the financial institution has taken.[18] The financial institution can insist that any assignment to it of a construction contract provide that any modification is a breach by the assignor.[19]

Code rule

We look next at some other problems involving the assignee's vulnerability to the obligor's defenses and claims.

---

[14]Brice v. Bannister, 3 Q.B.D. 569 (1878) (Bramwell, L.J.: though it seems to be the law, "it does seem to me a strange thing and hard on a man, that he should enter into a contract with another and then find that because the other has entered into some contract with a third, he, the first man, is unable to do that which it is reasonable and just he should do for his own good"). This did not, however, prevent the original parties to the contract from making a new contract if the obligor had terminated the earlier contract following a breach by the obligee.

[15]See the discussion of an assignment of a builder's right in §11.1 *supra*.

[16]Fricker v. Uddo & Taormina Co., 312 P.2d 1085, 1087 (Cal. 1957) (canning company that had contracted to buy farmer's tomato crop and had made advances to farmer after notification that he had assigned right to payment had burden of proving necessity).

[17]UCC 9-405(a).

[18]See UCC 9-405 cmt. 2 ("The ability ... to modify assigned contracts can be important especially in the case of government contracts and complex contractual arrangements (e.g., construction contracts) with respect to which modifications are customary."). When for example it becomes necessary for a government agency to cut back or modify existing contracts, comparable arrangements must be made promptly in hundreds and even thousands of subcontracts lying in many tiers below the prime contract . . . . This subsection gives the prime contractor (the account debtor) the right to make the required arrangements directly with his subcontractors without undertaking the task of procuring assents from the many banks to whom rights under the contracts may have been assigned.").

[19]UCC 9-405(a) ("assignment may provide that the modification or substitution is a breach of contract by the assignor").

§11.8.   Vulnerability of Assignee to Obligor's Defenses and Claims.
Every law student knows that "the assignee stands in the shoes of the assignor."[1]
For the most part, this homely metaphor is an accurate generalization.[2] It means
that the assignee (C) acquires no better rights against the obligor (A) than the
assignor (B) had. The assignee takes what the assignor had "warts and all," for
an assignment does not deprive the obligor of any defenses or claims arising
out of the agreement that the obligor could have asserted against the assignor
absent assignment. The obligor may assert these defenses and claims against
the assignee, regardless of whether the assignee knew of their existence at
the time of assignment or whether they had even come into existence at that
time.

Typical defenses

Thus the assignee is vulnerable to defenses of the obligor that affect the
enforceability of the obligor's agreement with the assignor. These include unenforceability for lack of consideration, reasons of public policy, or failure to satisfy
the statute of frauds.[3] They also include voidability for incapacity, mistake, misrepresentation, or duress.[4] Since the assignee is subject to all of the terms of the
contract between the obligor and the assignor, the assignee is also vulnerable to
defenses of the obligor that arise under those terms during the performance of
the agreement. These include nonoccurrence of a condition and failure of performance, whether the failure is a breach or is justifiable.[5] Since the assignor's
rights are vulnerable to such defenses from the time the agreement is made,
the assignee's rights are similarly vulnerable, despite the fact that the event
giving rise to the defense may not have occurred at the time of the assignment
or even at the time the obligor had notice of it.[6]

Typical claims

In addition, the assignee is subject to recoupment of any claims that the
obligor would have had against the assignor for damages for breach of contract,

---

§11.8   [1] James Talcott, Inc. v. H. Corenzwit & Co., 387 A.2d 350 (N.J. 1978) ("The Code has
continued the common law view that an assignee of a chose in action, such as a receivable, stands
in the shoes of the assignor.").

[2] UCC 9-404(a) ("rights of an assignee are subject to . . . all the terms of the agreement between
the account debtor and assignor and any defense or claim in recoupment arising from the transaction that gave rise to the contract"). *See* Restatement Second §336(1) ("the assignee acquires a
right against the obligor only to the extent that the obligor is under a duty to the assignor").

[3] Beck v. Sheldon, 181 N.E. 360 (N.Y. 1932) (mortgagor claimed lack of consideration). As to
the statute of frauds, see the discussion of other effects in §6.10 *supra*.

[4] Apple v. Edwards, 16 P.2d 700 (Mont. 1932) (buyer of goods claimed fraud). *See* Restatement
Second §337.

[5] Sponge Divers' Assn. v. Smith, Kline & French Co., 263 F. 70 (3d Cir. 1920) (buyer rejected
defective goods).

[6] James Talcott, Inc. v. H. Corenzwit & Co., *supra* note 1 ("It is immaterial whether the contract
defenses or claims [arising by virtue of the contract out of which the receivable was created] arose
before or after notice of the assignment."). Compare the rule governing performance rendered
by the obligor to the assignor as a defense. See the discussion of the effect of notification in §11.7
supra.

again regardless of whether the breach has occurred at the time of the assignment or even at the time of notice.[7] The claim is only good against the assignee to the extent that it diminishes or extinguishes the assignee's claim; it cannot be used to impose liability on the assignee[8] unless the assignee has assumed the assignor's duty of performance.[9] If, after a defense or claim has arisen but before the obligor learns of it, the obligor mistakenly renders performance to the assignee when not obligated to do so, some courts held that the obligor may have restitution against an assignee who has not changed position in reliance on the performance,[10] while others denied such claims.[11] Revision of Article 9 of the Uniform Commercial Code has adopted the latter solution.[12]

Recall the example of the retailer (B) that sells a $1,000 stereo to a consumer (A) on credit and assigns the right to payment to a financial institution (C).[13] If the stereo is defective, so that before assignment the consumer could have returned it and refused to pay the balance of the price for breach of warranty or fraud, the consumer can still do so after assignment. And the consumer who chooses to keep the stereo in spite of its defects and claims damages of, say, $300, can deduct this sum from the balance of the price and pay the financial institution only the difference.[14] That the financial institution may not have

Example of retail sale

[7] James Talcott, Inc. v. H. Corenzwit & Co., *supra* note 1 (buyer's claim against seller for breach of guaranty against drop in price of goods).

[8] Shepard v. Commercial Credit Corp., 183 A.2d 525 (Vt. 1962) (finance company not liable to buyer for damages due to defects in house trailer because "claim can only be allowed against the assignee to the extent that it offsets the assignee's claim").

[9] Cuchine v. H.O. Bell Inc., 682 P.2d 723 (Mont. 1984) (Code was not intended "to place the assignee of a contract in the position of being held a guarantor"). The assignee may assume at the time of assignment by promising the assignor to perform the assignor's duty. On such assumption agreements, see the discussion of assumption by a delegate in §11.11 *infra*.

[10] Farmers Acceptance Corp. v. DeLozier, 496 P.2d 1016 (Colo. 1972) (where contractor's progress payments to assignee exceeded amount to which subcontractor was entitled because of breach, contractor could recover excess from assignee where there was "no showing that [assignee] changed its position and made further loans to [subcontractor] on the basis of the payment received from [contractor]").

[11] Michelin Tires (Canada) v. First Natl. Bank, 666 F.2d 673 (1st Cir. 1981) (following Restatement of Restitution §14(2) in "denying restitution against an assignee for value who is without notice of the assignor's fraud").

[12] Uniform Commercial Code 9-404(b) & cmt. 3 (2000 Revision) (new provision "generally does not allow the account debtor the right to an affirmative recovery from an assignee"). The "discharge for value" rule, which denies restitution to one who has mistakenly paid a debt that another person owes to the recipient, affords a rationale for this solution in most cases. The assignee can assert the rule on the ground that the obligor has mistakenly paid a debt owed by the assignor to the assignee, the debt commonly secured by the assignment.

[13] See the discussion of a consumer sale in §11.1 *supra*.

[14] The consumer whose damages exceed the amount due the financial institution cannot recover this excess from it, though the consumer may be able to recover payments made before learning of the retailer's breach. Eachen v. Scott Hous. Sys., 630 F. Supp. 162 (M.D. Ala. 1986) (under FTC rule buyer of mobile home could recover from assignee on warranty claim up to amount paid).

been aware of any defenses or claims when it took the assignment will not affect the result.

Example of construction contract

Recall also the example of the builder (B) that contracts to build a building for $10,000,000 and assigns the right to progress payments from the owner (A) to a financial institution (C).[15] If the builder fails to finish the building, the financial institution has no right to recover from the owner, since substantial performance by the builder is a constructive condition of the owner's duty to pay. This is so even though, in contrast to the case of the assignment by the retailer, the breach by the builder does not occur until after the assignment to the financial institution and perhaps until after notice of the assignment to the owner—the builder's right to payment being conditioned from the outset on performance.

Use of promissory note

Dissatisfied with their vulnerability under these rules, financial institutions that were assignees of retailers sought to step out of the retailer's "shoes" and to free themselves of the consumer's defenses and claims.[16] Usually they did so by means of a negotiable promissory note. The consumer who bought on credit signed not only a contract, but also a note in which the consumer promised to pay the price to the retailer or holder. The retailer that assigned the right to payment indorsed the note, ordering that it be paid to the financial institution. Under the law of negotiable instruments, if the financial institution took the note for value, in good faith, and without notice of any defense of the consumer, it qualified as a *holder in due course*. As a holder in due course it could enforce the note against the consumer, free of defenses such as breach of warranty and fraud in the inducement.[17]

Use of waiver-of-defense clause

Instead of using a separate promissory note, financial institutions sometimes had retailers include in the contract of sale itself a clause known as a "waiver-of-defense" clause (sometimes a "hell-or-high-water" clause). Under such a clause the consumer agreed that, should the right to payment be assigned, the consumer would not set up any defenses against the assignee. Courts generally held that after the financial insitution had given value in reliance on such a clause, the consumer was precluded from asserting against the financial institution defenses, such as breach of warranty and fraud in the inducement, that the

---

[15]See the discussion of an assignment of a builder's right in §11.1 *supra*.

[16]That not all buyers involved were "consumers" in the usual sense of that term, see note 22 *infra*.

[17]A holder in due course takes an instrument free from "personal" defenses subject only to rare "real" defenses, such as fraud in the execution (see the discussion of fraud in the factum or execution in §4.10 *supra*) and duress by physical compulsion (see the discussion of physical compulsion or threat in §4.16 *supra*). UCC 3-305. In order to be a holder in due course, the financial institution must take "for value," "in good faith," and "without notice" of any claim or defense. UCC 3-302(a). In addition, the note must be negotiable and must be indorsed by the retailer.

consumer could have asserted against the retailer.[18] Financial institutions often preferred to use waiver-of-defense clauses to avoid some of the cumbersome formalities inherent in negotiable promissory notes.[19]

The argument for cutting off the consumer's defenses by either of these methods was an extension of the argument for free assignability.[20] Allowing the financial institution to take free of defenses encouraged it to take assignments from the retailer, which in turn encouraged the retailer to extend credit to the consumer. Most consumers, whose goods were not defective, would benefit from the greater availability and the lower cost of credit. Even the few consumers who bought defective goods would be able to recover from the retailer that had sold them.[21]

Argument for cutting off defenses

On behalf of the consumer, however, it was argued that it was far more burdensome for the consumer to take the offensive in an attempt to hold the retailer liable than it was for the consumer defensively to resist payment to the financial institution. Furthermore, there was an appreciable risk that a retailer that regularly sold shoddy goods might be insolvent by the time the consumer came to press a claim. It was contended that a financial institution typically had close and continuing connections with a retailer from which it took assignments. Indeed, in practice, it is difficult for the financial institution to avoid a close connection with a dealer that makes assignments to it. Since the relationship is ordinarily a continuing one, there is typically a master agreement and some arrangement for a fund to be retained by the financial institution to secure its right of recourse against the dealer. In addition, the financial institution will insist that the standard forms for contracts with customers as well as for assignments be its own. Because of this, it was argued, subjecting the financial institution to defenses would encourage it to police the retailer in order to ensure that the retailer was not selling shoddy goods. As the Supreme Court of Florida expressed it, "We believe the finance company is better able to bear the risk of the dealer's insolvency than the buyer and in a far better

Argument against cutting off defenses

---

[18] United States v. Troy-Parisian, 115 F.2d 224 (9th Cir. 1940) ("there would appear to be no good reason why [parties] may not by agreement impart to [their contract] limited elements of negotiability"). *Contra:* American Natl. Bank v. A.G. Sommerville Inc., 216 P. 376 (Cal. 1923) ("Parties may not impart the character of negotiability to any other writing not of itself a negotiable instrument").

[19] Since a negotiable instrument is symbolic of the debt, the debtor cannot safely pay without ascertaining that the creditor is in possession of the note and having the note cancelled or the payment noted on it. *See* UCC 3-601(b) (discharge of party's obligation "is not effective against a person acquiring rights of a holder in due course of the instrument without notice of the discharge"). See also the discussion of the effect of notification in §11.7 *supra.*

[20] See the discussion of the modern role of free assignability in §11.2 *supra. See generally* Gilmore, The Commercial Doctrine of Good Faith Purchase, 63 Yale L.J. 1057, 1062-72 (1954).

[21] *See* Kripke, Chattel Paper as a Negotiable Specialty Under the Uniform Commercial Code, 59 Yale L.J. 1209, 1214-22 (1950) (even "in the case of justified dissatisfaction, the seller is ordinarily able and willing to make adjustment [and if not] he is, of course, legally responsible").

Judicial decisions for consumers

position to protect his interests against unscrupulous and insolvent dealers."[22] The consumer-oriented view was ultimately to prevail.

The first victories for the consumer-oriented view came in the courts, which began to hold, in the early 1950s, that a financial institution that was closely connected with a retailer could not be a holder in due course[23] and was not protected by a waiver-of-defense clause.[24] These decisions fell short of giving the consumer optimum protection for, although the requisite close connection could usually be shown, the consumer had to show it in each case.

Statutes protecting consumers

By the early 1970s, most state legislatures had enacted statutes applicable to consumer transactions prohibiting negotiable promissory notes and waiver-of-defense clauses, limiting their effectiveness, or depriving them of effect altogether.[25] The Federal Trade Commission then promulgated a rule regulating such transactions and made its violation an unfair trade practice.[26] Under these laws, the closeness of the connection between the financial institution and the retailer is irrelevant. Whatever that connection, the financial institution is back in the shoes of the retailer and is subject to all the defenses and claims that could have been asserted against the retailer. If the consumer makes payments to the financial institution before discovering the defects in the goods, the consumer presumably has the same right to restitution from the institution that the consumer would have had at common law.[27] The statutes generally confer no right to restitution on the consumer.[28] The Code declines to take a position on the rights of consumers to assert defenses and claims, generally validating the use of notes and clauses "subject to law other than this article which establishes a different rule for an account debtor who is an individual

---

[22] Mutual Fin. Co. v. Martin, 63 So. 2d 649, 653 (Fla. 1953). *See* Kripke, Consumer Credit Regulation: A Creditor-Oriented Viewpoint, 68 Colum. L. Rev. 445, 469-73 (1968) ("the risk of cases of legitimate consumer dissatisfaction should be thrown on the financier [since it] is best able to force redress by maintaining an action over against the merchant or by charging withheld amounts in the financier's hands"), repudiating the same writer's earlier argument to the contrary, cited *supra* note 21.

[23] Mutual Fin. Co. v. Martin, *supra* note 22 (where finance company had been involved in transaction it "had such notice of . . . infirmity" in note given by grocer for freezer).

[24] Fairfield Credit Corp. v. Donnelly, 264 A.2d 547 (Conn. 1969) ("use of a waiver of defense clause is an attempt to impart the attributes of negotiability to an otherwise nonnegotiable instrument" and is contrary to "a very strong public policy in favor of protecting purchasers of consumer goods").

[25] *See* Cal. Civ. Code §1804.2; Uniform Consumer Credit Code §§3.307, 3.404. (As to the Uniform Consumer Credit Code, see the discussion of legislation as common in §4.29 *supra*.)

[26] 16 C.F.R. pt. 433.

[27] See the discussion of typical claims *supra*.

[28] The FTC rule, however, seems to contemplate claims against assignees. See *supra* note 26. That the consumer's right against the creditor does not exceed the amount paid, *see* Ford Motor Credit Co. v. Morgan, 536 N.E.2d 587 (Mass. 1989); Home Sav. Assn. v. Guerra, 733 S.W.2d 134 (Tex. 1987).

and who incurred the obligation primarily for personal, family, or household purposes."[29]

If the assignee is unable to enforce the right that has been assigned because of a defense of the obligor against the assignor, the assignee may have recourse against the assignor. Absent disclaimer, an assignor that assigns for value impliedly warrants that the right as assigned actually exists and is subject to no defenses or claims good against the assignor, other than those stated or apparent at the time of the assignment.[30] The assignor also warrants that it will do nothing to defeat or impair the value of the assignment and has no knowledge of any fact that would do so,[31] and it has been held that if the right assigned is conditional on performance by the assignor, this warranty imposes a duty on the assignor to take affirmative action to perform.[32] But the assignment does not of itself operate as a warranty by the assignor that the obligor is solvent or will perform, though the assignor may undertake such an obligation and in many transactions does so.[33]

Assignor's warranties against defenses

The preceding discussion has been limited to the availability to the obligor of defenses and claims against the assignor arising out of the obligor's agreement with the assignor. A different situation arises if the obligor seeks to offset against the assignee a claim against the assignor that did not arise out of that agreement. Statutes or rules of court generally permit a defendant to assert such a claim against a plaintiff by offset or counterclaim, even though it is not related to the plaintiff's claim.[34] Suppose, to take a simple illustration, that a debtor (A) that owes a creditor (B) $3,000 extends $1,000 worth of credit to the creditor. In doing so, the debtor may expect not to collect the $1,000 from the creditor, but simply to deduct it from the $3,000, paying the creditor the difference of $2,000.

Claims not arising out of agreeement distinguished

---

[29]UCC 9-403(e). Article 3 contains a similar provision. UCC 3-302(g) ("section is subject to any law limiting status as a holder in due course in particular classes of transactions").

[30]Bouknight v. Mitchell, 129 S.E. 134 (S.C. 1924) ("assignor 'without recourse' is charged with an implied warranty that the chose in action assigned is what it purports to be"). *See* Restatement Second §333(1). Generally, the assignor's warranties run only to the assignor's immediate assignee and are not transferred by subassignment. *See* Restatement Second §333(4). Damages for breach of warranty are based on the value that the right would have had if it had been as warranted.

[31]P.N. Gray & Co. v. Cavalliotis, 276 F. 565 (E.D.N.Y. 1921) ("assignor is held to have contracted that he will do no act to deprive the assignee of his rights under the assigned contract"), aff'd mem., 293 F. 1018 (2d Cir. 1923).

[32]Lonsdale v. Chesterfield, 662 P.2d 385 (Wash. 1983) (assignor's "failure to fulfill its obligation made the assigned rights . . . virtually worthless").

[33]Galbreath v. Wallrich, 102 P. 1085 (Colo. 1909) ("assignment of a . . . contract does not carry a warranty that it will be performed"). *See* Restatement Second §333(2). One who transfers a negotiable promissory note for consideration, with or without indorsement, makes warranties set out in UCC 3-416(a). Furthermore, the indorser of a note undertakes to pay it if the maker does not. UCC 3-415(a).

[34]*See* Graves Equip. v. M. DeMatteo Constr. Co., 489 N.E.2d 1010 (Mass. 1986) (distinguishing claims and defenses that arise "out of the terms of the . . . contract" from those that "arise independently of the contract"). We are not concerned with the assignee's right to offset against the obligor the right acquired by assignment.

It would not be just to allow the creditor to deprive the debtor of the right to offset this claim merely by assigning the right to $3,000 to an assignee (C). On the other hand, it would not be just to subject the assignee to all claims by the debtor, no matter when they arose. Jurisdictions differ, however, in balancing the respective interests of the obligor and the assignee.

Code and Restatement rules

Fortunately, Article 9 of the Code has achieved considerable uniformity by providing that the rights of an assignee of an account are subject to any defense or claim not arising from the contract between the debtor and the assignor if it "accrues" before the account debtor receives notification of the assignment.[35] The "assignee is subject to all such claims that accrue before, and free of all those that accrue after, notification." With respect to assignments not covered by the Code, the rule often depends on the legislation governing offset in the particular jurisdiction,[36] but the Restatement Second states a general rule based on that of the Code.[37]

From the assignee's vulnerability to the obligor's defenses and claims, we turn to the assignee's vulnerability to competing claims of ownership.

Vulnerability to "latent equities"

§11.9. Vulnerability of Assignee to Competing Claims of Ownership. Since a contract right is a form of property, it may, like any other form of property, be the subject of competing claims of ownership. Suppose that, at the time of assignment, the assignor's (B's) ownership of the right is already held in constructive trust for another person (X) or is subject to a power of avoidance by that person.[1] Does the assignee (C) of the right take subject to these claims of ownership? Since claims like these have their origins in equity, the question is often framed as whether the assignee takes subject to "latent equities."

Assignee protected

In the days when an assignee's interest was regarded as "equitable" in nature,[2] some courts held that the assignee took subject to latent equities.[3] It is a maxim of equity that, as between two competing equitable claims, "first in time is first

---

[35] UCC 9-404(a)(2).

[36] Denying offset: Cronkleton v. Hastings Theatre & Realty Corp., 278 N.W. 144 (Neb. 1938) (unrelated claims "arising against the assignor, after notice of the assignment, cannot be set off against the claim of the assignee"). Allowing offset: St. Louis Natl. Bank v. Gay, 35 P. 876 (Cal. 1894) (rejecting argument that "set-off is not available against an assignee unless it be due, payable, and suable at the time of notice of assignment").

[37] Restatement Second §336(2) (subjecting assignee to "any defense or claim of the obligor which accrues before the obligor receives notification of the assignment").

§11.9 [1] The rules discussed here apply if the right assigned is held in trust or constructive trust for or subject to a right of avoidance or an equitable lien of a person other than the obligor. *See* Restatement Second §343. They do not protect an assignee where this would impair rights of the obligor. *See* Restatement Second §343 cmt. *b*.

As to the protection afforded an obligor who is confronted with adverse claims by an assignee and another person and is unsure who is entitled to performance, *see* Restatement Second §339.

[2] See the discussions of recognition in equity and of the significance of history in §11.2 *supra*.

[3] Owen v. Evans, 31 N.E. 999 (N.Y. 1892) ("in the absence of an estoppel, an assignee of a mortgage takes only the interest of his assignor, subject to any latent equity").

in right,"[4] and the other person's equitable claim arose prior to the assignee's "equitable" interest under the assignment. Chancellor Kent, however, argued that the other person should not be allowed to set up a "secret equity," against the assignee, which "may not be able, with the utmost diligence, to ascertain it."[5] His view prevailed. Today the assignee's interest is regarded as "legal" in nature, and the assignee is protected by a rule, generally applicable to personal property, that one acquiring legal ownership takes free of that claim.[6] Thus, an assignee that is a good faith purchaser takes free of latent equities,[7] though an assignee that takes in bad faith, with notice, or without giving value would be subject to them.[8]

Consider the example of an assignee (C) that takes by assignment a right fraudulently acquired by the assignor (B) under a previous assignment from its original owner (X). (The assignment in question is therefore actually a sub-assignment from a subassignor (B) to a subassignee (C), the first assignment having been from the original owner of the right to the subassignor.) Prior to the assignment, the assignor's right was subject to the original owner's power of avoidance for fraud. But after assignment, if the assignee has taken in good faith, without notice, and for value, the original owner's power of avoidance is cut off, and the assignee holds the assigned right free from that power.

Example of fraud

A similar problem with competing claims of ownership arises when, after an assignor (B) has assigned a right for value to an assignee (C), the same assignor assigns the same right for value to a second assignee (D), which is unaware of the first assignment. Which assignee owns the right, the first or the second?[9] Though the losing assignee has a claim for breach of warranty against the assignor,[10] a damage claim against one of demonstrated duplicity is usually

Priority of competing assignees

---

[4] 1 J. Pomeroy, Equity Jurisprudence §§413-415 (1st ed. 1881) ("where there are equal equities, the first in order of time shall prevail").

[5] Murray & Winter v. Lylburn, 2 Johns. Ch. 441, 442 (N.Y. 1817).

[6] 1 J. Pomeroy, Equity Jurisprudence §§416, 417 (1st ed. 1881) ("where there is equal equity the law must prevail"). *See also* Gilmore, The Commercial Doctrine of Good Faith Purchase, 63 Yale L.J. 1057 (1954).

[7] Glass v. Springfield L.I. Cemetery Socy., 299 N.Y.S. 244 (App. Div. 1937) (when assignee "became a purchaser for value, his legal title was superior to equitable rights previously created in favor of third parties"). *See* Restatement Second §343.

[8] Fiberchem v. General Plastics Corp., 495 F.2d 737 (9th Cir. 1974) (though "there is some dispute whether or not an assignee for value takes his claim free from the equities of third persons against the assignor, of which the assignee had no notice, there is no dispute that the assignee takes his claim subject to the equities . . . where he has knowledge"). Under UCC 1-204 (2), a transfer as security for or in satisfaction of a preexisting debt is a transfer for value. *See* Restatement Second §338 cmt. *c.*

[9] If either assignment is revocable or voidable and the other is not, the latter will prevail. McKnight v. Rice, Hoppner, Brown & Brunner, 678 P.2d 1330 (Alaska 1984) (revocable assignment not entitled to priority).

[10] According to the Restatement Second, if the first assignee loses, the first assignee can hold the assignor for breach of a warranty "that he will do nothing to defeat or impair the value of the

of little value, and the issue of the priority between the claims of two assignees becomes critical.

Three rules

To the delight of contracts teachers, the courts fashioned no fewer than three colorfully captioned rules to resolve this issue. There was a "New York" rule, an "English" rule, and a "Massachusetts" or "four horsemen" rule.

New York rule

Under the New York rule, the first assignee prevailed: even if the second assignee obtained the performance, the first assignee had priority and could recover from the second assignee.[11] Sometimes courts justified this on the ground, seen earlier in connection with the discussion of latent equities,[12] that both assignees' rights were in nature equitable and therefore the first in time prevailed.[13] Sometimes courts justified the rule on the ground that by the first assignment the assignor had divested itself of all it had, so that nothing remained for it to transfer by a second assignment.[14]

English rule

Under the English rule, the first assignee prevailed unless the second assignee had notified the obligor of its assignment before the first assignee notified the obligor of its.[15] Courts following this rule sometimes argued that it had the desirable effect of encouraging an assignee to give prompt notice to the obligor, so that others might obtain information as to the ownership of the claim from the obligor.[16]

Massachusetts or four horsemen rule

Under the Massachusetts or four horsemen rule, the first assignee prevailed, unless the second assignee had done one of four acts: (1) received payment or other satisfaction of the obligation; (2) obtained a judgment against the obligor; (3) made a new contract with the obligor by novation; or (4) obtained possession

---

assignment." If the second assignee loses, the second assignee can hold the assignor for breach of warranties that the assignor "has no knowledge of any fact" that would "defeat or impair the value of the assignment" and that the right "is subject to no limitations . . . good against [the assignor] other than those stated or apparent." *See* Restatement Second §333, described in a footnote to the discussion of the liability of the assignor in §11.7 *supra*.

[11] Superior Brassiere Co. v. Zimetbaum, 212 N.Y.S. 473 (App. Div. 1925) (since "second assignee took nothing under the assignment, . . . the money he received he holds in trust for the benefit of the first assignee"). The first assignee might, however, be estopped to assert its priority if, for example, the first assignee had misled the second assignee by leaving a document evidencing the right in the hands of the assignor. Salem Trust Co. v. Manufacturers' Fin. Co., 264 U.S. 182 (1924) (dictum: "would be unconscionable to permit him to prevail over a later assignee whom he had misled").

[12] See the discussion of an assignee as protected *supra*.

[13] Salem Trust Co. v. Manufacturers' Fin. Co., *supra* note 11 ("if it be assumed that each bona fide purchaser takes merely an equity . . . , the first in time is best in right").

[14] Salem Trust Co. v. Manufacturers' Fin. Co., *supra* note 11 ("subsequent assignee takes nothing by his assignment, because the assignor has nothing to give").

[15] The English rule was formulated in Dearle v. Hall, 38 Eng. Rep. 475, 492 (Ch. 1828).

[16] Graham Paper Co. v. Pembroke, 56 P. 627 (Cal. 1899) ("an intending purchaser of the accounts . . . would have it in his power to ascertain from the debtors, by inquiry whether any prior assignment existed"). This rule did not accord well with the practice of non-notification financing described in the discussion of a commercial sale in §11.1 *supra*.

of a symbolic writing.[17] Both Restatements have endorsed this rule.[18] The commentary to the Restatement Second notes that the historical justification for allowing the second assignee to achieve priority by such acts was that "the right of an assignee was equitable and was not enforceable against a bona fide purchaser of the legal right," and that today "the doctrine of bona fide purchase has been extended in the interest of the security of transactions."[19]

Article 9 of the Code has wrought a major change in this body of law with a system by which a secured creditor can perfect a security interest in most kinds of personal property by filing in a government office a financing statement briefly describing that interest.[20] Because Article 9 is not limited to assignments of accounts for security, its rules on filing extend to outright sales of accounts as well.[21] Under the Code, in a contest between two assignees that have given value, the assignee that first files a financing statement covering its assignment prevails.[22] Thus the second assignee might achieve priority over the first assignee by filing first. This rule enables an assignee to rely on the filing system: if it checks the files before it takes an assignment and finds no other financing statement, it can, by filing immediately itself, get priority over any other assignee, even if the other assignee's assignment was prior in time.[23]

First-to-file rule of Article 9

---

[17] For one of the cases that caused this to be called the Massachusetts rule, *see* Rabinowitz v. People's Natl. Bank, 126 N.E. 289 (Mass. 1920) (since money paid by debtor was received by second assignee "as its own," first assignee could not recover it).

[18] Restatement Second §342; first Restatement §173. According to Restatement Second §326(1), the same rule applies to partial assignments. Because of the "equitable" nature of partial assignments (see the discussion of partial assignment in §11.3 *supra*), courts have sometimes treated them differently.

[19] Restatement Second §342 cmt. *e*. Giving priority to a second assignee that gets possession of a symbolic writing is justified "as an application of a broader doctrine of estoppel." Restatement Second §342 cmt. *f*.

[20] Roughly a decade before the Code was first promulgated, the United States Supreme Court had reached the startling conclusion that assignees who engaged in non-notification financing of accounts receivable in Pennsylvania, which followed the English rule, were not protected in bankruptcy. Corn Exch. Natl. Bank & Trust Co. v. Klauder, 318 U.S. 434 (1943) ("non-notification financing . . . has characteristics which make it impossible for us to conclude that it is to be distinguished from the secret liens Congress was admittedly trying to reach"). The reasoning was that, under the version of the Bankruptcy Act then in effect, the assignee's security interest in the accounts was not "perfected" because it was possible that a hypothetical second assignee (regardless of whether one actually existed) from the same assignor could have achieved priority over the first assignee by giving notice.

The question of the rights of an assignee in the likely event of the assignor's bankruptcy was of far greater practical importance than the question of the rights of an assignee in the unlikely event of the assignor's wrongful second assignment. State legislatures responded promptly and enacted statutes to protect the assignee. The Code replaces these statutes, instituting a filing system. *See* 1 G. Gilmore, Security Interests in Personal Property ch. 15 (1965).

[21] See the discussion of assignments and the Code in §11.2 *supra*.

[22] UCC 9-322(1)(a).

[23] Under the Code, the assignee may file a financing statement even before taking the assignment.

Scope of rule

Article 9 exempts from its "first-to-file" rule an assignment of accounts "which does not by itself or in conjunction with other assignments to the same assignee transfer a significant part of the assignor's outstanding accounts — assignments that no one would think of filing."[24] The commentary explains that this exception is "to save from *ex post facto* invalidation casual or isolated assignments."[25] Such an assignment, although within the scope of Article 9, is entitled to priority if it was made before a competing unfiled assignment, unless the second assignment was filed before the first was made.[26] However, an assignment of an account that is excluded from the scope of Article 9 or of a contract right other than an account is left to the conflicting common law rules on priority.[27]

Rights of creditors

Unlike the claimants discussed so far, an unsecured creditor has no interest in any specific property of the debtor. Generally, therefore, an assignee (C) is not vulnerable to claims of the assignor's (B's) creditors. However, an unsecured creditor (X) can, by an attachment, obtain an interest in specific property. If the attaching creditor obtains such an interest in a contract right before it is assigned to an assignee, the attaching creditor will prevail over the assignee, which takes subject to the attachment. But if the attaching creditor does not obtain its interest until after the assignment, the assignee generally takes free of the attachment.[28]

Pre-Code rules

Before the enactment of the Code, however, the assignee might have been precluded from taking advantage of this priority if the assignee failed to notify the obligor in time to prevent the obligor from paying the creditor's claim.[29] In some states, the notice had to reach the obligor in time to bring the assignment to the court's attention and prevent judgment in the attachment proceeding.[30] In other states, it was enough if it came at any time before the obligor had paid the creditor, even if judgment had already been entered, as long as the obligor could still assert the assignment as a defense in the proceeding.[31]

---

[24]UCC 9-309(2).

[25]UCC 9-309 cmt. 4.

[26]*See* 1 G. Gilmore, Security Interests in Personal Property §19.6 (1965); Coenen, Priorities in Accounts: The Crazy Quilt of Current Law and a Proposal for Reform, 45 Vand. L. Rev. 1061, 1102-03 (1992).

[27]See the discussion of exclusions from Article 9 in §11.2 *supra*.

[28]Greentree v. Rosenstock, 61 N.Y. 583 (1875) (attachment was "absolutely ineffectual" because assignor then had "no interest . . . in the debt or claim which had already been assigned by him"). *See* Restatement Second §341(1). An unsecured creditor is not regarded as a good faith purchaser but may be protected by estoppel. *See* Restatement Second §341 cmt. *a*. See also the discussion of the vulnerability of an equitable assignment in §11.5 *supra*.

[29]Houtz v. Daniels, 211 P. 1088 (Idaho 1922) (obligor paid sheriff before notice).

[30]Peterson v. Kingman & Co., 81 N.W. 847 (Neb. 1900) ("an order to a garnishee for the payment of money . . . is final and conclusive . . . , and the payment by a garnishee under such an order, even after notice of an assignment . . . would relieve him from any further liability").

[31]McDowell, Pyle & Co. v. Hopfield, 128 A. 742 (Md. 1925) (judgment should have been stricken out and assignee allowed to intervene where it "has not been paid, nor has any execution

Under the Code, conflicts between assignees and attaching creditors are generally resolved by reference to the filing system. A creditor becomes a "lien creditor" by attachment, and an assignee's interest, if unperfected, is subordinate to the rights of "a person that becomes a lien creditor before . . . the security interest . . . is perfected."[32] Therefore, if an assignment is one for which a financing statement must be filed in order to perfect the assignee's interest, it must be filed in order to give the assignee priority over an attaching creditor. If the assignment is governed by Article 9, but is not one for which a financing statement must be filed, the assignee's interest is automatically perfected without filing. An assignee that has priority over the assignor's attaching creditors generally has priority in the event of the assignor's bankruptcy.[33]

Code rule

From the subject of assignment we turn to that of delegation.

C. DELEGATION

§11.10. Delegability of Performance. The term *delegation* as used in this treatise refers to the act by which one owing a duty (B) manifests an intention to confer upon another person (C) the power to perform that duty.[1] If the delegating party accomplishes that intention, the delegation is said to be "effective." It is important not to confuse delegation with assignment. The term *delegate* should be used in connection with performance, while the term *assign* should be reserved for rights, though courts often fail to use these terms with precision.[2]

Meaning of *delegation*

No particular language is necessary for an effective delegation of performance. Thus, the parties may not observe the distinction between the terms *assign* and *delegate*, and language by which one purports to "assign" one's duties may suffice to effect a delegation.[3] Furthermore, it is not uncommon for a party

Language of delegation

---

been issued on it, and the garnishee . . . applied within the term to have it stricken"). *See* Restatement Second §341(2) (obligor who does not receive notification of the assignment until after he has lost his opportunity to assert the assignment as a defense . . . is discharged . . . to the extent of his satisfaction of the lien").

[32] UCC 9-317(a)(2). An assignee's interest is perfected when it has attached and when the assignee has filed, if filing is required. The assignee's interest attaches as soon as the assignor authenticates a security agreement and acquires the account and the assignee gives value. UCC 9-203.

[33] For a treatment of rights in bankruptcy, *see* J. White & R. Summers, Uniform Commercial Code ch. 32 (5th ed 2002).

§11.10 [1] See the discussion of terminology in §11.1 *supra*.

[2] For example, it has been incorrectly asserted that a right that is coupled with a duty cannot be assigned, when what is presumably meant by such loose statements is merely that the duty is a nondelegable one. Paige v. Faure, 127 N.E. 898 (N.Y. 1920) ("general rule is that rights arising out of a contract cannot be transferred if they are coupled with liabilities").

[3] Imperial Ref. Co. v. Kanotex Ref. Co., 29 F.2d 193 (8th Cir. 1928) ("transfer and assignment" held to delegate performance).

to purport to assign in general terms "the contract," and, under both Article 2 of the Code and the Restatement Second, such language ordinarily will delegate performance as well as assign rights.[4] If, however, the language or the situation indicates the contrary, as in the case of an assignment for security, an assignment of rights but no delegation of performance results.[5]

Party delegating remains bound

Even an effective delegation does not relieve the delegating party (B) of its duty; that requires either consent by the obligee (A) or performance by the delegate (C). As the Uniform Commercial Code makes clear, a delegation of performance does not relieve the delegating party of "any duty to perform" or of any "liability for breach."[6] While an obligee can rid itself of a right merely by making an effective assignment, an obligor cannot rid itself of a duty merely by making an effective delegation.[7] If obligors could do so, they could discharge their duties simply by finding obliging insolvents to whom performance could be delegated. In the situation of the owner of a business (B) that sells the business as a going concern to a buyer (C),[8] the seller seeks to assign its rights against the supplier (A) and delegate the performance due its customer (A') under long-term contracts. If the seller makes an effective assignment of its right against its supplier, the assignment extinguishes the right. However, even if the seller makes an effective delegation of the performance due its customer, the delegation does not extinguish the duty: the seller is still under the duty, despite the delegation of performance. If the delegating party (B) denies the duty, this denial is therefore a repudiation.[9] If the owner of a business dissolves it and delegates performance in this connection, the customer may be discharged because the customer has no effective recourse against the business.[10] Under the Code, the obligee (A) may treat any delegation of duties "as creating

---

[4]UCC-O 2-210(4); UCC-R 2-210(3); Restatement Second §328(1). Both the Code and the Restatement Second give the same effect to an assignment of "all my rights under the contract," a more questionable rule of interpretation.

[5]Chatham Pharmaceuticals v. Angier Chem. Co., 196 N.E.2d 852 (Mass. 1964) ("use of the words 'right, title and interest' does not necessarily show that the assignment was intended to include obligations"). If a delegation is found in such a case, an assumption of the duty by the delegate is usually implied. See the discussion of implied assumption in §11.11 *infra*.

[6]UCC-O 2-210(1); UCC-R 2-210(2)(a).

[7]First Am. Commerce Co. v. Washington Mut. Sav. Bank, 743 P.2d 1193 (Utah 1987) ("party who delegates his duties . . . is not relieved of his responsibilities").

[8]See the discussion of a sale of a business in §11.1 *supra*.

[9]Western Oil Sales Corp. v. Bliss & Wetherbee, 299 S.W. 637 (Tex. Commn. App. 1927) (when delegating party "repudiated all liability for future deliveries of oil, it committed an anticipatory breach").

[10]Arkansas Valley Smelting Co. v. Belden Mining Co., 127 U.S. 379 (1888) (where seller was to deliver ore and to be paid on basis of assay that was to be made by umpire in event of disagreement, and during time after delivery had no security for payment, "except in [buyer's] character and solvency, [seller] could not be compelled to accept the liability of any other").

reasonable grounds for insecurity" and may demand from the delegating party adequate assurance of due performance.[11]

From the perspective of the delegating party, the significance of an effective delegation is not that the delegation itself discharges the duty of the delegating party, but that the subsequent performance of that duty by the delegate will discharge the duty.[12] Thus, from the obligee's perspective, an effective delegation means that the obligee must accept performance by the delegate as performance of the duty owed by the delegating party. If the obligee were to refuse to accept performance by the delegate and insist on performance by the delegating party, the refusal would be a repudiation.[13]

Significance of delegation

Plainly, not every performance is delegable. If an obligor attempts to delegate a nondelegable performance, the purported delegation is not effective, and the obligee is entitled to insist on performance by the delegating party. The obligee's refusal to accept performance by the purported delegate is not then a repudiation. Though the purported delegation of a nondelegable performance is not in itself a repudiation,[14] if the delegating party then refuses to perform, insisting that the obligee accept performance by the purported delegate, this refusal will be a repudiation.[15]

Consequence of nondelegability

When is a performance nondelegable? Occasionally a performance is not delegable for reasons of public policy.[16] Sometimes the parties to a contract explicitly provide that a performance is not delegable.[17] But the question most commonly arises when the obligee claims that the *delectus personae*

Reasons for nondelegability

[11] UCC-O 2-210(5); UCC-R 2-210(2)(c). See the discussion of the right to assurance under the Code in §8.23 *supra*. *See* Restatement Second §251. This situation should be distinguished from that treated in the discussion of assumption by a delegate in §11.11 *infra*, in which the obligor is entitled to demand assurance from a delegate that has assumed the duty of the delegating party. An obligor that demands assurance from a delegate should not, by so doing, be taken to concede the delegability of performance.

[12] If a third person (C) offers performance to an obligee (A), but does not do so on behalf of the obligor (B), the obligor's duty is discharged only if the obligee accepts the performance in satisfaction. *See* Restatement Second §278(2).

[13] Devlin v. Mayor of New York, 63 N.Y. 8 (1875) (delegation of duty to sweep streets of New York "did not terminate the agreement or authorize its rescission or abandonment by the city").

[14] American Lithographic Co. v. Ziegler, 103 N.E. 909 (Mass. 1914) (immaterial that party to contract may have executed delegation of nondelegable duties, along with assignment of rights, where purported delegate never undertook performance and delegating party itself performed).

[15] Crane Ice Cream Co. v. Terminal Freezing & Heating Co., 128 A. 280 (Md. 1925) (when party goes out of business on transferring contract with nondelegable duty "his course is a repudiation of the obligations of the contract").

[16] Thus it has been held that performance under a public works contract is nondelegable. Delaware County Commrs. v. Diebold Safe & Lock Co., 133 U.S. 473 (1890) (it is "against public policy to permit municipal corporations, . . . in the construction of public works, to be embarrassed by subcontracts . . . to which they have never assented").

[17] UCC-O 2-210(1); UCC-R 2-210(2)(a). *See* Restatement Second §318(1). Anti-delegation clauses are not subject to the restrictions on anti-assignment clauses. See the discussion of a term prohibiting assignment in §11.4 *supra*. *See* Arnold Prods. v. Favorite Films Corp., 298 F.2d 540

("the choice of the person") was of sufficient importance to the obligee when the bargain was made that the performance should be considered nondelegable — the obligee should not be required to receive performance from anyone except the obligor.[18]

Test of delegability

Whether a performance is nondelegable for this reason is a question for the court. The test to be applied is necessarily imprecise. According to the Code and the Restatement Second, a performance is nondelegable to the extent that the obligee has a "substantial interest" in having the original promisor perform, or at least control performance.[19] In deciding whether this is the case, the court will consider all the circumstances of the delegation.

Extent to which performance is personal

One of the most significant of these circumstances is the extent to which the performance is "personal," in the sense that the recipient must rely on qualities such as the character, reputation, taste, skill, or discretion of the party that is to render it. For example, an artist who contracts to paint a portrait or a singer who contracts to sing in an opera cannot delegate performance, even though the delegate's performance might be superior to that of the delegating party.[20] Analogous circumstances have been held to preclude delegation under a wide variety of more commercial contracts,[21] including contracts in which one of the parties engages to use "best efforts"[22] or to exercise "good faith."[23] The principle is not confined to situations in which an individual will render the

---

(2d Cir. 1962) (anti-assignment clause not applicable where party "did not technically 'assign' its contract in its entirety, but merely delegated a part . . . of its duties").

[18] Poling v. Condon-Lane Boom & Lumber Co., 47 S.E. 279 (W. Va. 1904) (delegability of performance depends on whether "the *delectus personae* is material").

[19] UCC-O 2-210(1); UCC-R 2-210(2)(a); Restatement Second §318(2).

[20] Taylor v. Palmer, 31 Cal. 241 (1866) (dictum: "All painters do not paint portraits like Sir Joshua Reynolds, nor landscapes like Claude Lorraine [*sic*], nor do all writers write dramas like Shakespeare or fiction like Dickens. Rare genius and extraordinary skill are not transferable, and contracts for their employment are therefore personal, and cannot be assigned.").

[21] New England Cabinet Works v. Morris, 115 N.E. 315 (Mass. 1917) (contract "to design, manufacture and install the furniture and fixtures for a new store . . . involves personal trust and confidence [and] demands artistic knowledge, skill and training").

[22] Wetherell Bros. Co. v. United States Steel Co., 200 F.2d 761 (1st Cir. 1952) (duty of agent under exclusive sales agency contract "to use 'best endeavors' in promoting the sale of steel" in territory "presupposed a reliance upon the agent by the principal which rendered impossible the delegation of the agent's duties which was attempted").

[23] Paper Prod. Mach. Co. v. Safepack Mills, 131 N.E. 288 (Mass. 1921) (duty of patent licensors to cooperate with licensee by giving it "such advice . . . as may be necessary to enable it to use said machines and any improvements thereof to the best advantage" was not delegable).

The Uniform Commercial Code takes no position on the delegability of the seller's duty to deliver goods under an output contract if the seller sells the business, but the Code comments state that if "the contract continues, the output . . . in the hands of the new owner continue[s] to be measured by the actual good faith output . . . under the normal operation of the enterprise prior to sale." UCC 2-306 cmt. 4. Nevertheless, it is the delegate that is to exercise the good faith after delegation. For another possible analysis, see note 38 *infra*.

performance; it may preclude delegation by a corporation as well.[24] On the other hand, many kinds of performance are generally regarded as not involving enough taste, skill, or discretion to be nondelegable,[25] even if the obligee claims to prefer performance by the delegating party.[26] For example, a seller that contracts to deliver goods[27] or a builder that contracts to build a building can ordinarily delegate performance.[28]

Another significant circumstance is the degree of control that the delegating party can be expected to exercise over the delegate. A performance may be considered delegable if the delegating party is to remain in the business and supervise the performance.[29] But the same performance may be considered nondelegable if, as in the example given earlier of the sale of a business, the delegating party divests itself of the business and exercises no further control over the performance.[30] For example, while a builder can ordinarily delegate performance to subcontractors that are to work under the builder's supervision, the builder may not be able, on the sale of its business, to delegate performance to a successor that will not be under the builder's control.[31] Courts have been especially prone to find nondelegability if the delegating party is dissolving its business.[32] Occasionally, a delegation has been sustained on the ground that the

Degree of control retained

[24] New York Bank Note Co. v. Hamilton Bank Note Engraving & Printing Co., 73 N.E. 48 (N.Y. 1905) ("though there is no personal or human equation in the management of a corporation, there may be a legal equation that is of the utmost importance").

[25] Taylor v. Palmer, *supra* note 20 ("rare genius and extraordinary skill are not indispensable to the workmanlike digging down of a sand hill or the filling up of a depression to a given level, or the construction of brick sewers with manholes and covers, and contracts in such work are not personal, and may be assigned").

[26] Macke Co. v. Pizza of Gaithersburg, 270 A.2d 645 (Md. 1970) (duty of supplier to install and maintain cold drink vending machines in pizza shops was delegable, even though pizza shops may have chosen supplier "because they preferred the way it conducted its business").

[27] UCC-O 2-210(1); UCC-R 2-210(2).

[28] Taylor v. Palmer, *supra* note 20.

[29] Arnold Prods. v. Favorite Film Corp., *supra* note 17 (film distributor that was under duty to use "best efforts" to exploit films could delegate part of duties while maintaining supervisory powers).

[30] See the discussion of a sale of a business in §11.1 *supra*.

[31] New England Cabinet Works v. Morris, *supra* note 21 (duty was not delegable when delegate bought business of delegating party, though delegating party was retained as manager of factory where furniture and fixtures were being built).

[32] Arkansas Valley Smelting Co. v. Belden Mining Co., *supra* note 10; Wooster v. Crane & Co., 66 A. 1093 (N.J. Ch. 1907) (where New Jersey corporation was to publish schoolbooks and account to author for sales, its duty was not delegable to Arizona corporation, since author contracted with corporation "whose solvency and pecuniary responsibility is protected and maintained by all the safeguards found in [New Jersey] statute for that purpose, and she is entitled . . . to the benefit of the continuation of those safeguards").

An analogous problem may arise on a party's death. *See* Folquet v. Woodburn Pub. Schools, 29 P.2d 554 (Or. 1934) (party who contracted to transport children in school bus, "if he did not drive the bus himself, was to be intrusted with the duty of employing a trustworthy, competent,

delegate is under the same control as the delegating party was, as may happen if one is the corporate alter ego of the other.[33]

Restriction for benefit of obligee

This restriction on delegability rests on a concern for the justifiable expectations of the obligee, just as the analogous restriction on assignability rests on a concern for the justifiable expectations of the obligor,[34] at the time the contract was made. Because the restriction is to protect the obligee, the obligee can dispense with it. Even if the obligee has a substantial interest in having the delegating party perform or control performance, the delegation will be effective if the obligee agreed in the original contract that the duty would be delegable[35] or later consented to the delegation by accepting performance or otherwise.[36]

Performance that is condition

Disputes over the delegability of performance occasionally arise when, though the delegating party is under no duty to render the performance, that party's performance is a condition of the obligee's duty.[37] Courts apply the same test to determine the delegability of a performance required as a condition as they do to determine the delegability of performance of a duty. As the Restatement Second puts it, performance by a particular person is required "only to the extent that the obligor has a substantial interest in having that person perform or control the acts required."[38] If there is no substantial interest, the person whose performance is required as a condition can delegate performance to another person, and performance by the latter will satisfy the requirement.

---

and careful driver and to have supervision over him," so that when he died his duty could not be performed by his son as administrator).

[33] Fisher v. Berg, 290 P. 984 (Wash. 1930) (partnership that was under duty to construct wood-splitting machine could delegate duty to corporation organized by partners since, on behalf of corporation, they "superintended the construction of the machine"). *But cf.* New England Cabinet Works v. Morris, *supra* note 21.

[34] See the discussion of a restriction as for the benefit of the obligor in §11.4 *supra*.

[35] Baum v. Rock, 108 P.2d 230 (Colo. 1940) (contract provided that it was binding on parties' "successors and assigns").

[36] Bewley v. Miller, 341 A.2d 428 (D.C. 1975) (student who takes dance lessons from transferee after dance studio purports to transfer contract cannot contest effectiveness of delegation). Absent reliance, however, it would seem that the obligee could withdraw consent. As to the possibility that accepting performance may also amount to a novation, see the discussion of a proposal of a novation inferred from a repudiation in §11.11 *infra*.

[37] Of course, one party's performance of a duty is often a constructive condition of a duty of the other party. See the discussion of the preference for dependent promises in §8.9 *supra*.

[38] Restatement Second §319. Here, just as when performance of a duty is involved, delegability is subject to contrary agreement by the parties and to considerations of public policy. See the discussion of reasons for nondelegability *supra*.

It may be helpful to view a seller's transfer of an output contract or a buyer's transfer of a requirements contract as involving a delegation of the performance of a condition — the condition of the seller's having output or the buyer's having requirements. In the case of the output contract, for example, the seller's performance (delivery of goods) would ordinarily by itself be delegable. It is the condition on which quantity depends that causes the problem. See note 23 *supra* and the discussion of a material change in the obligor's duty in §11.4 *supra*.

We next turn to the situation in which a delegate has come under a duty to perform because of the delegate's assumption of that duty.

§11.11. Assumption and Novation. We have seen that an effective del- **Liability of** egation empowers the delegate (C) to tender on behalf of the delegating party **delegate** (B) the performance due the obligee (A) but leaves the delegating party liable to the obligee in the event of the delegate's nonperformance.[1] We now consider whether the delegate is also liable in the event of its nonperformance.

The mere delegation of a performance imposes no duty on the delegate **Delegation** to perform. If the delegate performs the duty, the duty is discharged. If the **imposes no** delegate does not perform the duty, the duty is not discharged, but any claim **liability** of the obligee for breach is against the delegating party and not against the delegate.[2] The delegate is under no duty to perform unless it has undertaken to do so.

Often, as part of the transaction delegating performance, the delegate **Assumption by** expressly promises the delegating party to perform that party's duties. The **delegate** delegate is then said to have *assumed* the duties of the delegating party. It follows from the delegate's assumption that the delegate is under a duty to the delegating party,[3] and it usually follows that the delegate is also under a duty to the obligee, as an intended beneficiary of the assumption agreement.[4] But though the delegate's assumption makes the delegate liable to the obligee, it does not discharge the duty to the obligee of the delegating party; and if the delegating party repudiates its duty, it is liable to the obligee.[5] Thus, as a result of the assumption, the delegate and the delegating party are now both under a duty to the obligee to render the same performance. But the obligee is entitled to only one performance, and, as between the delegate and the delegating party, it is the delegate that should render the performance because the delegate promised to do so by its assumption. The relationship is thus one of suretyship, in which the delegate is the principal and the delegating party

---

§11.11 [1]See the discussion of how a party delegating remains bound in §11.10 *supra*.

[2]Rochester Lantern Co. v. Stiles & Parker Press Co., 31 N.E. 1018 (N.Y. 1892) ("obligations of the contract still rested upon [delegating party], and resort could still be made to him for the payment [if delegate] did not pay").

[3]If the delegate fails to perform and the delegating party performs or is required to pay damages, the delegating party can recover from the delegate. Imperial Ref. Co. v. Kanotex Ref. Co., 29 F.2d 193 (8th Cir. 1928) (implied assumption: delegating party "having been forced to respond in damages for the breach of the contract, it could recover from [the delegate] the amount so paid"). *But cf.* UCC 9-402.

[4]Rose v. Vulcan Materials Co., 194 S.E.2d 521 (N.C. 1973) (implied assumption: obligee may sue delegate "as a third party beneficiary of his promise of performance"). The rights of the obligee as an intended beneficiary are determined by the scope of the assumption agreement and are subject to defenses of the delegate against the delegating party under that agreement. See the discussion of how a beneficiary is subject to defenses in §10.9 *supra*.

[5]Bashir v. Moayedi, 627 A.2d 997 (D.C. 1993) ("delegant cannot free herself from liability by delegating her duties of performance to another," even where the delegate assumes).

is the surety,[6] and all of the consequences of a suretyship relationship follow.[7] Furthermore, since the delegate is now bound to perform, the obligee should, in a proper case, be entitled to demand assurance of due performance from the delegate as well as from the delegating party.[8] The Code allows a party to a contract for the sale of goods to do this if the other party transfers the entire contract.[9]

Example of sale of business

As an illustration, recall the owner (B) that transfers a business as a going concern by selling the assets to a buyer (C), delegating to the buyer the performance due a customer (A′) under a long-term contract.[10] Because the mere delegation imposes no duty on the buyer to render the delegated performance,[11] the contract for the sale of assets commonly imposes such a duty on the buyer. This assumption by the buyer of the seller's duty to supply the customer makes the buyer liable to the customer as an intended beneficiary. In the event of nonperformance, the customer now has recourse against both the buyer, which, as an assuming delegate, has become the principal obligor, and the seller, which, as the delegating party, remains a surety.

Example of transfer of mortgaged property

Assumption agreements are commonplace when mortgaged land is sold. When the vendor delegates the payment of the mortgage to the purchaser, the vendor usually insists that the purchaser assume the mortgage, rather than merely take subject to it. The effect of the purchaser's assumption of the vendor's duty to pay the mortgage is to make the purchaser — an assuming grantee of the land — liable to the mortgagee as an intended beneficiary.[12] In the event of nonpayment, the mortgagee now has recourse against both the purchaser, which, as an assuming delegate, has become the principal obligor, and the vendor, which, as the delegating party, remains a surety.

Implied assumption

Even if a delegate does not promise in so many words to perform the duty of the delegating party, a court may infer such a promise from the delegate's

---

[6] Imperial Ref. Co. v. Kanotex Ref. Co., *supra* note 3 (as between delegating party and delegate, "a primary duty rested upon the latter company to perform the contract, and the [delegating party] stood toward the [delegate] in the nature of a surety for the performance of the contract").

[7] Thus, if the obligee extends the time for performance by the delegate, the delegating party may be discharged as surety. However, the promise of assumption is not within the suretyship provision of the statute of frauds.

[8] On the right to demand assurance generally, see the discussion of the right to an assurance under the Code in §8.23 *supra*. On the obligee's right to demand assurance from the delegating party, see the discussion of how a party delegating remains bound in §11.10 *supra*.

[9] UCC-O 2-210(5); UCC-R 2-210(2)(c). See the discussion of the right to assurance under the Code in §8.23 *supra*.

[10] See the discussion of the sale of a business in §11.1 *supra*.

[11] There are several exceptions if the assets of a corporation are transferred to another corporation. Welco Indus. v. Applied Companies, 617 N.E.2d 1129 (Ohio 1993) (listing four exceptions to general rule "that the purchaser of a corporation's assets is not liable for the debts and obligations of the seller corporation").

[12] See the discussion of the mortgage assumption cases in §10.2 *supra*.

conduct.[13] Thus, if a party transfers the entire contract, assigning rights as well as delegating performance,[14] an assumption of those duties by the transferee will be inferred from the acceptance of the transfer,[15] unless the language or the situation indicates the contrary.[16] Both Restatements declare this to be the law,[17] and the Uniform Commercial Code incorporates such a rule for contracts for the sale of goods.[18] However, a notorious New York case, decided well over half a century ago, refused to apply the rule of the first Restatement to a transfer by a purchaser under a contract for the sale of land,[19] and in deference to this case the Restatement Second declines to decide whether its rule covers such a case.[20]

Although neither an effective delegation by a delegating party nor an assumption by a delegate results in the discharge of the duty of the delegating party, a discharge may result if the obligee consents to it.[21] The transaction usually takes the form of a novation, in which the promise of the delegate (C) to perform the duty of the delegating party (B) is the consideration for the discharge of that duty by the obligee (A).[22] There may be a novation even though the duty is

Discharge by novation of delegating party's duty

---

[13] Massey-Ferguson Credit Corp. v. Brown, 567 P.2d 440 (Mont. 1977) ("close relation and participation between the assignor and assignee requires a departure from the general rule of law" and therefore assignee "impliedly assumed the contractual obligation of the assignor").

[14] Since there is no implied delegation of performance in the case of an assignment as security only (see the discussion of language of delegation in §11.10 *supra*), there is no assumption of duties in such a case. UCC 9-402.

[15] Imperial Ref. Co. v. Kanotex Ref. Co., *supra* note 3 (delegate "by accepting the assignment accepted the delegation of the duties [and] accepted the burdens with the benefits").

[16] For an unusual example of the use of circumstances to justify a departure from the general rule, *see* Chatham Pharmaceuticals v. Angier Chem. Co., 196 N.E.2d 852 (Mass. 1964).

[17] Restatement §164 ("Acceptance by the assignee . . . is interpreted . . . as a promise to the assignor to assume the performance of the assignor's duties."); Restatement Second §328(2) ("acceptance by an assignee . . . operates as a promise to the assignor to perform the assignor's unperformed duties").

[18] UCC-O 2-210(4); UCC-R 2-210(2)(b).

[19] Langel v. Betz, 164 N.E. 890 (N.Y. 1928) (rejecting rule stated in first Restatement as "a complete reversal of our present rule of interpretation" and adhering to rule that "no promise of the assignee to assume the assignor's duties is to be inferred from the acceptance of an assignment of a bilateral contract").

[20] Restatement Second §328, *Caveat* ("The Institute expresses no opinion as to whether the rule . . . applies to an assignment by a purchaser of his rights under a contract for the sale of land."). By way of rationalization, the commentary explains that when such a purchaser "assigns his rights, the assignment does not amount to an assumption . . . unless the contract of assignment so provides either expressly or by implication." *Id.* cmt. c.

[21] The consent of the obligee may be given before the delegation, as happens when it is part of the obligee's contract with the delegating party. J.R. Simplot Co. v. Chambers, 350 P.2d 211 (Idaho 1960) (parties agreed that their agreement for sale of mining claims could be assigned by buyer to any corporation controlled by buyer, and, on assumption by corporation and notice to sellers, buyer would be released).

[22] Alexander v. Angel, 236 P.2d 561 (Cal. 1951) (novation on assumption of mortgage). See the discussion of novation in §4.24 *supra*.

nondelegable.[23] However, more is required for a novation than the mere consent of the obligee to performance by the delegate. Such consent may suffice to preclude the obligee from claiming that performance is not delegable,[24] but it is not enough to discharge the duty of the delegating party.[25] For that, assent by the obligee to release the delegating party, in exchange for the new liability of the delegate, is required. Thus, in the example of the sale of a business, the mere consent of the customer (A′) to performance by the buyer of the business (C), instead of by the seller (B), will not amount to a novation that will discharge the duty of the seller to the customer; for that the customer must assent to the substitution of the buyer's duty in place of the seller's, thereby discharging the seller's duty.

Proposal of novation inferred from repudiation

The proposal of a novation need not be express.[26] Thus, according to the Restatement Second, if the delegate offers to perform after the delegating party has repudiated its liability as surety, a court will infer a proposal of novation. If the obligee accepts performance from the delegate without reserving its rights against the delegating party, the duty of the delegating party is discharged, and a similar duty of the delegate is substituted for it.[27]

---

[23] For a case in which an entirely new contract was made, *see* American Colortype Co. v. Continental Colortype Co., 188 U.S. 104 (1903) (Holmes, J.: "having the old contract [of employment] before them, the parties came together under a new agreement, which was determined by reference to the terms of that contract").

[24] See the discussion of restriction as for the benefit of the obligee in §11.10 *supra*.

[25] Vetter v. Security Continental Ins. Co., 567 N.W.2d 516 (Minn. 1997) (proof of novation under Illinois or Minnesota law requires "strong evidence of the parties' intention to release one obligor and substitute another").

[26] Barton v. Perryman, 577 S.W.2d 596 (Ark. 1979) ("intention need not be expressly declared, but may be found upon examining the surrounding circumstances").

[27] Restatement Second §329(2). An insistence by the delegating party that the obligee accept performance of a nondelegable duty by a purported delegate is a repudiation by the delegating party. However, it would make no sense to apply the Restatement Second rule to that situation, for there is no proposal of novation implicit in the delegate's offer of performance.

PART V
ENFORCEMENT OF PROMISES

Chapter 12

Remedies

A.　CONTRACT REMEDIES IN GENERAL

§12.1.　Purposes of Remedies.　Why do people keep their promises?[1] Sometimes the reason has little to do with the legal remedies available to the promisee of a broken promise. One may simply regard keeping promises as the "right" thing to do. Or one may fear that if one breaks one's promise the promisee will not keep the return promise, that the promisee and others will not deal with one in the future, or that one's general reputation will suffer.

　　It might be supposed that the law would add to these extra-legal compulsions a system of sanctions of its own, designed to compel promisors to keep their

Extra-legal compulsion

Purpose not compulsion

---

§12.1　[1] *See* E. Farnsworth, *Changing Your Mind* chs. 1 & 2 (1998).

promises. Somewhat surprisingly, our system of contract remedies rejects, for the most part, compulsion of the promisor as a goal. It does not impose criminal penalties on one who refuses to perform one's promise,[2] nor does it generally require one to pay punitive damages.[3] Our system of contract remedies is not directed at *compulsion* of *promisors* to *prevent* breach; it is aimed, instead, at *relief* to *promisees* to *redress* breach. Its preoccupation is not with the question: how can promisors be made to keep their promises? Its concern is with a different question: how can people be encouraged to deal with those who make promises? The result may sometimes be to compel a promisor to keep a promise, but this is only the incidental effect of a system designed to serve other ends. Perhaps it is more consistent with free enterprise to promote the use of contract by encouraging promisees to rely on the promises of others instead of by compelling promisors to perform their promises. In any event, along with the celebrated freedom to make contracts goes a considerable freedom to break them as well.[4]

Expectation interest

How do courts encourage promisees to rely on promises? Ordinarily they do so by protecting the expectation that the injured party had when making the contract by attempting to put that party in as good a position as it would have been in had the contract been performed, that is, had there been no breach. The interest measured in this way is called the *expectation interest* and is said to give the injured party the "benefit of the bargain."[5] The expectation interest is based not on the injured party's hopes at the time of making the contract, but on the actual value that the contract would have had to the injured party had it been performed. The expectation of the foolishly optimistic landowner who contracted to have an oil well dug is not the gusher that the landowner hoped for but the dry well that actually would have resulted. Since the circumstances

---

[2]Under a California statute, a contractor who "willfully" fails to make improvements for which he has been paid and "wrongfully diverts the funds" to another use is guilty of a "public offense" punishable by imprisonment and a fine. Cal. Penal Code §484b. The spirit of the offense, however, is that of obtaining money by fraud and not mere nonperformance. People v. Howard, 451 P.2d 401 (Cal. 1969).

[3]See §12.8 *infra*.

[4]There are, of course, other means than contract to plan for the future. An enterprise that does not wish to be subjected to the risks inherent in its supplier's freedom to break its contracts can sometimes assure itself of a source of supply without resorting to contract by acquiring its supplier or by having another enterprise in the same conglomerate acquire it.

[5]For a statement of the expectation interest, *see* UCC 1-305(a) ("remedies provided . . . must be liberally administered to the end that the aggrieved party may be put in as good a position as if the other party had fully performed"). For another statement, *see* Restatement Second §344. *Cf.* Contempo Design v. Chicago & Northeast Ill. Dist. Council, 226 F.3d 535 (7th Cir. 2000) (rule that "injured party is to be placed in as good a position as he would have been had the contract been performed . . . applies in the labor context"). The seminal article on the expectation, reliance, and restitution interests is Fuller & Perdue, The Reliance Interest in Contract Damages (pts. 1, 2), 46 Yale L.J. 52, 373 (1936, 1937).

at the time for performance, rather than those at the time of the making of the contract, are determinative, changes in the market adverse to the promisee that occur between the time of making and the time for performance diminish the promisee's expectation interest.

Measurement of damages by the expectation interest sometimes poses difficult problems of causation.[6] There is, of course, a fundamental requirement, similar to that imposed in tort cases, that the breach of contract be the cause in fact of the loss. If, therefore, one treats a breach as total and terminates the contract, one must show that had there been no breach one could have performed or tendered performance as required under the contract.[8] Breach may not be precluded, however, by the presence of other contributing causes[9] — multiple[10] or intervening.[11] Although the injured party's own failure to avoid loss may bar recovery for that loss, this is not thought of as a consequence of a requirement of causation but of a limitation under a "mitigation" rule.[12] In addition the expectation measure necessitates a prediction of what the injured party's situation would have been had the contract been performed.[13] In practice, difficult problems of causation that might otherwise

Causation and expectation

---

[6]See the discussion of damages for total breach in §8.15 *supra*. For the problems posed by conditions, see the discussions of a causal connection in §8.6 *supra* and of impetus in §12.15 *infra*.

[7]Wright v. St. Mary's Med. Ctr., 59 F. Supp. 2d 794 (S.D. Ind. 1999) (causation-in-fact "is generally a prerequisite to recovery in both contract . . . and tort"). An even more fundamental requirement, of course, is that the breach must have caused loss. For a notorious authority, *see* City of New Orleans v. Firemen's Charitable Assn., 9 So. 486 (La. 1891) (city could not recover any of money paid to association that failed to maintain required number of firemen, saving substantial expense, where it was not alleged that "fires were not extinguished as required" or that there was "any damage suffered by the city in consequence").

[8]See the discussion of termination after some time in §8.18 *supra*. See also the discussion of loss avoided in §12.9 *infra*.

[9]Although the same problems of multiple causes and of intervening causes that enliven the law of torts also arise in connection with contract damages, they are relatively less important than in the law of torts. On causation in tort, see the discussion of two rules in §12.14 *infra*.

[10]Krauss v. Greenbarg, 137 F.2d 569 (3d Cir. 1943) (if "number of factors are operating one may so predominate in bringing about the harm as to make the effect produced by others so negligible that they cannot be considered substantial factors and hence legal causes of the harm produced").

[11]Newsome v. Western Union Tel. Co., 69 S.E. 10 (N.C. 1910) (telegraph company not liable for raft hand's refusal to work when whisky did not arrive because company had garbled telegram ordering it).

[12]See the discussion of no "duty" to mitigate in §12.12 *infra*.

[13]McDonald v. John P. Scripps Newspaper, 257 Cal. Rptr. 473 (Ct. App. 1989) (contestant in spelling bee "lost because he misspelled a word, and it is irrelevant that he was defeated by a contestant who 'had no right to advance in the contest'"). See the discussion of relaxation of the rule §12.15 *infra*.

As to whether a buyer's damages for defective goods are limited if no alternative product was available, *see* Chatlos Sys. v. National Cash Register Corp., 670 F.2d 1304 (3d Cir. 1982) (no error in basing damages on difference between value of computer system as delivered and value of computer system that would have conformed to warranties, in spite of claim that it was not

arise from attempting such a prediction are often obviated by the requirements that loss be foreseeable and proved with reasonable certainty.[14] Furthermore, the injured party is not entitled to more than the contract terms
would have given,[15] and thus if the party in breach had the power to terminate on a stated period of notice, the injured party's damages are limited to that
period.[16] The rationale is that the breach was the termination and that it caused
the loss of profits that would have been made if proper notice of termination
had been given at the time of the breach and performance had continued for
the notice period provided in the contract.[17]

Reliance interest   At times, a court will enforce a promise by protecting the promisee's reliance
instead of the promisee's expectation.[18] The injured party may, for example,
have changed position in reliance on the contract by incurring expenses in
preparation or in performance. In that case, the court may attempt to put the
injured party back in the position in which that party would have been had the
contract not been made. The interest measured in this way is called the *reliance
interest*. It is useful to distinguish two kinds of reliance. The first, reliance that
consists of preparation for and performance under the contract in question,
has been called "essential" reliance.[19] It includes whatever is, in a sense, the
"price" that a party must pay for what it is to receive under the contract. The

---

possible to buy system that would have conformed for less than four times the price and that
this was like "substituting a Rolls Royce for a Ford"). *But see* Overstreet v. Norden Labs., 669
F.2d 1286 (6th Cir. 1982) (to recover consequential damages for breach of warranty as to horse
vaccine, buyer must establish that equivalently effective alternative product was available, for to
hold otherwise would be like allowing balding man to recover for breach of warranty that product
would prevent loss of hair). *See* E. Farnsworth, Changing Your Mind ch. 6 at 60 (1998).

[14] Stokes v. Roberts, 711 S.W.2d 757 (Ark. 1986) (sellers of business who used proceeds to
pay off home mortgage but were forced to again mortgage home when buyer broke contract by
stopping payment on check could not recover interest on new loan as incidental damages "resulting
from the breach" under UCC 2-710 because not "result of performance made in *reliance*" on
contract). See §§12.14, 12.15 *infra*.

[15] Central Bering Sea Fishermen's Assn. v. Anderson, 54 P.3d 271 (Alaska 2002) (rejecting
employee's claim that while contract was for only one year she "reasonably expected to fill a
long-term need").

[16] United Indus. Syndicate v. Western Auto Supply Co., 686 F.2d 1312 (8th Cir. 1982) (supplier
would be entitled "to recover lost profits . . . it reasonably would have made with [retailer] during
the six-month notice period, as well as certain reliance damages (out-of-pocket costs incurred in
expectation of the relationship continuing for at least six months)").

[17] This is a more generous measure of damages than that generally allowed when courts have
imposed a requirement that a franchisee or distributor be given reasonable notice in order to
make alternative arrangements. In those cases damages are commonly limited to the lost profits
on the delayed alternative arrangement on the rationale that the breach was not the termination
but rather the failure to give the required notice in advance of termination. See the discussion of
the franchise cases in §7.17 *supra*.

[18] *See* Leitzel, Reliance and Contract Breach, 52 Law & Contemp. Probs. 87 (1989).

[19] For the distinction between "essential" and "incidental" reliance, *see* Fuller & Perdue, The
Reliance Interest in Contract Damages (pt. 1), 46 Yale L.J. 52, 78 (1936).

second, reliance that consists of preparations for collateral transactions that a party plans to carry out when the contract in question is performed, has been called "incidental" reliance.

Consider a contract to build a store. If the owner repudiates after the builder has spent money on architect's drawings, labor, and materials, these expenditures are essential reliance. If the builder repudiates after the owner has spent money in buying a stock of goods and hiring employees, these expenditures are incidental reliance. In either case the reliance interest is ordinarily smaller than the expectation interest because, while the expectation interest takes account of the injured party's lost profit as well as reliance, the reliance interest includes nothing for lost profit.[20] In this connection it is important to understand that the law has not generally recognized yet another kind of reliance — reliance that consists in forgoing opportunities to make other contracts. In the example given, the builder may have passed up another job, and the owner may have passed up the possibility of hiring another builder in reliance on their contract. But the difficulties of proving this are obvious, and courts have not been receptive to claims based on this kind of reliance.[21] Situations in which damages have been measured by the reliance interest have characteristically been those in which damages measured by the full expectation are for some reason regarded as inappropriate and the court turns to the reliance interest as a lesser included component that will give a measure of relief.

Examples of reliance

Measuring damages by the reliance interest is often supposed to pose fewer problems of causation than measuring damages by the expectation interest. This may be true if reliance damages are limited to out-of-pocket loss. It is not true, however, if reliance damages are expanded to cover lost opportunities, for this necessitates another prediction, one of what opportunities, if any, the injured party would have seized had the contract in dispute not been made.

Causation and reliance

Sometimes a court will recognize a third interest in cases of breach of contract by granting restitution to the injured party. However, the object of restitution is not the enforcement of a promise, but an entirely distinct goal — the prevention of unjust enrichment. The focus is on the party in breach rather than on the injured party, and the attempt is to put the party in breach back in the position in which that party would have been had the contract not been made. The party in breach is required to disgorge what that party has received in money or services by, for example, returning the benefit to the injured party that conferred it. The interest of the injured party that is measured in this way is

Restitution interest

---

[20] This is not, however, true for the case of a losing contract, one under which the injured party would have sustained a loss instead of making a profit. See §§12.10, 12.12 *infra*.

[21] For an exception, *see* Dialist v. Pulford, 399 A.2d 1374 (Md. App. 1979) ("giving up one's livelihood in reliance on, in preparation for, and performance of, a contractual obligation can be as real a detriment as out of pocket expenditures"). That courts have not been receptive to such claims under §90, see footnote to discussion of Restatement Second §87(2) in §3.25 *supra*. *See also* §12.16 *infra*.

called the _restitution interest_. It is ordinarily smaller than either the expectation interest or the reliance interest. Although recovery measured by either of those interests takes account of cost incurred in conferring a benefit on the party in breach, the restitution interest includes neither the injured party's lost profit nor the part of that party's expenditures in reliance that conferred no benefit on the party in breach.[22]

Illustration of three interests

For a simple illustration of the three interests — expectation, reliance, and restitution — consider a contract by a builder to build a building on an owner's land for $100,000. If it would have cost the builder $90,000 to build the building, and the owner repudiates the contract before the builder has done anything in reliance on it, the builder's only loss is the $10,000 profit that the builder would have made. This is the builder's expectation interest, since this is the amount it will take to put the builder in as good a position as if the contract had been performed. Since the builder has done nothing in reliance and no benefit has been conferred on the owner, the builder's reliance and restitution interests are both zero.[23] If, however, the owner does not repudiate until the builder has spent $60,000 of the $90,000 it would have cost to build it, the builder's expectation interest is now $70,000, since this is the amount it will take to put the builder in as good a position as if the contract had been performed.[24] The builder's reliance interest is now $60,000, the amount spent on past performance. And if the benefit to the owner of the partly finished building is, say, $40,000, the builder's restitution interest is now $40,000.

What types of remedies are available to protect these interests?

Specific or substitutional

§12.2. Types of Remedies. The judicial remedies available for breach of contract can be characterized as "specific" or "substitutional."[1] Relief is said to be specific when it is intended to give the injured party the very performance that was promised, as when the court orders a defaulting seller of goods to

---

[22] For an exceptional case, in which the benefit to the defendant exceeded the loss to the claimaint, _see_ Olwell v. Nye & Nissen Co., 173 P.2d 652 (Wash. 1947) (plaintiff "waived" conversion and claimed restitution where defendant benefited from appropriation of plaintiff's machine, even though it had been placed in storage and was not damaged by defendant's use). It has been pointed out that the restitution interest has "two elements: (1) reliance by the promisee, (2) a resultant gain to the promisor . . . . In some cases a defaulting promisor may after his breach be left with an unjust gain which was not taken from the promisee (a third party furnished the consideration), or which was not the result of reliance by the promisee (the promisor violated a promise not to appropriate the promisee's goods)." Fuller & Perdue, The Reliance Interest in Contract Damages (pt. 1), 46 Yale L.J. 52, 54 (1936).

[23] The builder may have relied on the contract by forgoing opportunities to make other contracts but, as noted earlier, courts generally have not recognized this kind of reliance.

[24] This assumes that no part of the price has been paid to the builder and that the builder cannot salvage any part of what was acquired with the $60,000. For more detailed discussion, see §12.10 _infra_.

§12.2   [1] For a discussion of the array of remedies of varying severity available for breach of contract, _see_ E. Farnsworth, Changing Your Mind ch. 11 (1998).

deliver them to the buyer. Relief is said to be <u>substitutional</u> when it is intended to give the promisee something in substitution for the promised performance, as when the court awards a buyer of goods money damages instead of the goods.

Remedies legal or equitable

Judicial remedies for breach of contract can also be characterized as either "<u>legal</u>" or "<u>equitable</u>," depending on whether, before the merger of law and equity, they were available in the common law courts or in courts of equity. The principal legal remedy to enforce a promise is a judgment awarding a sum of money. This is usually substitutional relief, as when the sum is damages to compensate the injured party for breach; but it may also be specific, as when the sum is an amount due under the contract. The principal equitable remedy to enforce a contract is an order requiring specific performance of the contract or enjoining its nonperformance. This is specific relief.

Restitutionary remedies

Similar distinctions can be drawn among remedies designed to prevent unjust enrichment. Restitution may be accomplished by a legal remedy, a judgment awarding a sum of money. This is usually <u>substitutional</u>, as when the sum is an amount considered equal to the value of the benefit conferred on the party in breach. But it may also be <u>specific</u>, as when the sum is an amount that the injured party paid to the party in breach and that constitutes the very benefit conferred. Restitution may also be accomplished by an <u>equitable</u> remedy, an order requiring the return of property.[2] This is <u>specific relief</u>.

Other remedies

Other remedies in contract cases include replevin of a chattel, cancellation or reformation of a writing, and issuance of a declaratory judgment.[3] Arbitration, a nonjudicial remedy, may also be available.[4] Moreover, in some circumstances a party to a contract is empowered to protect itself or to obtain satisfaction by methods not involving recourse to a court, such as retaking goods or foreclosing on security.

What is the economic basis of this system of contract remedies?

§12.3. Economic Aspects. Economic theory is a useful adjunct to legal analysis in the field of contract remedies. The important role that contracts play in the economy has inspired much economic analysis, which tends, to a surprising extent, to confirm the choices that common law judges made without the benefit of such insights.[1]

Importance of economic theory

According to traditional economic theory, the mechanism of bargained-for exchange plays a vital role in the voluntary reallocation of goods, labor, and other resources in a socially desirable manner. The basic notion is that an economy will operate "efficiently" only to the extent that available goods and resources are

Role of exchange

---

[2]Other equitable restitutionary remedies include the constructive trust, the equitable lien, and subrogation. See §2.20 *supra*.

[3]For a brief discussion of declaratory judgments, *see* C. Wright & H. Kay, Law of Federal Courts §100 (6th ed. 2002).

[4]*See generally* T. Oehmke, Commercial Arbitration (3d ed. looseleaf).

§12.3 [1]The most frequently cited work is R. Posner, Economic Analysis of Law ch. 4 (6th ed. 2003).

utilized in their most productive manner. Ideally, each good must be consumed by the person who values it most highly, and each factor of production must be employed in the way that produces the most valued output. However, actual allocations of wealth rarely meet this test of efficiency, since assets are often owned by persons who place lower values on them than do others. Through voluntary agreements, in which individuals exchange assets that they own for others that they value more, society progresses toward the goal of economic efficiency. A bargained-for exchange from which both parties benefit is socially desirable in the sense that it results in a gain in efficiency by moving the assets that are exchanged to higher valued uses.

Contract unprofitable for one

Economic theory presupposes rational parties that strive to maximize their own welfare. Such parties will not freely enter into agreements that are detrimental to their own interests. Absent some impediment, such as mistake, misrepresentation, or duress, each party will place a value on the other's performance that is greater than the anticipated cost of its own performance. At the time the agreement is made, each party has reason to suppose that it will be profitable for that party. A party may, however, err in calculating the net benefit to be anticipated from performance of the agreement, or circumstances may change so as to disappoint that party's initial hopes. A contract that the party once thought would be profitable may turn out to be unprofitable. If it is still profitable for the other party, should the reluctant party be compelled to perform?

Problem of gain and loss

If nonperformance of the agreement would result in a gain by the reluctant party at the expense of a loss by the other party, the result of nonperformance is economically efficient only if the value of the gain to the reluctant party is greater than the value of the loss to the other party. However, since individuals differ in their value judgments, the gain and the loss cannot be simply compared in absolute terms. One of the principles that has been developed to overcome this difficulty states that a redistribution of wealth is desirable if the party that benefits values its gains more than the loser values its losses.[2] This principle can be applied to the redistribution of wealth that follows from a breach of contract and to the payment of damages for that breach. The party in breach may gain enough from the breach to have a net benefit, even though that party compensates the injured party for resulting loss, calculated according to the subjective preferences of the injured party. If this is so, nonperformance and the consequent reallocation of resources is socially desirable, and economic theory not only sanctions but encourages breach. The breach is often called an "efficient breach."[3] To prevent such a breach

[2]This is known as the Kaldor or Kaldor-Hicks criterion, initially stated in Kaldor, Welfare Propositions of Economics and Interpersonal Comparisons of Utility, 49 Econ. J. 549 (1939), and in Hicks, The Foundations of Welfare Economics, 49 Econ. J. 696 (1939).

[3]For judicial endorsement of the notion of efficient breach by one of its leading advocates, *see* Patton v. Mid-Continent Sys., 841 F.2d 742 (7th Cir. 1988) (Posner, J.: "Even if the breach is

by compelling performance would result in an undesirable wealth distribution, since the party in breach would lose more than the injured party would gain.

This notion accords remarkably with the traditional assumptions of the law of contract remedies.[4] The principal interest protected by that law is the expectation interest, measured by the amount of money required to put the injured party in as good a position as that party would have been in had the contract been performed.[5] This amount is the counterpart of the compensation that economic analysis suggests. The effect is to give the reluctant party an incentive to break the contract if, but only if, that party gains enough from the breach that it can compensate the injured party for its losses yet still retain some of the benefits from the breach. Since the goal is compensation and not compulsion, the promisor who could have performed, but chose not to for financial reasons, should not be dealt with harshly. Punitive damages should not be awarded for breach of contract because they will encourage performance when breach would be socially more desirable. "Willful" breaches should not be distinguished from other breaches. And specific performance should generally not be required, at least where compensation in damages is an adequate substitute for the injured party. All of these conclusions mirror traditional contract doctrine.[6]

This economic analysis is not without shortcomings.[7] First, its focus on the relative pecuniary benefits from breach leaves no place for notions of the sanctity of contract and the moral obligation to honor one's promises.[8] Second, analysis in economic terms assumes an ability to measure value with a certainty

Accords with law's assumptions

Shortcomings of economic analysis

---

deliberate, it is not necessarily blameworthy. The promisor may simply have discovered that his performance is worth more to someone else. If so, efficiency is promoted by allowing him to break his promise, provided he makes good the promisee's actual losses."). As to the impact of delivery of goods on the possibility of an efficient breach by the seller, *see* E. Farnsworth, Changing Your Mind ch. 12 (1998).

[4] E.I. DuPont de Nemours & Co. v. Pressman, 679 A.2d 436 (Del. 1996) (quoting this section of this treatise).

[5] See §12.1 *supra*.

[6] A particularly thorny question arises when a buyer for resale breaks a contract with the seller because the buyer's purchaser has broken its contract with the buyer. Allowing the seller an action against the purchaser for tortious interference with the seller's contract with the buyer would have a chilling effect on the purchaser's power to commit an efficient breach. *See* R.E. Davis Chem. Co. v. Diasonics, 826 F.2d 678 (1987) (denying recovery because claim "requires more than the knowledge that one's conduct is substantially certain to result in one party breaking its contract with another").

[7] On the limitations of economic analysis, *see* Macneil, Economic Analysis of Contractual Relations: Its Shortfalls and the Need for a "Rich Classificatory Apparatus," 75 Nw. U. L. Rev. 1018 (1981).

[8] See C. Fried, Contract as Promise 36 (1981) (conception of contract rooted in bargain "challenges my thesis that the basis of contract is promise by locating that basis now in a distinct collective policy, the furtherance of economic exchange").

that is often not possible in the judicial process. Third, the economic analysis suggested here may be affected by "transaction costs," such as the cost of negotiation and the costs of search.[9]

Impact of transaction costs

The impact of transaction costs has attracted considerable attention. Suppose, for example, that a seller, under contract to deliver specific goods to a buyer, is offered a better price for the goods from another buyer, which values the goods more highly than the first buyer and therefore should end up with the goods if efficiency is to be served. Under the notion of "efficient breach," it is desirable that the seller break the contract and sell the goods to the second buyer, using part of the difference in price to pay damages to the first buyer and keeping whatever is left of the difference. Only in this way, the argument runs, will the goods end up in the hands of the second buyer, which values them more highly than does the first buyer. But if transaction costs are ignored, the argument is doubly flawed for, under either of two scenarios, the second buyer will end up with the goods even if the seller is not permitted to break the contract. First, if the costs of search are ignored, even if the seller performs the contract, the first buyer will costlessly find the second buyer and sell it the goods for the higher price. Second, if the costs of negotiation are ignored, the seller will costlessly negotiate a release from the contract with the first buyer, enabling the seller to sell the goods to the second buyer for the higher price. These scenarios would result in different allocations, as between the seller and the first buyer, of the gain from the sale to the second buyer, but since in all scenarios the goods end up in the hands of the buyer that values them more highly, there is no difference in economic efficiency. In life, however, transaction costs are not negligible. Furthermore, thorough analysis must also take account of the costs inherent in negotiating the contract in the first instance, if parties feel compelled to insist on protective clauses to assure performance.[10] This is a particularly significant defect if the amount involved is small. However, the main thrust of the analysis and its support of traditional contract doctrine in this area are clear. And the lawyer who, acting in a client's interest, advises the client to break a contract or assists the client in breaking it is not liable to the aggrieved party.[11]

We now look at the availability of specific performance and injunction for the enforcement of contracts.

---

[9] The seminal work is Coase, The Problem of Social Cost, 3 J.L. & Econ. 1 (1960).

[10] *See* Goetz & Scott, Enforcing Promises: An Examination of the Basis of Contract, 89 Yale L.J. 1261, 1292-01 (1980), criticized in Birmingham, Notes on the Reliance Interest, 60 Wash. L. Rev. 217, 245-65 (1985), and in Farber, Contract Law and Modern Economic Theory, 78 Nw. U. L. Rev. 303, 306-10 (1983).

[11] Restatement (Third) of Law Governing Lawyers §57(3) (lawyer who advises client to break a contract "is not liable to a nonclient for interference with contract").

B. ENFORCEMENT BY SPECIFIC PERFORMANCE AND INJUNCTION

§12.4.   Historical Development of Equitable Relief. Although in some cases damages will permit the injured party to arrange an adequate substitute for the expected performance, specific relief is plainly better suited to the objective of putting the promisee in the position in which it would have been had the promise been performed.[1] There are, however, some situations in which specific relief is simply not possible. The promise may, for example, have been one to deliver particular goods that are defective, destroyed, or owned by a third person.[2] Even if specific relief is possible, performance will usually be delayed, and the passage of time may reduce its effectiveness.[3] But there remain many instances in which specific relief will be both feasible and timely.

Feasibility of specific relief

The common law courts did not generally grant specific relief for breach of contract. The usual form of relief at common law was substitutional, and the typical judgment declared that the plaintiff recover from the defendant a sum of money.[4] This, in effect, imposed a new obligation on the defendant for the breach of the old. This new obligation could be enforced even without cooperation on the defendant's part. If the sum was not paid, a writ of execution was issued, empowering the sheriff to seize and sell so much of the defendant's property as was required to pay the plaintiff. Of course if the promise was simply to pay a sum of money, the effect of such a judgment was to give the plaintiff specific relief. For example, if a seller had judgment for the price of goods delivered but not paid for, the seller had, in effect, specific relief.[5] And occasionally specific relief was granted by means of proprietary actions, in which a party asserted rights as owner of the property concerned. For example, if a buyer was granted replevin of goods sold to him but not delivered, the sheriff would seize them from the seller and turn them over to the buyer, and the judgment would declare that the buyer was entitled to

Substitutional relief at common law

---

§12.4 [1]*See* Farnsworth, Legal Remedies for Breach of Contract, 70 Colum. L. Rev. 1145, 1151-56 (1970) (from which this section of the treatise is adapted). However, substitutional relief could, in theory, be in kind rather than in money. *See* Wright, The Law of Remedies as a Social Institution, 18 U. Det. L.J. 376, 378 (1955) ("If I lose the ski poles I have borrowed from a friend, I buy a new pair and return these to him.").

[2]See footnote to the discussion of specific performance in §12.5 *infra*.

[3]Contract remedies are not usually available until breach has occurred, though in the exceptional case, where a party repudiates obligation in advance of the time for performance, specific relief may be given without delay. See §12.5 *infra*. And where a declaratory judgment is granted before the time for performance, it at least reinforces the extra-legal compulsions to perform, although it adds no legal compulsion.

[4]*See* Washington, Damages in Contract at Common Law (pt. 1), 47 L.Q. Rev. 345 (1931).

[5]On the enforcement in equity of decrees for payment of money, *see* W. Walsh, Treatise on Equity 62-63 (1930).

them.[6] But these instances were exceptional, and even when the common law courts granted specific relief, they were unwilling to exert pressure directly on the defendant to compel performance. The judgment was seen as a mere declaration of rights as between the parties, and the process for its execution was directed, not at the defendant, but at the sheriff, ordering the sheriff to put the plaintiff in possession of real or personal property or to seize the defendant's property and sell so much of it as was necessary to satisfy a money judgment.[7]

Specific relief in equity

Promises were enforced in equity in a very different way. Prior to the development of assumpsit by the common law courts in the sixteenth century, most of the cases brought before the chancellor were based on promises that would not have been enforceable at common law, and the question was whether they would nevertheless be enforced in equity. After the development of assumpsit, equity accepted the doctrine of consideration, the test for enforcement that had been developed by the rival common law courts. To this extent, the jurisdiction of equity in contract cases became concurrent with that of the common law courts, and its concern shifted from the enforceability of promises to the nature of their enforcement.[8] Claimants then sought relief from the chancellor as an alternative to the judgment for damages to which they were entitled at common law. Under the influence of canon law — for the early chancellors were usually clerics — decrees in equity came to take the form of the chancellor's personal command to the defendant to do or not to do something. The defendant that disobeyed could be punished not only for criminal contempt, at the instance of the court, but also for civil contempt, at the instance of the plaintiff. This put into the plaintiff's hands the extreme sanction of imprisonment, which might be supplemented by fines payable to the plaintiff and by sequestration of the defendant's goods.[9] So it was said that equity acted *in personam,* against the person of the defendant, while the law acted *in rem,* against the defendant's property.[10] But it did not follow that the chancellor stood ready to order every

[6] Since replevin was generally available only to the owner of property, the conventional rationale was that the ownership of the goods in the seller's possession had passed to the buyer. *See* Uniform Sales Act §66 (replaced by UCC-O 2-716(3) and UCC-R 2-716(4)).

[7] *See* C. Huston, The Enforcement of Decrees in Equity 7 (1915).

[8] H. McClintock, Principles of Equity 125-27 (2d ed. 1948); Walsh, Treatise on Equity 22-25 (1930).

[9] The development of those supplementary sanctions is traced in C. Huston, The Enforcement of Decrees in Equity 76-83 (1915); W. Walsh, Treatise on Equity 47-48 (1930). Huston notes the measures required "to coerce obedience from the stubborn seventeenth-century Englishman. Thus in 1598, after one Walter had been already subjected in vain to close imprisonment for some time, the court ordered him to perform within a fortnight 'which if he shall not do . . . then his Lordship mindeth without further delay not only to shut the defendant close prisoner but also to lay as many irons to him as he may bear.'" Id. at 47, citing Clerk v. Walter, Monro 718 (1598).

[10] For a discussion of the power of equity, to act *in rem, see* C. Huston, The Enforcement of Decrees in Equity 71-86 (1915). Declaratory relief, in which the court states the rights of the parties but does nothing further to enforce them, may encourage performance of promises by reinforcing the extra-legal compulsions.

defaulting promisor to perform its promise. Equitable relief was confined to special cases by both historical and practical limitations.

The most important historical limitation grew out of the circumstance that the chancellor had originally granted equitable relief in order to supply the deficiencies of the common law. Equitable remedies were therefore readily characterized as "extraordinary." When, during the long jurisdictional struggle between the two systems of courts, some means of accommodation was needed, an adequacy test was developed to prevent the chancellor from encroaching on the powers of the common law judges. Equity would stay its hand if the remedy of an award of damages at law was "adequate."[11] To this test was added the gloss that damages were ordinarily adequate — a gloss encouraged by the philosophy of free enterprise with its confidence that a market economy ought to enable the injured party to arrange a substitute transaction. As one writer put it:

Adequacy test

> The law, concerning itself more and more with merchandise bought or sold for money, with things having a definite and calculable exchange value, came to conceive that the money compensation, which was an entirely adequate remedy in the common case, and in many cases the only possible one when once the wrong complained of had been committed, was [generally] the only remedy available for their use . . . .[12]

So English courts came to regard money damages as the norm and specific relief as the deviation. Only for land, which English courts regarded with particular esteem, was a general exception made, on the ground that each parcel of land was "unique" so money damages were inadequate.[13] This strong preference of English courts for substitutional relief stands in sharp contrast to the preference of civil law systems, those derived from the Roman law, for specific relief.

A second historical limitation, or group of limitations, is based on the concept that equitable relief is discretionary.[14] Since the chancellor was to act according to "conscience" (which prompted the notorious charge that his conscience might vary with the length of his foot[15]), he might withhold relief if considerations of fairness or morality dictated. Gradually these equitable restrictions

Discretionary limitations

---

[11]According to Holdsworth, "It was not till the eighteenth century that it was settled that equity would only grant specific relief if damages were not an adequate remedy." 1 W. Holdsworth, History of English Law 457 (7th ed. 1956).

[12]C. Huston, The Enforcement of Decrees in Equity 74 (1915). See also the quotation from Holmes in a footnote to the discussion of the nature of the problem in §9.1 *supra*.

[13]See §12.6 *infra*.

[14]*See* Yorio, A Defense of Equitable Defenses, 51 Ohio St. L.J. 1201 (1990).

[15]" 'Tis all one, as if they should make his foot the standard for the measure we call a Chancellor's foot; what an uncertain measure this would be! One Chancellor has a long foot, another a short foot, a third an indifferent foot; 'tis the same thing in the Chancellor's conscience." J. Selden, Table Talk, as quoted in Gee v. Pritchard, 2 Swanst. 402, 414, 36 Eng. Rep. 670, 679 (Ch. 1818). *See* J. Selden, Table Talk 43 (J. Pollock ed. 1927).

became more precise and hardened into rules. Some of the most renowned are embodied in equity's colorful maxims: "one who seeks equity must do equity";[16] "one who comes into equity must come with clean hands";[17] and "equity aids the vigilant."[18] One of the most troublesome of these rules was the now discredited "mutuality of remedy" rule, under which the injured party's right to specific relief depended on whether it would have been available to the other party, had the breach been on the other side.[19]

Practical limitations

The practical limitations on specific relief in equity grew out of the problems inherent in coercing the defendant to perform its promise. In some cases, of course, specific relief does not require the defaulting promisor's cooperation. If, for example, the promise is to convey land, the court can transfer the title by virtue of its own decree, or it can be transferred by a deed executed by an officer of the court.[20] But there is no such simple solution if the performance is personal in nature, and courts have bridled at coercing such performances. They will not, for example, compel a singer to perform a promise to sing, although they have been willing to order the singer not to act inconsistently with the promise, by enjoining the singer from singing elsewhere.[21] Courts have also been reluctant to order performance if difficulties of supervision or enforcement are foreseen, as may be the case under a building contract, especially if the absence of clear standards may lead to conflict and unfairness. Moreover, the practical exigencies of drafting decrees to guide future conduct under the threat of the severe sanctions available for contempt have moved courts to require that contract terms be expressed with greater certainty if specific relief is to be ordered than if damages are to be awarded.[22]

---

[16] Hazzard v. Westview Golf Club, 217 A.2d 217, 225 (Me. 1966) (party seeking to set aside decree confirming sale should have applied promptly to court for stay of order); Eastern Motor Inns v. Ricci, 565 A.2d 1265 (R.I. 1989) (though "equity abhors a forfeiture," it "also abhors bad faith and dilatory action").

[17] *See* New York Football Giants v. Los Angeles Chargers Football Club, 291 F.2d 471 (5th Cir. 1961) (Giants, who had kept contract with Charles Flowers secret so he could play in Sugar Bowl, lacked "clean hands" and could not have him enjoined from playing with Chargers). *But see* Houston Oilers v. Neely, 361 F.2d 36 (10th Cir. 1966) (disagreeing with rule in Flowers's case if it "was intended to apply to every instance in which a contract is entered into with a college football player before a post-season game with an understanding that it be kept secret to permit that player to compete in the game").

[18] Swiss Oil Corp. v. Fyffe, 176 S.W.2d 398, 402 (Ky. 1943) (party seeking return of payments "could have discovered, from data in its exclusive possession, that the payments were not due"). A related equitable concept is that of laches, a prejudicial delay in the exercise of a right that operates as a bar to it.

[19] For a case invoking the rule to allow specific performance by a vendor of land, *see* Hopper v. Hopper, 16 N.J. Eq. 147 (1863). See the discussion of insecurity in §12.7 *infra*.

[20] This is by statute in many jurisdictions and by judicial decision in others. *See* Fed. R. Civ. P. 70.

[21] See §12.5 *infra*.

[22] See the discussion of indefiniteness in §12.7 *infra*.

Thus it came to be that, although the injured party can always claim damages for breach of contract, that party's right to specific relief as an alternative is much more limited. The historical development of parallel systems of law and equity may afford an adequate explanation for the reluctance of our courts to grant specific relief more widely, but it is scant justification for it.[23] A more rational basis can today be found in the severity of the sanctions available for enforcement of equitable orders. Nevertheless, the modern trend is clearly in favor of the extension of specific relief at the expense of the traditional primacy of damages.

Expansion of specific relief

The limits on specific relief that grew out of the parallel systems of law and equity in England are peculiar to the common law and are unknown in other legal systems. Therefore the Vienna Convention ignores those limits in its broad provisions under which a "buyer may require performance by the seller of his obligations"[24] and a "seller may require the buyer to pay the price, take delivery or perform his other obligations."[25] In order to placate common law countries, however, "a court is not bound to enter a judgment for specific performance unless the court would do so under its own law in respect of similar contracts of sale."[26] This means that if suit is brought in a common law country in a case governed by the Convention, specific performance may be denied even though it would be granted were jurisdiction obtained elsewhere and suit brought there. Although the UNIDROIT Principles proclaim the general availability of specific performance, this is undercut by an exception, accommodating the common law position, if the injured party "may reasonably obtain performance from another source."[27]

International solutions

We turn now to the forms that specific relief takes when it is available in equity.

§12.5. Forms: Specific Performance and Injunction. The most direct form of equitable relief for breach of contract is specific performance. By ordering the promisor to render the promised performance, the court attempts to produce, as nearly as is practicable, the same effect as if the contract had been performed.[1] A court will not order a performance that has become impossible,

Specific performance

---

[23] Civil law systems (those descended from Roman law) have, by and large, proceeded on the premise that specific relief should be generally available for breach of contract. *See* Dawson, Specific Performance in France and Germany, 57 Mich. L. Rev. 495 (1959).

[24] CISG 46(1).

[25] CISG 62.

[26] CISG 28.

[27] UNIDROIT Principles 7.2.2(c).

§12.5 [1] Dalton v. Educational Testing Serv., 663 N.E.2d 289 (N.Y. 1995) (Kaye, C.J., quoting this section of this treatise: where testing service breached duty of good faith by disallowing student's test score without considering material he submitted, he was entitled only to good faith consideration of material and not to validation of score).

unreasonably burdensome, or unlawful,[2] nor will it issue an order that can be frustrated by the defendant through exercise of a power of termination or otherwise.[3] Specific performance may be granted after there has been a breach of contract by either nonperformance or repudiation.[4]

Injunction

Instead of ordering specific performance, a court may, by injunction, direct a party to refrain from doing a specified act. If the performance due under the contract consists simply of forbearance, the effect of an injunction is to order specific performance.[5] Often, however, an injunction is used as an indirect means of enforcing a duty to act. Instead of ordering that the act be done, as a court would in granting specific performance, the court orders forbearance from inconsistent action. This is done most often in cases in which specific performance is objectionable on some ground that can be avoided by the use of an injunction. Difficulties in supervising compliance with the order may, for example, be fewer if an injunction is issued than if specific performance is ordered.[6]

Example of *Lumley v. Wagner*

The classic case is *Lumley v. Wagner*, arising out of a contract in which Johanna Wagner, an opera singer from the court of Prussia, agreed to sing exclusively for Benjamin Lumley, proprietor of Her Majesty's Theatre in London, for a period of three months. When Frederick Gye, proprietor of the Royal Italian Opera, Covent Garden, persuaded Wagner to break her contract with Lumley and sing at his theater instead, Lumley obtained an injunction restraining her from appearing at the proposed or any other concert during the contract period. She appealed, but the chancellor upheld issuance of the injunction. "It is true that I have not the means of compelling her to sing, but she has no cause of complaint if I compel her to abstain from the commission of an act which she has bound herself not to do, and thus possibly cause

---

[2] Brand v. Lowther, 285 S.E.2d 474 (W. Va. 1981) (error to grant specific performance of contract to sell corporation where not shown that wife "acquiesced or consented to her husband's promise to sell her stock").

[3] State ex rel. Schoblum v. Anacortes Veneer, 255 P.2d 379 (Wash. 1953) (alternative holding: specific performance of employment contract denied against employer who could nullify it by termination without cause). If the power of termination makes the promise illusory, there is no contract to be enforced. See §2.14 *supra*.

[4] If a party repudiates an obligation before the time for performance, a court may without delay order performance at the agreed time. Bonde v. Weber, 128 N.E.2d 883 (Ill. 1955) (where one party repudiates, the other may bring action for specific performance "notwithstanding the fact that time for performance . . . is in the future").

[5] Bauer v. Sawyer, 134 N.E.2d 329 (Ill. 1956) (doctor enjoined from breach of covenant not to compete with former partnership). This also holds true for duties of forbearance that are imposed by law, such as the duty not to interfere with the other party's performance of the contract.

[6] For a curious example, *see* Prospect Park & Coney Island R.R. v. Coney Island & Brooklyn R.R., 39 N.E. 17 (N.Y. 1894) (suit for specific performance of contract to run street cars to connect with plaintiff's trains, in which court enjoined defendant from operating any cars unless it performed contract).

her to fulfil her engagement."[7] A court will not, however, grant an injunction unless the remedy in damages would be inadequate. This requirement is met if the employee's services are unique or extraordinary, either because of special skill that the employee possesses — as in Wagner's case — or because of special knowledge that the employee has acquired of the employer's business.[8] Injunctions are especially common in connection with contracts in the worlds of sports[9] and entertainment.[10] Although courts often recite that the purpose of the injunction is to restrain the employee from working for a *competitor*,[11] this has not always been required.[12] Nor should an express provision for exclusive employment be required as long as this can be implied.[13]

In framing an order of specific performance or an injunction, the court can mold it to do justice as fully as is practicable. The order may be directed at the injured party as well as at the party in breach. It may be conditioned on some performance to be rendered by the injured party or by a third person, such as the payment of money to compensate for defects or the giving of security. It may even be conditioned on the injured party's assent to modification of the contract sought to be enforced. If the exact performance promised is very difficult to enforce or has become impossible, unreasonably burdensome, or unlawful, the court may order a performance that is only part of what was promised or is otherwise not identical with what was promised. Thus a vendor that cannot fully perform because of a deficiency in area or a defect in title may be ordered to transfer all that the vendor can.[14]

Framing the order

Along with any equitable relief by specific performance or injunction, a court may also award damages and grant other relief.[15] The fact that a plaintiff is itself in breach does not bar relief, unless the other party can treat the breach as total

Damages and other relief

---

[7] 42 Eng. Rep. 687, 693 (Ch. 1852). *See also* the discussion of personal service contracts in §12.7 *infra*.

[8] See §12.7 *infra*.

[9] Nassau Sports v. Peters, 352 F. Supp. 870 (E.D.N.Y. 1972) ("Recent decisions indicate that that requirement [of exceptional talent] is met prima facie in cases involving professional athletes.").

[10] Shubert Theatrical Co. v. Rath, 271 F. 827 (2d Cir. 1921) (theatrical manager granted injunction against acrobats).

[11] Shubert Theatrical Co. v. Rath, *supra* note 10 (acrobats "contracted with a rival manager to appear . . . in a rival theater").

[12] Mission Indep. School Dist. v. Diserens, 188 S.W.2d 568 (Tex. 1945) (declining to restrict doctrine to include only situations "where the parties were competitors and loss of business have resulted").

[13] American Broadcasting Cos. v. Wolf, 420 N.E.2d 363 (N.Y. 1981) (following later cases that hold that "injunction is warranted because the employee either expressly or by clear implication agreed not to work elsewhere").

[14] Nelson v. Gibe, 127 N.W. 304 (Mich. 1910) (purchaser entitled to deed for what vendor owned, although over one-third of lot sold did not belong to vendor).

[15] Brockel v. Lewton, 319 N.W.2d 173 (S.D. 1982) (where seller has wrongfully held over, buyers in action for specific performance "are entitled to a setoff against the purchase price for use and occupation during the holdover period").

and terminate the contract. In granting relief, however, the court will take account of any damages caused by the breach.[16] If the court orders a performance that is not identical with what was promised, it may order compensation for any deficiency. Thus, if a vendor is ordered to convey a tract that is deficient in area or defective in title, the purchaser will be compensated for the resulting claim for partial breach — in damages, by restitution of money already paid, or through an abatement of the price if not yet paid.[17] Because an order granting equitable relief seldom results in performance within the time required by the contract, damages for delay are often appropriate.[18] A court may grant a preliminary injunction to prevent an undesirable change in the situation before trial and may, in granting preliminary or final relief, require an indemnity against future harm. A claimant who sues for specific performance or an injunction and is denied that relief may be awarded damages or restitution in the same proceeding.

We next examine the adequacy test.

Reasons for test

§12.6. The Adequacy Test. As we have seen, it came to be recognized that equitable relief would not be granted if the legal remedy of damages was adequate to protect the injured party.[1] This historical limitation has persisted in spite of the merger of law and equity. It can be justified on economic as well as historical grounds. It has been argued that it "promotes efficiency by reducing the costs of negotiating contracts," since it "draws the line between specific performance and money damages in the way that most contracting parties would draw it were they free to make their own rules concerning remedies for breach and had they deliberated about the matter at the time of contracting."[2]

Tendency to liberalize

The tendency is, however, to liberalize the granting of specific performance and injunction by enlarging the classes of cases in which damages are regarded

---

[16]Cimina v. Bronich, 537 A.2d 1355 (Pa. 1988) (lessors entitled to payment of taxes).

[17]Shell Oil Co. v. Kelinson, 158 N.W.2d 724 (Iowa 1968) (purchaser entitled to abatement out of unpaid price).

[18]Wirth & Hamid Fair Booking v. Wirth, 192 N.E. 297 (N.Y. 1934) (damages for delay awarded, along with injunction against breach of covenant not to compete).

§12.6   [1]See §12.4 *supra*. The adequacy test is stated in terms of the adequacy of the damage remedy, rather than the adequacy of common law remedies in general. Common law remedies other than damages will seldom afford as complete relief as will specific performance. The effectiveness of replevin, for example, is reduced by rules allowing the defendant to post a bond instead of surrendering the goods sought to be replevied. The availability of such a common law remedy will not preclude a grant of equitable relief but may be considered by the court in the exercise of its discretion. In choosing the remedy best suited to the circumstances of the case, the court will also consider the availability of other equitable relief, such as a decree of reformation, rescission, cancellation, or specific restitution.

[2]Kronman, Specific Performance, 45 U. Chi. L. Rev. 351, 365 (1978). For an argument that "specific performance should be as routinely available as the damages remedy," *see* Schwartz, The Case for Specific Performance, 89 Yale L.J. 271 (1979).

as an inadequate remedy.[3] The contemporary approach is to compare remedies to determine which is more effective in affording suitable protection to the injured party's legally recognized interest, which is usually that party's expectation interest.[4] The concept of adequacy has thus tended to become relative, and the comparison more often leads to granting equitable relief than was historically the case. If the adequacy of the damage remedy is unclear, the combined effect of such other practical considerations as uncertainty of terms, insecurity as to the agreed exchange, and difficulty of enforcement may be considered.[5] The fact that damages would be an adequate remedy for failure to render one part of the promised performance does not preclude specific performance of the contract as a whole.[6] Nor does a provision for liquidated damages preclude the grant of specific performance or an injunction instead of or in addition to the award of such damages,[7] though a clear provision to the contrary will be given effect.[8]

Damages will not be adequate to protect the injured party's expectation if the loss caused by the breach cannot be estimated with sufficient certainty. Damages may then be nominal only, and they will not, in any case, give full compensation for the loss.[9] If the subject of the contract involves matters of taste or sentiment, as in contracts for the sale of works of art or heirlooms, it may be impossible to value the injured party's expectation in money.[10] This

Uncertainty of damages

---

[3]D. Laycock, The Death of the Irreparable Injury Rule (1991), reprinted in part in Laycock, The Death of the Irreparable Injury Rule, 103 Harv. L. Rev. 688 (1990) (arguing that specific performance is granted for reasons other than inadequacy of legal remedies).

[4]Sams v. Goff, 540 S.E.2d 532 (W. Va. 1999) (for "existence of a legal remedy to bar injunctive relief, it must appear that the legal remedy is as practical and efficient to secure the ends of justice and its prompt administration as injunctive relief").

[5]See §12.7 *infra*.

[6]Complete relief can be afforded in such a case in a single action, by a decree ordering performance of the entire contract, as long as the other requisites are met. Taylor v. Highland Park Corp., 42 S.E.2d 335 (S.C. 1947) ("where part of an entire contract relates to ordinary personal property and the rest to a subject matter, such as land, over which equity jurisdiction is commonly exercised, specific performance may be had of the whole contract, including the part that relates to personal property").

[7]Karpinski v. Ingrasci, 268 N.E.2d 751 (N.Y. 1971) (provision for payment of $40,000 for breach of covenant not to compete).

[8]Equitable relief has been refused where the contract contains a provision for payment of money as a true alternate performance. Doyle v. Ortega, 872 P.2d 721 (Idaho 1994) (only reasonable interpretation was that in case of "seller's failure to consummate the sale, the buyer is entitled only to the remedies stated in the default clause").

[9]See §12.15 *infra*. For an example involving contract beneficiaries, see the discussion of a gift promise in §10.7 *supra*.

[10]Morris v. Sparrow, 287 S.W.2d 583 (Ark. 1956) (specific performance granted cowboy who had been promised roping pony after training it). *See* UCC 2-716 cmt. 2 ("contracts for the sale of heirlooms or priceless works of art . . . were usually involved in the older case").

may be so even in the case of contracts of a more commercial character.[11] The breach of a contract to transfer shares of stock may deprive the buyer of control over the corporation that cannot be accurately valued in money.[12] The breach of a contract to sell a business may leave the buyer unable to prove damages based on prospective profits.[13] The breach of a requirements contract may cut off a vital supply of raw materials of inestimable worth.[14] The breach of a contract not to compete may cause losses that are impossible to quantify.[15] If the breach occurs when the contract still has many years to run, it may not be possible at the time of the trial to forecast loss that will result in the future.[16] In such situations equitable relief has often been granted.

Availability of substitute

A critical factor in determining whether damages are an adequate remedy is whether money can buy a substitute for the promised performance. If a substitute can readily be obtained, the damage remedy is ordinarily regarded as adequate. Because entering into a substitute transaction is a more efficient way of preventing further injury than is specific performance or an injunction, there is good reason to limit the injured party to damages in such a case. Furthermore, it is ordinarily in the interest of the injured party, as well as of the party in breach, to find a substitute. Damages will be awarded to compensate the injured party for any additional cost in arranging the substitute transaction, and interest will be allowed to compensate for any additional burden in financing the transaction. In some situations, however, no substitute is available, or its procurement would be unreasonably difficult or inconvenient or would impose serious financial burdens or risks on the injured party. If the performance consists of forbearance, as under a contract not to compete, no substitute is possible.[17] Patents and copyrights are unique, so there

---

[11] Tom Doherty Assocs. v. Saban Entertainment, 60 F.3d 27 (2d Cir. 1995) (where "availability of a product is essential to the life of the business *or* increases business of the plaintiff beyond sales of that product — for example, by attracting customers who make purchases of other goods while buying the product in question — the damages caused by the loss will be far more difficult to quantify than where sales of one of many products is the sole loss," and injunctive relief is therefore appropriate).

[12] Dominick v. Vassar, 367 S.E.2d 487 (Va. 1988) (specific performance of option to buy other half of shares in closely held corporation).

[13] Triple-A Baseball Club Assocs. v. Northwestern Baseball, 832 F.2d 214 (1st Cir. 1987) (contract for sale of minor league baseball franchise that was "unique in character and cannot be duplicated").

[14] *See* UCC 2-716 cmt. 2 (output and requirements contracts involving "particular or peculiarly available source or market present today the typical commercial specific performance situation"). An example is Laclede Gas Co. v. Amoco Oil Co., 522 F.2d 33 (8th Cir. 1975) (long-term requirements contract for propane).

[15] See the discussion of the rule of reason in §5.3 *supra*.

[16] Hunt Foods v. O'Disho, 98 F. Supp. 267 (N.D. Cal. 1951) (breach of five-year contract to sell peaches at average price for county with three more seasons to run).

[17] Karpinski v. Ingrasci, *supra* note 7.

is no substitute.[18] Shares of stock in a corporation may not be obtainable elsewhere.[19]

Land was viewed by English courts with particular esteem and was therefore singled out for special treatment.[20] Each parcel, however ordinary, was considered "unique," and its value was regarded as to some extent speculative. From this it followed that, if a vendor broke a promise to convey an interest in land, money would not enable the injured purchaser to buy a substitute, and specific performance would generally be granted. Under this traditional view, the purchaser has the right to specific performance, even if the purchaser has made a contract to resell the land to a third person.[21] A purchaser who cannot convey the land to another purchaser will be held for damages for breach of the resale contract, and, at least so it is argued, these damages cannot be accurately determined without litigation. Although the arguments for allowing the vendor specific performance when the purchaser defaults are less compelling, equity also granted the vendor relief.[22] The arguments run: because the value of land is to some extent speculative, it may be difficult for the vendor to prove damages with sufficient certainty;[23] even if the vendor can make this proof, the land may not be immediately convertible into money, depriving the vendor of funds with which to make other investments; and, until the vendor gets a judgment, the existence of the contract, even if broken by the purchaser, may impair the saleability of the land, making it difficult to sell.[24] But after the vendor has transferred the interest in the land to the purchaser and all that remains is for the purchaser to pay the price, a money judgment is an adequate remedy for the vendor. The traditional view that land contracts are generally specifically

---

[18] Conway v. White, 9 F.2d 863 (2d Cir. 1925) (patent).

[19] Medcom Holding Co. v. Baxter Travenol Laboratories, 984 F.2d 223 (7th Cir. 1993) ("contract for the sale of corporate stock not publicly traded can be specifically enforced on the ground that valuation is imprecise without an active market for the stock" and also because a contract to sell a business is one to sell "a unique asset").

[20] Kitchen v. Herring, 42 N.C. 190 (1851) ("principle in regard to land was adopted, not because it was fertile or rich in minerals, . . . but simply because it was *land* — a favorite and favored subject in England"). See the discussion of the adequacy test in §12.4 *supra*. For an interesting economic argument in support of the special treatment of land, *see* Bishop, The Choice of Remedy for Breach of Contract, 14 J. Legal Stud. 299, 305 (1985) (characterizing land as "distinctively the kind of subject matter in which a potential bidder can easily make an offer to the owner regardless of whether that owner is the original seller or the original buyer — the information cost of finding the owner is trivial").

[21] Justus v. Clelland, 651 P.2d 1206 (Ark. App. 1982) ("what the purchaser did with the property was of no concern to the vendor").

[22] Hopper v. Hopper, 16 N.J. Eq. 147 (1863) ("vendor may maintain his bill in all cases where the purchaser could sue for a specific performance").

[23] For another application of the argument that the value of land is difficult to determine, see footnote to the discussion of the alternative of reliance in §12.8 *infra*.

[24] The fact that specific performance is available to the purchaser was sometimes regarded as of some weight under the now-discarded doctrine of "mutuality of remedy." See §12.7 *infra*.

enforceable has been challenged and is particularly difficult to defend if the vendor is the injured party.[25]

Rules as to goods

The traditional attitude toward contracts for the sale of goods is quite the opposite of the attitude toward contracts for the sale of land. In a market economy it was supposed that, with rare exceptions for such "unique" items as heirlooms and objects of art, substantially similar goods were available elsewhere.[26] The trend, however, has been to relax this restriction on the availability of specific performance. The commentary to the Uniform Commercial Code explains that it "seeks to further a more liberal attitude than some courts have shown in connection with the specific performance of contracts of sale."[27] It goes on to assert that it introduces "a new concept of what are 'unique' goods" with a test of uniqueness that "must be made in terms of the total situation which characterizes the contract," adding that the buyer's "inability to cover is strong evidence" of the propriety of granting specific performance.[28] It notes that "where the unavailability of a market price is caused by a scarcity of goods of the type involved, a good case is normally made for specific performance under this Article."[29] But the text of the Code is more circumspect, stating only, "Specific performance may be decreed where the goods are unique or in other proper circumstances."[30] The Code does not reject the adequacy test, and specific performance remains the exception rather than the rule under contracts for the sale of goods.[31] If the seller fails to deliver the goods, the typical buyer must still content itself with money as a substitute.[32]

Effect of insolvency

Even if damages are adequate in other respects, they are not an effective remedy if they cannot be collected. If the injured party has already performed, and the party in breach is insolvent, specific performance may be against public policy because it would result in a transfer that would give the injured party a

---

[25]For an unusual case, in which the purchaser was the injured party, *see* Watkins v. Paul, 511 P.2d 781 (Idaho 1973) (where evidence fails to show that purchasers need the land for "any particular, unique purpose" but shows "that they may resell it for profit," specific performance would bring them "no greater relief than would damages").

[26]Block v. Shaw, 95 S.W. 806 (Ark. 1906) (buyer denied specific performance of contract for sale of cotton).

[27]UCC 2-716 cmt. 1.

[28]UCC 2-716 cmt. 2.

[29]UCC 2-713 cmt. 3.

[30]UCC 2-716(1). *See* UCC 1-305(a) (remedies provided "must be liberally administered to the end that the aggrieved party may be put in as good a position as if the other party had fully performed").

[31]*See* Dawson, Specific Performance in France and Germany, 57 Mich. L. Rev. 495 (1959) ("adequacy test is so much a part of our historical tradition that to get rid of it . . . will clearly require express legislation").

[32]Weathersby v. Gore, 556 F.2d 1247 (5th Cir. 1977) (buyer "could have acquired additional cotton on the open market when [farmer] informed him he would no longer perform").

preference over other creditors of the party in breach.[33] But if the contract is unperformed on both sides and provides for a fair exchange, performance of the contract will not result in a preferential transfer and may even benefit other creditors of the party in breach by improving that party's financial condition. In such cases, some courts have granted specific performance on the ground of the defendant's insolvency.[34]

Because the restraints on the availability of equitable relief have tradition- **Power of parties** ally been viewed as limitations on the court's jurisdiction, it has been generally supposed that the parties cannot enlarge the availability of specific perfor- mance or injunction by dispensing with the adequacy test or with the other criteria for such relief.[35] Revised Article 2, however, specifically gives effect to an agreement in a contract for the sale of goods other than a consumer contract that specific performance may be decreed, unless the only remaining obligation is to pay money.[36] Furthermore, a court may, in determining ade- quacy, take notice of facts recited in the contract, a thought that has not escaped the attention of contract drafters.[37] This limitation on the power of the parties does not apply if they wish to reduce the availability of equitable relief. The parties can eliminate the possibility of specific performance or injunction by providing for the payment of a sum of money as an alternative, as long as they make clear their intention to do so.[38]

We next examine the other considerations that enter into a decision to grant or withhold specific performance or an injunction, once the adequacy test is met.

§12.7. Other Limitations. In addition to the adequacy test, a num- **List of limitations** ber of other limitations restrict the availability of specific performance and injunction as contract remedies. The most important of these relate to indefi- niteness of terms, insecurity as to the agreed exchange, difficulty in enforcement or supervision, unfairness, and public policy. Even if these limitations bar

[33] Jamison Coal & Coke Co. v. Goltra, 143 F.2d 889 (8th Cir. 1944) (although insolvency is factor in determining whether remedy at law is adequate, "specific performance would enable plaintiff to obtain a preference over the other creditors").

[34] Proyectos Electronicos v. Alper, 37 Bankr. 931 (E.D. Pa. 1983) (requiring buyer "to cover would require it to pay for identical goods a second time and then stand in line with other unsecured creditors of the debtor").

[35] Stokes v. Moore, 77 So. 2d 331 (Ala. 1955) (dictum: "provision that "injunction may be issued . . . would serve to oust the inherent jurisdiction of the court to determine whether an injunction is appropriate").

[36] UCC-R 2-716(1)

[37] King Records v. Brown, 252 N.Y.S.2d 988 (App. Div. 1964) (recordings "substantiate the contract characterization of [singer's] services as unique and extraordinary").

[38] Sun Bank v. Lester, 404 So. 2d 141 (Fla. App. 1981) ("provision waiving specific performance as a remedy was valid"). See *supra* note 8.

specific relief, the contract is nevertheless enforceable and damages can be recovered for its breach.[1] We consider these five limitations in the order listed.

Indefiniteness   A court will not grant specific performance or an injunction to enforce a contract unless the terms of the contract are sufficiently definite to provide the basis for an appropriate order.[2] This requirement goes beyond the general requirement of definiteness, under which there is no contract at all unless the terms of the agreement "provide a basis for determining the existence of a breach and for giving an appropriate remedy."[3] A decree of specific performance or an injunction must be formulated with special precision because of the severity of the contempt sanction. The terms of a contract may be certain enough to provide the basis for the calculation of damages but not certain enough to enable a court to frame an order granting specific relief with the requisite precision. In that case, there is a contract — an enforceable agreement — but it is not enforceable by specific performance or injunction. As Learned Hand observed:

> This contract is so obscure, and, strictly taken, so incoherent, that nobody can be sure of its meaning . . . . Arguendo, we shall assume that these promises created a valid contract which could be enforced at law like any other; but it does not follow that equitable remedies would also be available . . . .[4]

As it does in applying the general requirement of definiteness, a court will first avail itself of the usual aids in dispelling uncertainties and determining the scope of the agreement. These include course of performance, course of dealing, usages, and the addition of terms supplied by law.[5] The court will refuse to grant specific relief only if, after the use of these aids, the contract is still too indefinite to enable it to frame an appropriate order.

Insecurity   A court will not compel performance if a substantial part of the return performance has not been rendered, unless the rendering of that part can

---

§**12.7**   [1] This distinction between enforcement at law and in equity where unfairness is shown has been criticized as a "moral curtain that, heavy with the mold of centuries, still hangs across our law, cutting off from the main body of the law the benefit of the system of moral principles that we call equity." Newman, The Renaissance of Good Faith in Contracting in Anglo-American Law, 54 Cornell L. Rev. 553, 554 (1969). The author points out, however, that in practice claimants who are denied specific relief rarely pursue to a successful conclusion actions for damages. Id. at 558-61. Since equitable relief is generally available only when the damage remedy is "inadequate," the alternative of an action at law may not be an attractive one for the plaintiff.

[2] Plantation Land Co. v. Bradshaw, 207 S.E.2d 49 (Ga. 1974) (contract for sale of real property).

[3] Restatement Second §33(2). For a more thorough discussion of the requirement of definiteness, see §3.27 *supra*.

[4] Bethlehem Engrg. Export Co. v. Christie, 105 F.2d 933, 934 (2d Cir. 1939).

[5] These aids are discussed in §3.28 *supra*.

be secured to the court's satisfaction.[6] A party in breach should not be compelled to perform unless assured of receiving what it bargained for in exchange. Even if, under the contract, the party in breach would have had to perform before the injured party, security for the injured party's performance may be desirable if the controversy has increased the risk that that performance will not be forthcoming. If the injured party has already committed itself by reliance on the contract, that party's own self-interest may afford adequate security. Otherwise, it is up to the court to devise a means of securing the exchange. Sometimes it can do this by conditioning its order on simultaneous performance by the injured party.[7] Thus many courts do not insist on tender as a prerequisite for a suit for specific performance of a contract for the sale of land,[8] though a contrary view persists.[9] If simultaneous performance advances the time for the injured party's performance, that party may be allowed a discount as compensation. If simultaneous performance is not feasible, the order may be conditioned on the injured party's giving appropriate collateral.[10] If there is reason to fear that the injured party will not render the agreed exchange, and if it is impossible to secure it, the order may be refused. It has sometimes been said that there is a requirement of "mutuality of remedy" and that equitable relief is not available to one party unless, as of the time the contract was made, it would have been available to the other party had the breach been on the other side.[11] This doctrine is now discredited. To the extent that it may have been based on the notion that a party in breach should not be compelled to perform without the assurance that the

---

[6] Sabin v. Rauch, 258 P.2d 991 (Ariz. 1953) ("if the possibility of his future performance is challenged, he must give such assurances as the court may require that he will completely perform when the time arrives").

[7] Morad v. Silva, 117 N.E.2d 290 (Mass. 1954) ("the decree fully protects the purchasers by making performance on their part conditional on concurrent performance in full" on the seller's part).

[8] Fleenor v. Church, 681 P.2d 1351 (Alaska 1984) (following Restatement Second §369 and holding that tender by purchaser was not required even though vendor had not repudiated).

[9] Century 21 All Western Real Estate & Inv. v. Webb, 645 P.2d 52 (Utah 1982) ("neither party can be said to be in default (and thus susceptible to a judgment for damages or a decree for specific performance) until the other party has tendered his own performance").

[10] Rego v. Decker, 482 P.2d 834 (Alaska 1971) ("In granting specific performance, the decree can be fashioned to provide that the plaintiff furnish adequate security for his agreed performance. In so doing, the courts are fulfilling their function of achieving justice between the parties without requiring additional or unnecessary litigation.").

[11] The doctrine appears to have gained currency from the statement that to be specifically enforced a contract "must be mutual, — that is to say, such that it might, at the time it was entered into, have been enforced by either of the parties against the other of them." E. Fry, Treatise on Specific Performance of Contracts §286 (1st ed. 1858).

agreed exchange will be rendered in return, this result can be accomplished by requiring security.[12]

Difficulty in enforcement

A court will not grant specific enforcement or an injunction if this would impose on it burdens of enforcement or supervision that are disproportionate to the advantages to be gained.[13] This limitation is most often invoked in connection with construction contracts. The burdens may be particularly heavy if judging the quality of the performance poses difficult problems or if supervision will be required over an extended period of time.[14] It has been suggested that "these ideas carried a load of snobbery, expressed in distaste for menial tasks — 'how can a master judge of repairs in husbandry?' "[15] Experience, including that in civil rights cases, shows that the burdens of enforcement or supervision are often not as great as feared, and courts have today become more willing to order structures to be built and facilities to be maintained. Particularly is this true when the contract involves construction followed by the sale or lease of the property.[16] As the New York Court of Appeals has written, "Modern writers think that the 'difficulty of enforcement' idea is exaggerated and that the trend is toward specific performance...."[17] The advantages to be gained from specific performance merit special consideration if the claimant's need is great or a substantial public interest is involved.[18]

---

[12]Morad v. Silva, *supra* note 7 ("even under the rule which rejects the mutuality principle specific performance may be refused 'if a substantial part of the agreed exchange . . . is not well secured' "). *See* Restatement Second §363 cmt. *c*.

[13]Lorch, Inc. v. Bessemer Mall Shopping Center, 310 So. 2d 872 (Ala. 1975) ("Special knowledge, skill and judgment is necessarily involved in selecting and investing in inventory, selecting, training, and compensating adequate personnel, and innumerable other day-to-day business decisions.").

[14]Suchan v. Rutherford, 410 P.2d 434 (Idaho 1966) ("Ordinarily equity will not grant a decree of specific performance of a contract the enforcement of which requires supervision by the court over an extended period of time.").

[15]Dawson, Specific Performance in France and Germany, 57 Mich. L. Rev. 495, 537 (1959), quoting from Rayner v. Stone, 28 Eng. Rep. 845, 846 (Ch. 1762). Consider also the remark by Chancellor Walworth, in a suit against an opera singer for specific performance: "I am not aware that any officer of this court has that perfect knowledge of the Italian language, or possesses that exquisite sensibility in the auricular nerve which is necessary to understand, and to enjoy with a proper zest, the peculiar beauties of the Italian opera, so fascinating to the fashionable world." De Rivafinoli v. Corsetti, 4 Paige Ch. 263, 270 (N.Y. 1833).

[16]Floyd v. Watson, 254 S.E.2d 687 (W. Va. 1979) ("agreement here includes a provision for conveyance of land, and therefore specific performance is proper").

[17]Grayson-Robinson Stores v. Iris Constr. Corp., 168 N.E.2d 377, 379 (N.Y. 1960) (arbitration award directing specific performance of construction contract confirmed).

[18]Laclede Gas Co. v. Amoco Oil Co., 522 F.2d 33 (8th Cir. 1975) ("public interest in providing propane to the retail customer is manifest, while any supervision required will be far from onerous").

A court will not grant specific performance of a contract to provide a service that is personal in nature.[19] This refusal is based in part on the difficulty of passing judgment on the quality of performance and is, to this extent, an application of the more general rule just discussed. It is also based on the undesirability of compelling the continuance of personal relations after disputes have arisen and confidence and loyalty have been shaken and the undesirability, in some instances, of imposing what might seem like involuntary servitude. These policies are relevant in determining what services are personal for the purpose of this limitation.[20] As already noted, even though specific performance is denied, an injunction may be granted if it will afford substantial protection to the injured party without offending these policies.[21] It must, however, be shown that the employee's services are unique or extraordinary, because of either special skill or special knowledge acquired from the employer.[22] But the purpose of such relief is not to enforce indirectly the duty to render the service; its purpose is merely to enforce an implied duty of forbearance from competition with the employer. An injunction will not be issued if its probable result is to force the employee to perform the contract by leaving the employee with no other reasonable means of making a living.[23] This limitation on specific performance at the instance of the employer, when personal service by the employee is involved, has also been held to preclude specific performance at the instance of the employee when personal supervision by the employer is involved.[24]

In addition to the limitations already discussed, which turn largely on practical considerations inherent in the nature of equitable relief, there are other limitations derived from the historical role of courts of equity as courts of

Personal service contracts

Unfairness

---

[19] Fitzpatrick v. Michael, 9 A.2d 639 (Md. 1939) (even absent an adequate remedy at law, equity will not specifically enforce contract for personal service as nurse, chauffeur, companion, guardian, and housekeeper, because "the mischief likely to result from the enforced continuance of the relationship incident to the service when it has become personally obnoxious to one of the parties is so great that the best interests of society require that the remedy be refused," and "courts have not the means or the ability to enforce such decrees").

[20] A service is not personal for this purpose unless it is nondelegable, but not every nondelegable performance is personal. *See* Wilson v. Sandstrom, 317 So. 2d 732 (Fla. 1975) (specific performance of contract to furnish greyhounds to race track not precluded "even if we assume that some personal service is involved in the requirement that the kennel owners produce their unique product"). As to delegability in general, see §11.10 *supra*.

[21] See §12.5 *supra*.

[22] Most of the cases involve contracts of entertainers or athletes. See the discussion of the example of *Lumley v. Wagner* in §12.5 *supra*. Compare the cases involving the use of injunction for direct enforcement of covenants not to compete. See §5.3 *supra*.

[23] *See* Restatement Second §367 cmt. *c*. If an injunction will probably result in performance of the contract, it should appear that the employer is prepared to continue the employment in good faith.

[24] Fitzpatrick v. Michael, note 19 *supra* ("court can no more compel [employer] to accept [employee's] services . . . than it could compel her to render them if he demanded them and she were unwilling to give them").

"conscience."[25] For example, equitable relief will not usually be granted to enforce a contract, other than an option contract on fair terms, that is binding solely because of a nominal payment or by reason of some formality, such as a seal or a signed writing.[26] However, the importance of these other limitations has been considerably lessened by the merger of law and equity, by the acceptance as part of the general law of contract of such originally equitable doctrines as unconscionability[27] and undue influence,[28] and by the liberalization of the rules on misrepresentation,[29] duress,[30] and mistake.[31] Nevertheless, the discretionary nature of equitable relief permits its denial when unfairness appears as a result of a combination of factors, even though no single doctrine alone makes the promise unenforceable.[32] The unfairness may not meet the requirements for unconscionability because it may have developed after the contract was made.[33] And it may present elements of incapacity, mistake, misrepresentation, duress, undue influence, impracticability of performance, frustration of purpose, or substantive unfairness in the exchange that fall short of what is required for relief under any one of those grounds.[34]

Public policy   Furthermore, specific performance or an injunction may be refused on the ground that the act or forbearance that would be compelled is against public policy, though the contract itself is not so offensive to public policy as to be unenforceable.[35] They may also be refused on the ground that, though the act

---

[25] See §12.4 *supra*. As to the precursors of the modern doctrine of unconscionability, see the discussion of policing in equity in §4.27 *supra*.

[26] See footnote to the discussion of the seal as distinct from consideration in §2.16 *supra*, and footnote to the effect of the abolition of the seal in §3.23 *supra*.

[27] See §4.28 *supra*.

[28] See §4.20 *supra*.

[29] See §§4.10-4.15 *supra*.

[30] See §§4.16-4.20 *supra*.

[31] See §§9.3, 9.4 *supra*.

[32] Bailey v. Musumeci, 591 A.2d 1316 (N.H. 1991) (when "party claims mistake as one of the factors weighing against a petition for specific performance, rather than as grounds for rescission of the contract, the [usual] criteria . . . need not be met"). For criticism of the result that the contract is still enforceable at law by the award of damages, see note 1 *supra*.

[33] Courts are not agreed as to the effect of a change of circumstances after the making of the contract on the availability of specific performance. *See* Bergstedt v. Bender, 222 S.W. 547 (Tex. Commn. App. 1920) (buyer denied specific performance of contract to sell $4,900 homestead for $1,500 plus right in seller to use it for life, where seller's immediate death made it "harsh and inequitable"). *But see* Tuckwiller v. Tuckwiller, 413 S.W.2d 274 (Mo. 1967) (specific performance granted of contract to devise farm in return for lifetime care, although transferor died shortly after contract was made).

[34] Stenehjem v. Kyn Jin Cho, 631 P.2d 482 (Alaska 1981) (substantive unfairness: purchaser denied specific performance of contract for sale of land because subordination provision did not provide vendors with adequate security). Often more than one of these factors is present. See the discussion of rare exceptions in §4.27 *supra*.

[35] Jamison Coal & Coke Co. v. Goltra, 143 F.2d 889 (8th Cir. 1944) ("A court of equity is not bound to shut its eyes to the character of champerty").

or forbearance that would be compelled is not against public policy, the use of compulsion to require that act or forbearance is against public policy. Examples are the rules under which a court will refuse to grant specific performance if to do so would impose on it a disproportionate burden,[36] will refuse to grant specific performance of a personal service contract,[37] and will refuse to grant specific performance if it would give the injured party a preference over other creditors with respect to the assets of an insolvent party in breach.[38]

Given the limited availability of specific performance and injunction, the rules governing the award of damages take on special importance. We turn to them next.

C.   ENFORCEMENT BY AWARD OF DAMAGES

§12.8.   Basic Principles of Damages.   The award of damages is the common form of relief for breach of contract. Virtually any breach gives the injured party a claim for damages for at least nominal damages, "to which," as a distinguished federal judge put it "for reasons we do not understand every victim of a breach of contract, unlike a tort victim, is entitled."[1] Thus, even if the breach caused no loss or if the amount of loss is not proved with sufficient certainty, the injured party can recover as damages a nominal sum, commonly six cents or a dollar, fixed without regard to loss. An award of nominal damages may, in the discretion of the court, carry with it an award of court costs. Costs are generally awarded if the injured party made a good faith effort to prove damages but failed, or if a significant right was involved, but not if maintenance of the action was frivolous or in bad faith. But unless a significant right is involved, a court will not reverse and remand a case for a new trial if only nominal damages could result.[2] In most successful actions for breach of contract, however, substantial damages are awarded.

The basic principle for the measurement of those damages is that of compensation based on the injured party's expectation. One is entitled to recover

Nominal damages

Right to expectation

---

[36] See note 12 *supra.*

[37] See note 18 *supra.*

[38] See the discussion of the effect of insolvency in §12.6 *supra.*

§12.8   [1] Chronister Oil Co. v. Unocal Ref. & Mktg., 34 F.3d 462, 466 (7th Cir. 1994) (Posner, C.J.).

There is an exception if the contract is not enforceable against the party in breach because of the statute of frauds. *See* the discussion of the meaning of *unenforceable* in §6.10 *supra.* Furthermore, in the case of a contract for transfer of an interest in land that is unenforceable under the statute, some kinds of reliance make the contract enforceable by specific performance, even though there is no claim for damages for breach. See the discussion of *Monarco v. Lo Greco* in §6.12 *supra.*

[2] Sessa v. Gigliotti, 345 A.2d 45 (Conn. 1973) ("we will not grant a new trial in order to entitle a plaintiff to recover merely nominal damages"). *See* Restatement Second §346 cmt. *b.*

an amount that will put one in as good a position as one would have been in had the contract been performed.[3] At least in principle, a party's expectation is measured by the actual worth that performance of the contract would have had to that party, not the worth that it might have had to some hypothetical reasonable person. Damages based on expectation should therefore take account of any circumstances peculiar to the situation of the injured party, including that party's own needs and opportunities, personal values, and even idiosyncrasies.[4] As we shall see shortly, however, there are important limitations on damages that often hold the injured party to a more objective valuation of its expectation. In addition, the basic principle is subject to the important qualification that the injured party cannot recover costs of litigation.[5]

Alternative of reliance

Lon Fuller pointed out that to allow recovery measured by expectation is to "'compensate' the plaintiff by giving him something he never had. This seems on the face of things a queer kind of compensation."[6] In *Flureau v. Thornhill*, an English case decided in 1776, the court chose instead to limit the injured party to recovery measured by reliance. That case held that recovery against a vendor who contracted to convey land, but was unable in good faith to make title, was limited to the expense incurred by the purchaser in reliance on the promise, including any down payment. The purchaser was not "entitled to any damages for the fancied goodness of the bargain, which he supposes he has lost."[7] Although the rule has persisted in England as to contracts for the sale of land and has found its way into the law of a number of states, the tendency even in these jurisdictions is to narrow its application.[8] In general, courts do not limit the injured party's recovery to reliance, but allow damages measured by expectation.[9]

Control of jury

This more generous measure of expectation is, however, severely qualified by rules that grew out of the attempts by judges during the nineteenth century to control the award of damages by juries. For roughly two centuries after the final

---

[3] See the discussion of the expectation interest in §12.1 *supra*.

[4] *See* Restatement Second §347 cmt. *b* (this requires, in principle, determination of the value "to the injured party himself and not . . . to some hypothetical reasonable person or on some market").

[5] Bunnett v. Smallwood, 793 P.2d 157 (Colo. 1990) ("non-breaching party to a release who successfully defends a lawsuit brought in violation of the agreement is not entitled to the award of attorney fees and costs absent contractual, statutory or rule authorization").

[6] Fuller & Perdue, The Reliance Interest in Contract Damages (pt. 1), 46 Yale L.J. 52, 52-53 (1936), criticized in Friedmann, The Performance Interest in Contract Damages, 111 L.Q. Rev. 628 (1995).

[7] 96 Eng. Rep. 635, 635 (C.P. 1776).

[8] Beard v. S/E Joint Venture, 581 A.2d 1275 (Md. 1990) (limiting *Flureau* in Maryland).

[9] Menzel v. List, 246 N.E.2d 742 (N.Y. 1969) (buyer of stolen Chagall entitled to $22,500 market price at time he had to surrender it to the true owner, not just to $4,000 he had paid, since "an injured buyer is not compensated when he recovers only so much as placed him in *statu quo ante*"). For more on reliance as a measure of damages, see §12.16 *infra*.

extension of assumpsit in *Slade's Case*[10] at the beginning of the seventeenth century, the common law courts paid little attention to this problem. At first they were intent on expanding their influence and, since trial by jury was a means of attracting litigants who might otherwise have gone elsewhere, they followed the popular course of leaving the assessment of damages in the hands of the jury. Gradually, however, the common law developed procedures for the control of the jury, including those by which the trial judge ruled on the admissibility of evidence, instructed the jurors on the law, and might set aside the jury's verdict after trial and grant a new trial before another jury. It was the last of these that was the most significant. Since the trial judge could order a new trial on the ground that the jury had disregarded the judge's advice by awarding excessive damages, the judge gained added assurance that judicial instructions would be given proper weight. From this it was only a short step to more direct control over the assessment of damages by specific instructions to the jury as to the amount to be allowed should there be recovery. Most important, the ruling of the trial judge on a motion for a new trial was a matter of law, which could be considered on appeal by a higher court. It was out of appeals from these rulings that the common law courts, toward the end of the eighteenth century, finally began to limit the body of principles that were to govern the award of damages for breach of contract.[11] To the general principle of recovery based on the promisee's expectation there emerged three important limitations that now serve as a basis not merely for instructing jurors, but for passing on the admissibility of evidence and for withdrawing some elements of damage from the jury's consideration altogether.

One of these limitations is that the injured party cannot recover damages for loss that could have been avoided if that party had taken appropriate steps to do so.[12] To take an obvious case, the builder who stubbornly continues work after the owner has repudiated the contract cannot recover for expenditures in doing work after the repudiation. A second limitation denies the injured party recovery for loss that the party in breach did not have reason to foresee as a probable result of the breach at the time the contract was made.[13] The classic, if apocryphal, case is that in which "a man going to be married to an heiress, his horse having cast a shoe on the journey, employed a blacksmith to replace it, who did the work so unskillfully that the horse was lamed, and, the rider not arriving in time, the lady married another" — the blacksmith would

Three limitations

---

[10] 76 Eng. Rep. 1074 (1602), decribed in the discussion of the supplanting of debt by *indebitatus assumpsit* in §1.6 *supra*.

[11] For a thorough discussion of this historical background, *see* Washington, Damages in Contract at Common Law (pts. 1, 2), 47 L.Q. Rev. 345 (1931), 48 L.Q. Rev. 90 (1932) (problem of formulating general principles of contract damages "can hardly be said to have received any substantial judicial attention" before nineteenth century).

[12] See §12.12 *infra*.

[13] See §12.14 *infra*.

not be liable for the loss of the marriage.[14] The third limitation is that the injured party cannot recover damages for loss beyond the amount proved with reasonable certainty.[15] The operation of this requirement of certainty within the framework of the procedure for new trial is said to have caused the body of rules for damages to develop more rapidly in contract than in tort.[16] The effect of these three limitations is to reduce the amount of damages recoverable under the general principle that the law protects the injured party's expectation.

No punitive damages

Furthermore, a court will not ordinarily award damages that are described as "punitive," intended to punish the party in breach, or sometimes as "exemplary," intended to make an example of that party.[17] No matter how reprehensible the breach, damages are generally limited to those required to compensate the injured party for lost expectation, for it is a fundamental tenet of the law of contract remedies that an injured party should not be put in a better position than had the contract been performed.[18] As Holmes said, "If a contract is broken the measure of damages generally is the same, whatever the cause of the breach."[19] The skeptical reader may well ask whether persons of judicial temperament are immune from the temptation to depart from a rule oblivious to blame,[20] and some exceptions to the rule will be suggested in the pages that

[14]Willes, J., in British Columbia etc. Saw Mill Co. v. Nettleship, 3 L.R. C.P. 499, 508 (1868). A similar illustration is one "where a Canon of the church, by reason of the nondelivery of a horse pursuant to agreement, was prevented from arriving at his residence in time to collect his tithes." Griffin v. Colver, 16 N.Y. 489, 493 (1858). This is evidently taken from the French writer Pothier. 1 R. Pothier, A Treatise on the Law of Obligations, or Contracts 91-92 (W. Evans trans. 1806).

[15]See §12.15 *infra*.

[16]*See* Washington, Damages in Contract at Common Law (pt. 2), 48 L.Q. Rev. 90, 90-93 (1932).

[17]A seminal case denying such damages is Addis v. Gramophone Co., [1909] A.C. 488 (H.L. 1909) (punitive damages denied for wrongful discharge of employee since "damages for breach of contract [are] in the nature of compensation, not punishment").

UCC 1-305(a) says that penal damages may be had only "as specifically provided" in the Code or by other rule of law. UCC 2-721 says that remedies for fraud "include all remedies available under this Article for non-fraudulent breach." Courts have disagreed as to the effect of this language on the availability of punitive damages for fraud.

[18]The New York Court of Appeals has gone so far as to take a minority position that an arbitrator has no power to award punitive damages despite the consent of the party liable. Garrity v. Lyle Stuart, Inc., 353 N.E.2d 793 (N.Y. 1976) (4-3: "The prohibition against an arbitrator awarding punitive damages is based on strong public policy indeed.").

The United States Supreme Court has held, as a matter of contract interpretation, that where the governing arbitration rules permitted an award of punitive damages, an express provision that "the laws of the State of New York" should govern did not incorporate *Garrity*. Mastrobuono v. Shearson Lehman Hutton, 514 U.S. 52 (1995) ("best way to harmonize the choice-of-law provision with the arbitration provision" is to read former as not including "special rules limiting the authority of arbitrators").

[19]Globe Ref. Co. v. Landa Cotton Oil Co., 190 U.S. 540, 544 (1903).

[20]*See* Lagerloef Trading Co. v. American Paper Prods. Co., 291 F. 947 (7th Cir. 1923) ("Repudiators of fair and solemn and binding promises are commercial sinners.").

follow.[21] Nevertheless, contract law is, in its essential design, a law of strict liability, and the accompanying system of remedies operates without regard to fault.

Punitive damages may, however, be awarded in tort actions,[22] and a number of courts have awarded them for a breach of contract that is in some respect tortious.[23] In an early application of this principle, punitive damages were assessed against public utilities and others engaged in furnishing a public service that were liable in tort for failing to discharge their obligations to the public.[24] Some courts impose punitive damages when the breach of contract is accompanied by an "independent" tort,[25] at least if the conduct is sufficiently outrageous to justify such damages.[26] Other courts impose them when the breach is accompanied by conduct that is "fraudulent," even in the absence of an independent tort that would justify punitive damages.[27] It was followed in Edens v. Goodyear Tire & Rubber Co., 858 F.2d 198 (4th Cir. 1988) ("false excuse for cancelling the lease" not enough). Courts have occasionally gone to considerable lengths to find the necessary tortious conduct. Where, for example, a customer had been unsuccessful after repeated efforts in having the dealer correct defects in a new car that were capable of correction, the Supreme Court of Indiana sustained an award of punitive damages up to the amount of $7,500 on the

Departures from rule

---

[21] See the discussions of the effect of willfulness in §12.13 *infra* and of reasonable certainty required in §12.15 *infra*, and the cases on willfulness cited in a footnote to the discussion of a promise of money or credit in §12.14 *infra*. Note also that the rule in Flureau v. Thornhill, *supra* note 7, is couched in terms of good faith.

[22] *See* Restatement (Second) of Torts §908 ("Punitive damages are damages, other than compensatory or nominal damages, awarded against a person to punish him for his outrageous conduct and to deter him and others like him from similar conduct in the future.").

[23] That evidence of the defendant's wealth may be admissible in such an action, *see* Cheney v. Palos Verdes Inv. Co., 665 P.2d 661 (Idaho 1983).

[24] Fort Smith & W. Ry. v. Ford, 126 P. 745 (Okl. 1912) (railroad's failure to transport purchaser of ticket to proper station was "not only a breach of contract and a violation of public duty by . . . a common carrier, but a willful, deliberate, conscious wrong"). Some courts have also granted punitive damages where the breach was of a fiduciary duty. Brown v. Coates, 253 F.2d 36 (D.C. Cir. 1958) (real estate broker who "holds himself out to public as worthy to be trusted for hire . . . warrants the imposition of punitive damages").

[25] Excel Handbag Co. v. Edison Bros. Stores, 630 F.2d 379 (5th Cir. 1980) (buyer's "conscious decision . . . to wrongfully take the goods and to withhold payment therefor for the purpose of forcing [seller] to relinquish some of its legal rights" was "an independent tort . . . committed willfully, wantonly, maliciously, or with conscious disregard for the legal rights of the injured party").

[26] Watkins v. Lundell, 169 F.3d 540 (8th Cir. 1999) (finding that party's "actions constituted 'willful and wanton disregard for the rights of [other party]' . . . satisfies the requirements for punitive damages under Iowa law").

[27] The landmark case, which laid down the "South Carolina rule," is Welborn v. Dixon, 49 S.E. 232 (S.C. 1904) (when "breach of contract is accompanied with a fraudulent act, the rule is well settled . . . that the defendant may be made to respond in punitive as well as in compensatory damages").

ground that "the jury could reasonably have found elements of fraud, malice, gross negligence or oppression mingled into the breach of warranty."[28] The trend both in judicial decisions and in legislation toward greater use of punitive damages for breach of contract has been most noticeable in consumer cases[29] and, in particular, with regard to claims against insurers for vexatious refusal to settle insurance claims.

Origins of bad faith breach

The first instances of this were "third party" cases in which a third party asserted a claim against the insured that greatly exceeded the policy limits, so that the insurer's self-interest in defending against the claim conflicted with the insured's interest in settling to avoid potential liability beyond those limits. Beginning in the late 1950s, courts, led by the Supreme Court of California, created a tort of "bad faith breach" as a means of imposing liability on insurers that refused to accept reasonable settlements in such cases.[30] Such a breach had all the consequences of a tort, notably the availability of punitive damages.[31] During the 1970s, the tort of "bad faith breach" was extended to "first party" cases, in which the wrong consisted in the insurer's unreasonable denial of its liability under the policy to the insured, and most,[32] though not all,[33] courts fell in line. Not until 1984, however, was there a serious suggestion that the new tort of bad faith breach might be extended beyond the insurance cases.

Rise of bad faith breach

The impetus for expansion came in 1984 with the opinion of the California Supreme Court in *Seaman's Direct Buying Service v. Standard Oil Company of California*, in which, remanding a case for erroneous jury instructions, the Supreme Court of California defined a new tort. The tort of bad faith breach of contract would occur where a party, "in addition to breaching the contract, . . . seeks to shield itself from liability by denying, in bad faith and without probable cause, that the contract exists." The court emphasized the "special relationship between insurer and insured, characterized by elements of public interest, adhesion, and fiduciary responsibility." But the court did not specify

---

[28] Hibschman Pontiac v. Batchelor, 362 N.E.2d 845, 848 (Ind. 1977) (ordering remittitur of $7,500 of $15,000 jury award under rule that damages must not "at first blush . . . appear to be outrageous and excessive").

[29] *See* Rice, Exemplary Damages in Private Consumer Actions, 55 Iowa L. Rev. 307 (1969).

[30] Seminal cases are Communale v. Traders & Gen. Ins. Co., 328 P.2d 198 (Cal. 1958) (insurer that fails to accept reasonable settlement offer from third party liable for entire judgment against insured though it exceeded policy limits); Crisci v. Security Ins. Co., 426 P.2d 173 (Cal. 1967) (recovery for mental distress allowed in addition to recovery in excess of policy limits).

[31] Other significant advantages to the plaintiff include the availability damages for emotional disturbance and of attorney's fees and a less demanding requirement of causation. The statute of limitations may, however, be shorter.

[32] Cases are reviewed in Best Place v. Penn Am. Ins. Co., 920 P.2d 334 (Haw. 1996) (breach of duty of good faith and fair dealing in first- and third-party insurance cases "gives rise to an independent tort cause of action," but punitive damages may not be awarded "unless the evidence reflects 'something more' than the conduct necessary to establish the tort").

[33] Federal Kemper Ins. Co. v. Hornback, 711 S.W.2d 844 (Ky. 1986) (declining to extend liability to "first party" cases).

what other relationships would be "deserving of similar legal treatment" and declined to pass on "the broad question" of when breach of a commercial contract "may give rise to an action in tort."[34] The case provoked much scholarly discussion and much litigation in intermediate appellate courts. Only Montana clearly followed California's lead.[35] Most courts declined to infringe on the freedom to keep or to break a contract traditionally afforded a party by the common law[36] and endorsed by the notion of efficient breach.[37]

In 1988, however, the California Supreme Court dealt a severe blow to the tort that it had spawned only a few years earlier, criticizing the "uncritical acceptance" by some California lower court decisions "of the insurance model into the employment context, without careful consideration of the fundamental policies underlying the development of tort and contract law in general or of significant differences between the insurer/insured and employer/employee relationships." The court concluded, "we are not convinced that a 'special relationship' analogous to that between insurer and insured should be deemed to exist in the usual employment relationship" and refused to apply *Seaman's* to an employer's discharge of an employee under an at-will employment.[38] Finally, in 1995, the California Supreme Court bowed to "the nearly unanimous criticism leveled at *Seaman's*" and overruled it "in favor of a general rule precluding tort recovery for noninsurance contract breach, at least in the absence of violation of 'an independent duty arising from principles of tort law.'" The court emphasized that nothing in its opinion "should be read as affecting the existing precedent governing enforcement of the implied covenant in insurance cases."[39] California thus rejoined the overwhelming majority of jurisdictions and restored the law in this area to the state in which it was had been a little over a decade before. California's rejection of the tort of bad faith breach, its own invention, makes it unlikely that the tort will now spread to other states.[40]

Fall of bad faith breach

---

[34]686 P.2d 1158, 1166, 1167 (1984).

[35]A leading Montana case that has inspired much litigation in that state is Nicholson v. United Pac. Ins. Co., 710 P.2d 1342 (Mont. 1985) (declining "to extend the breach of implied covenant to all contract breaches as a matter of law, as California has done," but holding that where party "acts arbitrarily, capriciously or unreasonably, that conduct exceeds the justifiable expectations" of other party and is bad faith breach).

[36]Bourgeous v. Horizon Healthcare Corp., 872 P.2d 852 (N.M. 1994) ("tort remedies are not available for breach of the implied covenant in an employment contract"). Rejection of the tort of bad faith breach does not, however, imply rejection of the implied duty of good faith imposed by the Code and by case law.

[37]Stop-N-Go of Madison v. UNO-VEN Co., 184 F.3d 672 (7th Cir. 1999) (quoting this section of this treatise but adding that "the breaching party must calculate the costs and benefits of the anticipated breach and . . . generally bears the risk of something going wrong"). On efficient breach, see §12.3 *supra*.

[38]Foley v. Interactive Data Corp., 765 P.2d 373, 393, 395 (Cal. 1988). *Foley* is described in the discussion of the public policy exception in §7.17 *supra*.

[39]Freeman & Mills Inc. v. Belcher Oil Co., 900 P.2d 669, 670-80 (Cal. 1995).

[40]See the discussion of the public policy exception in §7.17 *supra*.

Confining the concept of bad faith breach to the insurance cases, the Supreme court of Delaware explained in 1996:

> Market forces will not allow an employer consistently to treat valued employees in such a shabby manner as that presented here. An employer has an incentive to retain and motivate employees to achieve its mission . . . . Insurance is different. Once an insured files a claim, the insurer has a strong incentive to conserve its financial resources balanced against the effect on its reputation of a "hard-ball" approach.[41]

Rejection of the tort of bad faith breach does not, however, imply rejection of the implied duty of good faith imposed by the Code and by case law.

We now focus on the general measure of damages for breach of contract.

Significance of termination

§12.9. General Measure of Damages. How is the injured party's expectation to be measured in terms of money? What sum will put the injured party in as good a position as if the contract had been performed? The answer depends on whether the injured party has terminated the contract, refused to render any further return performance, and is claiming damages for total breach or has not terminated, stands ready to perform to render any remaining return performance, and is claiming damages for partial breach.

Damages for partial or total breach

If the injured party has not terminated the contract, damages need only compensate that party for the loss caused by the shortfall in the other party's performance. Thus if a builder has finished work on a building and been paid but has not done the work on time or in conformity with the contract, the owner is entitled to damages for partial breach.[1] And if the builder commits a breach while doing the work, the owner can continue performance and claim damages for partial breach, based on a calculation of the loss caused by the breach. But if the breach is material, the owner can choose instead to terminate, refuse to render any futher performance, and claim damages for total breach, based on a more complex calculation that takes account of savings as well as loss.[2] Claims for damages for partial and for total breach arise in myriad situations, some of which will be considered in later sections under such headings as avoidability, unforeseeability, and uncertainty. We examine in this section the general elements of a claim for damages, with emphasis on damages for total breach.

Claim for total breach: four elements

A claim of damages for total breach may have four elements because the breach may affect an injured party in four ways. First, the breach may cause that party loss in value. Second, it may cause that party other loss. Third, it may enable that party to avoid some cost. Fourth, it may enable that party to avoid

---

[41] E.I. DuPont de Nemours & Co. v. Pressman, 679 A.2d 436, 447 (Del. 1996).

§12.9 [1] As to the controversy over the calculation of such damages, *see* §12.13 *infra*.

[2] See the discussion of termination after some time in §8.18 *supra*.

some loss. The first two of these effects may also apply to an injured party's claim for partial breach. We take them up in order.

First, the breach may cause the injured party a loss by depriving that party, at least to some extent, of the performance expected under the contract. The difference between the value to the injured party of the performance that should have been received and the value to that party of what, if anything, actually was received will be referred to as the *loss in value*. If, for example, a buyer of goods has a claim for damages for partial breach because the goods were nonconforming, the *loss in value* equals the difference between the value to the buyer of the goods that were to have been delivered and the value of the goods that were actually delivered.[3] (In addition the Vienna Convention gives a buyer in this situation a right to price reduction, a remedy unknown to the common law, as an alternative to damages for partial breach.[4] If the buyer has a claim for damages for total breach because no goods were tendered or goods tendered were not accepted, the *loss in value* is simply the value to the injured party of the goods that were to have been tendered. In principle, since the court is attempting to measure the expectation of the injured party itself, the *loss in value* should be the loss to that party, not to some hypothetical reasonable person or on some market. In many situations the *loss in value* depends on the circumstances of the injured party or those of that party's enterprise.[5] If the injured party's expected advantage consists of the realization of profit, it may not be difficult to express that party's *loss in value* in terms of money. In other situations, such as those involving personal satisfaction, the task may be virtually impossible.[6] The expected advantage to an eccentric landowner of a bizarre sculpture that is to be executed on the land

1. Loss in value

---

[3] Under UCC 2-714(2) the general measure of damages for breach of warranty in the case of accepted goods is "the difference at the time and place of acceptance between the value of the goods accepted and the value they would have had if they had been as warranted."

[4] CISG 50 ("buyer may reduce the price in the same proportion as the value that the goods actually delivered had at the time of the delivery bears to the value that conforming goods would have had at that time"). This remedy, adapted from civil law systems, has its main impact when the market for the goods has fallen at the time of delivery or when the seller is not liable for the nonconformity. See the discussion of restitution in §9.9 *supra*.

[5] Wyatt v. School Dist. No. 104, 417 P.2d 221 (Mont. 1966) (school teacher entitled to damages for loss of rent-free living quarters as well as salary).

[6] Mieske v. Bartell Drug Co., 593 P.2d 1308 (Wash. 1979) (owners of movie film that was destroyed could recover for "actual or intrinsic value" to them though not for "unusual sentimental value" or "fanciful price" they might put on film "for their own special reasons").

For support for the principle stated in the text in connection with loss of publicity, *see* Restatement Second §344 ill. 3, based on Herbert Clayton & Jack Waller, Ltd. v. Oliver, [1930] A.C. 209 (H.L.) (actor who was to play leading role in musical comedy entitled to damages for loss of publicity), and Tolnay v. Criterion Film Prods., [1936] 2 All E.R. 1625 (K.B.) (authors, who were to write screenplay, entitled to damages for loss of publicity). *See also* Malik v. Bank of Credit & Commerce Intl., [1997] 3 All. E. R. 1 (H.L. 1997) (Lord Steyn: "there is no good reason why in the field of employment law recovery of financial loss in respect of damage to reputation caused by breach of contract is necessarily excluded").

may in principle be based on its value to the owner, rather than to others with more usual tastes, but in practice the owner will be hard put to establish this value.[7]

2. Other loss   Second, the breach may cause the injured party loss other than *loss in value*, and the party is also entitled to recovery for this, subject again to limitations such as that of unforeseeability. Such loss will be referred to as *other loss* and is sometimes said to give rise to "incidental" and "consequential" damages.[8] Incidental damages include additional costs incurred after the breach in a reasonable attempt to avoid loss, even if the attempt is unsuccessful.[9] If, for example, the injured party who has not received the promised performance pays a fee to a broker in a reasonable but unsuccessful attempt to obtain a substitute, that expense is recoverable.[10] Consequential damages include such items as injury to person or property caused by the breach. If, for example, services furnished to the injured party are defective and cause damage to that party's property, that loss is recoverable.[11] The terms used to characterize the loss should not, however, be critical, for the general principle is that all loss, however characterized, is recoverable.

Given the protection against excessive recovery afforded by the requirements of foreseeability and certainty, it is not easy to understand why American courts have been reluctant to recognize the principle. *See* Quinn v. Straus Broadcasting Group, 309 F. Supp. 1208 (S.D.N.Y. 1970) (announcer who was to be moderator of "talk show" not entitled to damages for loss of reputation); Amaducci v. Metropolitan Opera Assn., 304 N.Y.S.2d 322 (App. Div. 1969) (conductor could not recover damages to "good name, character and reputation").

[7] See the discussion of market price formulas in §12.12 *infra*.

[8] The term *consequential* is traditional (*see* §12.14 *infra*). The term *incidental* is a Code innovation. *See* Ohline Corp. v. Granite Mill, 849 P.2d 602 (Utah App. 1993) ("plain language of [UCC 2-715] includes overtime wages as 'any other reasonable expense incident to the delay or other breach' ").

Sellers have been denied recovery of consequential damages because UCC-O 2-710 makes no mention of them. Nobs Chem. v. Koppers Co., 616 F.2d 212 (5th Cir. 1980) (no recovery for seller's loss of discount from its supplier when buyer's breach reduced amount of seller's order).

UCC-R 2-710(2) rectifies this by giving the seller a right to consequential damages, but subsection (3) bars recovery of such damages from a consumer under a consumer contract. Consequential damages for a seller are also mentioned in UCC-R 2-706(1), 2-708, 2-709. Sellers are much less likely than buyers to have claims for consequential damages.

[9] Arcor v. Textron, 960 F.2d 710 (7th Cir. 1992) (buyer's costs in attempting to produce products for its customers after seller's breach resulted from reasonable efforts "to mitigate its damages by attempting to perform on its contracts").

[10] Fortin v. Ox-Bow Marina, 557 N.E.2d 1157 (Mass. 1990) (buyers of power boat could recover sales tax as incidental damages).

UCC 2-715(1) provides: "Incidental damages resulting from the seller's breach include expenses reasonably incurred in inspection, receipt, transportation and care and custody of goods rightfully rejected, any commercially reasonable charges, expenses or commissions in connection with effecting cover and any other reasonable expense incident to the delay or other breach."

[11] See UCC 2-715(2), under which the buyer can recover "consequential damages resulting from the seller's breach" including "injury to person or property proximately resulting from any breach of warranty."

What has been said in the two preceding paragraphs applies regardless of whether or not the injured party chooses to treat the breach as total. It applies to both claims for partial breach and claims for total breach. If the injured party does terminate the contract, however, the breach may have a third or a fourth effect because that party is relieved of the duty of rendering whatever remains of its own performance.[12] What is said in the two following paragraphs applies only to claims for total breach.

Effect of termination

Third, then, if the injured party terminates and claims damages for total breach, the breach may have a beneficial effect on that party by saving it the further expenditure that would otherwise have been incurred. This saving will be referred to as *cost avoided*. If, for example, the injured party is a builder that stops work after terminating a construction contract because of the owner's breach, the additional expenditure the builder saves is *cost avoided*.[13]

3. *Cost avoided*

Fourth, if the injured party terminates and claims damages for total breach, the breach may have a further beneficial effect on that party by allowing it to avoid some loss by salvaging and reallocating some or all of the resources that otherwise it would have had to devote to performance of the contract. The saving that results will be referred to as *loss avoided*. If, for example, the injured party is a builder that, after stopping work after terminating a construction contract, uses some of the leftover materials on another contract, the resulting saving to the builder is *loss avoided*. Or if the injured party is an employee who, after being wrongfully discharged by an employer, takes other employment, the net amount that has been earned or will be earned from that employment is *loss avoided*.[14] If the injured party has actually saved money, the saving is treated as *loss avoided* even though another person might not have been able to effect that saving. If, for example, the injured party happens to make especially favorable arrangements to dispose of leftover materials, and thereby avoids more loss than another person might have succeeded in

4. *Loss avoided*

---

[12]*See* Southern Colo. MRI v. Med-Alliance, 166 F.3d 1094 (10th Cir. 1999) (general rule is that "benefit to the plaintiff as a result of a breach reduces the plaintiff's damages accordingly," but proper not to subtract post-breach profits from damages based on market price). As to the injured party's power of termination for breach, see §8.18 *supra*. The injured party will have no saving if that party has fully performed or if, as is usually the case for the intended beneficiary of a gift promise, the injured party is not required to do anything.

[13]Allen, Heaton & McDonald v. Castle Farm Amusement Co., 86 N.W.2d 782 (Ohio 1949) (on defendant's repudiation after five months of contract for plaintiff to provide advertising for one year, "damages would include any compensation plaintiff would have received if the contract had been performed, less the value to plaintiff of its being relieved from performance during those seven months").

[14]Sutherland v. Wyer, 67 Me. 64 (1877) (earnings of actor after discharge subtracted).

Whether this principle applies to payments received by the injured party from "collateral sources," such as unemployment benefits in the case of a discharged employee, is a difficult question. The argument that payments should not be subtracted is less compelling here than in the case of a tort.

doing, the *loss avoided* will be based on the actual favorable arrangements.[15] Consistent with this, if, after breach, an event occurs that would have discharged the party in breach on grounds of impracticability of performance or frustration of purpose, damages are limited to the loss sustained prior to that event.[16] The injured party's recovery is not, however, affected by the saving that results from some event unrelated to not having to perform.[17]

General measure   The general measure of damages for total breach can therefore be expressed in terms of these four effects, two of which (*loss in value* and *other loss*) are adverse to the injured party and therefore increase damages, and two of which (*cost avoided* and *loss avoided*) are beneficial to the injured party and therefore decrease that party's damages.[18] Formula (A) therefore reads:

$$(\text{A}) \qquad \textit{general measure} = \textit{loss in value} + \textit{other loss}$$
$$- \textit{cost avoided} - \textit{loss avoided}$$

In the case of claim for damages for partial breach, only the first two terms apply. Under most agreements, one party, which will be referred to as the "supplier," is to furnish something characteristic of the type of contract, such as goods, land, or services, for which the other party, which will be referred to as the "recipient," is to pay a price in money. Typical pairs of suppliers and recipients include the seller and the buyer under a contract for the sale of goods, the vendor and the purchaser under a contract for the sale of land, the employee and the employer under an employment contract, and the builder and the owner under a construction contract. It is useful to distinguish cases in which the supplier is the injured party and asserts a claim for damages from those in which it is the recipient that is the injured party and asserts a claim for damages.

We begin with cases in which the supplier is the injured party.

Loss in value not a problem   **§12.10. Supplier's Damages.** Suppose that the recipient has broken the contract and the supplier has a claim for damages for total breach. Difficulty rarely arises in determining the *loss in value* to the supplier, for this is usually just

---

[15] Coast Trading Co. v. Cudahy Co., *supra* note 9 (where resale not commercially reasonable under UCC 2-706(1), seller limited to actual loss, if less than damages based on market price, under UCC 2-708(1)). See the discussions of loss actually avoided in §12.10 *infra* and in §12.11 *infra*.

[16] Model Vending v. Stanisci, 180 A.2d 393 (N.J. Super. 1962) (where fire after breach made rest of performance impossible, damages were limited to loss of profits before fire).

[17] Clydebank Engrg. & Shipbldg. Co. v. Yzquierdo y Castaneda, [1905] A.C. 6 (H.L. 1904) (contention that if warships had been delivered to Spanish government on time they would have been sunk with rest of Spanish fleet was "utterly absurd"), discussed in California & Hawaiian Sugar Co. v. Sun Ship, 794 F.2d 1433 (9th Cir. 1986).

[18] BVT Lebanon Shopping Center v. Wal-Mart Stores, 48 S.W.3d 132 (Tenn. 2001) (quoting Restatement Second § 347).

the amount of money not received from the recipient because of the breach.[1] If the supplier has fully performed, it simply recovers this sum, with interest to take account of late payment.[2] If the supplier has not fully performed, however, trouble comes in determining *cost avoided* and *loss avoided*. This is true, for example, of claims for damages by sellers of goods or land against buyers, by employees against employers, and by builders against owners. Contracts to build buildings and to manufacture goods are illustrative.

Suppose that a builder contracts to build a building on an owner's land for $100,000, not all of which has been paid by the owner. If the recipient (the owner) is the party in breach, and the supplier (the builder) as the injured party has used the breach as an excuse for terminating the contract, the *loss in value* to the builder will be simply that part of the $100,000 that remains unpaid, with a discount or interest to take account of early or late payment. The builder's *cost avoided* and *loss avoided*, however, are not so simply measured.

Example of building contract

If, for example, the owner repudiates before the builder has done anything by way of preparation or performance, the builder's *cost avoided* is what is saved by not having to build the building. If no part of the price has been paid, and the builder can prove that it would have cost $90,000 to build the building, the difference between the builder's *loss in value* ($100,000) and *cost avoided* ($90,000) is $10,000. Assuming for the moment that there is no *loss avoided* and no *other loss*, it is this sum to which the builder is entitled as damages. The same result follows in the case of a manufacturer that has contracted to manufacture and sell goods, if the buyer repudiates in similar circumstances. Now suppose, however, that before the owner repudiates, the builder has already spent $35,000, of which the builder later saves $5,000 by using on other jobs materials that are left over, and that the builder can prove that it would have cost $55,000 to finish the work. The difference between the builder's *loss in value* ($100,000) and the builder's *cost avoided* ($55,000) and *loss avoided* ($5,000) is $40,000. Assuming again that there is no other *loss avoided*, it is this

Cost avoided

---

§12.10   [1] There are bargains under which the supplier expects not only the payment of money, but the enhancement of experience, reputation, or good will, as in the case of a contract between the fledgling portrait painter and a distinguished subject. Recovery for such *loss in value*, although sound in principle, is generally precluded in practice by the requirement of certainty. See the discussion of loss in value in §12.9 *supra*.

Courts have generally refused to allow a wrongfully discharged lawyer to recover damages under the ordinary contract rule discussed here, which (assuming lost volume) would give the full contract price less expenses saved. It is reasoned that this rule would have a chilling effect on the client's power to discharge the lawyer. See footnote to the discussion of the contract price as a limit in §12.20 *infra*.

[2] Recovery of the price is often indiscriminately referred to as the recovery of "damages," although it amounts to specific relief, since "we speak of recovering damages even in the case of a liquidated debt. Obviously damages are not what is really recovered." Pound, Individual Interests of Substance — Promised Advantages, 59 Harv. L. Rev. 1, 3 (1945). Interest, on the other hand, is recovered in this instance as damages. *See* Restatement Second §354.

sum to which the builder is entitled as damages.[3] The same result follows in the case of a manufacturer that has contracted to manufacture and sell goods, if the buyer repudiates in similar circumstances.[4]

Alternative method

In practice, builders and manufacturers will often use an alternative method for calculating *cost avoided*. They will determine from their records what they have already spent (their *cost of reliance* on the contract), and will subtract this from their estimated *cost of complete performance*, commonly based on calculations made when they originally set the price — an estimate that is likely to be optimistic and favor the claimant.[5] In the example just given, this would mean subtracting $35,000 from an estimated $90,000, giving a *cost avoided* of $55,000. In other words:

$$cost\ avoided = cost\ of\ complete\ performance - cost\ of\ reliance$$

Substituting the right-hand side of this equation for *cost avoided* in Formula (A) for the general measure of damages, and remembering that the difference between *loss in value* and *cost of complete performance* is the builder's or manufacturer's expected profit, we get Formula (B) as an alternative to the general measure in Formula (A):

(B)   *supplier's damages = cost of reliance − loss avoided*

                                  + profit + other loss

Loss avoided

In the example given, the builder's or manufacturer's damages would be $35,000 (*cost of reliance*) less $5,000 (*loss avoided*) plus $10,000 (*profit*), or $40,000, assuming again that there is no other *loss avoided* and no *other loss*.[6] This is necessarily the same result reached under the other formula.[7]

---

[3]Blaine Econ. Dev. Auth. v. Royal Elec. Co., 520 N.W.2d 473 (Minn. App. 1994) (where builder has received no payments under construction contract, "Contract Price − Costs of Completion = Damages").

[4]Vitex Mfg. Corp v. Caribtex Corp., 377 F.2d 795 (3d Cir. 1967) (contract to process cloth).

[5]Peter Kiewit Sons' Co. v. Summit Constr. Co., 422 F.2d 242 (8th Cir. 1969) ("a new estimate of the cost of completion will generally be more reliable than the contractor's optimistic initial estimate").

[6]Warner v. McLay, 103 A. 113 (Conn. 1918) (builder can recover "his expenditures for work and labor supplied towards the completion of the contract" plus "the profit . . . if it had been fulfilled").

[7]Damages in such cases have occasionally been calculated in a third way. First, the fraction of the work done is determined by subtracting the *loss avoided* ($5,000) from the *cost of reliance* ($35,000) and dividing this difference by the *cost of complete performance* ($90,000). The contract price ($100,000) is then multiplied by this fraction (1/3). Second, the profit ($10,000) is multiplied by the fraction of the work not done (2/3). These two products are then added (1/3 × $100,000 + 2/3 × $10,000) to give the damages in the same amount as reached by the other two ways ($40,000). *See* Kehoe v. Rutherford, 27 A. 912 (N.J. Sup. 1893) (injured party can recover "for the work done, only such a proportion of the contract price as the fair cost of that work bore to the fair cost of the whole work required, and, in respect of the work not done, only such profit, if any, as he might have made by doing it").

In the example given, it was assumed that the builder or manufacturer saved $5,000 by using materials on other jobs. Is there always such a saving if, after the recipient's breach, the supplier uses materials and other resources that are left over to perform a new contract similar to the broken one? Is what is gained from the new contract always to be considered as something realized by the supplier's reallocation of resources from the first contract and therefore treated as *loss avoided*? A simple example is that of the employee under a contract of full-time employment, who takes another job after being wrongfully discharged. Since the employee could not have held both jobs, the amount that the employee has earned or will earn from the second job, with account being taken of any expenses required to realize that amount, is considered as if it were realized by the employee's reallocation of resources from the first contract and therefore is properly treated as *loss avoided*. The earnings on the second contract are subtracted in calculating damages on the first. Even if the second job is of a different kind than the first, it is nevertheless considered a substitute for the first.[8]

A similar result follows if the injured party is a seller that has contracted to **Resale by seller** sell a unique item and that, on the buyer's breach, resells it to a second buyer. The seller's proceeds on the second sale are properly treated as *loss avoided*, since the second sale is a substitute for the first, and is subtracted in calculating damages.[9] This result can be reached by subtracting the resale price from the contract price.[10] In more general terms:

(C) *supplier's damages = contract price − redisposition price + other loss*

In order for a sale to qualify as a resale for this purpose, it must be "made in good faith and in a commercially reasonable manner," and if it is it makes no difference that hindsight later shows that the seller might have gotten a better price.[11] A seller that resells promptly on the buyer's anticipatory repudiation is protected against a later market rise. The seller can recover actual loss in full, based on the difference between the contract price and his resale price, and is not limited to the difference between the contract price and the price on

---

[8] Erler v. Five Points Motors, 57 Cal. Rptr. 516 (Ct. App. 1967) (error to exclude evidence of employee's earnings from other automobile dealers after his discharge). Note that this result does not depend on the second job's being of the same type as the first, in contrast to the rule on avoidability. See the discussion of market price formulas in §12.12 *infra*.

[9] Famous Knitwear Corp. v. Drug Fair, 493 F.2d 251 (4th Cir. 1974) (case remanded because no findings of fact on whether reseller was "lost volume seller").

[10] UCC 2-706(1) (seller may recover difference between "contract price" and "resale price"). UCC 2-706(2) requires that the resale "be reasonably identified as referring to the broken contract." For the comparable provision of the Vienna Convention, *see* CISG 75.

[11] UCC 2-706. According to Comment 3, "Evidence of market or current prices . . . is relevant only on the question of whether the seller acted in a commercially reasonable manner in making the resale."

the risen market at the time for performance.[12] Resale is not mandatory, and if a substitute transaction does not qualify as a resale, the seller's damages are calculated without regard to that transaction.[13] The extent to which the Code rule on resale will be applied by analogy to non-Code cases is an open question.

Loss actually avoided

To the extent that a supplier has actually avoided loss by arranging a substitute transaction, the damages are reduced. This should be so even though the supplier has succeeded by an unusually favorable transaction in avoiding more loss than might reasonably have been expected.[14] Whether to subtract loss that the supplier might reasonably have been expected to avoid, but did not in fact avoid, is a different question, dealt with in a later section.[15]

Lost volume

The problem of the supplier's damages becomes more complex, however, if it is assumed that the supplier's own supply exceeds demand. Reconsider the example, given earlier, in which the owner repudiates the contract before the builder has done anything by way of preparation or performance. Suppose that the builder promptly makes a contract with another owner to build an identical building for $100,000, at a profit of $8,000. Is the second contract a substitute for the first, so that the $8,000 profit on the second should be treated as *loss avoided* and subtracted from the $10,000 damages to which the builder would otherwise be entitled, giving the builder only $2,000?[16] The builder will claim that had the first contract not been broken, the builder could and would have made both contracts — that the builder has "lost volume" as a result of the breach.[17] The same claim may be made by a manufacturer in similar circumstances, when manufacture of the goods is not begun, or is at least not completed, as a result of a breach.[18] And it may be made by a seller of

---

[12]UCC 2-706(1).

[13]UCC-R 2-706(7), a new provision parallel to that for buyers in UCC 2-712(3), makes this clear by providing that failure to resell cover does not bar seller "from any other remedy." This will usually mean that the seller's damages will be determined by the market price formula of UCC 2-708(1).

[14]Coast Trading Co. v. Cudahy Co., 592 1074 (9th Cir. 1979) (seller "should not be allowed to obtain a greater amount in Section 2-708 damages than the seller actually lost"). As to whether a similar rule applies to the buyer, see the discussion of loss actually avoided in §12.11 *infra*.

[15]See §12.12 *infra*.

[16]Any expenses incurred by the builder in obtaining the second contract would, in that case, be recoverable as incidental damages under *other loss*, if they were not already taken into account in the calculation of profit.

[17]It has been suggested that three conditions must be met for a showing of lost volume. First, at the time of the breach, the injured party "must have had the intention of maximizing his . . . volume." Second, the injured party must have had the "physical capacity to perform both his original contract . . . and another, similar contract with the first customer who comes along after . . . breach." Third, the injured party must not have recaptured (or been expected to recapture) "any lost volume by some adjustment in his manner of doing business which would have increased the demand for his product." Harris, A General Theory for Measuring Seller's Damages for Total Breach of Contract, 60 Mich. L. Rev. 577, 600-01 (1962).

[18]If the seller is to manufacture the goods to be sold and, after discontinuing their manufacture because of the breach, makes another contract to manufacture goods for a different buyer, the

goods that has bought the goods for resale rather than manufactured them. If the seller does not sell from stock on hand, and has not yet ordered the goods or cancels the order, the seller will claim to have lost volume as a result of the breach and seek recovery of the lost profit on the additional sale that the seller could and would have made but for the breach. Even the manufacturer that has completed the goods and disposed of them to another buyer, or the seller that has purchased the goods for resale from stock and disposed of them to another buyer, may claim to have lost volume as a result of the breach so that damages will not be reduced by what was realized on the second sale. Many courts have allowed the lost-volume supplier to recover damages for breach of the first contract with no reduction as a result of the second contract.[19]

If, in the example given, the builder can show or the court will assume that the builder could and would have expanded its business to take both contracts and make a combined profit of $18,000, but that as a result of the breach the builder has only one contract (the second one), on which the profit will be $8,000, the builder will be allowed to recover $10,000 damages on the first contract, with no subtraction for profit made on the second contract.[20] On similar reasoning, the seller that has bought for resale and can show the loss of a sale because of the buyer's breach will be allowed to recover the profit that would have been made on that sale, undiminished by whatever profit may have been made on a second contract.[21]

Examples of lost volume

---

situation is analogous to that of the builder. What the seller has reallocated is the capacity to manufacture goods, not the goods themselves. As to the choice between continuing and discontinuing manufacture on breach, see the discussion of completion of manufacture in §12.12 *infra*.

[19] As to the possibility that a seller might be limited to lost profits when it claimed greater damages based on fallen market price, see the discussion of the possibility of overcompensation in §12.12 *infra*.

[20] M & R Contractors & Builders v. Michael, 138 A.2d 350 (Md. 1958) ("building contractor normally has more than one project in progress at the same time").

So compelling is the assumption that a building contractor or subcontractor loses volume, that the assumption is often made even though the second contract is for the same work as the first contract. Grinnell Co. v. Voorhees, 1 F.2d 693 (3d Cir. 1924) (on breach by owner, contractor made contract with owner's successor to finish work).

It is sometimes argued that the contractor or subcontractor is entitled to recover with no deduction for the net profit on the second contract because a new risk is assumed on the second contract. But this encompasses too much, since it applies with equal force to any case where there is no lost volume.

[21] In original Article 2, UCC 2-708(2) appeared at first blush to be an exception only to UCC 2-708(1). *See* UCC-O 2-708(2) (if "measure of damages provided in subsection (1) is inadequate"). Revised Article 2 makes clear that UCC 2-708(2) is also an exception to the resale price formula of UCC 2-706(1). *See* UCC-R 2-708(2) (if "measure of damages provided in subsection (1) or in Section 2-706 is inadequate").

Whether the seller has lost volume does not depend on whether the goods are standard priced, although this is often the case. UCC-O 2-708(2) says at the end that the buyer is to be given "due credit for . . . proceeds of resale," which would appear to defeat the purpose of the provision. These words were held inapplicable to a retailer of a boat in Neri v. Retail Marine Corp., 285 N.E.2d 311 (N.Y. 1972). The court in *Neri* accepted the argument, based on legislative history,

Economics of lost volume

Cogent arguments can be mounted, however, to show that some suppliers that might at first appear to have lost volume have not in fact done so. For example, it has been argued that suppliers generally operate their enterprises at optimum volume and will not undertake additional contracts once they have attained this volume. If for this reason the supplier would not have made the second contract had there been no breach, the second contract should be regarded as a substitute for the first, and the profit on the second should be regarded as *loss avoided* and subtracted in the calculation of damages.[22] Some courts have facilitated this argument by placing on the injured party the burden of showing lost volume.[23]

Treatment of overhead

In calculating a price that will return a satisfactory net profit, a supplier allocates to each transaction over the course of a year a portion of the yearly expenses for such items as heat, electricity, insurance premiums, and property taxes. How should such expenses, commonly described as "overhead," be treated in calculating the supplier's damages? Sometimes the expenses described as overhead are variable costs, such as those for heat or electricity that can be turned off when performance is stopped after breach. Plainly these should be included in *cost avoided* in Formula (A), since they can be avoided after breach. Sometimes, however, the expenses described as overhead are fixed costs, such as insurance premiums or property taxes, that are unaffected when performance is stopped after breach. Equally plainly these should be ignored (i.e., left out) in the calculation of *cost avoided,* since they cannot be avoided after breach and should not decrease the supplier's damages.[24] In the case of a lost-volume supplier, the matter ends there, since a later contract has no effect on damages. In the case of a supplier that does not lose volume by making a second contract, such fixed costs should be ignored, not only in the calculation of *cost avoided* on the first contract, but also in the calculation of the *loss avoided* as a result of the second contract.[25]

Next we consider the measurement of the recipient's damages.

---

that these words were intended to apply only to proceeds of a manufacturer's sale of materials for salvage when manufacture was not completed because of the breach, as described in the discussion of stopping performance in §12.12 *infra*. In that situation, deduction of such proceeds is simply part of the calculation of the manufacturer's lost profit. The words are deleted in UCC-R 2-708(2).

[22] R.E. Davis Chem. Corp. v. Diasonics, 924 F.2d 709 (7th Cir. 1991) ("ample evidence to establish . . . status as lost volume seller"), following R.E. Davis Chem. Corp. v. Diasonics, 826 F.2d 678 (7th Cir. 1987) ("relevant questions include, not only whether the seller [a manufacturer] could have produced the breached units in addition to its actual volume, but also whether it would have been profitable for the seller to produce both units").

[23] Famous Knitwear Corp. v. Drug Fair, *supra* note 9.

[24] Sure-Trip v. Westinghouse Engrg., 47 F.3d 526 (2d Cir. 1995) (fixed overhead costs "are not properly deducted in calculating plaintiff's lost profits," but "variable expenses, defined as those additional costs necessarily incurred in performing the contract, must be deducted").

[25] If Formula (B) is used, fixed costs should be ignored not only in the calculation of *loss avoided*, but also in the calculation of *cost of reliance* and of *profit*.

§**12.11.   Recipient's Damages.** Suppose now that the supplier has broken the contract and the recipient has a claim for damages for total breach. Difficulty rarely arises in determining the *cost avoided* by the recipient, for this is usually just the amount of money, if any, that the recipient is excused from paying the supplier because of the breach. Trouble comes with *loss in value* and with *loss avoided*. This is true, for example, of claims for damages by buyers of goods or land against sellers, by employers against employees, and by owners against builders. Contracts to build buildings are illustrative.

Cost avoided **not a problem**

Suppose that a builder contracts to build a building on an owner's land for $100,000, not all of which has been paid by the owner.[1] If the supplier (the builder) is the party in breach, and the recipient (the owner) as the injured party has used the breach as an excuse for not paying the balance of the price, the *cost avoided* by the recipient will be simply that part of the $100,000 that remains unpaid. However, the recipient's *loss in value* and *loss avoided* are not so easily measured.

Example of construction contract

Whether the builder's breach prevents the completion of the building or results in a defective building, the loss in value to the owner will depend on the purpose to which the owner intended to put the building.[2] Often the purpose will have been to put it to profitable use in some collateral transaction, and, if that is so, the owner is entitled to recovery based on loss of profits from that transaction caused by the breach. Suppose that the building cannot be used by the owner.[3] If the owner is a developer who intended to sell the land with the building on it but now cannot, the *loss in value* will be based on the loss in income from that sale, account being taken of the costs of the sale. If the recipient is an investor that intended to rent the building but now cannot, the *loss in value* will be based on the loss in rental income, account being taken of the costs of renting. If the recipient is a manufacturer that intended to use the building as an addition to a factory but now cannot, the *loss in value* will be based on loss of income from manufacturing, account being taken of the costs of manufacture.[4] If, however, the recipient is a homeowner who intended to live in the building but now cannot, the loss in value will be much harder to measure in money. Problems similar to these arise in the case of any supplier who breaks a contract in like circumstances. Thus, if a seller repudiates a contract to deliver goods to a buyer for resale, which is thereby prevented from reselling them at

Loss in value

---

§**12.11**   [1] See the example of a construction contract in §8.15 *supra*.

[2] In the case of a defective building, there is also the possibility of *other loss* in the form of injury to person or property as a result of the defect.

[3] If the building is used, but less profitably, damages will be based on the loss in profits due to the diminished profitability.

[4] See the discussion of the limitations of unforeseeability and uncertainty in §§12.14 & 12.15 *infra*.

a profit, the buyer's *loss in value* is the profit that would have been made on that resale, account being taken of the costs of resale.[5]

Avoidance of *loss in value*

Often, however, the recipient can avoid part of this *loss in value*. The owner in the example given might do this by having another builder complete the building or correct the defect. The owner is then entitled to damages based on the difference, if any, between the value of the building as originally contracted for (*loss in value*) and that of the building as completed or corrected (*loss avoided*), account being taken of any loss due to delay, along with that due to any remaining deficiencies in the structure. The owner can also recover any additional amount required by the second contract beyond what the owner would have had to pay under the first as incidental damages included in *other loss*.[6]

Cover by buyer

If the recipient is a buyer that has not received goods to be delivered under a contract of sale, the buyer's comparable course of action is to "cover." As the Uniform Commercial Code explains in introducing this term, the buyer may "'cover' by making in good faith and without unreasonable delay any reasonable purchase of or contract to purchase goods in substitution for those due from the seller."[7] If the goods acquired by the buyer in the substitute or cover transaction have the same value as those due under the original contract, the buyer's damages are simply the "difference between the cost of cover and the contract price together with any incidental or consequential damages . . . but less expenses saved in consequence of the seller's breach."[8] In more general terms:

(D)   *recipient's damages = replacement price − contract price + other loss*

Courts have not always been willing to extend by analogy the Code's concept of damages based on a substitute transaction to contracts that do not involve a sale of goods.[9]

---

[5] Murarka v. Bachrack Bros., 215 F.2d 547 (2d Cir. 1954) (buyer for resale entitled to lost profits on resale of surplus parachutes).

[6] S & D Mech. Contractors v. Enting Water Conditioning Sys., 593 N.E.2d 354 (Ohio App. 1991) (contractor entitled to recover overhead expense when it "had to divert its own time and resources from other projects to correct the deficiencies created by [subcontractor's] breach").

[7] UCC 2-712(1). The word *cover* is an innovation of the Code. In some situations where the buyer has received defective goods, it may avoid loss by having the defects remedied. The buyer's damages are then based on the cost to remedy them. Revised Article 2 makes clear that this section applies to repudiaton as well as to nonperformance. UCC-R 2-712(1).

[8] UCC 2-712(2). Under the terminology used here, this difference (the additional amount spent to cover) would also be characterized as "incidental damages," included in *other loss*. For the comparable provision of the Vienna Convention, *see* CISG 75.

[9] *But see* Hughes Communications Galaxy v. United States, 271 F.3d 1060 (Fed. Cir. 2001) ("courts often award an analogous remedy for breach of service contracts," citing this section of this treatise); Handicapped Children's Educ. Bd. v. Lukaszewski, 332 N.W.2d 774 (Wis. 1983) (employer's damages based on cost of "replacement").

In order for a recipient's damages to be calculated in this manner, the replacement transaction must be an appropriate one. According to the Code commentary, the test "is whether at the time and place the buyer acted in good faith and in a reasonable manner, and it is immaterial that hindsight may later prove that the method of cover used was not the cheapest or most effective." Cover may consist of "goods not identical with those involved but commercially usable as reasonable substitutes under the circumstances."[10] What is an appropriate substitute will depend in part on what substitutes are available, and the mere fact that a substitute is of superior or inferior quality does not of itself preclude its being cover; any measurable difference in quality can be compensated for by a money allowance.[11] It has even been held that goods manufactured by the buyer itself may be treated as cover.[12] Where a buyer regularly engages in many purchases of a similar kind, the identification of particular purchases as cover may pose a difficult question of fact.[13] Cover is not mandatory, and if a substitute transaction does not qualify as cover, the buyer's damages are calculated without regard to that transaction.[14] A buyer that covers on the seller's anticipatory repudiation is protected against a later market slump. The buyer can recover actual loss in full, based on the difference between the higher cover price and the contract price, and is not limited to the difference between the price on the fallen market at the time for performance and the contract price.[15] The extent to which this Code rule will be applied by analogy to non-Code cases is an open question.

To the extent that a recipient has actually avoided loss by arranging a substitute transaction, damages are reduced. This should be so even though the recipient has succeeded by an unusually favorable substitute transaction in avoiding more loss than might reasonably have been expected.[16] Whether to

> **What is cover?**

> **Loss actually avoided**

---

[10]UCC 2-712 cmt. 2. Hughes Communications Galaxy v. United States, *supra* note 9 (as "victim of the breach, [commercial satellite owner] was within its rights to obtain commercially reasonable substitute launch services even if the substitute services were not identical").

[11]Handicapped Children's Educ. Bd. v. Lukaszewski, *supra* note 9 (only replacement teacher available, though having "less of an educational background, . . . had more teaching experience," and any "additional value" to employer "was imposed on it").

[12]Dura-Wood Treating Co. v. Century Forest Indus., 675 F.2d 745 (5th Cir. 1982) ("buyer should be able to cover by manufacturing goods in substitution for those due from the seller").

[13]That the question is one of fact, *see* Commonwealth Edison Co. v. Allied Chem. Nuclear Prods., 684 F. Supp. 1434 (N.D. Ill. 1988) (whether buyer's use of purchased uranium under the pre-existing contracts was cover is a "question of fact.").

[14]UCC 2-712(3) provides that failure to effect cover does not bar buyer "from any other remedy." This will usually mean that the buyer's damages will be determined by the market price formula of UCC 2-713. That failure to cover may bar recovery of consequential damages, see the discussion of making substitute arrangements in §12.12 *infra*.

[15]UCC 2-712(2). The buyer is not, however, protected if late in making the replacement purchase or if goods of a different sort are purchased as a replacement. See note 11 *supra*.

[16]Illinois Cent. R.R. v. Crail, 281 U.S. 57 (1930) (Stone, J.: it is a "basic principle underlying common law remedies that they shall afford only compensation for the injury suffered"). *See*

Lost volume

subtract loss that the recipient might reasonably have been expected to avoid, but did not in fact avoid, is a different question, dealt with in the next section of this treatise.[17]

Problems of lost volume arise in connection with the recipient's measure of damages, much as they do in connection with the supplier's measure of damages.[18] If a recipient is a buyer of goods for resale whose volume is limited by supply because it is exceeded by demand, the recipient may claim to have lost volume if the supplier does not deliver what the contract requires. If, after the breach, the buyer purchases another lot of goods that the buyer would have purchased and been able to dispose of at a profit had there been no breach, the buyer may assert that the second lot is not a substitute for the first. Damages would then be based on *loss in value* as measured by lost profit on resale, without deducting the profit on the second lot as *loss avoided*. The Code language, which limits "cover" to the purchase of "goods *in substitution for* those due from the seller," seems to permit this result under contracts for the sale of goods.[19] A similar result should follow in other transactions in which the recipient proves loss of volume.[20]

We now examine the limitations that courts have placed on the recovery of damages, beginning with that of avoidability.

General rule

§12.12. Avoidability as a Limitation. A court ordinarily will not compensate an injured party for loss that that party could have avoided by making efforts appropriate, in the eyes of the court, to the circumstances. A quaint English case from over three centuries ago makes this point. The plaintiff had contracted to carry goods to Ipswich and to deliver them to a place to be appointed by the defendant. When the plaintiff arrived in Ipswich, however, "the defendant delayed by the space of six hours the appointment of the place; insomuch that his horses being so hot . . . and standing in *aperto aere*, they

---

Restatement Second §347 cmt. *e*. The Code gives the buyer the right to "'cover' and have damages" based on cover price or "recover damages" based on market price. UCC-O 2-711(1)(a); UCC 2-711 (2)(d). UCC 2-713 cmt. 5 makes clear that the buyer has a right to recover damages based on market price "only when and to the extent that the buyer has not covered." Though UCC 2-712 cmt. 3 says that the buyer "is always free to choose" between cover and damages based on market price, this appears to be said in the context of whether the buyer can recover damages based on market price after failing to cover, not of whether the buyer can recover such damages after covering.

As to whether a similar rule applies to the seller, see the discussion of loss actually avoided in §12.10 *supra*. As to the buyer that buys substitute goods that are not considered to be cover because they are bought too late, see the discussion of the time for a substitute in §12.12 *infra*.

[17] See §12.12 *infra*.

[18] See the discussion of lost volume in §12.10 *supra*.

[19] UCC 2-712(1). (When the seller is the injured party, however, there is no comparable limitation on the meaning of *resale*. See UCC 2-706, 2-708.)

[20] The problems of showing lost volume are similar to those raised when the supplier is the injured party. See §12.10 *supra*.

died soon after." The plaintiff sued for damages, but the court denied recovery on the ground that "it was the plaintiff's folly to let the horses stand," for he "might have taken his horses out of the cart or laid down the [goods] any where in Ipswich."[1] The economic justification of such a rule is plain, for it encourages the injured party to act so as to minimize the wasteful results of breach.[2] Looked at in another way, the rule allows the obligor to call upon the obligee's efforts to reduce the cost of satisfying the obligor's duty to perform. The Third Circuit has suggested that if "both the plaintiff and the defendant have had equal opportunity to reduce the damages by the same act and it is equally reasonable to expect the defendant to minimize damages, the defendant is in no position to contend that the plaintiff failed to mitigate,"[3] but this view has not escaped criticism.[4] The limitation of avoidability applies to damages measured by reliance as well as to damages based on expectation.[5]

It is sometimes said that in such cases the injured party is under a "duty" to take appropriate steps to mitigate damages.[6] This is misleading, however, for the injured party incurs no liability to the party in breach by failing to take such steps. That party is simply precluded from recovering damages for loss that it could have avoided, had it taken such steps. Since the injured party is in some sense responsible for such loss, this conclusion might seem to be

No "duty" to mitigate

---

§12.12   [1]Vertue v. Bird, 84 Eng. Rep. 1000 (same case), 86 Eng. Rep. 200 (K.B. 1677).

[2]Shiffer v. Board of Educ., 224 N.W.2d 255 (Mich. 1974) ("principle of mitigation is a thread permeating the entire jurisprudence").

The common sense behind the principle is apparently not overpowering. A different rule was once applied to employees under employment contracts. See the discussion of "constructive service" *infra* note 23. Furthermore, a different rule traditionally prevails as to lessors under leases. Stonehedge Square Ltd. v. Movie Merchants, 715 A.2d 1082 (Pa. 1998) (though under law of contracts, aggrieved party must mitigate damages, "a non-breaching landlord whose tenant has abandoned the property in violation of the lease has no duty to mitigate damages"). That view might have some validity in those cases where there is simply a lease of the land alone with no covenants except the covenant to pay rent. But a modern business lease is predominantly an exchange of promises and only incidentally a sale of a part of the lessor's interest in the land."). *See* Frenchtown Square Partnership v. Lemstone, Inc., 791 N.E.2d 417 (Ohio 2003) (collecting cases "that are part of the modern trend" and holding that "duty to mitigate arises in all commercial leases"). *See also* UCC 2A-529.

[3]S.J. Groves & Sons Co. v. Warner Co., 576 F.2d 524, 530 (3d Cir. 1978).

[4]Cates v. Morgan Portable Bldg. Corp., 780 F.2d 683 (7th Cir. 1985) (Posner, J.: such a suggestion is "discordant with common law principles" by not preserving "buyer's incentive to consider a wide range of possible methods of mitigation of damages").

[5]Mahoney v. Delaware McDonald's Corp., 770 F.2d 123 (8th Cir. 1985) (damages should "exclude the amount [claimant] could have avoided by acting prudently" after repudiation).

[6]McClelland v. Climax Hosiery Mills, 169 N.E. 605 (N.Y. 1930) (Cardozo, C.J., concurring: when statement is made that "servant wrongfully discharged is 'under a duty' to the master to reduce the damages, if he can, what is meant is merely that if he unreasonably reject [other employment], he will not be heard to say that the loss of wages from then on shall be deemed the jural consequence of the earlier discharge"). Failure to mitigate damages is not, therefore, a breach of the more general duty of "good faith." See the discussion of the duty of good faith in §7.17 *supra*.

no more than a corollary of the requirement that an injured party's damages must have been caused by the other party's breach, but it is not commonly thought of in this way.[7] The burden of showing that the injured party could have, but has not, taken appropriate steps generally rests upon the party in breach,[8] an allocation of the burden that has often worked to the advantage of employees.[9]

What steps are appropriate

What steps the injured party is expected to take depends on the circumstances.[10] Just as the plaintiff who carried the goods to Ipswich could not recover for loss he could have avoided by taking his horses out of the cool Ipswich air, a buyer of oil that discovers that the barrels are leaking cannot recover for loss it could have avoided by transferring the oil to other available barrels,[11] and a baker that knowingly uses seriously defective flour cannot recover from the seller for loss due to claims by dissatisfied customers.[12] The injured party is not, however, expected to guard against unforeseeable risks[13] nor to take steps that involve undue burden, risk, or humiliation.[14] Furthermore, a party that takes steps that seemed reasonable at the time will not be judged by hindsight. As the Third Circuit has said:

> When a choice has been required between two reasonable courses, the person whose wrong forced the choice can not complain that one rather than the other was chosen. The rule of mitigation of damages may not be invoked by a contract breaker as a basis for hypercritical examination of the conduct of the injured party, or merely for the purpose of showing that the injured person might have taken steps which seemed wiser or would have been more advantageous to the defaulter. One is not obligated to exalt the interest of the defaulter to his own probable detriment.[15]

[7] See the discussion of causation and expectation in §12.1 *supra*.

[8] Cates v. Morgan Portable Bldg. Corp., *supra* note 4 ("cases make no distinction between the burden of proving mitigation of damages under the Uniform Commercial Code and under the common law of contract" and Illinois common law places burden on party in breach).

[9] Delliponti v. DeAngelis, 681 A.2d 1261 (Pa. 1996) (employer did not meet burden though employee only "made telephone inquiries regarding three job openings she read about in the newspaper").

[10] Restatement Second §350(1) bars recovery of "loss that the injured party could have avoided without undue risk, burden or humiliation." The Vienna Convention bars recovery of loss that could have been avoided by such measures as were "reasonable in the circumstances." CISG 77. *See* UNIDROIT Principles 7.4.8(1) ("reasonable steps").

[11] *See* Restatement Second §350 ill. 3.

[12] *See* Restatement Second §350 ill. 4.

[13] Slovick v. All Am. Bank, 516 N.E.2d 947 (Ill. App. 1987) (lender not expected to mitigate damages caused by unforeseeable bankruptcy).

[14] Bank One, Texas v. Taylor, 970 F.2d 16 (5th Cir. 1992) (one "is not required to 'make unreasonable personal outlays of money' . . . or to 'sacrifice a substantial right of his own'").

[15] In re Kellett Aircraft Corp., 186 F.2d 197, 198-99 (3d Cir. 1950).

The most significant questions regarding just what steps one is expected to take arise under claims for damages for total breach in connection with *cost avoided* by stopping performance and *loss avoided* by making substitute arrangements.

As to the *cost avoided* by stopping performance, once a party has reason to know that the other's return performance will not be forthcoming, the former is ordinarily expected to stop performing in order to avoid further cost. On this ground, a builder that had contracted with a county to construct a bridge for a county road was denied recovery for expenditures incurred after the county had decided not to build the road and notified the builder to stop.[16] Under the Uniform Commercial Code, a seller of goods to be manufactured "may cease manufacture and resell for scrap or salvage value" and recover damages including lost profit.[17] However, the injured party may continue to perform if it reasonably expects that the other party will perform as, for example, when the breach is accompanied by assurance that performance will nevertheless be forthcoming.[18] And even if the injured party is sure that the other party will not perform, there are instances in which the more sensible course is to complete performance rather than to stop it. For example, if a buyer breaks a contract to buy manufactured goods after manufacture has begun, the seller may be better able to avoid loss by continuing manufacture and selling the finished goods than by ceasing manufacture and attempting to salvage the work in progress.[19]

As to *loss avoided* by making substitute arrangements, the injured party is usually expected not merely to stop performance in order to avoid cost, but to take reasonable affirmative steps to make appropriate substitute arrangements to avoid loss.[20] An injured party that is the recipient can often obtain a suitable substitute on the market. If, for example, a seller fails to deliver goods, the buyer may be able to cover by buying goods in substitution for those due from the seller. If the buyer could with reasonable effort have covered, but did not do so, the amount of loss that could have been avoided is subtracted from the buyer's damages.[21] Or if an employee quits a job, the employer can find another suitable employee as a replacement. If the employer could with reasonable effort have

Stopping performance

Making substitute arrangements

---

[16]Rockingham County v. Luten Bridge Co., 35 F.2d 301 (4th Cir. 1929) (when "county gave notice to the plaintiff that it would not proceed with the project, plaintiff . . . had no right thus to pile up damages by proceeding with the erection of a useless bridge").

[17]UCC 2-704(2), 2-708(2).

[18]Steele v. J.I. Case Co., 419 P.2d 902 (Kan. 1966) (farmer that bought combines failed to take steps to avoid loss to wheat crop because of seller's continued assurances that it would repair them). See the discussion of the right to assurance under the Code in §8.23 *supra.*

[19]*See* UCC 2-704(2) and the discussion of completion of manufacture *infra.*

[20]That cover is not always required, *see* Leinenger v. Sola, 314 N.W.2d 39 (N.D. 1981) (keeping unbred cows and buying bull to breed them "was much cheaper than selling the cows at slaughter value and purchasing bred, late term cows as required by the contract"). As to the burden of proof, see the discussion of no "duty" to mitigate *supra.*

[21]UCC 2-715 (consequential damages resulting from the seller's breach do not include loss that could "reasonably be prevented by cover or otherwise").

found a replacement, but did not do so, the amount of loss that could have been avoided is subtracted from the employer's damages.[22] Similarly, an injured party that is the supplier can often dispose on the market of the performance that was to have been rendered under the contract. For example, an employee that is fired can often find another suitable job as a replacement. If such a supplier of services could with reasonable effort have found a replacement, but did not do so, the amount of loss that could have been avoided is subtracted from the supplier's damages.[23] In this case the limitation of avoidability yields a generally accepted rule that the employee's recovery is based on "the wage that would be payable during the remainder of the term reduced by the income which the discharged employee has earned, will earn, or could with reasonable diligence have earned during the unexpired term."[24]

Time for substitute   The injured party is expected to act promptly after learning that the other party's performance will not be forthcoming.[25] Though there is some authority that the injured party may choose to ignore a repudiation and await breach by nonperformance,[26] the better view holds that one is expected to act within a reasonable time after the repudiation[27] and that if one delays one bears

---

[22]Cook v. City of Chicago, 192 F.3d 693 (7th Cir. 1999) (Posner, C.J.: if corporation wrongfully terminated its million-dollar-a-year CEO, "he would not be performing his duty of mitigation if he took a full-time job as an adoption counselor in a no-kill cat shelter at . . . $15,000 a year").

[23]There was once respectable authority to the contrary, under what was known as the doctrine of "constructive service," formulated in the nineteenth-century English case of Gandall v. Pontigny, 171 Eng. Rep. 119 (K.B. 1816) (clerk who had been wrongfully discharged recovered for balance of term since "being willing to serve the residue, in contemplation of law he may be considered to have served the whole"). The doctrine was denounced in Howard v. Daly, 61 N.Y. 362 (1875) ("it encourages idleness and gives compensation to men to fold their arms and decline service, equal to those who perform with willing hands their stipulated amount of labor"). But see the rule on holders of public office in a footnote to the discussion of *loss avoided* in §12.9 *supra*.

[24]Hollwedel v. Duffy-Mott Co., 188 N.E. 266, 268 (N.Y. 1933). As to what one "has earned," see the discussion of *loss avoided* in §12.9 *supra*.

[25]For example, a buyer that covers must do so "without unreasonable delay" (UCC 2-712(1)), and the "general baseline" of the Code's market-price formula "uses as a yardstick the market in which the buyer would have obtained cover had he sought that relief" (UCC 2-713 cmt. 1).

[26]This was the prevailing rule as to contracts for the sale of goods prior to the Uniform Commercial Code. Reliance Cooperage Corp. v. Treat, 195 F.2d 1977 (8th Cir. 1952) (seller's anticipatory repudiation of contract to deliver barrel staves). See also the footnote to the discussion of urging retraction in §8.22 *supra*, quoting the dictum of Lord Cockburn in Frost v. Knight, L.R. 7 Ex. 711 (1872).

[27]This is consistent with UCC-O 2-723(1) (if "action based on anticipatory repudiation comes to trial before the time for performance," damages based on market price "shall be determined according to the price of such goods prevailing at the time when the aggrieved party learned of the repudiation."), and is supported by Cosden Oil & Chem. Co. v. Karl O. Helm Actiengesellsschaft, 736 F.2d 1064 (5th Cir. 1984) ("learned of the breach" means when "he learns of the repudiation plus a commercially reasonable time").

Revised Article 2 clarifies this by adding parallel provisions dealing with repudiation by buyer (UCC-R 2-708(1)(b) and by seller (UCC-R 2-713(1)(b)), each of which refers to "the expiration of a commercially reasonable time after the [aggrieved party] learned of the repudiation." UCC-O 2-723(1) is deleted.

the risk of any adverse change in the market during the period of the delay.[28] Conversely, if there is a favorable change in the market during the period of delay, the buyer should have the benefit of it. Thus an injured buyer that delays unreasonably in purchasing replacement goods should have damages based on the market price of replacement goods at the time when cover should have been effected, even if the market fell during the delay and enabled purchase for less than that price.[29] Even so, it can be argued that one is not expected to act after a breach by repudiation if one is still reasonably trying to get the other party to perform or to retract the repudiation, and that one is not expected to act after a breach by either repudiation or nonperformance if led by the other party's assurances to expect performance.[30]

In the case of contracts for the sale of goods, these rules on substitute arrangements are reflected in the standard formulas according to which a buyer's or seller's claim for damages for total breach is based on the difference between the contract price and the price on the market, when the injured party is expected to have arranged a substitute transaction for the purchase or sale of similar goods. The market-price formulas are, in effect, based on the loss that the injured party would have suffered had that party arranged the transaction as expected. If the buyer is the injured party, the market will often have risen, and the contract price is subtracted from the market price at which the buyer could have covered.[31] (Analogous rules have been applied to breach by a vendor of land[32] and by a seller of securities.[33]) If the seller of goods is the injured party, the market will often have fallen, and the market price at which the seller could have resold is subtracted from the contract price.[34] Under the better rule, just

Market price formulas

---

[28] Some cases have even refused to grant a reasonable time after the aggrieved party learns of the repudiation. Weiss v. Karch, 466 N.E.2d 155 (N.Y. 1984) (UCC 2-713(1) applied literally to sale of securities in cooperative corporation).

There may be a difficult question of fact as to which of a number of transactions is the substitute transaction if the injured party continuously engages in making similar transactions during the period in question.

[29] See Farnsworth, Legal Remedies for Breach of Contract, 70 Colum. L. Rev. 1145, 1190 n.190 (1970); Jackson, "Anticipatory Repudiation" and the Temporal Element of Contract Law: An Economic Inquiry into Contract Damages in Cases of Prospective Nonperformance, 31 Stan. L. Rev. 69, 115-16 (1978).

[30] See UCC 2-610 (aggrieved party may "for a commercially reasonable time await performance by the repudiating party").

[31] UCC 2-713 ("the measure of damages for non-delivery or repudiation by the seller is the difference between the market price at the time when the buyer learned of the breach and the contract price"). For the comparable rule under the Vienna Convention, see CISG 76(1).

[32] Cedar Point Apartments v. Cedar Point Inv. Corp., 756 F.2d 629 (8th Cir. 1985) ("[e]veryone agrees" that "damages are the difference between the fair market value of the land on the date fixed for the sale, and the price agreed to in the contract").

[33] Simon v. Electrospace Corp., 269 N.E.2d 21 (N.Y. 1971) (broker that did not receive promised stock limited to damages based on market price at time of breach).

[34] UCC 2-708(1) (damages for buyer's non-acceptance are based on difference between contract price and "market price at the time and place for tender"). Under UCC-R 2-706(7), a seller's

referred to, the relevant market price in the case of an anticipatory repudiation is the market price following the repudiation, not the market price at the time for delivery of the goods. Comparable rules are applied to other contracts, such as contracts for the sale of securities, where there is a market for the type of performance involved.[35] In more general terms:

(E)   *supplier's damages = contract price − price on redisposition market*
+ other loss

(F)   *recipient's damages = price on replacement market − contract price*
+ other loss

What market?   In speaking of "market price," it has been observed, "You always have to ask yourself, 'what market?'"[36] Here the market is the one in which the substitute transaction would have been arranged. Take as an example the buyer for resale that buys in one market and sells in another. If the seller breaks the contract, the buyer is expected to look to the market in which the buyer buys to find a substitute seller, and market price is the price in that market. If the buyer breaks the contract, the seller is expected to look to the market in which the seller sells to find a substitute buyer, and market price is the price in that market. This may not be the "spot" market, for, in the case of a contract for future delivery, the market should be that for a similar forward contract, and in the case of a long-term contract, the market should be that for a similar long-term contract.[37] Although, as noted earlier, the burden of showing that the injured party could have avoided the loss is ordinarily on the party in breach,[38] if there is a well-established market the burden of showing the market price is commonly placed on the injured party.[39]

---

failure to resell under UCC 2-706 "does not bar the seller from any other remedy," in particular damages based on market price. For the comparable rule under the Vienna Convention, *see* CISG 76(1).

[35] Simon v. Electrospace Corp., *supra* note 33.

[36] Lord Dunedin, in Charrington & Co. v. Wooder, [1914] A.C. 71, 84.

[37] Manchester Pipeline Corp. v. Peoples Natural Gas Co., 862 F.2d 1439 (10th Cir. 1988) ("damages should be calculated by reference to the difference between the . . . contract price and the market price of gas under a similar long term contract at the time [seller] learned of [buyer's] repudiation").

[38] See the discussion of no "duty" to mitigate *supra*.

[39] Lewis v. Nine Mile Mines, 886 P.2d 912 (Mont. 1994) ("mere speculative and conclusionary statements do not create a question of material fact" as to market price). This view is held with particular tenacity with respect to money. New York Life Ins. Co. v. Pope, 68 S.W. 851 (Ky. 1902) (injured party under contract to borrow money could recover only damages based on interest rate where he did not plead that he "could not have procured the loan from other sources").

The burden of proving market price is not always onerous, however. For example, when a vendor, after refusing to convey real property, sells it to another, the price on the second sale

A particularly vexing problem may arise when, in a sharply rising market, a seller breaks a contract to sell goods to a buyer that has already contracted to resell them. If the increase in the market price exceeds the buyer's expected profit on the resale, the seller may argue that the buyer's damages should be limited to that lost profit on the ground that damages based on market price will overcompensate the buyer.[40] This argument does not, however, take into account the buyer's potential liability under the resale contract for damages based on a similarly risen market. When this liability is added to the buyer's lost profit on the resale, no overcompensation will usually result.[41] Complications arise if the buyer's resale contract provides that the buyer is not liable if the seller fails to deliver, or if the purchaser from the buyer simply releases the buyer from liability. Courts have split over whether the buyer's damages should then be limited to its lost profit on the resale contract in order to avoid overcompensation.[42] If a court takes the former position, limiting the buyer's damages where overcompensation will result, it makes sense to place on the seller that broke the contract the burden of showing that use of a market-price will in fact result in overcompensation.[43]

Possibility of overcompensation

Whether an available alternative transaction is an appropriate substitute depends on many factors, including the similarity of the performance that the injured party will receive and the times and places at which they would

What is an appropriate substitute

---

has been used to show the market price of the property. Cedar Point Apartments v. Cedar Point Inv. Corp., *supra* note 32 (price for which land was actually sold is "fair proxy for the fair market value six months earlier"). And when an employee leaves an employer for a new job at a higher salary, that salary has been used to show the market price at which the first employer could obtain a replacement. Roth v. Speck, 126 A.2d 153 (D.C. 1956) (although employer did not "prove by expert testimony how much [hairdresser's] services would bring in the market," the amount he earned in subsequent employment "was some evidence of the value of [his] services and therefore of the cost of replacement").

[40] For an oft-cited case limiting recovery to lost profits, *see* Allied Canners & Packers v. Victor Packing Co., 209 Cal. Rptr. 60 (Ct. App. 1984) ("buyer has not been able to show that it will be liable in damages to the buyer on its forward contract, and there has been no finding of bad faith on the part of the seller").

A similar argument may be made by a buyer in the case of a sharp market drop when the seller has already contracted with a supplier. For a leading case under the Code involving breach by a buyer, *see* Nobs Chem. v. Koppers Co., 616 F.2d 212 (5th Cir. 1980) (interpretation that UCC 2-708(1) was intended "as a liquidated damage clause available to a plaintiff-seller regardless of his actual damages . . . is inconsistent with the code's basic philosophy").

[41] Tongish v. Thomas, 840 P.2d 471 (Kan. 1992) (*Allied Canners* [*supra* note 40] is "minority rule" with "only nominal support").

[42] See the cases cited in notes 40 & 41 *supra*. Cases decided before the Uniform Commercial Code generally refused to consider relationships with third parties. Iron Trade Prods. Co. v. Wilkoff Co., 116 A. 150 (Pa. 1922) (to consider evidence that "purchaser at such resale released plaintiff from all claim for damages . . . would inject collateral issues").

[43] See J. White & R. Summers, Uniform Commercial Code §7.12 (5th ed. 2000) (seller should not be limited to damages based on actual loss unless buyer can show that damages based on market price will overcompensate seller).

be rendered.[44] If discrepancies between the two transactions in these respects can be compensated for in damages, the alternative transaction may be treated as a partial substitute and damages awarded for the discrepancies.[45] If the party in breach itself offers to perform the contract on terms less favorable to the injured party, this may nevertheless be an offer of an appropriate substitute.[46] Such an offer is not one of an appropriate substitute, however, if it is conditioned on the injured party's surrender of any claim to damages.[47] Nor is it one of an appropriate substitute if acceptance of the offer would involve humiliation or otherwise result in a strained relationship, as may be the case if an employer offers to rehire an employee who has been fired.[48]

Lost volume

A similar transaction is not necessarily a "substitute" in the sense in which that word is used here, and if this is so the injured party need not take steps to arrange such a transaction. The mere fact that after breach the injured party could have made arrangements for the disposition of goods or services that that party was to supply does not necessarily mean that that party could have avoided loss by doing so. The injured party may claim that, but for the breach, it could and would have profitably entered into both transactions, as in the lost-volume situations discussed earlier where the question is whether an actual, rather than a hypothetical, transaction was a substitute.[49] In such a situation if a seller does not make a disposition of the goods that qualifies as a resale, this will not prevent the seller from recovering damages based on lost profit

[44]Parker v. Twentieth Century-Fox Film Corp., 474 P.2d 689 (Cal. 1970) (role for Shirley MacLaine as female lead in movie western was not appropriate substitute for role as female lead in movie musical).

[45]Utah Farm Prod. Credit Assn. v. Cox, 627 P.2d 62 (Utah 1981) (had debtor "been able to secure even a lesser loan from an alternative source . . . he may have been able to stave off the threat of foreclosure"). *See* Restatement Second §350 ill. 13 (injured party who can cover in market at another place recovers damages based on price in that market, together with cost of transportation).

[46]Lawrence v. Porter, 63 F. 62 (6th Cir. 1894) (buyer expected to accept seller's offer to deliver goods for cash at reduced price, rather than on credit, where the offer "was not coupled with any condition operating as an abandonment of the contract, nor as a waiver of any right of action for damages for the breach"). As to the distinction between such an offer and cure, see the discussion of what cure is not in §8.17 *supra*.

[47]Gilson v. F.S. Royster Guano Co., 1 F.2d 82 (3d Cir. 1924) (buyer not expected to accept seller's offer to deliver goods without credit term where it "meant a waiver of the plaintiff's claim for damages for the breach"). The statement in the text holds true even though the injured party might, after accepting the offer, later refuse to perform under the pre-existing duty rule or avoid the transaction for duress. See §§4.18, 4.21 *supra*.

[48]Voorhees v. Guyan Machinery Co., 446 S.E.2d 672 (W. Va. 1994) ("offer of reemployment by an employer will not diminish the employee's recovery if the offer is not accepted if circumstances are such as to render further association between the parties offensive or degrading to the employee").

[49]See the discussions of lost volume in §§12.10 and 12.11 *supra*.

rather than on the difference between contract and market price.[50] Similarly, a buyer as injured party can base its recovery on lost profit, rather than on the difference between the market price and the contract price, even if it does not acquire similar goods in a transaction that qualifies as cover, as in the case of the "jobber" that makes a commercially reasonable decision not to acquire goods after breach.[51]

Since the limitation of avoidability is intended to encourage the injured party to take appropriate steps to minimize damages, a difficult question is posed if that party has in good faith taken steps that seemed reasonable at the time but that, in retrospect, prove not to have been the most effective possible. Common sense dictates that an injured party that makes a reasonable, but to some extent unsuccessful, attempt to avoid loss, should not be penalized by being denied recovery for loss that could have been avoided if the attempt had been more successful.[52] Self-help of this kind should be encouraged. The Uniform Commercial Code therefore protects the injured party in several such situations.

Actual steps to avoid loss — self-help

Thus the seller of goods to be specially manufactured for the buyer may, on breach by the buyer, "in the exercise of reasonable commercial judgment for the purposes of avoiding loss and of effective realization either complete the manufacture and wholly identify the goods to the contract or cease manufacture and resell for scrap or salvage value or proceed in any other reasonable manner."[53] The injured seller's "reasonable commercial judgment" is to be respected and the seller is not held to a judgment based on hindsight.[54]

Completion of manufacture

The same principle informs the Code rules on resale and cover. As long as the injured seller resells "in good faith and in a commercially reasonable manner,"[55] or the injured buyer covers "by making in good faith" a "reasonable

Resale and cover

---

[50]Neumiller Farms v. Cornett, 368 So. 2d 272 (Ala. 1979) (sellers would have "to forego and advantageous opportunity" if they were required "to give priority to selling those potatoes allocated to Buyer's contract, rather than selling the unallocated portion of their inventory").

[51]Blair Internatl. v. LaBarge, Inc., 675 F.2d 954 (8th Cir. 1982) ("decision not to acquire the casing under the market situation . . . cannot be said to be commercially unreasonable").

[52]Restatement Second §350(2), analogizing from the Code, protects the injured party "to the extent that he has made reasonable but unsuccessful efforts to avoid a loss." *See* UNIDROIT Principles 7.4.8(2) (allowing recovery of "expenses reasonably incurred in attempting to reduce the harm").

[53]UCC 2-704(2). The deletion in UCC-R 2-708(2) of the final words of the original version of that subsection concerning "due allowance" for "proceeds of resale" does not affect the buyer's right to an allowance for the proceeds of resale in this situation. See footnote to the discussion of examples of lost volume in § 12.10 *supra*. That UCC 2-708(2) applies where there is no market for the goods, *see* Anchorage Centennial Dev. Co. v. Van Womer & Rodrigues, 443 P.2d 596 (Alaska 1968) ("no market for these made to order coins").

[54]*See* UCC 2-704 cmt. 2 (burden is on "buyer to show the commercially unreasonable nature of the seller's action in completing manufacture").

[55]See the discussion of resale by seller in §12.10 *supra*.

purchase or contract to purchase,"[56] the injured party can recover based on actual loss, regardless of the market price. The fact that hindsight shows that the injured seller could have sold for more or that the injured buyer could have bought for less is irrelevant, as long as that party acted reasonably. It would be well if these salutary changes in the law governing the sale of goods were applied by analogy to other types of contracts.[57]

We look now at an especially troublesome aspect of the limitation of avoidability that arises when a party seeks to recover damages based on the cost to complete performance or to remedy a defective performance.

Cost to remedy defect

§12.13.   Avoidability and Cost to Remedy Defect. An especially troublesome aspect of the limitation of avoidability may arise if the recipient is the injured party and seeks damages for partial breach based on the cost to remedy the defect in the other party's performance.[1] If the breach consists merely of incomplete, rather than defective, performance, the cost at which the recipient can arrange a substitute transaction to have the performance completed will ordinarily be less than the *loss in value* to the recipient. So the limitation of avoidability will have the effect of restricting the recipient to damages based on that lesser cost to complete performance, rather than on *loss in value*.[2] Suppose, for example, that a builder breaks a contract to construct a factory by failing to finish the roof, making the factory unusable. The owner cannot recover the relatively enormous loss resulting from the inability to use the factory, but is instead relegated to the relatively small amount that it will cost to get another builder to finish the roof.[3] Trouble may arise, however, if the performance under such a contract is defective, rather than merely incomplete. In that case, part of the cost to remedy the defect and complete the performance as agreed will probably be the cost of undoing some of the work already done. The total

---

[56] See the discussion of cover by buyer in §12.11 *supra*.

[57] Generally, however, the price at which a seller resells has been regarded as, at most, evidence of the market price. Williams v. Ubaldo, 670 A.2d 913 (Me. 1996) (evidence of price from subsequent sale of home is "probative of a property's fair market value").

§12.13   [1] The problem does not generally arise if the recipient is a buyer of goods that can resell defective goods and use the proceeds, together with damages based on difference in value, to buy goods that conform to the contract.

[2] Even in the situation in which the supplier is a seller of goods that fails to deliver in a rising market and the recipient is a buyer for resale that has already contracted to resell the goods for a fixed price, the buyer will ordinarily be expected to cover in the rising market rather than lose the profit on resale and be exposed to a claim by a purchaser on resale for damages. As to the situation in which the buyer's contract with a purchaser on resale gives the buyer a power of cancellation if the seller fails to deliver, see the discussion of the possibility of overcompensation in §12.12 *supra*.

[3] Louise Caroline Nursing Home v. Dix Constr. Corp., 285 N.E.2d 904 (Mass. 1972) ("such 'benefits of its bargain' as would derive from obtaining a building worth much more than the actual costs of construction are preserved if the building can be completed").

cost to remedy the defect may then exceed the *loss in value* to the injured party, so an award based on that cost would to that extent be a windfall.

Jacob & Youngs v. Kent is a striking example of this. A contractor built a $77,000 country residence for the owner, but inadvertently departed from the contract specifications by using plumbing pipe of Cohoes rather than of Reading manufacture. It was not disputed that the two types of pipe were identical in all characteristics except their origin. To have replaced the Cohoes pipe with Reading would not, therefore, have affected the market price of the house, although it would have required demolition of substantial parts of the structure. Judge Cardozo wrote for the New York Court of Appeals that

Example of *Jacob & Youngs*

> the measure of the allowance is not the cost of replacement, which would be great, but the difference in value, which would be either nominal or nothing . . . . The owner is entitled to the money which will permit him to complete, unless the cost of completion is greatly out of proportion to the good to be attained. When this is true, the measure is the difference in value.[4]

An English judge has read Cardozo's requirement that the cost of completion not be greatly out of proportion to the good to be obtained as indicating "the central importance of reasonableness" and as supporting the conclusion that if completion "is not the reasonable way of dealing with the situation, then diminution in value, if any, is the true measure of the plaintiff's loss."[5]

The Restatement Second states a similar rule, applicable if the "breach results in defective or unfinished construction and the loss in value is not proved with reasonable certainty." The owner is not limited to "the diminution in the market price of the property caused by the breach," but may recover damages based on "the reasonable cost of completing performance or of remedying the defects if that cost is not clearly disproportionate to the probable loss in value to him."[6] As under Cardozo's formulation, the trier of the facts need not measure the loss in value, but must only decide whether there is a clear disproportion between the cost to remedy the defect and the *loss in value*. In a situation like that in *Jacob & Youngs v. Kent*, it is reasonable to conclude that there is such a disproportion. There, the cost to complete has been substantially increased by the breach itself and consists in large part of the cost of undoing work already done and then redoing it, and only in small part does it consist of the cost of making improvements that directly affect the value to the owner.[7] *Loss in value*

Restatement Second rule

---

[4] 129 N.E. 889, 891 (1921), followed in Ruxley Electronics & Constrs. Ltd. v. Forsyth, [1995] 3 W.L.R. 118 (H.L. 1995) (swimming pool not constructed with specified depth).

[5] Ruxley Electronics & Constrs. Ltd. v. Forsyth, *supra* note 4, at 134 (Lord Lloyd of Berwick).

[6] Restatement Second §348(2), quoted with approval in Eastlake Constr. Co. v. Hess, 686 P.2d 465 (Wash. 1984) (Restatement formulation represents "sensible and workable approach to measuring damages in construction contract cases").

[7] *But cf.* Shell v. Schmidt, 330 P.2d 817 (Cal. App. 1958) (cost to remedy defect was proper where "it would not be necessary to undo any of the work").

to the owner is likely to be only a small fraction of the cost to complete, and damages measured by the diminution in market price are probably the better approximation of this loss. This is not, however, the case if serious structural defects make the building unsafe or otherwise unusable.[8]

Rules compared
The less generous measure of damages for partial breach, based on diminution in market price, is sometimes defended on the ground that allowing the more generous measure, based on cost to remedy the defect, would result in "economic waste."[9] This pejorative term is misleading, however, since even if the injured party is awarded an excessive amount of damages, that party will not ordinarily pay to have the defects remedied if to do so will cost the party more than the resulting increase in value.[10] The more generous measure will then result in a "windfall" to the injured party, but not in anything that can be described as "economic waste." On the other hand, the less generous measure may deprive the injured party of compensation for some of the *loss in value* if that loss is not fully reflected in the diminution in market price. Indeed, it may seem anomalous under the Restatement Second rule that the injured party may recover less if the cost to remedy the defect, and therefore the disproportion, is greater. Rather than accept the draconian choice between overcompensation through cost to remedy and undercompensation through diminution in market price, the trier of the facts ought to be allowed at least to fix an intermediate amount as its best estimate, in the light of all the circumstances, of the loss in value to the injured party.[11]

Example of
Groves v. John
Wunder
Some courts have suggested that the measure of recovery in these cases turns on whether the breach is inadvertent or intentional. In *Groves v. John Wunder Co.*, Groves, a company engaged in extracting gravel, agreed to give Wunder, a company similarly engaged, a lease including the right to excavate on a 24-acre industrial tract. Wunder paid $105,000 and promised to leave the property at a uniform grade. Wunder broke the contract by leaving the grade uneven. The problem of measuring Groves's damages was especially baffling because the contract stated no price for the grading. Had Wunder performed, the market price of the property upon termination of the lease would have been

---

[8]Prier v. Refrigeration Engrg. Co., 442 P.2d 621 (Wash. 1968) (owner could recover cost of reconstruction where necessary for usable ice rink that refrigeration contractor had contracted to install).

[9]County of Maricopa v. Walsh & Oberg Architects, 494 P.2d 44 (Ariz. App. 1972) ("The conceptual defense of economic waste has been recognized in Arizona.").

[10]*See* Restatement Second §348 cmt. *c*. For an English case in which the trial judge found as a fact that the homeowner's "stated intention of rebuilding the pool would not persist for long after the litigation had been concluded," *see* Ruxley Electronics & Constrs. Ltd. v. Forsyth, *supra* note 4, at 138. An owner can, however, provide in the contract that if defects are not corrected by the builder, the owner can have them corrected himself and then claim reimbursement from the builder. See the discussion of limits as to avoidability in §12.18 *supra*.

[11]*See* Farnsworth, Legal Remedies for Breach of Contract, 70 Colum. L. Rev. 1145, 1175 (1970).

$12,160, but for Groves to have had the grading done would have cost upwards of $60,000. Groves sued for damages measured by the higher figure, but was limited by the trial court to damages measured by the lower figure. On appeal, the Supreme Court of Minnesota held that the trial court erred in limiting Groves to damages measured by the diminution in market price. The court stressed the "willful" character of the breach and remarked that the "objective of this contract . . . was the improvement of real estate."[12] It evidently thought that the value to the owner of restoration was approximately $60,000. Groves submitted no evidence to support this, however, and it would not necessarily follow that this was so, even had the parties originally fixed $165,000 as the sum to be paid for the lease, with no restorative work, and later modified the agreements to reduce the sum to $105,000 and to include the restorative work.

The court's emphasis of the willful character of the breach as a basis for allowing the larger amount is of special interest. Suppose that at the end of the lease, Wunder had determined that it would cost $60,000 to grade the property as required by the contract, and that this would have increased the market price by only $12,160. Assuming no special value to Groves[13] other than that reflected in the market price, the only sensible course of action for Wunder, from an economic point of view, would have been to refuse to do the grading and instead to pay Groves $12,160.[14] It would be hard to justify awarding Groves the balance of $60,000 as damages in such a case on the ground that Wunder's breach was willful.[15] Had Groves attempted to prove that graded land had a special value to it, not reflected in the market price, this might have justified taking willfulness into account, but Groves made no such attempt. Other courts have declined to follow the decision in *Groves v. John Wunder Co.*, even when the breach might be characterized as "willful"[16] and willfulness

Effect of willfulness

---

[12]286 N.W. 235, 236, 238 (Minn. 1939).

[13]It would, for example, be possible to suppose that Groves owned adjacent land that could be used productively only if the tract were restored, but no such suggestion appears in the opinion.

[14]See the discussion of how economic analysis accords with the law's assumptions in §12.3 *supra*. This sum would fully compensate Groves for its loss if the discrepancy between the two figures were attributed to any of the following: (1) a mistake by Groves at the time the contract was made as to the effect of restoration on the market price; (2) a mistake by Wunder at the time the contract was made as to the cost of restoration; (3) increased expense of restoration caused by having left it until the end, rather than doing it along with removal of gravel; (4) a precipitous decline in the market price of the land after the contract was made due to the Depression. *See* R. Posner, Economic Analysis of Law 121 (6th ed. 2003).

[15]One of the objections to taking account of willfulness is that it is difficult to define in this context, but it certainly means something less than maliciousness, which would require that the breach be with the intent to harm the injured party. If the party in breach intended to break the contract at the time the contract was made, the remedies for fraud are available. See §4.14 *supra*. *See also* Restatement (Second) of Torts §530.

[16]A leading case is Peevyhouse v. Garland Coal & Mining Co., 382 P.2d 109 (Okl. 1963) (overturning trial court's award of $5,000 even though it was between the limits of $29,000, based on cost of promised restoration of farm after strip mining, and $300, based on market price. For

does not figure in the Restatement Second's damage formulation.[17] It should be noted, however, that in none of the cases denying recovery for cost to remedy the defect had the claimant actually incurred that cost. Furthermore, it has been argued that if a party commits an intentional breach that leaves the other party with a defective performance and a significant risk of undercompensation because of the lack of a damage remedy adequate to cover lost expectation, the party in breach ought to be required at least to disgorge any benefits gained from such an "abuse of contract."[18]

The next section deals with the second of the three main limitations on contract damages, that of foreseeability.

Historical background

§12.14. Unforeseeability as a Limitation. As we have seen, until the nineteenth century judges left the assessment of damages for breach of contract largely to the discretion of the jury.[1] With the advent of the industrial revolution, a solicitude for burgeoning enterprise led to the development of rules to curb this discretion and the "outrageous and excessive" verdicts to which it led. The limitation of unforeseeability is an apt example. Under this limitation, a party in breach is not liable for damages, whether for partial or for total breach, that the party did not at the time of contracting have reason to foresee as a probable result of the breach.[2] The development of such a limitation was encouraged by a realization that liability for unforeseeable loss might impose upon an entrepreneur a burden greatly out of proportion to the risk that the entrepreneur originally supposed was involved and to the corresponding benefit that the entrepreneur stood to gain.

Hadley v. Baxendale

The fountainhead of the limitation of foreseeability is the famous English case of *Hadley v. Baxendale*, which in 1854 laid down general principles that are still honored today. A grist mill was idle because the crankshaft of the steam

---

the background of *Peevyhouse*, *see* Maute, *Peevyhouse v. Garland Coal Co.* Revisited: The Ballad of Willie and Lucille, 89 Nw. U. L. Rev. 1341 (1995) (reporting that landowners negotiated for coal company's promise to do restorative work in return for their giving up standard advance payment for surface damage, usually equal to value of land before mining).

[17] On the relevance of willfulness, *see* Cohen, The Fault Lines in Contract Damages, 80 Va. L. Rev. 1225 (1994).

[18] *See* Laurin v. DeCarolis Constr. Co., 363 N.E.2d 675 (Mass. 1977) (where removal of gravel by vendor of land was "deliberate and wilful," recovery of fair market value of material removed "merely deprives the defendant of a profit wrongfully made, a profit which the plaintiff was entitled to make"). On abuse of contract, *see* Farnsworth, Your Loss or My Gain? The Dilemma of the Disgorgement Principle in Breach of Contract, 94 Yale L.J. 1339, 1392 (1985).

§12.14 [1] See §12.8 *supra*.

[2] That this limitation applies to a claim for damages based on reliance, see the discussion of the recipient as injured party in §12.16 *infra*. But it ought not to prevent a court from taking account of an unforeseeable saving to the injured party. For example, if an injured buyer spends $10,000 in reliance on the contract before a sudden turn of events occurs that would have caused the buyer to lose $5,000 if the buyer had had to perform the contract, the $5,000 that the buyer saved because of the breach should be subtracted from the $10,000, even though the saving was unforeseeable. Otherwise the damages would exceed the buyer's expectation.

engine that drove it was broken. The miller gave a carrier the broken shaft to take to its manufacturer so that a duplicate could be made to replace it. When the carriage was delayed, the reopening of the mill was delayed for several days, and the miller sued the carrier for loss of profits during this period. The miller had judgment on a jury verdict for lost profits, but on the carrier's appeal the court held that it was error to have left this matter to the jury, which ought not to have considered the lost profits at all.[3]

The rationale of the decision appears in Baron Alderson's noted statement of what came to be known as the two rules of *Hadley v. Baxendale.* The first rule was that the injured party may recover damages for loss that "may fairly and reasonably be considered [as] arising naturally, i.e., according to the usual course of things, from such breach of contract itself."[4] This assertion has occasioned little controversy. The second and more significant rule went to recovery of damages for loss other than that "arising naturally" — to recovery of what have come to be known as "consequential" damages.[5] It denied recovery of consequential damages unless the loss was "such as may reasonably be supposed to have been in the contemplation of both parties, at the time they made the contract as the probable result of the breach of it."[6] The court must have assumed that the miller had communicated to the carrier only the circumstance "that the article to be carried was the broken shaft of a mill, and that the plaintiffs were the millers of the mill."[7] The resulting loss of the miller's profits could not then have been in the contemplation of the carrier since, for all the carrier knew, the miller might have had a spare crankshaft as a replacement, or the machinery might have been defective in other respects, so that the carrier's delay would have had no effect upon the operation of the mill. Had the miller notified the carrier of all the circumstances, the result would presumably have been different. By introducing this requirement of "contemplation" for the recovery

Two rules

---

[3]156 Eng. Rep. 145 (Ex. 1854).

[4]156 Eng. Rep. at 151.

[5]*See* Nyquist v. Randall, 819 F.2d 1014 (11th Cir. 1987) ("lost profits may indeed be the quintessential example of 'consequential damages'"). Damages under the second rule are also sometimes called "special," while those under the first rule are called "general," but this is an unfortunate use of those terms. The terms *general* and *special* originated in, and are still properly applied to, the distinction between those losses that are so usual that they need not be specifically set out in the pleadings and those that are so unusual that they must be so set out; and it is best not to confuse problems of substantive liability with those of pleading.

It is not unusual for a supplier to include a provision excluding liability for such damages. *See* the discussion of applicability to limitation of remedies in §4.28 *supra.*

[6]156 Eng. Rep. at 151.

[7]156 Eng. Rep. at 151. The facts in the case are not entirely clear. The headnote states, among the facts that "appeared" at the court below, that "The plaintiffs' servant told the clerk that the mill was stopped, and that the shaft must be sent immediately." 156 Eng. Rep. at 147. And yet "it is reasonably plain from Alderson B's judgment that the court rejected this evidence," as the court pointed out in Victoria Laundry (Windsor) Ltd. v. Newman Indus. Ltd., [1949] 2 K.B. 528, 537. (Even so, one might ask whether the loss was unforeseeable.)

of consequential damages, the court imposed an important new limitation on the scope of recovery that juries could allow for breach of contract. The result was to impose a more severe limitation on the recovery of damages for breach of contract than that applicable to actions in tort or for breach of warranty, in which substantial or proximate cause is the test.[8]

Tacit agreement test

For a time it seemed that courts, both here and in England, might transform the contemplation test into an even stricter limitation. Some courts suggested that one was not liable for consequential damages unless, when one made the contract, one had made a "tacit agreement" to assume the risk of that liability. Mere notice to a party of circumstances making the loss foreseeable would not then be enough.[9] In the best known of the American cases to take this view, *Globe Refining Co. v. Landa Cotton Oil Co.*, Justice Holmes declared that "the extent of liability . . . should be worked out on terms which it fairly may be presumed [the defendant] would have assented to if they had been presented to his mind."[10] The underlying concept of damages as somehow based on agreement between the parties has not prevailed, however. The "tacit agreement" test has been generally rejected as overly restrictive and doctrinally unsound,[11] and it is explicitly condemned in the comments to the Uniform Commercial Code.[12]

Foreseeability test

The modern trend is, on the contrary, toward narrowing the limitation imposed by *Hadley v. Baxendale* by phrasing the test in terms of "foreseeability." The Restatement Second states: "Damages are not recoverable for loss that the party in breach did not have reason to foresee as a probable result of the breach when the contract was made."[13] It adds that loss may be foreseeable if, as under the first rule of *Hadley v. Baxendale*, it follows "in the ordinary course of events" or if, as under the second rule, it follows "as a result of special circumstances, beyond the ordinary course of events, that the party in breach

---

[8] As to tort, *see* Restatement (Second) of Torts §435. As to injury to person or property because of breach of warranty, *see* UCC 2-715(2)(b) ("proximately resulting from any breach of warranty"). Because of this difference, breach of warranty cases are not cited in this section. See also the discussion of causation and expectation in §12.1 *supra*.

[9] A leading English example is the statement of Bovill, C.J., in British Columbia etc. Saw Mill Co. v. Nettleship, L.R. 3 C.P. 499, 506 (1868), that the loss "must be something which could have been foreseen and reasonably expected, and to which he has assented expressly or impliedly by entering into the contract."

[10] 190 U.S. 540, 543 (1903).

[11] Arkansas continues to apply the tacit agreement test. Morrow v. First Natl. Bank, 550 S.W.2d 429 (Ark. 1977) (bank's promise to notify owners of coin collection as soon as safe deposit boxes were available did not amount to tacit agreement to be liable for theft from their home).

[12] UCC 2-715 cmt. 2 ("'tacit agreement' test for the recovery of consequential damages is rejected").

[13] Restatement Second §351. Article 74 of the Vienna Convention similarly provides that "damages may not exceed the loss which the party in breach foresaw or ought to have foreseen at the time of the conclusion of the contract").

had reason to know."[14] The party in breach need not have consented, even tacitly, to be liable for the loss. That party need only have been given notice of facts that made it foreseeable.[15] The parol evidence rule should not bar resort to extrinsic evidence for the limited purpose of showing that such notice has been given.[16]

In spite of the vagueness of the concept of foreseeability, a few general propositions can be asserted with some assurance. First, foreseeability is to be determined as of the time of the making of the contract and is unaffected by events subsequent to that time. The question is not what was foreseeable at the time of the breach, but what was foreseeable at the time of contracting.[17] Second, what must be foreseeable is only that the loss would result if the breach occurred. There is no requirement that the breach itself or the particular way that the loss came about be foreseeable.[18] Third, it is foreseeability only by the party in breach that is determinative. This is now accepted, even though Baron Alderson spoke of the contemplation "of both parties." Fourth, foreseeability has an objective character. When one makes a contract one takes the risk not only of those consequences that one actually did foresee,[19] but also of those that one ought reasonably to have foreseen.[20] Fifth, the loss need only have been foreseeable as a probable, as opposed to a necessary or certain, result of the breach.[21] Of course much depends on how broadly the court defines the

Meaning of foreseeability

---

[14] Restatement Second §351. The first of the phrases quoted in the text was taken by the Restatement from UCC 2-714(1) and the second from UCC 2-715(2)(a).

[15] It has been suggested that the rule "induces the party with knowledge of the risk either to take any appropriate precautions himself or, if he believes that the other party might be the more efficient preventer or spreader (insurer) of the loss, to reveal the risk to that party and pay him to assume it." R. Posner, Economic Analysis of Law 127 (6th ed. 2003). As to disclosure by recitals, see §12.18 *infra*.

[16] See the discussion of the parol evidence rule in §7.16 *supra*.

[17] Spang Indus. v. Aetna Cas. & Sur. Co., 512 F.2d 365 (2d Cir. 1975) ("it is essential under Hadley v. Baxendale and its Yankee progeny that the notice of the facts which would give rise to special damages in case of breach be given at or before the time the contract was made" but when the contract "provides that the time of performance is to be fixed at a later date, the knowledge of the consequences of a failure to perform is to be imputed to the defaulting party as of the time the parties agreed upon the date of performance"). See the discussion of freedom as to foreseeability in §12.18 *infra*.

[18] Spang Indus. v. Aetna Cas. & Sur. Co., *supra* note 17 (subcontractor liable for loss caused by "unforeseen delays").

[19] That the term *foreseeable* includes *foreseen*, *see* Kuehl v. Freeman Bros. Agency, 521 N.W.2d 714 (Iowa 1994) ("fact that this type of damage was in the minds of the parties when they entered into the contract can be discerned from the circumstances").

[20] Independent Mechanical Contractors v. Gordon T. Burke & Sons, 635 A.2d 487 (N.H. 1993) (general contractor "had reason to foresee that misassigning punch list items would probably harm [subcontractor's] reputation and economic prospects").

[21] Prutch v. Ford Motor Co., 618 P.2d 657 (Colo. 1980) ("defendant, in trying to add the ingredient of 'prior knowledge' to the 'foreseeability' concept, confuses 'foreseeable' with 'actually foreseen'"). On the degree of "foreseeability," *see* Spang Indus. v. Aetna Cas. & Sur. Co., *supra*

loss that must have been foreseeable. The magnitude of the loss need not have been foreseeable, and a party is not disadvantaged by its failure to disclose the profits that it expected to make from the contract. However, the mere circumstance that some loss was foreseeable may not suffice to impose liability for a particular type of loss that was so unusual as not to be foreseeable.[22] Aside from these general propositions, it is prudent to consider specific cases. Such cases frequently involve an issue of avoidability, for it is often questioned whether the injured party's inability to avoid the loss by arranging a substitute transaction was foreseeable. In the following discussion, the repudiation of a contract for the sale of goods will be taken as paradigmatic, but the conclusions are generally applicable to other kinds of breaches and to other types of contracts — for the sale of land, for services, for the lending of money, and the like. There is, however, a line of authority holding that damages for nonpayment by a recipient of such a performance (e.g., purchaser, recipient of services, borrower) are limited to interest.[23]

Seller as injured party

If the injured party is the seller, the requirement of foreseeability is rarely a problem. If the seller has or could have arranged a substitute transaction by reselling without loss of volume, the cause of loss will be a decline in the market, together with any expenses incurred in arranging a second sale. Courts have not asked whether such loss follows from the breach in the ordinary course.[24] They have not done so even when the injured seller has lost volume by the breach, so that loss turns on prospective profit on the broken contract. The same holds true if the injured party is a builder or other supplier instead of a seller.

Cover by buyer as injured party

Furthermore, if the injured party is the buyer rather than the seller, and if the buyer has or could have arranged a substitute transaction by covering, the requirement of foreseeability ordinarily poses no problem. In that case, the

---

note 17 (rule does not require that "damages must necessarily follow, but only that they are likely to follow"). It might be asked if the American requirement of foreseeability was not met in Hadley v. Baxendale itself.

The Convention on Contracts for the International Sale of Goods speaks of damages "which the party in breach foresaw or ought to have foreseen at the time of the conclusion of the contract . . . as a possible consequence of the breach." CISG art. 74. Compare this with the somewhat more restrictive language of UNIDROIT Principles 7.4.4, which refers to loss that a party foresaw or could reasonably have foreseen "as being *likely* to result" from nonperformance). *See* Delchi Carrier SpA v. Rotorex Corp., 71 F.3d 1024 (2d Cir. 1995) (explaining that "CISG requires that damages be limited by the familiar principle of foreseeability established in Hadley v. Baxendale" but failing to note that CISG says "possible" rather than "probable").

[22] In that case, of course, the injured party can recover for such loss as was foreseeable. Victoria Laundry (Windsor) Ltd. v. Newman Indus. Ltd., *supra* note 7 (*see* the discussion of buyer as manufacturer *infra*).

[23] The seminal case is Loudon v. Taxing Dist., 104 U.S. 771 (1881) ("all damages for delay in the payment of money owing upon contract are provided for in the allowance of interest, which is in the nature of damages for withholding money that is due").

[24] The Heron II, [1967] 3 All E.R. 686 (H.L.) (Lord Reid: in "any ordinary market prices are apt to fluctuate from day to day" and there "was an even chance that the fluctuation would be downwards").

cause of loss will be a rise in the market, together with any expenses incurred in arranging cover, and — as in the case in which the seller is the injured party — courts have not generally questioned that such loss follows from the breach in ordinary course. This is so even though the rise in the market was startling and extreme, and, as a perceptive analyst has pointed out, "some of the most extraordinary and most unpredictable losses resulting from breaches of contract are those due to unusual changes in market price."[25] Problems of foreseeability do not usually arise unless the injured party is a buyer who cannot cover, so that loss turns on loss of profits in collateral transactions that have been disrupted by the breach.[26] It is damage for this type of loss that is commonly characterized as "consequential." Since ours is a market economy, courts have traditionally begun with the assumption that there is ordinarily a market on which the buyer can cover. Therefore, losses resulting from the buyer's inability to cover do not follow from the breach in the ordinary course, and they are foreseeable by the seller only if the seller was aware of facts making the buyer's inability to cover itself foreseeable.[27] Occasionally this assumption has been virtually irrebuttable.

Promise of money or credit

If the injured party is a borrower under a contract to lend money or extend credit, it is sometimes supposed that "money is always in the market, and procurable at the lawful rate of interest," so the borrower can recover only the difference in the interest that the borrower would have to pay to borrow on that market and the interest that the borrower had contracted to pay.[28] But under the prevailing view, if the borrower can show that the inability to borrow elsewhere was foreseeable by the lender, the borrower can recover damages based on losses in collateral transactions.[29]

Profits on collateral transactions

Even if the borrower of money, buyer of goods, or other recipient can surmount the barrier of showing that the inability to cover was foreseeable, the

---

[25] J. Bonbright, The Valuation of Property 291 (1937). As to the possibility that the seller might succeed in claiming to be excused altogether from performing because of a sharp price rise, see §9.6 *supra*.

[26] Wullschleger & Co. v. Jenny Fashions, 618 F. Supp. 373 (S.D.N.Y. 1985) (not determinative that buyer did not tell seller it intended to make circle skirts since circle skirts were neither "unusual in the industry nor unique in any way").

[27] Marcus & Co. v. K.L.G. Baking Co., 3 A.2d 627 (N.J. 1939) (baking company that agreed to sell its used ovens not liable for buyer's profit on resale because not shown that "seller knew . . . that goods of like kind could not be procured elsewhere by the buyer for the performance of his sub-contract").

For a suggestion that UCC 2-715(2) changes this, *see* J. Perillo, Calamari & Perillo on Contracts §14-22 (5th ed. 2003).

No comparable problem arises with respect to the foreseeability of resale when the seller is the injured party, since the seller that cannot resell is entitled to force the goods on the buyer and recover the price under UCC 2-709(1)(b).

[28] Smith v. Parker, 45 N.E. 770, 772 (Ind. 1897).

[29] Stacy v. Merchants Bank, 482 A.2d 61 (Vt. 1984) (breach of contract) to lend money for dairy farming).

recipient must then show that loss of profits on collateral transactions was also foreseeable in order to recover for that loss.[30] Here it is helpful to distinguish the buyer that buys for resale and stands between manufacturer and consumer from the buyer that is a manufacturer.[31]

Buyer for resale

If the buyer is known by the seller to be buying for resale, a loss of profit within the normal range is foreseeable.[32] As the commentary to the Code expresses it, "In the case of sale of wares to one in the business of reselling them, resale is one of the requirements of which the seller has reason to know. . . . "[33] The seller is not, however, liable for lost profit to the extent that it is extraordinary.[34] Nor is the seller liable for losses that result from unusual terms in the buyer's resale contracts or from other circumstances of which the seller is ignorant.[35] But if the breach results in claims by third persons against the buyer, the seller is liable for the amount of any judgment against the buyer, together with reasonable expenditures in the litigation to the extent that they were foreseeable.[36] If the buyer settles such claims to avoid litigation, the buyer can recover the reasonable amount of that settlement, as well as the costs of making it.[37]

Buyer as manufacturer

If the buyer is not a buyer for resale but a manufacturer that is buying either capital goods or raw materials, it is much more difficult when the contract is made for the seller to foresee the loss of profit in collateral transactions that a breach may cause. Here "the provision of opportunities for gain may have

---

[30]Wells Fargo Bank v. United States, 88 F.3d 1012 (Fed. Cir. 1996) (bank's lost profits on other loans forgone when federal agency failed to honor commitment to guaranty construction loan were not foreseeable).

[31]The distinction is admittedly somewhat artificial, since even a manufacturer stands between the seller from which the manufacturer buys raw materials and the buyer to which the manufacturer sells the finished product.

[32]Appliances v. Queen Stove Works, 36 N.W.2d 121 (Minn. 1949) ("the seller's knowledge that the buyer is a dealer in the kind of goods purchased is sufficient to impute to the seller notice of the fact that the goods are intended for resale, and to charge him . . . with special damages based on the buyer's resale of the goods in the ordinary course of business, although the seller had no knowledge of any actual resale or specific customer").

[33]UCC 2-715 cmt. 6.

[34]Bockman Printing & Servs. v. Baldwin-Gregg, Inc., 572 N.E.2d 1094 (Ill. App. 1991) (manufacturer "had no reason to believe that [publishing company] would make quotes and enter contracts based upon [manufacturer's] promise" since reasonable skepticism "would require [publishing company] to wait until some initial indicia of success was demonstrated").

[35]Anna Ready Mix v. N.E. Pierson Constr. Co., 747 F. Supp. 1299 (S.D. Ill. 1990) ("Without detailed knowledge of [buyer's] financial situation, [seller] would have no reason to foresee that a breach . . . would cause [buyer] to become so thinly capitalized that it could not obtain a performance bond."). *But cf.* Krauss v. Greenberg, 137 F.2d 569 (3d Cir. 1943) (subcontractor "could have foreseen" that contractor would have been liable for liquidated damages under its contract with government).

[36]Verhagen v. Platt, 61 A.2d 892 (N.J. 1948) (expenses of litigation and settlement were recoverable).

[37]Verhagen v. Platt, *supra* note 36.

a snowball effect: opportunities breed further opportunities."[38] To the extent
that the manufacturer's loss of profits resulted from an intended use of the
goods that was abnormal, for example, the seller is not liable for that loss unless
the seller had reason to know of this special circumstance.[39] Nevertheless, a
manufacturer may recover substantial damages despite the rule in *Hadley v.
Baxendale,* as is shown in a noted English case that grew out of a contract made
shortly after World War II to sell a secondhand boiler. The seller, an engineering
company that did not sell boilers, knew only that boilers were in short supply
and that the buyer, a laundry, wanted to put the boiler into use "in the shortest
possible space of time." The boiler was damaged by the firm engaged by the
seller to prepare it for shipment, and delivery was delayed for five months
at a time when there was an "insatiable" demand for laundry services. The
buyer sued for its lost profit during that time. In holding that it was error to
deny recovery of profits altogether, the court held that, although the laundry
could not recover the profit that it would have made under some "particularly
lucrative" contracts of which the seller had no knowledge, it was not "precluded
from recovering some general . . . sum for loss of business . . . to be reasonably
expected."[40] Furthermore, a buyer that seeks damages for delay may be able
to meet the requirement of foreseeability by basing damages on rental value or
interest, rather than on lost profits, during the period of delay.[41]

In fact the question of foreseeability arises less frequently than might be supposed because sellers and other suppliers frequently provide that consequential
damages are not recoverable, regardless of whether they would be recoverable under the rule of *Hadley v. Baxendale.* The validity of such provisions is
discussed elsewhere in this treatise.[42]

Exclusion of consequential damages

A requirement of certainty also imposes severe constraints on recovery of
lost profits on collateral transactions. We turn to that requirement next.

§12.15.   Uncertainty as a Limitation. In the middle of the nineteenth
century, while English judges were introducing the requirement of foreseeability in order to control the discretion of juries in awarding contract damages,
American judges were engaged in fashioning an additional doctrine to the same
end—the requirement of certainty. This limitation has been characterized by
an authority on remedies as "probably the most distinctive contribution of the
American courts to the common law of damages."[1] As formulated in 1858 in a

Origin of the requirement

---

[38] H. Hart & A. Honoré, Causation in the Law 312 (2d ed. 1985).

[39] Cory v. Thames Ironworks & Shipbldg. Co., L.R. 3 Q.B. 181 (1868) (buyer's intended use
of derrick was "entirely novel and exceptional").

[40] Victoria Laundry (Windsor) Ltd. v. Newman Indus. Ltd., *supra* note 7, at 543.

[41] Hector Martinez & Co. v. Southern Pac. Transp. Co., 606 F.2d 106 (5th Cir. 1979) ("might
be quite foreseeable that deprivation of the machine's use . . . will cause a loss of rental value or
interest value"). See the discussion of the alternatives in case of delay in §12.15 *infra.*

[42] See §4.28 *supra.*

§12.15   [1] C. McCormick, Law of Damages 124 (1935).

leading New York case, the doctrine required damages for breach of contract to "be shown, by clear and satisfactory evidence, to have been actually sustained" and to "be shown with certainty, and not left to speculation or conjecture."[2] It thus imposed on the injured party a distinctly more onerous burden than that imposed in tort cases[3] and manifested a judicial reluctance to recognize interests that are difficult or impossible to measure in money.

Reasonable certainty required   Recent decades, however, have seen a relaxation of the requirement. Contemporary statements insist only on "reasonable certainty" rather than on certainty itself. The Restatement Second, for example, precludes recovery "for loss beyond an amount that the evidence permits to be established with reasonable certainty."[4] The comments to the Uniform Commercial Code explain that damages need not "be calculable with mathematical accuracy," are "at best approximate," and "have to be proved with whatever definiteness and accuracy the facts permit, but no more."[5] Doubts are generally resolved against the party in breach on the rationale, as Judge Amalya Kearse put it, that it is "not improper, given the inherent uncertainty, to exercise generosity in favor of the injured party rather than in favor of the breaching party."[6] Courts are therefore less demanding in applying the requirement if the breach was "willful," in spite of the general tenet that the amount of contract damages does not turn on the character of the breach.[7] Courts are also less demanding if it appears that, as in the case of claims for loss of "good will," proof with precision is inherently impossible.[8] Furthermore, should the injured party fail to prove some of its loss, it is not precluded from recovering for other loss that it does prove. Indeed, a few courts have taken the extreme view that one need only prove the "fact" as distinguished from the "extent" of the loss with reasonable certainty,[9] a

---

[2] Griffin v. Colver, 16 N.Y. 489, 491 (1858).

[3] See Restatement (Second) of Torts §912 ("with as much certainty as the nature of the tort and the circumstances permit"). Of course, to the extent that the uncertainty results because the breach occurs long before the time for performance, the difficulty in forecasting may be reduced or eliminated by delays in coming to trial.

[4] Restatement Second §352.

[5] 1-106 cmt. 1. See also UCC 2-715 cmt. 4 ("Loss may be determined in any manner which is reasonable under the circumstances.").

[6] United States Naval Inst. v. Charter Communications, 936 F.2d 692, 697 (2d Cir. 1991). For a similar view, see Locke v. United States, 283 F.2d 521, 524 (Ct. Cl. 1960) (one "who has wrongfully broken a contract should not be permitted to reap advantage from his own wrong by insisting on proof which by reason of his breach is unobtainable").

[7] See §12.8 supra.

[8] Delano Growers' Coop. Winery v. Supreme Wine Co., 473 N.E.2d 1066 (Mass. 1985) (if seller "reasonably knows that substantially impaired goods provided for resale could affect . . . established good will, the buyer's loss of good will" is recoverable).

[9] Bagwell Coatings v. Middle S. Energy, 797 F.2d 1298 (5th Cir. 1986) (endorsing "distinction between the amount of proof necessary to establish that a breach of contract is the proximate cause of some substantial damage of a particular kind" and "quantum of proof necessary to fix the amount of those damages").

relaxation of the rule that is tantamount to its abandonment. The impact of the requirement of certainty can be seen by considering the case of a repudiation of a contract for the sale of goods, in which the seller is representative of suppliers in general and the buyer of recipients.[10]

Where the injured party is the seller, the requirement of certainty is rarely a problem. If the seller has or could have resold without loss of volume, damages for total breach depend on either the price at which the goods were actually resold or the market price at which they could have been resold; and in either case no problem of proof ordinarily arises.[11] Furthermore, even in cases of lost volume, where the seller's damages depend on the profit that the seller would have made on the transaction in question, courts have rarely applied the requirement of certainty to preclude recovery.[12] The lost-volume seller that is to manufacture goods specially for the buyer usually encounters little difficulty in proving the cost or other loss avoided that is to be subtracted from the price fixed in the contract.[13] Courts have not been greatly troubled in these cases by such relatively minor uncertainties as those relating to allocation of overhead.[14] The results are similar if the injured party is a builder or other supplier rather than a seller.[15]

Seller as injured party

If the injured party is the buyer rather than the seller, the requirement of certainty ordinarily poses no problem if the buyer has or could have covered. In that case damages for total breach will depend on the actual cover price or the market price at which the buyer could have covered, and no problem as to proof ordinarily arises.[16] Problems of proof become serious only when the injured party is a buyer who cannot cover, so that damages depend on loss of profits in collateral transactions that have been disrupted by the breach.[17] In such cases the requirement of certainty, like that of foreseeability, is a "convenient means for keeping within the bounds of reasonable expectation the risk which

Buyer as injured party

---

[10]See the discussion of the meaning of *foreseeability* §12.14 *supra*.

[11]See the discussion of the seller as injured party in §12.14 *supra* for a similar point as to foreseeability.

[12]See the discussion of the seller as injured party in §12.14 *supra* for a similar point as to foreseeability.

[13]That the burden is on the injured party to prove the cost avoided, *see* Allen, Heaton & McDonald v. Castle Farm Amusement Co., 86 N.E.2d 782 (Ohio 1949) (contract to furnish advertising).

[14]On overhead, see §12.10 *supra*.

[15]Peter Kiewit Sons' Co. v. Summit Constr. Co., 422 F.2d 242 (8th Cir. 1969) (in action by subcontractor against general contractor, "only reasonable certainty, not absolute certainty, is required in estimating damages and . . . doubts are generally resolved against the party committing breach").

[16]See §12.12 *supra*.

[17]See the discussion of the buyer as injured party in §12.14 *supra* for a similar point as to foreseeability. If the buyer for resale is liable in turn to its purchasers on resale, the buyer is not required to wait until it has been held liable before recovering from the seller. S.G. Supply Co. v. Greenwood Intl., 769 F. Supp. 1430 (N.D. Ill. 1991) (seller liable for buyer's probable liability).

litigation imposes upon commercial enterprises."[18] If the test of foreseeability is met, but the court nevertheless concludes that liability would impose on the party in breach a risk disproportionate to the rewards that the party stood to gain by the contract, "the test of certainty is the most usual surrogate."[19] As in the case of the requirement of foreseeability, it is helpful to distinguish the buyer that buys for resale and stands between manufacturer and consumer from the buyer that is a manufacturer.

Buyer for resale   A buyer that buys a fixed quantity of goods for resale can often prove with reasonable certainty the loss on resale contracts that have been disrupted or prevented by the breach. A buyer that has already made resale contracts can show resale price, and a buyer that has not made resale contracts can show the market price, if there is one, at which the goods could have been resold.[20] Courts have not been much concerned with uncertainties in estimating incidental costs, such as delivery costs, or in allocating overhead for activities like merchandising and advertising. If, however, the buyer is to receive an indefinite quantity of goods over an extended period of time under a continuing relationship, as in the case of a distributorship or a requirements or output contract, the problems of proof are more acute, and courts have more often denied recovery.[21]

Buyer as manufacturer   If the buyer is not a buyer for resale but a manufacturer that is buying either capital goods or raw materials, the seller's breach may cause a loss of profit in collateral transactions that is much more difficult to prove.[22] It is in the cases of the loss of business opportunities by such buyers and similar recipients of services, land, and the like that the requirement of certainty has had its principal impact. The plethora of decisions applying the requirement of certainty to such cases cannot be reduced to a few simple rules. As in the case of foreseeability, much depends on the particular circumstances of the case and the judicial philosophy of the court. However, a few significant factors stand out. One is the length of time over which performance

---

[18]C. McCormick, Law of Damages 105 (1935).

[19]Fuller & Perdue, The Reliance Interest in Contract Damages (pt. 2), 46 Yale L.J. 373, 376 (1937).

[20]*See* J & J Farms v. Cargill, Inc., 693 F.2d 830 (8th Cir. 1982) (allowing "lost profits due to the decline of the market during the time the contaminated cattle were being tested," but not "lost profits from the marketing of *other* cattle which [buyer] could have purchased with the lost profits from the marketing of the contaminated cattle").

[21]Under a contract of exclusive agency for the sale of goods on commission, the agent can often prove with sufficient certainty the profits that would have been made, had the agent not been discharged, by proof of sales that the agent made in the territory before the breach or of sales made there by the principal after the breach. If, however, the agency is not an exclusive one, so that the agent's ability to withstand competition is in question, such a showing will be more difficult.

[22]Fleming Mfg. Co. v. Capitol Brick, 734 S.W.2d 405 (Tex. App. 1987) (loss of profit resulting from defective mold not proved with sufficient certainty where no proof of "existing contracts" or "normal market demand increases").

is to extend. Courts have been especially chary in allowing damages if the loss depends on price levels, buyer's requirements, or other highly variable circumstances that will not be known for some time.[23] A second factor is the newness of the injured party's enterprise. Courts have been notably hesitant to allow damages for loss of profits by a new venture[24] as opposed to an existing business with records of previous transactions on which forecasts of profits can be based,[25] and some courts have gone so far as to bar virtually any recovery of lost profits by a "new business."[26] A third factor is the speculative nature of the injured party's enterprise. Courts have been reluctant to permit recovery of prospective profits that depend on the public whim, as is thought to be particularly true under contracts for entertainment or sporting events. The New York Court of Appeals stressed this factor in holding that damages for lost profits were not recoverable for breach of a contract to build a domed stadium. "The economic facts of life, the whim of the general public and the fickle nature of popular support for professional athletic endeavors must be given great weight in attempting to ascertain damages 20 years in the future."[27] The "new business" rule has been largely abandoned,[28] however, and the mere presence of one or more of these three factors, however, should not prevent recovery if the injured party's proof meets the standard of reasonable certainty.

In several cases involving lost business opportunities, courts have shown a remarkable willingness at least to give the injured party a chance to prove loss of prospective profits. For example, the Fifth Circuit sustained an award of lost profits on non-advertised or collateral sales when a seller failed to deliver watches to be used as a "loss leader" item. The court held that the amount of the loss had been sufficiently established by data on past promotions combined with testimony from an expert economist that the

Relaxation of rule

---

[23]Center Chem. Co. v. Avril, Inc., 392 F.2d 289 (5th Cir. 1968) (loss of profits over remaining 16 years of 20-year contract to sell goods not proved with sufficient certainty).

[24]Brenneman v. Auto-Teria, 491 P.2d 992 (Or. 1971) (loss of profits by new car-wash business because of defective machine was not proved with sufficient certainty).

Recovery has been denied even where there is merely a delay in the opening of a new business, despite the fact that later profits can used as evidence. Evergreen Amusement Corp. v. Milstead, 112 A.2d 901 (Md. 1955) (delay in opening of drive-in theater).

[25]McDermott v. Middle East Carpet Co. Assoc., 811 F.2d 1422 (11th Cir. 1987) (lost profits can be recovered if new business "can show a 'track record' of profitability").

[26]Evergreen Amusement Corp. v. Milstead, *supra* note 24 (though court has not laid down a flat rule, "no case has permitted recovery of lost profits under comparable circumstances.").

[27]Kenford Co. v. County of Erie, 493 N.E.2d 234, 236 (N.Y. 1986).

[28]Humetrix, Inc. v. Gemplus S.C.A., 268 F.3d 910 (9th Cir. 2001) (though as "empirical matter, new businesses often cannot offer reliable proof of prospective profits," as "normative matter, if a business can offer reliable proof of profits, there is no reason to deprive it of the profits . . . merely because it is 'new'").

Impetus

planned promotion would provide similar results in the light of its special circumstances.[29]

The impetus for this relaxation has come from two sources. One is a more liberal rule laid down for the proof of such profits in private actions for treble damages under the antitrust laws. There the Supreme Court of the United States has imposed no requirement of certainty and has said instead that "the jury may make a just and reasonable estimate of the damage based on relevant data" since the "most elementary conceptions of justice and public policy require that the wrongdoer shall bear the risk of the uncertainty which his own wrong has created."[30] Even if no past history of profits is available in such actions, a "yardstick test" has been used to estimate profits by comparison with those of similar businesses.[31] The other source is the rule that allows a party to an aleatory contract[32] — such as one involving insurance or a game of chance — to recover damages based on the "value of the chance." Suppose, for example, that each of ten contestants in a contest has an equal chance of winning a $10,000 prize and one is denied the right to participate. Some courts will allow that contestant to recover $1,000, based on the value of the contestant's chance, although if allowed to participate the contestant would have won either $10,000 or nothing.[33] As applied to lost business opportunities, one court has said: "We are here concerned with the value of a chance for obtaining business and profits" and "where it is fairly measurable by calculable odds and by evidence bearing specifically on the probabilities, . . . the court should be allowed to value [the] lost opportunity."[34] An increased opportunity to offer proof of lost profits, combined with greater receptivity on the part of courts to proof by expert opinion and by sophisticated economic and financial data, can be expected to make it increasingly easy for claimants to meet the requirement of certainty.[35]

---

[29] Migerobe, Inc. v. Certina USA, 924 F.2d 1330, 1338 (5th Cir. 1991) ("Certina was peaking in name recognition" among buyer's customers and "Certina's strongest market was in the southeastern United States" where buyer's retail outlets were).

[30] Bigelow v. RKO Radio Pictures, 327 U.S. 251, 264, 265 (1946).

[31] Lehrman v. Gulf Oil Corp., 500 F.2d 659 (5th Cir. 1974) (damages based on "a study of the profits of business operations that are closely comparable").

[32] See the discussion of risk affecting imbalance in §2.11 *supra*.

[33] The classic case is Chaplin v. Hicks, [1911] 2 K.B. 786 (winner of preliminary round in beauty contest).

[34] Locke v. United States, *supra* note 6, at 524, 525. Chaplin v. Hicks, *supra* note 33, was cited in the *Air Technology* case, *supra* note 29. *But cf.* Scallon v. U.S. AG Ctr., 42 F. Supp. 2d 867 (N.D. Iowa 1999) (party to "hedge-to-arrive" contract could not recover "damages based on a 'lost chance to win' theory" where evidence established that he had no such chance because "no scenario . . . showed that he could obtain a profit").

[35] McDermott v. Middle East Carpet Co. Assoc., *supra* note 25 ("expert witness in economics" testified as to "natural life cycle of a manufacturing facility" and used "arithmetic and geometric models").

Furthermore, if the breach merely results in a delay or stoppage in the buyer's use of property for a period of time, rather than in outright abandonment of a venture, the loss may be measured by the rental value of the property for that period, not by the profits that would have been earned.[36] However, since rental value depends on what the property would command on the market and that, in turn, depends on the profits that it can be expected to yield, uncertainty as to profits may result in uncertainty as to rental value. As a last resort, if rental value is uncertain, a court may allow interest on the value of the property for the period that it is unproductive, provided that this can be proved with reasonable certainty.[37]

But what if, in spite of all this, the injured party cannot prove its expectation interest with sufficient certainty?

§12.16. Reliance as an Alternative Measure of Damages. As we saw in the preceding section, the requirement of certainty has its greatest impact on proof of lost profits. Nevertheless, a party that fails to meet the burden of proving prospective profits is not necessarily relegated to nominal damages. The requirement of certainty also applies to damages based on reliance. But a party that has relied on a contract can usually meet the burden of proving with sufficient certainty the extent of that reliance, even if unable to meet that burden as to profits. The injured party can then recover damages for total breach based on reliance, with deduction for any benefit received through salvage or otherwise.[1] This will not help a party that has done nothing in reliance on the contract. Nor will it allow a party to recover costs incurred *before* the contract was made.[2] But it does protect a significant interest of an injured party that has relied and is of particular importance if the *cost of reliance* is an appreciable part of the expectation interest. In this situation, as generally in contract law, the reliance interest is regarded as affording a means for giving some relief when the full expectation interest is for some reason inappropriate.

Sometimes the injured party is a supplier, such as a builder under a construction contract, that cannot prove lost profits with sufficient certainty. If the

> **Alternatives in case of delay**

> **Significance of alternative**

> **Supplier as injured party**

---

[36] *See* Restatement Second §348(1) (recovery based on "rental value of the property").

[37] *See* Restatement Second §348(1) ("interest on the value of the property").

The interest ought to be allowed on the value of the property as measured by its market price, which will, like rental value, depend on the profitability of the property. To the extent that the injured party merely incurs costs through payment of interest on money borrowed to finance the project or loss of the use of that party's own funds tied up in it, these are costs of reliance, these are reimbursable costs of reliance. See §12.16 *infra*.

§12.16 [1] DPJ Co. v. FDIC, 30 F.3d 247 (1st Cir. 1994) (quoting this section of this treatise and emphasizing that recovery is on the contract). *See* Restatement Second §349.

[2] DPJ Co. v. FDIC, *supra* note 1 ("pre-loan expenditures were not made in reliance upon the line of credit promise but were made in order to secure it," quoting this section). For a case arising out of Jack Dempsey's repudiation of a contract in order to train for his fight with Gene Tunney, *see* Chicago Coliseum Club v. Dempsey, 265 Ill. App. 542 (1932) (no recovery for expenses prior to signing agreement).

builder has already begun work when the owner repudiates, the builder can recover as damages any expenditures for labor and materials and other costs of preparation and part performance, even though the builder cannot prove lost profits.[3] The rationale suggested for this result is that the builder is entitled to use Formula (B), as for damages based on expectation interest, but may disregard the *profit* term.[4] The builder therefore recovers its *cost of reliance*, with deduction for any *loss avoided* through salvage or, because the limitation of avoidability applies to damages measured by reliance, for any loss that could have been avoided through salvage.[5] However, claims for recovery based on such essential reliance[6] are not common, since, as we saw in the preceding section, a supplier does not often encounter difficulty in proving lost profits.[7]

Recipient as injured party

Recovery based on incidental reliance is more significant in practice. An injured party that is a recipient, such as an entrepreneur attempting to establish a new business, will often encounter difficulty in proving lost profits on collateral transactions. If the recipient has relied on the contract by spending money or making commitments for advertising, acquiring premises and equipment, hiring employees, and the like, it is important to be able to recover these costs as damages if the breach frustrates the venture. Reliance has often been used as the basis for measuring recovery. An early example is *Nurse v. Barns*, a seventeenth-century English case in which an entrepreneur promised to pay £10 for the use of an owner's iron mills. When the owner denied him their use, the entrepreneur recovered £500 for the stock he had laid in.[8] Of course any benefit to the injured party from preparation should be deducted.[9] Damages measured by reliance have proved important in connection with such speculative ventures as the staging of an entertainment or sporting event[10] or the exhibition of a new machine at a trade fair.[11] Damages measured by reliance may, however, still be

---

[3]C.C. Haupt Hardware v. Long Mfg. Co., 148 N.W.2d 428 (Iowa 1967) (expenditures "in preparation and part performance are recoverable . . . when other measures fail").

[4]See the discussion of the alternative method in §12.10 *supra*. In the treatment of "overhead," fixed costs should not be included in the *cost of reliance*. See the treatment of overhead under Formula B in a footnote to the discussion of the treatment of overhead in §12.10 *supra*.

[5]See the discussion of the general rule in §12.12 *supra*.

[6]For the distinction between essential and incidental reliance, see the discussion of the reliance interest in §12.1 *supra*.

[7]See the discussion of the seller as injured party in §12.15 *supra*.

[8]83 Eng. Rep. 43 (K.B. 1664). American cases are L. Albert & Son v. Armstrong Rubber Co., 178 F.2d 182 (2d Cir. 1949) (contract to supply machines to recondition old rubber); Paola Gas Co. v. Paola Glass Co., 44 P. 621 (Kan. 1896) (contract to supply gas for glass factory to be built).

[9]Paola Gas Co. v. Paola Glass Co., *supra* note 8 ("any value or benefit to plaintiffs resulting from the work done [by them] must be deducted" and "the burden was on plaintiffs to prove this item").

[10]Chicago Coliseum Club v. Dempsey, *supra* note 2 (contract to stage heavyweight championship fight).

[11]Security Stove & Mfg. Co. v. American Ry. Express Co., 51 S.W.2d 572 (Mo. App. 1932) (contract to transport furnace for exhibition at trade fair).

denied if the party in breach did not have reason at the time the contract was made to foresee them as a probable result of the breach.[12]

Since it is a fundamental tenet of the law of contract damages that an injured party should not be put in a better position than if the contract had been performed,[13] this alternative measure of damages rests on the premise that the injured party's reliance interest is no greater than that party's expectation interest. The classic analysis of reliance losses puts it in this fashion: "We will not, in a suit for reimbursement for losses incurred in reliance on a contract knowingly put the plaintiff in a better position than he would have occupied had the contract been fully performed."[14] Therefore, to the extent that the party in breach can prove with reasonable certainty that the injured party's expectation interest was less than its reliance interest so that performance of the contract would have resulted in a net loss to that party rather than a net profit, the amount of that loss will be subtracted from the cost of reliance.[15] It will be more difficult for the party in breach to show this when the injured party is a recipient and the reliance is incidental, just as it is more difficult for the injured party to show lost profit in such a case.[16]

There is no objection in theory to combining recovery measured by the reliance interest with recovery for such lost profits as are proved with sufficient certainty. The problem in practice is to avoid excessive recovery through overlapping items. If the injured party is a supplier, excessive recovery can be avoided simply by adhering to Formula (B), which measures damages by the *cost of reliance* minus *loss avoided* plus *profit*,[17] and allowing recovery of lost profits only to the extent that they are proved with sufficient certainty. If the injured party is a recipient, however, more pains must be taken to avoid excessive recovery. For example, were the injured party to be allowed recovery of both advertising expenses and part of the gross income from the prospective collateral transactions promoted by that advertising, double recovery would result. This is because the injured party would have had to pay for advertising out of gross income and therefore should not, as a result of breach, get both the

*[margin note: **Effect of losing contract**]*

*[margin note: **Overlapping items of damage**]*

---

[12] Sitlington v. Fulton, 281 F.2d 552 (10th Cir. 1960) ("sellers could not have foreseen that the purchaser would buy cattle or incur expenses in planting crops and making improvements on the farm before obtaining complete possession").

[13] See the discussion of the right to expectation in §12.8 *supra*.

[14] Fuller & Perdue, The Reliance Interest in Contract Damages (pt. 1), 46 Yale L.J. 52, 79 (1936).

[15] L. Albert & Son v. Armstrong Rubber Co., *supra* note 8 ("the promisee may recover his outlay in preparation for the performance, subject to the privilege of the promisor to reduce it by as much as he can show that the promisee would have lost, if the contract had been performed").

[16] For more on losing contracts, see the discussion of the situation where the benefit is performance other than money in §12.20 *infra*.

[17] See the discussion of an alternative method in §12.10 *supra*.

cost of advertising and the gross income.[18] In cases in which the rental value of property or the interest on the value of that property is used as a measure of profitability excessive recovery will not result, since these turn not on the gross income but on the net profit that can be realized from the use of the property.[19]

We have considered the three traditional limitations of avoidability, unforeseeability, and uncertainty. Are these the only limitations on damages?

Nature of the problem

§12.17. Other Limitations, Including Emotional Disturbance. Sometimes a court is confronted with a large damage claim that seems greatly disproportionate to the modest consideration received by the party in breach. It may not seem just to require the party in breach to pay for all loss caused by the breach, even though that loss was foreseeable and has been proved with reasonable certainty. Would it have been right in *Hadley v. Baxendale*,[1] for example, to have held the carrier liable for the miller's profit if the carrier had been told at the time of contracting that the miller had no other crankshaft and if the miller had later proved lost profit with sufficient certainty? Some courts have balked at reaching such a conclusion.

Use of tacit agreement test

For a time many courts overtly used the tacit agreement test to justify their refusal to award damages to the full extent of the loss in such cases. In a leading case, a compress company sought to recover profits lost when a smelting company broke its contract to repair a compress. The Supreme Court of Arkansas denied recovery for lost profits, reasoning that "where the damages arise from special circumstances, and are so large as to be out of proportion to the consideration agreed to be paid for the services to be rendered under the contract, it raises a doubt at once as to whether the party would have assented to such a liability, had it been called to his attention."[2] However, the tacit agreement test has now generally been discarded and no longer affords a vehicle for limiting recovery in such cases.[3]

Covert solutions

Nevertheless, there remains a judicial reluctance to impose on a contracting party liability in an amount greatly disproportionate to the consideration received. The early cases usually involved common carriers and public utilities for, as Cardozo put it as to telegraph companies, "much may be said in favor of the social policy of a rule" relieving such defendants "of liabilities that might otherwise be crushing."[4] Statutorily sanctioned limitations on such liability, however, have now largely eliminated this risk.[5] Sometimes courts have cloaked their reluctance by so applying the test of foreseeability as to find that

---

[18]As to the treatment of overhead, *see* Autotrol Corp. v. Continental Water Sys. Corp., 918 F.2d 689 (7th Cir. 1990) (Posner, J.: "question of fact whether . . . overhead items allocated as a bookkeeping matter to a broken contract would in fact have been recovered in a substitute contract").

[19]See the discussion of alternatives in case of delay in §12.15 *supra*.

§12.17 [1]See §12.14 *supra*.

[2]Hooks Smelting Co. v. Planters' Compress Co., 79 S.W. 1052, 1056 (Ark. 1904).

[3]See the discussion of the tacit agreement test in §12.14 *supra*.

[4]Kerr S.S. Co. v. Radio Corp. of Am., 157 N.E. 140, 142 (N.Y. 1927) (telegraph company).

[5]See the discussion of exceptions as to negligence in §5.2 *supra*.

what was foreseeable becomes "unforeseeable."[6] Sometimes they have done so by a particularly rigorous application of the requirement of certainty.[7] Use of the requirements of foreseeability and certainty as surrogates for some other principle, however, has not contributed to clarity in dealing with this problem. What is the principle for which these limitations are surrogates?

Restatement Second §351(3) gives the following answer: "A court may limit damages for foreseeable loss by excluding recovery for loss of profits, by allowing recovery only for loss incurred in reliance, or otherwise if it concludes that in the circumstances justice so requires in order to avoid disproportionate compensation." Although this frank recognition of the judicial reluctance just described may be untraditional,[8] the qualification on the right to damages is analogous to that introduced in Restatement Second §90, under which the remedy granted for breach of a promise made enforceable by reliance "may be limited as justice requires."[9] Section 351(3), like §90, invites the court to evaluate the proper allocation of risks in determining what justice requires, an invitation that courts have begun to accept.[10]

A case that lends support to this approach is *Sullivan v. O'Connor*, which arose out of a contract under which a surgeon had agreed to perform plastic surgery to enhance the appearance of his patient's nose.[11] Instead, the surgery disfigured her nose, necessitated an additional operation, and caused her pain and suffering. The Supreme Judicial Court of Massachusetts explained that in such a case "an expectancy recovery may well be excessive" and said that the facts "suggest moderation as to the breadth of the recovery that should be permitted." It noted that "the fee paid by the patient to the doctor would usually be quite disproportionate to the putative expectancy recovery"; and it concluded that there was much to be said for limiting recovery to the patient's reliance interest, including "her out-of-pocket expenditures," damages "for the worsening of her condition, and for the pain, suffering and mental distress" resulting from the

Restatement Second rule

Example of Sullivan v. O'Connor

---

[6] Kerr S.S. Co. v. Radio Corp. of Am., *supra* note 4 (telegraph company not liable for lost profits caused by failure to send coded radiogram because it did not know its contents), followed in Evra Corp. v. Swiss Bank Corp., 673 F.2d 951 (7th Cir. 1982) (wire transfer). For a statutory limitation on *Hadley* in case of failure properly to execute a payment order, *see* UCC 4A-306.

[7] Winston Cigarette Mach. Co. v. Wells-Whitehead Tobacco Co., 53 S.E. 885 (N.C. 1906) (breach of very simple contract "might bring ruin upon the party in default, by leaving the damages to the unbridled discretion of the jury").

[8] A case cited in support is Lamkins v. International Harvester Co., 182 S.W.2d 203 (Ark. 1944) (no recovery for loss of profits caused by inability to run tractor at night due to failure to deliver lights). However, that case was decided under the "tacit agreement" rule, still applied in Arkansas, as indicated in the discussion of the use of the tacit agreement test *supra*.

[9] See the discussion of how recovery may be limited in §2.19 *supra*.

[10] Vitol Trading S.A. v. SGS Control Servs., 874 F.2d 76 (2d Cir. 1989) (noting "enormous disparity" between fee charged and "damage liability . . . allegedly assumed"); Postal Instant Press v. Sealy, 51 Cal. Rptr. 2d 365 (Ct. App. 1996) (noting similarity of Restatement Second limitation to that in California Civil Code).

[11] As to such contracts, *see* the discussion of the example of *Hawkins v. McGee* in §3.6 *supra*.

additional operation." It was not, however, required to decide whether the patient could "recover the difference in value between the nose as promised and the nose as it appeared after the operations," since she did not press her claim for that element of damage.[12] Unfortunately, few other courts have been equally frank in discussing this possibility of limiting recovery.

Emotional disturbance

A limitation more firmly rooted in tradition generally denies recovery for emotional disturbance (or "mental distress") resulting from breach of contract, even if the limitations of unforeseeability and uncertainty can be overcome.[13] Under Restatement Second §353, recovery for emotional disturbance is allowed, even absent bodily harm, if "the contract or the breach is of such a kind that serious emotional disturbance was a particularly likely result." It could be argued that the real basis of this rule is that such recovery is likely to result in disproportionate compensation, and that the rule could therefore be subsumed under the more general rule of Restatement Second §351(3). Whatever the basis of the limitation, courts have not applied it inflexibly. Some courts have looked to the nature of the contract and made exceptions, as under the Restatement Second rule, where serious emotional disturbance was a particularly likely result of breach.[14] Other courts have looked to the nature of the breach and allowed damages for emotional disturbance on the ground that the breach of contract was reprehensible,[15] perhaps amounting to a tort,[16] or that it caused bodily harm.[17]

We turn now from the rules that courts apply in granting relief for breach of contract to the power of the parties to vary those rules by agreement.

---

[12]296 N.E. 183, 185, 187-89 (Mass. 1973). See the treatment of the rule in Flureau v. Thornhill in the discussion of the alternative of reliance in §12.8 *supra*.

[13]Silva v. Albuquerque Assembly & Distrib. Freeport Warehouse Corp., 738 P.2d 513 (N.M. 1987) ("damages for emotional distress are not recoverable in an action for breach of an employment contract" by failing to maintain group health insurance "in the absence of a showing that the parties contemplated such damages at the time the contract was made").

Courts have generally rejected claims for emotional distress arising out of home construction. Erlich v. Menezes, 981 P.2d 978 (Cal. 1999) (building house is "likely to be the stuff of urban legends" and emotional suffering "derives from an inherently economic concern").

In Restatement Second §353, however, the analogy to the rule in §351(3) is not drawn.

[14]Prominent are the "casket" cases. Hirst v. Elgin Metal Casket Co., 438 F. Supp. 906 (D. Mont. 1977) (casket manufacturer liable for "mental suffering" caused by leakproof casket that leaked).

[15]Lutz Farms v. Asgrow Seed Co., 948 F.2d 638 (10th Cir. 1991) (where, because of defective seed, onion growers' "crop was a failure and [they] were forced into bankruptcy," they could recover damages for emotional distress caused by "willful or wanton breach").

[16]Chung v. Kaonohi Center Co., 618 P.2d 283 (Haw. 1980) (damages for "emotional distress and disappointment" recoverable where actions by shopping mall in denying lease for fast-food kitchen "were reprehensible and clearly amounted to wanton and/or reckless conduct sufficient to give rise to tort liability").

[17]Sullivan v. O'Connor, discussed *supra* (recovery allowed for "mental distress" resulting from additional operation).

§12.18. Liquidated Damages, Penalties, and Other Agreed Remedies. To what degree is the law of remedies for breach of contract amenable to contrary agreements by the parties? Compared with the extensive power that contracting parties have to bargain over their substantive contract rights and duties, their power to bargain over their remedial rights is surprisingly limited.[1] The most important restriction is the one denying them the power to stipulate in their contract a sum of money payable as damages that is so large as to be characterized as a "penalty."

The advantages of stipulating in advance a sum payable as damages are manifold. For both parties, stipulating a sum may facilitate the calculation of risks and reduce the cost of proof.[2] For the injured party, it may afford the only possibility of compensation for loss that is not susceptible of proof with sufficient certainty. For the party in breach, it may have the effect of limiting damages to the sum stipulated. For society as a whole, it may save the time of judges, juries, and witnesses, as well as the parties, and may cut the expense of litigation. These advantages are of special significance when the amount in controversy is small.

If, however, the stipulated sum is significantly larger than the amount required to compensate the injured party for its loss, the stipulation may have quite a different advantage to that party — an *in terrorem* effect on the other party that will deter breach by compelling performance. Enforcement of such a provision would allow the parties to depart from the fundamental principle that the law's goal on breach of contract is not to deter breach by compelling the promisor to perform, but rather to redress breach by compensating the promisee.[3] It is this departure that is proscribed when a courtcharacterizes such a provision as a penalty. Since it is the *in terrorem* effect that is objectionable, the proscription applies only if the stipulated sum is on the high, rather than the low, side of conventional damages, although a provision stipulating an "unreasonably small amount . . . might be stricken under the section on unconscionable contracts or clauses."[4] This hostile attitude toward penalties

Limited power over remedies

Reasons to fix damages

Principle of compensation

---

§12.18 [1] Absent legislation, parties' power over substantive rights and duties is subject only to the restraints imposed by public policy (see §5.1 *supra*) and unconscionability (see §4.28 *supra*).

[2] Wallace Real Estate Inv. v. Groves, 881 P.2d 1010 (Wash. 1994) (quoting this section of this treatise).

[3] Jaquith v. Hudson, 5 Mich. 123 (1858) ("principle of just compensation" must not be disregarded and courts "will not permit the parties by express stipulation, or any form of language, however clear the intent, to set it aside"). See the discussion of no punitive damages in §12.8 *supra*.

[4] UCC 2-718 cmt. 1. See the discussion of UCC 2-302 in §4.28 *supra*.

History as to penalties

is peculiar to common law countries and is not generally shared by other legal systems.[5] How did this hostile attitude come about?

The attitude can be traced back to the development of equitable relief in cases involving penal bonds, which were used to secure performance under contracts. A penal bond, originally a sealed instrument, took the form of a promise to pay a stated sum, coupled with a provision that this obligation was "null and void" if the promisor rendered the required performance under the contract.[6] The common law courts enforced such bonds literally and, if the promisor had not strictly performed as required by the contract, would give judgment against the promisor for the sum fixed in the bond, regardless of the amount of loss caused by the promisee by the breach. However, by the latter part of the seventeenth century, it had become settled that equity would enjoin collection of the penal sum by the promisee and send the case to trial at law for determination of the amount of actual loss caused by the breach. This equity practice led to the enactment of statutes in both England and the United States, requiring the promisee at common law to state the promisor's failure to perform and allowing the promisee recovery only for damages actually proved. The principles developed in connection with penal bonds were later extended to contractual penalties of all kinds.[7] In this way a distinction grew in contract provisions stipulating the amount of damages between those characterized as "penalties," and therefore condemned, and those characterized as "liquidated damages," and therefore permitted. With the development of a doctrine of unconscionability capable of coping with abusive stipulated damage provisions in the same way as other abusive provisions, however, it has become increasingly difficult to justify the peculiar historical distinction between liquidated damages and penalties.[8] Today the trend favors freedom of contract through

---

[5] For example, article 1152 of the French Civil Code provides that if the contract stipulates "a certain sum as damages, no larger or smaller amount can be awarded," but a 1975 amendment allows the judge to "reduce or increase the agreed penalty if it is plainly excessive or ridiculously small."

Because of the wide gulf between common law systems and other legal systems, the Vienna Convention contains no provision on the important subject of stipulated damages. Article 7.4.13 of the UNIDROIT Principles provides that an aggrieved party is entitled to recover a specified sum "irrespective of its actual harm," though the sum may be "reduced to a reasonable amount where it is grossly excessive in relation to the harm resulting from the non-performance and to the other circumstances." Whether this provision can have any effect on a mandatory rule such as the common law rule prohibiting penalties is an open question.

[6] A similar form is still in use, particularly if the promise is that of a third party, such as a surety company, that guarantees performance. In that case the stated sum serves as an upper limit of the third party's liability.

[7] See generally Lloyd, Penalties and Forfeitures, 29 Harv. L. Rev. 117 (1915).

[8] In 1977, California amended its Civil Code to make liquidated damage provisions "valid unless the party seeking to invalidate the provision establishes that the provision was unreasonable under the circumstances existing at the time the contract was made," except against a consumer in a consumer case. Cal. Civ. Code §1671.

the enforcement of stipulated damage provisions as long as they do not clearly disregard the principle of compensation.[9]

If a provision is condemned as a penalty, it is unenforceable. But the rest of the agreement stands, and the injured party is remitted to the conventional damage remedy for breach of that agreement, just as if the provision had not been included.[10] If the provision is sustained as one for liquidated damages, both parties are bound by it, and it displaces the conventional damage remedy for breach.[11] This is so whether it provides for damages that are larger or smaller than would otherwise have been awarded.[12] The same distinction is now often applied to clauses providing that a sum of money deposited as security shall be forfeit in the case of breach.[13]

Consequences of distinction

Once a distinction between penalties and liquidated damages had been recognized, there remained the considerable task of drawing the line between the two. The question is one of law for the court, but, as the New York Court of Appeals lamented in 1854, "the ablest judges have declared that they felt themselves embarrassed in ascertaining the principle on which the decisions [distinguishing penalties from liquidated damages] were founded."[14] By 1914, however, the Supreme Court of Errors of Connecticut was able to state, in *Banta v. Stamford Motor Co.*, three conditions for enforcement of a clause that are "clearly brought out in the opinions": (1) "the amount stipulated must be

Factors in distinction

Courts have occasionally suggested that the distinction between penalties and liquidated damages is questionable on economic grounds. *See* Lake River Corp. v. Carborundum Co., 769 F.2d 1284 (7th Cir. 1985) (Posner, J.: "like every other state, Illinois, untroubled by academic skepticism of the wisdom of refusing to enforce penalty clauses against sophisticated promisors, . . . continues steadfastly to insist on the distinction between penalties and liquidated damages").

For academic skepticism on economic grounds of the wisdom of refusing to enforce penalty clauses, *see* Goetz & Scott, Liquidated Damages, Penalties and the Just Compensation Principle, 77 Colum. L. Rev. 554 (1977) ("cost-benefit analysis suggests that the traditional penalty rule is anachronistic").

[9]Walter Motor Truck Co. v. State, 292 N.W.2d 321 (S.D. 1980) (recognizing "the modern tendency not to look with disfavor upon liquidated damage provisions").

[10]For a representative case holding a sum to be a penalty, *see* Rye v. Public Serv. Mut. Ins. Co., 315 N.E.2d 458 (N.Y. 1974) ($200 per day up to $100,000 for delay in completion of building complex). As to the divisibility of a penalty clause, see the discussion of the possibility of abuse in §5.8 *supra.*

[11]For a representative case, *see* Dave Gustafson & Co. v. State, 156 N.W.2d 185 (S.D. 1968) ($210 per day for delay in completion of $530,742 highway contract).

That other remedies are not necessarily excluded, *see* Baybank Middlesex v. 1200 Beacon Properties, 760 F. Supp. 957 (D. Mass. 1991) ("enforceable liquidated damages provision . . . does not preclude the plaintiffs from resorting to alternative remedies in order to collect what obligations are owed"). See also the discussion of the tendency to liberalize in §12.6 *supra.*

[12]That the injured party cannot recover more, *see* Fisher v. Schmeling, 520 N.W.2d 820 (N.D. 1994) (though contract provided that liquidated damages were "without prejudice to other rights and legal remedies," vendor was denied "opportunity to establish actual damages in excess of that sum").

[13]See the discussions of a buyer of goods and a purchaser of land in §8.14 *supra.*

[14]Cotheal v. Talmadge, 9 N.Y. 551, 553 (1854).

a reasonable one, that is to say, not greatly disproportionate to the presumable loss or injury"; (2) "the damages to be anticipated as resulting from the breach must be uncertain in amount or difficult to prove"; and (3) "there must have been an intent on the part of the parties to liquidate them in advance."[15]

1. Reasonableness of forecast

The most important of the three conditions listed by the Connecticut court in *Banta* is that the stipulated sum must be "a reasonable one" in the light of the "presumed loss."[16] The time as of which the forecast of loss must be judged to be reasonable has traditionally been regarded as the time when the contract was made, not the time when the breach occurred. Melvin Eisenberg has argued for a "second-look standard" on the ground that contracting parties systematically focus on provisions specifying the performance that each is to render and are therefore less attentive to provisions dealing with remedies for failure to render that performance,[17] and this view has some judicial support.[18] But courts have generally adhered to the view of the *Banta* court:

> The standard of measure here is not furnished by the plaintiff's actual loss or injury, as the event proved, but by the loss or injury which might reasonably have been anticipated at the time the contract was made . . . . It is the look forward and not backward that we are called upon to take . . . .[19]

On this reasoning, the injured party does not have to show actual loss and, indeed, that loss is irrelevant except to help show what loss was anticipated.[20] As explained by the Supreme Judicial Court of Massachusetts, "the 'single look' approach helps resolve disputes efficiently by making it unnecessary to wait until actual damages . . . are proved."[21] The traditional view is put to the test in the rare and extreme situation in which, although the forecast was reasonable when the contract was made, the injured party actually sustained no loss at all. Some courts have still adhered to the traditional view and enforced the provision as one for liquidated damages, weighing the practical advantages of upholding a forecast that seemed reasonable when made, over the disadvantages of allowing

---

[15]92 A. 665, 667 (Conn. 1914) (upholding $15 per day for delay in delivery of $5,500 yacht).

[16]This is suggested in the parallel formulations of the Uniform Commercial Code and the Restatement Second, which emphasize the reasonableness of the stipulated sum. UCC 2-718(1) ("an amount which is reasonable in the light of the anticipated or actual harm caused by the breach"); Restatement Second §356 ("an amount that is reasonable in the light of the anticipated or actual loss caused by the breach").

[17]Eisenberg, The Limits of Cognition and the Limits of Contract, 47 Stan. L. Rev. 211, 225-36 (1995).

[18]Hubbard Business Plaza v. Lincoln Liberty Life Ins. Co., 649 F. Supp. 1310 (D. Nev. 1986) (in Nevada, liquidated damages must not "be disproportionate to the actual damages").

[19]92 A. at 667.

[20]Kimbrough & Co. v. Schmitt, 939 S.W.2d 105 (Tenn. App. 1996) ("wide disparity between the stipulated damage amount and actual damages may indicate that a damage forecast was unreasonable").

[21]Kelly v. Marx, 705 N.E.2d 1114, 1117 (Mass. 1999).

a party to recover although it has sustained no loss.[22] Other courts have characterized the sum as a penalty,[23] even though this results in a somewhat arbitrary
distinction between the situations in which there is no loss at all and those in
which there is only a little loss.[24] In applying the requirement that the forecast
be a reasonable one, courts have usually treated the issue as a matter of law[25]
and have often resolved doubts in favor of unenforceability,[26] an unfortunate
reflection of the historical hostility toward attempts to stipulate damages.

The Uniform Commercial Code makes a slight shift from the traditional
stress on anticipated, rather than actual, loss by requiring only that the stipulated
amount be "reasonable in the light of the anticipated *or actual* harm caused by
the breach."[27] However, this says only that a stipulation might be upheld as one
for liquidated damages on the ground that the sum was reasonable in the light of
the actual loss, even though it was not reasonable in the light of the anticipated
loss. It does not say that the stipulation might be stricken as one for a penalty
on the ground that the sum was unreasonable in the light of the actual loss,
even though it was not unreasonable in the light of the anticipated loss.[28] Thus
a court should look to the actual loss to sustain provisions that might otherwise
be unenforceable, but not to strike down provisions that would otherwise be
enforceable. In this respect, the Code follows the trend favoring enforcement.

Code on actual loss

Since, under the traditional view, the reasonableness of the forecast is to
be judged as of the time of contracting, rather than the time of breach, a
question arises as to whether the forecast must be reasonable as to all possible

Relevance of actual breach

---

[22] California & Hawaiian Sugar Co. v. Sun Ship, 794 F.2d 1433 (9th Cir. 1986) ("in this case of
concurrent causation each defaulting contractor is liable" though "because both parties were in
default, [injured party] suffered no damage until one party performed").

[23] Norwalk Door Closer Co. v. Eagle Lock & Screw Co., 220 A.2d 263 (Conn. 1966) ($100,000
for seller's breach of contract to continue in business manufacturing door closers exclusively for
buyer was penalty where seller transferred business to subsidiary which with same management
took its place with no loss to buyer).

[24] Courts that take this view sometimes avoid applying it by finding that there was at least a
little loss. *See* Wassenaar v. Panos, 331 N.W.2d 357 (Wis. 1983) ("difficult to uphold the employer's
position that the employee suffered no harm").

[25] Lake River Corp. v. Carborundum Co., *supra* note 8 (whether provision "is a penalty clause
or a liquidated-damages clause is a question of law rather than fact").

[26] Lake River Corp. v. Carborundum Co., *supra* note 8 ("Illinois courts resolve doubtful cases
in favor of classification as a penalty").

A contrary view, however, is more in line with the trend toward supporting stipulated damage
clauses. *See* Wassenaar v. Panos, *supra* note 24 (putting "burden of proof on the challenger
is consistent with giving the nonbreaching party the advantage inherent in stipulated damages
clauses").

[27] UCC 2-718(1). The same language is carried over into Restatement Second §356, quoted
supra note 16. It is unclear whether actual loss includes loss that would be excluded from damages
because not foreseeable. As to leases, UCC 2A-504 speaks only of the "anticipated harm."

[28] Equitable Lumber Corp. v. IPA Land Dev. Corp., 344 N.E.2d 391 (N.Y. 1976) (case
remanded to determine whether stipulated sum was reasonable in light of either "damages to
be anticipated" or "actual" loss suffered).

breaches or just as to the breach that actually occurred.[29] The typical case is that of a "shotgun" or "blunderbuss" clause, one that fixes a single large sum for any breach, substantial or insubstantial. Under the prevailing view, such a clause is unenforceable, even in the case of a substantial breach, because it was not a reasonable forecast as to a hypothetical insubstantial breach.[30] It would make more sense to hold that the clause is enforceable as long as it is a reasonable forecast in the light of the breach that actually occurred, for, as one writer put it, the "defendant should not be given the loophole of escape that, if he had committed a different breach, the sum named would not have been reasonable."[31] The Code's reference to actual loss seems to support this.[32] It is uncertain whether the prevailing view will still be followed in the face of the trend toward increasing recognition of stipulated damage clauses.

2. Difficulty of proof of loss

The second of the three conditions listed by the court in *Banta*, that the "damages to be anticipated . . . must be uncertain in amount or difficult to prove," is still reiterated.[33] It is, for example, the usual basis for sustaining provisions that fix a lump sum for any substantial breach of a covenant not to compete, since the loss resulting from such a breach will almost inevitably be uncertain in amount and difficult to prove.[34] The traditional view is that uncertainty and difficulty are to be determined as of the time the contract was made, not at the time of the breach or of the trial.[35] If the advantages of stipulating damages include reducing costs of proof and compensating for loss that cannot be proved with sufficient certainty, in addition to facilitating the calculation of risks, there is good reason to accept uncertainty and difficulty at any of these

---

[29] National Emergency Servs. v. Wetherby, 456 S.E.2d 639 (Ga. App. 1995) ($25,000 for breach by doctor of covenant not to compete was penalty).

[30] Seidlitz v. Auerbach, 129 N.E. 461 (N.Y. 1920) (decision whether agreement provides for liquidated damages or a penalty is to be made "as of its date, not as of its breach").

[31] C. McCormick, Law of Damages §151 (1935). This result has sometimes been put on the ground of interpretation. Hackenheimer v. Kurtzmann, 138 N.E. 735 (N.Y. 1923) (clause in contract for transfer of business that provided for payment by seller of $50,000 "in case of breach" interpreted to apply only to "material interference with the good will of the business," which there was).

[32] UCC 2-718(1), quoted *supra* note 16, speaks of "the harm caused by *the* breach"). *See* Restatement Second §356, quoted *supra* note 16.

[33] Board of Trustees v. Johnson, 507 So. 2d 887 (Miss. 1987) (difficult to assess "loss arising from [doctor's] refusal to engage in family practice"). *See* Restatement Second §356 ("reasonable in the light of . . . the difficulties of proof of loss").

UCC-O 2-718(1) speaks of reasonableness "in the light of . . . the difficulties of proof of loss." Under UCC-R 2-718(1) the "difficulties of proof of loss" are relevant only in connection with a consumer contract. As to leases, UCC 2A-504 makes no mention of such difficulties.

[34] Williams v. Dakin, 22 Wend. 201 (N.Y. 1839) ("value of the good will or patronage of the paper, as well as the amount of injury which the purchasers might sustain by any interference with it, were wholly uncertain and incapable of estimation otherwise than by mere conjecture").

[35] Hutchison v. Tompkins, 259 So. 2d 129 (Fla. 1972) (better "to allow the liquidated damage clause to stand if the damages are not readily ascertainable at the time the contract is drawn, but to permit equity to relieve against the forfeiture if it appears unconscionable in light of the circumstances existing at the time of breach").

times as a factor in sustaining a stipulation. However, it is questionable whether uncertainty or difficulty should be a condition, as opposed to just a factor to be weighed along with others. Although the ease of forecasting and proving loss may make it incumbent on the parties to make a more accurate forecast if it is to be sustained as reasonable, there is little sense in upsetting an accurate forecast on the ground that the loss was neither uncertain in amount nor difficult to prove.[36] As the Supreme Court of Wisconsin explained, this second condition "is generally viewed as helpful in assessing the reasonableness of the clause," which is the third condition. "The greater the difficulty of estimating or proving damages, the more likely the stipulated damages will appear reasonable."[37]

Courts occasionally still allude, like the court in *Banta*, to the intention of the parties.[38] Thus the New York Court of Appeals has said that a "clause which provides for an amount plainly disproportionate to real damage is not intended to provide fair compensation but to secure performance by . . . compulsion."[39] These references are, however, fast disappearing, and there is no good reason why a stipulation should not be upheld as one for liquidated damages even though its purpose may have been compulsion. According to the Federal Circuit, "a liquidated damage clause is not rendered unlawful simply because the promisee hopes that it will have the effect of encouraging prompt performance."[40] Since the proscription is based on a policy against compulsion, the inquiry does not go to what the parties intended but rather to whether the effect of upholding the stipulation would be improperly to compel performance.[41] For this reason, the parties' characterization of the sum as "liquidated damages" is not controlling,[42] nor is their use of such words as "penalty" or "forfeit."[43]

3. Intention of the parties

The tension between the parties' freedom in shaping rights and duties and their lack of freedom in stipulating damages is shown by the cases involving alternative performances.[44] Although it is beyond the parties' power to provide

Alternative performances

---

[36]Wallace Real Estate Inv. v. Groves, *supra* note 2 (quoting this section of this treatise). The point may be of little practical importance, for in such a situation there is little reason to stipulate damages and, if the forecast is accurate, even less to argue over its enforceability.

[37]Wassenaar v. Panos, *supra* note 24, at 363.

[38]Walter Implement v. Focht, 730 P.2d 1340 (Wash. 1987) ("Courts will look to the intention of the parties to make an accurate assessment of the clause's purpose.").

[39]Truck Rent-A-Center v. Puritan Farms 2nd, 361 N.E.2d 1015, 1018 (N.Y. 1977).

[40]DJ Mfg. Corp. v. United States, 86 F.3d 1130, 1135 (Fed. Cir. 1996).

[41]Wassenaar v. Panos, *supra* note 24 (recent discussions of reasonableness test have generally discarded "subjective intent of the parties, because subjective intent has little bearing on whether the clause is objectively reasonable").

[42]Caesar v. Robinson, 67 N.E. 58 (N.Y. 1903) ("circumstance that deposit is described as liquidated damages "is not at all conclusive.").

[43]Brooks v. Bankson, 445 S.E.2d 473 (Va. 1994) ("use of a word such as 'forfeited' is not determinative").

[44]Chandler v. Doran Co., 267 P.2d 907 (Wash. 1954) (employer of plant manager gave employee an option to purchase plant but employer could release itself from duty under option by paying employee additional sums as salary and expenses).

for a penalty of, say, $10,000 in the case of a party's breach by failure to perform, they may be able to shape their substantive rights and duties by having that party promise to render that performance or, in the alternative, to pay $10,000. A party that fails to do either may then be held for breach of a duty to pay $10,000. Under such a provision, there is no right to specific performance of the promise that is the alternative to payment, whereas under a provision for liquidated damages there is, absent provision to the contrary, a right to specific performance of the promise for which damages have been stipulated.[45] The mere presence of such a provision to the contrary should not, however, be decisive in characterizing the provision. Courts have used the concept of alternative performances to sustain "take or pay" contracts under which natural gas pipeline companies agree to pay for a minimum quantity of gas whether they take it or not.[46] Such provisions are sometimes couched in terms of an "option" to pay rather than perform, but the form of the provision should not obscure the underlying issue of whether what is provided is in substance a penalty for nonperformance.

Premiums

The same tension is shown by the cases involving premiums to reward superior performance. Although it is beyond the parties' power to provide for a penalty of, say, $1,000 for every day's delay in performance, up to a maximum of $10,000, they can shape their substantive rights and duties through a provision for a premium by setting the completion date ten days later and providing that the price shall be increased by $1,000 for each day the work is finished early, up to a maximum of $10,000.[47] Presumably, a court could refuse to apply either of these rules if it found that the sum was merely a disguised penalty. One can, however, sympathize with the difficulties encountered by courts groping for criteria with which to draw the line in this area of tension.[48]

Provision for attorney's fees

A provision that simply attempts to add a sum to the injured party's actual damages is ordinarily an obvious penalty.[49] There is, however, no reason why the parties cannot liquidate damages due to one cause, for example, delay in delivery, so that they would be added to those due to another cause, for

---

[45]See the discussion of the tendency to liberalize in §12.6 *supra*.

[46]Prenalta Corp. v. Colorado Interstate Gas Co., 944 F.2d 677 (10th Cir. 1991) (collecting cases: "Because one of the alternative performances in a take-or-pay contract is the payment of money, courts have distinguished the 'pay' provision from a liquidated damages provision.").

[47]For a case in which the contract provided for such a premium, *see* Banta v. Stamford Motor Co., *supra* note 15 ($5 per day for advance delivery of $5,500 yacht).

[48]Chandler v. Doran Co., *supra* note 44 (determining whether contract contains true alternative promise is "problem which the text writers seem to agree is puzzling, and upon which the decided cases are in conflict").

[49]Jarro Bldg. Indus. Corp. v. Schwartz, 281 N.Y.S.2d 420 (Sup. Ct. 1967) ("If appellant here could recover both liquidated damages and actual damages, there would be no question that the 'liquidated damages' provision was a penalty.").

example, defective quality.[50] Furthermore, a provision allowing the injured party to recover attorney's fees and other legal expenses in addition to damages will be sustained, even though the injured party would not otherwise be entitled to recover them.[51] An attempt to fix a particular sum as attorney's fees or set out a formula for their calculation must meet the same test as a liquidated damages clause.[52]

It would seem that the parties should also be limited in their power to dispense with the limitation of avoidability that is imposed on damages. It ought not to be within the parties' power to frustrate the salutary policy that the limitation serves of discouraging wasteful activity by the injured party after breach.[53] But if the parties stipulate damages according to a formula that takes reasonable account of this policy, the stipulation will be upheld.[54] Thus a clause calling for reimbursement for expenses incurred by the injured party in completing performance itself may be sustained.[55]

Limits as to avoidability

Stipulated damage clauses in employment contracts have raised troublesome questions of avoidability. A common provision allows the wrongfully discharged employee to recover the salary for the balance of the term, undiminished by anything the employee may have earned or been able to earn in other employment. In *Wassenaar v. Panos* the Supreme Court of Wisconsin upheld such a provision, concluding that it was "reasonable under the totality of circumstances" because "in providing for stipulated damages, the parties to the contract could anticipate the types of damages not usually awarded by law," including consequential damages such as that for "permanent injury to professional reputation, loss of career development opportunities, and emotional stress" as well as "for

Example of employment contracts

---

[50]Construction Contracting & Mgt. v. McConnell, 815 P.2d 1161 (N.M. 1991) ("jury should . . . be instructed that the [liquidated delay damage] clause does not compensate the party for non-delay-related damages, such as the higher cost of the replacement contractor").

[51]Katz v. Van Der Noord, 546 So. 2d 1047 (Fla. 1989) (purchasers entitled to attorney fees from vendor under provision of contract even though contract was held to be rescinded). As to the rule in the absence of a provision, see the discussion of the right to expectation in §12.8 *supra.*

[52]Equitable Lumber Corp. v. IPA Land Dev. Corp., *supra* note 28 (case remanded to determine whether clause fixing attorney's fees of seller of goods at 30 percent of amount recovered was void as a penalty).

[53]Saxon Constr. & Mgt. Corp. v. Masterclean, 641 A.2d 1056 (N.J. Super. 1994) (refusing to enforce provision in subcontract giving subcontractor in breach the right to any excess of unpaid balance of contract price over contractor's cost to complete on ground that "it discourages the contractor from affirmatively seeking to minimize its losses by obtaining a substitute subcontractor at a lesser cost").

[54]Truck Rent-A-Center v. Puritan Farms 2nd, *supra* note 39 ("Since there was uncertainty as to whether [leased] trucks could be re-rented or sold [on lessee's wrongful termination of lease], the parties could reasonably set, as they did, the value of such mitigation at 50% of the amount the lessee was obligated to pay for rental of the trucks.").

[55]*But see* Eastern S.S. Lines v. United States, 112 F. Supp. 167 (Ct. Cl. 1953) (where ship owner did not restore ship, recovery was limited to diminished value).

injury to the employee's reputation."[56] Other cases have shown like tolerance for similar provisions.[57]

Freedom as to foreseeability

No such policy underlies the limitation of foreseeability, however, and if a party chooses to assume the risk of liability for unforeseeable loss, there is no reason why the party should not be allowed to do so by a clause to that effect. More commonly, however, the risk of loss that would otherwise have been unforeseeable is thrust on a party by notice from the other party of facts that make that loss foreseeable. Such notice may be given, for example, by a recital in the writing that embodies the contract itself or by a letter or a telephone call,[58] and the parol evidence rule should not preclude the use of extrinsic evidence to show that this has been done.[59]

We conclude this chapter with a consideration of restitution as a remedy for breach of contract.

D.   RESTITUTION AS A REMEDY FOR BREACH

Other aspects distinguished

§12.19.   Relation to Restitution in General. Restitution is a substantial subject with a literature of its own, and this treatise addresses only those aspects that are of special importance to the law of contracts. Many of these aspects have already been discussed in other chapters in connection with the rules on indefiniteness,[1] incapacity,[2] misrepresentation,[3] duress,[4] undue influence,[5] unenforceability on grounds of public policy,[6] the statute of frauds,[7]

---

[56] *Supra* note 24, at 361, 365-66.

[57] Cherry v. A-P-A Sports, 662 P.2d 200 (Colo. App. 1983) (upholding provision requiring lump sum payment to hockey coach on team's failure to exercise option to extend term and concluding "failure to mitigate damages is inapplicable here [because] plaintiff is not seeking damages for breach of contract"). For the related problem of take or pay contracts, *see* the discussion of alternative performances *supra*.

[58] Florafax Intl. v. GTE Mkt. Resources, 933 P.2d 282 (Okl. 1997) (clause in "contract itself expressly reflects the parties' contemplation of the recovery of lost profits"). Since no agreement is necessary, it seems misleading to characterize the rule of Hadley v. Baxendale, as is sometime done, a "penalty default rule." See the discussion of the burden of expression in §7.16 *supra*.

[59] See the discussions of the parol evidence rule in §7.16 *supra* and of the foreseeability test in §12.14 *supra*.

§12.19   [1] See the discussion of relief based on resitution in §3.30 *supra*.

[2] See §§4.5, 4.8 *supra*.

[3] See the discussion of the requirement of restitution in §4.15 *supra*.

[4] See the discussion of restitution in §4.19 *supra*.

[5] See the discussion of development in §4.20 *supra*.

[6] See §5.9 *supra*.

[7] See §6.11 *supra*.

nonoccurrence of a condition,[8] breach by repudiation and nonperformance,[9] mistake,[10] impracticability of performance,[11] frustration of purpose,[12] and contract beneficiaries.[13] There remains one other aspect of restitution that is of particular concern to the law of contracts — restitution to an injured party as a remedy for the other party's breach.

When a court grants this remedy for breach, the party in breach is required to account for a benefit that has been conferred by the injured party. Sometimes this is accomplished by requiring the party in breach to return the very benefit received and sometimes by requiring that party instead to pay a sum of money that represents the value of that benefit. In contrast to cases in which the court grants specific performance or awards damages as a remedy for breach, the effort is not to enforce the promise by protecting the injured party's expectation or reliance interest, but to prevent unjust enrichment of the party in breach by protecting the injured party's restitution interest. The objective is not to put the *injured* party in as good a position as that party would have been in if the contract had been performed, nor even to put the *injured* party back in the position that party would have been in if the contract had not been made. It is, rather, to put the party *in breach* back in the position that party would have been in if the contract had not been made.[14]

Effect as remedy for breach

Since the restitution interest is ordinarily the smallest of the three interests, the injured party will usually find restitution less attractive than enforcement of the other party's broken promise, either by specific relief or by an award of damages based on the injured party's expectation or reliance interest.[15] However, if the bargain has turned out to favor the party in breach rather than the injured party, the injured party may prefer restitution. Cases of this kind are rare since the party who is favored by the bargain has every reason to keep it, not to break it.

Reason for use as remedy

---

[8] See the discussion of duty discharged in §8.3 *supra*.

[9] See §8.14 *supra*.

[10] See the discussion of avoidance as a remedy in §9.3 *supra*.

[11] See the discussion of restitution in §9.9 *supra*.

[12] See the discussion of restitution in §9.9 *supra*.

[13] See the discussions of beneficiary against promisor and of promisee against promisor in §10.7 *supra*.

[14] But see the discussion of the exception in §12.20 *infra*.

[15] In one exceptional situation, that of the losing contract, the injured party prefers restitution because that party's restitution interest exceeds its expectation interest. See the discussion of the situation when the benefit is a performance other than money in §12.20 *infra*. In another exceptional situation, the injured party prefers restitution because it wants specific restitution of what the other party has received, rather than money damages, because the other party is financially insecure. Furthermore, in rare cases an injured party that has no claim for damages based on a repudiation until the time for performance has come may prefer an immediate claim in restitution. See note 18 *infra*.

Basic requirements

When such cases have arisen, however, courts have often granted restitution to the injured party.[16] The injured party uses the breach as a basis for claiming that its remaining duties under the contract are discharged, and that party pursues an alternative remedy that is generally regarded as inconsistent with relief based on the contract itself.[17] Restitution as a remedy for breach is therefore limited to cases in which the injured party has a claim for damages for total breach, so that that party's remaining duties are discharged. If the claim is only one for damages for partial breach, the injured party's remaining duties are not discharged, and restitution is not available as an alternative.[18] And if the injured party is precluded from treating a material breach as the basis of a claim for damages for total breach, the alternative remedy of restitution is unavailable.[19] As a condition of restitution, the injured party must return or account[20] for any benefit received.[21]

Specific restitution

Although courts sometimes refer to the injured party's remedy in these cases as based on "rescission" (i.e., avoidance) of the contract,[22] this description is inaccurate. This appears clearly if the injured party seeks specific restitution, the return of the very thing that has resulted in the benefit, rather than the recovery of the value of the benefit in money. Although specific restitution is often available to a party that has a claim to restitution as a remedy for breach,[23]

---

[16]City of Harker Heights v. Sun Meadows Land, 830 S.W.2d 313 (Tex. App. 1992) (restitution "is often an appropriate measure of recovery for breach of contract, for example in a case where the complaining party's expectation damages are too hard to measure"). See the discussion of the general principle in §12.20 *infra*.

[17]A few cases have allowed damages in addition to restitution. CBS v. Merrick, 716 F.2d 1292 (9th Cir. 1983) (error to refuse "to allow reliance damages"). That the mere choice of restitution by the injured party, through bringing suit or otherwise, does not necessarily bar relief based on the contract itself, *see* Restatement Second §378. See also the discussion of avoidance and ratification in §4.15 *supra*.

[18]Hibiscus Assocs. Ltd. v. Board of Trustees of Policemen & Firemen Sys., 50 F.3d 908 (11th Cir. 1995) (Florida law: term must be such an essential part of the bargain "that its breach destroys the entire contract"). As to the effect of divisibility, see the discussion of divisibility in §12.20 *infra*.

[19]This is not without exception, however, for if the other party repudiates the contract, the court should allow the injured party restitution even in those exceptional situations in which that party does not have a claim for damages for total breach. See the discussion of other types of relief in §8.20 *supra*.

[20]Utemark v. Samuel, 257 P.2d 656 (Cal. App. 1953) (seller of land entitled to reasonable rental value of land that buyer used before seller's breach).

[21]Bernstein v. Nemeyer, 570 A.2d 164 (Conn. 1990) (Peters, C.J.: "it is a condition of rescission and restitution that the plaintiff offer, as nearly as possible, to place the other party in the same situation that existed prior to the execution of the contract," and because of defendants' "great loss," plaintiffs could not have done this).

[22]*See* Earthinfo v. Hydrosphere Resource Consultants, *supra* note 18 ("extraordinary remedy of rescission and disgorgement of profits is justified"). Under the Uniform Commercial Code terminology, what the injured party does is "cancel." UCC 2-106(4) (cancellation "occurs when either party puts an end to the contract for breach by the other").

[23]Neenan v. Otis Elevator Co., 194 F. 414 (2d Cir. 1912) (transferee of patents failed to use invention as agreed).

courts do not grant it routinely, as they would in cases of avoidance. Thus, although a vendor of land entitled to avoid on the ground of misrepresentation is routinely entitled to have the deed cancelled and the land returned,[24] a vendor of land entitled to restitution as a remedy for the purchaser's breach[25] may not be granted specific restitution of the land itself.[26] A leading writer on restitution attributed the denial of specific restitution in that case to "the belief that such relief would interfere unduly with the certainty of titles to land."[27] Furthermore, if the performance of the grantee is support of the grantor for life, the difficulty of measuring recovery in money is great enough that specific restitution is generally allowed.[28] It has sometimes been stated that the "adequacy" test, developed in connection with specific performance, must be met if specific restitution is to be granted,[29] but this view has met with criticism.[30] Whatever the criteria for the grant or denial of specific restitution as a remedy for breach, the important point for our purposes is that it is not as generally available as it would be in a case of rescission in the sense of a true avoidance of the contract.

We now inquire into the availability of restitution as a remedy for breach.

§12.20. Availability for Breach. When can a party with a claim for damages for total breach have restitution as an alternative remedy? It is a principle of the law of contracts that damages should be based on the injured party's lost expectation. In the words of Amalya Kearse, speaking for the Second Circuit, because "the purpose of damages for breach of contract is to compensate the injured party for the loss caused by the breach . . . . those damages are generally measured by the plaintiff's actual loss."[1] On the other hand it is a principle of the law of restitution that one should not gain by one's own wrong. In the words of the Restatement of Restitution, "A person is not permitted to profit by his own wrong at the expense of another."[2] In many cases, the principles are mutually consistent. If, as usually happens, the injured party's lost expectation equals or exceeds the gain by the party in breach, damages based on expectation will strip the party in breach of all gain and make the injured party whole

General principle

---

[24]See the discussion of the requirement of restitution in §4.15 *supra.*

[25]It is important to realize that in the common case, in which the buyer's breach consists merely in the nonpayment of the price, the seller has no claim to restitution at all, but only one to the price. See the discussion of the case in which the benefit is full performance in §12.20 *infra.*

[26]City of Cleveland v. Herron, 131 N.E. 489 (Ohio 1921) ("mere failure of consideration . . . when unmingled with fraud or bad faith, is not sufficient").

[27]1 G. Palmer, Law of Restitution §4.19 (1978).

[28]Caramini v. Teguilias, 186 A. 482 (Conn. 1936) (specific restitution granted in case of "transfer of land in consideration of the promise of the grantee to support the grantor for life").

[29]*See* first Restatement §354 ("if the circumstances are such that other remedies are inadequate").

[30]The "adequacy" test is abandoned in Restatement Second §372.

§12.20 [1]United States Naval Inst. v. Charter Communications, 936 F.2d 692, 696 (2d Cir. 1991).

[2]Restatement of Restitution §3 (1937).

as well. But if the injured party's lost expectation is less than the gain realized by the party in breach, then damages based on expectation will not strip the party in breach of all gain. Will a court disregard the damage remedy based on lost expectation and instead require the party in breach to disgorge the benefit received? With an important exception, courts have done so, allowing restitution as an alternative remedy to that of damages unless the measurement of the amount of recovery would involve the court in problems that could be avoided by awarding expectation damages.[3]

Exception

The exception is made when the injured party seeks to require the party in breach to disgorge gain that has resulted not from the injured party's *performance* but rather from the other party's *breach*. Courts have refused to allow recovery for profits that the party in breach has obtained as a result of opportunities that would not have been available but for the breach, as where a seller breaks a contract and sells the goods to a third person for more than the contract price.

Effect on efficient breach

Restitution as a remedy for breach of contract is limited to benefits that are regarded as having somehow flowed from the injured party, a party that can be said to have "lost" something that the party in breach is being asked to "restore."[4] As we have seen, a contracting party that commits an efficient breach in order to engage in a more profitable transaction can generally retain what is left of the profit on that transaction after compensating the injured party for its lost expectation.[5] Even if a court requires the party in breach to disgorge the gain resulting from the injured party's performance, this may still leave the party in breach with some of the gain resulting from the breach. But a broader disgorgement principle, one that stripped the party in breach of all of the gain resulting from the breach, would make it impossible to commit an "efficient" breach. In this respect the restitutionary liability of a contracting party for breach of a contract duty differs importantly from that of a fiduciary for breach of a fiduciary duty. A fiduciary cannot commit an efficient breach. Just as the duty of good faith is more onerous for a fiduciary than for a contracting party,[6] so too the restitutionary liability of a fiduciary is more extensive than that of a contracting party. A trustee, for example, that violates its fiduciary

---

[3] For an exhaustive treatment of the question, *see* 1 G. Palmer, Law of Restitution ch. 4 (1978).

That restitution is available when a promise is enforceable because of reliance instead of bargain, *see* Restatement Second §373 cmt *a* & ill. 4. *See also* §90 cmt. *d*.

[4] *See* Farnsworth, Your Loss or My Gain? The Dilemma of the Disgorgement Principle in Breach of Contract, 94 Yale L.J. 1339, 1370-82 (1985). For a case discussing disgorgement of profits, *see* Earthinfo v. Hydrosphere Resource Consultants, 900 P.2d 113 (Colo. 1995) (buyer of products to be developed by computer software developer properly required to disgorge profits when it refused to pay agreed royalties). The profits in that case did not, however, result from the buyer's *breach* but rather from the *performance* of the injured party, the developer.

[5] See the discussion of the problem of gain and loss in §12.3 *supra*.

[6] See the discussion of the significance of discretion in §7.17 *supra*.

duty by using trust funds for its own purposes must disgorge all of gain from the improper use regardless of whether that gain came from the beneficiary or not.[7] A "mere" breach of contract is not regarded as a "wrong" that will justify such an extreme remedy.

Despite this exception, restitution is an important remedy for breach of con-   **Benefit is**
tract. It is helpful to begin analysis with the case in which the benefit conferred   **payment of money**
on the party in breach consists simply of the payment of money, as distinguished
from the case in which it consists of something other than money. The former
is the clearest case for restitution. If the injured party has paid part or all of
the price in advance for a performance that is not forthcoming, that party can
get restitution of what has been paid.[8] The injured party can do so even in the
face of the contention by the party in breach that, had the performance been
rendered, its value to the injured party would have been less than the price.
In the venerable case of *Bush v. Canfield*, a buyer made a $5,000 payment on
a contract for the sale of flour for a total price of $14,000. The seller broke
the contract by failing to deliver the flour, although the market price of the
flour at the time for delivery had dropped to $11,000. When the buyer sought
restitution of the $5,000, the seller contended that, because the buyer had been
spared a loss of $3,000 on the market, that sum should be subtracted from the
recovery. The court rejected the contention: "The defendant has violated his
contract; and it is not for him to say, that if he had fulfilled it, the plaintiffs would
have sustained a great loss, and that this ought to be deducted from the money
advanced."[9] The result would have been the same if the seller had tendered
defective flour and the buyer had rejected it after the market drop and then
sought restitution of what he had paid.[10] What a court does in such cases is to
grant specific restitution as a matter of law rather than of equity. The policy
favoring restitution is reinforced by the practical convenience to the court of
allowing recovery of the very sum of money paid, thereby avoiding the problems of measurement that would be required if damages were to be measured
by expectation. The right to restitution against a party in breach is not, however,
limited to cases in which the benefit consists simply of the payment of money.

Restitution against a party in breach may also be allowed when the benefit   **Benefit is**
consists of something other than money, even though this requires that the   **performance**
court measure the value of the benefit in money. Suppose that a builder con-   **other than money**
tracts to build a building for an owner for $1,000,000. After the builder has

---

[7]Snepp v. United States, 444 U.S. 507 (1980) (per curiam: CIA agent was fiduciary and therefore liable to disgorge profit from book published without required agency approval, regardless
of whether agency suffered any loss).

[8]Furthermore, an injured purchaser of land that has made improvements on the land that
remains in the hands of the vendor after its breach can have restitution for those improvements. Utemark v. Samuel, 257 P.2d 656 (Cal. App. 1953) (recovery measured by reasonable
cost of improvements, not merely "amount by which the improvements enhanced the value
of the property"). See the discussion of remedies on avoidance in §4.15 *supra*.

[9]2 Conn. 485, 488 (1818).

[10]On the right to reject, see the discussion of the perfect tender rule in §8.12 *supra*.

spent $500,000 in preparation and part performance, none of which can be salvaged, the owner repudiates the contract and the builder stops work.[11] As we have seen, if the builder cannot prove with sufficient certainty how much it would have cost to finish the job, and therefore cannot establish lost profit, the builder can still recover the $500,000 spent. The rationale for this result is that the builder can use the formula for damages based on lost expectation and can disregard the *profit* term.[12] Suppose, however, that the owner can prove with sufficient certainty that it would have cost the builder $600,000 to finish the job and that the builder would therefore have sustained a loss of $100,000, instead of a profit. There is no longer any reason to ignore the negative "profit" term in the case of such a "losing contract" since it is no longer uncertain. The $100,000 should be subtracted, giving only $400,000 in damages.[13] As far as the expectation measure of recovery is concerned, the breach does not shift to the party in breach a loss that would have been suffered by the injured party had the contract been fully performed. However, many courts have been willing to measure the benefit conferred on the party in breach by the injured party's performance under a losing contract up to the time of termination and then allow that party restitution of that sum, with a deduction for any payments received.[14] Even though the court must face the problem of measuring the benefit, if recovery were based on expectation the court would have to face the comparably difficult problem of measuring the expectation. Since the party who has broken the contract can scarcely complain if the more generous measure of benefit is chosen, benefit is measured, not by that party's net enrichment, but by that party's cost avoided, that is, by what it would have cost the party in breach to have obtained a similar performance from another person such as the injured party at the time and the place it was rendered.[15] Even if the party in breach abandons the enterprise and does not have the performance completed, this measure of benefit is used on the ground that what the injured party did was in the interest of the party in breach under the contract.[16] The

---

[11] If the builder did not stop work, the rule that precludes restitution for a benefit that has been conferred officiously (see the discussion of the meaning of *officious* in §2.20 *supra*) would apply to deny recovery for performance rendered after the repudiation. *See* Restatement Second §373 cmt. *e*. This gives a result analogous to that with respect to damages under the limitation of avoidability. See the discussion of stopping performance in §12.12 *supra*.

[12] See the discussion of the supplier as injured party in §12.16 *supra*.

[13] See the discussion of the effect of a losing contract in §12.16 *supra*.

[14] United States v. Algernon Blair, Inc., 479 F.2d 638 (4th Cir. 1973) (subcontractor can recover from contractor "the reasonable value of the services"); United States v. Zara Contracting Co., 146 F.2d 606 (2d Cir. 1944) (subcontractor can recover from contractor "the reasonable value of his performance").

[15] United States v. Algernon Blair, Inc., *supra* note 14 ("the standard for measuring the reasonable value of the services rendered is the amount for which such services could have been purchased from one in the plaintiff's position at the time and place the services were rendered").

[16] Acme Process Equip. Co. v. United States, 347 F.2d 509 (Ct. Cl. 1965) (manufacturer of rifles for government granted restitution when government cancelled contract, although no rifles

practical result in the example given is to allow the injured party to recover the $500,000 spent — the *cost of reliance* — not on the rationale that it is the reliance interest, but on the rationale that it is the restitution interest.[17] Since the injured party ordinarily need not specify a theory of recovery, that party can be reimbursed for expenses under a losing contract even if restitution is not explicitly sought.

Although the contract price can be evidence of the value of the benefit conferred, recovery in restitution may exceed the contract rate. Recovery is not limited to that fraction of the price that equals the fraction of the work that the injured party has done.[18] This is so even if the contract expresses the price in terms of an amount for each unit of performance. For example, if a contract for excavation expresses the price in terms of an amount for each cubic foot of earth, the injured party may have restitution in excess of that rate.[19] This makes especially good sense when the rate is constant, but the performance that was rendered before the breach was more burdensome than the average under the contract as a whole. Such would be the case under an excavation contract if the initial excavation were the hardest.[20]

Contract rate no limit

Occasionally, however, a losing contract is regarded as divisible for this purpose. This is usually disadvantageous to the injured party for, instead of getting restitution the value of the benefit conferred, that party is limited to an apportioned part of the unprofitable contract price for the part completed, with no claim for damages for the part not completed.[21] If, however, the completed

Divisibility

---

were delivered and nothing was created that added to the wealth of the government), rev'd on other grounds, 385 U.S. 138 (1966). As to the requirement that a benefit be conferred on the party in breach, see the discussion of limitations on restitution in §2.20 *supra*.

[17] See the discussions of the alternative method in §12.10 *supra* and of the effect of a losing contract in §12.16 *supra*. To the extent that the $500,000 included excessive expenditures, recovery in restitution should be reduced. However, since what another person would have charged for the performance rendered would have included an amount as profit, the actual expenditures should, at least in principle, be augmented by that amount.

[18] United States v. Western Cas. & Sur. Co., 498 F.2d 335 (9th Cir. 1974) (error to limit subcontractor to 40 percent of price where only 40 percent of work had been completed).

[19] United States v. Zara Contracting Co., *supra* note 14 ("under the better rule the contract price or the unit price per cubic yard of a construction or excavation contract does not limit recovery").

[20] For an interesting illustration of this, *see* Wellston Coal Co. v. Franklin Paper Co., 48 N.E. 888 (Ohio 1897) (buyer under one-year contract for coal at fixed price per ton took coal at times when market was high but refused to take it when market was low).

[21] Dibol & Plank v. E.H. Minott, 9 Iowa 403 (1859) (painter who agreed to paint ten houses for $70 each could recover only $280 plus any lost profit when owner allowed him to paint four; even though painter claimed that the reasonable value of painting each house exceeded $70). A mere provision for progress payments, however, does not make a contract divisible. See the discussion of time for performance distinguished in §8.13 *supra*.

part happens to be profitable and the uncompleted part unprofitable, this will give a larger recovery than would restitution.[22]

Benefit is full performance

Restitution will be denied if the injured party has fully performed, and all that remains is for the party in breach to pay a definite sum in money as the price of that performance.[23] If, in the example given, the builder has spent the full $1,100,000, and the owner has not paid the $1,000,000, recovery will be limited to the $1,000,000 promised, the limit of the builder's expectation. Here, to implement the policy favoring restitution would involve the court in problems of measurement, while recognition of the expectation interest requires it only to award a sum fixed by the parties.[24] Courts have, however, often been willing to grant restitution, even on full performance by the injured party, if the performance due from the party in breach is something other than the payment of a definite sum of money so that the problem of valuation cannot be avoided by awarding damages based on the expectation interest.[25]

Contract price as limit

A perplexing problem arises if the performance due from the party in breach is simply the payment of a sum of money, but the injured party has already spent more than that sum and not finished performance. Using the contract price as a ceiling on recovery in such a case will not entirely avoid problems of measurement of the benefit conferred on the party in breach, since that benefit must, at least in principle, be measured before it can be known whether the ceiling has been reached. On the other hand, not using the contract price as a ceiling on recovery may result in a more generous recovery for part performance than would have been allowed for full performance.[26] Although authority can

---

[22]Shapiro Engrg. Corp. v. Francis O. Day Co., 137 A.2d 695 (Md. 1958) (construction contract was divisible, so that builder could recover price apportioned to first part, which it had completed, with no deduction for any loss that it might have sustained if it had been allowed to perform second part).

[23]Oliver v. Campbell, 273 P.2d 15 (Cal. 1954) (lawyer who fully performed limited to $750 fee agreed upon, rather than $5,000 value of services); John T. Brady & Co. v. City of Stamford, 599 A.2d 370 (Conn. 1991) (Peters, C.J.: "work on the project was 99 percent complete" and after full performance "appropriate measure of the value of the benefit conferred upon the party in breach is [generally] the value that the parties themselves, in their contract, have assigned to that performance").

[24]This results in an anomaly that favors a party that puts money into the transaction. In Bush v. Canfield, described in the discussion of the benefit as payment of money *supra*, the buyer could have recovered the full $14,000 had this been paid before the seller's breach in a falling market. But if the seller had delivered the goods before being paid by the buyer, the seller could not have recovered the goods, or even their value, had the buyer failed to pay in a rising market. The seller would have been limited to recovery of the price.

[25]Coon v. Schoeneman, 476 S.W.2d 439 (Tex. Civ. App. 1972) (recovery based on value of work when injured party was to get as compensation an amount contingent on profits from sale of houses). This is the rule of Restatement Second §373(1) and is approved in 1 G. Palmer, Law of Restitution §4.3 (1978).

[26]This anomaly is illustrated by Oliver v. Campbell, *supra* note 23, in which the majority held that a lawyer was limited to the $750 fee agreed upon because he had finished performance, and

be found that the contract price is an upper limit on recovery in such a case,[27] there is also support for the contrary view.[28]

Furthermore, if a contract is unenforceable under the statute of frauds, a court should not unhesitatingly apply the rule that denies restitution if the contract has been fully performed by the injured party and all that remains is for the other to pay the price in money. No special problem is posed by the provisions relating to contracts that cannot be performed within a year or to contracts for the sale of goods or of an interest in real property since full performance makes such contracts enforceable.[29] The injured party can then recover the price just as if the statute had been satisfied in the first place. A problem arises, however, if full performance does not make the contract enforceable, as is the case, for example, under provisions in some states relating to contracts that cannot be performed within a lifetime.[30] To deny the injured party restitution for full performance of such a contract would leave that party without a remedy. Therefore, an exception should be made if an injured party that has fully performed has no remedy other than restitution, and full performance should not preclude restitution.[31]

Statute of frauds

---

the dissent contended that he was entitled to the $5,000 value of his services because he had not finished.

[27] Johnson v. Bovee, 574 P.2d 513 (Colo. App. 1978) (builder of house was *limited* by "the contract price as a ceiling on restitution").

[28] Southern Painting Co. v. United States, 222 F.2d 431 (10th Cir. 1955) (plumbing and heating subcontractor recovered $20,000 for part performance where contract price was $10,000). *See* 56 Am. L. Inst. Proc. 407-13 (1979).

[29] See the discussions of the sale of goods under the Code, of the land contract provision, and of the one-year provision in §6.9 *supra*.

[30] See the discussion of the lifetime provision in §6.4 *supra*.

[31] For a thorough discussion, *see* 2 G. Palmer, Law of Restitution §6.4 (1978). *See also* Restatement Second §375 cmt. *b*.

Biographical Appendix

The following are thumbnail biographies of some of the judges and scholars whose names appear in this treatise and who have had a special influence on contract law.

Bacon. Francis Bacon (1561–1626) was appointed attorney general in 1613 and several years later managed the dismissal of his bitter rival, Edward Coke, from King's Bench. Two years later he was made lord chancellor. In 1621, however, he was charged with bribery. He resigned his office, paid a heavy fine, and suffered brief imprisonment in the Tower of London. Among philosophers, he is remembered for his *Novum Organum* (1620), in which he argued that science is inductive. Lawyers still encounter his name in connection with *A Collection of Some Principal Rules and Maximes of the Common Law* (1597). *See generally* D. Coquillette, Francis Bacon (1992).

Braucher. Robert Braucher (1916–1981) was a decorated pilot during World War II before becoming a member of the Harvard law faculty, where he taught for a quarter of a century. He served as a Commissioner on Uniform State Laws and as Reporter for the Restatement (Second) until 1971, when he was appointed to the Supreme Judicial Court of Massachusetts.

Cardozo. Benjamin Nathan Cardozo (1870–1938) practiced in New York City after graduation from law school. He served as Judge and later Chief Judge of the Court of Appeals of New York and was appointed Associate Justice of the Supreme Court of the United States in 1932 to fill the vacancy left by Holmes. Of his contribution to the law of contracts, Professor Corbin has written: "It cannot be said that he made any extensive changes in the existing law of contract. To state the facts of the cases, the decision, and the reasoning of his opinion will not show the overthrow of old doctrine or the establishment of new. Instead, it will show the application of existing doctrines with wisdom and discretion; an application that does not leave those doctrines wholly unaffected, but one that carries on their evolution as is reasonably required by the new facts before the court. When Cardozo is through, the law is not exactly as it was before; but there has been no sudden shift or revolutionary change." Cardozo's best known jurisprudential work is a series of lectures entitled *The Nature of Judicial Process.*

Coke. Edward Coke (pronounced *Cook*) (1552–1634) rose to Attorney General in 1593 after serving as Solicitor General and Speaker of the House of Commons. He came to hold a favorable position in the court of James I and became Chief Justice of the Common Pleas in 1606 and Chief Justice of the King's Bench in 1613. He championed the cause of the common law in its struggle against the encroachments of royal prerogatives, including equity jurisdiction. His bitter rival, Sir Francis Bacon, helped to engineer his dismissal in 1616; but Coke got himself back on the Privy Council, and in 1620 was again elected to Parliament, where he was a leader of the opposition to James I and Charles I. Among his influential writings are his *Institutes,* which include his commentary on Littleton's *Tenures.*

Corbin. Arthur Linton Corbin (1874–1967) practiced law in Colorado for four years after his graduation from law school in 1899. He taught law, notably contracts, at the Yale Law School from 1903 until his retirement in 1943. He was Special Adviser and Reporter for the Chapter on Remedies of the Restatement of Contracts. His treatise on contracts is a classic.

Dawson. John Philip Dawson (1902–1985) spent almost his entire professional career in academic life. His teaching, first at Michigan, then at Harvard, and finally at Boston University, spanned half a century. His writing ranged over the areas of restitution, contracts, comparative law, and legal history. He authored books entitled *Unjust Enrichment: A Comparative Analysis, The Oracles of the Law,* and *Gifts and Promises: Continental and American Law Compared,* and collaborated on casebooks on restitution and contracts.

Easterbrook. Frank Easterbrook (1948–   ) served for several years in the Department of Justice and then joined the University of Chicago law faculty, where he made influential contributions to scholarship in the fields of corporate and antitrust law. In 1985 he was appointed to the United States Court of Appeals, Seventh Circuit.

Eisenberg. Melvin Eisenberg (1934–   ) practiced law in New York City and held several government posts before joining the law faculty of the University of California at Berkeley. He has written widely on contract and corporate law and served as Chief Reporter for the American Law Institute's Principles of Corporate Governance.

Friendly.   Henry Friendly (1903–1986) clerked for Brandeis and then practiced law in New York for thirty years before becoming a judge and later chief judge on the United States Court of Appeals, Second Circuit. He was admired for his keen mind and was considered by many the most learned judge of his generation. In *Federal Jurisdiction: A General View* (1973) he advocated a drastic pruning of the diversity jurisdiction of the federal courts.

Fuller.   Lon L. Fuller (1902–1978) had a long teaching career at Oregon, Illinois, Duke, and, for the final three decades, Harvard, where he taught contracts and jurisprudence. In philosophical works he presented alternatives to positivist attitudes toward law, sometimes using partly fanciful cases in imaginary and contrasting opinions, as in *The Case of the Speluncean Explorers*, 62 Harv. L. Rev. 616 (1949). He edited a contracts casebook, and his article, with one of his students, on the reliance interest in contract damages prompted an extensive reexamination of the remedial side of the subject.

Gilmore.   Grant Gilmore (1910–1982) taught French at Yale before earning his law degree and then taught law at Yale, and for a time Chicago, after a brief stint in Wall Street practice. During nearly four decades in academic life, he contributed to a casebook on contracts and a text on admiralty and authored a multivolume treatise on secured transactions and a provocative monograph entitled *The Death of Contract*.

Hand.   Learned Hand (1872–1961) was admitted to the practice of law in New York in 1897 and appointed to the United States District Court for the Southern District of New York in 1909 and to the United States Court of Appeals for the Second Circuit in 1924. He retired in 1951, after having sat on the federal bench longer than any other judge. Justice Cardozo called him "the greatest living American jurist" and he was so regarded by many of his contemporaries. His extrajudicial utterances may be sampled in *The Spirit of Liberty* and *The Bill of Rights*.

Holmes.   Oliver Wendell Holmes (1841–1935) practiced law in Boston, served briefly as professor of law at Harvard, and then for 20 years was Justice and later Chief Justice of the Supreme Judicial Court of Massachusetts. In 1902 he was appointed an Associate Justice of the United States Supreme Court, where the quality of his dissenting opinions won him the title, "the Great Dissenter." He resigned because of age in 1932. His judicial opinions and other writings did much to shape the law of contracts at the turn of the century. His most famous work is *The Common Law*, based on a series of lectures.

Kaye. Judith Kaye (1938–   ) practiced law for several years in New York City before becoming the first woman partner, specializing in commercial litigation, in a firm in that city. In 1983 she was appointed to the New York Court of Appeals, the first woman member of that court, and in 1993 she became its chief judge.

Kearse. Amalya Kearse (1937–   ) practiced in New York City, becoming the first African-American partner and the second woman partner in a leading law firm. In 1979 she was appointed to the United States Court of Appeals, Second Circuit. Her writing ranges from tax law to bridge, and she has held national and world contract bridge titles.

Kent. James Kent (1763–1847) augmented a meager income from law practice in New York City by serving as the first professor of law at Columbia College from 1794 to 1798. His lectures did not attract students, and in 1798 he accepted an appointment to the state Supreme Court, of which he later became Chief Judge. From 1814 to 1823 he was Chancellor of the New York Court of Chancery, where his opinions shaped American equity jurisprudence. After retirement, he briefly returned to Columbia but "got heartily tired of lecturing" and resigned to devote his time to an expansion of his lectures into a four-volume treatise, *Commentaries on American Law.* It was received with enthusiasm and became a classic on American Law.

Kozinski. Alex Kozinski (1950–   ) was born in Bucharest. After clerking for Chief Justice Burger, he practiced law in Los Angeles and Washington. In 1981 he was appointed to the United States Claims Court and in 1985 to the United States Court of Appeals, Ninth Circuit. He is a frequent contributor to legal and other publications.

Llewellyn. Karl Nickerson Llewellyn (1893–1962) practiced law in New York for two years and taught law at Yale for several years before becoming a member of the law faculty at Columbia in 1925. He remained there until 1951, when he joined the law faculty in Chicago. He was well known for his contributions to the field of jurisprudence, as a leader of the school of "legal realists," as well as to the fields of contracts and commercial law, serving as Chief Reporter for the Uniform Commercial Code. Soia Mentschikoff, Llewellyn's wife, was Associate Chief Reporter of the Code.

Mansfield. William Murray (1705–1793), a Scot and the first Earl of Mansfield, was a rival of the elder Pitt in school, in Parliament, and in politics. He favored strict measures with the American rebels. His friends included

Samuel Johnson and Alexander Pope, who helped him practice advocacy and later praised his eloquence in verse. He achieved greatness as a judge, being Lord Chief Justice from 1756 to 1788. In one important decision he discountenanced slave-holding in England, but he is remembered primarily because of his influence on commercial law.

Peters. Ellen Ash Peters (1930–   ) was a member of the faculty of the Yale Law School for over two decades, teaching and writing in the fields of contracts and commercial law and serving as an Adviser for the Restatement Second of Contracts. In 1978 she was appointed an associate justice of the Connecticut Supreme Court, becoming Chief Justice in 1984. For discussion of her decisions involving the Uniform Commercial Code, *see* Comment, 21 Conn. L. Rev. 753 (1989).

Posner. Richard Allen Posner (1939–   ), after clerking for Justice William Brennan and occupying several legal positions in the federal government, taught briefly at Stanford University Law School and then for over a decade at the University of Chicago Law School before his appointment to the United States Court of Appeals for the Seventh Circuit, where he became Chief Judge in 1993. A key figure in the development of the field of law and economics, his books include the influential *Economic Analysis of Law. See generally* Lake, Posner's Pragmatist Jurisprudence, 73 Neb. L. Rev. 545 (1994).

Story. Joseph Story (1779–1845) was appointed at age 32 from the Massachusetts legislature to the United States Supreme Court, the youngest person ever named to that Court. In 1829 he became concurrently a professor of law at Harvard, where he was a popular teacher, though given to long and eloquent ramblings that had little to do with his prepared lectures. His treatise on such subjects as equity jurisdiction and conflict of laws had enormous influence. In 1842 he wrote the opinion in *Swift v. Tyson,* which generated great controversy until it was overturned almost a century later in *Erie Railroad Co. v. Tompkins.* He also wrote poems, some of Chief Justice Marshall, his closest friend, and many of his 18 children. One of them, William, became a noted legal scholar and authored the first significant American treatise on contracts, before abandoning law practice to become a sculptor in Rome.

Traynor. Roger Traynor (1900–1983) was a member of the law faculty of the University of California at Berkeley for a decade, specializing in the law, before becoming Associate Justice of the Supreme Court of California in 1940. From 1964 to 1970 he served as its Chief Justice. Some of his opinions on contract law are discussed in Macaulay, Mr. Justice Traynor and the Law of Contracts, 13 Stan. L. Rev. 812 (1961).

Williston.   Samuel Williston (1861–1963) joined the faculty of Harvard Law School in 1890, after practicing law for a short period in Boston, and taught there until his retirement in 1938. His principal fields were contracts and sales. He was the drafter of several uniform acts, including the Uniform Sales Act, the predecessor of the sales article of the Uniform Commercial Code, and was Reporter for the Restatement of Contracts. His treatise on contracts is a classic. *See generally* Boyer, Samuel Williston's Struggle with Depression, 43 Buff. L. Rev. 1 (1994).

Table of Cases

References are to sections.

883

Index

Items may be indexed not only under the usual analytic headings but also under such generic headings as: Cases, real and hypothetical; Clauses; History; Persons in biographical appendix; Restatements of Contracts; Statutes; Uniform Commercial Code; Words and phases. References are to section and footnote numbers unless otherwise noted.

Index

Index

Moral turpitude, 5.1
Mortgage
  assumption, beneficiaries of, 10.7
  equitable lien, 11.5
  standard mortgage clause, 10.9
  statute of frauds
    land contract provision, 6.5
    suretyship provision, 6.3
  subject to, sale, 8.2-8.4; 8.6; 8.9
  three-cornered settlements, 8.10
Mutuality
  obligation, of, 3.2-3.4; 3.13
  remedy, of, 12.4
Mutual mistake. *See* Mistake

Necessaries, 4.5; 4.8
Necessary advances, 11.7
Negligence. *See* Fault
Negotiable instruments
  checks. *See* Checks
  claim settlements, in, 2.12
  consumer sales, in, 11.8
  drafts. *See* Checks
  holder in due course, 11.8
  integration under parol evidence rule, 7.3
  kinds of, 11.3 n.14
  promissory notes, 11.3 n.14
  statute of frauds and, 6.3
  symbolic writing, 4.25; 11.6
Nominal consideration, 2.11; 3.23
Nominal damages, 12.8
Nondisclosure. *See* Disclosure
Nonperformance. *See also* Performance
  assignor, as defense against, 11.8
  beneficiary, as defense against, 10.9
  breach. *See* Breach
  cure, 8.17; 8.18
  excused by frustration or impracticability, 9.9
  installments, contract to pay money in, 8.18
  prospective, 8.20-8.23
  termination for, 8.15; 8.18
No-oral-modification clause, 7.6; 8.5
Note, promissory, 11.3 n.14
Notice
  acceptance, of, 3.15
  assignment, of, 11.7
Novation, 4.24; 6.3; 10.7; 11.6; 11.11

Objective and subjective theories
  acceptance and, 3.13
  interpretation and, 7.9
  offer and, 3.10

Obligation. *See* Duty
Offer
  auction, 3.11
  bid as, 3.11
  counteroffer. *See* Counteroffer
  cross, 2.10
  death or incapacity
    offeree's, 3.11
    offeror's, 3.16; 3.18
  defined, 3.3; 3.10
  delay, effect of, 3.19
  disguised, 2.13
  firm, 3.23
  general, 3.10; 3.17; 3.19
  illusory promise and, 2.13
  invitation to make, 3.10
  irrevocable, 3.23
  lapse of. *See* Lapse of offer
  offeree, reaching, 3.10
  prize, of, 3.4
  promise, as, 3.3
  public, proposal to, 3.10
  quantity, failure to limit, 3.10
  quotation of price, 3.10
  recipients, failure to limit, 3.10
  rejection. *See* Revocation of offer
  reward, of, 2.10
  standing, 3.17
  what constitutes, 3.10; 4.26
  who can accept, 3.11
Offeree
  offer to reach, 3.10
  protection of, 3.23-3.26
Offeror as master of offer, 3.12; 3.13
Officiousness. *See* Restitution
Offset, 8.14 nn.13; 26; 8.15; 11.8
Omitted cases. *See* Implication
One-year provision of statute of frauds, 6.1; 6.4; 6.9
Opinion
  misrepresentation of, 4.14
  promise distinguished, 3.6
Opportunity costs. *See* Lost opportunities
Option contracts
  anticipatory repudiation of, 8.20
  bilateral contract, offer of, 3.25
  conditions under, 8.2; 8.5; 8.7
  consideration, supported by, 3.23
  purpose of, 9.1
  recitals, supported by, 4.34
  reliance, supported by, 3.23

Index